68,163,966
11,936,034
80,100,000
104,677,474
909,666,494
1,014,343,968

Accounting Principles

Eleventh Edition

C. ROLLIN NISWONGER, CPA, PhD

Professor of Accountancy
Miami University, Oxford, Ohio

PHILIP E. FESS, CPA, PhD

Professor of Accountancy
University of Illinois, Urbana

Published by

A30 **SOUTH-WESTERN PUBLISHING CO.**

CINCINNATI   WEST CHICAGO, ILL.   DALLAS   PELHAM MANOR, N.Y.
PALO ALTO, CALIF.   BRIGHTON, ENGLAND

ISBN: 0-538-01300-1

Library of Congress Catalog Card Number: 72-90237

7 8 9 K 7 6 5 4

Printed in the United States of America

Preface

Among the innovations characterizing recent editions of *Accounting Principles* have been subtle improvements in clarity and conciseness in expressing the principles, techniques, and uses of accounting. This new dimension has enhanced the reputation of *Accounting Principles* as the leader in integrating accounting principles and practices. The eleventh edition expands this dimension, enabling students not only to obtain a better understanding of the sources of financial information but also to improve their comprehension of the uses of such information.

The objectives of contemporary accounting, including a discussion of the increasing need for the measurement of social costs and benefits, are presented in the opening chapter, followed by an introduction to the underlying principles of accounting. Additional principles are discussed and their applications in business illustrated in each succeeding chapter. Questions, exercises, and problems are presented at the end of each chapter, enabling students to sharpen their skills through application of the principles studied.

Although the procedural aspects of accounting are minimized in this edition, recording and controlling techniques are described to the extent necessary to illuminate the principles. The selection and development of principles is designed to fulfill the needs of college students planning a career in accounting, as well as those studying business administration, liberal arts, law, or other disciplines.

Those familiar with earlier editions will recognize the continuance of many successful features. Some rearrangement has been made to improve the sequential order of subject matter, and more use has been made of diagrams, charts, and other illustrative devices. Both the corporate form and the sole proprietorship form of business enterprise are introduced in the first chapter, with basic differences in accounting for owners' equity being developed gradually in succeeding chapters. Other innovations adopted to keep pace with changes in the statutes, accounting techniques, and business operations include the presentation of certain schedules and reports in simulated computer print-out format (Chapter 11), introduction of the various methods of determining profit-sharing bonuses (Chapter 12), and illustration of income tax minimization through the employment of "income averaging" and the "maximum tax on earned income" (Chapter 23).

Quotations and citations of Opinions of the Accounting Principles Board and other authoritative publications have been more than doubled. The chapters devoted exclusively to corporations (Chapters 16, 17, 18) have been extensively revised to accord with the officially adopted interest method of amortizing bond discount and premium, the equity method of accounting for investments in common stock, and methods of disclosing changes in accounting principle. The discussion of the statement of changes in financial position has been rewritten to reflect current accounting practice (Chapter 26), and the prevailing accounting thought on both the purchase method and the pooling of interests method of consolidating statements is presented (Chapter 27). A brief description of the organization and operation of the recently created Financial Accounting Foundation is also presented (Appendix A).

As in past editions, the attention given to managerial uses of accounting data has continued to increase. For example, the material on perpetual inventory has been given greater emphasis and an explanation added of the difference in results between the periodic and perpetual systems obtained when *lifo* cost flow is employed (Chapter 8). There is a new section on responsibility accounting (Chapter 22) and a discussion of managerial uses of quantitative techniques, including new materials on linear programming and on the formula for economic order quantity (Chapter 25).

As in the preceding edition, the variety and volume of the questions, exercises, and problems presented at the end of each chapter provide a wide choice of subject matter and range of difficulty. They have been carefully written and revised to be both practical and comprehensive. An additional series of problems is provided (Appendix B) and selected specimen financial statements are reproduced (Appendix C). The working papers correlating with the problems are designed to relieve students of the burden of repetitive details in order that attention may be more effectively directed to mastery of the underlying concepts.

Four short practice sets, each requiring the recording, analysis, interpretation, and reporting of accounting data for a single month, are available for use in developing greater student proficiency or for review purposes. Workbooks of study guides, student check sheets, transparencies of solutions to problems, objective tests, examination problems, multiple-choice questions, and other teaching aids are also available.

The authors acknowledge with gratitude the helpful suggestions received from many teachers who have used earlier editions. Although space limitations prohibit a listing of all of those who have made significant contributions, we acknowledge with sincere thanks the detailed suggestions and recommendations submitted by Professors Joe J. Cramer, Jr., The Pennsylvania State University; Paul M. Fischer, The University of Wisconsin; John G. Helmkamp, Arizona State University; Frank J. Imke, Texas Tech University; George C. Mead, Michigan State University; Catherine E. Miles, Georgia State University; Harry R. Price, University of Miami; Warren L. Slagle, University of Tennessee; and Clayton R. Tidyman, California State University, Fresno. Our special thanks go to Professor Raymond C. Dockweiler, University of Missouri; Dean James H. MacNeill, Fordham University; and Professor Richard L. Nolan, Harvard University, for their assistance in preparing specific portions of the manuscript.

We are also grateful to the American Accounting Association and to the American Institute of Certified Public Accountants for permission to use materials from their publications.

C. Rollin Niswonger

Philip E. Fess

Contents

PART FOUR / DEFERRALS, ACCRUALS, PLANT ASSETS, AND INTANGIBLE ASSETS

CHAPTER NINE / DEFERRALS AND ACCRUALS   209

CHAPTER TEN / PLANT ASSETS AND INTANGIBLE ASSETS   235

PART FIVE / ACCOUNTING SYSTEMS

CHAPTER ELEVEN / SYSTEMS AND CONTROLS   264

CHAPTER TWELVE / PAYROLL SYSTEMS   296

PRACTICE SET 2 / MIDWEST APPLIANCE COMPANY

The narrative accompanies the set, which is available both with and without business papers. This set provides practice in accounting for a sole proprietorship using the voucher system.

CHAPTER THIRTEEN / SYSTEMS DESIGN AND AUTOMATED DATA PROCESSING   321

PART SIX / ACCOUNTING PRINCIPLES

CHAPTER FOURTEEN / CONCEPTS AND PRINCIPLES   344

PART SEVEN / PARTNERSHIPS AND CORPORATIONS

CHAPTER FIFTEEN / PARTNERSHIPS   369

PRACTICE SET 3 / KALAMAZOO HARDWARE CORPORATION

The narrative accompanies the set, which is available without business papers. This set provides practice in accounting for a corporation that operates a departmentalized business.

CHAPTER TWENTY / MANUFACTURING AND PROCESS COST SYSTEMS 508

CHAPTER TWENTY-ONE / JOB ORDER COST SYSTEMS 538

PRACTICE SET 4 / UPLAND MANUFACTURING COMPANY

The narrative accompanies the set, which is available without business papers. This set provides practice in accounting for a manufacturing business that uses a job order cost system.

CHAPTER TWENTY-TWO / BUDGETARY CONTROL AND STANDARD COST SYSTEMS 561

PART NINE / DECISION MAKING

CHAPTER TWENTY-THREE / INCOME TAXES AND THEIR EFFECT ON BUSINESS DECISIONS

CHAPTER TWENTY-FOUR / COST AND REVENUE RELATIONSHIPS FOR MANAGEMENT

CHAPTER TWENTY-FIVE / MANAGEMENT REPORTS AND SPECIAL ANALYSES

PART TEN / ADDITIONAL STATEMENTS AND ANALYSES

CHAPTER TWENTY-SIX / STATEMENT OF CHANGES IN FINANCIAL POSITION   669

CHAPTER TWENTY-SEVEN / CONSOLIDATED STATEMENTS AND OTHER STATEMENTS   697

CHAPTER TWENTY-EIGHT / FINANCIAL STATEMENT ANALYSIS   726

PART ELEVEN / APPENDIXES

Chapter 1

ACCOUNTING PRINCIPLES AND PRACTICES

CONTEMPORARY ACCOUNTING

Accounting is often characterized as "the language of business." The acceleration of change in our complex society has contributed to ever-increasing complexities in this "language," which is used in recording and interpreting basic economic data for individuals, businesses, governments, and other entities. Sound decisions, based on reliable information, are essential for the efficient distribution and use of the nation's scarce resources. Accounting, therefore, plays a very important role in our economic and social system.

Because of the wide range of accounting activity, there is no concise yet all-inclusive description of accounting. Accounting is concerned with processes of recording, sorting, and summarizing data related to business transactions and events. Such data are to a large extent, but not exclusively, of a financial nature and are frequently, but not always, stated in monetary terms. Accounting is more than this, however; it is also concerned with reporting and interpreting the data. Accounting has been defined rather broadly as:

> . . . the process of identifying, measuring, and communicating economic information to permit informed judgments and decisions by users of the information.[1]

Implicit in this definition is the requirement that accountants have a broad knowledge of the socioeconomic environment; without it they would be unable to identify and develop relevant information. Accordingly, the basic structure of accounting is influenced by such factors as the prevailing political situation, the various types of institutions that provide society with goods and services, and the legal privileges and restraints within which society lives.

---

[1] *A Statement of Basic Accounting Theory* (Evanston, Illinois: American Accounting Association, 1966), p. 1.

Characteristics of accounting information. Without exploring in detail the characteristics of the economic information provided by accounting, it is sufficient at this juncture to indicate that it is composed principally of financial data about business transactions, expressed in terms of money. Historical recording of transaction data may take various forms, such as pen or pencil markings made by hand, printing by various mechanical and electronic devices, or holes or magnetic impressions in cards or tape.

The mere records of transactions are of little use in making "informed judgments and decisions." The recorded data must be sorted and summarized before significant reports and analyses can be prepared. It is not the single transaction but the sum of all the operations of a day, week, month, or year that has significance. Some of the reports to enterprise managers and to others who need economic information may be made frequently; other reports are issued only at longer intervals. The usefulness of reports is often enhanced by various types of percentage and trend analysis.

The "raw materials" of accounting are composed to a large extent of business transaction data; various summaries, reports, and analyses are its primary "end products."

Users of accounting information. Accounting provides the techniques for accumulating and the language for communicating economic data to various categories of individuals and institutions. Owners and prospective owners of a business enterprise need to know about its financial status and its prospects for the future. Bankers and suppliers appraise the financial soundness of a business organization and weigh the risks involved before making loans or granting credit. Government agencies are concerned with the financial activities of business organizations for purposes of taxation and regulation. Employees and their union representatives are also vitally interested in the stability and the profitability of the organization that employs them.

The individuals most dependent upon and most involved with the end-products of accounting are those charged with the responsibility for directing the operations of enterprises. They are often referred to collectively as "management." The type of data needed by managers may vary with the size of the enterprise. The manager of a small business may need relatively little accounting information. As the size of a business unit increases, however, the manager becomes farther and farther removed from direct contact with day-to-day operations. He must be supplied with timely information about various aspects of the business, which may range from the determination of direct and indirect costs incurred in a job training program to cost projections for installations designed to reduce air or water pollution.

The relevant information for one category of users may differ markedly from that needed by other users. Once the user groups are identified, however, and the nature of the relevant data determined, the accountant is able to establish an information network to assist each group in forming judgments and making decisions regarding future actions.

RELATIONSHIP TO OTHER FIELDS

Individuals engaged in such areas of business as finance, production, marketing, personnel, and general management need not be expert accountants, but their effectiveness is enhanced if they have a good understanding of accounting principles. Everyone engaged in business activity, from the youngest employee to the manager and owner, comes into contact with accounting. The higher the level of authority and responsibility, the greater is the need for an understanding of accounting concepts and terminology.

Many employees with specialized training in nonbusiness areas also make use of accounting data and need to understand accounting principles and terminology. For example, an engineer responsible for selecting the most desirable solution to a technical manufacturing problem may consider cost accounting data to be the decisive factor. Lawyers use accounting data in tax cases and in lawsuits involving property ownership and damages from breach of contract. Governmental agencies rely on accounting data in evaluating the efficiency of government operations and for appraising the feasibility of proposed taxation and spending programs. Finally, every adult engages in business transactions and must necessarily be concerned with the financial aspects of his own life, and perhaps of others. Accounting plays an important role in modern society and, broadly speaking, it can be said that all citizens are affected by accounting. The closer the contact with financial activity, of course, the greater the need for an understanding of accounting concepts and terminology.

3

PROFESSION OF ACCOUNTANCY

Accountancy is a profession with stature comparable to that of law or engineering. The rapid development of accounting theory and technique during the current century has been accompanied by an ever-increasing number of professionally trained accountants. Among the factors contributing to this growth have been the increase in number, size, and complexity of business corporations; the imposition of new and increasingly complex taxes, particularly the federal income tax; and other restrictions imposed on business operations by governmental regulations.

Accountants who render accounting services on a fee basis, and staff accountants employed by them, are said to be engaged in *public accounting*. Accountants employed by a particular business firm or nonprofit organization, perhaps as chief accountant, controller, or financial vice president, are said to be engaged in *private accounting*.

Recognizing the need for reliable professional accounting service, all the states have enacted laws providing for the licensing of certified public accountants, commonly called CPAs. Only those individuals who have met the qualifications and received a license may engage in public practice as CPAs.

The qualifications required for the CPA certificate differ among the various states. A specified level of education is required, often the completion of a collegiate course of study in accounting. All states require that a candidate pass an examination prepared by the American Institute of Certified Public Accountants. The examination is administered twice a year, in May and November, and many states permit candidates to take the examination upon graduation from college or during the term in which they will complete the educational requirements. The examination, which occupies one afternoon and two all-day sessions, is divided into four parts: Accounting Theory, Accounting Practice, Auditing, and Business Law. Some states also require an examination in an additional subject, such as Rules of Professional Conduct. Most states do not permit successful candidates to practice as independent CPAs until they have had from one to three years' experience in public accounting or in employment considered equivalent.

In some of the states the practice of public accounting is not restricted solely to CPAs. In the absence of express statutory prohibition, any person may style himself as a public accountant, or PA. Details regarding requirements for practice as a CPA or PA in any particular state can be obtained from the respective state Board of Accountancy.

The scope of activities and responsibilities of private accountants varies quite widely. They are frequently referred to as administrative or executive accountants, or, if they are employed by a manufacturing concern, as industrial accountants. Various branches of federal, state, and local governments also employ accountants in increasing numbers.

Both public and private accounting have long been recognized as excellent training for top managerial responsibilities. Many executive positions in government and in industry are held by CPAs and others with education and experience in accounting.

SPECIALIZED ACCOUNTING FIELDS

As in many other areas of human activity in the twentieth century, a number of specialized fields in accounting have evolved. This tendency toward specialization has been caused in large measure by growth in size and complexity of business units, mounting taxes, and increasing regulation of business by law and by governmental agencies. These influences, together with rapid technological advances and accelerated economic growth, have created the need for accountants to acquire a high degree of expertise in various specialties.

General accounting and financial accounting apply to the overall accounting for an economic unit. This function is concerned with the recording of transactions for a business or other economic unit and the periodic preparation of statements from these records. The various general purpose and special purpose reports and statements prepared from the accounting records are used to impart useful information to managers, owners, creditors, governmental agencies, and the general public. Of particular importance to financial accountants are the established rules of accounting, termed "generally accepted accounting principles." It is incumbent upon corporate enterprises to abide by such principles in preparing their annual reports on profitability and financial status for their stockholders and the investing public. Comparability of annual reports is an essential element in the allocation of the nation's resources among business organizations in a socially desirable manner. The accounting principles and techniques that will be developed in this book are in large part included in financial accounting.

Auditing is a field of accounting activity that involves an independent review of general accounting. Auditing was the first service rendered by public accountants and is still one of their principal activities. These accountants examine the records supporting financial statements of an enterprise and express an opinion regarding the fairness and reliability of such statements. An essential element of "fairness and reliability" is adherence to generally accepted accounting principles. The auditing activity of independent CPAs is often referred to as their "attest" function. Most large corporations also employ their own staffs of *internal auditors*. One of the most important duties of internal auditors is to determine the extent to which the various operating divisions observe the policies and procedures prescribed by management.

Cost accounting emphasizes the determination and the control of costs. It is concerned primarily with the costs of manufacturing processes and of manufactured products, but increasing attention is being given to distribution costs. In addition, one of the principal functions of the cost accountant is to assemble and interpret cost data, both actual and prospective, for the use of management in controlling current operations and in planning for the future.

Management accounting employs both historical and estimated data in assisting management in day-to-day operations and in planning

5

future operations. It deals with specific problems that confront enterprise managers at various organizational levels. The management accountant is frequently concerned with identifying alternative courses of action and then helping to select the best one. For example, he may assist the company treasurer in preparing plans for future financing, or he may develop data for the use of the sales manager in determining the selling price to be placed on a new product. In recent years, public accountants have come to realize that their training and experience uniquely qualify them to advise management personnel on policies and administration. This rapidly growing field of specialization by CPAs is frequently called *management advisory services* or *administrative services*.

Tax accounting encompasses the preparation of tax returns and the consideration of the tax consequences of proposed business transactions or alternative courses of action. Accountants specializing in this field, particularly in the area of tax planning, must be familiar with the tax statutes affecting their employer or clients and also must keep up-to-date on administrative regulations and court decisions on tax cases.

Accounting systems is the special field concerned with the design and implementation of procedures for the accumulation and reporting of financial data. The systems accountant must devise appropriate "checks and balances" to safeguard business assets and, to the fullest possible extent, provide for information flow that will be efficient and helpful to management. It is essential that he also be knowledgeable about the uses and relative merits of various types of data processing equipment.

Budgetary accounting presents the plan of financial operations for a period and, through accounts and summaries, provides comparisons of actual operations with the predetermined plan. A combination of planning and controlling future operations, it is sometimes considered to be a part of management accounting.

Governmental accounting specializes in recording and reporting the transactions of political units, such as states and municipalities. It seeks to provide useful accounting information regarding the business aspects of public administration and helps to control the expenditure of public funds in accordance with statutory requirements.

Social accounting is the newest field of accounting and unquestionably the most difficult to describe succinctly. There have been increasing demands on the profession for measurement of social costs and benefits which have hitherto been considered to be unmeasurable. One of the engagements in this new field involved the measurement of traffic patterns in a densely populated section of the nation as part of a government study to determine the most efficient use of transportation funds, not only in terms of facilitating trade but also of assuring a good environment for the area's residents. Other innovative engagements have dealt with the optimum use of welfare funds in a large city, with the public use of state parks, with wildlife in state game reserves, and with statewide water and air pollution.

Accounting instruction, as a field of specialization, requires no explanation. However, in addition to teaching, accounting professors often engage in research, auditing, tax accounting, or other areas of accounting on a part-time or consulting basis.

There is some overlapping among the various specialized fields, and leaders in any particular field are likely to be well versed in related areas. There is also a considerable degree of specialization within particular specialties. For example, within the field of auditing one may become an expert in a particular classification such as department stores or public utilities; in tax accounting one may specialize in the problems of oil and gas producing companies; or in systems one may become an expert in electronic data processing equipment.

BOOKKEEPING AND ACCOUNTING

There is some confusion over the distinction between "bookkeeping" and "accounting." This is due in part to the fact that the two are related and that there is no universally accepted distinction between them.

In general, *bookkeeping* is the recording of business data in a prescribed manner. A bookkeeper may be responsible for keeping all of the records of a business or of only a minor segment, such as a portion of the customers' accounts in a department store. Much of the work of the bookkeeper is clerical in nature and is increasingly being accomplished through the use of mechanical and electronic equipment.

Accounting is primarily concerned with the design of the system of records, the preparation of reports based on the recorded data, and the interpretation of the reports. Accountants often direct and review the work of bookkeepers. The larger the firm, the greater is the number of gradations in responsibility and authority. The work of accountants at the beginning levels may include some bookkeeping. In any event, the accountant must possess a much higher level of knowledge, conceptual understanding, and analytical skill than is required of the bookkeeper.

PRINCIPLES AND PRACTICE

In accounting, as in the physical and biological sciences, experimentation and change are never-ending. Capable scholars devote their lives and their intellectual energies to the development of accounting principles. Experienced professional accountants contribute their best thinking to the solution of problems continually confronting their clients or employers. The several professional accounting associations regard research as a major activity. It is from such research that accounting principles evolve to form the underlying basis for accounting practice.

This book is devoted primarily to explanations of accounting principles and, to a lesser extent, to demonstrations of related practices or procedures. It is only through this duality of emphasis on the "why" of accounting as well as on the "how" that the full significance of accounting can be learned.

ROLE OF ACCOUNTING IN PLANNING AND EVALUATING RESULTS

Knowledge of the past performance of an enterprise is of additional value beyond its historical aspects; it is useful in planning future operations. Comparisons of past performance with current operations may reveal the means of accelerating favorable trends and reducing those that are unfavorable. For example, an increase in the volume of services or merchandise sold is a favorable indication. If the increase is accompanied by increases in costs and expenses of such magnitude that net income is decreased, the end result is, of course, unfavorable. The relevant factors responsible for the unfavorable results should be considered in planning future operations. Questions such as the following should be answered: Was the increased volume of sales attributable to excessive reductions in selling price? Did the cost of the merchandise increase without a comparable adjustment in selling price? What types of expenses increased and what were the causes of the increases? Which of the increases were unavoidable and which ones can be reduced in the future without adverse effects?

In the conduct of day-to-day operations management relies upon accounting for many needs of a more routine nature. For example, it is necessary to know the amount owed to each creditor and by each customer and the date each payment is due. Records of property are necessary in determining the amount and type of insurance that should be carried and in ascertaining the amount of any insured loss that may occur. Knowing when to place orders for merchandise and supplies, granting credit to customers, anticipating the amount of cash required at any particular time — these and many other essential items of information can be obtained in a timely and orderly manner only if adequate records are maintained and reports prepared.

Management is also dependent upon accounting records and reports in determining the extent to which actual performance agrees with the planned objectives. For example, the budgeting of revenues and expenses for a business would be of little value without frequent follow-up reports comparing actual performance with the budget.

The use of accounting information in decision making is by no means limited to management. Owners (stockholders) and prospective owners of corporate enterprises need to be informed periodically about their profitability and financial status in order to evaluate the relative attractiveness of alternative stock investments. Bankers and suppliers need information regarding the financial soundness of a business organization before making loans or granting credit. Various branches of federal, state, and local governments require reports in connection with income, property, sales, social security, and other taxes. One of the prerequisites to the issuance of securities by corporations is the filing of detailed reports on business operations and financial position with governmental agencies. Stock exchanges also require periodic reports from corporations whose stocks are listed. The foregoing reasons for preparing accounting reports for outsiders are merely illustrative; there are many others.

Thus far attention has been focused on business enterprises. Records and reports are also needed by those engaged in professional pursuits and even by persons who have retired from active participation in a business or profession. Agencies of federal, state, and local governments are required to report financial data to other agencies at a higher level of authority and also to the citizenry. Formulation of governmental programs and policies on ecology, welfare, housing, education, taxation, and many other areas are influenced to a considerable extent by accounting data. Appraisal of the degree of success of such programs would be haphazard and incomplete without historical records in monetary terms. For similar reasons, churches, educational institutions, and other organizations must maintain records and report on their financial transactions.

BUSINESS ENTITY CONCEPT

Accounting always applies to an economic organization or unit in society. Economic units include profit-making enterprises; governmental units, such as states, cities, and school districts; consumers, such as families and individuals; and nonprofit organizations, such as churches, hospitals, and clubs. Each economic unit has business transactions that must be recorded, sorted, summarized, and reported. The accounting must therefore apply to each unit.

The *business entity* concept does not mean, however, that accounting data for a particular unit cannot be combined with data for other similar units to obtain an overall picture. For example, accounting data accumulated by each airline in the country may be assembled to provide financial information about the entire airline industry. Similarly, figures for national income may be developed from the accounting records of many separate economic units.

Although accounting principles and techniques have been developed for all types of economic units, this textbook emphasizes those applicable to profit-making business enterprises. Such enterprises may be organized in a variety of ways. The principal forms of organization are sole proprietorship, partnership, and corporation. A *sole proprietorship* is a business that is owned entirely by one individual. A *partnership* is an enterprise owned by two or more individuals in accordance with a contractual arrangement among them. A *corporation* is a separate legal entity, organized in accordance with state or federal statutes, in which ownership is divided into shares of stock. The principal difference among the three types of organization, from the standpoint of accounting, lies in the nature of the ownership and in the legal rights and responsibilities related to it.

BUSINESS TRANSACTIONS

A *business transaction* is the occurrence of an event or of a condition that must be recorded. For example, the payment of a monthly telephone bill of $25, the purchase of $500 of merchandise on credit, and the acquisition of land and a store building for $100,000 are illustrative of the variety of business transactions.

The first two transactions are relatively simple: a payment of money in exchange for a service, and a promise to pay within a short time in exchange for commodities. The purchase of a building and the land on which it is situated is usually a more complex transaction. The total price agreed upon must be allocated between the land and the building, and the agreement usually provides for spreading the payment of a substantial part of the price over a period of years and for the payment of interest on the unpaid balance. There may be other provisions designed to safeguard the seller until the full price has been paid that are a part of the initial transaction and must be recorded.

It can readily be seen that a particular business transaction may lead to an event or a condition that constitutes another transaction. For example, the purchase of merchandise on credit described above will be followed by payment to the creditor, which is another transaction; and each time a portion of the merchandise is sold, another transaction occurs. Similarly, partial payments for the land and the building constitute additional transactions, as do periodic payments of interest on the debt. Each of these events must be recorded.

The fact that the life of the building acquired in the illustrative transaction is limited must also be given recognition in the records. The wearing-out of the building is not an exchange of goods or services between the business and an outsider, but it is nevertheless a significant condition that must be recorded. Transactions of this type, as well as others not directly related to outsiders, are sometimes referred to as *internal* transactions.

10

The system of records begins with the recording of each transaction. There are many different methods of recording transactions. For example, a sale of a service for cash may be recorded by a handwritten sales ticket, or it may be recorded by merely depressing the appropriate keys of a cash register. Regardless of the recording system used, the historical data thus accumulated provide the basis for the preparation of various summarizing reports. In addition, the supporting documents and other forms of evidence furnish a basis for subsequent review and verification by internal auditors, independent CPAs, and others.

BUSINESS TRANSACTIONS AND MONETARY AMOUNTS

When properties or services are purchased by a business, they are recorded at the price agreed upon in the business transaction. For example, if a business building is purchased for $50,000, that amount is used in the buyer's accounting records. The seller may have been asking $60,000 for the building up to the time of sale; the buyer may have initially offered $40,000 for it; the building may have been assessed at $35,000 for property tax purposes and insured for $45,000; and the buyer may have received an offer of $75,000 for the building the day after he acquired it. These latter amounts have no effect on the accounting records because they do not originate from an exchange transaction. The transaction price, or cost, of $50,000 determines the monetary amount at which the building is recorded.

Continuing the illustration, the $75,000 offer received by the buyer is an indication that it was a bargain purchase at $50,000. To record the building at $75,000, however, would give recognition to an illusory or unrealized profit. If the purchaser should accept the offer and sell the building for $75,000, he would, of course, realize a profit of $25,000 and the new owner would record the building at its $75,000 cost.

The determination of costs incurred and revenues earned is fundamental to accounting. In transactions between buyer and seller, both attempt to obtain the most favorable price, and it is only the amount agreed upon that is sufficiently objective for accounting purposes. If the monetary amounts at which properties were recorded were constantly revised upward and downward on the basis of mere offers, appraisals, and opinions, accounting reports would soon become so unstable and unreliable as to be meaningless.

ASSETS, LIABILITIES, AND CAPITAL

It is customary to refer to the properties owned by a business enterprise as *assets* and to refer to the rights or claims to the properties as *equities*. If the assets owned by a business amount to $100,000, the equities

11

in the assets must also amount to $100,000. The relationship between the two may be stated in the form of an equation, as follows:

$$Assets = Equities$$

Equities may be subdivided into two principal types: the rights of creditors and the rights of owners. The equities of creditors represent *debts* of the business and are called *liabilities*. The equity of the owners is called *capital*, or *owner's equity*. Expansion of the equation to give recognition to the two basic types of equities yields the following, which is known as the *accounting equation*:

$$Assets = Liabilities + Capital$$

It is customary to place "Liabilities" before "Capital" in the accounting equation because creditors have preferential rights to the assets. The residual claim of the owner or owners is sometimes given greater emphasis by transposing liabilities to the other side of the equation, yielding:

$$Assets - Liabilities = Capital$$

All business transactions, from the simplest to the most complex, can be stated in terms of their effect on the three basic elements of the accounting equation.

TRANSACTIONS AND THE ACCOUNTING EQUATION

The effect of changes in assets, liabilities, and capital on the accounting equation can be demonstrated by studying some typical transactions. As the basis of the illustration, assume that John King establishes a sole proprietorship to be known as King Taxi. Each transaction or group of similar transactions during the first month of operations is described below, followed by an illustration of its effect on the accounting equation.

Transaction (a)

King's first transaction is to deposit $9,000 in a bank account in the name of King Taxi. The effect of this transaction is to increase the asset cash by $9,000 and to increase capital, on the other side of the equation, by the same amount. After the transaction the equation for King Taxi will appear as follows:

Assets	Capital
Cash	John King, Capital
(a) 9,000	9,000

It should be noted that the equation relates only to the business enterprise. King's personal assets, such as his home and his personal bank account, and his personal liabilities are excluded from consideration. The business is treated as a distinct entity, with cash of $9,000 and owner's equity of $9,000.

Transaction (b)

King's next transaction in establishing the business is to purchase automobiles and other equipment, for which $7,400 in cash is paid. This transaction changes the composition of the assets but does not change the total. The items in the equation prior to this transaction, the effects of this transaction, and the new balances after the transaction are as follows:

	Assets			Capital
	Cash	+	Equipment	John King, Capital
Bal.	9,000			9,000
(b)	−7,400		+7,400	
Bal.	1,600		7,400	9,000

Transaction (c)

During the month King purchases $650 of gasoline, oil, and other supplies from various suppliers, agreeing to pay in the near future. This type of transaction is called a purchase *on account* and the liability created is termed an *account payable*. In actual practice each purchase would be recorded as it occurred and a separate record would be maintained for each creditor. The effect of this group of transactions is to increase assets and liabilities by $650, as indicated below:

	Assets					Liabilities	+	Capital
						Accounts		John King,
	Cash	+	Supplies	+	Equipment	Payable	+	Capital
Bal.	1,600				7,400			9,000
(c)			+650			+650		
Bal.	1,600		650		7,400	650		9,000

Transaction (d)

During the month $300 is paid to creditors on account, thereby reducing both assets and liabilities. The effect on the equation is as follows:

	Assets					Liabilities	+	Capital
						Accounts		John King,
	Cash	+	Supplies	+	Equipment	Payable	+	Capital
Bal.	1,600		650		7,400	650		9,000
(d)	− 300					−300		
Bal.	1,300		650		7,400	350		9,000

The principal objective of the owner of a business enterprise is to increase his capital by earning a net income. For John King this means that the assets he acquires from the sale of services must exceed the cost of supplies used, salaries incurred, and all other expenses of operating the business. In general, the amount charged to customers for goods or

13

services sold to them is called *revenue*.[2] Alternative terms may be used for particular types of revenue, such as *sales* for the sale of merchandise or business services, *fees earned* for charges by a physician to his patient, *rent earned* for the use of real estate or other property, and *fares earned* for King Taxi.

The excess of the revenue over the expenses incurred in earning the revenue is called *net income*. If the expenses of the enterprise exceed the revenue, the excess is a *net loss*. As it is ordinarily impossible to determine the exact amount of expense incurred in connection with each revenue transaction, it is considered satisfactory to determine the net income or the net loss for a specified period of time, such as a month or a year, rather than for each sale or small group of sales.

Transaction (e)

During the first month of operations King Taxi earned fares of $2,000, receiving the amount in cash. The total effect of these transactions is to increase cash by $2,000 and to yield revenue in the same amount. The revenue can be viewed as though it effected a $2,000 increase in capital. At the time expenses of the business are incurred, they are treated as offsets against revenue and hence as reductions in capital. In terms of the accounting equation, the effect of the receipt of cash for services performed is as follows:

	Assets				Liabilities +	Capital
	Cash +	Supplies +	Equipment		Accounts + Payable	John King, Capital
Bal.	1,300	650	7,400	=	350	9,000
(e)	+2,000					+ 2,000 Fares earned
Bal.	3,300	650	7,400		350	11,000

Instead of requiring the payment of cash at the time goods or services are sold, a business may make sales *on account*, allowing the customer to pay later. In such cases the firm acquires a claim against the customer called an *account receivable*. It is as much an asset as cash, and the revenue is realized in exactly the same manner as if cash had been immediately received. At a later date, when the money is collected, there is only an exchange of one asset for another, cash increasing and accounts receivable decreasing.

Transaction (f)

Various business expenses incurred and paid during the month were as follows: wages, $550; rent, $50; utilities, $25; miscellaneous, $75. The effect of this group of transactions is to reduce cash and to reduce capital, as indicated in the following manner:

---

[2] *Accounting Research and Terminology Bulletins*, "No. 2, Proceeds, Revenue, Income, Profit, and Earnings" (New York: American Institute of Certified Public Accountants, 1961), p. 34.

	Assets				Liabilities +	Capital
	Cash +	Supplies +	Equipment		Accounts Payable	+ John King, Capital
Bal.	3,300	650	7,400		350	11,000
(f)	− 700			=		− 550 Wages exp.
						− 50 Rent expense
						− 25 Utilities exp.
						− 75 Misc. expense
Bal.	2,600	650	7,400		350	10,300

Transaction (g)

At the end of the month it is determined that the cost of the supplies on hand is $250, the remainder ($650 − $250) having been used in the operations of the business. This reduction of $400 in supplies and capital may be shown as follows:

	Assets				Liabilities +	Capital
	Cash +	Supplies +	Equipment		Accounts Payable	+ John King, Capital
Bal.	2,600	650	7,400	=	350	10,300
(g)		−400				− 400 Supplies exp.
Bal.	2,600	250	7,400		350	9,900

Transaction (h)

As was the case with supplies, the automobiles and other equipment were used in the operations of the business. In spite of such usage throughout the month there is no discernible reduction in the quantity of the equipment, as was the case with supplies. It is obvious, however, that equipment does wear out with usage and that, in any event, its utility decreases with the passage of time. This decrease in utility is a business expense, which is called *depreciation*. The determination of the amount of depreciation expense associated with specific items of equipment requires the careful exercise of judgment in evaluating many factors. A discussion of the intricacies involved is left to a later chapter.

The effect of the recognition of depreciation expense is to decrease both assets and capital. For reasons that will become apparent in a later chapter, it is considered to be more useful to maintain a cumulative record of the recognized depreciation than to deduct it directly from the equipment. The effect on the equation of the recognition of depreciation expense estimated at $200 is as follows:

	Assets					Liabilities +	Capital
	Cash +	Sup- plies +	Equip- ment −	Accumu- lated Depre- ciation		Accounts Payable	+ John King, Capital
Bal.	2,600	250	7,400		=	350	9,900
(h)				+200			− 200 Depr. exp.
Bal.	2,600	250	7,400	200		350	9,700

Although the equipment balance of $7,400 is unchanged, the remaining unexpired cost of the asset after recognition of the depreciation expense is clearly only $7,200, shown as follows:

Equipment $7,400
Less accumulated depreciation.... 200 $7,200

It should be noted that accumulated depreciation appears on the left side of the equation as a subtraction from assets. Therefore, the $200 increase in accumulated depreciation, which is in effect a decrease in assets, is matched by the $200 of depreciation expense, which is a decrease in capital.

Transaction (i)

At the end of the month King withdraws from the business $500 in cash for his personal use. This transaction, which effects a decrease in cash and a decrease in capital, is the exact opposite of an investment in the business by the owner. The withdrawal is not a business expense, and it should be excluded from consideration in determining the net income from operations of the enterprise. The balances in the equation, the effect of the $500 withdrawal, and the new balances are as follows:

				Assets	Accumulated Depreciation −	=	Liabilities + Accounts Payable	Capital + John King, Capital
		Cash +	Sup-plies +	Equip-ment −				
Bal.		2,600	250	7,400	200		350	9,700
(i)	−	500						− 500 Drawing
Bal.		2,100	250	7,400	200		350	9,200

SUMMARY OF ILLUSTRATION

The business transactions of King Taxi are summarized in tabular form at the top of the next page. The transactions are identified by letter, and the balance of each item is shown after each transaction. The following observations, which apply to all types of businesses, should be noted:

1. The effect of every transaction can be stated in terms of increases and/or decreases in one or more of the elements of the accounting equation.
2. The equality of the two sides of the accounting equation is always maintained.

ACCOUNTING STATEMENTS

The principal accounting statements of a sole proprietorship are the *balance sheet* and the *income statement*. They are usually accompanied by a less important, but nevertheless useful, statement called the *capital statement*. The nature of the data presented in each statement, in general terms, is presented on the next page.

	Assets				= Liabilities +	Capital	
	Cash +	Sup-plies +	Equip-ment −	Accumu-lated Depre-ciation =	Accounts Payable +	John King, Capital	
(a)	+9,000					+ 9,000	
(b)	−7,400		+7,400				
	1,600		7,400			9,000	
(c)		+650			+650		
	1,600	650	7,400		650	9,000	
(d)	− 300				−300		
	1,300	650	7,400		350	9,000	
(e)	+2,000					+ 2,000	Fares earned
	3,300	650	7,400		350	11,000	
(f)	− 700					− 550	Wages exp.
						− 50	Rent expense
						− 25	Utilities exp.
						− 75	Misc. expense
	2,600	650	7,400		350	10,300	
(g)		−400				− 400	Supplies exp.
	2,600	250	7,400		350	9,900	
(h)				+200		− 200	Depr. expense
	2,600	250	7,400	200	350	9,700	
(i)	− 500					− 500	Drawing
	2,100	250	7,400	200	350	9,200	

Balance sheet

A list of the assets, liabilities, and capital of a business entity as of a specific date, usually at the close of the last day of a month.

Income statement

A summary of the revenue and the expenses of a business entity for a specific period of time, such as a month or a year.

Capital statement

A summary of the changes in capital of a business entity that have occurred during a specific period of time, such as a month or a year.

The basic features of the three statements and their interrelationships are illustrated on page 19. The data for the statements were taken from the summary of transactions of King Taxi presented in the preceding section.

An additional statement, often referred to as the *funds* statement or more formally as the *statement of changes in financial position*, is also useful in appraising a business enterprise. In recent years CPAs have considered it to be an essential part of financial reports to owners and creditors.[3] The preparation and interpretation of the funds statement will be considered in a later chapter after various basic concepts and principles have been explained and illustrated.

All financial statements should be identified by the name of the business, the title of the statement, and the date or period of time. The

17

---

[3] *Opinions of the Accounting Principles Board, No. 19,* "Reporting Changes in Financial Position" (New York: American Institute of Certified Public Accountants, 1971), par. 7.

data presented in the balance sheet are for a specific date; the data presented in the income statement, the capital statement, and the funds statement are for a period of time.

The use of indentions, captions, dollar signs, and rulings in the financial statements should be noted. They are employed to accentuate the several distinct sections of the various statements.

Balance sheet. The amounts of King Taxi's assets, liabilities, and capital at the end of the first month of operations appear on the last line of the summary on page 17. Minor rearrangements of these data and the addition of a heading yield the balance sheet illustrated on page 19. This form of balance sheet, with the liability and capital sections presented below the asset section, is called the *report form*. Another arrangement in common use lists the assets on the left and the liabilities and capital on the right. Because of its similarity to the account, a basic accounting device described in the next chapter, it is referred to as the *account form* of balance sheet.

It is customary to begin the asset section with cash, which is followed by receivables, supplies, and other assets, such as prepaid expenses, that will be converted into cash or consumed in the near future. The assets of a relatively permanent nature, such as equipment, buildings, and land, follow in that order.

In the liabilities and capital section of the balance sheet, it is customary to present the liabilities first, followed by capital. In the illustration on page 19 the liabilities are composed entirely of accounts payable. When there are two or more categories of liabilities, each should be listed and the total amount of liabilities presented in the following manner:

LIABILITIES

Notes payable..........................	$ 600
Accounts payable......................	1,500
Salaries payable.......................	100
Total liabilities.......................	$2,200

Income statement. Revenue earned and expenses incurred during the month were recorded in the equation as increases and decreases in capital, respectively. The details, together with net income in the amount of $700, are reported in the income statement on page 19.

The order in which the operating expenses are presented in the income statement varies among businesses. One of the arrangements commonly followed is to list them approximately in the order of size, beginning with the larger items. Miscellaneous expense is usually shown as the last item regardless of the relative magnitude of the item.

Capital statement. Comparison of the original investment of $9,000 at the beginning of the month with the $9,200 of capital reported in the

King Taxi
Balance Sheet
August 31, 1973

Assets				
Cash			$2 1 0 0 00	
Supplies			2 5 0 00	
Equipment	$7 4 0 0 00			
Less accumulated depreciation	2 0 0 00		7 2 0 0 00	
Total assets			$9 5 5 0 00	
Liabilities				
Accounts payable			$ 3 5 0 00	
Capital				
John King, capital			9 2 0 0 00	
Total liabilities and capital			$9 5 5 0 00	

Balance sheet —
sole proprietorship

19

King Taxi
Income Statement
For Month Ended August 31, 1973

Fares earned			$2 0 0 0 00	
Operating expenses:				
Wages expense	$ 5 5 0 00			
Supplies expense	4 0 0 00			
Depreciation expense	2 0 0 00			
Rent expense	5 0 00			
Utilities expense	2 5 00			
Miscellaneous expense	7 5 00			
Total operating expenses			1 3 0 0 00	
Net income			$ 7 0 0 00	

Income
statement

King Taxi
Capital Statement
For Month Ended August 31, 1973

Capital, August 1, 1973			$9 0 0 0 00	
Net income for the month	$ 7 0 0 00			
Less withdrawals	5 0 0 00			
Increase in capital			2 0 0 00	
Capital, August 31, 1973			$9 2 0 0 00	

Capital
statement

balance sheet at the end of the month reveals an increase in capital of $200. This net increase is composed of two significant changes in capital that occurred during the period: (1) net income of $700 and (2) withdrawals of $500 by the owner. This information is presented in the capital statement on page 19, which serves as a connecting link between the two principal statements.

Statements for corporations. Business enterprises with large aggregations of assets are usually organized as corporations with many stockholders. The corporate form is available, however, to small enterprises with a limited number of stockholders. If King Taxi had been organized as a corporation with ownership represented by shares of stock, its balance sheet at the end of the first month of operations would appear as follows:

King Taxi
Balance Sheet
August 31, 1973

Assets			
Cash			$2,100.00
Supplies			250.00
Equipment	$7,400.00		
Less accumulated depreciation	200.00	7,200.00	
Total assets			$9,550.00
Liabilities			
Accounts payable			$ 350.00
Capital			
Capital stock	$9,000.00		
Retained earnings	200.00		
Total capital		9,200.00	
Total liabilities and capital			$9,550.00

Balance sheet —
corporation

The only differences between the balance sheet above and the one illustrated on page 19 occur in the capital section. It is customary on corporation balance sheets to differentiate between the investment of the stockholders ($9,000) and the accumulated earnings retained in the business ($200). Also, the identity of the owners (stockholders) is not disclosed on corporation balance sheets.

The form of income statement employed by corporate enterprises is similar to the form applicable to sole proprietorships.

The report of changes in the capital of a corporation follows a somewhat different pattern from that of the capital statement of a sole proprietorship. In corporate enterprises the emphasis is on the changes in retained earnings that have occurred during the period. Such changes are reported in a "retained earnings" statement. If there have been

King Taxi
Retained Earnings Statement
For Month Ended August 31, 1973

Net income for the month			#	7	0	0	00
Less dividends				5	0	0	00
Retained earnings, August 31, 1973			#	2	0	0	00

Retained
earnings
statement

significant changes in capital stock during a period, such data should be reported in a separate additional statement. The details of minor changes in capital stock need not be reported.

Distributions of earnings to owners (stockholders) are called *dividends* rather than drawings or withdrawals and are so identified on the retained earnings statement above. Having been in existence only one month, King Taxi had no retained earnings at the beginning of the period. For subsequent periods there would normally be a beginning balance of retained earnings, and the usual format of the body of such a statement would conform to the following:

Retained earnings, January 1, 1974...................		$3,100
Net income for six months...................	$4,300	
Less dividends.............................	1,000	
Increase in retained earnings........................		3,300
Retained earnings, June 30, 1974....................		$6,400

QUESTIONS

1. Why is a knowledge of accounting concepts and terminology useful to all individuals engaged in business activities?

2. Distinguish between public accounting and private accounting.

3. Describe in general terms the requirements that an individual must meet to become a CPA.

4. Name some of the specialized fields of accounting activity.

5. What are the three principal forms of profit-making business organizations and in what principal respect do they differ, so far as accounting is concerned?

6. In what way are accounting reports of past performance useful to the owner or manager in making plans for the future?

7. What is meant by the *business entity* concept?

8. Discuss the meanings of the terms *business transaction* and *internal transaction*.

9. (a) Land with an assessed value of $25,000 for property tax purposes is acquired by a business enterprise for $35,000. At what amount should the land be recorded by the purchaser?

(b) Five years later the plot of land in (a) has an assessed value of $45,000 and the business enterprise receives an offer of $75,000 for it. Should the monetary amount assigned to the land on the business records now be increased and, if so, by what amount?

10. (a) An enterprise has assets of $40,000 and capital of $25,000. What is the total amount of its liabilities?
(b) An enterprise has liabilities of $20,000 and capital of $40,000. What is the total amount of its assets?
(c) An enterprise has assets of $25,000 and liabilities of $5,000. What is the amount of its capital?
(d) A corporation has assets of $200,000, liabilities of $50,000, and capital stock of $80,000. What is the amount of its retained earnings?

11. If a particular transaction increases a specific asset, what is the possible effect of the transaction on (a) other assets, (b) liabilities, (c) capital?

12. Apex Decorators completed a $4,000 painting contract in May for which they received full payment in June. (a) In which month was the revenue earned? (b) What was the effect of the receipt of the $4,000 in cash on the three elements in the accounting equation?

13. (a) A vacant lot acquired for $12,000, on which there is a balance owed of $2,000, is sold for $15,000 in cash. What is the effect of the sale on the total amount of the seller's (1) assets, (2) liabilities, (3) capital?
(b) After receiving the $15,000 cash in (a) the seller pays the $2,000 owed. What is the effect of the payment on the total amount of the seller's (1) assets, (2) liabilities, (3) capital?

14. Operations of a service enterprise for a particular month are summarized as follows:

Service sales: on account, $13,000; for cash, $8,000
Expenses incurred: on account, $6,000; for cash, $7,000

What was the amount of the enterprise's (a) revenue, (b) expenses, and (c) net income?

15. Financial statements are prepared for a sole proprietorship as of the end of September, the first month of operations. State whether the information reported is as of September 30 or for the entire month of September on the (a) income statement, (b) balance sheet, (c) capital statement.

16. What particular item of financial or operating data of a service enterprise, organized as a corporation, appears on (a) both the income statement and the retained earnings statement, and (b) both the balance sheet and the retained earnings statement?

17. If total assets have decreased by $2,000 during a period of time and capital has increased by $9,000 during the same period, what was the amount and direction (increase or decrease) of the period's change in total liabilities?

18. What is the term applied to distributions of earnings of a corporation to its stockholders?

19. The income statement of a sole proprietorship for the month of November indicates a net income of $2,000. During the same period the owner withdrew $2,500 in cash from the business for personal use. Would it be correct to say that the owner incurred a *net loss* of $500 during the month? Discuss.

20. If the total liabilities of the enterprise in Question 19 increased by $4,500 during the same month, and the owner made no additional investments in the business, what was the amount and direction of change (increase or decrease) in total assets during the month?

EXERCISES

1-1. The following selected transactions were completed during the month of October by a service enterprise organized as a sole proprietorship:

(1) Paid rent for October, $400.
(2) Purchased equipment on account, $2,000.
(3) Purchased supplies for cash, $150.
(4) Purchased a car for cash for the personal (rather than business) use of the owner of the enterprise, $2,700.
(5) Received cash from cash customers, $610.
(6) Charged customers for services sold on account, $390.
(7) Paid creditors on account, $700.
(8) Received cash on account from charge customers, $200.
(9) Paid cash to owner for personal use, $300.
(10) Determined by taking an inventory that $95 of supplies had been used during the month.

Indicate the effect of each transaction on the accounting equation by listing the numbers identifying the transactions, (1) through (10), in a vertical column, and inserting at the right of each number the appropriate letter from the following list:

(a) Increase in one asset, decrease in another asset.
(b) Increase in an asset, increase in a liability.
(c) Increase in an asset, increase in capital.
(d) Decrease in an asset, decrease in a liability.
(e) Decrease in an asset, decrease in capital.

1-2. Dexter Corporation, engaged in a service business, completed the following selected transactions during the period:

(1) Charged customers for services sold on account.
(2) Paid a creditor on account.
(3) Issued additional capital stock, receiving cash.
(4) Paid telephone expense.
(5) Purchased equipment on account.
(6) Paid cash dividends to stockholders.
(7) Returned defective equipment originally purchased on account and not yet paid for.
(8) Received cash on account from charge customers.
(9) Paid cash to a customer to correct an overcharge for services.
(10) Estimated depreciation for the month.

Using a tabular form with four column headings entitled Transaction, Assets, Liabilities, and Capital, respectively, indicate the effect of each transaction, using + for increase and − for decrease.

1-3. Summary financial data for April of a sole proprietorship engaged in a service business are presented in equation form on the next page. Each line designated by a number indicates the effect of a transaction on the equation. Each increase and decrease in capital affects net income except transaction (8).

(a) Describe each transaction.
(b) What is the amount of net decrease in cash during the month?
(c) What is the amount of net increase in capital during the month?
(d) What is the amount of the net income for the month?
(e) How much of the net income of the month was retained in the business?

23

	Cash	+ Supplies	+ Equipment	Accumulated − Depreciation	= Liabilities	+ Capital
Bal.	2,500	1,000	6,000	1,500	= 1,200	6,800
(1)	− 400		+ 400			
(2)		+ 100			+ 100	
(3)	+1,900					+1,900
(4)	− 700				− 700	
(5)	− 500					− 500
(6)		− 300				− 300
(7)				+ 100		− 100
(8)	− 400					− 400
Bal.	2,400	800	6,400	1,600	600	7,400

1-4. Summary balance sheet data, exclusive of the amount of capital, for four different sole proprietorships, A, B, C, and D, at the beginning and end of a year are as follows:

	Total Assets	Total Liabilities
Beginning of the year.	$ 85,000	$20,000
End of the year......	100,000	10,000

On the basis of the above data and the additional information for the year presented below, determine the net income (or loss) of each company for the year. (Suggestion: First determine the amount of increase or decrease in capital during the year.)

Company A: The owner had made no additional investments in the business and no withdrawals from the business.

Company B: The owner had made no additional investments in the business but had withdrawn $11,000.

Company C: The owner had made an additional investment of $28,000 but had made no withdrawals.

Company D: The owner had made an additional investment of $10,000 and had withdrawn $18,000.

1-5. Cummings Corporation manufactures a product at a unit cost of 60 cents and sells it at a unit price of $1. Annual sales have averaged 1,000,000 units and total annual operating expenses have been approximately $220,000. On the basis of a study of markets, costs, and expenses it is concluded (1) that reduction of the selling price to 90 cents would result in a 50% increase in the number of units sold, (2) that a 50% increase in production would result in a cost reduction of 6 cents a unit, (3) that a 50% increase in volume would be accompanied by a 25% increase in operating expenses, and (4) that the increased volume would not necessitate the investment of additional funds in the business.

Assuming the correctness of the study, determine whether the reduction in price would increase or decrease net income and the amount, presenting your report in tabular form. (Suggestion: First present data for current operations, in the form of an income statement, followed by data for proposed operations, in similar format.)

PROBLEMS

The following additional problems for this chapter are located in Appendix B: 1-2B, 1-3B.

1-1A. On November 1 of the current year Carl Holt established an enterprise under the name Holt Realty. Transactions completed during the month were as follows:

(a) Opened a business bank account with a deposit of $2,000.
(b) Paid office rent for the month, $200.
(c) Purchased equipment (desk, chairs, filing cabinet, etc.) for $1,500, paying cash of $900, with the balance on account.
(d) Purchased supplies (stationery, stamps, pencils, ink, etc.) for cash, $80.
(e) Earned sales commissions, receiving cash, $1,200.
(f) Paid creditor on account, $150.
(g) Paid automobile expenses (including rental charge) for month, $120, and miscellaneous expenses, $75.
(h) Paid cash to Holt for personal use, $300.
(i) Estimated depreciation on the equipment to be $30.
(j) Determined by taking an inventory that the cost of supplies used was $8.

Instructions:

(1) Record the transactions and the balances after each transaction, using the following tabular headings:

Assets				Liabilities		Capital
			Accumulated	= Accounts	+	Carl Holt,
Cash +	Supplies +	Equipment −	Depreciation	Payable		Capital

Indicate the nature of each increase and decrease in capital subsequent to the initial investment by appropriate notations at the right of each change.

(2) Prepare an income statement for November, a capital statement for November, and a balance sheet as of November 30.

1-2A. On January 1, the *beginning* of the current year, Lane Corporation had capital stock of $50,000 and retained earnings of $29,000. During the year the corporation paid cash dividends of $20,000. The amounts of the corporation's assets and liabilities at December 31, the *end* of the current year, and of its revenue and expenses for the year ended on that date are as stated below, listed in alphabetical order.

Accounts payable......................	$ 4,720
Accounts receivable....................	10,610
Accumulated depreciation — building....	2,710
Accumulated depreciation — equipment..	3,240
Advertising expense....................	3,940
Building...............................	59,600
Cash..................................	7,440
Depreciation expense — building.........	990
Depreciation expense — equipment.......	1,310
Equipment.............................	17,820
Insurance expense.....................	870
Land..................................	5,300
Miscellaneous expense.................	1,320

25

Prepaid insurance......................	1,850
Salaries payable.......................	460
Salary expense........................	30,210
Sales.................................	85,360
Supplies..............................	1,350
Supplies expense......................	1,920
Taxes expense........................	10,800
Taxes payable........................	2,310
Utilities expense.....................	2,470

Instructions:

(1) Prepare an income statement for the current year ending December 31, exercising care to include each item of expense listed.
(2) Prepare a retained earnings statement for the current year ending December 31.
(3) Prepare a balance sheet as of December 31 of the current year. There was no change in the amount of capital stock during the year.

1-3A. B. J. Shaw operates a sole proprietorship known as Aladdin Dry Cleaners. The actual work of dry cleaning is done by another company at wholesale rates. The assets and the liabilities of the business on June 1 of the current year are as follows: Cash, $1,600; Accounts Receivable, $450; Supplies, $80; Equipment, $5,100; Accumulated Depreciation, $800; Accounts Payable, $970. Business transactions during June are summarized below.

(a) Paid rent for the month, $180.
(b) Purchased supplies on account, $50.
(c) Received cash from cash customers for dry cleaning sales, $1,800.
(d) Paid creditors on account, $810.
(e) Charged customers for dry cleaning sales on account, $590.
(f) Received monthly invoice for dry cleaning expense for June (to be paid on July 10), $1,070.
(g) Paid the following: wages expense, $250; truck expense, $70; utilities expense, $40; miscellaneous expense, $60.
(h) Purchased an item of equipment on account, $150.
(i) Received cash from customers on account, $510.
(j) Paid personal expenses by checks drawn on the business, $320, and withdrew $150 in cash for personal use.
(k) Reimbursed a customer $60 for a garment lost by the cleaning company, which agreed to deduct the amount from the invoice received in transaction (f).
(l) Determined by taking an inventory the cost of supplies used during the month, $15.
(m) Estimated depreciation of truck and other equipment for the month, $85.

Instructions:

(1) State the assets, liabilities, and capital as of June 1 in equation form similar to that shown in this chapter.
(2) Record, in tabular form below the equation, the increases and decreases resulting from each transaction, indicating the new balances after each transaction. Explain the nature of each increase and

decrease in capital by an appropriate notation at the right of the amount.

(3) Prepare (a) an income statement, (b) a capital statement, and (c) a balance sheet.

1-4A. City Parcel Service, Inc., was organized as a corporation on October 1 of the current year. The transactions of the business enterprise for its first three months, ending on December 31, are summarized below.

(a) Received and deposited in a bank account cash
    received from stockholders for capital stock.... $25,000

(b) Purchased a delivery service that had been operating as a sole proprietorship, in accordance with details presented below.

Assets acquired by the corporation:

Accounts receivable......................	$ 4,500	
Truck supplies........................	900	
Office supplies........................	100	
Trucks...............................	20,000	$25,500

Liabilities assumed by the corporation:

Accounts payable.......................		2,000

Payment to be made as follows:

Cash....................................	$19,500	
Two non-interest-bearing notes payable of $2,000 each, due at three-month intervals..	4,000	$23,500

(c) Charged parcel service sales to customers on account.................................	$21,000
(d) Purchased truck supplies on account..........	2,800
(e) Purchased office supplies for cash............	150
(f) Received cash from customers on account.....	17,900
(g) Paid creditors on account....................	3,000
(h) Paid first of the two notes payable...........	2,000
(i) Paid taxes in advance......................	800
(j) Paid insurance premiums in advance.........	960
(k) Purchased truck supplies on account..........	220
(l) Paid wages expense........................	7,700
(m) Paid rent expense.........................	600
(n) Paid utilities expense......................	190
(o) Paid repairs expense.......................	420
(p) Paid miscellaneous expenses.................	135
(q) Paid cash dividends to stockholders...........	2,000
(r) Truck supplies used........................	1,620
(s) Office supplies used........................	25
(t) Depreciation of trucks......................	950
(u) Insurance expired.........................	510
(v) Taxes expired.............................	200

27

Instructions:

(1) List the following captions in a single line at the top of a sheet turned sideways.

Cash	+	Accounts Receivable	+	Truck Supplies	+	Office Supplies	+	Prepaid Insurance	+	Prepaid Taxes	+	Trucks

−	Accumulated Depreciation	=	Notes Payable	+	Accounts Payable	+	Capital Stock	+	Retained Earnings	Retained Earnings Notations

(2) Record the original investment in the corporation and the remaining transactions in the appropriate columns, identifying each by letter. Indicate increases by + and decreases by −. *Do not determine the new balances of the items after each transaction.* In the space for retained earnings notations, identify each revenue and expense item and dividends paid to stockholders.

(3) Insert the final balances in each column and determine that the equation is in balance at December 31, the end of the period.

(4) Prepare the following: (a) income statement for the three months, (b) retained earnings statement for the three months, and (c) balance sheet as of December 31.

Chapter 2

THE ACCOUNTING CYCLE

RECORDING TRANSACTIONS

The nature of transactions and their effect on business enterprises were illustrated in the preceding chapter by the use of the accounting equation, Assets = Liabilities + Capital (+ Revenues − Expenses). Although transactions can be analyzed and recorded in terms of their effect on the equation, such a format is not practicable as a design for actual accounting systems.

The transactions completed by an enterprise during a fiscal period may effect increases and decreases in a great many different asset, liability, capital, revenue, and expense items. In order to have day-to-day information available when needed and to be able to prepare timely periodic financial statements, it is necessary to maintain a separate record for each different item. For example, it is necessary to have a form devoted solely to recording increases and decreases in cash, another form devoted exclusively to recording increases and decreases in supplies, another devoted to equipment, etc. The form traditionally used for this purpose is called an *account.* A group of related accounts that comprise a complete unit, such as all of the accounts of a specific business enterprise, is referred to as a *ledger*.

Familiarity with the manner in which increases and decreases are recorded in accounts is prerequisite to an understanding of the system known as double-entry accounting.

NATURE OF AN ACCOUNT

The simplest form of an account has three parts: (1) a title, which is the name of the item recorded in the account; (2) a space for recording increases in the amount of the item, in terms of money; and (3) a space for recording decreases in the amount of the item, also in monetary terms. This form of an account, illustrated on the next page, is known as a *T account* because of its similarity to the letter T.

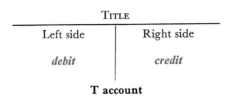

	TITLE	
Left side		Right side
debit		*credit*

T account

The left side of the account is called the *debit* side and the right side is called the *credit* side.[1] The word *charge* is sometimes used as a synonym for debit. Amounts entered on the left side of an account, regardless of the account title, are called *debits* or *charges* to the account, and the account is said to be *debited* or *charged*. Amounts entered on the right side of an account are called *credits*, and the account is said to be *credited*.

	CASH	
	3,000	500
	2,500	1,000
	4,000	2,500
4,300	*9,500*	300
		900
		5,200

In the illustration at the left, receipts of cash during a period of time have been listed vertically on the debit side of the cash account. The cash payments for the same period have been listed in similar fashion on the credit side of the account. A memorandum total of the cash receipts for the period to date may be inserted below the last debit at any time the information is desired. The figures should be small, and written in pencil, in order to avoid mistaking the amount for an additional debit. (The procedure is sometimes referred to as *pencil footing*.) The total of the cash payments may be inserted on the credit side in a similar manner. Subtraction of the smaller sum from the larger, $9,500 — $5,200, in the illustration, yields the amount of cash on hand, which is called the *balance* of the account. The cash account in the illustration has a balance of $4,300, which may be inserted in pencil figures next to the larger pencil footing, which identifies it as a *debit balance*. If a balance sheet were to be prepared at this time, the amount of cash reported thereon would be $4,300.

RELATIONSHIP OF ACCOUNTS TO THE BALANCE SHEET

The manner of recording data in the accounts, and the relationship of accounts to the balance sheet are presented below and on page 31.

Assume that H. T. Ross establishes a business venture, to be known as Ross TV Service, by initially depositing $3,200 cash in a bank account for the use of the enterprise. Immediately after the deposit, the balance sheet for the business, in account form, would contain the following information:

Assets		Capital	
Cash......................	$3,200	H. T. Ross, capital...........	$3,200

[1]Often abbreviated as *Dr.* for "debit" and *Cr.* for "credit," derived from the Latin *debere* and *credere*.

The effect of the transaction on accounts in the ledger can be described as a $3,200 debit to Cash and a $3,200 credit to H. T. Ross, Capital. The information can also be stated in a formalized manner by listing the title of the account and the amount to be debited, followed by a similar listing, below and to the right of the debit, of the title of the account and the amount to be credited. This form of presentation is called a *journal entry*, and is illustrated as follows:

Cash..	3,200
H. T. Ross, Capital.......................................	3,200

The data in the journal entry are transferred to the appropriate accounts by a process known as *posting*. The accounts after posting the above journal entry appear as follows:

CASH	H. T. ROSS, CAPITAL
3,200	3,200

Note that the amount of the cash, which is reported on the left side of the account form of balance sheet, is posted to the left (debit) side of Cash. The owner's equity in the business, which is reported on the right side of the balance sheet is posted to the right (credit) side of H. T. Ross, Capital. When other assets are acquired, the increases will be recorded as debits to the appropriate accounts; and as capital is increased or liabilities are incurred, the increases will be recorded as credits.

For the second illustration assume that after opening the checking account Ross purchased equipment and tools at a cost of $2,400. He paid $1,400 in cash and agreed to pay the remaining $1,000 within thirty days. After this transaction the data reported in the balance sheet would be as follows:

Assets		Liabilities	
Cash......................	$1,800	Accounts payable.............	$1,000
Equipment.................	2,400	Capital	
		H. T. Ross, capital............	3,200
Total assets..................	$4,200	Total liabilities and capital.....	$4,200

The effect of the transaction can be described as a $2,400 debit (increase) to Equipment, a $1,400 credit (decrease) to Cash and a $1,000 credit (increase) to Accounts Payable. The same information can be presented in the form of the journal entry appearing below. (An entry composed of two or more debits or of two or more credits is called a *compound journal entry*.)

Equipment..	2,400	
Cash..		1,400
Accounts Payable....................................		1,000

After the journal entry for the second transaction has been posted, the accounts of Ross TV Service appear as follows:

CASH		ACCOUNTS PAYABLE	
3,200	1,400		1,000

EQUIPMENT		H. T. ROSS, CAPITAL	
2,400			3,200

Note that the effect of the transaction was to increase one asset account, decrease another asset account, and increase a liability account. Note also that although the amounts, $2,400, $1,400, and $1,000, are different, the equality of debits and credits was maintained.

CLASSIFICATION OF ACCOUNTS

Accounts in the ledger are customarily classified according to a common characteristic: assets, liabilities, capital, revenues, and expenses. In addition there may be subgroupings within the major categories. The classifications and accounts characteristically employed by a small service enterprise are described in the paragraphs that follow. Additional classes and accounts are introduced in later chapters.

ASSETS. Any physical thing (tangible) or right (intangible) that has a money value is an asset. Assets are customarily divided into distinctive groups for presentation on the balance sheet. The two groups occurring most frequently are (1) *current assets* and (2) *plant assets*. These two categories and the most common individual accounts in each are discussed in the paragraphs that follow.

Current assets. Cash and other assets that may reasonably be expected to be realized in cash or sold or consumed usually within a year or less through the normal operations of the business are called *current assets*. In addition to cash, the assets in this group usually owned by a service business are notes receivable and accounts receivable, and supplies and other prepaid expenses.

Cash is any medium of exchange that a bank will accept at face value; it includes bank deposits, currency, checks, bank drafts, and money orders. *Notes receivable* are claims against debtors evidenced by a written promise to pay a certian sum in money at a definite time to the order of a specified person or to bearer. *Accounts receivable* are claims against debtors, less formal than notes, that arise from sales of services or merchandise on account. *Prepaid expenses* include supplies on hand and advance payments of expenses such as insurance and property taxes.

Plant assets. Tangible assets used in the business that are of a relatively fixed or permanent nature are called *plant assets* or *fixed assets*. With the exception of land, such assets gradually wear out or otherwise lose their usefulness with the passage of time; they are said to *depreciate*. The amount of *depreciation expense* of an accounting period cannot be determined with the same degree of exactitude that applies to many other types of expense. Some of the methods of computing depreciation, which are described in a later chapter, require the use of the original cost of a plant asset over its entire life. The original cost is also required in preparing income tax and other reports. Accordingly, it is customary to record the decrease in plant assets as credits in *accumulated depreciation* accounts rather than in the plant asset accounts.

Typical titles for accounts in this category are: Equipment, Accumulated Depreciation — Equipment, Buildings, Accumulated Depreciation — Buildings, and Land. Instead of a single account for equipment or buildings, additional accounts may be employed, based on function, such as Delivery Equipment, Store Equipment, and Office Equipment, with related accounts for accumulated depreciation.

LIABILITIES. Liabilities are debts owed to outsiders (creditors) and are frequently described on the balance sheet by titles that include the word "payable." The two categories occurring most frequently are: (1) *current liabilities* and (2) *long-term liabilities*.

Current liabilities. Liabilities that will be due within a short time (usually one year or less) and that are to be paid out of current assets are called *current liabilities*. The most common liabilities in this group are *notes payable* and *accounts payable*, which are exactly like their receivable counterparts except that the debtor-creditor relationship is reversed. Other current liability accounts commonly found in the ledger are Salaries Payable, Interest Payable, and Taxes Payable.

Long-term liabilities. Liabilities that will not be due for a comparatively long time (usually more than one year) are called *long-term liabilities* or *fixed liabilities*. As they come within the one-year range and are to be paid, such liabilities become current. If the obligation is to be renewed rather than paid at maturity, however, it would continue to be classed as long-term. When payment of a long-term debt is to be spread over a number of years, the installments due within one year from a balance sheet date are classed as a current liability. When notes are accompanied by security in the form of a mortgage, the obligation may be referred to as *mortgage notes payable* or *mortgage payable*.

CAPITAL. *Capital* is the term applied to the owner's equity in the business. It is a residual claim against the assets of the business after the total liabilities are deducted. Other commonly used terms for capital are

33

owner's equity and *net worth* (*stockholders' equity, shareholders' equity,* and *shareholders' investment* in referring to a corporation).

REVENUE. *Revenue* is the gross increase in capital attributable to business activities. It results from the sale of merchandise, the performance of services for a customer or a client, the rental of property, the lending of money, and other business and professional activities entered into for the purpose of earning income. Revenue from sales of merchandise or sales of services are often identified merely as *sales*. Other terms employed to identify sources of revenue include *professional fees, commissions revenue, fares earned,* and *interest income.* If an enterprise has different types of revenue, a separate account should be maintained for each.

EXPENSE. Costs that have been consumed in the process of producing revenue are *expired costs* or *expenses*. The number of expense categories and individual expense accounts maintained in the ledger varies with the nature and the size of an enterprise. A large business with authority and responsibility spread among many employees may use an elaborate classification and hundreds of accounts as an aid in controlling expenses. For a small service business of the type assumed here, a modest number of expense accounts is satisfactory.

34

DEBIT AND CREDIT

Balance sheet accounts. Earlier in the chapter it was observed that the left side of asset accounts is used for recording increases and the right side is used for recording decreases. It was also observed that the right side of liability and capital accounts is used to record increases. It naturally follows that the left side of such accounts is used to record decreases. The left side of all accounts, whether asset, liability, or capital, is called *debit* and the right side is called *credit*. Consequently, a debit may signify either an increase or a decrease, depending on the nature of the account, and a credit may likewise signify either increase or decrease, depending on the nature of the account. The rules of debit and credit may therefore be stated as follows:

DEBIT may signify:	**CREDIT** may signify:
Increase in asset accounts	Decrease in asset accounts
Decrease in liability accounts	Increase in liability accounts
Decrease in capital accounts	Increase in capital accounts

The rules of debit and credit may also be stated in relationship to the accounting equation and the account form of balance sheet as in the diagram at the top of the next page.

Every business transaction affects a minimum of two accounts. Regardless of the complexity of a transaction or the number of accounts affected, the sum of the debits is always equal to the sum of the credits.

BALANCE SHEET

ASSETS	LIABILITIES

ASSET ACCOUNTS		LIABILITY ACCOUNTS	
Debit for increases	Credit for decreases	Debit for decreases	Credit for increases

CAPITAL

CAPITAL ACCOUNTS	
Debit for decreases	Credit for increases

This equality of debit and credit for each transaction is inherent in the equation $A = L + C$. It is also because of this duality that the system is known as "double-entry accounting."

Income statement accounts. The theory of debit and credit in its application to revenue and expense accounts is based on the relationship of these accounts to capital. The net income or the net loss for a period, as reported on the income statement, is the net increase or the net decrease in capital resulting from operations.

Revenue increases capital; and just as increases in capital are recorded as credits, increases in revenues during an accounting period are recorded as credits.

Expenses have the effect of decreasing capital; and just as decreases in capital are recorded as debits, increases in expense accounts are recorded as debits. Although debits to expense accounts signify *decreases in capital*, they may also be referred to as *increases in expense*. The usual practice is to consider debits to expense accounts in the positive sense (increases in expense) rather than in the negative sense (decreases in capital). The rules of debit and credit as applied to revenue and expense accounts are shown in the diagram below.

CAPITAL ACCOUNTS

DEBIT *Decreases in capital*		CREDIT *Increases in capital*	
EXPENSE ACCOUNTS		REVENUE ACCOUNTS	
Debit for increases	Credit for decreases	Debit for decreases	Credit for increases

At the end of an accounting period the revenue and expense account balances are reported in the income statement. Periodically, usually at

35

the end of the accounting year, all revenue and expense account balances are transferred to a summarizing account and the accounts are then said to be *closed*. The balance in the summarizing account, which is the net income or net loss for the period, is then transferred to the capital account (to the retained earnings account of a corporation), and the summarizing account is also closed. Because of this periodic closing of these accounts, they are sometimes called *temporary capital* or *nominal* accounts. The balances of the accounts reported in the balance sheet are carried forward from year to year and because of their greater permanence are sometimes referred to as *real* accounts.

Drawing account. The owner of a successful enterprise organized as a sole proprietorship may from time to time withdraw cash from the business for his personal use. It is the customary practice if the owner devotes full time to the business or if the business is his principal source of income. Such withdrawals are recorded as debits to an account bearing the owner's name followed by *Drawing* or *Personal*. Debits to the account may be considered either as decreases in capital (negative sense) or as increases in drawings (positive sense).

Dividends account. The dividends account of a corporation is comparable to the drawing account of a sole proprietorship. Distributions of earnings to the stockholders are debited to *Dividends*, and the account is periodically closed to the retained earnings account. Debits to the account may be regarded either as decreases in capital (negative sense) or as increases in dividends (positive sense).

Normal balances. The sum of the increases recorded in an account is customarily equal to or greater than the sum of the decreases recorded in the account; consequently, the normal balances of all accounts are positive rather than negative. For example, the total debits (increases) in an asset account will ordinarily be greater than the total credits (decreases); thus, asset accounts normally have debit balances. It is entirely possible, of course, for the debits and the credits in an account to be equal, in which case the account is said to be *in balance*.

The rules of debit and credit, and the normal balances of the various types of accounts are summarized below. Note that the drawing, divi-

Type of Account	Increase	Decrease	Normal Balance
Asset	Debit	Credit	Debit
Liability	Credit	Debit	Credit
Capital			
Capital, Capital Stock, Retained Earnings	Credit	Debit	Credit
Drawing, Dividends	Debit	Credit	Debit
Revenue	Credit	Debit	Credit
Expense	Debit	Credit	Debit

dends, and expense accounts are considered in the positive sense. Increases in these accounts, which represent decreases in capital, are recorded as debits.

When an account that normally has a debit balance actually has a credit balance, or vice versa, it is an indication of an accounting error or of an unusual situation. For example, a credit balance in the office equipment account could result only from an accounting error. On the other hand, a debit balance in an account payable account could result from an overpayment.

FLOW OF ACCOUNTING DATA

The flow of accounting data from the time a transaction occurs to its recording in the ledger may be diagrammed as follows:

Business TRANSACTION occurs	→	Business DOCUMENT prepared	→	Entry recorded in JOURNAL	→	Entry posted to LEDGER

The initial record of each transaction, or of a group of similar transactions, is evidenced by a business document such as a sales ticket, a check stub, or a cash register tape. On the basis of the evidence provided by the business document, the transactions are entered in chronological order in a journal. The amounts of the debits and the credits in the journal are then transferred or posted to the accounts in the ledger.

37

TWO-COLUMN JOURNAL

The basic features of a journal entry were illustrated earlier when introducing the use of debit and credit. There is great variety in both the design of journals and the number of different journals that can be employed by an enterprise. The standard form of two-column journal is illustrated on page 38. Instead of such a single all-purpose two-column journal, a business may use a number of multicolumn journals, restricting each to a single type of transaction. Examples of more sophisticated journal systems are discussed and illustrated in later chapters. Means by which business documents or automated processing devices may entirely supplant journals is also discussed. However, the two-column journal is still widely used. It also serves as a valuable device in analyzing transactions.

The process of recording a transaction in a journal is called *journalizing*. The procedures employed for the two-column journal are as follows:

1. Recording the date:
   a. Year is inserted at top only of date column of each page, except when the year date changes.

JOURNAL   PAGE *14*

	DATE	DESCRIPTION	POST. REF.	DEBIT	CREDIT	
1	*1973 Nov 1*	Cash		1 4 3 5 50		1
2		Sales			1 4 3 5 50	2
3		Cash sales for the day.				3
4						4
5	1	Supplies		1 4 0 00		5
6		Accounts Payable			1 4 0 00	6
7		On account from Apex Co.				7
8						8
9	1	Advertising Expense		2 0 0 00		9
10		Cash			2 0 0 00	10
11		Quarter page in Troy News.				11
12						12

Standard form
of the
two-column
journal

b. Month is inserted on first line only of date column of each page, except when the month date changes.

c. Day is inserted in date column on first line used for each transaction, regardless of number of transactions during the day.

2. Recording the debit:
Title of account to be debited is inserted at extreme left of the description column and amount is entered in the debit column.

3. Recording the credit:
Title of account to be credited is inserted below the account debited, moderately indented, and the amount is entered in the credit column.

4. Writing explanation:
Brief explanations may be written below each entry, moderately indented. Some accountants prefer that the explanation be omitted if the nature of the transaction is obvious. It is also permissible to omit a lengthy explanation of a complex transaction if it is feasible to substitute a reference to the related business document.

It should be noted that all transactions are recorded only in terms of debits and credits to specific accounts. The titles used in the entries should correspond exactly to the titles of the accounts in the ledger. For example, a desk purchased for use in the office should be entered as a debit to Office Equipment, not to "desks purchased," and cash received should be entered as a debit to Cash, not to "cash received."

The line following an entry is left blank in order to clearly separate each entry. The column headed Post. Ref. (posting reference) is not used until the debits and credits are posted to the appropriate accounts in the ledger.

TWO-COLUMN ACCOUNT

Accounts in the simple **T** form are used primarily for illustrative purposes. The addition of special rulings to the T form yields the standard two-column form illustrated at the top of the next page.

ACCOUNT *Cash*   ACCOUNT NO. 11

DATE	ITEM	POST. REF.	DEBIT	DATE	ITEM	POST. REF.	CREDIT
1973 Nov. 1	Balance	✓	4736 00	1973 Nov. 1		14	200 00
1		14	1435 50	1		14	987 75
3	4,374.50	14	948 00	3		14	38 00
			7119 50	3		14	1519 25
							2745 00

Standard form of the two-column account

FOUR-COLUMN ACCOUNT

The standard two-column account form distinguishes to the greatest possible extent between debit entries and credit entries. It is primarily because of this feature that the T form is used at the beginning of introductory accounting courses. In actual practice there has been a tendency for account forms with balance columns to replace the simpler T form, though the latter is still widely used.

ACCOUNT *Cash*   ACCOUNT NO. 11

DATE	ITEM	POST. REF.	DEBIT	CREDIT	BALANCE DEBIT	BALANCE CREDIT
1973 Nov. 1	Balance	✓			4736 00	
1		14	1435 50		6171 50	
1		14		200 00	5971 50	
1		14		987 75	4983 75	
3		14	948 00		5931 75	
3		14		38 00	5893 75	
3		14		1519 25	4374 50	

Standard form of the four-column account

39

The principal advantage of the four-column form lies in its provision for clearly displaying the amount and the debit-credit nature of account balances. The possibilities of confusion and errors when listing account balances on the trial balance (discussed later in this chapter) are thus minimized. The single date column and the contiguity of the debit and credit columns also facilitate both the scanning of an account and the careful examination of its details.

When posting machines are used with the four-column form, the new balance of an account is automatically computed and printed in the proper column after each posting. The account balance is thus always readily available. The same procedure may be followed when the posting is done manually. An alternative is to postpone the computation of the balance until all postings for the month have been completed. When this is done, only the final month-end balance is inserted in the appropriate balance column. The exact procedure adopted in a particular situation will depend upon such factors as the accessibility of adding machines and the desirability of having current account balances readily available at all times.

POSTING

In many accounting systems much or all of the posting to the ledger is done by the use of mechanical or electronic equipment designed for the purpose. When the posting is performed manually, the debits and credits in the journal may be posted sequentially as they occur or, if a considerable number of items is to be posted at one time, all of the debits may be posted first, followed by the credits. The posting of a debit journal entry or a credit journal entry to an account in the ledger is performed as follows:

1. Record the amount and the date of the entry in the account.
2. Insert the number of the journal page in the posting reference column of the account.
3. Insert the account number in the posting reference column of the journal.

The foregoing procedures are illustrated below by the posting of a debit to the cash account. The posting of a credit follows the same sequence of procedures.

40

Diagram
of the
posting
of a debit

CHART OF ACCOUNTS

The number of accounts maintained by a specific enterprise is affected by the nature of its operations, its volume of business, and the extent to which details are needed for taxing authorities, managerial decisions, credit purposes, etc. For example, one enterprise may have separate accounts for Executive Salaries, Office Salaries, and Sales Salaries, while another may find it satisfactory to record all types of salaries in a single salary expense account.

Insofar as possible, the order of the accounts in the ledger should agree with the order of the items in the balance sheet and the income statement. The accounts are numbered to permit indexing and also for use as posting references in the journal.

Although accounts in the ledger may be numbered consecutively as in the pages of a book, a flexible system of indexing is preferable. In the chart of accounts illustrated below, each account number has two digits. The first digit indicates the major division of the ledger in which the account is placed. Accounts beginning with 1 represent assets; 2, liabilities; 3, capital; 4, revenue; and 5, expenses. The second digit indicates the position of the account within its division. A numbering system of this type has the advantage of permitting the later insertion of new accounts in their proper sequence without disturbing the other account numbers. For a large enterprise with a number of departments or branches, it is not unusual for each account number to have four or more digits.

BALANCE SHEET ACCOUNTS	INCOME STATEMENT ACCOUNTS
1. Assets	*4. Revenue*
11 Cash	41 Sales
12 Accounts Receivable	
14 Supplies	*5. Expenses*
15 Prepaid Rent	51 Salary Expense
18 Printing Equipment	52 Supplies Expense
19 Accumulated Depreciation	53 Rent Expense
	54 Depreciation Expense
	59 Miscellaneous Expense
2. Liabilities	
21 Accounts Payable	
22 Salaries Payable	
3. Capital	
31 Charles Bell, Capital	
32 Charles Bell, Drawing	
33 Income Summary	

Chart
of accounts
for Bell
Print Shop

ILLUSTRATIVE PROBLEM

The transactions of a hypothetical business enterprise for a month are used to illustrate the recording process. The sequence of steps to be followed in analyzing each part of a transaction is as follows:

1. Determine whether the item affected is asset, liability, capital, revenue, or expense.
2. Determine whether the item affected increases or decreases.
3. Determine whether the effect should be recorded as a debit or as a credit.

After a transaction is analyzed in accordance with the foregoing outline, the entry is journalized and posted to the accounts in the ledger.

In order to restrict the length of the illustration and to reduce repetition, some of the transactions are stated as a summary. For example, sales of services for cash are ordinarily recorded on a daily basis, but in the illustration summary totals are given only at the middle and end of the month. Similarly, all sales of services on account during the month are summarized as a single transaction; in practice each sale would be recorded separately.

Oct 2. Charles Bell operated a printing business in his home workshop on a part-time basis. He decided to move to rented quarters as of October 2 and to devote full time to the business, which was to be known as Bell Print Shop. The following assets were invested in the enterprise: cash, $1,100; accounts receivable, $600; supplies, $400; and printing equipment, $4,200. There were no liabilities transferred to the business.

Analysis: The four asset accounts Cash, Accounts Receivable, Supplies, and Printing Equipment increase and are debited for $1,100, $600, $400, and $4,200 respectively. The owner's equity in these assets is equal to the sum of the assets, or $6,300; hence Charles Bell, Capital is credited for that amount. (The manner in which individual accounts for customers are maintained is considered in a later chapter.)

JOURNAL
PAGE 1

	DATE	DESCRIPTION	POST. REF.	DEBIT	CREDIT	
	1973					
1	Oct. 2	Cash	11	1 1 0 0 00		1
2		Accounts Receivable	12	6 0 0 00		2
3		Supplies	14	4 0 0 00		3
4		Printing Equipment	18	4 2 0 0 00		4
5		Charles Bell, Capital	31		6 3 0 0 00	5

(*The ledger to which the illustrative entries are posted is presented on pages 45 and 46.*)

Oct. 2. Paid $600 on a lease rental contract, the payment representing three months' rental.

Analysis: The asset acquired in exchange for the cash payment is the right to use the property for three months. The asset Prepaid Rent increases and is debited for $600; the asset Cash decreases and is credited for $600. (When rent for a single month is prepaid it is customarily debited to the rent expense account at the time of payment, thus avoiding the necessity of transferring the amount from Prepaid Rent to Rent Expense at the close of the fiscal period.)

6						6
7	2	Prepaid Rent	15	6 0 0 00		7
8		Cash	11		6 0 0 00	8

Oct. 3. Purchased additional printing equipment on account from Miller Equipment Co. for $1,800.

Analysis: The asset Printing Equipment increases and is therefore debited for $1,800. The liability Accounts Payable increases and is credited for $1,800. (The manner in which individual accounts for creditors are maintained is considered in a later chapter.)

9											9
10		3	Printing Equipment	18	1	8 0 0	00				10
11			Accounts Payable	21				1	8 0 0	00	11

Oct. 4. Received $525 from customers in payment of their accounts.

Analysis: The asset Cash increases and is debited for $525; the asset Accounts Receivable decreases and is credited for $525.

12											12
13		4	Cash	11		5 2 5	00				13
14			Accounts Receivable	12					5 2 5	00	14

Oct. 6. Paid $38 for a newspaper advertisement.

Analysis: Expense accounts are subdivisions of capital. Increases in expense are decreases in capital; hence an expense account is debited for $38. The asset Cash was decreased by the transaction; therefore that account is credited for $38. (Miscellaneous Expense is debited because total expenditures for advertising during a fiscal period are expected to be relatively minor.)

15											15
16		6	Miscellaneous Expense	59		3 8	00				16
17			Cash	11					3 8	00	17

43

Oct. 10. Paid $400 to Miller Equipment Co. to apply on the $1,800 debt owed them.

Analysis: This payment decreases the liability Accounts Payable, so that account is debited for $400. It also decreases the asset Cash, which is credited for $400.

18											18
19		10	Accounts Payable	21		4 0 0	00				19
20			Cash	11					4 0 0	00	20

Oct. 13. Paid part-time assistants $320 for two weeks' salary.

Analysis: Similar to transaction of October 6.

21											21
22		13	Salary Expense	51		3 2 0	00				22
23			Cash	11					3 2 0	00	23

Oct. 16. Received $960 cash from sales for the first half of October.

Analysis: Cash increases and is debited for $960. The revenue account Sales, which is a subdivision of capital, increases and is credited for $960.

24											24
25		16	Cash	11		9 6 0	00				25
26			Sales	41					9 6 0	00	26

Oct. 20. Paid $350 for supplies.

Analysis: The asset Supplies increases and is debited for $350; the asset Cash decreases and is credited for $350.

27									27
28	20	Supplies	14	3 5 0 00					28
29		Cash	11			3 5 0 00			29

Oct. 27. Paid part-time assistants $320 for two weeks' salary.

Analysis: Similar to transaction of October 6.

30									30
31	27	Salary Expense	51	3 2 0 00					31
32		Cash	11			3 2 0 00			32

Oct. 31. Paid $20 for telephone bill for the month.

Analysis: Similar to transaction of October 6.

33									33
34	31	Miscellaneous Expense	59	2 0 00					34
35		Cash	11			2 0 00			35

Oct. 31. Paid $45 for electric bill for the month.

Analysis: Similar to transaction of October 6.

36									36
37	31	Miscellaneous Expense	59	4 5 00					37
38		Cash	11			4 5 00			38

Oct. 31. Received $1,070 from sales for the second half of October.

Analysis: Similar to transaction of October 16.

JOURNAL   PAGE   2

	DATE	DESCRIPTION	POST. REF.	DEBIT	CREDIT	
1	1973 Oct. 31	Cash	11	1 0 7 0 00		1
2		Sales	41		1 0 7 0 00	2

Oct. 31. Sales on account totaled $510 for the month.

Analysis: The asset Accounts Receivable increases and is debited for $510. The revenue account Sales increases and is credited for $510. (Note that the revenue is earned even though no cash is received; the claim against the customers is as much an asset as cash. As customers pay their accounts later, Cash will be debited and Accounts Receivable will be credited.)

3									3
4	31	Accounts Receivable	12	5 1 0 00					4
5		Sales	41			5 1 0 00			5

Oct. 31. Bell withdrew $500 for his personal use.

Analysis: The transaction resulted in a decrease in the amount of capital invested in the business and is recorded by a $500 debit to Charles Bell, Drawing; the decrease in business cash is recorded by a $500 credit to Cash.

6						6
7	31	Charles Bell, Drawing	32	5 0 0 00		7
8		Cash	11		5 0 0 00	8

After all of the entries for the month have been posted, the ledger will appear as shown below and on page 46. Tracing each entry from the journal to the accounts in the ledger will give a clear understanding of the posting process.

In practice, each account would appear on a separate page in the ledger. They are numbered in accordance with the chart shown on page 41. However, some of the accounts listed in the chart are not shown in the illustrative ledger. The additional accounts will be used later when completing the work of the accounting cycle.

ACCOUNT Cash   ACCOUNT NO. 11

DATE	ITEM	POST. REF.	DEBIT	CREDIT	BALANCE DEBIT	BALANCE CREDIT
1973 Oct. 2		1	1 1 0 0 00		1 1 0 0 00	
2		1		6 0 0 00	5 0 0 00	
4		1	5 2 5 00		1 0 2 5 00	
6		1		3 8 00	9 8 7 00	
10		1		4 0 0 00	5 8 7 00	
13		1		3 2 0 00	2 6 7 00	
16		1	9 6 0 00		1 2 2 7 00	
20		1		3 5 0 00	8 7 7 00	
27		1		3 2 0 00	5 5 7 00	
31		1		2 0 00	5 3 7 00	
31		1		4 5 00	4 9 2 00	
31		2	1 0 7 0 00		1 5 6 2 00	
31		2		5 0 0 00	1 0 6 2 00	

ACCOUNT Accounts Receivable   ACCOUNT NO. 12

DATE	ITEM	POST. REF.	DEBIT	CREDIT	BALANCE DEBIT	BALANCE CREDIT
1973 Oct. 2		1	6 0 0 00		6 0 0 00	
4		1		5 2 5 00	7 5 00	
31		2	5 1 0 00		5 8 5 00	

ACCOUNT Supplies   ACCOUNT NO. 14

DATE	ITEM	POST. REF.	DEBIT	CREDIT	BALANCE DEBIT	BALANCE CREDIT
1973 Oct. 2		1	4 0 0 00		4 0 0 00	
20		1	3 5 0 00		7 5 0 00	

Ledger —
Bell Print Shop

ACCOUNT   Prepaid Rent   ACCOUNT NO.   15

DATE	ITEM	POST. REF.	DEBIT	CREDIT	BALANCE DEBIT	BALANCE CREDIT
1973 Oct. 2		1	6 0 0 00		6 0 0 00	

ACCOUNT   Printing Equipment   ACCOUNT NO.   18

DATE	ITEM	POST. REF.	DEBIT	CREDIT	BALANCE DEBIT	BALANCE CREDIT
1973 Oct. 2		1	4 2 0 0 00		4 2 0 0 00	
3		1	1 8 0 0 00		6 0 0 0 00	

ACCOUNT   Accounts Payable   ACCOUNT NO.   21

DATE	ITEM	POST. REF.	DEBIT	CREDIT	BALANCE DEBIT	BALANCE CREDIT
1973 Oct. 3		1		1 8 0 0 00		1 8 0 0 00
10		1	4 0 0 00			1 4 0 0 00

ACCOUNT   Charles Bell, Capital   ACCOUNT NO.   31

DATE	ITEM	POST. REF.	DEBIT	CREDIT	BALANCE DEBIT	BALANCE CREDIT
1973 Oct. 2		1		6 3 0 0 00		6 3 0 0 00

46

ACCOUNT   Charles Bell, Drawing   ACCOUNT NO.   32

DATE	ITEM	POST. REF.	DEBIT	CREDIT	BALANCE DEBIT	BALANCE CREDIT
1973 Oct. 31		2	5 0 0 00		5 0 0 00	

ACCOUNT   Sales   ACCOUNT NO.   41

DATE	ITEM	POST. REF.	DEBIT	CREDIT	BALANCE DEBIT	BALANCE CREDIT
1973 Oct. 16		1		9 6 0 00		9 6 0 00
31		2		1 0 7 0 00		2 0 3 0 00
31		2		5 1 0 00		2 5 4 0 00

ACCOUNT   Salary Expense   ACCOUNT NO.   51

DATE	ITEM	POST. REF.	DEBIT	CREDIT	BALANCE DEBIT	BALANCE CREDIT
1973 Oct. 13		1	3 2 0 00		3 2 0 00	
27		1	3 2 0 00		6 4 0 00	

ACCOUNT   Miscellaneous Expense   ACCOUNT NO.   59

DATE	ITEM	POST. REF.	DEBIT	CREDIT	BALANCE DEBIT	BALANCE CREDIT
1973 Oct. 6		1	3 8 00		3 8 00	
31		1	2 0 00		5 8 00	
31		1	4 5 00		1 0 3 00	

Ledger —
Bell Print Shop
(concluded)

TRIAL BALANCE

From time to time the equality of debits and credits in the ledger should be verified. In any event the verification should be performed at the end of each accounting period. Such a verification, which is called a *trial balance*, may be in the form of an adding machine tape or in the form illustrated below. The summary listing of both the balances and the titles of the accounts is also useful in preparing the income statement and balance sheet.

Bell Print Shop

Trial Balance

October 31, 1973

Cash	1 0 6 2 00	
Accounts Receivable	5 8 5 00	
Supplies	7 5 0 00	
Prepaid Rent	6 0 0 00	
Printing Equipment	6 0 0 0 00	
Accounts Payable		1 4 0 0 00
Charles Bell, Capital		6 3 0 0 00
Charles Bell, Drawing	5 0 0 00	
Sales		2 5 4 0 00
Salary Expense	6 4 0 00	
Miscellaneous Expense	1 0 3 00	
	1 0 2 4 0 00	1 0 2 4 0 00

47

Trial balance —
Bell Print Shop

As the first step in preparing the trial balance, the balance of each account in the ledger should be determined. If two-column accounts are used, memorandum pencil footings and balances are inserted in accordance with the procedure illustrated on page 39. If the four-column account form is employed, the balance of each account must be indicated in the appropriate balance column on the same line as the last posting to the account. (In the illustrative ledger the balances were extended after each posting.)

PROOF PROVIDED BY THE TRIAL BALANCE

The trial balance does not provide complete proof of the accuracy of the ledger. It indicates only that the *debits* and the *credits* are *equal*. This proof is of value, however, because errors frequently affect the equality of debits and credits. If the two totals of a trial balance are not equal, it is probably due to one or more of the following types of errors:

1. Error in preparing the trial balance, such as:
   a. One of the columns of the trial balance was incorrectly added.
   b. The amount of an account balance was incorrectly recorded on the trial balance.

       c. A debit balance was recorded on the trial balance as a credit, or vice versa, or a balance was omitted entirely.

    2. Error in determining the account balances, such as:

       a. A balance was incorrectly computed.

       b. A balance was entered in the wrong balance column.

    3. Error in recording a transaction in the ledger, such as:

       a. An erroneous amount was posted to the account.

       b. A debit entry was posted as a credit, or vice versa.

       c. A debit or a credit posting was omitted.

Among the types of errors that will not cause an inequality in the trial balance totals are the following:

    1. Failure to record a transaction or to post a transaction.

    2. Recording the same erroneous amount for both the debit and the credit parts of a transaction.

    3. Recording the same transaction more than once.

    4. Posting a part of a transaction to the wrong account.

It is readily apparent that care should be exercised both in recording transactions in the journal and in posting to the accounts. The desirability of accuracy in determining account balances and reporting them on the trial balance is equally obvious.

DISCOVERY OF ERRORS

The existence of errors in the accounts may be ascertained in a variety of ways: through audit procedures, through chance discovery, or through the medium of the trial balance. If the debit and the credit totals of the trial balance are not in agreement, the exact amount of the difference between the totals should be determined before proceeding to search for the error.

The amount of the difference between the two totals of the trial balance sometimes gives a clue to the type or the location of the error. For example, a difference of 10, 100, or 1,000 between two totals is frequently the result of an error in addition. A difference between totals can also be due to the omission of a debit or a credit posting or, if it is divisible evenly by 2, to the posting of a debit as a credit, or vice versa. For example, if the debit and the credit totals of a trial balance are $20,640 and $20,236 respectively, the difference of $404 may indicate that a credit posting of that amount was omitted or that a credit of $202 was erroneously posted as a debit.

Two other common types of errors are known as *transpositions* and *slides*. A transposition is the erroneous rearrangement of digits, such as writing $542 as $452 or $524. In a slide the entire number is erroneously moved one or more spaces to the right or the left, such as writing $542.00 as $54.20 or $5,420.00. If an error of either type has occurred and there are no other errors, the discrepancy between the two trial balance totals will be evenly divisible by 9.

A preliminary examination along the lines suggested by the preceding paragraphs will frequently disclose the error. If it does not, the general procedure is to retrace the various steps in the accounting process, beginning with the last step and working back to the original entries in the journal. While there are no rigid rules governing this check or audit, the following plan is suggested:

1. Double check the totals that were obtained for the trial balance by re-adding the columns.
2. Compare the listings in the trial balance with the balances shown in the ledger, making certain that no accounts have been omitted.
3. Recompute the balance of each account in the ledger.
4. Trace the postings in the ledger back to the journal, placing a small check mark by the item in the ledger and also in the journal. If the error is not found, scrutinize each account to see if there is an entry without a check mark; do the same with the entries in the journal.
5. Verify the equality of the debits and the credits in the journal.

Ordinarily, errors that have caused the trial balance totals to be unequal will be discovered before completing all of the procedures outlined above.

49

QUESTIONS

1. Differentiate between an account and a ledger.

2. Name the three parts of a "T" account.

3. Do the terms *debit* and *credit* signify increase or decrease, or may they signify either? Explain.

4. Describe the assets that compose the current assets category.

5. As of the time a balance sheet is being prepared a business enterprise owes a mortgage note payable of $20,000, the terms of which provide for monthly payments of $1,000. How should the liability be classified on the balance sheet?

6. Identify each of the following accounts as asset, liability, capital, revenue, or expense, and state in each case whether the normal balance is a debit or a credit: (a) Accounts Payable, (b) Salary Expense, (c) Interest Income, (d) J. T. Cassidy, Capital, (e) Cash, (f) Notes Payable, (g) Supplies, (h) J. T. Cassidy, Drawing, (i) Rent Expense, (j) Sales.

7. What is the effect (increase or decrease) of debits to expense accounts, (a) in terms of capital, (b) in terms of expense?

8. Differentiate between real accounts and temporary capital accounts.

9. Rearrange the following in proper sequence: (a) business document prepared, (b) entry posted to ledger, (c) entry recorded in journal, (d) business transaction occurs.

10. Assuming that during the month a business enterprise has a substantial number of transactions affecting each of the accounts listed below, state for each account whether it is likely to have (a) debit entries only, (b) credit entries only, or (c) both debit and credit entries.

(1) Cash   (5) Miscellaneous Expense
(2) Accounts Payable   (6) Joel Klein, Drawing
(3) Sales   (7) Notes Receivable
(4) Accounts Receivable   (8) Interest Income

11. Lee Baird Company adheres to a policy of depositing all cash receipts in a bank account and making all payments by check. The cash account as of July 31 has a credit balance of $115 and there is no undeposited cash on hand. (a) Assuming that there were no errors in journalizing or posting, what is the explanation of this unusual balance? (b) Is the $115 credit balance in the cash account an asset, a liability, capital, a revenue, or an expense?

12. Describe the three procedures required to post the credit portion of the following journal entry (Sales is Account No. 41).

JOURNAL   PAGE 15

19—				
June	20	Accounts Receivable..............	160	
		Sales.........................		160

13. Describe in general terms the sequence of accounts in the ledger.

14. Bancroft Decorators performed services for a specific customer in December for which the fee was $450; payment was received in the following January. (a) Was the revenue earned in December or January? (b) What accounts should be debited and credited in (1) December and (2) January?

15. As of January 1 the capital account of a sole proprietorship had a credit balance of $10,000. During the year the owner's withdrawals totaled $9,000 and the business incurred a net loss of $2,000; there were no additional investments in the business. Assuming that there have been no recording errors, will the balance sheet prepared at December 31 balance? Explain.

16. During the month a business corporation received $110,000 in cash and paid out $100,000 in cash. Do the data indicate that the corporation earned net income of $10,000 during the month? Explain.

17. (a) Describe the form known as a trial balance. (b) What proof is provided by a trial balance?

18. In preparing a trial balance an account balance of $500 is listed as $5,000 and an account balance of $2,100 is listed as $1,200. Identify the transposition and the slide.

19. In recording a purchase of supplies of $75 for cash, both debit and credit were journalized and posted as $57. (a) Would this error cause the trial balance to be out of balance? (b) Would the answer be the same if the $75 entry had been journalized correctly and the debit to Supplies had been posted correctly but the credit to Cash had been posted as $57?

20. Indicate which of the following errors, each considered individually, would cause the trial balance totals to be unequal:

(a) A payment of $340 for equipment was posted as a debit of $300 to Equipment and a credit of $340 to Cash.

(b) A fee of $150 earned and due from a client was not debited to Accounts Receivable or credited to a revenue account because the cash had not been received.

(c) A withdrawal of $100 by the owner was journalized and posted as a debit of $10 to Salary Expense and a credit of $10 to Cash.

(d) A receipt of $80 from an account receivable was journalized and posted as a debit of $80 to Cash and a credit of $80 to Sales.

(e) A payment of $140 to a creditor was posted as a credit of $140 to Accounts Payable and a credit of $140 to Cash.

EXERCISES

2-1. The City Telephone Answering Service has the following accounts in its ledger: Cash; Accounts Receivable; Supplies; Office Equipment; Accounts Payable; Sue Nelson, Capital; Sue Nelson, Drawing; Fees Earned; Rent Expense; Advertising Expense; Utilities Expense; Miscellaneous Expense.

Record the following transactions completed during the month of May of the current year in a two-column journal:

May 1. Paid rent for the month, $150.
3. Paid cash for supplies, $18.
10. Purchased office equipment on account, $590.
15. Received cash from customers on account, $375.
21. Paid advertising expense, $28.
26. Paid creditor on account, $300.
28. Withdrew cash for personal use, $250.
29. Paid telephone bill for the month, $39.
30. Fees earned and billed to customers for the month, $810.
31. Paid for repairs to typewriter, $15.
31. Paid electricity bill for the month, $21.

2-2. Eight transactions are recorded in the T accounts presented below. Indicate for each debit and each credit: (a) the type of account affected (asset, liability, capital, revenue, or expense) and (b) whether the account was increased (+) or decreased (−). Answers should be presented in the following form; transaction (1) is given as an example:

Transaction	Account Debited		Account Credited	
	Type	Effect	Type	Effect
(1)	asset	+	capital	+

CASH

(1)	6,000	(2)	500
(8)	1,000	(3)	700
		(4)	100
		(6)	600
		(7)	300

EQUIPMENT

(2)	2,500		

ALAN GREEN, DRAWING

(7)	300		

ACCOUNTS RECEIVABLE

(5)	1,600	(8)	1,000

ACCOUNTS PAYABLE

(6)	600	(2)	2,000

SERVICE REVENUE

		(5)	1,600

SUPPLIES

(4)	100		

ALAN GREEN, CAPITAL

		(1)	6,000

OPERATING EXPENSES

(3)	700		

51

2-3. List the following accounts in the order in which they should appear in the ledger of R. M. Littler Corporation:

(1) Accounts Receivable
(2) Accounts Payable
(3) Cash
(4) Equipment
(5) Miscellaneous Expense
(6) Interest Payable

(7) Capital Stock
(8) Sales
(9) Salary Expense
(10) Prepaid Insurance
(11) Mortgage Note Payable
(12) Retained Earnings

2-4. The accounts (all normal balances) in the ledger of Sun Realty, Inc., as of August 31 of the current year are listed below in alphabetical order. The balance of the cash account has been intentionally omitted. Prepare a trial balance, listing the accounts in proper sequence, inserting the missing figure for cash.

Accounts Payable	3,100	Land	8,000
Accounts Receivable	8,900	Miscellaneous Expense	1,200
Buildings	125,000	Mortgage Note Payable	
Capital Stock	75,000	(due 1985)	24,000
Cash	X	Prepaid Insurance	1,600
Cleaning Expense	900	Retained Earnings	62,100
Dividends	15,000	Salary Expense	7,500
Equipment	35,000	Supplies	800
Fees Earned	45,000	Utilities Expense	1,700

2-5. The preliminary trial balance of Malone Company presented below does not balance. In reviewing the ledger and other records you discover the following: (1) the debits and credits in the cash account total $18,480 and $14,980 respectively; (2) a payment of $400 to a creditor on account was not posted to the cash account; (3) a receipt of $500 from a customer on account was not posted to the accounts receivable account; (4) the balance of the equipment account is $4,500; (5) each account had a normal balance. Prepare a corrected trial balance.

Malone Company
Trial Balance
April 30, 19—

Cash	3,700	
Accounts Receivable	4,100	
Prepaid Insurance		600
Equipment	5,400	
Accounts Payable		3,000
Salaries Payable	400	
Dennis Malone, Capital		5,800
Service Revenue		6,200
Salary Expense	2,800	
Advertising Expense		300
Miscellaneous Expense	500	
	16,900	15,900

2-6. The following errors occurred in posting from a two-column journal:
(1) A debit of $250 to Supplies was posted as $520.
(2) An entry debiting Salary Expense and crediting Cash for $300 was not posted.
(3) A debit of $410 to Equipment was posted twice.
(4) A debit of $90 to Accounts Receivable was posted as a credit.
(5) A credit of $80 to Accounts Payable was not posted.

(6) A credit of $100 to Accounts Receivable was posted to Sales.

(7) A credit of $50 to Cash was posted as $500.

Considering each case individually (i.e. assuming that no other errors had occurred) indicate: (a) by "yes" or "no" whether the trial balance would be out of balance; (b) if answer to (a) is "yes," the amount by which the trial balance totals would differ; and (c) the column of the trial balance that would have the larger total. Answers should be presented in the following form; error (1) is given as an example:

Error	(a) Out of Balance	(b) Difference	(c) Larger Total
(1)	yes	$270	debit

PROBLEMS

The following additional problems for this chapter are located in Appendix B: 2-1B, 2-3B, 2-4B, 2-6B.

2-1A. Henry L. Dalton established an enterprise to be known as Dalton Decorators, on June 16 of the current year. During the remainder of the month he completed the following business transactions:

June 16. Dalton transferred cash from a personal bank account to an account to be used for the business, $2,900.

16. Purchased supplies for cash, $80.

16. Purchased a truck for $3,800, paying $800 cash and giving a note payable for the remainder.

17. Purchased equipment on account, $410.

18. Paid rent for period of June 16 to end of month, $125.

19. Received cash for job completed, $225.

22. Purchased supplies on account, $280.

23. Paid wages of employees, $500.

25. Paid premiums on property and casualty insurance, $304.

26. Paid creditor for equipment purchased on June 17, $410.

27. Recorded sales on account and sent invoices to customers, $3,075.

28. Received cash for job completed, $271. This sale had not been recorded previously.

29. Received an invoice for truck expenses, to be paid in July, $58.

29. Paid utilities expense, $29.

29. Paid miscellaneous expenses, $31.

30. Received cash from customers on account, $2,025.

30. Paid wages of employees, $500.

30. Withdrew cash for personal use, $600.

Instructions:

(1) Open a ledger of two-column accounts for Dalton Decorators, using the following titles and account numbers: Cash, 11; Accounts Receivable, 12; Supplies, 13; Prepaid Insurance, 14; Truck, 16; Equipment, 18; Notes Payable, 21; Accounts Payable, 22; Henry L. Dalton, Capital, 31; Henry L. Dalton, Drawing, 32; Sales, 41; Wages Expense, 51; Rent Expense, 53; Truck Expense, 54; Utilities Expense, 55; Miscellaneous Expense, 59.

(2) Record each transaction in a two-column journal, referring to the above list of accounts or to the ledger in selecting appropriate account titles to be debited and credited. (Do *not* insert the account numbers in the journal at this time.)

(continued)

53

(3) Post the journal to the ledger, inserting appropriate posting references as each item is posted.

(4) Determine the balances of the accounts in the ledger, pencil footing all accounts having two or more debits or credits. A memorandum balance should also be inserted in accounts having both debits and credits, in the manner illustrated on page 39. For accounts with entries on one side only (such as Sales) there is no need to insert the memorandum balance in the item column. Accounts containing only a single debit and a single credit (such as Accounts Receivable) need no pencil footings; the memorandum balance should be inserted in the appropriate item column. Accounts containing a single entry only (such as Prepaid Insurance) need neither a pencil footing nor a memorandum balance.

(5) Prepare a trial balance for Dalton Decorators as of June 30.

2-2A. Neil G. Runyon, M.D., completed the following transactions in the practice of his profession during May of the current year:

May 2. Paid office rent for May, $525.
    4. Purchased equipment on account, $1,600.
    5. Received cash on account from patients, $3,600.
    9. Purchased X-ray film and other supplies on account, $85.
   11. One of the items of equipment purchased on May 4 was defective. It was returned with the permission of the supplier, who agreed to reduce the account for the amount charged for the item, $90.
   12. Paid cash for renewal of property insurance policy, $190.
   16. Sold X-ray film to another doctor at cost, as an accommodation, receiving cash, $63.
   17. Paid cash to creditors on account, $1,500.
   20. Discovered that the balance of the cash account and of the accounts payable account as of May 1 were overstated by $25. A payment of that amount to a creditor in April had not been recorded. Journalize the $25 payment as of May 20.
   23. Received cash in payment of services (on a cash basis) to patients during May, $3,125.
   25. Paid invoice for laboratory analyses, $210.
   27. Paid cash from business bank account for personal and family expenses, $1,400.
   30. Paid salaries of receptionist and nurses, $1,600.
   30. Paid gas and electricity expense, $162.
   30. Paid water expense, $29.
   31. Recorded fees charged to patients on account for services performed in May, $2,035.
   31. Paid telephone expense, $62.
   31. Paid miscellaneous expenses, $120.

Instructions:

(1) Open a ledger of accounts with balance columns for Dr. Runyon as of May 1 of the current year. The accounts and their balances (all normal balances) as of May 1 are listed below. Enter the balances in the appropriate balance columns and place a check mark (√) in the posting reference column. Cash, 11, $2,732; Accounts Receivable, 12, $6,125; Supplies, 13, $290; Prepaid Insurance, 14, $380; Equipment, 18, $18,045; Accounts Payable, 22, $705; Neil G. Runyon, Capital, 31, $26,867; Neil G. Runyon, Drawing, 32; Professional Fees, 41; Salary Expense, 51; Rent Expense, 53;

Laboratory Expense, 55; Utilities Expense, 56; Miscellaneous Expense, 59. (It is advisable to verify the equality of the debit and credit balances in the ledger before proceeding with the next instruction.)

(2) Record each transaction in a two-column journal.

(3) Post the journal to the ledger, extending the month-end balances to the appropriate balance columns after all posting is completed.

(4) Prepare a trial balance as of May 31.

(5) Assuming that the supplies expense, insurance expense, and depreciation expense (which have not been recorded) amount to a total of $290 for the month, determine the following amounts:

(a) Net income for the month of May.

(b) Increase or decrease in capital during the month of May.

(c) Capital as of May 31.

If the working papers correlating with the textbook are not used, omit Problem 2-3A.

2-3A. The following records of Ace TV Service are presented in the working papers:

Journal containing entries for the period January 1–31.

Ledger to which the January entries have been posted.

Preliminary trial balance as of January 31, which does not balance.

Locate the errors, supply the information requested, and prepare a corrected trial balance, proceeding in accordance with the detailed instructions presented below. The balances recorded in the accounts as of January 1 and the entries in the journal are correctly stated. If it is necessary to correct any posted amounts in the ledger, a line should be drawn through the erroneous figure and the correct amount inserted above. Although corrections to memorandum pencil footings and balances are ordinarily accomplished through erasures, any such errors discovered may be corrected by crossing out the erroneous amount and substituting the correct figure. Corrections or other notations may be inserted on the preliminary trial balance in any manner desired. It is not necessary to complete all of the instructions if equal trial balance totals can be obtained earlier. However, the requirements of instructions (9) and (10) should be completed in any event.

Instructions:

(1) Verify the totals of the preliminary trial balance, inserting the correct amounts in the schedule provided in the working papers.

(2) Compute the difference between the trial balance totals.

(3) Determine whether the difference obtained in (2) is evenly divisible by 9.

(4) If the difference obtained in (2) is an even number, determine half the amount.

(5) Scan the amounts in the ledger to determine whether a posting has been omitted or erroneously posted to the wrong side of an account.

(6) Compare the listings in the trial balance with the memorandum balances appearing in the ledger.

(7) Verify the accuracy of the memorandum footings and balances of each account in the ledger.

(8) Trace the postings in the ledger back to the journal, using small check marks to identify items traced. (Correct any memorandum amounts in the ledger that may be necessitated by errors in posting.)

(9) Journalize as of January 31 the payment of $12.80 for telephone

service. The bill had been paid on January 31 but was inadvertently omitted from the journal. Post to the ledger. (Revise any memorandum amounts necessitated by posting this entry.)

(10) Prepare a new trial balance.

2-4A. The following business transactions were completed by Outdoor Theatre Corporation during June of the current year:

June 3. Received and deposited in a bank account $30,000 cash received from stockholders for capital stock.

4. Purchased the Valley Drive-In Theatre for $50,000, allocated as follows: equipment, $20,000; buildings, $13,000; land, $17,000. Paid $15,000 in cash and gave a mortgage note for the remainder.

5. Paid premiums for property and casualty insurance policies, $1,430.

7. Paid for June billboard and newspaper advertising, $425.

8. Purchased supplies, $290, and equipment, $1,300, on account.

9. Cash received from admissions for the week, $2,200.

11. Paid miscellaneous expense, $87.

15. Paid semimonthly wages, $1,800.

16. Cash received from admissions for the week, $2,480.

16. Entered into a contract for the operation of the refreshment stand concession at a rental of 10% of the concessionaire's sales, with a guaranteed minimum of $300 a month, payable in advance. Received cash of $150 as the advance payment for the second half of the month of June.

18. Paid miscellaneous expenses, $58.

20. Returned portion of equipment purchased on June 8 to the supplier, receiving full credit for its cost, $225.

22. Paid cash to creditors on account, $1,235.

23. Cash received from admissions for the week, $2,610.

24. Purchased supplies for cash, $37.

25. Paid for advertising leaflets for June, $51.

28. Recorded invoice of $2,175 for rental of film for June. Payment is due on July 5.

29. Paid electricity and water bills, $309.

30. Paid semimonthly wages, $2,100.

30. Cash received from admissions for remainder of the month, $2,742.

30. Recorded additional amount owed by the concessionaire for the second half of June; sales for that period totaled $1,850. Rental charges in excess of the advance payment of $150 are not due and payable until July 10.

Instructions:

(1) Open a ledger of four-column accounts for Outdoor Theatre Corporation, using the following account titles and numbers: Cash, 11; Accounts Receivable, 12; Prepaid Insurance, 13; Supplies, 14; Equipment, 17; Buildings, 18; Land, 19; Accounts Payable, 21; Mortgage Note Payable, 24; Capital Stock, 31; Admissions Income, 41; Concession Income, 42; Wages Expense, 51; Film Rental Expense, 52; Advertising Expense, 53; Electricity & Water Expense, 54; Miscellaneous Expense, 59.

(2) Record the transactions in a two-column journal.

(3) Post the journal to the ledger, extending the month-end balances to the appropriate balance columns after all posting is completed.

(4) Prepare a trial balance as of June 30.

(5) Determine the following:

(a) Amount of total revenue recorded in the ledger.

(b) Amount of total expenses recorded in the ledger.

(c) Amount of net income for June, assuming that additional unrecorded expenses were as follows: Supplies expense, $125; Insurance expense, $70; Depreciation expense — equipment, $190; Depreciation expense — buildings, $85; Interest expense (on mortgage note), $175.

(d) The understatement or overstatement of net income for June that would have resulted from failure to record the invoice for film rental until it was paid in July. (See transaction of June 28.)

(e) The understatement or overstatement of liabilities as of June 30 that would have resulted from failure to record the invoice for film rental in June. (See transaction of June 28.)

2-5A. Keller Realty, Inc., acts as an agent in buying, selling, renting, and managing real estate. The account balances at the end of July of the current year are presented below.

Account Balances, July 31

11	Cash	3,127	
12	Accounts Receivable	6,024	
13	Prepaid Insurance	916	
14	Office Supplies	125	
16	Automobiles	19,000	
17	Accumulated Depr. — Automobiles		6,600
18	Office Equipment	5,920	
19	Accumulated Depr. — Office Equip.		690
21	Accounts Payable		297
31	Capital Stock		10,000
32	Retained Earnings		5,575
33	Dividends	1,000	
41	Revenue from Fees		33,815
51	Salary and Commission Expense	16,908	
52	Rent Expense	1,400	
53	Advertising Expense	938	
54	Automobile Expense	1,272	
59	Miscellaneous Expense	347	

The following business transactions were completed by Keller Realty, Inc., during August of the current year.

Aug. 1. Paid rent for month, $280.

2. Purchased office supplies on account, $125.

4. Purchased office equipment on account, $810.

10. Received cash from clients on account, $4,219.

12. Paid insurance premium on automobiles, $652.

15. Paid salaries and commissions, $1,690.

15. Recorded revenue earned and billed to clients during first half of month, $3,415.

16. Discovered an error in computing a commission; received cash from the salesman for the overpayment, $20.

18. Paid creditors on account, $612.

20. Received cash from clients on account, $2,310.

23. Paid advertising expense, $206.

24. Returned an item of office equipment purchased on May 4, receiving full credit for its cost, $55.

28. Paid automobile expenses, $243.

57

Aug. 29. Paid miscellaneous expenses, $62.
    31. Recorded revenue earned and billed to clients during second half of month, $3,391.
    31. Paid salaries and commissions, $1,687.
    31. Paid dividend, $1,000.

Instructions:

(1) Open a ledger of four-column accounts for the accounts listed; record the balances in the appropriate balance columns as of August 1, write "Balance" in the item section, and place a check mark (√) in the posting reference column.
(2) Record the transactions for August in a two-column journal.
(3) Post to the ledger, extending the month-end balances to the appropriate balance columns after all posting is completed.
(4) Prepare a trial balance of the ledger as of August 31.

2-6A. The following trial balance for Reliable Household Services as of October 31 of the current year does not balance because of a number of errors:

Cash.............................	1,870	
Accounts Receivable...............	2,220	
Supplies.........................	930	
Prepaid Insurance.................	214	
Equipment.......................	6,940	
Notes Payable....................		1,200
Accounts Payable.................		640
George Reed, Capital.............		3,620
George Reed, Drawing.............	100	
Sales............................		14,700
Wages Expense....................	4,600	
Rent Expense.....................	500	
Advertising Expense..............	31	
Gas, Electricity, and Water Expense.	192	
	17,607	20,160

In the process of comparing the amounts in the trial balance with the ledger, recomputing the balances of the accounts, and comparing the postings with the journal entries, the errors described below were discovered.

(a) The balance of cash was overstated by $100.
(b) A cash payment of $190 was posted as a credit to Cash of $910.
(c) A debit of $60 to Accounts Receivable was not posted.
(d) A return of $120 of defective supplies was erroneously posted as a $210 credit to Supplies.
(e) An insurance policy acquired at a cost of $148 was posted as a credit to Prepaid Insurance.
(f) A debit of $300 in Notes Payable was overlooked when determining the balance of the account.
(g) The balance of Accounts Payable was understated by $100.
(h) A debit of $300 for a withdrawal by the owner was posted as a credit to the capital account.
(i) The balance of $310 in Advertising Expense was entered as $31 in the trial balance.
(j) Miscellaneous Expense, with a balance of $418, was omitted from the trial balance.

Instructions:

Prepare a corrected trial balance as of October 31 of the current year.

Chapter 3

COMPLETION OF THE ACCOUNTING CYCLE

TRIAL BALANCE AND ACCOUNTING STATEMENTS

The summary of the ledger at the end of an accounting period, as set forth in the trial balance, is a convenient starting point in the preparation of financial statements. Assuming no errors in journalizing or posting, many of the amounts listed are acceptable for presentation on the income statement, balance sheet, and capital statement respectively. For example, the balance of the cash account is ordinarily the amount of that asset owned by the enterprise on the last day of the accounting period. Similarly, the balance in Accounts Payable is likely to be the total amount of that type of liability owed by the enterprise on the last day of the accounting period.

The assumption of correctness of trial balance amounts is not necessarily applicable to every account listed on the trial balance. The amounts listed on the trial balance for prepaid assets are ordinarily overstated. The reason for the overstatement is that the day-to-day usage or expiration of such assets has, for reasons of practicability, not been recorded. For example, the balance in the supplies account represents the cost of the inventory of supplies at the beginning of the period plus the cost of those acquired during the period. Some of the supplies would inevitably have been consumed during the period; hence, the balance listed on the trial balance is overstated. In the same manner, the balance in Prepaid Insurance represents the beginning balance plus the cost of insurance policies acquired during the period, and no entries were made from day to day for the premiums as they expired. The effect on the ledger of not recording the daily reduction in prepaid assets is twofold: (1) asset accounts are overstated and (2) expense accounts are understated.

Other data needed for the financial statements may be entirely omitted from the trial balance because of revenue or expense applicable to the period that has not been recorded. For example, salary expense incurred between the last payday and the end of the accounting period would not ordinarily be recorded in the accounts because salaries are customarily recorded only when they are paid. However, such accrued salaries are an expense of the period because the services were rendered during the period; they also represent a liability as of the last day of the period because they are owed to the employees.

MIXED ACCOUNTS AND BUSINESS OPERATIONS

An account with a balance that is partly a balance sheet amount and partly an income statement amount is sometimes referred to as a *mixed account*. Again using the supplies account to illustrate, the balance reported on the trial balance is composed of two elements: the inventory of supplies at the end of the period, which is an **unexpired cost** (asset), and the supplies used during the period, which is an **expired cost** (expense). Before financial statements can be prepared at the end of the period, it is necessary to determine the portion of the balance that is an asset and the portion that is an expense.

The amount of the asset can be determined by counting the quantity of each of the various commodities, multiplying each quantity by the unit cost of that particular commodity, and totaling the dollar amounts thus obtained. The resulting figure represents the amount of the supplies inventory (asset). The excess of the balance in the supplies account over the supplies inventory is the cost of the supplies consumed (expense).

Instead of recording the cost of supplies and other prepaid expenses as assets at the time of purchase, they may be recorded initially as expenses. This alternative treatment will be considered in a later chapter. Meanwhile, all expenditures that include prepayments of expense of future periods will be assumed to be initially recorded as assets as in the foregoing examples.

Prepayments of expenses applicable solely to a particular accounting period are sometimes made at the beginning of the period to which they apply. When this is the case, the expenditure is ordinarily recorded as an expense rather than as an asset. The expense account debited will be a mixed account during the accounting period, but it will be wholly expense at the end of the period. For example, if rent for the month of March is paid on March 1, it is almost entirely an asset at the time of payment. The asset expires gradually from day to day, and at the end of the month the entire amount has become an expense. Therefore, if the expenditure is initially recorded as a debit to Rent Expense, no additional attention need be given to the matter at the close of the period.

ADJUSTING PROCESS

The entries required at the end of an accounting period to record internal transactions are called *adjusting entries*. In a broad sense they may be said to be corrections to the ledger. But the necessity for bringing the ledger up-to-date is a planned part of the accounting procedure; it is not caused by errors. The term "adjusting entries" is therefore more appropriate than "correcting entries."

The illustrations of adjusting entries that follow are based on the ledger of Bell Print Shop. T accounts are used for illustrative purposes and the adjusting entries, which are presented directly in the accounts, appear in bold face type to differentiate them from items that were posted during the month.

Prepaid expenses. According to Bell's trial balance appearing on page 47, the balance in the supplies account on October 31 is $750. Some of these supplies (paper, ink, etc.) have been used during the past month and some are still in stock. If the amount of either is known, the other can be readily determined. It is more practicable to determine the cost of the supplies on hand at the end of the month than it is to keep a record of those used from day to day. Assuming that the inventory of supplies on October 31 is determined to be $230, the amount to be transferred from the asset account to the expense account is computed as follows:

Supplies available (balance of account).......	$750
Supplies on hand (inventory)................	230
Supplies used (amount of adjustment)......	$520

Increases in expense accounts are recorded as debits and decreases in asset accounts are recorded as credits. Hence the adjusting entry required is a debit to Supplies Expense of $520 and a credit to Supplies of $520. After the adjustment, the asset account has a debit balance of $230 and the expense account has a debit balance of $520.

SUPPLIES			SUPPLIES EXPENSE	
Oct. 2	400	**Oct. 31 520** →	**Oct. 31 520**	
20	350			
	750			

The debit balance of $600 in Bell's prepaid rent account represents a prepayment on October 2 of rent for three months, October, November, and December. At the end of October, the rent expense account should be increased (debited) and the prepaid rent account should be decreased (credited) by $200, the rental for one month. The adjusting entry is illustrated in the T accounts below.

PREPAID RENT			RENT EXPENSE	
Oct. 2	600	**Oct. 31 200** →	**Oct. 31 200**	

The prepaid rent account now has a debit balance of $400, which is an asset; the rent expense account has a debit balance of $200, which is an expense.

61

If the foregoing adjustments for supplies and rent were not recorded, the financial statements prepared as of October 31 would be erroneous to the following extent: (1) income statement, expenses understated and net income overstated by $720; (2) balance sheet, assets overstated and capital overstated by $720; (3) capital statement, net income and ending capital overstated by $720.

Plant assets. As was explained earlier, all plant assets except land depreciate. The adjusting entry to record depreciation is similar to those illustrated in the preceding section in that there is a transfer from an asset account to an expense account. The amount to be transferred to expense, however, must be based on estimate rather than on verifiable facts, as in the case of expiration of rent and other prepaid expenses. Because of this and the desire to present on the balance sheet both the original cost and the cumulative amount of depreciation, the reduction of the asset is credited to an account titled Accumulated Depreciation.

The adjusting entry to record depreciation for October is illustrated in the T accounts below. The estimated amount of depreciation[1] for the month is assumed to be $50.

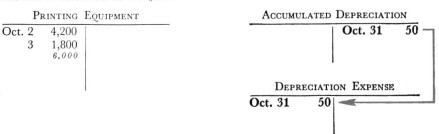

The accumulated depreciation account is called a *contra asset* account. The $50 increase in the account represents a subtraction from the cost recorded in the corresponding asset account. The asset account and the related contra asset account are component parts of the asset, the difference between the two balances being customarily referred to as the *book value* of the asset.

The balances in both the asset and contra asset accounts, together with the book value, may be presented on the balance sheet in the following manner.

Plant assets:
Printing equipment.............. $6,000
Less accumulated depreciation...   50 $5,950

Accrued expenses (liabilities). It is customary practice to pay for some types of services in advance of their use, such as insurance and rent. There are other types of services for which payment is not made until

---

[1]Methods of estimating depreciation will be presented in a later chapter.

after the service has been performed. An example of this type of situation, which is known as an _accrual_, is services performed by employees. The wage or salary expense accrues hour by hour and day by day, but payment is made only weekly, biweekly, or in accordance with some other periodic time interval. If the last day of a pay period does not coincide with the last day of the accounting period, the accrued expense and the related liability must be recorded in the accounts by an adjusting entry.

The data in the T accounts below were taken from the ledger of Bell Print Shop. The debits of $320 on October 13 and 27 in the salary expense account were biweekly payments on alternate Fridays for the payroll periods ended on those days. The salaries earned on Monday and Tuesday, October 30 and 31, amount to $68. This amount is an additional expense of October and it is therefore debited to the salary expense account. It is also a liability as of October 31 and it is therefore credited to Salaries Payable.

SALARIES PAYABLE			SALARY EXPENSE		
	Oct. 31	68	Oct. 13	320	
			27	320	
				640	
			31	68	

After the adjustment, the debit balance of the salary expense account is $708, which is the actual expense for the month; the credit balance of $68 in Salaries Payable is the amount of the liability for salaries owed as of October 31. If no adjusting entry for the accrual is recorded, the effect on the financial statements prepared as of October 31 would be as follows: (1) income statement, expenses understated and net income overstated by $68; (2) balance sheet, liabilities understated and capital overstated by $68; (3) capital statement, net income and ending capital overstated by $68.

63

WORK SHEET FOR FINANCIAL STATEMENTS

Before journalizing and posting adjustments similar to those just described, it is necessary to determine and assemble the relevant data. For example, it is necessary to determine the cost of supplies on hand and the salaries accrued at the end of the period. Such details, as well as other compilations of data, preliminary drafts of financial statements, and other facilitating analyses prepared by accountants are characterized generally as _working papers_.

A particular type of working paper frequently employed by accountants as a preliminary to the preparation of financial statements has come to be called a _work sheet_. Its use reduces the possibility of overlooking the need for an adjustment, provides a convenient means of verifying arithmetical accuracy, and provides for the arrangement of data in a logical form.

The work sheet for Bell Print Shop is presented on the next page. The three lines at the top identify (1) the enterprise, (2) the nature of the form, and (3) the period of time involved. The form has a column for account titles and eight money columns, arranged in four pairs of debit and credit columns. The principal headings of the four sets of money columns are as follows:

1. Trial Balance   3. Income Statement
2. Adjustments   4. Balance Sheet

Trial balance columns.   The trial balance data may be assembled directly on the work sheet form or it may be prepared on another sheet first and then copied on the work sheet form.

Adjustments columns.   Both the debit and the credit portions of an adjustment should be inserted on the appropriate lines before proceeding to another adjustment. Cross-referencing the related debit and credit of each adjustment by letters is useful to anyone who may have occasion to review the work sheet; it is also helpful later when recording the adjusting entries in the journal. The sequence of adjustments is immaterial except that there is a time and accuracy advantage in following the order in which the adjustment data are assembled. If titles of accounts to be adjusted do not appear in the trial balance, they should be inserted below the trial balance totals as they are needed.

The adjusting entries for Bell Print Shop were explained and illustrated by T accounts earlier in the chapter. In practice the adjustments are inserted directly on the work sheet on the basis of the data assembled by the accounting department.

Explanatory notes for the entries in the adjustments columns of the work sheet (next page) follow.

(a) *Supplies.* The supplies account has a debit balance of $750; the cost of the supplies on hand at the end of the period is $230; therefore, the supplies expense for October is the difference between the two amounts, or $520. The adjustment is entered by writing (1) *Supplies Expense* in the Account Title column, (2) *$520* in the Adjustments Debit column on the same line, and (3) *$520* in the Adjustments Credit column on the line with Supplies.

(b) *Rent.* The prepaid rent account has a debit balance of $600, which represents a payment for three months beginning with October; therefore, the rent expense for October is $200. The adjustment is entered by writing (1) *Rent Expense* in the Account Title column, (2) *$200* in the Adjustments Debit column on the same line, and (3) *$200* in the Adjustments Credit column on the line with Prepaid Rent.

Bell Print Shop

Work Sheet

For Month Ended October 31, 1973

ACCOUNT TITLE	TRIAL BALANCE DEBIT	TRIAL BALANCE CREDIT	ADJUSTMENTS DEBIT	ADJUSTMENTS CREDIT	INCOME STATEMENT DEBIT	INCOME STATEMENT CREDIT	BALANCE SHEET DEBIT	BALANCE SHEET CREDIT	
Cash	1062 00						1062 00		1
Accounts Receivable	585 00						585 00		2
Supplies	750 00			(a) 520 00			230 00		3
Prepaid Rent	600 00			(b) 200 00			400 00		4
Printing Equipment	6000 00						6000 00		5
Accounts Payable		1400 00						1400 00	6
Charles Bell, Capital		6300 00						6300 00	7
Charles Bell, Drawing	500 00						500 00		8
Sales		2540 00				2540 00			9
Salary Expense	640 00		(d) 68 00		708 00				10
Miscellaneous Expense	103 00				103 00				11
	10240 00	10240 00							12
Supplies Expense			(a) 520 00		520 00				13
Rent Expense			(b) 200 00		200 00				14
Depreciation Expense			(c) 50 00		50 00				15
Accumulated Depreciation				(c) 50 00				50 00	16
Salaries Payable				(d) 68 00				68 00	17
			838 00	838 00	1581 00	2540 00	8777 00	7818 00	18
Net Income					959 00			959 00	19
					2540 00	2540 00	8777 00	8777 00	20

Eight-column work sheet

65

(c) *Depreciation.* Depreciation of the printing equipment for the month is estimated at $50. This expired portion of the cost of the equipment is both an expense and a reduction in the asset. The adjustment is entered by writing (1) *Depreciation Expense* in the Account Title column, (2) *$50* in the Adjustments Debit column on the same line, (3) *Accumulated Depreciation* in the Account Title column, and (4) *$50* in the Adjustments Credit column on the same line.

(d) *Salaries.* Salaries accrued but not paid at the end of October amount to $68. This is an increase in expense and an increase in liabilities. The adjustment is entered by writing (1) *$68* in the Adjustments Debit column on the same line with Salary Expense, (2) *Salaries Payable* in the Account Title column, and (3) *$68* in the Adjustments Credit column on the same line.

The final step in completing the Adjustments columns is to prove the equality of debits and credits by totaling and ruling the two columns.

Income statement and balance sheet columns. The data in the trial balance columns are combined with the adjustments data and extended to one of the remaining four columns. The amounts of assets, liabilities, capital, and drawing (or dividends) are extended to the balance sheet columns, and the revenues and expenses are extended to the income statement columns. This procedure must be applied to the balance of each account listed, beginning at the top and proceeding down the page in sequential order.

In the illustrative work sheet, the first account listed is Cash and the balance appearing in the trial balance is $1,062. With there being no adjustments to Cash, the trial balance amount should be extended to the appropriate column. Cash is an asset, it is listed on the balance sheet, and it has a debit balance. Accordingly, the $1,062 amount is extended to the debit column of the balance sheet section. The balance of Accounts Receivable is extended in similar fashion. Supplies has an initial debit balance of $750 and a credit adjustment (decrease) of $520. The amount to be extended is therefore the remaining debit balance of $230. The same procedure is continued until all account balances, with or without adjustment as the case may be, have been extended to the appropriate columns. The balances of the capital and drawing accounts are extended to the balance sheet section, even though they are reported on the capital statement.

After all of the balances have been extended, each of the four columns is totaled. The amount of the net income or the net loss for the period is then determined by ascertaining the amount of the difference between the totals of the two income statement columns. If the credit column total is greater than the debit column total, the excess is the net income.

For the work sheet presented on page 65, the computation of net income is as follows:

Total of credit column (revenue)...............	$2,540
Total of debit column (expenses)...............	1,581
Net income (excess of revenue over expenses)..	$ 959

Revenue and expense accounts, which are in reality subdivisions of capital, are temporary in nature. They are used during the accounting period to facilitate the accumulation of detailed operating data. After they have served their purpose, the net balance will be transferred to the capital account (or the retained earnings account) in the ledger. This transfer is accomplished on the work sheet by entries in the income statement debit column and the balance sheet credit column, as illustrated on page 65. If there had been a net loss instead of a net income, the amount would have been entered in the income statement credit column and the balance sheet debit column.

After the final entry on the work sheet, each of the four statement columns is totaled to verify the arithmetic accuracy of the amount of net income or net loss transferred from the income statement to the balance sheet. The totals of the two income statement columns must be equal, as must the totals of the two balance sheet columns. The form of work sheet illustrated may be expanded by the addition of a pair of columns solely for capital statement (or retained earnings statement) data. However, because of the very few items involved, this variation is not illustrated.[2]

67

FINANCIAL STATEMENTS

The income statement, capital statement, and balance sheet prepared from the work sheet of Bell Print Shop appear on page 69. Their basic forms correspond to the statements presented in Chapter 1. Some minor variations are illustrated; others will be introduced from time to time in later chapters. The remaining portions of this section are devoted to the sources of the data and the manner in which they are reported on the statements.

Income statement. The work sheet is the source of all of the data reported on the income statement. The sequence of expenses may be altered in order to present them in the order of magnitude.

Capital statement. The amount listed on the work sheet as the capital of a sole proprietorship does not necessarily represent the account balance at the beginning of the accounting period. The proprietor may have invested additional assets in the business during the period. Hence,

---

[2]If there are a great many adjustments, it may be advisable to insert a section entitled Adjusted Trial Balance between the trial balance section and the income statement section. The arithmetic of combining the data may then be verified before extending balances to the statement sections. Other variations in form may be introduced to meet special requirements or to accord with the preferences of the particular user.

it is necessary to refer to the account in the ledger to determine the beginning balance and any additional investments. The amount of net income (or loss) is taken from the balance sheet columns of the work sheet, and the amount of the withdrawals during the period also appears in the balance sheet section. The final balance of capital is then determined arithmetically.

The form of the capital statement can be modified to meet the circumstances of any particular case. In the illustration on the next page, the amount withdrawn by the owner was less than the net income. If the withdrawals had exceeded the net income, the order of the two items could have been reversed and the difference between the two deducted from the beginning capital.

Other factors, such as additional investments or a net loss, also necessitate modifications in form, as in the following example:

Capital, January 1, 19--	$35,000.00	
Additional investment during the year .	6,000.00	
Total.		$41,000.00
Net loss for the year.	$ 8,000.00	
Withdrawals.	3,600.00	
Decrease in capital.		11,600.00
Capital, December 31, 19--		$29,400.00

In an incorporated business it is necessary to differentiate between changes in capital stock and changes in retained earnings. If the change in the amount of capital stock issued during the period is significant, a capital stock statement should be prepared; otherwise such a statement is unnecessary. (The reporting of changes in retained earnings is discussed below.)

Balance sheet. The balance sheet illustrated on the next page was expanded by the addition of subcaptions for current assets, plant assets, and current liabilities. If there were any liabilities that were not due until more than a year from the balance sheet date, they would be listed under the caption of "long-term liabilities." The work sheet is the source of all of the data reported on the balance sheet with the exception of the amount of the sole proprietor's capital, which can be obtained from the capital statement.

The capital section of the balance sheet of a corporation is subdivided into capital stock and retained earnings; the amount to be reported for the latter is obtained from the retained earnings statement.

Retained earnings statement. The basic form of a retained earnings statement for a corporation is illustrated on page 21. If dividend payments are debited to Dividends, the amount will appear on the work sheet. However, some accountants prefer to debit dividends directly to Retained Earnings. When this is the case, it is necessary to refer to the

Bell Print Shop
Income Statement
For Month Ended October 31, 1973

Sales		$2,540.00
Operating expenses:		
Salary expense.	$708.00	
Supplies expense.	520.00	
Rent expense.	200.00	
Depreciation expense.	50.00	
Miscellaneous expense	103.00	
Total operating expenses.		1,581.00
Net income.		$ 959.00

Income statement

Bell Print Shop
Capital Statement
For Month Ended October 31, 1973

Capital, October 2, 1973.		$6,300.00
Net income for the month.	$959.00	
Less withdrawals.	500.00	
Increase in capital		459.00
Capital, October 31, 1973		$6,759.00

Capital statement

69

Bell Print Shop
Balance Sheet
October 31, 1973

Assets

Current assets:		
Cash.	$1,062.00	
Accounts receivable	585.00	
Supplies.	230.00	
Prepaid rent.	400.00	
Total current assets.		$2,277.00
Plant assets:		
Printing equipment.	$6,000.00	
Less accumulated depreciation . .	50.00	5,950.00
Total assets.		$8,227.00

Liabilities

Current liabilities:		
Accounts payable.	$1,400.00	
Salaries payable.	68.00	
Total liabilities		$1,468.00

Capital

Charles Bell, capital		6,759.00
Total liabilities and capital		$8,227.00

Balance sheet

ledger to ascertain the beginning balance of Retained Earnings and the amount of the dividends debited during the period.

JOURNALIZING AND POSTING ADJUSTING ENTRIES

At the end of the fiscal period the adjusting entries appearing in the work sheet are recorded in the journal and posted to the ledger, bringing the ledger into agreement with the data reported on the financial statements. The adjusting entries are dated as of the last day of the accounting period, even though they are usually recorded at a later date. Each entry may be supported by an explanation, but a suitable caption above the first adjusting entry, as in the illustration below, is sufficient. A brief explanation of each separate entry serves no useful purpose and, on the other hand, a detailed explanation would needlessly duplicate working papers and other basic documents available in the files.

The adjusting entries in the journal of Bell Print Shop are presented below. The accounts to which they have been posted appear in the ledger beginning on page 73. To facilitate identification, each adjusting entry is identified in the item section of the accounts. It is not necessary that this be done in actual practice.

JOURNAL   PAGE 2

	DATE	DESCRIPTION	POST. REF.	DEBIT	CREDIT	
10						10
11		Adjusting Entries				11
12	Oct. 31	Supplies Expense	52	5 2 0 00		12
13		Supplies	14		5 2 0 00	13
14						14
15	31	Rent Expense	53	2 0 0 00		15
16		Prepaid Rent	15		2 0 0 00	16
17						17
18	31	Depreciation Expense	54	5 0 00		18
19		Accumulated Depreciation	19		5 0 00	19
20						20
21	31	Salary Expense	51	6 8 00		21
22		Salaries Payable	22		6 8 00	22

Adjusting
entries

JOURNALIZING AND POSTING CLOSING ENTRIES

The revenue, expense, and drawing (or dividends) accounts are temporary accounts employed in classifying and summarizing changes in capital during the accounting period. At the end of the period the net effect of the balances in these accounts must be recorded in the permanent account. The balances must also be removed from the temporary accounts so that they will be ready for use in accumulating data for the following accounting period. Both of these objectives are accomplished by a series of entries called *closing entries*.

An account titled Income Summary is used for summarizing the data in the revenue and expense accounts. It is employed only at the end of the accounting period and is both opened and closed during the closing process. Other account titles used for the summarizing account are Expense and Revenue Summary, Profit and Loss Summary, and Income and Expense Summary.

Four entries are required to close the temporary accounts of a sole proprietorship at the end of the period. They are as follows:

1. Each revenue account is debited for the amount of its balance, and Income Summary is credited for the total revenue.
2. Each expense account is credited for the amount of its balance, and Income Summary is debited for the total expense.
3. Income Summary is debited for the amount of its balance (net income), and the capital account is credited for the same amount. (Debit and credit are reversed if there is a net loss.)
4. The drawing account is credited for the amount of its balance, and the capital account is debited for the same amount.

After the closing entries have been journalized, as illustrated below, and posted to the ledger, the balance in the capital account will correspond to the amounts reported on the capital statement and balance sheet. In addition, the revenue, expense, and drawing accounts will be closed (in balance). The process of closing is illustrated by the flow chart presented on page 72.

71

JOURNAL   PAGE 2

	DATE		DESCRIPTION	POST. REF.	DEBIT	CREDIT	
23							23
24			Closing Entries				24
25	Oct.	31	Sales	41	2 5 4 0 00		25
26			Income Summary	33		2 5 4 0 00	26
27							27
28		31	Income Summary	33	1 5 8 1 00		28
29			Salary Expense	51		7 0 8 00	29
30			Miscellaneous Expense	59		1 0 3 00	30
31			Supplies Expense	52		5 2 0 00	31
32			Rent Expense	53		2 0 0 00	32
33			Depreciation Expense	54		5 0 00	33
34							34
35		31	Income Summary	33	9 5 9 00		35
36			Charles Bell, Capital	31		9 5 9 00	36
37							37
38		31	Charles Bell, Capital	31	5 0 0 00		38
39			Charles Bell, Drawing	32		5 0 0 00	39

Closing entries

	1		
SALES	INCOME SUMMARY		
2,540	960	1,581	2,540
	1,070	959	3
	510		CHARLES BELL, CAPITAL
			500	6,300
		CHARLES BELL, DRAWING	4		959
SALARY EXPENSE	500	500
320	708
320	
68	
SUPPLIES EXPENSE	
520	520
		2
RENT EXPENSE	
200	200
DEPRECIATION EXPENSE	
50	50

1 Transfers revenue to Income Summary.

2 Transfers expenses to Income Summary.

MISCELLANEOUS EXPENSE	
38	103
20	
45	

3 Transfers net income to Capital.

4 Transfers drawings to Capital.

72

The procedure for closing the temporary accounts of a corporation differ only slightly from the outline above. Income Summary is closed (entry 3) to Retained Earnings, and Dividends is closed (entry 4) to Retained Earnings.

The account titles and amounts needed in journalizing the closing entries may be obtained from any one of three sources: (1) work sheet, (2) income and capital statements, and (3) ledger. When the work sheet is used, the data for the first two entries are taken from the income statement columns; the amount for the third entry is the net income or net loss appearing at the bottom of the work sheet; and reference to the drawing account balance appearing in the balance sheet column of the work sheet supplies the information for the fourth, and final, entry.

The ledger of Bell Print Shop after the adjusting and closing entries have been posted is presented on pages 73–75. Each posting of an adjusting entry and a closing entry is identified in the item section of the account as an aid to the student. It is not necessary that this be done in actual practice.

ACCOUNT Cash   **ACCOUNT NO.** 11

DATE	ITEM	POST. REF.	DEBIT	CREDIT	BALANCE DEBIT	BALANCE CREDIT
1973 Oct. 2		1	1 1 0 0 00		1 1 0 0 00	
2		1		6 0 0 00	5 0 0 00	
4		1	5 2 5 00		1 0 2 5 00	
6		1		3 8 00	9 8 7 00	
10		1		4 0 0 00	5 8 7 00	
13		1		3 2 0 00	2 6 7 00	
16		1	9 6 0 00		1 2 2 7 00	
20		1		3 5 0 00	8 7 7 00	
27		1		3 2 0 00	5 5 7 00	
31		1		2 0 00	5 3 7 00	
31		1		4 5 00	4 9 2 00	
31		2	1 0 7 0 00		1 5 6 2 00	
31		2		5 0 0 00	1 0 6 2 00	

ACCOUNT Accounts Receivable   **ACCOUNT NO.** 12

DATE	ITEM	POST. REF.	DEBIT	CREDIT	BALANCE DEBIT	BALANCE CREDIT
1973 Oct. 2		1	6 0 0 00		6 0 0 00	
1		1		5 2 5 00	7 5 00	
31		2	5 1 0 00		5 8 5 00	

ACCOUNT Supplies   **ACCOUNT NO.** 14

DATE	ITEM	POST. REF.	DEBIT	CREDIT	BALANCE DEBIT	BALANCE CREDIT
1973 Oct. 2		1	4 0 0 00		4 0 0 00	
20		1	3 5 0 00		7 5 0 00	
31	Adjusting	2		5 2 0 00	2 3 0 00	

ACCOUNT Prepaid Rent   **ACCOUNT NO.** 15

DATE	ITEM	POST. REF.	DEBIT	CREDIT	BALANCE DEBIT	BALANCE CREDIT
1973 Oct. 2		1	6 0 0 00		6 0 0 00	
31	Adjusting	2		2 0 0 00	4 0 0 00	

ACCOUNT Printing Equipment   **ACCOUNT NO.** 18

DATE	ITEM	POST. REF.	DEBIT	CREDIT	BALANCE DEBIT	BALANCE CREDIT
1973 Oct. 2		1	4 2 0 0 00		4 2 0 0 00	
3		1	1 8 0 0 00		6 0 0 0 00	

73

Ledger after the accounts have been adjusted and closed

ACCOUNT Accumulated Depreciation   ACCOUNT NO. 19

DATE		ITEM	POST. REF.	DEBIT	CREDIT	BALANCE	
						DEBIT	CREDIT
1973 Oct.	31	Adjusting	2		5 0 00		5 0 00

ACCOUNT Accounts Payable   ACCOUNT NO. 21

DATE		ITEM	POST. REF.	DEBIT	CREDIT	BALANCE	
						DEBIT	CREDIT
1973 Oct.	3		1		1 8 0 0 00		1 8 0 0 00
	10		1	4 0 0 00			1 4 0 0 00

ACCOUNT Salaries Payable   ACCOUNT NO. 22

DATE		ITEM	POST. REF.	DEBIT	CREDIT	BALANCE	
						DEBIT	CREDIT
1973 Oct.	31	Adjusting	2		6 8 00		6 8 00

ACCOUNT Charles Bell, Capital   ACCOUNT NO. 31

DATE		ITEM	POST. REF.	DEBIT	CREDIT	BALANCE	
						DEBIT	CREDIT
1973 Oct.	2		1		6 3 0 0 00		6 3 0 0 00
	31	Closing	2		9 5 9 00		7 2 5 9 00
	31	Closing	2	5 0 0 00			6 7 5 9 00

ACCOUNT Charles Bell, Drawing   ACCOUNT NO. 32

DATE		ITEM	POST. REF.	DEBIT	CREDIT	BALANCE	
						DEBIT	CREDIT
1973 Oct.	31		2	5 0 0 00		5 0 0 00	
	31	Closing	2		5 0 0 00	—	—

ACCOUNT Income Summary   ACCOUNT NO. 33

DATE		ITEM	POST. REF.	DEBIT	CREDIT	BALANCE	
						DEBIT	CREDIT
1973 Oct.	31	Closing	2		2 5 4 0 00		2 5 4 0 00
	31	Closing	2	1 5 8 1 00			9 5 9 00
	31	Closing	2	9 5 9 00		—	—

ACCOUNT Sales   ACCOUNT NO. 41

DATE		ITEM	POST. REF.	DEBIT	CREDIT	BALANCE	
						DEBIT	CREDIT
1973 Oct.	16		1		9 6 0 00		9 6 0 00
	31		2		1 0 7 0 00		2 0 3 0 00
	31		2		5 1 0 00		2 5 4 0 00
	31	Closing	2	2 5 4 0 00		—	—

Ledger
after the
accounts have
been adjusted
and closed —
continued

ACCOUNT Salary Expense   **ACCOUNT NO.** 51

DATE		ITEM	POST. REF.	DEBIT	CREDIT	BALANCE DEBIT	BALANCE CREDIT
1973 Oct.	13		1	3 2 0 00		3 2 0 00	
	27		1	3 2 0 00		6 4 0 00	
	31	Adjusting	2	6 8 00		7 0 8 00	
	31	Closing	2		7 0 8 00	—	—

ACCOUNT Supplies Expense   **ACCOUNT NO.** 52

DATE		ITEM	POST. REF.	DEBIT	CREDIT	BALANCE DEBIT	BALANCE CREDIT
1973 Oct.	31	Adjusting	2	5 2 0 00		5 2 0 00	
	31	Closing	2		5 2 0 00	—	—

ACCOUNT Rent Expense   **ACCOUNT NO.** 53

DATE		ITEM	POST. REF.	DEBIT	CREDIT	BALANCE DEBIT	BALANCE CREDIT
1973 Oct.	31	Adjusting	2	2 0 0 00		2 0 0 00	
	31	Closing	2		2 0 0 00	—	—

ACCOUNT Depreciation Expense   **ACCOUNT NO.** 54

DATE		ITEM	POST. REF.	DEBIT	CREDIT	BALANCE DEBIT	BALANCE CREDIT
1973 Oct.	31	Adjusting	2	5 0 00		5 0 00	
	31	Closing	2		5 0 00	—	—

ACCOUNT Miscellaneous Expense   **ACCOUNT NO.** 59

DATE		ITEM	POST. REF.	DEBIT	CREDIT	BALANCE DEBIT	BALANCE CREDIT
1973 Oct.	6		1	3 8 00		3 8 00	
	31		1	2 0 00		5 8 00	
	31		1	4 5 00		1 0 3 00	
	31	Closing	2		1 0 3 00	—	—

Ledger after the accounts have been adjusted and closed — concluded

75

As the entry to close an account is posted, a line should be inserted in both balance columns opposite the final entry, as illustrated by Charles Bell, Drawing and the remaining temporary accounts. Transactions affecting the accounts in the following period will be posted in the spaces immediately below the closing entry.

POST-CLOSING TRIAL BALANCE

The final procedure of the accounting cycle is the preparation of a post-closing trial balance. Its purpose is to assure that the ledger is in balance at the beginning of the new accounting period. The items on the post-closing trial balance should correspond exactly with those reported on the balance sheet.

A post-closing trial balance is illustrated below. A common practice is to proceed directly from the ledger to the preparation of adding machine listings, omitting the more formalized procedure. The adding machine tapes then become the post-closing trial balance.

Bell Print Shop

Post-Closing Trial Balance

October 31, 1973

Cash	1 0 6 2 00	
Accounts Receivable	5 8 5 00	
Supplies	2 3 0 00	
Prepaid Rent	4 0 0 00	
Printing Equipment	6 0 0 0 00	
Accumulated Depreciation		5 0 00
Accounts Payable		1 4 0 0 00
Salaries Payable		6 8 00
Charles Bell, Capital		6 7 5 9 00
	8 2 7 7 00	8 2 7 7 00

Post-closing trial balance

FISCAL YEAR

The maximum length of an accounting period is ordinarily one year, which includes a complete cycle of the seasons and of business activities. Income and property taxes are also based on yearly periods and thus require that annual reckonings be made.

The annual accounting period adopted by an enterprise is known as its *fiscal year*. Fiscal years ordinarily begin with the first day of the particular month selected and end on the last day of the twelfth month hence. The period most commonly adopted is the calendar year, but other periods are not infrequently elected, particularly by incorporated businesses.

The long-term financial history of a business enterprise may be depicted by a succession of balance sheets, prepared at yearly intervals. The history of operations for the intervening periods is presented in a series of income statements. If the life of a business enterprise is represented by a line moving from left to right, a series of balance sheets and income statements may be diagrammed as follows:

| Balance Sheet dated Dec. 31, 1972 | Balance Sheet dated Dec. 31, 1973 | Balance Sheet dated Dec. 31, 1974 | Balance Sheet dated Dec. 31, 1975 |

THE LIFE OF A BUSINESS

| Income Statement for Fiscal Year 1973 | Income Statement for Fiscal Year 1974 | Income Statement for Fiscal Year 1975 |

ACCOUNTING CYCLE

The principal accounting procedures of a fiscal period have been presented in this and the preceding chapter. The sequence of procedures is frequently called the *accounting cycle*. It begins with the analysis and the journalizing of transactions and ends with the post-closing trial balance. The most significant output of the cycle is, of course, the financial statements.

An understanding of all phases of the accounting cycle is essential as a foundation for further study of accounting principles and the uses of accounting data by management. The following outline summarizes the basic phases of the cycle:

1. Transactions are analyzed.
2. Transactions are journalized and posted to the ledger.
3. Trial balance is prepared.
4. Data needed to adjust the accounts are assembled.
5. Work sheet is prepared.
6. Financial statements are prepared.
7. Adjusting entries are journalized and posted to the ledger.
8. Closing entries are journalized and posted to the ledger.
9. Post-closing trial balance is prepared.

77

INTERIM STATEMENTS

In order to reduce the number of transactions and physical space requirements in the illustrative case of Bell Print Shop, the accounting cycle covered only a single month. Most business enterprises close the temporary capital accounts at the end of each fiscal year rather than at the end of each month.

Analyzing and recording transactions (phases 1 and 2 of the accounting cycle) are performed on a continuous basis throughout the fiscal year, regardless of when the accounts are closed. It is also customary to prepare a trial balance (phase 3) at the end of each month or oftener. When monthly (*interim*) financial statements (phase 6) are to be prepared, the adjustment data are assembled (phase 4) and a work sheet is completed (phase 5) as of the end of each month.

The amounts of the asset and liability accounts appearing in the balance sheet section of the work sheet are the balances as of the last day of the interim period. On the other hand, the amounts of the revenue and expense items appearing in the income statement section of the work sheet are cumulative from the beginning of the fiscal year. To illustrate, assume that the fiscal year of a hypothetical enterprise is the calendar year. The work sheet prepared at the end of February provides data for an income statement for the two-month period, January–February, and data for a balance sheet as of February 28(29); the work sheet at the end of March provides data for an income statement for the three-month period, January–March, and data for a balance sheet as of March 31; and so on throughout the year. Data for the income statement for one month only are then obtained by subtracting from the amount of each revenue and expense of the current cumulative income statement the corresponding amount from the preceding cumulative income statement. Continuing the illustration, if sales are reported on the cumulative January–March income statement at $190,000 and on the cumulative January–February income statement at $120,000, the sales reported on the March income statement will be $70,000 ($190,000–$120,000). The amount of each expense incurred in March and of the net income for March is determined in the same manner.

The capital or retained earnings statement customarily presents cumulative data from the beginning of the fiscal year, but statements for single months can be readily prepared.

CORRECTION OF ERRORS

Occasional errors in journalizing and posting transactions are inevitable. Procedures employed to correct errors in the journal and ledger vary according to the nature of the error and the phase of the accounting cycle in which it is discovered.

When an error in an account title or amount in the journal is discovered before the entry is posted, the correction may be effected by drawing a line through the error and inserting the correct title or amount immediately above. If a debit journal entry is erroneously posted as a credit, or vice versa, or if the amount of the posting is in error, the correction may be accomplished in a similar manner. If there is any likelihood of questions arising later, the person responsible may initial the correction as in the illustration at the top of the next page.

When an account has been erroneously debited or credited in the journal and the item has been posted, it is preferable to journalize and post a correcting entry. For example, if at the end of March it is discovered that a cash purchase of office equipment for $500 on March 5 had been journalized and posted as a debit to Office Supplies and a credit to Cash, the error should be corrected by an additional entry in the journal. Before attempting to formulate a correcting entry, it is

ACCOUNT Miscellaneous Expense   ACCOUNT NO. 59

DATE	ITEM	POST. REF.	DEBIT	CREDIT	BALANCE DEBIT	BALANCE CREDIT
1973 Oct. 6	*DC*	1	~~3 8 00~~ ~~3 8 0 00~~		~~3 8 00~~ ~~3 8 0 00~~	

Account with corrected posting

advisable to establish clearly both (1) the debit(s) and credit(s) of the entry in which the error occurred and (2) the debit(s) and credit(s) that should have been recorded. T accounts may be helpful in making this analysis, as in the example below.

Entry in which error occurred:

OFFICE SUPPLIES   CASH
        500 | | 500

Entry that should have been recorded:

OFFICE EQUIPMENT   CASH
        500 | | 500

Comparison of the two sets of T accounts reveals that the erroneous debit of $500 to Office Supplies may be corrected by a $500 credit to that account and that Office Equipment should be debited for $500. The following correcting entry is then journalized and posted:

79

JOURNAL   PAGE 18

	DATE	DESCRIPTION	POST. REF.	DEBIT	CREDIT	
1	1973 Mar. 31	Office Equipment	18	5 0 0 00		1
2		Office Supplies	15		5 0 0 00	2
3		To correct erroneous debit to				3
4		Office Supplies on March 5.				4
5		See invoice from Allen				5
6		Supply Company. CRN				6

Correcting entry

Although there is some latitude in the techniques employed to correct errors, the explanations should be sufficiently clear to be readily understood by anyone examining the records.

QUESTIONS

1. What is the nature of the balance in the supplies account at the end of the accounting period (a) before adjustment? (b) after adjustment?

2. What is the term usually employed in referring to (a) unexpired costs? (b) expired costs?

3. Which of the following services are customarily paid for only after they have become an expired cost: (a) property and casualty insurance, (b) water, (c) services of employees, (d) rent, (e) electric power?

4. If the effect of the credit portion of an adjusting entry is to decrease the balance of an asset account, which of the following statements describes the effect of the debit portion of the entry: (a) decreases the balance of a liability account? (b) increases the balance of an expense account? (c) decreases the balance of an expense account?

5. Does every adjusting entry have an effect on the determination of the amount of net income for a period? Explain.

6. On October 1, an enterprise pays the October rent on the building that it occupies. (a) Do the rights acquired at October 1 represent an asset or an expense? (b) What is the justification for debiting Rent Expense at the time of payment?

7. (a) Explain the purpose of the two accounts: Depreciation Expense and Accumulated Depreciation. (b) What is the normal balance of each account? (c) Is it customary for the balances of the two accounts to be equal in amount? (d) In what financial statements, if any, will each account appear?

8. How is the *book value* of a plant asset determined?

9. At the end of January, the first month of the fiscal year, the usual adjusting entry transferring expired insurance to an expense account is inadvertently omitted. Which items will be erroneously stated, because of the error, on (a) the income statement for January and (b) the balance sheet as of January 31? Also indicate whether the items in error will be overstated or understated.

10. Accrued salaries of $800 owed to employees for December 30 and 31 are not taken into consideration in preparing the financial statements for the fiscal year ended December 31. Which items will be erroneously stated, because of the error, on (a) the income statement for the year and (b) the balance sheet as of December 31? Also indicate whether the items in error will be overstated or understated.

11. Assume that the error in question 10 was not corrected and that the $800 of accrued salaries was included in the first salary payment in January. Which items will be erroneously stated, because of failure to correct the initial error, on (a) the income statement for January and (b) the balance sheet as of January 31?

12. Is the work sheet a substitute for the financial statements? Discuss.

13. What type of accounts are closed by transferring their balances to Income Summary (a) as a credit, (b) as a debit?

14. To what account is the income summary account closed (a) in a sole proprietorship, (b) in a corporation?

15. To what account in the ledger of a corporation is the account "Dividends" periodically closed?

16. Identify the accounts in the following list that should be closed to Income Summary at the end of the fiscal year: (a) Accounts Payable, (b) Accumulated Depreciation, (c) Cash, (d) Depreciation Expense, (e) Insurance Expense, (f) R. Nash, Drawing, (g) R. Nash, Capital, (h) Office Equipment, (i) Prepaid Insurance, (j) Salary Expense, (k) Sales, (l) Supplies.

17. Are adjusting and closing entries in the journal dated as of the last day of the fiscal period or as of the day the entries are actually made? Explain.

18. Which of the following accounts in the ledger of a corporation will ordinarily appear in the post-closing trial balance: (a) Accounts Receivable, (b) Accumulated Depreciation, (c) Capital Stock, (d) Cash, (e) Depreciation Expense, (f) Dividends, (g) Equipment, (h) Prepaid Insurance, (i) Retained Earnings, (j) Sales, (k) Utilities Expense?

19. At what time intervals are the temporary capital accounts ordinarily closed and a new cycle begun?

20. For an enterprise that closes its temporary capital accounts annually as of June 30, the end of its fiscal year, what period will be covered by the income statement prepared from the work sheet as of November 30?

EXERCISES

3-1. The balance in the prepaid insurance account before adjustment at the end of the year is $1,460. Journalize the adjusting entry required under each of the following alternatives: (a) the amount of insurance expired during the year is $610; (b) the amount of unexpired insurance applicable to future periods is $610.

3-2. A business enterprise pays weekly salaries of $4,500 on Friday for a five-day week ending on that day. Journalize the necessary adjusting entry at the end of the fiscal period, assuming that the fiscal period ends (a) on Monday, (b) on Thursday.

3-3. On January 2 of the current year a business enterprise pays $720 to the city for taxes (license fees) for the coming year. The same enterprise is also required to pay an annual tax (on property) at the end of the year. The estimated amount of the current year's property tax allocable to January is $95. (a) Journalize the two adjusting entries required to bring the accounts affected by the two taxes up-to-date as of January 31. (b) What is the amount of tax expense for the month of January?

3-4. After all revenues and expenses have been closed at the end of the fiscal year, Income Summary has a debit of $140,000 and a credit of $125,000. As of the same date Eric Mason, Capital has a credit balance of $95,000 and Eric Mason, Drawing has a debit balance of $9,000. (a) Journalize the entries required to complete the closing of the accounts. (b) State the amount of Mason's capital at the end of the period.

3-5. Selected accounts from the ledger of Gibson's, Incorporated, for the current fiscal year ended December 31 are presented in T form below. Prepare a retained earnings statement for the year.

CAPITAL STOCK				DIVIDENDS			
		Jan. 1	200,000	Mar. 15	2,000	Dec. 31	10,000
				June 15	2,000		
				Sept. 15	2,000		
				Dec. 15	4,000		

RETAINED EARNINGS				INCOME SUMMARY			
Dec. 31	10,000	Jan. 1	70,000	Dec. 31	165,000	Dec. 31	210,000
		Dec. 31	45,000	31	45,000		

3-6. Selected accounts from the ledger of Shafer & Company for the current fiscal year ended June 30 are presented in T form below. Prepare a capital statement for the year.

FRED SHAFER, CAPITAL				FRED SHAFER, DRAWING	
June 30	10,000	July 1	42,000	Sept. 30	3,000	June 30	10,000
		June 30	7,000	Dec. 30	2,000		
				Mar. 30	5,000		

INCOME SUMMARY			
June 30	63,000	June 30	70,000
30	7,000		

3-7. A number of errors in journalizing and posting transactions are described below. Present the journal entries to correct the errors.

(a) Rent of $300 paid for the current month was recorded as a debit to Prepaid Insurance and a credit to Cash.

(b) Equipment of $1,500 purchased on account was recorded as a debit to Buildings and a credit to Cash.

(c) Payment of $400 cash to L. B. North, owner of the enterprise, for his personal use was recorded as a debit to Salary Expense and a credit to Cash.

(d) Cash of $160 received from a customer on account was recorded as a $610 debit to Cash and credit to Accounts Receivable.

(e) A $30 cash payment for utilities expense was recorded as a debit to Supplies and a credit to Cash.

PROBLEMS

The following additional problems for this chapter are located in Appendix B: 3-1B, 3-2B, 3-3B.

3-1A. The trial balance of Ventura Laundromat at December 31, the end of the current fiscal year, and data needed to determine year-end adjustments are presented below and on the next page.

Ventura Laundromat
Trial Balance
December 31, 19—

Cash	1,198	
Laundry Supplies	1,965	
Prepaid Insurance	574	
Laundry Equipment	22,700	
Accumulated Depreciation		5,600
Accounts Payable		315
Helen Walsh, Capital		13,006
Helen Walsh, Drawing	6,120	
Laundry Revenue		23,820
Wages Expense	7,335	
Rent Expense	1,320	
Utilities Expense	1,025	
Miscellaneous Expense	504	
	42,741	42,741

Adjustment data:
(a) Inventory of laundry supplies at December 31 . $ 210
(b) Insurance premiums expired during the year . . 305
(c) Depreciation on equipment during the year . . . 1,810
(d) Wages accrued but not paid at December 31 . . 77

Instructions:
(1) Record the trial balance on an eight-column work sheet.
(2) Complete the work sheet.
(3) Prepare an income statement, a capital statement (no additional investments were made during the year), and a balance sheet.
(4) On the basis of the adjustments data in the work sheet, journalize the adjusting entries.
(5) On the basis of the data in the work sheet or in the income and capital statements, journalize the closing entries.
(6) Compute the following:
(a) Percent of net income to sales.
(b) Percent of net income to the capital balance at the beginning of the year.

3-2A. As of June 30, the end of the current fiscal year, the accountant for Vance Company prepared a trial balance, journalized and posted the adjusting entries, prepared an adjusted trial balance, prepared the statements, and completed the other procedures required at the end of the accounting cycle. The two trial balances as of June 30, one before adjustments and the other after adjustments, are presented below.

83

Vance Company
Trial Balance
June 30, 19—

	Unadjusted		Adjusted	
Cash	1,720		1,720	
Supplies	2,365		575	
Prepaid Rent	3,500		1,650	
Prepaid Insurance	405		230	
Automobile	4,900		4,900	
Accumulated Depr. — Automobile		825		1,875
Equipment	14,100		14,100	
Accumulated Depr. — Equipment		3,675		5,000
Accounts Payable		460		540
Salaries Payable		—		130
Taxes Payable		—		65
Arthur Vance, Capital		12,950		12,950
Arthur Vance, Drawing	10,500		10,500	
Service Fees Earned		35,900		35,900
Salaries Expense	14,710		14,840	
Rent Expense	—		1,850	
Supplies Expense	—		1,790	
Depreciation Expense — Equipment . .	—		1,325	
Depreciation Expense — Automobile .	—		1,050	
Utilities Expense	595		675	
Taxes Expense	575		640	
Insurance Expense	—		175	
Miscellaneous Expense	440		440	
	53,810	53,810	56,460	56,460

Instructions:

(1) Present the eight journal entries that were required to adjust the accounts at June 30. None of the accounts was affected by more than one adjusting entry.

(2) Present the journal entries that were required to close the accounts at June 30.

(3) Prepare a capital statement for the fiscal year ended June 30. There were no additional investments during the year.

If the working papers correlating with this textbook are not used, omit Problem 3-3A.

3-3A. The ledger and trial balance of Todd Machine Repairs as of October 31, the end of the first month of its current fiscal year, are presented in the working papers. The accounts had been closed on September 30.

Instructions:

(1) Complete the eight-column work sheet. Data needed to determine the necessary adjusting entries are as follows:

Inventory of supplies at October 31................	$312.00
Insurance premiums expired during October........	81.60
Depreciation on the truck during October..........	170.00
Depreciation on equipment during October.........	115.00
Wages accrued but not paid at October 31.........	108.00

(2) Prepare an income statement, a capital statement, and a balance sheet.

(3) Journalize and post the adjusting entries, inserting balances in the accounts affected.

(4) Journalize and post the closing entries. Indicate closed accounts by inserting a line in both balance columns opposite the closing entry. Insert the new balance of the capital account.

(5) Prepare a post-closing trial balance.

3-4A. Columbia Lanes, Inc., prepares interim statements at the end of each month and closes its accounts annually as of December 31. The interim income statement for the three months ended March 31 of the current year, the trial balance at April 30 of the current year, and the adjustment data needed at April 30 are presented below and on page 85. (Corporation income tax is excluded from consideration.)

Columbia Lanes, Inc.
Income Statement
For Three Months Ended March 31, 19—

Bowling revenue......................		$27,134
Operating expenses:		
Salaries and wages expense...........	$ 8,950	
Depreciation expense — equipment....	2,700	
Advertising expense.................	1,100	
Utilities expense.....................	780	
Depreciation expense — building......	675	
Repairs expense.....................	640	
Supplies expense....................	305	
Insurance expense...................	255	
Miscellaneous expense...............	810	
Total operating expenses...........		16,215
Net income.........................		$10,919

Columbia Lanes, Inc.
Trial Balance
April 30, 19—

Cash...........................	4,620	
Prepaid Insurance....................	985	
Supplies........................	1,320	
Equipment.......................	130,700	
Accumulated Depreciation — Equipment.		26,400
Building........................	75,950	
Accumulated Depreciation — Building...		9,800
Land...........................	12,000	
Accounts Payable....................		2,300
Capital Stock.....................		100,000
Retained Earnings..................		70,725
Dividends.......................	2,500	
Bowling Revenue...................		34,792
Salaries and Wages Expense...........	11,620	
Advertising Expense.................	1,410	
Utilities Expense...................	1,020	
Repairs Expense....................	772	
Miscellaneous Expense...............	1,120	
	244,017	244,017

Adjustment data at April 30:

(a)	Insurance expired for the period January 1–April 30..........	$ 340
(b)	Inventory of supplies on April 30............................	910
(c)	Depreciation of equipment for the period January 1–April 30...	3,600
(d)	Depreciation of building for the period January 1–April 30.....	900
(e)	Accrued salaries and wages on April 30.....................	215

Instructions:

(1) Record the trial balance on an eight-column work sheet.
(2) Complete the work sheet.
(3) Prepare an interim income statement for the four months ended April 30.
(4) Prepare an interim retained earnings statement for the four months ended April 30. (See page 21 for form of statement.)
(5) Prepare an interim balance sheet as of April 30.
(6) On the basis of the income statement for the four-month period and the income statement for the three-month period, prepare an interim income statement for the month of April.
(7) Compute the percent of net income to revenue for:
  (a) The three-month period ended March 31.
  (b) The four-month period ended April 30.
  (c) The month of April.
(8) Compute the percent of net income for the four-month period ended April 30 to total capital as of the beginning of the fiscal year. The capital stock account remained unchanged during the four-month period.

3-5A. The selected transactions and errors described below relate to the accounts of Oakwood Co. during the current fiscal year:

March 15. Richard T. Bryant established the business with the investment of $17,000 in cash and $1,100 in equipment, on which there was a balance owed of $450. The account payable is to be recorded in the ledger of the enterprise.

May 20. Discovered that $45 of supplies returned to the supplier for credit had been journalized and posted as a debit to Cash and a credit to Prepaid Insurance. Payment had not been made for the supplies.

June 10. Discovered that cash of $410, received from a customer on account, had been journalized and posted as a debit to Cash and a credit to Commissions Earned.

July 25. Received $620 payment on a note receivable ($600) and interest income ($20).

Aug. 10. Acquired land and a building to be used as an office at a contract price of $25,000, of which $2,000 was allocated to the land. The property was encumbered by a mortgage of $10,000. Paid the seller $15,000 in cash and agreed to assume the responsibility for paying the mortgage note.

Sept. 20. Discovered that a withdrawal of $850 by the owner had been debited to Miscellaneous Expense.

Oct. 10. Discovered that a cash payment of $73 for prepaid insurance had been journalized and posted as a debit to Supplies of $37 and a credit to Cash of $37.

Nov. 9. Paid the quarterly installment due on the principal of the mortgage note, $750, and the quarterly interest, $200.

Instructions:

Journalize the transactions and the corrections in a two-column journal. When there are more than two items in an entry, present the entry in compound form.

Chapter 4

ACCOUNTING FOR SALES AND CASH RECEIPTS

SPECIAL JOURNALS

Innumerable devices and techniques are available for processing transaction media. The recording, classifying, and summarizing of data may be accomplished manually or by the use of mechanical, electrical, or electronic equipment. Manually operated systems are easier to understand and more adaptable to learning through practice; therefore, special journals designed for manual operation are described and illustrated in this and the following chapter. More advanced techniques are explored in later chapters.

In the two preceding chapters all transactions were initially recorded in a two-column journal, then posted individually to the appropriate accounts in the ledger. The impracticability of applying such detailed procedures to large numbers of transactions of a repetitive nature is readily apparent. One of the simplest methods of reducing the processing time and the attendant expense is to expand the two-column journal to a multi-column journal. Each money column added to the general purpose journal is restricted to the recording of transactions affecting a specified account. For example, a special column could be reserved solely for recording debits to the cash account and another special column could be used only for recording credits to the cash account. The addition of the two special columns would eliminate the writing of "Cash" in the journal for every receipt and payment of cash. Furthermore, there would be no need to post each individual debit and credit to the cash account. Instead, the "Cash Dr." and "Cash Cr." columns could be totaled periodically and only the totals posted, yielding additional economies. In a similar manner special columns could be added for recording credits to sales, debits and credits to accounts receivable and accounts payable, and for other entries of a repetitive nature. Although the maximum number of columns that may be effectively used in a single journal is not subject to exact determination, there is an optimum

87

beyond which the journal would become unwieldy. Also, the possibilities of errors in recording become greater as the number of columns and the width of the page increases.

An all-purpose multicolumn journal is frequently satisfactory for a small business enterprise that requires the services of only one book-keeper. If the volume of transactions is sufficient to require two or more bookkeepers, the use of a single journal is usually not practicable. The next logical development in expanding the system is to replace an all-purpose journal with a number of *special journals*, each designed to record a single type of transaction. Of course, special journals would be needed only for the types of transactions that occur frequently. Most enterprises have many transactions in which cash is received and many in which cash is paid out; hence, it is common practice to employ a special journal for recording cash receipts and another special journal for recording cash payments. An enterprise that sells services or merchandise to customers on account might advantageously employ a special journal designed solely for recording such transactions. Conversely, a business that does not extend credit would have no need for such a journal.

In addition to variations among enterprises in the number and type of special journals employed, there are also many possible variations in the design of any particular journal. For example, the accounting systems of both a retail clothing store and an insurance agency would need to provide for the expeditious recording of cash receipts, but the cash receipts journal designed for one of the businesses would not be suitable for the other.

MERCHANDISING

The special journals described and illustrated in this and the following chapter are designed for use by a business engaged in the buying and selling of merchandise. Familiarity with the nature of the operations of an enterprise is prerequisite to understanding its accounting system. Accordingly, some of the discussion that follows is devoted to the usual customs and practices applicable to merchandising businesses.

Merchandising activities may ordinarily be classified as *wholesale* or *retail*. Manufacturers, producers, and importers usually sell their goods to wholesalers, to brokers, or directly to retailers. Wholesale merchants sell to retailers and sometimes to large consumers, such as schools and hospitals. Retail merchants sell to consumers.

The number, purpose, and design of the special journals used by merchandising enterprises will of necessity vary, depending upon the needs of the particular enterprise. In the typical firm of moderate size the transactions that occur most frequently and the special journals in which they are recorded are listed at the top of the next page.

TRANSACTION:		RECORDED IN:
Sale of merchandise		
on account	⟶	Sales journal
Receipt of cash from		
any source	⟶	Cash receipts journal
Purchase of merchandise or other item		
on account	⟶	Purchases journal
Payment of cash for		
any purpose	⟶	Cash payments journal

Although most of the transactions of a typical merchandising business fit one of the four categories listed above, there are always some that do not. Provision must also be made for the recording of correcting, adjusting, and closing entries. The two-column form illustrated in earlier chapters can be used for all such miscellaneous entries that do not "fit" in any of the special journals. The two-column form is commonly referred to as the *general journal* or simply as the *journal*.

SALES

Sales of merchandise by a merchandising business are typically identified merely as *Sales*. The number of individual sales transactions completed is typically quite large in relationship to other transactions. Some businesses sell merchandise for cash only, others sell only on a credit basis, and still others have many transactions of both types.

Sales of merchandise for cash result in a debit to Cash and a credit to Sales. The customary practice is to record *cash sales* in the cash receipts journal. Sales of merchandise *on account* result in a debit to Accounts Receivable and a credit to Sales and should be recorded in the sales journal. A sale of supplies, plant assets, or other items acquired for use in the business (i.e. not as merchandise for resale) must be recorded by a debit to the Cash or appropriate receivable account and a credit to the supplies account or other account for the asset that is being sold. Such transactions should be recorded in the cash receipts journal or the general journal, depending upon the terms of sale; they must not be recorded in the sales journal.

TRADE DISCOUNTS

Manufacturers and wholesalers of certain types of commodities frequently grant substantial reductions from the *list price* quoted in their catalogs. Such reductions in price are called *trade discounts*. Trade discounts are a convenient method of making revisions in prices without the necessity of reprinting catalogs. As prices fluctuate, new schedules of discounts may be issued. Trade discounts may also be used to make price differentials among different classes of customers. For example, a manufacturer may use two different schedules of discounts, one of which applies to wholesalers and the other to retailers.

There is no need to record list prices and their related trade discounts in the accounts. For example, the seller of an article listed at $100 with a trade discount of $40 would record the transaction as a sale of $60. Similarly, the buyer would record the transaction as a purchase of $60. For accounting purposes it is only the agreed price, which in the example is $60, that is significant. Trade discounts have been described here in order to more readily distinguish between them and another type of discount discussed in later paragraphs.

PROCEDURES FOR SALES ON ACCOUNT

Every sale is made in response to an order received from a customer. An order given a retail store is usually oral; an order given a manufacturing, a wholesale, or a mail-order business is ordinarily written. There are many methods of handling orders and of recording sales, the routines varying with the type and the size of the business.

In a retail business a *sales ticket* is usually prepared for a sale on account. Sales tickets are usually prepared in duplicate or triplicate. One copy is given to the customer, one copy is sent to the accounting department for use as the basis of an entry in the sales journal, and one copy may be used as the salesman's personal record of his sales or for such other purposes as the organization of the business requires.

In a manufacturing, a wholesale, or a mail-order business, a written order is received from a customer or from the salesman who obtained the order from the customer. After the order has been approved by the credit department, it is sent to the billing department, where the invoice is prepared. At least two copies of a *sales invoice* are made by the billing department. The original is sent to the customer, and the carbon copy is sent to the accounting department for use as the basis of an entry in the sales journal. Sometimes additional copies of the invoice are made for the use of different departments of the business. For example, the credit department may desire a copy for use in following up the payment of the invoice, or the shipping department may need a copy as authorization to ship the goods. A typical sales invoice is illustrated on the next page.

CONTROLLING ACCOUNTS AND SUBSIDIARY LEDGERS

When illustrating credit transactions with customers in earlier chapters, the debits and credits to the customer were recorded in the single account "Accounts Receivable." Consideration of procedures associated with maintaining an individual account receivable for each credit customer was purposely postponed until this point.

INVOICE   **No. 615**

MIDTOWN *Electric* CORPORATION
1200 SAN VICENTE BLVD.
LOS ANGELES, CALIFORNIA 90019

SOLD TO
R. A. Barnes, Inc.
814 Glenview
Pasadena, California 91109

Date October 2, 1973

Terms 2/10, n/30

Shipped Via Express Collect

QUANTITY	DESCRIPTION	PRICE	TOTAL
6	Transformers, Model 392 E	40.00	240.00
12	Switches, Model 719 J	5.00	60.00
50	Resistors, Model 420 K	1.00	50.00
			350.00

Sales invoice

It is possible to delete from the ledger the single account for accounts receivable and substitute a separate account for each individual credit customer. However, such an arrangement is not satisfactory when there are a substantial number of credit customers. The ledger would be cumbersome, the likelihood of posting errors would be increased, and the preparation of the trial balance and the statements delayed.

When there is a substantial number of individual accounts with a common characteristic, such as accounts with credit customers, it is customary to place them in a separate ledger called a *subsidiary ledger*. The principal ledger, which contains all of the balance sheet and income statement accounts, is then referred to as the *general ledger*. In order to facilitate the preparation of a trial balance and the discovery of errors, each subsidiary ledger is represented in the general ledger by a single summarizing account which is called a *controlling account*. Each controlling account may be said to *control* its related subsidiary ledger.

The controlling account for credit customers is Accounts Receivable, which is located in the general ledger. The individual accounts with such customers comprise a subsidiary ledger called the *accounts receivable ledger* or *customers ledger*.

The special journals in which numerous transactions affecting customer's accounts are recorded are designed in such a way as to facilitate the posting of monthly totals to the controlling account, Accounts Receivable, and the posting of the individual transactions to the accounts receivable ledger. The basic techniques of posting a sales journal are depicted in the flow chart presented at the top of the next page.

91

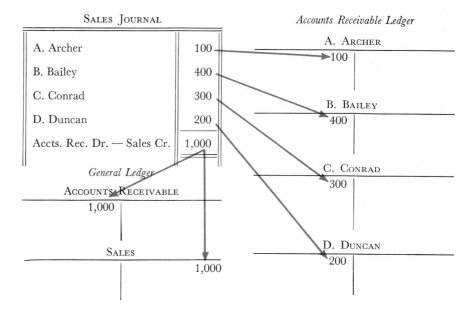

Flow of data
from sales
journal to
ledgers

The total of the sales journal is posted both as a $1,000 debit to Accounts Receivable and a $1,000 credit to Sales in the general ledger. The individual debits to Archer, Bailey, Conrad, and Duncan are also posted to their respective accounts in the accounts receivable ledger. It is evident that the sum of the debits to the four individual accounts in the subsidiary ledger is equal to the single $1,000 debit to the controlling account in the general ledger.

SALES JOURNAL

The sales journal is used solely for recording *sales of merchandise on account*. As was indicated earlier, sales of merchandise for cash are recorded in the cash receipts journal. Sales of assets not a part of the stock in trade are recorded in the cash receipts journal or the general journal.

The sales journal of Midtown Electric Corporation is illustrated on page 93. The sales invoice illustrated on page 91 is recorded on the first line. The invoice number (615) is recorded in order to facilitate future reference to the supporting document if questions concerning the transaction should arise. The customer's name (R. A. Barnes, Inc.) is recorded in the Account Debited column, and the invoice total ($350) is recorded in the amount column, which represents both a debit to Accounts Receivable and a credit to Sales.

POSTING THE SALES JOURNAL

Unlike the numbering system for accounts in the general ledger, the accounts in the accounts receivable ledger are usually arranged alpha-

SALES JOURNAL PAGE 35

	DATE		INVOICE NO.	ACCOUNT DEBITED	POST. REF.	ACCTS. REC. DR. SALES CR.	
1	1973 Oct.	2	615	R. A. Barnes, Inc.	√	3 5 0 00	1
2		3	616	Standard Supply Co.	√	1 6 0 4 00	2
3		5	617	David T. Mattox	√	3 0 5 00	3
4		9	618	R. A. Barnes, Inc.	√	1 3 9 6 00	4
5		10	619	Adler Company	√	7 5 0 00	5
6		17	620	R. E. Hamilton, Inc.	√	8 6 5 00	6
7		23	621	Cooper & Co.	√	1 5 0 2 00	7
8		26	622	Tracy & Lee, Inc.	√	2 6 0 00	8
9		27	623	Standard Supply Co.	√	1 9 0 8 00	9
10		31				8 9 4 0 00	10
11						(1 1 3) (4 1 1)	11

Sales journal after posting

betically, providing ready access when posting, and making it possible to insert new accounts and remove inactive accounts without disturbing the general sequence. Postings to the accounts should be made at frequent intervals. Daily posting distributes the work load. It also provides current account balances, which is advantageous when considering requests for additional credit or when answering inquiries. The source of the entry in the sales journal is indicated in the posting reference column of the account by the letter "S" and the appropriate page number. As each debit to a customer's account is posted, a check mark (√) is inserted in the posting reference column of the sales journal.

93

A customer's account with a posting from the sales journal above is illustrated below. Inasmuch as the balances in customer's accounts are normally debit balances, there is no need for the four-column account form illustrated earlier. When a customer's account is overpaid and a credit balance occurs, such fact should be indicated by an asterisk or parentheses in the Balance column. When an account is in balance, a line may be drawn in the Balance column, as illustrated on page 103.

NAME Adler Company
ADDRESS 7608 Melton Ave., Los Angeles, California 90025

DATE		ITEM	POST. REF.	DEBIT	CREDIT	BALANCE
1973 Oct.	10		S35	7 5 0 00		7 5 0 00

An account in the accounts receivable ledger

At the end of each month the amount column of the sales journal is added and the total posted as a debit to Accounts Receivable and a credit to Sales. The respective account numbers are then inserted below the total to indicate that the posting has been completed. The procedure is illustrated by the sales journal above and the two general ledger accounts presented on the next page.

ACCOUNT	Accounts Receivable							ACCOUNT NO.	113	

DATE		ITEM	POST. REF.	DEBIT	CREDIT	BALANCE	
						DEBIT	CREDIT
1973 Oct.	1	Balance	✓			5 2 6 0 00	
	31		S35	8 9 4 0 00		14 2 0 0 00	

ACCOUNT	Sales							ACCOUNT NO.	411	

DATE		ITEM	POST. REF.	DEBIT	CREDIT	BALANCE	
						DEBIT	CREDIT
1973 Oct.	1	Balance	✓				108 2 3 6 00
	31		S35		8 9 4 0 00		117 1 7 6 00

Accounts receivable account and sales account in the general ledger after the sales journal has been posted

SALES RETURNS AND ALLOWANCES

Merchandise sold may be returned by the customer (*sales return*) or, because of defects or for other reasons, the customer may be allowed a reduction from the original price at which the goods were sold (*sales allowance*). If the return or allowance is related to a sale on account, the seller usually issues to the customer a *credit memorandum* indicating the amount for which the customer is to be credited and the reason therefor. A typical credit memorandum is illustrated below.

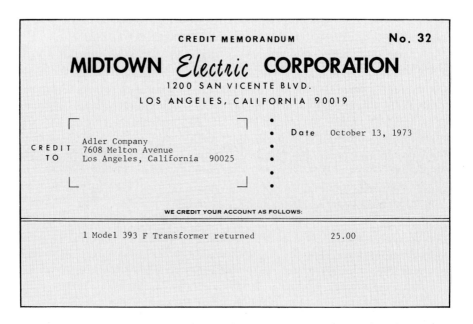

Credit memorandum

The effect of a sales return or allowance is a reduction in sales revenue and a reduction in cash or accounts receivable. If the sales account is debited, however, the balance of the account at the end of the period will represent net sales, and the volume of returns and allowances will not be disclosed. Because of the loss in revenue resulting from allowances, and the various expenses (transportation, unpacking, repairing, etc.) related to returns, it is advisable that management be informed of the magnitude of such transactions. It is therefore preferable to debit an account entitled Sales Returns and Allowances. If the original sale had been made for cash, the amount of the refund is recorded as a credit to Cash. Otherwise the remainder of the transaction is recorded by a credit to Accounts Receivable (in the general ledger) and to the specific customer (in the subsidiary ledger).

Midtown Electric Corporation issued two credit memorandums during the month. They were recorded in the general journal as shown below.

JOURNAL   PAGE 18

	DATE		DESCRIPTION	POST. REF.	DEBIT	CREDIT	
1	1973 Oct.	13	Sales Returns and Allowances	412	2 5 00		1
2			Accounts Receivable - Adler Company	113 ✓		2 5 00	2
3			Credit Memo No. 32.				3
33		28	Sales Returns and Allowances	412	6 5 00		33
34			Accounts Receivable - Cooper & Co.	113 ✓		6 5 00	34
35			Credit Memo No. 33.				35

General journal entries for sales returns and allowances

95

Note that in each transaction both the controlling account and the customer's account are credited. As an indication that the amount must be posted to both the general ledger and the subsidiary ledger, a diagonal line should be placed in the posting reference column *at the time the entry is recorded in the general journal*. When the credit is posted to the customer's account, a check mark is inserted at the right of the diagonal line. The number of the accounts receivable controlling account is inserted at the left in accordance with the usual routine of posting to that account in the general ledger. After the posting has been completed, the accounts affected appear as reproduced at the top of the following page.

If the volume of credit memorandums issued is substantial, the general journal may be expanded by inserting special columns to record debits to Sales Returns and Allowances and credits to Accounts Receivable. Alternatively, an additional journal such as the one illustrated at the bottom of the next page may be employed. The recording and posting routines for this special journal are the same as those that apply to the sales journal.

It should be noted that in each of the foregoing illustrations the amount of the credit memorandums was credited both to Accounts

GENERAL LEDGER

ACCOUNT   Accounts Receivable   ACCOUNT NO.   113

DATE	ITEM	POST. REF.	DEBIT	CREDIT	BALANCE DEBIT	BALANCE CREDIT
1973 Oct. 1	Balance	✓			5 2 6 0 00	
13		J18		2 5 00	5 2 3 5 00	
28		J18		6 5 00	5 1 7 0 00	

ACCOUNT   Sales Returns and Allowances   ACCOUNT NO.   412

DATE	ITEM	POST. REF.	DEBIT	CREDIT	BALANCE DEBIT	BALANCE CREDIT
1973 Oct. 1	Balance	✓			2 3 6 5 00	
13		J18	2 5 00		2 3 9 0 00	
28		J18	6 5 00		2 4 5 5 00	

ACCOUNTS RECEIVABLE LEDGER

NAME   Adler Company

ADDRESS   7608 Melton Ave., Los Angeles, California 90025

DATE	ITEM	POST. REF.	DEBIT	CREDIT	BALANCE
1973 Oct. 10		S35	7 5 0 00		7 5 0 00
13		J18		2 5 00	7 2 5 00

NAME   Cooper & Co.

ADDRESS   57 LaBrea Ave., Los Angeles, California 90036

DATE	ITEM	POST. REF.	DEBIT	CREDIT	BALANCE
1973 Oct. 23		S35	1 5 0 2 00		1 5 0 2 00
28		J18		6 5 00	1 4 3 7 00

96

Accounts receivable account, sales returns and allowances account, and customers' accounts after the posting of sales returns and allowances

SALES RETURNS AND ALLOWANCES JOURNAL   PAGE 2

DATE	CR. MEMO. NO.	ACCOUNT CREDITED	POST. REF.	SALES RET. & ALLOW. DR. ACCTS. REC. CR.
1973 Nov. 2	12	Ralph Boyer	✓	142 00
6	13	Morrow & Co.	✓	150 00
29	26	J. R. Field Co.	✓	13 00
30				1,762 50
				(412) (113)

Sales returns and allowances journal

Receivable and to the customer's account. If merchandise is returned or an allowance is granted after the customer has made full payment of his account, the seller may elect to make a cash refund instead of crediting the customer's account. In such cases the entire transaction would be recorded in the cash payments journal, which is considered in the following chapter.

BUSINESS DOCUMENTS AS JOURNALS

Instead of recording each merchandise sale on account in a sales journal, many businesses use carbon copies of sales invoices as the posting medium. Postings to the customers' accounts are made directly from each carbon copy, and the total amount for the month is determined from an adding machine listing of all of the duplicate invoices. The total amount thus obtained provides the basis for an entry in the general journal debiting Accounts Receivable and crediting Sales.

The use of duplicate sales invoices as a journal may effect a material savings in bookkeeping expenses, particularly if the volume of sales transactions is substantial. Not only is the necessity of copying the name of the customer and other details in the sales journal avoided, but the elimination of this intermediate step also reduces the number of errors and the amount of time devoted to their detection and correction. In addition, posting to customers' accounts can be facilitated by dividing invoices into a number of alphabetical groupings and assigning each segment to a particular posting clerk.

The same system can be employed with equal effectiveness in accounting for returns and allowances, carbon copies of the credit memorandums becoming in effect the sales returns and allowances journal.

97

CASH RECEIPTS

All transactions that increase the amount of cash are recorded in a cash receipts journal. Cash may be received from a variety of sources, such as investments in the business by the owner, receipts from cash sales, collections from customers to whom sales have been made on account, and collections of principal and interest on notes receivable. In a typical merchandising business the most frequent sources of cash receipts are likely to be cash sales and collections from customers on account.

Before describing the form and the use of the cash receipts journal, it is desirable that consideration be given to the nature of the agreement between a business enterprise and its customers.

CREDIT TERMS

The arrangements agreed upon by the seller and the buyer as to when payments for commodities are to be made are called the *credit terms*. If payment is required immediately upon delivery, the terms are said to be "cash" or "net cash." Otherwise, the buyer is allowed a specified time, known as the *credit period*, in which to pay.

There is considerable variation in credit periods. Retailers may require that all purchases by customers in one month be paid for by a particular date in the succeeding month. They sometimes stipulate that purchases made after a particular date, such as the 25th, will not be included in the billing for that month but will be carried over to the succeeding month. They may also have special "budget" and "lay-away" terms.

Among manufacturers and wholesalers it is usual for the credit period to begin with the date of the sale as evidenced by the date of the invoice. If payment is due within a stated number of days after the date of the invoice, for example 30 days, the terms are said to be "net 30 days,"[1] which may be written as "n/30." If payment is due by the end of the month in which the sale was made, it may be expressed as "n/eom."

CASH DISCOUNTS

As a means of encouraging payment before the expiration of the credit period, a discount may be offered for the early payment of cash. Thus the expression "2/10, n/30" means that, while the credit period is 30 days, the debtor may deduct 2% of the amount of the bill if payment is made in 10 days from the date of the invoice. This deduction is known as a *cash discount*. For example, assume a sales invoice totaling $500 dated July 6, with credit terms of 2/10, n/30. If the buyer mails his check on or before July 16, he may deduct $10 from the invoice and pay $490. If he wishes to wait the full credit term, he should mail his check for $500, or otherwise deliver it, not later than August 5.

From the seller's point of view, cash discounts are known as *sales discounts*; the purchaser refers to them as *purchases discounts*. At one time cash discounts were considered to be similar to interest for the use of money and were accordingly treated as an expense by the seller and as revenue by the buyer. Today, however, when cash discounts are offered by the seller, it is with the expectation that the customer will pay within the discount period. In effect the seller is offering to make the sale for the invoice price reduced by the amount of the cash discount. Therefore, it is customary for the seller to view cash discounts as a reduction of sales revenue and for the buyer to consider them as a deduction from the quoted price of the commodity purchased.

CASH RECEIPTS JOURNAL

Inasmuch as the cash receipts journal is designed for the recording of all incoming cash, it obviously should contain a special column entitled Cash Dr. The number and titles of the other columns will be governed

[1]The word "net" in this context does not have the usual meaning of a remainder after all relevant deductions, have been subtracted, as in "net sales," "net income," etc.

by the frequency of the various types of transactions in which cash is received. Receipts of cash by Midtown Electric Corporation that occur most frequently are from cash sales and collections from retailers to whom sales have been made on 2/10, n/30 terms. There are also occasional receipts of cash from various other sources. Accordingly, the cash receipts journal illustrated below has the following columns:

For credits — Sundry Accounts, Sales, Accounts Receivable
For debits — Sales Discount, Cash

CASH RECEIPTS JOURNAL   PAGE 14

	DATE		ACCOUNT CREDITED	POST. REF.	SUNDRY ACCOUNTS CR.	SALES CR.	ACCOUNTS RECEIVABLE CR.	SALES DISCOUNT DR.	CASH DR.	
1	1973 Oct.	2	Notes Receivable	112	4 00 00				4 12 00	1
2			Interest Income	811	12 00					2
3		5	R. A. Barnes, Inc.	✓			8 00 00	16 00	7 84 00	3
4		6	Fogarty & Jacobs	✓			6 25 00	12 50	6 12 50	4
5		7	Sales	✓		1 70 0 00			1 70 0 00	5
6		10	David T. Mattox	✓			6 00 00	12 00	5 88 00	6
7		13	Standard Supply Co.	✓			16 04 00	32 08	15 71 92	7
8		14	Sales	✓		1 63 2 00			1 63 2 00	8
9		17	Adler Company	✓			7 25 00	14 50	7 10 50	9
10		19	R. E. Hamilton, Inc.	✓			18 50 00		18 50 00	10
11		21	Sales	✓		1 92 0 30			1 92 0 30	11
12		23	Purchases	511	36 20				36 20	12
13		24	B. C. Wallace Corporation	✓			2 00 00		2 00 00	13
14		27	R. E. Hamilton, Inc.	✓			8 65 00	17 30	8 47 70	14
15		28	Sales	✓		2 08 6 00			2 08 6 00	15
16		31	Sales	✓		4 23 40			4 23 40	16
17		31			4 48 20	7 76 1 70	72 69 00	1 04 38	15 37 4 52	17
18					(✓)	(411)	(113)	(413)	(111)	18

99

Cash receipts journal after posting

The Sundry Accounts Cr. column is used for recording credits to any account for which there is no special column. For example, as of October 2, in the illustration, the receipt of $412 in payment of an interest-bearing note[2] was recorded by a credit to Notes Receivable of $400 and a credit to Interest Income of $12, both amounts being entered in the Sundry Accounts Cr. column. The posting references for the notes receivable and interest income accounts were inserted later, at the time the amounts were posted.

The Sales Cr. column is used for recording sales of merchandise for cash. Each individual sale is recorded on a cash register, and the totals thus accumulated are recorded in the cash receipts journal daily, weekly, or at other regular intervals. This is illustrated by the entry of October 7 recording weekly sales and cash receipts of $1,700. Inasmuch

[2] It is not necessary to maintain a subsidiary ledger for notes receivable, the note itself containing all essential information. Detailed consideration of notes is postponed to later chapters.

as the total of the Sales Cr. column will be posted at the end of the month, a check mark was inserted in the posting reference column to indicate that the $1,700 item needed no further attention.

Credits to customers' accounts for payments of invoices are recorded in the Accounts Receivable Cr. column. The amount of the cash discount granted, if any, is recorded in the Sales Discount Dr. column, and the amount of cash actually received is recorded in the Cash Dr. column. The entry on October 5 illustrates the use of these columns. Cash in the amount of $784 was received from R. A. Barnes, Inc., in payment of their account of $800, the cash discount being 2% of $800 or $16. The Post. Ref. column was left blank until the credit of $800 was posted to the R. A. Barnes, Inc., account in the subsidiary ledger, at which time a check mark was inserted.

It should be noted that when a debtor has returned merchandise or has been granted an allowance, the discount should be computed on the amount of the invoice reduced by the amount of the credit memorandum. For example, on October 17 a check for $710.50 was received from Adler Company. Reference to the account receivable, reproduced on page 103, reveals a debit of $750 (sale), a credit of $25 (sales return), and a balance of $725. Deduction of the cash discount of $14.50 (2% of $725) from the account balance yields cash of $710.50.

POSTING THE CASH RECEIPTS JOURNAL

Each amount in the Sundry Accounts Cr. column of the cash receipts journal is posted to the appropriate account in the general ledger at any time during the month, and the posting is indicated by writing the account number in the posting reference column. At regular intervals the amounts in the Accounts Receivable Cr. column are posted to the customers' accounts in the subsidiary ledger and check marks are placed in the posting reference column to indicate that they have been posted and need no further attention. None of the individual amounts in the remaining three columns of the cash receipts journal is posted.

At the end of the month all the amount columns are footed and ruled as shown in the illustration. To check the accuracy of the footings, the equality of debits and credits should be proved by use of an adding machine or a listing similar to that shown below.

DEBIT TOTALS		CREDIT TOTALS	
Sales Discount	$ 104.38	Sundry Accounts.....	$ 448.20
Cash..............	15,374.52	Sales..............	7,761.70
		Accounts Receivable.	7,269.00
	$15,478.90		$15,478.90

Inasmuch as each amount in the Sundry Accounts Cr. column has been posted individually to general ledger accounts, the total of the column is not posted. A check mark may be inserted below this column total to indicate that no further action is necessary. The totals of the other four columns are posted to the appropriate accounts in the general ledger and their account numbers are inserted below the totals to indicate that the posting has been completed.

In terms of posting procedures, there are three distinct types of columns in the cash receipts journal. They may be described as follows:

1. Individual entries posted to general ledger accounts, column total not posted:

    Sundry Accounts Cr. column

2. Individual entries not posted, column total posted to a general ledger account:

    Sales Cr. column
    Sales Discount Dr. column
    Cash Dr. column

3. Individual entries posted to subsidiary ledger accounts, column total posted to the corresponding general ledger controlling account:

    Accounts Receivable Cr. column

The flow of data from the cash receipts journal to the ledgers of Midtown Electric Corporation is illustrated in the diagram below.

101

CASH RECEIPTS JOURNAL

ACCOUNT CREDITED	P. R.	SUNDRY ACCOUNTS CR.	SALES CR.	ACCOUNTS RECEIV- ABLE CR.	SALES DISCOUNT DR.	CASH DR.
Notes Receivable	112	400.00				412.00
Interest Income	811	12.00				
R. A. Barnes, Inc.	√			800.00	16.00	784.00
Fogarty & Jacobs	√			625.00	12.50	612.50
Sales	√		1,700.00			1,700.00
David T. Mattox	√			600.00	12.00	588.00
Sales	√		423.40			423.40
		448.20	7,761.70	7,269.00	104.38	15,374.52

Accounts Receivable Ledger

General Ledger

Notes Receivable 400.00

Accounts Receivable 7,269.00

Sales Discount 104.38

Each individual entry is posted to the credit of an account in the accounts receivable ledger, making a total of $7,269.00.

Interest Income 12.00

Sales 7,761.70

Cash 15,374.52

Flow of data from cash receipts journal to ledgers

ACCOUNTS RECEIVABLE CONTROL AND SUBSIDIARY LEDGER

During October the following postings were made to Accounts Receivable in the general ledger of Midtown Electric Corporation:

DEBITS

Oct. 31 Total sales on account (from sales journal). $8,940.00

CREDITS

Oct. 13 A sales return (from general journal)................	25.00
Oct. 28 A sales return (from general journal)................	65.00
Oct. 31 Total credits resulting from cash received on account (from cash receipts journal)........................	7,269.00

The controlling account with its opening balance, the foregoing postings, and the balances is shown below.

ACCOUNT   Accounts Receivable   ACCOUNT NO.   113

DATE	ITEM	POST. REF.	DEBIT	CREDIT	BALANCE	
					DEBIT	CREDIT
1973 Oct. 1	Balance	✓			5 2 6 0 00	
13		J18		2 5 00	5 2 3 5 00	
28		J18		6 5 00	5 1 7 0 00	
31		S35	8 9 4 0 00		14 1 1 0 00	
31		CR14		7 2 6 9 00	6 8 4 1 00	

Accounts receivable account in the general ledger at the end of the month

As indicated earlier it is the usual practice to post to customers' accounts in the subsidiary ledger at frequent intervals. If the accounts are kept up-to-date, they can be relied upon in deciding whether to grant additional credit, and inquiries from customers about the status of their accounts can be answered promptly. There is also an obvious advantage in spreading the posting over the month rather than allowing it to accumulate until the end of the month.

The accounts receivable ledger of Midtown Electric Corporation after the posting of all entries for the month is shown on the following pages.

The sum of the balances of the accounts in the accounts receivable ledger should be compared periodically with the balance of the accounts receivable account in the general ledger. This is customarily done at the end of each month at the same time that the trial balance is prepared. If the subsidiary ledger and the controlling account are not in agreement, the error must be found and corrected. As in the case of the trial balance, however, arithmetic equality is not an absolute guarantee of correctness. For example, the erroneous posting of a credit for cash received from a particular customer as a credit to another customer's account would not be revealed by this comparison.

The balances in the subsidiary ledger accounts may be summarized by use of an adding machine, or a schedule of accounts receivable similar to the one illustrated on page 104 may be prepared. Note that the total of the schedule, $6,841, is in agreement with the balance of the accounts receivable account shown above.

NAME   Adler Company

ADDRESS   7608 Melton Ave., Los Angeles, California 90025

DATE		ITEM	POST. REF.	DEBIT	CREDIT	BALANCE
1973 Oct.	10		S35	7 5 0 00		7 5 0 00
	13		J18		2 5 00	7 2 5 00
	17		CR14		7 2 5 00	——

NAME   R. A. Barnes, Inc.

ADDRESS   814 Glenview, Pasadena, California 91109

DATE		ITEM	POST. REF.	DEBIT	CREDIT	BALANCE
1973 Sept.	27		S34	8 0 0 00		8 0 0 00
Oct.	2		S35	3 5 0 00		1 1 5 0 00
	5		CR14		8 0 0 00	3 5 0 00
	9		S35	1 3 9 6 00		1 7 4 6 00

NAME   Cooper & Co.

ADDRESS   57 LaBrea Ave., Los Angeles, California 90036

DATE		ITEM	POST. REF.	DEBIT	CREDIT	BALANCE
1973 Oct.	23		S35	1 5 0 2 00		1 5 0 2 00
	28		J18		6 5 00	1 4 3 7 00

NAME   Fogarty & Jacobs

ADDRESS   1001 State Street, Burbank, California 91503

DATE		ITEM	POST. REF.	DEBIT	CREDIT	BALANCE
1973 Sept.	28		S34	6 2 5 00		6 2 5 00
Oct.	6		CR14		6 2 5 00	——

NAME   R. E. Hamilton, Inc.

ADDRESS   91 S. Spring, Los Angeles, California 90012

DATE		ITEM	POST. REF.	DEBIT	CREDIT	BALANCE
1973 Sept.	19		S34	1 8 5 0 00		1 8 5 0 00
Oct.	17		S35	8 6 5 00		2 7 1 5 00
	19		CR14		1 8 5 0 00	8 6 5 00
	27		CR14		8 6 5 00	——

NAME   David T. Mattox

ADDRESS   8050 Broadway, Burbank, Californa 91503

DATE		ITEM	POST. REF.	DEBIT	CREDIT	BALANCE
1973 Sept.	29		S34	6 0 0 00		6 0 0 00
Oct.	5		S35	3 0 5 00		9 0 5 00
	10		CR14		6 0 0 00	3 0 5 00

103

Accounts
receivable
ledger at the end
of the month

NAME Standard Supply Co.

ADDRESS 40 West Fourth Street, Los Angeles, California 90019

DATE		ITEM	POST. REF.	DEBIT	CREDIT	BALANCE
1973 Oct.	3		S35	1 6 0 4 00		1 6 0 4 00
	13		CR14		1 6 0 4 00	
	27		S35	1 9 0 8 00		1 9 0 8 00

NAME Tracy & Lee, Inc.

ADDRESS 1500 Santa Ana Blvd., Los Angeles, California 90002

DATE		ITEM	POST. REF.	DEBIT	CREDIT	BALANCE
1973 Oct.	26		S35	2 6 0 00		2 6 0 00

NAME B. C. Wallace Corporation

ADDRESS 412 Maple Ave., Los Angeles, California 90013

DATE		ITEM	POST. REF.	DEBIT	CREDIT	BALANCE
1973 Aug.	24		S33	1 3 8 5 00		1 3 8 5 00
Oct.	24		CR14		2 0 0 00	1 1 8 5 00

Accounts receivable ledger at the end of the month — concluded

Midtown Electric Corporation
Schedule of Accounts Receivable
October 31, 1973

R. A. Barnes, Inc.	$1,746
Cooper & Co.	1,437
David T. Mattox	305
Standard Supply Co.	1,908
Tracy & Lee, Inc.	260
B. C. Wallace Corporation	1,185
Total accounts receivable	$6,841

Schedule of accounts receivable

DELIVERY OF MERCHANDISE SOLD

The terms of a sales agreement include an implied or expressed provision concerning the cost of delivering the goods to the buyer. If the seller is to assume the cost of transportation, the terms are said to be *FOB* (free on board) *destination;* if the buyer is to absorb the cost, the terms are stated as *FOB shipping point.*

If the agreement provides that the seller is to bear the delivery costs, the payments to airlines, trucking companies, and other carriers are debited to Delivery Expense, Transportation Out, or a similarly titled account. The total of such costs incurred during a period is reported on the seller's income statement as a selling expense.

On the other hand, if the agreement provides that the buyer is to bear the delivery costs and the buyer pays the carrier upon delivery, the seller's responsibility ceases when the carrier takes custody of the merchandise.

PREPAYMENT OF DELIVERY CHARGES

It is not unusual for the seller to prepay transportation charges on merchandise sold even though the terms are FOB shipping point. The seller may do so as an accommodation to the customer, or it may be the only procedure practicable, as in the case of postage charges on goods shipped by parcel post. In all such situations the postage or other delivery costs to be borne by the purchaser should be listed on the sales invoice as a separate item and the invoice total (sale plus transportation) debited to the customer's account.

A sales journal designed to accommodate such transactions is illustrated below. The amount recorded in the Accounts Receivable Dr. column and posted to the customer's account is the sum of the sale plus the prepaid delivery charges.

SALES JOURNAL   PAGE 43

DATE	IN-VOICE NO.	ACCOUNT DEBITED	POST. REF.	ACCOUNTS RECEIV-ABLE DR.	DELIVERY EXPENSE CR.	SALES CR.
1973 Nov. 1	2477	Reed Corporation	√	820 00	20 00	800 00
30				26,925 00	525 00	26,400 00
				(113)	(615)	(411)

Sales journal designed for charging prepaid transportation costs to customers

The amount of the delivery charge is recorded in the sales journal as a *credit* to Delivery Expense rather than as a credit to Sales. The actual payment of cash to the carrier by the seller is a separate transaction; it will be recorded in the cash payments journal as a *debit* to Delivery Expense and a credit to the cash account. If the sale terms are uniformly FOB shipping point, all of the prepaid delivery costs will be passed on to customers. Consequently, the amount paid to carriers will be exactly the same as the total delivery costs charged to customers, and the amount of the debits and the credits to Delivery Expense will be equal. However, if some of the sales are on an FOB destination basis, the delivery expense account will have a debit balance after all related transactions have been recorded and posted. To illustrate, assume that in addition to the $525 charged to customers in November for prepaid delivery expense (see sales journal above), additional payments were made for the delivery of merchandise sold on an FOB destination basis. Assume further that the total delivery cost incurred for outgoing shipments in the same month was $657. The data may be analyzed as shown at the top of the next page.

Total amount paid for delivery of outgoing shipments of merchandise
 DEBITS to Delivery Expense.................................... $657
Amount of delivery charges debited to customers' accounts (terms
 FOB shipping point)
 CREDITS to Delivery Expense................................ 525
Amount of delivery charges not debited to customers' accounts (terms
 FOB destination)
 DEBIT BALANCE in Delivery Expense........................ $132

The excess of the total cost over the amount passed on to customers yields a debit balance of $132 of delivery expense for the month. It is an operating expense of the business.

When delivery costs are prepaid as an accommodation (FOB shipping point) on sales that are subject to a cash discount, the discount should be computed on the amount of the sale only; the buyer is not entitled to a discount on the transportation charges advanced by the seller. For example, assuming that the $800 sale recorded on the first line of the sales journal on page 105 is subject to a 2% discount and that payment is received within the discount period. The amount of the sales discount and the remittance may be determined in the following manner:

Debit to Reed Corporation, including prepaid transportation . $820
Amount of sale to Reed Corporation...................... $800
Rate of sales discount.................................... 2%
Amount of sales discount................................. 16
Cash received.. $804

In order to facilitate computation of the discount, a memorandum notation of the amount of transportation added to an invoice should be inserted in the item section of the customer's account when posting the sales journal.

SALES TAXES

Many business enterprises are required by state or city statute to collect sales taxes from their customers and remit to the taxing authority. Such taxes may be levied only on the sale of tangible commodities or they may also apply to the sale of specified services, such as dry cleaning, shoe repairs, and property rentals. They are often imposed only upon retail sales or sales to consumers, with sales of certain commodities exempted from tax. For example, in some jurisdictions there is no tax on the sale of food for consumption off the premises of the seller. Sales of gasoline, cigarettes, and other specified commodities may be subjected to a special tax by the state and consequently be exempted from the general sales tax.

Sales taxes are levied as a percent of all sales except those specifically exempted. The tax may be assessed against the seller, who may in turn charge it to his customers, or the statutes may specifically impose the tax upon the purchaser but require the seller to collect it. In either case, procedures should be adopted to assure collection of the tax and the timely transmittal of tax returns accompanied by remittances.

COLLECTION OF SALES TAXES

Liability for a sales tax is ordinarily incurred at the time the sale is made, regardless of the terms of payment. The seller therefore collects the tax at the time of a cash sale and charges the customer's account for the tax when credit is granted. The sales account should be credited only for the amount of the sale, the tax being credited to Sales Tax Payable. For example, a sale of $100 on account subject to a tax of 3% would be recorded as a debit of $103 to Accounts Receivable and credits of $100 to Sales and $3 to Sales Tax Payable.

In preparing sales invoices the sales tax should be listed as a separate item. If a sales journal is employed for sales on account, a special column should be provided for recording the credit to Sales Tax Payable. Provision for differentiating between taxable sales and exempt sales may also be made if necessary. Arrangements for recording decreases in the tax liability account attributable to sales returns and allowances can be made in a similar manner.

The sales tax collected on a cash sale is ordinarily recorded separately in the cash register. When this is not possible, the money received for the tax may be physically separated until the close of the day and then counted. Special columns for recording the amount of exempt sales and the sales tax liability can be added to the cash receipts journal.

Variations from the system outlined above can be made where necessary to provide all data needed in preparing periodic tax returns. As payments of the tax are made, usually on a monthly, quarterly, or semiannual basis, they are recorded as debits to Sales Tax Payable and credits to Cash.

QUESTIONS

1. Should the following transactions be recorded in a sales journal like that illustrated on page 93: (a) sale of merchandise for cash; (b) sale of vacant land (plant asset) no longer needed? Give reasons for answers.

2. What is considered to be the sales price of an item of merchandise with a list price of $200 and subject to a trade discount of 30%?

3. What is the general term applied: (a) to the single summarizing accounts receivable account and (b) to the ledger comprising the individual customers' accounts?

4. In recording 1,000 sales of merchandise on account during a single month, how many times will it be necessary to write "Sales" (a) if each transaction, including sales, is recorded individually in a two-column general journal; (b) if each sale is recorded in a sales journal?

5. How many individual postings to Sales for the month would be required in Question 4 if the procedure described in (a) had been used; if the procedure described in (b) had been used?

6. Why is it advisable to maintain an account for sales returns and allowances when the same net result may be obtained by debiting returns and allowances directly to the sales account?

7. In posting the general journal entry appearing below the bookkeeper posted correctly to Shaw's account but failed to post to the controlling account.

| Nov. | 12 | Sales Returns and Allowances................ | 412 | 76 | |
| | | Accounts Receivable — M. L. Shaw........ | ✓ | | 76 |

(a) How will the error be discovered? (b) Describe the procedure that is designed to prevent oversights of this type.

8. What is the meaning of (a) 2/10, n/30; (b) n/eom; (c) n/30?

9. What is the term applied to cash discounts by (a) the seller, (b) the buyer?

10. What is the amount of the cash discount allowable on a sale of $1,050, terms 1/10, n/30, on which a credit memo for $50 was issued prior to payment?

11. (a) What is the normal balance of Sales Discount? (b) Is it an asset, expense, or contra revenue account?

12. The debits and credits from three related transactions are presented in the T accounts below. Describe each transaction.

CASH		ACCOUNTS RECEIVABLE			SALES	
(c) 2,450		(a) 2,600	(b) 100			(a) 2,600
			(c) 2,500			

SALES RETURNS & ALLOWANCES		SALES DISCOUNT	
(b) 100		(c) 50	

13. A customer who has paid his account in full returns merchandise for credit. A credit memorandum for $40 is issued, recorded, and posted. (a) Is the $40 balance of the customer's account a debit or a credit balance? (b) Is the balance of the account an asset, liability, revenue, or expense?

14. What does a check mark (✓) in the posting reference column of the cash receipts journal illustrated in this chapter signify (a) when the account credited is an account receivable; (b) when the account credited is Sales?

15. After receiving payment from a customer, within the discount period, of the amount due on a sale of $100, terms 2/10, n/30, the seller consents to the return of the entire shipment. (a) What is the amount of the refund owed to the customer? (b) What accounts should be debited and credited to record the return and the refund?

16. Assuming the use of the sales journal and the cash receipts journal illustrated in this chapter and a two-column general journal, indicate the journal in which each of the following should be recorded:

(a) Investment of additional cash in the business by the owner.
(b) Sale of supplies on account, at cost, to a competitor.
(c) Receipt of cash refund for an overcharge on an insurance premium.
(d) Issuance of a credit memorandum to a customer.
(e) Adjustment of Salaries Payable at the end of the year.
(f) Sale of merchandise on account.
(g) Sale of merchandise for cash.
(h) Closing of the owner's drawing account at the end of the year.
(i) Receipt of cash in payment of principal and interest on a note.

17. Who bears the transportation costs when the terms of sale are (a) FOB destination, (b) FOB shipping point?

18. Merchandise is sold on account to a customer for $1,000, terms FOB shipping point, 2/10, n/30, the seller paying the transportation costs of $40. Determine the following: (a) amount of the sale, (b) amount debited to the customer's account, (c) amount of the cash discount, (d) amount of the remittance due within the discount period.

19. A business that sells to in-state customers on FOB destination terms and to out-of-state customers on FOB shipping point terms prepays the delivery charges on all sales. (a) What is the normal balance of the delivery expense account before closing at the end of the period? (b) Is the balance of the account related to the in-state customers or to the out-of-state customers? (c) Is the balance of the account an asset, liability, revenue, or expense?

109

20. A sale of merchandise on account for $100 is subject to a 3% sales tax. (a) Should the sales tax be recorded at the time of sale or when payment is received? (b) What is the amount of the sale? (c) What is the amount debited to the customer's account? (d) What is the title of the account to which the $3 is credited?

21. It is discovered that a cash sale subject to a sales tax of 5% was recorded in the cash register as a sale of $147, which included the correct amount of sales tax. (a) Was the sales tax 5% of $147, which amounts to $7.35? (b) If $7.35 is not the amount of the sales tax, how can the correct amount be determined?

EXERCISES

4-1. During the month of September a merchandising enterprise issues 976 sales invoices, totaling $152,300 and 27 credit memorandums for returns and allowances, totaling $536. Postings to the customers ledger are made directly from carbon copies of the invoices and credit memorandums and the totals are journalized in two entries at the end of the month. Present the two general journal entries for September.

4-2. Record the following transactions in the form of general journal entries:

Nov. 10. Sold merchandise to a customer for $900, terms FOB shipping point,

2/10, n/30, charging the customer an additional $30 for prepaid delivery costs.
14. Issued a credit memorandum for $60 to the customer for merchandise returned.
20. Received a check for the amount due from the sale to the customer.

4-3. For each of the following sales on account determine (a) the amount to be recorded for the sale, and (b) the correct amount of the remittance.

	Invoice Date	List Price	Trade Discount	Credit Terms	Payment Date
(1)	April 6	$1,500	20%	2/10, n/30	April 16
(2)	April 10	1,000	30%	1/10, n/30	April 20
(3)	April 17	1,900	—	2/10, n/30	April 26
(4)	April 23	750	50%	1/10, n/30	May 23

4-4. Determine for each sale described below, each of which is subject to terms of 2/10, n/30, (a) the amount of the cash discount and (b) the correct amount of the remittance if the account is paid within the discount period. Assume that all credit memorandums were received by the buyer before payment was made.

	Amount of Sale	Transportation Terms	Prepaid Transportation	Credit Memorandum
(1)	$ 570	FOB shipping point	$30	$40
(2)	750	FOB destination	20	10
(3)	1,100	FOB shipping point	—	30
(4)	1,400	FOB shipping point	50	—

4-5. During its first three months of operations, a retail merchandising business failed to differentiate between the amount of its sales and the amount of a 4% sales tax charged on all sales. All credits to the sales account and debits to the sales returns and allowances account included the sales tax. Permission is granted by the state tax department to estimate the net amount of tax charged to customers during the quarter. Balances in the sales account and the sales returns and allowances account at the end of the three-month period are $98,476.10 and $932.78 respectively. (a) Determine as accurately as possible the amount of sales tax debited to customers' accounts, credited to customers' accounts, and the net debit. (b) Present the general journal entry necessary to record the liability for sales tax and to correct errors in the other accounts affected by the transactions.

4-6. Present the general journal entries necessary to correct each of the errors described below. Assume that the incorrect entries had been posted and that the errors are discovered in the same fiscal period in which they occurred.

(a) Cash refund of $15 received for an overcharge on a purchase of office equipment was recorded as a sale of merchandise for cash.
(b) A cash sale of $50 to R. B. Borden was recorded as a sale to him on account.
(c) A remittance of $30 received from J. Rudd on account was recorded as a cash sale.
(d) A $400 sale to George Matson on account, FOB shipping point, with prepaid delivery expense of $25, was recorded as a $425 debit to Matson (and Accounts Receivable) and a $425 credit to Sales.
(e) A cash receipt of $990 ($1,000 less 1% discount) from Hall Corp. was recorded as a $990 debit to Cash and a $990 credit to Hall Corp. (and Accounts Receivable).

PROBLEMS

The following additional problems for this chapter are located in Appendix B: 4-1B, 4-2B, 4-3B.

4-1A. Hammond Trading Co. was established in September of the current year. Its sales of merchandise on account and related returns and allowances during the remainder of the month are described below. Terms of all sales were n/30, FOB destination.

Sept. 17. Sold merchandise on account to Superior Corp., Invoice No. 1, $640.
    18. Sold merchandise on account to Matson & Palmer, Invoice No. 2, $720.
    20. Sold merchandise on account to Carter & Co., Invoice No. 3, $1,160.
    22. Issued Credit Memorandum No. 1 for $40 to Matson & Palmer for merchandise returned.
    22. Sold merchandise on account to B. J. Weaver Co., Invoice No. 4, $1,650.
    25. Sold merchandise on account to R. T. Jordan, Inc., Invoice No. 5, $870.
    26. Issued Credit Memorandum No. 2 for $50 to Superior Corp. for merchandise returned.
    27. Sold merchandise on account to Matson & Palmer, Invoice No. 6, $1,030.
    28. Issued Credit Memorandum No. 3 for $30 to B. J. Weaver Co. for damages to merchandise caused by faulty packing.
    30. Sold merchandise on account to Carter & Co., Invoice No. 7, $290.

Instructions:

(1) Open the following accounts in the general ledger, using the account numbers indicated: Accounts Receivable, 113; Sales, 411; Sales Returns and Allowances, 412.
(2) Open the following accounts in the accounts receivable ledger: Carter & Co.; R. T. Jordan, Inc.; Matson & Palmer; Superior Corp.; B. J. Weaver Co.
(3) Record the transactions for September, posting to the customers' accounts in the accounts receivable ledger and inserting the balance *immediately* after recording each entry. Use a sales journal similar to the one illustrated on page 93 and a two-column general journal.
(4) Post the general journal and the sales journal to the three accounts opened in the general ledger, inserting the account balances only after the last postings.
(5) (a) What is the sum of the balances of the accounts in the subsidiary ledger?
      (b) What is the balance of the controlling account?

If the working papers correlating with the textbook are not used, omit Problem 4-2A.

4-2A. Three journals, the accounts receivable ledger, and portions of the general ledger of York Company are presented in the working papers. Sales invoices and credit memorandums were entered in the journals by an assistant. Terms of sales on account are 2/10, n/30, FOB shipping point. Transactions in which cash and notes receivable were received during May of the current year are as follows:

May 1. Received $1,225 cash from John Hill & Co. in payment of April 22 invoice, less discount.

2. Received $814 cash in payment of a $800 note receivable and interest of $14.

Post transactions of May 1, 3, and 4 to accounts receivable ledger.

8. Received $1,764 cash from Daniel G. Weber in payment of April 29 invoice, less discount.
9. Received $900 cash from James B. Riley Corp. in payment of April 9 invoice, no discount.

Post transactions of May 8, 9, 10, 12, and 15 to accounts receivable ledger.

15. Cash sales for first half of May totaled $8,164.
17. Received $350 cash refund for return of defective equipment purchased for cash in April.
19. Received $1,127 cash from John Hill & Co. in payment of balance due on May 10 invoice, less discount.
22. Received $637 cash from James B. Riley Corp. in payment of May 12 invoice, less discount.

Post transactions of May 18, 19, 22, 23, 24, 25, and 26 to accounts receivable ledger.

29. Received $11 cash for sale of store supplies at cost.
30. Received $238 cash and a $700 note receivable from H. L. Abbott, Inc., in settlement of the balance due on the invoice of May 3, no discount. (Record receipt of note in the general journal.)
31. Cash sales for second half of May totaled $9,138.

Post transactions of May 30 to accounts receivable ledger.

Instructions:

(1) Record the cash receipts in the cash receipts journal and the note in the general journal. *Before recording a receipt of cash on account, determine the balance of the customer's account.* Post the entries from the three journals, in date sequence, to the *accounts receivable* ledger in accordance with the instructions inserted in the narrative of transactions. Insert the new balance after each posting to an account.
(2) Post the appropriate individual entries from the cash receipts journal and the general journal to the *general* ledger.
(3) Add the columns of the sales journal and the cash receipts journal and post the appropriate totals to the *general* ledger. Insert the balance of each account after the last posting.
(4) Prepare a schedule of the accounts receivable as of May 31 and compare the total with the balance of the controlling account.

4-3A. Transactions related to sales and cash receipts completed by Hatcher Company during the period January 16–31 of the current year are described below. The terms of all sales on account are 2/10, n/30, FOB shipping point, with delivery charges prepaid and debited to the customers' accounts.

Jan. 16. Received cash from Boyd & Cole for the balance due on its account, less discount.
17. Issued Invoice No. 497 to Todd & Co., $2,193; delivery, $38; total, $2,231.
18. Issued Invoice No. 498 to T. B. Porter Co., $1,850; delivery, $36; total, $1,886.
19. Issued Invoice No. 499 to Henry Kirk, $1,242; delivery, $31; total, $1,273.

Post all journals to the accounts receivable ledger.

22. Received cash from Henry Kirk for the balance owed on January 16; no discount.
24. Issued Credit Memo No. 23 to Todd & Co., $43.
24. Issued Invoice No. 500 to T. B. Porter Co., $1,317; delivery, $25; total, $1,342.
25. Received $918 cash in payment of a $900 note receivable and interest of $18.

Post all journals to the accounts receivable ledger.

27. Received cash from Todd & Co. for the balance due on invoice of January 17, less discount.
28. Received cash from T. B. Porter Co. for invoice of January 18, less discount.
29. Issued Invoice No. 501 to Boyd & Cole, $2,200; delivery, $66; total, $2,266.
31. Recorded cash sales for the second half of the month, $6,810.
31. Issued Credit Memo No. 24 to Boyd & Cole, $65.

Post all journals to the accounts receivable ledger.

Instructions:

(1) Open the following accounts in the general ledger, inserting the balances indicated, as of January 1:

111 Cash.............	$1,973	412 Sales Returns and Allowances.	———
112 Notes Receivable...	2,000	413 Sales Discount..............	———
113 Accounts Receivable	3,654	615 Delivery Expense...........	———
411 Sales.............	———	811 Interest Income...........	———

113

(2) Open the following accounts in the accounts receivable ledger, inserting the balances indicated, as of January 16: Boyd & Cole, $1,193, including a delivery charge of $43; Henry Kirk, $1,651, including a delivery charge of $51; T. B. Porter Co.; Todd & Co. Make a notation of the amount of the delivery charges in the item section of the first two accounts.

(3) Insert the amounts stated below in a sales journal similar to the one illustrated on page 105, a sales returns and allowances journal similar to the one illustrated on page 96, and a cash receipts journal similar to the one illustrated on page 99. Insert on the first line of each journal "Jan. 16 Totals Forwarded √" and the following dollar figures in the amount columns, reading from left to right:

Sales journal: 3,468; 68; 3,400
Sales ret. & allow. journal: 26
Cash receipts journal: 217; 6,230; 4,252; 63; 10,636

(4) Record the transactions for the remainder of January, posting to the *accounts receivable* ledger and inserting the balances, at the points indicated in the narrative of transactions. *Determine the balance in the customer's account before recording a cash receipt.*

(5) Add the columns of the journals and post the individual entries and totals to the general ledger. Insert account balances after the last posting.

(6) Determine that the subsidiary ledger agrees with the controlling account.

4-4A. The statutes of the state in which Kenyon Markets Co. is located require that retailers collect a sales tax of 4% on all sales to consumers except on certain items, such as seeds and fertilizers, and on sales to governmental units, such as public schools, cities, and counties. They provide further that in the event the amount charged to customers is less than 4% of net taxable sales, the deficiency must be borne by the retailer. Payments for each calendar quarter are payable by the end of the month following the quarter.

The March 31 and June 30 balances of Kenyon Markets Co. accounts related to the sales tax are presented below. The sales tax expense of $28 as of March 31 represents the deficiency in the amount of sales tax charged to customers during the first quarter of the year. The sales tax payable of $4,094 as of March 31, which includes the $28 deficiency, was paid on April 30. The sales tax payable of $4,957 as of June 30 is the amount charged to customers during the second quarter of the year. No adjustment has been made for any deficiency to be borne by Kenyon Markets Co. for the second quarter of the year. The company closes its accounts on December 31.

	Balance	
Account	March 31	June 30
Sales Tax Payable................	$ 4,094	$ 4,957
Sales.........................	106,530	236,860
Sales Returns and Allowances.......	1,840	4,020
Sales Tax Expense (Jan. 1–Mar. 31).	28	28

Supplementary records indicate that for the period April 1–June 30 nontaxable sales amounted to $3,460 and returns and allowances on nontaxable sales amounted to $210. These amounts are included in the June 30 balances of Sales and Sales Returns and Allowances respectively.

Instructions:

(1) Determine the amount of the total liability for sales tax for the period April 1–June 30, identifying all figures and presenting them in good order.

(2) Determine the sales tax expense (deficiency in amount of tax charged to customers) for the period April 1–June 30.

(3) Present the entry as of June 30 to record the sales tax expense and the additional liability for sales taxes for the period April 1–June 30.

(4) On the basis of the ledger information presented above, determine the amount of the net taxable sales for the *first* quarter of the year.

Chapter 5

ACCOUNTING FOR PURCHASES AND CASH PAYMENTS

PURCHASING PROCEDURES

The procedures followed in purchasing activities vary considerably among different types of business enterprises, and in accordance with the volume of such activities. The owner of a small retail store may do all of the buying, in many cases placing orders with salesmen who periodically call at his place of business. In large enterprises all procedures related to ordering merchandise and other assets for use in the business are ordinarily concentrated in one or more specialized departments. Purchasing departments maintain catalogs and other data on quality and prices, on reliability of various suppliers, on current price trends, and other information which promotes the efficient operation of all buying activities.

To avoid misunderstanding, all orders for merchandise, equipment, supplies, or other assets should be in writing. An order may be written on a form supplied by the vendor, or the buyer may use his own forms. The original of the purchase order is sent to the supplier; it is his authorization to deliver the items listed at the prices specified. A duplicate copy of the order should be retained as evidence of what was ordered and of the other terms stipulated.

The seller usually mails an invoice to the buyer at about the time the goods are shipped. From the viewpoint of the seller, the invoice is a *sales invoice*; the buyer refers to it as a *purchase invoice*. An invoice should contain the names and the addresses of both the buyer and the seller; the date of the transaction; the terms; the method of shipment; and the quantities, descriptions, and prices of the goods. An invoice from Arnold Electronics Supply in response to a purchase order of Midtown Electric Corporation is shown on the next page.

The invoice form illustrated is a standard form recommended by the National Association of Purchasing Agents. It is divided into three

```
┌─────────────────────────────────────────────────────────────────────────────────┐
│  ARNOLD ELECTRONICS SUPPLY              FOR CUSTOMER'S USE ONLY                    │
│                                                                                   │
│      7900 MARKET STREET           Register No.        │ Voucher No.               │
│  SAN FRANCISCO, CALIFORNIA 94131  ─────────────────────────────────────           │
│                                   F. O. B. Checked                                │
│  Customer's                       ─────────────────────────────────────           │
│  Order No. & Date 412  Oct. 9, 1973   Refer to        Terms Approved │ Price Approved│
│                                   Invoice No. 106-8                   │  H. H.      │
│  Requisition No.                  ─────────────────────────────────────           │
│                                   Calculations Checked                            │
│  Contract No.          Invoice Date Oct. 11, 1973      C. R. S.                    │
│                           Vendor's Nos.   Transportation                          │
│  SOLD Midtown Electric Corporation     ─────────────────────────────────           │
│   TO  1200 San Vicente Blvd.          Freight Bill No.    │   Amount               │
│       Los Angeles, California 90019   Material Received                           │
│  Shipped to                           10/13 19 73  M.a.S.  Rec. Cl.               │
│   and                                  Date    Signature   Title                  │
│  Destination  Same                    Satisfactory and Approved                   │
│  Date Shipped Oct. 11, 1973 From San Francisco  Prepaid or Collect?               │
│                                       Adjustments                                 │
│  Car Initials and No.    F. O. B. Los Angeles    Prepaid                          │
│  How Shipped and                      Accounting Distribution                     │
│  Route Western Trucking Co.           ─────────────────────────────────           │
│  Terms 2/15, n/30       Made in U. S. A.  Audited      │ Final Approval           │
│                                          J. H. C.                                 │
└─────────────────────────────────────────────────────────────────────────────────┘
```

QUANTITY	DESCRIPTION	UNIT PRICE	AMOUNT
20	392E Transformers	30.00 ✓	600.00 ✓
43	719J Switches	2.50 ✓	107.50 ✓
7	824L Switches	2.50 ✓	17.50 ✓
25	406P Capacitors	4.00 ✓	100.00 ✓
10	215J Reactors	15.00 ✓	150.00 ✓
10	115R Chassis	40.00 ✓	400.00 ✓
4	274T Turntables	45.00 ✓	180.00 ✓
			1,555.00 ✓

116

Invoice

distinct sections: (1) upper left section for miscellaneous details of the terms of the transaction; (2) lower section for quantity, description, unit price, and amount; and (3) upper right section for use by the purchaser as a record that various comparisons and verifications have been made.

The purchase invoice is ordinarily received before the shipment arrives. The correctness of the terms, quantities, prices, and other details on the invoice should be verified by comparison with the corresponding data on the carbon copy of the purchase order. Arithmetic details of extensions, the invoice total, and the amount of discount allowable should also be verified.

Upon arrival of the commodities the receiving department should determine the quantity of each item received, making note of any substitutions and damage in transit. The receiving department may be supplied with a copy of the purchase invoice for use in making this verification. A preferable alternative, however, is to send the receiving department an incomplete copy of the purchase order or invoice, with quantities, unit prices, and amounts omitted. As the receiving department employee determines the quantity of each item, he inserts the figures on the incomplete document, which then becomes the *receiving report*. The quantities and item descriptions indicated on the receiving report are then compared with the invoice. Discrepancies between the two are investigated and appropriate action taken. Such independent verification is an important element of internal control over purchasing activities.

In summary, the following verifications should be completed and appropriate actions taken before a purchase invoice is approved for payment:

1. Determine that the invoice conforms to the purchase order.
2. Determine that all arithmetic details, such as extensions, total amount, and amount of discount, are correct.
3. Ascertain that commodities listed on the invoice have been received.

PURCHASES JOURNAL

Property most frequently purchased on account by a trading concern is of the following types: (1) merchandise for resale to customers, (2) supplies for use in conducting the business, and (3) equipment and other plant assets. Because of the variety of assets acquired on credit terms, the purchases journal should be designed to accommodate the recording of everything purchased on account. The number and the purpose of the special columns provided in the journal depend upon the nature of the business and the frequency of purchases of the various assets. The form of purchases journal used by Midtown Electric Corporation is illustrated on pages 118 and 119.

For each transaction recorded in the purchases journal, the credit is entered in the Accounts Payable Cr. column. The next three columns are used in accumulating debits to the particular accounts most frequently affected.

The Purchases Dr. column is for merchandise bought for resale. A more exact title for the column and the account to which the total is posted would be Merchandise Purchases. It is customary, however, to employ the shorter account title, Purchases. The purpose of the Store Supplies Dr. and Office Supplies Dr. columns is readily apparent. If supplies of these two categories were bought only infrequently, the two columns could be omitted from the journal.

The final set of columns, under the principal heading Sundry Accounts Dr., is used to record acquisitions, on account, of items not provided for in the special debit columns. The title of the account to be debited is entered in the Account column and the amount is entered in the Amount column; the account number is inserted in the Post. Ref. column at the time of posting.

CONTROLLING ACCOUNT AND SUBSIDIARY LEDGER

The necessity for maintaining a separate account for each creditor is evident. Although it would be possible to keep these accounts in the

117

PURCHASES JOURNAL

	DATE		ACCOUNT CREDITED	POST. REF.	ACCOUNTS PAYABLE CR.	
1	1973 Oct.	2	Video-Audio Co.	✓	7 2 4 00	1
2		3	Marsh Electronics, Inc.	✓	4 0 6 00	2
3		7	Parker Supply Co.	✓	5 7 00	3
4		9	Marsh Electronics, Inc.	✓	2 0 8 00	4
5		11	Dunlap Electric Corp.	✓	6 2 3 00	5
6		13	Arnold Electronics Supply	✓	1 5 5 5 00	6
7		14	Walton Manufacturing Co.	✓	9 1 0 00	7
8		16	Office Equipment Distributors	✓	9 7 0 00	8
9		19	Tri-State Distributors	✓	1 0 0 0 00	9
10		21	Walton Manufacturing Co.	✓	1 6 5 00	10
11		25	Parker Supply Co.	✓	3 2 00	11
12		27	Dunlap Electric Corp.	✓	3 7 5 00	12
13		31			7 0 2 5 00	13
14					(211)	14

Purchases journal — left page

general ledger, it is ordinarily preferable, for convenience and control purposes, to segregate them in a subsidiary ledger. The account in the general ledger that summarizes the debits and the credits to the individual accounts in the subsidiary ledger is entitled Accounts Payable. It is a controlling account. The subsidiary ledger may be referred to as the *accounts payable ledger* or *creditors ledger*.

POSTING THE PURCHASES JOURNAL

At frequent intervals the amounts in the Accounts Payable Cr. column are posted to the creditors' accounts in the subsidiary ledger. As each posting is completed, a check mark is placed in the posting reference column of the purchases journal at the left of the amount posted.

The three-column account form ordinarily used for the accounts payable ledger is designed to disclose at all times the balance owed each creditor. The accounts are arranged alphabetically so as to permit easy access and a loose-leaf binder is used to facilitate the insertion of new accounts and the withdrawal of inactive accounts.

As each item is posted to a creditor's account, the source of the entry is recorded in the posting reference column of the account by the letter "P" and the page number of the purchases journal. The account with Arnold Electronics Supply, taken from the accounts payable ledger of Midtown Electric Corporation is presented below as an example.

NAME   Arnold Electronics Supply

ADDRESS   7900 Market Street, San Francisco 94131

DATE		ITEM	POST. REF.	DEBIT	CREDIT	BALANCE
1973 Oct.	13		P19		1 5 5 5 00	1 5 5 5 00

An account in the accounts payable ledger

PURCHASES JOURNAL   PAGE 19

	PURCHASES DR.	STORE SUPPLIES DR.	OFFICE SUPPLIES DR.	SUNDRY ACCOUNTS DR.			
				ACCOUNT	POST. REF.	AMOUNT	
1	724 00						1
2	406 00						2
3		31 00	26 00				3
4	208 00						4
5	623 00						5
6	1555 00						6
7	910 00						7
8				Office Equipment	122	970 00	8
9	1000 00						9
10				Store Equipment	121	165 00	10
11		25 00	7 00				11
12	375 00						12
13	5801 00	56 00	33 00			1135 00	13
14	(511)	(115)	(116)			(✓)	14

Purchases journal — right page

At the end of the month, the purchases journal is totaled and ruled in the manner illustrated on page 118 and above. Before it is posted to the general ledger, the equality of the debits and the credits should be verified. This may be done on an adding machine tape or by a listing similar to the following:

DEBIT TOTALS		CREDIT TOTALS	
Purchases...........	$5,801.00	Accounts Payable....	$7,025.00
Store Supplies.......	56.00		
Office Supplies......	33.00		
Sundry Accounts....	1,135.00		
	$7,025.00		$7,025.00

The total of the Accounts Payable Cr. column is posted to the accounts payable account in the general ledger and the posting reference is indicated below the column total. The totals of the Purchases Dr., Store Supplies Dr., and Office Supplies Dr. columns are posted in a similar manner. Each individual amount in the Sundry Accounts Dr. section is posted to the appropriate account in the general ledger, the posting reference being entered at the left of the amount. The total of the column is not posted. A check mark is therefore placed below the $1,135 total to indicate that no action is required.

Postings were made to six accounts in the general ledger of Midtown Electric Corporation. Three of the accounts are presented at the top of the next page. The debit of $970 to Office Equipment was posted from the Sundry Accounts Dr. column of the purchases journal; the credit of $7,025 to Accounts Payable and the debit of $5,801 to Purchases were posted as totals from the Accounts Payable Cr. and Purchases Dr. columns respectively.

119

ACCOUNT Office Equipment · **ACCOUNT NO.** 122

DATE	ITEM	POST. REF.	DEBIT	CREDIT	BALANCE DEBIT	BALANCE CREDIT
1973 Oct. 1	Balance	✓			4 6 0 0 00	
16		P19	9 7 0 00		5 5 7 0 00	

ACCOUNT Accounts Payable · **ACCOUNT NO.** 211

DATE	ITEM	POST. REF.	DEBIT	CREDIT	BALANCE DEBIT	BALANCE CREDIT
1973 Oct. 1	Balance	✓				6 2 7 5 00
31		P19		7 0 2 5 00		13 3 0 0 00

ACCOUNT Purchases · **ACCOUNT NO.** 511

General ledger
accounts after
posting from
purchases journal

DATE	ITEM	POST. REF.	DEBIT	CREDIT	BALANCE DEBIT	BALANCE CREDIT
1973 Oct. 1	Balance	✓			89 1 2 8 00	
31		P19	5 8 0 1 00		94 9 2 9 00	

The flow of data from the purchases journal to the ledgers is presented graphically in the following diagram.

PURCHASES JOURNAL

ACCOUNT CREDITED	P.R.	ACCTS. PAYABLE CR.	PUR-CHASES DR.	STORE SUP. DR.	OFFICE SUP. DR.	SUNDRY ACCOUNTS DEBIT ACCOUNT	P.R.	AMOUNT
Video-Audio Co.	✓	724	724					
Marsh Electronics	✓	406	406					
Parker Supply Co.	✓	57		31	26			
Walton Mfg. Co.	✓	165				Store Equip.	121	165
Parker Supply Co.	✓	32		25	7			
Dunlap Electric Corp.	✓	375	375					
		7,025	5,801	56	33			1,135

Accounts Payable Ledger

General Ledger

Accounts Payable 7,025 · Store Supplies 56 · Office Supplies 33

Each individual entry is posted to the credit of an account in the accounts payable ledger, making a total of $7,025.

Purchases 5,801 · Store Equipment 165

Flow of data from
purchases journal
to ledgers

Two procedures revealed by the flow diagram should be particularly emphasized:

1. Postings are made from the purchases journal to both (a) accounts in the subsidiary ledger and (b) accounts in the general ledger.
2. The sum of the postings to individual accounts in the subsidiary ledger equals the columnar total posted to the controlling account in the general ledger.

RETURNS AND ALLOWANCES

When merchandise or other commodities purchased are returned or a price adjustment is requested, the purchaser usually communicates with the seller in writing. The details may be stated in a letter or the debtor may use his own *debit memorandum* form. This form, illustrated below, is a convenient medium for informing the creditor of the amount to be debited to his account in the buyer's ledger and the reasons for the return or price reduction.

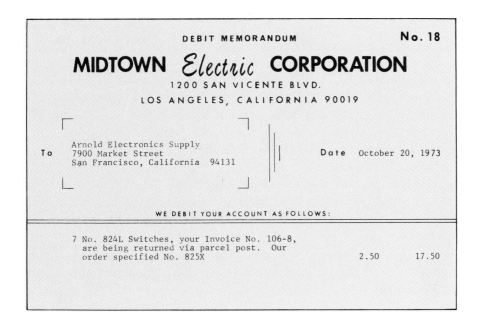

DEBIT MEMORANDUM   No. 18

MIDTOWN *Electric* CORPORATION
1200 SAN VICENTE BLVD.
LOS ANGELES, CALIFORNIA 90019

To
    Arnold Electronics Supply
    7900 Market Street
    San Francisco, California 94131

Date October 20, 1973

WE DEBIT YOUR ACCOUNT AS FOLLOWS:

7 No. 824L Switches, your Invoice No. 106-8,
are being returned via parcel post. Our
order specified No. 825X   2.50   17.50

Debit
memorandum

The debtor may use a copy of the debit memorandum as the basis for an entry or he may await confirmation from the creditor, which is usually in the form of a *credit memorandum*. In either event, both the creditor's account and the controlling account must be debited and the account to which the commodities were originally debited must be credited. For example, if the return or the allowance relates to merchandise purchased for resale to customers, the amount of the cost reduction is credited to Purchases. On the other hand, if the reduction is in the cost of some other commodity, such as office equipment, the credit is made to Office Equipment.

During October, Midtown Electric Corporation issued two debit memorandums, one for a return of merchandise and the other for an allowance granted on office equipment that deviated somewhat from the stipulated specifications. The entries may be recorded in a two-column general journal as illustrated at the top of the next page.

JOURNAL   PAGE 18

	DATE		DESCRIPTION	POST. REF.	DEBIT	CREDIT	
17	Oct.	20	Accounts Payable - Arnold Electronics Supply	211 ✓	1 7 50		17
18			Purchases	511		1 7 50	18
19			Debit Memo No. 18.				19
37		29	Accounts Payable - Office Equip. Distributors	211 ✓	2 0 00		37
38			Office Equipment	122		2 0 00	38
39			Debit Memo No. 19.				39

General journal entries for returns and allowances on commodities purchased

It should be noted that the debit portions of the entries are posted to the accounts payable account in the general ledger (No. 211), and also to the respective creditors' accounts in the subsidiary ledger (✓). The necessity for posting the debits to two different accounts is indicated, at the time these entries are journalized, by drawing a diagonal line in the posting reference column. The account numbers and check marks are inserted, in the usual manner, at the time the entries are posted.

In both of the examples above the creditors' accounts were debited for the amount of the debit memorandums. When the return or the allowance is granted after the invoice has been paid, the settlement may be made in cash. In such cases the transaction is recorded in the cash receipts journal as a debit to Cash and a credit to the appropriate account.

Significant losses in revenue and additional operating expenses caused by returns and allowances usually affect the seller to a much greater extent than the buyer. Hence, there is ordinarily no need for accumulating separately the amount of reductions in purchases of merchandise attributable to returns and allowances. However, if the total dollar volume of merchandise purchase returns and allowances is thought to be significant, a separate account, Purchases Returns and Allowances, can be maintained.

PURCHASES INVOICES AS A JOURNAL

Many business enterprises dispense with a formal purchases journal, replacing it with the invoices themselves. When this system is used, the original invoices become the basis for posting credits to the individual accounts in the subsidiary ledger. As each credit is posted, an appropriate notation of the fact is stamped or written on the invoice. At the end of each month, the data on all invoices received during that month are summarized and an entry is made in the general journal debiting the appropriate general ledger accounts and crediting the accounts payable account. For example, if the summary lists purchases of merchandise, $8,612, office supplies, $340, store supplies, $218, and office equipment,

$670, the general journal entry at the end of the month would be as follows:

Nov.	30	Purchases.....................	8,612	
		Office Supplies................	340	
		Store Supplies................	218	
		Office Equipment..............	670	
		Accounts Payable............		9,840

CREDIT TERMS AND CASH DISCOUNTS

Purchases on account from some suppliers may be on what is termed a *net cash* basis, which means that payment is to be made immediately following delivery of the commodities. Other suppliers may grant credit for varying lengths of time, sometimes with a cash discount allowed for early payment. The payment of accounts as they come due is an important determinant of credit ratings. It is also important that advantage be taken of all available cash discounts, even though it may be necessary to borrow the money with which to make the payment. For example, assume that an invoice for $1,000, with terms of 2/10, n/30, is to be paid within the discount period with funds borrowed for the remaining 20 days of the credit period. If an annual interest rate of 6% is assumed, the net savings to the purchaser is $16.73, determined as follows:

Discount of 2% on $1,000................	$20.00
Interest for 20 days, at rate of 6%, on $980.	3.27
Savings effected by borrowing...........	$16.73

Payments on account are ordinarily made by use of the mails. For purposes of determining timeliness of payment, the customary business practice is to consider the date of the postmark as the date of payment. The possible time lag of as much as several days for delivery of the remittance is likely to be no more than the time lag between the date of the purchase invoice and the day it is received by the purchaser.

There are various systems designed to assure payment within the discount period or on the last day of the credit period. A simple but effective method is to file each unpaid invoice according to the earliest date that consideration should be given to its payment. The file may be composed of a group of folders, numbered from 1 to 31, the numbers representing days of a month.

To illustrate the foregoing, assume that a purchase invoice dated October 10, with terms of 2/10, n/30, is received on October 12. After the appropriate verifications are completed, the invoice is placed in File No. 20 so that it will be considered for payment on October 20, the last day of the discount period.

On October 20 this invoice, together with all other invoices requiring consideration on that date, will be taken from File No. 20 by the treasurer or other person responsible for making disbursements. Each invoice in the folder will then either be paid or be refiled in the appropriate folder. If the October 10 invoice is not paid on October 20, consideration should again be given to its payment on November 9, which is the last day of the credit period. Accordingly, it should be refiled in File No. 9. The maintenance of such a system is also helpful in determining the amount of cash that should be available each day in the near future. This control feature may in turn yield benefits in the form of a reduction in the amount of interest expense on short-term loans or increased revenue from investing excess cash in income-yielding securities.

CASH PAYMENTS JOURNAL

The criteria for determining the special columns to be provided in the cash payments journal are the same as for other journals illustrated earlier, namely, the nature of the transactions to be recorded and the frequency of their occurrence. It is necessary, of course, to have a Cash Cr. column. Payments to creditors on account are usually sufficiently frequent to require columns for Accounts Payable Dr. and Purchases Discount Cr. The cash payments journal illustrated below has these three columns and an additional column for Sundry Accounts Dr.

124

CASH PAYMENTS JOURNAL   PAGE 16

	DATE	CK. NO.	ACCOUNT DEBITED	POST. REF.	SUNDRY ACCOUNTS DR.	ACCOUNTS PAYABLE DR.	PURCHASES DISCOUNT CR.	CASH CR.	
1	1973 Oct. 2	312	Purchases	511	275 00			275 00	1
2	4	313	Store Equipment	121	350 00			350 00	2
3	12	314	Marsh Electronics, Inc.	✓		406 00	4 06	401 94	3
4	12	315	Sales Salaries	611	560 00			560 00	4
5	12	316	Office Salaries	711	180 00			180 00	5
6	14	317	Misc. General Expense	715	26 40			26 40	6
7	16	318	Prepaid Insurance	117	84 00			84 00	7
8	18	319	Marsh Electronics, Inc.	✓		208 00	2 08	205 92	8
9	20	320	M. B. Heath Co.	✓		1850 00		1850 00	9
10	21	321	Sales Returns and Allowances	412	62 00			62 00	10
11	23	322	Video-Audio Co.	✓		1600 00		1600 00	11
12	23	323	Purchases	511	89 20			89 20	12
13	24	324	Tri-State Distributors	✓		2300 00		2300 00	13
14	24	325	Walton Manufacturing Co.	✓		525 00		525 00	14
15	26	326	Sales Salaries	611	560 00			560 00	15
16	26	327	Office Salaries	711	180 00			180 00	16
17	26	328	Arnold Electronics Supply	✓		1537 50	30 75	1506 75	17
18	26	329	Advertising Expense	613	86 00			86 00	18
19	27	330	Misc. Selling Expense	617	41 50			41 50	19
20	28	331	Office Equipment	122	900 00			900 00	20
21	31				3394 10	8426 50	36 89	11783 71	21
22					(✓)	(211)	(512)	(111)	22
23									23

Cash payments journal after posting

If payments for one or more specific operating expenses were sufficiently numerous, other special columns could be added to the journal.

All payments by Midtown Electric Corporation are made by check. As each transaction is recorded in the cash payments journal, the related check number is entered in the column at the right of the Date column. The check numbers provide a convenient cross-reference, and their use also is helpful in controlling cash payments. A review of the Check No. column from time to time will disclose any failure to record a payment.

The Sundry Accounts Dr. column is used to record debits to any account for which there is no special column. For example, on October 2 Midtown Electric Corporation paid $275 for a cash purchase of merchandise. The transaction was recorded by writing "Purchases" in the space provided and $275 in the Sundry Accounts Dr. and the Cash Cr. columns. The posting reference (511) was inserted later, at the time the debit was posted.

Debits to creditors' accounts for invoices paid are recorded in the Accounts Payable Dr. column. If there is no cash discount, the amount recorded in the Cash Cr. column will be the same as the debit to the creditor. If a discount is allowed, the credit to Cash will be correspondingly less. Cash discounts taken on merchandise purchased for resale are recorded in the Purchases Discount Cr. column. For example, the payment to Marsh Electronics, Inc., on October 12 was recorded as a debit to Accounts Payable of $406, a credit to Purchases Discount of $4.06, and a credit to Cash of $401.94.

At frequent intervals during the month, the amounts entered in the Accounts Payable Dr. column are posted to the creditors' accounts in the accounts payable ledger. Check marks are placed in the posting reference column of the cash payments journal to indicate that the amounts have been posted. The items in the Sundry Accounts Dr. column are also posted to the appropriate accounts in the general ledger at frequent intervals and the posting is indicated by writing the account numbers in the posting reference column of the cash payments journal.

At the end of the month the cash payments journal is ruled, each of the money columns is footed, and the equality of debits and credits is determined as follows:

DEBIT TOTALS		CREDIT TOTALS	
Sundry Accounts...	$ 3,394.10	Purchases Discount.	$ 36.89
Accounts Payable..	8,426.50	Cash.............	11,783.71
	$11,820.60		$11,820.60

A check mark is placed below the total of the Sundry Accounts Dr. column to indicate that it is not posted. As each of the totals of the other three columns is posted to a general ledger account, the appropriate posting references are inserted below the column totals.

125

ACCOUNTS PAYABLE CONTROL AND SUBSIDIARY LEDGER

During October the following postings were made to Accounts Payable in the general ledger of Midtown Electric Corporation:

CREDITS TO ACCOUNTS PAYABLE

Oct. 31 Total purchases on account (from purchases journal)... $7,025.00

DEBITS TO ACCOUNTS PAYABLE

Oct. 20 A return of merchandise (from general journal)........ 17.50
29 An allowance on office equipment (from general journal). 20.00
31 Total debits resulting from cash payments on account (from cash payments journal).................... 8,426.50

The controlling account with its opening balance, the foregoing postings, and the resulting balances is shown below.

ACCOUNT   Accounts Payable   ACCOUNT NO.   211

DATE	ITEM	POST. REF.	DEBIT	CREDIT	BALANCE DEBIT	BALANCE CREDIT
1973 Oct. 1	Balance	✓				6 2 7 5 00
20		J18	1 7 50			6 2 5 7 50
29		J18	2 0 00			6 2 3 7 50
31		P19		7 0 2 5 00		13 2 6 2 50
31		CP16	8 4 2 6 50			4 8 3 6 00

Accounts payable account in the general ledger at the end of the month

The accounts payable ledger of Midtown Electric Corporation, after posting the October entries, is shown below and on the next page.

NAME   Arnold Electronics Supply
ADDRESS   7900 Market Street, San Francisco, California 94131

DATE	ITEM	POST. REF.	DEBIT	CREDIT	BALANCE
1973 Oct. 13		P19		1 5 5 5 00	1 5 5 5 00
20		J18	1 7 50		1 5 3 7 50
26		CP16	1 5 3 7 50		

NAME   Dunlap Electric Corporation
ADDRESS   521 Scottsdale Blvd., Phoenix, Arizona 85004

DATE	ITEM	POST. REF.	DEBIT	CREDIT	BALANCE
1973 Oct. 11		P19		6 2 3 00	6 2 3 00
27		P19		3 7 5 00	9 9 8 00

NAME   M. B. Heath Co.
ADDRESS   9950 Ridge Ave., Los Angeles, California 90048

DATE	ITEM	POST. REF.	DEBIT	CREDIT	BALANCE
1973 Sept. 21		P18		1 8 5 0 00	1 8 5 0 00
Oct. 20		CP16	1 8 5 0 00		—

Accounts payable ledger at the end of the month

NAME   Marsh Electronics, Inc.

ADDRESS   650 Wilson, Portland, Oregon 97209

DATE	ITEM	POST. REF.	DEBIT	CREDIT	BALANCE
1973 Oct. 3		P19		4 0 6 00	4 0 6 00
9		P19		2 0 8 00	6 1 4 00
12		CP16	4 0 6 00		2 0 8 00
18		CP16	2 0 8 00		

NAME   Office Equipment Distributors

ADDRESS   4872 Webster, Oakland, California 94609

DATE	ITEM	POST. REF.	DEBIT	CREDIT	BALANCE
1973 Oct. 16		P19		9 7 0 00	9 7 0 00
29		J18	2 0 00		9 5 0 00

NAME   Parker Supply Co.

ADDRESS   142 West 8th, Los Angeles, California 90014

DATE	ITEM	POST. REF.	DEBIT	CREDIT	BALANCE
1973 Oct. 7		P19		5 7 00	5 7 00
25		P19		3 2 00	8 9 00

NAME   Tri-State Distributors

ADDRESS   8876 Montgomery, San Francisco, California 94111

DATE	ITEM	POST. REF.	DEBIT	CREDIT	BALANCE
1973 Sept. 26		P18		2 3 0 0 00	2 3 0 0 00
Oct. 19		P19		1 0 0 0 00	3 3 0 0 00
24		CP16	2 3 0 0 00		1 0 0 0 00

NAME   Video-Audio Co.

ADDRESS   1200 Capitol Ave., Sacramento, California 95814

DATE	ITEM	POST. REF.	DEBIT	CREDIT	BALANCE
1973 Sept. 25		P18		1 6 0 0 00	1 6 0 0 00
Oct. 2		P19		7 2 4 00	2 3 2 4 00
23		CP16	1 6 0 0 00		7 2 4 00

NAME   Walton Manufacturing Co.

ADDRESS   9554 W. Colorado Blvd., Pasadena, California 91107

DATE	ITEM	POST. REF.	DEBIT	CREDIT	BALANCE
1973 Sept. 28		P18		5 2 5 00	5 2 5 00
Oct. 14		P19		9 1 0 00	1 4 3 5 00
21		P19		1 6 5 00	1 6 0 0 00
24		CP16	5 2 5 00		1 0 7 5 00

127

Accounts payable ledger at the end of the month — concluded

After all posting has been completed for the month, the sum of the balances in the creditors ledger should be compared with the balance of the accounts payable account in the general ledger. If the controlling account and the subsidiary ledger are not in agreement, the error or errors must be located and corrected. The balances of the individual creditors' accounts may be summarized on an adding machine tape, or a schedule like the one below may be prepared. The total of the schedule, $4,836, agrees with the balance of the accounts payable account shown on page 126.

Midtown Electric Corporation
Schedule of Accounts Payable
October 31, 1973

Dunlap Electric Corporation	$ 998
Office Equipment Distributors	950
Parker Supply Co.	89
Tri-State Distributors.	1,000
Video-Audio Co.	724
Walton Manufacturing Co.	1,075
Total accounts payable.	$4,836

Schedule of
accounts payable

TRANSPORTATION ON INCOMING SHIPMENTS

The cost of merchandise acquired for resale includes the transportation charges for delivery of the goods. Similarly, the cost of plant assets, supplies, and other items purchased includes the cost of transporting them from the seller to the buyer. This is true, in a general sense, regardless of the agreement as to who shall pay the transportation company. Businesses that quote prices FOB destination, making no specific charge for delivery, must of necessity provide for recoupment of transportation costs when establishing their schedule of selling prices.

When assets are purchased on FOB shipping point terms, the related freight, express, postage, or other transportation costs borne by the buyer should be debited to the same account to which the commodities are debited. Thus, transportation charges on merchandise purchased for resale should be debited to Purchases, transportation charges on store equipment should be debited to Store Equipment, etc. If the buyer pays the transportation company directly, the delivery charges are recorded when such payment is made. If the seller pays the delivery costs and adds them to the invoice, the entire amount of the invoice, including transportation, is debited by the buyer to the appropriate account.

Some enterprises maintain an account titled Freight In or Transportation In for accumulating all separately charged delivery costs on merchandise purchased for resale to customers. If such merchandise is invariably purchased on an FOB shipping point basis, the data thus accumulated may be useful in determining the amount of transportation cost allocable to the merchandise inventory at the end of the accounting period. On the other hand, if much of the merchandise is purchased on FOB destination terms, the percentage relationship of the balance of the freight-in account to the balance of the purchases account at the end of the period is not significant. The important consideration, in this regard, is that every reasonable effort be made to buy at the lowest possible delivered price. This can be accomplished only through efficient management of the purchasing department. Each time a purchase order is to be issued, consideration must be given not only to the quoted price but also to the transportation and discount terms.

QUESTIONS

1. (a) Name two commonly used business forms described in this chapter that are the basis for accounting entries. (b) Name a business form that facilitates but does not represent a completed business transaction.

2. How can an invoice be both a purchase invoice and a sales invoice?

3. The commodities described below were purchased on account by a retail hardware store. Indicate the title of the account to which each purchase should be debited.

(a) One dozen snow shovels
(b) One gross pads of sales tickets
(c) Adding machine for office use
(d) Six refrigerators
(e) Two-year fire insurance policy on merchandise
(f) Three display cases
(g) Four cartons of light bulbs

4. Comment on the relative merits of the two systems described below of verifying and reporting the receipt of merchandise purchased.

(a) The purchase invoice is sent to the receiving department. The receiving department indicates agreement between the quantities received and the quantities appearing on the invoice by inserting a check mark opposite each item. Any discrepancies are indicated.
(b) An incomplete copy of the purchase order, on which quantities, unit prices, and amounts do not appear, is sent to the receiving department. The receiving department inserts the actual quantities received opposite each description on the incomplete purchase order.

5. (a) Under what circumstances described in this chapter should a diagonal line be inserted in the posting reference column opposite an entry in a two-column general journal? (b) Should the diagonal line be inserted at the time the entry is journalized or at the time the entry is posted?

6. Which is more likely to cause the greater amount of expense to be incurred by an enterprise, merchandise returned to it by customers (sales returns) or merchandise returned by it to suppliers (purchases returns)? Discuss.

7. Assuming that the ledger does not contain an account entitled "Purchases Returns and Allowances," indicate the titles of the accounts that should be credited for return of the following commodities purchased on account: (a)

Store supplies purchased for use in the business. (b) Merchandise purchased for resale. (c) Equipment purchased for use in the office.

8. During the current month the following errors occurred in recording transactions in the purchases journal or in posting therefrom. How will each error come to the attention of the bookkeeper other than by chance discovery?

(a) A credit of $300 to B. B. Clawson, Inc., was posted as $30.
(b) An invoice for office equipment of $320 was recorded as $230.
(c) An invoice for merchandise of $250 from Sumer Corp. was recorded as having been received from Sumner Co., another supplier.
(d) The accounts payable column of the purchases journal was underadded by $100.

9. The accounts payable and cash columns in the cash payments journal were unknowingly underadded by $100 at the end of the month. (a) Assuming no other errors in recording or posting, will the error cause the trial balance totals to be unequal? (b) Will the creditors ledger agree with the accounts payable controlling account?

10. The debits and credits from three related transactions are presented in the T accounts below. (a) Describe each transaction. (b) What is the rate of the cash discount and on what amount was it computed?

CASH				ACCOUNTS PAYABLE		
		(3)	1,176	(2)	200	(1) 1,400
				(3)	1,200	

PURCHASES				PURCHASES DISCOUNT		
(1)	1,400	(2)	200			(3) 24

11. If the amount paid within the discount period on an invoice subject to a 2% discount is $829.57, how could the amount of the debit to the account payable be determined arithmetically?

12. In recording a cash payment the bookkeeper enters the correct amount of $700 in the Accounts Payable Dr. column and the correct amount of $693 in the Cash Cr. column but omits the entry for Purchases Discount. How will this error come to his attention other than by chance discovery?

13. A dealer in appliances purchases an item of merchandise priced at $300, terms FOB shipping point, subject to a 2% cash discount; he also pays $7 for transportation. (a) What is the total cost of the item before considering the discount? (b) If the invoice is paid within the discount period, what is the *net* cost of the item?

14. A retailer is considering the purchase of 10 units of a specific commodity from either of two suppliers. Their offers are as follows:

A: $50 a unit, total of $500, 2/10, n/30, plus transportation costs of $30.
B: $55 a unit, total of $550, 2/10, n/30, no charge for transportation.

Which of the two offers, A or B, yields the lower price?

15. The commodities listed below are purchased FOB shipping point. Indicate the respective accounts to which the incoming transportation cost should be debited. (a) Desk and chair for use in the office. (b) Supplies for use in selling. (c) Merchandise purchased for resale.

EXERCISES

5-1. Determine the amount to be paid in full settlement of each of the following invoices, assuming that credit for returns and allowances was received prior to payment and that all invoices were paid within the discount period.

	Purchase Invoice			Returns and Allowances
	Merchandise	Transportation	Terms	
(a)	$1,500	—	FOB shipping point, 2/10, n/30	$100
(b)	1,200	$50	FOB shipping point, 1/10, n/30	—
(c)	800	—	FOB destination, n/30	60
(d)	1,400	40	FOB shipping point, 2/10, n/30	50
(e)	760	—	FOB destination, 2/10, n/30	10

5-2. Burton & Co. uses its purchase invoices as its purchases journal. Summarization of the invoices for the month of June yields the following totals for the various categories of commodities purchased on account: merchandise for resale, $65,412; store supplies, $274; office supplies, $63; office equipment, $1,840. Prepare the general journal entry that should be made on the basis of this information.

5-3. Osborn Corp. purchases merchandise from Ryan Co., on account, $1,200, terms FOB shipping point, 2/10, n/30. Ryan Co. adds transportation charges of $30 to the invoice. Osborn Corp. returns some of the merchandise, receiving a credit memorandum for $70, and then pays the amount due within the discount period. Present Osborn Corp.'s entries, in general journal form, to record (a) the purchase, (b) the merchandise return, and (c) the payment. (Osborn Corp. does not maintain a separate account for the recording of purchases returns and allowances.)

131

5-4. Present entries in general journal form for the following related transactions of Graham Decorators, recording merchandise purchases returns and allowances in the purchases account:

(a) Purchased $900 of drapery fabrics from Wabash Mills on account, terms 2/10, n/30.
(b) Paid the amount owed on the invoice within the discount period.
(c) Discovered that many of the fabrics were not colorfast and returned items with an invoice price of $350, receiving credit.
(d) Purchased an additional $300 of fabrics from Wabash Mills on account, terms 2/10, n/30.
(e) Received a check for the balance owed from the return in (c), after deducting for the purchase in (d).

5-5. Present the general journal entries necessary to correct each of the errors described below, assuming that the incorrect entries had been posted and that the corrections are recorded in the same period in which the errors occurred.

(a) A $60 cash purchase of merchandise from Newton Co. had been recorded as a purchase on account.
(b) The $75 cost of faulty office equipment returned to the supplier had been credited to Purchases.
(c) Transportation costs of $40 incurred on store equipment purchased for use in the business had been charged to Purchases.
(d) The payment of a $1,500 invoice for merchandise, less 2% discount, to Walker Corp. had been recorded as a $1,470 debit to Walker Corp. (and Accounts Payable) and a $1,470 credit to Cash.

PROBLEMS

The following additional problems for this chapter are located in Appendix B: 5-2B, 5-3B, 5-4B.

5-1A. Purchases on account and related returns and allowances completed by Valley Book Store during April of the current year are described below.

April 3. Purchased merchandise on account from Arden Stationery Co., $118.70.
  4. Purchased merchandise on account from Gilbert Publishing Co., $565.
  6. Received a credit memorandum from Arden Stationery Co. for merchandise returned, $12.50.
  10. Purchased office supplies on account from Nash Supply Corp., $19.70.
  12. Purchased office equipment on account from King Equipment Co., $488.60.
  13. Purchased merchandise on account from Arden Stationery Co., $245.10.
  18. Purchased merchandise on account from Trenton Publishers, $373.40.
  19. Received a credit memorandum from Nash Supply Corp. for office supplies returned, $5.30.
  20. Purchased merchandise on account from Richter Press, Inc., $416.
  24. Received a credit memorandum from Gilbert Publishing Co. as an allowance for damaged merchandise, $25.
  25. Purchased store supplies on account from Nash Supply Corp., $43.80.
  27. Purchased merchandise on account from Trenton Publishers, $242.10.
  28. Purchased office supplies on account from Nash Supply Corp., $22.50.

Instructions:

(1) Open the following accounts in the general ledger and enter the balances as of April 1:

114 Store Supplies	$ 132.50	211 Accounts Payable	$ 1,502.50
115 Office Supplies	68.40	511 Purchases	16,486.20
122 Office Equipment	4,720.00		

(2) Open the following accounts in the accounts payable ledger and enter the balances in the balance columns as of April 1: Arden Stationery Co., $176.30; Gilbert Publishing Co., $742; King Equipment Co.; Nash Supply Corp.; Richter Press, Inc.; Trenton Publishers, $584.20.

(3) Record the transactions for April, posting to the creditors' accounts in the accounts payable ledger immediately after each entry. Use a purchases journal similar to the one illustrated on pages 118 and 119 and a two-column general journal.

(4) Post the general journal and the purchases journal to the accounts in the general ledger.

(5) (a) What is the sum of the balances in the subsidiary ledger?
    (b) What is the balance of the controlling account?

5-2A. Scottsdale Toggery Shop was established in July of the current year. Transactions related to purchases, returns and allowances, and cash payments during the remainder of the month are described below.

July 16. Purchased store equipment on account from Ritter Supply Corp., $9,300.
  16. Issued Check No. 1 in payment of rent for July, $400.

17. Purchased merchandise on account from Vanguard Clothes, Inc., $1,350.
17. Issued Check No. 2 in payment of store supplies, $56, and office supplies, $31.
19. Purchased merchandise on account from Lane Clothing Co., $2,692.
20. Purchased merchandise on account from Brady & Co., $1,800.
21. Received a credit memorandum from Lane Clothing Co. for returned merchandise, $42.

Post the journals to the accounts payable ledger.

24. Issued Check No. 3 to Ritter Supply Corp. in payment of invoice of $9,300.
25. Received a credit memorandum from Brady & Co. for defective merchandise, $37.
26. Issued Check No. 4 to Vanguard Clothes, Inc., in payment of invoice of $1,350, less 2% discount.
27. Issued Check No. 5 to a cash customer for merchandise returned, $19.
28. Issued Check No. 6 to Lane Clothing Co. in payment of the balance owed, less 2% discount.
28. Purchased merchandise on account from Brady & Co., $927.

Post the journals to the accounts payable ledger.

29. Purchased the following from Ritter Supply Corp. on account: store supplies, $42; office supplies, $36; office equipment, $3,850.
30. Issued Check No. 7 to Brady & Co. in payment of invoice of $1,800, less the credit of $37.
30. Purchased merchandise on account from Vanguard Clothes, Inc., $3,769.
31. Issued Check No. 8 in payment of incoming transportation charges on merchandise delivered during July, $214.
31. Issued Check No. 9 in payment of sales salaries, $1,025.
31. Received a credit memorandum from Ritter Supply Corp. for defect in office equipment, $25.

133

Post the journals to the accounts payable ledger.

Instructions:

(1) Open the following accounts in the general ledger, using the account numbers indicated.

111	Cash	412	Sales Returns and Allowances
116	Store Supplies	511	Purchases
117	Office Supplies	512	Purchases Discount
121	Store Equipment	611	Sales Salaries
122	Office Equipment	712	Rent Expense
211	Accounts Payable		

(2) Open the following accounts in the accounts payable ledger: Brady & Co.; Lane Clothing Co.; Ritter Supply Corp.; Vanguard Clothes, Inc.

(3) Record the transactions for July, using a purchases journal similar to the one illustrated on pages 118 and 119, a cash payments journal similar to the one illustrated on page 124, and a two-column general journal. Post to the *accounts payable ledger* at the points indicated in the narrative of transactions.

(4) Post the appropriate individual entries to the *general ledger.* (Sundry Accounts columns of the purchases journal and the cash payments journal; both columns of the general journal.)

(5) Add the columns of the purchases journal and the cash payments journal, and post the appropriate totals to the general ledger. (Because of omission from the problem of transactions related to cash receipts, the cash account in the ledger will have a credit balance.)

(6) Prepare a schedule of accounts payable.

If the working papers correlating with the textbook are not used, omit Problem 5-3A.

5-3A. Fresno Specialty Co. uses carbon copies of its sales invoices as a sales journal, posting to the accounts receivable ledger directly from the invoices. At the end of the month the invoices are totaled and the appropriate entry is recorded in the general journal and posted to the general ledger. Purchases on account are recorded in a similar manner, the invoices being used as a purchases journal.

Invoices for the month of March, the first month of the current fiscal year, are listed and summarized below.

Sales Invoices

Mar.	4. Henry Parker Co.	$ 2,200
	6. Waldon & Kline, Inc.	875
	10. A. Clark & Co.	1,830
	16. Hamilton Corp.	736
	17. A. Clark & Co.	2,762
	22. Waldon & Kline, Inc.	1,670
	Total	$10,073

134

Purchases Invoices

Mar.	2. T. Altman & Co.; store supplies, $105; office supplies, $36.	$ 141
	3. Kirby Corp.; merchandise	2,710
	11. Dixon-Elliott, Inc.; merchandise	2,300
	18. Quincy Manufacturing Co.; store equipment	3,100
	19. Scott & Young, Inc.; merchandise	869
	29. T. Altman & Co.; store supplies	28
	31. Dixon-Elliott, Inc.; merchandise	1,374
	Total	$10,522
Analysis:	Purchases	$ 7,253
	Store supplies	133
	Office supplies	36
	Store equipment	3,100
	Total	$10,522

The other transactions completed during the month have already been recorded in a cash receipts journal, a cash payments journal, and a four-column general journal with special columns for debits to Sales Returns and Allowances and credits to Accounts Receivable. The three journals are presented in the working papers. The accounts receivable ledger, the accounts payable ledger, and the general ledger are also presented in the working papers, with March 1 balances. There have been no postings to any of the accounts during the month of March.

Instructions:

(1) Post the sales invoices to the accounts receivable ledger and the purchases invoices to the accounts payable ledger. The posting

reference columns of the accounts in the subsidiary ledgers may be left blank.

(2) Post the appropriate entries in the three journals to the accounts receivable ledger and the accounts payable ledger, in the following order: (a) general journal, (b) cash receipts journal, (c) cash payments journal. (If the customary practice of daily posting were followed, the postings would be in chronological order; imperfect date sequence is immaterial in this problem. It is also unnecessary to extend the account balance after each posting.)

(3) Record the appropriate sales and purchases data (see summaries of the sales invoices and purchases invoices) in the four-column general journal. Add each of the four columns.

(4) Post all entries in the Sundry Accounts columns of the three journals to the general ledger, proceeding in the order indicated in instruction (2).

(5) Post the appropriate columnar totals of the three journals, proceeding in the order indicated in instruction (2).

(6) Prepare a trial balance of the general ledger.

(7) Determine the sum of the balances in (a) the accounts receivable ledger and (b) the accounts payable ledger; compare the amounts with the balances of the related accounts in the general ledger.

5-4A. The transactions completed by Snyder's during June, the first month of the current fiscal year, were as follows:

135

June 1. Issued Check No. 595 for June rent, $600.
2. Purchased merchandise on account from Roth-Engle Corp., $2,225.
3. Purchased equipment on account from Gibson Supply, Inc., $1,930.
3. Issued Invoice No. 627 to L. B. Shannon, Inc., $843.
5. Received check for $2,646 from Allen & Cramer in payment of $2,700 invoice, less discount.
5. Issued Check No. 596 for miscellaneous selling expense, $97.
5. Received credit memorandum from Roth-Engle Corp. for merchandise returned to them, $75.
8. Issued Invoice No. 628 to Zimmer Corp., $1,800.
9. Issued Check No. 597 for $3,430 to Bader Manufacturing Co. in payment of $3,500 balance, less 2% discount.
9. Received check for $833 from Hartman & Co. in payment of $850 invoice, less discount.
10. Issued Check No. 598 to Layton & Co. in payment of invoice of $797, no discount.
10. Issued Invoice No. 629 to Allen & Cramer, $2,930.
11. Issued Check No. 599 to Ward & Halter, Inc., in payment of account, $1,322, no discount.
12. Received check from L. B. Shannon, Inc., on account, $922, no discount.
14. Issued credit memorandum to Allen & Cramer for damaged merchandise, $130.
15. Issued Check No. 600 for $2,107 to Roth-Engle Corp. in payment of $2,150 balance, less 2% discount.
15. Issued Check No. 601 for $438 for cash purchase of merchandise.
15. Cash sales for June 1–15, $4,269.
17. Purchased merchandise on account from Layton & Co., $2,365.
18. Received check for return of merchandise that had been purchased for cash, $19.

18. Issued Check No. 602 for miscellaneous general expense, $171.
22. Purchased the following on account from Gibson Supply, Inc.: store supplies, $23; office supplies, $42.
22. Issued Check No. 603 in payment of advertising expense, $275.
23. Issued Invoice No. 630 to Hartman & Co., $2,482.
24. Purchased the following on account from Bader Manufacturing Co.: merchandise, $935; store supplies, $26.
25. Issued Invoice No. 631 to Zimmer Corp., $1,860.
25. Received check for $2,744 from Allen & Cramer in payment of $2,800 balance, less discount.
26. Issued Check No. 604 to Gibson Supply, Inc., in payment of invoice of June 3, $1,930, no discount.
29. Issued Check No. 605 to Frank Snyder as a personal withdrawal, $750.
30. Issued Check No. 606 for monthly salaries as follows: sales salaries, $1,450; office salaries, $650.
30. Cash sales for June 16–30, $3,918.
30. Issued Check No. 607 for transportation on commodities purchased during the month as follows: merchandise, $127; equipment, $48.

Instructions:

(1) Open the following accounts in the general ledger, entering the balances indicated as of June 1:

111	Cash	$ 6,840	411	Sales
113	Accounts Receivable	4,472	412	Sales Returns and Allow.
114	Merchandise Inventory	25,960	413	Sales Discount
115	Store Supplies	215	511	Purchases
116	Office Supplies	145	512	Purchases Discount
117	Prepaid Insurance	1,320	611	Sales Salaries
121	Equipment	19,827	612	Advertising Expense
121.1	Accumulated Depreciation	4,394	619	Miscellaneous Selling Exp.
211	Accounts Payable	5,619	711	Office Salaries
311	Frank Snyder, Capital	48,766	712	Rent Expense
312	Frank Snyder, Drawing		719	Miscellaneous General Exp.

136

(2) Record the transactions for June, using a sales journal (as on page 93), a purchases journal (as on pages 118 and 119), a cash receipts journal (as on page 99), a cash payments journal (as on page 124), and a 2-column general journal. The terms of all sales on account are FOB shipping point, 2/15, n/60. Assume that an assistant makes daily postings to the individual accounts in the accounts receivable ledger and the accounts payable ledger.

(3) Post the appropriate individual entries to the general ledger.

(4) Add the columns of the special journals and post the appropriate totals to the general ledger.

(5) Prepare a trial balance.

(6) Balances in the accounts in the subsidiary ledgers as of June 30 are listed below. Verify the agreement of the ledgers with their respective controlling accounts.

    Accounts Receivable: Balances of $2,482; $843; $3,660.
    Accounts Payable: Balances of $961; $65; $2,365.

Chapter 6

PERIODIC REPORTING

Although many business enterprises prepare interim statements on a monthly or quarterly basis, a complete cycle of business operations is usually assumed to recur every twelve months. At yearly intervals throughout the life of a business enterprise the operating data for the fiscal year must be summarized and reported for the use of managers, owners, creditors, various governmental agencies, and other interested persons. Summaries of the various assets of the enterprise on the last day of the fiscal year, together with the status of the equities of creditors and owners, must also be reported. The ledger, which contains the basic data for the reports, must then be brought up-to-date through appropriate adjusting entries. Finally, the accounts must be prepared to receive entries for transactions that will occur in the following year. The sequence of year-end procedures may be varied to a minor extent but in general the following outline is typical:

1. Prepare a trial balance of the general ledger.
2. Determine that each subsidiary ledger is in agreement with the related controlling account in the general ledger.
3. Review the accounts to determine which ones should be adjusted, and compile the data necessary for making the adjustments.
4. Prepare a work sheet from the unadjusted trial balance and the data for the adjustments.
5. Prepare financial statements from the data in the work sheet.
6. Journalize the adjusting entries and post to the general ledger.
7. Journalize the closing entries and post to the general ledger.
8. Prepare a post-closing trial balance of the general ledger.
9. Journalize the reversing entries required to facilitate the recording of transactions in the following year, and post to the general ledger.

Although the summarizing and reporting procedures presented in this chapter are similar in broad outline to those discussed in an earlier chapter, there are a number of differences. For businesses that purchase

137

and sell merchandise, consideration must be given to the inventory of commodities on hand at the beginning and at the end of the period. In addition, the use of subsidiary ledgers for accounts receivable and accounts payable necessitates verifications that were not required in the less complex situations discussed in earlier chapters. The relationship between certain adjusting entries at the close of a year and entries for transactions in the following year is also considered in this chapter, as well as variations in trial balance preparation.

MERCHANDISE INVENTORY ADJUSTMENTS

Purchases of merchandise during a period and the inventory adjustment at the end of the period could be recorded in much the same manner as purchases of supplies and the related year-end adjustment. If such a procedure were followed, the balance in the account Merchandise at the beginning of the period would represent the cost of the merchandise on hand at that time; during the period the cost of merchandise purchased would be debited to the same account. At the end of the period an adjusting entry would be made to transfer the cost of the merchandise sold to an account so named, leaving the ending inventory of merchandise as the balance of the asset account. Because of the greater significance of merchandise transactions, however, it is customary to accumulate detailed data about the cost of merchandise sold. Such details may be presented on the income statement in the following manner:

Cost of merchandise sold:

Merchandise inventory, January 1, 1973........		$ 19,700
Purchases.................................	$105,280	
Less purchases discount.....................	1,525	
Net purchases.............................		103,755
Merchandise available for sale...............		$123,455
Less merchandise inventory, December 31, 1973.		22,150
Cost of merchandise sold..................		$101,305

The most efficient method of making the foregoing data readily available is to maintain a separate account in the ledger entitled Merchandise Inventory. Purchases of merchandise during the period are then debited to the account entitled Purchases. Related cash discounts, transportation in, and returns and allowances may also be recorded directly in the purchases account or in separate accounts, in accordance with the principles and procedures presented in the preceding chapter.

At the end of the period it is necessary to remove from Merchandise Inventory the amount representing the inventory at the beginning of the period and to replace it with the amount representing the inventory at the end of the period. This is accomplished by two adjusting entries. The first entry transfers the beginning inventory to Income Summary. Inasmuch as this beginning inventory is part of the cost of merchandise sold, it is debited to Income Summary. It is also a subtraction from the asset account Merchandise Inventory and hence is credited to that account. The first adjusting entry is as follows:

| Dec. | 31 | Income Summary..................... | 19,700 | |
| | | Merchandise Inventory.............. | | 19,700 |

The second of the two adjusting entries debits the cost of the merchandise inventory at the end of the fiscal period to the asset account Merchandise Inventory. The credit portion of the entry effects a deduction of the unsold merchandise from the total cost of the merchandise available for sale during the period. In terms of the illustration of the partial income statement on page 138, the credit portion of the second entry accomplishes the subtraction of $22,150 from $123,455 to yield the $101,305 cost of merchandise sold. The second adjusting entry is as follows:

| Dec. | 31 | Merchandise Inventory.............. | 22,150 | |
| | | Income Summary................... | | 22,150 |

The effect of the two inventory adjustments is indicated by the following T accounts, Merchandise Inventory and Income Summary:

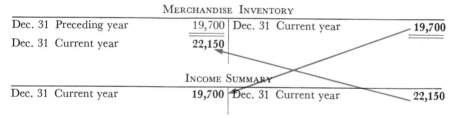

MERCHANDISE INVENTORY

| Dec. 31 Preceding year | 19,700 | Dec. 31 Current year | 19,700 |
| Dec. 31 Current year | 22,150 | | |

INCOME SUMMARY

| Dec. 31 Current year | 19,700 | Dec. 31 Current year | 22,150 |

In the accounts, the inventory of $19,700 at the end of the preceding year (beginning of current year) has been transferred to Income Summary as a part of the cost of merchandise available for sale. It is replaced by a debit of $22,150, the merchandise inventory at the end of the current year; the credit of the same amount to Income Summary is a deduction from the cost of merchandise available for sale.

TRIAL BALANCE AND ADJUSTMENTS ON THE WORK SHEET

After year-end posting of the various journals has been completed, a trial balance of the general ledger is taken and conformity between each subsidiary ledger and its related controlling account verified. Any discrepancies should of course be corrected before proceeding with the adjusting entries.

The trial balance for Midtown Electric Corporation as of December 31, 1973, appears on the work sheet presented on pages 140 and 141. It differs slightly from trial balances illustrated earlier. All the accounts

Midtown Electric Corporation
Work Sheet
For Year Ended December 31, 1973

	ACCOUNT TITLE	TRIAL BALANCE DEBIT	TRIAL BALANCE CREDIT	ADJUSTMENTS DEBIT	ADJUSTMENTS CREDIT	INCOME STATEMENT DEBIT	INCOME STATEMENT CREDIT	BALANCE SHEET DEBIT	BALANCE SHEET CREDIT	
1	Cash	8590 00						8590 00		1
2	Accounts Receivable	6880 00						6880 00		2
3	Merchandise Inventory	19700 00		(b) 22150 00	(a) 19700 00			22150 00		3
4	Store Supplies	970 00			(c) 420 00			550 00		4
5	Office Supplies	480 00			(d) 200 00			280 00		5
6	Prepaid Insurance	1560 00			(e) 910 00			650 00		6
7	Store Equipment	10200 00						10200 00		7
8	Accumulated Depreciation - Store Equipment		4600 00		(f) 1100 00				5700 00	8
9	Office Equipment	5570 00						5570 00		9
10	Accumulated Depreciation - Office Equipment		2230 00		(g) 490 00				2720 00	10
11	Building	51000 00						51000 00		11
12	Accumulated Depreciation - Building		9400 00		(h) 1500 00				10900 00	12
13	Land	6000 00						6000 00		13
14	Accounts Payable		7420 00						7420 00	14
15	Salaries Payable				(i) 296 00				296 00	15
16	Mortgage Note Payable		9000 00						9000 00	16
17	Capital Stock		40000 00						40000 00	17
18	Retained Earnings		13256 00						13256 00	18
19	Dividends	4000 00						4000 00		19
20	Income Summary			(a) 19700 00	(b) 22150 00	19700 00	22150 00			20
21	Sales		167736 00				167736 00			21
22	Sales Returns and Allowances	2140 00				2140 00				22
23	Sales Discount	1822 00				1822 00				23

#	Account	Trial Balance Dr	Trial Balance Cr	Adjustments Dr	Adjustments Cr	Income Statement Dr	Income Statement Cr	Balance Sheet Dr	Balance Sheet Cr
24	Purchases	105280 00				105280 00			
25	Purchases Discount		1525 00				1525 00		
26	Sales Salaries	19820 00		(i) 224 00		20044 00			
27	Advertising Expense	3460 00				3460 00			
28	Depreciation Expense - Store Equipment			(f) 1100 00		1100 00			
29	Insurance Expense - Selling			(e) 580 00		580 00			
30	Store Supplies Expense			(c) 420 00		420 00			
31	Miscellaneous Selling Expense	230 00				230 00			
32	Office Salaries	5960 00		(i) 72 00		6032 00			
33	Taxes Expense	1810 00				1810 00			
34	Depreciation Expense - Building			(h) 1500 00		1500 00			
35	Depreciation Expense - Office Equipment			(g) 490 00		490 00			
36	Insurance Expense - General			(e) 330 00		330 00			
37	Office Supplies Expense			(d) 200 00		200 00			
38	Miscellaneous General Expense	310 00				310 00			
39	Rent Income		1200 00				1200 00		
40	Interest Expense	585 00				585 00			
41		256367 00	256367 00	4676 00	4676 00	166033 00	192611 00	115870 00	89292 00
42	Net Income					26578 00			26578 00
43						192611 00	192611 00	115870 00	115870 00

141

Work sheet

in the ledger are listed in sequential order, including titles of accounts that have no balances. This variation in format has the advantage of listing accounts in the order in which they will be used when the statements are prepared. If additional accounts are needed in making the necessary adjustments, their titles can be inserted below the trial balance totals in the manner illustrated in an earlier chapter.

The data needed for adjusting the accounts of Midtown Electric Corporation are summarized as follows:

Merchandise inventory as of December 31, 1973............		$22,150
Inventories of supplies as of December 31, 1973:		
Store supplies.................................		550
Office supplies................................		280
Insurance expired during 1973 on:		
Merchandise and store equipment....................	$580	
Office equipment and building.....................	330	910
Depreciation during 1973 on:		
Store equipment................................		1,100
Office equipment...............................		490
Building......................................		1,500
Salaries accrued on December 31, 1973:		
Sales salaries.................................	$224	
Office salaries................................	72	296

Explanations of the adjusting entries in the work sheet appearing on pages 140 and 141 are given in the paragraphs that follow.

Merchandise inventory. The $19,700 balance of merchandise inventory appearing in the trial balance represents the amount of the inventory at the end of the preceding year (beginning of the current year). It is a part of the merchandise available for sale during the year and is hence transferred to Income Summary, where it will be combined with the net cost of merchandise purchased during the year. (Entry (a) on the work sheet.)

The merchandise on hand at the end of the current year, as determined by a physical inventory, amounts to $22,150. It is an asset and must be debited to the asset account Merchandise Inventory. It must also be deducted from the cost of merchandise available for sale (beginning inventory plus net purchases) to yield the cost of the merchandise sold. These objectives are accomplished by debiting Merchandise Inventory and crediting Income Summary. (Entry (b) on the work sheet.)

Supplies. The $970 balance of the store supplies account in the trial balance is the aggregate cost of supplies on hand at the beginning of the year plus store supplies purchased during the year. The physical inventory at the end of the year indicates store supplies on hand totaling $550. The excess of $970 over the inventory of $550 is $420, which is the cost of the store supplies consumed during the period. The accounts are adjusted by debiting Store Supplies Expense and crediting Store Supplies for $420. (Entry (c) on the work sheet.) The adjustment for office supplies consumed is determined in the same manner. (Entry (d) on the work sheet.)

Prepaid insurance. The adjustment for insurance expired is similar to the adjustment for supplies consumed. The balance in Prepaid Insurance is the amount prepaid at the beginning of the year plus the additional premium costs incurred during the year. Analysis of the various insurance policies reveals that a total of $910 in premiums has expired, of which $580 is applicable to merchandise and store equipment and $330 is applicable to office equipment and building. Insurance Expense — Selling is debited for $580, Insurance Expense — General is debited for $330, and Prepaid Insurance is credited for $910. (Entry (e) on the work sheet.)

Depreciation of plant assets. The expired cost of a plant asset is debited to a depreciation expense account and credited to an accumulated depreciation account. A separate account for the expense and for the accumulation is maintained for each plant asset account. Thus, the adjustment for $1,100 depreciation of the store equipment is recorded by a debit to Depreciation Expense — Store Equipment and a credit to Accumulated Depreciation — Store Equipment for $1,100. The adjustments for depreciation of the office equipment and for depreciation of the building are recorded in a similar manner. (Entries (f), (g), and (h) on the work sheet.)

143

Salaries payable. The liability for the salaries earned by employees but not yet paid is recorded by a credit of $296 to Salaries Payable and debits to Sales Salaries and Office Salaries of $224 and $72 respectively. (Entry (i) on the work sheet.)

COMPLETING THE WORK SHEET

After all necessary adjustments are entered on the work sheet, the two Adjustments columns are totaled to prove the equality of debits and credits.

The process of extending the balances to the statement columns is accomplished most expeditiously by beginning with Cash at the top and proceeding down the work sheet, item by item, in sequential order. An exception to the usual practice of extending only the account balances should be noted. Both the debit and credit amounts for Income Summary are extended to the Income Statement columns. Inasmuch as both the amount of the debit adjustment (beginning inventory of $19,700) and the amount of the credit adjustment (ending inventory of $22,150) are needed in preparing the income statement, no purpose would be served by determining and extending only the single balancing amount ($22,150 − $19,700).

After all of the items have been extended into the statement sections of the work sheet, the four columns are totaled and the net income or net loss is determined. In the illustration the difference between the credit and the debit columns of the Income Statement section is $26,578, the amount of the net income. The difference between the debit and the credit columns of the Balance Sheet section is also $26,578, which is the increase in capital resulting from net income. Agreement between the two balancing amounts is evidence of debit-credit equality and arithmetical accuracy.

PREPARATION OF STATEMENTS AND SUPPORTING SCHEDULES

The income statement, the retained earnings statement, and the balance sheet are prepared from the account titles and the data in the statement sections of the work sheet.

Formal schedules of accounts receivable and accounts payable are sometimes prepared from the respective subsidiary ledgers. They may be useful to management in reviewing customer accounts for credit purposes and in preparing reports for credit-rating agencies.

INCOME STATEMENT

The accompanying income statement for Midtown Electric Corporation, a merchandising business, is somewhat more complex than the income statements illustrated in earlier chapters. Because of its numerous subsections and intermediate summary figures, it is sometimes called the *multiple-step* form. The *single-step* form, in which the total of all expired costs is deducted as a single figure from the total of all revenues, is illustrated in a later chapter.

In practice, there is considerable variation in the amount of detail presented in income statements. For example, instead of reporting separately gross sales and the related returns, allowances, and discounts, the statement may begin with net sales. Similarly, the supporting data for the determination of the cost of merchandise sold may be omitted from the statement. The various sections of a conventional multiple-step income statement for a mercantile enterprise are discussed briefly in the paragraphs that follow.

Revenue from sales. The total of all charges to customers for merchandise sold, both for cash and on account, is reported in this section. Sales returns and allowances and sales discounts are deducted from the gross amount to yield net sales.

Cost of merchandise sold. The determination of this important figure was explained and illustrated earlier in the chapter. Other descriptive terms frequently employed are *cost of goods sold* and *cost of sales*.

Midtown Electric Corporation
Income Statement
For Year Ended December 31, 1973

Revenue from sales:			
Sales		$167,736	
Less: Sales returns and allowances. . . .	$ 2,140		
Sales discount.	1,822	3,962	
Net sales			$163,774
Cost of merchandise sold:			
Merchandise inventory, January 1, 1973. .		$ 19,700	
Purchases	$105,280		
Less purchases discount	1,525		
Net purchases		103,755	
Merchandise available for sale.		$123,455	
Less merchandise inventory, Dec. 31, 1973		22,150	
Cost of merchandise sold.			101,305
Gross profit on sales			$ 62,469
Operating expenses:			
Selling expenses:			
Sales salaries.	$ 20,044		
Advertising expense	3,460		
Depreciation expense--store equipment .	1,100		
Insurance expense--selling.	580		
Store supplies expense.	420		
Miscellaneous selling expense	230		
Total selling expenses.		$ 25,834	
General expenses:			
Office salaries	$ 6,032		
Taxes expense	1,810		
Depreciation expense--building.	1,500		
Depreciation expense--office equipment.	490		
Insurance expense--general.	330		
Office supplies expense	200		
Miscellaneous general expense	310		
Total general expenses.		10,672	
Total operating expenses.			36,506
Income from operations.			$ 25,963
Other income:			
Rent income		$ 1,200	
Other expense:			
Interest expense.		585	615
Net income.[1]			$ 26,578

Income statement

145

Gross profit on sales. The excess of the net revenue from sales over the cost of merchandise sold is called *gross profit on sales* or *gross margin*. It is termed *gross* because operating expenses must be deducted from it.

Operating expenses. The operating expenses of a business may be classified under any desired number of headings and subheadings. In a retail business of the kind that has been used for illustrative purposes,

[1]This amount is further reduced by corporation income tax. The discussion of income taxes levied on corporate entities is reserved for later chapters.

it is usually satisfactory to classify operating expenses as either *selling* or *general*.

Expenses that are incurred directly and entirely in connection with the sale of merchandise are known as *selling expenses*. They include such expenses as salaries of the sales force, store supplies used, depreciation of store equipment, and advertising.

Expenses incurred in the general operations of the business are known as *general expenses* or *administrative expenses*. Examples of these expenses are office salaries, depreciation of office equipment, and office supplies used. Expenses that are partly connected with selling and partly connected with the general operations of the business may be divided between the two categories. In a small business, however, mixed expenses such as rent, insurance, and taxes are commonly reported as general expenses.

Expenses of relatively small amount that cannot be identified with the principal accounts are usually accumulated in accounts entitled Miscellaneous Selling Expense and Miscellaneous General Expense.

Income from operations. The excess of gross profit on sales over total operating expenses is called *income from operations*, or *operating income*. The amount of the income from operations and its relationship to capital investment and to net sales are important factors in judging the efficiency of management and the degree of profitability of an enterprise. If operating expenses should exceed gross profit, the excess is designated *loss from operations*.

Other income. Revenue from sources other than the principal activity of a business is classified as *other income*, or *nonoperating income*. In a merchandising business this category often includes income from interest, rent, dividends, and gains resulting from the sale of plant assets.

Other expense. Expenses that cannot be associated definitely with operations are identified as *other expense*, or *nonoperating expense*. Interest expense that results from financing activities and losses incurred in the disposal of plant assets are examples of items reported in this section.

The two categories of nonoperating items are offset against each other on the income statement. If the total of other income exceeds the total of other expense, the difference is added to income from operations; if the reverse is true, the difference is subtracted from income from operations.

Net income. The final figure on the income statement is labeled *net income* (or *net loss*). It is the net increase in capital resulting from profit-making activities. (As noted on the preceding page, the reporting of corporation income tax is discussed later.)

BALANCE SHEET AND RETAINED EARNINGS STATEMENT

The form of the balance sheet for a merchandising business is basically the same as that for a service enterprise illustrated in an earlier chapter. There may be a larger number of both assets and liabilities to report, as in the accompanying balance sheet for Midtown Electric Corporation. The manner in which the mortgage note payable is reported should be noted. The $9,000 balance of this account in the ledger is divided between the $1,500 installment due within a year, which is classified as a current liability, and the remaining $7,500, which is classified as a long-term liability.

Midtown Electric Corporation
Balance Sheet
December 31, 1973

147

Assets

Current assets:			
Cash		$ 8,590	
Accounts receivable		6,880	
Merchandise inventory		22,150	
Store supplies		550	
Office supplies		280	
Prepaid insurance		650	
Total current assets			$39,100
Plant assets:			
Store equipment	$10,200		
Less accumulated depreciation	5,700	$ 4,500	
Office equipment	$ 5,570		
Less accumulated depreciation	2,720	2,850	
Building	$51,000		
Less accumulated depreciation	10,900	40,100	
Land		6,000	
Total plant assets			53,450
Total assets			$92,550

Liabilities

Current liabilities:			
Accounts payable		$ 7,420	
Mortgage note payable (current portion)		1,500	
Salaries payable		296	
Total current liabilities			$ 9,216
Long-term liabilities:			
Mortgage note payable (final payment, 1979)			7,500
Total liabilities			$16,716

Capital

Capital stock		$40,000	
Retained earnings		35,834	
Total capital			75,834
Total liabilities and capital			$92,550

Balance
sheet

```
                    Midtown Electric Corporation
                     Retained Earnings Statement
                  For Year Ended December 31, 1973
```

Retained earnings, January 1, 1973		$13,256
Net income for the year.	$26,578	
Less dividends	4,000	
Increase in retained earnings.		22,578
Retained earnings, December 31, 1973		$35,834

Retained earnings statement

```
                    Midtown Electric Corporation
                    Schedule of Accounts Receivable
                         December 31, 1973
```

Adler Company	$ 320
R. A. Barnes, Inc.	1,280
Cooper & Co.	516
Fogarty & Jacobs.	402
R. E. Hamilton, Inc.	1,310
David T. Mattox	745
Standard Supply Co.	97
Tracy & Lee, Inc.	1,883
B. C. Wallace Corporation	327
Total accounts receivable	$6,880

Schedule of accounts receivable

```
                    Midtown Electric Corporation
                     Schedule of Accounts Payable
                         December 31, 1973
```

Arnold Electronics Supply	$2,316
Dunlap Electric Corporation	1,193
Marsh Electronics, Inc.	975
Office Equipment Distributors	210
Parker Supply Co.	55
Tri-State Distributors.	2,114
Walton Manufacturing Co.	557
Total accounts payable.	$7,420

Schedule of accounts payable

The form of the retained earnings statement[1] is not affected by the nature of the business operations. The statement summarizes the changes in the account during the fiscal period and serves as a connecting link between the income statement and the balance sheet.

ADJUSTING ENTRIES

The analyses required to formulate the adjustments were completed during the process of preparing the work sheet. It is therefore unnecessary to refer again to the basic data when recording the adjusting entries in the general journal. After the entries are posted, the balances of all

---

[1]A capital statement for a sole proprietorship is illustrated on page 19.

asset, liability, revenue, and expense accounts correspond exactly to the amounts reported in the financial statements. The adjusting entries for Midtown Electric Corporation are presented below.

	DATE		DESCRIPTION	POST. REF.	DEBIT	CREDIT	
1			Adjusting Entries				1
2	1973 Dec.	31	Income Summary	313	19 7 0 0 00		2
3			Merchandise Inventory	114		19 7 0 0 00	3
4							4
5		31	Merchandise Inventory	114	22 1 5 0 00		5
6			Income Summary	313		22 1 5 0 00	6
7							7
8		31	Store Supplies Expense	615	4 2 0 00		8
9			Store Supplies	115		4 2 0 00	9
10							10
11		31	Office Supplies Expense	716	2 0 0 00		11
12			Office Supplies	116		2 0 0 00	12
13							13
14		31	Insurance Expense - Selling	614	5 8 0 00		14
15			Insurance Expense - General	715	3 3 0 00		15
16			Prepaid Insurance	117		9 1 0 00	16
17							17
18		31	Depreciation Expense - Store Equipment	613	1 1 0 0 00		18
19			Accumulated Depreciation - Store Equip.	122		1 1 0 0 00	19
20							20
21		31	Depreciation Expense - Office Equipment	714	4 9 0 00		21
22			Accumulated Depreciation - Office Equip.	124		4 9 0 00	22
23							23
24		31	Depreciation Expense - Building	713	1 5 0 0 00		24
25			Accumulated Depreciation - Building	126		1 5 0 0 00	25
26							26
27		31	Sales Salaries	611	2 2 4 00		27
28			Office Salaries	711	7 2 00		28
29			Salaries Payable	213		2 9 6 00	29

JOURNAL   PAGE 28

Adjusting entries

CLOSING ENTRIES

The closing entries are recorded in the general journal immediately following the adjusting entries. All of the temporary capital accounts are cleared of their balances, reducing them to zero. The final effect of closing out such balances is a net increase or a net decrease in the retained earnings account. The closing entries for Midtown Electric Corporation are illustrated on the next page.

The effect of each of the four closing entries journalized on the preceding page may be described as follows:

1. The first entry closes all income statement accounts with *credit* balances by transferring the total to the *credit* side of Income Summary.

	DATE		DESCRIPTION	POST. REF.	DEBIT	CREDIT	
1			Closing Entries				1
2	1973 Dec.	31	Sales	411	167 7 3 6 00		2
3			Purchases Discount	512	1 5 2 5 00		3
4			Rent Income	812	1 2 0 0 00		4
5			Income Summary	313		170 4 6 1 00	5
6							6
7		31	Income Summary	313	146 3 3 3 00		7
8			Sales Returns and Allowances	412		2 1 4 0 00	8
9			Sales Discount	413		1 8 2 2 00	9
10			Purchases	511		105 2 8 0 00	10
11			Sales Salaries	611		20 0 4 4 00	11
12			Advertising Expense	612		3 4 6 0 00	12
13			Depreciation Expense - Store Equipment	613		1 1 0 0 00	13
14			Insurance Expense - Selling	614		5 8 0 00	14
15			Store Supplies Expense	615		4 2 0 00	15
16			Miscellaneous Selling Expense	619		2 3 0 00	16
17			Office Salaries	711		6 0 3 2 00	17
18			Taxes Expense	712		1 8 1 0 00	18
19			Depreciation Expense - Building	713		1 5 0 0 00	19
20			Depreciation Expense - Office Equip.	714		4 9 0 00	20
21			Insurance Expense - General	715		3 3 0 00	21
22			Office Supplies Expense	716		2 0 0 00	22
23			Miscellaneous General Expense	719		3 1 0 00	23
24			Interest Expense	911		5 8 5 00	24
25							25
26		31	Income Summary	313	26 5 7 8 00		26
27			Retained Earnings	311		26 5 7 8 00	27
28							28
29		31	Retained Earnings	311	4 0 0 0 00		29
30			Dividends	312		4 0 0 0 00	30

150

Closing
entries

2. The second entry closes all income statement accounts with *debit* balances by transferring the total to the *debit* side of Income Summary.
3. The third entry closes Income Summary by transferring its balance to Retained Earnings.
4. The fourth entry closes Dividends by transferring its balance to Retained Earnings.

The income summary account, as it will appear after the merchandise inventory adjustments and the closing entries have been posted, is presented on the next page. Each item in the account is identified as an aid to understanding; such notations are not an essential part of the posting procedure.

After the closing of all temporary capital accounts, only the accounts for assets, contra assets, liabilities, and capital remain with balances. The balances of these accounts in the ledger will correspond exactly with the amounts appearing on the balance sheet presented on page 147.

| ACCOUNT | Income Summary | | | | | | | ACCOUNT NO. | 313 | | |

ACCOUNT   Income Summary   ACCOUNT NO.   313

DATE		ITEM	POST. REF.	DEBIT	CREDIT	BALANCE	
						DEBIT	CREDIT
1973 Dec.	31	Mer. inv., Jan. 1	J28	19 7 0 0 00		19 7 0 0 00	
	31	Mer. inv., Dec. 31	J28		22 1 5 0 00		2 4 5 0 00
	31	Revenue, etc.	J29		170 4 6 1 00		172 9 1 1 00
	31	Expense, etc.	J29	146 3 3 3 00			26 5 7 8 00
	31	Net income	J29	26 5 7 8 00			

Income summary account

POST-CLOSING TRIAL BALANCE

As indicated at the beginning of this chapter, the first step in the year-end summarizing procedures is the taking of a trial balance of the general ledger. After the adjusting and closing entries have been recorded, it is advisable to take another trial balance to verify the debit-credit equality of the ledger at the beginning of the following year. This post-closing trial balance may be composed of two adding machine listings, one for the debit balances and the other for the credit balances, or its details may be set forth in a more formal fashion, as the trial balance reproduced below.

Midtown Electric Corporation
Post-Closing Trial Balance
December 31, 1973

	Debit	Credit
Cash	8 5 9 0 00	
Accounts Receivable	6 8 8 0 00	
Merchandise Inventory	22 1 5 0 00	
Store Supplies	5 5 0 00	
Office Supplies	2 8 0 00	
Prepaid Insurance	6 5 0 00	
Store Equipment	10 2 0 0 00	
Accumulated Depreciation - Store Equipment		5 7 0 0 00
Office Equipment	5 5 7 0 00	
Accumulated Depreciation - Office Equipment		2 7 2 0 00
Building	51 0 0 0 00	
Accumulated Depreciation - Building		10 9 0 0 00
Land	6 0 0 0 00	
Accounts Payable		7 4 2 0 00
Salaries Payable		2 9 6 00
Mortgage Note Payable		9 0 0 0 00
Capital Stock		40 0 0 0 00
Retained Earnings		35 8 3 4 00
	111 8 7 0 00	111 8 7 0 00

Post-closing trial balance

REVERSING ENTRIES

Some of the adjusting entries recorded at the close of a fiscal year have a significant effect on otherwise routine transactions that occur in the following year. A typical example is the adjusting entry for accrued salaries owed to employees at the end of the year. The wage or salary expense of an enterprise and the accompanying liability to employees actually accumulates or accrues day by day, or even hour by hour, during any part of the fiscal year. Nevertheless, the customary practice of recording the expense only at the time of payment is more efficient. When salaries are paid weekly, an entry debiting Salary Expense and crediting Cash will be recorded 52 or 53 times during the year. If there has been an adjusting entry for accrued salaries at the end of the year, however, the first payment of salaries in the following year will include such year-end accrual. In the absence of some special provision, it would be necessary to debit Salaries Payable for the amount owed for the earlier year and Salary Expense for the portion of the payroll that represents expense for the later year.

In order to illustrate the situation, assume the following four facts for an enterprise that pays salaries weekly and ends its fiscal year on December 31:

1. Salaries are paid on Friday for the five-day week ending on Friday.
2. The balance in Salary Expense as of Friday, December 27, is $62,500.
3. Salaries accrued for Monday and Tuesday, December 30 and 31, total $500.
4. Salaries paid on Friday, January 3, of the following year total $1,200.

The foregoing data may be presented in diagrammatic form as follows:

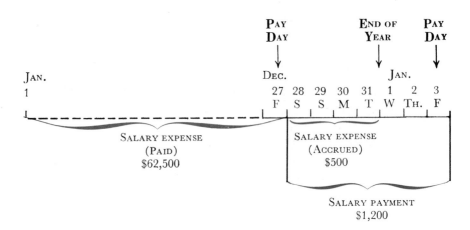

The adjusting entry to record the accrued salary expense and salaries payable for Monday and Tuesday, December 30 and 31, is as follows:

| Dec. | 31 | Salary Expense........................ | 611 | 500 | |
| | | Salaries Payable................... | 213 | | 500 |

After the adjusting entry has been posted, Salary Expense will have a debit balance of $63,000 ($62,500 + $500) and Salaries Payable will have a credit balance of $500. After the closing process is completed, the account Salary Expense is in balance and ready for entries of the following year, but Salaries Payable continues to have a credit balance of $500. As matters now stand it would be necessary to record the $1,200 payroll on January 3 as a debit of $500 to Salaries Payable and a debit of $700 to Salary Expense. This means that the employee who records payroll entries must not only record this particular payroll in a different manner from all other weekly payrolls for the year, but that he must also refer back to the adjusting entries in the journal or the ledger to determine the amount of the $1,200 payment to be debited to each of the two accounts.

The need to refer to earlier entries and to divide the debit between two accounts can be avoided by recording a *reversing* entry as of the first day of the following fiscal period. As the term implies, such an entry is the exact reverse of the adjusting entry to which it relates. The amounts are the same and the accounts debited and credited are the same; they are merely reversed. Continuing with the illustration, the reversing entry for the accrued salaries is as follows:

153

| Jan. | 1 | Salaries Payable.................... | 213 | 500 | |
| | | Salary Expense.................. | 611 | | 500 |

The effect of the reversing entry is to transfer the $500 liability from Salaries Payable to the credit side of Salary Expense. The real nature of the $500 balance is unchanged; it remains a liability. When the payroll is paid on January 3, Salary Expense will be debited and Cash will be credited for $1,200, the entire amount of the weekly salaries. After the entry is posted, Salary Expense will have a debit balance of $700, which is the amount of expense incurred in January. The sequence of entries, including adjusting, closing, and reversing entries, may be traced in the accounts reproduced on the next page.

The year-end procedures for Midtown Electric Corporation are completed by journalizing and posting the reversing entry for accrued salaries. The entry is presented below.

JOURNAL PAGE 29

DATE		DESCRIPTION	POST. REF.	DEBIT	CREDIT	
32		Reversing Entry				32
33	1974					33
34	Jan. 1	Salaries Payable	213	2 9 6 00		34
35		Sales Salaries	611		2 2 4 00	35
36		Office Salaries	711		7 2 00	36

Reversing entry

ACCOUNT **SALARY EXPENSE**   ACCOUNT No. 611

DATE		ITEM	POST. REF.	DEBIT	CREDIT	BALANCE DEBIT	BALANCE CREDIT
1973 Jan.	5		CP36	1,240		1,240	
Dec.	6		CP80	1,300		58,440	
	13		CP81	1,450		59,890	
	20		CP83	1,260		61,150	
	27		CP84	1,350		62,500	
	31	Adjusting	J8	500		63,000	
	31	Closing	J9		63,000	—	—
1974 Jan.	1	Reversing	J9		500		500
	3		CP85	1,200		700	

ACCOUNT **SALARIES PAYABLE**   ACCOUNT No. 213

DATE		ITEM	POST. REF.	DEBIT	CREDIT	BALANCE DEBIT	BALANCE CREDIT
1973 Dec.	31	Adjusting	J8		500		500
1974 Jan.	1	Reversing	J9	500		—	—

154

After the reversing entry is posted, the account Salaries Payable is in balance and the liabilities for sales and office salaries appear as credits in the respective expense accounts. The entire amount of the first payroll in January will be debited to the salary expense accounts and the balances of the accounts will then automatically represent the expense of the new period.

QUESTIONS

1. Does the fact that the trial balance is in balance at the end of the year prove that all transactions for the year have been recorded correctly? Discuss.

2. In the following equations identify the items designated by X:

(a) Purchases $-$ X = Net purchases.
(b) Merchandise inventory (beginning) $+$ X = Merchandise available for sale.
(c) Merchandise available for sale $-$ X = Cost of merchandise sold.
(d) Sales $-$ (X $+$ X) = Net sales.
(e) Net sales $-$ cost of merchandise sold = X.

3. The account Merchandise Inventory is listed at $30,000 on the trial balance (before adjustments) as of January 31, the end of the first month in the current fiscal year. Which of the following phrases describes the item correctly?

(a) Inventory of merchandise at January 31, end of the month.
(b) Purchases of merchandise during January.

(c) Merchandise available for sale during January.
(d) Inventory of merchandise at January 1, beginning of the month.
(e) Cost of merchandise sold during January.

4. The data presented below appear in a work sheet as of December 31, the end of the fiscal year.

	ADJUSTMENTS		INCOME STATEMENT	
	DR.	CR.	DR.	CR.
Income Summary	(a) 20,000	(b) 30,000	20,000	30,000

(a) To what account was the $20,000 credited in adjustment (a)?
(b) To what account was the $30,000 debited in adjustment (b)?
(c) What was the amount of the merchandise inventory at January 1, the beginning of the fiscal year?
(d) What amount will be listed for merchandise inventory on the balance sheet at December 31, the end of the fiscal year?
(e) If the totals of the Income Statement columns of the work sheet are $200,000 debit and $260,000 credit, what is the amount of the net income?
(f) Would the amount determined to be net income be affected by extending only the net amount of $10,000 ($30,000 − $20,000) into the Income Statement credit column?

5. For the fiscal year net sales were $350,000 and net purchases were $250,000. Merchandise inventory at the beginning of the year was $40,000 and at the end of the year it was $30,000. Determine the following amounts:

155

(a) Merchandise available for sale.
(b) Cost of merchandise sold.
(c) Gross profit on sales.
(d) Merchandise inventory listed on the balance sheet as of the end of the year.

6. Before adjustment at September 30, the end of the fiscal year, the salary expense account has a debit balance of $160,000. The amount of salary accrued (owed but not paid) on the same date is $1,500. Indicate the necessary (a) adjusting entry, (b) closing entry, and (c) reversing entry.

7. At the end of the current fiscal year there is a balance of $34,000 in Mortgage Note Payable. Terms of the note require the payment of $1,000 a month. On the balance sheet as of this date indicate the amount of the mortgage note that should be reported (a) as a current liability and (b) as a long-term liability.

8. The expenses described below were incurred by a merchandising enterprise during the year. In which of the following expense sections of the income statement should each be reported: (a) selling, (b) general, (c) other?

(1) Depreciation expense — office equipment.
(2) Gasoline and oil used in delivery truck.
(3) Advertising materials used.
(4) Fire insurance premiums expired on store equipment.
(5) Interest expense on notes payable.
(6) Salary of the general manager.
(7) Salary of the salesmen.
(8) Heating and lighting expense.

9. On what two financial statements of a corporation are each of the following items reported: (a) net income for the period and (b) balance of retained earnings at the end of the period?

10. What is the effect of closing the revenue, expense, and dividends accounts of a corporation at the end of a fiscal year?

11. Immediately after the year-end entries have been recorded, the account Salary Expense has a credit balance of $1,380. Assuming that there have been no errors, does the balance represent an asset, expense, revenue, liability, contra asset, or contra revenue?

12. As of February 1, the first day of the fiscal year, Salary Expense has a credit balance of $900. On February 4, the first payday in the year, salaries of $2,300 are paid. (a) Is the salary expense for February 1–4 $900, $1,400, $2,300, or $3,200? (b) What entry should be made to record the payment on February 4?

13. Why is it advisable, after closing the accounts at the end of a year, to reverse the adjusting entries that had been made for accrued salaries and other accrued expenses?

14. At the end of fiscal year A, an incorporated enterprise owes $2,800 in taxes for which no adjusting entry is made. Early in the following year, fiscal year B, taxes expense of $3,200, which includes the $2,800 accrual, is paid. The payment in fiscal year B was recorded by a debit of $3,200 to Taxes Expense and a credit of the same amount to Cash. Indicate the effect of the error (assuming it is not corrected) on each of the following, stating (a) the amount, and (b) whether an under-or-over-statement:

(1) Net income for fiscal year A.
(2) Net income for fiscal year B.
(3) Total assets, total liabilities, retained earnings, at end of fiscal year A.
(4) Total assets, total liabilities, retained earnings, at end of fiscal year B.

156

EXERCISES

6-1. On the basis of the following data, journalize (a) the adjusting entries at June 30, the close of the current fiscal year and (b) the reversing entry on July 1, the first day of the following year.

(1) Merchandise inventory: July 1 (beginning) $25,700; June 30 (ending) $23,200.
(2) Office supplies account balance before adjustment, $320; office supplies physical inventory, June 30, $70.
(3) The prepaid insurance account before adjustment on June 30 has a balance of $2,340. An analysis of the policies indicates that $760 of premiums has expired during the year.
(4) Sales salaries are uniformly $2,500 for a five-day work week, ending on Friday. The last payday of the year was Friday, June 26.

6-2. At the beginning of the year the merchandise inventory was $38,000; during the year net purchases of merchandise amounted to $173,000; the inventory of merchandise at the end of the year is $33,400. Determine the following:

(a) Merchandise available for sale.
(b) Cost of merchandise sold.

6-3. Selected account titles and related amounts appearing in the Income Statement and Balance Sheet columns of the work sheet of the Hamilton Corporation for December 31 are listed in alphabetical order below.

Accum. Depr. — Bldg.....	$ 19,600	Purchases Discount........	$ 2,800
Capital Stock............	100,000	Rent Income.............	2,400
Dividends...............	8,000	Retained Earnings........	26,300
General Expenses (total)...	27,600	Salaries Payable..........	950
Merchandise Inv. (1/1)....	56,000	Sales....................	320,000
Merchandise Inv. (12/31)..	48,300	Sales Discount...........	2,300
Prepaid Insurance........	2,100	Sales Returns and Allow...	4,400
Purchases...............	197,000	Selling Expenses (total)....	52,300

(a) Prepare an income statement for the year.
(b) Determine the amount of retained earnings to be reported in the balance sheet at the end of the year.
(c) Journalize the entries to adjust the merchandise inventory.
(d) Journalize the closing entries. Controlling accounts are maintained in the general ledger for selling expenses and general expenses.

6-4. Two or more items are omitted in each of the following tabulations of income statement data. Determine the amounts of the missing items, identifying them by letter.

Sales	Sales Returns	Net Sales	Beginning Inventory	Net Purchases	Ending Inventory	Cost of Merchandise Sold	Gross Profit on Sales
$55,000	$3,000	(a)	$14,000	$40,000	(b)	$38,000	(c)
46,000	(d)	$44,000	9,000	28,000	$ 8,000	(e)	(f)
92,000	(g)	92,000	(h)	74,000	14,000	(i)	$20,000
81,000	2,000	79,000	18,000	62,000	(j)	(k)	21,000

6-5. Portions of the salary expense account of an enterprise are presented below. (a) Indicate the nature of the entry (payment, adjusting, closing, reversing) from which each numbered posting was made. (b) Present in general journal form the complete entry from which each numbered posting was made.

SALARY EXPENSE

DATE		ITEM	POST REF.	DR.	CR.	BALANCE	
						DR.	CR
19—							
Jan.	6		CP 18	1,500		1,500	

DATE		ITEM	POST REF.	DR.	CR.	BALANCE	
						DR.	CR
Dec.	27	(1)	CP 37	2,100		92,300	
	31	(2)	J 12	800		93,100	
	31	(3)	J 13		93,100	——	——
19—							
Jan.	1	(4)	J 13		800		800
	3	(5)	CP 38	2,000		1,200	

PROBLEMS

The following additional problems for this chapter are located in Appendix B: 6-1B, 6-2B, 6-4B.

6-1A. The accounts in the ledger of Butler, Inc., with the unadjusted balances on June 30, the end of the current fiscal year, are as follows:

Cash..........................	$ 5,220	Income Summary..............	——
Accounts Receivable............	23,700	Sales.........................	$210,000
Merchandise Inventory..........	52,300	Purchases.....................	133,000
Prepaid Insurance..............	2,510	Sales Salaries.................	22,000
Store Supplies.................	620	Advertising Expense............	2,310
Store Equipment...............	24,600	Depreciation Expense —	
Accum. Depreciation —		Store Equipment............	——
Store Equipment.............	2,400	Delivery Expense..............	1,600
Accounts Payable...............	6,100	Store Supplies Expense.........	——
Salaries Payable................	——	Rent Expense..................	8,400
Capital Stock..................	50,000	Office Salaries.................	7,200
Retained Earnings..............	20,840	Insurance Expense..............	——
Dividends.....................	4,000	Misc. General Expense..........	1,650
		Loss on Disposal of Equip........	230

The data needed for year-end adjustments on June 30 are as follows:

Merchandise inventory on June 30..	$51,400	
Insurance expired during the year . . .	1,130	
Store supplies inventory on June 30.	250	
Depreciation for the current year . . .	1,950	
Accrued salaries on June 30:		
Sales salaries.............	$320	
Office salaries............	110	430

Instructions (corporation income tax is excluded from consideration):
(1) Prepare an eight-column work sheet for the fiscal year ended June 30, listing all of the accounts in the order given.
(2) Prepare an income statement.
(3) Prepare a retained earnings statement.
(4) Prepare a balance sheet.
(5) Compute the following:
  (a) Percent of income from operations to sales.
  (b) Percent of net income to total capital as of the beginning of the year.

If the working papers correlating with this textbook are not used, omit Problem 6-2A.

6-2A. The general ledger of Plaza Appliances, Inc., with account balances as of December 1, is presented in the working papers. The company's journals, in which transactions for the month of December have been recorded, are also presented in the working papers. The fiscal year ends on December 31.

Instructions (corporation income tax is excluded from consideration):
(1) Post the journals to the general ledger accounts, following the order indicated below and at the top of the next page. Balances need not be inserted in the balance columns of the accounts until all journals have been posted. Assume that entries to the subsidiary ledgers have been posted by an assistant.

POSTING ORDER
(a) Individual items in Sundry Accounts columns:
  (1) General Journal, (2) Purchases Journal, (3) Cash Receipts Journal, (4) Cash Payments Journal.

(b) Column totals:
(1) Sales Journal, (2) Purchases Journal, (3) Cash Receipts
Journal, (4) Cash Payments Journal.
(2) Complete the trial balance as of December 31. The account titles are
listed on an eight-column work sheet presented in the working papers.
(3) Complete the work sheet. Adjustment data are:

Merchandise inventory at December 31.	$41,430
Insurance expired during the year......	1,526
Store supplies on hand at December 31.	336
Depreciation for the current year on:	
Store equipment..................	1,600
Office equipment..................	392
Accrued taxes at December 31.........	3,200

(4) Prepare an income statement, a retained earnings statement,
and a balance sheet.
(5) Journalize the adjusting entries and post.
(6) Journalize the closing entries and post. Indicate closed accounts
by inserting a line in both balance columns.
(7) Complete the post-closing trial balance presented in the working
papers.
(8) Journalize the reversing entry or entries as of January 1 and post.

6-3A. The accounts and their balances in the ledger of The Jackson Corporation on August 31 of the current year are as follows:

Cash........................	$ 21,200	Sales Ret. and Allow...........	$ 3,300
Accounts Receivable...........	42,500	Purchases....................	232,600
Merchandise Inventory.........	61,700	Purchases Discount............	2,930
Prepaid Insurance.............	2,130	Sales Salaries.................	35,600
Store Supplies................	720	Rent Expense — Selling........	5,400
Office Supplies................	390	Depreciation Expense —	
Store Equipment..............	21,400	Store Equipment..........	——
Accum. Depreciation —		Insurance Expense — Selling.....	——
Store Equipment...........	7,200	Store Supplies Expense.........	——
Office Equipment.............	8,300	Misc. Selling Expense..........	960
Accumulated Depreciation —		Office Salaries.................	17,300
Office Equipment...........	1,800	Taxes Expense.................	16,400
Accounts Payable.............	31,600	Rent Expense — General.......	1,200
Salaries Payable..............	——	Depreciation Expense —	
Mortgage Note Payable (due 1982)	12,000	Office Equipment...........	——
Capital Stock.................	60,000	Insurance Expense — General....	——
Retained Earnings.............	11,570	Office Supplies Expense........	——
Dividends....................	12,000	Miscellaneous General Expense...	1,440
Income Summary..............	——	Gain on Disposal of Plant Assets..	800
Sales........................	357,600	Interest Expense..............	960

The data for year-end adjustments on August 31 are as follows:

Merchandise inventory on August 31.	$59,200	
Insurance expired during the year:		
Allocable as selling expense..	$840	
Allocable as general expense.	430	1,270
Inventory of supplies on August 31:		
Store supplies..................		320
Office supplies.................		150
Depreciation for the year:		
Store equipment................		2,050
Office equipment...............		630
Salaries payable on August 31:		
Sales salaries.............	$460	
Office salaries............	210	670

Instructions (corporation income tax is excluded from consideration):

(1) Prepare a work sheet for the fiscal year ended August 31, listing all accounts in the order given.
(2) Prepare an income statement.
(3) Prepare a retained earnings statement.
(4) Prepare a balance sheet.
(5) Journalize the adjusting entries.
(6) Journalize the closing entries.
(7) Journalize the reversing entries as of September 1.

6-4A. A portion of the work sheet of Mark Olson Co. for the current year ending November 30 is presented below.

Account Title	Income Statement Debit	Income Statement Credit	Balance Sheet Debit	Balance Sheet Credit
Cash..			13,200	
Accounts Receivable...........................			37,900	
Merchandise Inventory.........................			48,000	
Prepaid Rent.................................			1,500	
Prepaid Insurance............................			1,360	
Supplies.....................................			420	
Store Equipment..............................			17,700	
Accumulated Depr. — Store Equip..............				4,800
Office Equipment.............................			3,900	
Accumulated Depr. — Office Equip.............				1,610
Accounts Payable.............................				25,600
Sales Salaries Payable........................				360
Mortgage Note Payable........................				15,000
Mark Olson, Capital..........................				49,410
Mark Olson, Drawing..........................			12,000	
Income Summary..............................	52,500	48,000		
Sales..		300,000		
Sales Returns and Allowances.................	3,100			
Purchases....................................	198,000			
Purchases Discount...........................		2,200		
Sales Salaries................................	26,200			
Delivery Expense.............................	5,300			
Supplies Expense.............................	720			
Depreciation Expense — Store Equip..........	1,710			
Miscellaneous Selling Expense.................	860			
Office Salaries...............................	11,600			
Rent Expense................................	6,000			
Insurance Expense............................	1,540			
Depreciation Expense — Office Equip..........	950			
Miscellaneous General Expense................	1,320			
Interest Expense.............................	1,200			
	311,000	350,200	135,980	96,780

Instructions:

(1) From the partial work sheet presented above, determine the eight entries that appeared in the adjustments columns and present them in general journal form. The only accounts affected by more than a single adjusting entry were Merchandise Inventory and Income Summary. The balance in Prepaid Rent before adjustment was $7,500, representing a prepayment for 15 months' rent at $500 a month.
(2) Determine the following:
  (a) Amount of net income for the year.
  (b) Amount of the owner's capital at the end of the year.

160

Chapter 7

RECEIVABLES AND PAYABLES

USE OF CREDIT IN BUSINESS

The extension of credit plays an important role in the operations of many business enterprises. Credit may be granted on open account or on the basis of a formal instrument of credit such as a *promissory note*. The use of the latter is customary for credit periods in excess of sixty days, as in sales of equipment on the installment plan, and for transactions of relatively large dollar amounts. Promissory notes may also be used in settlement of an open account and in borrowing or lending money.

From the point of view of the creditor, a claim evidenced by a note has some advantages over a claim in the form of an account receivable. By signing a note, the debtor acknowledges the debt and agrees to pay it in accordance with the terms specified. It is therefore a stronger legal claim in the event of court action. It is also more liquid than an open account because the holder may transfer it to a creditor in settlement of a debt or to a bank or other financial agency in exchange for cash.

When relatively large sums are borrowed for an appreciable period of time, the borrower may be required to furnish some type of security. The practice is also followed when payments for substantial purchases of land, buildings, or equipment are to be spread over a number of years. One of the most frequently employed types of security is a mortgage, which gives the creditor a lien, or claim, on property owned by the debtor. In the event that the debtor (mortgagor) defaults on his obligation, the creditor (mortgagee) may, under specified conditions, take possession of the property or force its sale to satisfy his claim. When a note secured by a mortgage is fully paid, the lien is canceled.

Increased assurance of the payment of individual notes or accounts may also be provided through the pledging of specific assets such as marketable securities, notes and accounts receivable, and inventories. Assets that are pledged may not be disposed of by the debtor until the related debt has been paid or the proceeds from their disposition are used in settlement of the obligation.[1]

CLASSIFICATION OF RECEIVABLES

The term *receivables* includes all money claims against individuals, organizations, or other debtors. They are acquired by a business enterprise in various types of transactions, the most common being the sale of merchandise or services on a credit basis. Accounts and notes receivable originating from sales transactions are sometimes referred to as *trade receivables*. In the absence of other descriptive words or phrases, accounts and notes receivable may be assumed to have originated from sales in the usual course of the business.

Other receivables of not infrequent occurrence include interest receivable, loans to officers or employees, and loans to affiliated companies. In order to facilitate their classification and presentation on the balance sheet, a general ledger account should be maintained for each type of receivable, with appropriate subsidiary ledgers.

All receivables that are expected to be realized in cash within a year are presented in the current assets section of the balance sheet. Those that are not currently collectible, such as long-term loans, should be listed under the caption "Investments" below the current assets section.

The importance of accounts and notes receivable to specific enterprises varies with the volume of credit sales and the length of the credit period. For many businesses the revenue from sales of their products on a credit basis is the largest factor influencing the amount of net income. Claims against customers may also represent a substantial percentage of the total amount of their current assets.

CLASSIFICATION OF PAYABLES

Payables are, of course, the opposite of receivables; they are debts owed by an enterprise to its creditors. Money claims against a firm may originate in numerous ways, such as purchases of merchandise or services on a credit basis, loans from banks, purchases of equipment, and purchases of marketable securities. At any particular moment of time a business may also owe its employees for wages or salaries accrued, banks or other creditors for interest accrued on notes, and governmental agencies for taxes.

Liabilities that are due and payable within a year are presented in the current liability section of the balance sheet. Those that are not payable until a more distant future date are listed as long-term liabilities. When a mortgage note payable or other long-term liability is payable in

---

[1]Special problems related to the issuance and acquisition of long-term notes and bonds are discussed in Chapter 18.

periodic installments, the portion due within one year should be listed as a current liability.

In addition to known liabilities of a definite or reasonably approximate amount, there may be potential obligations that will materialize only if certain events occur in the future. Such liabilities, which are termed *contingent* liabilities, should be disclosed either on the financial statements or in accompanying notes. The nature of the contingency and, if the events should occur, the magnitude of the obligation are important considerations in assessing the ability of an enterprise to meet its commitments.

PROMISSORY NOTES

A promissory note, frequently referred to simply as a *note*, is a written promise to pay a sum certain in money on demand or at a definite time. As in the case of a check, it must be payable to the order of a particular person or firm, or to bearer. It must also be signed by the person or firm that makes the promise. The one to whose order the note is payable is called the *payee*, and the one making the promise is called the *maker*. In the note illustrated below, Connor Equipment Company is the payee and Arrow Corporation is the maker.

$ 2,500.00	DAYTON, OHIO ___October 2___ 19 73
Sixty days	AFTER DATE ___We___ PROMISE TO PAY TO
THE ORDER OF Connor Equipment Company	
Two thousand five hundred 00/100 ------------------------- DOLLARS	
PAYABLE AT Merchants National Bank	
VALUE RECEIVED WITH INTEREST AT 7%	ARROW CORPORATION
No. 14 DUE December 1, 1973	H. B. Lane
	TREASURER

Interest-bearing note

The enterprise owning a note refers to it as a *note receivable* and records it as an asset at its face amount; the maker of a note refers to it as a *note payable* and records it as a liability at its face amount. Thus, the note in the illustration would be recorded in the ledger of Connor Equipment Company as a $2,500 debit in Notes Receivable and in the ledger of Arrow Corporation as a $2,500 credit in Notes Payable.

A note that provides for the payment of interest for the period between the issuance date and the due date is called an *interest-bearing* note. If a note makes no provision for interest, it is said to be *non-interest bearing*. In such cases, however, interest may be charged at the legal rate for any time that the note remains unpaid after it is due. The interest that a debtor is obliged to pay is an expense and is called *interest expense*. The interest that a creditor is entitled to receive is revenue and is called *interest income.*

DETERMINING INTEREST

Interest rates are customarily stated in terms of a period of a year, regardless of the actual period of time involved. Thus the interest on $2,000 for a year at 8% would be $160 (8% of $2,000); the interest on $2,000 for one fourth of a year at 8% would be $40 (¼ of $160).

Notes covering a period of time longer than a year ordinarily provide that the interest be paid semiannually, quarterly, or at some other specified interval. The time involved in commercial credit transactions is usually less than a year, and the interest provided for by a note is payable at the time the note is paid. In computing interest for a period of less than a year, agencies of the federal government use the actual number of days in the year; for example, 90 days is considered to be 90/365 of a year. The usual commercial practice is to use 360 as the denominator of the fraction; thus 90 days is considered to be 90/360 of a year.

The basic formula for computing interest is as follows:

$$\text{Principal} \times \text{Rate} \times \text{Time} = \text{Interest}$$

To illustrate the application of the formula, assume a note for $900, payable in 20 days with interest at 7%. The interest would be $3.50, computed as follows:

$$\$900 \times \frac{7}{100} \times \frac{20}{360} = \$3.50 \text{ interest}$$

One of the commonly used shortcut methods of computing interest is called the 60-day, 6% method. The 6% annual rate is converted to the effective rate of 1% for a 60-day period (60/360 of 6%). Accordingly, the interest on any amount for 60 days at 6% is determined by moving the decimal point in the principal two places to the left. For example, the interest on $1,342 at 6% for 60 days is $13.42. The amount obtained by moving the decimal point must be adjusted (1) for interest rates greater or less than 6% and (2) for periods of time greater or less than 60 days.

Comprehensive interest tables are available and are commonly used by financial institutions and other enterprises that require frequent interest calculations. Nevertheless, the student of business should be sufficiently conversant with the mechanics of interest computations to employ them with complete accuracy and to recognize significant errors in interest determinations that come to his attention.

When the term of a note is expressed in months instead of in days, each month may be considered as being 1/12 of a year, or, alternatively, the actual number of days in the term may be counted. For example, the interest on a 3-month note dated June 1 could be computed on the basis of 3/12 of a year or on the basis of 92/360 of a year. It is the usual commercial practice to employ the first method, while banks usually charge interest for the exact number of days. For the sake of simplicity, the usual commercial practice will be assumed in all cases.

DETERMINING DUE DATE

The period of time between the issuance date and the maturity date of a short-term note may be expressed in either days or months. When the term of a note is expressed in days, the due date is the specified number of days after its issuance and may be determined as follows:

1. Subtract the date of the note from the number of days in the month in which it is dated.
2. Add as many full months as possible without exceeding the number of days in the note, counting the full number of days in these months.
3. Subtract the sum of the days obtained in *1* and *2* from the number of days in the note.

To illustrate, the due day of a 90-day note dated March 16 may be determined as follows:

```
Term of the note.................  90
March (days).............  31
Date of note.............  16
                          ___
    Remainder.................  15
April (days).................  30
May (days)...................  31
                                ___
Total.........................  76
Due date, June...............  14
                                ===
```

When the term of a note is expressed as a specified number of months after the issuance date, the due date is determined by counting the number of months from the issuance date. Thus, a 3-month note dated June 5 would be due on September 5. In those cases in which there is no date in the month of maturity that corresponds to the issuance date, the due date becomes the last day of the month. For example, a 2-month note dated July 31 would be due on September 30.

NOTES PAYABLE AND INTEREST EXPENSE

When the volume of notes payable is relatively small, there is no need for a subsidiary ledger. A file of carbon copies of all notes issued should be maintained; details of each note may also be entered on a single line of a multi-column supplementary record.

Notes may be issued to creditors in temporary satisfaction of an account payable created earlier, or they may be issued at the time merchandise, equipment, or other assets are purchased. To illustrate the former, assume that an enterprise, which owes F. B. Murray Co. $1,000

165

on an overdue account, issues a 90-day, 8% note for $1,000 in liquidation of the account. The transaction is recorded by the following entry in the general journal:

June	6	Accounts Payable — F. B. Murray Co.......	1,000	
		Notes Payable.........................		1,000
		Issued a 90-day, 8% note on account.		

The payee may hold the note until maturity, or he may transfer it by endorsement to his bank or to a creditor. In any event, on the due date the note is ordinarily presented by the holder at the maker's place of business or other location specified in the note. Upon payment, the holder surrenders the note to the maker. The effect of paying the $1,000 note recorded in the entry above may be presented in general journal form as follows:

Sept.	4	Notes Payable...........................	1,000	
		Interest Expense.........................	20	
		Cash...................................		1,020

In practice, the foregoing transaction would be recorded in the cash payments journal rather than in the general journal. Because of its greater simplicity and clarity, the general journal format will continue to be used to illustrate entries throughout the remainder of the chapter.

There are numerous variations in interest and repayment terms when borrowing money from banks. The most direct procedure is for the borrower to issue an interest-bearing note for the amount of the loan. For example, assuming that on September 19 a firm borrows $4,000 from the First National Bank, the loan being evidenced by its 90-day, 7% note, the effect of the transaction is as follows:

| Sept. | 19 | Cash................................... | 4,000 | |
| | | Notes Payable......................... | | 4,000 |

On the due date of the note, ninety days later, the borrower owes $4,000, the face amount of the note, and interest of $70. The accounts affected by the payment are as follows:

Dec.	18	Notes Payable...........................	4,000	
		Interest Expense.........................	70	
		Cash...................................		4,070

Discounting notes payable. A variant of the bank loan transaction just illustrated is to issue a non-interest-bearing note for the amount that is to be paid at maturity. When this plan is followed, the interest is deducted from the maturity value of the note and the borrower receives the remainder. The deduction of interest from a future value is termed *discounting*. The rate used in computing the interest may be termed the *discount rate*, the deduction may be referred to as the *discount*, and the net amount available to the borrower is called the *proceeds*.

To illustrate the discounting of a note payable, assume that on August 10 an enterprise issues to a bank an $8,000, 90-day, non-interest-bearing note and that the bank discount rate is 6½%. The amount of the discount is $130 and the proceeds $7,870. The debits and credit required to record the transaction follow:

```
Aug. 10   Cash.................................   7,870
          Interest Expense..........................   130
          Notes Payable............................          8,000
```

It should be observed that the above note payable is recorded at its face value, which is also its maturity value, and that the interest expense is recorded at the time the note is issued. When the note is paid, the entry is as follows:

```
Nov.  8   Notes Payable............................   8,000
          Cash.................................          8,000
```

NOTES RECEIVABLE AND INTEREST INCOME

The typical retail enterprise makes most of its sales for cash or on account. If the account of a customer becomes delinquent, the creditor may insist that the account be converted into a note. In this way the debtor may be given an extension of time, and if the creditor needs additional funds, he may endorse and transfer the note to his bank. Notes may also be received by retail firms that sell merchandise on long-term credit. For example, a dealer in household appliances may require a down payment at the time of sale and accept a note or a series of notes for the remainder. Such arrangements usually provide for monthly payments. Wholesale firms and manufacturers are likely to receive notes more frequently than retailers, although here, too, much depends upon the nature of the product and the length of the credit period.

When a note is received from a customer to apply on his account, the facts are recorded by debiting the notes receivable account and crediting the accounts receivable controlling account and the account of the customer from whom the note is received. It is not necessary to maintain a subsidiary ledger for notes receivable because the notes themselves provide detailed information.

To illustrate, assume that the account of Norton & Co., which has a debit balance of $900, is past due. A 20-day, 8% note for that amount, dated April 23, is accepted in settlement of the account. The entry to record the transaction is as follows:

167

```
Apr. | 23 | Notes Receivable.........................|  900 |
     |    |    Accounts Receivable — Norton & Co......|      | 900
     |    |       Received a 20-day, 8% note dated    |      |
     |    |       April 23.                           |      |
```

Upon receipt of the principal and interest due on the above note, the following debits and credits are recorded in the cash receipts journal:

May 13	Cash..	904
	Notes Receivable.........................	900
	Interest Income..........................	4

Discounting notes receivable. Instead of being retained by the holder until maturity, notes receivable may be transferred to a bank by endorsement. The discount (interest) charged is computed on the maturity value of the note for the period of time that will elapse between the date of the transfer and the due date of the note. The amount of the proceeds paid to the endorser is the excess of the maturity value over the discount. Two examples will illustrate discounting operations, one for a non-interest-bearing note and the other for an interest-bearing note.

Non-interest-bearing note. Assume that among the notes receivable held by an enterprise is a 90-day non-interest-bearing note for $1,350, dated August 21, and that the note is discounted at a bank on September 20 at the rate of 7%. The data may be tabulated as follows:

Face value of note dated Aug. 21.......................		$1,350.00
Maturity value of note due Nov. 19.....................		$1,350.00
Discount period — Sept. 20 to Nov. 19...........	60 days	
Discount on maturity value — 60 days at 7%.............		15.75
Proceeds..		$1,334.25

The effect of the transaction, which would be recorded in the cash receipts journal, is as follows:

Sept. 20	Cash............................	1,334.25	
	Interest Expense......................	15.75	
	Notes Receivable.................		1,350.00

Interest-bearing note. Assume that a 90-day, 6% note receivable for $1,800, dated November 8, is discounted on December 3 at the rate of 7%. The data used in determining the effect of the transaction are as follows:

Face value of note dated Nov. 8.......................		$1,800.00
Interest on note — 90 days at 6%......................		27.00
Maturity value of note due Feb. 6.....................		$1,827.00
Discount period — Dec. 3 to Feb. 6.............	65 days	
Discount on maturity value — 65 days at 7%.............		23.09
Proceeds..		$1,803.91

The same information is presented graphically in the flow diagram illustrated at the top of the next page. In reading the data, follow the direction of the arrows.

Face Value	plus	Maturity Value
$1,800 ———————→ $27.00 interest ————————→ =		$1,827.00

Nov. 8   90 days   Feb. 6

Proceeds	minus	
$1,803.91 = ◄———— $23.09 discount ◄————		$1,827.00

Dec. 3   65 days   Feb. 6

The excess of the proceeds from discounting the note, $1,803.91, over its face value, $1,800 is recorded as interest income. The entry for the transaction, in general journal form, is as follows:

Dec. 3 Cash............................... 1,803.91
            Notes Receivable.................. 1,800.00
            Interest Income................... 3.91

It should be observed that the proceeds from discounting an interest-bearing note receivable may be less than the face value. When this occurs, the excess of the face value over the proceeds is recorded as interest expense. The amount and direction of the difference between the interest rate and the discount rate will affect the result, as will the relationship between the full term of the note and the length of the discount period.

169

Contingent liability. In the absence of a qualification limiting his responsibility, the endorser of a note is committed to paying the bank or other endorsee if the maker should default. Accordingly, the discounting of a note receivable creates a contingent liability that continues in effect until the due date. If the maker pays the promised amount at maturity, the contingent liability is discharged without any action on the part of the endorser. If, on the other hand, the maker defaults and the endorser is notified in accordance with legal requirements, the liability becomes an actual one.

The nature and amount of the contingency should be disclosed on the balance sheet or in an accompanying notation somewhat as follows: "As of [balance sheet date] the company was contingently liable for notes receivable discounted in the amount of [amount]." It should be noted that it is only the amount of the unmatured notes discounted as of the balance sheet date that is significant. The number of such notes may represent only a minor portion of the total volume of short-term notes that were discounted during the year. The amount of the contingent liability can ordinarily be determined from a memorandum record of amounts, due dates, and other pertinent data for each note.

DISHONORED NOTES RECEIVABLE

If the maker of a note fails to pay his obligation on the due date, the note is said to be *dishonored*. A dishonored note receivable ceases to be negotiable, and for that reason the holder ordinarily transfers the claim, including any interest due, to the accounts receivable account. For example, if the $900, 20-day, 8% note received and recorded on April 23 (page 167) had been dishonored at maturity, the entry to charge the note, including the interest, back to the customer's account would have been as follows:

May	13	Accounts Receivable — Norton & Co........	904	
		Notes Receivable......................		900
		Interest Income.......................		4
		Dishonored note and interest.		

If there had been some assurance that the maker would pay the note within a relatively short time, action could have been postponed until the matter was resolved. However, for future guidance in extending credit it may be desirable that the customer's account in the subsidiary ledger disclose the dishonor of the note.

When a discounted note receivable is dishonored, the holder ordinarily notifies the endorser of such fact and requests payment. If the presentation for payment and notification of dishonor are timely, the endorser is legally obligated to pay the amount due on the note. The entire amount paid to the holder by the endorser, including the interest, should be debited to the account receivable of the maker. To illustrate, assume that the $1,800, 90-day, 6% note discounted on December 3 (page 168) is dishonored at maturity by the maker, Pryor & Co. The entry to record the payment by the endorser, in general journal form, would be as follows:

Feb.	6	Accounts Receivable — Pryor & Co.......... 1,827	
		Cash..................................	1,827

In some cases the holder of a dishonored note submits to the endorser a notarized statement of the facts of the dishonor. The fee for this statement, known as a *protest fee*, is charged to the endorser, who in turn charges it to the maker of the note. If there had been a protest fee of $2 in connection with the dishonor and the payment recorded above, the debit to the maker's account and the credit to Cash would have been $1,829.

UNCOLLECTIBLE ACCOUNTS

When merchandise or services are sold without the immediate receipt of cash, a portion of the claims against customers ordinarily proves to be uncollectible. This is usually the case regardless of the care used in granting credit and the efficacy of the collection procedures employed.

The operating expense incurred because of the failure to collect receivables is variously termed an expense or a loss from *uncollectible accounts, doubtful accounts,* or *bad debts.*[2]

There is no single general rule for determining when an account or a note becomes uncollectible. The fact that a debtor fails to pay his account in accordance with the sales contract or dishonors a note on the due date does not necessarily indicate uncollectibility. Bankruptcy of the debtor is one of the most positive indications of partial or complete worthlessness of a receivable. Other evidence includes discontinuance of the debtor's business, disappearance of the debtor, failure of repeated attempts to collect, and the barring of collection by the statute of limitations.

There are two generally accepted methods of accounting for receivables that are deemed to be uncollectible. The *allowance* method, which is sometimes referred to as *reserve* method, makes advance provision for uncollectible receivables. The other procedure, called the *direct write-off* or *direct charge-off* method, recognizes the expense only when specific accounts are judged to be worthless.

ALLOWANCE METHOD OF ACCOUNTING FOR UNCOLLECTIBLES

Most large business enterprises provide currently for the amount of their trade receivables estimated to become uncollectible in the future. The advance provision for future uncollectibility is effected by an adjusting entry at the end of the fiscal period. As with all periodic adjustments, the entry serves a dual purpose. In this instance it provides for (1) the reduction of the value of the receivables to the amount of cash expected to be realized from them in the future and (2) the allocation to the current period of the expected expense resulting from such reduction.

Assumed data for a new business firm will be used to explain and illustrate the allowance method. The enterprise began business in August and elected to adopt the calendar year as its fiscal year. The accounts receivable account, which is reproduced at the top of the next page, has a balance of $105,000 at the end of the period.

Among the individual customers' accounts comprising the $105,000 balance in Accounts Receivable are a number of balances which are a varying number of days past due. No specific accounts are determined to be wholly uncollectible at this time, but it appears inevitable that some will be collected only in part and that others are likely to become entirely worthless. Based on a careful study, it is estimated that a total of $3,000 will eventually prove to be uncollectible. The amount expected to be realized from the accounts receivable is accordingly $105,000 —

---

[2]If both notes and accounts are involved, both may be included in the title, as in "uncollectible notes and accounts expense," or the general term "uncollectible receivables expense" may be substituted. Because of its wide usage and simplicity, "uncollectible accounts expense" will be used in this book.

Account ACCOUNTS RECEIVABLE   Account No. 114

DATE		ITEM	POST. REF.	DEBIT	CREDIT	BALANCE DEBIT	BALANCE CREDIT
19--							
Aug.	31		S3	20,000		20,000	
Sept.	30		S6	25,000		45,000	
	30		CR4		15,000	30,000	
Oct.	31		S10	40,000		70,000	
	31		CR7		25,000	45,000	
Nov.	30		S13	38,000		83,000	
	30		CR10		23,000	60,000	
Dec.	31		S16	75,000		135,000	
	31		CR13		30,000	105,000	

$3,000, or $102,000, and the $3,000 reduction in value is the uncollect-ible accounts expense for the period.

It is obvious that the $3,000 reduction in accounts receivable cannot be identified with specific customers' accounts in the subsidiary ledger and should therefore not be credited to the controlling account in the general ledger. The customary practice is to employ a *contra asset* account entitled Allowance for Doubtful Accounts. The adjusting entry to record the expense and the reduction in the asset is presented below, followed by the two accounts to which the entry is posted.

		Adjusting Entry			
Dec.	31	Uncollectible Accounts Expense.......	717	3,000	
		Allowance for Doubtful Accounts . . .	114.1		3,000

Account UNCOLLECTIBLE ACCOUNTS EXPENSE   Account No. 717

DATE		ITEM	POST. REF.	DEBIT	CREDIT	BALANCE DEBIT	BALANCE CREDIT
19--							
Dec.	31	Adjusting	J4	3,000		3,000	

Account ALLOWANCE FOR DOUBTFUL ACCOUNTS   Account No. 114.1

DATE		ITEM	POST. REF.	DEBIT	CREDIT	BALANCE DEBIT	BALANCE CREDIT
19--							
Dec.	31	Adjusting	J4		3,000		3,000

The debit balance of $105,000 in Accounts Receivable is the face amount of the total claims against customers on open account, and the credit balance of $3,000 in Allowance for Doubtful Accounts is the amount to be deducted from Accounts Receivable to determine their expected realizable value. The $3,000 reduction in the asset was transferred to uncollectible accounts expense, which will in turn be closed to the income summary account.

Uncollectible accounts expense is reported on the income statement as either selling expense or general expense, depending upon the department responsible. Credits and collections may be the responsibility of the sales department or of an independent department within the general administrative framework.

The accounts receivable may be listed on the balance sheet at the net amount of $102,000 with a parenthetical notation disclosing the amount of the allowance, or the details may be presented as shown on the partial balance sheet below.

Richards Company
Balance Sheet
December 31, 19--

Assets

Current assets:		
Cash.......		$ 21,600
Accounts receivable........	$105,000	
Less allowance for doubtful accounts.......	3,000	102,000

When the allowance account includes provision for doubtful notes as well as accounts, it should be deducted from the total of Notes Receivable and Accounts Receivable.

Write-offs to the allowance account. When an account is deemed to be uncollectible, it is written off against the allowance account as in the following entry:

Jan.	21	Allowance for Doubtful Accounts........	110	
		Accounts Receivable — John Parker...		110
		To write off the uncollectible account.		

As additional accounts or portions of accounts are determined during the year to be uncollectible, they are written off against Allowance for Doubtful Accounts in the same manner. Instructions for write-offs should originate with the credit manager or other designated official. The authorizations, which should always be written, serve as objective evidence in support of the accounting entry.

Naturally enough, the total amount written off against the allowance account during the period will rarely be exactly equal to the amount in the account as of the beginning of the period. The allowance account will have a credit balance at the end of the period if the write-offs during the period amount to less than the beginning balance; it will have a debit balance if the write-offs exceed the beginning balance. After the year-end adjusting entry is recorded, the allowance account will have a credit balance.

An account receivable that has been written off against the allowance account may subsequently be collected. In such cases the account should be reinstated by an entry that is the exact reverse of the write-off entry. For example, assume that the account of $110 written off in the preceding journal entry is later collected. The entry to reinstate the account would be as follows:

June	10	Accounts Receivable — John Parker.....	110	
		Allowance for Doubtful Accounts.....		110
		To reinstate account written off earlier in the year.		

The cash received in payment would be recorded in the cash receipts journal as a receipt on account. Although it is possible to combine the reinstatement and the receipt of cash into a single debit and credit, the entries in the customer's account, with an appropriate notation, provide useful credit information.

Estimating uncollectibles. The estimate of uncollectibles at the end of the fiscal period is based on past experience modified by forecasts of future business activity. When the trend of general sales volume is upward and there is relatively full employment, the magnitude of the expense should ordinarily be less than when the trend is in the opposite direction. The estimate is customarily based on either (1) the amount of sales for the entire fiscal period or (2) the amount and the age of the receivable accounts at the end of the fiscal period.

Estimate based on sales. Accounts receivable are acquired as a result of sales on account. The volume of such sales during the year may therefore be used as an indication of the probable amount of the accounts that will be uncollectible. For example, if it is known from past experience that about 1% of charge sales will be uncollectible and the charge sales for a particular year amount to $300,000, the adjusting entry for uncollectible accounts at the end of the year would be as follows:

		Adjusting Entry		
Dec.	31	Uncollectible Accounts Expense.........	3,000	
		Allowance for Doubtful Accounts......		3,000

Instead of charge sales, total sales (including those made for cash) may be used in developing the percentage. The total sales figure is obtainable from the ledger without the necessity for the analysis that may be required to determine charge sales. If the ratio of sales on account to cash sales does not change materially from year to year, the results obtained will be equally satisfactory. For example, if in the example above the balance of the sales account at the end of the year is assumed to be $400,000, the application of ¾ of 1% to that amount would also yield an estimate of $3,000.

If it becomes apparent over a period of time that the amount of the write-offs is consistently greater or less than the amount provided by the adjusting entry, the percentage applied to sales data should be revised accordingly. A newly established business enterprise, having no record of credit experience, may obtain data on the probable amount of the expense from trade association journals and other publications containing information on credit and collections.

Estimate based on analysis of receivables. The process of analyzing the receivable accounts is sometimes called *aging the receivables.* The base point for determining age is the due date of the account. The number and breadth of the time intervals used will vary according to the credit terms granted to customers. A portion of a typical analysis is presented below.

CUSTOMER	BALANCE	NOT DUE	1–30	31–60	61–90	91–180	181–365	over 365
Ashby & Co.....	$ 150			$ 150				
B. T. Barr.......	610					$ 350	$ 260	
Brock Co........	470	$ 470						
J. Zimmer Co....	160							160
Total.........	$86,300	$75,000	$4,000	$3,100	$1,900	$1,200	$ 800	$ 300

Analysis of accounts receivable

The analysis is completed by adding the columns to determine the total amount of receivables in each age group. A sliding scale of percentages, based on experience, is next applied to obtain the estimated amount of uncollectibles in each group. The manner in which the data may be assembled is illustrated below.

ESTIMATED UNCOLLECTIBLE ACCOUNTS

AGE INTERVAL	BALANCE	PERCENT	AMOUNT
Not due........................	$75,000	2%	$1,500
1–30 days past due..............	4,000	5	200
31–60 days past due.............	3,100	10	310
61–90 days past due.............	1,900	20	380
91–180 days past due............	1,200	30	360
181–365 days past due...........	800	50	400
Over 365 days past due..........	300	80	240
Total......................	$86,300		$3,390

Estimate of uncollectible accounts

The estimate of uncollectible accounts, $3,390 in the above example, is the amount to be deducted from accounts receivable in order to yield their expected realizable value. It is thus the amount of the desired balance of the allowance account after adjustment. The excess of this figure over the balance of the allowance account before adjustment is the amount of the current provision to be made for uncollectible accounts expense.

To continue the illustration, assume that the allowance account has a credit balance of $510 before adjustment. The amount to be added to this balance is therefore $3,390 − $510, or $2,880, and the adjusting entry is as follows:

			Adjusting Entry		
Dec.	31	Uncollectible Accounts Expense.	2,880	
		Allowance for Doubtful Accounts.		2,880

After the adjusting entry is posted, the balance in the allowance account will be $3,390, which is the desired amount. If the allowance account before the year-end adjustment had had a debit balance of $300, the amount of the adjustment would have been $3,390 (the desired balance) + $300 (the negative balance), or $3,690.

The use of the analysis-of-receivables method of determining the uncollectible accounts expense yields a more reasoned estimate of the current realizable value of the receivables and is frequently preferred over the percent of sales method. An inadequate or excessive provision in one period automatically influences the amount of the adjustment for the succeeding period. The percent of sales method lacks this relatively automatic device for keeping the amount of the estimated expense close to the actual net write-offs.

DIRECT WRITE-OFF METHOD OF ACCOUNTING FOR UNCOLLECTIBLES

If an enterprise sells most of its merchandise or services on a cash basis, the amount of its expense from uncollectible accounts is ordinarily minor in relation to its revenue. The amount of its receivables at any time is also likely to represent a relatively small portion of its total current assets. These observations are based on the assumption that the credit period is short, which would be usual if sales are preponderantly on a cash basis, and that credit policies and collection procedures are adequate. The nature of the service or the product sold and the type of clientele may also have an important bearing on collection experience. For example, an enterprise that sells most of its output on account to a small number of companies, all of which are financially strong, will incur little, if any, expense from inability to collect its accounts.

In such situations, as well as in many small business and professional enterprises, it is satisfactory to defer recognition of uncollectibility until the period in which specific accounts are deemed to be worthless and are actually written off as an expense. Accordingly, there is no necessity for an allowance account or for an adjusting entry at the end of the period. The entry to write off an account when it is believed to be uncollectible is as follows:

May	10	Uncollectible Accounts Expense	42	
		Accounts Receivable — D. L. Ross		42
		To write off uncollectible account.		

If an account that has been written off is collected later, the account should be reinstated. If the recovery is in the same fiscal year as the write-off, the earlier entry should be reversed to reinstate the account. To illustrate, assume that the account written off in the May 10 entry above is collected in November of the same fiscal year. The entry to reinstate the account would be as follows:

Nov.	21	Accounts Receivable — D. L. Ross	42	
		Uncollectible Accounts Expense		42
		To reinstate account written off earlier in the year.		

The receipt of cash in payment of the reinstated amount would be recorded in the cash receipts journal in the usual manner.

When an account that has been written off is collected in a subsequent fiscal year, it may be reinstated by an entry like that just illustrated. An alternative is to credit some other appropriately titled account, such as Recovery of Uncollectible Accounts Written Off. The credit balance in such an account at the end of the year may then be reported on the income statement as a deduction from Uncollectible Accounts Expense, or the net expense only may be reported. Such amounts are likely to be minor in relationship to net income.

QUESTIONS

1. What are "trade receivables?"

2. In what section should a three-year note receivable from the president of X Corporation be listed on X Corporation's balance sheet?

3. What are the advantages, to the creditor, of a note receivable in comparison to an account receivable?

4. The unpaid balance of a mortgage note payable is $40,000 at the close of the current fiscal year. The terms of the note provide for monthly principal payments of $500. How should the liability for the principal be presented on the balance sheet as of this date?

5. A business firm is contesting a suit for damages of a substantial amount brought by a supplier for alleged breach of contract. Is this a contingent liability of the defendant? If so, should it be disclosed in financial reports issued during the period of litigation? Discuss.

6. Name the two parties to a promissory note and state the title of the account each would use in recording the note.

7. If a note provides for payment of principal of $1,000 and interest at the rate of 7%, will the interest amount to $70? Explain.

8. The following questions refer to a 30-day, 6% note for $2,000, dated July 20: (a) What is the face value of the note? (b) What is the amount of interest payable at maturity? (c) What is the maturity value of the note? (d) What is the due date of the note?

9. A business enterprise issues a 60-day, 8% note for $900 to a creditor on account. Give in general journal form the entries to record (a) the issuance of the note and (b) the payment of the note at maturity, including interest of $12.

10. In borrowing money from a bank an enterprise issues a non-interest-bearing note, which the bank discounts at 7%. Does the maker incur a contingent liability? Explain.

11. The payee of a 90-day, 6% note for $2,000, dated May 10, endorses it to his bank on May 20. The bank discounts the note at 8%, paying the endorser $1,993.91. Identify or determine the following, as they relate to the note: (a) face value, (b) maturity value, (c) due date, (d) number of days in the discount period, (e) proceeds, (f) interest income or expense recorded by payee, (g) amount payable to the bank if the maker should default.

12. A discounted note receivable is dishonored by the maker and the endorser pays the bank the face of the note, $800, the interest, $16, and a protest fee of $2. What entry should be made to record the payment?

13. Of the $135,000 of notes receivable discounted to a bank by an enterprise during the year, $110,000 have matured by the end of the year. What is the amount of the endorser's contingent liability for notes receivable discounted at the close of the year?

14. The series of six transactions recorded in the T accounts below were related to a sale to a customer on account and payment of the amount owed. Describe each transaction briefly.

Cash			Notes Receivable			Accounts Receivable		
(4)	795	(5) 808	(3)	800	(4) 800	(1)	815	(2) 15
(6)	810					(5)	808	(3) 800
								(6) 808

Sales			Interest Income			Interest Expense		
(2)	15	(1) 815			(6) 2	(4)	5	

15. Which of the two methods of accounting for uncollectible accounts provides for recognition of the expense at the earlier date?

16. What kind of an account (asset, liability, etc.) is Allowance for Doubtful Accounts, and is its normal balance a debit or a credit?

17. Give the adjusting entry to increase Allowance for Doubtful Accounts by $3,100.

18. The $240 balance of an account owed by a customer is considered to be uncollectible and is to be written off. Give the entry to record the write-off in the general ledger (a) assuming that the allowance method is used and (b) assuming that the direct write-off method is used.

19. After accounts are adjusted and closed at the end of the fiscal year, Accounts Receivable has a balance of $185,000 and Allowance for Doubtful Accounts has a balance of $3,000.

(a) What is the expected realizable value of the accounts receivable?
(b) If an account receivable of $100 is written off against the allowance account, what will be the expected realizable value of the accounts receivable after the write-off, assuming that no other changes in either account have occurred in the meantime?

20. A firm has consistently adjusted its allowance account at the end of the fiscal year by adding a fixed percent of the period's net sales on account. After six years the balance in Allowance for Doubtful Accounts has become disproportionately large in relationship to the balance in Accounts Receivable. Give two possible explanations.

179

EXERCISES

7-1. Determine the interest on the following notes:

Face Amount	Number of Days	Interest Rate
(a) $ 750.00	30	6%
(b) $1,300.00	75	7%
(c) $ 938.50	68	$6\frac{1}{2}\%$
(d) $2,145.00	54	8%

7-2. Meeker Corporation issues a 60-day, 8% note for $2,400, dated March 2, to Ballard Co. on account.
(a) Determine the due date of the note.
(b) Determine the amount of interest to be paid on the note at maturity.
(c) Present entries, in general journal form, to record the following:
(1) Issuance of the note by the maker.
(2) Receipt of the note by the payee.
(3) Payment of the note at maturity.
(4) Receipt of payment of the note at maturity.

7-3. Drake Co. issues a 120-day, non-interest-bearing note for $24,000 to Merchants Bank and Trust Co., which the bank discounts at 7%. Present the maker's entries, in general journal form, to record (a) issuance of the note and (b) payment of the note at maturity.

7-4. In negotiating a 90-day loan, an enterprise has the option of either (1) issuing a $40,000, non-interest-bearing note that will be discounted at the rate of 8%, or (2) issuing a $40,000 note bearing interest at the rate of 8% that will be accepted at face value.

(a) Determine the amount of the interest expense for each option.
(b) Determine the amount of the proceeds for each option.
(c) Indicate the option that is more favorable to the borrower.

7-5. On July 1 Northgate Plaza purchases land for $70,000 and a building for $850,000, paying $220,000 cash and issuing an 8% note for the balance, secured by a mortgage on the property. The terms of the note provide for fourteen semiannual payments of $50,000 on the principal plus the interest accrued from the date of the preceding payment. Present the entry, in general journal form, to record (a) the transaction on July 1, (b) the payment of the first installment on December 31, and (c) the payment of the second installment the following June 30.

7-6. T. J. Tyler, Inc., holds a 90-day, 7% note for $3,600, dated September 4, that was received from a customer on account. On November 3, the note is discounted at the First National Bank at the rate of 8%.

(a) Determine the maturity value of the note.
(b) Determine the number of days in the discount period.
(c) Determine the amount of the discount.
(d) Determine the amount of the proceeds.
(e) Present the entry, in general journal form, to record the discounting of the note on November 3.

7-7. Record the following transactions, each in general journal form, in the accounts of Mitchell Company.

June   1. Received an $1,800, 60-day, 7% note dated June 1 from Beckett Corp. on account.
July   1. Discounted the note at Citizens State Bank, discount rate 8%.
   31. The note is dishonored; paid the bank the amount due on the note plus a protest fee of $2.
Aug. 30. Received the amount due on the dishonored note plus interest for 30 days at 7% on the total amount debited to Beckett Corp. on July 31.

7-8. At the end of the current year, the accounts receivable account has a debit balance of $90,000 and net sales for the year total $760,000. Determine the amount of the adjusting entry to record the provision for doubtful accounts under each of the following assumptions:

(a) The allowance account before adjustment has a *credit* balance of $640.
   (1) Uncollectible accounts expense is estimated at 3/4 of 1% of net sales.
   (2) Analysis of the accounts in the customers ledger indicates doubtful accounts of $6,200.
(b) The allowance account before adjustment has a *debit* balance of $320.
   (1) Uncollectible accounts expense is estimated at 1/2 of 1% of net sales.
   (2) Analysis of the accounts in the customers ledger indicates doubtful accounts of $3,700.

PROBLEMS

The following additional problems for this chapter are located in Appendix B: 7-1B, 7-2B, 7-3B, 7-4B.

7-1A. The following were selected from among the transactions completed by McCann Co. during the current year:

Jan. 12. Purchased merchandise on account from Price & Co., $750.

22. Paid Price & Co. for the invoice of January 12, less 2% discount.

Feb. 10. Purchased merchandise on account from M. S. Taylor Co., $1,200.

Mar. 12. Issued a 30-day, 8% note for $1,200 to M. S. Taylor Co. on account.

Apr. 11. Paid M. S. Taylor Co. the amount owed on the note of March 12.

May 26. Issued a 60-day, non-interest-bearing note for $10,000 to First National Bank. The bank discounted the note at the rate of 7%.

July 25. Paid First National Bank the amount due on the note of May 26.

Aug. 8. Borrowed $3,000 from Merchants National Bank, issuing a 60-day, 7½% note for that amount.

Oct. 7. Paid Merchants National Bank the interest due on the note of August 8 and renewed the loan by issuing a new 30-day, 7½% note for $3,000. (Record both the debit and the credit to the notes payable account.)

Nov. 6. Paid Merchants National Bank the amount due on the note of October 7.

Dec. 1. Purchased office equipment from Globe Co. for $5,900, paying $900 and issuing a series of ten 8% notes for $500 each, coming due at 30-day intervals.

31. Paid the amount due Globe Co. on the first note in the series issued on December 1.

181

Instructions:

(1) Record the transactions in general journal form.

(2) Determine the total amount of interest accrued as of December 31 on the nine notes owed to Globe Co.

(3) Assume that a single note for $5,000 had been issued on December 1 instead of the series of ten notes, and that its terms required principal payments of $500 each 30 days, with interest at 8% on the principal balance before applying the $500 payment. Determine the amount that would have been due and payable on December 31.

7-2A. The following were selected from among the transactions completed by R. A. Staley Co. during the current year:

Jan. 8. Sold merchandise on account to Marshall Co., $1,080.

18. Accepted a 30-day, 7% note for $1,080 from Marshall Co. on account.

Feb. 17. Received from Marshall Co. the amount due on the note of January 18.

Mar. 10. Sold merchandise on account to Horn & Rusk, $1,400, charging an additional $30 for prepaid transportation costs.

20. Received from Horn & Rusk the amount due on the invoice of March 10, less 2% discount.

Apr. 28. Loaned $400 cash to John Ward, receiving a 30-day, 8% note.

May 28. Received the interest due from John Ward and a new 60-day, 8% note as a renewal of the loan. (Record both the debit and the credit to the notes receivable account.)

July 27. Received from John Ward the amount due on his note.

Aug. 16. Sold merchandise on account to B. T. Frost Corp., $3,000.

Sept. 17. Received from B. T. Frost Corp. a 60-day, 8% note for $3,000, dated September 15.

     25. Discounted the note from B. T. Frost Corp. at the Bank of Commerce at 7%.

Nov. 14. Received notice from Bank of Commerce that B. T. Frost Corp. had dishonored its note. Paid the bank the maturity value of the note.

Dec. 4. Received from B. T. Frost Corp. the amount owed on the dishonored note, plus interest for 20 days at 8% computed on the maturity value of the note.

Instructions:

    Record the transactions in general journal form.

7-3A. The transactions, adjusting entries, and closing entries described below are related to uncollectible accounts. All were completed during the current fiscal year ended December 31.

Jan. 26. Wrote off the $405 balance owed by Walsh Corp., which has no assets.

Apr. 10. Reinstated the amount of Harold Martin that had been written off in the preceding year and received $90 cash in full payment.

July 17. Received 8% of the $600 balance owed by Bruner & Co., a bankrupt, and wrote off the remainder as uncollectible.

Oct. 3. Reinstated the account of Roger Kirk that had been written off two years earlier and received $72 cash in full payment.

Dec. 27. Wrote off the following accounts as uncollectible (compound entry): Mark Alden, $310; Easton & Sharp, $762; Osgood Corp., $980; J. B. White, Inc., $525.

    31. On the basis of an analysis of the $123,580 of accounts receivable, it was estimated that $3,410 will be uncollectible. Recorded the adjusting entry.

    31. Recorded the entry to close the appropriate account to Income Summary.

Instructions:

(1) Open the following selected accounts, recording the credit balance indicated as of January 1 of the current fiscal year:

      114.1   Allowance for Doubtful Accounts. $3,200

      313   Income Summary. . . . . ——

      718   Uncollectible Accounts Expense. . ——

(2) Record in general journal form the transactions and the adjusting and closing entries described above. After each entry, post to the three selected accounts affected and extend the new balances.

(3) Determine the expected realizable value of the accounts receivable as of December 31.

(4) Assuming that, instead of basing the provision for uncollectible accounts on an analysis of receivables, the adjusting entry on December 31 had been based on an estimated loss of 1/2 of 1% of net sales for the year of $800,000, determine the following:

    (a) Uncollectible accounts expense for the year.

    (b) Balance in the allowance account after the adjustment of December 31.

    (c) Expected realizable value of the accounts receivable as of December 31.

If the working papers correlating with the textbook are not used, omit Problem 7-4A.

7-4A. The transactions presented on the next page, all of which are related to receivables and payables, were selected from among the transactions completed by Fletcher Co. during the current fiscal year.

182

Jan. 9. Issued to Holton Co. a 2-month, 8% note for $4,200, on account.

 22. Received from Rialto Co. a 90-day, non-interest-bearing note for $3,000, dated January 21, on account.

Feb. 20. Discounted at Manufacturers Trust Co. at 7% the note received from Rialto Co., dated January 21.

Mar. 9. Issued Check No. 515 to Holton Co. in payment of the note issued on January 9.

 18. Received from Long & Co. the amount due on a March 8 invoice for $1,800, less 2% discount.

Apr. 4. Wrote off against the allowance account the $175 owed by Grant & Son.

 24. Borrowed $5,000 from Manufacturers Trust Co., issuing a 7%, 90-day note.

May 12. Received from Apex, Inc., a 90-day, 7% note for $2,400, dated May 11, on account.

 18. Purchased land for a building site from Modern Development Co. for $46,000, issuing Check No. 598 for $10,000 and a 7% mortgage note for the balance. The contract provides for payments of $4,000 of principal plus accrued interest at intervals of six months. (Record entire transaction in the Cash Payments Journal.)

June 10. Discounted at First State Bank at 8% the note received from Apex, Inc., dated May 11.

July 3. Received from Corbin's, Inc., on account a 30-day, 6% note for $600, dated July 2.

 23. Issued Check No. 657 to Manufacturers Trust Co. for the amount due on the note dated April 24.

Aug. 1. Corbin's, Inc., dishonored its note dated July 2. Charged the principal and interest to its account.

 10. Received notice from First State Bank that Apex, Inc., had dishonored the note due on August 9. Issued Check No. 703 for the amount due on the note, plus a protest fee of $3.

Sept. 2. Received from Corbin's, Inc., the amount due on the note dishonored on August 1, plus $3.02 interest for 30 days on the maturity value of the note.

 15. Reinstated the account of Fred Lee that had been written off against the allowance account in the preceding year, and received cash in full payment, $82.

Oct. 9. Received from Apex, Inc., the amount due on the note dishonored on August 9, plus $28.53 interest for 60 days.

Nov. 18. Issued Check No. 815 for principal and interest due on the mortgage note issued on May 18.

Instructions:

(1) Record the selected entries in the three journals provided in the working papers: Cash Receipts, Cash Payments, and a General Journal. No posting is required.

(2) At the end of the year, Accounts Receivable has a debit balance of $110,400. The distribution of the accounts, by age intervals, is presented in the working papers, together with the percent of each class estimated to be uncollectible. Determine the amount of the accounts estimated to be uncollectible.

(3) Prior to adjustment at the end of the year, Allowance for Doubtful Accounts has a credit balance of $548. Record the adjusting entry in the general journal as of December 31.

(4) Present the data on accounts receivable as they will appear in the balance sheet as of December 31.

183

7-5A. Universal Sales Co. has just completed its fourth year of operations. The direct write-off method of recording uncollectible accounts expense has been employed during the entire period. Because of substantial increases in sales volume and amount of uncollectible accounts, the firm is considering the possibility of changing to the allowance method. Information is requested as to the effect that an annual provision of 1/2 of 1% of sales would have had on the amount of uncollectible accounts expense reported for each of the past four years. It is also considered desirable to know what the balance of Allowance for Doubtful Accounts would have been at the end of each year. The following data have been obtained from the accounts:

Year	Sales	Uncollectible Accounts Written Off	Year of Origin of Accounts Receivable Written Off as Uncollectible			
			1st	2d	3d	4th
1st	$500,000	$ 200	$ 200			
2d	600,000	2,400	2,100	$ 300		
3d	800,000	3,300	400	2,400	$ 500	
4th	900,000	3,600		200	2,600	$ 800
			$2,700	$2,900		

Instructions:

(1) Assemble the desired data, using the following columnar captions:

	Uncollectible Accounts Expense			Balance of
Year	Expense Actually Reported	Expense Based on Estimate	Increase in Amount of Expense	Allowance Account, End of Year

(2) Advise management as to whether the estimate of 1/2 of 1% of sales appears to be reasonably close to the actual experience with uncollectible accounts originating during the first two years.

7-6A. The Osborn Co. received the notes described below during the last three months of the current fiscal year. Notes (1), (2), (3), and (4) were discounted on the dates and at the rates indicated.

Date	Face Amount	Term	Interest Rate	Date Discounted	Discount Rate
(1) Oct. 8	$2,400	60 days	—	Oct. 18	7%
(2) Oct. 22	1,600	30 days	6%	Nov. 1	8%
(3) Nov. 14	1,920	90 days	7%	Nov. 19	8%
(4) Nov. 17	1,800	30 days	8%	Dec. 7	7%
(5) Dec. 6	2,000	60 days	6%	—	—
(6) Dec. 21	4,200	60 days	8%	—	—

Instructions:

(1) Determine for each note (a) the due date and (b) the amount of interest due at maturity, identifying each note by number.
(2) Determine for each of the first four notes (a) the maturity value, (b) the discount period, (c) the discount, (d) the proceeds, and (e) the interest income or interest expense, identifying each note by number.
(3) Present, in general journal form, the entries to record the discounting of notes (1) and (2) at a bank.
(4) Assuming that notes (5) and (6) are held until maturity, determine for each the amount of interest earned (a) in the current fiscal year and (b) in the following fiscal year.

Chapter 8

MERCHANDISE INVENTORY

***

The term *inventories* is used to designate merchandise held for sale in the normal course of business and also materials in the process of production or held for such use. This chapter is devoted to problems arising in the determination of the inventory of merchandise purchased for resale, commonly called *merchandise inventory*. Consideration will be given in a later chapter to inventories of raw materials and partially processed materials of a manufacturing enterprise.

Merchandise is one of the most active elements in the operation of wholesale and retail businesses, being continuously purchased and sold. The sale of merchandise provides the principal source of revenue for such enterprises. In determining net income, the cost of merchandise sold is the largest deduction from sales; in fact, it is customarily larger than all other deductions combined. In addition, a substantial portion of a merchandising firm's resources is invested in inventory; it is frequently the largest of the current assets.

Inventory determination plays an important role in matching expired costs with revenues of the period. As was explained and illustrated in Chapter 6, the total cost of merchandise available for sale during a period of time must be divided into two elements at the end of the period. The cost of the merchandise determined to be in the inventory will appear on the balance sheet as a current asset; the other element, which is the cost of the merchandise sold, will be reported on the income statement as a deduction from net sales to yield gross profit on sales. An error in the determination of the inventory figure at the end of the period will cause an equal misstatement of gross profit and net income in the income statement, and the amount reported for both assets and capital in the balance sheet will be incorrect by the same amount. The effects of understatements and overstatements of merchandise inventory at the end of the period are demonstrated below by three sets of severely

185

condensed income statements and balance sheets. The first statements are based on a correct inventory determination, in the second set of statements the inventory has been understated by $8,000, and in the third set the inventory has been overstated by $7,000. In each case the merchandise available for sale is assumed to be $140,000.

1. Inventory at end of period correctly stated at $20,000.

INCOME STATEMENT FOR THE YEAR		BALANCE SHEET AT END OF YEAR	
Net sales.....................	200,000	Merchandise inventory.........	**20,000**
Cost of merchandise sold.......	**120,000**	Other assets.................	80,000
Gross profit...............	80,000	Total....................	100,000
Expenses...................	55,000		
Net income...............	**25,000**	Liabilities...................	30,000
		Capital.....................	**70,000**
		Total....................	100,000

2. Inventory at end of period incorrectly stated at $12,000; **understated by $8,000.**

Net sales.....................	200,000	Merchandise inventory.........	**12,000**
Cost of merchandise sold.......	**128,000**	Other assets.................	80,000
Gross profit...............	72,000	Total....................	92,000
Expenses...................	55,000		
Net income...............	**17,000**	Liabilities...................	30,000
		Capital.....................	**62,000**
		Total....................	92,000

3. Inventory at end of period incorrectly stated at $27,000; **overstated by $7,000.**

Net sales.....................	200,000	Merchandise inventory.........	**27,000**
Cost of merchandise sold.......	**113,000**	Other assets.................	80,000
Gross profit...............	87,000	Total....................	107,000
Expenses...................	55,000		
Net income...............	**32,000**	Liabilities...................	30,000
		Capital.....................	**77,000**
		Total....................	107,000.

Note that in the illustration the total amount of merchandise cost to be accounted for was constant at $140,000; it was the manner in which the cost was allocated that varied. The variations in allocating the $140,000 of merchandise cost are summarized as follows:

	MERCHANDISE AVAILABLE		
	TOTAL	INVENTORY	SOLD
1. Inventory correctly stated.................	$140,000	$20,000	$120,000
2. Inventory understated by $8,000............	140,000	12,000	128,000
3. Inventory overstated by $7,000.............	140,000	27,000	113,000

The effect of the erroneous allocations on net income, assets, and capital may also be summarized. Comparison of the amounts reported on the preceding page in financial statements *2* and *3* with the comparable amounts reported in financial statement *1* yields the following:

	NET INCOME	ASSETS	CAPITAL
2. Ending inventory understated $8,000	Understated $8,000	Understated $8,000	Understated $8,000
3. Ending inventory overstated $7,000	Overstated $7,000	Overstated $7,000	Overstated $7,000

It should be noted that the inventory at the end of one period becomes the inventory for the beginning of the following period. Thus, if the inventory is incorrectly stated at the end of the period, the net income of that period will be misstated and so will the net income of the following period. The amount of the two misstatements will be equal and in opposite directions. Therefore, the effect on net income of an incorrectly stated inventory, if uncorrected, is limited to the period of the error and the following period. At the end of this following period, assuming no additional errors, both assets and capital will be correctly stated.

Elements of the foregoing analyses are closely related to the various inventory systems and methods presented hereinafter. A thorough understanding of the effect of inventories on the determination of net income, as presented in the foregoing examples, will be helpful.

INVENTORY SYSTEMS

187

There are two principal systems of inventory accounting, *periodic* and *perpetual*. When the periodic system is employed, only the revenue from sales is recorded each time a sale is made; no entries are made to credit the inventory account or the purchases account for the cost of the merchandise that has been sold. Consequently, it is only by a detailed listing of the merchandise on hand (called a *physical inventory*) at the close of an accounting period that the cost of the inventory can be determined. Ordinarily, it is feasible to take a complete physical inventory only at the end of the fiscal year. When the merchandise inventory can be determined only by a physical measurement at specified intervals, the system can be characterized as *periodic*. In earlier chapters dealing with sales and purchases of merchandise, the use of the periodic system has always been assumed.

In contrast to the periodic system, the *perpetual* inventory system employs accounting records that continuously disclose the amount of the inventory. A separate account for each type of merchandise is maintained in a subsidiary ledger. Increases in inventory items are recorded as debits to the appropriate accounts, and decreases are recorded as credits; the balances of the accounts are called the *book* inventories of the items on hand. Regardless of the care with which the perpetual inventory records are maintained, it is necessary to test their accuracy by taking a physical inventory of each type of commodity at least once a year. The records are then compared with the actual quantities and any discrepancies corrected.

The periodic inventory system of accounting is ordinarily used by retail enterprises that sell a great variety of low unit cost merchandise, such as groceries, hardware, and drugs. The expense of maintaining perpetual inventory records is likely to be prohibitive in such cases. Firms selling a relatively small number of high unit cost items, such as office equipment, automobiles, or fur garments, are more likely to employ the perpetual system.

Although much of the discussion that follows is applicable to both systems, the use of the periodic inventory system will be assumed. Later in the chapter, consideration will be given to principles and procedures related exclusively to the perpetual inventory system.

DETERMINING ACTUAL QUANTITIES IN THE INVENTORY

The first stage in the process of "taking" an inventory is the determination of the quantity of each type of merchandise owned by the enterprise. Where the periodic system is used, the counting, weighing, and measuring should be done at the end of the accounting period. In order to accomplish this, the inventory crew may work during the night, or business operations may be suspended until the count is completed.

The details of the specific procedures for determining quantities and assembling the data vary considerably among companies. A common practice is to employ teams composed of two persons; one person counts, weighs, or otherwise determines quantity, and the other lists the description and the quantity on inventory sheets. The quantity indicated for high-cost items is verified by a third person at some time during the inventory-taking period. It is also advisable for the third person to verify other items selected at random from the inventory sheets.

All of the merchandise owned by the business on the inventory date, and only such merchandise, should be included in the inventory. It may be necessary to examine sales and purchase invoices of the last few days of the accounting period and the first few days of the ensuing period to determine who has legal title to merchandise in transit on the inventory date. When goods are purchased or sold FOB shipping point, title ordinarily passes to the buyer when the goods are shipped. When the terms are FOB destination, title usually does not pass to the buyer until the commodities are delivered. To illustrate, assume that merchandise purchased FOB shipping point is shipped by the seller on the last day of the buyer's fiscal period. The merchandise does not arrive until the following period and hence is not available for "counting" by the inventory crew. Such merchandise should nevertheless be included in the buyer's inventory because title has passed. It is also evident that a debit to Purchases and credit to Accounts Payable should be recorded by the buyer as of the end of the period, rather than recording it as a transaction of the following period.

Another example, although less common, will further emphasize the importance of scrutinizing transactions involving shipments of merchandise. Manufacturers sometimes ship merchandise on a consignment basis to retailers who act as the manufacturer's agent when selling the merchandise. The manufacturer retains title until the commodities are sold. Obviously, such unsold merchandise is a part of the manufacturer's (consignor's) inventory even though he does not have physical possession. It is just as obvious that the retailer (consignee) should not list the consigned merchandise on his inventory sheets.

DETERMINING THE COST OF INVENTORY

The cost of merchandise inventory is composed of the purchase price and all expenditures incurred in acquiring such merchandise, including transportation, customs duties, and insurance. The purchase price can be readily determined, as may some of the other costs. Those that are difficult to associate with specific inventory items may be prorated on some equitable basis. Minor costs that are difficult to allocate may be excluded entirely from inventory cost and treated as operating expenses of the period.

189

If purchases discounts are treated as a deduction from purchases on the income statement, they should also be deducted from the purchase price of items in the inventory. If it is not feasible to determine the exact amount of discount applicable to each inventory item, a pro rata amount of the total discount for the period may be deducted instead. For example, if net purchases and purchases discount for the period amount to $200,000 and $3,000 respectively, the discount represents $1\frac{1}{2}\%$ of net purchases. If the inventory cost, before considering cash discount, is $30,000, the amount may be reduced by $1\frac{1}{2}\%$, or $450, to yield an inventory cost of $29,550.

One of the most significant complications in determining inventory cost arises when identical units of a particular commodity have been acquired at various unit cost prices during the period. When such is the case, it is necessary to determine the unit prices to be associated with the items still on hand. The exact nature of the problem and its relationship to the determination of net income and inventory cost are indicated by the illustration that follows.

Assume that during the fiscal year three identical units of Commodity X were available for sale to customers, one of which was in the inventory at the beginning of the year. Details as to the dates of purchase and the costs per unit are shown at the top of the next page.

Commodity X		Units	Cost
Jan. 1	Inventory......	1	$ 9
Mar. 4	Purchase.......	1	13
May 9	Purchase.......	1	14
	Total	3	$36
	Average cost per unit		$12

During the period two units of Commodity X were sold, leaving a single unit in the inventory at the end of the period. Information is not available as to which two of the three units were sold and which unit remains. Consequently it becomes necessary to adopt an arbitrary assumption as to the *flow of costs* of merchandise through the enterprise. The three most common assumptions employed in determining the cost of the merchandise sold are as follows:

1. Cost flow is in the order in which the expenditures were made.
2. Cost flow is in the reverse order in which the expenditures were made.
3. Cost flow is an average of the expenditures for merchandise.

Details of the cost of the two units of Commodity X assumed to be sold and the cost of the one unit remaining, determined in accordance with each of these assumptions, are presented below.

	Commodity X Costs		
	Units Available	Units Sold	Unit Remaining
1. In order of expenditures...............	$36	−($ 9 + $13) =	$14
2. In reverse order of expenditures	36	−(14 + 13) =	9
3. In accordance with average of expenditures	36	−(12 + 12) =	12

In actual practice it may be possible to identify units with specific expenditures if both the variety of merchandise carried in stock and the volume of sales are relatively small. Ordinarily, however, specific identification procedures are too laborious and costly to justify their use. It is customary, therefore, to adopt one of the three generally accepted costing methods, each of which is also acceptable in determining income subject to the federal income tax.

First-in, first-out method. The first-in, first-out (*fifo*) method of costing inventory is based on the assumption that costs should be charged against revenue in the order in which they were incurred. Hence the inventory remaining is assumed to be composed of the most recent costs. The illustration of the application of this method is based on the following data for a particular commodity:

Jan. 1	Inventory............	200 units at $ 9.....	$ 1,800
Mar. 10	Purchase............	300 units at 10.....	3,000
Sept. 21	Purchase............	400 units at 11.....	4,400
Nov. 18	Purchase............	100 units at 12.....	1,200
	Available for sale during year.	1,000................	$10,400

The physical count on December 31 indicates that 300 units of the commodity are on hand. In accordance with the assumption that the inventory is composed of the most recent costs, the cost of the 300 units is determined as follows:

Most recent costs, Nov. 18.......100 units at $12.......	$1,200
Next most recent costs, Sept. 21 ..200 units at 11.......	2,200
Inventory, Dec. 31..........300.................	**$3,400**

Deduction of the inventory of **$3,400** from the $10,400 of merchandise available for sale yields **$7,000** as the cost of merchandise sold, which represents the earliest costs incurred for this commodity.

In most businesses there is a tendency to dispose of commodities in the order of their acquisition. This would be particularly true of perishable merchandise and goods in which style or model changes are frequent. Thus the fifo method is generally in harmony with the physical movement of merchandise in an enterprise. To the extent that this is the case, the fifo method approximates the results that would be obtained by specific identification of costs.

Last-in, first-out method. The last-in, first-out (*lifo*) method is based on the assumption that the most recent costs incurred should be charged against revenue. Hence the inventory remaining is assumed to be composed of the earliest costs. Based on the illustrative data presented in the preceding section, the cost of the inventory is determined in the following manner:

Earliest costs, Jan. 1............200 units at $ 9.......	$1,800
Next earliest costs, Mar. 10......100 units at 10.......	1,000
Inventory, Dec. 31..........300.................	**$2,800**

Deduction of the inventory of **$2,800** from the $10,400 of merchandise available for sale yields **$7,600** as the cost of merchandise sold, which represents the most recent costs incurred for this particular commodity.

The use of the lifo method was originally confined to the relatively rare situations in which the units sold were taken from the most recently acquired stock. Its use has greatly increased during the past few decades, and it is now often employed when it is not in conformity with the physical flow of commodities.

Weighted average method. The weighted average method is based on the assumption that costs should be charged against revenue on the basis of an average, taking into consideration the number of units acquired at each price. The same average unit cost is employed in computing the cost of the merchandise remaining in the inventory. The weighted average is determined by dividing the total costs of a commodity available for sale by the total number of units of that commodity available for sale. Assuming the same cost data as in the preceding illustrations,

191

the weighted average cost of the 1,000 units and the cost of the inventory are determined as follows:

Weighted average cost. . . . $10,400 ÷ 1,000 = $10.40 per unit
Inventory, Dec. 31 . . . . . . 300 units at $10.40 . . . . $3,120

Deduction of the inventory of **$3,120** from the $10,400 of merchandise available for sale yields **$7,280** as the cost of merchandise sold, which represents the average of the costs incurred for this commodity.

For businesses in which various purchases of identical units of a commodity are mingled, the weighted average method has some relationship to the physical flow of commodities.

Comparison of inventory costing methods. Each of the three alternative methods of costing inventories under the periodic system is based on a different assumption as to the flow of costs. If the cost of commodities and the prices at which they were sold remained perfectly stable, all three methods would yield the same results. Prices do fluctuate, however, and as a consequence the three methods will ordinarily yield different amounts for both (1) the inventory at the end of the period and (2) the cost of the merchandise sold and net income reported for the period. The examples presented in the preceding sections illustrated the effect of rising prices. They may be summarized as follows:

	FIRST-IN, FIRST-OUT	LAST-IN, FIRST-OUT	WEIGHTED AVERAGE
Merchandise available for sale			
Merchandise inventory, December 31	3,400	2,800	3,120
Cost of merchandise sold	$ 7,000	$ 7,600	$ 7,280

In comparing and evaluating the results obtained in the illustration, it should be borne in mind that both the amount reported as net income and the amount reported as inventory are affected. The method that yields the lowest figure for the cost of merchandise sold will yield the highest figure for gross profit and net income reported on the income statement; it will also yield the highest figure for inventory reported on the balance sheet. Conversely, the method that yields the highest figure for the cost of merchandise sold will yield the lowest figure for gross profit and net income and the lowest figure for inventory.

During periods of consistently rising prices, the use of first-in, first-out yields the highest possible amount of net income. The reason for this effect is that business enterprises tend to increase their selling prices in accordance with market trends, regardless of the fact that merchandise in stock may have been acquired before the price increase. In periods of declining prices the effect is reversed, and the fifo method yields the lowest possible net income. The principal criticism of the fifo method is this tendency to accentuate the effect of inflationary and deflationary

192

trends on reported income. On the other hand, the amount reported for inventory on the balance sheet will closely approximate its current replacement cost.

During periods of consistently rising prices, the use of last-in, first-out yields the lowest possible amount of net income. The reason for this effect is that the cost of the most recently acquired units most nearly approximates the expenditure required to replace the units sold. In periods of declining prices, the effect is reversed and the lifo method yields the highest possible net income. The principal justification for lifo is this tendency to minimize the effect of price trends on reported net income. A criticism of the general use of lifo is its complete lack of relationship to the physical flow of merchandise in most enterprises. The amount reported for inventory on the balance sheet may also be quite far removed from current replacement cost. If there is little change in the physical composition of the inventory from year to year, the inventory cost reported remains nearly constant, regardless of extreme changes in price levels.

The weighted average method of inventory costing is, in a sense, a compromise between fifo and lifo. The effect of price trends is averaged, both in the determination of net income and the determination of inventory cost. For any given series of acquisitions, the weighted average cost will be the same regardless of the direction of price trends. For example, a complete reversal of the sequence of acquisitions and unit costs presented in the illustration on page 190 would not affect the reported net income or the inventory cost. The time required to assemble the data is likely to be greater for the weighted average method than for the other two methods. The additional expense incurred could be significant if there are numerous purchases of a wide variety of merchandise items.

The foregoing comparisons indicate the importance attached to the selection of the inventory costing method. The method adopted must be consistently followed from year to year, except where there is a valid reason for a change. The effect of any change in method and the reason for the change should be fully disclosed in the financial statements for the fiscal period in which the change occurred.

Throughout the discussion of inventory costing there has been an assumption that the commodities on hand were salable in a normal manner. Because of imperfections, shop wear, style changes or other causes, there may be items that are not salable except at prices below cost. Such merchandise should be valued at estimated selling price less any direct cost of disposition, such as sales commission.

VALUATION AT THE LOWER OF COST OR MARKET

An alternative to valuing inventory at cost is to compare cost with market price and use the lower of the two. It should be borne in mind

193

that regardless of the method used it is first necessary to determine the cost of the inventory. "Market," as used in the phrase *lower of cost or market* or *cost or market, whichever is lower*, is interpreted to mean the cost to replace the merchandise on the inventory date. To the extent practicable, the market or replacement price should be based on quantities typically purchased from the usual source of supply. In the discussion that follows, the salability of the merchandise in a normal manner will be assumed. The valuation of articles that have to be sold at a price below cost would be determined by the method described in the preceding paragraph.

If the replacement price of an item in the inventory is lower than its cost, there is almost certain to be an accompanying decline in the selling price. Recognition of the price decline in valuing the item reduces the gross profit (and net income) for the period in which the decline occurred. There is also an inherent presumption that when the item is sold in the following period at a reduced price, the sale should yield approximately the normal gross profit. To illustrate, assume that particular merchandise with a unit cost of $70 has sold during the period at $100, yielding a gross profit of $30 a unit, or 30% of sales. Assume also that there is a single unit of the commodity in the inventory at the end of the year and that meanwhile the replacement price has declined to $63. Under such circumstances it would be reasonable to expect that the selling price would also decline, if indeed it had not already done so. Assuming a reduction in selling price to $90, the gross profit based on replacement cost of $63 would be $27, which is also 30% of selling price. Accordingly, valuation of the unit in the inventory at $63 reduces net income of the past period by $7 and permits a normal gross profit of $27 to be realized on its sale in the following period. If the unit had been valued at its original cost of $70, the net income determined for the past year would have been $7 greater, and the net income attributable to the sale of the item in the following period would have been $7 less.

It would be possible to apply the lower of cost or market basis (1) to each item in the inventory, (2) to major classes or categories, or (3) to the inventory as a whole. The first procedure is the one customarily followed in practice, and it is the only one of the three that is acceptable for federal income tax purposes. To illustrate the application of the lower of cost or market to individual items, assume that there are 400 identical units of Commodity A in the inventory, each acquired at a unit cost of $10.25. If at the inventory date the commodity would cost $10.50 to replace, the cost price of $10.25 would be multiplied by 400 to determine the inventory value. On the other hand, if the commodity could be replaced at $9.50 a unit, the replacement price of $9.50 would be used for valuation purposes. The tabulation at the top of the next page illustrates one of the forms that may be followed in assembling inventory data.

Although the column for total cost is not essential, it permits the measurement of the reduction in inventory attributable to market declines. When the amount of the market decline is known ($450 in the illustration), it may be reported as a separate item on the income statement. Otherwise, the market decline will be included in the amount reported as the cost of merchandise sold and will reduce gross profit by a

		UNIT COST	UNIT MARKET	TOTAL	
					LOWER
DESCRIPTION	QUANTITY	PRICE	PRICE	COST	OF C OR M
Commodity A	400	$10.25	$ 9.50	$ 4,100	$ 3,800
Commodity B	120	22.50	24.10	2,700	2,700
Commodity C	600	8.00	7.75	4,800	4,650
Commodity D	280	14.00	14.00	3,920	3,920
Total..........				$15,520	$15,070

corresponding amount. In any event, the amount reported as net income will not be affected; it will be the same regardless of whether or not the amount of the market decline is determined and separately stated.

As with the method elected for the determination of inventory cost (fifo, lifo, or weighted average), the method elected for inventory valuation (cost, or lower of cost or market) must be followed consistently from year to year. Both methods of valuation are acceptable in determining income for federal income tax purposes, except that when the last-in, first-out procedure is employed, the inventory must be stated at cost.

195

RETAIL METHOD OF INVENTORY COSTING

The *retail inventory* method of inventory costing is widely used by retail businesses, particularly department stores. It is employed in connection with the periodic system of inventories and is based on the relationship of the cost of merchandise available for sale to the retail price of the same merchandise. The retail prices of all merchandise acquired are accumulated in supplementary records, and the inventory at retail is determined by deducting sales for the period from the retail price of the goods that were available for sale during the period. The inventory at retail is then converted to cost on the basis of the ratio of the cost of the merchandise available for sale to the selling price of the merchandise available for sale.

Determination of inventory by the retail method is illustrated at the top of the next page.

There is an inherent assumption in the retail method that the composition or "mix" of the commodities in the ending inventory, in terms of per cent of cost to selling price, is comparable to the entire stock of merchandise available for sale. For example, in the illustration above it is un-

	COST	RETAIL
Merchandise inventory, January 1......................	$19,400	$ 36,000
Purchases in January (net)..............................	42,600	64,000
Merchandise available for sale..........................	$62,000	$100,000

Ratio of cost to retail price:

$$\frac{\$62,000}{\$100,000} = 62\%$$

Sales for January (net)...................................	70,000
Merchandise inventory, January 31, at retail price...........	$ 30,000
Merchandise inventory, January 31, at estimated cost price ($30,000 × 62%)	$ 18,600

likely that the retail price of every item was composed of exactly 62% cost and 38% gross profit margin. It is assumed, however, that the weighted average of the cost percentages of the merchandise in the inventory ($30,000) is the same as in the merchandise available for sale ($100,000). Where the inventory is composed of different classes of merchandise with significantly different gross profit rates, the cost percentages and the inventory should be developed separately for each section or department.

The use of the retail method does not eliminate the necessity for taking a physical inventory at the end of the year. However, the items are recorded on the inventory sheets at their selling prices instead of their cost prices. The physical inventory at selling price is then converted to cost by applying the ratio of the cost of merchandise available for sale to the selling price of the same merchandise. To illustrate, assume that the data presented in the example above are for an entire fiscal year rather than for the first month of the year only. If the physical inventory taken on December 31, priced at retail, totaled $29,000, it would be this amount rather than the $30,000 in the illustration that would be converted to cost. Accordingly, the inventory at cost would be $17,980 ($29,000 × 62%) instead of $18,600 ($30,000 × 62%).

One of the principal advantages of the retail method is that it provides inventory figures for use in preparing interim statements. Department stores and similar merchandisers customarily determine gross profit and operating income each month but take a physical inventory only once a year. In addition to facilitating frequent income determinations, a comparison of the computed inventory total with the physical inventory total, both at retail prices, will disclose the extent of inventory shortages and the consequent need for corrective measures.

PERPETUAL INVENTORY SYSTEM

The use of a perpetual inventory system for merchandise provides the most effective means of control over this important asset. Although it is

196

possible to maintain a perpetual inventory in memorandum records only or to limit the data to quantities, a complete set of records integrated with the general ledger is preferable. The basic feature of the system is the recording of all merchandise increases and decreases in a manner somewhat similar to the recording of increases and decreases in cash. Just as receipts of cash are debited to Cash so are purchases of merchandise debited to Merchandise Inventory. Similarly, sales or other reductions of merchandise are recorded in a manner comparable to that employed for reductions in Cash, that is, by credits to Merchandise Inventory. Thus, just as the balance of the cash account indicates the amount of cash presumed to be on hand, so the balance of the merchandise inventory account represents the amount of merchandise presumed to be on hand.

Unlike cash, merchandise is a heterogeneous mass of commodities. Details of the cost of each type of merchandise purchased and sold, together with such related transactions as returns and allowances, must be maintained in a subsidiary ledger, with a separate account for each type. Thus an enterprise that stocks five hundred types of merchandise would need five hundred individual accounts in its *inventory ledger*. The flow of costs through a subsidiary account is illustrated below. There was a beginning inventory, three purchases, and six sales of the particular commodity during the year covered. The number of units on hand after each transaction, together with total cost and unit prices appears in the inventory section of the account.

Commodity 127B							
	PURCHASED		SOLD		INVENTORY		
DATE	QUANTITY	TOTAL COST	QUANTITY	TOTAL COST	QUANTITY	TOTAL COST	UNIT PRICE
Jan. 1					10	200	20
Feb. 4			7	140	3	60	20
Mar. 10	8	168			3	60	20
					8	168	21
Apr. 22			4	81	7	147	21
May 18			2	42	5	105	21
Aug. 30	10	220			5	105	21
					10	220	22
Oct. 7			4	84	1	21	21
					10	220	22
Nov. 11			8	175	3	66	22
Dec. 13	10	230			3	66	22
					10	230	23
18			3	66	10	230	23

Perpetual inventory account

With a perpetual system, as in a periodic system of inventory determination, it is necessary to identify the item sold with a specific group or to employ a cost flow assumption. In the foregoing illustration the first-in, first-out flow method of costing was used. Note that after the 7 units of the commodity were sold on February 4 there was a remaining inventory of 3 units at $20 each. The 8 units purchased on March 10 were acquired at a unit cost of $21, instead of $20, and hence could not be combined with the 3 units. The inventory after the March 10 purchase is therefore reported on two lines, 3 units at $20 each and 8 units at $21 each. Next, it should be noted that the $81 cost of the 4 units sold on April 22 is composed of the remaining 3 units at $20 each and 1 unit at $21. Finally, the 10 units of the commodity in the inventory at the end of the period is composed of the last units acquired, which were purchased at $23 each.

When the last-in, first-out flow method of costing is strictly applied to a perpetual inventory system, the unit cost prices assigned to the ending inventory will not necessarily be those associated with the earliest unit costs of the period. The unit costs for the ending inventory will vary from those obtained by use of the periodic costing system if at any time the number of units of a commodity sold exceeds the number previously purchased during the same period. This situation is not unusual, and when it occurs, the excess quantity sold is deducted from the opening inventory balance. An example of such a temporary reduction of the inventory appears in the perpetual inventory account illustrated on page 197. The cost of the 7 units of the commodity sold on February 4 reduced the opening inventory to 3 units priced at $20 each. They were replaced on March 10 but at a unit price of $21 instead of $20. Application of the last-in, first-out method to the data in the illustration, using the periodic inventory system, would yield an ending inventory of 10 units at $20, which corresponds to the opening inventory. Redetermination of balances in the illustrative perpetual inventory account, however, yields a last-in, first-out inventory composed of 3 units at $20 each and 7 units at $23 each. This is an obvious departure from the underlying purpose of the lifo costing method, which is to deduct the current cost of merchandise from current sales revenue. One method of avoiding pricing problems of this type is to maintain the perpetual inventory accounts throughout the period in terms of quantities only, inserting the cost data at the end of the period. Another variation in procedure is to record both quantities and costs in the subsidiary accounts during the period, thus providing data needed for interim statements; any required adjustments are then made to price the inventory at the end of the year at the earliest costs and to apply the most recent costs against the year's sales revenue.

The weighted average method of cost flow can be applied to the perpetual system, though in a somewhat modified form. Instead of determining a weighted average price for each type of commodity at the end of a period, an average unit price is computed each time a purchase is made. The unit price so computed is then used to determine the cost of the items sold until another purchase is made. This averaging technique is called a *moving average*.

In earlier chapters, sales of merchandise were recorded by debits to the cash or accounts receivable account and credits to the sales account. The cost of the merchandise sold was not determined for each sale. It was determined only periodically by means of a physical inventory. In contrast to the periodic system, the perpetual system provides the cost data related to each sale. The cost data for sales on account may be accumulated in a special column inserted in the sales journal. Each time merchandise is sold on account the amount entered in the "cost" column represents a debit to Cost of Merchandise Sold and a credit to Merchandise Inventory. Similar provisions can be made for cash sales. To illustrate sales on account under the perpetual inventory system, assume that the monthly total of the cost column of the sales journal is $140,000 and that the monthly total of the sales column is $210,000. The effect on the general ledger accounts is indicated by the two entries below, in general journal form.

Cost of Merchandise Sold........................	140,000	
Merchandise Inventory........................		140,000
Accounts Receivable...........................	210,000	
Sales.......................................		210,000

The control feature is the most important advantage of the perpetual system. The inventory of each class of merchandise is always readily available in the subsidiary ledger. A physical count of any class of merchandise can be made at any time and compared with the balance of the subsidiary account to determine the existence and seriousness of any shortages. When a shortage is discovered, an entry is made debiting Inventory Shortages and crediting Merchandise Inventory for the cost. If the balance of the inventory shortages account at the end of a fiscal period is relatively minor, it may be included in miscellaneous general expense on the income statement. Otherwise it may be separately reported in the general expense section.

In addition to the usefulness of the perpetual inventory system in the preparation of interim statements, the subsidiary ledger can be an aid in maintaining inventory quantities at an optimum level. Frequent comparisons of quantity balances with predetermined maximum and minimum levels facilitate both (1) the timely reordering of merchandise to avoid the loss of sales and (2) the avoidance of excessive accumulation of inventory.

PRESENTATION OF MERCHANDISE INVENTORY ON THE BALANCE SHEET

Merchandise inventory is customarily presented on the balance sheet immediately below receivables. Both the method of determining the cost

199

of the inventory (lifo, fifo, or average) and the method of valuing the inventory (cost, or lower of cost or market) should be disclosed. Both are significant to the reader. The details may be disclosed by a parenthetical notation or a footnote. The use of a parenthetical notation is illustrated by the following partial balance sheet:

Brewster Company
Balance Sheet
December 31, 1973

Assets

Current assets:

Cash...		$19,400
Accounts receivable.............................	$80,000	
Less allowance for doubtful accounts..............	3,000	77,000
Merchandise inventory — at lower of cost (first-in, first-out method) or market..........................		216,300

It is not unusual for large enterprises with diversified activities to use different costing and pricing methods for different segments of their inventories. The following note from the balance sheet of a merchandising chain is illustrative: "Merchandise inventories in stores are stated at the lower of cost or market, as calculated by the retail method of inventory. Merchandise in warehouses and in transit and food products inventories in restaurants are stated at cost."

GROSS PROFIT METHOD OF ESTIMATING INVENTORIES

When perpetual inventories are maintained or when the retail inventory method is used, the inventory on hand may be closely approximated at any time without the necessity of a physical count. In the absence of these devices, the inventory may be estimated by the *gross profit* method, which utilizes an estimate of the gross profit realized on sales during the period.

If the rate of gross profit on sales is known, the dollar amount of sales for a period can be divided into its two components: (1) gross profit and (2) cost of merchandise sold. The latter may then be deducted from the cost of merchandise available for sale to yield the estimated inventory of merchandise on hand.

To illustrate this method, assume that the inventory on January 1 is $17,000, that net purchases during the month amount to $9,000, that net sales during the month amount to $15,000, and finally that gross profit is *estimated* to be 30% of net sales. The inventory on January 31 may be estimated as shown at the top of the next page.

The estimate of the rate of gross profit is ordinarily based on the actual rate for the preceding year, adjusted for any known changes in markups during the current period. Inventories estimated in this

Merchandise inventory, January 1.............		$17,000
Purchases in January (net)...................		9,000
Merchandise available for sale................		$26,000
Sales in January (net)........................	$15,000	
Less estimated gross profit ($15,000 × 30%)..	**4,500**	
Estimated cost of merchandise sold............		10,500
Estimated merchandise inventory, January 31		**$15,500**

manner are useful in preparing interim statements. The method may also be employed in establishing an estimate of the cost of merchandise destroyed by fire.

QUESTIONS

1. The merchandise inventory at the end of the year was inadvertently over-stated by $5,000. (a) Did the error cause an overstatement or an understatement of the net income for the year? (b) Which items on the balance sheet at the end of the year were overstated or understated as a result of the error?

2. The $5,000 inventory error in Question 1 was not discovered and the inventory at the end of the following year was correctly stated. (a) Will the earlier error cause a $5,000 overstatement or understatement of the net income for the following year? (b) Which items on the balance sheet at the end of the following year will be overstated or understated by $5,000 as a result of the error in the earlier year?

3. (a) Differentiate between the periodic system and the perpetual system of inventory determination. (b) Which system ordinarily is more costly to maintain?

4. What is the meaning of the terms: (a) physical inventory; (b) book inventory?

5. In which of the following types of businesses would a perpetual inventory system be practicable: (a) retail drug store, (b) wholesale office machine distributor, (c) retail hardware store, (d) retail furrier, (e) retail florist, and (f) restaurant?

6. When does title to merchandise ordinarily pass from the seller to the buyer if the terms of shipment are (a) FOB shipping point; (b) FOB destination?

7. Purchases of merchandise for the year totaled $200,000 and purchases discounts for the same period, which are considered to be reductions in cost, amounted to $1,900. If the cost of the merchandise inventory at the end of the year, before considering the purchases discount, is $60,000, what would be a reasonable amount of purchases discount to deduct from the purchase price of the inventory?

8. Do the terms *fifo* and *lifo* refer to techniques employed in determining quantities of the various classes of merchandise on hand? Explain.

9. Does the term *first-in* in the fifo method mean that the items in the inventory are assumed to be those that were acquired first? Explain.

10. Under which method of cost flow are (a) the most recent costs assigned to inventory; (b) the earliest costs assigned to inventory; (c) average costs assigned to inventory?

11. The following lots of a particular commodity were available for sale during the year:

Beginning inventory . . . . 30 units at $18
First purchase . . . . 50 units at $19
Second purchase . . . . 25 units at $20

The firm uses the periodic system and there are 20 units of the commodity on hand at the end of the year.   (a) What is their unit cost according to fifo? (b) What is their unit cost according to lifo? (c) Is the weighted average unit cost $19?

12. If merchandise inventory is being valued at cost and the price level is consistently rising, which of the three methods of costing, fifo, lifo, or weighted average, will yield (a) the highest inventory cost, (b) the lowest inventory cost, (c) the largest net income, (d) the smallest net income?

13. An enterprise using "cost" as its method of inventory valuation proposes to value at $325 a group of items having a total cost of $500. On what basis could this reduction in value be justified?

14. Which of the three methods of inventory costing, fifo, lifo, or weighted average, will in general yield an inventory cost most nearly approximating current replacement cost?

15. In the phrase *lower of cost or market*, what is meant by market?

16. The cost of a particular inventory item is $100, the current replacement cost is $95, and the selling price is $140. At what amount should the item be included in the inventory according to the lower of cost or market basis?

17. Under which, if any, of the following systems or methods of inventory determination is a periodic physical inventory unnecessary: (a) periodic inventory system, (b) perpetual inventory system, (c) retail inventory method, (d) gross profit method?

18. An enterprise using a perpetual inventory system sells merchandise to a customer on account for $500; the cost of merchandise was $350. (a) What are the effects of the transaction on general ledger accounts? (b) What is the amount and direction of the net change in the amount of assets and capital resulting from the transaction?

19. What are the three most important advantages of the perpetual inventory system over the periodic system?

20. When inventory is valued at cost and the periodic system of inventory determination is used, does the amount reported on the income statement as *cost of merchandise sold* ordinarily include an unknown amount of write-downs for shop wear, the cost of stolen merchandise, and costs attributable to other shortages? Discuss.

21. Is it possible that the expense incurred in maintaining a perpetual inventory system might be greater than the benefits derived through reduction of inventory shortages caused by theft, negligence, and other causes? Discuss.

EXERCISES

8-1. The beginning inventory and the purchases of Commodity F33A during the year were as follows:

Commodity F33A

Jan. 1	Inventory................	15 units at	$11.50
Apr. 12	Purchase.................	20 units at	12.00
July 7	Purchase.................	12 units at	11.70
Nov. 2	Purchase.................	16 units at	12.30

There are 18 units of Commodity F33A in the physical inventory at December 31 (the periodic system is used). Determine the inventory cost and the cost of merchandise sold by three methods, presenting your answers in the following form:

	Cost	
Inventory Method	Merchandise Inventory	Merchandise Sold
(1) First-in, first-out	$	$
(2) Last-in, first-out		
(3) Weighted average		

8-2. On the basis of the data presented below, determine the value of the inventory at the lower of cost or market. Assemble the data in the form illustrated on page 195, in order that the inventory reduction attributable to price declines may be ascertained.

Commodity	Inventory Quantity	Unit Cost	Unit Market
10A	200	$10.50	$10.00
11B	100	22.00	22.50
12C	400	15.00	16.00
13D	300	21.00	20.00
14E	200	15.50	15.00

8-3. On the basis of the following data, estimate the cost of the merchandise inventory at June 30 by the retail method:

		Cost	Retail
June 1	Merchandise inventory..	$143,680	$207,500
June 1–30	Purchases (net)........	85,400	124,500
June 1–30	Sales (net)............		110,000

8-4. Beginning inventory, purchases, and sales data for Commodity 179-G are presented below. The enterprise maintains a perpetual inventory system, costing by the first-in, first-out method. Determine the cost of the merchandise sold in each sale and the inventory balance after each sale, presenting the data in the form illustrated on page 197.

May 1	Inventory....................	15 units at $20	
5	Sold........................	9 units	
15	Purchased...................	10 units at $21	
18	Sold........................	7 units	
25	Sold........................	5 units	
30	Purchased...................	15 units at $22	

8-5. Beginning inventory, purchases, and sales data for Commodity P21X for June are presented below.

Inventory, June 1 . . . . 15 units at $10
Sales, June 12 . . . . 7 units
          18 . . . . 5 units
          26 . . . . 8 units
Purchases, June 9 . . . . 10 units at $11
          20 . . . . 10 units at $12

(a) Assuming that the perpetual inventory system is used, costing by the last-in, first-out method, determine the cost of the inventory balance at June 30.

(b) Assuming that the periodic inventory system is used, costing by the last-in, first-out method, determine the cost of the 15 units in the physical inventory at June 30.

(c) Determine the amount of the difference between the inventory cost in (a) and (b), and explain the reason for the difference.

8-6. The merchandise inventory of Caldwell Company was destroyed by fire on March 7. The following data were obtained from the accounting records:

Jan. 1	Merchandise inventory	$25,000
Jan. 1–March 7	Purchases (net)	16,500
	Sales (net)	32,000
	Estimated gross profit rate	40%

Estimate the cost of the merchandise destroyed.

204

PROBLEMS

The following additional problems for this chapter are located in Appendix B: 8-1B, 8-2B, 8-3B, 8-4B, 8-5B.

8-1A. Lewis Stereo World employs the periodic inventory system. Details regarding their inventory of television sets at January 1, purchase invoices during the year, and the inventory count at December 31 are summarized below.

Model	Inventory Jan. 1	Purchase Invoices 1st	Purchase Invoices 2d	Purchase Invoices 3d	Inventory Count Dec. 31
A17	5 at $ 60	6 at $ 63	4 at $ 63	5 at $ 66	7
C35	7 at 110	8 at 109	5 at 112	6 at 114	6
G40	2 at 149	4 at 145	2 at 147	2 at 149	3
K10	4 at 200	4 at 205	6 at 208	4 at 210	4
Q19	6 at 260	4 at 263	6 at 270	4 at 272	6
T70	——	2 at 300	2 at 310	——	2
W23	6 at 356	4 at 351	9 at 340	3 at 330	5

Instructions:

(1) Determine the cost of the inventory on December 31 by the first-in, first-out method. Present data in columnar form, using the columnar headings indicated below. If the inventory of a particular model is composed of an entire lot plus a portion of another lot acquired at a different unit price, use a separate line for each lot.

Model	Quantity	Unit Cost	Total Cost

(2) Determine the cost of the inventory on December 31 by the last-in, first-out method, following the procedures indicated in instruction (1).

(3) Determine the cost of the inventory on December 31 by the weighted average method, using the columnar headings indicated in instruction (1).

8-2A. The beginning inventory of Commodity 717B and data on purchases and sales for a three-month period are presented below.

April	1	Inventory...... 5 units at $14.00	$ 70.00
	10	Purchase.......10 units at 14.25	142.50
	12	Sale.......... 6 units at 20.00	120.00
	27	Sale.......... 4 units at 20.00	80.00
May	6	Purchase....... 8 units at 14.50	116.00
	7	Sale.......... 5 units at 20.00	100.00
	14	Sale.......... 2 units at 20.00	40.00
	25	Purchase....... 7 units at 15.00	105.00
June	6	Sale.......... 6 units at 21.00	126.00
	12	Sale.......... 3 units at 21.00	63.00
	15	Purchase.......10 units at 15.25	152.50
	20	Sale.......... 5 units at 22.00	110.00

Instructions:

(1) Record the inventory, purchase, and cost of merchandise sold data in a perpetual inventory record similar to the one illustrated on page 197, using the first-in, first-out method.

(2) Determine the total sales and the total cost of Commodity 717B sold for the period, and express their effect on the general ledger by two entries in general journal form. Assume that all sales were on account.

(3) Determine the gross profit from sales of Commodity 717B for the period.

(4) Determine the cost of the inventory at June 30, assuming that the periodic system of inventory had been employed and that the inventory cost had been determined by the last-in, first-out method.

8-3A. Selected data on merchandise inventory, purchases, and sales for the Hamilton Co. and the Parker Co. are presented below.

HAMILTON CO.

	Cost	Retail
Merchandise inventory, April 1.....	$294,975	$445,650
Transactions during April:		
Purchases.....................	90,700 }	
Purchases discount.............	810 }	146,450
Sales........................		180,500
Sales returns and allowances......		3,200

PARKER CO.

Merchandise inventory, July 1.............	$195,500
Transactions during July and August:	
Purchases...........................	310,900
Purchases discount...................	2,900
Sales...............................	405,000
Sales returns and allowances...........	4,100
Estimated gross profit rate.............	34%

205

Instructions:

(1) Determine the estimated cost of the merchandise inventory of the Hamilton Co. on April 30 by the retail method, presenting details of the computations.

(2) Estimate the cost of the merchandise inventory of the Parker Co. on August 31 by the gross profit method, presenting details of the computations.

If the working papers correlating with the textbook are not used, omit Problem 8-4A.

8-4A. Data on the physical inventory of W. Nelson and Co. as of June 30, the close of the current fiscal year, are presented in the working papers. The quantity of each commodity on hand has been determined and recorded on the inventory sheet; unit market prices have also been determined as of June 30 and recorded on the sheet. The inventory is to be determined at cost and also at the lower of cost or market, using the first-in, first-out method. Quantity and cost data from the last purchase invoice of the year and the next-to-the-last purchase invoice are summarized below.

	Last Purchase Invoice		Next-to-the-Last Purchase Invoice	
Description	Quantity Purchased	Unit Cost	Quantity Purchased	Unit Cost
31FT	50	$ 20	30	$ 19
1542E	75	9	100	10
OP37	25	210	25	220
SE72	300	11	200	10
31VX	40	45	60	47
57ABC	175	15	125	15
WD71	12	400	10	425
C775	500	6	500	7
814B	90	8	60	7
259LC	5	250	4	260
XX75	25	225	25	220
1954D	300	13	200	12
BD111	8	48	10	47
AD65	175	8	100	9
G17H	360	5	220	5
KK22	100	29	100	28
PX86	96	20	120	21
MK630	50	90	30	92

Instructions:

Record the appropriate unit costs on the inventory sheet and complete the pricing of the inventory. When there are two different unit costs applicable to a commodity, proceed as follows:

(1) Draw a line through the quantity and insert the quantity and unit cost of the last purchase.

(2) On the following line insert the quantity and unit cost of the next-to-the-last purchase. The first item on the inventory sheet has been completed as an example.

8-5A. The preliminary income statement of Garner Company presented below was prepared before the accounts were adjusted or closed at the end of the fiscal year. The company uses the periodic inventory system.

Garner Company
Income Statement
For Year Ended June 30, 19—

Sales (net)...............................		$252,300
Cost of merchandise sold:		
Merchandise inventory, July 1, 19—.........	$ 52,120	
Purchases (net).........................	185,650	
Merchandise available for sale.............	$237,770	
Less merchandise inventory, June 30, 19—...	47,750	
Cost of merchandise sold.................		190,020
Gross profit on sales.......................		$ 62,280
Operating expenses.........................		40,710
Net income................................		$ 21,570

The following errors in the ledger and on inventory sheets were discovered by the independent CPA retained to conduct the annual audit:

(a) A number of errors were discovered in pricing inventory items, in extending amounts, and in footing inventory sheets. The net effect of the corrections, exclusive of those described below, was to decrease by $1,500 the amount stated as the ending inventory on the income statement above.

(b) A purchase invoice for merchandise of $500, dated June 29, had been received and correctly recorded, but the merchandise was not received until July 3 and had not been included in the June 30 inventory. Title had passed to Garner Company on June 29.

(c) A purchase invoice for merchandise of $950, dated June 28, was not received until July 1 and had not been recorded by June 30. However, the merchandise, to which title had passed, had arrived and had been included in the June 30 inventory.

(d) A sales order for $1,200, dated June 30, had been recorded as a sale on that date, but title did not pass to the purchaser until shipment was made on July 2. The merchandise, which had cost $900, was excluded from the June 30 inventory.

(e) A sales invoice for $2,000, dated June 30, had not been recorded. The merchandise was shipped on June 30, FOB shipping point, and its cost, $1,450, was excluded from the June 30 inventory.

(f) An item of office equipment, received on June 30, was erroneously included in the June 30 merchandise inventory at its cost of $350. The invoice had been recorded correctly.

Instructions:

(1) Journalize the entries necessary to correct the general ledger accounts as of June 30, inserting the identifying letters in the date column. All purchases and sales were made on account.

(2) Determine the correct inventory for June 30, beginning your analysis with the $47,750 shown on the preliminary income statement. Assemble the corrections in two groupings, "Additions" and "Deductions," allowing six lines for each group. Identify each correction by the appropriate letter.

(3) Prepare a revised income statement.

207

8-6A. The unadjusted trial balance of L & L Imports, distributor of imported motor bicycles, as of the end of the current fiscal year, is as follows:

L & L Imports
Trial Balance
September 30, 19—

Cash.................................	13,260	
Accounts Receivable..........................	18,350	
Allowance for Doubtful Accounts...............		325
Merchandise Inventory.......................	45,700	
Equipment.................................	22,500	
Accumulated Depreciation — Equipment........		12,500
Accounts Payable...........................		28,650
L. S. Lamb, Capital.........................		38,860
L. S. Lamb, Drawing........................	12,000	
Sales......................................		227,400
Purchases..................................	148,400	
Operating Expenses (control account)...........	46,800	
Interest Income.............................		250
Interest Expense............................	975	
	307,985	307,985

Data needed for adjustments at September 30:

(a) Merchandise inventory at September 30, at lower of cost (first-in, first-out method) or market, $49,750.

(b) Uncollectible accounts expense is estimated at $1,087 for current year.

(c) Depreciation on equipment for current year is $1,000.

(d) Accrued wages on September 30, $400.

Instructions:

(1) Journalize the necessary adjusting entries.

(2) Prepare (a) an income statement, (b) a capital statement, and (c) a balance sheet in report form, without the use of a conventional work sheet.

Chapter 9

DEFERRALS AND ACCRUALS

ACCOUNTING AND PERIODIC REPORTS

Data on revenues earned and expenses incurred by a business enterprise are periodically assembled and reported in the form of an income statement. Such statements always cover a definite period of time, such as a specific month, quarter, half-year, or year. The periodic matching of revenues and expenses yields the amount of net income or net loss, which is of great significance to management, owners, creditors, and others who may be interested in the enterprise. In addition, the matching process yields the amounts of assets, liabilities, and capital to be reported on the balance sheet as of the end of the period, which is also significant to interested parties.

When cash is received for a revenue within the same period that the revenue is earned, there is no question about the period to which the revenue relates. Similarly, when an expense is paid during the period in which the benefits from the service are received, there can be no doubt concerning the period to which the expense should be allocated. Problems of allocation are encountered when there are time differentials between the earning of revenues or the occurrence of expenses and the recognition of their respective effects on assets and equities.

The use of adjusting entries in facilitating the allocation of expenses to appropriate periods was demonstrated in earlier chapters. Deferrals and accruals of various expenses, including insurance, supplies, taxes, wages, and uncollectible accounts, have been described and illustrated. This chapter is devoted to further consideration of deferrals and accruals of expenses and also of revenues. The underlying purpose of their recognition is to achieve a fair statement of all revenues and expenses for a period of time and a fair statement of all assets and equities as of the last day of the period.

CLASSIFICATION AND TERMINOLOGY

Many kinds of revenues and expenses may require deferral or accrual in particular circumstances. When such is the case they are recorded as adjusting entries on the work sheet used in preparing financial statements. If the work sheet is for the fiscal year, the adjustments are also journalized and posted to the ledger. For interim statements, the adjustments may appear only on the work sheet.

The following characteristic of all adjustments should be noted in the explanations and illustrations of this chapter: Every adjusting entry affects both a balance sheet account and an income statement account. To illustrate, assume that the effect of the credit portion of a particular adjusting entry is to increase a liability account (balance sheet). It follows that the effect of the debit portion of the entry will be either (1) to increase an expense account (income statement) or (2) to decrease a revenue account (income statement). In no case will an adjustment affect only an asset and a liability (both balance sheet) or only an expense and a revenue (both income statement).

Deferral. A deferral is a postponement of the recognition of an expense already paid or of a revenue already received.

Deferred expenses expected to benefit a relatively short period of time are listed on the balance sheet among the current assets, where they are often described as *prepaid expenses.* Long-term prepayments properly chargeable to the operations of several years are presented on the balance sheet in a section often described as *deferred charges.*

Deferred revenues may be listed on the balance sheet as a current liability, where they are often described as *unearned revenues* or *revenues received in advance.* If a relatively long period of time is involved, they are presented on the balance sheet in a section often described as *deferred credits.*

Accrual. An accrual is an expense or a revenue that gradually increases with the passage of time. Unrecorded accruals must be given accounting recognition when financial statements are prepared.

Accrued expenses may also be described on the balance sheet as *accrued liabilities,* or reference to the accrual may be omitted from the title, as in "Wages payable." The liabilities for accrued expenses are ordinarily due within a year and are listed as current liabilities.

Accrued revenues may also be described on the balance sheet as *accrued assets,* or reference to the accrual may be omitted from the title, as in "Interest receivable." The amounts receivable for accrued revenues are usually due within a short time and are classified as current assets.

PREPAID EXPENSES (DEFERRAL)

Prepaid expenses are commodities and services purchased for consumption that are unconsumed at the end of the accounting period. The portion of the asset that has been used during the period has become an expense; the remainder will not become an expense until some time in the future. Prepaid expenses include such items as prepaid insurance, prepaid rent, prepaid advertising, prepaid interest, and various types of supplies.

At the time a prepaid expense is acquired, it may be debited either to an asset account or to an expense account. The two alternative systems are explained and illustrated in the paragraphs that follow. It should be understood that in any particular situation either alternative may be elected. The difference between the systems is entirely procedural; their effect on the financial statements is identical.

Prepaid expenses recorded initially as assets. Insurance premiums or other consumable services or supplies may be debited to asset accounts when purchased, even though all or a part of them is expected to be consumed during the accounting period. The amount actually used is then determined at the end of the period and the accounts adjusted accordingly.

To illustrate, assume that the prepaid insurance account has a balance of $1,034 at the close of the year. This amount represents the unexpired insurance at the beginning of the year plus the total of premiums on policies purchased during the year. Assume further that $406 of insurance premiums is ascertained to have expired during the year. The adjusting entry to record the $406 decrease of the asset and the corresponding increase in expense is as follows:

		Adjusting Entry			
Dec.	31	Insurance Expense..................	716	406	
		Prepaid Insurance................	118		406

After this entry has been posted, the two accounts affected appear as shown at the top of the next page.

After the $406 of expired insurance is transferred to the expense account, the balance of $628 remaining in Prepaid Insurance represents the cost of premiums on various policies that apply to future periods. The $406 expense appears on the income statement for the period and the $628 asset appears on the balance sheet as of the end of the period.

Prepaid expenses recorded initially as expenses. The alternative to the system just illustrated is to debit the costs to an appropriate expense account at the time of the expenditure. It may be considered the preferable procedure for recording the discount on notes payable issued to

ACCOUNT PREPAID INSURANCE   ACCOUNT No. 118

DATE		ITEM	POST. REF.	DEBIT	CREDIT	BALANCE DEBIT	BALANCE CREDIT
1973							
Jan.	1	Balance	√			650	
Mar.	18		CP6	110		760	
Aug.	26		CP16	180		940	
Nov.	11		CP21	94		1,034	
Dec.	31	Adjusting	J17		406	628	

ACCOUNT INSURANCE EXPENSE   ACCOUNT No. 716

DATE		ITEM	POST. REF.	DEBIT	CREDIT	BALANCE DEBIT	BALANCE CREDIT
1973							
Dec.	31	Adjusting	J17	406		406	

banks, which are ordinarily for a period of from 30 to 90 days. If the interest deducted by the bank is debited to Interest Expense at the time the funds are borrowed and if the notes are paid by the end of the fiscal year, no adjusting entry is necessary. When one or more discounted notes are still outstanding on the last day of the year, however, the portion of the interest applicable to the following period should be deducted from the expense account and transferred to the asset account by means of an adjusting entry.

To illustrate this alternative system, assume that during the year four non-interest-bearing notes payable were discounted and that in each case the discount was debited to Interest Expense. Three of the notes became due and were paid during the year. The fourth, a $12,000, 90-day note, had been issued on December 1 at a discount of $180.

As of the last day of the fiscal year, only 30 days of the 90-day term of the $12,000 note have elapsed. Therefore only $60 ($\frac{1}{3}$ of $180) of the discount is an expense of the year; the remaining $120 ($\frac{2}{3}$ of $180) will become an expense during the first 60 days of the following year. The entry to transfer the $120 to the asset account is as follows:

		Adjusting Entry			
Dec.	31	Prepaid Interest....................	117	120	
		Interest Expense..................	911		120

After the adjusting entry has been posted, the asset account and the expense account appear as shown at the top of the next page.

The remaining balance of $359 in Interest Expense is the amount of expense for the year and appears on the income statement. The balance of $120 in Prepaid Interest is reported in the balance sheet as a current asset.

ACCOUNT PREPAID INTEREST   ACCOUNT No. 117

DATE		ITEM	POST. REF.	DEBIT	CREDIT	BALANCE	
						DEBIT	CREDIT
1973 Dec.	31	Adjusting	J17	120		120	

ACCOUNT INTEREST EXPENSE   ACCOUNT No. 911

DATE		ITEM	POST. REF.	DEBIT	CREDIT	BALANCE	
						DEBIT	CREDIT
1973 Feb.	5		CR3	50		50	
May	15		CR8	144		194	
June	10		CR10	105		299	
Dec.	1		CR20	180		479	
	31	Adjusting	J17		120	359	

During the first 60 days of the following year, the prepaid interest on the loan becomes interest expense at the rate of $2 a day ($120 ÷ 60). It would be possible, though obviously unnecessary, to record a $2 transfer from the asset account to the expense account on each of the 60 days. Another possibility would be to wait until the 60 days had elapsed and then transfer the entire $120 from the asset account to the expense account. If there were additional notes payable on which interest had been prepaid, a similar transfer would be required each time a note became due.

In such situations, the most efficient means of assuring proper allocations in the ensuing period is to add *reversing entries* to the summarizing procedures. Their use eliminates the necessity of referring back to earlier adjustment data and lessens the possibilities of error. The effect of the reversing entry for the prepayment is to transfer the entire balance of the asset account to the expense account immediately after the temporary accounts have been closed for the period. Continuing with the illustration, the reversing entry is as follows:

213

			Reversing Entry				
Jan.	1	Interest Expense.....................	911	120			
		Prepaid Interest..................	117			120	

After the reversing entry has been posted, the prepaid interest account and the interest expense account appear as shown on the next page.

It should be noted that the reversing entry does not change the essential nature of the $120, only its location in the ledger. It is prepaid interest on January 1, just as it was prepaid interest on December 31.

ACCOUNT **PREPAID INTEREST**   ACCOUNT No. 117

DATE		ITEM	POST. REF.	DEBIT	CREDIT	BALANCE DEBIT	BALANCE CREDIT
1973 Dec.	31	Adjusting	J17	120		120	
1974 Jan.	1	Reversing	J18		120	——	——

ACCOUNT **INTEREST EXPENSE**   ACCOUNT No. 911

DATE		ITEM	POST. REF.	DEBIT	CREDIT	BALANCE DEBIT	BALANCE CREDIT
1973 Feb.	5		CR3	50		50	
May	15		CR8	144		194	
June	10		CR10	105		299	
Dec.	1		CR20	180		479	
	31	Adjusting	J17		120	359	
	31	Closing	J17		359	——	——
1974 Jan.	1	Reversing	J18	120		120	

However, it will become an expense before the close of the ensuing year, and hence no further attention needs to be given to the item.

Comparison of the two systems. The two systems of recording prepaid expenses and the related entries at the end of an accounting period are summarized below.

Prepaid expense **recorded initially as an asset:**

     Adjusting — Transfers amount *used* to appropriate **expense** account.
     Closing — Closes balance of expense account.
     Reversing — **Not required.**
     (Amount prepaid at beginning of new period is in the asset account.)

Prepaid expense **recorded initially as an expense:**

     Adjusting — Transfers amount *unused* to appropriate **asset** account.
     Closing — Closes balance of expense account.
     Reversing — Transfers amount *unused* back to **expense** account.
     (Amount prepaid at beginning of new period is in the expense account.)

Either of the two systems may be adopted for all of the prepaid expenses of an enterprise, or one system may be used for prepayment of certain types of expenses and the other system for other types. Initial debits to the asset account appear to be particularly logical for prepayments of insurance, which are typically for periods of from one to three years. On the other hand, interest charges on notes payable are usually for short periods; some charges may be recorded when a note is issued (as in the illustration); other charges may be recorded when a note is paid; and few, if any, of the debits for interest may require adjustment at the end of the period. It therefore seems logical to record all interest charges initially by debiting the expense account rather than the asset account.

As was noted earlier, the amount reported as expense in the income statement and as asset on the balance sheet will not be affected by the system employed. To avoid confusion the system adopted by an enterprise for each particular type of prepaid expense should be followed consistently from year to year.

UNEARNED REVENUES (DEFERRAL)

Revenue received during a particular period may be only partly earned by the end of the period. Items of revenue that are received in advance represent a liability that may be termed *unearned revenue*. The portion of the liability that is discharged during the period through delivery of commodities or services has been earned; the remainder will be earned in the future. For example, magazine publishers ordinarily receive advance payment for subscriptions extending for periods ranging from a few months to a number of years. At the end of an accounting period, the portion of the receipts applicable to future periods has not been earned and should appear in the balance sheet as a liability.

Other examples of unearned revenue are rent received in advance on property owned, interest deducted in advance on notes receivable, premiums received in advance by an insurance company, tuition received in advance by a school, an annual retainer fee received in advance by an attorney, and amounts received in advance by an advertising firm for advertising services to be rendered in the future.

By accepting advance payment for a commodity or service, a business commits itself to furnish the commodity or the service at some future time. At the end of the accounting period, if some portion of the commodity or the service has been furnished, part of the revenue has been earned. The earned portion appears in the income statement. The unearned portion represents a liability of the business to furnish the commodity or the service in a future period and is reported in the balance sheet as a liability. As in the case of prepaid expenses, two systems of accounting are explained and illustrated.

Unearned revenues recorded initially as liabilities. When revenue is received in advance, it may be credited to a liability account. To illustrate, assume that on October 1 a business rents a portion of its building for a period of one year, receiving $3,600 in payment for the entire term of the lease. Assume also that the transaction was originally recorded by a debit to Cash and a credit to the liability account Unearned Rent. On December 31, the end of the fiscal year, one fourth of the amount has been

215

earned and three fourths of the amount remains a liability. The entry to record the revenue and reduce the liability appears as follows:

		Adjusting Entry				
Dec.	31	Unearned Rent.....................	218	900		
		Rent Income.....................	812		900	

After this entry has been posted, the unearned rent account and the rent income account appear as follows:

ACCOUNT UNEARNED RENT   ACCOUNT No. 218

DATE		ITEM	POST. REF.	DEBIT	CREDIT	BALANCE DEBIT	BALANCE CREDIT
1973 Oct.	1		CR8		3,600		3,600
Dec.	31	Adjusting	J17	900			2,700

ACCOUNT RENT INCOME   ACCOUNT No. 812

DATE		ITEM	POST. REF.	DEBIT	CREDIT	BALANCE DEBIT	BALANCE CREDIT
1973 Dec.	31	Adjusting	J17		900		900

After the amount earned, $900, is transferred to Rent Income, the balance of $2,700 remaining in Unearned Rent is a liability to render a service in the future, and it therefore appears as a current liability in the balance sheet. Rent Income is reported in the Other Income section of the income statement.

Unearned revenues recorded initially as revenues. Instead of being credited to a liability account, unearned revenue may be credited to a revenue account as the cash is received. To illustrate this alternative, assume the same facts as in the preceding illustration, except that the transaction was originally recorded on October 1 by a debit to Cash and a credit to Rent Income. On December 31, the end of the fiscal year, three fourths of the balance in Rent Income is still unearned and the remaining one fourth has been earned. The entry to record the transfer to the liability account appears as follows:

		Adjusting Entry				
Dec.	31	Rent Income......................	812	2,700		
		Unearned Rent..................	218		2,700	

After this entry has been posted, the unearned rent account and the rent income account appear as shown at the top of the next page.

216

ACCOUNT **UNEARNED RENT**   ACCOUNT No. 218

DATE		ITEM	POST. REF.	DEBIT	CREDIT	BALANCE	
						DEBIT	CREDIT
1973 Dec.	31	Adjusting	J17		2,700		2,700

ACCOUNT **RENT INCOME**   ACCOUNT No. 812

DATE		ITEM	POST. REF.	DEBIT	CREDIT	BALANCE	
						DEBIT	CREDIT
1973 Oct.	1		CR8		3,600		3,600
Dec.	31	Adjusting	J17	2,700			900

The unearned rent of $2,700 is listed as a current liability in the balance sheet, and the rent income of $900 is reported in the income statement.

The $2,700 of unearned rent at the end of the year will be earned during the following year. If it is transferred to the income account by a *reversing* entry immediately after the accounts are closed, no further action will be needed either month by month or at the end of the nine-month period. Furthermore, since the $3,600 rent was credited initially to the income account, all such payments received in the following year will presumably be treated in a similar fashion. If a reversing entry is not made, there may be balances in both the liability account and the income account at the end of the following year, necessitating analysis of both accounts and causing possible confusion. The reversing entry for the unearned rent, which is the exact reverse of the adjusting entry, is as follows:

		Reversing Entry				
Jan.	1	Unearned Rent.....................	218	2,700		
		Rent Income.....................	812		2,700	

After the foregoing entry is posted to the two accounts, they will appear as shown at the top of the next page.

At the beginning of the new fiscal year, there is a credit balance of $2,700 in Rent Income. Although the balance is in reality a liability at this time, it will become revenue before the close of the year. Whenever a revenue account needs adjustment for an unearned amount at the end of a period, the adjusting entry should be reversed after the accounts have been closed.

217

ACCOUNT   **UNEARNED RENT**   ACCOUNT No. 218

DATE		ITEM	POST. REF.	DEBIT	CREDIT	BALANCE DEBIT	BALANCE CREDIT
1973 Dec.	31	Adjusting	J17		**2,700**		2,700
1974 Jan.	1	Reversing	J18	2,700		—	—

ACCOUNT   **RENT INCOME**   ACCOUNT No. 812

DATE		ITEM	POST. REF.	DEBIT	CREDIT	BALANCE DEBIT	BALANCE CREDIT
1973 Oct.	1		CR8		3,600		3,600
Dec.	31	Adjusting	J17	2,700			900
	31	Closing	J17	900		—	—
1974 Jan.	1	Reversing	J18		2,700		2,700

Comparison of the two systems. The two systems of recording unearned revenue and the related entries at the end of the accounting period are summarized below.

Unearned revenue **recorded initially as a liability:**

> Adjusting — Transfers amount *earned* to appropriate **revenue** account.
> Closing — Closes balance of revenue account.
> Reversing — **Not required.**
> (Amount unearned at beginning of new period is in the liability account.)

Unearned revenue **recorded initially as revenue:**

> Adjusting — Transfers amount *unearned* to appropriate **liability** account.
> Closing — Closes balance of revenue account.
> Reversing — Transfers amount *unearned* back to **revenue** account.
> (Amount unearned at beginning of new period is in the revenue account.)

Either of the systems may be adopted for all revenues received in advance, or the first system may be used for advance receipts of certain types of revenue and the second system for other types. The results obtained are the same under both systems, but it is not advisable to shift back and forth arbitrarily from one system to the other.

ACCRUED LIABILITIES

Some expenses accrue from day to day but for obvious reasons are ordinarily recorded only when they are paid. Examples are salaries paid to employees and interest paid on notes payable. The amounts of such accrued but unpaid items at the end of the fiscal period are both an expense and a liability. It is for this reason that such accruals are referred to variously as *accrued liabilities* or *accrued expenses*.

To illustrate the adjusting entry for an accrued liability, assume that on December 31, the end of the fiscal year, the salary expense account has a debit balance of $32,300. During the year salaries have been paid each Friday for the five-day week then ended. For this particular fiscal year, December 31 falls on Wednesday. Reference to the records of the business reveals that the salary accrued for these last three days of the year amounts to $575. The entry to record the additional expense and the liability is as follows:

		Adjusting Entry			
Dec.	31	Salary Expense......................	611	575	
		Salaries Payable...................	214		575

After the adjusting entry has been posted to the two accounts, they appear as follows:

Account **SALARIES PAYABLE** Account No. 214

DATE		ITEM	POST. REF.	DEBIT	CREDIT	BALANCE	
						DEBIT	CREDIT
1973 Dec.	31	Adjusting	J17		575		575

Account **SALARY EXPENSE** Account No. 611

DATE		ITEM	POST. REF.	DEBIT	CREDIT	BALANCE	
						DEBIT	CREDIT
1973 Dec.	31	Balance	√			32,300	
	31	Adjusting	J17	575		32,875	

219

The accrued salaries of $575 recorded in Salaries Payable will appear in the balance sheet of December 31 as a current liability. The balance of $32,875 now recorded in Salary Expense will appear in the income statement for the year ended December 31.

When the weekly salaries are paid on January 2 of the following year, part of the payment will discharge the liability of $575 and the remainder will represent salary expense incurred in January. In order to avoid the necessity of analyzing the payment, a reversing entry is made at the beginning of the new year. The effect of the entry, which is illustrated below, is to transfer the credit balance in the salaries payable account to the credit side of the salary expense account.

		Reversing Entry			
Jan.	1	Salaries Payable.....................	214	575	
		Salary Expense....................	611		575

After the reversing entry has been posted, the salaries payable account and the salary expense account appear as follows:

ACCOUNT SALARIES PAYABLE   ACCOUNT No. 214

DATE		ITEM	POST. REF.	DEBIT	CREDIT	BALANCE DEBIT	BALANCE CREDIT
1973 Dec.	31	Adjusting	J17		575		575
1974 Jan.	1	Reversing	J18	575		—	—

ACCOUNT SALARY EXPENSE   ACCOUNT No. 611

DATE		ITEM	POST. REF.	DEBIT	CREDIT	BALANCE DEBIT	BALANCE CREDIT
1973 Dec.	31	Balance	√			32,300	
	31	Adjusting	J17	575		32,875	
	31	Closing	J18		32,875	—	—
1974 Jan.	1	Reversing	J18		575		575

220

The liability for salaries on December 31 now appears as a credit in Salary Expense. Assuming that the salaries paid on Friday, January 2, amount to $710, the debit to Salary Expense will automatically record the discharge of the liability of $575 and an expense of $135 ($710 − $575).

The discussion of the treatment of accrued salary expense is illustrative of the method of handling accrued liabilities in general. If, in addition to accrued salaries, there are other accrued liabilities at the end of a fiscal period, separate liability accounts may be set up for each type. When these liability items are numerous, however, a single account entitled Accrued Payables or Accrued Liabilities may be used. All accrued liabilities may then be recorded as credits to this account instead of to separate accounts.

Because of peculiarities in the timing of their accrual and payment, the adjusting process applicable to property taxes is frequently more complicated than it is for salaries and interest. Accounting for property taxes is described and illustrated later in this chapter.

ACCRUED ASSETS

All assets belonging to the business at the end of an accounting period and all revenues earned during the period should be recorded in the ledger. But during a fiscal period it is customary to record some types of revenue only as the cash is received; consequently, at the end of the period there may be items of revenue that have not been recorded. In such cases it is necessary to record the amount of the accrued revenue by debiting an asset account and crediting a revenue account. Because of the dual nature of such accruals, they are referred to variously as *accrued assets* or *accrued revenues*.

To illustrate the adjusting entry for an accrued asset, assume that on December 31, the end of the fiscal year, the interest income account has a credit balance of $584. Assume further that on the same date the business owns three short-term, interest-bearing notes accepted from customers. The three notes are for varying amounts and have varying due dates in January and February of the succeeding year. The total interest accrued on the three notes from their respective issuance dates to December 31 is determined to be $167. The entry to record this increase in the amount owed by the debtors and the additional revenue earned on the notes is as follows:

		Adjusting Entry			
Dec.	31	Interest Receivable..................	114	167	
		Interest Income..................	811		167

After this entry has been posted, the interest receivable account and the interest income account appear as follows:

ACCOUNT **INTEREST RECEIVABLE** ACCOUNT No. 114

DATE		ITEM	POST. REF.	DEBIT	CREDIT	BALANCE DEBIT	BALANCE CREDIT
1973 Dec.	31	Adjusting	J17	167		167	

ACCOUNT **INTEREST INCOME** ACCOUNT No. 811

DATE		ITEM	POST. REF.	DEBIT	CREDIT	BALANCE DEBIT	BALANCE CREDIT
1973 Dec.	31	Balance	√				584
	31	Adjusting	J17		167		751

The accrued interest of $167 recorded in Interest Receivable will appear in the balance sheet of December 31 as a current asset. The credit balance of $751 now recorded in Interest Income will appear in the Other Income section of the income statement for the year ended December 31.

When the amount due on each of the three notes is collected in the succeeding year, part of the interest received will effect a reduction of the interest receivable and the remainder will represent revenue for the new year. To avoid the inconvenience of analyzing each receipt of interest in the new year, a reversing entry is made immediately after the accounts are closed. The effect of the entry, which is illustrated below, is to transfer the debit balance in the interest receivable account to the debit side of the interest income account.

		Reversing Entry			
Jan.	1	Interest Income.....................	811	167	
		Interest Receivable...............	114		167

After this entry has been posted, the interest receivable account and the interest income account appear as follows:

ACCOUNT INTEREST RECEIVABLE   ACCOUNT No. 114

DATE		ITEM	POST. REF.	DEBIT	CREDIT	BALANCE DEBIT	BALANCE CREDIT
1973 Dec.	31	Adjusting	J17	167		167	
1974 Jan.	1	Reversing	J18		167	—	—

ACCOUNT INTEREST INCOME   ACCOUNT No. 811

DATE		ITEM	POST. REF.	DEBIT	CREDIT	BALANCE DEBIT	BALANCE CREDIT
1973 Dec.	31	Balance	√				584
	31	Adjusting	J17		167		751
	31	Closing	J17	751		—	—
1974 Jan.	1	Reversing	J18		167	167	

The interest accrued on the three notes receivable as of December 31 now appears as a debit in Interest Income. At the time each note matures and the payment is received from the maker, the entire amount of the interest received will be credited to Interest Income. The credit will in part represent a reduction in the receivable of $167 and in part a revenue of the new period. If, for example, one of the three notes held on December 31 is for the face amount of $5,000 with interest at 6% for 90 days, the total amount of interest received at maturity will be $75. The entire $75 will be credited to Interest Income regardless of the amount representing collection of a receivable and the amount representing revenue of the new period.

The treatment of interest accrued on notes receivable illustrates the method of handling accrued assets in general. If, in addition to accrued interest, there are other accrued assets at the end of a fiscal period,

222

separate accounts may be set up. Each of these accounts will be of the same nature as the account with interest receivable. When such items are numerous, a single account entitled Accrued Receivables or Accrued Assets may be used. All accrued assets may then be recorded as debits to this account.

ACCOUNTING FOR PROPERTY TAXES

The various types of taxes levied on businesses by federal, state, and local governments frequently amount to a substantial total tax expense. It is usually the responsibility of the accounting department to prepare the required tax reports, to design the procedure for recording taxes in the accounts, and to prescribe the manner of reporting taxes in the financial statements. In designing the procedure for recording property taxes, a unique combination of deferral and accrual accounting may be employed.

The liability for annual property taxes is usually incurred on a particular day of the year specified by the laws of the taxing jurisdiction. The period covered by the tax may be the year just ended, the year just begun, or some other twelve-month period, depending upon the tax laws applicable. Inasmuch as the governmental services to which the tax relates are received during an entire year, it is logical to allocate the expense equitably over the twelve months benefited.

The selection of the particular twelve-month period for allocation is complicated by the fact that the exact amount of the tax assessment may not be known until several months after the liability attaches to the property. A difference between the fiscal year of the taxpayer and the fiscal year of the taxing authority may also complicate the problem. Various methods of accounting for property taxes are acceptable, provided the method selected is followed consistently from year to year.

The method to be described here provides for monthly allocation over the fiscal year of the taxing authority for which the tax is levied.[1] Two alternative procedural patterns may be followed: (1) interim adjustments may be recorded solely on working papers, with any required year-end adjustments being recorded in the accounts, or (2) adjustments may be recorded in the accounts at the end of each month. Because of the cumulative nature of the adjustments for property taxes, the second alternative is frequently used. It will be used in the illustration that follows. The allocations reported in the interim and year-end financial statements will be the same regardless of which procedure is adopted. The illustration is based on the facts described at the top of the next page.

223

---

[1]Recommended by *Accounting Research and Terminology Bulletins — Final Edition*, "No. 43, Restatement and Revision of Accounting Research Bulletins" (New York: American Institute of Certified Public Accountants, 1961), Chapter 10, par. 14.

Fiscal year of the business enterprise: January 1, 1973 to December 31, 1973.
Fiscal year of the taxing authority: July 1, 1973 to June 30, 1974.
Tax statement received: October 15, 1973.
Tax paid in equal installments on November 10, 1973 and May 10, 1974.

The adjustments data and related transactions are described below, followed by the related entries, in each case in general journal form.

At the end of July the taxpayer estimates that the property tax assessment for the 1973–74 fiscal year of the taxing authority will be $3,240. The amount to be accrued as of July 31, 1974 is therefore $270 ($3,240 ÷ 12) and the entry to record the accrual in the taxpayer's accounts is as follows:

		Adjusting Entry		
July	31	Property Tax Expense.....................	270	
		Property Tax Payable..................		270

An entry for the same amount is recorded as of the last day of August and again on September 30, by which time there is a balance of $810 (3 × $270) in the property tax payable account.

On October 15 a tax statement for $3,480 is received, half of which is payable on November 10. The correct amount of the accrual apportionable to each of the past three months is therefore $290 ($3,480 ÷ 12) instead of $270. Ordinarily the difference between the actual and the estimated monthly expense is not material. In any event, the underestimate or overestimate is corrected in the adjusting entry for the month in which the actual amount of the tax becomes known. The amount of the accrual to be recorded at the end of October is therefore determined as follows:

Amount of tax allocable to July, Aug., Sept. and Oct., 4×$290	$1,160
Amount of tax allocated to July, Aug. and Sept., 3 × $270...	810
Tax allocation for October...............................	$ 350

The $350 allocation for October may also be computed by adding the $60 deficiency (3 × $20) for the first three months to the regular October monthly allocation of $290. The adjusting entry as of October 31 is as follows:

		Adjusting Entry		
Oct.	31	Property Tax Expense.....................	350	
		Property Tax Payable..................		350

One half of the tax bill, $1,740, is paid on November 10. Of this amount, $1,160 is in payment of the accrual and $580 represents a deferral. The entry to record the payment is as follows, in general journal form:

Nov.	10	Property Tax Payable.....................	1,160	
		Prepaid Property Tax.....................	580	
		Cash......................................		1,740

At the end of November, and again at the end of December, the following adjusting entry is made:

		Adjusting Entry			
Nov.	30	Property Tax Expense......................	290		
		Prepaid Property Tax.....................		290	

At December 31, the end of the fiscal year for the business enterprise, one half of the 1973–74 property tax has been charged to expense and there is neither a tax accrual nor a tax deferral recorded in the accounts. The legal obligation for the entire tax of 1973–74 was created in 1973, but the usual accounting treatment is to spread the cost ratably over the period to which the tax relates. If it were considered necessary to report the accrual of the second half of the tax bill as a liability on the balance sheet at December 31, 1973, it would also be necessary to report a deferral of equal amount as an asset.

The adjusting entries and the entry for payment of the second half of the tax bill during January through June of the following year would be similar to those presented for the period July through December. There would, however, be no need to estimate the property tax assessment; the monthly charges to expense would be uniformly $290.

225

QUESTIONS

1. Classify the following items as (a) prepaid expense, (b) unearned revenue, (c) accrued asset, or (d) accrued liability.

   (1) Supplies on hand.
   (2) Subscriptions collected in advance by a publisher.
   (3) Interest earned but not received.
   (4) Interest owed but not yet due.
   (5) Portion of fee earned but not yet received.
   (6) Taxes owed but payable in the following period.
   (7) Receipts from sale of meal tickets by a restaurant.
   (8) Receipts from sale of season tickets for a series of concerts.
   (9) A three-year premium paid on a fire insurance policy.
  (10) Property taxes paid in advance.
  (11) Life insurance premiums received by an insurance company.
  (12) Salary owed but not yet due.

2. From time to time during the fiscal year, an enterprise makes advance payment of premiums on three-year and one-year property insurance policies. (a) At the close of such fiscal year will there be a deferral or an accrual? (b) Which of the following types of accounts will be affected by the related adjusting entry at the end of the fiscal year: (1) asset, (2) liability, (3) revenue, (4) expense?

3. (a) Is it almost a certainty that a business enterprise will always have prepaid property and casualty insurance at the end of each fiscal year? Explain.

(b) Is it almost a certainty that a business enterprise that occasionally discounts short-term notes payable at its bank will always have prepaid interest at the end of each fiscal year? Explain.

(c) Would it be logical to record prepayments of the type referred to in (a) as assets and prepayments of the type referred to in (b) as expenses? Discuss.

4. On January 3 an enterprise receives $12,000 from a tenant as rent for the current calendar year. The fiscal year of the enterprise is from April 1 to March 31. (a) Will the adjusting entry for the rent as of March 31 of the current year be a deferral or an accrual? (b) Which of the following types of accounts will be affected by the adjusting entry as of March 31: (1) asset, (2) liability, (3) revenue, (4) expense? (c) How much of the $12,000 rent should be allocated to the current fiscal year ending March 31?

5. On June 30, the end of its fiscal year, an enterprise owes salaries of $800 for an incomplete payroll period. On the first payday in July, salaries of $2,200 are paid. (a) Is the $800 a deferral or an accrual as of June 30? (b) Which of the following types of accounts will be affected by the related adjusting entry: (1) asset, (2) liability, (3) revenue, (4) expense? (c) How much of the $2,200 salary payment should be allocated to July?

6. At the end of the fiscal year an enterprise holds a 90-day interest-bearing note receivable accepted from a customer sixty days earlier. (a) Will the interest on the note as of the end of the year represent a deferral or an accrual? (b) Which of the following types of accounts will be affected by the related adjusting entry at the end of the fiscal year: (1) asset, (2) liability, (3) revenue, (4) expense? (c) Assuming that the note is held until maturity, what fraction of the total interest should be allocated to the year in which the note is collected?

7. The debit portion of a particular adjustment is to an asset account. (a) If the adjustment is for a deferral, which of the following types of accounts will be credited: (1) asset, (2) liability, (3) revenue, (4) expense? (b) If the adjustment is for an accrual, which of the following types of accounts will be credited: (1) asset, (2) liability, (3) revenue, (4) expense?

8. Each of the following debits and credits represents one half of an adjusting entry. Name the title of the account that would be used for the remaining half of the entry.

(a) Interest Income is debited.
(b) Prepaid Insurance is credited.
(c) Interest Payable is credited.
(d) Office Supplies is debited.
(e) Unearned Rent is debited.
(f) Unearned Subscriptions is credited.

9. The interest accrued on a $6,000 note payable at the end of the year is $80. In the following year the note is paid, including interest of $240. (a) Give the adjusting entry that should be made at the end of the year. (b) Give the entry for payment of the note and interest, assuming (1) that the adjusting entry for $80 had been reversed and (2) that the adjusting entry had not been reversed.

10. There are balances in each of the following accounts after adjustments have been made at the end of the fiscal year. Identify each as (a) asset, (b) liability, (c) revenue, or (d) expense.

(1) Prepaid Interest
(2) Rent Expense
(3) Prepaid Insurance
(4) Insurance Expense
(5) Unearned Rent
(6) Interest Expense
(7) Salary Expense
(8) Interest Income
(9) Supplies
(10) Rent Income
(11) Interest Payable
(12) Interest Receivable

11. The accountant for a real estate brokerage and management company adheres to the following uniform procedures in recording certain transactions:

(1) Premiums on fire insurance are debited to Prepaid Insurance.
(2) Supplies purchased are debited to Supplies Expense.
(3) Management fees, which are collected for one year in advance, are credited to Management Fees when received.

Assuming that an adjusting entry is required for each of the foregoing at the end of the fiscal year, (a) give the accounts to be debited and credited for each adjustment and (b) state whether or not each of the adjusting entries should be reversed as of the beginning of the following year.

12. How is it possible to determine from a trial balance before adjustments whether a particular type of prepaid expense has been recorded initially as an asset or as an expense?

227

13. Explain how the reversing of adjustments for accrued assets and accrued liabilities facilitates the recording of transactions.

14. If a particular type of revenue typically collected in advance is invariably credited to an income account at the time received, why should the year-end adjusting entry be reversed?

15. The status of the accounts listed below is as of the beginning of the fiscal year, after reversing entries have been posted but before any transactions have occurred. Identify each balance as (a) an asset or (b) a liability.

(1) Salary Expense, credit balance of $1,150.
(2) Supplies Expense, debit balance of $75.
(3) Interest Income, debit balance of $285.
(4) Unearned Rent, credit balance of $2,500.
(5) Prepaid Insurance, debit balance of $640.

16. At the end of the first month of the year, the Olympic Company estimates that its property taxes for such year will amount to $9,000. Give the adjusting entry to be recorded by Olympic Company.

17. During the first three months of the year, Hanson Co. records accruals of estimated property tax of $400 a month. The tax statement received in the fourth month is for $5,040, which means that the actual tax accrual is $420 a month. Give the adjusting entry to be recorded at the end of the fourth month.

18. At the time of payment of $6,600 for the semiannual property tax, the property tax payable account has a credit balance of $4,400. Give the entry to record the $6,600 payment.

EXERCISES

9-1. The store supplies inventory of R. N. Nolan Company at the beginning of the fiscal year is $425, purchases of store supplies during the year total $1,450, and the inventory at the end of the year is $385.

(a) Set up T accounts for Store Supplies and Store Supplies Expense, and record the following directly in the accounts, employing the system of initially recording store supplies as an asset (identify each entry by number): (1) opening balance; (2) purchases for the period; (3) adjusting entry at end of the period; (4) closing entry.

(b) Set up T accounts for Store Supplies and Store Supplies Expense, and record the following directly in the accounts, employing the system of initially recording store supplies as an expense (identify each entry by number): (1) opening balance; (2) purchases for the period; (3) adjusting entry at end of the period; (4) closing entry.

9-2. The salary expense account has a balance of $77,420 as of August 26.

(a) Present entries in general journal form for the following:

Aug. 31. Recorded accrued salaries, $1,215.
  31. Closed the salaries expense account.
Sept. 1. Recorded a reversing entry for accrued salaries.
  2. Recorded salaries paid, $1,640.

(b) Answer the following questions:

(1) What is the balance of the salary expense account on September 1?
(2) Is the balance of the salary expense account on September 1 an asset, a liability, a revenue, or an expense?
(3) What is the balance of the salary expense account on September 2?
(4) Of the $1,640 salary payment on September 2, how much is expense of September?
(5) If there had been no reversing entry on September 1, how should the debit for the salary payment of September 2 have been recorded?

9-3. In their first year of operations, the Midwest Publishing Co. receives $340,000 from advertising contracts and $280,000 from magazine subscriptions, crediting the two amounts to Advertising Revenue and Circulation Revenue respectively. At the end of the year, the deferral of advertising revenue amounts to $72,500 and the deferral of circulation revenue amounts to $93,000. (a) If no adjustments are made at the end of the year, will revenue for the year be overstated or understated, and by what amount? (b) Present the adjusting entries that should be made at the end of the year. (c) Present the entries to close the two revenue accounts. (d) Present the reversing entries if appropriate.

9-4. (a) Present entries in general journal form for the following:

Nov. 1. Issued to Stone Co., on account, a $12,000, 90-day, 8% note dated November 1.
Dec. 31. Recorded an adjusting entry for accrued interest on the note of November 1.
  31. Closed the interest expense account. The only entry in this account originated from the above adjustment.
Jan. 1. Recorded a reversing entry for accrued interest.
  30. Paid Stone Co. $12,240 on the note due today.

(b) What is the balance in Interest Expense after the entry of January 30?
(c) How many days' interest on $12,000 at 8% does the amount reported in (b) represent?

9-5. Because of a lack of consistency by the bookkeeper in recording the payment of premiums on property and casualty insurance, there are balances in both the asset and expense accounts at the end of the year before adjustments. Prepaid Insurance has a debit balance of $1,480 and Insurance Expense has a debit balance of $950. You ascertain that the total amount of insurance premiums allocable to future periods is $1,625.

(a) Assuming that you will instruct the bookkeeper to record all future insurance premiums as an expense, present journal entries: (1) to adjust the accounts, (2) to close the appropriate account, and (3) to reverse the adjusting entry if appropriate.
(b) Assuming that you will instruct the bookkeeper to record all future insurance premiums as an asset, present journal entries: (1) to adjust the accounts, (2) to close the appropriate account, and (3) to reverse the adjusting entry if appropriate.
(c) (1) What is the amount of insurance expense for the year?
    (2) What is the amount of prepaid insurance at the close of the year?

9-6. The entries in the following account identified by numbers are related to the summarizing process at the end of the year. (a) Identify each entry as adjusting, closing, or reversing and (b) present for each entry the title of the account to which the **related** debit or credit was posted.

INTEREST INCOME

DATE		ITEM	DEBIT	CREDIT	BALANCE DEBIT	BALANCE CREDIT
Jan.	1	(1)	180		180	
	1	(2)		120	60	
Jan. to Dec.	1 31	Transactions during the year		960		900
	31	(3)		90		990
	31	(4)	45			945
	31	(5)	945		—	—
Jan.	1	(6)	90		90	
	1	(7)		45	45	

PROBLEMS

The following additional problems for this chapter are located in Appendix B: 9-1B, 9-2B, 9-3B, 9-4B, 9-7B.

9-1A. The accounts listed at the top of the next page appear in the ledger of Carson Company at December 31, the end of the current fiscal year. None of the year-end adjustments have been recorded.

The following information relating to adjustments at December 31 is obtained from physical inventories, supplementary records, and other sources:

(a) Interest accrued on notes receivable at December 31, $70.
(b) Inventory of supplies at December 31, $120.

113 Interest Receivable....	$——	411 Rental Income........	$99,760
114 Supplies..............	345	511 Salary and Commissions	
115 Prepaid Insurance.....	1,270	Expense............	18,900
116 Prepaid Advertising....	——	513 Advertising Expense....	3,100
117 Prepaid Interest.......	——	514 Insurance Expense.....	——
213 Salaries and Commissions		515 Supplies Expense......	——
Payable............	——	611 Interest Income.......	345
215 Unearned Rent........	——	711 Interest Expense.......	420
313 Income Summary......	——		

(c) The insurance record indicates that $490 of insurance has expired during the year.

(d) Of a prepayment of $500 for advertising space in a local newspaper, 75% has been used and the remainder will be used in the following year.

(e) A short-term non-interest-bearing note payable was discounted at a bank in December. The amount of the total discount of $200 applicable to December is $60.

(f) Salaries and commissions accrued at December 31, $650.

(g) Rent collected in advance that will not be earned until the following year, $5,400.

Instructions:

(1) Open the accounts listed and record the balances in the appropriate balance columns, as of December 31.

(2) Journalize the adjusting entries and post to the appropriate accounts after each entry, extending the balances. Identify the postings by writing "Adjusting" in the item columns.

(3) Prepare a compound journal entry to close the revenue accounts and another compound entry to close the expense accounts.

(4) Post the closing entries, inserting a short line in both balance columns of accounts that are closed. Identify the postings by writing "Closing" in the item columns.

(5) Prepare the reversing journal entries that should be made on January 1 and post to the appropriate accounts after each entry, inserting a short line in both balance columns of accounts that are now in balance. Write "Reversing" in the item columns.

9-2A. Reese Co. closes its accounts annually as of December 31, the end of the fiscal year. All relevant data regarding notes payable and related interest from November 21 through February 19 of the following year are presented below. (All notes are dated as of the day they are issued.)

Nov. 21. Issued a $4,500, 8%, 90-day note on account.

Dec. 1. Issued a $6,000, 8%, 60-day note on account.

12. Paid principal, $5,000, and interest, $100, on note payable due today.

16. Borrowed $12,000 from First National Bank, issuing a 7%, 60-day note.

31. Recorded an adjusting entry for the interest accrued on the notes dated November 21, December 1, and December 16. There are no other notes outstanding on this date.

31. Recorded the entry to close the interest expense account.

Jan. 1. Recorded a reversing entry for the accrued interest.

12. Issued a $9,000, 8%, 30-day note on account.

30. Paid $6,080 on the note issued on December 1.

Feb. 11. Paid $9,060 on the note issued on January 12.
    14. Paid $12,140 on the note issued on December 16.
    19. Paid $4,590 on the note issued on November 21.

Instructions:

(1) Open accounts for Interest Payable (Account No. 214) and Interest Expense (Account No. 711), and record a debit balance of $1,125 in the latter account as of November 21 of the current year.

(2) Present entries in general journal form to record the transactions and other data described above, posting to the two accounts after each entry affecting them.

(3) If the reversing entry had not been recorded as of January 1, indicate how each interest payment in January and February should be allocated. Submit the data in the following form:

Note (Face Amount)	Total Interest Paid	Dr. Interest Payable	Dr. Interest Expense
$ 6,000	$	$	$
9,000			
12,000			
4,500			
Total	$	$	$

(4) Do the February 19 balances of Interest Payable and Interest Expense obtained by use of the reversing entry technique correspond to the balances that would have been obtained by the more laborious process of analyzing each payment?

If the working papers correlating with the textbook are not used, omit Problem 9-3A.

9-3A. Allen Company prepares interim financial statements at the end of each month and closes its accounts annually on December 31. Its income statement for the two-month period, January and February of the current year, is presented in the working papers. In addition, the trial balance of the ledger as of one month later is presented on an eight-column work sheet in the working papers. Data needed for adjusting entries at March 31, the end of the three-month period, are as follows:

(a) Uncollectible accounts expense is estimated at ½ of 1% of net sales for the three-month period.

(b) Estimated merchandise inventory at March 31, $57,425.

(c) Insurance expired during the three-month period:
    Allocable as selling expense, $210.
    Allocable as general expense, $95.

(d) Estimated inventory of store supplies at March 31, $275.

(e) Depreciation for the three-month period:
    Store equipment, $450.
    Office equipment, $135.

(f) Estimated property tax of $140 a month for January and February was recorded in the accounts. The tax statement, which was received in March, indicates a liability of $1,800 for the calendar year.

(g) Salaries accrued at March 31:
    Sales salaries, $280.
    Office salaries, $85.

(h) The notes payable balance of $15,000 is composed of the following: $9,000, 90-day, non-interest-bearing note discounted at Winters Trust

Co. on March 1. The $180 discount was debited to Interest Expense. (Record adjustment in work sheet before considering the other note.) $6,000, 6-month, 8% note dated December 1 of the preceding year. (Accrue interest for 4 months.)

Instructions:

(1) Complete the eight-column work sheet for the three-month period ended March 31 of the current year.
(2) Prepare an income statement for the three-month period, using the last three-column group of the nine-column form in the working papers.
(3) Prepare an income statement for the month of March, using the middle three-column group of the nine-column form in the working papers.
(4) Prepare a capital statement for the three-month period. There were no additional investments during the period.
(5) Prepare a balance sheet as of March 31.
(6) Determine the amount of interest expense on each note allocable to the month of March and compare the total with the amount reported as interest expense in the income statement for March.

9-4A. The Roberson Co. prepares interim statements at the end of each month and closes its accounts annually on December 31. Property taxes are assessed for fiscal years beginning on July 1 and ending on June 30. Selected transactions and property tax allocations for the period July 1 to December 31 of one year and of January 1 to June 30 of the following year are presented below.

July 31. Property tax allocation for July based on estimated property tax of $9,900 for the taxing authority's fiscal year beginning July 1.
Sept. 30. Property tax allocation for September, based on tax statement dated September 20 indicating a tax assessment of $8,940.
Oct. 15. Paid first half of tax assessment, $4,470.
    31. Property tax allocation for October.
Dec. 31. Property tax allocation for December.
Jan. 31. Property tax allocation for January.
May 15. Paid second half of tax assessment, $4,470.
    31. Property tax allocation for May.
June 30. Property tax allocation for June.

Instructions:

(1) Present in general journal form the entries to record the selected tax allocations and payments, assuming in all cases that appropriate entries have been recorded in the accounts for all intervening months.
(2) Indicate the amount of prepaid property tax and property tax payable that would be reported on the balance sheets prepared as of (a) November 30, (b) December 31, and (c) April 30. In each case list the section in which the item would appear (Current assets, etc.), the account title (Prepaid Property Tax, etc.), and the amount.

9-5A. The information presented on the next page was obtained from a review of the ledger (before adjustments) and other records of Wright Company at the close of the current fiscal year ended December 31:

(a) Notes Receivable has a debit balance of $17,500 at December 31. The two notes on hand, both of which were accepted at face value, are as follows:

Date	Face	Term	Interest Rate
Nov. 16	$10,000	90 days	8%
Dec. 16	7,500	60 days	8%

(b) As advance premiums have been paid on insurance policies during the year they have been debited to Prepaid Insurance, which has a balance of $1,194 at December 31. Details of premium expirations are as follows:

Policy No.	Premium Cost per Month	Period in Effect During Year
247P	$15	Jan. 1–June 30
765O	16	July 1–Dec. 31
817CF	10	Jan. 1–Dec. 31
3318Y	12	Jan. 1–Mar. 31
4146D	14	Apr. 1–Dec. 31

(c) Prepaid Advertising has a debit balance of $2,860 at December 31, which represents the advance payment on April 1 of a yearly contract for a uniform amount of space in 52 consecutive issues of a weekly publication. As of December 31, advertisements had appeared in 39 issues.

(d) As office supplies have been purchased during the year, they have been debited to Office Supplies Expense, which has a balance of $440 at December 31. The inventory of supplies on hand at that date totals $135.

(e) Rent Expense has a debit balance of $7,800 on December 31, which includes rent of $600 for January of the following year, paid on December 31.

(f) Mortgage Note Payable has a credit balance of $30,000 at December 31. Interest at the rate of 7% is payable semiannually on July 31 and January 31. No entry has been made for the interest accrued since the last semiannual payment on July 31.

(g) Unearned Rent has a credit balance of $3,300 composed of the following: (1) January 1 balance of $600, representing rent prepaid for three months, January through March, and (2) a credit of $2,700 representing advance payment for twelve months rent at $225 a month, beginning with April.

Instructions:

(1) Determine the amount of each adjustment, identifying all principal figures used in the computations.

(2) Journalize the adjusting entries as of December 31 of the current fiscal year, identifying each entry by letter.

(3) Journalize the reversing entries that should be made as of January 1 of the succeeding fiscal year, identifying each entry by the corresponding letter used in (2).

9-6A. Transactions related to advertising and rent are presented below and on the next page. Accounts are adjusted and closed only at December 31, the end of the fiscal year.

Advertising

Jan. 1. Debit balance of $900 (allocable to January–March).
June 1. Payment of $4,800 (allocable at $400 a month, for 12 months beginning June 1).

Rent

Jan. 1. Credit balance of $6,700 ($2,500 allocable to January–May; $4,200 allocable to January–June).

233

June 1. Receipt of $6,300 (allocable at $525 a month, for 12 months beginning June 1).

July 1. Receipt of $8,400 (allocable at $700 a month, for 12 months beginning July 1).

Instructions:

(1) Open accounts for Prepaid Advertising, Advertising Expense, Unearned Rent, and Rent Income. Employing the system of initially recording prepaid expense as an asset and unearned revenue as a liability, record the following directly in the accounts: (a) opening balances as of January 1; (b) transactions of June 1 and July 1; (c) adjusting entries at December 31; (d) closing entries at December 31; and (e) reversing entries at January 1, if appropriate. Identify each entry in the item section of the accounts as balance, transaction, adjusting, closing, or reversing, and extend the balance after each entry.

(2) Open a duplicate set of accounts and follow the remaining instructions in Instruction (1), except to employ the system of initially recording prepaid expense as an expense and unearned revenue as a revenue.

(3) Determine the amounts that would appear in the balance sheet at December 31 as asset and liability respectively, and in the income statement for the year as expense and revenue respectively, according to the system employed in Instruction (1) and the system employed in Instruction (2). Present your answers in the form shown below.

System	Asset	Expense	Liability	Revenue
Instruction (1)	$	$	$	$
Instruction (2)				

9-7 A. Selected accounts from the ledger of Lowell Co., with the account balances before and after adjustment, at the close of the fiscal year are presented below:

	Unadjusted Balance	Adjusted Balance		Unadjusted Balance	Adjusted Balance
Interest Receivable ...	$ —	$ 150	Rent Income........	$ 9,100	$ 8,400
Supplies.............	1,240	510	Wages Expense......	24,425	24,750
Prepaid Insurance....	1,860	1,220	Supplies Expense....	—	730
Prepaid Property Tax.	300	—	Property Tax Expense	3,100	3,400
Prepaid Interest......	—	80	Insurance Expense...	—	640
Wages Payable.......	—	325	Interest Income.....	400	550
Interest Payable......	—	40	Interest Expense.....	360	320
Unearned Rent......	—	700			

Instructions:

(1) Journalize the adjusting entries that were posted to the ledger at the close of the fiscal year.

(2) Insert the letter "R" in the date column opposite each adjusting entry that should be reversed as of the first day of the following fiscal year.

Chapter 10

PLANT ASSETS AND INTANGIBLE ASSETS

NATURE OF PLANT ASSETS

"Long-lived" is a general term that may be applied to assets of a relatively fixed or permanent nature owned by a business enterprise. Such assets that are tangible in nature, used in the operations of the business, and not held for sale in the ordinary course of the business are classified on the balance sheet as *plant assets* or *fixed assets*. Other descriptive titles frequently employed are *property*, *plant*, and *equipment*, used either singly or in various combinations. The properties most frequently included in plant assets may be described in more specific terms as equipment, furniture, tools, machinery, buildings, and land. Although there is no standard criterion as to the minimum length of life necessary for classification as plant assets, they must be capable of repeated use and are ordinarily expected to last more than a year. However, the asset need not actually be used continuously or even frequently. Items of standby equipment held for use in the event of a breakdown of regular equipment or for use only during peak periods of activity are included in plant assets.

Assets acquired for purposes of resale in the normal course of business cannot be characterized as plant assets regardless of their durability or the length of time they are held. Thus, undeveloped land or other real estate acquired as a speculation should not be classified as plant assets. When equipment or machines are removed from service and held for sale, they cease to be plant assets.

INITIAL COSTS OF PLANT ASSETS

The initial cost of a plant asset includes all expenditures *necessary* to get it in place and ready for use. Expenditures for sales tax, transportation charges, insurance on the asset while in transit, special foundations, and installation costs should be added to the purchase price of the related plant asset. Similarly, when a secondhand asset is purchased, the initial costs of getting it ready for use, such as expenditures for new parts, repairs, and painting, are properly chargeable to the asset account. On the other hand, costs associated with the acquisition of plant assets that do not increase their utility should be excluded from the asset account. Expenditures resulting from carelessness or errors in installing the asset, from vandalism, or from other abnormal occurrences do not increase the utility of the asset and should be allocated to the period as an expense.

The cost of constructing a building includes the fees paid to architects and engineers for plans and supervision, insurance during construction, and all other necessary expenditures applicable to the project. Interest incurred during the construction period on money borrowed to finance a building project should be treated as an expense. It is a payment for the use of funds rather than an essential cost of the building.

The cost of land includes not only the negotiated price but broker's commissions, title fees, surveying fees, and other expenditures connected with securing title. If delinquent real estate taxes are assumed by the buyer, they also are chargeable to the land account. If unwanted buildings are located on land acquired for a plant site, the cost of their razing or removal, less any salvage recovered, is properly chargeable to the land account. The cost of leveling or otherwise permanently changing the contour is also an additional cost of the land.

Other expenditures related to the land may be charged to Land, Buildings, or Land Improvements, depending upon the circumstances. If the property owner bears the initial cost of paving the public street bordering his land, either by direct payment or by special tax assessment, the paving may be considered to be as permanent as the land. On the other hand, the cost of constructing walkways to and around the building may be added to the building account if the walkways are expected to last as long as the building. Expenditures for improvements that are neither as permanent as the land nor directly associated with the building may be segregated in a land improvements account and depreciated in accordance with their varying life spans. Some of the more usual items of this nature are trees and shrubs, fences, outdoor lighting systems, and paved parking areas.

NATURE OF DEPRECIATION

With the passage of time, all plant assets except land[1] lose their capacity to yield services. The several factors that contribute in varying degrees to the inexorable decline in utility are wear, deterioration, inadequacy, and obsolescence. Accordingly, the cost of such assets

[1]Land is here assumed to be used only as a site. Consideration will be given later in the chapter to land acquired for its mineral deposits or other natural resources.

should be transferred to the related expense accounts in a systematic manner during their expected useful life. This periodic cost expiration is called *depreciation*.

The factors contributing to decline in utility may be divided into two categories, *physical* depreciation, which includes wear attributable to use and deterioration from the action of the elements, and *functional* depreciation, which includes inadequacy and obsolescence. A plant asset becomes inadequate if its capacity is not sufficient to meet the demands of increased production. A plant asset is obsolete if the commodity that it produces is no longer in demand or if a newer machine can produce a commodity of superior quality or at a material reduction in cost. The continued acceleration of technological progress during this century has made obsolescence an increasingly important component of depreciation. Although the several factors comprising depreciation can be defined, it is not feasible to identify them when recording depreciation expense.

The meaning of the term "depreciation" as used in accounting is frequently misunderstood because the same term is also commonly used in business to connote a decline in the market value of an asset. The amount of unexpired cost of plant assets reported in the balance sheet is not likely to agree with the amount that could be realized from their sale. Plant assets are held for use in the enterprise rather than for sale. It is assumed that the enterprise will continue indefinitely as a going concern. Consequently the decision to dispose of a plant asset is based primarily on its utility to the enterprise, rather than the amount that could be realized from its sale.

Another common misunderstanding is that depreciation accounting automatically provides the cash required to replace plant assets as they wear out. The cash account is neither increased or decreased by the periodic entries that transfer the cost of plant assets to depreciation expense accounts. The misconception is doubtless attributable to the fact that, unlike most expenses, depreciation expense does not require an equivalent outlay of cash in the period in which the expense is recorded.

RECORDING DEPRECIATION

Depreciation may be recorded by an entry at the end of each month, or the adjustment may be postponed until the end of the fiscal year. The portion of the entry that records the decrease in the plant asset is credited to a *contra asset* account entitled Accumulated Depreciation or Allowance for Depreciation.[2] The use of a contra asset account permits the original

237

---

[2]Until fairly recent years, the term "Reserve for Depreciation" was used to describe the contra asset account. Because the older term was often misunderstood by readers of financial statements, it has been supplanted to a great extent, but still appears, particularly in the accounting literature.

cost to remain undisturbed in the plant asset account, which facilitates the computation of periodic depreciation, the listing of both cost and accumulated depreciation on the balance sheet, and the reporting required for property tax and income tax purposes.

An exception to the general procedure of recording depreciation monthly or annually is made when a plant asset is sold, traded in, or scrapped. In order to record the disposal properly, it is necessary to know not only the cost of the item but also the amount of its related accumulated depreciation. Hence, it is advisable to record the additional depreciation on the item for the current period before recording the transaction disposing of the asset. A further advantage of recording the depreciation at the time the accounts are relieved of the asset is that no additional attention need be given the transaction later when determining the amount of the periodic depreciation adjustment.

DETERMINING DEPRECIATION

The first factor to be considered in computing the periodic depreciation of a plant asset is its cost. The other two factors to be considered are the length of life of the asset and its market value at the time it is permanently retired from service. It is evident that neither of these two factors can be accurately determined until the asset is retired; they must be estimated at the time the asset is placed in service.

The estimated market value of a depreciable asset as of the time of its removal from service is variously termed *residual, scrap, salvage,* or *trade-in* value. The excess of cost over the estimated residual value is the amount that is to be recorded as depreciation expense during the asset's life. When residual value is expected to be insignificant in comparison with the cost of the asset, it is frequently ignored in computing depreciation.

There are no hard-and-fast rules for estimating either the period of usefulness of an asset or its residual value at the end of such period. The two factors, which are interrelated, may be affected to a considerable degree by management policies. The estimates of a company that provides its salesmen with a new automobile every year will differ from those of a firm that retains its cars for three years. Such variables as climate, frequency of use, maintenance, and minimum standards of efficiency will also affect the estimates.

Life estimates for depreciable assets are available in various trade association and other publications. Revenue Procedure 62-21, issued by the Internal Revenue Service (IRS) in 1962, provided depreciation "guidelines" classified according to the following types of enterprises: (1) business in general, (2) manufacturing, (3) transportation, communication, and public utilities, and (4) other nonmanufacturing. The lives suggested in the guidelines were applicable to about seventy-five

238

broad classes of assets. The guideline method of estimating depreciation was liberalized by legislation in 1971, followed by the issuance of Revenue Procedure 72-10 in 1972. The system is now referred to as the Asset Depreciation Range (ADR) system.

A much earlier publication of the IRS, identified as Bulletin F, provides life estimates of individual assets for more than a hundred industries and, in some instances, estimates for composite groups. For example, the individual life estimates for office equipment vary from 5 years for typewriters to 50 years for safes and vaults; the composite estimate for office equipment as a group is 15 years. The estimates contained in the IRS publications are suggestive rather than mandatory.

In addition to the many factors that may influence the life estimate of an asset, there is considerable latitude in the degree of exactitude used in the computation. A calendar month is ordinarily the smallest unit of time employed. When this time interval is adopted, all assets placed in service or retired from service during the first half of a month are treated as if the event had occurred on the first day of that month. Similarly, all plant asset additions and reductions during the second half of a month are considered to have occurred on the last day of that month. In the absence of any statement to the contrary, this practice will be assumed throughout this chapter.

It is not necessary that an enterprise employ a single method of computing depreciation for all classes of its depreciable assets. The methods adopted by management for use in the accounts and financial statements may also differ from the methods employed in determining income taxes and property taxes. The four methods used most frequently, *straight-line*, *units-of-production*, *declining-balance*, and *sum-of-the-years-digits*, are described and illustrated.

239

Straight-line method. The straight-line method of determining depreciation provides for equal periodic charges to expense over the estimated life of the asset. To illustrate this method, assume the cost of a depreciable asset to be $15,000, its estimated residual value to be $3,000, and its estimated life to be 10 years. The annual depreciation is computed as follows:

$$\frac{\$15,000 - \$3,000}{10 \text{ years}} = \$1,200 \text{ annual depreciation}$$

The annual depreciation of $1,200 would be prorated for the first and the last partial years of use. Assuming a fiscal year ending on December 31 and first use of the asset on September 15, the depreciation for that fiscal year would be $400 (4 months). If usage had begun on September 16, the depreciation for the year would be $300 (3 months).

The estimated life of a plant asset is frequently converted to an annual *depreciation rate* stated in the form of a percentage. It is usually assumed that the rate is applied to the cost of the asset rather than to the depreciable amount (cost less residual value). Thus, in the above example, the annual depreciation rate based on cost is $1,200 ÷ $15,000, or 8%. If the rate were to be applied to the depreciable amount, it would be $1,200 ÷ ($15,000 − $3,000), or 10%. If residual values are nominal in relationship to cost and are to be excluded from consideration, an estimated life can be converted directly to an annual rate. Thus, a life of 50 years can be said to be equivalent to a rate of 2%, 20 years to be equivalent to 5%, 8 years to be equivalent to 12½%, and so on.

The straight-line method is widely used. In addition to its simplicity, it provides a reasonable allocation of costs to periodic revenue when usage is relatively uniform from period to period.

Units-of-production method. The units-of-production method relates depreciation to the estimated productive capacity of the asset. Depreciation is first computed for an appropriate unit of production, such as hours, miles, or number of operations. The depreciation for each period is then determined by multiplication of the unit depreciation by the number of units used during the period. To illustrate, assume that a machine with a cost of $21,000 and estimated residual value of $1,000 is expected to have an estimated life of 40,000 hours. The depreciation for a unit of one hour is computed as follows:

$$\frac{\$21,000 - \$1,000}{40,000 \text{ hours}} = \$.50 \text{ an hour depreciation}$$

Assuming that the machine was in operation for 2,000 hours during a particular year, the depreciation for that year would be $.50 × 2,000, or $1,000.

When the amount of usage of a plant asset varies considerably from year to year, the units-of-production method is more logical than the straight-line method. It may yield fairer allocations of cost against periodic revenue.

Declining-balance method. The declining-balance method yields a declining periodic depreciation charge over the estimated life of the asset. Of several variants in technique, the most common is to apply double the straight-line depreciation rate, computed without regard to residual value, to the cost of the asset less its accumulated depreciation. Thus, for an asset with an estimated life of five years the rate would be double the straight-line rate of 20%, or 40%. The double rate is then applied to the cost of the asset for the first year of its use and thereafter to the declining book value (cost minus accumulated depreciation). The method is illustrated by the tabulation presented at the top of the next page.

Year	Cost	Accumulated Depreciation at Beginning of Year	Book Value at Beginning of Year	Rate	Depreciation for Year	Book Value at End of Year
1	$10,000	—	$10,000	40%	$4,000.00	$6,000.00
2	10,000	$4,000	6,000	40%	2,400.00	3,600.00
3	10,000	6,400	3,600	40%	1,440.00	2,160.00
4	10,000	7,840	2,160	40%	864.00	1,296.00
5	10,000	8,704	1,296	40%	518.40	777.60

It should be noted that estimated residual value is not considered in determining the depreciation rate. It is also ignored in computing periodic depreciation, except that the asset should not be depreciated below the estimated residual value. In the foregoing example it was assumed that the estimated residual value at the end of the fifth year approximates the book value of $777.60. If the residual value had been estimated at $1,000, the depreciation for the fifth year would have been $296 instead of $518.40.

There was an implicit assumption in the foregoing illustration that the first use of the asset coincided with the beginning of the fiscal year. This would seldom occur in actual practice, however, and would necessitate a slight variation in the computation for the first partial year of use. If the asset in the example had been placed in service at the end of the third month of the fiscal year, only the pro rata portion of the first full year's depreciation, $9/12 \times (40\% \times \$10,000)$, or $3,000, would be allocated to the first fiscal year. The method of computing the depreciation for subsequent years would not be affected. Thus, the depreciation for the second fiscal year, to continue the illustration, would be $40\% \times (\$10,000 - \$3,000)$, or $2,800.

The declining-balance method is widely used in computing depreciation for purposes of the federal income tax. Acceleration of the "write-off" of the asset reduces the income tax expense in the earlier years and correspondingly increases the amount of funds available to pay for the asset or for other purposes. The method is appropriate for accounting and financial reporting purposes in situations in which the decline in productivity or earning power of the asset is proportionately greater in the early years of its use than in later years. Further justification for its use is based on the tendency of repairs to increase with the age of an asset. The reduced amounts of depreciation in later years are therefore offset to some extent by increased maintenance expenses.

Sum-of-the-years-digits method. The sum-of-the-years-digits method yields results similar to those obtained by use of the declining-balance method. The periodic charge for depreciation declines steadily over the estimated life of the asset because a successively smaller fraction is applied each year to the original cost of the asset less the estimated residual value.

241

The denominator of the fraction, which remains constant, is the sum of the digits representing the years of life. The numerator of the fraction, which changes each year, is the number of remaining years of life. Thus, for an asset with an estimated life of 5 years the denominator[3] is $5 + 4 + 3 + 2 + 1$, or 15; for the first year the numerator is 5, for the second year 4, and so on. The method is illustrated by the following depreciation schedule for an asset with an assumed cost of $16,000, residual value of $1,000, and life of 5 years:

Year	Cost Less Residual Value	Rate	Depreciation for Year	Accumulated Depreciation at End of Year	Book Value at End of Year
1	$15,000	5/15	$5,000	$ 5,000	$11,000
2	15,000	4/15	4,000	9,000	7,000
3	15,000	3/15	3,000	12,000	4,000
4	15,000	2/15	2,000	14,000	2,000
5	15,000	1/15	1,000	15,000	1,000

When the first use of the asset does not coincide with the beginning of a fiscal year, it is necessary to allocate each full year's depreciation between the two fiscal years benefited. Assuming that the asset in the example was placed in service after three months of the fiscal year had elapsed, the depreciation for that fiscal year would be $9/12 \times (5/15 \times \$15,000)$, or $3,750. The depreciation for the second year would be $4,250, computed as follows:

$$3/12 \times (5/15 \times \$15,000) \dots\dots\dots\dots \quad \$1,250$$
$$9/12 \times (4/15 \times \$15,000) \dots\dots\dots\dots \quad 3,000$$

Total, second fiscal year $4,250

Comparison of depreciation methods. The straight-line method provides for uniform periodic charges to depreciation expense over the life of the asset. The declining-balance method and the sum-of-the-years-digits method provide for a declining periodic charge to expense over the life of the asset. The latter methods are frequently referred to as *accelerated depreciation* methods because they provide for higher depreciation charges in the early years of use of the asset and lower depreciation charges in the later years. The periodic depreciation charges for these three methods, based on an item with a cost of $15,000, an estimated life of 5 years, and no residual value, are depicted graphically at the top of the next page.

The units-of-production method provides for periodic charges to depreciation expense that may vary considerably from year to year depending upon the amount of usage of the asset.

---

[3]The denominator can also be determined from the following formula where S = sum of the digits and N = number of years of estimated life:

$$S = N\left(\frac{N+1}{2}\right)$$

242

Straight-line method	Declining-balance method	Sum-of-the-years-digits method

Comparison of depreciation methods

CAPITAL AND REVENUE EXPENDITURES

In addition to the initial cost of acquiring a plant asset, other costs related to its efficiency or capacity may be incurred from time to time during its service life. It is often difficult to recognize the difference between expenditures that add to the utility of the asset for more than one accounting period and those that benefit only the period in which they are incurred. Costs that add to the utility for more than one period are chargeable to an asset account or to a related accumulated depreciation account; they are termed *capital expenditures*. Expenditures that benefit only the current period are chargeable to expense accounts; they are referred to as *revenue expenditures*.

Expenditures for an addition to a plant asset clearly constitute capital expenditures. For example, the cost of installing an air conditioning unit in an automobile or of adding a wing to a building should be debited to the respective asset accounts. It is equally clear that expenditures for maintenance and repairs of a recurring nature should be classified as revenue expenditures. Thus, the cost of replacing spark plugs in an automobile or of repainting a building should be debited to appropriate expense accounts. In less obvious situations, several criteria may be considered in classifying the expenditures.

Expenditures that increase operating efficiency or capacity for the remaining useful life of an asset should be capitalized; that is, they should be treated as capital expenditures. For example, if the power unit attached to a machine is replaced by one of greater capacity, the cost and the accumulated depreciation applicable to the old motor should be removed from the accounts and the cost of the new one added to the asset account.

Expenditures that increase the useful life of an asset beyond the original estimate are also capital expenditures. They should be debited to the accumulated depreciation account, however, rather than to the asset account. To illustrate, assume that a machine with an estimated

243

life of ten years is substantially rebuilt at the end of its seventh year of use, and that the extraordinary repairs are expected to extend the life of the machine an additional three years beyond the original estimate. In such circumstances the expenditures may be said to restore or "make good" a portion of the depreciation accumulated in prior years, and it is therefore appropriate that they be debited to the accumulated depreciation account.

When the cost of improvements or extraordinary repairs is substantial or when there is a material change in estimated life, the periodic depreciation allocable to future periods should be redetermined on the basis of the new book value of the asset and the new estimate of the remaining useful life.

Expenditures that are minor in amount are usually treated as repair expense even though they may have the characteristics of capital expenditures. The consequent saving in time and clerical expenses justifies the sacrifice of a small degree of accuracy. Some businesses establish a minimum amount required to classify an item as a capital expenditure.

DISPOSAL OF PLANT ASSETS

Plant assets that are no longer useful may be discarded, sold, or applied toward the purchase of other plant assets. The details of the entry to record the disposal will vary, but in all cases it is necessary to remove the book value of the asset from the accounts. This is accomplished by debiting the appropriate accumulated depreciation account for the total depreciation to the date of disposal and crediting the asset account for the cost of the asset.

A plant asset should not be removed from the accounts solely because it has been depreciated for the full period of its estimated life. If the asset is still useful to the enterprise, the cost and accumulated depreciation should remain in the ledger. Otherwise the accounts would contain no evidence of the continued existence of such plant assets and the control function of the ledger would be impaired. In addition, the cost and the accumulated depreciation data on such assets are frequently needed in reporting for property tax and income tax purposes.

Discarding plant assets. When plant assets are no longer useful to the business and have no market value, they are discarded. If the asset has been fully depreciated, no loss is realized. To illustrate, assume that an item of equipment acquired at a cost of $1,000 became fully depreciated at December 31, the close of the preceding fiscal year, and is now to be discarded as worthless. The entry to record the disposal is illustrated at the top of the next page.

Mar.	24	Accumulated Depreciation — Equipment....	1,000	
		Equipment............................		1,000
		To write off equipment discarded.		

If the accumulated depreciation applicable to the $1,000 of discarded equipment had been less than $1,000, there would have been a loss on its disposal. Furthermore, it would have been necessary to record depreciation for the three months of use in the current period before recording the disposal. To illustrate these variations, assume that annual depreciation on the equipment is computed at 10% of cost and that the accumulated depreciation balance is $767 after the annual adjusting entry at the end of the preceding year. The entry to record depreciation of $25 for the three months of the current period is as follows:

Mar.	24	Depreciation Expense — Equipment........	25	
		Accumulated Depreciation — Equipment..		25
		To record current depreciation on equip-		
		ment discarded.		

The equipment is then removed from the accounts and the loss is recorded by the following entry:

245

Mar.	24	Accumulated Depreciation — Equipment....	792	
		Loss on Disposal of Plant Assets............	208	
		Equipment............................		1,000
		To write off equipment discarded.		

Ordinary losses and gains on the disposal of plant assets are non-operating items and may be reported in the Other Expense and Other Income sections, respectively, of the income statement.

Sale of plant assets. The entry to record the sale of a plant asset is similar to the entries illustrated in the preceding section, except that the cash or other asset received must also be recorded. If the selling price exceeds the book value of the asset, the transaction results in a gain; if the selling price is less than the book value, there is a loss. To illustrate various possibilities, assume that equipment acquired at a cost of $10,000 and depreciated at the annual rate of 10% of cost is sold for cash on October 12 of the eighth year of its use. The accumulated depreciation in the account as of the preceding December 31 is $7,000. The entry to record the depreciation for the nine months of the current year is illustrated at the top of the next page.

Oct.	12	Depreciation Expense — Equipment.........	750	
		Accumulated Depreciation — Equipment.		750
		To record current depreciation on equipment sold.		

After recording the current depreciation, the book value of the asset is $2,250. Entries to record the sale, in general journal form, are presented below, under three different assumptions as to selling price.

Sold at book value, for $2,250. *No gain or loss.*

Oct. 12	Cash..................................	2,250	
	Accumulated Depreciation—Equipment........	7,750	
	Equipment..............................		10,000

Sold below book value, for $1,000. *Loss of $1,250.*

Oct. 12	Cash..................................	1,000	
	Accumulated Depreciation—Equipment........	7,750	
	Loss on Disposal of Plant Assets...............	1,250	
	Equipment..............................		10,000

Sold above book value, for $3,000. *Gain of $750.*

Oct. 12	Cash..................................	3,000	
	Accumulated Depreciation—Equipment........	7,750	
	Equipment..............................		10,000
	Gain on Disposal of Plant Assets.............		750

246

Exchange of plant assets. Old equipment is frequently traded in for new equipment having a similar use. The trade-in allowance is deducted from the price of the new equipment, and the balance owed ("boot") is paid in accordance with the credit terms. If the trade-in allowance granted by the seller is greater than the book value of the asset traded in, there is a gain on disposal; if it is less than the book value, there is a loss.

The Internal Revenue Code (IRC) requires that gains and losses from such transactions not be recognized for income tax purposes if (1) the asset acquired by the taxpayer is similar in use to the asset given in exchange and (2) any boot involved is given (rather than received) by the taxpayer. The gain or loss not recognized affects the cost basis of the plant asset acquired and the amount of depreciation expense deductible in subsequent years. Both methods of recording an exchange are illustrated below, based on the following data:

Equipment traded in (old):

Cost of old equipment.......................		$4,000
Accumulated depreciation at end of preceding year.	$2,800	
Depreciation for current year (to be recorded)..	400	3,200
Book value at date of exchange................		$ 800

Equipment acquired (new):

Price of new equipment......................		$5,000
Trade-in allowance on old equipment..........		1,100
Cash paid (boot)............................		$3,900

Current depreciation of $400 would be recorded in the usual manner before proceeding to record the details of the acquisition and trade-in.

Gain or loss recognized on exchange. The amount of the gain or loss realized on trading in the old equipment may be determined as follows:

Trade-in allowance on old equipment...........	$1,100
Book value of old equipment at date of exchange.	800
Gain on exchange.............................	$ 300

The compound entry to record the exchange of the old asset for the new, the payment of cash, and the gain realized, in general journal form, is as follows:

June 19 Accumulated Depreciation — Equipment....	3,200	
Equipment..............................	5,000	
Equipment............................		4,000
Cash.................................		3,900
Gain on Disposal of Plant Assets..........		300

Gain or loss not recognized on exchange. When the gain or loss is not recognized as such, it is given effect in determining the cost basis of the new asset. The computation may be made by either of two methods: (1) deduct the unrecognized gain or add the unrecognized loss to the price of the new asset or (2) add the boot given to the book value of the old asset. The two methods are illustrated below, based on the transaction data presented earlier in this section.

(1)	Price of new equipment...........	$5,000
	Less unrecognized gain on exchange.	300
	Cost of new equipment...........	$4,700

(2)	Book value of old equipment.......	$ 800
	Boot given (cash paid)...........	3,900
	Cost of new equipment...........	$4,700

The compound entry to record the exchange and the payment of cash, in general journal form, is as follows:

June 19 Accumulated Depreciation — Equipment.....	3,200	
Equipment.............................	4,700	
Equipment............................		4,000
Cash.................................		3,900

The nonrecognition of gain or loss at the time of the exchange is in reality a postponement. The amount of periodic depreciation on the new equipment allowable for federal income tax purposes is based on a cost of $4,700 rather than on the quoted price of $5,000. The unrecognized gain of $300 at the time of the exchange will be matched by a reduction of $300 in the total amount of depreciation expense allowed during the life of the asset.

The complications that arise from having two different cost bases for a plant asset, one in the ledger and the other for income tax purposes, can be avoided by adopting the tax method of recording exchanges. This is frequently done where the effect on data reported in the financial statements is not material.

SUBSIDIARY LEDGERS FOR PLANT ASSETS

When depreciation is to be computed individually on a substantial number of assets comprising a functional group, it is advisable to maintain a subsidiary ledger. To illustrate, assume that an enterprise owns about 200 individual items of office equipment with an aggregate cost of approximately $100,000. Unless the business is newly organized, the equipment would have been acquired over a number of years. The individual cost, estimated residual value, and estimated life would vary in any case, and the composition of the group will continually change as a result of acquisitions and disposals.

There are many variations in the form of subsidiary records for depreciable assets. Multicolumn analysis sheets may be employed, or a separate ledger account may be maintained for each asset. The form should be designed to provide spaces for recording the acquisition and the disposal of the asset, the depreciation charged each period, the accumulated depreciation to date, and any other pertinent data desired. An example of a subsidiary ledger account for a plant asset is illustrated below:

PLANT ASSET RECORD

Account No. 123-215

Item: Bookkeeping machine General Ledger Account: Office Equipment
Serial No. AT 47-3926 Description: Accounts receivable posting
From Whom Purchased: Hamilton Office Machines Co., Inc.
Estimated Life 10 years Estimated Scrap or Trade-In Value $500 Depreciation per Year $240

DATE MO.	DAY	YR.	EXPLANATION	ASSET DEBIT	CREDIT	BALANCE	ACCUMULATED DEPRECIATION DEBIT	CREDIT	BALANCE	BOOK VALUE
4	8	73		2,900		2,900				2,900
12	31	73						180	180	2,720
12	31	74						240	420	2,480

An account in the office equipment ledger

The number assigned to the account illustrated is composed of the number of the office equipment account in the general ledger (123) followed by the number assigned to the specific item of office equipment purchased (215). An identification tag or plaque with the corresponding account number is attached to the asset. Depreciation for the year in which the asset was acquired, computed for nine months on a straight-line basis, is $180; for the following year it is $240. These amounts, together with the corresponding amounts from all other accounts in the subsidiary ledger, provide the figures for the respective year-end adjusting entries debiting the depreciation expense account and crediting the accumulated depreciation account.

The sum of the asset balances and the sum of the accumulated depreciation balances in all of the accounts should be compared periodically with the balances of their respective controlling accounts in the general ledger. When a particular asset is disposed of, the asset section of the subsidiary account is credited and the accumulated depreciation section is debited, reducing the balances of both sections to zero. The account is then removed from the ledger and filed for possible future reference.

Subsidiary ledgers for plant assets are useful to the accounting department in (1) determining the periodic depreciation expense, (2) recording the disposal of individual items, (3) preparing tax returns, and (4) preparing insurance claims in the event of insured losses. The forms may also be expanded to provide spaces for accumulating data on the operating efficiency of the asset. Such information as frequency of breakdowns, length of time out of service, and cost of repairs is useful in comparing similar equipment produced by different manufacturers. When new equipment is to be purchased, the data are useful to management in deciding upon size, model, and other specifications and the best source of supply.

Regardless of whether subsidiary equipment ledgers are maintained, plant assets should be inspected periodically in order to ascertain their state of repair and whether or not they are still in use.

DEPRECIATION BASED ON AVERAGES

In the preceding illustrations, depreciation has been computed on each individual plant asset and, unless otherwise stated, this procedure will be assumed in the problem materials at the end of the chapter. An alternative procedure is to determine depreciation for entire groups of assets by use of a single rate. The basis for grouping may be similarity in life estimates or other common characteristics, or it may be broadened to include all assets within a functional class, such as office equipment.

When depreciation is computed on the basis of a composite group of assets of differing life spans, it is necessary to develop a rate based on averages. This may be done by (1) computing the annual depreciation

249

for each asset, (2) determining the total annual depreciation, and (3) dividing the sum thus obtained by the total cost of the assets. The procedure is illustrated below.

ASSET No.	COST	RESIDUAL VALUE	ESTIMATED LIFE	ANNUAL DEPRECIATION
101	$ 20,000	$4,000	10 years	$ 1,600
102	15,600	1,500	15 years	940
147	41,000	1,000	8 years	5,000
Total	$473,400			$49,707

Composite rate: **$49,707 ÷ $473,400 = 10.5%**

Although new assets of varying life spans and residual values will be added to the group and old assets will be retired from time to time, the "mix" is assumed to remain relatively unchanged. Accordingly, a depreciation rate based on averages (10.5% in the illustration) also remains unchanged for an indefinite time in the future.

When a composite rate is used, it may be applied against total asset cost on a monthly basis, or some reasonable assumption may be made regarding the timing of increases and decreases in the group. A common practice is to assume that all additions and retirements have occurred uniformly throughout the year; the composite rate is then applied to the average of the beginning and the ending balances of the account. Another acceptable averaging technique is to assume that all additions and retirements during the first half of the year occurred as of the first day of the year, and that all additions and retirements during the second half occurred on the last day of the year.

When assets within the composite group are retired, no gain or loss should be recognized. Instead, the asset account is credited for the cost of the asset and the accumulated depreciation account is debited for the excess of cost over the amount realized from the disposal. Any deficiency in the amount of depreciation recorded on the shorter-lived assets is presumed to be balanced by excessive depreciation on the longer-lived assets.

Regardless of whether depreciation is computed for each individual unit or for composite groups, the periodic depreciation charge is based on estimates. The effect of obsolescence and inadequacy on the life of plant assets is particularly difficult to forecast. Any system that provides for the allocation of depreciation in a systematic and rational manner fulfills the requirements of good accounting.

DEPRECIATION OF PLANT ASSETS OF LOW UNIT COST

Subsidiary ledgers are not ordinarily maintained for classes of plant assets that are composed of numerous individual items of low unit cost.

250

Hand tools and other portable equipment of small size and value are typical examples. Because of hard usage, breakage, and pilferage, such assets may be relatively short-lived and require constant replacement. In such circumstances the usual depreciation methods are impracticable. One common method of determining cost expiration is to take a periodic inventory of the items on hand, estimate their fair value based on original cost, and transfer the remaining amount from the asset account to an appropriately titled account, such as Tools Expense. Other categories to which the same method is often applied are dies, molds, patterns, and spare parts.

REPORTING PLANT ASSETS AND DEPRECIATION EXPENSE IN THE FINANCIAL STATEMENTS

The balance of each major class of depreciable assets should be disclosed in the financial statements or in notes thereto, together with the related accumulated depreciation, either by major class or in total.[4] A more compact arrangement than that employed in earlier chapters is illustrated below:

Dexter Custom Cabinets
Balance Sheet
December 31, 19--

Assets				
Total current assets...				$262,500
		ACCUMULATED	BOOK	
Plant assets:	COST	DEPRECIATION	VALUE	
Office equipment.............	$ 20,000	$ 3,000	$ 17,000	
Factory equipment...........	250,000	92,000	158,000	
Buildings....................	100,000	26,000	74,000	
Land......................	10,000	—	10,000	
Total plant assets...........	$380,000	$121,000		259,000

When the classes of plant assets are too numerous to permit such detailed listing on the balance sheet, a single figure may be presented, supported by a separate schedule.

The amount of depreciation expense for the period should be set forth separately on the income statement or disclosed in some other manner. A general description of the method or methods used in computing depreciation should also accompany the financial statements.[5]

---

[4]*Opinions of the Accounting Principles Board, No. 12*, "Omnibus Opinion—1967" (New York: American Institute of Certified Public Accountants, 1967), par. 5.
[5]*Opinions of the Accounting Principles Board, No. 22*, "Disclosure of Accounting Policies" (New York: American Institute of Certified Public Accountants, 1972), par. 13.

DEPLETION

The cost of metal ores and other minerals removed from the earth is called *depletion*. The amount of the periodic cost allocation is based on the relationship of the cost to the estimated magnitude of the mineral deposit, and the quantity extracted during the particular period. To illustrate, assume that the cost of certain mineral rights is $400,000 and that the deposit is estimated at 1,000,000 tons of ore of uniform grade. The depletion rate is accordingly $400,000 ÷ 1,000,000, or $.40 a ton. If 90,000 tons are mined during the year, the depletion, amounting to $36,000, would be recorded by the following entry:

			Adjusting Entry		
Dec.	31	Depletion Expense......................	36,000		
		Accumulated Depletion.................		36,000	

The accumulated depletion account is a contra asset account and is presented in the balance sheet as a deduction from the cost of the mineral deposit.

In determining income subject to the federal income tax, the IRC permits, with certain limitations, a depletion deduction equal to a specified percent of gross income from the extractive operations. Thus for income tax purposes it is possible for aggregate depletion deductions to exceed the cost of the property. The percentage allowance for oil and gas wells is 22%. Percentage allowances for mines and other natural deposits range from 5% to 22%. Detailed examination of the tax law and regulations regarding "percentage depletion" is beyond the scope of this discussion. The subject is introduced here because of frequent references to percentage depletion, particularly of oil wells, in the financial press.

INTANGIBLE ASSETS

Long-lived assets useful in the operations of an enterprise that are not held for sale and have no physical qualities are usually classified as *intangible assets*. The basic principles applicable to the accounting for intangible assets are similar to those described earlier for plant assets. The major concerns are the determination of the initial costs and the recognition of periodic cost expiration, called *amortization*, attributable to the passage of time or a decline in utility.

Intangible assets are ordinarily presented in the balance sheet as a separate section following plant assets. Intangible assets frequently include patents, copyrights, and goodwill.

Patents. Manufacturers may acquire exclusive rights to produce and sell commodities with one or more unique features. Such rights are evidenced by *patents*, which are issued to inventors by the federal government. They continue in effect for 17 years. An enterprise may obtain patents on new products developed in its own research laboratories or it may purchase patent rights from others. The initial cost of purchased patents should be debited to an asset account and then written off, or amortized, over the years of its expected usefulness. This period of time may be less than the remaining legal life of the patent, and the expectations are also subject to change in the future.

To illustrate, assume that at the beginning of its fiscal year an enterprise acquires for $100,000 a patent granted six years earlier. Although the patent will not expire for another eleven years, it is expected to be of value for only five years. The entry to amortize the patent at the end of the fiscal year is as follows:

			Adjusting Entry		
Dec.	31	Amortization of Patents...................	20,000		
		Patents.............................		20,000	

Continuing the illustration, assume that after two years of use it appears that the patent will cease to have value at the end of an additional two years. The cost to be amortized in the third year would be the balance of the asset account, $60,000, divided by the remaining two years, or $30,000.

The cost of obtaining patents from the government is usually nominal. The cost of the experimental work leading to the development of a new product may be substantial and in theory should be treated as an asset in the same manner as patent rights purchased from others. In practice, however, the effort required to obtain a reasonably fair cost figure for each patent may be such as to make it impracticable. A number of research projects may be in process simultaneously, work on some projects may extend over a number of years, and, perhaps most important of all, there is ordinarily no assurance of ultimate success of a project. Accordingly, many enterprises treat their normally recurring expenditures for research and development as current operating expenses.

253

Copyrights. The exclusive right to publish and sell a literary, artistic, or musical composition is obtained by a *copyright*. Copyrights are issued by the federal government and extend for 28 years with the privilege of renewal for a like term. The costs assigned to a copyright include all costs of creating the work plus the cost of obtaining the copyright. A copyright that is purchased from another should be recorded at the price paid for it. Because of the uncertainty regarding the useful life of a copyright, it is usually amortized over a relatively short period of time.

Goodwill. In the sense that it is used in business, *goodwill* is an intangible asset that attaches to a business as a result of such favorable factors as location, product superiority, reputation, and managerial skill. Its existence is evidenced by the ability of the business to earn a rate of return on the investment that is in excess of the normal rate for other firms in the same line of business.

Accountants are in general agreement that goodwill should be recognized in the accounts only if it can be objectively determined by an event or transaction, such as a purchase or sale. Accountants also agree that the value of goodwill eventually disappears and that the recorded costs should be amortized over the years during which the goodwill is expected to be of value. The period of amortization should not, however, exceed 40 years.[6]

QUESTIONS

1. Which of the following qualities of an asset are characteristic of *plant assets?*

(a) Long-lived.
(b) Intangible.
(c) Held for sale in normal course of business.
(d) Used continuously in operations of the business.
(e) Capable of repeated use in operations of the business.
(f) Tangible.

2. Indicate which of the following expenditures incurred in connection with the acquisition of a lathe should be charged to the asset account: (a) insurance while in transit, (b) freight charges, (c) sales tax on purchase price, (d) new parts to replace those damaged in unloading, (e) cost of special foundation, (f) fee paid to factory representative for assembling and adjusting.

3. Which of the following expenditures incurred in connection with the purchase of a secondhand printing press should be debited to the asset account: (a) new parts to replace those worn out, (b) freight charges, (c) interest on funds borrowed to make the purchase, (d) installation costs?

4. In order to increase its parking area, Country Fair Shopping Center acquired adjoining land for $40,000 and a building located on the land for $15,000. The net cost of razing the building and leveling the land after deducting amounts received from sale of salvaged building materials, was $1,500. What accounts should be debited for (a) the $40,000, (b) the $15,000, (c) the $1,500?

5. Are the amounts at which plant assets are reported on the balance sheet their approximate market values as of the balance sheet date? Discuss.

---

[6]*Opinions of the Accounting Principles Board, No. 17,* "Intangible Assets" (New York: American Institute of Certified Public Accountants, 1970), par. 29.

6. (a) Describe the nature of depreciation as the term is used in accounting. (b) Does the recognition of depreciation in the accounts provide a special cash fund for the replacement of plant assets?

7. What three factors must be considered in computing the periodic depreciation of a plant asset?

8. (a) What is the nature of the account Accumulated Depreciation? (b) What is the normal balance of the account? (c) Do credits to the account increase or decrease the account balance? (d) What is meant by the term *book value*, as applied to a plant asset? (e) Do credits to Accumulated Depreciation increase or decrease the book value of plant assets?

9. Why is it advisable, when a plant asset is to be sold, traded in, or scrapped, to first record depreciation on the asset for the current period?

10. Convert each of the following life estimates to a straight-line depreciation rate, stated as a percent, assuming that residual value of the plant asset is to be ignored: (a) 4 years, (b) 5 years, (c) 8 years, (d) 10 years, (e) 20 years, (f) 25 years, (g) 40 years.

11. A plant asset with a cost of $15,000 has an estimated residual value of $1,500 and an estimated life of 10 years. (a) What is the amount of the annual depreciation, computed by the straight-line method? (b) The amount of the annual depreciation is what percent of the cost of the asset?

12. The declining-balance method, at double the straight-line rate, is to be used for an asset with a cost of $6,000, estimated residual value of $400, and estimated life of 10 years. What is the depreciation for the first fiscal year, assuming that the asset was placed in service at the beginning of the year?

255

13. An asset with a cost of $11,250, an estimated residual value of $750, and an estimated life of 6 years is to be depreciated by the sum-of-the-years-digits method. (a) What is the denominator of the depreciation fraction? (b) What is the amount of depreciation for the first full year of use? (c) What is the amount of depreciation for the second full year of use?

14. Differentiate between capital expenditures and revenue expenditures.

15. Immediately after a used truck is acquired, a new motor is installed and the tires are replaced at a total cost of $600. Is this a capital expenditure or a revenue expenditure?

16. For a number of subsidiary plant ledger accounts of an enterprise, the balance in accumulated depreciation is exactly equal to the cost of the asset. (a) Is it permissible to record additional depreciation on the assets if they are still in use? (b) When should an entry be made to remove the cost and accumulated depreciation from the accounts?

17. In what sections of the income statement are gains and losses from the disposal of plant assets presented?

18. A plant asset priced at $25,000 is acquired by trading in a similar asset and paying cash for the remainder. (a) Assuming the trade-in allowance to be $7,000, what is the amount of "boot" given? (b) Assuming the book value of the asset traded in to be $5,000, what is the amount of gain or loss on the exchange? (c) What is the cost basis of the new asset for the computation of depreciation for federal income tax purposes?

19. The cost of a composite group of equipment is $250,000 and the annual depreciation, computed on the individual items, totals $25,000. (a) What is the composite straight-line depreciation rate? (b) What would the rate be if the total depreciation amounted to $20,000 instead of $25,000?

20. What is the term applied to the periodic charge for ore removed from a mine?

21. What is the term applied to the periodic write-off of the cost of intangible assets?

22. (a) Over what period of time should the initial cost of a patent be amortized? (b) For what period of time is a patent granted?

EXERCISES

10-1. An item of equipment acquired on January 7 at a cost of $105,000 has an estimated life of 20 years. Assuming that it will have no residual value, determine the depreciation for each of the first two years (a) by the straight-line method, (b) by the declining-balance method, using twice the straight-line rate, and (c) by the sum-of-the-years-digits method.

10-2. A diesel-powered generator with a cost of $50,000 and estimated salvage value of $5,000 is expected to have a useful operating life of 150,000 hours. During April the generator was operated 520 hours. Determine the depreciation for the month.

10-3. Balances in Trucks and Accumulated Depreciation — Trucks at the end of the year prior to adjustment are $39,900 and $22,100 respectively. Details of the subsidiary ledger are presented below. (a) Determine the depreciation rates per mile and the amount to be credited to the accumulated depreciation section of each of the subsidiary accounts for the current year. (b) Present the general journal entry to record depreciation for the year.

Truck No.	Cost	Residual Value	Useful Life in Miles	Accumulated Depreciation at Beginning of Year	Miles Operated During Year
1	$ 9,500	$ 400	140,000	$4,550	20,000
2	8,800	1,000	150,000	6,700	12,000
3	7,600	500	100,000	6,350	14,000
4	14,000	1,200	200,000	4,500	25,000

10-4. A plant asset acquired at the beginning of the fiscal year at a cost of $17,800 has an estimated trade-in value of $1,600 and an estimated useful life of 8 years. Determine the following: (a) the amount of annual depreciation by the straight-line method, (b) the amount of depreciation for the second year computed by the declining-balance method (at twice the straight-line rate), (c) the amount of depreciation for the second year computed by the sum-of-the-years-digits method.

10-5. An item of equipment acquired at a cost of $7,500 has an estimated residual value of $500 and an estimated life of 4 years. It was placed in service on March 29 of the current fiscal year, which ends on December 31. Determine the depreciation for the current fiscal year and for the following fiscal year (a) by the declining-balance method, at twice the straight-line rate, and (b) by the sum-of-the-years-digits method.

10-6. A number of major structural repairs completed at the beginning of the current fiscal year at a cost of $80,000 are expected to extend the life of a building ten years beyond the original estimate. The original cost of the building was $400,000 and it has been depreciated by the straight-line method for 25 years. Residual value is expected to be negligible and has been ignored. The related accumulated depreciation account after the depreciation adjustment at the end of the preceding year is $250,000. (a) What has the amount of annual depreciation been in past years? (b) To what account should the $80,000 be debited? (c) What is the book value of the building after the repairs have been recorded? (d) What is the amount of depreciation for the current year, using the straight-line method (assume that the repairs were completed at the very beginning of the year)?

10-7. On September 27 Austin Co. acquired a new data processing machine with a list price of $37,500, receiving a trade-in allowance of $2,700 on old equipment of a similar type, paying cash of $6,800, and giving a note for the remainder. The following information about the old equipment is obtained from the account in the office equipment ledger: cost, $18,250; accumulated depreciation on December 31, the close of the preceding fiscal year, $12,100; annual depreciation, $2,200. Present entries, in general journal form, to record the following: (a) current depreciation on the old equipment to date of trade-in, (b) the transaction on September 27, assuming that gain or loss is to be recognized, (c) the transaction on September 27, assuming that gain or loss is not to be recognized.

10-8. On the first day of the fiscal year a delivery truck with a list price of $6,500 was acquired in an exchange transaction in which there was a gain of $800. The new truck is to be depreciated over 5 years by the straight-line method, assuming a trade-in value of $500. Determine the following: (a) annual depreciation, assuming that the gain was recognized, (b) annual depreciation assuming that the gain was not recognized, (c) the quantitative effect of the unrecognized gain on the annual depreciation computed in (b).

10-9. Details of a plant asset account for the fiscal year ended December 31 are presented below. A composite depreciation rate of 11% is applied annually to the account. Determine the depreciation for the year according to each of the following assumptions: (a) that all additions and retirements have occurred uniformly throughout the year and (b) that additions and retirements during the first half of the year occurred on the first day of the year and those during the second half occurred on the last day of the year.

FACTORY EQUIPMENT

Jan. 1	Balance	226,700	Apr. 3		8,500
Feb. 27		6,700	June 17		2,900
May 11		3,400	Nov. 25		6,400
Aug. 8		11,800			
Oct. 31		2,700			

10-10. On July 1 of the current fiscal year ending December 31, Hart Company acquired a patent for $50,000 and mineral rights for $150,000. The patent, which expires in 13 years, is expected to have value for 5 years; the mineral deposit is estimated at 600,000 tons of ore of uniform grade. Present entries to record the following for the current year: (a) amortization of the patent, (b) depletion, assuming that 60,000 tons were mined during the year.

PROBLEMS

The following additional problems for this chapter are located in Appendix B: 10-1B, 10-2B, 10-3B, 10-4B, and 10-6B.

10-1A. The following expenditures and receipts are related to land, land improvements, and buildings acquired for use in a business enterprise. The receipts are identified by an asterisk.

(a)	Cost of real estate acquired as a plant site: Land........	$ 50,000
	Building......	30,000
(b)	Fee paid to attorney for title search....................	425
(c)	Delinquent real estate taxes on property, assumed by purchaser..	3,500
(d)	Cost of razing and removing the building..............	4,000
(e)	Architect's and engineer's fees for plans and supervision...	49,000
(f)	Premium on 1-year insurance policy during construction..	4,500
(g)	Cost of land fill and grading.........................	1,750
(h)	Paid to building contractor for new building...........	700,000
(i)	Cost of repairing windstorm damage during construction..	1,500
(j)	Cost of paving parking lot to be used by customers.......	3,500
(k)	Cost of trees and shrubbery, planted..................	750
(l)	Special assessment paid to city for extension of water main to the property.....................................	500
(m)	Real estate taxes accrued during construction...........	2,150
(n)	Interest accrued on building loan during construction....	18,000
(o)	Cost of floodlights on parking lot, installed.............	1,250
(p)	Cost of repairing vandalism damage during construction..	250
(q)	Proceeds from sale of salvage materials from old building..	800*
(r)	Money borrowed to pay building contractor...........	450,000*
(s)	Proceeds from insurance company for windstorm damage.	1,400*
(t)	Refund of premium on insurance policy (f) canceled after 11 months.......................................	300*
		$418,575

Instructions:

(1) Assign each expenditure and receipt (indicate receipts by an asterisk) to Land (permanently capitalized), Land Improvements (limited life), Building, or "Other Accounts." Identify each item by letter and list the amounts in columnar form, as follows:

Item	Land	Land Improvements	Building	Other Accounts
	$	$	$	$

(2) Total the amount columns.

10-2A. An item of new equipment acquired at a cost of $50,000 at the beginning of a fiscal year has an estimated life of 5 years and an estimated trade-in value of $5,000. The manager requested information (details given in Instruction 1) regarding the effect of alternative methods on the amount of depreciation expense deductible each year for federal income tax purposes.

Upon the basis of the data presented to the manager in accordance with Instruction 1, the declining-balance method was elected. In the first week of the fifth year the equipment was traded in for similar equipment priced at $72,500. The trade-in allowance on the old equipment was $7,500, cash of $15,000 was paid, and a note payable was issued for the balance.

Instructions:

(1) Determine the annual depreciation for each of the estimated 5 years of use, the accumulated depreciation at the end of each year, and the book value of the equipment at the end of each year by (a) the straight-line method, (b) the declining-balance method (at twice the straight-line rate), and (c) the sum-of-the-years-digits method. The following columnar headings are suggested for each schedule:

Year	Depreciation Expense	Accumulated Depreciation End of Year	Book Value End of Year

(2) Present the debits and credits required, in general journal form, to record the exchange at the beginning of the fifth year, assuming that the gain or loss on the disposal is to be recognized.

(3) Present the debits and credits required, in general journal form, to record the exchange at the beginning of the fifth year, assuming that the gain or loss on the disposal is not to be recognized.

(4) What is the cost basis of the new equipment, for purposes of computing the amount of depreciation allowable for income tax purposes?

(5) Assuming that the trade-in allowance had been $5,000 instead of $7,500, determine the cost basis of the new equipment for purposes of computing the amount of depreciation allowable for income tax purposes, solving by two methods.

259

If the working papers correlating with the textbook are not used, omit Problem 10-3A.

10-3A. Printing Impressions Co. maintains a subsidiary equipment ledger for the printing equipment and accumulated depreciation accounts in the general ledger. A small portion of the subsidiary ledger, the two controlling accounts, and a general journal are presented in the working papers. The company computes depreciation on each individual item of equipment. Transactions and adjusting entries affecting the printing equipment are described below.

1973

Aug. 2. Purchased a power cutter (Model D, Serial No. 7170C) from Monroe Typograph Co. on account for $4,800. The estimated life of the asset is 10 years, it is expected to have no residual value, and the straight-line method of depreciation is to be used. (This is the only transaction of the year that directly affected the printing equipment account.)

Dec. 31. Recorded depreciation for the year in subsidiary accounts 125-77 to 125-79, and inserted the new balances. (An assistant recorded the depreciation and the new balances in accounts 125-1 to 125-76.)

31. Journalized and posted the annual adjusting entry for depreciation on printing equipment. The depreciation for the year recorded in subsidiary accounts 125-1 to 125-76 totaled $16,027 to which was added the depreciation entered in accounts 125-77 to 125-79.

1974

Apr. 27. Purchased a Model 210 rotary press from Bower Press, Inc., priced at $27,620, giving the Model C8 flatbed press (Account No. 125-77) in exchange plus $7,620 cash and a series of eight $1,500 notes payable, maturing at 6-month intervals. The estimated life of the new press is 10 years, it is expected to have a residual value of $2,000, and the straight-line method of depreciation is used. (Recorded depreciation to date in 1974 on item traded in; gain or loss on the disposal was not recognized.)

Instructions:

(1) Journalize the transaction of August 2. Post to Printing Equipment in the general ledger and to Account No. 125-79 in the subsidiary ledger.

(2) Journalize the adjusting entries required on December 31 and post to Accumulated Depreciation — Printing Equipment in the general ledger.

(3) Journalize the entries required by the purchase of printing equipment on April 27. Post to Printing Equipment and to Accumulated Depreciation — Printing Equipment in the general ledger and to Accounts Nos. 125-77 and 125-80 in the subsidiary ledger.

(4) If the rotary press purchased on April 27 had been depreciated by the declining-balance method, at twice the straight-line rate, determine the depreciation on this press for the fiscal years ending (a) December 31, 1974 and (b) December 31, 1975.

10-4A. The following transactions, adjusting entries, and closing entries were completed by Baxter Furniture Co. during a 3-year period. All are related to the use of delivery equipment. The declining-balance method (twice the straight-line rate) of depreciation is used.

1973

Mar. 3. Purchased a used delivery truck for $2,900, paying cash.

10. Paid $220 for major repairs to the truck.

Oct. 28. Paid garage $45 for miscellaneous repairs to the truck.

Dec. 31. Recorded depreciation on the truck for the fiscal year. The estimated life of the truck is 4 years, with a trade-in value of $325.

31. Closed the appropriate accounts to the income summary account.

1974

June 27. Traded in the used truck for a new truck priced at $5,735, receiving a trade-in allowance of $1,700 and paying the balance in cash. (Record depreciation to date in 1974; gain or loss on exchange is not to be recognized.)

Dec. 21. Paid garage $35 for miscellaneous repairs to the truck.

31. Recorded depreciation on the truck. It has an estimated trade-in value of $625 and an estimated life of 5 years.

31. Closed the appropriate accounts to the income summary account.

1975
Sept. 25. Purchased a new truck for $4,800, paying cash.
Oct. 29. Sold the truck purchased in 1974 for $2,600. (Record depreciation.)
Dec. 31. Recorded depreciation on the remaining truck. It has an estimated trade-in value of $800 and an estimated life of 6 years.
  31. Closed the appropriate accounts to the income summary account.

Instructions:

(1) Open the following accounts in the ledger:

122 Delivery Equipment
122.1 Accumulated Depreciation — Delivery Equipment
616 Depreciation Expense — Delivery Equipment
617 Truck Repair Expense
912 Loss on Disposal of Plant Assets

(2) Record the transactions and the adjusting and closing entries in general journal form. Post to the accounts and extend the balances after each posting.

10-5A. The recording errors described below occurred and were discovered during the current year.

(a) A $175 charge for incoming transportation on an item of factory equipment was debited to Purchases.

(b) The $120 cost of repairing factory equipment damaged in the process of installation was charged to Factory Equipment.

(c) The cost of a razed building, $7,500, was charged to Loss on Disposal of Plant Assets. The building and the land on which it was located had been acquired at a total cost of $25,000 ($17,500 debited to Land, $7,500 debited to Building) as a parking area for the adjacent plant.

(d) The fee of $900 paid to the wrecking contractor to raze the building in (c) was debited to Miscellaneous Expense.

(e) Property taxes of $1,150 on the real estate in (c) paid during the year and debited to Property Tax Expense included $550 for taxes that were delinquent at the time the property was acquired.

(f) The $550 cost of a major motor overhaul expected to prolong the life of a truck one year beyond the original estimate was debited to Delivery Equipment. The truck was acquired new three years earlier.

(g) The $2,500 cost of repainting the interior of a building was debited to Building. The building had been owned and occupied for five years.

(h) The sale of an electric typewriter for $150 was recorded by a $150 credit to Office Equipment. The original cost of the machine was $700 and the related balance in Accumulated Depreciation at the beginning of the current year was $410. Depreciation of $35 accrued during the current year, prior to the sale, had not been recorded.

Instructions:

Journalize the entries necessary to correct the errors during the current year. Identify each entry by letter.

10-6A. The trial balance of Alco Corporation at the end of the current fiscal year, before adjustments, is reproduced at the top of the next page.

Data needed for year-end adjustments:

(a) Merchandise inventory at June 30, $92,425.

(b) Insurance and other prepaid operating expenses expired during the year, $1,970.

261

Alco Corporation
Trial Balance
June 30, 19—

Cash..	19,120	
Accounts Receivable............................	22,034	
Allowance for Doubtful Accounts................		1,100
Merchandise Inventory..........................	91,625	
Prepaid Expenses...............................	6,480	
Office Equipment...............................	7,110	
Accumulated Depreciation — Office Equipment....		2,972
Store Equipment................................	25,750	
Accumulated Depreciation — Store Equipment.....		12,137
Delivery Equipment.............................	24,330	
Accumulated Depreciation — Delivery Equipment.		7,145
Buildings......................................	106,000	
Accumulated Depreciation — Buildings..........		44,520
Land..	24,700	
Accounts Payable...............................		51,350
Notes Payable (short-term).....................		10,000
Capital Stock..................................		100,000
Retained Earnings..............................		48,200
Dividends......................................	5,000	
Sales (net)....................................		947,350
Purchases (net)................................	743,240	
Operating Expenses (control account)...........	148,760	
Interest Expense...............................	625	
	1,224,774	1,224,774

(c) Estimated uncollectible accounts at June 30, $1,750.

(d) Depreciation is computed at composite rates on the average of the beginning and the ending balances of the plant asset accounts. The beginning balances and rates are as follows:

Office equipment, $6,890; 8%   Delivery equipment, $25,170; 20%
Store equipment, $24,250; 10%   Buildings, $90,000; 2½%

(e) Accrued liabilities at the end of the year, $1,135, of which $125 is for interest on the notes and $1,010 is for wages and other operating expenses.

Instructions (corporation income tax is excluded from consideration):

(1) Prepare an income statement for the current year.

(2) Prepare a balance sheet in report form, presenting the plant assets in the manner illustrated in this chapter.

10-7 A. In each of the following selected transactions it is assumed that subsidiary equipment ledgers are maintained and that the fiscal year ends on December 31. Depreciation is recorded only at the end of each year, except for depreciation on items disposed of during the year.

(a) Jan. 5. Paid $7,000 for replacing the roof on a building. It is estimated that the new roof will extend the life of the building from an original estimate of 25 years to a total life of 30 years. Details from the subsidiary ledger are as follows: cost, $200,000; accumulated depreciation on preceding December 31, $120,000; age of building, 15 years.

(b) Jan. 10. Discarded a duplicating machine (office equipment), realizing no salvage. Details from the subsidiary ledger are as follows: cost, $325; accumulated depreciation, $325.

(c) Feb. 22. Discarded store equipment, realizing no salvage. Details from the subsidiary ledger are as follows: cost, $720, accumulated depreciation on preceding December 31, $625; annual depreciation, $72.

(d) Apr. 4. Traded in an old delivery truck for a new one priced at $5,000, receiving a trade-in allowance of $700 and paying the balance in cash. Data on the old truck are as follows: cost, $4,000, accumulated depreciation on preceding December 31, $3,250; annual depreciation, $1,000. Gain or loss is to be recognized.

(e) July 1. Sold 8 desks (office equipment) for cash, $120. The desks were identical and had been acquired at the same time. Details from the subsidiary ledger are as follows: total cost, $1,300, total accumulated depreciation on preceding December 31, $1,080; total annual depreciation, $80.

(f) Sept. 28. Traded in a refrigerated display case (store equipment) for a new one priced at $1,750, receiving a trade-in allowance of $250 and giving a note for the balance. Data on the old equipment are as follows: cost, $1,200; accumulated depreciation on preceding December 31, $928; annual depreciation, $96. Gain or loss is not to be recognized.

Instructions:

(1) Present entries, all in general journal form, to record the transactions and, where appropriate, to accrue the depreciation for the partial year preceding the transaction. Identify each entry by letter.

(2) Determine the depreciation on the building affected by entry (a) for the year in which the roof was replaced, using the straight-line method and assuming no residual value.

(3) Determine the depreciation on the new store equipment recorded in entry (f), using the declining-balance method (twice the straight-line rate) for (a) the remainder of the year and (b) the following year. The expected useful life of the display case is 8 years.

263

Chapter 11

SYSTEMS AND CONTROLS

ACCOUNTING SYSTEMS

One of the areas of specialization in accounting is the design and installation of accounting systems. In developing principles of accounting in earlier chapters, attention has been focused to a large extent on analysis and recording of accounting data, preparation of financial statements, and uses of accounting data by management. Consideration has also been given, however, to some aspects of accounting systems, such as documentary evidence of transactions, charts of accounts, journals, special journals, ledgers, and subsidiary ledgers. This chapter is devoted primarily to the basic concepts of accounting systems.

An accounting system should assure the availability of data required by management in conducting the affairs of an enterprise and in reporting to owners, creditors, and other interested parties. Consequently, a properly designed accounting system must provide for (1) efficient accumulation, recording, and reporting of data, (2) measurement of all phases of a firm's operations, (3) assignment of authority and responsibility, and (4) prevention of errors and fraud. Beyond these fundamental requirements there are an infinite number of variations in the details of accounting systems. Each system must be designed to fit the nature of the individual enterprise, the volume of transactions of various types, and the number and the capacities of the personnel.

INTERNAL CONTROL

In a small business it is possible for the owner-manager to personally supervise the employees and direct the affairs of the business. As the number of employees and the complexities of an enterprise increase, it becomes more difficult for management to maintain contact with all phases of operations. As a firm grows, management finds it necessary to delegate authority and to place more reliance on the accounting system in controlling operations.

Plans and procedures designed to meet the need for controlling operations are called *internal control*. It comprises the plan of organization and the related methods and procedures adopted within an enterprise to (1) safeguard its assets, (2) produce accurate accounting data, (3) contribute to efficient operation, and (4) encourage adherence to management policies. In a broad sense, internal control also includes such activities as motion and time study, quality control, and statistical analysis. The portion of internal control related to the accounting system is sometimes referred to as *internal check*.

Some degree of internal control is needed in all businesses. For example, the requirement that each cash sale be recorded by depressing the appropriate keys on a cash register is a fundamental part of internal control. The use of sales tickets, sales invoices, and other documentary evidences of transactions is also a part of internal control. The details of a system of internal control will of necessity vary with the nature and the size of a firm. There are, however, a number of broad principles that should be considered.

Competent personnel and rotation of duties. All accounting systems require people to perform prescribed duties. Obviously, a system can be only as good as the people who perform these duties. Therefore, all employees should be adequately trained and supervised in the performance of their duties. Whenever feasible, clerical employees should be rotated from job to job. The knowledge that other employees may perform their duties at a later date tends to discourage deviations from prescribed procedures. Rotation also helps to disclose any irregularities that may occur. For these same reasons, all employees should be required to take annual vacations, with their duties assigned to others during their absence.

Assignment of responsibility. If employees are to work efficiently, it is essential that their responsibilities be clearly defined. There should be no overlapping or undefined areas of responsibility. For example, if a particular cash register is to be used by two or more sales clerks, each one should be assigned a separate cash drawer and register key. Thus, daily proof of the handling of cash can be obtained for each clerk. Similarly, if several employees are assigned to posting entries to customers' accounts, each employee should be assigned to a particular alphabetical section so that errors can be traced to the person responsible for the error.

Separation of responsibility for related operations. To minimize the possibility of inefficiency, errors, and fraud, responsibility for a sequence of related operations should be divided among two or more persons. For example, no single individual should be authorized to order merchandise, verify the receipt of the goods, and pay the supplier. To do so would invite such abuses as placing orders with a supplier on the basis of

265

friendship rather than on price, quality, and other objective factors; perfunctory verification of the quantity and the quality of goods received; conversion of goods to the personal use of the employee; carelessness in verifying the validity and the accuracy of invoices; and payment of fictitious invoices. When the responsibility for purchasing, receiving, and paying are divided among three persons or departments, the possibilities of such abuses are minimized. The documentary evidence of the work of each department, including purchase orders, receiving reports, and invoices should be routed to the accounting department for comparison and recording.

It should be noted that the "checks and balances" provided by distributing responsibility among various departments requires no duplication of effort. The work of each department, as evidenced by the business documents that it prepares, must "fit" with those prepared by the other departments.

Separation of operations and accounting. Responsibility for maintaining the accounting records should be separated from the responsibility for operations and custody of assets. In this way the accounting records can serve as an independent check on operations. For example, the cashier who receives remittances from customers on account should not have access to the journals or the ledgers. Separation of the two functions reduces the possibilities of errors and defalcations.

Proofs and security measures. Proofs and security measures should be utilized to safeguard business assets and assure reliable accounting data. This principle applies to a wide variety of techniques and procedures, such as the use of controlling accounts and subsidiary ledgers; the use of a bank account and other safekeeping measures for cash, investments, and other valuable documents; and the use of various types of mechanical equipment. Cash registers are widely employed in making the initial record of cash sales. The conditioning of the public to observe the amount recorded as the sale or to accept a printed receipt from the salesclerk increases the machine's effectiveness as a part of internal control. Other devices with a similar feature include gasoline pumps and automatic counters in city buses.

The use of fidelity insurance is also an aid to internal control. It insures against losses caused by fraud on the part of employees who are entrusted with company assets and serves as a psychological deterrent to the misappropriation of assets.

Independent review. To determine whether the other internal control principles are being effectively applied, the system should be periodically reviewed and evaluated by internal auditors who are independent of the employees responsible for operations. The auditors should report any weaknesses and recommend changes to correct them. For example, a review of cash disbursements may disclose that invoices were not paid within the discount period, even though sufficient cash was available.

CONTROL OVER CASH

Because of the high value of money in relation to its mass, its easy transferability, and other obvious characteristics, it is the asset most susceptible to improper diversion and use by employees. In addition, a great many transactions either directly or indirectly affect its receipt or payment. It is therefore essential that cash be effectively safeguarded by special controls. The most important of these controls are described in the sections that follow.

BANK ACCOUNT

Most businesses deposit all cash receipts in a bank and make all payments by checks drawn against the bank account. The forms used by the depositor in connection with a bank account are signature card, deposit ticket, check, and record of checks drawn.

Signature card. At the time an account is opened, an identifying number is assigned to the account and the bank requires that a *signature card* be signed by each individual authorized to sign checks drawn on the account. The card is used by the bank to determine the authenticity of the signature on checks presented to it for payment.

Deposit ticket. The details of a deposit are listed by the depositor on a printed form supplied by the bank. *Deposit tickets* may be prepared in duplicate, in which case the carbon copy is stamped or initialed by the bank's teller and given to the depositor as a receipt. There are alternative procedures to the use of a duplicate deposit ticket, but all systems provide the depositor with written evidence of the date and total amount of the deposit.

Check. A *check* is a written instrument signed by the depositor, ordering the bank to pay a specified sum of money to a designated person or to his order. There are three parties to a check: the *drawer*, the one who signs the check; the *drawee*, the bank on which the check is drawn; and the *payee*, the one to whose order the check is drawn. When checks are issued to pay obligations, they are recorded as credits to Cash even though they are not presented to the drawer's bank until some later time. Conversely, when checks are received from customers, they are recorded as debits to Cash, on the assumption that the customer has sufficient funds on deposit.

Check forms may be obtained in a variety of styles. The name and the address of the depositor are often printed on each check, and the checks are usually serially numbered to facilitate the depositor's internal control. Banks that employ automatic sorting and posting equipment provide check forms on which the bank's identification number and the depositor's account number are printed along the lower margin in magnetic ink. (When the check is presented for payment, the amount for which it is drawn is inserted next to the account number, also in magnetic ink.)

Record of checks drawn. A memorandum record of the basic details of a check should be prepared at the time the check is written. The record may be in the form of a stub from which the check is detached or it may be in the form of a small booklet designed to be kept with the check forms. Both types of record also provide spaces for recording deposits and the current bank balance.

Business firms may prepare a carbon copy of each check drawn and then use it as a basis for recording the transaction in the cash payments journal. Checks issued to a creditor on account are frequently accompanied by a notification of the specific invoice that is being paid. The purpose of such notification, sometimes called a *remittance advice*, is to assure proper credit in the accounts of the creditor. Misunderstandings are less likely to occur and the possible need for exchanges of correspondence is minimized. The invoice number or other descriptive data may be inserted in spaces provided on the face or the back of the check, or on an attachment to the check as in the illustration on the next page.

The payee detaches the portion of the check containing the remittance information before depositing the check at his bank. The detached portion may then be used by the payee as documentary evidence of the details of the cash receipt.

BANK STATEMENT

Although there are some variations in procedure, banks ordinarily maintain an original and a carbon copy of all checking accounts. When this is done, the original becomes the statement of account that is mailed to the depositor, usually at the end of each month. Like any account with a customer or a creditor, the bank statement begins with the opening balance, lists debits (deductions by the bank) and credits (additions by the bank), and ends with the balance at the close of the period. Accompanying the bank statement are the depositor's checks received by the bank during the period, arranged in the order of payment. The *paid* or *canceled* checks are perforated or stamped "Paid" together with the date of payment.

Debit or credit memorandums describing other entries on the depositor's account may also be enclosed with the statement. For example,

		363
HARTMAN COMPANY		
813 Monroe Street		

HARTMAN COMPANY
813 Monroe Street

Detroit, Michigan _____ May 15 ____ 19 73   9-42
                                                    720

Pay to the Order of ____ Roland Supply Company _____ $ 514.80

Five hundred fourteen 80/100------------------------------------ Dollars

AMERICAN NATIONAL BANK
    of DETROIT

C. P. White Treasurer

Carl M. Hartman Vice President

⑆0720⑈0042⑆ ⑆627⑈042⑈

- -

DETACH THIS PORTION BEFORE CASHING

DATE	DESCRIPTION	GROSS AMOUNT	DEDUCTIONS	NET AMOUNT
5/15/73	Invoice No. 727401	520.00	5.20	514.80
		HARTMAN COMPANY		

269

Check and
remittance advice

the bank may have debited the depositor's account for service charges or for deposited checks returned because of insufficient funds; or it may have credited the account for receipts from notes receivable left for collection or for bank loans to the depositor. A typical bank statement is illustrated on the next page.

BANK RECONCILIATION

When all cash receipts are deposited in the bank and all payments are made by check, the cash account is often entitled Cash in Bank. This account in the depositor's ledger is the reciprocal of the account with the depositor in the bank's ledger. Cash in Bank in the depositor's ledger is an asset with a debit balance, and the account with the depositor in the bank's ledger is a liability with a credit balance.

It might seem that the two balances should be equal in amount, but they are not likely to be equal on any specific date because of either or both of the following: (1) delay by either party in recording transactions, and (2) errors by either party in recording transactions.

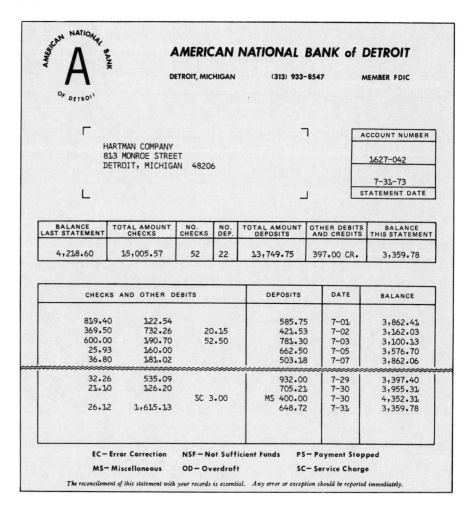

AMERICAN NATIONAL BANK of DETROIT

DETROIT, MICHIGAN   (313) 933-8547   MEMBER FDIC

HARTMAN COMPANY
813 MONROE STREET
DETROIT, MICHIGAN 48206

ACCOUNT NUMBER
1627-042
7-31-73
STATEMENT DATE

BALANCE LAST STATEMENT	TOTAL AMOUNT CHECKS	NO. CHECKS	NO. DEP.	TOTAL AMOUNT DEPOSITS	OTHER DEBITS AND CREDITS	BALANCE THIS STATEMENT
4,218.60	15,005.57	52	22	13,749.75	397.00 CR.	3,359.78

CHECKS AND OTHER DEBITS			DEPOSITS	DATE	BALANCE
819.40	122.54		585.75	7-01	3,862.41
369.50	732.26	20.15	421.53	7-02	3,162.03
600.00	190.70	52.50	781.30	7-03	3,100.13
25.93	160.00		662.50	7-05	3,576.70
36.80	181.02		503.18	7-07	3,862.06
32.26	535.09		932.00	7-29	3,397.40
21.10	126.20		705.21	7-30	3,955.31
		SC 3.00	MS 400.00	7-30	4,352.31
26.12	1,615.13		648.72	7-31	3,359.78

EC— Error Correction   NSF—Not Sufficient Funds   PS— Payment Stopped

MS— Miscellaneous   OD— Overdraft   SC— Service Charge

The reconcilement of this statement with your records is essential. Any error or exception should be reported immediately.

Bank statement

Ordinarily, there is a time lag of one day or more between the date a check is written and the date that it is presented to the bank for payment. If the depositor mails deposits to his bank or uses the night depository, a time lag between the date of the deposit and the date that it is recorded by the bank is also probable. On the other hand, the bank may debit or credit the depositor's account for transactions about which the depositor will not be informed until later. Examples are service or collection fees charged by the bank and the proceeds of notes receivable sent to the bank for collection.

In order to determine the reasons for any discrepancy and to correct any errors that may have been made by the bank or the depositor, the depositor should *reconcile* the bank statement with his own records. The bank reconciliation is divided into two major sections: one section begins with the balance according to the bank statement and ends with the adjusted balance; the other section begins with the balance according to the depositor's records and also ends with the adjusted balance. The two amounts designated as the adjusted balance must be in exact agreement. The form and the content of the bank reconciliation is outlined below.

Bank balance according to bank statement................		xx
Add: Additions by depositor not on bank statement........	xx	
Bank errors.....................................	xx	xx
	—	—
		xx
Deduct: Deductions by depositor not on bank statement....	xx	
Bank errors..................................	xx	xx
	—	—
Adjusted balance.......................................		xx
		=
Bank balance according to depositor's records..............		xx
Add: Additions by bank not recorded by depositor.........	xx	
Depositor errors.................................	xx	xx
	—	—
		xx
Deduct: Deductions by bank not recorded by depositor.....	xx	
Depositor errors..............................	xx	xx
	—	—
Adjusted balance.......................................		xx
		=

To achieve a maximum of internal control, the bank reconciliation should be prepared by an employee who does not engage in or record bank transactions. Errors or irregularities discovered should be reported to the chief accountant, controller, or other supervisory official.

The procedures described in the following paragraphs are employed in locating the reconciling items and determining the adjusted balance of Cash in Bank:

1. Individual deposits listed on the bank statement are compared with unrecorded deposits appearing in the preceding reconciliation and with deposit receipts or other records of deposits. Deposits not recorded by the bank are added to the balance according to the bank statement.

2. Paid checks returned by the bank are arranged in numerical order and are compared with outstanding checks appearing on the preceding reconciliation and with checks listed in the cash payments journal. Checks issued that have not been returned by the bank are outstanding and are deducted from the balance according to the bank statement.

3. Bank credit memorandums are traced to the cash receipts journal. Credit memorandums not recorded in the cash receipts journal are added to the balance according to the depositor's records.

4. Bank debit memorandums are traced to the cash payments journal. Debit memorandums not recorded in the cash payments journal are deducted from the balance according to the depositor's records.

5. Errors discovered during the process of making the foregoing comparisons are listed separately on the reconciliation. For example, if the

271

amount for which a check was drawn had been recorded erroneously, the amount of the error should be added to or deducted from the balance according to the depositor's records. Similarly, errors by the bank should be added to or deducted from the balance according to the bank statement.

Illustration. The bank statement for Hartman Company reproduced on page 270 indicates a balance of $3,359.78 as of July 31. The balance in Cash in Bank in Hartman Company's ledger as of the same date is $2,242.99. Application of the procedures outlined above reveals the following reconciling items:

1. Deposit of July 31 not recorded on bank statement . . . . $ 816.20
2. Checks outstanding: No. 812, $1,061.00; No. 878, $435.39; No. 883, $48.60 . . . . 1,544.99
3. Note collected by bank (credit memorandum) not recorded in cash receipts journal 400.00
4. Bank service charges (debit memorandum) not recorded in cash payments journal 3.00
5. Check No. 879 for $732.26 to Belden Co. on account recorded in cash payments journal as $723.26 . . . . 9.00

The bank reconciliation based on the bank statement and the reconciling items above is shown below:

Hartman Company
Bank Reconciliation
July 31, 1973

Balance per bank statement		$3,359.78
Add: Deposit of July 31, not recorded by bank		816.20
		$4,175.98
Deduct: Outstanding checks		
No. 812	$1,061.00	
No. 878	435.39	
No. 883	48.60	1,544.99
Adjusted balance		**$2,630.99**
Balance per depositor's records		$2,242.99
Add: Note collected by bank		400.00
		$2,642.99
Deduct: Bank service charges	$3.00	
Error in recording Check No. 879	9.00	12.00
Adjusted balance		**$2,630.99**

Bank reconciliation

ENTRIES BASED ON BANK RECONCILIATION

Bank memorandums not recorded by the depositor and depositor's errors revealed by the bank reconciliation necessitate entries in the accounts. The entries may be recorded in the appropriate special journals if they have not already been posted for the month, or they may be recorded in the general journal.

The entries for Hartman Company, based on the bank reconciliation shown on the preceding page, are as follows:

July	31	Cash in Bank............................	400	
		Notes Receivable........................		400
		Note collected by bank.		
	31	Miscellaneous General Expense............	3	
		Accounts Payable — Belden Co.............	9	
		Cash in Bank............................		12
		Bank service charges and error in recording Check No. 879.		

It should be noted that the data necessary for these adjustments are provided by the section of the bank reconciliation that begins with the balance per depositor's records.

After the foregoing entries are posted, the cash in bank account will have a debit balance of $2,630.99, which agrees with the adjusted balance shown on the bank reconciliation. This is the amount of cash available for use as of July 31 and the amount that would be reported on the balance sheet on that date.

INTERNAL CONTROL OF CASH RECEIPTS

A bank account is one of the principal devices for maintaining control over cash. To achieve maximum effectiveness, all cash received must be deposited in the bank and all payments must be made by checks drawn on the bank or from special cash funds. When such a system is strictly adhered to, there is a double record of cash, one maintained by the business and the other by the bank.

Department stores and other retail businesses ordinarily receive cash from two principal sources: (1) over the counter from cash customers and (2) by mail from charge customers making payments on account. At the close of the business day each salesclerk counts the cash in his cash drawer and records the amount on a memorandum form. An employee from the cashier's department removes the cash register tapes on which total receipts were recorded for each cash drawer, counts the cash, and compares the total with the memorandum and the tape, noting any discrepancies. The cash is then taken to the cashier's office and the tapes and memorandum forms are forwarded to the accounting department, where they become the basis for entries in the cash receipts journal.

The employees who open incoming mail compare the amount of cash received with the amount shown on the accompanying remittance advice to be certain that the two amounts agree. If there is no separate remittance advice, an employee prepares one on a form designed for such use. All cash received, usually in the form of checks and money orders, is sent to the cashier's department where it is combined with the receipts from cash sales and a deposit ticket is prepared. The remittance advices are delivered to the accounting department where they become the basis for entries in the cash receipts journal and for posting to the customers' accounts in the subsidiary ledger.

The duplicate deposit tickets or other bank receipt forms obtained by the cashier are forwarded to the controller or other financial officer, who compares the total amount with that reported by the accounting department as the total debit to Cash in Bank for the period.

CASH SHORT AND OVER

The amount of cash actually received during a day often does not agree with the record of cash receipts. Whenever there is a difference between the record and the actual cash and no error can be found in the record, it must be assumed that the mistake occurred in making change. The cash shortage or overage is recorded in an account entitled Cash Short and Over. A common method for handling such mistakes is to include in the cash receipts journal a Cash Short and Over Debit column into which all cash shortages are entered, and a Cash Short and Over Credit column into which all cash overages are entered. For example, if the actual cash received from cash sales is less than the amount indicated by the cash register tally, the entry in the cash receipts journal would include a debit to Cash Short and Over. An example of a complete entry, in general journal form, follows:

Cash in Bank..............................	720.10	
Cash Short and Over........................	1.90	
Sales...................................		722.00

If there is a debit balance in the cash short and over account at the end of the fiscal period, it is an expense and may be included in "Miscellaneous general expense" on the income statement. If there is a credit balance, it is revenue and may be listed in the "Other income" section. If the balance becomes larger than may be accounted for by minor errors in making change, the management should take corrective measures.

CASH CHANGE FUNDS

Retail stores and other businesses that receive cash directly from customers must maintain a fund of currency and coins in order to make change. The fund may be established by drawing a check for the required amount, debiting the account Cash on Hand and crediting Cash in Bank. No additional charges or credits to the cash on hand account are necessary unless the amount of the fund is to be increased or decreased. At the close of each business day the total amount of cash received during the day is deposited and the original amount of the change fund is retained. The desired composition of the fund is maintained by exchanging bills or coins for those of other denominations at the bank.

INTERNAL CONTROL OF CASH PAYMENTS

It is common practice for business enterprises to require that every payment of cash be evidenced by a check signed by a designated official. As an additional control some firms require two signatures on all checks or only on checks over a specified amount. The use of a check protector that produces an indelible and unalterable amount on the check is also common.

When the owner of a business has personal knowledge of all goods and services purchased, he may sign checks with the assurance that the creditors have complied with the terms of their contracts and that he is paying the exact amount of the obligation. Such all-encompassing knowledge of affairs by disbursing officials is seldom possible, however. In enterprises of even moderate size the responsibility for issuing purchase orders, inspecting commodities received, and verifying contractual and arithmetical details of invoices is divided among the employees of various departments. It is desirable, therefore, to coordinate these related activities and to link them with the ultimate issuance of checks to creditors. One of the most effective systems employed for this purpose is known as the *voucher system*.

275

BASIC FEATURES OF THE VOUCHER SYSTEM

A voucher system is composed of records, methods, and procedures employed in (1) verifying and recording liabilities and (2) paying and recording cash payments. As in all areas of accounting systems and internal controls, many variations in detail are possible. The discussion and the illustrations that follow refer to a merchandising enterprise of moderate size with separate departments for purchasing, receiving, accounting, and disbursing.

A voucher system employs (1) vouchers, (2) a voucher register, (3) a file for unpaid vouchers, (4) a check register, and (5) a file for paid vouchers.

Vouchers. The term *voucher* is widely used in accounting. In a general sense it means any document that serves as evidence of authority to pay cash, such as an invoice approved for payment, or as evidence that cash has been paid, such as a canceled check. The term has a narrower meaning when applied to the voucher system: a voucher is a special form on which is recorded pertinent data about a liability and the particulars of its payment.

A voucher form is illustrated on the opposite page. The face of the voucher provides space for the name and the address of the creditor, the date and the number of the voucher, and basic details of the invoice or other supporting document, such as the vendor's invoice number and the amount and the terms of the invoice. One half of the back of the voucher is devoted to the account distribution and the other half to summaries of the voucher and the details of payment. Spaces are also provided for the signature or initials of various employees.

Vouchers are customarily prepared by the accounting department on the basis of an invoice or a memorandum that serves as evidence of the expenditure. This is usually done only after the following comparisons and verifications have been completed and noted on the invoice:

1. Comparison of the invoice with a copy of the purchase order to verify quantities, prices, and terms.
2. Comparison of the invoice with the receiving report to verify receipt of the items billed.
3. Verification of the arithmetical accuracy of the invoice.

After all data except details of payment have been inserted, the invoice or other supporting evidence is attached to the face of the voucher, which is then folded with the account distribution and summaries on the outside. The voucher is then presented to the designated official or officials for final approval.

Voucher register. After approval by the designated official, each voucher is recorded in a journal known as a *voucher register*. It is similar to and replaces the purchases journal described in Chapter 5.

A typical form of a voucher register is illustrated on pages 278 and 279. The vouchers are entered in numerical sequence, each being recorded as a credit to Accounts Payable (sometimes entitled Vouchers Payable) and as a debit to the account or accounts to be charged for the expenditure.

When a voucher is paid, the date of payment and the number of the check are inserted in the appropriate columns in the voucher register. The effect of such notations is to provide a ready means of determining at any time the amount of an individual unpaid voucher or of the total amount of unpaid vouchers.

Unpaid voucher file. An important characteristic of the voucher system is the requirement that a voucher be prepared for each expenditure. In fact, a check may not be issued except in payment of a properly authorized voucher. Vouchers may be paid immediately after they are prepared or at a later date, depending upon the circumstances and the credit terms.

After a voucher has been recorded in the voucher register, it is filed in an unpaid voucher file, where it remains until it is paid. The amount

VOUCHER

JANSEN AUTO SUPPLIES, INC.

Date July 1, 1973   Voucher No.   451

Payee   Allied Manufacturing Company

      683 Fairmont Road

      Chicago, Illinois 60630

DATE	DETAILS	AMOUNT
June 28, 1973	Invoice No. 4693-C FOB Chicago, 2/10, n/30	450.00

Attach Supporting Documents

Voucher — face

277

ACCOUNT DISTRIBUTION			VOUCHER No. 451		
Debit	**Amount**		Date 7-1-73 Due 7-8-73		
Purchases	450	00	**Payee**		
Supplies			Allied Manufacturing Company		
Advertising Expense			683 Fairmont Road		
Delivery Expense			Chicago, Illinois 60630		
Misc. Selling Expense			**Voucher Summary**		
Misc. General Expense			Amount	450	00
			Adjustment		
			Discount	9	00
			Net	441	00
			Approved R. G. Davis Controller		
			Recorded T. N.		
			Payment Summary		
			Date 7-8-73		
			Amount 441.00		
			Check No. 863		
Credit Accounts Payable	450	00	Approved C. S. Reed Treasurer		
			Recorded B. W. RM		
Distribution Approved C. B. White					

Voucher — back

Voucher register (computer print-out)

	DATE	VOU. NO.	PAYEE	PAID DATE	CK. NO.	ACCOUNTS PAYABLE CR.	PURCHASES DR.	
1	19--							1
2	July	1 451	Allied Mfg. Co.	7-8	863	450 00	450 00	2
3		1 452	Adams Realty Co.	7-1	856	600 00		3
4		2 453	Foster Publications	7-2	857	52 50		4
5		3 454	Benson Express Co.	7-3	859	36 80	24 20	5
6		3 455	Office Outfitters			784 20		6
7		3 456	Moore & Co.	7-11	866	1,236 00	1,236 00	7
8		6 457	J. L. Brown Co.	7-6	860	22 50		8
9		6 458	Turner Corp.			395 30	395 30	9
27		31 477	Central Motors			112 20		27
28		31 478	Petty Cash	7-31	883	48 60		28
29		31				15,551 60	11,640 30	29
30						(212)	(511)	30

due on each voucher represents the credit balance of an account payable, and the voucher itself is comparable to an individual account in a subsidiary accounts payable ledger; accordingly, a separate subsidiary ledger is unnecessary.

All voucher systems include some provision for efficiently determining the vouchers to be paid each day. The method of filing invoices by due date described in Chapter 5 is equally acceptable for filing vouchers. It brings to the attention of the disbursing official the vouchers that are to be paid on each day. It also provides management with a convenient means of continuously forecasting the amount of cash needed to meet maturing obligations.

When a voucher is to be paid, it is removed from the unpaid voucher file and a check is issued in payment. The date, the number, and the amount of the check are listed on the back of the voucher for use in recording the payment in the check register. Paid vouchers and the supporting documents are often run through a canceling machine to prevent accidental or intentional reuse.

An exception to the general rule that vouchers be prepared for all expenditures may be made for bank charges evidenced by debit memorandums or notations on the bank statement. For example, such items as bank service charges, safe-deposit box rentals, and returned NSF (Not Sufficient Funds) checks may be charged to the depositor's account without either a formal voucher or a check. For large expenditures, such as the repayment of a bank loan, a supporting voucher may be prepared, if desired, even though a check is not written. The paid note may

	STORE SUPPLIES DR.	ADV. EXP. DR.	DEL. EXP. DR.	MISC. SELLING EXP. DR.	MISC. GENERAL EXP. DR.	SUNDRY ACCOUNTS DR. ACCOUNT	POST. REF.	AMOUNT	
1									1
2									2
3						Rent Expense	712	600 00	3
4		52 50							4
5			12 60						5
6	34 20					Office Equipment	122	750 00	6
7									7
8					22 50				8
9									9
27			112 20						27
28	4 30		16 20	19 50	8 60				28
29	59 80	176 40	286 10	48 30	64 90			3,275 80	29
30	(116)	(612)	(613)	(618)	(718)			(√)	30

Voucher register (computer print-out)

then be attached to the voucher as evidence of the obligation. All bank debit memorandums are, of course, the equivalent of checks as evidence of payment.

Check register. The payment of a voucher is recorded in a *check register*, an example of which is illustrated on the next page. The check register is a modified form of the cash payments journal and is so called because it is a complete record of all checks. It is customary to record all checks in the check register in sequential order, including occasional checks that are voided because of an error in their preparation.

Each check issued is in payment of a voucher that has previously been recorded as an account payable in the voucher register. The effect of each entry in the check register is consequently a debit to Accounts Payable and a credit to Cash in Bank (and Purchases Discount, when appropriate).

The memorandum columns for Bank Deposits and Bank Balance appearing in the illustration of the check register are optional. They provide a convenient means of determining the cash available at all times.

When check forms with a remittance advice are prepared in duplicate, the carbon copies retained may constitute the check register. At the end of each month summary totals can be readily obtained for accounts payable debit, purchases discount credit, and cash credit, and the entry recorded in the general journal. If the volume of checks issued is substantial, a significant savings in clerical expenses may be effected by eliminating the copying of data in a columnar check register.

279

	DATE	CK. NO.	PAYEE	VOU. NO.	ACCOUNTS PAYABLE DR.	PURCHASES DISCOUNT CR.	CASH IN BANK CR.	BANK DEPOSITS	BALANCE	
1	19--								8,743 10	1
2	July	1 856	Adams Realty Co.	452	600 00		600 00	1,240 30	9,383 40	2
3		2 857	Foster Publications	453	52 50		52 50		9,330 90	3
4		2 858	Hill and Davis	436	1,420 00	14 20	1,405 80	865 70	8,790 80	4
5		3 859	Benson Exp. Co.	454	36 80		36 80	942 20	9,696 20	5
22		30 879	Voided							22
23		30 880	Stone & Co.	460	14 30		14 30		9,521 80	23
24		30 881	Evans Corp.	448	1,015 00		1,015 00	765 50	9,272 30	24
25		31 882	Graham & Co.	469	830 00	16 60	813 40		8,458 90	25
26		31 883	Petty Cash	478	48 60		48 60	938 10	9,348 40	26
27		31			17,322 90	198 20	17,124 70			27
28					(212)	(513)	(111)			28

Check register (computer print-out)

Paid voucher file. After payment, vouchers are customarily filed in numerical sequence in a paid voucher file. They are then readily available for examination by employees or independent auditors requiring information about a specific expenditure. Eventually the paid vouchers are destroyed in accordance with the firm's policies concerning the retention of records.

Voucher system and management. The voucher system not only provides effective accounting controls but also aids management in discharging other responsibilities. For example, the voucher system provides greater assurance that all payments are in liquidation of valid liabilities. In addition, current information is always available for use in determining future cash requirements, which in turn enables management to make the maximum use of cash resources. Invoices on which cash discounts are allowed can be paid within the discount period and other invoices can be paid on the final day of the credit period, thus minimizing costs and maintaining a favorable credit standing. Seasonal borrowing for working capital purposes can also be planned more accurately, with a consequent saving in interest costs.

PURCHASES DISCOUNT

In preceding chapters, purchases of merchandise were recorded at the invoice price, and cash discounts taken were credited to the purchases discount account at the time of payment. There are two opposing views on how such discounts should be reported in the income statement.

The most widely accepted view, which has been followed in this textbook, is that purchases discounts should be reported as a deduction

280

from purchases. For example, the cost of merchandise with an invoice price of $1,000, subject to terms of 2/10, n/30, is recorded initially at $1,000. If payment is made within the discount period, the discount of $20 reduces the cost to $980. If the invoice is not paid within the discount period, the cost of the merchandise remains $1,000. This treatment of purchases discounts may be attacked on the grounds that the date of payment should not affect the cost of a commodity; the additional payment required beyond the discount period adds nothing to the value of the commodities purchased.

The second view reports discounts taken as "other income." In terms of the example above, the cost of the merchandise is considered to be $1,000 regardless of the time of payment. If payment is made within the discount period, revenue of $20 is considered to be realized. The objection to this procedure lies in the recognition of revenue from the act of purchasing and paying for a commodity. Theoretically, an enterprise might make no sales of merchandise during an accounting period and yet might report as revenue the amount of cash discounts taken.

A major disadvantage of recording purchases at the invoice price and recognizing purchases discounts at the time of payment is that this method does not measure the cost of failing to take discounts. Efficiently managed enterprises maintain sufficient cash to pay within the discount period all invoices subject to a discount, and view the failure to take a discount as an inefficiency. To measure the cost of this inefficiency, purchases invoices may be recorded at the net amount, assuming that all discounts will be taken. Any discounts not taken are then recorded in an expense account entitled Discounts Lost. This method measures the cost of failure to take cash discounts and gives management an opportunity to take remedial action. Again assuming the same data, the invoice for $1,000 would be recorded as a debit to Purchases of $980 and a credit to Accounts Payable for the same amount. If the invoice is not paid until after the discount period has expired, the entry, in general journal form, would be as follows:

Accounts Payable	980	
Discounts Lost	20	
Cash in Bank		1,000

When this method is employed with the voucher system, all vouchers are prepared and recorded at the net amount. Any discount lost is noted on the related voucher and recorded in a special column in the check register when the voucher is paid.

Another advantage of this treatment of purchases discounts is that all merchandise purchased is recorded initially at the net price and hence no subsequent adjustments to cost are necessary. An objection, however, is that the amount reported as accounts payable in the balance sheet may be less than the amount necessary to discharge the liability.

281

PETTY CASH

In most businesses there is a frequent need for the payment of relatively small amounts, such as to the postman for postage due, to a deliveryman for transportation charges, or to an employee for the purchase of urgently needed supplies at a nearby retail store. Payment by check in such cases would result in delay, annoyance, and excessive expense of maintaining the records. Yet because these small payments may occur frequently and therefore amount to a considerable total sum, it is desirable to retain close control over such payments. This may be accomplished by maintaining a special cash fund that is designated *petty cash*.

In establishing a petty cash fund, the first step is to estimate the amount of cash needed for disbursements of relatively small amounts during a specified period such as a week or a month. If the voucher system is used, a voucher is then prepared for this amount and it is recorded in the voucher register as a debit to Petty Cash and a credit to Accounts Payable. The check drawn to pay the voucher is recorded in the check register as a debit to Accounts Payable and a credit to Cash in Bank.

The money obtained from "cashing" the check is placed in the custody of a specific employee who is authorized to disburse the fund in accordance with stipulated restrictions as to maximum amount and purpose. Each time a disbursement is made from the fund, the employee records the essential details on a receipt form, obtains the signature of the payee as evidence of the payment, and adds his own signature or initials. A typical petty cash receipt is illustrated below.

```
┌─────────────────────────────────────────────────────────────┐
│                   PETTY CASH RECEIPT                         │
│                                                             │
│   NO. __121__              DATE __August 1, 1973__          │
│                                                             │
│   PAID TO ____Metropolitan Times____      AMOUNT            │
│                                          ┌──────┐           │
│   FOR _____Daily newspaper_____       │ 3│70 │           │
│                                          └──────┘           │
│   CHARGE TO ___Miscellaneous General Expense___            │
│                                                             │
│   PAYMENT RECEIVED:                                         │
│       S.O.Hall        APPROVED BY   N.E.R.                 │
└─────────────────────────────────────────────────────────────┘
```

Petty cash
receipt

When the amount of money in the petty cash fund is reduced to the predetermined minimum amount, the fund is replenished. If the voucher system is used, the accounts debited on the replenishing voucher are those indicated by a summary of expenditures. The voucher is then recorded in the voucher register as a debit to the various expense and asset accounts and a credit to Accounts Payable. The entry is similar to that on line 28 of the voucher register on pages 278 and 279. The check in payment of the voucher is recorded in the check register in the usual manner, as shown on line 26 of the illustration on page 280.

After the petty cash fund has been replenished, the fund will be restored to its original amount. It should be noted that the sole entry in the petty cash account will be the initial debit unless at some later time the standard amount of the fund is increased or decreased.

Because disbursements are not recorded in the accounts until the fund is replenished, petty cash funds and other special funds that operate in a similar manner should always be replenished at the close of an accounting period. The amount of money actually in the fund will then agree with the balance in the related fund account, and the expenses and the assets for which payment has been made will be recorded in the proper period.

OTHER CASH FUNDS

Cash funds may also be established to meet other special needs of a business. For example, money advanced to a salesman for travel expenses may be accounted for in the same manner as petty cash. A standard amount is advanced; then upon receipt of expense reports from the salesman, the expenses are recorded and the fund is replenished. A similar procedure may be used to provide a working fund for a sales office located in another city. The amount of the fund may be deposited in a local bank and the sales representative may be authorized to draw checks for payment of rent, salaries, and other operating expenses. Each month the representative sends the invoices, bank statement, paid checks, bank reconciliation, and other business documents to the home office. The data are audited, the expenditures are recorded, and a reimbursing check is returned for deposit in the local bank.

283

CONTROL OVER NONCASH ITEMS

Earlier chapters have discussed the use of subsidiary records for recording and controlling such items as accounts receivable, equipment, and accounts payable. Perpetual inventory records assist in the management and control of inventory. Two other useful devices that represent an elaboration of the accounting system are described below.

Note registers. The notes receivable and notes payable accounts in the general ledger are primarily summarizing devices. They are not designed for recording detailed information about the terms of each note and its disposition. If numerous notes are received from customers or issued to creditors, it is customary to record the details of each note in a notes receivable register or a notes payable register.

The initial recording is made in the register at the time a note is given or received, showing the details of the note, such as name of maker or payee, place of payment, amount, term, interest rate, and due date. Daily reference to the due date section directs attention to which notes, if any, are due for payment or are to be presented for collection.

Insurance registers. An important means of safeguarding a firm's investment in plant assets is through insurance against losses from fire, windstorm, and other casualties. Potential losses resulting from injury to customers or employees while on the business premises, from dishonesty of employees, and from business interruptions caused by fire are only a few of the many other risks that may need to be insured against. The responsibility for appropriate insurance coverage ordinarily rests with the treasurer, controller, or other accounting officer. It is also the responsibility of the accounting department to determine and to record the amount of insurance expense applicable to each accounting period.

The contract between the insurer and the insured is called the *insurance policy*, and the amount paid for the contract is called the *insurance premium*. Insurance policies are written for a definite amount and for a definite period of time, most commonly for one or three years. The amount of insurance that should be carried on a particular asset does not necessarily correspond to its original cost or book value. The reproduc-

284

INSURANCE

DATE OF POLICY	POLICY NO.	INSURER	PROPERTY OR PURPOSE	AMOUNT	TERM	EXPIRATION DATE	UNEXPIRED PREMIUM
1970							
Mar. 5	24983	Midland Fire	Equipment	15,000	3	3/5/73	18 96
June 4	6179A	Acme Fire & Cas.	Merchandise	20,000	3	6/4/73	77 75
Oct. 28	723BB	Evans Fire & Cas.	Building	30,000	3	10/28/73	190 00
1972							
Oct. 1	9674	Columbia Fire & Cas.	Public Liability	100,000	1	10/1/73	94 50
1973							
Mar. 5	37468	Midland Fire	Equipment	15,000	3	3/5/76	378 36
May 26	2694Y	Liberty Auto	Delivery Equipment		1	5/26/74	542 40
June 4	96423	Acme Fire & Cas.	Merchandise	25,000	3	6/4/76	706 32
Oct. 1	11731	Columbia Fire & Cas.	Public Liability	100,000	1	10/1/74	129 00
28	9847	U.S. Fire	Building	35,000	1	10/28/74	250 80

Insurance register (computer print-out)

tion cost of the asset less accumulated depreciation thereon is a better criterion of the appropriate coverage. In any event, the insured cannot recover more than the cash value of the loss incurred.

A large firm may have literally hundreds of insurance policies in effect. For even a small business the number may be considerable. The review of insurance coverage and the determination of periodic insurance expense are facilitated by the use of a multicolumn form termed an *insurance register*.

An insurance register for a small business is illustrated below and at the bottom of page 284. The data for the insurance policies in effect at the beginning of the year are taken from the register for the preceding year; policies acquired during the year are recorded in the order of their acquisition. At the end of each month the insurance expense for that month is determined by adding the appropriate column. For example, the November expiration column in the illustration is totaled at the end of that month and an adjusting entry debiting Insurance Expense and crediting Prepaid Insurance for $106.98 is recorded in the general journal.

At the end of the year the Total Expired Premium column and the two unexpired premium columns are added. The total of the first Unexpired Premium column should agree with the total debits to Prepaid Insurance, the Total Expired Premium column should agree with the credits to the account, and the total of the second Unexpired Premium column should agree with the balance of Prepaid Insurance after all adjustments have been posted.

285

REGISTER — 1973

					EXPIRED PREMIUM									UNEXPIRED PREMIUM
JAN.	FEB.	MAR.	APR.	MAY	JUNE	JULY	AUG.	SEPT.	OCT.	NOV.	DEC.		TOTAL	
9 48	9 48												18 96	—
15 55	15 55	15 55	15 55	15 55									77 75	—
19 00	19 00	19 00	19 00	19 00	19 00	19 00	19 00	19 00	19 00				190 00	—
10 50	10 50	10 50	10 50	10 50	10 50	10 50	10 50	10 50					94 50	—
		10 51	10 51	10 51	10 51	10 51	10 51	10 51	10 51	10 51	10 51		105 10	273 26
					45 20	45 20	45 20	45 20	45 20	45 20	45 20		316 40	226 00
					19 62	19 62	19 62	19 62	19 62	19 62	19 62		137 34	568 98
									10 75	10 75	10 75		32 25	96 75
										20 90	20 90		41 80	209 00
54 53	54 53	55 56	55 56	55 56	104 83	104 83	104 83	104 83	105 08	106 98				

Insurance register (computer print-out)

QUESTIONS

1. Name four requisites of a properly designed accounting system.

2. (a) What is the meaning of *internal control*? (b) What is *internal check*?

3. Why should the responsibility for a sequence of related operations be divided among different persons?

4. How does a policy of rotating clerical employees from job to job aid in strengthening internal control?

5. The ticket seller at a motion picture theater doubles as ticket taker for a few minutes each day while the ticket taker is on a "break." Which principle of internal control is violated in this situation?

6. Why should the responsibility for maintaining the accounting records be separated from the responsibility for operations?

7. The bookkeeper pays all obligations by prenumbered checks. What are the strengths and the weaknesses in the internal control over cash disbursements in this situation?

8. The bookkeeper has the responsibility of determining the accounts receivable to be written off as uncollectible. Which principle of internal control is violated in this situation?

9. When checks are received, they are recorded as debits to Cash, the assumption being that the drawer has sufficient funds on deposit. What entry should be made if a check received from a customer and deposited is returned by the bank for lack of sufficient funds (NSF)?

10. What is the purpose of preparing a bank reconciliation?

11. Identify each of the following reconciling items as: (a) an addition to the balance per bank statement, (b) a deduction from the balance per bank statement, (c) an addition to the balance per depositor's records, or (d) a deduction from the balance per depositor's records. (None of the transactions reported by bank debit and credit memorandums have been recorded by the depositor.)
   (1) Outstanding checks, $872.41.
   (2) Check of a customer returned by bank to depositor because of insufficient funds, $30.
   (3) Deposit in transit, $213.64.
   (4) Check for $100 charged by bank as $10.
   (5) Note collected by bank, $750.
   (6) Bank service charge, $4.95.
   (7) Check drawn by depositor for $75 recorded in check register as $57.

12. Which of the reconciling items listed in Question 11 will require an entry in the depositor's accounts?

13. The procedures employed by the Parkside Food Mart for over-the-counter receipts are as follows: Each salesclerk counts the cash in his cash drawer at the close of business. He then removes the cash register tape and prepares the memorandum daily cash form, noting any discrepancies. An employee from the cashier's office counts the cash, compares the total with the memorandum, and takes the cash to the cashier's office. (a) Indicate the weak link in internal control. (b) How can the weakness be corrected?

14. The procedures employed by Fowler Company for mail receipts are as follows: Mailroom employees send all remittances and remittance advices to the cashier. The cashier deposits the cash in the bank and forwards the remittance advices and duplicate deposit slips to the accounting department. (a) Indicate the weak link in internal control. (b) How can the weakness be corrected?

15. The combined cash count of all cash registers at the close of business is $3.95 less than the cash sales indicated by the cash register tapes. (a) In what account is the cash shortage recorded? (b) Are cash shortages debited or credited to this account?

16. What is meant by the term "voucher" as applied to the voucher system?

17. Before a voucher for the purchase of merchandise is approved for payment, three documents should be compared to verify the accuracy of the liability. Name these three documents.

18. (a) When the voucher system is employed, is the accounts payable account in the general ledger a controlling account? (b) Is there a subsidiary creditors ledger?

19. In what order are vouchers ordinarily filed (a) in the unpaid voucher file, and (b) in the paid voucher file? Give reasons for answers.

287

20. Merchandise with an invoice price of $5,000 is purchased subject to terms of 2/10, n/30. Determine the cost of the merchandise according to each of the following systems:
- (a) Discounts taken are treated as deductions from the invoice price.
  - (1) The invoice is paid within the discount period.
  - (2) The invoice is paid after the discount period has expired.
- (b) Discounts taken are treated as other income.
  - (1) The invoice is paid within the discount period.
  - (2) The invoice is paid after the discount period has expired.
- (c) Discounts allowable are treated as deductions from the invoice price regardless of when payment is made.
  - (1) The invoice is paid within the discount period.
  - (2) The invoice is paid after the discount period has expired.

21. What account or accounts are debited when recording the voucher (a) establishing a petty cash fund and (b) replenishing a petty cash fund?

22. The petty cash account has a debit balance of $300. At the end of the accounting period there is $93 in the petty cash fund along with petty cash receipts totaling $207. Should the fund be replenished as of the last day of the period? Discuss.

23. As the newly appointed controller of a company established thirty years ago, you are responsible for maintaining appropriate fire and windstorm insurance coverage on plant assets. A review of the insurance policies in force indicates that the assets are insured for their approximate book values. Assuming that the company wishes to be fully insured against losses from fire and windstorm, do you consider the current amount of coverage to be adequate? Discuss.

EXERCISES

11-1. The following data are accumulated for use in reconciling the bank account of F. W. Williams Company for May.

(a) Balance per bank statement at May 31, $3,471.50.
(b) Balance per depositor's records at May 31, $3,186.30.
(c) Checks outstanding, $594.65.
(d) Deposit in transit not recorded by bank, $312.40.
(e) Bank debit memorandum for service charges, $6.05.
(f) A check for $45 in payment of a voucher was erroneously recorded in the check register as $54.

Prepare a bank reconciliation.

11-2. Using the data presented in Exercise 11-1, prepare in general journal form the entry or entries that should be made by the depositor.

11-3. Accompanying a bank statement for Thomas Lumber Company, Inc., is a debit memorandum for $611.50 representing the principal ($600), interest ($8), and protest fee ($3.50) on a discounted note that had been dishonored by C. M. Barr Co. The depositor had been notified by the bank at the time of the dishonor but had made no entries. Present the necessary entry by the depositor, in general journal form.

11-4. Record in general journal form the following selected transactions, indicating above each entry the name of the journal in which it should be recorded. Assume the use of a voucher register similar to that illustrated on pages 278 and 279 and a check register similar to that illustrated on page 280. All invoices are recorded at invoice price.

May 1. Recorded Voucher No. 617 for $900, payable to Evans Office Equipment Co., for office equipment purchased on terms n/30.
     5. Recorded Voucher No. 621 for $1,200, payable to Walters Co., for merchandise purchased on terms 2/10, n/30.
     15. Issued Check No. 790 in payment of Voucher No. 621.
     16. Recorded Voucher No. 630 for $81.15 to replenish the petty cash fund for the following disbursements: Store Supplies, $24.35; Office Supplies, $22.47; Miscellaneous Selling Expense, $17.73; and Miscellaneous General Expense, $16.60.
     17. Issued Check No. 792 in payment of Voucher No. 630.
     19. Recorded Voucher No. 635 for $125, payable to *Elgin Times*, for advertising appearing in yesterday's newspaper.
     25. Issued Check No. 800 in payment of Voucher No. 635.
     31. Issued Check No. 805 in payment of Voucher No. 617.

11-5. Prepare in general journal form the entries to record the following:

(a) Voucher No. 325 is prepared to establish a petty cash fund of $100.
(b) Check No. 320 is issued in payment of Voucher No. 325.
(c) The amount of cash in the petty cash fund is now $18.20. Voucher No. 352 is prepared to replenish the fund, based on the following summary of petty cash receipts: Office Supplies, $20.25; Miscellaneous Selling Expense, $35.72; Miscellaneous General Expense, $25.53.
(d) Check No. 348 is issued by the disbursing officer in payment of Voucher No. 352. The check is cashed and the money is placed in the fund.

11-6. Record in general journal form the following transactions:

(a) Voucher No. 1 is prepared to establish a change fund of $150.
(b) Check No. 1 is issued in payment of Voucher No. 1.
(c) Determined cash sales for the day, according to the cash register tapes, to be $599.45 and cash on hand to be $748.20. A bank deposit ticket was prepared for $598.20.

11-7. Record in general journal form the following related transactions, assuming that invoices for commodities purchased are recorded at their net price after deducting the allowable discount:

Apr. 6. Voucher No. 827 is prepared for merchandise purchased from Allen Supply Co., $2,500, terms 1/10, n/30.
     7. Voucher No. 828 is prepared for merchandise purchased from Baskin Co., $5,000, terms 2/10, n/30.
    17. Check No. 901 is issued, payable to Baskin Co., in payment of Voucher No. 828.
May   6. Check No. 927 is issued, payable to Allen Supply Co., in payment of Voucher No. 827.

289

PROBLEMS

The following additional problems for this chapter are located in Appendix B: 11-1B, 11-2B, 11-3B, 11-5B.

11-1A. The cash in bank account for L. M. Curtis, Inc., at December 31 of the current year indicated a balance of $8,670.81 after both the cash receipts journal and the check register for December had been posted. The bank statement indicated a balance of $10,871.60 on December 31. Comparison of the bank statement and the accompanying canceled checks and memorandums with the records revealed the following reconciling items:

(a) Checks outstanding totaled $3,011.28.
(b) A deposit of $1,717.24 representing receipts of December 31 had been made too late to appear on the bank statement.
(c) The bank had collected for L. M. Curtis, Inc., $1,020 on a note left for collection. The face of the note was $1,000.
(d) A check for $58 returned with the statement had been recorded in the check register as $85. The check was for the payment of an obligation to Doyle Equipment Company for the purchase of office equipment on account.
(e) A check drawn for $15 had been erroneously charged by the bank as $150.
(f) Bank service charges for December amounted to $5.25.

Instructions:

(1) Prepare a bank reconciliation.
(2) Journalize the necessary entries. The accounts have not been closed. The voucher system is used.

11-2A. Roth Company had the following vouchers in its unpaid voucher file at May 31 of the current year:

Due Date	Voucher No.	Creditor	Date of Invoice	Amount	Terms
June 3	810	Carr, Inc.	May 24	$1,200	1/10, n/30
June 12	805	Hunt Co.	May 13	450	n/30
June 21	815	Ames Co.	May 22	840	n/30

The vouchers prepared and the checks issued during the month of June were as follows:

VOUCHERS

Date	Voucher No.	Payee	Amount	Terms	Distribution
June 1	826	L. West Co.	$ 400	2/10, n/30	Purchases
3	827	Orr Supply	1,375	n/30	Store equipment
5	828	B. B. Lee, Inc.	700	1/10, n/30	Purchases
9	829	Neff and Son	36	cash	Store supplies
12	830	Mason Co.	1,100	2/10, n/30	Purchases
17	831	Root Co.	450	2/10, n/30	Purchases
18	832	Cook Co.	725	n/30	Office equipment
19	833	Ryan Trust Co.	5,075		Note payable, $5,000 Interest, $75
19	834	W. Feld Co.	600	2/10, n/30	Purchases
22	835	Kane Supply	85	cash	Store supplies
25	836	Morton Courier	64	cash	Advertising expense
27	837	Myers Co.	250	1/10, n/30	Purchases
29	838	Petty Cash	76		Office supplies, $26 Store supplies, $21 Delivery expense, $8 Miscellaneous selling expense, $13 Miscellaneous general expense, $8

CHECKS

Date	Check No.	Payee	Voucher Paid	Amount
June 3	902	Carr, Inc.	810	$1,188
9	903	Neff and Son	829	36
11	904	L. West Co.	826	392
12	905	Hunt Co.	805	450
15	906	B. B. Lee, Inc.	828	693
19	907	Ryan Trust Co.	833	5,075
21	908	Ames Co.	815	840
22	909	Kane Supply	835	85
22	910	Mason Co.	830	1,078
25	911	Morton Courier	836	64
27	912	Root Co.	831	441
29	913	W. Feld Co.	834	588
29	914	Petty Cash	838	76

Instructions:

(1) Set up a four-column account for Accounts Payable, Account No. 211, and record the balance of $2,490 as of June 1.

290

(2) Record the June vouchers in a voucher register similar to the one illustrated in this chapter, with the following amount columns: Accounts Payable Cr., Purchases Dr., Store Supplies Dr., Office Supplies Dr., and Sundry Accounts Dr. Purchase invoices are recorded at the gross amount.

(3) Record the June checks in a check register similar to the one illustrated in this chapter, but omit the Bank Deposits and Balance columns. After each check is recorded in the check register, the date and check number should be inserted in the appropriate columns of the voucher register. (Assume that notations for payment of May vouchers are made in the voucher register for May.)

(4) Total and rule the registers and post to the accounts payable account.

(5) Prepare a schedule of unpaid vouchers.

If the working papers correlating with the textbook are not used, omit Problem 11-3A.

11-3A. Portions of the following accounting records of P. D. Connors Co. are presented in the working papers:

Voucher Register	General ledger accounts:
Check Register	Prepaid Insurance
General Journal	Notes Payable
Insurance Register	Accounts Payable
Notes Payable Register	

Expenditures, cash disbursements, and other selected transactions completed during the period March 24–31 of the current year are described below.

Mar. 24. Recorded Voucher No. 627 payable to Powers Co. for merchandise, $2,750, terms 2/10, n/30. (Purchase invoices are recorded at the gross amount.)

24. Issued Check No. 938 to Bowers Co. in payment of Voucher No. 615 for $2,000, less cash discount of 2%.

26. Issued a 60-day, 7% note (No. 52), dated today to Walters Co. in settlement of Voucher No. 611, $6,500. The note is payable to Miami County Bank.

26. Recorded Voucher No. 628 payable to United Automobile Insurance Co. for the following insurance policy, dated today: No. 4593C, automobiles, 1 year, $1,122.

26. Issued Check No. 939 in payment of Voucher No. 628.

26. Recorded Voucher No. 629 payable to First National Bank for note payable (No. 48), $5,000.

26. Issued Check No. 940 in payment of Voucher No. 629.

28. Recorded Voucher No. 630 payable to Gates Co. for merchandise, $3,125, terms n/30.

28. Recorded Voucher No. 631 payable to Ogden Gazette for advertising, $320.

28. Issued Check No. 941 in payment of Voucher No. 631.

29. Recorded Voucher No. 632 payable to Petty Cash for $170.80, distributed as follows: Office Supplies, $44.35; Advertising Expense, $11.40; Delivery Expense, $30.95; Miscellaneous Selling Expense, $54.30; Miscellaneous General Expense, $29.80.

29. Issued Check No. 942 in payment of Voucher No. 632.

31. Issued Check No. 943 to Troy Products Co. in payment of Voucher No. 612 for $2,800, less cash discount of 2%.

Mar. 31. Recorded Voucher No. 633 payable to Wilcox Insurance Co. for the following insurance policy, dated today: No. F613, building, $100,000, 3 years, $1,836.

31. Issued Check No. 944 in payment of Voucher No. 633.

After the journals are posted at the end of the month, the cash in bank account has a debit balance of $15,865.90.

The bank statement indicates a March 31 balance of $22,200.40. Comparison of paid checks returned by the bank with the check register reveals that Nos. 939, 943, and 944 are outstanding. Check No. 889 for $720, which appeared on the February reconciliation as outstanding, is still outstanding. A debit memorandum accompanying the bank statement indicates a charge of $87.50 for a check drawn by L. M. Parker, a customer, which was returned because of insufficient funds.

Instructions:

(1) Record the transactions for March 24–31 in the appropriate journals. Immediately after recording a transaction, post individual items, where appropriate, to the three general ledger accounts given.

(2) Enter the necessary notations in the notes payable register and the insurance register, rounding insurance expirations to the nearest month.

(3) Total and rule the voucher register and the check register, and post totals to the accounts payable account.

(4) Complete the schedule of unpaid vouchers. (Compare the total with the balance of the accounts payable account as of March 31.)

(5) Prepare a bank reconciliation and journalize any necessary entries.

(6) Total the Expired Premium column for March in the insurance register, journalize the adjusting entry, and post to the prepaid insurance account. (Determine the balance of prepaid insurance as of March 31 from the columns in the insurance register and compare it with the balance of the prepaid insurance account as of the same date.)

(7) Determine the amount of interest accrued as of March 31 on notes payable (Nos. 50 and 52). (Assume 28 days in February.)

(8) Determine the amount of interest prepaid as of March 31 on notes payable (No. 51). (The non-interest-bearing note was discounted by the bank.)

11-4A. R. W. Hoffman Company has just adopted the policy of depositing all cash receipts in the bank and of making all payments by check in conjunction with the voucher system. The following transactions were selected from those completed in June of the current year:

June 1. Recorded Voucher No. 1 to establish a petty cash fund of $150 and a change fund of $500.

1. Issued Check No. 740 in payment of Voucher No. 1.

2. Recorded Voucher No. 3 to establish an advance to salesmen fund of $750.

2. Issued Check No. 742 in payment of Voucher No. 3.

6. The cash sales for the day according to the cash register tapes totaled $1,784.55. The combined count of all cash on hand (including the change fund) totaled $2,285.75.

June 15. Recorded Voucher No. 27 to reimburse the petty cash fund for the following disbursements, each evidenced by a petty cash receipt:

> June 3. Store supplies, $12.50.
> 4. Express charges on merchandise purchased, $9.40.
> 7. Office supplies, $17.45.
> 9. Telegram charges, $1.75 (Misc. Selling Expense).
> 10. Office supplies, $10.50.
> 11. Postage stamps, $16 (Office Supplies).
> 12. Repair to adding machine, $11.25 (Misc. General Expense).
> 15. Postage due on special delivery letter, $.25 (Miscellaneous General Expense).
> 15. Repair to typewriter, $9.55 (Misc. General Expense).
> 15. Express charges on merchandise purchased, $12.40.

15. Issued Check No. 768 in payment of Voucher No. 27.
22. The cash sales for the day according to the cash register tapes totaled $1,541.92. The count of all cash on hand totaled $2,038.52.
27. Recorded Voucher No. 43 to replenish the advances to salesmen fund for the following expenditures for travel: Dan Stark, $210; Oliver West, $105.50; Lee Boland, $290.70.
27. Issued Check No. 781 in payment of Voucher No. 43.

Instructions:

Record the above transactions in general journal form.

11-5A. Downs Company employs the voucher system in controlling expenditures and disbursements. All cash receipts are deposited in a night depository after banking hours each Wednesday and Friday. The data required to reconcile their bank statement as of June 30 of the current year have been abstracted from various documents and records and are reproduced below. To facilitate identification the sources of the data are printed in capital letters.

CASH IN BANK ACCOUNT
Balance as of June 1 . . . . $5,172.40
CASH RECEIPTS JOURNAL
Total of Cash in Bank Debit column for month of June. . . . 6,021.29
DUPLICATE DEPOSIT TICKETS

Date and amount of each deposit in June:

Date	Amount	Date	Amount	Date	Amount
June 2	$545.27	June 14	$715.25	June 23	$591.69
7	657.30	16	749.89	28	742.12
9	782.29	21	620.84	30	616.64

CHECK REGISTER
Number and amount of each check issued in June:

Check No.	Amount	Check No.	Amount	Check No.	Amount
722	$ 58.41	729	$315.04	736	$320.13
723	32.00	730	32.87	737	272.10
724	361.04	731	627.59	738	617.56
725	631.21	732	300.60	739	89.49
726	517.62	733	759.62	740	54.20
727	74.30	734	Void	741	511.21
728	266.29	735	315.40	742	147.76

Total amount of checks issued in June. $6,304.44

293

BANK STATEMENT FOR JUNE
Balance as of June 1 . . . . $5,144.84
Deposits and other credits 6,629.17
Checks and other debits 5,453.32
Balance as of June 30 . . . . $6,320.69

Date and amount of each deposit in June:

Date	Amount	Date	Amount	Date	Amount
June 1	$714.52	June 10	$782.29	June 22	$620.84
3	545.27	15	715.25	24	591.69
8	657.30	17	749.89	29	742.12

CHECKS ACCOMPANYING BANK STATEMENT FOR JUNE
Number and amount of each check, rearranged in numerical sequence:

Check No.	Amount	Check No.	Amount	Check No.	Amount
690	$ 64.23	726	$517.62	735	$315.40
720	410.93	727	47.30	736	320.13
721	89.50	728	266.29	737	272.10
722	58.41	729	315.04	739	89.49
723	32.00	730	32.87	741	511.21
724	361.04	731	627.59	742	147.76
725	631.21	732	300.60		

BANK MEMORANDUMS ACCOMPANYING BANK STATEMENT FOR JUNE
Date, description, and amount of each memorandum:

Date	Description	Amount
June 12	Bank credit memo for note collected:	
	Principal	$ 500.00
	Interest	10.00
21	Bank debit memo for check returned because of insufficient funds	39.55
30	Bank debit memo for service charges	3.05

BANK RECONCILIATION FOR PRECEDING MONTH

Downs Company
Bank Reconciliation
May 31, 19—

Balance per bank statement		$5,144.84
Add: Deposit of May 31, not recorded by bank		714.52
		$5,859.36
Deduct: Outstanding checks:		
No. 690	$ 64.23	
718	122.30	
720	410.93	
721	89.50	686.96
Adjusted balance		$5,172.40
Balance per depositor's records		$5,175.35
Deduct: Service charges		2.95
Adjusted balance		$5,172.40

Instructions:

(1) Prepare a bank reconciliation as of June 30. If errors in recording deposits or checks are discovered, assume that the errors were made by the depositor.
(2) Journalize the necessary entries. The accounts have not been closed.
(3) What is the amount of cash in bank that should appear on the balance sheet as of June 30?

11-6A. John Cullum and Sons was organized on July 1 of the current year. The voucher system is not used. The following transactions are selected from those completed during July:

July 2. Purchased $5,000 of merchandise from Howard Industries, terms 1/10, n/30. Purchase invoices are recorded at the net price after deducting allowable cash discounts.

2. Issued a check for $198 to the American Insurance Company in payment of Policy No. F1727, dated July 1, covering public liability for one year in the amount of $200,000.

3. Issued a check to Sentry Insurance Co. in payment of the premiums on the following insurance policies, all dated July 1:

Policy No.	Property	Amount	Term	Premium
9172	Merchandise	$25,000	1 year	$180
9173	Building	50,000	3 years	684
437C	Delivery Equipment		1 year	504

12. Purchased $2,500 of merchandise from Palmer Co., terms 2/10, n/30.
18. Issued a check to the Parkland Guaranty Insurance Co. for $144 in payment of the premium on Policy No. 4265, dated July 16, covering fidelity insurance for one year in the amount of $10,000.
21. Paid the amount due Palmer Co. for invoice of July 12.
28. Issued a check for $100 to Worden's Garage in payment of the balance due on charges of $450 for repair of a delivery truck damaged in a collision earlier in the month. Sentry Insurance Co. paid $350 of the charge in accordance with the terms of Policy No. 437C, which has a $100 deductible clause on collision damage.
31. Paid the amount due Howard Industries for invoice of July 2.

Instructions:

(1) Record the transactions in general journal form.
(2) Record the relevant data for the current year in an insurance register similar to the one illustrated on pages 284 and 285. In allocating insurance expirations, round all expirations to the nearest one-half month.
(3) Journalize the insurance adjustment as of July 31.
(4) Considering only those insurance policies included above:
   (a) What will be the total amount of insurance expense for the current year ending December 31?
   (b) What will be the amount of unexpired insurance that will appear on the balance sheet at December 31 of the current year?

Chapter 12

PAYROLL SYSTEMS

OBJECTIVES OF PAYROLL SYSTEMS

The volume of expenditures for labor costs and related payroll taxes has a significant effect on the net income of most business enterprises. Although the degree of importance of such expenses varies widely, it is not uncommon for a business to expend nearly a third of its sales revenue for payroll and labor-related expenses. Accordingly, it is important that the payroll segment of the accounting system provides safeguards to insure that payments are in accord with management's general plans and its specific authorizations.

All employees of a firm expect and are entitled to receive their remuneration at regular intervals following the close of each payroll period. Regardless of the number of employees and of intricacies in computing the amounts to be paid, the payroll system must be designed to process the necessary data quickly and accurately and pay the correct amount to each employee. It is essential that the system provide adequate safeguards against overpayments, payments to fictitious persons, and other misappropriations of funds.

Various federal, state, and local laws require that employers accumulate certain specified data in their payroll records of a summary nature not only for payroll periods but also for each individual employee. Periodic reports of such data must be submitted to the appropriate governmental agencies and remittances made for amounts withheld from employees and for taxes levied on the employer. The records must be retained for specified periods of time and be available for inspection by those responsible for enforcement of the laws. In addition, payroll data may be useful in negotiations with labor unions, in settling employee grievances, and in determining entitlement to vacations, sick leaves, and retirement pensions.

EMPLOYER-EMPLOYEE RELATIONSHIP

Persons who perform remunerative services for a business enterprise may be classified either as employees or as independent contractors. Payroll systems are concerned only with employees and the records, reports, remuneration, taxes, etc., associated with the employer-employee relationship. The relationship of employer and employee generally exists when the person for whom the services are performed has the right to control and direct the individual in the performance of his services. Accordingly, salesclerks and bookkeepers in a retail store are unquestionably employees. Similarly, an accountant occupying the position of controller of a corporation is an employee. On the other hand, a public accountant or CPA engaged to audit the accounting records of a business chooses his own means of performing the services and is not subject to the control and guidance of his client. He is an independent contractor rather than an employee. In similar fashion an attorney working in the tax department of a corporation would be an employee, but an attorney engaged to negotiate a particular contract or defend a particular lawsuit would be an independent contractor.

Payments to independent contractors for services are usually referred to as *fees* or *charges*. Such payments are not part of the payroll system and are not subject to withholding or to the payroll taxes levied on employers.

297

TYPES OF REMUNERATION OF EMPLOYEES

The term *salary* is usually applied to payment for managerial, administrative, or similar services. The rate of salary is ordinarily expressed in terms of a month or a year. Remuneration for manual labor, both skilled and unskilled, is commonly referred to as *wages* and is stated on an hourly, weekly, or piecework basis. In practice, the terms salary and wages are often used interchangeably.

The basic salary or wage of an employee may be supplemented by commissions, bonuses, profit sharing, or cost-of-living adjustments. The form in which remuneration is paid generally has no effect on the manner in which it is treated by either the employer or the employee. Although payment is usually in terms of cash, it may be in other media such as securities, notes, lodging, or other property or services.

MEASUREMENT OF EMPLOYEE EARNINGS

Salary and wage rates are determined, in general, by agreement between the employer and the employees. Enterprises engaged in interstate commerce must also conform to the requirements of the Federal Fair Labor Standards Act. Employers covered by this legislation, which is commonly known as the "wages and hours law," are required to pay a minimum rate of $1\frac{1}{2}$ times the regular rate for all hours worked in excess of 40 hours per week. Exemptions from the requirements are provided for executive, administrative, and certain supervisory positions. Premium rates for overtime or for working at night or other less desirable times are fairly common, even when not required by law, and the premium rates may be as much as twice the base rate.

The computation of the earnings of an employee is illustrated below. It is assumed that Harold B. Ashton is employed at the rate of $5.50 per hour for the first 40 hours in the weekly pay period and at $8.25 ($5.50 + $2.75) per hour for any additional hours. His time card reveals that he worked 44 hours during the week ended November 21. His earnings for that week are computed as follows:

Earnings at base rate............	40 × $5.50	$220.00
Earnings at overtime rate........	4 × $8.25	33.00
Total earnings........................		$253.00

The foregoing computations can be stated in generalized arithmetic formulas or *algorithms*. If the hours worked during the week are less than or equal to ($\leq$) 40, the formula may be expressed by the following equation, where E represents total earnings, H represents hours worked, and R represents hourly rate:

$$E = H \times R$$

The foregoing equation cannot be used to determine the earnings of an employee who has worked more than ($>$) 40 hours during the week because the overtime rate differs from the basic rate. The expansion of the equation to incorporate the additional factor of overtime yields the following:

$$E = 40\,R + 1.5\,R\,(H - 40)$$

The two equations can be expressed graphically in the following algorithm:

If	*Then*
$H \leq 40$	$E = H \times R$
$H > 40$	$E = 40R + 1.5R(H - 40)$

After the value of H and R are known for each employee at the conclusion of a payroll period, the earnings of each employee can be computed accurately and speedily. Application of the standardized procedure of the algorithm to mechanized or electronic processing equipment makes it possible to process routinely a payroll regardless of the number of employees.

Many enterprises pay their employees an annual bonus in addition to their regular salary or wage. The amount of the bonus is often based on the productivity of the employees, as measured by the net income of the enterprise. Such profit-sharing bonuses are part of the employee's earnings subject to withholding and payroll taxes; they are deductible expenses of the enterprise in determining income subject to the federal income tax.

The method used in determining the amount of a profit-sharing bonus is ordinarily stipulated in the agreement between the employer and the employees. When the amount of the bonus is measured by a specified percentage of income, there are four basic formulas for the computation. The percentage may be applied (1) to income before deducting the bonus and income taxes, (2) to income after deducting the bonus but before deducting income taxes, (3) to income before deducting the bonus but after deducting income taxes, or (4) to net income after deducting both the bonus and income taxes.

Determination of a 10% bonus according to each of the four methods is illustrated below, based on the assumption that the employer's income before deducting the bonus and income taxes amounts to $100,000, and that income taxes are levied at the rate of 40% of income. Bonus and income taxes are abbreviated as B and T respectively.

299

(1) *B based on income before deducting B and T.*
$$B = .10 \,(\$100,000)$$
$$\text{Bonus} = \$10,000$$

(2) *B based on income after deducting B but before deducting T.*
$$B = .10 \,(\$100,000 - B)$$
Simplifying: $\quad B = \$10,000 - .10B$
Transposing: $\quad 1.10B = \$10,000$
$$\text{Bonus} = \$9,090.91$$

(3) *B based on income before deducting B but after deducting T.*
B equation: $\quad B = .10 \,(\$100,000 - T)$
T equation: $\quad T = .40 \,(\$100,000 - B)$
Substituting for T in the B equation and solving for B:
$$B = .10 \,[\$100,000 - .40 \,(\$100,000 - B)]$$
Simplifying: $\quad B = .10 \,(\$100,000 - \$40,000 + .40B)$
Simplifying: $\quad B = \$10,000 - \$4,000 + .04B$
Transposing: $\quad .96B = \$6,000$
$$\text{Bonus} = \$6,250$$

(4) *B based on net income after deducting B and T.*
B equation: $\quad B = .10 \,(\$100,000 - B - T)$
T equation: $\quad T = .40 \,(\$100,000 - B)$
Substituting for T in the B equation and solving for B:
$$B = .10 \,[\$100,000 - B - .40 \,(\$100,000 - B)]$$
Simplifying: $\quad B = .10 \,(\$100,000 - B - \$40,000 + .40B)$
Simplifying: $\quad B = \$10,000 - .10B - \$4,000 + .04B$
Transposing: $\quad 1.06B = \$6,000$
$$\text{Bonus} = \$5,660.38$$

With the amount of the bonus possibilities ranging from the high of $10,000 to the low of $5,660.38, the importance of strict adherence to the agreement is evident. If the bonus is to be shared by all of the employees, the agreement must also provide for the manner by which the bonus is divided among them. If no distinction is made between classes of employees (managerial, clerical, etc.), the allocation would ordinarily be based on the relationship of each employee's salary or wage for the year to the total salaries and wages of the enterprise.

DEDUCTIONS FROM EMPLOYEE EARNINGS

The total earnings of an employee for a payroll period are frequently referred to as the *gross pay*. From it is subtracted one or more *deductions* to arrive at the *net pay*, which is the amount the employer is obligated to pay the employee. The deductions of widest applicability and usually of greatest magnitude are for federal taxes. Deductions may also be required for state or local income taxes and for contributions to state unemployment compensation programs. Other deductions may be authorized by individual employees.

FICA tax. Most employers are required by the Federal Insurance Contributions Act (FICA) to withhold a portion of the earnings of each of their employees. The amount withheld is the employees' contribution to the combined federal programs for old-age and disability benefits, insurance benefits to survivors, and health insurance for the aged (medicare). With very few exceptions, employers are required to withhold from each employee a tax at a specified rate on earnings up to a specified amount paid in the calendar year.[1] Although both the schedule of future tax rates and the maximum amount subject to tax are revised frequently by Congress, such changes have no effect on the basic outline of the payroll system. For purposes of illustration, a rate of 6% on maximum annual earnings of $12,000, or a maximum annual tax of $720, will be assumed.

Federal income tax. Except for certain types of employment, all employers are required to withhold a portion of the earnings of their employees for payment of the employees' liability for federal income tax. The amount required to be withheld from each employee varies in accordance with the amount of his gross pay, marital status, and the estimated deductions and exemptions to which he will be entitled when filing his annual income tax return. The withholding can be computed in accordance with either the "percentage" method, which necessitates the determination of taxable earnings and multiplication by the appro-

[1]As of December 31, 1972 the Internal Revenue Code specifies for 1973 a tax rate of 5.85% on maximum earnings of $10,800, with the maximum subject to tax increasing to $12,000 in 1974. The rate is scheduled to increase to 6.05% in 1978.

priate tax rate, or by the "wage-bracket" method, which is a one-step operation utilizing tables of predetermined withholding amounts.

Other deductions. Deductions from gross earnings for payment of taxes are compulsory; neither the employer nor the employee has any choice in the matter. In addition, however, there may be other deductions authorized by individual employees or by the union representing them. For example, an employee may authorize deductions of specified amounts for the purchase of United States savings bonds, for contributions to a United Fund or other charitable organization, for payment of premiums on various types of employee insurance, or for the purchase of a retirement annuity. The union contract may also require the deduction of union dues or other deductions for group benefits.

COMPUTATION OF EMPLOYEE NET PAY

Gross earnings for a payroll period less the payroll deductions yields the amount to be paid to the employee, which is frequently called the *net* or *take home* pay. The amount to be paid Harold B. Ashton is $203.90, based on the following summary:

Gross earnings for the week............		$253.00
Deductions:		
FICA tax........................	$ 6.90	
Federal income tax...............	30.70	
U.S. savings bonds................	6.50	
United Fund.....................	5.00	
Total deductions.................		49.10
Net pay..........................		$203.90

As has been indicated, there is a ceiling on the annual earnings subject to the FICA tax, and consequently the amount of the annual tax is also limited. Therefore, when determining the amount of FICA tax to withhold from an employee for a payroll period, it is necessary to refer to one of the following cumulative amounts:

(1) Employee gross earnings for the year prior to the current payroll period, or

(2) Employee tax withheld for the year prior to the current payroll period.

To continue with the Ashton illustration, reference to his earnings record indicates cumulative earnings of $11,885 prior to the current week's earnings of $253. The amount of the current week's earnings subject to tax is therefore the maximum of $12,000 − $11,885, or $115, and the FICA tax to be withheld is 6% of $115, or $6.90. Alternatively, the determination could be based on the amount of FICA tax withheld from Ashton prior to the current payroll period. This amount, according to the employee record, is $713.10 and the amount to be withheld is the maximum of $720 − $713.10, or $6.90.

301

Unlike the FICA tax, there is no ceiling on the amount of earnings subject to withholding for income taxes and hence no need to consider the cumulative earnings. The amount of federal income tax withheld, $30.70, was determined by reference to official withholding tax tables issued by the Internal Revenue Service. The deductions for the purchase of bonds and for the charitable contribution were in accordance with Ashton's specific authorizations.

As in the determination of gross earnings where overtime rates are a factor, the computation of some deductions can be generalized in the form of algorithms. The algorithm for the determination of the FICA tax deduction, based on the maximum deduction approach, is presented below, where E represents current period's earnings, F represents current period's FICA deduction, and f represents cumulative FICA deductions prior to the current period.

If	*Then*
$f + (.06E) \leq \$720$	$F = .06E$
$f + (.06E) > \$720$	$F = \$720 - f$

An alternative generalization of the method of determining FICA deductions, based on the maximum taxable earnings approach, is illustrated at the top of the next page in the form of a *decision diagram*. The additional symbol "e" represents cumulative earnings prior to the current period.

The elements of the decision diagram are merely examples of standardized instructions that can be applied to computations involving

PAYROLL FOR WEEK ENDING

NAME	TOTAL HOURS	EARNINGS REGULAR	EARNINGS OVERTIME	EARNINGS TOTAL	TAXABLE EARNINGS UNEMPLOY- MENT COMP.	TAXABLE EARNINGS FICA
ASHTON, HAROLD B.	44	220.00	33.00	253.00		115.00
BALLARD, MARY	40	232.00		232.00	232.00	232.00
DAVIS, JOHN T.	41	160.00	6.00	166.00		166.00
DRAKE, PAUL W.		300.00		300.00		
WILLIAMS, ROSE V.	40	140.00		140.00	60.00	140.00
YORK, HENRY J.		220.00		220.00	220.00	220.00
		6,512.20	360.00	6,872.20	1,763.20	5,110.50

Miscellaneous Deductions: AR — Accounts Receivable

Payroll register

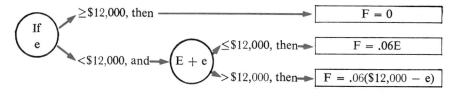

numerous variables. They are employed in many situations as an aid to routine processing of repetitive data, regardless of whether the processing is performed manually, mechanically, or electronically.

COMPONENTS OF PAYROLL SYSTEMS

Although complex organizational structures may necessitate the use of detailed subsystems, the major components common to most payroll systems are the *payroll register*, *paycheck*, and *employee's earnings record*. The framework for the illustrations and discussion here are relatively uncomplicated; in actual practice many modifications might be introduced.

PAYROLL REGISTER

The term *payroll* may be used to refer to the total amount paid to employees for a specified period. It is also often applied to the multi-column form used in assembling and summarizing the data needed at the end of each payroll period, a form referred to more specifically as the *payroll register*. Its design varies in accordance with variations in the number and classes of employees, the extent to which automation is employed, and the type of equipment used. A form suitable for a small number of employees is illustrated below and at the bottom of page 302.

303

NOVEMBER 21, 19--

	DEDUCTIONS				PAID		ACCOUNTS DEBITED	
FICA TAX	FEDERAL INCOME TAX	U.S. SAVINGS BONDS	MISCEL-LANEOUS	TOTAL	NET AMOUNT	CHECK NO.	SALES SALARY EXPENSE	OFFICE SALARY EXPENSE
6.90	30.70	6.50	UF 5.00	49.10	203.90	1136	253.00	
13.92	26.90	3.25	UF 4.00	48.07	183.93	1137		232.00
9.96	13.50		AR 16.50	39.96	126.04	1138		166.00
	40.20	20.00	UF 25.00	85.20	214.80	1139	300.00	
8.40	11.50	5.00		24.90	115.10	1170	140.00	
13.20	25.00	10.00	UF 15.00	63.20	156.80	1171		220.00
306.63	642.60	270.50	UF 182.00 AR 16.50	1,418.23	5,453.97		5,894.80	977.40

UF — United Fund

Payroll register

The nature of most of the data appearing in the illustrative payroll register is evident from the columnar headings. Number of hours worked and earnings and deduction data are inserted in the appropriate columns. The sum of the deductions applicable to an employee is then deducted from the total earnings to yield the amount to be paid. Recording the check numbers in the payroll register as the checks are written eliminates the need to maintain other detailed records of the payments.

The last two columns of the payroll register are used to accumulate the total wages or salaries to be charged to the expense accounts. This process is usually termed *payroll distribution*. If there is an extensive account classification of labor expense, the charges may be analyzed on a separate payroll distribution sheet.

The two columns under the general heading of Taxable Earnings are used in accumulating data needed to compute the employer's payroll taxes discussed later in the chapter.

The format of the illustrative payroll register and of most variants facilitates the determination of arithmetic accuracy prior to issuance of checks to employees and formal recording of the summary amounts. Specifically, all columnar totals except those in the Taxable Earnings columns should be cross-verified. The miscellaneous deductions must also be summarized by account classification. The tabulation that follows illustrates the method of cross-verification. In practice the amounts would be listed by means of an adding machine, taking the figures directly from the payroll register.

Earnings:		
Regular......................	$6,512.20	
Overtime.....................	360.00	
Total......................		$6,872.20
Deductions:		
FICA tax.....................	$ 306.63	
Federal income tax.............	642.60	
U.S. savings bonds.............	270.50	
United Fund..................	182.00	
Accounts receivable............	16.50	
Total......................		1,418.23
Paid — net amount..............		$5,453.97
Accounts debited:		
Sales Salary Expense............		$5,894.80
Office Salary Expense...........		977.40
Total (as above).............		$6,872.20

The payroll register may be used as a posting medium in a manner similar to that in which the voucher register and check register are used. Alternatively, it may be used as a supporting record in a manner similar to that in which the insurance register and the note registers are used. In the latter case the payroll data will be posted to the ledger accounts through the medium of a compound journal entry such as the following, which is based on the payroll register appearing at the bottom of pages 302 and 303.

Nov.	21	Sales Salary Expense....................	5,894 80		
		Office Salary Expense..................	977 40		
		FICA Tax Payable..................		306 63	
		Employees Income Tax Payable.......		642 60	
		Bond Deductions Payable.............		270 50	
		United Fund Deductions Payable......		182 00	
		Accounts Receivable — John T. Davis..		16 50	
		Salaries Payable.....................		5,453 97	
		Payroll for week ended November 21..			

The total expense incurred for the services of employees is recorded by the debits to the salary accounts. Amounts withheld from employees' earnings have no effect on the debits to the salary expense accounts. Of the six credits in the compound entry, five represent increases in specific liability accounts and one represents a decrease in the accounts receivable account.

PAYCHECK

One of the principal outputs of the system is a series of payroll checks at the conclusion of each payroll period. The data needed for this purpose are provided by the payroll register, each line of which applies to an individual employee. It is possible to prepare the checks solely by reference to the net amount column of the register. However, the customary practice is to provide each employee with a statement of the details of the computation. Employers are required to do so in some states. The statement may be entirely separate from the check or it may be in the form of a detachable stub attached to the check.

EMPLOYEE'S EARNINGS RECORD

The necessity of having the cumulative amount of each employee's earnings readily available at the close of each payroll period was discussed earlier. Without such information or the related data on the cumulative amount of FICA tax previously withheld there would be no means of determining the appropriate amount to withhold from current earnings. It is essential therefore that detailed records be maintained for each employee.

A portion of an employee's earnings record is illustrated at the bottom of pages 306 and 307. The relationship between this record and the payroll register can be readily observed by tracing the amounts entered on Ashton's earnings record for November 21 back to its source, which is the first line of the payroll register illustrated at the bottom of pages 302 and 303.

In addition to spaces for recording data for each payroll period and the cumulative total of earnings, there are spaces for quarterly totals and the yearly total. These totals are used in various reports for tax, insurance, and other purposes. Copies of one such annual report, known as Form W-2, Wage and Tax Statement, must be submitted to each employee as well as to the Internal Revenue Service. The source of the amounts inserted in the statement illustrated on page 308 was the employee's earnings record reproduced below and at the bottom of the next page.

EMPLOYEE'S

NAME Ashton, Harold B.

ADDRESS 1986 Belmont Street   **PHONE** 531-1149

Lakewood, Ohio   44112

MARRIED √   **PER DAY** _____

SINGLE _____   **NUMBER OF EXEMPTIONS** 4   **PAY RATE** $220.00   **WEEK** √

MONTH _____

306

OCCUPATION Salesman   **EQUIVALENT HOURLY RATE** $5.50

LINE NO.	PERIOD ENDED	TOTAL HOURS	EARNINGS			
			REGULAR	OVERTIME	TOTAL	CUMULATIVE TOTAL
39	Sept. 26	42	220.00	16.50	236.50	10,320.75
THIRD QUARTER			2,640.00	495.00	3,135.00	
40	Oct. 3	43	220.00	24.75	244.75	10,565.50
46	Nov. 14	45	220.00	41.25	261.25	11,885.00
47	Nov. 21	44	220.00	33.00	253.00	12,138.00
48	Nov. 28	43	220.00	24.75	244.75	12,382.75
49	Dec. 5	42	220.00	16.50	236.50	12,619.25
50	Dec. 12	44	220.00	33.00	253.00	12,872.25
51	Dec. 19	41	220.00	8.25	228.25	13,100.50
52	Dec. 26	40	220.00		220.00	13,320.50
FOURTH QUARTER			2,860.00	486.75	3,346.75	
YEARLY TOTAL			11,440.00	1,880.50	13,320.50	

Employee's earnings record

CHARACTERISTICS OF INPUT DATA

Attention thus far has been directed to the end product or *output* of a payroll system, namely the payroll register, the checks payable to individual employees, the earnings records for each employee, and reports for tax and other purposes. The basic data entering the payroll system are sometimes called the *input* of the system. Input data that remain relatively unchanged and do not need to be reintroduced into the system for each payroll period are characterized as *constants*; those that differ from period to period are *variables*.

EARNINGS RECORD

soc. sec. no. 259-08-8114   EMPLOYEE NO. 15

DATE EMPLOYED June 15, 1966

DATE OF BIRTH April 22, 1940

DATE EMPLOYMENT TERMINATED

307

| DEDUCTIONS | | | | | PAID | | LINE NO. |
FICA TAX	FEDERAL INCOME TAX	U.S. BONDS	OTHER		TOTAL	NET AMOUNT	CHECK NO.	
14.19	28.90	6.50			49.59	186.91	866	39
188.10	396.80	84.50	AR	22.50	691.90	2,443.10		
14.69	30.70	6.50	UF	5.00	56.89	187.86	901	40
15.68	32.10	6.50			54.28	206.97	1101	46
6.90	30.70	6.50	UF	5.00	49.10	203.90	1136	47
	30.70	6.50			37.20	207.55	1172	48
	28.90	6.50	UF	5.00	40.40	196.10	1220	49
	30.70	6.50			37.20	215.80	1254	50
	27.30	6.50			33.80	194.45	1285	51
	27.30	6.50			33.80	186.20	1323	52
100.75	405.70	84.50	UF	15.00	605.95	2,740.80		
720.00	1,622.70	338.00	AR UF	22.50 15.00	2,718.20	10,602.30		

Employee's earnings record

Wage and
tax statement

Constants include such data for each employee as name and social security number, marital status, number of income tax exemptions claimed, rate of pay, functional category (office, sales, etc.), and department where employed. The FICA tax rate, maximum earnings subject to tax, and various tax tables are also constants which apply to all employees. The variable data for each employee include the number of hours or days worked during each payroll period, days of sick leave with pay, vacation credits, and cumulative amounts of earnings and taxes withheld. If salespersons are employed on a commission basis, the amount of their sales would also vary from period to period. The forms used in initially recording both the constant and the variable data vary widely according to the complexities of the payroll system and the processing methods employed.

PAYROLL SYSTEM DIAGRAM

The flow of data within segments of an accounting system may be shown by diagrams such as the one illustrated on the next page. It depicts the interrelationships of the principal components of the payroll system described in this chapter. The requirement of constant updating of the employee's earnings record is indicated by the dotted line.

INTERNAL CONTROLS FOR PAYROLL SYSTEMS

The considerable volume of data required and the computations necessary to determine the amount of each paycheck is evident. As the number of employees and the mass of data increase, the number of individuals required to manage and process payroll data likewise increases. Such characteristics, together with the relative magnitude of labor costs in most businesses, are indicative of the need for controls that will assure the reliability of the data and minimize the opportunity for misappropriation of funds.

308

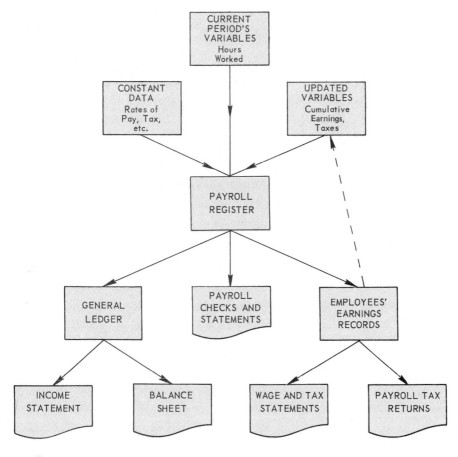

Flow diagram of
a payroll system

309

The expenditure and cash disbursement controls discussed in the preceding chapter are of course applicable to payrolls. Thus, the use of the voucher system and the requirement that all payments be supported by vouchers are desirable. The addition or deletion of names on the payroll should be supported by written authorizations from the personnel department. It is also essential that employees' attendance records be controlled in such a manner as to prevent errors and abuses. Perhaps the most basic and widely used records are "In and Out" cards whereby employees indicate, often by "punching" a time clock, their time of arrival and departure. Employee identification cards or badges are also widely used in this connection to assure that all salaries and wages paid are paid to the proper individuals.

Employees may be paid (1) by checks drawn on the regular bank account, (2) by the use of currency, or (3) by special payroll checks drawn on a special bank account designated for this purpose.

Regular bank account. When employees are paid by checks drawn on the regular bank account and the voucher system is employed, it is necessary to prepare a voucher for the net amount to be paid the employees. The voucher is then recorded in the voucher register as a debit to Salaries Payable and a credit to Accounts Payable, and payment is recorded in the check register in the usual manner. If the voucher system is not used, the payment would be recorded merely by a debit to Salaries Payable and a credit to Cash.

It should be understood, of course, that the general journal entry derived from the payroll register, which is illustrated on pages 302 and 303, would precede the entries just described. It should also be noted that the entire amount paid may be recorded as a single item regardless of the number of employees. There is no need to record each check separately in the check register because all of the details are available in the payroll register for future reference.

Currency. Currency is sometimes used as the medium of payment when the payroll is paid each week or when the business location or the time of payment are such that banking or check-cashing facilities are not readily available to employees. In such cases a single check, payable to Payroll, is drawn for the entire amount to be paid. The check is then cashed at the bank and the money is inserted in individual payroll envelopes. The procedures for recording the payment correspond to those outlined in the preceding section.

When payment is made in currency, each employee should be required to sign a receipt which serves as evidence of payment.

Special bank account. Most employers with a large number of employees use a special bank account and payroll checks designed specifically for the purpose. After the data for the payroll period have been recorded and summarized in the payroll register, a single check for the total amount to be paid is drawn on the firm's regular bank account and deposited in a special account. The individual payroll checks are then drawn against the special payroll account, and the numbers of the payroll checks are inserted in the payroll register.

The use of special payroll checks makes it possible to relieve the treasurer or other executives of the task of signing a large number of regular checks each payday. The responsibility for signing payroll checks may be assigned to the paymaster, or mechanical means of signing the checks may be employed. Another advantage of this system is that the task of reconciling the regular bank statement is simplified. The paid payroll checks are returned by the bank separately from regular checks and are accompanied by a statement of the special bank account. Any balance shown on the bank's statement will correspond to the sum of the payroll checks outstanding because the amount of each deposit is exactly the same as the total amount of checks drawn. The recording procedures are the same as when checks on the regular bank account are used.

EMPLOYER'S PAYROLL TAXES

Thus far the discussion of taxes has been confined to those levied against employees and withheld by employers. Most employers are subject to federal and state taxes based on the amount of remuneration earned by their employees. Such taxes constitute an operating expense of the business and may in the aggregate amount to a relatively substantial sum.

FICA tax. Employers are required to contribute to the Federal Insurance Contributions Act program for each employee. The tax rate and the maximum amount of remuneration of an employee entering into an employer's tax base correspond to those applicable to employees, which for purposes of illustration are assumed to be 6% and $12,000 respectively.

Federal unemployment compensation tax. Unemployment insurance provides temporary relief to those who become unemployed as a result of economic forces beyond their control and also tends to encourage full employment. Types of employment subject to the unemployment insurance program are similar to those covered by the FICA tax. The tax is levied on employers only, rather than on both employers and employees, and is applicable only to the first $4,200 of remuneration of each covered employee during a calendar year. The funds collected by the federal government are not paid out as benefits to the unemployed but are allocated among the states for use in administering state programs.

State unemployment compensation tax. The amounts paid as benefits to unemployed persons are obtained, for the most part, by taxes levied upon employers only. A very few states also require employee contributions. The rates of tax and the tax base vary, and in most states employers who provide steady employment for their employees are awarded reduced rates. The employment experience and the status of each employer's tax account are reviewed annually, and the merit ratings and tax rates are revised accordingly.

RECORDING AND PAYING PAYROLL TAXES

Each time the payroll register is prepared, the amounts of all employees' current earnings entering the tax base are listed in the respective taxable earnings columns. As explained earlier, the cumulative amounts of each employee's earnings just prior to the current period are available in the employee's earnings record.

311

According to the payroll register illustrated on pages 302 and 303, for the week ended November 21, the amount of remuneration subject to FICA tax was $5,110.50 and the amount subject to state and federal unemployment compensation taxes was $1,763.20. Multiplication by the respective tax rates assumed to be applicable yields the following amounts:

FICA tax............................	$306.63
State unemployment compensation tax.....	31.74
Federal unemployment compensation tax...	8.82
Total payroll taxes expense.............	$347.19

The general journal entry to record the payroll tax expense for the week and the liability for the taxes accrued is as follows:

Nov.	21	Payroll Taxes Expense	347	19		
		FICA Tax Payable..................			306	63
		State Unemployment Tax Payable.....			31	74
		Federal Unemployment Tax Payable...			8	82
		Payroll taxes for the week ended November 21.				

Payment of the liability for each of the taxes is recorded in the same manner as the payment of other liabilities. Employers are required to compute and report all payroll taxes on the calendar year basis regardless of the fiscal year they may employ for financial reporting and income tax purposes. Details of the federal income tax and FICA tax withheld from employees are combined with the employer's FICA tax on a single return filed each quarter, accompanied by the amount of tax due. Earlier payments, on a weekly, semimonthly, or monthly basis, are required when the combined taxes exceed certain specified minimums. Unemployment compensation tax returns and payments are required by the federal government on an annual basis. Earlier payments, on a quarterly basis, are required when the tax exceeds a certain minimum. Unemployment compensation tax returns and payments are required by most states on a quarterly basis.

ACCRUAL OF PAYROLL TAXES

All payroll taxes levied against employers become liabilities at the time the related remuneration is *paid* to employees, rather than at the time the liability to the employees is incurred. Observance of this requirement may create a problem of expense allocation among periods of time. To illustrate the situation, assume that an enterprise using the calendar year as its fiscal year pays its employees on Friday for a weekly payroll period ending the preceding Wednesday, the two-day lag between Wednesday and Friday being required to process the payroll. Regardless of the day of the week on which the year ends, there will be some accrued wages; if it ends on a Thursday, the accrual will cover a full week plus an extra day. Logically, the unpaid wages and the related payroll taxes should both be charged to the period that benefited from the services performed by the employees. On the other hand, there is legally no liability for the payroll taxes until the wages are paid in January, when a new cycle of earnings subject to tax is begun. The distortion of net income that would result from failure to accrue the payroll taxes might well be inconsequential. The practice adopted should, of course, be followed consistently.

QUESTIONS

1. What is the distinction between an employee and an independent contractor? Why is it necessary to make this distinction?

2. (a) Identify the federal taxes that most employers are required to withhold from employees. (b) Give the titles of the accounts to which the amounts withheld are credited.

3. If an employee is granted a "profit-sharing bonus," is the amount of the bonus (a) part of the employee's earnings and (b) deductible as an expense of the enterprise in determining the federal income tax?

4. What is *net* or *take home* pay?

313

5. Why is salary expense measured by the gross amount of the payroll rather than the net amount actually paid to employees?

6. For which of the following payroll related taxes is there a ceiling on the annual earnings subject to the tax: (a) FICA tax, (b) federal income tax, (c) federal unemployment compensation tax?

7. Indicate the principal functions served by the employee's earnings record.

8. What is the source of the information needed to prepare the Wage and Tax Statements (Form W-2) that must be distributed to employees after the close of the calendar year?

9. Explain how a payroll system that is properly designed and operated tends to give assurance (a) that wages paid are based upon hours actually worked, and (b) that payroll checks are not issued to fictitious employees.

10. The following questions are based on the assumption that the employer pays his employees in currency and that the pay envelopes are prepared by an employee rather than by the bank: (a) Why would it be advisable to obtain from the bank the exact amount of money needed for a payroll? (b) How could the exact number of each bill and coin denomination needed be determined efficiently in advance?

11. An employer who pays in currency draws a check for $27,910.32 for the payroll of November 21. After the money is inserted in the envelopes for the 120 employees, there remains $12 in currency. Assuming that the arithmetical accuracy of the payroll register has been determined and that the amounts of net pay stated on the pay envelopes agree with the payroll register, what should be done to locate the error?

12. The following questions are based on the assumption of a weekly payroll period and the use of a special bank account for payroll: (a) At what times should deposits be made in the account? (b) How is the amount of the deposit determined? (c) Is it necessary to have in the general ledger an account entitled "Cash in Bank — Special Payroll Account"? Explain. (d) The bank statement for the payroll bank account for the month ended April 30 indicates a bank balance of $678.12. Assuming that the bank has made no errors, what does this amount represent?

13. Identify the payroll taxes levied against employers.

14. The Larson Company uses the voucher system and for each weekly pay period prepares a voucher for the net amount to be paid to employees. (a) Should this voucher be prepared before the individual payroll checks are distributed to the employees? Explain. (b) At the time the weekly payroll voucher is prepared, should a voucher also be prepared for the liability for taxes withheld from employees? Explain.

15. Prior to the last weekly payroll period of the calendar year, the cumulative earnings of employees A and B are $11,850 and $12,140 respectively. Their earnings for the last completed payroll period of the year, which will be paid in January, are $200 each. If the amount of earnings subject to FICA tax is $12,000 and the tax rate is 6%, (a) what will be the employer's FICA tax on the two salary amounts of $200 each; (b) what is the employer's total FICA tax expense for employees A and B for the calendar year just ended?

16. Do payroll taxes levied against employers become liabilities at the time the liabilities to employees for wages are incurred or at the time the wages are paid?

EXERCISES

12-1. Develop an algorithm, in the form illustrated in this chapter, to compute the amount of each employee's weekly earnings subject to state unemployment compensation tax. Assume that the tax is 2.3% on the first $4,200 of each employee's earnings during the year and that the following symbols are to be used:

e — Cumulative earnings subject to state unemployment compensation tax prior to current week

E — Current week's earnings

S — Amount of current week's earnings subject to state unemployment compensation tax

12-2. Oliver Kinney is employed at the rate of $5.60 per hour, with time and a half for all hours in excess of 40 worked during a week. Data to be considered in preparing the payroll register, Kinney's paycheck, and his earnings record for the current week ended October 26 are as follows: hours worked, 45; federal income tax withheld, $32.60; cumulative earnings for year prior to current week, $11,810.50; FICA tax withheld prior to current week, $708.63. Compute the following for the week ended October 26: (a) Kinney's earnings; (b) FICA tax to be withheld (6% on maximum of $12,000); (c) net amount to be paid.

12-3. The general manager of a business enterprise is entitled to an annual profit-sharing bonus of 5%. For the current year income before bonus and income taxes is $63,000 and income taxes are estimated at 40% of income before income taxes. Determine the amount of the bonus assuming that (a) the bonus is based on income before deductions for bonus and income taxes, (b) the bonus is based on income after deduction for bonus but before deduction for income taxes, (c) the bonus is based on income after deduction for income taxes but before deduction for bonus, and (d) the bonus is based on net income after deduction for both bonus and income taxes.

12-4. In the following summary of columnar totals of a payroll register, some amounts have been intentionally omitted:

Earnings:

(1) At regular rate.....	——	(7) Medical insurance	$	280.77
(2) At overtime rate....	$ 810.70	(8) Total deductions.		2,105.21
(3) Total earnings.....	——	(9) Net amount paid.		12,725.43

Deductions:

Accounts debited:

(4) FICA tax..........	484.60	(10) Factory Wages...	——
(5) Income tax withheld	1,185.84	(11) Sales Salaries....	4,661.79
(6) Union dues........	——	(12) Office Salaries....	1,350.08

(a) Determine the totals omitted in lines (1), (3), (6), and (10). (b) Present the general journal entry to record the payroll. (c) Present, in general journal form, the entry to record the voucher for the payroll. (d) Present, in general journal form, the entry to record the payment of the payroll. (e) From the data given in this exercise and your answer to part (a), would you conclude that this payroll was paid sometime during the first few weeks of the calendar year? Explain.

315

12-5. According to a summary of the payroll register of Norris and Co. for the four weekly payrolls paid in August, the amount of earnings was $130,000, of which $20,000 was not subject to FICA tax and $95,000 was not subject to state and federal unemployment taxes. (a) Determine the employer's payroll taxes expense for the month using the following rates: FICA, 6%; state unemployment, 2.5%; federal unemployment, .5%. (b) Present the general journal entry to record the accrual of payroll taxes for the month.

12-6. The employees' earnings records for the calendar year for the Fletcher Optical Service yield the information below:

Employee	Cumulative Earnings
Allison, Paul	$13,100
Dawson, Edith	6,750
Garner, Marie	12,500
Johns, Ralph	4,900
Paulson, James	8,780
Reese, Norman	2,150
	$48,180

The FICA tax during the year was levied at the rate of 6% on the first $12,000 of earnings, and unemployment insurance rates were 1.8% for the state and .5% for the federal on the first $4,200 of earnings. (a) Compute the total amount of payroll taxes borne by the employees. (b) Compute the total amount of payroll taxes borne by the employer. (c) What percentage of the employer's total payroll costs was represented by payroll taxes?

PROBLEMS

The following additional problems for this chapter are located in Appendix B: 12-1B, 12-2B, 12-3B, 12-5B.

12-1A. The Conley Corporation has seven employees. They are paid on an hourly basis, receiving time-and-one-half pay for all hours worked in excess of 40 a week. The record of time worked for the week ended December 12 of the current year, together with other relevant information, is summarized below:

Name	Total Hours	Hourly Rate	Income Tax Withheld	Bond Deductions	Cumulative Earnings, December 5
A	40	$3.25	$ 9.90	$1.50	$ 6,220
B	44	3.50	15.10	1.75	6,770
C	24	2.90	3.40	——	2,125
D	42	5.25	23.10	——	11,900
E	45	5.00	26.90	7.50	12,150
F	40	4.25	16.70	2.00	8,220
G	48	5.20	34.50	1.75	4,140

In addition to withholdings for income tax, FICA tax, and bond purchases, $22 is to be withheld from B for partial payment of his account receivable.

A and C are office employees; the others are salesmen. The following tax rates and limitations are assumed: FICA, 6% on maximum of $12,000; state unemployment (employer only), 2.2% on maximum of $4,200; federal unemployment, .5% on maximum of $4,200.

Instructions:

(1) Prepare the payroll register for the week, using a form like the one illustrated on pages 302 and 303.

(2) Journalize the entry to record the payroll for the week.

(3) The company uses a voucher system and pays by regular check. Give the necessary entries in *general journal form* to record the payroll voucher and the issuance of the checks.

(4) Complete the payroll register by inserting the check numbers, beginning with No. 876.

(5) Journalize the entry to record the employer's payroll taxes for the week.

If the working papers correlating with the textbook are not used, omit Problem 12-2A.

12-2A. The payroll register for Bell and Powell Company for the week ending November 27 of the current fiscal year is presented in the working papers.

Instructions:

(1) Journalize the entry to record the payroll for the week.

(2) Assuming the use of a voucher system and payment by regular check, present the entries, in *general journal form*, to record the payroll voucher and the issuance of the checks to employees.

(3) Journalize the entry to record the employer's payroll taxes for the week. Assume the following tax rates: FICA, 6%; state unemployment, 2.4%; federal unemployment, .5%.

(4) Present the entries, in *general journal form*, to record the following

transactions selected from those completed by Bell and Powell Company:

Dec. 14. Prepared a voucher, payable to First National Bank, for employees income taxes, $933.40, and FICA taxes, $697.12, on salaries paid in November.

14. Issued a check to First National Bank in payment of the above voucher.

12-3A. The following information relative to the payroll for the week ended December 30 was abstracted from the payroll register and other records of Becker Transportation, Inc.:

Salaries:		Deductions:	
Sales salaries	$30,650	Income tax withheld	$3,855
Warehouse salaries	7,140	U.S. savings bonds	310
Office salaries	4,325	Group insurance	170
	$42,115	FICA tax withheld is assumed to total the same amount as the employer's tax.	

Tax rates assumed:

FICA, 6%
State unemployment (employer only), 2%
Federal unemployment, .5%

Instructions:

317

(1) Assuming that the payroll for the last week of the year is to be paid on December 31, present the following entries:
  (a) December 30, to record the payroll. Of the total payroll for the last week of the year, $20,710 is subject to FICA tax and $2,630 is subject to unemployment compensation taxes.
  (b) December 30, to record the employer's payroll taxes on the payroll to be paid on December 31.

(2) Assuming that the payroll for the last week of the year is to be paid on January 2 of the following fiscal year, present the following entries:
  (a) December 31, to record the payroll.
  (b) January 2, to record the employer's payroll taxes on the payroll to be paid on January 2.

12-4A. The following accounts, with the balances indicated, appear in the ledger of K. N. Doyle and Co. on December 1 of the current year:

214	Salaries Payable	——
215.1	FICA Tax Payable	$ 616.30
215.2	Employees Federal Income Tax Payable	876.45
215.3	Employees State Income Tax Payable	101.75
215.4	State Unemployment Tax Payable	150.70
215.5	Federal Unemployment Tax Payable	347.73
216.1	Bond Deductions Payable	312.50
216.2	Medical Insurance Payable	525.00
611	Sales Salary Expense	91,632.60
711	Officers Salary Expense	37,800.00
712	Office Salary Expense	8,690.30
719	Payroll Taxes Expense	6,500.55

The following transactions relating to payroll, payroll deductions, and payroll taxes occurred during December:

Dec. 1. Prepared Voucher No. 818, payable to Busey National Bank, for $187.50 to purchase United States savings bonds for employees.
2. Issued Check No. 929 in payment of Voucher No. 818.
12. Prepared Voucher No. 840 for $1,492.75, payable to Busey National Bank, for the amount of employees' federal income tax and FICA tax due on December 15.
12. Issued Check No. 948 in payment of Voucher No. 840.
14. Prepared a general journal entry to record the biweekly payroll. A summary of the payroll record follows:

> Deductions: FICA tax, $136.10; federal income tax withheld, $624.60; state income tax withheld, $64.50; bond deductions, $86.75; medical insurance deductions, $90

> Salary distribution: sales, $4,130; officers, $1,685; office, $740

> Net amount: $5,553.05

14. Prepared Voucher No. 851, payable to Payroll Bank Account, for the net amount of the biweekly payroll.
14. Issued Check No. 958 in payment of Voucher No. 851.
16. Prepared Voucher No. 854, payable to United Insurance Co., for $525, the semiannual premium on the group medical insurance policy.
17. Issued Check No. 961 in payment of Voucher No. 854.
28. Prepared a general journal entry to record the biweekly payroll. A summary of the payroll record follows:

> Deductions: FICA tax, $82.48; federal income tax withheld, $568.90; state income tax withheld, $59.75; bond deductions, $81.25

> Salary distribution: sales, $3,827; officers, $1,685; office, $740

> Net amount: $5,459.62

28. Prepared Voucher No. 886, payable to Payroll Bank Account, for the net amount of the biweekly payroll.
29. Issued Check No. 994 in payment of Voucher No. 886.
30. Prepared Voucher No. 887, payable to Busey National Bank, for $112.50 to purchase United States savings bonds for employees.
30. Issued Check No. 996 in payment of Voucher No. 887.
30. Prepared Voucher No. 888 for $101.75 payable to Busey National Bank, for the amount of employees' state income tax due on December 31.
30. Issued Check No. 997 in payment of Voucher No. 888.
31. Prepared a general journal entry to record the employer's payroll taxes on earnings paid in December. Taxable earnings for the two payrolls, according to the payroll records, are as follows: subject to FICA tax, $3,643; subject to unemployment compensation tax, $819.20. Assume the following tax rates: FICA, 6%; state unemployment, 2.2%; federal unemployment, .5%.

Instructions:

(1) Open the accounts listed and enter the account balances as of December 1.

(2) Record the transactions, using a voucher register, a check register, and a general journal. The only amount columns needed in the voucher register are Accounts Payable Cr. and Sundry Accounts Dr. (subdivided into Account, Post. Ref., and Amount). The only

amount columns needed in the check register are Accounts Payable Dr. and Cash in Bank Cr. After each entry, post to the accounts opened in the ledger and extend the new balances to the appropriate balance column.

(3) Journalize the adjusting entry on December 31 to record salaries for the incomplete payroll period. Salaries accrued are as follows: sales salaries, $375; officers salaries, $160; office salaries, $75. Post to the accounts.

(4) Journalize the entry to close the salary expense and payroll taxes expense accounts to Income Summary and post to the accounts.

(5) Journalize the entry on January 1 to reverse the adjustment of December 31 and post to the accounts.

12-5A. Putman Company began business on January 2 of last year. Salaries were paid to employees on the last day of each month and both FICA tax and federal income tax were withheld in the required amounts. All required payroll tax reports were filed and the correct amount of payroll taxes was remitted by the company for the calendar year. Before the Wage and Tax Statements (Form W-2) could be prepared for distribution to employees and filing with the Internal Revenue Service, the employees' earnings records were inadvertently destroyed.

Data on dates of employment, salary rates, and employees' income taxes withheld, which are summarized below, were obtained from personnel records and payroll registers. None of the employees resigned or were discharged during the year and there were no changes in salary rates. The FICA tax was withheld at the rate of 6% on the first $12,000 of salary.

319

Employee	Date First Employed	Monthly Salary	Monthly Income Tax Withheld
A	Jan. 2	$1,100	$140.10
B	Mar. 1	540	56.30
C	Jan. 2	870	97.20
D	Oct. 16	560	68.10
E	Jan. 2	1,000	117.00
F	Feb. 1	460	52.10
G	July 1	720	78.00

Instructions:

(1) Determine the amounts to be reported on each employee's Wage and Tax Statement (Form W-2) for the year, arranging the data in the following form:

Employee	Gross Earnings	Federal Income Tax Withheld	Earnings Subject to FICA Tax	FICA Tax Withheld

(2) Determine the total FICA tax withheld from employees during the year.

(3) Determine the following payroll taxes for the year incurred and paid by the employer: (a) FICA; (b) state unemployment compensation at 1.8% on first $4,200; (c) federal unemployment compensation at .5% on first $4,200; (d) total.

(4) In a manner similar to the illustrations in this chapter, develop four algorithms to describe the computations required to determine the four amounts in part (1), using the following symbols:

n = Number of payroll periods
g = Monthly gross earnings
f = Monthly federal income tax withheld
G = Total gross earnings
F = Total federal income tax withheld
T = Total earnings subject to FICA tax
S = Total FICA tax withheld

Chapter 13

SYSTEMS DESIGN AND AUTOMATED DATA PROCESSING

ACCOUNTING SYSTEM COMPONENTS

In a general sense an accounting system may be said to encompass the entire network of communications employed by a business organization to provide for its informational requirements. Indeed, there are frequent references to accounting systems as the "total informational system" of an enterprise. It is essential therefore that this communications network be designed to provide useful information to all interested parties on a timely basis.

The variety of types of information collected, summarized, and reported through accounting systems has increased markedly in recent years and will probably continue to increase. Regardless of the volume of data to be processed, however, there are certain broad principles that should be considered in the installation of an accounting system. Attention in this chapter is directed first to these broad principles. The various data processing methods — manual, mechanical, and electronic — which can be utilized to meet the informational needs of the individual enterprise are then presented.

The basic components of an accounting system are the forms, records, procedures, and data processing methods employed to obtain the various reports needed by the enterprise. *Forms* are the media initially used in recording transactions, such as sales invoices, vouchers, and bank checks. *Records* include ledgers, journals, registers, and other media used for compilations of data. Various *procedures* designed to safeguard business assets and control expenditures were described in the two preceding chapters. Although the *data processing methods* described and illustrated in earlier chapters were to a great extent manual in nature, there have been numerous references to data processing equipment. The *reports* to which attention has heretofore been primarily directed have been the principal financial statements. Many other statements and analyses are based on accounting data, a number of which are described and illustrated in later chapters. Reports may be characterized as the end product of the accounting system.

ACCOUNTING SYSTEM INSTALLATION AND REVISION

Prerequisite to designing and installing the accounting system of an enterprise is a thorough knowledge of its operations. At the time a business is organized, however, there are likely to be many undeterminable factors that will affect such facets of the system as the types and design of the forms needed, the number and titles of the accounts required, and the exact procedures to be employed. It is also quite common for a firm to expand its already successful operations into new areas not originally contemplated, to increase its volume of transactions, to employ additional personnel, and in other ways to "outgrow" its accounting system.

Many large business enterprises maintain an almost continuous review of their accounting system and may constantly be engaged in changing some portion of it. The task of revising an accounting system, either in its entirety or only in part, is composed of three phases: (1) *analysis*, (2) *design*, and (3) *implementation*.

322

Systems analysis. The objective of systems analysis is the determination of informational needs, the sources of such information, and the deficiencies in procedures and data processing methods currently employed. The analysis ordinarily begins with a review of organizational structure and job descriptions of the personnel affected, followed by a study of the forms, records, procedures, processing methods, and reports used by the enterprise. A detailed description of the system employed by the enterprise, including specific instructions to personnel and minute details of procedures, is of considerable value to the systems analyst in his fact-finding review. Such a compilation is usually referred to as the firm's *Systems Manual*.

In addition to assessing the shortcomings of the current system, the analyst should determine management's plans for changes in operations (volume, products, territories, etc.) in the foreseeable future.

Systems design. Accounting systems are altered as a result of the type of analysis described above. The design of the new system may involve only minor changes from the existing system, such as revision of a particular form and the related procedures and processing methods, or it may constitute a complete revision of the entire system. Systems designers must have a general knowledge of the merits of various types of data processing equipment, and the capacity to evaluate various alternatives.

Although successful systems design depends to a large extent upon the creativity, imagination, and general capabilities of the designer, observance of the following broad principles is essential:

1. The value of the information produced should be at least equal to the cost of obtaining it.
2. The internal control features should be adequate to safeguard assets and assure reliability of data.
3. There should be sufficient flexibility to accommodate increases in volume of data and changes in operating procedures and data processing methods without major disturbances to the existing system.

Systems implementation. The final phase of the creation or revision of an accounting system is to carry out, or implement, the proposals. New or revised forms, records, procedures, and equipment must be installed, and any that are no longer applicable must be withdrawn. All personnel responsible for operating the system must be carefully trained and closely supervised until satisfactory efficiency is achieved.

A major revision for a large organization, such as a change from manual processing to electronic processing, is customarily accomplished gradually over a protracted period rather than all at once. With such a procedure there is less likelihood that the flow of reliable data will be seriously impeded during the critical phase of implementation. Weaknesses and conflicting or unnecessary elements in the design may also become apparent during the implementation phase. They are more easily detected and remedied when changes in a system are adopted gradually, and the chaos that might otherwise occur is thereby avoided.

323

FLOW CHARTS

One of the principal devices used in systems analysis, design, and implementation is known as a *flow chart.* Such charts depict in graphic form the major data processing operations that are to be performed in accounting for a particular transaction or series of closely related transactions. They are helpful in visualizing the outline of a system and the relationships between the major processes to be performed. Symbols commonly employed in preparing flow charts are illustrated at the top of the next page. The term "processing," as it is employed in charting, usually refers to procedural matters as well as processing methods.

Flow charts are usually arranged so as to be read from top to bottom, the direction of flow being indicated by arrows. The nature of the process or phase of processing is usually written inside the rectangle. Similarly, when a decision is required at some point in the processing, the factors to be considered are described within the diamond symbol. To a large extent, decisions are connected with comparisons of two items of data. If they "match," the decision is to proceed with a particular process; if

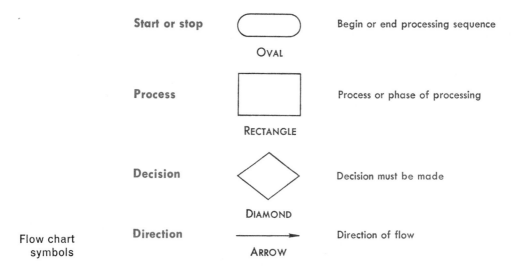

Start or stop — OVAL — Begin or end processing sequence

Process — RECTANGLE — Process or phase of processing

Decision — DIAMOND — Decision must be made

Flow chart
symbols

Direction — ARROW — Direction of flow

the desired relationship is lacking, the decision is to proceed in some other manner.

The flow chart presented on page 325 depicts the principal processes involved in posting debits to accounts receivable from sales invoices. An employee begins the process by arranging in alphabetical order the copies of sales invoices issued during the preceding day. The customer's name on the first invoice is then compared with the name on the first account in the accounts receivable ledger. If they match, the relevant information is posted to the account. If the names are not the same, successive pages of the ledger are examined until the appropriate account is reached. After posting the sales invoice, the employee proceeds to the next invoice and repeats the process until all invoices have been posted.

In preparing the illustrative flow chart it was assumed that no more than one invoice per day is issued to any customer and that an account form is prepared and inserted in the ledger each time credit is extended to a new customer. If the circumstances were otherwise the chart would need to be revised accordingly. The chart could also be expanded by adding data required for implementing a program of systems revision. It would be necessary to identify the equipment to be employed and to include detailed instructions on such procedures as the alphabetization of invoices, the removal and return of ledger pages, and the disposition of the invoices after posting.

DATA PROCESSING METHODS

With pencil, paper, and sufficient time, one or more persons can process all of the data needed by an enterprise. If the business requirements for data are few, manually kept records may serve reasonably well. But as an enterprise becomes larger and more complex, manual processing becomes too costly and time-consuming. Therefore, the tendency is to replace manual effort with machines that both reduce the cost and accelerate the processing of data.

Some of the more common machines are the typewriter, cash register, adding machine, calculator, and bookkeeping machine. The efficiency of the typewriter is increased merely by using carbon paper. Cash registers can record and accumulate totals for credit sales, cash sales, sales taxes, and receipts on account. The use of adding machines and calculators speeds up processing and minimizes the annoyance and the expense caused by arithmetical errors. Conventional bookkeeping machines, which have movable carriages and keyboards similar to those of a typewriter and accumulating devices similar to adding machines, are commonly used in journalizing transactions and posting to ledger accounts. For example, both an account receivable account and the sales journal can be placed in the machine together so that sales transactions can be recorded in the sales journal and debits can be posted to the accounts receivable ledger simultaneously. The sales journal remains in the machine until all sales for the day are recorded and posted to customers' accounts. The total credit to Sales and debit to Accounts Receivable for the day and the cumulative total for the month and the year to date are then automatically recorded. Similar techniques are employed for recording cash received on account and posting the credits to the customers' accounts. Additional forms may also be inserted in the machine with the accounting records so that monthly statements for customers can be prepared simultaneously with the recording of sales and cash receipts.

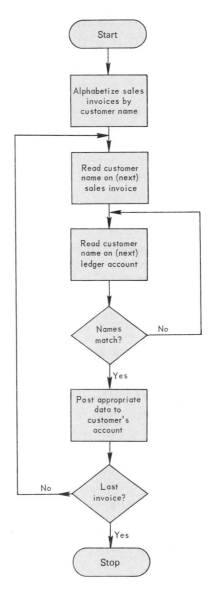

325

Flow chart — posting debits to customers' accounts

Although bookkeeping machines and other mechanical equipment speed up the accounting process and reduce the clerical costs of processing data, large enterprises need equipment that can process data even more expeditiously. This latent demand has stimulated the development of ever more elaborate mechanical devices and increasingly sophisticated electronic equipment. There has also been an accompanying trend toward bringing the cost of the services of such equipment down to levels that can be afforded by medium or smaller-size enterprises.

Automated data processing (ADP) is the general term applied to the processing of data by mechanical or electronic equipment (sometimes referred to as "hardware") that operates with a minimum of manual intervention. When all of the equipment employed by a processing system operates electronically, it may be termed *electronic data processing* (EDP). Much of the expansion of the role of accounting in systems design and installation has been made possible by the development and ever-widening use of automated data processing equipment.

It may be well to note that manual processing of data may be the most efficient method for some particular businesses and for some particular procedures. In any event a solid background of basic principles and an understanding of the general framework of accounting are prerequisites to any meaningful consideration of automated data processing.

326

NATURE OF AUTOMATED EQUIPMENT

A wide variety of automation equipment is produced by numerous manufacturers. It is an area noted for rapid technological progress and continuous innovation. Any detailed cataloging of the available equipment would be of little value for our purposes here. There are, however, some characteristics common to all automated systems that should be understood at the outset.

It is customary to subdivide automated data processing systems generally into three major parts: (1) input, (2) processing, and (3) output. *Input* refers to the raw data introduced into the system. The forms used to introduce the data into the system in preparation for processing are called the *input media*. The *processing* portion of a system is concerned largely with the processing equipment that manipulates the data in the desired manner. Information emitted by the system is the *output*. The forms used for various summary figures and reports are the *output media*.

Automated data processing systems may employ various combinations of input media, processing equipment, and output media. Such variables as the nature and the volume of data to be processed, the significance of speed and operating costs, and the type of output desired will influence the type of installation. The relationship of input media, processing equipment, and output media is indicated by the diagram on the next page.

INPUT MEDIA ⟶ PROCESSING EQUIPMENT ⟶ OUTPUT MEDIA

CHECK WITH
MAGNETIC
INK FIGURES

MAGNETIC INK
CHARACTER PROCESSOR

PUNCHED CARDS

DOCUMENT
WITH OPTICAL
CHARACTERS

OPTICAL
CHARACTER READER

PUNCHED PAPER TAPE

PUNCHED CARDS

PUNCHED CARD
MACHINE

MAGNETIC TAPE

PUNCHED PAPER TAPE

MAGNETIC DISKS

MAGNETIC TAPE

ELECTRONIC COMPUTER

30139
17
646553
3013917
1962
46553

CATHODE RAY TUBE

MAGNETIC DISKS

PRINTED MATTER

327

Automated
data
processing

INPUT MEDIA

Data to be processed automatically must be translated into special symbols and transcribed on a medium that can be read by the processing equipment. Input media may be prepared from sales tickets, purchases invoices, and other conventional business documents, or the input for a particular process may be the output media of some other phase of processing. The most common forms of input media are paper with symbols printed in magnetic ink or optical characters, punched cards, punched paper tape, magnetic tape, and magnetic disks.

Magnetic ink is commonly employed on check forms. The data in magnetic ink appear as numerical symbols printed along the lower margin of the check, as illustrated on page 269. The first set of symbols at the left identifies the Federal Reserve district and the drawee bank. The second set of symbols is the account number assigned to the drawer (depositor). The amount for which the check is drawn is inserted later at the right of the account number by the bank first receiving it. Many banks employ a similar system of encoding on their deposit tickets and other memorandums, with additional symbols to designate service charges and other special data.

328

Optical characters are employed in much the same manner as are magnetic ink characters. Data to be read optically may be printed in special type fonts similar in design to magnetic ink characters. A common use of optical characters is in the preparation of sales invoices where the special type font impressions are made from gasoline and other credit card forms.

Punched cards may be prepared for internal use only or they may be used as basic business documents as well as input media for the processing equipment. Checks issued by business firms, particularly those used for payroll or payment of dividends, are frequently of the punched card type. The admonition not to "fold, spindle, or otherwise mutilate" is frequently encountered, not only on checks but on punched card invoices and statements of account designed to be returned to the issuer.

Punched paper tape is employed as an input medium for internal use only, particularly when data must be transmitted from one business location to another, as from a branch to the central office. For example, details of sales orders received at one location may be recorded in the form of holes in the tape, which may then be used to transmit the data, by use of teletype, to one or more other locations. The data at the receiving end may also be produced in the form of punched tape or in other media, which in turn may be used to issue shipping instructions, prepare invoices, and perform other functions.

Magnetic tape is employed in much the same manner as punched paper tape. Data in magnetic form can be compressed into a much smaller area and thus reduce handling and storage expense. The speed of transmission and processing is also much greater than can be achieved with punched tape or punched cards.

Magnetic disks are used primarily as an input medium for internal use. Data is recorded on and read from both sides of the disk, which resembles a phonograph record. The advantages of magnetic disks are the speed with which the data can be transmitted into the processing equipment and the large amount of data that can be recorded on a single disk.

PROCESSING EQUIPMENT

Four of the most common types of processing equipment for automated systems are magnetic ink character processors, optical character readers, punched card machines, and electronic equipment.

Magnetic ink character processors. The most common application of magnetic ink character processors is by commercial banks. When magnetic ink character processors are fully employed, the recording of all entries to depositors' accounts, computation of service charges, and preparation of monthly statements are completely automated.

329

Optical character readers. The optical character reader reads specially designed characters in much the same manner as the magnetic ink character processor senses the impulses generated from magnetized characters. Optical character readers are employed by many oil companies to "read" the sales invoices received from their service stations representing sales made on account. When optical character readers are fully employed, the recording of all entries to customers' accounts and the preparation of monthly statements are completely automated.

Punched card machines. The earliest efforts in the development of large-scale mechanization of data processing were based on the use of punched cards. The standard-size card contains 80 vertical columns; a smaller, compact version contains 96 vertical columns. Each column has ten numbers (0 through 9) which may be used for recording numerical data. There are two additional positions in each column for use in coding alphabetical information or for other special purposes. The holes are punched in accordance with a predetermined code designed for the particular system, and the various machines are adjusted or "wired" to manipulate the data in the desired manner. An installation of punched card equipment, also referred to as unit record equipment, is composed of a series of machines, each of which performs a specific operation. Those most frequently employed, known as key punch, sorter, reproducer, collator, calculator, and tabulator, are briefly described in the paragraphs that follow.

The original data are recorded on the cards by a *key punch* which utilizes a keyboard similar to that of a typewriter. The simplest models punch holes only. Other models are capable of printing both alphabetical and numerical characters along the top of the card simultaneously with the punching operation, thus facilitating the manual reading of the card when the need arises.

One of the commonest processes applied to a group of punched cards is performed by a *sorter*. By successive "passes" through the sorter, cards may be placed in alphabetical or numerical sequence or classified into an almost unlimited number of subgroupings. Cards containing specified data can also be quickly selected without disturbing the sequence of the remaining group. The most efficient sorters can process cards at the rate of 2,000 per minute.

All or portions of data already punched on cards can be automatically transferred to a new set of cards by a *reproducer*. It is also used to convert manually made marks on a card into punched holes in the same card.

330

A *collator* is used to insert new cards at the proper point in an already existing group of appropriately arranged cards. Two separate groups of cards may also be merged together into a unified group.

A *calculator* performs basic arithmetical computations of addition, subtraction, multiplication, and division on the numerical data punched in a card. The computation is almost instantaneous and the resulting amount is converted to punched holes in the same card.

The final stage in a sequence of punched card processes is usually performed by a *tabulator*, which converts to printed matter the data punched in the cards. All or selected portions of the data on a card may be printed in a single horizontal line, with as many as 120 characters to a line. The sequence of the data on the line can differ from the sequence on the punched cards, and it is also possible to obtain subtotals by groups of cards or to omit details and print only subtotals and totals. A typical tabulator prints about 150 lines per minute.

Punched card equipment, arranged in appropriate sequence, can be used to process most accounting data. Human intervention is required only in preparing the punched cards, instructing the equipment, and transferring the cards from one machine to another. "Instructing" the equipment consists of the setting of dials or the wiring of control panels to achieve the proper flow and summarization of data.

Electronic computers. The creation and continued development of electronic computers may be subdivided into three periods or "generations," beginning about 1955, 1960, and 1965 respectively. During the first generation the circuitry was composed of vacuum tubes. The speed of operations attained during this period was approximately five hundred additions per minute. The second generation was characterized by the replacement of vacuum tubes by transistors. In addition to eliminating the problems caused by the heat generated by vacuum tubes, the space required for the equipment was reduced and the speed of operation was increased approximately tenfold. The circuitry of the present, or third, generation of computers is composed of silicon chips, with a further enhancement of speed and efficiency. Some models are capable of adding two ten-digit numbers in less than a millionth of a second.

Electronic computers are composed of three basic components: (1) storage unit, (2) arithmetic unit, and (3) control unit. The *storage* unit of a computer, also referred to as the *memory*, accepts and retains the data needed to perform an operation. The *arithmetic* unit performs the operations of addition, subtraction, multiplication, and division. In addition, it is capable of performing a logical operation. The usual situation involving logic requires the comparison of one number with another and the determination of whether the two numbers are the same or, if not, which number is the larger. On the basis of the results of the comparison, the computer proceeds to the next appropriate processing step. The *control* unit directs the flow of data into, through, and out of the computer in accordance with a set of instructions called a *program*. By following the program, which can be stored within a computer, the electronic computer provides an uninterrupted flow of processing from the input data at the beginning to the output data at the end.

331

Electronic computers employ codes and symbols that are unlike the numerical and alphabetical characters used in ordinary communication. The "machine language" used is not uniform for the various "brands" of computers, which causes difficulties in writing programs of broad applicability. The problem was alleviated by the creation of *common* or *symbolic* languages, which enable programmers to write instructions in English and algebraic terms. Three of the widely used common languages are known as FORTRAN (*FOR*mula *TRAN*slation), COBOL (*CO*mmon *B*usiness *O*riented *L*anguage), and PL/1 (*P*rogramming *L*anguage *1*).

After a program is expressed in terms of a common language, it is converted by means of a *compiler* into the machine language of the particular computer employed. For example, an addition operation is designated by FORTRAN as "+," by COBOL as "ADD," and by PL/1 as "+." Reference to the compiler for a particular computer model indicates that these symbols are translated into the operating code "0400."

Although punched cards and punched tape can be used as input media for electronic computers, magnetic tape or magnetic disks are more commonly used because of the greater speed with which a computer can sense the magnetic signals. Some magnetic tape and magnetic disks are capable of input speeds approximately 100 times faster than those possible with punched cards. Various types of equipment can be connected with an electronic computer to produce output media in the form desired. High-speed printers are capable of printing in excess of 1,000 lines per minute.

OUTPUT MEDIA

The output of processing equipment is ordinarily in the form of punched cards, punched paper tape, magnetic tape, magnetic disks, or data displayed on a cathode ray tube or printed on paper, depending upon the use that is to be made of the data. Punched cards, punched paper tape, magnetic tape, and magnetic disks may be used as input at a later date or in other parts of the system. For example, if monthly statements of account for customers are produced by a particular process employing punched cards, the process may simultaneously produce a punched card for the end-of-month balance of each account. At the end of the following month the cards are merged with the punched cards for current sales, returns, and cash receipts data, and the month-end processing routine repeated. A cathode ray tube is similar to a television picture tube. Output in the form of printed material is frequently referred to as "print-out."

AUTOMATED DATA PROCESSING FACILITIES

The potential uses of automated equipment in accounting are innumerable. However, because of its high cost the purchase or renting of such equipment is practicable only when there is a large and continuous mass of data to be processed. Businesses whose requirements are not sufficient to justify the high cost may obtain the advantages of ADP by using a data processing service center. Such centers provide both the necessary equipment and the operating personnel and charge a fee for their services.

A growing practice is for two or more business enterprises to purchase or rent equipment on a cooperative basis. Time-sharing systems are ordinarily composed of a centrally located, highly efficient computer, with input and output terminals for each of the cooperating firms. The terminals can be linked to the computer by teletype, telephone, or other means of communication. In a typical time-sharing system, contact with the computer can be established merely by dialing the appropriate telephone number, connecting the telephone with the terminal, and typing an encoded message on the terminal keyboard.

Input   Processing   Output

International Business Machines Corporation

An electronic
computer system

APPLICATIONS OF AUTOMATED EQUIPMENT

Although in recent years the processing of data has become highly automated for many enterprises, the basic principles and objectives of accounting have not changed. The form of financial statements is not affected, documents to evidence transactions are still essential, and sound principles of internal control and systems design are still relevant. Automation may affect the form of accounting records and the sequence of processing. Less time is required to process accounting data, and additional analyses helpful to management can be produced. Illustrative uses of automated equipment in accounting systems are briefly described in the paragraphs that follow.

333

Accounts receivable. A common method of processing accounts receivable is described in the following outline:

1. A master card is prepared for each customer's account, holes being punched for the name, address, and any other desired information.
2. A combination typewriter and card punch is used to prepare simultaneously conventional sales invoices and punched cards, the sales invoices being sent to customers and the cards becoming the input media for additional processing.
3. The punched cards for sales are sorted alphabetically by customer and are merged with the master accounts receivable cards.
4. As remittances are received and allowances granted, cards are appropriately punched, sorted, and merged with the other punched cards.
5. At the end of the month, the punched cards are processed by a tabulator that prints the monthly statements of account and punches new cards with the ending balances. The cards representing debits and credits to the accounts during the month are removed and the new balance cards are merged with the master cards, ready for transactions of the following month.

Although the foregoing outline was restricted to the processing of accounts receivable, it should be noted that the cards punched for sales, sales allowances, and cash receipts will also be used to determine the monthly transaction totals. Additional processing of the cards representing sales can yield analyses of sales by product, territory, salesman, magnitude, and various combinations of such factors. If appropriate data regarding the product are recorded on the same cards, they can also be used as a part of a perpetual inventory system.

Perpetual inventories. The use of punched card or electronic equipment in maintaining perpetual inventory records is quite common. The principal processes involved in a punched card system are as follows:

1. A master card is prepared for each commodity, holes being punched to identify the commodity, its color, unit size or weight, or other descriptive data, storage location, and any other information desired.
2. The inventory of each commodity is punched on a separate card as of the date the system is installed, each card being keyed to its related master card. Quantities only may be recorded, or unit cost and total cost may also be punched.
3. Each time the inventory of a commodity increases by purchase or sales return, or decreases by sale or other cause, the data are recorded by punched holes in a card, also keyed to the master card.
4. The cards representing the beginning inventory and the individual transactions are merged with the master cards at appropriate intervals.
5. The inventory of any particular commodity can be determined at any time by passing the master card and its related cards through a tabulator. The tabulator prints only the final inventory quantity and cost, or if desired the details of each transaction can be printed, in sequential order.
6. At the close of each month the entire group of inventory records is tabulated and a complete inventory listing printed. The cards representing the beginning inventory and the increases and decreases for the month are removed and new inventory cards are automatically punched and merged with their master cards.

When an electronic computer is used to process perpetual inventory data, magnetic tape may be used as the input medium instead of punched cards. The processing phases may also vary somewhat from the foregoing outline in order to achieve a more automatic updating of inventory quantities and more frequent inventory listings.

Either the punched card or the electronic computer system can be extended to improve control over inventory quantities and thereby minimize investment, reduce losses from obsolescence, and improve ability to fill sales orders without delay. For each commodity in the inventory it is necessary to determine the most economical quantity to be purchased in a single order and the minimum quantity to be maintained. After the data on these factors are merged with the data on actual inventory flow, the equipment is programmed to make the necessary comparisons and initiate purchasing activity by preparing purchase orders.

Payrolls. Automation is often applied to payroll systems because of the mass of data to be manipulated, the frequently recurring and routine natures of the processing, and the importance of speed and accuracy. Employees' hourly rates of pay ordinarily remain unchanged for a number of payroll periods, and the withholding structures for FICA tax and income tax usually remain constant for an entire year. Such data can be punched in cards or stored in the memory unit of a computer.

The preceding chapter described and illustrated the computation of gross earnings, computation of tax and other deductions, determination of net pay, preparation of the payroll register, preparation of the payroll check, and updating of each employee's earnings record. All of these processes can be performed mechanically or electronically. In addition, the data needed for determination of the employer's payroll taxes and for reports to governmental agencies and employees can be accumulated automatically by the same equipment.

INTEGRATED DATA PROCESSING

The systematization of processing operations in such a manner as to eliminate retranscriptions of data and to minimize the rehandling and resorting of data from one stage to the next is termed *integrated data processing* (IDP). The term may be applied to a particular segment of the operations of an enterprise or to its entire operations. A totally integrated system, in the strictest sense, would require only the introduction of transaction data and a complete program into the accounting system. All of the processing would then be automatic, and the required business documents, such as checks, sales invoices, and tax reports, and all financial statements and schedules, would be printed without human intervention. It is readily apparent that a high degree of integration requires an exacting coordination of the manual, mechanical, and electronic processing devices employed.

Highly sophisticated data processing systems usually employ an electronic computer with (1) a memory unit of large capacity and (2) the capability of manipulating heterogeneous financial data in random order. Large memory capacity within the computer permits continuous accumulation of new data, comparisons with related data, issuance of the necessary instructions and documents, and restorage for further use. A hypothetical merchandising enterprise will be assumed in describing the principal features of an integrated data processing system.

When a purchase order is received from a customer, all of the pertinent data, such as name and address, quantity and description of the items ordered, and delivery instructions, are recorded on magnetic tape. This is the input for this part of the system. Acting upon instructions stored in the memory unit, the output unit prints the customer's name and address on a sales invoice and a shipping order. The quantity and description data for each commodity ordered are automatically transmitted to an electronic computer where comparisons are made with the perpetual inventory record, which is also contained in the memory unit. If the supply of a commodity on hand is sufficient to fill the order, its description, quantity, and sales price are printed on the invoice, and the inventory data in the memory unit are adjusted accordingly. The new inventory balance of the item is then compared with the reorder quantity recorded in the memory unit. If a reorder is indicated, a purchase order for disposition by the purchasing department is printed automatically. The sales data and cost of merchandise sold data for each transaction are also accumulated and stored within the system.

If the quantity of a commodity on hand is not sufficient to fill the customer's order, the lesser quantity and its sales price are recorded on the invoice, the inventory record is modified, and the sales data and the cost of merchandise sold data are added to the existing balances. In addition, the reason for shipping the smaller quantity is printed on the invoice and a "back order" is printed for the remaining quantity. Later, when the back-ordered goods become available, a sales invoice and a shipping order for the quantity necessary to complete the original order are automatically prepared.

The foregoing processes are repeated for each commodity ordered by the purchaser. After the data for the last item have been processed, the total amount of the sale is printed on the invoice. This amount is then tentatively added to the balance of the appropriate customer's account in the memory unit and the sum compared with the credit limit previously stored in the memory unit. If the credit limit is not exceeded, the addition to the account balance is confirmed and the sales invoice and shipping order are released. All of the required computations and comparisons are accomplished so rapidly that the printing of the invoice and shipping order appear to be uninterrupted.

When a customer's account balance plus the amount of a sale exceeds the credit limit, the invoice and shipping order are routed to the credit department for consideration. If the sale is approved, the documents are released for disposition in the usual manner. If the credit department does not approve the sale, the sales data are reintroduced into the system with instructions to reverse the earlier processes.

The only visible output from the processing of a routine sales transaction are the sales invoice and the shipping order. The updated account receivable and the perpetual inventory records remain in the memory unit. The general ledger accounts affected by the transaction, namely Accounts Receivable, Sales, Merchandise Inventory, and Cost of Merchandise Sold, are also brought up-to-date in the memory unit.

When cash is received on account, the details are introduced into the system by means of magnetic tape. The balances of the individual customers' accounts are automatically revised and the cumulative balances of the general ledger accounts are brought up-to-date.

Details of purchases transactions, cash disbursements, and related data are processed automatically in a similar manner. The individual accounts with creditors are debited and credited, the inventory records are debited for merchandise purchased, and the amounts of assets acquired and expenses incurred are automatically added to the preceding balances of the appropriate general ledger accounts. When a creditor's account is due for payment, the account balances affected by the payment, including purchases discount, are revised and the output unit automatically prints a disbursement check ready for signature. Payrolls are also processed automatically and the output unit automatically prints the payroll checks.

If information is needed at any time about a specific item, such as the balance owed a particular creditor or the inventory of a particular commodity, it can be extracted from the system almost instantly. At the end of the month the general ledger accounts, the trial balance, and the financial statements are printed automatically. Whenever desired, the equipment can produce a printed list of the balances in any of the subsidiary ledgers, an aging schedule of the receivables, the individual withholding tax forms for employees, and analyses of sales and other data in the memory unit.

337

Computers can also be an integral part of a *management information system* which provides data for use by management in controlling current operations and planning for the future. Actual operating results can be compared with predetermined plans and the variances automatically determined. Historical accounting data in the memory unit can also be compared with input data in the memory unit representing various hypothetical future conditions. Output media in the form of reports indicating the expected effect of alternative courses of action are thus provided for management's use in making decisions.

The most advanced integrated data processing systems for manufacturing enterprises combine engineering and scientific tasks with the processing of financial data. For example, by introducing into the system all data on orders received, job specifications, quantities to be produced, materials required, production priorities, and other relevant factors, the system can be programmed to prepare the production orders for each department. If the results of production are also introduced, the system can monitor the manufacturing operations and prepare up-to-the-minute reports on the progress of production and deviations from the scheduled operations.

Automation has affected requirements for clerical personnel, and its continued development will undoubtedly further reduce the need for manual processing. On the other hand, the demand for accountants needed to assist in the analysis, design, and implementation of automated systems continues to exceed the available supply, and the shortage is expected to continue into the foreseeable future.

QUESTIONS

1. Describe, in general terms, an accounting system.

2. What is the objective of systems analysis?

3. What type of information is contained in a *Systems Manual*?

4. Why should the essential features of internal control be incorporated in the design of all accounting systems?

5. Discuss how cash registers can be used to strengthen internal control over receipts from cash sales.

6. What is meant by the term *flow chart*?

7. What does the "diamond" flow chart symbol signify?

8. Employees who are 55 years of age or older at the time they are first employed by Axis Corporation are not eligible to participate in the company's pension plan. Other employees qualify for the plan in the 250th week of their employment and their required contributions to the pension fund are deducted from gross earnings in computing the amount of the weekly payroll checks. The portion of the flow chart related to determination of pension fund participation is presented below, with statements omitted from three of the symbols.

338

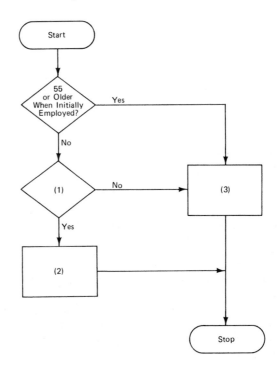

Which of the following statements represents the items identified by number in the flow chart? (a) Deduct pension fund contribution. (b) Print ineligibility notation on payroll check. (c) Employed more than 249 weeks.

9. Briefly describe (a) input, (b) processing, and (c) output, as they relate to automated data processing systems.

10. Included with monthly bills sent to its customers by the East Central Telephone Company is a punched card. The customer is instructed to return the card with his check. (a) What purpose is served by the punched card? (b) What information do you think should be punched in the card?

11. Discuss the primary function performed by each of the following punched card machines: (a) reproducer, (b) collator, (c) tabulator.

12. Name and describe the function of each of the three basic components of electronic computers.

13. Describe the logical operations performed by the arithmetic unit of an electronic computer.

14. What is a computer *program*?

15. Describe the basic function of the *compiler*.

16. Why is magnetic tape often preferred over punched cards and punched paper tape as input media for electronic computers?

17. Why is the processing of payrolls especially well suited to the use of automated data processing equipment?

18. What do the following initials represent: (a) ADP, (b) EDP, (c) IDP?

339

EXERCISES

13-1. The E. M. North Company is a wholesaler of major household appliances. Design a form that can be used as a perpetual inventory record to indicate the quantity, unit costs, and total cost of each commodity on hand. The form is also to be used by management as an aid in reordering merchandise, as a check on the storage personnel, and as an aid in taking a physical inventory. Assume that each commodity received is listed on a receiving report prepared by the receiving department and that each commodity sold is listed on a sales invoice.

13-2. A large retail store initiates a procedure requiring that all purchase orders for merchandise be issued by its newly created purchasing department. A purchase order is to be prepared upon the receipt of a purchase requisition from the various merchandising departments. All incoming invoices and shipments are to be verified by the receiving department and the merchandise is to be stored or routed to the appropriate sales department. Purchase orders are to be issued in quintuplicate. List the original and each of the four copies and indicate for each its distribution and any special instructions or purpose.

13-3. In reviewing the current income statement of Ralph Terry, Incorporated, a medium-size merchandising enterprise, it was noted that the amount of purchases discount was disproportionately small in comparison with earlier periods. Further investigation revealed that in spite of a sufficient bank balance a significant amount of available cash discounts had been lost because of failure to make timely payments. In addition, it was discovered that several purchases invoices had been paid twice.

Outline procedures for the payment of vendors' invoices that will minimize the possibility of losing available cash discounts and of paying an invoice a second time.

13-4. Mason Company maintains on magnetic tape a master file of inventory items. The file contains in commodity number sequence the commodity number and unit cost price for each item of merchandise. Another magnetic tape contains the commodity number and number of units sold (sales record) for the current period, also in commodity number sequence.

Construct a flow chart of the following computer operations: read a commodity number from the sales record; read commodity numbers from the master file until the commodity number on the master file is the same as the number from the sales record; multiply the unit cost price obtained from the master file by the number of units sold as indicated by the sales record; print the commodity number, units sold, unit cost price, and total cost price of the sale; and continue the process until the last entry on the sales record has been read and the details of the cost of the sale have been printed.

13-5. One of the features of Walker Wholesale Company's integrated data processing system is automatic approval or rejection of customers' orders to purchase commodities on credit terms.

Accounts receivable and the credit limit established for each customer are stored in the memory unit of an electronic computer. As orders are received from customers, the computer operator actuates the stored program instructing the computer to add the total of the prospective sale to the customer's account balance, compare the resulting total with the credit limit, and print a rejection or approval notice.

Prepare a flow chart of the following computer operations: secure account balance for customer; add amount of sale to account balance; secure credit limit for customer; determine if credit limit is exceeded; and print notice of rejection or approval of credit.

13-6. Clifford Company employs a computer in preparing sales invoices. One of the functions performed by the computer is the determination of whether or not the customer is entitled to a 5% quantity discount from list price granted when the total amount of an order exceeds $500.

Construct a flow chart of the following computer operations: add list price amounts of each commodity described on the sales invoice to determine the total; print the total of the list price amounts on the invoice; determine if a quantity discount is allowable; multiply the total of the list price amounts by 5%, if appropriate; print amount of quantity discount, if appropriate; subtract amount of quantity discount from the total of the list price amounts, if appropriate; print net amount of the invoice, if appropriate.

PROBLEMS

The following additional problems for this chapter are located in Appendix B: 13-1B, 13-2B, 13-4B.

13-1A. Allen Company is a newly organized enterprise. The list of asset, liability, and capital accounts to be opened in the general ledger is presented below, arranged in alphabetical order. The accounts are to be arranged in balance sheet order and account numbers assigned. Each account number is to be composed of three digits; the first digit is to indicate the major classification ("1" for assets, etc.), the second digit is to indicate the subclassification ("11" for current assets, etc.) and the third digit is to identify the specific account ("111" for Cash in Bank, etc.).

Accounts Payable	Merchandise Inventory
Accounts Receivable	Mortgage Note Payable (long-term)
Accumulated Depr. — Building	Office Equipment
Accumulated Depr. — Office Equip.	Office Supplies
Accumulated Depr. — Store Equip.	Petty Cash
Allowance for Doubtful Accounts	Prepaid Insurance
Building	Prepaid Taxes
Cash in Bank	Retained Earnings
Capital Stock	Salaries and Commissions Payable
Dividends	Store Equipment
Interest Payable	Store Supplies
Land	Taxes Payable

Instructions:

Construct a chart of accounts for the accounts listed.

13-2A. Dixon Springs Power and Light Co. employs an automated system for billing customers for electric current. There are two rate structures, commercial and residential. A master file of customers is maintained on punched cards, with name, address, and appropriate rate structure indicated. At the end of each billing period the meter readers are given prepunched and printed cards containing the name, address, and last meter reading for each customer on their route. The current meter readings are recorded on the cards by the meter readers with a special pencil. The reproducer converts the pencil markings to holes in the card and the cards are then matched by the collator against the master file to assure that a current billing card has been prepared for each customer. The current billing cards are then processed by an electronic computer that computes the amount of the billing and prints the sales journal. The journal is then subjected to clerical review before processing is continued.

Instructions:

Construct a flow chart of the following computer operations: read a current billing card; compute the amount of billing, including provision to employ the appropriate rate structure; print an entry in the sales journal; and continue the processing until the last current billing card has been processed.

13-3A. Tall Men is a men's retail clothing store in Troy, Iowa. The enterprise employs a full-time sales staff of four people, each on a combined salary and commission basis. Sales are made for cash and on account, and are subject to a sales tax.

Instructions:

(1) Identify the various types of data, such as name and address of company, for which provision should be made in the printed sales

tickets for the enterprise, and the purpose served by each item. Use the following headings in presenting your recommendations.

Type of Data   Purpose of Data

(2) Design a sales ticket for Tall Men.

If the working papers correlating with the textbook are not used, omit Problem 13-4A.

13-4A. Foster Supply Company employs punched card machines in processing much of its accounting data. This problem requires the manual processing of a portion of the data normally processed by the machines.

Instructions:

(1) Remove from the working papers and separate the 15 punched cards. Note that the cards numbered 1–3 represent customers' account balances at April 30, the cards numbered 4–6 represent receipts on account from customers at various dates during May, and the cards numbered 7–15 represent sales made to customers on account at various dates in May. Record on the top line of the cards numbered 13–15 the following additional sales data:

	Customer No.	Date	Salesman No.	Invoice No.	Commodity No.	Quantity Sold	Unit Sales Price	Amount
13.	115	5/20	3	17189	212	50	5.00	250.00
14.	110	5/25	1	17190	202	200	1.75	350.00
15.	115	5/30	3	17191	208	100	1.25	125.00

(2) Sort the cards into numerical order according to customer number.
(3) Sort the cards for each customer according to date, placing the earliest date on top.
(4) Using the data recorded on the cards, prepare the three customers' statements of account.
(5) Resort cards numbered 7–15 into numerical order according to salesman number. Prepare for the sales manager a report of sales by salesmen during May.
(6) Resort cards numbered 7–15 into numerical order by commodity number. Prepare for the store manager, who also acts as buyer, a report of the quantity of each commodity sold during May.

13-5A. The Simpson Company maintains its customers ledger on magnetic tape. Each day the data for sales, sales returns and allowances, and cash receipts are recorded on the tape. At the end of each month the tape is used in preparing a statement of account for each customer, detailing the beginning balance, debits, credits, and ending balance. In addition to the statement of account, a delinquency letter is prepared for all customers whose ending balance includes sales charges that are more than two months old.

Instructions:

Construct a flow chart of the following computer operations performed at the end of the month: read a customer's beginning balance, debits and credits for the month, and ending balance; determine if the account is delinquent; print a delinquency letter, if appropriate; print a statement of account; and continue the procedure until the last customer's statement of account and delinquency letter have been printed.

13-6A. One of the programming languages designed for use with electronic computers of medium size is called BASIC (**B**eginner's **A**ll-purpose **S**ymbolic **I**nstruction **C**ode). Computer programs expressed in BASIC are composed of a series of instructions, called *statements*, presented in the order in which each operation is to be performed.

To illustrate the format of such a program, assume that the computer is to be instructed to add a series of pairs of numbers, designated as A and B, and print the total of each pair. Assume further that the pairs of numbers are as follows: 8, 11, 20, 110, 980.5, 1210.4. The six statements required to complete the requisite program are presented below.

Statement 1	READ	A, B	Statement 4	PRINT	X
Statement 2	DATA	8, 11, 20, 110, 980.5, 1210.4	Statement 5	GO TO 1
Statement 3	LET	X = A + B	Statement 6	END

Statement 1 instructs the computer to READ the values of A and B, which are presented in statement 2 as DATA. Statement 3, the LET instruction, indicates the manner in which the data are to be manipulated. Statement 4 instructs the computer to PRINT the results of the computation. After the sum (19) of the first two numbers (8 + 11) is printed, statement 5 instructs the computer to GO TO statement 1 and repeat the process for the next pair of numbers. After the sums 130 (20 + 110) and 2190.9 (980.5 + 1210.4) are printed, the END of the program is indicated by statement 6.

343

Instructions:

Construct a program of six statements, in BASIC, to compute and print the net pay for each of the following employees:

Employee No.	Total Hours Worked	Hourly Rate	Income Tax Withheld	FICA Tax Withheld
101	40	$7.50	$40.20	$18.00
102	40	5.55	25.50	13.32
105	20	4.50	4.80	5.40
107	18	4.75	4.20	5.13
108	40	6.75	34.50	16.20

The BASIC symbol used to indicate subtraction is the minus sign (−); multiplication is indicated by an asterisk (*). Although in general the letter designation of the variables in a program is completely arbitrary, the following letters should be used:

A   Total hours worked
B   Hourly rate
C   Income tax withheld

D   FICA tax withheld
X   Net amount to be paid

Chapter 14

CONCEPTS AND PRINCIPLES

NEED FOR CONCEPTS AND PRINCIPLES

The historical development of accounting practice has been closely related to the economic development of the country. In the earlier stages of the American economy a business enterprise was very often managed by its owner and the accounting records and reports were used primarily by the owner-manager in conducting the business. Bankers and other lenders often relied more heavily on their personal relationship with the owner than on financial statements as the basis for making loans for business purposes. If a substantial amount was owed to a bank or supplier, the creditor frequently participated in management decisions.

As business organizations grew in size and complexity, "management" and "outsiders" became more clearly differentiated. From the latter group, which includes owners (stockholders), creditors, government, labor unions, customers, and the general public, came the demand for accurate financial information for use in judging the performance of management. In addition, as the size and complexity of the business unit increased, the accounting problems involved in the issuance of financial statements became more and more complex. With these developments came an awareness of the need for a framework of concepts and generally accepted accounting principles.

DEVELOPMENT OF CONCEPTS AND PRINCIPLES

Users of financial statements need a basic understanding of the principles underlying the preparation of such statements if they are to interpret them properly. It is equally evident that accountants must have a thorough knowledge of these principles and that they must be in substantial agreement as to the meaning and the importance of the guides and the standards that, collectively, comprise them.

Responsibility for the development of accounting principles has rested primarily on practicing accountants and accounting teachers, working both independently and as groups under the sponsorship of such organizations as the American Accounting Association, the American Institute of Certified Public Accountants, the National Association of Accountants, and the Financial Executives Institute. These principles are also influenced by business practices and customs, ideas and beliefs of the users of the financial statements, governmental agencies such as the Securities and Exchange Commission, stock exchanges, and other business groups.

Various terms are employed by accountants in referring to a particular accounting standard. In addition to *principle* and *concept*, the terms *standard*, *axiom*, *assumption*, *postulate*, *convention*, *tenet*, and *doctrine* are frequently encountered in accounting literature. An examination of the similarities and the differences in meaning of these terms is not essential to the understanding of the particular principles that will be discussed in this chapter; they are mentioned only for the sake of completeness.

It should be borne in mind that the word "principle" as used in this context does not have the same authoritativeness as universal principles or natural laws relating to the study of astronomy, physics, or other physical sciences. Accounting principles have been developed by man to enhance the usefulness of accounting data in an ever-changing society. They represent the best possible guides, based on reason, observation, and experimentation, to the achievement of the desired results. The selection of the best single method, or of several equally good methods, among a number of alternatives, has come about gradually, and in some subject matter areas a clear consensus is still lacking. These principles are continually reexamined and revised to keep pace with the increasing complexity of business operations. General acceptance among the members of the accounting profession is the criterion for determining an accounting principle.

Many accounting principles have been introduced and integrated with discussions in earlier chapters. The remainder of this chapter is devoted to the underlying assumptions, concepts, and principles of the greatest importance and widest applicability. Attention will also be directed to applications of principles to specific situations in order to facilitate better understanding of accounting practices.

BUSINESS ENTITY

The *business entity* concept assumes that a business enterprise is separate and distinct from the persons who supply the assets it uses. This is true regardless of the legal form of the business organization. The accounting equation, Assets = Equities, or Assets = Liabilities + Capital, is an expression of the entity concept; it is as if the business itself owns the assets and in turn owes the various claimants. Thus, the accounting process is primarily concerned with the enterprise as a productive economic unit and only secondarily with the investor as a claimant to the assets.

The business entity concept employed in accounting for a sole proprietorship is distinct from the legal concept of a sole proprietorship. The nonbusiness assets, liabilities, revenues, and expenses of a sole proprietor are excluded from the business accounts. If a sole proprietor owns two or more dissimilar enterprises, each one is customarily treated as a separate entity for accounting purposes. Legally, however, a sole proprietor is personally liable for all of his business debts and may be required to use nonbusiness assets to satisfy the business creditors. Conversely, business assets are not immune from claims of the sole proprietor's personal creditors.

Differences between the business entity concept and the legal nature of other forms of business organization will be considered in later chapters. For accounting purposes, however, revenues and expenses of any enterprise are viewed as affecting the business assets and liabilities, not the owners' assets and liabilities.

GOING CONCERN

Only in rare instances is a business organized with the expectation of remaining in existence for only a specified period of time. In most cases there is no means of foretelling the length of life of an enterprise, and so an assumption must be made. The nature of the assumption will affect the manner of recording some of the business transactions, which in turn will affect the data reported in the financial statements.

It is customary to assume that a business entity has a reasonable expectation of continuing in business at a profit for an indefinite period of time. This assumption that an enterprise is a *going concern* provides much of the justification for recording plant assets at acquisition cost and depreciating them in a systematic manner without reference to their current realizable values. It is pointless to report plant assets on the balance sheet at their estimated realizable values if there is no immediate expectation of selling them. This is true regardless of whether the current market value of the plant assets is less than their book value or greater than their book value. If the firm continues to use the assets, the fluctuation in market value causes no gain or loss, nor does it enhance or diminish the usefulness of the assets. Thus, if the going-concern assumption is a valid concept, the investment in plant assets will serve the purpose for which it was made — the investment in the assets will be recovered even though they may be individually marketable only at a loss.

The going-concern assumption similarly supports the treatment of prepaid expenses as assets, even though they may be virtually unsalable. To illustrate, assume that on the last day of its fiscal year a wholesale firm receives from a printer a $20,000 order of sales catalogs. In the absence of the assumption that the firm is to continue in business, the catalogs would be merely scrap paper and the value reported for them on the balance sheet would be negligible.

A less direct effect of the going-concern concept is that it helps to focus attention on the determination of net income rather than on the valuation of assets. The earning power of an enterprise is more significant than the market value of its individual assets in judging the overall worth of a business. Because of this emphasis on earnings, the accountant directs his attention to the proper allocation of revenues and expenses to the current period and needs not to be concerned with determining the market value of assets that will not be sold.

When there is conclusive evidence that a specific business entity has a limited life, the accounting procedures should be appropriate to the expected terminal date of the entity. The financial statements should also clearly disclose the limited life of the enterprise. Such modifications in the application of normal accounting procedures may become necessary for business organizations in receivership or bankruptcy.

OBJECTIVE EVIDENCE

Entries in the accounting records and data reported on financial statements must be based on objectively determined evidence. Without close adherence to this principle, the confidence of the many users of the financial statements could not be maintained. For example, objective evidence such as invoices and vouchers for purchases, bank statements for the amount of cash in bank, and physical counts for merchandise on hand supports much of accounting. Such evidence is completely objective and is subject to verification.

Evidence is not always conclusively objective, for there are numerous occasions in accounting where judgments, estimates, and other subjective factors must be taken into account. In such situations, the most objective evidence available should be used. For example, the provision for doubtful accounts is an estimate of the losses expected from failure to collect sales made on account. Estimation of this amount should be based on such objective factors as past experience in collecting accounts receivable and reliable forecasts of future business activities. To provide accounting reports that can be accepted with confidence, evidence should be developed that will minimize the possibility of error and intentional bias or fraud.

UNIT OF MEASUREMENT

All business transactions are recorded in terms of money. Other pertinent information of a nonfinancial nature may also be recorded, such as the description of assets acquired, the terms of purchase and sale contracts, and the purpose, amount, and term of insurance policies. But it is only through the record of dollar amounts that the diverse transactions and activities of a business may be measured, reported, and periodically compared. Money is both the common factor of all business transactions and the only practicable unit of measurement that can be employed to achieve homogeneity of financial data.

The generally accepted use of the monetary unit for accounting for and reporting the activities of an enterprise has two major limitations: (1) it restricts the scope of accounting reports and (2) it assumes a stability of the measurement unit.

Scope of accounting reports. Many factors affecting the activities and the future prospects of an enterprise cannot be expressed in monetary terms. In general, accounting does not attempt to report such factors. For example, information regarding the capabilities of the management, the state of repair of the plant assets, the effectiveness of the employee welfare program, the attitude of the labor union, the effectiveness of anti-pollution measures, and the relative strengths and weaknesses of the firm's principal competitors cannot be expressed in monetary terms. Although such matters are important to those concerned with enterprise operations, at the present time accountancy does not assume responsibility for reporting information of this kind.

Stability of monetary unit. As a unit of measurement the dollar is far inferior to such quantitative standards as the pound, quart, or meter, which have remained unchanged for centuries. The instability of the purchasing power of the dollar is well-known, and the disruptive effect of inflation on accounting reports during the past few decades is acknowledged by accountants. However, up to the present time this declining value of the unit of measurement generally has not been given recognition in the accounts or in conventional financial statements.

To indicate the nature of the problem, assume that the plant assets acquired by an enterprise for $100,000 twenty years ago are now to be replaced with similar assets which at present price levels will cost $200,000. Assume further that during the twenty-year period the plant assets had been fully depreciated and that the net income of the enterprise had amounted to $300,000. Although the initial outlay of $100,000 for the plant assets was recovered, the amount represents only one half of the cost of replacing the assets. Instead of considering the current value of the new assets to have increased to double the value of two decades earlier, the dollars recovered can be said to have declined to one half of their earlier value. From either point of view, the firm has suffered a loss in purchasing power which is tantamount to a loss of capital. In addition, $100,000 of the net income reported during the period might be said to be illusory inasmuch as it must be used to replace the assets.

The use of a monetary unit that is assumed to be stable insures objectivity. In spite of the inflationary trend in the United States, historical-dollar financial statements are considered to be superior to statements based on movements of the general price level. However, there has been a growing belief among accountants that in many cases the basic historical-cost statements should be supplemented by general price-level statements.[1] This subject will be discussed again in a later chapter.

ACCOUNTING PERIOD

A complete and accurate picture of the degree of success achieved by an enterprise cannot be obtained until it discontinues operations, converts its assets into cash, and pays off its debts. Then, and only then, is it possible to determine with finality its net income. But innumerable decisions regarding the business must be made by management and interested outsiders throughout the period of its existence, and it is therefore necessary to prepare periodic reports on operations, financial position, and changes in financial position.

Reports may be prepared upon the completion of a particular job or project, but more often they are prepared at specified time intervals. For a number of reasons, including custom and various legal requirements, the maximum interval between reports is one year.

This element of periodicity creates many of the problems of accountancy. The fundamental problem is the determination of periodic net income. For example, the necessity for adjusting entries discussed in earlier chapters is directly attributable to the division of an enterprise into arbitrary time periods. Problems of inventory costing, of recognizing the uncollectibility of receivables, and of selecting depreciation methods are also directly related to the periodic measurement process. Furthermore, it should be noted that the amounts of the assets and the equities reported on the balance sheet will also be affected by the methods employed in determining net income. For example, the particular cost flow assumption employed in determining the cost of merchandise sold during the accounting period will have a direct effect on the amount of cost assigned to the remaining inventory.

349

MATCHING REVENUE AND EXPIRED COSTS

During the early stages of accounting development, accountants viewed the balance sheet as the principal financial statement. Over the years the emphasis has shifted to the income statement as the users of

---

[1]Evidenced by *Statement of the Accounting Principles Board, No. 3*, "Financial Statements Restated for General Price-Level Changes" (New York: American Institute of Certified Public Accountants, 1969).

the financial statements have become more concerned with the results of operations of a business than with its financial position.

The determination of periodic net income is a twofold problem involving (1) the revenue recognized during the period and (2) the expired costs to be allocated to the period. It is thus a problem of matching revenues and expired costs, the residual amount being the provisional net income or net loss for the period.

RECOGNITION OF REVENUE

Revenue is measured by the amount charged to customers for merchandise delivered or services rendered to them. The problem created by periodicity is one of timing; at what point is the revenue realized? For any particular accounting period, the question is whether revenue items should be recognized and reported as such in the current period or whether their recognition should be postponed to a future period.

Various criteria are acceptable for determining when revenue is realized. In any case the criteria adopted should be reasonably in accord with the terms of the contractual arrangements with the customer and based insofar as possible on objective evidence. The criteria most frequently used are described in the remaining paragraphs of this section.

Point of sale. It is customary to consider revenue from the sale of commodities as being realized at the time title passes to the buyer. At this point the sale price has been agreed upon, the buyer acquires the right of ownership in the commodity, and the seller has an enforceable claim against the buyer. The realization of revenue from the sale of services may be determined in a somewhat similar manner, although there is frequently a time lag between the time of the initial agreement and the completion of the service. For example, assume that a contract provides that certain repair services be performed, either for a specified price or on a time and materials basis. The price or terms agreed upon in the initial contract does not constitute revenue until the work has been performed.

Theoretically, revenue from the production and sale of commodities and services emerges continuously as effort is expended. As a practical matter, however, it is ordinarily not possible to make an objective determination until both (1) the contract price has been agreed upon and (2) the seller has completed his portion of the contract.

Receipt of payment. The recognition of revenue may be postponed until payment is received. When this criterion is adopted, revenue is considered to be earned at the time the cash is collected, regardless of when the sale was made. The cash basis is widely used by physicians, attorneys, and other enterprises in which professional services are the source of revenue. It has little theoretical justification but has the practical advantage of simplicity of operation and avoidance of the problem of estimating losses from uncollectible accounts. Its acceptability as a fair method of timing the recognition of revenue from personal services is influenced somewhat by the fact that it may be used in determining income subject to the federal income tax. It is not an appropriate method of measuring revenue from the sale of commodities.

Installment method. In some businesses, especially in the retail field, it is common to make sales on the installment plan. In the typical installment sale, the purchaser makes a down payment and agrees to pay the remainder in specified amounts at stated intervals over a period of time. The seller may retain technical title to the goods or may take other means to facilitate repossession in the event the purchaser defaults on his payments. Despite such provisions, installment sales should ordinarily be treated in the same manner as any other sale on account, in which case the revenue is considered to be realized at the point of sale.[2]

In exceptional cases where the circumstances are such that the collection of receivables is not reasonably assured, an alternate method of determining revenue may be used.[3] The alternative is to consider each receipt of cash to be composed of partial payment of two elements: (1) cost of the merchandise sold and (2) gross profit on the sale.

As a basis for illustration, assume that the following data are for the first year of operations of a dealer in household appliances:

Installment sales	$300,000
Cost of merchandise sold	180,000
Gross profit on sales	$120,000
Per cent of gross profit to sales, $\dfrac{\$120,000}{\$300,000}$	40%
Cash collected on installment sales during the year	$140,000

According to the point-of-sale method of recognizing revenue, the entire $300,000 is recognized and the gross profit reported for the year is $120,000. According to the installment method, the amount of gross profit recognized is based on the amount of cash collected, which was $140,000. The gross profit reported for the year is then $56,000 (40% of $140,000). The remaining gross profit of $64,000 ($120,000 − $56,000) is shown on the balance sheet at the end of the year as a deferred credit. Continuing the illustration, assume that an additional $100,000 is collected on the first year's installment sales during the following year. The gross profit to be recognized in the second year would be $40,000

351

---

[2]*Opinions of the Accounting Principles Board, No. 10,* "Omnibus Opinion — 1966" (New York: American Institute of Certified Public Accountants, 1966), par. 12.
[3]*Ibid.*

(40% of $100,000) and the amount deferred would be $24,000 ($64,000 − $40,000).

Degree of contract completion. Enterprises engaged in large construction projects may devote several years to the completion of a particular contract. In order to illustrate a situation of this nature, assume that a contractor engages in a project that will require three years to complete, for which he is to receive $50,000,000. Assume also that the total cost to be incurred, which will also be spread over the three-year period, is estimated at $44,000,000. According to the point-of-sale criterion, neither the revenue nor the related costs would be recognized until the project is completed and, therefore, the entire net income from the contract would be reported in a single year.

Whenever the total cost of a long-term contract and the extent of progress can be reasonably estimated, it is preferable to consider the revenue as being earned over the entire life of the contract.[4] The amount of revenue to be recognized in any particular period is then determined on the basis of the estimated percentage of the contract that has been completed during the period. The estimated percentage of completion can be developed by comparing incurred costs with the most recent estimates of total costs or by estimates by engineers, architects or other qualified personnel of the progress of the work performed. To continue with the illustration, assume that by the close of the first fiscal year the contract is estimated to be one-fourth completed. The amount of revenue recognized for the year would be ¼ of $50,000,000, or $12,500,000. The costs incurred during the period (rather than ¼ of the original cost estimate of $44,000,000) would then be deducted from the $12,500,000 of revenue recognized to determine the income from the contract.

There is, of course, an element of subjectivity, and hence of possible error, in the determination of the amount of revenue earned by the degree-of-contract-completion method. The financial statements may be more informative, however, in spite of estimates, than they would be if none of the revenue were recognized until completion of the contract. The method used should be noted on the financial statements.

A situation somewhat comparable to long-term construction contracts arises in connection with revenue from rentals, loans, and other services that are definitely measurable on a time basis. Neither the point of sale, the receipt of payment, nor the installment method is an appropriate criterion for determining the emergence of revenue from such sources. Both the amount of total revenue to be earned and the period over which it is to be earned are readily ascertainable. For example, if a

---

[4]*Accounting Research and Terminology Bulletins — Final Edition*, "No. 45, Long-term Construction-type Contracts" (New York: American Institute of Certified Public Accountants, 1961), par. 15.

building is leased for a period of 3 years at a rental of $36,000, the revenue is realized at the rate of $1,000 a month. Whether the rent is received in a lump sum at the beginning of the lease, in installments over the life of the lease, or at its termination is irrelevant in determining the amount of revenue realized. In accordance with the concept of the going concern, it is assumed that the owner will supply the use of the building during the term of the lease and that the lessee will fulfill his part of the contract.

ALLOCATION OF COSTS

Properties and services acquired by an enterprise are generally recorded at cost. "Cost" is the amount of cash or equivalent given to acquire the property or the service. If property other than cash is given to acquire properties or services, the cost is the cash equivalent of the property given. When the properties or the services acquired are sold or consumed, the costs are deducted from the related revenue to determine the amount of net income or net loss. The costs of properties or services acquired that are on hand at any particular time represent assets. Such costs may also be referred to as "unexpired costs." As the assets are sold or consumed, they become "expired costs" or "expenses."

Theoretically, it is possible to assign all costs to each specific product sold or each service rendered. If this were done, the net income of an enterprise could be measured in terms of units of output. In practice, however, it would be difficult and costly to fragmentize cost allocations to such a degree. As stated earlier in this chapter, the determination of expired revenue and expired costs on a periodic time basis is satisfactory.

The techniques of determining and recording cost expirations have been described and illustrated in earlier chapters. In general, there are two approaches to cost allocations: (1) compute the amount of the expired cost or (2) compute the amount of the unexpired cost. For example, it is customary to determine the portion of plant assets that have expired. After recording the depreciation for the period, the balances of the plant asset accounts minus the balances of the related accumulated depreciation accounts represent the unexpired cost of the assets. The alternative approach must be employed for merchandise and supplies unless perpetual inventory records are maintained. If the cost of the merchandise or supplies on hand at the close of the period is determined by taking a physical inventory, the remaining costs in the related accounts are assumed to have expired. It might appear that the first approach emphasizes expired costs and the second emphasizes unexpired costs. This is not the case, however, as the selection of the method is based on convenience or practicability.

Many of the costs allocable to a period are treated as an expense at the time of incurrence because they will be wholly expired at the end

353

of the period. For example, when a monthly rent is paid at the beginning of a month, the cost incurred is unexpired and hence it is an asset; but since the cost incurred will be wholly expired at the end of the month, it is customary to charge the rental directly to the appropriate expense account, thus avoiding the necessity for an additional entry later. The proper allocation of costs among periods is the paramount consideration; any one of a variety of accounting techniques may be employed in achieving this objective.

ADEQUATE DISCLOSURE

Financial statements and their accompanying footnotes or other explanatory materials should contain all of the pertinent data believed essential to the reader's understanding. Criteria for standards of disclosure are of necessity nebulous and indefinite. They are often based on value judgments rather than on objective facts.

The usefulness of financial statements is enhanced by the use of headings and subheadings and by merging items in significant categories. For example, detailed information as to the amount of cash in various special and general funds, the amount on deposit in each of several banks, and the amount invested in a variety of marketable government securities is not needed by the reader of financial statements. Such information displayed on the balance sheet would impede rather than aid understanding. On the other hand, if the terms of significant loan agreements provide for a secured claim through a mortgage on an asset, the details should be disclosed.

Some of the matters that accountants agree should be adequately disclosed in financial statements or accompanying notes are briefly described and illustrated in the following paragraphs. The illustrations quoted were taken from corporations' annual reports to stockholders, where they appeared in a section variously titled "Statement of Accounting Practices," "Principles Reflected in Financial Statements," and "Notes to Financial Statements."

Accounting methods employed. When there are several acceptable alternative methods that could have a significant effect on amounts reported on the statements, the particular method adopted should be disclosed. Examples include inventory cost flow and pricing methods, depreciation methods, treatment of research and development expenditures, and various criteria of revenue recognition. There is considerable variation in the format used to disclose accounting methods employed. One form is to use a separate "Summary of Significant Accounting Policies" preceding the notes to financial statements or as the initial note.[5]

---

[5]*Opinions of the Accounting Principles Board, No. 22,* "Disclosure of Accounting Policies" (New York: American Institute of Certified Public Accountants, 1972), par. 15.

Note 1 — Summary of significant accounting policies:

Inventories. Inventories are carried at cost (about half under the last-in, first-out method and the remainder under the first-in, first-out method), which is substantially less than current market value.

Depreciation. With minor exceptions, depreciation of domestic properties is computed using the sum-of-the-years-digits method. Depreciation of foreign properties is generally computed using the straight-line method.

Research and development. Research and development expenditures, including process development and product application development costs, are expensed in the year incurred.

Changes in accounting estimates. There are numerous situations in accounting where the use of estimates is necessary. These estimates should be revised when additional information or subsequent developments permit better insight or improved judgment upon which to base the estimates. If the effect of such a change on net income is material, it should be disclosed in the financial statements for the year in which the change is adopted.[6]

Note 5 — Change in service lives of property:

Effective July 1, 19—, the Company revised its estimates of remaining useful lives of certain machinery and equipment. The revision resulted primarily from a change in conditions and not from a change in accounting principles. As a result of this revision, net income increased $246,000 from what it would have been if the estimated lives had not changed.

355

Contingent liabilities. Contingent liabilities arising from discounted notes receivable, litigation, guarantees of products, possible tax assessments, or other causes should be disclosed.

Note E — Commitments and contingent liabilities:

. . . In addition, there are several legal actions pending against the Company. A purported class action is pending in the Supreme Court of the State of New York seeking injunctive relief and $4,001,000,000 for damages suffered as a result of air pollution from the Company's generating plants. Counsel of the Company is of the opinion that the injunctive relief requested will not be granted and that this is not a proper class action under the reported decisions as to New York law. The Attorney General of the State of New York has also commenced an action against the Company alleging that [named a specified installation] is damaging the ecology of the Hudson River. The complaint seeks damages in the amount of $5,000,000 and an injunction against the operation of this plant in such a manner as to damage the river.

Events subsequent to date of statements. Events occurring or becoming known after the close of the period that may have a significant effect on

---

[6]*Opinions of the Accounting Principles Board, No. 20,* "Accounting Changes" (New York: American Institute of Certified Public Accountants, 1971), pars. 31–33.

the financial statements should be disclosed.[7] For example, if an enterprise should suffer a crippling loss from a fire or other catastrophe between the end of the year and the issuance of the statements, the facts should be disclosed. Similarly, such occurrences as the issuance of bonds or capital stock, or the purchase of another business enterprise after the close of the period should be made known if they have a significant effect on the company.

> Note 18 — Subsequent events:
>
> In April 19—, the Company's Almirante Division (Panama) experienced heavy rains and resultant flooding. As a consequence, banana cultivations and farm installations were damaged. However, property and crop losses cannot be accurately assessed for some time. The Company has insurance coverage, with certain deductibles, on property and installations but not on crop losses. Interruptions in near-term shipping schedules are not expected to be extensive, nor will any serious shortage of fruit result.

CONSISTENCY

A number of accepted alternative principles affecting the determination of income statement and balance sheet amounts have been presented in earlier sections of the text. Recognizing that different methods may be used under varying circumstances, some guide or standard is needed to assure a high degree of comparability of the periodic financial statements of an enterprise. It is common practice to compare an enterprise's current income statement and balance sheet with the statements of the preceding year.

The amount and the direction of change in net income and financial position from period to period is highly significant to the reader and may greatly influence his decisions. Therefore, interested persons should be able to assume that the successive financial statements of an enterprise are based consistently on the same generally accepted accounting principles. If the principles are not applied consistently, the trends indicated could be the result of changes in the accounting principles employed rather than the result of changes in business conditions or managerial effectiveness.

The concept of consistency does not completely prohibit changes in the accounting principles employed. Changes are permissible when it is believed that adoption of a different principle will more fairly state net income and financial position. Examples of changes in accounting principle include a change in the method of inventory pricing, a change in depreciation method for previously recorded assets, a change in the method of accounting for long-term construction contracts, and a change in accounting for research and development costs. Consideration of

[7]*Statement on Auditing Procedure, No. 47,* "Subsequent Events" (New York: American Institute of Certified Public Accountants, 1971).

changes in accounting principle must of necessity be accompanied by consideration of the general rule for disclosure of such changes, which is as follows:

> The nature of and justification for a change in accounting principle and its effect on income should be disclosed in the financial statements of the period in which the change is made. The justification for the change should explain clearly why the newly adopted accounting principle is preferable.[8]

There are various methods of reporting the effect of a change in accounting principle on net income. The cumulative effect of the change on net income may be reported on the income statement of the period in which the change is adopted. In some cases the effect of the change could be applied retroactively to past periods by presenting revised income statements for the earlier years affected. Further consideration of the methods of disclosure is reserved for a later chapter.

It should be observed that the application of the consistency concept does not require that a specific accounting method be applied uniformly throughout an enterprise. It is not unusual for large enterprises to use different costing and pricing methods for different segments of their inventories. For example, a department store might apply the lower of cost or market, on a first-in, first-out basis, to the merchandise inventory in some departments and employ cost, on a last-in, first-out basis, in determining the inventory of other departments.

357

MATERIALITY

In adhering to generally accepted accounting principles, the accountant must consider the relative importance of any event, accounting procedure, or change in procedure that affects items on the financial statements. Absolute accuracy in accounting and full disclosure in reporting are not ends in themselves, and there is no need to exceed the limits of practicability. The determination of what is significant and what is unimportant requires the exercise of judgment; precise criteria cannot be formulated.

To determine materiality, the size of an item and its nature must be considered in relationship to the size and the nature of other items. The erroneous classification of a $10,000 asset on a balance sheet exhibiting total assets of $10,000,000 would probably be immaterial. If the assets totaled only $100,000, however, it would certainly be material. If the $10,000 represented a note receivable from an officer of the enterprise, it might well be material even in the first assumption. If the amount of the loan was increased to $100,000 between the close of the period and

---

[8]*Opinions of the Accounting Principles Board, No. 20,* "Accounting Changes" (New York: American Institute of Certified Public Accountants, 1971), par. 17.

the issuance of the statements, both the nature of the item at the balance sheet date and the subsequent increase in amount would require disclosure.

The concept of materiality may be applied to procedures employed in recording transactions. As was stated in an earlier chapter, minor expenditures for plant assets may be treated as an expense of the period rather than as an asset. The saving in clerical costs is justified if the practice does not materially affect the financial statements. In establishing a dollar amount as the dividing line between a revenue expenditure and a capital expenditure, consideration would need to be given to such factors as: (1) amount of total plant assets, (2) amount of plant assets in relationship to other assets, (3) frequency of occurrence of expenditures for plant assets, (4) nature and expected life of plant assets, and (5) probable effect on the amount of periodic net income reported.

Custom and practicality also influence criteria of materiality. Corporate financial statements seldom report the cents amounts or even the hundreds of dollars. A common practice is to round to the nearest thousand. For large corporations there is an increasing tendency to report financial data in terms of millions, carrying figures to one decimal; for example, an amount stated in millions as $907.4 may be read as nine hundred seven million, four hundred thousand.[9]

A technique known as "whole-dollar" accounting, which is employed by some businesses, eliminates the cents amounts from accounting entries wherever possible and at the earliest practicable point in the accounting sequence. There are some accounts, such as those with customers and creditors, in which it is not feasible to round to the nearest dollar. Nevertheless, the technique yields savings in office costs and improved productivity. The errors introduced into other accounts by rounding the amounts of individual entries at the time of recording tend to be compensating in nature, and the amount of the final error is not material.

It should not be inferred from the foregoing that whole-dollar accounting encourages or condones errors. The unrecorded cents are not lost; they are merely reported in a manner that reduces bookkeeping costs without materially affecting the accuracy of accounting data.

CONSERVATISM

Periodic statements are of necessity affected to a considerable degree by the selection of accounting procedures and other value judgments. Historically, accountants have tended to be conservative, and in selecting among alternatives they often favored the method or the procedure that yielded the lesser amount of net income or of asset value. This attitude of conservatism was frequently expressed in the admonition to "anticipate

[9]Examples are presented in Appendix C.

no profits and provide for all losses." For example, it is acceptable to price merchandise inventory at lower of cost or market. If market price is higher than cost, the higher amount is ignored in the accounts and, if presented in the financial statements, is presented parenthetically. Such an attitude of pessimism has been due in part to the need for an offset to the optimism of business management. It could also be argued that potential future losses to an enterprise from poor management decisions would be lessened if net income and assets were understated.

Current accounting thought has shifted somewhat from this philosophy of conservatism. Conservatism is no longer considered to be a dominant factor in selecting among alternatives. Revenue should be recognized when realized, and expired costs should be matched against revenue in accordance with principles based on reason and logic. The element of conservatism may be considered only when other factors affecting a choice of alternatives are neutral. The concepts of objectivity, consistency, disclosure, and materiality take precedence over conservatism, and the latter should be a factor only where the others do not play a significant role.

CONTINUING DEVELOPMENT OF ACCOUNTING PRINCIPLES

Accounting, like most disciplines, has evolved gradually over many years. Accounting principles are continually being examined and refined in an effort to improve accounting practice and to keep it abreast of changes in economic and social conditions, in the legal environment, and in methods of business operation. Many individual accountants, professional accounting associations, and governmental agencies have contributed to the development of accounting principles.

Among the oldest and most influential organizations of accountants are the American Accounting Association (AAA), the American Institute of Certified Public Accountants (AICPA), the Financial Executives Institute (FEI), and the National Association of Accountants (NAA). Each group publishes a periodical journal for its members and other subscribers. They also issue other publications from time to time in the form of research studies, technical opinions, and monographs. There are several additional national organizations of accountants, as well as many state societies and local chapters of the national and state organizations. Each one provides forums for the interchange of ideas and discussion of accounting principles.

One of the earliest attempts by an accounting organization to formulate general principles was published by the AAA in 1936 under the title "A Tentative Statement of Accounting Principles Underlying Corporate Financial Statements."[10] A mere five pages in length, it has been followed

359

---

[10] *The Accounting Review* (Evanston, Illinois: American Accounting Association, 1936), Vol. XI, No. 2, pp. 187–191.

by five additional complete statements and thirteen supplements. The latest in the series, entitled *A Statement of Basic Accounting Theory*,[11] was published as a hundred-page volume in 1966.

Another indication of the efforts of an accounting organization to formulate general principles is the publication of three recent research studies and a statement by the AICPA. Two of the research studies, "The Basic Postulates of Accounting"[12] and "A Tentative Set of Broad Principles for Business Enterprises,"[13] were attempts to delineate the accounting principles that should be adhered to as generally accepted. The third study, entitled "Inventory of Generally Accepted Accounting Principles for Business Enterprises,"[14] was a listing of the principles that were generally accepted in actual practice. These exploratory studies provided a basis for consideration, discussion and experimentation, culminating in the issuance by the Accounting Principles Board (APB) in 1970 of a 105 page statement, entitled "Basic Concepts and Accounting Principles Underlying Financial Statements of Business Enterprises." The purpose of the statement is

> . . . to provide a basis for enhanced understanding of the broad fundamentals of financial accounting. It is also intended to provide a basis for guiding the future development of financial accounting. To achieve these purposes the Statement (1) discusses the nature of financial accounting, the environmental forces that influence it, and the potential and limitations of financial accounting in providing useful information, (2) sets forth the objectives of financial accounting and financial statements, and (3) presents a description of present generally accepted accounting principles.[15]

The organization and operation of the recently created "Financial Accounting Standards Board" are described in Appendix A.

Of the various governmental agencies with an interest in the development of accounting principles, the Securities and Exchange Commission (SEC) has undoubtedly been the most influential. Opinions on accounting policies and practices that are to be observed in the preparation of financial statements and the other reports filed with the Commission are published as *Accounting Series Releases*.

---

[11]*A Statement of Basic Accounting Theory* (Evanston, Illinois: American Accounting Association, 1966).

[12]Maurice Moonitz, *The Basic Postulates of Accounting*, Accounting Research Study No. 1 (New York: American Institute of Certified Public Accountants, 1961).

[13]Robert Sprouse and Maurice Moonitz, *A Tentative Set of Broad Accounting Principles for Business Enterprises*, Accounting Research Study No. 3 (New York: American Institute of Certified Public Accountants, 1961).

[14]Paul Grady, *Inventory of Generally Accepted Accounting Principles for Business Enterprises*, Accounting Research Study No. 7 (New York: American Institute of Certified Public Accountants, 1965).

[15]*Statement of the Accounting Principles Board, No. 4*, "Basic Concepts and Accounting Principles Underlying Financial Statements of Business Enterprises" (New York: American Institute of Certified Public Accountants, 1970), par. 2.

QUESTIONS

1. Accounting principles are broad guides to accounting practice. (a) Who has the responsibility for the development of accounting principles? (b) How are accounting principles developed? (c) Of what significance is acceptability in the development of accounting principles? (d) Why must accounting principles be continually reexamined and revised?

2. (a) Would the accountant for a sole proprietorship record in the accounts the personal assets and liabilities of the proprietor? Explain. (b) Would a banker considering a loan to a sole proprietorship have any interest in the amount and the nature of the personal assets and liabilities of the proprietor? Explain.

3. Plant assets are reported on the balance sheet of Thompson Company at a total cost of $500,000 less accumulated depreciation of $150,000. (a) Is it possible that the assets might realize considerably more or considerably less than $350,000 if the business were discontinued and the assets were sold separately? (b) Why aren't plant assets reported on the balance sheet at their estimated market values?

4. During the current year a mortgage note payable for $150,000 issued by W. J. Wilkens Corporation ten years ago becomes due and is paid. Assuming that the general price level has increased by 50% during the ten-year period, did the loan result in an increase or decrease in Wilkens Corporation's purchasing power? Explain.

361

5. A machine with a cost of $40,000 and accumulated depreciation of $37,000 will soon need to be replaced by a similar machine that will cost $55,000. (a) At what amount should the machine presently owned be reported on the balance sheet? (b) What amount should management use in planning for the cash required to replace the machine?

6. Conventional financial statements do not give recognition to the instability of the purchasing power of the dollar. How can the effect of the fluctuating dollar on business operations be presented to users of the financial statements?

7. During January merchandise costing $7,000 was sold for $10,000 in cash. Because the purchasing power of the dollar has declined, it will cost $7,500 to replace the merchandise. (a) What is the amount of gross profit on sales in January? (b) Assuming that all operating expenses for the month are paid in cash and that the owner withdraws cash for the amount of net income, would there be enough cash remaining from the $10,000 of sales to replace the merchandise sold? Discuss.

8. If it were unnecessary to prepare annual financial statements during the life of a business enterprise, would there be any necessity for recording the annual adjusting entry for depreciation expense?

9. At which point is revenue from sales of merchandise on account more commonly recognized, time of sale or time of cash receipt?

10. Merchandise costing $70,000 was sold on the installment plan for $100,000 during the current year. The down payments and the installment payments received during the current year total $30,000. What is the amount of gross profit considered to be realized in the current year (a) applying the point-of-sale principle of revenue recognition and (b) the installment method of accounting?

11. During the current year, the Kent Construction Company obtained a contract to build an apartment building. The total contract price was $5,000,000 and the estimated construction costs were $4,000,000. During the current year the project was estimated to be 30% completed and the costs incurred totalled $1,250,000. Under the degree-of-contract-completion method of recognizing revenue, what amount of (a) revenue, (b) cost, and (c) income should be recognized from the contract for the current year?

12. On August 8 of the current year, Lambert Realty acquired a ten-acre tract of land for $100,000. Before the end of the year $35,000 was spent in subdividing the tract and in paving streets. The market value of the land at the end of the year was estimated at $150,000. Although no lots were sold during the year, the income statement for the year reported revenue of $50,000, expenses of $35,000, and net income of $15,000 from the project. Were generally accepted accounting principles followed? Discuss.

13. Lowell Company constructed a warehouse at a cost of $25,000 after a local contractor had submitted a bid of $27,500. The building was recorded at $27,500 and income of $2,500 was recognized. Were generally accepted accounting principles followed? Discuss.

362

14. Rowland Company purchased equipment for $150,000 at the beginning of a fiscal year. The equipment could be sold for $160,000 at the end of the fiscal year. It was proposed that since the equipment was worth more at the end of the year than at the beginning of the year, (a) no depreciation should be recorded for the current year and (b) the gain of $10,000 should be recorded. Discuss the propriety of the proposals.

15. If significant changes are made in the accounting principles applied from one period to the next, why should the effect of these changes be disclosed in the financial statements?

16. You have just been employed by a relatively small merchandising business that records its revenues only when cash is received and its expenses only when cash is paid. You are aware of the fact that the enterprise should record its revenues and expenses on the accrual basis. Would changing to the accrual basis violate the principle of consistency? Discuss.

17. The Parker Company has used the straight-line method of computing depreciation for many years. For the current year, the sum-of-the-years-digits method was used and depreciation expense totaled $60,000; net income was $100,000. Depreciation computed by the straight-line method would have been $40,000. (a) What is the quantitative effect of the change in method on the net income for the current year? (b) Is the effect of the change material? (c) Should the effect of the change in method be disclosed in the financial statements?

18. The accountant for a large wholesale firm charged the acquisition of a pencil sharpener to an expense account, even though the asset had an estimated useful life of 5 years. What concept supports this treatment of the expenditure?

19. In 1950 the Dexter Corporation acquired a building with a useful life of 40 years, which it depreciated by the declining-balance method. Is this practice conservative (a) for the year 1950 and (b) for the year 1989? Explain.

EXERCISES

14-1. Indicate for each of the following the amount of revenue that should be reported for the current year and the amount that should be postponed to a future period. Give a reason for your answer.

(a) Thirty days before the close of the current fiscal year, $60,000 was loaned at 7% for 90 days.

(b) Sixty days before the close of the current fiscal year, a $30,000, 90-day non-interest-bearing note was accepted at a discount of 7%. Proceeds in the amount of $29,475 were given to the maker of the note.

(c) Merchandise on hand at the close of the current fiscal year costing $72,500 is expected to be sold in the following year for $110,000.

(d) Salesmen submitted orders in the current year for merchandise for delivery in the following year. The merchandise had a cost of $7,250 and a selling price of $11,100.

(e) Season tickets for a series of five concerts were sold for $60,000. Two concerts were played during the current year.

(f) Cash of $5,000 was received in the current year on the sale of gift certificates to be redeemed in merchandise in the following year.

(g) Leased a tract of land on the first day of the third month of the current year, receiving one year's rent of $6,000.

(h) The contract price for building a bridge is $6,000,000. During the current year, the first year of construction, the bridge is estimated to be 20% completed and the costs incurred totaled $925,000. Revenue is to be recognized by the degree-of-contract-completion method.

14-2. Keck's makes all sales on the installment plan. Data related to merchandise sold during the current fiscal year are as follows:

Sales..	$400,000
Cash received on the $400,000 of installment contracts.	190,000
Merchandise inventory, beginning of year............	64,700
Merchandise inventory, end of year.................	65,200
Purchases.....................................	240,500

Determine the amount of gross profit that would be recognized for the current fiscal year according to (a) the point-of-sale method and (b) the installment method of recognizing revenue.

14-3. Properties and services acquired by an enterprise are generally recorded at cost. For each of the following, determine the cost:

(a) A machine was purchased for $10,000 under terms of n/30, FOB shipping point. The freight amounted to $175 and installation costs totaled $200.

(b) Chandler Company purchased $350 of materials and supplies and paid a carpenter $275 to build a showcase. A similar showcase would cost $700 if purchased from a manufacturer.

(c) An adjacent tract of land was acquired for $17,500 to provide additional parking for customers. The structures on the land were removed at a cost of $1,100. The salvage from the structures was sold for $500. The cost of grading the land was $400.

363

14-4. The cost of the merchandise inventory at the close of the first fiscal year of operations, according to three different methods, is as follows: fifo, $50,000; average, $47,500; lifo, $45,900. If the average-cost method is employed, the net income reported will be $40,000. (a) What will be the amount of net income reported if the fifo method is adopted? (b) What will be the amount of net income reported if the lifo method is adopted? (c) Which of the three methods is the most conservative? (d) Is the particular method adopted of sufficient materiality to require disclosure in the financial statements?

14-5. Salesmen for the Miller Company receive a commission of 10% of sales, the amount due on sales of one month being paid in the middle of the following month. At the close of each of the first three years of operations, the accountant failed to record accrued sales commissions expense as follows: first year, $4,500; second year, $8,000; third year, $11,000. In each case the commissions were paid during the first month of the succeeding year and were charged as an expense of that year. Accrued sales commissions expense was properly recorded at the end of the fourth year. (a) Determine the amount by which net income was overstated or understated for each of the four years. (b) Determine the items on the balance sheet that would have been overstated or understated, and the amount, as of the end of each of the four years as a result of the errors.

14-6. Of the following matters, considered individually, indicate those that are material and that should be disclosed either on the financial statements or in accompanying explanatory notes:

(a) A change in accounting principles adopted in the current year increased the amount of net income that would otherwise have been reported from $650,000 to $800,000.
(b) A manufacturing company employs the first-in, first-out cost flow assumption and prices its inventory at the lower of cost or market.
(c) A company is facing litigation involving restraint of trade. Damages might amount to $1,500,000. Annual net income reported in the past few years has ranged from $4,000,000 to $5,000,000.
(d) Between the end of its fiscal year and the date of publication of the annual report, a fire destroyed a portion of the plant. The loss is estimated at $15,000 and is fully covered by insurance. The net income for the year is $1,750,000.

14-7. McGraw Company sells most of its products on a cash basis but extends short-term credit to some of its customers. Invoices for sales on account are placed in a file and are not recorded until cash is received, at which time the sale is recorded in the same manner as a cash sale. The net income reported for the first three years of operations was $40,000, $55,000, and $45,000 respectively. The total amount of the uncollected sales invoices in the file at the end of each of the three years was $4,000, $5,750, and $5,000. In each case the entire amount was collected during the first month of the succeeding year. (a) Determine the amount by which net income was overstated or understated for each of the three years. (b) Determine the items on the balance sheet that were overstated or understated, and the amount, as of the end of each year.

14-8. Each of the statements presented at the top of the next page represents a decision made by the accountant. State whether or not you agree with his decision. Support your answer with reference to generally accepted accounting principles that are applicable in the circumstances.

(a) In preparing the balance sheet, detailed information as to the amount of cash on deposit in each of several banks was omitted. Only the total amount of cash under a caption "Cash in banks" was presented.

(b) Merchandise transferred to other parties on a consignment basis and not sold is included in merchandise inventory.

(c) Used electronic data processing equipment, with an estimated four-year life and no salvage value, was purchased early in the current fiscal year for $150,000. Since the company planned to purchase new equipment costing $300,000 to replace this equipment at the end of four years, depreciation expense of $75,000 was recorded for the current year. The depreciation expense thus provided for one fourth of the cost of the replacement.

(d) Land, used as a parking lot, was purchased 10 years ago for $25,000. Since its market value is now $45,000, the land account is debited for $20,000 and a gain account is credited for a like amount. The gain is presented as an "Other income" item in the income statement.

(e) All minor expenditures for office equipment are charged to an expense account.

PROBLEMS

The following additional problems for this chapter are located in Appendix B: 14-1B, 14-3B, 14-4B, 14-6B.

14-1A. You are engaged to review the accounting records of Simpson Company prior to closing of the revenue and expense accounts as of December 31, the end of the current fiscal year. The following information comes to your attention during the review:

(a) No interest has been accrued on a $30,000, $7\frac{1}{2}\%$, 90-day note receivable, dated November 1 of the current year.

(b) Accounts receivable include $1,500 owed by Yoder and Co., a bankrupt. There is no prospect of collecting any of the receivable. The allowance method of accounting for receivables is employed.

(c) Merchandise inventory on hand at December 31 of the current year has been recorded in the accounts at cost, $71,250. Current market price of the inventory is $73,100.

(d) The store supplies account has a balance of $1,200. The cost of the store supplies on hand at December 31, as determined by a physical count, was $525.

(e) Since net income for the current year is expected to be considerably less than it was for the preceding year, depreciation on equipment has not been recorded. Depreciation for the year on equipment, determined in a manner consistent with the preceding year, amounts to $19,500.

(f) Land recorded in the accounts at a cost of $25,000 was appraised at $40,000 by two expert appraisers.

(g) The company is being sued for $50,000 by a customer who claims damages for personal injury apparently caused by a defective product. Company attorneys feel extremely confident that the company will have no liability for damages resulting from this case.

Instructions:

Journalize any entries required to adjust or correct the accounts, identifying each entry by letter.

14-2A. Carriage Lane Furniture Company makes all sales on the installment basis and recognizes revenue at the point of sale. Condensed income statements and the amounts collected from customers for each of the first three years of operations are given below.

	First Year	Second Year	Third Year
Sales........................	$190,000	$285,000	$297,500
Cost of merchandise sold........	114,000	159,600	172,550
Gross profit on sales............	$ 76,000	$125,400	$124,950
Operating expenses............	62,500	87,100	90,500
Net income..................	$ 13,500	$ 38,300	$ 34,450
Collected from sales of first year.	$ 72,000	$ 68,000	$ 50,000
Collected from sales of second year........		100,000	95,000
Collected from sales of third year..................			110,000

Instructions:

Determine the amount of net income that would have been reported in each of the three years if the installment method of recognizing revenue had been employed, ignoring the possible effects of uncollectible accounts on the computation. Present figures in good order.

14-3A. Wright Construction Company began construction on three contracts during 1973. The contract prices and construction activities for 1973, 1974, and 1975 were as follows:

		1973		1974		1975	
Contract	Contract Price	Costs Incurred	Percent Completed	Costs Incurred	Percent Completed	Costs Incurred	Percent Completed
A	$2,500,000	$1,100,000	55%	$ 960,000	45%	—	—
B	4,000,000	640,000	20%	1,920,000	60%	$ 695,000	20%
C	3,000,000	234,000	10%	702,000	30%	1,170,000	50%

Instructions:

Determine the amount of revenue and the income to be recognized for each of the following years from the contracts: 1973, 1974, and 1975. Revenue is to be recognized by the degree-of-contract-completion method. Present computations in good order.

14-4A. Sweeney Company was organized on January 1, 1972. During its first three years of operations, the company determined uncollectible accounts expense by the direct write-off method, the cost of the merchandise inventory at the end of the period by the first-in, first-out method, and depreciation expense by the straight-line method. The amounts of net income reported and the amounts of the foregoing items for each of the three years were as follows:

	First Year	Second Year	Third Year
Net income reported..........	$22,500	$33,750	$40,000
Uncollectible accounts expense.	350	1,250	2,500
Ending merchandise inventory.	38,000	41,500	43,750
Depreciation expense........	7,300	7,500	7,750

The firm is considering the possibility of changing to the following methods in determining net income for the fourth and subsequent years: provision for doubtful accounts through the use of an allowance account, last-in, first-out inventory, and declining-balance depreciation at twice the straight-line rate. In order to consider the probable future effect of these changes on the determination of net income, the management requests that net income of the past three years be recomputed on the basis of the proposed methods. The uncollectible accounts expense, inventory, and depreciation expense, for the past three years, computed in accordance with the proposed methods, are as follows:

	First Year	Second Year	Third Year
Uncollectible accounts expense.	$ 1,050	$ 1,450	$ 2,000
Ending merchandise inventory.	36,750	39,500	40,250
Depreciation expense.........	14,600	13,200	12,100

Instructions:

Recompute the net income for each of the three years, presenting the figures in an orderly manner.

14-5A. Glenn Martin Television Sales employs the installment method of recognizing gross profit for sales made on the installment plan. Details of a particular installment sale, amounts collected from the purchaser, and the repossession of the item sold are presented below.

First year:
 Sold for $750 a color television set having a cost of $600 and received a down payment of $150.
Second year:
 Received twelve monthly payments of $25 each.
Third year:
 The purchaser defaulted on the monthly payments, the set was repossessed, and the remaining 12 installments were canceled. The set was estimated to be worth $275.

Instructions:

(1) Determine the gross profit to be recognized in the first year.
(2) Determine the gross profit to be recognized in the second year.
(3) Determine the gain or the loss to be recognized from the repossession of the set.

14-6A. Frank Monroe owns and manages The Art Mart on a full-time basis. He also maintains the accounting records. At the close of the first year of operations, he prepared the following income statement and balance sheet.

The Art Mart
Income Statement
For Year Ended December 31, 19—

Sales.....................		$70,000
Purchases.................		61,750
Gross profit on sales.......		$ 8,250
Operating expenses:		
Salary expense............	$ 8,600	
Rent expense.............	4,875	
Utilities expense..........	1,600	
Miscellaneous expense.....	1,150	
Total operating expenses.		16,225
Net loss..................		$ 7,975

The Art Mart
Balance Sheet
December 31, 19—

Cash............................	$ 3,025
Equipment.......................	4,000
Frank Monroe....................	$ 7,025

Because of the large net loss reported by the income statement, Monroe is considering discontinuing operations. Before making a decision, he asks you to review the accounting methods employed and, if material errors are found, to prepare revised statements. The following information is elicited during the course of the review:

(a) The only transactions recorded have been those in which cash was received or disbursed.
(b) The accounts have not been closed for the year.
(c) The business was established on January 4 by an investment of $10,000 in cash by the owner. An additional investment of $5,000 was made in cash on July 1.
(d) The equipment listed on the balance sheet at $4,000 was purchased for cash on January 5. Equipment purchased July 1 for $1,500 in cash was debited to Purchases. Equipment purchased on December 28 for $2,500 for which a 90-day non-interest-bearing note was issued, was not recorded.

(e) Depreciation on equipment has not been recorded. The equipment is estimated to have a useful life of 10 years and no salvage value. (Use straight-line method.)
(f) Accounts receivable from customers at December 31 total $3,850.
(g) Uncollectible accounts are estimated at $235.
(h) The merchandise inventory at December 31, as nearly as can be determined, has a cost of $12,500.
(i) A total of $4,400 is owed to merchandise creditors on account at December 31.
(j) Insurance premiums of $750 were debited to Miscellaneous Expense during the year. The unexpired portion at December 31 is $350.
(k) Supplies of $900 purchased during the year were debited to Purchases. An estimated $300 of supplies were on hand at December 31.
(l) Rent Expense includes an advance payment of $375 for the month of January in the subsequent year.
(m) Salaries owed but not paid on December 31 total $425.
(n) The classification of operating expenses as "selling" and "general" is not considered to be sufficiently important to justify the cost of the analysis.
(o) The proprietor made no withdrawals during the year.

Instructions:

(1) On the basis of the financial statements presented above, prepare an unadjusted trial balance as of December 31, on an eight-column work sheet.
(2) Record the adjustments and the corrections in the Adjustments columns and complete the work sheet.
(3) Prepare an income statement, a capital statement, and a balance sheet.

Chapter 15

PARTNERSHIPS

PARTNERSHIP ORGANIZATION AND OPERATION

The Uniform Partnership Act, which has been adopted by more than three fourths of the states, defines a partnership as "an association of two or more persons to carry on as co-owners a business for profit." The partnership form of business organization is widely used for comparatively small businesses that wish to take advantage of the combined capital, managerial talent, and experience of two or more persons. In many cases, the alternative to securing the amount of investment required or the various skills needed to operate a business is to adopt the corporate form of organization, which is discussed in later chapters. The corporate form of organization is sometimes not available, however, to certain professions because of restrictions in state statutes or in professional codes of ethics. Hence, a group of physicians, attorneys, or certified public accountants that wishes to band together to practice a profession frequently organize as a partnership. Medical and legal partnerships composed of 20 or more partners are not unusual, and the number of partners in some CPA firms exceeds 500.

The partnership characteristics that have accounting implications are described in the following paragraphs.

Limited life. Dissolution of a partnership occurs whenever a partner ceases to be a member of the firm for any reason, including withdrawal, bankruptcy, incapacity, or death. Similarly, admission of a new partner to the firm dissolves the old partnership. In the event of dissolution, a new partnership must be formed if the operations of the business are to be continued without interruption. This is the usual situation with professional partnerships; their composition may change frequently through admissions of new partners and retirements of others.

Unlimited liability. Each partner is individually liable to creditors for debts incurred by the partnership. Thus, if a partnership becomes

369

insolvent, the partners are required to contribute sufficient personal assets to settle the debts of the partnership.

Co-ownership of property. The property invested in a partnership by a partner becomes the property of all the partners jointly. Upon dissolution of the partnership and distribution of its assets, each member's claim against the assets is measured by the amount of the balance in his capital account.

Participation in income. Net income and net loss are distributed among the partners in accordance with their agreement. In the absence of any agreement, all partners share equally. If the agreement specifies profit distribution but is silent as to losses, the losses are shared in the same manner as profits.

Articles of partnership. A partnership is created by a voluntary contract containing all the elements essential to any other enforceable contract. It is not necessary that this contract be in writing, nor even that its terms be specifically expressed orally. However, good business practice dictates that the contract should be in writing and should clearly express the intentions of the partners. The contract, known as the *articles of partnership* or *partnership agreement*, should contain provisions regarding such matters as the amount of investment to be made, limitations on withdrawals of funds, the manner in which net income and net loss are to be divided, and the admission and withdrawal of partners.

ACCOUNTING FOR PARTNERSHIPS

Most of the day-to-day accounting for a partnership is the same as the accounting for any other form of business organization. The system described in earlier chapters may be employed by a partnership with little modification. For example, the journals described may be used without alteration and the chart of accounts, with the exception of drawing and capital accounts for each partner, does not differ from the chart of accounts of a similar business conducted by a single owner. It is in the areas of the formation, income distribution, dissolution, and liquidation of partnerships that transactions peculiar to partnerships arise. The remainder of the chapter is devoted to the accounting principles and procedures applicable in these areas.

RECORDING INVESTMENTS

A separate entry is made for the investment of each partner in a partnership. The various assets contributed by a partner are debited to the proper asset accounts; if liabilities are assumed by the partnership, the appropriate liability accounts are credited; and the partner's capital account is credited for the net amount.

To illustrate the entry required to record an initial investment, assume that George M. Allen and James D. Barker, who are sole owners of competing hardware stores, agree to combine their enterprises in a partnership. Each is to contribute specified amounts of cash and other business assets. It is also agreed that the partnership is to assume the liabilities of the individual businesses. The entry to record the assets contributed and the liabilities transferred by George M. Allen, in general journal form, is as follows:

Apr. 1	Cash	7,200	
	Accounts Receivable	16,300	
	Merchandise Inventory	28,700	
	Store Equipment	5,400	
	Office Equipment	1,500	
	Allowance for Doubtful Accounts		1,500
	Accounts Payable		2,600
	George M. Allen, Capital		55,000

The monetary amounts at which the noncash assets are stated are those agreed upon by the partners. In arriving at an appropriate amount for such assets, particular consideration should be given to their market price at the time of the formation of the partnership. The values agreed upon represent the acquisition cost to the new accounting entity created by the formation of the partnership. These amounts may differ from the balances appearing in the accounts of the separate businesses before the partnership was organized. For example, the store equipment stated at $5,400 in the entry above may have had a book value of $3,500, appearing in Allen's ledger at its original cost of $10,000 with accumulated depreciation of $6,500.

Equipment contributed to the partnership may be recorded at the amount of the original cost to the partner, with a credit to the accumulated depreciation account for the amount necessary to bring the book value into agreement with the value assigned by the partners. For example, the store equipment invested by Allen could have been recorded at $10,000, with an offsetting credit to the accumulated depreciation account for $4,600, effecting a book value of $5,400. But the preferred practice is to record only the net amount agreed upon, as it represents the acquisition cost to the partnership.

Receivables contributed to the partnership are recorded at their face amount, with a credit to a contra account if provision is to be made for possible future uncollectibility. Ordinarily only accounts with reasonable chances of collection are transferred to the partnership and those believed to have little, if any, value are not acceptable to the other partner(s). Again referring to the illustrative entry above, the accounts receivable on Allen's ledger may have totaled $17,600, of which $1,300 was considered to be worthless. The remaining $16,300 of receivables

371

was recorded in the partnership accounts by a debit to Accounts Receivable and by debits to the individual accounts in the subsidiary ledger. Provision for possible future uncollectibility of the accounts receivable contributed to the partnership by Allen was recorded by a credit of $1,500 to Allowance for Doubtful Accounts.

DIVISION OF NET INCOME OR NET LOSS

As in the case of a sole proprietorship, the net income of a partnership may be said to include a return for the services of the owners, for the capital invested, and for economic or pure profit. A partner is not legally an employee of the partnership, nor is his capital contribution a loan. If each of two partners is to contribute equal services and amounts of capital, an equal sharing in partnership net income would be equitable. But if one partner is to contribute a larger portion of capital than the other, his greater contribution should be taken into consideration in the arrangements for dividing net income. Or, if the services of one partner are much more valuable to the partnership than those of the other, provision for unequal service contributions should be given recognition in their agreement.

To illustrate the division of net income and the accounting for this division, two possible agreements are to be considered. It should be noted that division of the net income or the net loss among the partners in exact accordance with their partnership agreement is of the utmost importance. If the agreement is silent on the matter, the law provides that all partners share equally, regardless of differences in amounts of capital contributed or of time devoted to the business. The partners may, however, make any agreement they wish in regard to the division of net income and net losses.

Income division recognizing services of partners. As a means of recognizing differences in ability and in amount of time devoted to the business, articles of partnership often provide for the allocation of a portion of net income to the partners in the form of a salary allowance. The articles may also provide for withdrawals of cash by the partners in lieu of salary payments. A clear distinction must therefore be made between the allocation of net income, which is credited to the capital accounts, and payments to the partners, which are debited to the drawing accounts.

As a basis for illustration, assume that the articles of partnership of Stone and Thomas provide for monthly salary allowances of $1,000 and $800 respectively, with the balance of the net income to be divided equally, and that the net income for the year is $30,000. A report of the division of net income may be presented as a separate statement accompanying the balance sheet and the income statement, or it may be added at the bottom of the income statement. Assuming that the latter procedure is adopted, the lower part of the income statement would appear as follows:

Net income..........			$30,000

Division of net income:	J. M. STONE	R. D. THOMAS	TOTAL
Salary allowance................	$12,000	$ 9,600	$21,600
Remaining income...............	4,200	4,200	8,400
Net income.....................	$16,200	$13,800	$30,000

The division of net income is recorded as a closing entry, regardless of whether or not the partners actually withdraw the amounts of their salary allowances. The entry for the division of net income is as follows:

Dec.	31	Income Summary..................	30,000	
		J. M. Stone, Capital.............		16,200
		R. D. Thomas, Capital...........		13,800

If Stone and Thomas had withdrawn their salary allowances monthly, the withdrawals would have accumulated as debits in the drawing accounts during the year. At the end of the year, the debit balances of $12,000 and $9,600 in their respective drawing accounts would be transferred to their respective capital accounts.

Income division recognizing services of partners and investment. Partners may agree that the most equitable plan of income sharing is to allow salaries commensurate with the services rendered and also to allow interest on the capital investments. The remainder is then shared in an arbitrary ratio. To illustrate, assume that Stone and Thomas (1) are allowed monthly salaries of $1,000 and $800 respectively; (2) are allowed interest at 7% on capital balances at January 1 of the current fiscal year which amounted to $40,000 and $25,000 respectively; and (3) divide the remainder of net income equally. The division of $30,000 net income for the year could then be reported on the income statement as follows:

373

Net income......			$30,000

	J. M. STONE	R. D. THOMAS	TOTAL
Salary allowance................	$12,000	$ 9,600	$21,600
Interest allowance................	2,800	1,750	4,550
Remaining income...............	1,925	1,925	3,850
Net income.....................	$16,725	$13,275	$30,000

On the basis of the information in the foregoing income statement, the entry to close the income summary account would be recorded in the general journal as follows:

Dec.	31	Income Summary..................	30,000	
		J. M. Stone, Capital.............		16,725
		R. D. Thomas, Capital...........		13,275

In the illustrations presented thus far, the net income has exceeded the sum of the allowances for salary and interest. It is obvious that this may not always be the case. If the net income is less than the total of the special allowances, the "remaining balance" will be a negative figure that must be divided among the partners as though it were a net loss. The effect of this situation may be illustrated by assuming the same salary and interest allowances as in the preceding illustration but changing the amount of net income to $20,000. The salary and interest allowances to Stone total $14,800 and the comparable figure for Thomas is $11,350. The sum of these amounts, $26,150, exceeds the net income of $20,000 by $6,150. It is therefore necessary to deduct $3,075 (½ of $6,150) from each partner's share to arrive at the net income, as indicated below.

Net income... $20,000

	J. M. STONE	R. D. THOMAS	TOTAL
Salary allowance	$12,000	$ 9,600	$21,600
Interest allowance.................	2,800	1,750	4,550
Total........................	$14,800	$11,350	$26,150
Excess of allowances over income.....	3,075	3,075	6,150
Net income.......................	$11,725	$ 8,275	$20,000

In closing Income Summary at the end of the year, $11,725 would be credited to J. M. Stone, Capital, and $8,275 would be credited to R. D. Thomas, Capital.

PARTNERS' SALARIES AND INTEREST TREATED AS EXPENSES

Although the traditional view among accountants is to treat salary and interest allowances as allocations of net income, as in the foregoing illustrations, some prefer to treat them as expenses of the enterprise. According to this view, the partnership is treated as a distinct legal entity and the partners are considered to be employees and creditors of the firm. When salaries for partners' services and interest on partners' investments are viewed as expenses of the enterprise, withdrawals of the agreed amount are charged to expense accounts rather than to the partners' drawing accounts. The expense accounts are then closed into the income summary account, and the remaining net income is allocated among the partners in the agreed ratio. The amounts paid to partners that are considered to be salary expense and interest expense should be specifically identified as such on the income statement. Regardless of whether partners' salary and interest are treated as expenses of the partnership or as a division of net income, the total amount allocated to each partner will be the same.

STATEMENTS FOR PARTNERSHIPS

Details of the division of net income should be disclosed in the financial statements prepared at the end of the fiscal period. This may be done by adding a section to the income statement, which has been illustrated in the preceding pages, or the data may be presented in a separate statement.

Details of the changes in partnership capital during the period should also be presented in a capital statement. The purposes of the statement and the data included in it correspond to those of the capital statement of a sole proprietorship. There are a number of variations in form, one of which is illustrated below.

Stone and Thomas
Capital Statement
For Year Ended December 31, 19—

	J. M. STONE	R. D. THOMAS	TOTAL
Capital, January 1, 19—................	$40,000	$25,000	$ 65,000
Additional investment during the year.....		5,000	5,000
	$40,000	$30,000	$ 70,000
Net income for the year................	16,725	13,275	30,000
	$56,725	$43,275	$100,000
Withdrawals during the year............	15,000	12,500	27,500
Capital, December 31, 19—............	$41,725	$30,775	$ 72,500

Capital
statement

375

Under the Internal Revenue Code, enterprises organized as partnerships are not distinct entities and are not required to pay federal income taxes. Instead, the individual partners must report their distributive shares of partnership income on their personal tax returns. However, data on the distributive shares of each partner, as well as a summary of revenue and expense and other financial details of partnership operations, must be reported annually on official "information return" forms. If the agreement requires the payment of salaries or interest to partners regardless of the amount of net income of the enterprise, such payments must be reported on the partnership information return as an expense. The partners are required, in turn, to combine the amounts thus received with their distributive shares of net income so that, despite the method, all income is reported for taxation by the individual partners.

PARTNERSHIP DISSOLUTION

One of the basic characteristics of the partnership form of organization is its limited life. Any change in the personnel of the membership results in the dissolution of the partnership. Thus, admission of a new partner effects the dissolution of the old firm. Similarly, death, bankruptcy, or withdrawal of a partner causes dissolution.

Dissolution of the partnership is not necessarily followed by the winding up of the affairs of the business. For example, a partnership composed of two partners may admit an additional partner. Or if one of three partners in a business withdraws, the remaining two partners may continue to operate the business. In all such cases, a new partnership is formed and new articles of partnership should be prepared.

ADMISSION OF A PARTNER

An additional person may be admitted to a partnership enterprise only with the consent of all the current partners. It does not follow, however, that a partner cannot dispose of part or all of his interest in the firm without the consent of the remaining partners. Under common law, if a partner assigned his interest in the partnership to an outside party, the partnership was automatically dissolved. Under the Uniform Partnership Act, a partner can dispose of part or all of his interest in the firm without the consent of the remaining partners. The person who buys the interest acquires the selling partner's rights to share in net income and assets upon liquidation. He does not automatically become a partner, however, and has no voice in partnership affairs unless he is admitted to the firm.

An additional person may be admitted to a partnership through either of two procedures:

1. Purchase of an interest from one or more of the current partners.
2. Contribution of assets to the partnership.

When the first procedure is followed, the capital interest of the incoming partner is obtained from current partners, and neither the total assets nor the total capital of the business is affected. When the second procedure is followed, both the total assets and the total capital of the business are increased.

ADMISSION BY PURCHASE OF AN INTEREST

When an additional person is admitted to a firm by purchasing an interest from one or more of the partners, he pays the purchase price directly to the selling partners. Payment is for partnership equity owned by the partners as individuals, and hence the cash or other consideration paid is not recorded in the accounts of the partnership. The only entry required is the transfer of the appropriate amounts of capital from the capital accounts of the selling partners to the capital account established for the incoming partner.

As an example, assume that partners Abbott and Beck have capital balances of $50,000 each. On June 1, each of them sells one fifth of his capital interest to Carson for $10,000 in cash. The only entry required in the partnership accounts is as shown at the top of the following page.

June	1	John Abbott, Capital.................	10,000		
		Henry Beck, Capital.	10,000		
		Roger Carson, Capital..............			20,000

The effect of the transaction on the partnership accounts is presented in the following diagram:

The foregoing entry is made regardless of the amount paid by Carson for the one-fifth interest. If the firm had been earning a high rate of return on the investment and Carson had been very eager to obtain the one-fifth interest, he might have paid considerably more than $20,000. Had other circumstances prevailed, he might have acquired the one-fifth interest for considerably less than $20,000. In either event, the entry to transfer the capital interests would not be affected.

After the admission of Carson, the total capital of the firm is $100,000, in which he has a one-fifth interest, or $20,000. It does not necessarily follow that he will be entitled to a similar share of the partnership net income. Division of net income or net loss will be in accordance with the new partnership agreement.

ADMISSION BY CONTRIBUTION OF ASSETS

Instead of buying an interest from the current partners, the incoming partner may contribute assets to the partnership. In this case both the assets and the capital of the firm are increased. To illustrate, assume that Logan and Macy are partners with capital accounts of $35,000 and $25,000 respectively. On June 1, Nichols invests $20,000 cash in the business, for which he is to receive an ownership equity of $20,000. The entry to record this transaction, in general journal form, is:

June	1	Cash....................................	20,000	
		William Nichols, Capital................		20,000

The essential difference between the circumstances of the admission of Nichols above and of Carson in the preceding example may be observed by comparing the diagram at the top of the next page with the one above.

With the admission of Nichols, the total capital of the new partnership becomes $80,000, of which he has a one-fourth interest, or $20,000. The extent of his participation in partnership net income will be governed by the articles of partnership.

PARTNERSHIP ACCOUNTS

NET ASSETS			LOGAN, CAPITAL	
60,000				35,000
20,000				

	NICHOLS, CAPITAL		MACY, CAPITAL	
		20,000		25,000

Revaluation of assets. If the partnership assets are not fairly stated in terms of current market price at the time of admission of a new partner, the accounts may be adjusted accordingly. The net amount of the increases and decreases in asset values are then allocated to the capital accounts of the old partners in accordance with their income-sharing ratio. To illustrate, assume that in the preceding illustration for the Logan and Macy partnership the balance of the merchandise inventory account had been $14,000 and the current replacement price had been $17,000. Prior to the admission of Nichols the revaluation would be recorded as follows, assuming that Logan and Macy share equally in net income:

June	1	Merchandise Inventory...............	3,000	
		George Logan, Capital..............		1,500
		Thomas Macy, Capital.............		1,500

If a number of assets are revalued, the adjustments may be debited or credited to a temporary account entitled Asset Revaluations. After all adjustments are made, the net balance of the account is closed to the capital accounts.

It is important that the assets be stated in terms of current prices at the time of admission of a new partner. Failure to recognize current prices may result in participation by the new partner in gains or losses attributable to the period prior to his admission to the partnership.

Goodwill. When a new partner is admitted to a partnership, goodwill attributable to either the old partnership or to the incoming partner may be recognized. Although there are various methods of estimating goodwill, such factors as the respective shares owned by the partners and the relative bargaining abilities of the partners will influence the final determination. The amount of goodwill agreed upon is recorded as an asset, with a corresponding addition to the appropriate capital accounts.

To illustrate the recognition of goodwill to the old partners, assume that on March 1 the partnership of Joyce and Keller admits Long, who is to contribute cash of $15,000. After the tangible assets of the old partnership have been adjusted to current market prices, the capital balances of Joyce and Keller are $20,000 and $24,000 respectively. The parties agree, however, that the enterprise is worth $50,000. The excess of $50,000 over the capital balances of $44,000 ($20,000 + $24,000) indicates the existence of $6,000 of goodwill, which should be allocated to the capital accounts of the original partners in accordance with their income-sharing agreement.

The entries to record the goodwill and the admission of the new partner, assuming that the original partners share equally in net income, are as follows, in general journal form:

Mar. 1 Goodwill............................. 6,000
       F. G. Joyce, Capital..................   3,000
       G. N. Keller, Capital.................   3,000

    1 Cash............................... 15,000
       W. J. Long, Capital..................   15,000

If a partnership admits a new partner who is expected to improve the fortunes of the firm, the parties might agree to recognize this high earnings potential. To illustrate, assume that William Evans is to be admitted to the partnership of Cowen and Dodd for an investment of $30,000. If the parties agree to recognize $5,000 of goodwill attributable to Evans, the entry to record his admission is as follows, in general journal form:

July 1 Cash............................... 30,000
       Goodwill............................ 5,000
       William Evans, Capital...............   35,000

379

WITHDRAWAL OF A PARTNER

When a partner retires or for some other reason wishes to withdraw from the firm, one or more of the remaining partners may purchase his interest and the business may be continued without apparent interruption. In such cases, settlement for the purchase and sale is made between the partners as individuals. The only entry required by the partnership is a debit to the capital account of the partner withdrawing and a credit to the capital account of the partner or partners acquiring the interest.

If the settlement with the withdrawing partner is made by the partnership, the effect is to reduce the assets and the capital of the firm. In order to determine the ownership equity of the withdrawing partner, the asset accounts should be adjusted to bring them into agreement with current market prices. The net amount of the adjustments should be allocated among the capital accounts of the partners in accordance with the income ratio. In the event that the cash or the other available assets are insufficient to make complete payment at the time of withdrawal, a liability account should be credited for the balance owed to the withdrawing partner

DEATH OF A PARTNER

The death of a partner effects the dissolution of the partnership. In the absence of any contrary agreement, the accounts should be closed as of the date of death, and the net income for the fractional part of the year should be transferred to the capital accounts. It is not unusual, however, for the partnership agreement to stipulate that the accounts remain open to the end of the fiscal year or until the affairs are wound up, if that should occur earlier. The net income of the entire period is then allocated, as provided by the agreement, to the respective periods occurring before and after dissolution.

The balance in the capital account of the deceased partner is then transferred to a liability account with his estate. The surviving partner or partners may continue the business or the affairs may be wound up. If the former course is followed, the procedures for settling with the estate will conform to those outlined earlier for the withdrawal of a partner from the business.

LIQUIDATION OF A PARTNERSHIP

When a partnership goes out of business, it customarily sells most of the assets, pays the creditors, and distributes the remaining cash or other assets to the partners in accordance with their claims. The winding-up process may be referred to generally as *liquidation*. Although liquidation refers specifically to the payment of liabilities, it is often used in a broader sense to include the entire winding-up process.

When the ordinary business activities are discontinued preparatory to liquidation, the accounts should be adjusted and closed in accordance with the customary procedures of the periodic summary. The only accounts remaining open then will be the various asset, contra asset, liability, and capital accounts.

The sale of the assets is referred to as *realization*. As cash is realized, it is applied first to the payment of the claims of creditors. After all liabilities have been paid, the remaining cash is distributed to the partners based on their ownership equities as indicated by their capital accounts.

If the assets are sold piecemeal, the liquidation process may extend over a considerable period of time. This creates no special problem, however, if the distribution of cash to the partners is postponed until all of the assets have been sold. As a basis for illustration, assume that Alden, Beeler, and Craig decide to liquidate their partnership. Their income-sharing ratio is 5:3:2. After discontinuing the ordinary business operations and closing the accounts, the summary of the general ledger shown at the top of the next page is prepared.

Accounting for the liquidation will be illustrated by three examples based on the foregoing statement of facts. In all cases it will be assumed that all noncash assets are disposed of in a single transaction and that all liabilities are paid at one time. This is merely for the sake of brevity. In addition, Assets and Liabilities will be used as account titles in place of

Cash..	$11,000
All noncash assets	64,000
All liabilities	$ 9,000
J. Alden, Capital................................	22,000
B. Beeler, Capital...............................	22,000
H. Craig, Capital...............................	22,000
Total.....................................	$75,000 $75,000

the various asset, contra asset, and liability accounts that in actual practice would be affected by the transactions.

Gain on realization. Alden, Beeler, and Craig sell all noncash assets for $72,000, realizing a gain of $8,000 ($72,000 − $64,000). The gain is divided among the capital accounts in the income-sharing ratio of 5:3:2, the liabilities are paid, and the remaining cash is distributed to the partners according to the balances in their capital accounts. A tabular summary of the transactions follows:

					CAPITAL		
		OTHER			J. ALDEN	B. BEELER	H. CRAIG
	CASH +	ASSETS =	LIABILITIES +		50% +	30% +	20%
Balances before realization......	$11,000	$64,000	$ 9,000		$22,000	$22,000	$22,000
Sale of assets and division of gain.	+72,000	−64,000			+ 4,000	+ 2,400	+ 1,600
Balances after realization.......	$83,000		$ 9,000		$26,000	$24,400	$23,600
Payment of liabilities..........	− 9,000		−9,000				
Balances....................	$74,000				$26,000	$24,400	$23,600
Distribution of cash to partners..	−74,000				−26,000	−24,400	−23,600

381

The entries to record the several steps in the liquidation procedure are as follows, in general journal form:

Sale of assets

Cash.......................................	72,000	
Assets......................................		64,000
Loss and Gain on Realization.........................		8,000

Division of gain

Loss and Gain on Realization............................	8,000	
J. Alden, Capital.......................................		4,000
B. Beeler, Capital......................................		2,400
H. Craig, Capital.......................................		1,600

Payment of liabilities

Liabilities..	9,000	
Cash...		9,000

Distribution of cash to partners

J. Alden, Capital.......................................	26,000	
B. Beeler, Capital......................................	24,400	
H. Craig, Capital.......................................	23,600	
Cash...		74,000

In the foregoing illustration, the distribution of the cash among the partners was determined by reference to the balances of their respective capital accounts after the gain on realization had been allocated. Under no circumstances should the income-sharing ratio be used as a basis for distributing the cash.

Loss on realization; no capital deficiencies. Assume that in the foregoing example Alden, Beeler, and Craig dispose of all noncash assets for $44,000, incurring a loss of $20,000 ($64,000 − $44,000). The various steps in the liquidation of the partnership are summarized as follows:

	Cash	+	Other Assets	=	Liabilities	+	J. Alden 50%	+	B. Beeler 30%	+	H. Craig 20%
							Capital				
Balances before realization......	$11,000		$64,000		$ 9,000		$22,000		$22,000		$ 22,000
Sale of assets and division of loss.	+44,000		−64,000				−10,000		− 6,000		− 4,000
Balances after realization.......	$55,000				$ 9,000		$12,000		$16,000		$18,000
Payment of liabilities..........	− 9,000				− 9,000						
Balances..................	$46,000						$12,000		$16,000		$18,000
Distribution of cash to partners..	−46,000						−12,000		−16,000		−18,000

The entries required to record the liquidation are presented below, in general journal form.

Sale of assets

Cash...	44,000	
Loss and Gain on Realization..........................	20,000	
Assets..		64,000

Division of loss

J. Alden, Capital.......................................	10,000	
B. Beeler, Capital......................................	6,000	
H. Craig, Capital.......................................	4,000	
Loss and Gain on Realization.........................		20,000

Payment of liabilities

| Liabilities... | 9,000 | |
| Cash... | | 9,000 |

Distribution of cash to partners

J. Alden, Capital.......................................	12,000	
B. Beeler, Capital......................................	16,000	
H. Craig, Capital.......................................	18,000	
Cash...		46,000

Loss on realization; capital deficiency. In the preceding illustration, the capital account of each partner was more than sufficient to absorb his share of the loss from realization. Each partner shared in the distribution of cash to the extent of the remaining credit balance in his capital account. The share of the loss chargeable to a partner may be such that it exceeds his ownership equity. The resulting debit balance in his capital account, which is referred to as a *deficiency*, is a claim of the partnership against the partner. Pending collection from the deficient partner, the partnership cash will not be sufficient to pay the other partners in full. In such cases the available cash should be distributed in such a manner that, if the claim against the deficient partner cannot be collected, each of the remaining capital balances will be sufficient to absorb the appropriate share of the deficiency.

To illustrate a situation of this type, assume that Alden, Beeler, and Craig sell all of the noncash assets for $10,000, incurring a loss of $54,000 ($64,000 − $10,000). It is readily apparent that the portion of the loss allocable to Alden, which is $27,000 (50% of $54,000), exceeds the $22,000 balance in his capital account. This $5,000 deficiency is a potential loss to Beeler and Craig and must be tentatively divided between them in their income-sharing ratio of 3:2 (3/5 and 2/5). The capital balances remaining represent their claims on the partnership cash. The computations may be summarized in the manner presented below:

383

CAPITAL

	J. Alden 50%	B. Beeler 30%	H. Craig 20%	Total
Balances before realization..........	$ 22,000	$ 22,000	$ 22,000	$ 66,000
Division of loss on realization........	−27,000	−16,200	−10,800	−54,000
Balances after realization...........	$− 5,000	$ 5,800	$ 11,200	$ 12,000
Division of potential additional loss...	5,000	− 3,000	− 2,000	
Claims to partnership cash..........		$ 2,800	$ 9,200	$ 12,000

The complete summary of the various transactions that have occurred thus far in the liquidation may then be reported, in the form illustrated earlier, as follows:

CAPITAL

	CASH +	OTHER ASSETS =	LIABIL- ITIES +	J. ALDEN 50% +	B. BEELER 30% +	H. CRAIG 20%
Balances before realization......	$11,000	$64,000	$ 9,000	$22,000	$22,000	$22,000
Sale of assets and division of loss.	+10,000	−64,000		−27,000	−16,200	−10,800
Balances after realization.......	$21,000		$ 9,000	$ 5,000 (Dr.)	$ 5,800	$11,200
Payment of liabilities...........	− 9,000		− 9,000			
Balances....................	$12,000			$ 5,000 (Dr.)	$ 5,800	$11,200
Distribution of cash to partners..	−12,000				− 2,800	− 9,200
Balances....................				$ 5,000 (Dr.)	$ 3,000	$ 2,000

The entries to record the liquidation to this point, in general journal form, are shown at the top of the next page.

Sale of assets

Cash...	10,000	
Loss and Gain on Realization............................	54,000	
Assets...		64,000

Division of loss

J. Alden, Capital......................................	27,000	
B. Beeler, Capital.....................................	16,200	
H. Craig, Capital......................................	10,800	
Loss and Gain on Realization............................		54,000

Payment of liabilities

Liabilities...	9,000	
Cash...		9,000

Distribution of cash to partners

B. Beeler, Capital.....................................	2,800	
H. Craig, Capital......................................	9,200	
Cash...		12,000

The affairs of the partnership are not completely wound up until the claims among the partners are settled. Payments to the firm by the deficient partner are credited to his capital account. Any uncollectible deficiency becomes a loss and is written off against the capital balances of the remaining partners. Finally, the cash received from the deficient partner is distributed to the other partners in accordance with their ownership claims.

To continue with the illustration, the capital balances remaining after the $12,000 cash distribution are as follows: Alden, $5,000 debit; Beeler, $3,000 credit; Craig, $2,000 credit. The entries for the partnership, in general journal form, under three different assumptions as to final settlement are presented below and at the top of the next page.

If Alden pays the entire amount of his $5,000 deficiency to the partnership (no loss), the final entries will be:

Receipt of deficiency

Cash...	5,000	
J. Alden, Capital....................................		5,000

Distribution of cash to partners

B. Beeler, Capital.....................................	3,000	
H. Craig, Capital......................................	2,000	
Cash...		5,000

If Alden pays $3,000 of his deficiency to the partnership and the remainder is considered to be uncollectible ($2,000 loss), the final entries will be:

Receipt of part of deficiency

Cash...	3,000	
J. Alden, Capital....................................		3,000

Division of loss

B. Beeler, Capital....................................	1,200	
H. Craig, Capital....................................	800	
J. Alden, Capital....................................		2,000

Distribution of cash to partners

B. Beeler, Capital....................................	1,800	
H. Craig, Capital....................................	1,200	
Cash...		3,000

If Alden is unable to pay any part of his $5,000 deficiency ($5,000 loss), the loss to the other partners will be recorded by the following entry:

Division of loss

B. Beeler, Capital....................................	3,000	
H. Craig, Capital....................................	2,000	
J. Alden, Capital....................................		5,000

It should be noted that the type of error most likely to occur in the liquidation of a partnership is improper distribution of cash among the partners. Errors of this type result from confusing the distribution of cash with the division of gains and losses on realization.

Gains and losses on realization result from the disposal of assets to outsiders; they represent changes in partnership capital and should be divided among the capital accounts in the same manner as net income or net loss from ordinary business operations, namely, in the income-sharing ratio.

On the other hand, the distribution of cash (or other assets) to the partners is an entirely different matter and has no direct relationship to the income-sharing ratio. Distribution of assets to the partners upon liquidation is the exact reverse of contribution of assets by the partners at the time the partnership was established. The amount that a partner is entitled to receive from the firm is equal to the credit balance in his capital account after all gains and losses on realization have been divided and appropriate allowance has been made for any additional potential losses.

QUESTIONS

1. Is it possible for a partner to lose a greater amount than the amount of his investment in the partnership enterprise? Explain.

2. Adams, Barr, and Cook are contemplating the formation of a partnership in which Adams is to invest $20,000 and devote one-half time, Barr is to invest $40,000 and devote one-fourth time, and Cook is to make no investment and devote full time. Would Cook be correct in assuming that inasmuch as he is not contributing any assets to the firm, he is risking nothing? Explain.

3. As a part of his initial investment, a partner contributes store equipment that had been recorded in his accounts at a cost of $40,000 and on which the accumulated depreciation had totaled $18,000. The partners agree on a valuation of $30,000. How should the store equipment be recorded in the accounts of the partnership?

4. All partners agree that accounts receivable of $10,000 invested by a partner will be collectible to the extent of 95%. How should the accounts receivable be recorded in the general ledger of the partnership?

5. (a) What two principal factors should be considered in arriving at an agreement for the distribution of net income and net loss between the partners? (b) In the absence of a specific agreement on the matter, how should the periodic net income or net loss be divided?

6. (a) What accounts are debited and credited to record a partner's cash withdrawal in lieu of salary? (b) What accounts are debited and credited to record the division of net income among partners at the end of the fiscal year? (c) The articles of partnership provide for a salary allowance of $1,000 per month to partner X. If X withdrew only $900 per month, would this affect his share of the partnership net income?

7. (a) What is the purpose of providing for the allocation of a portion of partnership net income to the partners in the form of a salary and/or interest allowance? (b) What is the ultimate effect on the total amount of each partner's equity in the partnership if salary and/or interest allowances are treated as expenses rather than as distributions of net income?

8. Must a partnership file a federal income tax return and pay federal income taxes? Explain.

9. Davis, a partner in the firm of Davis, Eaton, and Foster, sells his investment (capital balance of $30,000) to Reynolds. (a) Does the withdrawal of Davis dissolve the partnership? (b) Are Eaton and Foster required to admit Reynolds as a partner?

10. Differentiate between the admission of a new partner to a partnership (a) by purchase of an interest from another partner and (b) by contribution of assets to the partnership.

11. Gilbert and Harris are partners who share in net income equally and have capital balances of $25,000 and $15,000 respectively. Gilbert, with the consent of Harris, sells one half of his interest to Yost. What entry is required by the partnership if the sale price is (a) $10,000? (b) $15,000?

12. Why is it important to state all partnership assets in terms of current prices at the time of the admission of a new partner?

13. When a new partner is admitted to a partnership and goodwill is attributable to the old partnership, how should the amount of the goodwill be allocated to the capital accounts of the original partners?

14. (a) Differentiate between "dissolution" and "liquidation" of a partnership. (b) What is the meaning of "realization" when used in connection with liquidation of a partnership?

15. In the liquidation process, (a) how are losses and gains on realization divided among the partners, and (b) how is cash distributed among the partners?

16. J and K are partners, sharing gains and losses equally. At the time they decide to terminate the partnership, their capital balances are $45,000 and $35,000 respectively. After all noncash assets are sold and all liabilities are paid, there is a cash balance of $90,000. (a) What is the amount of gain or loss on realization? (b) How should the gain or the loss be divided between J and K? (c) How should the cash be divided between J and K?

17. A, B, and C share equally in net income and net loss. After selling all of the assets for cash, dividing the losses on realization, and paying liabilities, the balances in the capital accounts are as follows: A, $6,000, Dr.; B, $12,000, Cr.; C, $8,000, Cr. (a) What is the amount of cash on hand? (b) How should the cash be distributed?

18. X, Y, and Z are partners sharing income 2:1:2. After distribution of the firm's loss from liquidation, X's capital account has a debit balance of $7,500. If X is personally bankrupt and unable to pay any of the $7,500, how will the loss be divided between Y and Z?

EXERCISES

15-1. Lee Jacobs and Dan Kane decide to form a partnership by combining the assets of their separate businesses. Jacobs contributes the following assets to the partnership: cash $4,500; accounts receivable with a face amount of $22,500 and an allowance for doubtful accounts of $1,200; inventory with a cost of $19,750; and equipment with a cost of $32,000 and accumulated depreciation of $16,000. The partners agree that $500 of the accounts receivable are completely worthless and are not to be accepted by the partnership, that $1,000 is a reasonable allowance for the uncollectibility of the remaining accounts, that the inventory is to be recorded at the current market price of $20,250, and that the equipment is to be priced at $10,000. Present the entry, in general journal form, to record Jacobs' investment in the partnership accounts.

15-2. Lewis and Myers form a partnership with investments of $45,000 and $30,000 respectively. Determine their participation in net income of $33,000 for the year under each of the following assumptions: (a) no agreement concerning division of income; (b) divided in the ratio of their original capital investments; (c) interest at the rate of 8% allowed on original investments and the remainder divided in the ratio of 2:1; (d) salary allowances of $12,000 and $9,000 and the balance divided equally; (e) allowance of interest at the rate of 8% on original investments, salary allowances of $12,000 and $9,000 respectively, and the remainder divided equally.

15-3. Determine the participation of Lewis and Myers in a net income of $15,000 for the year according to each of the five assumptions as to income division listed in Exercise 15-2.

15-4. The capital accounts of Fred Neff and John Olson have balances of $22,500 and $30,000 respectively on January 1, the beginning of the current fiscal year. On April 10, Neff invested an additional $2,500. During the year Neff and Olson withdrew $7,800 and $9,000 respectively, and net income for the year was $20,000. The articles of partnership make no reference to the division of net income. (a) Present the journal entries to close (1) the income summary account and (2) the drawing accounts. (b) Prepare a capital statement for the current year.

15-5. The capital accounts of Donald Reed and James Scott have balances of $30,000 and $40,000 respectively. Oliver Ashby and Alfred Brooks are to be admitted to the partnership. Ashby purchases one third of Reed's interest for $12,000 and one fifth of Scott's interest for $9,600. Brooks contributes $20,000 cash to the partnership, for which he is to receive an ownership equity of $20,000. (a) Present the entries in general journal form to record the admission to the partnership of (1) Ashby and (2) Brooks. (b) What are the capital balances of each partner after the admission of Ashby and Brooks?

15-6. Howard Case is to retire from the partnership of Case and Associates as of June 30, the end of the current fiscal year. After closing the accounts, the capital balances of the partners are as follows: Howard Case, $50,000; Eric Doyle, $35,000; and John Edwards, $20,000. They have shared net income and net losses in the ratio of 3:2:1. The partners agree that the merchandise inventory should be increased by $2,500 and that the allowance for doubtful accounts should be increased by $1,000. Case agrees to accept an interest-bearing note for $25,000 in partial settlement of his ownership equity. The remainder of his claim is to be paid in cash. Doyle and Edwards are to share in the ratio of 2:1 in the net income or net loss of the new partnership. Present entries in general journal form to record (a) the adjustment of the assets to bring them into agreement with current fair prices and (b) the withdrawal of Case from the partnership.

15-7. Brush and Carver, with capital balances of $12,500 and $17,500 respectively, decide to liquidate the partnership. After selling the noncash assets and paying the liabilities, there is $10,000 of cash remaining. If the partners share income and losses equally, how should the cash be distributed?

15-8. Paul Farley, Dan Glover, and Fred Hill arrange to import and sell orchid corsages for a university dance. They agree to share the net income or net loss on the venture equally. Farley and Glover advance $30 and $20 respectively of their own funds to pay for advertising and other expenses. After collecting for all sales and paying creditors, they have $170 in cash. (a) How should the money be distributed? (b) Assuming that they have only $20 instead of $170, how should the money be distributed? (c) Assuming that the money was distributed as determined in (b), do any of the three have claims against another and, if so, how much?

15-9. After closing the accounts preparatory to liquidating the partnership, the capital accounts of Getty, Hart, and Inman are $21,000, $26,000, and $13,000 respectively. Cash and noncash assets total $11,000 and $79,000 respectively. Amounts owing to creditors total $30,000. The partners share income and losses in the ratio of 2:2:1. The noncash assets are sold and sufficient cash is available to pay all of the creditors except one for $5,000. Determine how the claim of the creditors should be settled. Present a summary of the transactions in the form illustrated in the chapter.

PROBLEMS

The following additional problems for this chapter are located in Appendix B: 15-1B, 15-2B, 15-5B.

15-1A. John Reed and Peter Shaw have decided to form a partnership. They have agreed that Reed is to invest $30,000 and that Shaw is to invest $20,000. Reed is to devote full time to the business and Shaw is to devote one-half time. The following plans for the division of income are being considered:

(a) Equal division.
(b) In the ratio of original investments.
(c) In the ratio of time devoted to the business.
(d) Interest of 6% on original investments and the remainder in the ratio of 2:1.
(e) Interest of 6% on original investments, salaries of $10,000 to Reed and $5,000 to Shaw, and the remainder equally.
(f) Plan (e), except that Reed is also to be allowed a bonus equal to 10% of the amount by which net income exceeds the salary allowances.

Instructions:

Determine the division of net income under each of the following assumptions: net income of $27,000 and net income of $12,000. Present the data in tabular form, using the following columnar headings:

	$27,000		$12,000	
Plan	Reed	Shaw	Reed	Shaw

15-2A. On May 1 of the current year G. H. Vance and A. R. Watt form a partnership.

Vance invests certain business assets at valuations agreed upon, transfers business liabilities, and contributes sufficient cash to bring his total capital to $30,000. Details regarding the book values of the business assets and liabilities, and the agreed valuations, follow:

	Vance's Ledger Balance	Agreed Valuation
Accounts Receivable....................	$ 9,600	$ 9,600
Allowance for Doubtful Accounts.........	500	750
Merchandise Inventory.................	17,000	17,500
Equipment...........................	25,000⎫	13,750
Accumulated Depreciation — Equipment..	8,000⎭	
Accounts Payable.....................	7,900	7,900
Notes Payable........................	5,000	5,000

Watt agrees to invest merchandise inventory priced at $15,000 and $5,000 in cash.

The articles of partnership include the following provisions regarding the division of net income: interest on original investment at 8%, salary allowances of $7,200 and $9,600 respectively, and the remainder equally.

Instructions:

(1) Give the entries, in general journal form, to record the investments of Vance and Watt in the partnership accounts.

(2) Prepare a balance sheet as of May 1, the date of formation of the partnership.

(3) After adjustments and the closing of revenue and expense accounts at April 30, the end of the first full year of operations, the income summary account has a credit balance of $26,200 and the drawing accounts have debit balances of $7,000 (Vance) and $9,200 (Watt). Present the journal entries to close the income summary account and the drawing accounts at April 30.

15-3A. The accounts in the ledger of Rush and Scott, attorneys-at-law, with the balances on December 31, the end of the current fiscal year after adjustments have been recorded, are as follows:

Cash	$ 4,125
Accounts Receivable	6,750
Supplies	525
Building	37,500
Accumulated Depreciation — Building	12,250
Office Equipment	8,750
Accumulated Depreciation — Office Equipment	1,500
Land	6,500
Accounts Payable	600
Salaries Payable	750
Dennis Rush, Capital	26,000
Dennis Rush, Drawing	17,500
Louis Scott, Capital	15,000
Louis Scott, Drawing	12,700
Professional Fees	70,500
Salary Expense	26,750
Depreciation Expense — Building	1,500
Property Tax Expense	950
Heating and Lighting Expense	800
Depreciation Expense — Office Equipment	625
Supplies Expense	500
Miscellaneous Expense	1,125

Instructions:

(1) Prepare an income statement for the current fiscal year indicating the division of net income. The articles of partnership provide for salary allowances of $18,000 to Rush and $12,000 to Scott; that each partner be allowed 8% on his capital balance at the beginning of the fiscal year; and that the remaining net income or net loss be divided equally. An additional investment of $5,000 was made by Scott during the year.

(2) Prepare a capital statement for the current fiscal year.

(3) Prepare a balance sheet as of the end of the current fiscal year.

15-4A. T. R. Mayer and A. C. Nolan have operated a successful firm for many years, sharing net income and net losses equally. E. M. Owens is to be admitted to the partnership on June 1 of the current year in accordance with the following agreement:

(a) Assets and liabilities of the old partnership are to be valued at their book values as of May 31, except for the following:

Accounts receivable amounting to $500 are to be written off and the allowance for doubtful accounts is to be increased to 5% of the remaining accounts.

Merchandise inventory is to be priced at $29,900.
Equipment is to be priced at $40,000.
(b) Goodwill of $10,000 is to be recognized as attributable to the firm of Mayer and Nolan.
(c) Owens is to purchase $15,000 of Nolan's ownership interest for $17,500 cash and to contribute $5,000 cash to the partnership for total ownership equity of $20,000.
(d) The income-sharing ratio of Mayer, Nolan, and Owens is to be 2:1:1.

The post-closing trial balance of Mayer and Nolan as of May 31 follows:

Mayer and Nolan
Post-Closing Trial Balance
May 31, 19—

Cash	2,250	
Accounts Receivable	9,500	
Allowance for Doubtful Accounts		400
Merchandise Inventory	28,700	
Prepaid Insurance	580	
Equipment	49,950	
Accumulated Depreciation — Equipment		14,700
Accounts Payable		4,280
Notes Payable		5,000
T. R. Mayer, Capital		33,800
A. C. Nolan, Capital		32,800
	90,980	90,980

391

Instructions:

(1) Present general journal entries as of May 31 to record the revaluations, using a temporary account entitled Asset Revaluations. The balance in the accumulated depreciation account is to be eliminated.
(2) Present the additional entries, in general journal form, to record the remaining transactions relating to the formation of the new partnership. Assume that all transactions occur on June 1.
(3) Present a balance sheet for the new partnership as of June 1.

15-5A. Ryan, Shay, and Todd decide to discontinue business operations as of May 31 and liquidate their partnership. The firm's post-closing trial balance at that date is reproduced at the top of the next page.
The partners share net income and losses in the ratio 2:2:1. The realization and liquidation transactions are summarized as follows:

(a) Collected $6,600 of accounts receivable; the remainder are worthless.
(b) Collected $5,000 on notes receivable.
(c) Sold the merchandise for $21,300 cash.
(d) Realized $400 cash from cancellation of the insurance policies.
(e) Sold the supplies for $375 cash.
(f) Sold the equipment for $5,500 cash.
(g) Sold the land and building for $29,000, purchaser paying $9,000 cash and assuming the mortgage note. The mortgage holder released the partners from further liability.
(h) Paid miscellaneous expenses in connection with the sale of the assets, $500. (Charge to Loss and Gain on Realization.)
(i) Distributed the loss on realization to the partners' capital accounts.

Ryan, Shay, and Todd
Post-Closing Trial Balance
May 31, 19—

Cash...	7,525	
Accounts Receivable............................	7,950	
Allowance for Doubtful Accounts.................		750
Notes Receivable...............................	5,000	
Merchandise Inventory..........................	25,500	
Prepaid Insurance..............................	475	
Supplies.......................................	450	
Equipment.....................................	11,500	
Accumulated Depreciation — Equipment...........		5,450
Building.......................................	32,000	
Accumulated Depreciation — Building............		12,000
Land..	6,000	
Accounts Payable..............................		7,500
Mortgage Note Payable.........................		20,000
Alan Ryan, Capital............................		21,200
John Shay, Capital.............................		18,500
Lee Todd, Capital.............................		11,000
	96,400	96,400

(j) Paid the accounts payable in full.
(k) Distributed remaining cash to the partners.

Instructions:

(1) Open T accounts for Cash; Loss and Gain on Realization; Alan Ryan, Capital; John Shay, Capital; and Lee Todd, Capital, and record the May 31 balances in the respective accounts.
(2) Present entries, in general journal form, to record the liquidation, posting to the appropriate T accounts after each journal entry. (None of the five T accounts should have a balance after the final entry is posted.)
(3) Assuming that there had been a net loss of $46,250, instead of the amount determined above, prepare a complete summary of the liquidation in the form illustrated in the chapter. No entries are required.
(4) Assuming that there had been a net loss of $49,250, instead of the amount determined above, prepare a complete summary of the liquidation in the form illustrated in the chapter. No entries are required.

15-6A. On the date the partners in the firm of Bowen, Cox, and Davis decide to liquidate the partnership, the partners have capital balances of $60,000, $45,000, and $30,000 respectively. The cash balance is $15,000, the book value of noncash assets total $145,000, and liabilities total $25,000. The partners share income and losses in the ratio of 3:2:2.

Instructions:

Prepare a summary of the liquidation, in the form illustrated in this chapter, for each of the assumptions described in (1), (2), (3), and (4) below.

(1) All of the noncash assets are sold for $180,000 in cash, the creditors are paid, and the remaining cash is distributed to the partners.

(2) All of the noncash assets are sold for $75,000 in cash, the creditors are paid, and the remaining cash is distributed to the partners.

(3) All of the noncash assets are sold for $26,000 in cash, the creditors are paid, and the remaining cash is distributed to the partners,
    After the available cash is paid to the partners:
    (a) The partner with the debit capital balance pays the amount owed to the firm.
    (b) The additional cash is distributed.

(4) All of the noncash assets are sold for $12,000 in cash, the creditors are paid, and the remaining cash is distributed to the partners.
    After the available cash is paid to the partners:
    (a) The partner with the debit capital balance pays 75% of his deficiency to the firm.
    (b) The additional cash is distributed.
    (c) The remaining partners absorb the remaining deficiency as a loss.

Chapter 16

CORPORATIONS — ORGANIZATION AND OPERATION

CHARACTERISTICS OF A CORPORATION

In the Dartmouth College Case in 1819, Chief Justice Marshall stated: "A corporation is an artificial being, invisible, intangible, and existing only in contemplation of the law." The concept underlying this definition has become the foundation for the prevailing legal doctrine that a corporation is an artificial person, created by law and having a distinct existence separate and apart from the natural persons who are responsible for its creation and operation. Almost all large business enterprises in the United States are organized as corporations.

Corporations may be classified as *profit* or *nonprofit*. *Profit* corporations are engaged in business activities; they depend upon profitable operations for their continued existence. *Nonprofit* corporations include those organized for recreational, educational, charitable, or other philanthropic purposes; they depend for their continuation upon dues from their members or upon gifts and grants from the public at large. Profit corporations whose ownership equity is widely distributed are sometimes referred to as *public corporations*;[1] those whose ownership equity is confined to a small group are called *close corporations*. Regardless of their nature or purpose, corporations are created in accordance with state or federal statutes and are separate legal entities.

As a legal entity, the corporation has certain characteristics that distinguish it from other types of business organizations. The most important characteristics with accounting implications are described briefly in the following paragraphs.

Separate legal existence. The corporation may acquire, own, and dispose of property in its corporate name. It may also incur liabilities and enter into other types of contracts in accordance with the provisions of its *charter* (also called *articles of incorporation*).

---

[1] The term may also be applied to incorporated municipalities which are supported by taxes and by revenues from such services as waste removal, water, and electric power.

Transferable units of ownership. The ownership of a corporation, of which there may be several categories or classes, is divided into transferable units known as *shares of stock*. Each share of stock of a particular class has the same rights and privileges as every other share of the same class. The *stockholders* (also called *shareholders*) may buy and sell shares without interfering with the activities of the corporation. The millions of transactions that occur daily on stock exchanges are independent transactions between buyers and sellers. Thus, in contrast to the partnership, the life term of the corporation is not affected by changes in ownership.

Limited liability of stockholders. A corporation is responsible for its own acts and obligations, and therefore its creditors ordinarily may not look beyond the assets of the corporation for satisfaction of their claims. Thus, the financial loss that a stockholder may suffer is limited to the amount of his investment. The phenomenal growth of the corporate form of business would not have been possible without this limited liability feature.

Working organization. The stockholders, who are the owners of the corporation, exercise control over the management of corporate affairs indirectly by electing a *board of directors*. The board of directors meets from time to time to determine the corporate policies and to select the officers who manage the corporation. The chart at the right depicts the organizational structure of a corporation.

Organizational structure of a corporate enterprise

395

Additional taxes. A corporation is required to pay a charter fee to the state at the time of its organization and annual taxes thereafter. If the corporation does business in states other than the one in which it is incorporated, it may also be required to pay annual taxes to such states. The earnings of a corporation are subject to the federal income tax. When the remaining earnings are distributed to stockholders as dividends, they are again taxed as income to the individuals receiving them.

Under certain conditions specified in the Internal Revenue Code, corporations with not more than ten stockholders may elect to be treated in a manner similar to a partnership for income tax purposes. Corporations electing this optional treatment do not pay federal income taxes. Instead, its stockholders include their distributive shares of corporate income in their own taxable income, regardless of whether the income is distributed to them.

Governmental regulation. Being creatures of the state and being owned by stockholders who possess limited liability, corporations have less freedom of action than sole proprietorships and partnerships. There may be restrictions in such matters as ownership of real estate, retention of earnings, and purchase of its own stock.

CORPORATE CAPITAL

The owners' equity in a corporation is commonly called *capital, stockholders' equity, shareholders' equity,* or *shareholders' investment.* As was indicated in Chapter 1, the stockholders' equity section of corporation balance sheets is divided into subsections based on the source of the capital. The two principal sources are (1) investments contributed by the stockholders and (2) net income retained in the business. The capital acquired from the stockholders, sometimes referred to as *paid-in capital,* is recorded in accounts maintained for each class of stock. If there is only one class of stock, the account is entitled Common Stock or Capital Stock. At the close of the fiscal year, the balance in the income summary account is transferred to Retained Earnings. The dividends account, to which distributions of net income to stockholders have been debited, is also closed to Retained Earnings. The stockholders' equity section of the balance sheet presented below illustrates the two principal subdivisions of capital.

Stockholders' Equity

Paid-in capital:	
Common stock......................................	$150,000
Retained earnings..................................	30,000
Total stockholders' equity............................	$180,000

If the occurrence of net losses results in a debit balance in the retained earnings account, it is termed a *deficit.* In the stockholders' equity section of the balance sheet a deficit would be deducted from paid-in capital to yield total stockholders' equity.

A number of years ago the term customarily applied to "retained earnings" was *earned surplus,* but most accountants avoid the use of it now in financial statements. Because of its connotation of an excess, or something left over, "surplus" was sometimes erroneously interpreted by readers of financial statements to mean "cash available for dividends." There are a number of acceptable variants of "retained earnings," among which are *earnings retained for use in the business, earnings reinvested in the business, earnings employed in the business,* and *accumulated earnings.*

CHARACTERISTICS OF STOCK

The general term applied to the shares of ownership of a corporation is *capital stock.* The number of shares that a corporation is *authorized* to issue is set forth in its charter. The term *issued* is applied to the shares issued to the stockholders. A corporation may, under various circumstances discussed later in the chapter, reacquire some of the stock that it has issued. The stock remaining in the hands of the stockholders is then referred to as the stock *outstanding*.

The shares of capital stock are frequently assigned an arbitrary monetary figure, known as *par*. The par amount is printed on the *stock certificate*, which is the evidence of ownership issued to the stockholder. Stock may also be issued without par, in which case it is known as *no-par* stock. Many states provide that no-par stock must be assigned a *stated value* by the board of directors, which makes it similar to par stock.

Because of the limited liability feature, the creditors of a corporation have no claim against the personal assets of stockholders. To afford some protection to the creditors, the law requires that some specific minimum contribution by the stockholders be retained by the corporation for the protection of its creditors. This amount, called *legal capital*, varies among the states but ordinarily includes the par or stated value of the shares.

Classes of stock. The principal basic rights that accompany ownership of a share of stock are (1) the right to vote, (2) the right to share in distributions of earnings, (3) the right to maintain the same fractional interest in the corporation by purchasing a proportionate number of shares of any additional issuances of stock (*preemptive right*), and (4) the right to share in assets upon liquidation.

If a corporation issues only common stock, each share has equal rights. In order to appeal to a broader investment market, a corporation may provide for one or more classes of stock with various preferential rights. The preference usually relates to the right to share in distributions of earnings. Such stock is called *preferred stock* or *preference stock*.

The board of directors has the sole authority to distribute earnings to the stockholders. When such action is taken the directors are said to *declare a dividend*. A corporation cannot guarantee that its operations will be profitable and hence it cannot guarantee dividends to its stockholders. Furthermore, the directors have wide discretionary powers in determining the extent to which earnings should be retained by the corporation to provide for expansion, to offset possible future losses, or to provide for other contingencies.

A corporation with both preferred stock and common stock may declare dividends on the common only after it meets the requirements of the stipulated dividend on the preferred (which may be stated in monetary terms or as a percent of par). To illustrate, assume that a corporation has 1,000 shares of preferred stock and 4,000 shares of common stock outstanding, and that the preferred has a prior claim to an annual $6 dividend. Assume also that in the first three years of operations net income was $12,000, $25,000, and $50,000 respectively. The directors authorize the retention of a portion of each year's earnings and the distribution of the remainder. Details are presented in the following tabulation:

	First Year	Second Year	Third Year
Net income	$12,000	$25,000	$50,000
Amount retained	5,000	10,000	15,000
Amount distributed	$ 7,000	$15,000	$35,000
Preferred dividend (1,000 shares)	6,000	6,000	6,000
Common dividend (4,000 shares)	$ 1,000	$ 9,000	$29,000
Dividends per share:			
Preferred	$6.00	$6.00	$6.00
Common	$ .25	$2.25	$7.25

Participating and nonparticipating preferred stock. In the foregoing illustration the holders of preferred stock received an annual dividend of $6 per share in each of the three years, in contrast to the common stockholders, whose annual per share dividends were $.25, $2.25, and $7.25 respectively. It is apparent from the example that holders of preferred stock have relatively greater assurance than common stockholders of receiving dividends regularly. On the other hand, holders of common stock have the potentiality of receiving larger dividends than preferred stockholders. The preferred stockholders' preferential right to dividends is ordinarily limited to a specified amount, which was assumed to be the case in the example. Such stock is said to be *nonparticipating*.

Preferred stock which provides for the possibility of dividends in excess of a specified amount is said to be *participating*. Preferred shares may participate with common shares to varying degrees, and the contract must be examined to determine the extent of this participation. To illustrate, assume that the contract covering the preferred stock of the corporation in the preceding illustration provides that if the total dividends to be distributed exceed the regular preferred dividend and a comparable dividend on common, the preferred shall share ratably with the common in the excess. In accordance with such terms, the $35,000 dividend distribution in the third year would be allocated as follows:

	Preferred Dividend	Common Dividend	Total Dividends
Regular dividend to preferred (1,000 x $6)	$ 6,000	—	$ 6,000
Comparable dividend to common (4,000 x $6)	—	$24,000	24,000
Remainder to 5,000 shares ratably	1,000	4,000	5,000
Total	$ 7,000	$28,000	$35,000
Dividends per share	$7	$7	

Cumulative and noncumulative preferred stock. As was indicated in the preceding section, most preferred stock is nonparticipating. Provision is usually made, however, to assure the continuation of the preferential dividend right if at any time the directors *pass* (do not declare) the usual dividend. This is accomplished by providing that dividends may not be paid on the common stock if any preferred dividends are in arrears. Such preferred stock is known as *cumulative*. To illustrate, assume that a corporation has outstanding 5,000 shares of cumulative preferred 7% stock of $100 par and that dividends have been passed for the preceding two years. In the current year no dividend may be declared on the common stock unless the directors first declare preferred dividends of $70,000 for the past two years and $35,000 for the current year. Preferred stock not having this cumulative right is called *noncumulative*.

Other preferential rights. Thus far the discussion of preferential rights of preferred stock has related to dividend distributions. Preferred stock may also be given a preference over common stock in its claim to assets upon liquidation of the corporation. If the assets remaining after payment of creditors are not sufficient to return the capital contributions of both classes of stock, payment would first be made to the preferred stockholders and any balance remaining would go to the common stockholders. Another customary difference between preferred stock and common stock is that the former may have no voting rights. It is not unusual for a corporation to have more than one class of preferred stock, with differences as to the amount of dividends, priority of claims upon liquidation, and voting rights. In any particular case the rights of a class of stock may be determined by reference to the charter, the stock certificate, or some other abstract of the agreement.

399

ISSUING STOCK AT PAR

The entries to record the investment of capital in a corporation are similar to those of other types of business organizations in that cash and other assets received are debited and any liabilities assumed are credited. The credit to capital differs, however, in that there are accounts for each class of stock. To illustrate, assume that a corporation, with an authorization of 5,000 shares of preferred stock of $100 par and 50,000 shares of common stock of $20 par, issues one half of each authorization at par for cash. The entry to record the stockholders' investment and the receipt of the cash, in general journal form, is as follows:

Cash	750,000	
Preferred Stock		250,000
Common Stock		500,000

The capital stock accounts (Preferred Stock, Common Stock) are controlling accounts. It is necessary to maintain records of the name and the address of each stockholder and the number of shares held in order to issue dividend checks, proxy forms, and financial reports. The accounts with individual stockholders are kept in a subsidiary ledger known as the *stockholders ledger*.

ISSUING STOCK AT A PREMIUM OR DISCOUNT

Par stock is often issued by a corporation at a price other than par. When it is issued for more than par, the excess of the contract price over par is termed a *premium*. When it is issued at a price that is below par, the difference is called a *discount*. Thus, if stock with a par of $50 is issued at $60, the amount of the premium is $10; if the same stock is issued at $45, the amount of the discount is $5.

Theoretically, there is no reason for a newly organized corporation to issue stock at a price other than par. The par designation is merely a part of the plan of dividing capital into a number of units of ownership. Hence, a group of persons investing their funds in a new corporation might all be expected to pay par for the shares. The fortunes of an enterprise do not remain static, however, even when it is still in the process of organizing. The changing prospects for its future success may affect the price per share at which the incorporators can secure additional investors.

A need for additional capital may arise long after a corporation has become established. Losses during the early period may have depleted working capital or the operations may have been sufficiently successful to warrant a substantial expansion of plant and equipment. If the funds are to be obtained by the issuance of additional stock, it is apparent that the current price at which the original stock is selling in the market will affect the price that can be obtained for the new shares.

Generally speaking, the price at which stock can be sold by a corporation is influenced by (1) the financial condition, the earnings record, and the dividend record of the corporation, (2) its potential earning power, (3) the availability of money for investment purposes, and (4) general business and economic conditions and prospects.

Premium on stock. When capital stock is issued at a premium, cash or other assets are debited for the amount received, the stock account is credited for par, and a premium account is credited for the amount of the premium. For example, if a hypothetical corporation issues 1,000 shares of $50 par preferred stock at $54, the entry to record the transaction would be as follows, in general journal form:

Cash..	54,000	
Preferred Stock...................................		50,000
Premium on Preferred Stock......................		4,000

The premium of $4,000 is a part of the investment of the stockholders and is therefore a part of paid-in capital. It is distinguished from the capital stock account because ordinarily it is not a part of legal capital and in many states may be used as a basis for dividends to stockholders. However, if the premium is returned to stockholders as a dividend at a later date, it should be made quite clear that the dividend is a return of paid-in capital rather than a distribution of earnings.

Discount on stock. Some states do not permit the issuance of stock at a discount; in others, it may be done only under specified conditions. When stock is issued at less than its par, it is considered to be fully paid as between the corporation and the stockholder. In some states, however, the stockholders are contingently liable to creditors for the amount of the discount; that is, if the corporation is liquidated and the assets are insufficient to pay creditors in full, the stockholders may be assessed for an additional contribution up to the amount of the discount on their stock.

When capital stock is issued at a discount, cash or other assets are debited for the amount received, a discount account is debited for the amount of the discount, and the capital stock account is credited for par. For example, if the same hypothetical corporation issues 20,000 shares of $25 par common stock at $22, the entry to record the transaction would be as follows, in general journal form:

Cash..	440,000	
Discount on Common Stock.........................	60,000	
Common Stock...................................		500,000

401

The discount of $60,000 is a contra paid-in capital account and must be offset against Common Stock to arrive at the amount actually invested by the holders of common stock. The discount should not be listed on the balance sheet as an asset, nor should it be amortized against revenue as though it were an expense.

The manner in which premiums and discounts may be presented in the stockholders' equity section of the balance sheet is illustrated below, based on the two illustrative entries above.

Stockholders' Equity

Paid-in capital:			
Preferred 7% stock, cumulative, $50 par			
(1,000 shares authorized and issued)...	$ 50,000		
Premium on preferred stock............	4,000	$ 54,000	
Common stock, $25 par (50,000 shares			
authorized, 20,000 shares issued)......	$500,000		
Less discount on common stock.........	60,000	440,000	
Total paid-in capital...............		$494,000	
Retained earnings......................		76,000	
Total stockholders' equity...............			$570,000

The stockholders' equity section appearing at the top of the next page illustrates the reporting of a deficit and some variations in terminology from that in the foregoing example.

Shareholders' Equity

Paid-in capital:

Preferred 7% stock, cumulative, $25 par (10,000 shares authorized and issued).	$ 250,000	
Excess of issuance price of stock over par	20,000	$ 270,000
Common stock, $10 par (200,000 shares authorized, 100,000 shares issued).....	$1,000,000	
Excess of par over issuance price of stock	100,000	900,000
Total paid in by stockholders........		$1,170,000
Less deficit...........................		55,000
Total shareholders' equity..............		$1,115,000

ISSUING STOCK FOR ASSETS OTHER THAN CASH

When capital stock is issued in exchange for assets other than cash, such as land, buildings, and equipment, the assets acquired should be recorded at their fair market price or at the fair market price of the stock issued. The determination of the values assigned to the assets is the responsibility of the board of directors. It is not always possible to make an objective determination, but if shares of stock are also being issued for cash at about the same time, the price of the stock may provide an indication of the proper valuation of the assets.

As a basis for illustration, assume that a corporation acquired buildings and land in exchange for 20,000 shares of its $10 par common stock, for which the average current market price is $13. An independent appraisal of the assets indicates a current value of approximately $220,000 for the buildings and $40,000 for the land. The transaction could be recorded as follows:

Dec.	5	Buildings...............................	220,000	
		Land...................................	40,000	
		Common Stock........................		200,000
		Premium on Common Stock............		60,000

NO-PAR STOCK

In the early days of rapid industrial expansion and increasing use of the corporate form of business organization, it was customary to assign a par of $100 to shares of stock. It is not surprising that unsophisticated investors, mistakenly considering "par value" to be the equivalent of "value," were often induced to invest in mining and other highly speculative enterprises by the simple means of offering $100 par stock at "bargain" prices. Another misleading practice was the use of par in assigning highly inflated values to assets acquired in exchange for stock. For example, stock with a total par of $1,000,000 might be issued in exchange for patents, mineral rights, or other properties with a conservatively estimated value of $50,000. The assets would be recorded at the full par of $1,000,000, whereas in reality the stock had been issued at a discount of $950,000. Balance sheets that were "window-dressed" in this manner were obviously deceptive.

It was to combat such abuses and also to eliminate the troublesome discount liability of stockholders that stock without par was conceived. The issuance of stock without par was first permitted by New York in 1912. At present its use is authorized in nearly all of the states.

Over the years questionable practices in the issuance of securities have to a considerable degree been eliminated. Today federal and state laws and rules imposed by organized stock exchanges and governmental agencies such as the Securities and Exchange Commission combine to protect the investor from misrepresentations that were not uncommon in earlier days.

In most states both preferred and common stock may be issued without a par designation. However, preferred stock is usually assigned a par. When no-par stock is issued, the entire proceeds may be credited to the capital stock account, even though the issuance price varies from time to time. For example, if at the time of organization a corporation issues no-par common stock at $18 a share and at a later date issues additional shares at $16, the transactions could be recorded as follows, in general journal form:

403

1. Original issuance of 10,000 shares of no-par common at $18:

Cash....................................	180,000	
Common Stock............................		180,000

2. Subsequent issuance of 1,000 shares of no-par common at $16:

Cash....................................	16,000	
Common Stock............................		16,000

The laws of some states require that the entire proceeds from the issuance of no-par stock be regarded as legal capital. The entries above are in conformity with this principle, which also conforms to the original concept of no-par stock. In other states no-par stock may be assigned a stated value per share, and the excess of the proceeds over the stated value may be credited to Paid-In Capital in Excess of Stated Value. Assuming that in the example above the stated value is $10 and the board of directors wishes to credit the common stock for stated value, the transactions would be recorded as follows, in general journal form:

1. Original issuance of 10,000 shares of no-par common, stated value $10, at $18:

Cash....................................	180,000	
Common Stock............................		100,000
Paid-In Capital in Excess of Stated Value.......		80,000

2. Subsequent issuance of 1,000 shares of no-par common, stated value $10, at $16:

Cash....................................	16,000	
Common Stock............................		10,000
Paid-In Capital in Excess of Stated Value.......		6,000

It is readily apparent that the accounting for no-par stock with a stated value may follow the same pattern as the accounting for par stock.

SUBSCRIPTIONS AND STOCK ISSUANCE

In some situations involving the initial issue of capital stock or subsequent issuances where the stockholders have waived the preemptive right, a corporation may sell its stock to an *underwriter*. The underwriter then resells the shares to investors at a price high enough to provide him with a profit from the sale. Under these circumstances, the corporation is relieved of the task of marketing the stock; it receives the entire amount of cash without delay and can proceed immediately with its plans for the use of the funds.

In other situations a corporation may sell its stock directly to investors. Ordinarily the investor first enters into an agreement with the corporation to *subscribe* to shares at a specified price per share. The terms may provide for payment in full at some future date or for installment payments over a period of time.

The amount of the subscriptions represents an asset to the corporation. When stock is subscribed for at par, the subscription price is debited to the asset account Stock Subscriptions Receivable and credited to the capital stock account Stock Subscribed. If there is more than one class of stock, a subscriptions receivable account and a stock subscribed account should be maintained for each class.

When stock is subscribed for at a price above or below par, the stock subscriptions receivable account is debited for the subscription price rather than par. The stock subscribed account is credited at par, and the difference between the subscription price and par is debited to a discount account or credited to a premium account, as the case may be.

The stock subscriptions receivable account is a controlling account. The individual accounts with each subscriber are maintained in a subsidiary ledger known as a *subscribers ledger*. It is used in much the same manner as the accounts receivable ledger.

After a subscriber completes his agreed payments, the corporation issues the stock certificate. The stock subscribed account is then debited for the total par of the shares issued, and the capital stock account is credited for the same amount.

As the basis for illustrating the entries for subscriptions and stock issuance, assume that the newly organized Carson Corporation receives subscriptions, collects cash, and issues stock certificates in accordance with the transactions given below and on page 405. The required entries, in general journal form, appear after the statement of the transaction.

1. Received subscriptions to 10,000 shares of $20 par common stock from various subscribers at $21 per share, with a down payment of 50% of the subscription price.

```
March 1 Common Stock Subscriptions Receivable..    210,000
             Common Stock Subscribed............             200,000
             Premium on Common Stock..........              10,000

       1 Cash.............................    105,000
             Common Stock Subscriptions Receivable          105,000
```

2. Received 25% of subscription price from all subscribers.

```
May   1 Cash.............................     52,500
             Common Stock Subscriptions Receivable           52,500
```

3. Received final 25% of subscription price from all subscribers and issued the stock certificates.

```
July   1 Cash.............................     52,500
             Common Stock Subscriptions Receivable           52,500

       1 Common Stock Subscribed.............    200,000
             Common Stock.....................              200,000
```

A balance sheet prepared after the transactions of March 1 would list the subscriptions receivable as a current asset and the stock subscribed and the premium as paid-in capital. While it is true that the entire amount has not been "paid-in" in cash, the claim against the subscribers is an asset of equivalent value. The presentation of the items in the balance sheet of the Carson Corporation as of March 1 is illustrated below.

Carson Corporation
Balance Sheet
March 1, 19--

Assets		Stockholders' Equity	
Current assets:		Paid-in capital:	
Cash...................	$105,000	Common stock subscribed..	$200,000
Common stock subscriptions		Premium on common stock.	10,000
receivable.............	105,000		
Total assets...............	$210,000	Total stockholders' equity....	$210,000

After all the subscriptions have been collected, the common stock subscriptions receivable account will have a zero balance. The stock certificates will then be issued and the common stock subscribed account will have a zero balance. It should be noted that the ultimate effect of the series of transactions is a debit to Cash of $210,000, a credit to Common Stock of $200,000, and a credit to Premium on Common Stock of $10,000.

TREASURY STOCK

A corporation may reacquire some of its own outstanding stock by purchase or by donation from its stockholders. It may also accept shares of its own stock in payment of a debt owed by a stockholder, which in essence is much the same as acquisition by purchase. The term *treasury stock* may be applied only to (1) stock of the issuing corporation, (2) that has been issued as fully paid, (3) that has been subsequently reacquired by the corporation, and (4) that has not been canceled or reissued.

Treasury stock is not an asset. A corporation cannot own a part of itself. Treasury stock has no voting rights, it does not have the preemptive right to participate in additional issuances of stock, nor does it generally participate in cash dividends. When a corporation purchases its own stock, it is returning capital to the stockholders from whom the purchase was made. If stockholders donate stock to the corporation, the total capital of the corporation is not affected; only the number of shares outstanding is reduced.

Corporations occasionally list treasury stock on the balance sheet as an asset. The justification for such treatment is that the stock can be reissued and is thus comparable to an investment in the stock of another corporation. The same argument might well be extended to authorized but unissued stock, which is obviously indefensible. It is generally agreed among accountants that treasury stock should not be reported as an asset.

PURCHASED TREASURY STOCK

Although there are some legal restrictions on the practice, corporations may in general purchase shares of their own stock from stockholders. There are various reasons why a corporation may buy its own stock. For example, it may be to provide shares for resale to employees, for reissuance to employees as a bonus or in accordance with stock purchase agreements, or to support the market price of the stock. There are several methods of accounting for the purchase and the resale of treasury stock. A commonly used method, known as the *cost basis*, is illustrated in the following paragraphs.

When the stock is purchased, the account Treasury Stock is debited for its cost. The par and the price at which the stock was originally issued are ignored. When the stock is resold, Treasury Stock is credited at the price paid for it, and the difference between the price paid and the selling price is debited or credited to an account entitled Paid-In Capital from Sale of Treasury Stock.

As a basis for illustration, assume that the paid-in capital of a hypothetical corporation is composed of common stock issued at a premium, detailed as follows:

Common Stock, $25 par (20,000 shares authorized and issued) $500,000
Premium on Common Stock 25,000

The assumed transactions involving treasury stock and the required entries in general journal form are as follows:

1. Purchased 1,000 shares of treasury stock at $40; total $40,000.

| Treasury Stock.................................... | 40,000 | |
| Cash.. | | 40,000 |

2. **Sold 200 shares of treasury stock at $50; total $10,000.**

Cash..	10,000	
Treasury Stock....................................		8,000
Paid-In Capital from Sale of Treasury Stock..........		2,000

3. **Sold 200 shares of treasury stock at $36; total $7,200.**

Cash..	7,200	
Paid-In Capital from Sale of Treasury Stock............	800	
Treasury Stock....................................		8,000

The additional capital obtained through the sale of treasury stock is reported in the paid-in capital section of the balance sheet, and the cost of the treasury stock held by the corporation is deducted from the total of the capital accounts. After the three foregoing transactions were completed, the stockholders' equity section of the balance sheet would appear as shown below.

Stockholders' Equity

Paid-in capital:		
Common stock, $25 par (20,000 shares authorized and issued).............	$500,000	
Premium on common stock..........	25,000	$525,000
From sale of treasury stock...........		1,200
Total paid-in capital..............		$526,200
Retained earnings...................		120,000
Total.............................		$646,200
Deduct treasury stock (600 shares at cost).		24,000
Total stockholders' equity..............		$622,200

407

The stockholders' equity section of the balance sheet indicates that 20,000 shares of stock were issued, of which 600 are held as treasury stock. The number of shares outstanding is therefore 19,400. If cash dividends were declared at this time, the declaration would apply to 19,400 shares. Similarly, 19,400 shares could be voted at a stockholders' meeting.

If sales of treasury stock result in a net decrease in paid-in capital, the decrease may be reported on the balance sheet as a reduction of paid-in capital or it may be debited to the retained earnings account.

DONATED TREASURY STOCK

Stockholders occasionally donate shares of stock to the issuing corporation for resale. This may occur when a corporation that has issued large blocks of stock in exchange for plant and equipment, an invention, mineral rights, or other noncash assets is in need of working capital and encounters difficulty in finding subscribers willing to invest cash equal to the par of the stock. As a means of avoiding the difficulty of selling new stock at a discount, the original stockholders may donate a portion of their stock to the corporation and the corporation may then resell it at any price without the purchaser incurring a contingent liability to creditors. The donating stockholders may actually incur little financial sacrifice by their action.

One of the acceptable methods of accounting for donated stock requires no entry at the time of the donation, except for a memorandum of the number of shares. As the treasury stock is sold, the proceeds are credited to a paid-in capital account entitled Donated Capital.

As a basis for illustration, assume that a corporation originally issued 50,000 shares of $25 par common stock at par for oil properties. The stockholders then donate 10,000 shares to the corporation, which the corporation resells for cash. The entries required, in general journal form, and the paid-in capital section of the balance sheet after each entry are as follows:

1. Issued 50,000 shares of $25 par common stock for oil properties.

Oil Properties................................	1,250,000	
Common Stock............................		1,250,000

Paid-in capital:
Common stock, $25 par (200,000 shares authorized, 50,000 shares issued)	$1,250,000

2. Received 10,000 shares of stock from stockholders.

(Memo) Received 10,000 shares as a donation.

Paid-in capital:
Common stock, $25 par (200,000 shares authorized, 50,000 shares issued less 10,000 shares of treasury stock acquired by donation)........	$1,250,000

3. Sold treasury stock at $20 per share for cash.

Cash......................................	200,000	
Donated Capital..........................		200,000

Paid-in capital:
Common stock, $25 par (200,000 shares authorized, 50,000 shares issued)...............	$1,250,000	
Donated capital...........................	200,000	
Total paid-in capital.....................		$1,450,000

EQUITY PER SHARE

The amount appearing on the balance sheet as total stockholders' equity can be stated in terms of the equity allocable to a single share of stock. Another term frequently used in referring to *equity per share* is *book value*. The latter term is not only less descriptive; it may also be misleading because of its connotation of "worth." It may be said to be an accurate measure of value only to the extent that it represents the amount that would be distributed for a share of stock if the corporation were to liquidate without incurring any expenses, losses, or gains in disposing of its assets and paying its liabilities.

When there is only one class of stock, the equity per share is determined by dividing total stockholders' equity by the number of shares outstanding. For a corporation with both preferred and common stock, it is necessary first to allocate the total equity between the two classes. In making the allocation, consideration must be given to the liquidation rights of the preferred stock, including any participating and cumulative dividend features. After allocating the total to the two classes, the equity per share of each class may then be determined by dividing the respective amounts by the related number of shares outstanding. To illustrate, assume that as of the close of the current fiscal year a corporation has both preferred and common shares outstanding, that there are no preferred dividends in arrears, and that the preferred stock is entitled to receive $105 upon liquidation. The assumed amounts comprising stockholders' equity at the same time and the computation of equity per share are as follows:

STOCKHOLDERS' EQUITY

Preferred 7% stock, cumulative, $100 par (1,000 shares outstanding)	$100,000
Premium on preferred stock	2,000
Common stock, $10 par (50,000 shares outstanding)	500,000
Premium on common stock	50,000
Retained earnings	253,000
Total equity	$905,000

ALLOCATION OF TOTAL EQUITY TO PREFERRED
AND COMMON STOCK

Total equity	$905,000
Allocated to preferred stock:	
Liquidation price	105,000
Allocated to common stock	$800,000

EQUITY PER SHARE

Preferred stock: $105,000 ÷ 1,000 shares = $105 per share
Common stock: $800,000 ÷ 50,000 shares = $ 16 per share

If in the foregoing illustration it is assumed that the preferred stock is entitled to dividends in arrears in the event of liquidation, and that there is an arrearage of two years, the computations would be as shown below and at the top of the next page.

ALLOCATION OF TOTAL EQUITY TO PREFERRED
AND COMMON STOCK

Total equity		$905,000
Allocated to preferred stock:		
Liquidation price	$105,000	
Dividends in arrears	14,000	119,000
Allocated to common stock		$786,000

EQUITY PER SHARE

Preferred stock: $119,000 ÷ 1,000 shares = $119.00 per share
Common stock: $786,000 ÷ 50,000 shares = $ 15.72 per share

Equity per share, particularly of common stock, is frequently stated in corporation reports to stockholders and quoted in the financial press. It is one of the many factors affecting the *market price*, that is, the price at which a share is bought and sold at a particular moment. However, it should be noted that earning capacity, dividend rates, and prospects for the future usually affect the market price of listed stocks to a much greater extent than does equity per share. So-called "glamour" stocks may at times sell at more than ten times the amount of the equity per share. On the other hand, stock in corporations that have suffered severe declines in earnings or whose future prospects appear to be unfavorable may sell at prices which are substantially less than the equity per share.

ORGANIZATION COSTS

Expenditures incurred in organizing a corporation, such as legal fees, taxes and fees paid to the state, and promotional costs, are charged to an intangible asset account entitled Organization Costs. Although such costs have no realizable value upon liquidation, they are as essential as plant and equipment, for without the expenditures the corporation could not have been created. If the life of a corporation is limited to a definite period of time, the organization costs should be amortized over the period by annual charges to an expense account. However, at the time of incorporation the length of life of most corporations is indeterminate.

There are two possible extreme viewpoints on the appropriate accounting for organization costs and other intangibles of indeterminate life. One extreme would consider the cost of intangibles as a permanent asset until there was convincing evidence of loss in value. The other extreme would consider the cost of intangibles as an expense in the period in which the cost is incurred. The practical solution to the problem is expressed in the following quotation:

. . . . Allocating the cost of goodwill or other intangible assets with an indeterminate life over time is necessary because the value almost inevitably becomes zero at some future date. Since the date at which the value becomes zero is indeterminate, the end of the useful life must necessarily be set arbitrarily at some point or within some range of time for accounting purposes.[2]

The Internal Revenue Code permits the amortization of organization costs ratably over a period of not less than sixty months beginning with the month the corporation commences business. Inasmuch as the magni-

[2]*Opinions of the Accounting Principles Board, No. 17*, "Intangible Assets" (New York: American Institute of Certified Public Accountants, 1970), par. 23.

410

tude of such costs is relatively minor in relation to total assets and the effect on net income is ordinarily not significant, amortization of organization costs over sixty months is generally accepted in accounting practice.

QUESTIONS

1. Why are most large business enterprises organized as corporations?

2. Why is it said that the earnings of a corporation are subject to "double taxation"? Discuss.

3. What is the distinction, if any, between owners' equity of sole proprietorships, partnerships, and corporations as to each of the following: (a) nature, (b) source, and (c) financial statement presentation?

4. The retained earnings account of a corporation at the beginning of the year had a credit balance of $50,000. The only other entry in the account during the year was a debit of $70,000 transferred from the income summary at the end of the year. (a) What is the term applied to the $70,000 debit? (b) What is the balance in retained earnings at the end of the year? (c) What is the term applied to the balance determined in (b)?

5. The charter of a corporation provides for the issuance of a maximum of 100,000 shares of common stock. The corporation issued 60,000 shares of common stock and two years later it reacquired 1,000 shares. After the reacquisition what is the number of shares (a) authorized, (b) issued, and (c) outstanding?

6. Of two corporations organized at approximately the same time and engaged in competing businesses, one issued $10 par common stock and the other issued $25 par common stock. Do the par designations provide any indication as to which stock is preferable as an investment?

7. Differentiate between common stock and preferred stock.

8. What is (a) participating preferred stock and (b) cumulative preferred stock?

9. What are some of the factors that influence the market price of a corporation's stock?

10. When a corporation issues stock at a premium, does the premium constitute income? Explain.

11. The stockholders' equity section of a corporation balance sheet is composed of the following items:

Preferred 7% stock..........	$400,000		
Premium on preferred stock...	40,000	$440,000	
Common stock.............	$600,000		
Discount on common stock...	20,000	580,000	$1,020,000
Retained earnings...........		180,000	$1,200,000

Determine the following amounts: (a) paid-in capital attributable to preferred stock, (b) paid-in capital attributable to common stock, (c) earnings retained for use in the business, and (d) total stockholders' equity.

12. Land with an estimated fair market price of $63,000 is acquired by a newly organized corporation for 600 shares of its $100 par, 7% preferred stock, for which there is no established market. (a) At what value should the land be recorded? (b) What accounts and amounts should be credited to record the transaction?

13. (a) In what respect does treasury stock differ from unissued stock? (b) What is the preferred manner of presenting purchased treasury stock on the balance sheet?

14. A corporation purchases 1,000 shares of its own $10 par common stock for $13,000, recording it at cost. (a) What effect does this transaction have on revenue or expense of the period? (b) What effect does it have on stockholders' equity?

15. The treasury stock in Question 14 is resold for $15,000. (a) What is the effect on revenue of the period? (b) What is the effect on stockholders' equity?

16. A corporation that had issued 50,000 shares of $20 par common stock subsequently reacquired 2,000 shares, which it now holds as treasury stock. If the board of directors declares a cash dividend of $1 per share, what will be the total amount of the dividend?

17. Stockholders of a corporation donated 1,000 shares of no-par common stock to the corporation. The corporation then resold these shares for cash at $20 per share. What entry is made for (a) the receipt of the stock and (b) the sale of the stock?

18. The par of the common stock of Hill Oil Corporation is $25. The current equity per share is $38.20 and the market price per share is $64. Suggest reasons for the comparatively high market price in relation to par and to equity per share.

19. (a) What type of expenditure is charged to the organization costs account? (b) Give examples of such expenditures.

20. Identify each of the accounts listed below as asset, liability, stockholders' equity, revenue, or expense, and indicate the normal balance of each.

(1) Common Stock
(2) Common Stock Subscribed
(3) Common Stock Subscriptions Receivable
(4) Discount on Preferred Stock
(5) Donated Capital
(6) Organization Costs
(7) Paid-In Capital from Sale of Treasury Stock
(8) Preferred Stock
(9) Premium on Common Stock
(10) Retained Earnings
(11) Treasury Stock

EXERCISES

16-1. Broadhurst, Inc., has stock outstanding as follows: 5,000 shares of 7%, $100 par, cumulative, nonparticipating preferred and 40,000 shares of $50 par common. During its first five years of operations, the following amounts were distributed as dividends: first year, none; second year, $27,000; third year, $63,000; fourth year, $120,000; fifth year, $161,000. Determine the dividends per share on each class of stock for each of the five years.

412

16-2. The outstanding stock of People's Service Company is composed of 5,000 shares of 6%, $100 par, participating preferred stock and 25,000 shares of no-par common stock. The preferred stock is entitled to participate equally with the common, share for share, in any dividend distributions which exceed the regular preferred dividend and a $3 a share common dividend. The directors declare dividends of $150,000 for the current year. Determine the amount of the dividend per share on (a) the preferred stock and (b) the common stock.

16-3. On August 10, the Marine Corporation issued for cash 8,000 shares of no-par common stock (with a stated value of $10) at $15, and on August 19 it issued for cash 500 shares of $100 par preferred stock at $107. (a) Give the entries, in general journal form, for August 10 and August 19. (b) What is the total amount invested by all stockholders as of August 19?

16-4. On September 1 the Colvin Company received its charter authorizing 50,000 shares of $25 par common stock. On November 1 the corporation received subscriptions to 10,000 shares of stock at $30. Cash for one half of the subscription price accompanied the subscriptions. On February 1 the remaining half was received from all subscribers and the stock was issued. (a) Present entries, in general journal form, to record the transactions of November 1. (b) Present entries, in general journal form, to record the transactions of February 1. (c) By what amount did the corporation's capital increase on September 1, November 1, and February 1? (d) Name two controlling accounts used in the transactions above and the related subsidiary ledgers.

16-5. Lewisdale Products, Inc., with an authorization of 5,000 shares of preferred stock and 50,000 shares of common stock, completed several transactions involving its capital stock on April 30, the first day of operations. The trial balance at the close of the day follows:

Cash.	90,000	
Common Stock Subscriptions Receivable .	240,000	
Buildings	110,000	
Land	10,000	
Preferred 6% Stock, $50 par		100,000
Premium on Preferred Stock		20,000
Common Stock, $25 par		75,000
Premium on Common Stock		55,000
Common Stock Subscribed		200,000
	450,000	450,000

413

All shares within each class of stock were sold or subscribed at the same price, the preferred stock was issued in exchange for the buildings and the land, and no cash was received on the unissued common stock subscribed. (a) Present the three compound entries, in general journal form, to record the transactions summarized in the trial balance. (b) Prepare the stockholders' equity section of the balance sheet as of April 30.

16-6. The Activity Center, Inc., was organized on January 2 of the current year with an authorization of 1,000 shares of cumulative preferred 7% stock, $20 par, and 10,000 shares of $10 par common stock.

(a) Record in general journal form the following selected transactions completed during the first year of operations:

Jan. 2. Sold 2,000 shares of common stock at par for cash.

2. Issued 150 shares of common stock to an attorney in payment for his legal fees for organizing the corporation.

Sept. 8. Issued 5,000 shares of common stock in exchange for land, buildings, and equipment with fair market prices of $4,500, $36,200, and $24,300 respectively.

Nov. 13. Sold 500 shares of preferred stock at $18 for cash.

(b) Prepare the stockholders' equity section of the balance sheet as of December 31, the end of the current year. The net income for the year amounted to $1,700.

16-7. The capital accounts of Cumberly-Evers, Inc., are as follows: Preferred 4% Stock, $50 par, $250,000; Common Stock, $15 par, $1,500,000; Premium on Common Stock, $150,000; Premium on Preferred Stock, $20,000; Retained Earnings, $545,000. (a) Determine the equity per share of each class of stock, assuming that the preferred stock is entitled to receive $53 upon liquidation. (b) Determine the equity per share of each class of stock assuming that the preferred stock is to receive $53 plus dividends in arrears in the event of liquidation, and that only the dividends for the current year are in arrears.

16-8. The following items were listed in the stockholders' equity section of the balance sheet on June 30: Common stock, $30 par (25,000 shares outstanding), $750,000; Discount on common stock, $10,000; Retained earnings, $210,000. On July 1 the corporation purchased 500 shares of its stock at $62.50. (a) Determine the equity per share of stock on June 30. (b) Present the entry, in general journal form, to record the purchase of the stock on July 1. (c) Determine the equity per share on July 1.

16-9. The following items were listed in the stockholders' equity section of the balance sheet on August 31: Preferred stock, $20 par, $160,000; Common stock, $10 par, $500,000; Premium on preferred stock, $8,000; Deficit, $67,000. On September 1 the board of directors voted to dissolve the corporation immediately. A short time later, after all noncash assets were sold and liabilities were paid, cash of $526,000 remained for distribution to stockholders. (a) Determine the equity per share on August 31 of (1) preferred stock and (2) common stock, assuming that preferred stock is entitled to preference in liquidation to the extent of 110% of par. (b) Determine the amount of the $526,000 that will be distributed for each share of (1) preferred stock and (2) common stock. (c) Explain the reason for the difference between the common stock equity per share on August 31 and the amount of the cash distribution per common share.

PROBLEMS

The following additional problems for this chapter are located in Appendix B: 16-2B, 16-3B, 16-5B.

16-1A. Interstruct Corp. was organized by Wakely, Travers, and Rich. The charter authorizes 75,000 shares of common stock with a par of $5. The following transactions affecting stockholders' equity were completed during the first year of operations:

(a) Issued 12,000 shares of stock at par to Wakely for cash.

(b) Purchased land and a building from Travers. The building is encumbered by an 8%, 19-year mortgage of $25,000, and there is accrued interest of $400 on the mortgage note at the time of the purchase. It is agreed that the land is to be priced at $11,000 and the building at $42,000, and that Travers is to accept stock at par for his equity. The corporation agreed to assume responsibility for paying the mortgage note and the accrued interest.

(c) Purchased equipment from Rich for $32,000. Rich accepted a 9-month, 6% note for $8,000 and 4,800 shares of stock for the equipment.

(d) Issued 600 shares of stock at par to Rich for promotional services rendered in connection with the organization of the corporation.

(e) Issued 6,700 shares of stock at $6 to various investors for cash.

Instructions:

(1) Prepare entries in general journal form to record the transactions presented above.

(2) Prepare the stockholders' equity section of the balance sheet as of the end of the first year of operations. Net income for the year amounted to $41,700 and dividends of 50¢ per share were declared and paid during the year.

16-2A. The annual dividends declared by Churchill Fabrics, Inc., during a six-year period are presented in the table below. During the entire period the outstanding stock of the company was composed of 2,000 shares of cumulative, participating, 6% preferred stock, $100 par, and 25,000 shares of common stock, $20 par. The preferred stock contract provides that the preferred stock shall participate in distributions of additional dividends after allowance of a $1.50 dividend per share on the common stock, the additional dividends to be divided among common and preferred shares on the basis of the total par of the stock outstanding.

Year	Total Dividends	Preferred Dividends Total	Preferred Dividends Per Share	Common Dividends Total	Common Dividends Per Share
1970	$ 6,000				
1971	38,000				
1972	39,500				
1973	84,500				
1974	56,500				
1975	77,500				

Instructions:

(1) Determine the total dividends and the per share dividends declared on each class of stock for each of the six years, using the headings presented above. There were no dividends in arrears on January 1, 1970.

(2) Determine the average annual dividend per share for each class of stock for the six-year period.

(3) Assuming that the preferred stock was sold at 120 and the common stock was sold at par at the beginning of the six-year period, determine the percentage return on initial shareholders' investment based on the average annual dividend per share (a) for preferred stock, and (b) for common stock.

16-3A. Selected data from the balance sheets of six corporations, identified by letter, are presented below:

A. Common stock, $20 par...... $1,300,000
    Premium on common stock...   118,000
    Deficit...................   40,000

B. Preferred 7% stock, $100 par. $ 500,000
    Premium on preferred stock..   45,000
    Common stock, $50 par......   1,000,000
    Discount on common stock...   75,000
    Deficit...................   120,000

Preferred stock has prior claim to assets on liquidation to the extent of par.

C. Preferred 5% stock, $50 par.. $ 300,000
    Common stock, $100 par.....   1,100,000
    Premium on common stock...   110,000
    Retained earnings..........   176,000

Preferred stock has prior claim to assets on liquidation to the extent of par.

D. Preferred 6% stock, $30 par.. $ 600,000
    Premium on preferred stock..   50,000
    Common stock, $10 par......   1,750,000
    Deficit...................   375,000

Preferred stock has prior claim to assets on liquidation to extent of 110% of par.

E. Preferred 8% stock, $50 par.. $ 400,000
    Common stock, $25 par......   1,250,000
    Premium on common stock...   100,000
    Retained earnings..........   80,000

Dividends on preferred stock are in arrears for 3 years including the dividend passed during the current year. Preferred stock is entitled to par plus unpaid cumulative dividends upon liquidation to the extent of the retained earnings.

F. Preferred 6% stock, $25 par.. $ 750,000
    Discount on preferred stock...   50,000
    Common stock, $5 par.......   1,500,000
    Retained earnings..........   80,000

Dividends on preferred stock are in arrears for 2 years including the dividend passed during the current year. Preferred stock is entitled to par plus unpaid cumulative dividends upon liquidation, regardless of the availability of retained earnings.

Instructions:

Determine for each corporation the equity per share of each class of stock, presenting the total stockholders' equity allocated to each class and the number of shares outstanding.

16-4A. The following accounts and their balances appear in the ledger of Modern Means, Inc., on April 30 of the current year:

Preferred 5% Stock, par $20 (50,000 shares authorized, 24,000 shares issued)......	$ 480,000
Premium on Preferred Stock............	24,000
Common Stock, par $10 (250,000 shares authorized, 130,000 shares issued).....	1,300,000
Premium on Common Stock............	110,000
Retained Earnings (debit balance).......	70,000

At the annual stockholders meeting on May 6, the chairman of the board of directors presented a plan for modernizing operations at a cost of $750,000. The plan provided (a) that the corporation borrow $225,000, (b) that the stockholders purchase 15,000 shares of the unissued preferred stock at par, and (c) that 25,000 of the common shares outstanding be donated to the corporation for resale. The plan was approved by the stockholders and accomplished by the following transactions:

May 17. Received 25,000 shares of common stock from stockholders.
    20. Issued 15,000 shares of preferred stock at $20, receiving cash.
    20. Sold all of the treasury stock for $260,000.
    31. Borrowed $225,000 from National Insurance, giving a 7% mortgage note.

Instructions:

Assuming for the purpose of the problem that no other transactions occurred during May:

(1) Prepare, in general journal form, the entries to record the foregoing transactions, recording receipt of the treasury stock by a memorandum entry.
(2) Prepare the stockholders' equity section of the balance sheet as of May 17.
(3) Prepare the stockholders' equity section of the balance sheet as of May 31.

16-5A. The stockholders' equity and related accounts appearing in the ledger of Ellsworth Engineering Corporation on November 1, the beginning of the current fiscal year, are listed below.

Preferred 8% Stock Subscriptions Receivable..	$ 110,000
Preferred 8% Stock, $100 par (25,000 shares authorized, 15,000 shares issued).........	1,500,000
Preferred 8% Stock Subscribed (3,000 shares).	300,000
Premium on Preferred Stock............	70,000
Common Stock, $25 par (500,000 shares authorized, 200,000 shares issued).........	5,000,000
Premium on Common Stock..............	800,000
Retained Earnings......................	2,160,000

During the year the corporation completed a number of transactions affecting the stockholders' equity. They are summarized below.

(a) Received balance due on preferred stock subscribed and issued the certificates.
(b) Purchased 5,000 shares of treasury common for $210,000.
(c) Received subscriptions to 4,000 shares of preferred 8% stock at $102, collecting one third of the subscription price.
(d) Sold 2,000 shares of treasury common for $92,000.

(e) Issued 35,000 shares of common stock at $44, receiving cash.
(f) Sold 1,000 shares of treasury common for $40,000.

Instructions:

(1) Prepare entries, in general journal form, to record the transactions
listed above. Identify each entry by letter. (The use of T
accounts for stockholders' equity accounts will facilitate the
determination of the amounts needed in recording some of the
transactions and in completing instruction (2).)

(2) Prepare the stockholders' equity section of the balance sheet as
of October 31. Net income for the year amounted to $840,000.
Cash dividends declared and paid during the year totaled $510,000.

16-6A. Microplastics was organized on October 15 of the current year and
prepared its first financial statements as of the following September 30, the date
that had been adopted as the end of the fiscal year. The balance sheet prepared
by the bookkeeper as of September 30 is presented below. You are retained by
the board of directors to audit the accounts and to prepare a revised balance
sheet.

Microplastics
Balance Sheet
October 15 to September 30, 19—

Assets		Liabilities	
Cash...................	$ 17,400	Accounts payable.........	$ 29,700
Accounts receivable.......	46,300	Preferred stock...........	60,000
Merchandise inventory....	73,800	Common stock..........	200,000
Prepaid insurance........	250		
Treasury preferred stock...	15,000		
Equipment.............	109,000		
Discount on common stock.	10,000		
Retained earnings (deficit).	17,950		
Total assets.............	$289,700	Total liabilities..........	$289,700

The relevant facts developed during the course of your engagement are:

(a) Stock authorized: 1,000 shares of $100 par, 8% preferred and 10,000
shares of $25 par common.

(b) Stock issued: 600 shares of fully paid preferred at $110 and 5,000 shares
of fully paid common at $23. The premium on preferred stock was
credited to Retained Earnings.

(c) Stock subscribed but not issued: 3,000 shares of common at par, on
which all subscribers have paid two thirds of the subscription price.
Unpaid subscriptions are included in accounts receivable, and are
collectible in sixty days.

(d) The company reacquired 150 shares of the issued preferred stock at $108.
The difference between par and the price paid was debited to Retained
Earnings. (It is decided that the treasury stock is to be recorded at cost.)

(e) Land costing $22,000, which is to be used as a future building site, was
charged to Equipment.

(f) No depreciation has been recognized. The equipment is to be depreciated for one-half year by the straight-line method, using an estimated
life of 10 years.

(g) Organization costs of $600 were charged to Advertising Expense. (None of the organization costs is to be amortized until next year, the first full year of operations.)

(h) Included in merchandise inventory is $400 of office supplies.

(i) No dividends have been declared or paid.

(j) In balancing the common stockholders ledger with the common stock control account, it was discovered that the account with Patricia Gleason contained a posting for an issuance of 50 shares, while the carbon copy of the stock certificate indicated that 500 shares had been issued. The stock certificate was found to be correct.

Instructions:

(1) Prepare general journal entries where necessary to record the corrections. Corrections of net income may be recorded as adjustments to retained earnings.

(2) Prepare a six-column work sheet with columns for (a) balances per balance sheet, (b) corrections, and (c) corrected balances. In listing the accounts, leave an extra line blank following the retained earnings account.

(3) Prepare a balance sheet in report form as of the close of the fiscal year.

419

Chapter 17

CORPORATIONS — STOCKHOLDERS' EQUITY, EARNINGS, AND DIVIDENDS

CLASSIFICATION OF STOCKHOLDERS' EQUITY

As has been indicated, the stockholders' equity section of the balance sheet is divided into two major subdivisions, "paid-in capital" and "retained earnings." Although in practice there is wide variation in the amount of detail presented and the descriptive captions employed, sources of significant amounts of capital should be adequately disclosed.

The emphasis on disclosure and clarity of expression by the accounting profession has been relatively recent. In earlier days it was not unusual to present only the amount of the par of the preferred and common stock outstanding and a balancing amount described merely as "Surplus." Readers of the balance sheet could only assume that par represented the amount paid in by stockholders and that surplus represented retained earnings. Although it was possible for a "surplus" of $1,000,000, for example, to be composed solely of retained earnings, it could represent paid-in capital from premiums on stock issued or even an excess of $1,200,000 of such premiums over an accumulated deficit of $200,000 of retained earnings.

The term "capital surplus" was also frequently employed in the past to describe the portion of paid-in capital that exceeded the par or stated value of the capital stock. It is generally agreed that the term "surplus," either alone or with such words as "capital," "paid-in," or "earned," should not be used as a descriptive caption in financial statements.[1] Nevertheless, the terms are still encountered occasionally in corporate financial reports and, of course, in accounting literature; their significance should be understood by students of business.

PAID-IN CAPITAL

The principal credits to paid-in capital accounts result from the issuance of stock. If par stock is issued at a price above or below par,

---

[1] *Accounting Research and Terminology Bulletins — Final Edition*, "Accounting Terminology Bulletins, No. 1, Review and Résumé" (New York: American Institute of Certified Public Accountants, 1961), par. 69.

the difference is recorded in a separate premium or discount account. It is also not uncommon to employ two accounts in recording the issuance of no-par stock, one for the stated value and the other for the excess over stated value. Other accounts for paid-in capital discussed in the preceding chapter were Paid-In Capital from Sale of Treasury Stock and Donated Capital.

Paid-in capital may also originate from donated real estate and redemptions of a corporation's own stock. Civic organizations sometimes give land or land and buildings to a corporate enterprise as an inducement to locate in the community. In such cases the assets are recorded in the corporate accounts at fair market value, with a credit to Donated Capital. Preferred stock contracts may give to the issuing corporation the right to redeem the stock at varying redemption prices at varying future dates. If the redemption price paid to the stockholder is greater than the original issuance price, the excess is considered to be a distribution of retained earnings. On the other hand, if the amount paid is less than the amount originally received by the corporation, the difference is a retention of capital and should be credited to Paid-In Capital from Preferred Stock Redemption or similarly titled account.

As with other sections of the balance sheet, there are numerous variations in terminology and arrangement of the paid-in capital section. The details of each class of stock, including related stock premium or discount, are commonly listed first, followed by the other paid-in capital accounts. Instead of describing the source of each amount in excess of par or stated value, a common practice is to combine all such accounts into a single amount. It is then listed below the capital stock accounts and described as "Additional paid-in capital," "Capital in excess of par (or stated value) of shares," or by a similarly descriptive phrase. Some of the variations in terminology and arrangement are illustrated by the three examples shown below and on page 422.

421

Stockholders' Equity

Paid-in capital:			
Common stock, $20 par (50,000 shares authorized, 40,000 shares issued)	$800,000		
Premium on common stock	128,000	$928,000	
From stock redemption		30,000	
From sale of treasury stock		10,000	
Total paid-in capital			$968,000

Capital

Paid-in capital:			
Common stock, $20 par (50,000 shares authorized, 40,000 shares issued)		$800,000	
Excess of issuance price of stock over par	$128,000		
From donation	30,000		
From transactions in own stock	10,000	168,000	
Total paid-in capital			$968,000

Shareholders' Investment

Contributed capital:
Common stock, $20 par (50,000 shares authorized,
40,000 shares issued)........................ $800,000
Additional paid-in capital..................... 168,000
Total contributed capital.................... $968,000

CORPORATE EARNINGS AND INCOME TAXES

The determination of the net income or net loss of a corporation is comparable, in most respects, to that of other forms of business organization. Unlike sole proprietorships and partnerships, however, corporations are distinct legal entities and in general are subject to the federal income tax and in many cases to income taxes levied by states or other political subdivisions. Although the discussion that follows is restricted to the income tax levied by the federal government, the basic concepts apply also to state and local income taxes.

Income tax expense should be allocated to the fiscal year in which the related income is earned. Most corporations are required to estimate the amount of their federal income tax and make advance payments, usually in four installments during the year in which the income is earned.

After the close of the fiscal year the tax liability, based on taxable income, is compared with the total amount of the advance payments. If an additional amount is owed, it may be paid in two equal installments, the first when the tax return is filed 2½ months after the close of the fiscal year and the second installment 3 months later. The entry to record additional tax liability as of the close of a fiscal year coinciding with the calendar year would be as follows:

| Dec. | 31 | Income Tax........................ | 26,139 | |
| | | Income Tax Payable............... | | 26,139 |

If the amount of the advance payments exceeds the tax liability based on actual income, the amount of the overpayment would be debited to a receivable account and credited to Income Tax.

Income tax returns and related records and documents are subject to review by the taxing authority, usually for a period of three years after the return is filed. Consequently, the determination made by the taxpayer is provisional rather than final. In recognition of the possibility of an assessment for a tax deficiency, the liability for income taxes is sometimes described in the current liability section of the balance sheet as "Estimated income tax payable" or "Provision for income tax."

Because of its substantial magnitude in relationship to net income, income tax is frequently reported on the income statement as a special deduction, as illustrated at the top of the next page.

Dunbar Corporation
Income Statement
For Year Ended December 31, 19—

Sales	$920,000
Income before income tax	$180,000
Income tax	79,900
Net income	$100,100

INCOME TAX ALLOCATION

The *taxable income* of a corporation, determined in accordance with the Internal Revenue Code and governmental regulations, frequently differs substantially from the amount of income (before income tax) determined from the accounts and reported to stockholders in the income statement. Differences between the two may arise from one or more of the following situations:

1. Revenue from a specified source is excludable from taxable income or an expense for a specified purpose is not deductible in determining taxable income. Example: Interest received on tax-exempt municipal bonds.
2. A deduction allowed in determining taxable income for which there is no actual expenditure and hence no expense. Example: Excess of the deduction for percentage depletion of oil wells over depletion expense based on cost.
3. The method elected in determining the amount of a specified revenue or expense for income tax purposes differs from the method employed in determining net income for reporting purposes. Example: Declining-balance depreciation at twice the straight-line rate elected in determining taxable income and straight-line depreciation employed for reporting purposes.
4. The manner prescribed for the treatment of a specified revenue or expense in determining taxable income is contrary to generally accepted accounting principles and hence not acceptable in determining net income for reporting purposes. Example: Revenue to be earned in future years received in advance must be included in taxable income in the year received, which is contrary to the basic accounting principle that such revenue be allocated among the years benefited.

Details of the items contributing to the discrepancy between taxable income and net income must be disclosed in a section of the income tax return entitled "Reconciliation of Income per Books with Income per Return." The reconciling items are readily identifiable and quantifiable for purposes of the tax return. However, those arising from a difference in accounting methods must also be given recognition in corporate financial statements.

Differences resulting from the first two situations described above cause no problem of financial reporting. Differences caused by the third

423

and fourth situations are largely attributable to differences in accounting methods, which in turn are related to differences in the timing of revenue and expense recognition. The remainder of this section is devoted to such timing differences and their related effect on the amount of income tax reported in corporate financial statements.

To illustrate the effect of timing differences, assume that a corporation that sells its product on the installment basis recognizes the revenue at the time of sale, and maintains its accounts accordingly. At the close of its first year of operations, the income before income tax according to the ledger is $300,000. Realizing the advantage of reducing current income tax, the corporation elects the installment method of determining revenue, which yields taxable income of only $100,000. Assuming an income tax rate of 45%, the income tax on $300,000 of income would amount to $135,000 but the income tax actually due for the year would be only $45,000 (45% of $100,000). The $90,000 difference between the two amounts is attributable to the timing difference in recognizing revenue. It represents a deferment of $90,000 of income tax to future years. As the installment accounts receivable are collected in later years, the additional $200,000 of income will be included in taxable income and the $90,000 deferment will become a tax liability of those years. The situation may be summarized as follows:

Income before income tax according to ledger	$300,000	
Income tax based on $300,000 at 45%		$135,000
Taxable income according to tax return	$100,000	
Income tax based on $100,000 at 45%		45,000
Income tax deferred to future years		**$ 90,000**

If the $90,000 of deferred income tax were not recognized in the accounts, the income statement for the first year of operations would report the following:

Income before income tax	$300,000
Income tax	45,000
Net income	$255,000

Failure to allocate the additional income tax of $90,000 to the year in which the revenue was earned may be viewed as an overstatement of net income and an understatement of liabilities of $90,000. To ignore this additional expense of $90,000 and the accompanying deferred liability of $90,000 would be considered by most accountants to be erroneous and unacceptable. It is considered preferable to allocate the income tax to the period in which the related income is earned. In accordance with this view, the income tax reported on the financial statements will be the total tax expected to result from the net income of the year regardless of when the tax will become an actual liability.[2] Application of this latter viewpoint to the illustrative data yields the following results, stated in terms of a journal entry:

Income Tax	135,000	
Income Tax Payable		45,000
Deferred Income Tax Payable		90,000

Continuing with the illustration, the $90,000 in Deferred Income Tax Payable will be transferred to Income Tax Payable as the remaining $200,000 of income becomes taxable in subsequent years. If, for example, $120,000 of untaxed income of the first year of the corporation's operations becomes taxable in the second year, the effect would be as follows, stated as a journal entry:

Deferred Income Tax Payable	54,000	
Income Tax Payable		54,000

Installment sales of the corporation in succeeding years will continue to result in additional differences between taxable and reported income, and an accompanying deferment of tax liability. Thus the balance in the deferred income tax payable account will fluctuate from year to year.

ERRORS AND ADJUSTMENTS OF THE CURRENT PERIOD

425

Accounting errors of a fiscal year that are discovered and corrected within the same fiscal year were discussed in Chapter 3. The procedure recommended there for correcting erroneous entries that have been posted to the ledger is summarized as follows: (1) set forth the entire entry in which the error occurred by the use of memorandum T accounts or a journal entry; (2) set forth the entry that should have been made, using a second set of T accounts or a journal entry; and (3) formulate the debits and credits required to bring the erroneous entry in (1) into agreement with the correct entry in (2).

The correction of current errors is entirely a matter of technique, no question of principle being involved. After the correction has been made, the account balances are the same as they would have been in the absence of error, and, more importantly, the information communicated through the income statement and the balance sheet is unaffected.

PRIOR PERIOD ADJUSTMENTS, EXTRAORDINARY ITEMS, AND CHANGES IN ACCOUNTING PRINCIPLE

It is sometimes necessary to revise the amount reported as net income of prior periods because of errors or changes in accounting principle. "Errors in financial statements result from mathematical mistakes, mistakes in the application of accounting principles, or oversight or

---

[2]*Opinions of the Accounting Principles Board, No. 11,* "Accounting for Income Taxes" (New York: American Institute of Certified Public Accountants, 1967).

misuse of facts that existed at the time the financial statements were prepared."[3] Extraordinary gains and losses, which are accorded special treatment in the income statement, result from "events and transactions which have occurred during the current period, which are of an extraordinary nature. . . ."[4] A change in accounting principle, which also should be accorded special treatment in the income statement, "results from adoption of a generally accepted accounting principle different from the one used previously for reporting purposes."[5]

For many years there were two conflicting points of view concerning the proper reporting of prior period adjustments, extraordinary items, and changes in accounting principle. According to the *current operating performance* viewpoint, only the ordinary normal recurring operations of an enterprise should be reported in the income statement. To avoid erroneous interpretations of operating performance resulting from distortions of net income, it was considered preferable to report material nonrecurring items in the retained earnings statement. Contrastingly, the *all-inclusive* viewpoint required that all revenue and expense items recorded in the current period be reported in the income statement for such period, with material items of a nonrecurring nature appropriately identified. By so doing the aggregate of the periodic net income reported over the entire life of an enterprise would be reported in the income statement.

There is now substantial agreement among professional accountants that the all-inclusive viewpoint, with minor variations, is preferable. The generally accepted position on the subject is discussed briefly in the subsections that follow.

Prior period adjustments. Minor errors resulting from the use of estimates inherent in the accounting process are normal and tend to be recurring. For example, relatively insignificant adjustments in the current period for amounts provided for income taxes of one or more prior periods are not unusual. Similarly, annual provisions for the uncollectibility of receivables tend to be somewhat inadequate or somewhat excessive. The amounts recorded as uncollectible accounts expense in the current period seldom agree with the actual experience, which is also influenced by economic events occurring subsequent to the current period.

Under certain specified circumstances the correction of a material[6] error related to a prior period or periods may be excluded from the determination of net income of the current period. Corrections of this

---

[3]*Opinions of the Accounting Principles Board, No. 20,* "Accounting Changes" (New York: American Institute of Certified Public Accountants, 1971), par. 13.
[4]*Opinions of the Accounting Principles Board, No. 9,* "Reporting the Results of Operations" (New York: American Institute of Certified Public Accountants, 1966), par. 21.
[5]*Opinions of the Accounting Principles Board, No. 20, op. cit.,* par. 7.
[6]Review discussion of "Materiality" beginning on page 357.

type are ordinarily referred to as *prior period adjustments*. The criteria for identifying circumstances that justify exclusion from the current income statement are as follows:

> . . . material adjustments which (a) can be specifically identified with and directly related to the business activities of particular prior periods, and (b) are not attributable to economic events occurring subsequent to the date of the financial statements for the prior period, and (c) depend primarily on determinations by persons other than management and (d) were not susceptible of reasonable estimation prior to such determination.[7]

A correction treated as a prior period adjustment should be reported as an adjustment of the balance of retained earnings at the beginning of the period in which the correction is made. If financial statements are presented only for the current period, the effect of the adjustment on the net income of the preceding period should also be disclosed. If income statements for prior periods are presented in the annual report, which is preferable, the effect of the adjustment on each statement should be disclosed.[8]

Corrections applicable to prior periods that meet the criteria for a prior period adjustment are rare in modern financial accounting. Annual audits by independent public accountants, combined with the internal control features of accounting systems, minimize the possibilities of errors justifying such treatment.

427

Extraordinary items. Unusual gains or losses may result from events or transactions which are significantly different from the typical or customary business activities of an enterprise. For example, a material gain or loss on the sale of an entire plant or other significant segment of a business would be an extraordinary gain or loss. Similarly, the sale of an investment not acquired for resale, or the loss of assets from floods, earthquakes, or other catastrophes not ordinarily covered by insurance are events of an unusual nature. Extraordinary items of significant amount should be reported in a special section of the income statement located immediately prior to the amount described as "Net income."

Changes in accounting principle. The concept of consistency and its relationship to changes in accounting methods were discussed in Chapter 14. A change from one generally accepted accounting principle or method (such as *fifo*) to another generally accepted principle or method (such as *lifo*) should be disclosed in the financial statements of the period in which the change is made. In addition to describing the nature of the change, the justification for the change should be stated and the effect of the change on net income should be disclosed.

---

[7] *Opinions of the Accounting Principles Board, No. 9, op. cit.*, par. 23.
[8] *Ibid.*, pars. 18 and 26. Also *Opinions of the Accounting Principles Board, No. 20, op. cit.*, pars. 36 and 37.

The generally accepted procedures for disclosing the effect on net income of a change in principle are as follows: (1) Report the cumulative effect of the change on net income of prior periods as a special item on the income statement, and (2) Report the effect of the change on net income of the current period. If statements for prior periods are presented in conjunction with the current statements, the effect of the change in principle should also be applied retroactively to the prior periods and reported either on the face of the statements or in accompanying notes.

The amount of the cumulative effect on net income of prior periods should be reported in a special section of the income statement located immediately prior to the amount described as "Net income." If an extraordinary item or items are reported on the statement, the amount related to the change in principle should follow the extraordinary items.

The procedures described above should be modified for a change from the lifo assumption for inventory costing to another method or for a change in the method of accounting for long-term construction contracts. For these changes in principle the cumulative effect on prior years' income is not reported as a special item on the income statement. Instead, the newly adopted principle should be applied retroactively to the income statements of the prior periods and the effect on income disclosed, either on the face of the statements or in accompanying notes. Financial statements of subsequent periods need not repeat the disclosures.[9]

Allocation of related income tax. The amount reported as a prior period adjustment, an extraordinary item, or the cumulative effect of a change in accounting principle should be net of the related income tax. The amount of income tax allocable to each item may be disclosed on the face of the appropriate financial statement or by an accompanying note.

The manner in which extraordinary items and the cumulative effect of a change in accounting principle may be presented in the income statement is illustrated at the top of the next page. Many variations in terminology and format are possible.

The explanatory note in support of the change in accounting principle might be phrased somewhat as follows:

Note A. Depreciation of property, plant, and equipment has been computed by the straight-line method at all manufacturing facilities in [current year]. Prior to [current year], depreciation of equipment for one of the divisions had been computed on the double-declining balance method. In [current year] the straight-line method was adopted for this division in order to achieve uniformity and to more appropriately match the remaining depreciation

428

---

[9]*Opinions of the Accounting Principles Board, No. 20, ibid.,* pars. 27 and 28.

AMR Corporation
Income Statement
For Year Ended August 31, 19—

Net sales...		$9,600,950
Income before income tax............................		$1,310,000
Income tax...		620,000
Income before extraordinary items and cumulative effect of a change in accounting principle		$ 690,000
Extraordinary items:		
Gain on sale of investments, net of applicable income tax of $60,000.......................................	$130,000	
Loss on sale of branch plant facilities, net of applicable income tax of $48,000............................	52,000	78,000
Cumulative effect on prior years of changing to a different depreciation method (Note A).......................		92,000
Net income...		$ 860,000

charges with the estimated economic utility of such assets. Pursuant to Opinion 20 of the Accounting Principles Board of the American Institute of Certified Public Accountants, this change in depreciation has been applied retroactively to prior years. The effect of the change was to increase income before extraordinary items for [current year] by approximately $30,000. The adjustment of $92,000 (after reduction for income tax of $88,000) to apply retroactively the new method is also included in income for [current year].[10]

429

EARNINGS PER SHARE

Data on earnings per share of common stock are ordinarily reported by corporations to their stockholders, by the financial press to the general public, and by various statistical services to their subscribers. For many stockholders, and for investors generally, it is frequently the item of greatest interest contained in corporate annual reports.

The effect of nonrecurring additions or deductions to income of a period should be considered in computing earnings per share; otherwise a single per share amount based on net income would be misleading. To illustrate this point, assume that the corporation whose partial income statement appears on page 430 reported net income of $750,000 for the preceding year, with no nonrecurring items. Assume also that its capital stock was composed of 200,000 common shares outstanding during the entire two-year period. If the earnings per share of $3.75 ($750,000 ÷ 200,000) of the preceding year were compared with the earnings per share of $4.30 ($860,000 ÷ 200,000) of the current year, it would appear that operations had improved substantially. The per share amount for the current year comparable to $3.75 is in reality $3.45 ($690,000 ÷ 200,000), which indicates a downward trend in normal operations.

---

[10] *Adapted from a corporate annual report.*

Data on earnings per share should be presented in conjunction with the income statement, and if nonrecurring items are reported on the statement the per share amounts should be presented for (1) income before nonrecurring items, (2) each category of nonrecurring items (net of applicable income tax), and (3) net income.[11] The per share data may be shown parenthetically or appended at the bottom of the statement, as in the illustration below.

AMR Corporation
Income Statement
For Year Ended August 31, 19—

Income before extraordinary items and cumulative effect of a change in accounting principle...	$690,000
Net income	$860,000
Earnings per share:	
Income before extraordinary items and cumulative effect of a change in accounting principle...	$3.45
Extraordinary items...	.39
Cumulative effect on prior years of changing to a different depreciation method...	.46
Net income..	$4.30

430

The computation of earnings per share should give effect to variations in number of shares outstanding, stock dividends, stock splits, conversion of preferred stock and many other complexities of the capital structure of some businesses. The concern here is with the basic concept; further consideration is left for advanced courses.

APPROPRIATION OF RETAINED EARNINGS

The amount of a corporation's retained earnings available for distribution to its shareholders may be restricted by action of the board of directors. The amount restricted, which is called an *appropriation* or a *reserve*, remains a part of retained earnings and should be so classified in the financial statements. An appropriation can be effected by transferring the desired amount from Retained Earnings to a special account designating its purpose, such as Appropriation for Plant Expansion.

Appropriations may be initiated by the directors, or they may be required by law or contract. Some states require that a corporation retain earnings equal to the amount paid for treasury stock. For example, if a corporation with accumulated earnings of $100,000 purchases shares of its own issued stock for $40,000, the corporation would not be permitted to pay more than $60,000 in dividends. The restriction is equal to the $40,000 paid for the treasury stock and assures that legal

---

[11]*Opinions of the Accounting Principles Board, No. 15,* "Earnings per Share" (American Institute of Certified Public Accountants, 1969) as amended by *Opinions of the Accounting Principles Board, No. 20.*

capital will not be impaired by declaration of dividends. The entry to record the appropriation would be:

Apr.	24	Retained Earnings....................	40,000	
		Appropriation for Treasury Stock.....		40,000

When a portion or all of an appropriation is no longer needed, the amount should be transferred back to the retained earnings account. Thus, if the corporation in the above illustration sells the treasury stock, the appropriation would be terminated by the following entry:

Nov.	10	Appropriation for Treasury Stock.......	40,000	
		Retained Earnings.................		40,000

When a corporation borrows a substantial amount through issuance of bonds or long-term notes, the agreement may provide for restrictions on dividends until the debt is paid. The contract may stipulate that retained earnings equal to the amount borrowed be restricted during the entire period of the loan, or it may require that the restriction be built up by annual appropriations. For example, assume that a corporation borrows $500,000 on ten-year bonds. If equal annual appropriations were to be made over the life of the bonds, there would be a series of ten entries, each in the amount of $50,000, debiting Retained Earnings and crediting an appropriation account entitled Appropriation for Bonded Indebtedness. Even if the bond agreement did not require the restriction on retained earnings, the directors might deem it advisable to establish the appropriation. In that case it would be a *discretionary* rather than a *contractual* appropriation. The entries would be identical in either case.

It must be clearly understood that the appropriation account is not directly related to any particular group of asset accounts. Its existence does not imply that there is an equivalent amount of cash or other assets set aside in a special fund. The appropriation serves the purpose of restricting dividends, but it does not assure that the cash that might otherwise be distributed as dividends will not be invested in additional inventories or other assets, or used to reduce liabilities.

Appropriations of retained earnings may be accompanied by a segregation of equivalent amounts of cash or marketable securities, in which case the appropriation is said to be *funded*. Accumulation of such funds is discussed in the next chapter.

There are other purposes for which the directors may consider appropriations desirable. Expansion of plant facilities was mentioned earlier. Some companies with properties widely scattered geographically may assume their own risk of losses from fire, windstorm, and other casualties rather than obtain protection from insurance companies. In

431

such cases the appropriation account would be entitled Appropriation for Self-Insurance. An appropriation of this nature is likely to be permanent, although its amount may vary as the total value of properties, the extent of fire protection, etc. fluctuates. If a loss should occur, it should be debited to a special loss account rather than to the appropriation account. It is definitely a loss of the particular period and should be reported in the income statement. A company may also earmark earnings for other specific contingencies, such as inventory price declines or an adverse decision on a pending law suit.

The details of retained earnings may be presented in the balance sheet in the manner illustrated below. The item designated "Unappropriated" is the balance of the retained earnings account.

```
Retained earnings:
  Appropriated:
    For plant expansion....................... $50,000
  Unappropriated.............................   80,000
    Total retained earnings..................         $130,000
```

It is not essential that restrictions on retained earnings be formalized in the ledger. However, compliance with legal requirements and with contractual restrictions is essential, and the nature and the amount of all restrictions should always be disclosed in the balance sheet. For example, the appropriations data appearing in the foregoing illustration could be presented in the form of a note accompanying the balance sheet. Such an alternative might also be employed as a means of simplifying or condensing the balance sheet even though appropriation accounts are maintained in the ledger. The alternative balance sheet presentation, including the note, might appear as shown below:

```
Retained earnings (see note)....................................... $130,000
```

Note: Retained earnings in the amount of $50,000 are appropriated for expansion of plant facilities; the remaining $80,000 is unrestricted.

NATURE OF DIVIDENDS

A dividend is a distribution by a corporation to its shareholders. It is ordinarily on a pro rata basis for all shares of a particular class. In most cases dividends represent distributions from retained earnings. In many states dividends may be declared from the excess of paid-in capital over par or stated value, but such dividends are unusual. The term *liquidating dividend* is applied to a distribution out of paid-in capital when a corporation permanently reduces its operations or winds up its affairs completely. The discussion that follows will be concerned with dividends based on accumulated earnings.

Dividends may be paid in cash, in stock of the company, in scrip, or in other property. The discussion in this chapter will be concerned mainly with the two most common types of dividends — *cash dividends* and *stock dividends* (stock of the company issuing the dividend).

Ordinarily there are three prerequisites to paying a cash dividend: (1) sufficient unappropriated retained earnings, (2) sufficient cash, and (3) formal action by the board of directors. A substantial amount of accumulated earnings does not necessarily indicate that a corporation is able to pay dividends; there must also be sufficient cash over and above working capital needs. The amount of retained earnings is not directly related to cash; the former represents net income of past periods retained in the business, but the cash provided by the net income may have been used to purchase plant assets, to reduce liabilities, or for other purposes. The directors of a corporation are not compelled by law to declare dividends even when both retained earnings and cash appear to be sufficient. When a dividend has been declared, however, it becomes a liability of the corporation.

Seasoned corporations with a wide distribution of stock usually try to maintain a stable dividend record. They may retain a substantial portion of earnings in good years in order to be able to continue dividend payments in lean years. Dividends may be paid once a year or on a semiannual or quarterly basis. The tendency is to pay quarterly dividends on both common and preferred stock. In particularly good years the directors may declare an "extra" dividend on common stock. It may be paid at one of the usual dividend dates or at some other date. The designation "extra" indicates that the board of directors does not anticipate an increase in the amount of the "regular" dividend.

There are three different dates related to a dividend declaration: (1) the date of declaration, (2) the date of record, and (3) the date of payment. The first is the date the directors take formal action declaring the dividend, the second is the date as of which ownership of shares is to be determined, and the third is the date payment is to be made. For example, on October 11 the board of directors declares a quarterly cash dividend to stockholders of record as of the close of business on October 21, payable on November 15. Notices of dividend declarations are usually reported in financial publications and newspapers.

The liability for the dividend is recorded on the declaration date, as it is incurred when the formal action is taken by the directors. No entry is required on the date of record; it merely fixes the date for determining the identity of the stockholders entitled to receive the dividend. The period of time between the record date and the payment date is provided to permit completion of the postings to the stockholders ledger and preparation of the dividend checks. The liability of the corporation is paid by the mailing of the checks.

433

Dividends on cumulative preferred stock do not become a liability of the corporation until formal action is taken by the board of directors. However, dividends in arrears at a balance sheet date should be disclosed by a footnote, a parenthetical notation, or a segregation of retained earnings similar to the following:

Retained earnings:
Required to meet dividends in arrears on preferred stock . $30,000
Remainder, unrestricted 16,000
Total retained earnings $46,000

CASH DIVIDENDS

Dividends payable in cash are by far the most usual form of dividend. Dividends on common stock are usually stated in terms of dollars and cents rather than as a percentage of par. Dividends on preferred stock may be stated either in monetary terms or as a percentage of par. For example, the annual dividend rate on a particular $100 par preferred stock may be stated as either $6 or 6%.

Corporations ordinarily follow a fixed pattern of dividend payment dates, such as January 15, April 15, July 15, and October 15, or March 30, June 30, September 30, and December 30. Assuming a sufficient balance in retained earnings, including estimated net income of the current year, the directors ordinarily consider the following factors in determining whether to pass a dividend or declare a particular amount:

1. The company's working capital position.
2. Resources needed for planned expansion or replacement of facilities.
3. Maturity dates of large liabilities.
4. Future business prospects of the company and forecasts for the industry and the economy generally.

To illustrate the entries required in the declaration and the payment of cash dividends, assume that on December 1 the board of directors declares the regular quarterly dividend of $1.50 on the 5,000 shares of $100 par, 6% preferred stock outstanding (total dividend of $7,500), and a quarterly dividend of 25¢ on the 100,000 shares of $10 par common stock outstanding (total dividend of $25,000). Both dividends are to stockholders of record on December 10, and checks are to be issued to stockholders on January 2. The entry to record the declaration of the dividends is as follows:

| Dec. | 1 | Cash Dividends. . . . . | 32,500 | |
| | | Cash Dividends Payable. . . . . | | 32,500 |

The balance in Cash Dividends would be transferred to Retained Earnings as a part of the closing process and Cash Dividends Payable would be listed on the balance sheet as a current liability. Payment of the liability on January 2 would be recorded in the usual manner as a debit of $32,500 to Cash Dividends Payable and a credit to Cash.

STOCK DIVIDENDS

A pro rata distribution of shares of stock to stockholders, accompanied by a transfer of retained earnings to paid-in capital accounts, is called a *stock dividend*. Such distributions are usually in common stock and are issued to holders of common stock. It is possible to issue common stock to preferred stockholders or vice versa, but such stock dividends are too unusual to warrant their consideration here.

Stock dividends are quite unlike cash dividends in that there is no distribution of cash or other corporate assets to the stockholders. They are ordinarily issued by corporations that "plow back" (retain) earnings for use in acquiring new facilities or for expanding their operations.

The effect of a stock dividend on the capital structure of the issuing corporation is to transfer accumulated earnings to paid-in capital. The statutes of most states require that an amount equivalent to the par or stated value of a stock dividend be transferred from the retained earnings account to the common stock account. Compliance with this minimum requirement is considered by accountants to be satisfactory for a closely held corporation; their stockholders are presumed to have sufficient knowledge of the corporation's affairs to recognize the true import of the dividend. However, many investors in the stock of widely held corporations are often less knowledgeable. An analysis of this latter situation, and the widely accepted viewpoint of professional accountants has been expressed as follows:

> . . . many recipients of stock dividends look upon them as distributions of corporate earnings and usually in an amount equivalent to the fair value of the additional shares received. Furthermore, it is to be presumed that such views of recipients are materially strengthened in those instances, which are by far the most numerous, where the issuances are so small in comparison with the shares previously outstanding that they do not have any apparent effect upon the share market price and, consequently, the market value of the shares previously held remains substantially unchanged. The committee therefore believes that where these circumstances exist the corporation should in the public interest account for the transaction by transferring from earned surplus to the category of permanent capitalization . . . an amount equal to the fair value of the additional shares issued. Unless this is done, the amount of earnings which the shareholder may believe to have been distributed to him will be left, except to the extent otherwise dictated by legal requirements, in earned surplus subject to possible further similar stock issuances or cash distributions.[12]

To illustrate the issuance of a stock dividend in accordance with the procedure recommended above, assume the following balances in the

435

---

[12]*Accounting Research and Terminology Bulletins — Final Edition*, "No. 43, Restatement and Revision of Accounting Research Bulletins" (New York: American Institute of Certified Public Accountants, 1961), Ch. 7, Sec. B, par. 10.

stockholders' equity accounts of a hypothetical corporation as of December 15:

Common Stock, $10 par (2,000,000 shares issued). $20,000,000
Premium on Common Stock.................. 4,000,000
Retained Earnings......................... 28,500,000

On December 15 the board of directors declares a 5% stock dividend (100,000 shares, $1,000,000 par), to be issued on January 10. Assuming the average of the high and low market prices on the declaration date to be $22 a share, the entry to record the declaration would be as follows:

Dec.	15	Stock Dividends......................	2,200,000	
		Stock Dividends Distributable.......		1,000,000
		Premium on Common Stock.........		1,200,000

The $2,200,000 debit in Stock Dividends would be transferred to Retained Earnings as a part of the closing process and the issuance of the stock certificates would be recorded on January 10 by the following entry:

| Jan. | 10 | Stock Dividends Distributable......... | 1,000,000 | |
| | | Common Stock.................... | | 1,000,000 |

The effect of the stock dividend is to transfer $2,200,000 from the retained earnings account to paid-in capital accounts and to increase by 100,000 the number of shares outstanding. There is no change in the assets, liabilities, or total stockholders' equity of the corporation. If financial statements are prepared between the date of declaration and the date of issuance, the stock dividends distributable account should be listed in the paid-in capital section of the balance sheet.

The issuance of the additional shares does not affect the total amount of a stockholder's equity nor of his proportionate interest in the corporation. The effect of the stock dividend on the accounts of the hypothetical corporation and on the equity of a stockholder owning 1,000 shares is demonstrated by the following tabulation:

THE CORPORATION	BEFORE STOCK DIVIDEND	AFTER STOCK DIVIDEND
Common stock.............	$20,000,000	$21,000,000
Premium on common stock...	4,000,000	5,200,000
Retained earnings..........	28,500,000	26,300,000
Total stockholders' equity.	$52,500,000	$52,500,000
Number of shares outstanding.	2,000,000	2,100,000
Equity per share............	$26.25	$25.00
A STOCKHOLDER		
Number of shares owned.....	1,000	1,050
Total equity.............	$26,250	$26,250
Portion of corporation owned.	.05%	.05%

STOCK SPLITS

Corporations sometimes reduce the par or stated value of their common stock and issue a proportionate number of additional shares. Such a procedure is called a *stock split* or *stock split-up*. For example, a corporation with 10,000 shares of $50 par stock outstanding may reduce the par to $25 and increase the number of shares to 20,000. A stockholder who owned 100 shares before the split would own 200 shares after the split. There are no changes in the balances of any of the corporation's accounts, hence no entry is required. The primary purpose of a stock split is to reduce the market price per share and encourage more investors to enter the market for the company's shares.

DIVIDENDS AND TREASURY STOCK

Cash or property dividends are not paid on treasury stock. To do so would place the corporation in the position of earning income through dealing with itself, an obvious fiction. Accordingly, the total amount of a cash (or property) dividend should be based on the number of shares outstanding at the record date. To illustrate, assume the following balances in the stockholders' equity accounts of a corporation:

Common Stock, $10 par (100,000 shares issued).	$1,000,000 cr.
Retained Earnings.	1,600,000 cr.
Treasury Stock (2,000 shares at cost).	42,000 dr.

437

If the corporation declares a cash dividend of $1 a share, it is computed on the basis of the 98,000 shares outstanding (100,000 − 2,000) and the dividend will total $98,000.

When a corporation holding treasury stock declares a stock dividend, the number of shares to be issued may be based either on (1) the number of shares outstanding or (2) the number of shares issued. If the above hypothetical corporation declares a 5% stock dividend and adopts the first method, it will issue 4,900 shares (5% of 98,000) to its stockholders. If the second method is adopted, the corporation will issue a total of 5,000 shares (5% of 100,000); 4,900 shares to its stockholders and 100 shares to itself. Regardless of the method of computation used, the monetary amount of the treasury stock remains unchanged at its original cost of $42,000. However, if the second alternative is adopted the average cost of the treasury stock will decrease from $21 a share ($42,000 ÷ 2,000) to $20 a share ($42,000 ÷ 2,100).

The issuance of stock dividends on treasury stock is theoretically sound because the percentage relationship of the treasury stock to the total issuance remains unchanged. In practice, however, either method of determining the total amount of the dividend is satisfactory. In most cases the number of shares held as treasury stock represents a small percent of the number of shares issued and the rate of dividend is also ordinarily small, so that the difference between the end results is usually not significant.

There is no legal, theoretical, or practical reason for excluding treasury stock when computing the number of shares to be issued in a stock split. The reduction in par or stated value would apply to all shares of the class, including the unissued, issued, and treasury shares. If, for example, the above hypothetical corporation were to reduce the par of its stock from $10 to $5 in a two-for-one split, it would increase the number of its shares by 100,000, of which 98,000 would be issued to stockholders and 2,000 would be added to the treasury shares.

RETAINED EARNINGS STATEMENT

The retained earnings statement illustrated in Chapter 1 reported only the changes in the account balance attributable to earnings and dividends for the period. When there are accounts for appropriations, it is customary to divide the statement into two major sections: (1) appropriated and (2) unappropriated. The first section is composed of an analysis of all appropriation accounts, beginning with the opening balance, listing the additions or the deductions during the period, and ending with the closing balance. The second section is composed of an analysis of the retained earnings account and is similar in form to the first section. The final figure on the statement is the total retained earnings as of the last day of the period; it corresponds to the amount reported in the balance sheet as of that date.

To illustrate the form of the statement and the sources from which the information is obtained, the pertinent accounts of a corporation and its retained earnings statement for a fiscal year are presented below and on the following page.

ACCOUNT **APPROPRIATION FOR PLANT EXPANSION** ACCOUNT No. 3202

DATE		ITEM	DEBIT	CREDIT	BALANCE	
					DEBIT	CREDIT
Jan.	1	Balance				30,000
Dec.	31	Retained earnings		25,000		55,000

ACCOUNT **RETAINED EARNINGS** ACCOUNT No. 3301

DATE		ITEM	DEBIT	CREDIT	BALANCE	
					DEBIT	CREDIT
Jan.	1	Balance				113,300
Dec.	31	Income summary		100,000		213,300
	31	Appropriation for plant expansion	25,000			188,300
	31	Cash dividends	47,500			140,800

438

ACCOUNT CASH DIVIDENDS   ACCOUNT No. 3302

DATE		ITEM	DEBIT	CREDIT	BALANCE	
					DEBIT	CREDIT
Mar.	20		9,875		9,875	
June	19		9,875		19,750	
Sept.	18		9,875		29,625	
Dec.	18		17,875		47,500	
	31	Retained earnings		47,500	——	——

Douglas Corporation
Retained Earnings Statement
For Year Ended December 31, 19—

Appropriated:			
Appropriation for plant expansion, balance January 1, 19—..............................		$ 30,000	
Additional appropriation (see below)............		25,000	
Retained earnings appropriated, December 31, 19—			$ 55,000
Unappropriated:			
Balance, January 1, 19—......................	$113,300		
Net income for the year......................	100,000	$213,300	
Cash dividends declared......................	$ 47,500		
Transfer to appropriation for plant expansion (see above)...................................	25,000	72,500	
Retained earnings unappropriated, December 31, 19—.....................................			140,800
Total retained earnings, December 31, 19—.......			$195,800

439

Retained earnings statement

There are many possible variations in the form of the retained earnings statement. It may also be appended to the income statement to form a combined statement of income and retained earnings, which is illustrated in Chapter 27. The details of any significant changes in paid-in capital during the period should also be presented, either as a separate paid-in capital statement or in notes to other financial statements.[13]

QUESTIONS

1. Name the titles of the two principal subdivisions of the stockholders' equity section of a corporate balance sheet.

2. If a corporation is given land as an inducement to locate in a particular community, (a) how should the amount of the debit to the land account be determined, and (b) what is the title of the account that should be credited for the same amount?

---

[13]*Opinions of the Accounting Principles Board, No. 12*, "Omnibus Opinion — 1967" (New York: American Institute of Certified Public Accountants, 1967), par. 10.

3. (a) What is the term that has generally replaced earned surplus on the balance sheet? (b) Is the term capital surplus recommended as a balance sheet caption describing premiums on stock and other miscellaneous sources of paid-in capital?

4. For a corporation with five different paid-in capital accounts in addition to its account for par of the stock issued, what is an acceptable alternative to listing each balance separately on the balance sheet?

5. A corporation that has paid $100,000 of federal income tax during the year on the basis of its estimated income determines at the end of the year that it owes an additional $15,000 for the year. What entry should be recorded as of the end of the year?

6. An amount described as "Provision for income tax" appears on the balance sheet of a corporation. (a) In which section of the balance sheet would it logically appear? (b) What other descriptive term might be considered to be more accurately descriptive?

7. The income before income tax reported on the income statement for the year is $200,000. Because of timing differences in accounting and tax methods the taxable income for the same year is $150,000. Assuming an income tax rate of 50% state (a) the amount of income tax to be deducted from the $200,000 on the income statement, (b) the amount of the actual income tax that should be paid for the year, and (c) the amount of the deferred income tax liability.

8. Classify each of the revenue and expense items listed below as either (a) normally recurring or (b) extraordinary. Assume that the amount of each item is material.

(1) Gain on sale of an investment not acquired for resale
(2) Uncollectible accounts expense
(3) Salaries of executives
(4) Uninsured earthquake loss
(5) Depreciation expense on plant asset

9. A building with a book value of $100,000, owned by a business enterprise, was completely destroyed by an explosion. How should the loss, which was uninsured, be reported in the income statement, assuming that the amount is material?

10. A corporation reports earnings per share of $3.20 for the most recent year and $2.70 for the preceding year. The $3.20 includes $.80 per share gain from the sale of a substantial segment of the business. (a) Should the composition of the $3.20 be disclosed in the financial report? (b) What is the amount for the most recent year that is comparable to the $2.70 earnings per share of the preceding year? (c) On the basis of the limited information presented would you conclude that operations had improved or retrogressed?

11. Appropriations of retained earnings may be (a) required by law, (b) required by contract, or (c) made at the discretion of the board of directors. Give an illustration of each type of appropriation.

12. A credit balance in Retained Earnings does not represent cash. Explain.

13. The board of directors of Preston Corporation votes to appropriate $100,000 of retained earnings for plant expansion. What is the effect of their action on

(a) cash, (b) total retained earnings, and (c) retained earnings available for dividends?

14. The dates in connection with the declaration of a cash dividend are December 30, January 10, and January 30. Identify each date.

15. A corporation with both cumulative preferred stock and common stock outstanding has a substantial credit balance in the retained earnings account at the beginning of the current fiscal year. Although net income for the current year is sufficient to pay the preferred dividend of $40,000 each quarter and a common dividend of $100,000 each quarter, the board of directors declares dividends only on the preferred stock. Suggest possible reasons for passing the dividends on the common stock.

16. Describe alternative methods of reporting dividends in arrears on cumulative preferred stock on the balance sheet.

17. State the effect of the following actions by a corporation on its assets, liabilities, and stockholders' equity: (a) declaration of a cash dividend, (b) payment of the cash dividend declared in (a), (c) declaration of a stock dividend, (d) issuance of stock certificates for the stock dividend declared in (c), (e) authorization and issuance of stock certificates in a stock split.

18. An owner of 100 shares of MRT Corporation common stock receives a stock dividend of 10 shares. (a) What is the effect of the stock dividend on the equity per share of his stock? (b) How does the total equity of his 110 shares compare with the total equity of his 100 shares before the stock dividend?

441

19. A corporation with 25,000 shares of no-par common stock issued, of which 1,000 shares are held as treasury stock, declares a cash dividend of $1 a share. What is the total amount of the dividend?

20. A 10% stock dividend declared by the corporation in Question 19 would amount to what number of shares? Give two alternatives.

21. If a corporation with 1,000 shares of treasury stock has a 3-for-1 stock split (2 additional shares for each share issued), what will be the number of treasury shares after the split?

EXERCISES

17-1. Present entries, in general journal form, to record the selected transactions of Caldwell Corporation described below.

Apr. 15. Paid the first installment of the estimated income tax for the current fiscal year ending December 31, $60,000. No entry had been made to record the liability.

June 15. Paid the second installment of $50,000. (Same note as above.)

Dec. 31. Recorded the additional income tax liability for the year just ended and the deferred income tax liability, based on the two transactions above and the data listed below:

Income tax rate....................................	50%
Income for the year before income tax................	$500,000
Taxable income according to the tax return...........	450,000
Third installment paid on September 15..............	45,000
Fourth installment paid on December 15.............	55,000

17-2. Prior to adjusting and closing the accounts at June 30, the end of the current fiscal year, the accountant discovered the following errors related to such year. Present the entry to correct each error.

(a) A purchase of $600 of office equipment on account was debited to Office Supplies and credited to Accounts Payable.

(b) In recording a purchase of Store Equipment on June 20 for which a note payable was given, Accounts Payable was credited for $7,500.

(c) Office equipment that had cost $5,000 and on which $4,000 of depreciation had accumulated at the time of sale was sold for $400. The transaction was recorded by a debit to Cash and a credit to Sales for $400.

(d) The declaration of a cash dividend of $6,000 had been recorded as a debit to Interest Expense and a credit to Interest Payable. Payment of the dividend had been recorded as a debit to Interest Payable and a credit to Cash.

17-3. On the basis of the data listed below, from the records of Harris Corporation for the current fiscal year ended June 30, prepare an income statement, including an analysis of earnings per share in the form illustrated in this chapter. There were 10,000 shares of $10 par common stock outstanding throughout the year.

Sales....................................	$475,000
Cost of merchandise sold...................	324,000
Uninsured flood loss.......................	20,000
Selling expenses..........................	58,600
General expenses.........................	23,400
Income tax reduction applicable to flood loss.	9,600
Income tax applicable to ordinary income....	25,900
Interest expense..........................	1,500

17-4. A corporation purchased for cash 2,000 shares of its own $10 par common stock at $22 a share. In the following year it sold 500 of the treasury shares at $25 a share for cash. (a) Present the entries in general journal form (1) to record the purchase (treasury stock is recorded at cost) and (2) to provide for the appropriation of retained earnings. (b) Present the entries in general journal form (1) to record the sale of the stock and (2) to reduce the appropriation.

17-5. The dates in connection with a cash dividend of $40,000 on a corporation's common stock are June 9, June 20, and July 1. Present the entries, in general journal form, required on each date.

17-6. The balance sheet of Wagner Company indicates common stock (25,000 shares authorized), $25 par, $250,000; premium on common stock, $60,000; and retained earnings, $152,000. The board of directors declares a 10% stock dividend when the market price of the stock is $51 a share. (a) Present entries to record (1) the declaration of the dividend, capitalizing an amount equal to market value and (2) the issuance of the stock certificates. (b) Determine the equity per share (1) before the stock dividend and (2) after the stock dividend. (c) Donald Clark owned 100 shares of the common stock before the stock dividend was declared. Determine the total equity of his holdings (1) before the stock dividend and (2) after the stock dividend.

17-7. The board of directors of the Pearson Corporation authorized the reduction of par of its common shares from $50 to $10, increasing the number of outstanding shares to 1,000,000. The market price of the stock immediately before the stock split is $165 a share. (a) Determine the number of outstanding shares prior to the stock split. (b) Present the entry required to record the stock split. (c) At approximately what price would a share of stock be expected to sell immediately after the stock split?

17-8. Benton Corporation reports the following results of transactions affecting net income and retained earnings for its first fiscal year of operations ending on August 31:

Income before income tax........	$162,400
Income tax....................	76,200
Cash dividends declared..........	30,000
Appropriation for plant expansion.	20,000

Prepare a retained earnings statement for the first fiscal year ended August 31.

PROBLEMS

The following additional problems for this chapter are located in Appendix B: 17-1B, 17-2B, 17-4B, 17-5B.

17-1A. Differences in accounting methods between those applied to its accounts and financial reports and those used in determining taxable income yielded the following amounts during the first four years of a corporation's operations:

	First Year	Second Year	Third Year	Fourth Year
Income before income tax.	$200,000	$220,000	$230,000	$210,000
Taxable income..........	150,000	180,000	240,000	230,000

The income tax rate for each of the four years was 45% of taxable income and each year's taxes were promptly paid.

Instructions:
(1) Determine for each year the amounts described in the following columnar captions, presenting the information in the form indicated:

Year	Income Tax Deducted on Income Statement	Income Tax Payments for the Year	Deferred Income Tax Payable	
			Year's Addition (Deduction)	Year-End Balance

(2) Total the first three amount columns.

17-2A. Selected transactions completed by the Sawyer Corporation during the current fiscal year are as follows:

Jan. 15. Purchased 1,000 shares of own common stock at $25, recording the stock at cost. (Prior to the purchase there were 30,000 shares of $10 par common stock outstanding.)

Apr. 8. Discovered that a receipt of $400 cash on account from A. L. Hayes had been posted in error to the account of A. L. Haynes. The transaction was recorded correctly in the cash receipts journal.

443

May 10. Declared a semiannual dividend of $1.50 on the 10,000 shares of preferred stock and a 50¢ dividend on the common stock to stockholders of record on May 25, payable on June 8.

June 8. Paid the cash dividends.

Sept. 30. Sold 500 shares of treasury stock at $30, receiving cash.

Nov. 10. Declared semiannual dividends of $1.50 on the preferred stock and 50¢ on the common stock. In addition, a 5% common stock dividend was declared on the common stock outstanding, to be capitalized at the fair market value of the common stock which is estimated at $32.

Dec. 8. Paid the cash dividends and issued the certificates for the common stock dividend.

　　　31. Recorded $78,600 additional federal income tax allocable to net income for the year. Of this amount, $69,000 is a current liability and $9,600 is deferred.

　　　31. The board of directors authorized the appropriation necessitated by the holding of treasury stock.

Instructions:

Record the transactions above in general journal form.

17-3A. The retained earnings accounts of Haven Corporation for the current fiscal year ended December 31 are as follows:

ACCOUNT **APPROPRIATION FOR PLANT EXPANSION**　　　　　ACCOUNT No. 3201

DATE		ITEM	DEBIT	CREDIT	BALANCE DEBIT	BALANCE CREDIT
Jan.	1	Balance				200,000
Dec.	31	Retained earnings	50,000			150,000

ACCOUNT **APPROPRIATION FOR BONDED INDEBTEDNESS**　　　　ACCOUNT No. 3202

DATE		ITEM	DEBIT	CREDIT	BALANCE DEBIT	BALANCE CREDIT
Jan.	1	Balance				150,000
Dec.	31	Retained earnings		30,000		180,000

ACCOUNT **RETAINED EARNINGS**　　　　　　　　　　　　ACCOUNT No. 3301

DATE		ITEM	DEBIT	CREDIT	BALANCE DEBIT	BALANCE CREDIT
Jan.	1	Balance				385,000
Dec.	31	Income summary		162,400		547,400
	31	Appropriation for plant expansion		50,000		597,400
	31	Appropriation for bonded indebtedness	30,000			567,400
	31	Cash dividends	70,000			497,400
	31	Stock dividends	90,000			407,400

444

Account **CASH DIVIDENDS**   Account No. 3302

DATE		ITEM	DEBIT	CREDIT	BALANCE	
					DEBIT	CREDIT
May	30		35,000		35,000	
Nov.	30		35,000		70,000	
Dec.	31	Retained earnings		70,000	——	——

Account **STOCK DIVIDENDS**   Account No. 3303

DATE		ITEM	DEBIT	CREDIT	BALANCE	
					DEBIT	CREDIT
Nov.	30		90,000		90,000	
Dec.	31	Retained earnings		90,000	——	——

Instructions:

Prepare a retained earnings statement for the fiscal year ended December 31.

17-4A. The following data were selected from the records of Judson, Inc., for the current fiscal year ended September 30:

Merchandise inventory (October 1).............	$ 71,300
Merchandise inventory (September 30).........	65,200
Advertising expense..........................	11,400
Depreciation expense — store equipment........	4,100
Sales......................................	690,000
Sales salaries..............................	58,300
Sales commissions...........................	27,250
Office salaries..............................	23,600
Purchases..................................	422,100
Rent expense...............................	18,000
Delivery expense............................	3,500
Store supplies expense.......................	950
Office supplies expense.......................	760
Insurance expense...........................	2,800
Depreciation expense — office equipment........	1,420
Miscellaneous selling expense..................	2,400
Miscellaneous general expense.................	2,970
Interest expense............................	2,150
Uninsured flood loss.........................	20,000
Gain on sale of investments...................	30,000
Income tax:	
Net of amounts allocable to extraordinary items.	42,000
Reduction applicable to uninsured flood loss....	9,600
Applicable to gain on sale of investments.......	9,000

445

Instructions:

Prepare an income statement, concluding with a section for earnings per share in the form illustrated in this chapter. There were 10,000 shares of common stock (no preferred) outstanding throughout the year.

17-5A. The stockholders' equity accounts of Malden Enterprises, Inc., with balances on January 1 of the current fiscal year are as follows:

Common Stock, stated value $5 (100,000 shares
    authorized, 80,000 shares issued)............ $400,000
Paid-In Capital in Excess of Stated Value...... 180,000
Appropriation for Retirement of Debt......... 25,000
Appropriation for Treasury Stock............. 14,000
Retained Earnings......................... 136,000
Treasury Stock (2,000 shares, at cost)......... 14,000

The following selected transactions occurred during the year:

Jan. 10. Paid cash dividends of 30¢ per share on the common stock. The dividend had been properly recorded when declared on December 10 of the preceding fiscal year.
Mar. 15. Sold all of the treasury stock for $30,000 cash.
Apr. 4. Issued 5,000 shares of common stock for $75,000 cash.
    4. Received land with an estimated fair market value of $15,000 from the Midwest Industrial Park Council as a donation.
June 15. Declared a 4% stock dividend on common stock, to be capitalized at the market price of the stock, which is $16 a share.
July 10. Issued the certificates for the dividend declared on June 15.
Nov. 8. Purchased 2,000 shares of treasury stock for $34,000.
Dec. 15. Declared a 30¢ per share dividend on common stock.
    15. The board of directors authorized the addition of $50,000 to the appropriation for retirement of debt.
    15. Increased the appropriation for treasury stock to $34,000.
    31. Closed the credit balance of the income summary account, $113,150.
    31. Closed the two dividends accounts to Retained Earnings.

Instructions:

(1) Open T accounts for the stockholders' equity accounts listed and enter the balances as of January 1. Also open T accounts for the following: Paid-In Capital from Sale of Treasury Stock; Donated Capital; Stock Dividends Distributable; Stock Dividends; Cash Dividends.
(2) Prepare entries in general journal form to record the selected transactions and post to the eleven selected accounts.
(3) Prepare the stockholders' equity section of the balance sheet as of December 31 of the current fiscal year.

17-6A. The stockholders' equity section of the balance sheet of Durban Company as of December 31, the close of the fiscal year, is presented below.

Stockholders' Equity

Paid-in capital:
Common stock, $20 par (50,000 shares
  authorized, 40,000 shares issued less
  2,500 shares of treasury stock acquired
  by donation)..................... $800,000
Premium on common stock............ 160,000
    Total paid-in capital............... $960,000
Retained earnings:
Appropriated for expansion........... $125,000
Unappropriated.................... 390,000
    Total retained earnings............   515,000
Total stockholders' equity.............. $1,475,000

The selected transactions described below occurred during the following fiscal year.

Jan. 20. Sold all of the treasury stock for $70,000.

Mar. 12. Issued 5,000 shares of stock in exchange for land and buildings with an estimated fair market value of $30,000 and $240,000 respectively. The property was encumbered by a mortgage of $130,000 and the company agreed to assume the responsibility for paying the mortgage note.

June 28. Declared a cash dividend of 40¢ per share to stockholders of record on July 12, payable on July 31.

July 31. Paid the cash dividend declared on June 28.

Aug. 15. Received additional land for a plant site valued at $23,000 from the Parkway Industrial Development Council as a donation.

Dec. 15. Issued 1,000 shares of stock to officers as a salary bonus. Market price of the stock is $30 a share. (Debit Officers Salaries.)

   30. Declared a 5% stock dividend on the stock outstanding to stockholders of record on January 12, to be issued on January 31. The stock dividend is to be capitalized at the market price of $30 a share.

   30. Increased the appropriation for expansion by $25,000.

   31. After closing all revenue and expense accounts, Income Summary has a credit balance of $126,000. Closed the account.

   31. Closed the two dividends accounts to Retained Earnings.

Instructions:

(1) Open T accounts for the accounts appearing in the stockholders' equity section of the balance sheet and enter the balances as of January 1. Also open T accounts for the following:
   Donated Capital   Cash Dividends
   Stock Dividends Distributable   Stock Dividends

(2) Prepare entries in general journal form to record the transactions and post to the eight selected accounts.

(3) Prepare the stockholders' equity section of the balance sheet as of December 31, the close of the fiscal year.

(4) Prepare a retained earnings statement for the fiscal year ended December 31.

447

Chapter 18

CORPORATIONS — LONG-TERM LIABILITIES AND INVESTMENTS

FINANCING CORPORATIONS

The acquisition of cash and other assets by a corporation through the issuance of its stock has been discussed in earlier chapters. Expansion of corporate enterprises through the retention of earnings, in some instances accompanied by the issuance of stock dividends, has also been explored. In addition to these two methods of obtaining relatively permanent funds, corporations may also borrow money on a long-term basis through the issuance of notes or bonds. Long-term notes may be issued to relatively few lending agencies or to a single investor such as an insurance company. Bonds are ordinarily sold to underwriters (dealers and brokers in securities) who in turn sell them to investors. Although the discussion that follows will be confined to bonds, the accounting principles involved apply equally to long-term notes.

When funds are borrowed through the issuance of bonds, there is a definite commitment to pay interest and to repay the principal at a specified future date. Bondholders are creditors of the issuing corporation and their claims for interest and for repayment of principal rank ahead of the claims of stockholders.

Many factors influence the incorporators or the board of directors in deciding upon the best means of obtaining funds. The subject will be limited here to a brief illustration of the effect of different financing methods on the income of a corporation and its common stockholders. To illustrate, assume that three different plans for financing a $4,000,000 corporation are under consideration by its organizers, and that in each case the securities will be issued at their par or face amount. The incorporators estimate that the enterprise will earn $680,000 annually, before deducting interest on the bonds and income tax estimated at 50% of income. The tabulation on the next page indicates the amount of earnings that would be available to common stockholders under each of the three plans.

	PLAN 1	PLAN 2	PLAN 3
6% bonds........................	—	—	$2,000,000
7% preferred stock, $50 par...........	—	$2,000,000	1,000,000
Common stock, $10 par..............	$4,000,000	2,000,000	1,000,000
Total.........................	$4,000,000	$4,000,000	$4,000,000
Earnings before interest and income tax..	$ 680,000	$ 680,000	$ 680,000
Deduct interest on bonds.............	—	—	120,000
Income before income tax...........	$ 680,000	$ 680,000	$ 560,000
Deduct income tax..................	340,000	340,000	280,000
Net income......................	$ 340,000	$ 340,000	$ 280,000
Dividends on preferred stock..........	—	140,000	70,000
Available for dividends on common stock.	$ 340,000	$ 200,000	$ 210,000
Earnings per share on common stock..	$ .85	$ 1.00	$ 2.10

If Plan 1 is adopted and the entire financing is from the issuance of common stock, the earnings per share on the common stock would be $.85 per share. Under Plan 2, the effect of using 7% preferred stock for half of the capitalization would result in $1 earnings per common share. The issuance of 6% bonds in Plan 3 with the remaining capitalization split between preferred and common stock would yield a return of $2.10 per share on common stock.

Obviously, under the assumed conditions Plan 3 would be the most attractive for common stockholders. If the anticipated earnings should increase beyond $680,000, the spread between the yield to common stockholders under Plan 1 and Plan 3 would become even greater. But if successively smaller amounts of earnings are assumed, the comparative attractiveness of Plan 2 and Plan 3 decreases. This is illustrated by the tabulation below, in which earnings, before deducting interest and income tax, are assumed to be $280,000 instead of $680,000.

449

	PLAN 1	PLAN 2	PLAN 3
6% bonds........................	—	—	$2,000,000
7% preferred stock, $50 par...........	—	$2,000,000	1,000,000
Common stock, $10 par..............	$4,000,000	2,000,000	1,000,000
Total.........................	$4,000,000	$4,000,000	$4,000,000
Earnings before interest and income tax..	$ 280,000	$ 280,000	$ 280,000
Deduct interest on bonds.............	—	—	120,000
Income before income tax...........	$ 280,000	$ 280,000	$ 160,000
Deduct income tax..................	140,000	140,000	80,000
Net income......................	$ 140,000	$ 140,000	$ 80,000
Dividends on preferred stock..........	—	140,000	70,000
Available for dividends on common stock.	$ 140,000	—	$ 10,000
Earnings per share on common stock..	$ .35	—	$ .10

The preceding analysis focused attention on the effect of the different plans on earnings per share of common stock. There are other factors that must be considered when evaluating different methods of financing. The issuance of bonds represents a fixed annual interest charge that must be paid, in contrast to dividends, which are subject to corporate control. Provision must also be made for the eventual repayment of the principal amount of the bonds, in contrast to the absence of any such obligation to stockholders. On the other hand, a decision to finance entirely by an issuance of common stock would require substantial investment by a single stockholder or small group of stockholders to assure their control of the corporation.

CHARACTERISTICS OF BONDS

When a corporation issues bonds, it executes a contract with the bondholders known as a *bond indenture* or *trust indenture*. The entire issue is divided into a number of individual bonds, which may be of varying denominations. Ordinarily the principal of each bond, also referred to as the *face value*, is $1,000 or a multiple thereof. The interest on bonds may be payable at annual, semiannual, or quarterly intervals. Most bonds provide for payment on a semiannual basis.

Registered bonds may be transferred from one owner to another only by endorsement on the bond certificate, and the issuing corporation must maintain a record of the name and the address of each bondholder. Interest payments are made by check to the owner of record. Title to *bearer bonds*, which are also referred to as *coupon bonds*, is transferred merely by delivery and the issuing corporation is unaware of the identity of the bondholders. Interest coupons for the entire term, in the form of checks or drafts payable to bearer, are attached to the bond certificate. At each interest date the holder detaches the appropriate coupon and presents it at his bank, receiving cash or a credit to his account.

When all bonds of an issue mature at the same time, they are called *term bonds*. If the maturities are spread over several dates, they are called *serial bonds*. For example, one tenth of an issue of $1,000,000, or $100,000, may mature eleven years from the issuance date, another $100,000 may mature twelve years from the issuance date, and so on until the final $100,000 matures at the end of the twentieth year. Bonds that may be exchanged for other securities under specified conditions are called *convertible bonds*. If the issuing corporation reserves the right to redeem the bonds before maturity, they are referred to as *callable bonds*.

A *secured bond* is one that gives the bondholder a claim on particular assets in the event that the issuing corporation fails to meet its obligations on the bonds. The properties mortgaged or pledged may be specific buildings and equipment, the entire plant, or stocks and bonds of other companies owned by the debtor corporation. Bonds issued on the basis of the general credit of the corporation are called *debenture bonds*.

ACCOUNTING FOR BONDS PAYABLE

When a corporation issues bonds, it typically incurs two distinct obligations: (1) to pay the face amount of the bonds at a specified maturity date, and (2) to pay periodic interest at a specified percentage of the face amount. The interest rate specified in the bond indenture is called the *contract* or *coupon* rate, which may differ from the *market* or *effective* rate at the time the bonds are issued. If the market rate is higher than the contract rate, the bonds will sell at a *discount*, or less than their face amount. Conversely, if the market rate is lower than the contract rate the bonds will sell at a *premium*, or more than their face amount.

To illustrate the foregoing, assume that on January 1 a corporation issues for cash $100,000 of 7%, five-year bonds, with interest of $3,500 payable semiannually. The amount received for the bonds will be the sum of (1) the *present value* of $100,000 to be repaid in 5 years plus (2) the *present value* of 10 semiannual interest payments of $3,500 each. The present value of the two items are influenced by the market rate of interest for similar bonds. The issuance price of the bonds is computed in the paragraphs that follow according to various assumptions as to the market rate of interest.

Bonds issued at face amount. If the market rate of interest is exactly the same as the contract rate, the bonds will sell for their face amount. The present value of the 7% five-year bonds, assuming that the market rate is also 7%, can be determined as follows:

451

Present value of $100,000 due in 5 years, at 7% compounded semi-annually..	$ 70,892
Present value of 10 semiannual interest payments of $3,500, at 7% compounded semiannually....................................	29,108
Total present value of the bonds............................	**$100,000**

The basic data for the present values listed above were obtained from compound interest tables. The details of the computations need not concern the student at this juncture; an understanding of the concept of present value is essential, however. The discounting of a bond issue to determine its present value is comparable to the discounting of a note receivable to determine its proceeds (see page 168). The latter is less complex because for a short-term note the interest is not compounded and there is a single interest payment at maturity instead of a series of interest payments.

In the above illustration the first of the two present values, $70,892, is the value of $100,000 five years hence, discounted back to the present at the rate of 7% compounded semiannually. If the bond indenture provided that no separate interest payments would be made during the entire 5-year period, the bonds would be worth only $70,892 at the time of their issuance. To express the concept from a somewhat different point of view, if $70,892 were presently invested with interest to accumulate at the rate of 7%, compounded semiannually, the sum accumulated at the end of 5 years would be $100,000.

The second of the two present value figures, $29,108, is the total value of the ten $3,500 payments, discounted back to the present at the rate of 7% compounded semiannually. It is the sum of the present value of the first interest payment of $3,500 discounted for ½ year, plus the present value of the second interest payment of $3,500 discounted for 1 year, plus the present value of the third interest payment of $3,500 discounted for 1½ years, and so on for each payment, with the tenth payment of $3,500 being discounted for 5 years. Alternatively, the $29,108 can be viewed as the amount deposited now at 7% that would yield ten semiannual withdrawals of $3,500 each, the original deposit of $29,108 being reduced to zero by the final withdrawal.

The entry to record the issuance of the illustrative bonds, in general journal form, is:

```
Jan. 1   Cash.......................................   100,000
             Bonds Payable.............................              100,000
```

At six-month intervals following the issuance of the bonds the interest payment of $3,500 is recorded in the usual manner by a debit to Interest Expense and a credit to Cash. At the maturity date the payment of the principal sum of $100,000 would be recorded by a debit to Bonds Payable and a credit to Cash.

Bonds issued at a discount. If the market rate of interest is 8%, the illustrative 7% bonds will sell at a discount. The present value of the 7%, five-year bonds, assuming a market rate of 8%, is determined as follows:

Present value of $100,000 due in 5 years, at 8% compounded semiannually.........	$67,557
Present value of 10 semiannual interest payments of $3,500, at 8% compounded semiannually.........	28,388
Total present value of the bonds.........	$95,945

It is customary to record the bonds at their face amount, necessitating a separate contra account for the discount. The entry to record the issuance of the bonds, in general journal form, is as follows:

```
Jan. 1   Cash.......................................   95,945
             Discount on Bonds Payable..................    4,055
             Bonds Payable.............................              100,000
```

The $4,055 discount must be amortized as additional interest expense over the five-year life of the bonds. There are two methods of allocating bond discount to the various periods. The simpler of the two methods, sometimes referred to as *straight line*, provides for amortization of discount or premium in equal periodic amounts. Application of this method to the illustration would yield amortization of 1/10 of $4,055, or $405.50, each half year. The amount of the interest expense on the bonds would remain constant for each half year at $3,500 plus $405.50, or $3,905.50.

The more complex method, which is considered to be preferable,[1] is sometimes called the *interest* method. It provides for a constant rate of interest on the *carrying amount* (also called *book value*) of the bonds at the beginning of each period. The interest rate employed in the computation is the market rate as of the date the bonds were issued, and the carrying amount of the bonds is their face amount minus the unamortized discount or plus the unamortized premium. The difference between the interest expense computed in this manner and the amount of the periodic interest payment is the amount of discount or premium to be amortized for the period.[2] Application of this method to the illustration yields the data tabulated below. Note that the interest rates indicated are applicable to one-half year and that all computed amounts have been rounded to dollars.

Interest Payment	A Interest Paid $3\frac{1}{2}\%$ of Face Amount	B Interest Expense 4% of Bond Carrying Amount	C Discount Amortization (B–A)	D Unamortized Discount (D–C)	E Bond Carrying Amount ($100,000–D)
				$4,055	$ 95,945
1	$3,500	$3,838 (4% of $95,945)	$338	3,717	96,283
2	3,500	3,851 (4% of $96,283)	351	3,366	96,634
3	3,500	3,865 (4% of $96,634)	365	3,001	96,999
4	3,500	3,880 (4% of $96,999)	380	2,621	97,379
5	3,500	3,895 (4% of $97,379)	395	2,226	97,774
6	3,500	3,911 (4% of $97,774)	411	1,815	98,185
7	3,500	3,927 (4% of $98,185)	427	1,388	98,612
8	3,500	3,945 (4% of $98,612)	445	943	99,057
9	3,500	3,962 (4% of $99,057)	462	481	99,519
10	3,500	3,981 (4% of $99,519)	481	—	100,000

453

Amortization of discount on bonds payable

The following salient details should be observed in reviewing the above tabulation:

1. The interest paid (column A) remains constant at $3\frac{1}{2}\%$ of $100,000, the face amount of the bonds.

2. The interest expense (column B) is computed at 4% of the bond carrying amount at the beginning of each period, yielding a gradually increasing amount.

3. The excess of the periodic interest expense over the periodic interest payment of $3,500 is the amount of discount to be amortized (column C).

4. The unamortized discount (column D) decreases from the initial balance, $4,055, to a zero balance at maturity.

---

[1]*Opinions of the Accounting Principles Board, No. 21*, "Interest on Receivables and Payables" (New York: American Institute of Certified Public Accountants, 1971), par. 15.
[2]*Opinions of the Accounting Principles Board, No. 12*, "Omnibus Opinion — 1967" (New York: American Institute of Certified Public Accountants, 1967), par. 16.

5. The carrying amount (column E) increases from $95,945, the amount received for the bonds, to $100,000 at maturity.

The entry to record the first interest payment and the amortization of the related amount of discount in general journal form is as follows:

July 1	Interest Expense	3,838	
	Discount on Bonds Payable		338
	Cash		3,500

As an alternative to recording the amortization each time the interest is paid, it may be recorded only at the end of the year. When this procedure is adopted, each interest payment is recorded as a debit to Interest Expense and a credit to Cash. In terms of the illustration, the entry to amortize the discount at the end of the first year would then be a debit to Interest Expense and a credit to Discount on Bonds Payable of $689 ($338 + $351), assuming that the calendar year was also the fiscal year of the corporation.

Bonds issued at a premium. If the market rate of interest is 6%, the illustrative 7% bonds will sell at a premium. Present value data for the 7%, five-year bonds, assuming a market rate of 6%, are presented below:

Present value of $100,000 due in 5 years, at 6% compounded semi-annually	$ 74,409
Present value of 10 semiannual interest payments of $3,500 at 6% compounded semiannually	29,856
Total present value of the bonds	**$104,265**

The entry to record the issuance of the bonds, in general journal form, is as follows:

Jan. 1	Cash	104,265	
	Bonds Payable		100,000
	Premium on Bonds Payable		4,265

Procedures for amortization of the premium and determination of the periodic interest expense are basically the same as those employed for the bonds issued at a discount. Application of the interest method of amortization yields the data tabulated on the next page. The following salient details should be observed in reviewing the tabulation:

1. The interest paid (column A) remains constant at $3\frac{1}{2}\%$ of $100,000, the face amount of the bonds.
2. The interest expense (column B) is computed at 3% of the bond carrying amount at the beginning of each period, yielding a gradually decreasing amount.
3. The excess of the periodic interest paid over the interest expense is the amount of premium to be amortized (column C).
4. The unamortized premium (column D) decreases from the initial balance, $4,265, to a zero balance at the maturity date of the bonds.

Interest Payment	A Interest Paid $3\frac{1}{2}\%$ of Face Amount	B Interest Expense 3% of Bond Carrying Amount	C Premium Amortization (A–B)	D Unamortized Premium (D–C)	E Bond Carrying Amount ($100,000+D)
				$4,265	$104,265
1	$3,500	$3,128 (3% of $104,265)	$372	3,893	103,893
2	3,500	3,117 (3% of $103,893)	383	3,510	103,510
3	3,500	3,105 (3% of $103,510)	395	3,115	103,115
4	3,500	3,093 (3% of $103,115)	407	2,708	102,708
5	3,500	3,081 (3% of $102,708)	419	2,289	102,289
6	3,500	3,069 (3% of $102,289)	431	1,858	101,858
7	3,500	3,056 (3% of $101,858)	444	1,414	101,414
8	3,500	3,042 (3% of $101,414)	458	956	100,956
9	3,500	3,029 (3% of $100,956)	471	485	100,485
10	3,500	3,015 (3% of $100,485)	485	—	100,000

Amortization of premium on bonds payable

5. The carrying amount (column E) decreases from $104,265, the amount received for the bonds, to $100,000 at maturity.

The entry to record the first interest payment and the amortization of the related amount of premium is as follows, in general journal form:

July 1	Interest Expense..............................	3,128	
	Premium on Bonds Payable...................	372	
	Cash.......................................		3,500

BALANCE SHEET PRESENTATION OF BONDS PAYABLE

455

Bonds payable are typically reported on the balance sheet as long-term liabilities. If there are two or more bond issues, separate accounts should be maintained and the details of each should be reported on the balance sheet or in a supporting schedule or notes. As the maturity date of bonds comes within one year of the balance sheet date, they should be transferred to the current liability classification if they are to be paid out of current assets. If they are to be paid with segregated funds or if they are to be replaced with another bond issue, they should remain in the noncurrent category and their anticipated liquidation disclosed in an explanatory note.

It was formerly customary to report discount on bonds payable on the balance sheet as an asset under the caption "Deferred Expenses" or "Deferred Charges." Similarly, a premium was ordinarily reported as a liability under the caption "Deferred Credits." Earlier editions of this textbook, as well as other publications, expressed some criticism of the customary practice. It is now officially recognized that discount on bonds payable is not an asset and premium on bonds payable is not a liability separable from the bond issue. The balance in a discount account should be reported in the balance sheet as a deduction from the related bonds payable; conversely, the balance in a premium account should be reported as an addition to the related bonds payable.[3] The description of the bonds (terms, security, due date, etc.) should also

---

[3]*Opinions of the Accounting Principles Board, No. 21, op. cit.*, par. 16.

include the effective interest rate, either in the financial statements or accompanying notes.[4]

BOND SINKING FUND

The bond indenture may provide that funds for the payment of bonds at maturity be accumulated over the life of the issue. The amounts set aside are kept separate from other assets in a special fund called a *sinking fund*. Cash deposited in the fund is ordinarily invested in income-producing securities. The periodic deposits plus the earnings on the investments should approximately equal the face amount of the bonds at maturity. Control over the fund may be exercised by the corporation or by a *trustee*, which is usually a financial corporation.

When cash is transferred to the sinking fund, an account called Sinking Fund Cash is debited and Cash is credited. The purchase of investments is recorded by a debit to Sinking Fund Investments and a credit to Sinking Fund Cash. As interest or dividends on the investments are received, the cash is debited to Sinking Fund Cash and Sinking Fund Income is credited.

To illustrate the accounting for a bond sinking fund, assume that a corporation issues $100,000 of 10-year bonds dated January 1, with the provision that equal annual deposits be made in the bond sinking fund at the end of each of the 10 years. The fund is expected to be invested in securities that will yield approximately 5% per year. Reference to compound interest tables indicates that annual deposits of $7,950 are sufficient to provide a fund of approximately $100,000 at the end of 10 years. Typical transactions and the related entries affecting a sinking fund are illustrated below in general journal form. It should be noted that they represent only a few of the numerous transactions that might occur during the 10-year period.

Deposit of cash in the fund

A deposit is made at the end of each of the 10 years.

Entry: Sinking Fund Cash........................... 7,950
      Cash....................................... 7,950

Purchase of investments

The time of purchase and the amount invested at any one time vary, depending upon market conditions and the unit price of securities purchased.

Entry: Sinking Fund Investments..................... 7,800
      Sinking Fund Cash.......................... 7,800

Receipt of income from investments

Interest and dividends are received at different times during the year. The amount earned per year increases as the fund increases. The entry summarizes the receipt of income for the year on the securities purchased with the first deposit.

Entry: Sinking Fund Cash........................... 396
      Sinking Fund Income........................ 396

---

[4]*Ibid.*

Sale of investments

Investments may be sold from time to time and the proceeds reinvested. Prior to maturity, all investments are converted into cash. The entry records the sale of all securities at the end of the tenth year.

Entry: Sinking Fund Cash............................ 88,225
          Sinking Fund Investments.................... 87,750
          Gain on Sale of Investments.................. 475

Payments of bonds

The cash available in the fund at the end of the tenth year is composed of the following:

Proceeds from sale of investments (above)........	$ 88,225
Income earned in tenth year..................	4,395
Last annual deposit...........................	7,950
Total.....................................	$100,570

The entry records the payment of the bonds and the transfer of the remaining sinking fund cash to the cash account.

Entry: Bonds Payable............................. 100,000
          Cash.. 570
          Sinking Fund Cash......................... 100,570

In the illustration the amount of the fund exceeded the amount of the liability by $570. This excess was transferred to the regular cash account. If the fund had been less than the amount of the liability, for example $99,500, the regular cash account would have been drawn upon for the $500 deficiency.

Sinking fund income represents earnings of the corporation and is reported in the income statement as "Other income." The cash and the securities comprising the sinking fund are classified in the balance sheet as "Investments," which ordinarily appears immediately below the current assets section.

457

RESTRICTION OF DIVIDENDS

The restriction of dividends during the life of a bond issue is another means of increasing the assurance that the obligation will be paid at maturity. Assuming that the corporation in the preceding example is required by the bond indenture to appropriate $10,000 of retained earnings each year for the 10-year life of the bonds, the following entry would be made annually:

Dec. 31 Retained Earnings......................... 10,000
           Appropriation for Bonded Indebtedness...... 10,000

As was indicated in the preceding chapter, an appropriation has no direct relationship to a sinking fund; each is independent of the other. When there is both a fund and an appropriation for the same purpose, the appropriation may be said to be *funded*.

BOND REDEMPTION

Callable bonds are redeemable by the issuing corporation within the period of time and at the price specified in the bond indenture. Ordinarily the call price is above face value. If the market rate of interest declines subsequent to issuance of the bonds, the corporation may sell new bonds at a lower interest rate and use the funds to redeem the original issue. The reduction of future interest expense is always an incentive to bond redemption. A corporation may also redeem all or a portion of its bonds before maturity by purchasing them on the open market.

When a corporation redeems bonds at a price below their carrying amount, the corporation realizes a gain; if the price is in excess of carrying amount, a loss is incurred. To illustrate redemption, assume that on June 30 a corporation has a bond issue of $100,000 outstanding, on which there is an unamortized premium of $4,000. The corporation has the option of calling the bonds at 105, which it exercises on this date. The entry to record the redemption, in general journal form, is:

June 30	Bonds Payable..........................	100,000	
	Premium on Bonds Payable...............	4,000	
	Loss on Redemption of Bonds..............	1,000	
	Cash..................................		105,000

If the bonds were not callable, the corporation might purchase a portion on the open market. Assuming that the corporation purchases one fourth ($25,000) of the bonds at 96 on June 30, the entry to record the redemption would be as follows, in general journal form:

June 30	Bonds Payable..........................	25,000	
	Premium on Bonds Payable................	1,000	
	Cash..................................		24,000
	Gain on Redemption of Bonds...........		2,000

It should be noted that only the portion of the premium relating to the bonds redeemed is written off. The excess of the carrying amount of the bonds purchased, $26,000, over the cash paid, $24,000, is recognized as a gain.

INVESTMENTS IN STOCKS AND BONDS

The issuance of stocks and bonds, the declaration and the payment of dividends, and other related transactions have thus far been discussed from the standpoint of the issuing corporation. Whenever a corporation records a transaction between itself and the owners of its stock or bonds, there is a reciprocal entry in the accounts of the investor. In this and the following sections of the chapter, attention will be given to the principles underlying the accounting for investments in stocks and bonds.

Investments in corporate securities may be made by individuals, partnerships, industrial corporations, financial corporations such as banks and life insurance companies, and other types of organizations. Some investors are attracted to stocks by the prospects of future price appreciation and increasing dividends, while others prefer the greater safety of principal and certainty of interest afforded by bonds.

Corporate securities may be purchased directly from the issuing corporation or from other investors. Stocks and bonds may be *listed* on an organized exchange, or they may be *unlisted*, in which case they are said to be bought and sold *over the counter*. The services of a broker are usually employed in buying and selling both listed and unlisted securities. The record of transactions on stock exchanges is reported daily in the financial pages of newspapers. This record usually includes data on the volume of sales and the high, low, and closing prices for each security traded during the day. Prices for stocks are quoted in terms of fractional dollars, $1/8$ of a dollar being the usual minimum fraction. Some low-priced stocks are sold in lower fractions of a dollar, such as $1/16$ or $1/32$. A price of $40^3/8$ per share means $40.375; a price of $40^1/2$ means $40.50; and so on. Prices for bonds are quoted as a percentage of the face amount; thus the price of a $1,000 bond quoted at $104^1/2$ would be $1,045.

The cost of securities purchased includes not only the amount paid to the seller but also other costs incident to the purchase, such as broker's commission and postage charges for delivery. When bonds are purchased between interest dates, the purchaser pays the seller the interest accrued from the last interest payment date to the date of purchase. The amount of the interest paid should be debited to Interest Income, as it is an offset against the amount that will be received at the next interest date. To illustrate, assume that a $1,000 bond is purchased at 102 plus a brokerage fee of $5.30 and accrued interest of $10.20. The entry to record the transaction, in general journal form, is presented below. It should be noted that the cost of the bond is recorded in a single account, i.e., the face amount of the bond and the premium paid are not recorded in separate accounts.

459

Apr. 2	Investment in Taylor Co. Bonds..............	1,025.30	
	Interest Income.........................	10.20	
	Cash...................................		1,035.50

When stocks are purchased between dividend dates, there is no separate charge for the pro rata amount of the dividend. Dividends do not accrue from day to day, since they become an obligation of the issuing corporation only when they are declared by the board of directors. The prices of stocks may be affected by the anticipated dividend as the usual declaration date approaches, but this anticipated dividend is only one of many factors that influence stock prices.

TEMPORARY INVESTMENTS

A corporation may have on hand an amount of cash considerably in excess of its immediate requirements, but it may believe that this cash will be needed in operating the business, possibly within the coming year. Rather than allow this excess cash to lie idle until it is actually needed, the corporation may invest all or a portion of it in income-yielding securities. Such securities are known as *temporary investments* or *marketable securities*. Although they may be retained as an investment for a number of years, they continue to be classified as temporary provided: (1) that the securities can be readily sold for cash at any time and (2) that management intends to sell them at such time as the enterprise needs additional cash in carrying on its normal operations.

Securities held as temporary investments are classified on the balance sheet as current assets. They may be listed after "Cash" or combined with cash and described as "Cash and marketable securities," or more specifically as "Cash and certificates of deposit," "Cash and U.S. Government securities," etc. It has been customary to report them at cost unless their market value has declined substantially, in which case they could be valued at the lower of cost or market. A variant has been to retain valuation at cost, with market value stated parenthetically.

Unrealized increases and decreases in the value of securities are not reported as gains and losses for income tax purposes. When securities are sold, the gain or the loss to be recognized for tax purposes is determined by comparing the proceeds from the sale (selling price less commission, etc.) with the cost.

LONG-TERM INVESTMENTS

Investments that are not intended as a ready source of cash in the normal operations of the business are known as *long-term investments*. A business may make long-term investments simply because it has cash that it cannot use in its normal operations, but a corporation is more likely to make long-term investments for other reasons.

It is not unusual for a corporation to purchase stocks or bonds as a means of establishing or maintaining business relations with the issuing company. Such investments are ordinarily held for an indefinite period and are not sold so long as the relationship remains satisfactory. Corporations may also acquire all or a substantial portion of the voting stock of another corporation in order to control its activities. Similarly, a corporation may organize a new corporation for the purpose of marketing a new product or for some other business reason, receiving stock in exchange for the assets transferred to the new corporation. Cash and securities in bond sinking funds are also considered long-term investments, as they are accumulated for the purpose of paying the bond liability.

Securities held as long-term investments are listed in the balance sheet under the caption "Investments," which ordinarily follows the current assets. As with other assets acquired, they are initially recorded at their cost. The nature of any subsequent adjustments to cost vary, depending on the type of security and the relationship between the owner and the issuing corporation. Declines in market value subsequent to acquisition are ordinarily ignored unless the amount is material and is expected to be relatively permanent, in which case an adjustment may be made or the facts disclosed parenthetically or in an accompanying note.

INCOME FROM INVESTMENTS IN STOCKS

Cash dividends declared on capital stock held as a temporary investment may be recorded as a debit to Dividends Receivable and a credit to Dividend Income. The receivable account is then credited when the cash is received. A common alternative is to postpone recognition of the receivable and the income until the dividend income becomes taxable, which occurs when the cash is received.

A dividend in the form of additional shares of stock is ordinarily not income and hence no entry is necessary beyond a notation as to the additional number of shares acquired. The receipt of a stock dividend does, however, affect the *carrying amount* (also called *basis*) of each share of stock. Thus, if a 5-share common stock dividend is received on 100 shares of common stock originally purchased for $4,200 ($42 per share), the unit carrying amount of the 105 shares becomes $4,200 ÷ 105, or $40 per share.

When a corporation owns a sufficient portion of the voting stock of another corporation to exercise significant influence over its operating and financial policies, accounting recognition should be given to the earnings as well as the dividends associated with the stock. The procedures employed in such situations are referred to collectively as the *equity* method of accounting for investments in common stock. The basic features of the equity method are as follows:

1. The investor records its share of the periodic net income of the investee (company whose stock it owns) as an increase in the investment account and as revenue of the period. Conversely, loss for a period is recorded as a decrease in the investment and a loss of the period.

2. The investor records its share of cash or property dividends on the stock as a decrease in the investment account and an increase in the appropriate asset accounts.

To illustrate the foregoing, assume that as of the beginning of the fiscal years of Acme Corporation and Barr Corporation, Acme acquires 60% of the common (voting) stock of Barr for $280,000 in cash, that

461

Barr reports net income of $50,000 for the year, and that Barr declared and paid $20,000 in cash dividends during the year. Entries in the accounts of the investor to record these transactions are presented below, in general journal form.

1. *Record purchase of 60% of Barr Corp. common stock for $280,000 cash*

Entry: Investment in Barr Corp. Stock. 280,000
   Cash   280,000

2. *Record 60% of Barr Corp. net income of $50,000*

Entry: Investment in Barr Corp. Stock. 30,000
   Income of Barr Corp.   30,000

3. *Record 60% of cash dividends of $20,000 paid by Barr Corp.*

Entry: Cash 12,000
   Investment in Barr Corp. Stock.   12,000

The combined effect of recording 60% of Barr Corporation's income and the dividends received was to increase Cash by $12,000, Investment in Barr Corp. Stock by $18,000, and Income of Barr Corp. by $30,000. If the investment had represented a relatively minor percentage instead of 60% of Barr Corporation's outstanding stock, the cost method of accounting would probably have been employed, with only the $12,000 of dividends received being recognized as income from the investment.

However, the equity method of accounting for investments in common stock may be preferable to the cost method even though the investor holds 50% or less of the voting stock of the investee. The criterion is the ability of the investor to influence the policies and affairs of the investee to a significant degree. Evidence of such ability includes, but is not limited to, representation on the board of directors, material intercompany transactions, and interchange of managerial personnel. Guidelines to be applied in making the election are as follows:

> In order to achieve a reasonable degree of uniformity in application, the Board concludes that an investment (direct or indirect) of 20% or more of the voting stock of an investee should lead to a presumption that in the absence of evidence to the contrary an investor has the ability to exercise significant influence over an investee. Conversely, an investment of less than 20% of the voting stock of an investee should lead to a presumption that an investor does not have the ability to exercise significant influence unless such ability can be demonstrated.[5]

INCOME FROM INVESTMENTS IN BONDS

Interest received on bond investments is recorded by a debit to Cash and a credit to Interest Income. At the close of a fiscal year the interest accrued should be recorded by a debit to Interest Receivable and a credit

---

[5]*Opinions of the Accounting Principles Board, No. 18*, "The Equity Method of Accounting For Investments in Common Stock" (New York: American Institute of Certified Public Accountants, 1971), par. 17.

to Interest Income. The adjusting entry should be reversed after the accounts are closed so that all receipts of bond interest during the following year may be recorded without the necessity of referring back to the adjustment data.

The price paid for bonds by investors may be substantially greater or less than their face amount or their original issuance price. If a bond issued when interest rates were relatively low is purchased at a time when interest rates are higher, the price paid may be substantially less than the face amount. Conversely, if the movement of interest rates has been in the opposite direction, the price of a bond may be substantially higher than its face amount. The length of the period of time to maturity will materially affect the price differential, as will conversion and callable provisions, and the financial condition of the debtor.

Differences between the cost and the face amount of bonds acquired as temporary investments need not be amortized over the period held. However, the discount or premium on bonds purchased with the expectation of holding them to maturity should be amortized over their remaining life. The procedures for determining the amount of amortization each period corresponds to those described and illustrated on pages 452 to 455.

As a basis for illustrating the transactions associated with long-term investments in bonds, assume that $50,000 of 5% bonds of Webb Corporation, due in 8¾ years, are purchased on July 1 to yield approximately 7%, paying $43,540 plus interest of $625 accrued from April 1, the date of the last semiannual interest payment. Entries in the accounts of the purchaser at the time of purchase and for the remainder of the fiscal year, ending December 31, are presented below and at the top of the next page, in general journal form.

463

July 1 Payment for bonds and accrued interest

Cost of $50,000 of Webb Corp. bonds..............		$43,540
Interest accrued on $50,000 at 5%, April 1–July 1 (3 months)......................................		625
Total.....................................		$44,165

Entry: Investment in Webb Corp. Bonds............	43,540	
Interest Income........................	625	
Cash................................		44,165

October 1 Receipt of semiannual interest

Interest on $50,000 at 5%, April 1–October 1 (6 months).		$ 1,250

Entry: Cash....................................	1,250	
Interest Income.......................		1,250

December 31 Adjusting entries

Interest accrued on $50,000 at 5%, October 1–December 31 (3 months)...................................		$ 625

Entry: Interest Receivable 625
              Interest Income   625

Discount to be amortized by interest method, July 1–
December 31 (6 months) .... $ 276

Entry: Investment in Webb Corp. Bonds 276
              Interest Income   276

The entries in the interest income account in the above illustration may be summarized as follows:

July 1	Paid accrued interest — 3 months	$ (625)
Oct. 1	Received interest payment — 6 months	1,250
Dec. 31	Recorded accrued interest — 3 months	625
31	Recorded amortization of discount — 6 months	276
	Interest earned — 6 months	$1,526

SALE OF INVESTMENTS

When shares of stock that have been held as temporary or long-term investments are sold, the investment account is credited for the carrying amount of the shares sold and the cash or appropriate receivable account is debited for the proceeds (sales price less commission and other selling costs). The gain or loss on the sale is recorded in an account entitled Gain on Sale of Investments or Loss on Sale of Investments.

A sale of bonds held as temporary investments is recorded in much the same manner as a sale of stocks. However, in addition to the sale proceeds the seller receives the interest accrued since the last interest payment date. When bonds purchased at a discount or premium and held as a long-term investment are sold, the amount of the credit to the investment account is the carrying amount of the bonds rather than their initial cost.

To illustrate the recording of a sale of bonds held as a long-term investment, assume that the Webb Corporation bonds of the preceding example are sold for $47,350 plus accrued interest on June 30, seven years after their purchase. The carrying amount of the bonds (cost plus amortized discount) as of January 1 of the year of sale is $47,953. The entries to record the amortization of discount for the current year and the sale of the bonds are presented below, in general journal form.

June 30 Amortization of discount for current year

Discount to be amortized, January 1–June 30 .... $ 428

Entry: Investment in Webb Corp. Bonds 428
              Interest Income   428

June 30 Receipt of interest and sale of bonds

Interest accrued on $50,000 at 5%, April 1–June 30
(3 months) .... $ 625

Carrying amount of bonds on January 1 of current year .	$47,953	
Discount amortized in current year..................	428	
Carrying amount of bonds on June 30...............	$48,381	
Proceeds of sale...................................	47,350	
Loss on sale......................................	$ 1,031	

Entry:	Cash......................................	47,975	
	Loss on Sale of Investments.................	1,031	
	Interest Income.........................		625
	Investment in Webb Corp. Bonds..........		48,381

CORPORATION FINANCIAL STATEMENTS

Examples of retained earnings statements, the stockholders' equity section of balance sheets, and sections of income statements affected by the corporate form of organization have been presented in preceding chapters. A complete balance sheet of a corporation, containing items discussed in this and preceding chapters, is illustrated on page 466.

Some of the many variations in the form of corporation financial statements have been described and illustrated; additional possibilities will be presented in later chapters. Attention has also been directed to many of the alternatives in terminology used to describe items in the statements. Although accountants and others engaged in various business pursuits are likely to prefer certain forms and terms over other alternatives, it is important that they understand the import of the alternatives. Selected statements from the annual reports of a number of corporations are presented in Appendix C.

465

AUDITORS' REPORT

Responsibility for the form and content of financial statements issued to stockholders and creditors rests primarily with the principal officers of a corporation. Before issuing the annual statements all publicly held corporations, as well as many other corporations, engage independent public accountants, usually CPAs, to conduct an *examination*. Upon completion of the examination, which for large corporations may engage the time of scores of accountants for several weeks or longer, the auditors prepare a *report* (at one time called *certificate*) which then accompanies the financial statements. A typical report briefly describes the scope of the auditors' examination and their opinion as to the fairness of the statements. The phraseology used in the report illustrated at the top of page 467 conforms with general usage.[6]

In most instances the auditors can render a report such as the one illustrated, which may be said to be "unqualified." However, it is

---

[6]*Statements on Auditing Procedure, No. 50,* "Reporting on the Statement of Changes in Financial Position" (New York: American Institute of Certified Public Accountants, 1971). par. 3.

Logan Corporation
Balance Sheet
December 31, 19--

Assets

Current assets:			
Cash...		$ 51,379	
Marketable securities, at cost (market price, $78,000).		70,000	
Accounts and notes receivable....................	$156,000		
Less allowance for doubtful receivables..........	6,000	150,000	
Inventories, at lower of cost (first-in, first-out) or market....................................		192,880	
Prepaid expenses..............................		12,000	
Total current assets.........................			$ 476,259
Investments:			
Bond sinking fund.............................		$ 53,962	
Investment in affiliated company.................		140,000	
Total investments...........................			193,962

	Cost	Accumulated Depreciation	Book Value	
Plant assets:				
Machinery and equipment............	$ 764,400	$166,200	$598,200	
Buildings...........................	220,000	79,955	140,045	
Land.............................	50,000	---	50,000	
Total plant assets.................	$1,034,400	$246,155		788,245

Intangible assets:			
Goodwill......................................		$100,000	
Organization costs............................		18,000	
Total intangible assets.......................			118,000
Total assets....................................			$1,576,466

Liabilities

Current liabilities:			
Accounts payable..............................		$108,810	
Income tax payable...........................		30,500	
Dividends payable.............................		24,000	
Accrued liabilities..............................		11,400	
Total current liabilities.......................			$ 174,710
Long-term liabilities:			
Debenture 6% bonds payable, due December 31, 19--		$250,000	
Less unamortized discount....................		5,600	244,400
Deferred credits:			
Deferred income tax payable....................			25,500
Total liabilities....................................			$ 444,610

Stockholders' Equity

Paid-in capital:			
Common stock, $20 par (50,000 shares authorized, 20,000 shares issued).......................		$400,000	
Premium on common stock.......................		320,000	
Total paid-in capital.........................			$720,000
Retained earnings:			
Appropriated:			
For bonded indebtedness.............	$ 60,000		
For plant expansion.................	150,000	$210,000	
Unappropriated...............................		201,856	
Total retained earnings.......................		411,856	
Total stockholders' equity.........................			1,131,856
Total liabilities and stockholders' equity.............			$1,576,466

Balance
sheet of a
corporation

To the Stockholders of Logan Corporation:

We have examined the balance sheet of Logan Corporation as of December 31, 19-- and the related statements of income and retained earnings and changes in financial position for the year then ended. Our examination was made in accordance with generally accepted auditing standards, and accordingly included such tests of the accounting records and such other auditing procedures as we considered necessary in the circumstances.

In our opinion, the aforementioned financial statements present fairly the financial position of Logan Corporation at December 31, 19--, and the results of its operations and the changes in its financial position for the year then ended, in conformity with generally accepted accounting principles applied on a basis consistent with that of the preceding year.

Cincinnati, Ohio
January 28, 19--

Allen & White
Certified Public Accountants

Auditors' report

possible that accounting methods employed by a client do not conform with generally accepted accounting principles or that a client has not been consistent in the application of principles. In such cases a "qualified" opinion may be rendered, in which the exception is briefly described and sometimes presented in greater detail in a separate note. If the effect of the departure from accepted principles or change in principles is sufficiently material, the opinion may be "adverse."

467

The reporting responsibilities of independent CPAs in attesting to the fairness of financial statements is described as follows:

The report shall either contain an expression of opinion regarding the financial statements, taken as a whole, or an assertion to the effect that an opinion cannot be expressed. When an over-all opinion cannot be expressed, the reasons therefor should be stated. In all cases where an auditor's name is associated with financial statements the report should contain a clear-cut indication of the character of the auditor's examination, if any, and the degree of responsibility he is taking.[7]

Professional accountants cannot disregard the foregoing auditing standard without seriously jeopardizing their reputations. Indeed, they also risk legal action by persons who may suffer loss from reliance on erroneous statements for which they have rendered an opinion.

QUESTIONS

1. Contrast the status of interest on bonds payable and cash dividends on stock in determining the income tax of corporations making such payments.

2. How are interest payments made to holders of (a) registered bonds and (b) bearer or coupon bonds?

---

[7]*Statements on Auditing Procedure, No. 33*, "Auditing Standards and Procedures" (New York: American Institute of Certified Public Accountants, 1963), Chapter 10, par. 1.

3. Differentiate between term bonds and serial bonds.

4. Explain the meaning of each of the following terms as they relate to a bond issue: (a) callable, (b) convertible, (c) secured, and (d) debenture.

5. Describe the two distinct obligations incurred by a corporation when issuing bonds.

6. A corporation issues $500,000 of 7% coupon bonds to yield interest at the rate of 7½%. (a) Was the amount of cash received from the sale of the bonds greater than $500,000 or less than $500,000? (b) Identify the following terms related to the bond issue: (1) face amount, (2) contract rate of interest, (3) market rate of interest, (4) maturity amount, (5) effective rate of interest, and (6) coupon rate of interest.

7. What is the present value of $100 due in 6 months, if the market rate of interest is 8%?

8. If the bonds payable account has a balance of $500,000 and the premium on bonds payable account has a balance of $31,400, what is the carrying amount of the bonds?

9. The following data are related to a $200,000, 7% bond issue for a selected semiannual interest period:

Bond carrying amount at beginning of period.	$196,000
Interest paid at end of period.	7,000
Interest expense allocable to the period.	7,840

(a) Were the bonds issued at a discount or at a premium? (b) What is the balance of the discount or premium account at the beginning of the period? (c) How much amortization of discount or premium is allocable to the period?

10. Indicate the title of (a) the account to be debited and (b) the account to be credited in the entry for amortization of (1) discount on bonds payable and (2) premium on bonds payable.

11. Under what circumstances would Bonds Payable be reported in the balance sheet as a current liability?

12. Indicate how the following accounts should be reported in the balance sheet: (a) Discount on Bonds Payable, and (b) Premium on Bonds Payable.

13. What is the purpose of a bond sinking fund?

14. What is the purpose of establishing an appropriation of retained earnings for bonded indebtedness?

15. When there is both a fund and an appropriation for bonded indebtedness, what is the additional descriptive term that may be applied to the appropriation?

16. Under what caption would each of the following accounts be reported on the balance sheet: (a) Sinking Fund Cash; (b) Sinking Fund Investments; (c) Appropriation for Bonded Indebtedness?

17. Bonds Payable has a balance of $100,000 and Premium on Bonds Payable has a balance of $2,000. If the issuing corporation redeems the bonds at 104, what is the amount of gain or loss on redemption?

18. The quoted price of Acme Corp. bonds on August 1 is 101¼. On the same day the interest accrued is 2% of the face amount. (a) Does the quoted price include accrued interest? (b) If $10,000 face amount of Acme Corp. bonds is purchased on August 1 at the quoted price what is the cost of the bonds, exclusive of commission?

19. When stocks are purchased between dividend dates, does the purchaser pay the seller the dividend accrued since the last dividend payment date? Explain.

20. Under what caption should each of the following be reported on the balance sheet: (a) securities held as a temporary investment; (b) securities held as a long-term investment?

21. An investor sells a $10,000 bond of X Corp., carried at $9,500, for $10,500 plus accrued interest of $300. The broker remits the balance due after deducting a commission of $50. Indicate the debits and credits required to record the transaction.

22. A stockholder owning 10 shares of Baron Co. common stock acquired at a total cost of $660 receives a common stock dividend of 1 share. What is the carrying amount per share after the stock dividend?

EXERCISES

18-1. Two companies are financed as follows:

	Able Co.	Best, Inc.
Bonds Payable, 8% (issued at face value)	$ 250,000	$500,000
Convertible Preferred 7% Stock	250,000	500,000
Common Stock, $50 par	1,000,000	500,000

Income tax is estimated at 50% of income. Determine for each company the earnings per share of common stock, assuming the income before bond interest and income tax for each company to be (a) $115,000, (b) $155,000, and (c) $265,000.

18-2. The Osborn Company issued $1,000,000 of 10-year, 8% callable bonds on June 1, 1973, with interest payable on June 1 and December 1. The fiscal year of the company is the calendar year. Present entries, in general journal form, for the following selected transactions:

1973
June 1. Issued the bonds for cash at their face amount.
Dec. 1. Paid the interest.
     31. Recorded accrued interest for one month (round to nearest dollar).
     31. Closed the interest expense account.
1974
Jan. 1. Reversed the adjusting entry for accrued interest.
June 1. Paid the interest.
1978
June 1. Called the bond issue at 104, the rate provided in the bond indenture. (Omit entry for payment of interest.)

18-3. On the first day of its fiscal year, Merced Corporation issued $500,000 of 10-year, 9% bonds at an effective interest rate of 8%, receiving cash of $533,975. Interest is payable semiannually.

    (a) Present the entries, in general journal form, to record the following:
        (1) Sale of the bonds.
        (2) First semiannual interest payment. (Amortization of premium is to be recorded annually.)
        (3) Amortization of $2,328 of premium at the end of the first year.
    (b) Determine the amount of the bond interest expense for the first year.

18-4. The Paragon Corporation issued $500,000 of 20-year bonds on the first day of the fiscal year. The bond indenture provides that a sinking fund be accumulated by 20 annual deposits of $17,000, beginning at the end of the first year, and that dividends be restricted by annual appropriations of retained earnings, each equal to 1/20 of the maturity value of the bonds.

Present the entries, in general journal form, to record the following selected transactions related to the bond issue:

    (a) The required amount is deposited in the sinking fund.
    (b) Investments in securities from the first sinking fund deposit total $16,810.
    (c) The required appropriation is made at the end of the year.
    (d) The sinking fund earned $843 during the year following the first deposit (summarizing entry).
    (e) The bonds are paid at maturity and excess cash of $1,640 in the fund is transferred to the cash account.

18-5. On April 10, Leander Corporation acquired 100 shares of Fox Electric Co. common stock at 46⅝ plus commission and postage charges of $40. On July 25, a cash dividend of $1 per share and a 10% stock dividend were received. On November 10, 40 shares were sold at 48¼ less commission and postage charges of $23. Present entries in general journal form to record (a) purchase of the stock, (b) receipt of the dividends, and (c) sale of the 40 shares.

18-6. Present entries, in general journal form, to record the selected transactions of Morton Corporation described below. The fiscal year of the company is the calendar year.

    (a) Purchased for cash $100,000 of JBT Corporation 6% bonds at 93 plus accrued interest of $1,000.
    (b) Received first semiannual interest.
    (c) Amortized $620 discount on the bond investment at the end of the year.
    (d) Sold the bonds at 95½ plus accrued interest of $1,500. The bonds were carried at $96,894 at the time of the sale.

18-7. On the basis of the following data, prepare an income statement for the Banner Company for the current fiscal year ended June 30, indicating earnings per share for the 20,000 shares of common stock (no preferred stock) outstanding during the year:

Cost of merchandise sold	$580,000
Selling expenses	102,300
General expenses	71,400
Gain on sale of stock in affiliated corporation	100,000
Income tax (including $30,000 applicable to extraordinary gain on sale of stock in affiliated corporation)	127,000
Sales	976,000
Interest expense	6,500

PROBLEMS

The following additional problems for this chapter are located in Appendix B: 18-1B, 18-2B, 18-3B, 18-5B.

18-1A. The board of directors of Witter Electronics is planning an expansion of plant facilities expected to cost $2,000,000. The board is undecided about the method of financing this expansion and has two plans under consideration:

Plan A. Issue $2,000,000 of 20-year, 8% bonds at face amount.

Plan B. Issue an additional 50,000 shares of no-par common stock at $40 per share.

The condensed balance sheet of the company at the end of the most recent fiscal year is presented below.

Witter Electronics
Balance Sheet
December 31, 19--

Assets		Liabilities and Capital	
Current assets..........	$1,170,000	Current liabilities.......	$1,020,000
Plant assets.............	4,830,000	Common stock (100,000 shares issued).........	3,500,000
		Retained earnings.......	1,480,000
Total assets...........	$6,000,000	Total liabilities and capital	$6,000,000

Net income has remained relatively constant over the past several years. The expansion program is expected to increase yearly income before bond interest and income tax, from $660,000 to $960,000. Assume an income tax rate of 50%.

Instructions:

(1) Prepare a tabulation indicating the expected earnings per share on common stock under each plan.

(2) List factors other than earnings per share that the board should consider in evaluating the two plans.

(3) Which plan offers the greater benefit to the present stockholders? Give reasons for your opinion.

18-2A. The following transactions were completed by Central Gas Co.:

1973

Sept. 30. Issued $1,000,000 of 20-year, 7% callable bonds dated September 30, 1973, for cash of $901,036. Interest is payable semiannually on September 30 and March 31.

Dec. 31. Recorded the adjusting entry for interest payable.

   31. Recorded amortization of $521 discount on the bonds.

   31. Closed the interest expense account.

1974

Jan. 1. Reversed the adjusting entry for interest payable.

Mar. 31. Paid the semiannual interest on the bonds.

Sept. 30. Paid the semiannual interest on the bonds.

Dec. 31. Recorded the adjusting entry for interest payable.

   31. Recorded amortization of $2,167 discount on the bonds.

   31. Closed the interest expense account.

471

1988
Sept. 30. Called the bonds at 101¼. Recorded amortization of discount for the 9-month period, $4,809, leaving a balance of $40,554 in the discount account. Recorded the redemption of the bonds.

Instructions:

(1) Record the foregoing transactions in general journal form.
(2) Indicate the amount of the interest expense in (a) 1973 and (b) 1974.
(3) Determine the effective interest rate (divide the interest expense for 1973 by the bond carrying amount at time of issuance) and express as an annual rate.
(4) Determine the carrying amount of the bonds as of December 31, 1974.

18-3A. During 1973 and 1974 Valley Construction Company completed the transactions described below, relating to its $2,000,000 issue of 10-year, 9% bonds dated March 1, 1973. Interest is payable on March 1 and September 1. The corporation's fiscal year is the calendar year.

1973
Mar. 1. Sold the bond issue for $2,135,903 cash.
Sept. 1. Paid the semiannual interest on the bonds.
Dec. 31. Recorded the adjusting entry for interest payable.
      31. Recorded amortization of $7,728 of bond premium.
      31. Deposited $126,000 in a bond sinking fund.
      31. Appropriated $166,667 of retained earnings for bonded indebtedness.
      31. Closed the interest expense account.

1974
Jan. 1. Reversed the adjustment for interest payable.
      8. Purchased various securities with sinking fund cash, cost $125,420.
Mar. 1. Paid the semiannual interest on the bonds.
Sept. 1. Paid the semiannual interest on the bonds.
Dec. 31. Recorded the receipt of $7,520 of income on sinking fund securities, depositing the cash in the sinking fund.
      31. Recorded the adjusting entry for interest payable.
      31. Recorded amortization of $9,940 of bond premium.
      31. Deposited $152,000 cash in the sinking fund.
      31. Appropriated $200,000 of retained earnings for bonded indebtedness.
      31. Closed the interest expense account.

Instructions:

(1) Record the foregoing transactions in general journal form.
(2) Prepare a columnar table, using the headings presented below, and list the information for each of the two years.

					Account Balances at End of Year		
					Sinking Fund		Appropriation
	Bond Interest Expense	Sinking Fund Income	Bonds	Premium			for Bonded
Year	for Year	for Year	Payable	on Bonds	Cash	Investments	Indebtedness

18-4A. The board of directors of Miramar, Inc., has asked you to review the rough draft of the balance sheet presented on the next page.

During the course of your review and examination of the accounts and records, you assemble the following relevant data:

(a) Marketable securities are stated at cost; the market price is $94,100.
(b) Accounts receivable, equipment, buildings, land, and goodwill are stated at cost. Provisions for doubtful accounts and depreciation have

Miramar, Inc.
Balance Sheet
June 30, 19——

Assets

Current assets:

Cash..............................		$ 97,600	
Marketable securities..................		90,000	
Investment in affiliated company.......		156,300	
Treasury stock.......................	$ 25,750		
Deduct reserve for treasury stock purchased.........................	25,750	——	
Accounts receivable..................	$167,500		
Deduct accounts payable............	130,500	37,000	
Inventories..........................	$245,000		
Deduct reserve for possible price declines..........................	15,000	230,000	
Discount on bonds payable............		25,000	
Total current assets.................			$ 635,900

Plant assets:

Equipment...........................		$375,000	
Buildings............................	$450,000		
Deduct reserve for plant expansion...	100,000	350,000	
Land................................		70,000	
Goodwill............................		45,000	
Prepaid expenses.....................		12,500	
Total plant assets..................			852,500
Total assets.........................			$1,488,400

Liabilities

Cash dividends payable.................		$ 21,000	
Stock dividends distributable............		12,000	
Accrued liabilities......................		15,600	
Bonds payable........................	$500,000		
Deduct bond sinking fund.............	311,400	188,600	
Total liabilities........................			$ 237,200

Stockholders' Equity

Paid-in capital:

Common stock.......................		$620,000	

Retained earnings and reserves:

Premium on common stock............	$ 64,000		
Reserve for doubtful accounts..........	18,500		
Reserve for depreciation — equipment..	132,000		
Reserve for depreciation — buildings....	115,000		
Reserve for income taxes..............	52,600		
Retained earnings....................	249,100	631,200	
Total stockholders' equity..............			1,251,200
Total liabilities and stockholders' equity...			$1,488,400

473

been recorded correctly. The investment in the affiliated company is accounted for by the equity method.

(c) Treasury stock is composed of 1,000 shares purchased at 25¾ a share.

(d) Inventories are stated at the lower of cost (first-in, first-out) or market.

(e) The stock dividend distributable represents a 2% stock dividend declared on June 30.

(f) Bonds payable (20-year) are due 7 years from the balance sheet date. They are secured by a first mortgage and bear 6½% interest.

(g) The common stock is $20 par; 50,000 shares are authorized, 31,000 shares have been issued.

(h) The reserve for income taxes is the balance due on the estimated liability for taxes on income of the current fiscal year ended June 30.

Instructions:

Present a revised balance sheet in good order. Titles of items should be changed and additional descriptive data inserted where appropriate.

18-5A. The following transactions relate to certain securities acquired by Burton and Company, whose fiscal year ends on December 31:

1973

Apr.   1. Purchased $100,000 of Farr Company 10-year, 8% coupon bonds dated April 1, 1973, directly from the issuing company for $107,106.

June 25. Purchased 600 common shares of Link Corporation at 44¼ plus commission and other costs of $225.

Sept. 15. Received the regular cash dividend of 50¢ a share on Link Corporation stock.

Oct.   1. Deposited the coupons for semiannual interest on Farr Company bonds.

Dec. 15. Received the regular cash dividend of 50¢ plus an extra dividend of 75¢ a share on Link Corporation stock.

      31. Recorded the adjustment for interest receivable on the Farr Company bonds.

      31. Recorded the amortization of premium of $381 on the Farr Company bonds.

(Assume that all intervening transactions and adjustments have been recorded properly, and that the number of bonds and shares of stocks owned have not changed from December 31, 1973, to December 31, 1976.)

1977

Jan.   1. Reversed the adjustment of December 31, 1976, for interest receivable on the Farr Company bonds.

Mar. 15. Received the regular cash dividend of 50¢ a share and a 5% stock dividend on the Link Corporation stock.

Apr.   1. Deposited coupons for semiannual interest on the Farr Company bonds.

June   1. Sold one half of the Farr Company bonds at 102⅜ plus accrued interest (round interest to dollars). The broker deducted $202.50 for commission, etc., remitting the balance. Before recording the sale, record premium amortization of $135 on one half of the bonds, reducing the carrying amount of those bonds to $52,361.

      15. Received the regular cash dividend at the new rate of 60¢ a share on the Link Corporation stock.

Sept. 2. Sold 100 shares of Link Corporation stock at 51¾. The broker deducted commission and other costs of $45, remitting the balance.

Oct.   1. Deposited coupons for semiannual interest on the remaining Farr Company bonds.

Dec. 31. Recorded the adjustment for interest receivable on the remaining Farr Company bonds.

31. Recorded the amortization of premium of $331 on the remaining Farr Company bonds.

Instructions:

(1) Record the foregoing transactions in general journal form.

(2) Determine the amount of interest earned on the bonds in 1973.

(3) Determine the amount of interest earned on the bonds in 1977.

18-6A. The accounts in the ledger of Nash Company, Inc., with the balances on December 31, the end of the current fiscal year, are as follows:

Cash	$ 78,600
Accounts Receivable	164,500
Allowance for Doubtful Accounts	1,200
Merchandise Inventory	175,000
Prepaid Insurance	9,400
Store Supplies	4,450
Bond Sinking Fund	89,850
Store Equipment	390,000
Accumulated Depreciation — Store Equipment	120,000
Office Equipment	185,000
Accumulated Depreciation — Office Equipment	73,625
Organization Costs	8,000
Accounts Payable	64,900
Interest Payable	——
Income Tax Payable	——
First Mortgage 8% Bonds Payable	200,000
Premium on Bonds Payable	9,985
Deferred Income Tax Payable	16,400
Common Stock, $10 par	250,000
Premium on Common Stock	50,000
Appropriation for Bonded Indebtedness	115,000
Dividends	25,000
Retained Earnings	117,560
Income Summary	——
Sales	1,800,000
Purchases	1,325,000
Purchases Discount	16,300
Sales Salaries and Commissions	115,000
Advertising Expense	30,200
Depreciation Expense — Store Equipment	——
Store Supplies Expense	——
Miscellaneous Selling Expense	9,650
Office and Officers' Salaries	108,000
Rent Expense	40,000
Depreciation Expense — Office Equipment	——
Uncollectible Accounts Expense	——
Insurance Expense	——
Miscellaneous General Expense	6,400
Interest Expense	12,000
Sinking Fund Income	4,180
Rent Income	2,400
Uninsured Loss from Vandalism	12,500
Income Tax	53,000

475

The data needed for year-end adjustments on December 31 are as follows:

Merchandise inventory on December 31 (at cost, first-in, first-out)...	$192,000
Uncollectible accounts expense is estimated at ½ of 1% of sales...	—
Insurance expired during the year............................	4,850
Store supplies inventory on December 31......................	1,900
Depreciation for the current year on:	
Store equipment..	19,600
Office equipment...	12,100
Interest on bonds is payable on April 1 and October 1...........	—
Bonds payable are due on April 1 of the sixth year from the current year. Premium to be amortized...........................	1,225
Additional income tax due for the current year................	3,200

Instructions:

(1) Prepare an eight-column work sheet for the fiscal year ended December 31.

(2) Prepare an income statement, indicating per share data where appropriate. The reduction in income tax applicable to the uninsured loss from vandalism is $6,000; hence, the income tax applicable to income before extraordinary items is $62,200.

(3) Prepare a retained earnings statement. The balance of unappropriated retained earnings on January 1 was $137,560; the appropriation for bonded indebtedness was increased by $20,000 in December.

(4) Prepare a balance sheet. There were 25,000 shares of stock authorized and issued during the entire year.

Chapter 19

DEPARTMENTS AND BRANCHES

SEGMENTATION OF OPERATIONS

The activities of many business enterprises are performed by separate segments such as departments, divisions, and branches. It is also not unusual for the units of an operating entity to be organized as separate corporations, with common ownership of the stock and common management at the top. Selection of the organizational structure and the segmentation is often affected by size, volume of business, diversity of activity, and geographic distribution of operations. In any event the managers of segmented enterprises need accounting reports designed to aid them in planning, controlling, and evaluating the performance of the various segments.

Segmentation may occur in service enterprises as well as in businesses engaged primarily in merchandising or manufacturing activities. Segmented accounting reports are useful to management regardless of the type of activity. A merchandising enterprise is used as the basis for discussion and illustration in this chapter. The special accounting concepts and procedures applicable to multiple corporations with common ownership are discussed in a later chapter.

ACCOUNTING FOR DEPARTMENTAL OPERATIONS

Departmental accounting is more likely to be used by a large business than by a small one. Some degree of departmentalization may be employed by a small enterprise, however. For example, the owner of a one-man real estate and property insurance agency could account separately for real estate commissions and for insurance commissions. Analysis of the division of his time between the two activities and of his revenue and expenses by type of activity may indicate the desirability of devoting more time to one department and less to the other.

Departmental accounting for a large enterprise is likely to be both feasible and desirable. In a modern department store, for example, there are a number of distinct departments, each under the control of a departmental manager. Departmentalization of accounting and reporting facilitates the assignment of responsibility for departmental operations to departmental managers. It assists top management both in evaluating the relative operating efficiencies of individual departments and in planning future operations.

ACCOUNTING REPORTS FOR DEPARTMENTAL OPERATIONS

Accounting reports for departmental operations are generally limited to income statements. Although departmental income statements are not ordinarily issued to stockholders or others outside the management group, the trend is toward imparting more information along such lines. The degree to which departmental accounting may be adopted for a merchandising enterprise varies. Analysis of operations by departments may end with the determination of gross profit on sales or it may extend through the determination of net income. An income statement that includes a departmental breakdown of revenue and expenses categorized by responsibility for the incurrence of costs has been widely used in recent years. The most common departmental income statements are described in the paragraphs that follow.

GROSS PROFIT BY DEPARTMENTS

For a merchandising enterprise, the gross profit on sales is one of the most significant figures in the income statement. Since the sales and the cost of merchandise sold are both, to a large extent, controlled by departmental management, the reporting of gross profit by departments is useful in cost analysis and control. In addition, such reports assist management in directing its efforts toward obtaining a mix of sales that will maximize profits. After studying the reports, management may decide to change sales or purchases policies, curtail or expand operations, or shift personnel to achieve a higher gross profit for each department. Caution must be exercised in the use of such reports to insure that proposed changes affecting gross profit do not have an adverse effect on net income. For example, a change that increases gross profit but results in an even greater increase in operating expenses would decrease net income.

In order to determine gross profit on sales by departments, it is necessary to determine by departments each element entering into gross profit. There are two basic methods of doing this: (1) setting up departmental accounts and identifying each element by department at the time of the transaction, or (2) maintaining only one account for the element and then allocating it among the departments at the time the income statement is prepared. Ordinarily, the first method is used unless the time required in analyzing each transaction is too great. Allocation among departments at the end of a period is likely to yield less accurate results than the first method, but some degree of accuracy may be sacrificed to obtain a commensurate saving of time and expense.

The elements that must be departmentalized in order to determine gross profit by departments are merchandise inventory, purchases, sales, and the related cash discounts and returns and allowances. Departmental accounts may be maintained for each element so that the entries may be classified by department at the time the transactions are recorded. This can be accomplished by providing special departmental columns in the appropriate journals. For example, in a furniture store that sells furniture and carpeting, the sales journal may have a credit column for Furniture Sales and a credit column for Carpet Sales. To facilitate the journalizing of departmental transactions, the supporting documents such as sales invoices, vouchers, and cash register readings must identify the department affected by each transaction. Postings to departmental accounts from the special journals follow the procedures described in earlier chapters.

An income statement showing gross profit by departments for the York Company, which has two sales departments, appears on page 480. For illustrative purposes, the operating expenses are shown in condensed form; ordinarily they would be listed in detail.

479

NET INCOME BY DEPARTMENTS

Departmental reporting of income may be extended to various points, such as gross profit less selling expenses (gross selling profit), gross profit less all operating expenses (operating income), income before income tax, or net income. The underlying principle is the same for all degrees of departmentalization, namely, to assign to each department the related revenues and that portion of the expenses incurred for its benefit.

Some expenses may be easily identified with the department benefited. For example, if each salesperson is restricted to a particular sales department, the sales salaries may be assigned to the appropriate departmental salary accounts each time the payroll is prepared. On the other hand, the salaries of company officers, executives, and office personnel are not identifiable with specific sales departments and must therefore be allocated on an equitable basis.

Many accountants prefer to apportion all expenses to departments only at the end of the accounting period. When this is done, there is no need for departmental expense accounts in the general ledger and fewer postings are required. The apportionments may be made on a work sheet, which serves as the basis for preparing the departmental income statement.

480

Income statement
departmentalized
through
gross profit

York Company
Income Statement
For Year Ended December 31, 19--

	Department A	Department B	Total
Revenue from sales:			
Sales	$280,000	$120,000	$400,000
Less sales returns and allowances	7,600	3,100	10,700
Net sales	$272,400	$116,900	$389,300
Cost of merchandise sold:			
Merchandise inventory, January 1, 19--	$ 40,300	$ 30,700	$ 71,000
Purchases	$152,900	$ 87,300	$240,200
Less purchases discount	2,800	1,300	4,100
	150,100	86,000	236,100
Merchandise available for sale	$190,400	$116,700	$307,100
Less merchandise inventory, December 31, 19--	41,900	39,100	81,000
Cost of merchandise sold	148,500	77,600	226,100
Gross profit on sales	$123,900	$ 39,300	$163,200
Operating expenses:			
Selling expenses			$ 54,700
General expenses			53,900
Total operating expenses			108,600
Income from operations			$ 54,600
Other expense:			
Interest expense			1,200
Income before income tax			$ 53,400
Income tax			19,132
Net income			$ 34,268

APORTIONMENT OF OPERATING EXPENSES

As was indicated in the preceding section, some operating expenses are directly identifiable with particular departments and some are not. When operating expenses are allocated, they should be apportioned to the respective departments as nearly as possible in accordance with the cost of services rendered to them. Determining the amount of an expense chargeable to each department is not always a simple matter. In the first place, it requires the exercise of judgment; and accountants of equal ability may well differ in their opinions as to the proper basis for apportionment. Second, the cost of collecting data for use in making an apportionment must be kept within reasonable bounds; consequently, information that is readily available and is substantially reliable may be used in lieu of more accurate information that would be more costly to collect.

To illustrate the apportionment of operating expenses, assume that the York Company extends its departmentalization through income from operations. The company's operating expenses for the calendar year and the methods used in apportioning them are presented in the paragraphs that follow.

Sales Salaries is apportioned to the two departments in accordance with the distributions shown in the payroll records. Of the $42,000 total in the account, $27,000 is chargeable to Department A and $15,000 is chargeable to Department B.

Advertising Expense, covering billboard advertising and newspaper advertising, is apportioned according to the amount of advertising incurred for each department. The billboard advertising totaling $2,000 emphasizes the name and the location of the company. This expense is allocated on the basis of sales, the assumption being that this basis represents a fair allocation of billboard advertising to each department. Analysis of the newspaper space costing $7,000 indicates that 65% of the space was devoted to Department A and 35% to Department B. The apportionment of the total advertising expense is indicated in the tabulation below.

	TOTAL		DEPARTMENT A		DEPARTMENT B	
Sales — dollars..........	$400,000		$280,000		$120,000	
Sales — percent..........	100%		70%		30%	
Billboard advertising....		$2,000		$1,400		$ 600
Newspaper space—percent.	100%		65%		35%	
Newspaper advertising..		7,000		4,550		2,450
Advertising expense		$9,000		$5,950		$3,050

Depreciation of Store Equipment is apportioned in accordance with the average cost of the equipment in each of the two departments. The computations for the apportionment of the depreciation expense are given below.

	TOTAL	DEPARTMENT A	DEPARTMENT B
Cost of store equipment:			
January 1................	$13,600	$ 8,800	$ 4,800
December 31..............	14,400	8,000	6,400
Total.................	$28,000	$16,800	$11,200
Average.................	$14,000	$ 8,400	$ 5,600
Percent.................	100%	60%	40%
Depreciation expense.........	$ 1,650	$ 990	$ 660

Officers' Salaries and *Office Salaries* are apportioned on the basis of the relative amount of time devoted to each department by the officers and by the office personnel. Obviously, this can be only an approximation. The number of sales transactions may have some bearing on the matter, as may billing and collection procedures and other factors such as promotional campaigns that might vary from period to period. Of the total officers' salaries of $26,000 and office salaries of $9,000, it is estimated that 60%, or $15,600 and $5,400 respectively, is chargeable to Department A and that 40%, or $10,400 and $3,600 respectively, is chargeable to Department B.

Rent Expense and *Heating and Lighting Expense* are usually apportioned on the basis of the floor space devoted to each department. In apportioning rent expense for a multistory building, differences in the value of the various floors and locations may be taken into account. For example, the space near the main entrance of a department store is more valuable than the same amount of floor space located far from the elevator on the sixth floor. For York Company, rent expense is apportioned on the basis of floor space used because there is no significant difference in the value of the floor areas used by each department. In allocating heating and lighting expense, it is assumed that the number of lights, their wattage, and the extent of use are uniform throughout the sales departments. If there are major variations and the total lighting expense is material, further analysis and separate apportionment may be advisable. The rent expense and the heating and lighting expense are apportioned as follows:

	TOTAL	DEPARTMENT A	DEPARTMENT B
Floor space, square feet........	160,000	104,000	56,000
Percent...................	100%	65%	35%
Rent expense..............	$7,200	$4,680	$2,520
Heating and lighting expense.	$2,400	$1,560	$ 840

Property Tax Expense and *Insurance Expense* are related primarily to the value of the merchandise inventory and the store equipment. Although there are differences in the cost of such assets, their assessed value for tax purposes, and their value for insurance purposes, the cost is most readily available and is considered to be satisfactory as a basis for apportioning these expenses. The computation of the apportionment follows:

	TOTAL	DEPARTMENT A	DEPARTMENT B
Merchandise inventory:			
January 1.................	$ 71,000	$40,300	$30,700
December 31.............	81,000	41,900	39,100
Total.................	$152,000	$82,200	$69,800
Average................	$ 76,000	$41,100	$34,900
Average cost of store equipment			
(computed previously)......	14,000	8,400	5,600
Total.....................	$ 90,000	$49,500	$40,500
Percent.................	100%	55%	45%
Property tax expense........	$ 3,300	$ 1,815	$ 1,485
Insurance expense..........	$ 1,900	$ 1,045	$ 855

Uncollectible Accounts Expense, Miscellaneous Selling Expense, and Miscellaneous General Expense are apportioned on the basis of sales. Although the uncollectible accounts expense may be apportioned on the basis of an analysis of accounts receivable written off, it is assumed that the expense is closely related to sales. The miscellaneous selling and general expenses are apportioned on the basis of sales, the assumption being that this is a reasonable measure of the benefit to each department. The computation of the apportionment follows:

483

	TOTAL	DEPARTMENT A	DEPARTMENT B
Sales......................	$400,000	$280,000	$120,000
Percent...................	100%	70%	30%
Uncollectible accounts expense	$ 2,000	$ 1,400	$ 600
Miscellaneous selling expense.	$ 2,050	$ 1,435	$ 615
Miscellaneous general expense	$ 2,100	$ 1,470	$ 630

An income statement presenting income from operations by departments for York Company appears on page 484. The amounts for sales and cost of merchandise sold are presented in condensed form. Details could be reported, if desired, in the manner illustrated by the income statement on page 480.

DEPARTMENTAL MARGIN APPROACH TO INCOME REPORTING

Not all accountants agree as to the merits of the type of departmental analysis discussed in the preceding section. Many caution against complete reliance on such departmental income statements on the grounds that the use of arbitrary bases in allocating expenses are likely to yield incorrect amounts of departmental operating income. In addition, objection may be made to the reporting of operating income by departments on the grounds that departments are not independent operating units, but segments of a single enterprise, and that therefore no single department of a business can by itself earn an income. For these reasons the format

484

York Company
Income Statement
For Year Ended December 31, 19--

	DEPARTMENT A		DEPARTMENT B		TOTAL	
Net sales		$272,400		$116,900		$389,300
Cost of merchandise sold		148,500		77,600		226,100
Gross profit on sales		$123,900		$ 39,300		$163,200
Operating expenses:						
Selling expenses:						
Sales salaries	$ 27,000		$ 15,000		$ 42,000	
Advertising expense	5,950		3,050		9,000	
Depreciation expense — store equipment	990		660		1,650	
Miscellaneous selling expense	1,435		615		2,050	
Total selling expenses		$ 35,375		$ 19,325		$ 54,700
General expenses:						
Officers' salaries	$ 15,600		$ 10,400		$ 26,000	
Office salaries	5,400		3,600		9,000	
Rent expense	4,680		2,520		7,200	
Property tax expense	1,815		1,485		3,300	
Heating and lighting expense	1,560		840		3,300	
Uncollectible accounts expense	1,400		600		2,400	
Insurance expense	1,045		855		2,000	
Miscellaneous general expense	1,470		630		1,900	
Total general expenses		32,970		20,930		2,100
Total operating expenses		68,345		40,255		53,900
Income (loss) from operations		$ 55,555		$ (955)		108,600
						$ 54,600
Other expense:						
Interest expense						1,200
Income before income tax						$ 53,400
Income tax						19,132
Net income						$ 34,268

Income statement
departmentalized
through
income from
operations

of income statements of segmented businesses may follow a somewhat different format than the one illustrated on page 484. The alternative form emphasizes the contribution of each department to the expenses incurred on behalf of the business as a unified whole. Income statements prepared in this alternative form are said to follow the *departmental margin* or *contribution margin* approach to income reporting.

Preliminary to the preparation of an income statement in the departmental margin format, it is necessary to differentiate between operating expenses that are *direct* and those that are *indirect*. The two categories may be described in general terms as follows:

Direct expense — Operating expenses directly traceable to or incurred for the sole benefit of a specific department and ordinarily subject to the control of the department manager.

Indirect expense — Operating expenses incurred for the entire enterprise as a unit and hence not subject to the control of individual department managers.

The details of departmental sales and cost of merchandise sold are presented on the income statement in the usual manner. The direct expenses of each department are then deducted from the related departmental gross profit on sales, yielding balances which are identified as *departmental margin*. The remaining expenses, including the indirect operating expenses, are not departmentalized; they are reported singly below the total departmental margin.

An income statement in the departmental margin format for the York Company is presented on page 486. The basic revenue, cost, and expense data for the period are identical with those reported in the earlier illustration. The expenses identified as "direct" are sales salaries, property tax, uncollectible accounts, insurance, depreciation, and the newspaper advertising portion of advertising. The billboard portion of advertising, which is for the benefit of the business as an indivisible unit, as well as officers' and office salaries, and the remaining operating expenses, are identified as "indirect." Although a $955 net loss from operations is reported for Department B on page 484, a departmental margin of $18,250 is reported for the same department on page 486.

DEPARTMENTAL MARGIN ANALYSIS AND CONTROL

Thus far in this chapter, as in earlier chapters, the importance of controlling expenses as an essential element of profit maximization has been emphasized. The value of the departmental margin approach to income reporting derives largely from its emphasis on the assignment of responsibility for control. Elements of an accounting system that provide the means for such control, such as departmental margin income statements, are sometimes referred to as *responsibility accounting*.

485

York Company
Income Statement
For Year Ended December 31, 19--

	DEPARTMENT A		DEPARTMENT B		TOTAL	
Net sales................	....	$272,400	....	$116,900	....	$389,300
Cost of merchandise sold...	....	148,500	....	77,600	....	226,100
Gross profit on sales........	....	$123,900	....	$ 39,300	....	$163,200
Direct departmental expenses:						
Sales salaries............	$27,000	....	$15,000	....	$42,000	....
Advertising expense......	4,550	....	2,450	....	7,000	....
Property tax expense.....	1,815	....	1,485	....	3,300	....
Uncollectible accounts expense.............	1,400	....	600	....	2,000	....
Insurance expense......	1,045	....	855	....	1,900	....
Depreciation expense — store equipment.......	990	....	660	....	1,650	....
Total direct departmental expenses.....	....	36,800	....	21,050	....	57,850
Departmental margin......	....	$ 87,100	....	$ 18,250	....	$105,350
Indirect expenses:						
Officers' salaries.........	....	....	....	....	$26,000	....
Office salaries...........	....	....	....	....	9,000	....
Rent expense...........	....	....	....	....	7,200	....
Heating and lighting expense.............	....	....	....	....	2,400	....
Advertising expense.....	....	....	....	....	2,000	....
Miscellaneous selling expense.............	....	....	....	....	2,050	....
Miscellaneous general expense.............	....	....	....	....	2,100	....
Total indirect expenses	....	....	....	....	....	50,750
Income from operations...	....	....	....	....	....	$ 54,600
Other expense:						
Interest expense.........	....	....	....	....	....	1,200
Income before income tax	....	....	....	....	....	$ 53,400
Income tax.............	....	....	....	....	....	19,132
Net income.............	....	....	....	....	....	$ 34,268

Income statement
departmentalized
through
departmental
margin

With departmental margin analysis the manager of each department can be held accountable for the operating expenses traceable to his department. A reduction in the direct expenses of a department will have a favorable effect on the contribution made by that department to the indirect expenses and hence to the net income of the enterprise.

The departmental margin income statement may also be useful to management in formulating fundamental plans for future operations. For example, this type of analysis can be employed when the discontinuance of a particular operation or department is being considered. If a specific department yields a departmental margin, it generally should be retained even though the allocation of the indirect operating expenses to departments would indicate a net loss for such department. This observation is based upon the assumption that the department in question represents a relatively minor segment of the enterprise. Its termination, therefore, would not cause any significant reduction in the volume of indirect expenses. For example, if an enterprise occupying a rented three-story building is divided into twenty departments, each occupying about the same amount of space, termination of the least thriving department would probably not cause any reduction in rent or other occupancy expenses. The space vacated would probably be absorbed by the remaining nineteen departments. On the other hand, if the enterprise were divided into three departments, each occupying approximately equal areas, the discontinuance of one could result in vacating an entire floor and consequently materially reduce occupancy expenses. When the departmental margin analysis is applied to problems of this type, consideration should be given to the organizational structure and to related proposals for the use of released space.

To illustrate the application of the departmental margin approach to long-range planning, assume that an enterprise with six departments has earned $70,000 before income tax during the past year, which is fairly typical of recent operations. Assume also that recent income statements, in which all operating expenses are allocated, indicate that Department F has been incurring losses, the net loss having amounted to $5,000 for the past year. Departmental margin analysis indicates that, in spite of the losses, Department F should not be discontinued unless there is sufficient assurance that a commensurate increase in the gross profit of other departments or a decrease in indirect expenses can be effected. The analysis, considerably condensed, may be presented as follows:

487

Proposal to Discontinue Department F
January 25, 19--

	CURRENT OPERATIONS			DISCONTINUANCE OF
	DEPARTMENT F	DEPARTMENTS A–E	TOTAL	DEPARTMENT F
Sales..................	$100,000	$900,000	$1,000,000	$900,000
Cost of merchandise sold....	70,000	540,000	610,000	540,000
Gross profit on sales........	$ 30,000	$360,000	$ 390,000	$360,000
Direct departmental expenses	20,000	210,000	230,000	210,000
Departmental margin......	$ 10,000	$150,000	$ 160,000	$150,000
Indirect expenses..........			90,000	90,000
Income before income tax..			$ 70,000	$ 60,000

Departmental analysis — discontinuance of unprofitable department

The analysis shows a possible reduction of $10,000 in net income (the amount of the departmental margin for Department F) if Department F is discontinued. There are also other factors that may need to be considered. For example, there may be problems regarding the displacement of sales personnel. Or customers attracted by the least profitable department may make substantial purchases in other departments, so that discontinuance of that department may adversely affect the sales of other departments.

The foregoing discussion of departmental income statements has suggested various ways in which income data may be made useful to management in making important policy decisions. It should be kept in mind that the format selected for the presentation of income data to management must be that which will be most useful under the circumstances for evaluating, controlling, and planning departmental operations.

BRANCH OPERATIONS

Just as a firm may add a new department in an effort to increase its sales and income, it also may open new stores (branches) in different locations with the same objective in mind. Among the types of retail businesses in which branch operations were first successfully developed on a major scale were variety, grocery, and drugstores. There are a number of large corporations with hundreds or thousands of retail branches distributed over a large area. In addition to the national chain store organizations, there are many of a regional or local nature. The growth of suburban shopping centers in recent years has added materially to the number of firms, especially department stores, that have expanded through the opening of branches.

Although commonly associated with retailing, branch operations are also carried on by banking institutions, service organizations, and many types of manufacturing enterprises. Regardless of the nature of the business, each branch ordinarily has a branch manager. Within the framework of general policies set by top management, the branch manager may be given wide latitude in conducting the business of the branch. Data concerning the volume of business handled and the profitability of operations at each location are essential as a basis for decisions by the principal executives. It is also necessary to maintain a record of the assets at the branch locations and of liabilities incurred by each branch.

The remainder of this chapter deals with the central office and the single branch of a merchandising business. The fundamental considerations are not materially affected, however, by a multiplicity of branches or by the particular type of business.

SYSTEMS FOR BRANCH ACCOUNTING

There are various systems of accounting for branch operations. The system may be highly centralized, with the accounting for the branch done at the home office. Or the system may be almost completely decentralized, with the branch responsible for the detailed accounting and only summary accounts carried for the branch by the home office. Or the system may vary between these two extremes. Many variations are possible, but the two methods of branch accounting described in the following paragraphs are typical.

Centralized system. The branch may prepare only the basic records of its transactions, such as sales invoices, time tickets for employees, and vouchers for liabilities incurred. Copies of all such documents are forwarded to the home office, where they are recorded in appropriate journals in the usual manner. When this system is used, the branch has no journals or ledgers. If the operating results of the branch are to be determined separately, which is normally the case, separate branch accounts for sales, cost of merchandise sold, and expenses must be maintained in the home office ledger. It is apparent that the principles of departmental accounting will apply in such cases, the branch being treated as a department.

One important result of centralizing the bookkeeping activities at one location may be substantial savings in office expense. There is also greater assurance of uniformity in accounting methods employed. On the other hand, there is some likelihood of delays and inaccuracies in submitting data to the home office, with the result that periodic reports on the operations of a branch may not be available when needed.

Decentralized system. When the accounting for branches is decentralized, each branch maintains its own accounting system with journals and ledgers. The account classification for assets, liabilities, revenues, and expenses in the branch ledger conforms to the classification employed by the home office. The accounting processes are comparable to those of an independent business, except that the branch does not have capital accounts. A special account entitled Home Office takes the place of the capital accounts. The process of preparing financial statements and adjusting and closing the accounts is substantially the same as for an independent enterprise. It is this system of branch accounting to which the remainder of the chapter will be devoted.

UNDERLYING PRINCIPLES OF DECENTRALIZED BRANCH ACCOUNTING

When the branch has a ledger with a full complement of accounts, except capital accounts, it is apparent that there must be some tie-in between the branch ledger and the general ledger at the home office. The properties at the branch are a part of the assets of the entire enterprise, and liabilities incurred at the branch are similarly liabilities of the enterprise as a whole. Although the accounting system at the branch is much

489

like that of an independent company, the fact remains that the branch is not a separate entity but only a segment of the business.

The tie-in between the home office and the branch is accomplished by the control-account-subsidiary-ledger technique, with an added modification that makes the branch ledger a self-contained unit. The basic features of the system are shown in the chart below:

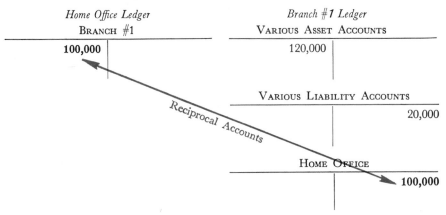

Home Office Ledger
BRANCH #1

| 100,000 | |

Branch #1 Ledger
VARIOUS ASSET ACCOUNTS

| 120,000 | |

VARIOUS LIABILITY ACCOUNTS

| | 20,000 |

Reciprocal Accounts

HOME OFFICE

| | 100,000 |

In the home office ledger, the account Branch #1 has a debit balance of $100,000. This balance represents the sum of the assets minus the sum of the liabilities recorded in the ledger at the branch. The various asset and liability accounts in the branch ledger are represented in the chart by one account for all assets ($120,000) and one account for all liabilities ($20,000). In order to make the branch ledger self-balancing, an account entitled Home Office is added. It has a credit balance of $100,000. The two accounts, Branch #1 in the home office ledger and Home Office in the branch ledger, have equal but opposite balances and are known as *reciprocal accounts*. The home office account in the branch ledger replaces the capital accounts that would be used if the branch were a separate entity. Actually, the account represents the portion of the capital of the home office that is invested in the branch.

When the home office sends assets to the branch, it debits Branch #1 for the totals and credits the appropriate asset accounts. Upon receiving the assets, the branch debits the appropriate asset accounts and credits Home Office. To illustrate, assume that branch operations are begun by sending $10,000 in cash to the newly appointed branch manager. The entries in the two ledgers are presented in the accounts illustrated at the top of the next page.

When the branch disburses the cash, it records the transactions as though it were an independent entity. For example, if the branch purchases office equipment for $4,000, paying cash, it debits Office Equipment and credits Cash. No entry is required by the home office because there is no change in the amount of the investment at the branch.

490

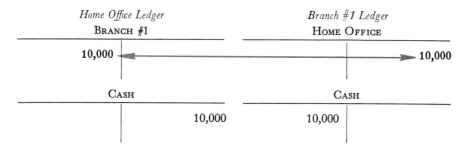

As the branch incurs expenses and earns revenues, it records the transactions in the usual manner. Such transactions do affect the amount of the total investment of the home office at the branch, but recognition of the change is postponed until the accounts are closed at the end of the accounting period. At that time the income summary account in the branch is closed to the account Home Office. If operations have resulted in an operating income, the account Home Office will be credited. In the home office an operating income at the branch is recorded by a debit to Branch #1 and a credit to Branch Operating Income. For an operating loss the entries would be just the reverse.

In a merchandising enterprise all or a substantial part of the stock in trade of the branch may be supplied by the home office. A shipment of merchandise from the home office is recorded by the home office by debiting Branch #1 and crediting Shipments to Branch #1. The branch records the transaction by debiting Shipments from Home Office and crediting Home Office. It is evident from the accounts below that the two shipments accounts are also reciprocal accounts.

491

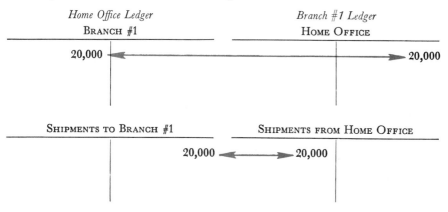

The account Shipments to Branch #1 is a contra account representing a reduction in Merchandise Inventory and Purchases in the home office ledger. Shipments from Home Office, in the branch ledger, is comparable to a purchases account. Both accounts are temporary in nature and are periodically closed to the respective income summary accounts.

ILLUSTRATION OF DECENTRALIZED BRANCH ACCOUNTING

A series of entries illustrating the underlying principles applicable to branch accounting on a decentralized basis is presented below and on page 493. The illustration begins with the opening of a branch and continues with operations covering a complete accounting period. Typical transactions between the home office and the branch, and between the branch and outsiders, are considered. Transactions between the home office and outsiders are ignored unless they affect the branch. A summary of transactions, together with the entries in the home office records and the branch records, is presented below in general journal form.

Transactions	Home Office Records	Branch Records

(1) The home office established Branch #1, sending $10,000 in cash and $30,000 in merchandise.	Branch #1 40,000
	  Cash 10,000
	  Shipments to
	  Branch #1 30,000
		Cash 10,000
		Shipments from
		Home Office 30,000
		  Home Office 40,000

(2) The branch purchased on account merchandise costing $10,000.		Purchases . . . . .10,000 Accounts Pay . . . 10,000
(3) The branch sold merchandise for $16,000 in cash and for $8,000 on account.		Cash . . . . .16,000 Accounts Rec . . . . . . 8,000 Sales 24,000
(4) The branch paid operating expenses amounting to $3,500.		Operating Exp . . . . 3,500 Cash 3,500
(5) The branch collected $6,000 on accounts receivable.		Cash . . . . 6,000 Accounts Rec . . . 6,000
(6) The branch paid $1,000 on accounts payable.		Accounts Pay . . . . . . 1,000 Cash 1,000

(7) The branch sent $20,000 in cash to the home office.	Cash 20,000
	  Branch #1 20,000
		Home Office 20,000
		  Cash 20,000

The entries to adjust and close the accounts of the branch at the end of the accounting period, together with the entries in the records of the home office to record the operating income of the branch, are presented at the top of page 493.

After the foregoing entries have been posted, the home office accounts affected and the branch ledger accounts appear as shown on pages 493 and 494.

Adjusting & Closing	Home Office Records	Branch Records

(a) To record the ending merchandise inventory of the branch.		Mdse. Inventory...22,000
		  Income
		    Summary....... 22,000

(b) To close the sales account of the branch.		Sales............24,000
		  Income
		    Summary....... 24,000

(c) To close the cost and expense accounts of the branch.		Income Summary..43,500
		  Shipments from
		    Home Office.... 30,000
		    Purchases....... 10,000
		    Operating Exp... 3,500

(d) To close the income summary account in the records of the branch and to record the operating income of the branch in the records of the home office.	Branch #1........ 2,500
	  Branch Operating
	    Income........ 2,500
		Income Summary.. 2,500
		  Home Office.... 2,500

493

Home Office Ledger	Branch Ledger

CASH (Home Office)

(7)	20,000	(1)	10,000

Other cash transactions of the home office would also be recorded in the account above.

CASH (Branch)

(1)	10,000	(4)	3,500
(3)	16,000	(6)	1,000
(5)	6,000	(7)	20,000
		Balance	7,500
	32,000		32,000
Balance	7,500		

ACCOUNTS RECEIVABLE

(3)	8,000	(5)	6,000
		Balance	2,000
	8,000		8,000
Balance	2,000		

MERCHANDISE INVENTORY

(a)	22,000		

Home Office Ledger	Branch Ledger

ACCOUNTS PAYABLE

(6)	1,000	(2)	10,000
Balance	9,000		
	10,000		10,000
		Balance	9,000

BRANCH #1 | HOME OFFICE

(1)	40,000	(7)	20,000	(7)	20,000	(1)	40,000
(d)	2,500	Balance	22,500	Balance	22,500	(d)	2,500
	42,500		42,500		42,500		42,500
Balance	22,500					Balance	22,500

BRANCH OPERATING INCOME | INCOME SUMMARY

		(d)	2,500	(c)	43,500	(a)	22,000
				(d)	2,500	(b)	24,000
					46,000		46,000

Branch Operating Income will be closed to the home office income summary account.

SALES

(b)	24,000	(3)	24,000

SHIPMENTS TO BRANCH #1 | SHIPMENTS FROM HOME OFFICE

		(1)	30,000	(1)	30,000	(c)	30,000

Shipments to Branch #1 is a deduction from merchandise inventory and purchases. It will be closed to the home office income summary account.

PURCHASES

(2)	10,000	(c)	10,000

OPERATING EXPENSES

(4)	3,500	(c)	3,500

BRANCH FINANCIAL STATEMENTS

Branch financial statements differ from those of a separate business entity in two minor respects. In the branch income statement, shipments from the home office appear in the cost of merchandise sold section following purchases. In the branch balance sheet the account Home Office takes the place of the capital accounts. Statements for the branches are used only by management and are not published.

COMBINED STATEMENTS FOR HOME OFFICE AND BRANCH

The income statement based on the home office ledger reports details of sales, cost of merchandise sold, expenses, and income or loss from home office operations in the usual manner. The operating income or loss of each branch is then listed, and the operating results for the entire enterprise are reported. The assets section of the balance sheet prepared from the home office ledger will include the controlling accounts for the various branches. The nature and the amounts of the various assets and liabilities at the branch locations will not be disclosed. The home office statements, together with financial statements for each individual branch, serve a useful purpose for management, but they are obviously unsuitable for presentation to stockholders and creditors.

495

Accordingly, it is necessary to combine the data on the income statements of the home office and the branches to form one overall income statement. The data on the balance sheets of the home office and of the various branches are also combined to form one balance sheet for the enterprise. The preparation of the combined statements is facilitated by the use of work sheets. The work sheets are similar in that each has a column for the home office account balances, a column for the account balances of each branch, a set of columns headed "Eliminations," and a final column to which the combined figures are extended.

The work sheet for the combined income statement and the related income statement, as prepared from the work sheet, of Taylor Corporation are presented on the next page. The account Shipments from Home Office is canceled by a credit in the Eliminations column, and the account Shipments to Branch #1 is canceled by a debit in the Eliminations column. These eliminations are necessary in the preparation of a combined statement reporting the home office and the branch as a single operating unit. The two accounts merely record a change in location of merchandise within the company.

The work sheet for the combined balance sheet and the related balance sheet, as prepared from the work sheet, of Taylor Corporation are presented on page 497. The reciprocal account Branch #1 is canceled by a credit elimination, and the reciprocal account Home Office is canceled by a debit elimination.

Taylor Corporation
Work Sheet for Combined Income Statement
For Month Ended March 31, 19 — —

	HOME OFFICE	BRANCH #1	ELIMINATIONS		COMBINED INCOME STATEMENT
			DEBIT	CREDIT	
Sales......................	47,000	24,000			71,000
Cost of merchandise sold:					
Mdse. inv., March 1........	41,000				41,000
Purchases.................	52,000	10,000			62,000
	93,000				
Shipments from home office..		30,000		30,000	
Less shipments to branch #1..	30,000		30,000		
Mdse. available for sale......	63,000	40,000			103,000
Less mdse. inv., March 31 ...	35,000	22,000			57,000
Cost of merchandise sold.....	28,000	18,000			46,000
Gross profit on sales...........	19,000	6,000			25,000
Total expenses...............	10,500	3,500			14,000
Net income.................	8,500	2,500	30,000	30,000	11,000

Taylor Corporation
Income Statement
For Month Ended March 31, 19 — —

Sales...			$71,000
Cost of merchandise sold:			
Merchandise inventory, March 1, 19 — —....................		$ 41,000	
Purchases..		62,000	
Merchandise available for sale..........................		$103,000	
Less merchandise inventory, March 31, 19 — —...............		57,000	
Cost of merchandise sold............................			46,000
Gross profit on sales....................................			$25,000
Total expenses.......................................			14,000
Net income...			$11,000

SHIPMENTS TO BRANCH BILLED AT SELLING PRICE

In the foregoing discussion and illustrations, the billing for merchandise shipped to the branch has been assumed to be at cost price. When all or most of the merchandise handled by the branch is supplied by the home office, it is not unusual for billings to be made at selling price. An advantage of this procedure is that it provides a convenient control over inventories at the branch. The branch merchandise inventory at the beginning of a period (at selling price), plus shipments during the period (at selling price), less sales for the period yields the ending inventory (at selling price). Comparison of the physical in-

Taylor Corporation
Work Sheet for Combined Balance Sheet
March 31, 19—

	HOME OFFICE	BRANCH #1	ELIMINATIONS		COMBINED BALANCE SHEET
			DEBIT	CREDIT	
Debit balances:					
Cash.....................	53,000	7,500			60,500
Accounts receivable.........	46,000	2,000			48,000
Merchandise inventory......	35,000	22,000			57,000
Prepaid insurance..........	250				250
Branch #1.................	22,500			22,500	
Equipment...............	15,000				15,000
Total.................	171,750	31,500			180,750
Credit balances:					
Accumulated depreciation...	3,000				3,000
Accounts payable..........	28,000	9,000			37,000
Home office...............		22,500	22,500		
Common stock............	100,000				100,000
Retained earnings.........	40,750				40,750
Total.................	171,750	31,500	22,500	22,500	180,750

Taylor Corporation
Balance Sheet
March 31, 19—

Assets

Cash..		$ 60,500
Accounts receivable.......................................		48,000
Merchandise inventory...................................		57,000
Prepaid insurance..		250
Equipment..	$15,000	
Less accumulated depreciation........................	3,000	12,000
Total assets..		$177,750

Liabilities and Capital

Accounts payable...		$ 37,000
Common stock...	$100,000	
Retained earnings.......................................	40,750	140,750
Total liabilities and capital.............................		$177,750

ventory taken at selling prices with the book amount discloses any discrepancies. A significant difference between the physical and the book inventories indicates a need for remedial action by the management.

When shipments to the branch are billed at selling prices, no gross profit on sales will be reported on the branch income statement. The merchandise inventory on the branch balance sheet will also be stated at the billed (selling) price of the merchandise on hand. In combining the branch statements with the home office statements, it is necessary to convert the data back to cost by eliminating the markup from both the shipments accounts and the inventory accounts.

ANALYSES OF OPERATING SEGMENTS

As business units grow ever larger and more diversified, the need for analysis of operations becomes increasingly important. It is necessary to account separately for the various segments that make up the larger unit. Departments and branches are two such segments. Accounting procedures can also be established for other segments of operations such as sales territories and individual products. The accounting procedures for sales territories would follow the principles of departmental accounting, each territory being treated as a department.

Business operations are often analyzed in terms of individual products. For the merchandising enterprise, accounting procedures similar to those illustrated for departmental operations could be employed. For the manufacturing enterprise the accounting process would be extended to include the various costs that are necessary in the manufacture of the product. Product cost data are essential in the evaluation of past manufacturing operations, in establishing effective control over costs, and in providing the information useful to management in making decisions. The accounting concepts and procedures applicable to manufacturing operations are discussed in subsequent chapters.

498

QUESTIONS

1. Departmental income statements are ordinarily not included in the published annual reports issued to stockholders and other parties outside the business enterprise. For whom are they prepared?

2. The newly appointed general manager of a department store is studying the income statements presenting gross profit by departments in an attempt to adjust operations to achieve the highest possible gross profit for each department. (a) Suggest ways in which an income statement departmentalized through gross profit can be used in achieving this goal. (b) Suggest reasons why caution must be exercised in using such statements.

3. For each of the following types of expenses, select the allocation basis listed that is most appropriate for use in arriving at operating income by departments:

Expense:	Basis of allocation:
(a) Insurance	(1) Physical space occupied
(b) Uncollectible accounts	(2) Departmental sales
(c) Sales salaries	(3) Cost of inventory and equipment
(d) Heating and lighting	(4) Time devoted to department

4. Differentiate between a direct and an indirect operating expense.

5. Indicate whether each of the following operating expenses incurred by Reed Department Store is a direct or an indirect expense:

(a) Office salaries   (d) Salesmen's commissions
(b) Rent on building   (e) President's salary
(c) Depreciation of store equipment   (f) Property tax

6. What term is applied to the dollar amount representing the excess of departmental gross profit over direct departmental expenses?

7. Recent income statements departmentalized through income from operations report operating losses for Department S, a relatively minor segment of the business. Management studies indicate that discontinuance of Department S would not affect sales of other departments or the volume of indirect expenses. Under what circumstances would the discontinuance of Department S result in a decrease of net income of the enterprise?

8. A portion of the income statement departmentalized through income from operations for the year just ended is presented below in condensed form.

	Department A
Net sales..............	$ 75,000
Cost of merchandise sold.	45,000
Gross profit on sales.....	$ 30,000
Operating expenses......	40,000
Loss from operations....	$(10,000)

The operating expenses of Dept. A include $15,000 for indirect expenses.
It is estimated that the discontinuance of Department A would not have affected the sales of the other departments nor have reduced the indirect expenses of the enterprise. Assuming the accuracy of these estimates, what would have been the effect on the income from operations of the enterprise if Department A had been discontinued?

499

9. Where are the journals and ledgers detailing the operations of a branch maintained in (a) a centralized system for branch accounting and (b) a decentralized system?

10. What is the nature of reciprocal accounts employed in branch accounting?

11. For each of the following accounts appearing in the home office ledger, name the reciprocal account in the branch ledger: (a) Dixon Branch; (b) Shipments to Dixon Branch.

12. In the branch ledger, what is the name of the account that takes the place of the capital accounts common to separate accounting entities?

13. What accounts are debited and credited (a) to close the income summary account in the accounts of the Evendale Branch and (b) to record the operating income of the Evendale Branch in the home office accounts?

14. Where, in the branch income statement, is the amount of shipments from the home office reported?

15. In the work sheet for a combined income statement for the home office and its Oakbrook Branch, what item is eliminated as an offset to shipments from home office?

16. In the work sheet for a combined balance sheet for the home office and its Country Fair Branch, what item is eliminated as an offset to Country Fair Branch?

17. After the accounts are closed, the asset accounts at Branch #1 total $125,000; the contra asset accounts total $15,000; and liabilities to outsiders total $12,000. (a) What is the title of the remaining account in the branch ledger and what is the amount of its balance? (b) What is the title of the reciprocal account in the home office ledger and what is the amount of its balance? (c) Do these reciprocal items appear in the combined balance sheet?

18. At the close of each accounting period Coleman Company charges each of its branches with interest on the net investment in the branch. At the end of the current year the home office debited the branch accounts for various amounts and credited Interest Income for a total of $17,500. The branches make comparable entries, debiting Interest Expense and crediting Home Office. How should the interest expense and the interest income be treated on the work sheet for the combined income statement?

19. During the first year of operations of the Greater Ames Branch, the home office shipped merchandise that had cost $140,000 to the branch. The branch was billed for the selling price of $200,000, which would yield a gross profit of 30% of sales. Branch net sales for the year totaled $150,000 (all sales were at the billed price). (a) What should be the amount of the branch ending physical inventory at billed prices? (b) Assuming that there are no inventory shortages at the branch, what is the cost of the ending inventory? (c) Which of the two amounts should be added to the home office inventory for presentation in the combined balance sheet? (d) How much gross profit will be reported in the branch income statement?

500

EXERCISES

19-1. K. L. Kerns Company occupies a two-story building. The departments and the floor space occupied by each are as follows:

Receiving and Storage...	basement.....	6,000 sq. ft.
Department 1..........	basement.....	6,000 sq. ft.
Department 2..........	first floor......	2,400 sq. ft.
Department 3..........	first floor......	4,800 sq. ft.
Department 4..........	first floor......	4,800 sq. ft.
Department 5..........	second floor...	3,000 sq. ft.
Department 6..........	second floor...	9,000 sq. ft.

The building is leased at an annual rental of $44,000, allocated to the floors as follows: basement, 20%; first floor, 50%; second floor, 30%. Determine the amount of rent to be apportioned to each department.

19-2. Reese Company apportions depreciation expense on equipment on the basis of the average cost of the equipment, and apportions property tax expense on the basis of the combined total of average cost of the equipment and average cost of the merchandise inventories. Depreciation expense on equipment amounted to $20,000 and property tax expense amounted to $5,000 for the year. Determine the apportionment of the depreciation expense and the property tax expense based on the data presented at the top of the next page.

Departments	Average Cost Equipment	Inventories
Service:		
1	$ 60,000	
2	40,000	
Sales:		
A	100,000	$200,000
B	120,000	230,000
C	80,000	170,000
Total	$400,000	$600,000

19-3. Johnson Sporting Goods is considering discontinuance of one of its twelve departments. If operations in Department A are discontinued, it is estimated that the indirect operating expenses and the level of operations in the other departments will not be affected.

Data from the income statement for the past year ended December 31, which is considered to be a typical year, are presented below.

	Department A		Departments B–L	
Sales.............................		$36,500		$504,000
Cost of merchandise sold...........		20,500		295,400
Gross profit on sales...............		$16,000		$208,600
Operating expenses:				
Direct expenses.................	$12,000		$108,000	
Indirect expenses...............	6,000	18,000	72,000	180,000
Income (loss) before income tax.....		$(2,000)		$ 28,600

(a) Prepare an estimated income statement for the current year ending December 31, assuming the discontinuance of Department A. (b) On the basis of the data presented, would it be advisable to retain Department A?

19-4. Morris Company maintains sales offices in several cities. The home office provides the sales manager at each office with a working fund of $5,000 with which to meet payrolls and to pay other office expenses. Prepare the entries, in general journal form, for the home office to record the following:

(a) Sent a check to establish a $5,000 fund for Branch No. 5.
(b) Sent a check to replenish the fund after receiving a report from Branch No. 5 indicating the following disbursements: sales salaries, $2,200; office salaries, $1,000; rent, $750; utilities expense, $195; miscellaneous general expense, $75.

19-5. Prepare the entries, in general journal form, for the Paxton Branch to record the following selected transactions.

May 1. The home office sent to the branch: cash, $1,500; equipment, $1,200; merchandise at cost, $3,500.
4. The branch purchased merchandise on account from an outside firm, $2,500.
10. The branch sold merchandise: for cash $3,150; on account, $2,250.
11. The branch paid accounts payable, $2,500.
17. The branch received merchandise at cost from the home office, $2,500.
20. The branch collected $2,000 on account.
24. The branch paid operating expenses, $525.
28. The branch sent the home office cash, $2,400.
31. The branch reported an operating income of $1,050.

501

19-6. Present the entries, in general journal form, for the home office to record the appropriate transactions in Exercise 19-5.

19-7. Reed Department Store maintains accounts entitled Fox Valley Branch and Morris Branch. Each branch maintains an account entitled Home Office. The Fox Valley Branch received instructions from the home office to ship to the Morris Branch merchandise costing $2,750 that had been received from the home office. Give the general journal entry to record the transfer of the merchandise in the records of (a) the home office, (b) the Fox Valley Branch, and (c) the Morris Branch.

19-8. During the year, the home office shipped merchandise that had cost $270,000 to the branch. The branch was billed for $360,000, which was the selling price of the merchandise. No merchandise was purchased from any outside sources. Branch net sales for the year totaled $345,000. All sales were made at the billed price. Merchandise on hand at the beginning of the period totaled $74,000 at the billed price. Merchandise on hand at the end of the period as determined by physical count was $86,500 at the billed price. Determine the amount, at the billed price, of any discrepancy between the book amount and the physical count of inventory.

PROBLEMS

The following additional problems for this chapter are located in Appendix B: 19-1B, 19-2B, 19-5B.

19-1A. Wooden and Co. operates two sales departments: Department A for men's clothing and Department B for women's clothing. The trial balance shown at the top of the next page was prepared at the end of the current fiscal year after all adjustments, including the adjustments for merchandise inventory, were recorded and posted.

Merchandise inventories at the beginning of the year were as follows: Department A, $21,500; Department B, $37,000.

The bases to be used in apportioning expenses, together with other essential information, are as follows:

Sales salaries — payroll records: Department A, $15,900; Department B, $23,500.

Advertising expense — usage: Department A, $3,500; Department B, $6,500.

Depreciation expense — average cost of equipment. Balances at beginning of year: Department A, $17,000; Department B, $21,250. Balances at end of year: Department A, $19,000; Department B, $22,750.

Store supplies expense — requisitions: Department A, $450; Department B, $600.

Office salaries — Department A, 40%; Department B, 60%.

Rent expense and heating and lighting expense — floor space: Department A, 1,800 sq. ft.; Department B, 2,700 sq. ft.

Property tax expense and insurance expense — average cost of equipment plus average cost of merchandise inventory.

Uncollectible accounts expense, miscellaneous selling expense, and miscellaneous general expense — volume of gross sales.

Instructions:

Prepare an income statement departmentalized through income from operations.

Wooden and Co.
Trial Balance
July 31, 19—

Cash	70,575	
Accounts Receivable	92,450	
Merchandise Inventory — Department A	22,500	
Merchandise Inventory — Department B	39,000	
Prepaid Insurance	2,350	
Store Supplies	525	
Store Equipment	41,750	
Accumulated Depreciation — Store Equipment		24,750
Accounts Payable		32,200
Income Tax Payable		7,500
Common Stock		100,000
Retained Earnings		87,300
Cash Dividends	20,000	
Income Summary	58,500	61,500
Sales — Department A		300,000
Sales — Department B		600,000
Sales Returns and Allowances — Department A	2,200	
Sales Returns and Allowances — Department B	8,050	
Purchases — Department A	245,600	
Purchases — Department B	499,250	
Sales Salaries	39,400	
Advertising Expense	10,000	
Depreciation Expense — Store Equipment	9,000	
Store Supplies Expense	1,050	
Miscellaneous Selling Expense	900	
Office Salaries	10,000	
Rent Expense	9,600	
Heating and Lighting Expense	3,600	
Property Tax Expense	2,400	
Insurance Expense	1,600	
Uncollectible Accounts Expense	1,050	
Miscellaneous General Expense	600	
Interest Income		900
Income Tax	22,200	
	1,214,150	1,214,150

19-2A. Eaton's, a department store, has 18 departments. Those with the least sales volume are Department C and Department N, which were established about a year ago on a trial basis. The board of directors feels that it is now time to consider the retention or the termination of these two departments. The adjusted trial balance, severely condensed, as of January 31, the end of the first month of the current fiscal year, is presented at the top of the next page. January is considered to be a typical month. The income tax accrual has no bearing on the decision and is excluded from consideration.

Instructions:

(1) Prepare an income statement for January departmentalized through departmental margin.

(2) State your recommendations concerning the retention of Departments C and N, giving reasons.

Eaton's
Trial Balance
January 31, 19—

Current Assets.............................	503,975	
Plant Assets..............................	415,050	
Accumulated Depreciation — Plant Assets.....		188,150
Current Liabilities........................		152,750
Common Stock............................		350,000
Retained Earnings.........................		179,375
Cash Dividends...........................	28,000	
Sales — Department C......................		17,950
Sales — Department N......................		12,200
Sales — Other Departments.................		825,800
Cost of Merchandise Sold — Department C....	13,025	
Cost of Merchandise Sold — Department N....	9,200	
Cost of Merchandise Sold — Other Departments	538,700	
Direct Expenses — Department C............	3,925	
Direct Expenses — Department N............	4,750	
Direct Expenses — Other Departments........	120,300	
Indirect Expenses.........................	83,700	
Interest Expense..........................	5,600	
	1,726,225	1,726,225

If the working papers correlating with the textbook are not used, omit Problem 19-3A.

19-3A. A work sheet for a combined income statement and a work sheet for a combined balance sheet for W. T. Cox and Co. and its Lincoln Branch for the current fiscal year ended June 30 are presented in the working papers. Data concerning account titles and amounts have been entered on the work sheets. The amounts on the work sheet for the combined income statement were taken from the adjusted trial balance, and the income of the branch had not been recognized in the revenue accounts of the home office. On the work sheet for the combined balance sheet, the amount in the Lincoln Branch account was adjusted to give effect to the income of the branch for the current year.

Instructions:

(1) Enter the proper amounts in the "Eliminations" columns and complete the work sheets.

(2) Prepare a combined income statement and a combined balance sheet.

19-4A. The data shown at the top of the next page relating to revenue and expenses are obtained from the ledger of Midstate Corporation on June 30, the end of the current fiscal year.

Other essential data are:

Sales salaries and commissions — Salesmen are paid a basic salary plus 5% of sales. Basic salaries for Department A, $26,000; Department B, $17,000.

Advertising expense — All advertising expense was incurred for brochures distributed within each department advertising specific products. Usages: Department A, $5,530; Department B, $4,445.

Depreciation expense — Average cost of store equipment: Department A, $48,000; Department B, $32,000.

Uncollectible accounts expense — Departmental managers are responsible

	Debit	Credit
Sales — Department A......................		$450,000
Sales — Department B.		275,000
Cost of Merchandise Sold — Department A.....	$297,000	
Cost of Merchandise Sold — Department B.....	173,250	
Sales Salaries and Commissions..............	79,250	
Advertising Expense.........................	9,975	
Depreciation Expense — Store Equipment......	9,000	
Miscellaneous Selling Expense................	750	
Administrative Salaries......................	27,500	
Rent Expense...............................	12,600	
Utilities Expense............................	5,200	
Uncollectible Accounts Expense..............	3,625	
Insurance Expense..........................	2,400	
Miscellaneous General Expense..............	550	
Interest Expense............................	1,800	
Income Tax.................................	43,500	

for the granting of credit on the sales made by their respective departments. Uncollectible accounts expense is estimated at ½% of sales.

Insurance expense — Based on average cost of store equipment plus average cost of merchandise inventory. Average cost of merchandise inventory was $51,000 for Department A and $49,000 for Department B.

Instructions:

(1) Prepare an income statement departmentalized through departmental margin.
(2) Determine the rate of gross profit on sales for each department.
(3) Determine the rate of departmental margin to sales for each department.

19-5A. H. K. Martin and Son opened a branch office in Alton on April 1 of the current year. Summaries of transactions, adjustments, and year-end closing for branch operations of the current year ended December 31 are described below.

(a) Received cash advance, $25,000, and merchandise (billed at cost), $85,000, from the home office.
(b) Purchased equipment on account, $20,000.
(c) Purchased merchandise on account, $115,000.
(d) Sales on account, $110,000; cash sales, $80,000.
(e) Received cash from customers on account, $95,000.
(f) Paid operating expenses, $19,450 (all expenses are charged to Operating Expenses, a controlling account).
(g) Paid creditors on account, $115,000.
(h) Sent $40,000 cash to home office.
(i) Recorded accumulated depreciation, $700, and allowance for doubtful accounts, $350.
(j) Merchandise inventory at December 31, $52,200.
(k) Closed revenue and expense accounts.

Instructions:

(1) Present, in general journal form, the entries for the branch to record the foregoing. Post to the following T accounts: Cash, Accounts Receivable, Allowance for Doubtful Accounts, Merchandise Inventory, Equipment, Accumulated Depreciation, Accounts Payable, Home Office, Income Summary, Sales, Shipments from

505

Home Office, Purchases, and Operating Expenses.

(2) Prepare an income statement for the year and a balance sheet as of December 31 for the branch.

(3) Present, in general journal form, the entries required on the home office records. Post to a T account entitled Alton Branch.

19-6A. The board of directors of Edwards Corporation has tentatively decided to discontinue operating Department C, which has incurred a net loss for several years. Condensed revenue and expense data for the most recent year ended June 30 are presented on the following page. Bases used in allocating operating expenses among departments are described below.

Expense	Basis
Sales commissions	Actual: 8% of net sales
Advertising expense	Actual: all advertising consists of brochures distributed by the various departments advertising specific products
Depreciation expense	Average cost of store equipment used
Miscellaneous selling expense	Amount of net sales
Administrative salaries	Each of the 10 departments apportioned an equal share
Rent expense	Floor space occupied
Utilities expense	Floor space occupied
Insurance and property tax expense	Average cost of equipment used plus average cost of inventory
Miscellaneous general expense	Amount of net sales

Instructions:

Prepare a brief statement of your recommendation to the board, supported by such schedule(s) as you think will be helpful to them in reaching a decision.

Edwards Corporation
Income Statement
For Year Ended June 30, 19—

	Department C	Other Departments	Total
Net sales	$ 62,500	$940,000	$1,002,500
Cost of merchandise sold	41,300	595,000	636,300
Gross profit on sales	$ 21,200	$345,000	$ 366,200
Operating expenses:			
Selling expenses:			
Sales commissions	$ 5,000	$ 75,200	$ 80,200
Advertising expense	2,750	25,500	28,250
Depreciation expense — store equipment	1,900	20,900	22,800
Miscellaneous selling expense	875	13,160	14,035
Total selling expenses	$ 10,525	$134,760	$145,285
General expenses:			
Administrative salaries	$ 8,750	$ 78,750	$ 87,500
Rent expense	2,950	22,150	25,100
Utilities expense	2,400	16,025	18,425
Insurance and property tax expense	1,800	18,000	19,800
Miscellaneous general expense	625	9,400	10,025
Total general expenses	16,525	144,325	160,850
Total operating expenses	27,050	279,085	306,135
Income (loss) from operations	$ (5,850)	$ 65,915	$ 60,065
Other income:			
Interest income			1,000
Income before income tax			$ 61,065
Income tax			22,950
Net income			$ 38,115

Chapter 20

MANUFACTURING AND PROCESS COST SYSTEMS

MANUFACTURING OPERATIONS

Manufacturers employ labor and use machinery to convert materials into finished products. In thus changing the form of commodities, their activities differ from those of merchandisers. The furniture manufacturer, for example, converts lumber and other materials into furniture. The furniture dealer in turn purchases the finished goods from the manufacturer and sells them without additional processing.

Some functions of manufacturing companies are similar to those of merchandising organizations, such as selling, administration, and financing. The accounting procedures for these functions are identical for both types of enterprises.

Accounting procedures for a manufacturing business must also provide for the accumulation of the accounting data identified with the production processes. Additional ledger accounts are required and the accounting system must establish internal control over the manufacturing operations. Periodic reports to management and other interested parties must include data that will be useful in measuring the efficiency of manufacturing operations and in guiding future operations.

CONCEPTS OF COST AND EXPENSE

The amount of cash paid or liability incurred for a commodity or service is referred to as the *cost* of the item. As the commodity or service is consumed in the operations of a business enterprise, its cost is said to expire. An expiration of cost is ordinarily called an *expense*. For example, as office equipment is used, the expiration of its cost is periodically recognized in the accounts as depreciation expense. The unexpired portion of its cost is the excess of the balance of the plant asset account over its related accumulated depreciation account. The expenses (expired costs) of an enterprise are reported periodically in the income statement as deductions from revenue.

The cost of merchandise acquired for resale to customers is treated somewhat differently from the cost of commodities and services that will be consumed during operations. The cost of merchandise, which is a composite of invoice prices and various additions and deductions to cover such items as delivery charges, allowances, and cash discounts, does not expire, in the usual sense. The merchandise is sold rather than consumed, and the amount sold is referred to as the "cost of merchandise sold."

Determination of the cost of the merchandise available for sale and the cost of the merchandise sold is infinitely more complex for a manufacturing enterprise than for a merchandising business. The cost of manufacturing a commodity is composed not only of the cost of tangible materials but of the many costs incurred in transforming the materials into a finished product ready for sale. This chapter and the next two are concerned principally with the determination and control of the costs incurred in manufacturing operations.

INVENTORIES OF MANUFACTURING ENTERPRISES

Manufacturing businesses maintain three inventory accounts instead of a single merchandise inventory account. Separate accounts are maintained for (1) goods in the state in which they are to be sold, (2) goods in the process of manufacture, and (3) goods in the state in which they were acquired. These inventories are called respectively *finished goods*, *work in process*, and *materials*. The balances in the inventory accounts may be presented in the balance sheet in the following manner:

Inventories:
Finished goods	$300,000	
Work in process	55,000	
Materials	123,000	$478,000

The finished goods inventory and work in process inventory are composed of three separate categories of manufacturing costs: *direct materials*, *direct labor*, and *factory overhead*. Direct materials represent the delivered cost of the materials that enter directly into the finished product. Direct labor represents the wages of the workmen who convert the materials into a finished product. Factory overhead includes all of the remaining costs of operating the factory, such as taxes, insurance, depreciation, and maintenance related to factory plant and equipment, supplies used in the factory but not entering directly into the finished product, and wages for factory supervision.

GENERAL ACCOUNTING FOR MANUFACTURING OPERATIONS

Although the accounting procedures applicable to manufacturing operations are likely to be more complex than those employed in trading operations, the range in the degree of complexity is quite broad. If only

509

a single product or several similar products are manufactured, and if the manufacturing processes are neither complicated nor numerous, the accounting system may be fairly simple. In such cases the periodic system of inventory accounting employed in merchandising may be extended to the three inventories described in the preceding section, and the manufacturing accounts may be summarized periodically in an account entitled Manufacturing Summary. It is to such a relatively simple situation that attention will first be directed.

STATEMENT OF COST OF GOODS MANUFACTURED

Inasmuch as manufacturing activities differ materially from selling and general administration activities, it is customary to segregate the two groups of accounts in the summarizing process at the end of the accounting period. In addition, the manufacturing group is usually reported in a separate statement in order to avoid a lengthy and complicated income statement. The data reported in the separate statement are those needed to determine the cost of the goods (merchandise) manufactured during the period. It is therefore comparable to that section of the income statement of a trading concern that presents the net cost of merchandise purchased. The relationship between the statement of cost of goods manufactured and the income statement is illustrated on the next page.

The amount listed for the work in process inventory at the beginning of the period is composed of the estimated cost of the direct materials, the direct labor, and the factory overhead applicable to the inventory of partially processed products at the close of the preceding period.

The cost of the direct materials placed in production is determined by adding to the beginning inventory of materials the net cost of the direct materials purchased and deducting the ending inventory. The amount listed for direct labor is determined by reference to the direct labor account. The factory overhead costs, which are determined by referring to the ledger, are listed individually either as a part of the statement of cost of goods manufactured or on a separate schedule. The sum of the costs of direct materials placed in production, the direct labor, and the factory overhead represents the total manufacturing costs incurred during the period. Addition of this amount to the beginning inventory of work in process yields the total cost of the work that has been in process during the period. The estimated cost of the ending inventory of work in process is then deducted to yield the cost of goods manufactured.

PERIODIC PROCEDURES

The process of adjusting the periodic inventory and other accounts of a manufacturing business is similar to that for a merchandising enterprise.

Sullivan Manufacturing Company
Income Statement
For Year Ended December 31, 19--

Sales		$415,100
Cost of goods sold:		
Finished goods inventory, January 1, 19-- . .	$ 38,500	
Cost of goods manufactured.	294,675	
Cost of finished goods available for sale . .	$333,175	
Less finished goods inventory, December 31,		
19--.	51,000	
Cost of goods sold.		282,175

Income statement

Sullivan Manufacturing Company
Statement of Cost of Goods Manufactured
For Year Ended December 31, 19--

Work in process inventory, January 1, 19--		$ 25,000
Direct materials:		
Direct materials inventory, January 1, 19--.	$ 32,000	
Direct materials purchases	120,800	
Cost of direct materials available for use.	$152,800	
Less direct materials inventory, December 31, 19--.	28,725	
Cost of direct materials placed in production	$124,075	
Direct labor	98,750	
Factory overhead:		
Indirect labor	$19,300	
Depreciation of factory equipment. .	17,600	
Heat, light, and power	11,800	
Factory maintenance.	8,000	
Property taxes	4,000	
Depreciation of buildings.	3,000	
Amortization of patents.	2,500	
Insurance expired.	2,100	
Factory supplies used.	1,000	
Miscellaneous factory costs.	2,050	
Total factory overhead	71,350	
Total manufacturing costs.		294,175
Total work in process during period. .		$319,175
Less work in process inventory, December 31, 19--.		24,500
Cost of goods manufactured		$294,675

Statement of cost of goods manufactured

511

Adjustments to the merchandise inventory account are replaced by adjusting entries for each of the three inventory accounts, direct materials, work in process, and finished goods. The first two accounts are adjusted through Manufacturing Summary, and the third is adjusted through Income Summary.

In closing the accounts at the end of the accounting period, the temporary accounts that appear in the statement of cost of goods manufactured are closed to Manufacturing Summary. The final balance of this account, which represents the cost of goods manufactured during the period, is then closed to Income Summary. The remaining temporary accounts (sales, expenses, etc.) are then closed to Income Summary in the usual manner.

The relationship of the manufacturing summary account to the income summary account is illustrated below. Note that the balance transferred from the manufacturing summary account to the income summary account, $294,675, is the same as the final figure reported on the statement of cost of goods manufactured.

MANUFACTURING SUMMARY

Dec. 31 Work in Pro. Inv., Jan. 1	25,000	Dec. 31 Work in Pro. Inv., Dec. 31	24,500
31 Direct Mat. Inv., Jan. 1	32,000	31 Direct Mat. Inv., Dec. 31	28,725
31 Direct Mat. Purchases	120,800	31 To Income Sum.	294,675
31 Direct Labor	98,750		
31 Factory Overhead	71,350		
	347,900		347,900

INCOME SUMMARY

Dec. 31 Fin. Goods Inv., Jan. 1	38,500	Dec. 31 Fin. Goods Inv., Dec. 31	51,000
31 From Manufac. Sum.	294,675		

The work sheet used in preparing financial statements for a merchandising business, which was illustrated in Chapter 6, may be expanded for the manufacturing enterprise to include the addition of a pair of columns for the statement of cost of goods manufactured.

COST ACCOUNTING

Cost accounting achieves greater accuracy in the determination of costs than is possible with a general accounting system such as that described in the preceding sections. Cost accounting procedures also permit far more effective control by supplying data on the costs incurred by each factory department and the unit cost of manufacturing each type of product. Such procedures provide not only data useful to management in minimizing costs but also other valuable information about production methods to employ, quantities to produce, product lines to "push," and sales prices to charge.

There are two principal types of cost systems, *process cost* and *job order cost*. Each of the two systems is widely used, and a manufacturer may employ a process cost system for some of its departments or products and a job order cost system for others.

Under process cost systems, the costs are accumulated for each of the various departments or processes within the factory. A process system is best utilized by manufacturers of homogeneous units of product that are not distinguishable from each other during a continuous production process.

Job order cost systems provide for a separate record of the cost of each particular quantity of product that passes through the factory. They are best suited to industries that manufacture commodities to fill special orders from customers and to industries that produce hetero-geneous lines of products for stock.

PROCESS COST SYSTEMS

Companies manufacturing a homogeneous mass such as cement or flour do so on a continuous basis. The manufacturing costs incurred are accumulated for each manufacturing department or process. The cost elements are identified first with the separate processes and then with the physical output of these processes. For example, the cost of producing a ton of cement equals the sum of costs incurred in each separate process divided by the number of tons produced. Other industries that use pro-cess cost accounting include ink, paint, soap, and paper manufacturing.

FLOW OF COSTS IN PROCESS COST SYSTEMS

Perpetual inventory accounts for materials, work in process, and finished goods are requisites of a process cost accounting system. Each of these accounts is debited for all additions and is credited for all de-ductions. The balance of each account thus represents the inventory on hand.

All expenditures incidental to manufacturing move through the work in process account, the finished goods account, and eventually into the cost of goods sold account. The flow of costs through the perpetual in-ventory accounts and into the cost of goods sold account is exemplified by the diagram presented below:

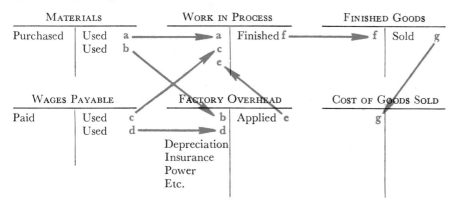

Flow of costs through perpetual inventory accounts

Materials and factory labor used in production are classified as direct and indirect. The materials and the factory labor used directly in the process of manufacturing are debited to Work in Process (**a** and **c** in the diagram). The materials and the factory labor used that do not enter directly into the finished product are debited to Factory Overhead (**b** and **d** in the diagram). Examples of indirect materials are oils and greases, abrasives and polishes, cleaning supplies, gloves, molding sand, drilling soap, and brushes. Examples of indirect labor are salaries of supervisors, inspectors, material handlers, watchmen, and janitors. The appropriate amount of factory overhead costs, which include depreciation, insurance, power, taxes, and other indirect manufacturing costs as well as indirect materials and indirect labor, are transferred to Work in Process (**e** in the diagram). The costs of the goods finished are transferred from Work in Process to Finished Goods when they are finished (**f** in the diagram) and thence to Cost of Goods Sold when they are sold (**g** in the diagram).

The number of accounts presented in the flow chart was severely restricted. In practice, separate work in process accounts and factory overhead accounts are maintained for each department or *cost center* in the factory. There is ordinarily a separate account in a subsidiary ledger for each type of material used in manufacturing, controlled by the account Materials. Similarly, if numerous commodities are manufactured, an account for each type may be maintained in a subsidiary ledger, controlled by the account Finished Goods.

SERVICE DEPARTMENTS AND PROCESS COSTS

In a factory with a number of processes, there may be one or more *service departments* that do not process the materials directly. They render services for the benefit of other production departments. The costs that they incur, therefore, are part of the total manufacturing costs and must be charged to the processing departments. Service departments include such departments as the factory office, the power plant, and the maintenance and repair shop.

The services rendered by a service department give rise to internal transactions between it and the processing departments benefited. These internal transactions are recorded periodically in order to charge the factory overhead accounts of the processing departments with their share of the costs incurred by the service departments. The period usually chosen is a month, although a different period of time may be used. To illustrate, assume that the Power Department produced 300,000 kilowatt-hours during the month at a total cost of $6,000, or 2¢ per kilowatt-hour ($6,000 ÷ 300,000). The factory overhead accounts for the departments that used the power are accordingly charged for power at the 2¢ rate. Assuming that during the month Department 1 used 100,000 kwh and Department 2 used 200,000 kwh, the accounts affected by the interdepartmental transfer of cost would appear as follows:

POWER DEPARTMENT

Fuel	2,400	To Factory Overhead—Dept. 1	2,000
Wages	1,700	To Factory Overhead—Dept. 2	4,000
Depreciation	600		
Maintenance	500		
Insurance	400		
Taxes	300		
Miscellaneous	100		
	6,000		6,000

| FACTORY OVERHEAD — DEPT. 1 | | FACTORY OVERHEAD — DEPT. 2 | |
| Power | 2,000 | Power | 4,000 |

Some service departments render services to other service departments. For example, the power department may supply electric current to light the factory office and to operate various bookkeeping and office machines. At the same time the factory office provides general supervision for the power department, maintains its payroll records, buys its fuel, and so on. In such cases the costs of the department rendering the greatest service to other service departments may be distributed first, ignoring the fact that it receives benefits from other service departments.

515

PROCESSING COSTS

The accumulated costs transferred from preceding departments and the costs of direct materials and direct labor incurred in each processing department are debited to the related work in process account. Each work in process account is also debited for its portion of the factory overhead. The costs incurred are summarized periodically, usually at the end of the month. The costs applicable to the output of each department during the month are then transferred to the next processing department or to Finished Goods, as the case may be. This flow of costs through a work in process account is illustrated below:

WORK IN PROCESS — DEPARTMENT 2

10,000 units at $1.20 from Dept. 1	12,000		To Dept. 3, 10,000 units	20,000
Direct labor	4,600		$\text{Cost per unit } \dfrac{\$20,000}{10,000} = \$2$	
Factory overhead	3,400	8,000		
		20,000		20,000

The three debits in the account above may be grouped into two distinct categories: (1) direct materials or partially processed materials received from another department, which in this case is composed of

10,000 units received from Department 1 with a total cost of $12,000, and (2) direct labor and factory overhead applied in Department 2, which in this case totaled $8,000. This second group of costs is called the *processing cost.*

Again referring to the illustration, all of the 10,000 units were completely processed in Department 2 and passed on to Department 3. The $2 unit cost of the product transferred to Department 3 is composed of Department 1 cost of $1.20 ($12,000 ÷ 10,000 units) and processing cost of $.80 ($8,000 ÷ 10,000 units) incurred in Department 2.

FACTORY OVERHEAD

The identification of factory overhead with specific processing departments is usually more difficult than identification of costs of a more direct nature. The cost of the direct materials physically entering a processing department can be determined and recorded on requisition forms. Similarly, the cost of direct labor can be identified with the department in which the labor is performed, and records maintained on time tickets. On the other hand, many items of factory overhead are incurred for the factory as a whole and are only indirectly related to the activity of the processing departments. The problem is further complicated by the fact that some items of factory overhead cost are relatively fixed in amount, while others tend to vary in accordance with changes in the volume of production.

The factory overhead costs incurred can be accumulated in their respective accounts until the end of the fiscal year and then apportioned among departments on some equitable basis. Such a procedure may be quite acceptable from the standpoint of accuracy, but it is usually highly unsatisfactory in terms of timeliness. Cost data must be available currently throughout the year if they are to be useful to management. If a shorter time period, such as a month, is selected for allocations of overhead, the costs per unit of product manufactured may fluctuate so greatly as to be meaningless. Such fluctuations may be caused by substantial variations in the number of units produced monthly, by the effect of seasonal variation in climatic conditions or other uncontrollable factors, or by a combination of factors.

The difficulties inherent in sole reliance on actual overhead costs can be overcome by the use of estimates. Advance estimates of the magnitude of overhead costs are combined with advance estimates of the volume of factory activity to yield measures called *predetermined factory overhead rates.* The use of such rates permits significant comparisons of unit product costs from month to month. In addition, management is able to make monthly comparisons of the amount of factory overhead actually incurred with the amount charged to processes by use of the predetermined rates.

Predetermined factory overhead rates. Factory overhead rates are determined by relating the estimated amount of factory overhead for each department for the forthcoming year to some common activity base, one that will equitably apply the factory overhead costs to the goods manufactured. The common bases include direct labor costs, direct labor hours, and machine hours. For example, if it is estimated that the total factory overhead costs for a particular department for the year will be $48,000 and that the total direct labor cost for that department will be $60,000, an overhead rate of 80% ($48,000 ÷ $60,000) may be applied to the direct labor cost incurred within the department during the year.

The actual factory overhead costs incurred are debited to the factory overhead accounts. The amounts of factory overhead costs applied to production are credited to the factory overhead accounts and debited to the work in process accounts. Assuming that the direct labor cost in Department 7 during a month is $5,000 and that the predetermined departmental overhead rate is 80%, the entry to apply factory overhead to production is as follows:

```
Work in Process — Department 7.......................  4,000
    Factory Overhead — Department 7....................          4,000
```

Inevitably, factory overhead costs applied and actual factory overhead costs incurred during a particular period will differ. If the amount applied exceeds the actual costs, the factory overhead account will have a credit balance and the overhead is said to be *overapplied* or *overabsorbed;* if the amount applied is less than the actual costs, the account will have a debit balance and the overhead is said to be *underapplied* or *underabsorbed.* Both situations are illustrated in the account presented below.

517

FACTORY OVERHEAD — DEPARTMENT 7

DATE		ITEM	DEBIT	CREDIT	BALANCE DEBIT	BALANCE CREDIT
May	1	Balance				300
	31	Costs incurred	4,510			
	31	Costs applied		4,000	210	

Underapplied Balance ———

Overapplied Balance ———

Disposition of factory overhead balances. The balances in the factory overhead accounts are carried forward from month to month until the end of the year. The net amount of the balances is reported on interim balance sheets as either a deferred charge (net underapplied balance) or a deferred credit (net overapplied balance).

The nature of the balance in the factory overhead account for a particular department (underapplied or overapplied), as well as the amount, will fluctuate during the year. If there is a decided trend in either direction and the amount is substantial, the reason should be determined. If the variation is caused by alterations in manufacturing methods or by substantial changes in production goals, it may be advisable to revise the factory overhead rate. The accumulation of a large underapplied balance is more serious than a trend in the opposite direction and may indicate inefficiencies in production methods, excessive expenditures, or a combination of factors.

Despite any corrective actions that may be taken to avoid an underapplication or overapplication of factory overhead, the accounts will ordinarily have balances at the end of the fiscal year. Since the sum of the balances represents the underapplied or overapplied factory overhead applicable to the operations of the year just ended, it is not proper to report it in the year-end balance sheet as a deferred charge or a deferred credit to manufacturing costs of the following year.

There are two principal alternatives for disposing of the balances of factory overhead at the end of the year: (1) by allocation of the balances among work in process, finished goods, and cost of goods sold accounts on the basis of the total amounts of applied factory overhead included in those accounts at the end of the year, or (2) by transfer of the balances to the cost of goods sold account. Theoretically only the first alternative is sound because it represents a correction of the estimated overhead rates and brings the accounts into agreement with the costs actually incurred. On the other hand, considerable time and expense may be required to make the allocation and to revise the unit costs of the work in process and finished goods inventories. Furthermore, in most manufacturing enterprises a very large proportion of the total manufacturing costs for the year pass through the work in process and the finished goods accounts into the cost of goods sold account before the end of the year. Therefore, unless the total amount of the underapplied or overapplied balances is substantial, it is satisfactory to transfer them to Cost of Goods Sold.

INVENTORIES OF PARTIALLY PROCESSED MATERIALS

Preceding illustrations assumed that all materials entering a process were completely processed at the end of the accounting period. In such cases the determination of unit costs is quite simple. The total of costs transferred from other departments, direct materials, direct labor, and factory overhead charged to a department is divided by the number of units completed and passed on to the next department or to finished goods. Frequently, however, some partially processed materials remain in various stages of production in a department at the close of a period. In this case, the processing costs must be allocated between the units that have been completed and transferred to the next process and those that are only partially completed and remain within the department.

To allocate direct material and transferred costs between the output completed and transferred to the next process and inventory of goods within the department, it is necessary to determine the manner in which the materials are placed in production. For some products, it is necessary to have all materials on hand before any work commences. For other products, materials may be added to production in relatively the same proportion as processing costs are incurred. In still other situations, materials may enter the process at relatively few points, which may or may not be evenly spaced throughout the process.

In order to allocate the processing costs between the output completed and transferred to the next process and the inventory of goods within the process, it is necessary to determine (1) the number of *equivalent units* of production during the period and (2) the *processing cost per equivalent unit* for the same period. The equivalent units of production are the number of units that would have been produced if there had been no inventories within the process either at the beginning or the end of the period. To illustrate, assume that there is no inventory of goods in process in a particular processing department at the beginning of the period, that 1,000 units of materials enter the process during the period, and that at the end of the period all of the units are 75% completed. The equivalent production in the processing department for the period would be 750 units (75% of 1,000). Assuming further that the processing costs incurred during the period totaled $15,000, the processing cost per equivalent unit would be $20 ($15,000 ÷ 750).

519

Ordinarily there is an inventory of partially processed units in the department at the beginning of the period, some units are completed during the period and transferred to the next department, and other units are partially processed and remain in the inventory at the end of the period. To illustrate the computation of equivalent units under such circumstances, the following data are assumed for Department 5:

Inventory within Department 5 on March 1:	600 units, ⅓ completed.
Completed in Department 5 and transferred to finished goods during March:	4,000 units, completed.
Inventory within Department 5 on March 31:	1,000 units, ⅖ completed.

The equivalent units of production may be determined as follows:

To process units in inventory on March 1:	600 units × ⅔......	400
To process units started and completed in March:	4,000 units − 600 units	3,400
To process units in inventory on March 31:	1,000 units × ⅖......	400
Equivalent units of production in March............................		4,200

Continuing with the illustration, the next step is to allocate the costs incurred in Department 5 between the units completed during March and those remaining in process at the end of the month. If materials (including transferred costs) were used and processing costs were incurred uniformly throughout the month, the total costs of the process would be divided by 4,200 units to obtain the unit cost. On the other hand, if all materials were introduced at the beginning of the period, the full materials cost per unit must be assigned to the uncompleted units. The processing costs would then be allocated to the finished and the uncompleted units on the basis of equivalent units of production. Entries in the account below are based on the latter assumption.

WORK IN PROCESS — DEPARTMENT 5

DATE		ITEM	DEBIT	CREDIT	BALANCE DEBIT	BALANCE CREDIT
Mar.	1	Bal. 600 units, ⅓ completed.			1,160	
	31	Dept. 4, 4,400 units at $1 ...	4,400		5,560	
	31	Direct labor.............	6,000		11,560	
	31	Factory overhead.........	4,500		16,060	
	31	Goods finished, 4,000 units..		14,060		
	31	Bal. 1,000 units, ⅖ completed................			2,000	

The processing costs incurred in Department 5 during March total $10,500 ($6,000 + $4,500). The equivalent units of production for March, determined on the preceding page, is 4,200. The processing cost per equivalent unit is therefore $2.50 ($10,500 ÷ 4,200). Of the $16,060 debited to Department 5, $14,060 was transferred to Finished Goods and $2,000 remained in the account as work in process inventory. The computation of the allocations to finished goods and to inventory is illustrated below:

GOODS FINISHED DURING MARCH

600 units:	Inventory on March 1, ⅓ completed...............	$1,160
	Processing cost in March:	
	600 × ⅔, or 400 units at $2.50..................	1,000
	Total......................................	$ 2,160
	(Unit cost: $2,160 ÷ 600 = $3.60)	
3,400 units:	Materials cost in March, at $1 per unit..............	$3,400
	Processing cost in March:	
	3,400 at $2.50 per unit........................	8,500
	Total......................................	11,900
	(Unit cost: $11,900 ÷ 3,400 = $3.50)	
4,000 units:	Goods finished during March..........................	$14,060

PROCESS 5 INVENTORY ON MARCH 31

1,000 units:	Materials cost in March, at $1 per unit..............	$1,000
	Processing cost in March:	
	1,000 × ⅖, or 400 at $2.50.....................	1,000
1,000 units:	Department 5 Inventory on March 31....................	$ 2,000

COST OF PRODUCTION REPORT

A report is prepared periodically for each processing department, summarizing (1) the units for which the department is accountable and the disposition of these units and (2) the costs charged to the department and the allocation of these costs. This report, termed the *cost of production report*, may be used as the source of the computation of unit production costs and the allocation of the processing costs in the general ledger to the finished and the uncompleted units. More importantly, the report is used as a means of controlling costs. Each department head is held responsible for the units entering production and the costs incurred in his department. Any variations in unit product costs from one month to another are carefully scrutinized and the causes of significant variations are determined.

The cost of production report based on the data presented in the preceding section for Department 5 is illustrated on the next page.

JOINT PRODUCTS

When two or more commodities of significant value are produced from a single principal direct material, the products are termed *joint products*. Similarly, the costs incurred in the manufacture of joint products are called *joint costs*. Common examples of joint products are gasoline, naphtha, kerosene, paraffin, benzine, and other related commodities, all of which emerge from the processing of crude oil.

In management decisions concerning the production and sale of joint products, only the relationship of the total revenue to be derived from the entire group to their total production cost is relevant. Nothing is to be gained from an allocation of joint costs to each individual product because one product cannot be produced without the others. A decision to produce a joint product is in effect a decision to produce all of the products.

For one purpose, namely inventory valuation for periodic income statements, it is necessary to make an arbitrary allocation of joint costs among the joint products. One common method of allocation is the *market (sales) value* method. Its essential feature is the assignment of costs to the various products in accordance with their relative sales values. To illustrate, assume that 10,000 units of Product X and 50,000 units of Product Y were produced at a total cost of $63,000. The sales values of the two products and the allocation of the joint costs are presented at the top of page 523.

Inasmuch as joint products emerge from the processing of a common parent material, the assignment of cost to each separate product cannot be based on actual expenditures. It is impossible to determine the amount of cost incurred in the manufacture of each separate product.

Avery Manufacturing Company
Cost of Production Report — Department 5
For the Month Ended March 31, 19--

Quantities:
Charged to production:
In process, March 1   600
Received from Department 4   4,400
Total units to be accounted for   5,000

Units accounted for:
Transferred to finished goods   4,000
In process, March 31   1,000
Total units accounted for   5,000

Costs:
Charged to production:
In process, March 1 . . . . $ 1,160

March costs:
Direct materials from Department 4 ($1 per unit).   4,400

Processing costs:
Direct labor . . . . $ 6,000
Factory overhead   4,500
Total processing costs ($2.50 per unit)   10,500
Total costs to be accounted for $16,060

Costs allocated as follows:

Transferred to finished goods:
600 units at $3.60 . . . . $ 2,160
3,400 units at $3.50   11,900
Total cost of finished goods $14,060

In process, March 31:
Direct materials (1,000 units at $1) . . . . $ 1,000
Processing costs (1,000 units × ⅖ × $2.50)   1,000
Total cost of inventory in process, March 31   2,000
Total costs accounted for $16,060

Computations:

Equivalent units of production:
To process units in inventory on March 1:
600 units × ⅔   400
To process units started and completed in March:
4,000 units − 600 units   3,400
To process units in inventory on March 31:
1,000 units × ⅖   400
Equivalent units of production   4,200

Unit processing cost:
$10,500 ÷ 4,200 . . . . $ 2.50

522

Cost of
production
report

Joint Product	Units Produced	Joint Costs	Sales Value Per Unit	Total Sales Value
X	10,000	$63,000	$3.00	$30,000
Y	50,000		1.20	60,000
Total sales value				$90,000

Allocation of joint costs:

X $\dfrac{30,000}{90,000} \times \$63,000$ $21,000

Y $\dfrac{60,000}{90,000} \times \$63,000$ 42,000

Unit cost:

X $21,000 ÷ 10,000 units $2.10

Y $42,000 ÷ 50,000 units 84

By apportioning joint costs on the basis of relative sales values, it is assumed that the cost of producing an item is proportional to its sales value.

BY-PRODUCTS

If one of the products resulting from a process has little value in relation to the principal product or joint products, it is known as a *by-product*. The emergence of a by-product is only incidental to the manufacture of the principal product or joint products. By-products may be leftover materials, such as sawdust and scraps of wood in a lumber mill; or they may be separated from the material at the beginning of production, as in the case of cottonseed from raw cotton.

The amount of manufacturing cost ordinarily assigned to a by-product is the sales value of the by-product reduced by any additional costs necessary to complete and sell it. The amount of cost thus determined is removed from the appropriate work in process account and transferred to a finished goods inventory account. To illustrate, assume that for a particular period the costs accumulated in Department 4 total $24,400, and that during the same period of time 1,000 units of by-product B, having an estimated value of $200, emerge from the processing in Department 4. Finished Goods — Product B would be debited for $200 and Work in Process — Department 4 would be credited for the same amount, as illustrated in the accounts below.

Work in Process — Department 4		Finished Goods — Product B	
24,400	200 ———————→	200	

The accounting for the costs remaining in the work in process account and for the sale of the by-product would follow the usual procedures.

ILLUSTRATION OF PROCESS COST ACCOUNTING

To illustrate further the procedures that have been described, the following facts are assumed: The Howell Manufacturing Company manufactures one principal product designated Product A. The manufacturing activity begins in Department 1, where all materials enter production. The materials remain in Department 1 for a relatively short time and there is ordinarily no inventory of work in process in that department at the end of the accounting period. A by-product, designated Product B, is also produced in Department 1. From Department 1 the materials comprising the principal product are transferred to Department 2. In Department 2 there are usually inventories at the end of the accounting period. Separate factory overhead accounts are maintained for Departments 1 and 2. Factory overhead is applied at 80% and 50% of direct labor cost respectively for Departments 1 and 2. There are two service departments, Maintenance and Power.

The trial balance of the general ledger on January 1, the first day of the fiscal year, is presented below.

Howell Manufacturing Company
Trial Balance
January 1, 19 – –

Cash...	18,500	
Accounts Receivable..................................	15,000	
Finished Goods — Product A (1,000 units at $11.50)	11,500	
Finished Goods — Product B (600 pounds at $.50)............	300	
Work in Process — Department 2 (800 units, ½ completed)....	7,800	
Materials	12,000	
Prepaid Expenses	2,150	
Plant Assets	310,000	
Accumulated Depreciation — Plant Assets....................		95,000
Accounts Payable..		21,180
Wages Payable..		1,400
Common Stock...		200,000
Retained Earnings		59,670
	377,250	377,250

In order to reduce the illustrative entries to a manageable number and to avoid repetition, the transactions and the adjustments for the month of January are stated as summaries. In practice, the transactions would be recorded from day to day in various journals. The descriptions of the transactions, followed in each case by the entry in general journal form, are presented below and on pages 525–527.

(a) Materials purchased and prepaid expenses incurred on account.

Entry: Materials..	33,500	
Prepaid Expenses.................................	1,100	
Accounts Payable.............................		34,600

(b) Materials requisitioned for use by the various factory departments.

Entry: Maintenance Department......................... 400
Power Department............................. 2,000
Factory Overhead — Department 1.................. 1,240
Factory Overhead — Department 2................. 900
Work in Process — Department 1................... 19,900
Materials...................................... 24,440

(c) Labor used by the various factory departments.

Entry: Maintenance Department......................... 1,200
Power Department............................. 1,500
Factory Overhead — Department 1.................. 950
Factory Overhead — Department 2................. 700
Work in Process — Department 1................... 8,300
Work in Process — Department 2.................. 12,600
Wages Payable................................. 25,250

(d) Costs and expenses incurred on account by the various factory departments and by the sales and administrative divisions.

Entry: Maintenance Department......................... 200
Power Department............................. 300
Factory Overhead — Department 1.................. 600
Factory Overhead — Department 2................. 400
Selling Expenses................................ 5,000
General Expenses................................ 4,500
Accounts Payable............................. 11,000

(e) Expiration of prepaid expenses chargeable to the various factory departments and to the sales and administrative divisions.

Entry: Maintenance Department......................... 100
Power Department............................. 250
Factory Overhead — Department 1.................. 450
Factory Overhead — Department 2................. 350
Selling Expenses................................ 300
General Expenses................................ 200
Prepaid Expenses.............................. 1,650

(f) Depreciation chargeable to the various factory departments and to the sales and administrative divisions.

Entry: Maintenance Department......................... 100
Power Department............................. 350
Factory Overhead — Department 1.................. 600
Factory Overhead — Department 2................. 900
Selling Expenses................................ 200
General Expenses................................ 100
Accumulated Depreciation — Plant Assets.......... 2,250

(g) Distribution of Maintenance Department costs to other factory departments on the basis of maintenance services rendered.

Entry: Power Department............................. 100
Factory Overhead — Department 1.................. 900
Factory Overhead — Department 2................. 1,000
Maintenance Department........................ 2,000

(h) Distribution of Power Department costs to factory processing departments on the basis of kwh supplied.

Entry: Factory Overhead — Department 1.................. 1,800
Factory Overhead — Department 2.................. 2,700
Power Department............................. 4,500

(i) Application of factory overhead costs to work in process accounts at predetermined rates of 80% and 50% of direct labor cost, respectively, for Departments 1 and 2. See transaction (c).

Entry: Work in Process — Department 1.................... 6,640
Work in Process — Department 2.................... 6,300
 Factory Overhead — Department 1................   6,640
 Factory Overhead — Department 2................   6,300

(j) Transfer of production costs from Department 1 to Department 2 and to Product B (by-product). 4,100 units were fully processed and 800 pounds of Product B, valued at 50¢ per pound, were produced. There is no work in process remaining in Department 1 at the end of the month.

Allocation of total costs of $34,840 charged to Department 1:

Product B, 800 × $.50...........................	$ 400
Transferred to Department 2.......................	34,440
Total costs..................................	$34,840

Unit cost of product transferred to Department 2:

$34,440 ÷ 4,100..................................	$ 8.40

Entry: Finished Goods — Product B...................... 400
Work in Process — Department 2.................. 34,440
 Work in Process — Department 1................   34,840

(k) Transfer of production costs from Department 2 to Finished Goods. 4,000 units were completed, and the remaining 900 units were ⅔ completed at the end of the month.

Equivalent units of production:

To process units in inventory on January 1:	
800 × ½.....................................	400
To process units started and completed in January:	
4,000 − 800..................................	3,200
To process units in inventory on January 31:	
900 × ⅔.....................................	600
Equivalent units of production in January...............	4,200

Processing costs:

Direct labor (c)...................................	$12,600
Factory overhead (i)..............................	6,300
Total processing costs.............................	$18,900

Unit processing costs:

$18,900 ÷ 4,200..................................	$ 4.50

Allocation of costs of Department 2:

Units started in December, completed in January:		
Inventory on January 1, 800 units ½ completed.......	$ 7,800	
Processing costs in January, 400 at $4.50.............	1,800	
Total ($9,600 ÷ 800 = $12 unit cost).............		$ 9,600
Units started and completed in January:		
From Department 1, 3,200 units at $8.40.............	$26,880	
Processing costs, 3,200 at $4.50....................	14,400	
Total ($41,280 ÷ 3,200 = $12.90 unit cost).........		41,280
Total transferred to Product A..................		$50,880

Units started in January, ⅔ completed:

From Department 1, 900 units at $8.40	$ 7,560	
Processing costs, 600 at $4.50	2,700	
Total work in process — Department 2		10,260
Total costs charged to Department 2		$61,140

Entry: Finished Goods — Product A	50,880	
Work in Process — Department 2		50,880

(l) Cost of goods sold.

Product A, 3,800 units:

1,000 units at $11.50	$11,500	
800 units at $12.00	9,600	
2,000 units at $12.90	25,800	
Total cost of Product A sold		$46,900

Product B, 1,000 pounds:

1,000 pounds at $.50		500
Total cost of goods sold		$47,400

Entry: Cost of Goods Sold	47,400	
Finished Goods — Product A		46,900
Finished Goods — Product B		500

(m) Sales on account.

Entry: Accounts Receivable	71,100	
Sales		71,100

(n) Cash received on account.

Entry: Cash	70,000	
Accounts Receivable		70,000

(o) Cash disbursed.

Entry: Accounts Payable	50,000	
Wages Payable	22,000	
Cash		72,000

527

A chart of the flow of costs from the service and processing department accounts into the finished goods accounts and thence to the cost of goods sold account is illustrated on page 528. Entries in the accounts are identified by letters to facilitate comparison with the summary journal entries presented above.

After recording and posting the foregoing entries, the trial balance of the ledger is as shown on page 529.

On the balance sheet at January 31, the net underapplied factory overhead of $550 would appear as a deferred charge. The balance in the cost of goods sold account would appear on the income statement as a deduction from sales.

528

Flow of costs
through process
cost accounts

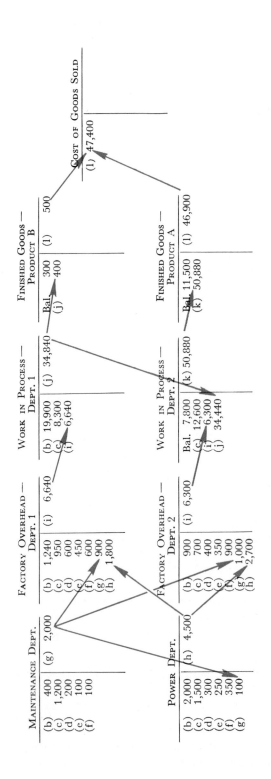

Howell Manufacturing Company
Trial Balance
January 31, 19--

Cash..	16,500	
Accounts Receivable.............................	16,100	
Finished Goods — Product A (1,200 units at $12.90).........	15,480	
Finished Goods — Product B (400 pounds at $.50)............	200	
Work in Process — Department 2 (900 units, ⅔ completed)....	10,260	
Materials..	21,060	
Prepaid Expenses.................................	1,600	
Plant Assets.....................................	310,000	
Accumulated Depreciation — Plant Assets...................		97,250
Accounts Payable.................................		16,780
Wages Payable....................................		4,650
Common Stock....................................		200,000
Retained Earnings................................		59,670
Sales..		71,100
Cost of Goods Sold...............................	47,400	
Factory Overhead — Department 1.......................		100
Factory Overhead — Department 2.......................	650	
Selling Expenses..................................	5,500	
General Expenses.................................	4,800	
	449,550	449,550

QUESTIONS

1. Name the three inventory accounts for a manufacturing business and describe what each balance represents at the end of an accounting period.

2. Name and describe the three categories of manufacturing costs included in the cost of finished goods and the cost of work in process.

3. Which of the following would be included in factory overhead cost? (a) insurance on factory building, (b) depreciation of machinery, (c) direct labor, (d) machinery repairs, (e) advertising, (f) factory rent, (g) factory foreman's salary.

4. (a) Name the two principal types of cost accounting systems. (b) How are the manufacturing costs accumulated under each system?

5. Distinguish between direct and indirect materials used in the process of manufacturing.

6. (a) How does a service department differ from a processing department? (b) Give two examples of a service department.

7. In the manufacture of 8,000 units of a product, direct materials cost incurred was $24,000, direct labor cost incurred was $20,000, and factory overhead applied was $12,000. (a) What is the total processing cost? (b) What is the processing cost per unit? (c) What is the total manufacturing cost? (d) What is the manufacturing cost per unit?

8. Why do many manufacturing enterprises use predetermined factory overhead rates?

9. (a) How are predetermined factory overhead rates determined? (b) Name three common bases used in determining rates.

10. Factory employees in Department 3 of the Collins Manufacturing Co. are paid widely varying wage rates. In such circumstances, would direct labor hours or direct labor cost be the more equitable base for applying factory overhead to the production of the department? Explain.

11. (a) What is (1) overapplied factory overhead and (2) underapplied factory overhead? (b) If the factory overhead account for Department 4 has a debit balance, was factory overhead underapplied or overapplied?

12. On interim balance sheets, where would the amount of (a) net overapplied factory overhead or (b) net underapplied factory overhead appear?

13. At the end of a fiscal year there was a relatively minor balance in each of the factory overhead accounts. What is the simplest, yet satisfactory procedure for the disposition of the balances in the accounts?

14. (a) What is meant by the term "equivalent units"? (b) If Department 1 had no work in process at the beginning of the period, 1,000 units were completed during the period, and 500 units were 50% completed at the end of the period, what was the number of equivalent units of production for the period?

15. The information concerning production in Department 1 for June is presented below. All direct materials are placed in process at the beginning of production. Determine the number of units in work in process inventory at the end of the month.

WORK IN PROCESS — DEPARTMENT 1

DATE		ITEM	DEBIT	CREDIT	BALANCE DEBIT	BALANCE CREDIT
June	1	Bal. 1,000 units, ½ completed			4,500	
	30	Direct material, 3,000 units..	6,150		10,650	
	30	Direct labor..............	12,400		23,050	
	30	Factory overhead.........	3,150		26,200	
	30	Goods finished, 3,500 units..		23,550		
	30	Bal. _____ units, ⅗ completed			2,650	

16. What is the most important purpose of the cost of production report?

17. Distinguish between a joint product and a by-product.

18. Department 5 produces two products. How should the costs be allocated (a) if the products are joint products and (b) if one of the products is a by-product?

19. Watson Company manufactures Products A and B and By-Product C from Process X. In deciding whether or not to continue producing and selling Products A, B, and C, it is not necessary to allocate the joint costs between the products. Explain.

EXERCISES

20-1. The accounts listed below were selected from the pre-closing trial balance at June 30, the end of the current fiscal year, of Jacobs Forging Company.

Sales..	$595,500
Finished Goods Inventory..............................	47,500
Work in Process Inventory.............................	22,500
Direct Materials Inventory.............................	30,000
Direct Materials Purchases............................	127,500
Direct Labor..	157,500
Factory Overhead (control)............................	110,250
Selling Expense (control).............................	45,200
General Expense (control).............................	51,600
Interest Expense.....................................	9,500

Inventories at June 30 were as follows:

Finished Goods......................................	$ 45,000
Work in Process.....................................	31,750
Direct Materials.....................................	26,000

Prepare a statement of cost of goods manufactured.

20-2. On the basis of the data presented in Exercise 1, prepare journal entries on June 30 to:

(a) Adjust the inventory accounts.
(b) Close the appropriate accounts to Manufacturing Summary.
(c) Close Manufacturing Summary.

20-3. The Reese Manufacturing Company manufactures two products. The entire output of Department 1 is transferred to Department 2. Part of the fully processed goods from Department 2 are sold as Product A and the remainder are transferred to Department 3 for further processing into Product B. The service department, Factory Office, provides service for each of the processing departments.

Prepare a chart of the flow of costs from the service and processing department accounts into the finished goods accounts and then into the cost of goods sold account. The relevant accounts are presented below.

Factory Office	Work in Process — Department 2
Factory Overhead — Department 1	Work in Process — Department 3
Factory Overhead — Department 2	Finished Goods — Product A
Factory Overhead — Department 3	Finished Goods — Product B
Work in Process — Department 1	Cost of Goods Sold

20-4. The Conley Company manufactures a single product by a continuous process, involving five production departments. The records indicate that $52,200 of direct materials were issued to and $67,600 of direct labor incurred by Department 1 in the manufacture of the product; the factory overhead rate is 80% of direct labor cost; work in process in the department at the beginning of the period totaled $21,400; and work in process at the end of the period totaled $22,500.

Prepare general journal entries to record (a) the flow of costs into Department 1 during the period for (1) direct materials, (2) direct labor, and (3) factory overhead; (b) the transfer of production costs to Department 2.

20-5. The chief cost accountant for Morgan Tool and Die estimates total factory overhead cost for Department 2 for the year at $64,000 and total direct labor

531

cost at $160,000. During January, actual direct labor cost totaled $14,500 and factory overhead cost incurred totaled $5,650. (a) What is the factory overhead rate based on direct labor cost? (b) Prepare the entry to apply factory overhead to production for January. (c) What is the balance of the account Factory Overhead — Department 2 at January 31? (d) Does the balance in (c) represent overapplied or underapplied factory overhead?

20-6. The charges to Work in Process — Department 1 for a period, together with information concerning production, are presented below. All direct materials are placed in process at the beginning of production.

WORK IN PROCESS — DEPARTMENT 1

1,000 units, 70% completed.....	8,900	To Dept. 2, 2,600 units........	30,580
Direct materials, 1,600 at $5.....	8,000		
Direct labor.................	9,120		
Factory overhead.............	4,560		
	30,580		30,580

Determine the following, presenting your computations: (a) equivalent units of production, (b) processing cost per equivalent unit of production, (c) total and unit cost of product started in prior period and completed in the current period, and (d) total and unit cost of product started and completed in the current period.

20-7. Prepare a cost of production report for the Finishing Department of Benson Manufacturing Company for the month of April of the current fiscal year, using the following data:

Inventory, April 1, 2,000 units, ¾ completed..............	$20,200
Materials from the Plating Department, 5,000 units.........	35,000
Direct labor for April.................................	11,000
Factory overhead for April.............................	9,900
Goods finished during April (includes units in process, April 1), 5,500 units..	—
Inventory April 30, 1,500 units, ½ completed.............	—

20-8. The charges to Work in Process — Department 3, together with units of product completed during the period, are indicated in the following account:

WORK IN PROCESS — DEPARTMENT 3

From Department 2...........	8,290	By-product P, 500 units
Direct labor.................	12,200	Joint product A, 2,500 units
Factory overhead.............	9,760	Joint product B, 5,000 units

There is no inventory of goods in process at either the beginning or the end of the period. The value of P is $.50 a unit; A sells at $8 a unit and B sells at $6 a unit.

Allocate the costs to the three products and determine the unit cost of each, presenting your computations.

PROBLEMS

The following additional problems for this chapter are located in Appendix B: 20-1B, 20-2B, 20-4B, 20-6B.

If the working papers correlating with the textbook are not used, omit Problem 20-1A.

20-1A. The work sheet for Creative Builders, Inc., for the current year ended December 31 is presented in the working papers. Data concerning account titles, trial balance amounts, and selected adjustments have been entered on the work sheet.

Instructions:

(1) Enter the six adjustments required for the inventories on the work sheet. Additional adjustment data are:

Finished goods inventory at December 31.................	$52,300
Work in process inventory at December 31...............	37,550
Direct materials inventory at December 31..............	31,750

(2) Complete the work sheet.
(3) Prepare a statement of cost of goods manufactured.
(4) Prepare an income statement.

20-2A. Lipman Company manufactures Product A. Material M is placed in process in Department 1 where it is ground and partially refined. The output of Department 1 is transferred to Department 2, where Material N is added at the beginning of the process and the refining is completed. On June 1, Lipman Company had the following inventories:

Finished goods (2,000 units)...........................	$48,000
Work in process — Department 1........................	—
Work in process — Department 2 (1,000 units, 2/5 completed)	20,550
Materials..	13,700

Departmental accounts are maintained for factory overhead and there is one service department, factory office. Manufacturing operations for the month of June are summarized as follows:

(a) Materials purchased on account.....................	$17,200
(b) Materials requisitioned for use:	
Material M....................................	$11,050
Material N....................................	5,600
Indirect materials — Department 1................	625
Indirect materials — Department 2................	410
(c) Labor used:	
Direct labor — Department 1.....................	$22,500
Direct labor — Department 2.....................	12,250
Indirect labor — Department 1...................	1,450
Indirect labor — Department 2...................	800
Factory office.................................	400
(d) Miscellaneous costs incurred on account:	
Department 1...................................	$ 2,750
Department 2...................................	1,875
Factory office.................................	975
(e) Expiration of prepaid expenses:	
Department 1...................................	$ 375
Department 2...................................	310
Factory office.................................	75

(f) Depreciation charged on plant assets:
    Department 1 . . . . $ 5,000
    Department 2   3,200
    Factory office   250

(g) Distribution of factory office costs:
    Department 1 .60% of total factory office costs
    Department 2 .40% of total factory office costs

(h) Application of factory overhead costs:
    Department 1 . . . . .50% of direct labor cost
    Department 2 . . . . .60% of direct labor cost

(i) Production costs transferred from Department 1 to Department 2: 2,800 units were fully processed and there was no inventory of work in process in Department 1 at June 30.

(j) Production costs transferred from Department 2 to finished goods: 3,000 units were fully processed including the inventory at June 1. 800 units were ¼ completed at June 30.

(k) Cost of goods sold during June:
    2,900 units (use the first-in, first-out method in crediting the finished goods account).

Instructions:

Prepare entries in general journal form to record the foregoing operations. Identify each entry by letter.

20-3A. The trial balance of Cameron Electronics, Incorporated, at January 31, the end of the first month of the current fiscal year is presented below and at the top of the next page.

Cameron Electronics, Incorporated
Trial Balance
January 31, 19––

Cash	49,250	
Marketable Securities	25,000	
Accounts Receivable	80,500	
Allowance for Doubtful Accounts		4,100
Finished Goods — Product P1	34,200	
Finished Goods — Product P2	45,700	
Work in Process — Department 1	7,400	
Work in Process — Department 2	10,750	
Work in Process — Department 3	15,300	
Materials	30,750	
Prepaid Insurance	6,500	
Office Supplies	2,150	
Office Equipment	29,500	
Accumulated Depreciation — Office Equipment		11,300
Machinery & Equipment	185,000	
Accumulated Depreciation — Machinery & Equipment		80,500
Buildings	550,000	
Accumulated Depreciation — Buildings		266,000
Land	80,000	
Patents	24,000	
Accounts Payable		62,400
Wages Payable		7,700
Income Tax Payable		3,760
Mortgage Note Payable (due 1985)		100,000

Common Stock ($20 par)........................		500,000
Retained Earnings.............................		127,250
Sales..		225,500
Cost of Goods Sold............................	151,750	
Factory Overhead — Department 1.................	250	
Factory Overhead — Department 2.................		50
Factory Overhead — Department 3.................	150	
Selling Expenses...............................	35,750	
General Expenses..............................	20,500	
Interest Expense..............................	500	
Interest Income...............................		100
Income Tax...................................	3,760	
	1,388,660	1,388,660

Instructions:

(1) Prepare an income statement.

(2) Prepare a balance sheet.

20-4A. Ryan Company manufactures Product A by a series of four processes, all materials being introduced in Department 1. From Department 1 the materials pass through Departments 2, 3, and 4, emerging as finished Product A. All inventories are priced at cost by the first-in, first-out method.

The balances in the accounts Work in Process — Department 4 and Finished Goods were as follows on March 1:

Work in Process — Department 4

  600 units, ⅓ completed............................. $11,050

Finished Goods

  1,000 units at $23.50 a unit......................... 23,500

The following costs were charged to Work in Process — Department 4 during March:

Direct materials transferred from Department 3: 2,500 units

  at $16 a unit...................................... $40,000

Direct labor....................................... 12,480

Factory overhead................................... 8,320

During the month of March, 2,200 units of A were completed and 2,000 units were sold. Inventories on March 31 were as follows:

Work in process — Department 4: 900 units, ⅔ completed

Finished Goods: 1,200 units

Instructions:

(1) Determine the following, presenting the computations in good order:

  (a) Equivalent units of production for Department 4 during March.

  (b) Unit processing cost for Department 4 for March.

  (c) Total and unit cost of Product A started in a prior period and finished in March.

  (d) Total and unit cost of Product A started and finished in March.

  (e) Total cost of goods transferred to finished goods.

  (f) Work in process inventory for Department 4, March 31.

  (g) Cost of goods sold (indicate number of units and unit costs).

  (h) Finished goods inventory, March 31.

(2) Prepare a cost of production report for Department 4 for March.

20-5A. Clark Products manufactures joint products X and Y. Materials are placed in production in Department 1 and after processing are transferred to

535

Department 2, where more materials are added. The finished products emerge from Department 2. There are two service departments, Factory Office, and Maintenance and Repair.

There were no inventories of work in process at either the beginning or the end of July. Finished goods inventories at July 1 were as follows:

Product X, 500 units . . . . $ 4,250
Product Y, 900 units 11,250

Transactions related to manufacturing operations for the month of July in summary form are as follows:

(a) Materials purchased on account, $17,250.

(b) Miscellaneous costs and expenses incurred on account: Department 1, $450; Department 2, $625; Factory Office, $250; and Maintenance and Repair, $400.

(c) Materials requisitioned for use: Department 1, $10,100 ($9,750 entered directly into the products); Department 2, $6,950 ($6,500 entered directly into the products); Maintenance and Repair, $450.

(d) Labor costs incurred: Department 1, $5,450 ($5,000 entered directly into the products); Department 2, $7,050 ($6,250 entered directly into the products); Factory Office, $550; Maintenance and Repair, $1,750.

(e) Expiration of various prepaid expenses: Department 1, $50; Department 2, $75; Factory Office, $75; and Maintenance and Repair, $125.

(f) Depreciation charged on plant assets: Department 1, $600; Department 2, $850; Factory Office, $125; and Maintenance and Repair, $175.

(g) Factory office costs allocated on the basis of man-hours worked: Department 1, 600 hours; Department 2, 1,200 hours; Maintenance and Repair, 200 hours.

(h) Maintenance and repair costs allocated on the basis of services rendered: Department 1, 40%; Department 2, 60%.

(i) Factory overhead applied to production at the predetermined rates: 70% and 80% of direct labor cost for Departments 1 and 2 respectively.

(j) Output of Department 1: 1,500 units.

(k) Output of Department 2: 1,000 units of Product X and 2,250 units of Product Y. Unit selling price is $15 for Product X and $20 for Product Y.

(l) Sales on account: 1,100 units of Product X at $15 and 2,100 units of Product Y at $20. Credits to the finished goods accounts are to be priced in accordance with the first-in, first-out method.

Instructions:

Present entries in general journal form to record the transactions; identifying each by letter. Include as an explanation for entry (k) the computations for the allocation of the production costs for Department 2 to the joint products, and as an explanation for entry (l) the units and the unit costs for each product sold.

20-6A. A process cost system is used to record the costs of manufacturing Product M-407, which requires a series of four processes. The inventory of Work in Process — Department 4 on May 1 and debits to the account during May were as follows:

Balance, 1,500 units, 2/3 completed . . . . $ 7,200
From Department 3, 7,500 units 24,375
Direct labor 12,000
Factory overhead 9,600

During May the 1,500 units in process on May 1 were completed, and of the 7,500 units entering the department, all were completed except 1,200 units, which were ⅓ completed.

Charges to Work in Process — Department 4 for the month of June were as follows:

From Department 3, 7,000 units......................... $21,350
Direct labor... 12,425
Factory overhead....................................... 9,940

During June the units in process at the beginning of the month were completed, and of the 7,000 units entering the department, all were completed except 1,400 units, which were ½ completed.

Instructions:

(1) Set up an account for Work in Process — Department 4. Enter the balance as of May 1 and record the debits and the credits in the account for May. Present computations for determination of (a) equivalent units of production, (b) unit processing cost, (c) cost of goods finished, differentiating between units started in the prior period and units started and finished in May, and (d) work in process inventory.

(2) Record the transactions for June in the account. Present the computations listed in instruction (1).

(3) Determine the difference in unit cost between the product started and completed in May and the product started and completed in June. Determine also the amount of the difference attributable collectively to operations in Departments 1 through 3 and the amount attributable to operations in Department 4.

537

Chapter 21

JOB ORDER COST SYSTEMS

JOB ORDER AND PROCESS COSTS DISTINGUISHED

A process cost accounting system is best suited to manufacturing situations where the processes are continuous and the products are homogeneous. A job order cost accounting system is most appropriate where the product is made to customers' orders or specifications and the identity of each job or order is kept separate. It is also appropriate when standard products are manufactured in batches rather than on a continuous basis. The most significant difference between the job order cost system and the process cost system is that the job order cost system requires the identification of the costs incurred by individual jobs within the manufacturing processes.

The basic concepts of the job order cost system are illustrated in this chapter. To simplify the illustration, a nondepartmentalized operation is assumed. In factories with departmentalized operations, costs are accumulated in factory overhead and work in process accounts maintained for each department.

The discussion of the job order cost system directs considerable attention to the source documents that serve as the basis for the entries in the cost system and to the managerial uses of cost accounting in planning and controlling business operations. Many of the methods, procedures, and managerial applications presented in this chapter in relation to job order cost systems apply equally to process cost systems. An example is the accounting system for the acquisition, storage, and issuance of materials described in the following section.

MATERIALS

Procedures employed in the procurement and issuance of materials vary considerably among manufacturers and even among departments of a particular manufacturer. The discussion that follows is confined to the basic principles, however, and will disregard relatively minor variations and details.

Some time in advance of the date that production of a particular commodity is to begin, the department responsible for scheduling informs the purchasing department of the materials that will be needed by means of *purchase requisitions*. The purchasing department then orders appropriate quantities of materials not already in stock by issuing *purchase orders* to suppliers. After the goods have been received and inspected, the receiving department personnel prepare a *receiving report* indicating the quantity received and their condition. Quantities, unit costs, and total costs of the goods billed, as reported on the supplier's invoice, are then compared with the purchase order and the receiving report to make sure that the amounts billed agree with the materials ordered and received. After such verifications the invoice is recorded in the voucher register or purchases journal as a debit to Materials and a credit to Accounts Payable.

The account Materials in the general ledger is a controlling account. An individual account for each type of material is maintained in a subsidiary ledger called the *materials ledger*. Details as to quantity and cost of materials received are recorded in the materials ledger on the basis of the receiving reports or purchase invoices. A typical form of materials ledger account is illustrated below.

539

Material No. 23						Reorder Point *1,000*			
Received			Issued			Balance			
Rec. Report No.	Quantity	Amount	Mat. Req. No.	Quantity	Amount	Date		Quantity	Amount	Unit Price
						Jan.	1	1,200	600 00	50
			672	500	250 00		4	700	350 00	50
196	3,000	1,620 00					8	700 3,000	350 00 1,620 00	50 54
			704	800	404 00		18	2,900	1,566 00	54

Materials ledger account

The accounts in the materials ledger may also be used as an aid in maintaining appropriate inventory quantities of stock items. Frequent comparisons of quantity balances with predetermined reorder points enable management to avoid costly idle time caused by lack of materials. The subsidiary ledger form may also include columns for recording quantities ordered and dates of the purchase orders.

Materials are transferred from the storeroom to the factory in response to *materials requisitions*, which may be issued by the manufacturing department concerned or by a central scheduling department. A typical materials requisition is illustrated below. Storeroom personnel record the issuances on the requisition by inserting the physical quantity data. Transfer of responsibility for the materials is evidenced by the signature or initials of the storeroom and factory personnel concerned. The materials requisition is then routed to the materials ledger clerk who inserts unit prices and amounts.

540

Materials Requisition

Job No. 62   Requisition No. 704

Authorized by J. W. Adams   Date January 17, 19--

Description	Quantity Authorized	Quantity Issued	Unit Price	Amount
Material No. 23	800	700	$.50	$350
		100	.54	54
Total issued				$404

Issued by L. P.   Received by P. P.

Materials requisition

The completed requisition serves as the basis for posting quantities and dollar data to the materials ledger accounts. In the illustration the first-in, first-out pricing method was employed. A summary of the materials requisitions completed during the month serves as the basis for transferring the cost of materials from the controlling account in the general ledger to the controlling accounts for work in process and factory overhead. The flow of materials into production is illustrated by the entry shown below.

Work in Process	6,500	
Factory Overhead	420	
Materials		6,920

The perpetual inventory system for materials has three important advantages: (1) it provides for prompt and accurate charging of materials to jobs and factory overhead, (2) it permits the work of inventory-taking to be spread out rather than concentrated at the end of a fiscal period, and (3) it facilitates the disclosure of inventory shortages or other irregularities. As physical quantities of the various materials are determined, the actual inventories are compared with the balances of the respective subsidiary ledger accounts. The causes of significant discrepancies between the two should be determined and the responsibility therefor assigned to specific individuals. Remedial action can then be taken.

FACTORY LABOR

Unlike materials, factory labor is not tangible, nor is it acquired and stored in advance of its use; hence, there is no perpetual inventory account for labor. The two principal objectives in accounting for labor are (1) determination of the correct amount to be paid each employee for each payroll period, and (2) appropriate allocation of labor costs to factory overhead and individual job orders.

The amount of time spent by an employee in the factory is ordinarily recorded on *clock cards*, which are also referred to as *in-and-out cards*. The amount of time spent by each employee and the labor cost incurred for each individual job, or for factory overhead, are recorded on *time tickets*. A typical time ticket form is illustrated below.

541

TIME TICKET

Employee Name ___John Kane___   No. 4521

Employee No. ___240___   Date ___January 18, 19--___

Description of work ___Finishing___   Job No. ___62___

Time Started	Time Stopped	Hours Worked	Hourly Rate	Cost
10:00	12:00	2	$4.50	$9.00
1:00	2:00	1	4.50	4.50

Total cost $13.50

Approved by ___A. C.___

Time ticket

The total time reported on each employee's time tickets for a payroll period is compared with the time reported on his clock cards as an internal check on the accuracy of payroll disbursements. A summary of the time tickets at the end of each month serves as the basis for recording the labor costs incurred. The flow of labor costs into production is illustrated by the following entry:

Work in Process...............................	5,000	
Factory Overhead	1,100	
Wages Payable................................		6,100

FACTORY OVERHEAD

Although it is possible to allocate the actual factory overhead costs among the various jobs, the difficulties and disadvantages of so doing are comparable to those discussed in connection with process cost systems. The use of a predetermined factory overhead rate is helpful to management in preparing bids on contract work and in quoting firm prices on special jobs. Such price determinations are especially important for job order manufacturers if many of their products are manufactured to individual specifications. In addition, the use of a predetermined factory overhead rate permits determination of the total cost of a job shortly after the job is completed. Timely reporting enables management to make whatever adjustments seem necessary in pricing and manufacturing to achieve the best combination of revenue and cost on future jobs.

Amounts of factory overhead applied to work in process are recorded periodically. The flow of factory overhead (80% of direct labor cost) into production is illustrated in the following entry:

Work in Process................................	4,000	
Factory Overhead		4,000

WORK IN PROCESS

Costs incurred for the various jobs are debited to Work in Process. The charges to the account that were illustrated in the three preceding sections may be summarized as follows:

Direct Materials, $6,500 — Work in Process debited and Materials credited; data obtained from summary of materials requisitions.

Direct Labor, $5,000 — Work in Process debited and Wages Payable credited; data obtained from summary of time tickets.

Factory Overhead, $4,000 — Work in Process debited and Factory Overhead credited; data obtained by applying overhead rate to direct labor cost (80% of $5,000).

Ordinarily a number of jobs are in various stages of production at all times. The work in process account is a controlling account that contains summary information only. The details concerning the costs incurred on each job order are accumulated in a subsidiary ledger known as the *cost ledger*. Each account in the cost ledger, called a *job cost sheet*, has spaces for recording all direct materials and direct labor chargeable to the job and for the application of factory overhead at the predetermined rate. Postings to the job cost sheets are made from materials requisitions and time tickets or from summaries of these documents.

Upon completion of a job, the data on the related job cost sheet are summarized, the unit cost of the finished product is computed, and the sheet is removed from the cost ledger. A summary of the job cost sheets completed during the month provides the basis for an entry debiting Finished Goods and crediting Work in Process.

A work in process account and a summary of the four cost sheets in the related subsidiary ledger are presented below.

WORK IN PROCESS

DATE		ITEM	DEBIT	CREDIT	BALANCE DEBIT	BALANCE CREDIT
May	1	Balance			1,500	
	31	Direct materials	6,500		8,000	
	31	Direct labor	5,000		13,000	
	31	Factory overhead	4,000		17,000	
	31	Jobs completed		15,960	1,040	

543

COST LEDGER

Job No. 71 (Summary)

Balance.....................	1,500
Direct Materials..............	1,000
Direct Labor..................	1,200
Factory Overhead............	960
	4,660

Job No. 73 (Summary)

Direct Materials..............	3,000
Direct Labor..................	2,000
Factory Overhead............	1,600
	6,600

Job No. 72 (Summary)

Direct Materials..............	2,000
Direct Labor..................	1,500
Factory Overhead............	1,200
	4,700

Job No. 74 (Summary)

Direct Materials..............	500
Direct Labor..................	300
Factory Overhead............	240
	1,040

The relationship between the work in process controlling account and the subsidiary cost ledger may be observed in the tabulation presented on the next page. The data is taken from the accounts illustrated above.

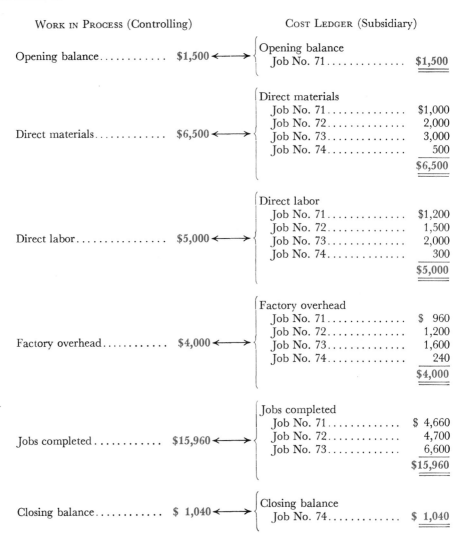

WORK IN PROCESS (Controlling)   COST LEDGER (Subsidiary)

Opening balance.......... $1,500 ←→	Opening balance Job No. 71............. $1,500

Direct materials........... $6,500 ←→	Direct materials
	  Job No. 71............. $1,000
	  Job No. 72............. 2,000
	  Job No. 73............. 3,000
	  Job No. 74............. 500
	  $6,500

Direct labor............... $5,000 ←→	Direct labor
	  Job No. 71............. $1,200
	  Job No. 72............. 1,500
	  Job No. 73............. 2,000
	  Job No. 74............. 300
	  $5,000

Factory overhead........... $4,000 ←→	Factory overhead
	  Job No. 71............. $ 960
	  Job No. 72............. 1,200
	  Job No. 73............. 1,600
	  Job No. 74............. 240
	  $4,000

Jobs completed........... $15,960 ←→	Jobs completed
	  Job No. 71............. $ 4,660
	  Job No. 72............. 4,700
	  Job No. 73............. 6,600
	  $15,960

Closing balance........... $ 1,040 ←→	Closing balance Job No. 74............. $ 1,040

The data in the foregoing cost ledger were presented in summary fashion for illustrative purposes. A form of job cost sheet providing for the current accumulation of cost elements entering into a job order and for a summary at the time the job is completed is presented on the next page for Job No. 72.

When Job No. 72 was completed, the direct materials costs and the direct labor costs were totaled and entered in the Summary column. Factory overhead was added at the predetermined rate of 80% of the direct labor cost, and the total cost of the job was determined. The total cost of the job, $4,700, divided by the number of units produced, 5,000, yielded a unit cost of $.94 for the Type C Containers produced.

Upon the completion of Job No. 72, the job cost sheet was removed from the cost ledger and filed for future reference. At the end of the ac-

Job No. 72					Date	May 7, 19--	
Item 5,000 Type C Containers					Date wanted	May 23, 19--	
For Stock					Date completed	May 21, 19--	

Direct Materials		Direct Labor				Summary	
Mat. Req. No.	Amount	Time Summary No.	Amount	Time Summary No.	Amount	Item	Amount
834	400.00	2202	83.60	2248	22.50	Direct	
838	500.00	2204	108.40	2250	87.30	materials	2,000.00
841	700.00	2205	67.00	2253	55.40	Direct labor	1,500.00
864	400.00	2210	129.00			Factory	
		2211	98.30		1,500.00	overhead	
	2,000.00	2213	107.20			(80% of	
		2216	110.00			direct	
		2222	77.60			labor cost)	1,200.00
		2224	217.40				
		2225	106.30			Total cost	4,700.00
		2231	53.20				
		2234	45.20			No. of units	
		2237	70.00			finished	5,000
		2242	61.60			Cost per unit	.94

Job cost sheet

545

counting period, the sum of the total costs on all cost sheets completed during the period is determined and the following entry is made:

```
Finished Goods.................................  15,960
    Work in Process..............................        15,960
```

The remaining balance in the work in process account represents the total costs charged to the uncompleted job cost sheets.

FINISHED GOODS AND COST OF GOODS SOLD

The finished goods account is a controlling account. The related subsidiary ledger, which has an account for each kind of commodity produced, is called the *finished goods ledger* or *stock ledger*. Each account in the subsidiary finished goods ledger provides columns for recording the quantity and the cost of goods manufactured, the quantity and the cost of goods shipped, and the quantity, the total cost, and the unit cost of goods on hand. An account in the finished goods ledger is illustrated on the next page.

Just as there are various methods of pricing materials entering into production, there are various methods of determining the cost of the finished goods sold. In the illustration, the first-in, first-out method is used. The quantities shipped are posted to the finished goods ledger from

Item: Type C Container									
MANUFACTURED			SHIPPED			BALANCE			
JOB ORDER No.	QUAN-TITY	AMOUNT	SHIP. ORDER No.	QUAN-TITY	AMOUNT	DATE	QUAN-TITY	AMOUNT	UNIT PRICE
						May 1	2,000	1,960 00	98
			643	2,000	1,960 00	8	—	—	–
72	5,000	4,700 00				21	5,000	4,700 00	94
			646	2,000	1,880 00	23	3,000	2,820 00	94

Finished goods
ledger account

a copy of the shipping order or other memorandum. The finished goods ledger clerk then records on the shipping order the unit price and the total amount of the commodity sold. A summary of the cost data on these shipping orders becomes the basis for the following entry:

Cost of Goods Sold.................................... 15,084
    Finished Goods..................................... 15,084

546

If goods are returned by a buyer and put back in stock, it is necessary to debit Finished Goods and credit Cost of Goods Sold for the cost.

SALES

For each sale of finished goods it is necessary to maintain a record of both the cost price and the selling price of the goods sold. As indicated above, the cost data may be recorded on the shipping orders. The sales journal may be expanded by the addition of a column for recording the total cost of the goods billed, the total of the column being posted at the end of the month as a debit to Cost of Goods Sold and a credit to Finished Goods. The total of the sales price column is posted at the end of the month as a debit to Accounts Receivable and a credit to Sales.

ILLUSTRATION OF JOB ORDER COST ACCOUNTING

To illustrate further the procedures described, the following facts are assumed: The Rockford Manufacturing Co. employs a job order cost accounting system. The trial balance of the general ledger on January 1, the first day of the fiscal year, is given at the top of the following page.

A summary of the transactions and the adjustments for the month of January, followed in each case by the related entry in general journal form, is presented on pages 547–549. In practice the transactions would be recorded from day to day in various journals.

Rockford Manufacturing Co.
Trial Balance
January 1, 19--

Cash...	85,000	
Accounts Receivable................................	73,000	
Finished Goods....................................	40,000	
Work in Process...................................	20,000	
Materials...	30,000	
Prepaid Expenses..................................	2,000	
Plant Assets......................................	850,000	
Accumulated Depreciation — Plant Assets..............		473,000
Accounts Payable..................................		70,000
Wages Payable....................................		15,000
Common Stock....................................		500,000
Retained Earnings.................................		42,000
	1,100,000	1,100,000

(a) Materials purchased and prepaid expenses incurred on account.
Summary of receiving reports:

Material A............	$ 20,000
Material B............	17,000
Material C...........	12,000
Material D...........	13,000
Total...............	$ 62,000

Entry: Materials................................... 62,000
      Prepaid Expenses............................. 1,000
        Accounts Payable........................... 63,000

547

(b) Materials requisitioned for use.
Summary of requisitions:

BY USE

Job No. 1001..........	$ 12,000	
Job No. 1002..........	26,000	
Job No. 1003..........	22,000	$ 60,000
Factory Overhead......		3,000
Total................		$ 63,000

BY TYPES

Material A............	$ 16,000	
Material B............	18,000	
Material C...........	15,000	
Material D...........	14,000	
Total...............		$ 63,000

Entry: Work in Process............................. 60,000
      Factory Overhead........................... 3,000
        Materials.................................. 63,000

(c) Factory labor used.
Summary of time tickets:

Job No. 1001..........	$ 60,000	
Job No. 1002..........	30,000	
Job No. 1003..........	10,000	$100,000

Factory Overhead......	20,000	
Total...............	$120,000	

Entry: Work in Process............................. 100,000
       Factory Overhead........................... 20,000
          Wages Payable........................... 120,000

(d) Costs and expenses incurred on account for the factory and by the sales and administrative divisions.

Entry: Factory Overhead........................... 56,000
       Selling Expenses........................... 25,000
       General Expenses........................... 10,000
          Accounts Payable........................ 91,000

(e) Expiration of prepaid expenses chargeable to factory and to the sales and administrative divisions.

Entry: Factory Overhead........................... 1,000
       Selling Expenses........................... 100
       General Expenses........................... 100
          Prepaid Expenses........................ 1,200

(f) Depreciation chargeable to factory and to sales and administrative divisions.

Entry: Factory Overhead........................... 7,000
       Selling Expenses........................... 200
       General Expenses........................... 100
          Accumulated Depreciation — Plant Assets...... 7,300

548

(g) Application of factory overhead costs to jobs at the rate of 90% of direct labor cost. See transaction (c).
Summary of factory overhead applied:

Job No. 1001 (90% of $60,000).	$ 54,000
Job No. 1002 (90% of $30,000).	27,000
Job No. 1003 (90% of $10,000).	9,000
Total....................	$ 90,000

Entry: Work in Process............................. 90,000
          Factory Overhead........................ 90,000

(h) Jobs completed.
Summary of completed job cost sheets:

Job No. 1001................	$146,000
Job No. 1002................	83,000
Total.....................	$229,000

Entry: Finished Goods............................. 229,000
          Work in Process......................... 229,000

(i) Sales on account and cost of goods sold.
Summary of sales invoices and shipping orders:

	SALES PRICE	COST PRICE
Product X........	$ 19,600	$ 15,000
Product Y.......	165,100	125,000
Product Z........	105,300	80,000
Total...........	$290,000	$220,000

Entry: Accounts Receivable.......................... 290,000
    Sales...................................... 290,000

Entry: Cost of Goods Sold.......................... 220,000
    Finished Goods............................ 220,000

(j) Cash received and disbursed.

Entry: Cash...................................... 300,000
    Accounts Receivable........................ 300,000

Entry: Accounts Payable............................ 190,000
    Wages Payable 125,000
    Cash...................................... 315,000

The flow of costs through the manufacturing accounts, together with summary details of the subsidiary ledgers, is illustrated on the following page. Entries in the accounts are identified by letters to facilitate comparisons with the foregoing summary journal entries.

The trial balance taken from the general ledger of the Rockford Manufacturing Co. on January 31 is as follows:

Rockford Manufacturing Co.
Trial Balance
January 31, 19——

Cash..	70,000	
Accounts Receivable...........................	63,000	
Finished Goods................................	49,000	
Work in Process...............................	41,000	
Materials.....................................	29,000	
Prepaid Expenses..............................	1,800	
Plant Assets..................................	850,000	
Accumulated Depreciation — Plant Assets........		480,300
Accounts Payable..............................		34,000
Wages Payable.................................		10,000
Common Stock..................................		500,000
Retained Earnings.............................		42,000
Sales...		290,000
Cost of Goods Sold............................	220,000	
Factory Overhead..............................		3,000
Selling Expenses..............................	25,300	
General Expenses..............................	10,200	
	1,359,300	1,359,300

549

The balances of the three inventory accounts, Materials, Work in Process, and Finished Goods, represent the respective inventories on January 31. Each account controls a subsidiary ledger. A comparison of the balances of the general ledger accounts with their respective subsidiary ledgers is presented at the top of page 551.

In order to simplify the illustration, only one work in process account and one factory overhead account have been used. Ordinarily a manufacturing business has several processing departments, each requiring

550

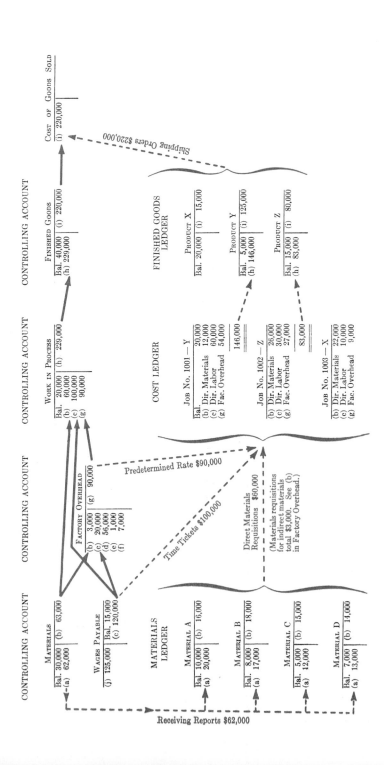

Flow of costs
through job
order cost
accounts

Controlling Accounts		Subsidiary Ledgers	
ACCOUNT	BALANCE	ACCOUNT	BALANCE
Materials.............	$29,000 ⟷	Material A.......... $14,000 Material B.......... 7,000 Material C.......... 2,000 Material D......... 6,000 $29,000	
Work in Process........	$41,000 ⟷	Job No. 1003................	$41,000
Finished Goods.........	$49,000 ⟷	Product X........... $ 5,000 Product Y........... 26,000 Product Z.......... 18,000 $49,000	

separate work in process and factory overhead accounts. In the foregoing illustration, one predetermined rate was used in applying the factory overhead to jobs. In a factory with a number of processing departments, a single factory overhead rate may not provide accurate product costs and effective cost control. A single rate for the entire factory cannot take into consideration such factors as differences among departments in the nature of their operations and in amounts of factory overhead incurred. In such cases, each factory department should have a separate factory overhead rate. For example, in a factory with twenty distinct operating departments, one department might have an overhead rate of 110% of direct labor cost, another a rate of $4 per direct labor hour, another a rate of $3.50 per machine hour, and so on.

551

QUESTIONS

1. Which type of cost system, process or job order, would be best suited for each of the following: (a) paint manufacturer, (b) printing shop, (c) flour milling company, (d) shipbuilder, (e) automobile manufacturer? Give reasons for your answers.

2. What purpose is served by (a) the purchase requisition and (b) the purchase order?

3. Briefly discuss how the purchase order, purchase invoice, and receiving report can be used to assist in controlling cash disbursements made for materials acquired.

4. What document is the source for (a) debiting the accounts in the materials ledger, and (b) crediting the accounts in the materials ledger?

5. Briefly discuss how the accounts in the materials ledger can be used as an aid in maintaining appropriate inventory quantities of stock items.

6. How does use of the materials requisition help control the issuance of materials from the storeroom?

7. The beginning balance, a purchase, and an issuance to production of a particular type of material are described below in chronological sequence. What is the cost of the materials issued to production determined by (a) the first-in, first-out method and (b) the last-in, first-out method?

Beginning balance................ 250 pounds at $1.00 per pound
Purchase....................... 300 pounds at $1.05 per pound
Issued to production.............. 100 pounds

8. Discuss the major advantages of a perpetual inventory system over a periodic system for materials.

9. If a perpetual inventory system is used, is it necessary to take a physical inventory? Discuss.

10. Differentiate between the clock card and the time ticket.

11. Discuss how the predetermined factory overhead rate can be used in job order cost accounting to assist management in pricing jobs.

12. What name is given to the individual accounts in the cost ledger?

13. Describe the source of the data for debiting Work in Process for (a) direct materials, (b) direct labor, and (c) factory overhead.

14. What document serves as the basis for posting to (a) the direct materials section of the job cost sheet and (b) the direct labor section of the job cost sheet?

15. What account is the controlling account for (a) the materials ledger, (b) the cost ledger, and (c) the finished goods ledger or stock ledger?

16. In a factory with several processing departments, a separate factory overhead rate is often determined for each department. Why is a single factory overhead rate often inadequate in such circumstances?

EXERCISES

21-1. The balance of Material C on May 1 and the receipts and issuances during May are presented below.

Balance, May 1, 150 units at $9.00

Received during May:
  May 4, 400 units at $9.00
  May 11, 200 units at $9.50
  May 25, 300 units at $10.00

Issued during May:
  May 6, 200 units for Job No. 617
  May 18, 300 units for Job No. 627
  May 27, 250 units for Job No. 639

Determine the cost of each of the three issuances using (a) the first-in, first-out method and (b) the last-in, first-out method.

21-2. The issuances of materials for the current month are presented below.

Requisition No.	Material	Job No.	Amount
822	C-11	299	$4,125
823	B-6	302	1,780
824	E-22	General factory use	520
825	A-10	297	1,225
826	A-16	302	2,750

Present the general journal entry to record the issuances of materials.

21-3. A summary of the time tickets for the current month follows:

Job No.	Amount	Job No.	Amount
917	$1,150	921	$2,200
918	775	922	575
920	2,100	Indirect labor	1,100

Present the general journal entry to record the factory labor costs incurred.

21-4. The Bower Manufacturing Company applies factory overhead to jobs on the basis of machine hours for work performed in Department 1 and on the basis of direct labor dollars for work performed in Department 2. Estimated factory overhead costs, direct labor costs, and machine hours for the year, and actual factory overhead costs, direct labor costs, and machine hours for January are presented below. Departmental accounts are maintained for work in process and factory overhead.

	Department 1	Department 2
Estimated factory overhead costs for year....	$33,000	$36,000
Estimated direct labor costs for year........		$45,000
Estimated machine hours for year..........	30,000 hrs.	
Actual factory overhead costs for January....	$ 2,690	$ 3,125
Actual direct labor costs for January........		$ 3,800
Actual machine hours for January..........	2,500 hrs.	

553

(a) Determine the factory overhead rate for Department 1. (b) Determine the factory overhead rate for Department 2. (c) Prepare the general journal entry to apply factory overhead to production for January. (d) Determine the balances of the departmental factory overhead accounts as of January 31 and indicate whether the amounts represent overapplied or underapplied factory overhead.

21-5. The following account appears in the ledger after only part of the postings have been completed for the month of March:

WORK IN PROCESS

Balance, March 1	7,700	
Direct Materials	24,350	
Direct Labor	38,000	
Factory Overhead	32,400	

Jobs finished during March are summarized below.

Job No. 430..........	$21,250	Job No. 435..........	$11,750
Job No. 433..........	29,700	Job No. 436..........	30,200

(a) Prepare the general journal entry to record the jobs completed and (b) determine the cost of the unfinished jobs at March 31.

21-6. Davidson Products began manufacturing operations on July 1. The cost sheets for the four jobs entering production during the month are presented below, in summary form. Jobs Nos. 1 and 3 were completed during the month, and all costs applicable to them were recorded on the related cost sheets. Jobs Nos. 2 and 4 are still in process at the end of the month, and all applicable costs except factory overhead have been recorded on the related cost sheets. In addition to the materials and labor charged directly to the jobs, $450 of indirect materials and $1,250 of indirect labor were used during the month.

Job No. 1		Job No. 2	
Direct Material............	4,850	Direct Material............	11,500
Direct Labor..............	4,000	Direct Labor..............	6,600
Factory Overhead.........	2,400	Factory Overhead.........	
Total.................	11,250		

Job No. 3		Job No. 4	
Direct Material............	7,800	Direct Material............	3,200
Direct Labor..............	6,200	Direct Labor..............	1,800
Factory Overhead.........	3,720	Factory Overhead.........	
Total.................	17,720		

Prepare an entry, in general journal form, to record each of the following operations for the month (one entry for each operation):

(a) Direct and indirect materials used.
(b) Direct and indirect labor used.
(c) Factory overhead to be applied (a single overhead rate is used, based on direct labor cost).
(d) Jobs Nos. 1 and 3 completed.

PROBLEMS

The following additional problems for this chapter are located in Appendix B: 21-1B, 21-2B, 21-5B.

21-1A. Watson Printing Company uses a job order cost system. The following data summarize the operations related to production for July, the first month of operations.

(a) Materials purchased on account, $17,600.
(b) Materials requisitioned and factory labor used:

	Materials	Factory Labor
Job No. 1.............................	$1,475	$ 900
Job No. 2.............................	2,350	1,750
Job No. 3.............................	2,600	1,300
Job No. 4.............................	3,660	2,700
Job No. 5.............................	1,150	850
Job No. 6.............................	1,225	950
For general factory use...............	425	600

(c) Factory overhead costs incurred on account, $3,375.

(d) Depreciation of machinery and equipment, $1,100.
(e) The factory overhead rate is 50% of direct labor cost.
(f) Jobs completed: Nos. 1, 2, 4, and 5.
(g) Jobs Nos. 1, 2, and 4 were shipped and customers were billed for $3,800, $6,600, and $11,100 respectively.

Instructions:

(1) Prepare entries in general journal form to record the foregoing summarized operations.
(2) Open T accounts for Work in Process and Finished Goods and post the appropriate entries, using the identifying letters as dates.
    Insert memorandum account balances as of the end of the month.
(3) Prepare a schedule of unfinished jobs to support the balance in the work in process account.
(4) Prepare a schedule of completed jobs on hand to support the balance in the finished goods account.

If the working papers correlating with the textbook are not used, omit Problem 21-2A.

21-2A. Carter Furniture Company repairs, refinishes, and reupholsters furniture. A job order cost system was installed recently to facilitate (1) the determination of price quotations to prospective customers, (2) the determination of actual costs incurred on each job, and (3) cost reductions.

In response to a prospective customer's request for a price quotation on a job, the estimated cost data are inserted on an unnumbered job cost sheet. If the offer is accepted, a number is assigned to the job and the costs incurred are recorded in the usual manner on the job cost sheet. After the job is completed, reasons for the variances between the estimated and actual costs are noted on the sheet. The data are then available to management in evaluating the efficiency of operations and in preparing quotations on future jobs.

On July 12, an estimate of $250 for reupholstering a couch was given to James Cole. The estimate was based upon the following data:

Estimated direct materials:	
11 yards at $10 per yard...............................	$110
Estimated direct labor:	
12 hours at $5 per hour..................................	60
Estimated factory overhead (50% of direct labor cost).........	30
Total estimated costs....................................	$200
Markup (25% of production costs).........................	50
Total estimate...	$250

On July 17, the couch was picked up from the residence of James Cole at 2408 Melrose Drive, Wilbur Heights, with a commitment to return it on July 31. The job was completed on July 29.

The materials requisition and time tickets related to the job are summarized below:

Materials Requisition No.	Description	Amount
298	11 yards at $10	$110
299	1 yard at $10	10

Time Ticket No.	Description	Amount
611	8 hours at $5	$ 40
612	5 hours at $5	25

Instructions:
(1) Complete that portion of the job order cost sheet that would be completed when the estimate is given to the customer.
(2) Assign number 635-R to the job, record the costs incurred, and complete the job order cost sheet. In commenting upon the variances between actual costs and estimated costs, assume that 1 yard of material was spoiled and that the factory overhead rate has been proved to be satisfactory.

21-3A. The trial balance of the general ledger of Rowe Manufacturing Corporation as of January 31, the end of the first month of the current fiscal year, is as follows:

Rowe Manufacturing Corporation
Trial Balance
January 31, 19—

Cash..	43,700	
Accounts Receivable...........................	79,500	
Finished Goods................................	62,800	
Work in Process...............................	15,700	
Materials......................................	26,900	
Plant Assets...................................	278,000	
Accumulated Depreciation — Plant Assets........		68,550
Accounts Payable..............................		47,700
Wages Payable.................................		8,800
Capital Stock..................................		250,000
Retained Earnings.............................		122,125
Sales..		87,600
Cost of Goods Sold............................	64,500	
Factory Overhead..............................	175	
Selling and General Expenses...................	13,500	
	584,775	584,775

As of the same date, balances in the accounts of selected subsidiary ledgers are as follows:

Finished goods ledger:
    Commodity A, 900 units, $10,800; Commodity B, 2,000 units, $40,000; Commodity C, 1,200 units, $12,000.
Cost ledger:
    Job No. 925, $15,700.
Materials ledger:
    Material X, $15,200; Material Y, $10,800; Material Z, $900.

The transactions completed during February are summarized as follows:
(a) Materials were purchased on account as follows:

Material X..	$22,600
Material Y..	7,000
Material Z..	500

(b) Materials were requisitioned from stores as follows:

Job No. 925, Material X, $4,700; Material Y, $3,000.......	$ 7,700
Job No. 927, Material X, $12,500; Material Y, $6,200.....	18,700
Job No. 928, Material X, $6,400; Material Y, $2,000......	8,400
For general factory use, Material Z.....................	650

(c) Time tickets for the month were chargeable as follows:

Job No. 925.........	$ 7,500	Job No. 928.........	$ 5,000
Job No. 927.........	12,500	Indirect labor.......	3,200

(d) Various factory overhead charges of $13,150 were incurred on account.

(e) Selling and general expenses of $12,100 were incurred on account.

(f) Depreciation on factory plant and equipment of $2,500 was recorded.

(g) Factory payroll checks for $27,700 were issued.

(h) Payments on account were $57,500.

(i) Factory overhead was applied to jobs at 80% of direct labor cost.

(j) Jobs completed during the month were as follows: Job No. 925 produced 3,000 units of Commodity A; Job No. 927 produced 2,000 units of Commodity B.

(k) Total sales on account were $97,700. The goods sold were as follows (use first-in, first-out method): 2,500 units of Commodity A; 2,200 units of Commodity B; 400 units of Commodity C.

(l) Cash of $93,500 was received on accounts receivable.

Instructions:

(1) Open T accounts for the general ledger, the finished goods ledger, the cost ledger, and the materials ledger. Record directly in these accounts the balances as of January 31, identifying them as "Bal." Record the quantities as well as the dollar amounts in the finished goods ledger.

(2) Prepare entries in general journal form to record the February transactions. After recording each transaction, post to the T accounts, using the identifying letters as dates. When posting to the finished goods ledger, record quantities as well as dollar amounts.

(3) Take a trial balance.

(4) Prepare schedules of the account balances in the finished goods ledger, the cost ledger, and the materials ledger.

(5) Prepare an income statement (to the point of income before income tax) for the two months ended February 28.

21-4A. The trial balance of W. L. Brown, Inc., at the end of the eleventh month of the current year is presented on the following page.

Transactions completed during December and adjustments required on December 31 are summarized as follows:

(a) Materials purchased on account...............			$24,750
(b) Materials requisitioned for factory use:			
Direct......................................		$22,250	
Indirect....................................		275	22,525
(c) Factory labor costs incurred:			
Direct......................................		$12,000	
Indirect....................................		1,100	13,100
(d) Other costs and expenses incurred on account:			
Factory overhead...........................		$ 6,025	
Selling expenses............................		5,650	
General expenses...........................		2,125	13,800
(e) Cash disbursed:			
Accounts payable...........................		$41,000	
Wages payable..............................		14,400	
Dividends payable..........................		3,000	58,400
(f) Applied factory overhead at a predetermined rate:			
75% of direct labor cost......................			

W. L. Brown, Inc.
Trial Balance
November 30, 19—

Cash.	35,400	
Accounts Receivable.	56,500	
Allowance for Doubtful Accounts.		2,150
Finished Goods.	88,950	
Work in Process.	24,900	
Materials.	41,200	
Prepaid Insurance.	4,100	
Factory Equipment.	190,000	
Accumulated Depreciation — Factory Equipment.		50,000
Office Equipment.	35,800	
Accumulated Depreciation — Office Equipment.		5,500
Accounts Payable.		40,860
Income Tax Payable.		11,700
Cash Dividends Payable.		3,000
Wages Payable.		2,500
Interest Payable.		———
Mortgage Note Payable (due 1985).		75,000
Common Stock ($10 par).		200,000
Retained Earnings.		62,565
Cash Dividends.	6,000	
Income Summary.		———
Sales.		642,500
Cost of Goods Sold.	503,700	
Factory Overhead.	550	
Selling Expenses.	62,900	
General Expenses.	24,950	
Interest Expense.	4,125	
Income Tax.	16,700	
	1,095,775	1,095,775

(g) Total cost of jobs completed.		44,150
(h) Sales, all on account:		
Selling price.		70,000
Cost price.		51,525
(i) Cash received on account.		65,500
(j) Depreciation charged:		
Factory equipment.		1,000
Office equipment.		200
(k) Insurance expired:		
Chargeable to factory.	$ 150	
Chargeable to selling expenses.	25	
Chargeable to general expenses.	20	195
(l) Uncollectible accounts receivable written off.		800
(m) Additional income tax recorded.		4,800
(n) Interest accrued on mortgage note payable recorded		375

(o) Analysis of accounts in customers ledger indicated doubtful accounts of $1,900. Adjusted the allowance account.

(p) Balance in Factory Overhead closed to Cost of Goods Sold.

Instructions:

(1) Open T accounts and record the initial balances indicated in the November 30 trial balance, identifying each as "Bal."
(2) Record the transactions and the adjustments directly in the accounts, using the identifying letters in place of dates.
(3) Record the necessary year-end closing entries directly in the accounts, using a capital "C" to designate these entries.
(4) Prepare an income statement for the year ended December 31, 19—.
(5) Prepare a balance sheet as of December 31, 19—.

21-5A. Selected accounts for Holmes Products are presented below. For the purposes of this problem, some of the debits and credits have been omitted.

ACCOUNTS RECEIVABLE

May 1	Balance	33,500	May 31	Collections	40,600
31	Sales	(A)			

MATERIALS

May 1	Balance	7,600	May 31	Requisitions	(B)
31	Purchases	12,100			

WORK IN PROCESS

May 1	Balance	7,100	May 31	Goods finished	(E)
31	Direct materials	(C)			
31	Direct labor	20,000			
31	Factory overhead	(D)			

FINISHED GOODS

May 1	Balance	18,100	May 31	Cost of goods sold	(G)
31	Goods finished	(F)			

FACTORY OVERHEAD

May 1	Balance	125	May 31	Applied (70% of direct	
1–31	Costs incurred	13,675		labor cost)	(H)

COST OF GOODS SOLD

May 31	(I)	

SALES

	May 31	(J)

Selected balances at May 31:

Accounts receivable.............................	$37,500
Finished goods.................................	17,100
Work in process...............................	7,250
Materials.....................................	5,750

Materials requisitions for May included $500 of materials issued for general factory use. All sales are made on account, terms n/30.

Instructions:
(1) Determine the amounts represented by the letters (A) through (J), presenting your computations.
(2) Determine the amount of factory overhead overapplied or underapplied as of May 31.

Chapter 22

BUDGETARY CONTROL AND STANDARD COST SYSTEMS

ACCOUNTING AIDS TO MANAGEMENT

The individuals charged with the responsibility of organizing and directing the operations of a business enterprise are often referred to collectively as the "management." The basic functions of management are frequently classified as (1) planning and (2) control. *Planning* is the process of selecting realistically attainable business objectives and formulating the general policies and the specific directions needed to achieve such objectives. *Control* encompasses the procedures designed to assure the conformity of actual operations with management's plans.

Effective planning and control are requisites of good business management and successful operations. When the owner of a business can personally supervise every phase of operations, he can perform the basic functions of management with minimum recourse to accounting data. Direct supervision of all phases of operations by a single individual is seldom possible, however, and it is necessary to establish a chain of management command from the chief executive down to department foremen. Under such circumstances, accounting data are indispensable in providing each management level with the financial and operating data needed to achieve sound planning and effective control.

Various uses of accounting data by management have been described in earlier chapters. The value of financial statements in appraising past operations and planning for the future has been emphasized. Attention has been directed to the principles of internal control designed to safeguard assets, assure accurate accounting data, encourage adherence to management policies, and increase efficiency. The role of cost accounting in planning production and controlling costs has been described. This chapter is devoted to budgeting and standard costs, two additional accounting tools designed to assist management in planning and controlling operations.

561

NATURE AND OBJECTIVES OF BUDGETING

The essentials of *budgeting* are (1) the establishment of specific goals for future operations and (2) the periodic comparison of actual results with these goals. Although budgeting is commonly associated with profit-making enterprises, its wide applicability in other areas should be noted. Budgeting plays an important role in operating most instrumentalities of government, ranging from rural school districts and small villages to gigantic agencies of the federal government. It is also an integral part of the operations of churches, hospitals, and other nonprofit institutions. Individuals and family units frequently employ budgeting techniques as an aid to careful management of resources.

A *budget* is a formal written statement of management's plans for the future, expressed in financial terms. A budget charts the course of future action. Thus, it serves management in the same manner that the architect's blueprints assist the builder and the navigator's flight plan aids the pilot. A budget, like a blueprint and a flight plan, should contain sound, attainable objectives.

BUDGETING AND MANAGEMENT

Each of management's primary functions is directly served by budgeting. If the budget is to contain sound, attainable goals, planning must be based on careful study, investigation, and research. Reliance by management on data thus obtained lessens the role of hunches and intuition in managing a business enterprise.

In order to be effective, managerial planning must be accompanied by control. The control feature of budgeting lies in periodic comparisons as disclosed by *budget performance reports* between planned objectives and actual performance. This "feedback" enables management to seek corrective action for areas where significant variations between the budget and actual performance are reported. The role of accounting is to assist management in the investigation phase of budget preparation, to translate management's plans into financial terms, and to prepare budget performance reports and related analyses.

BUDGETING PROCEDURES

The responsibility for developing and directing the budget process is ordinarily assigned to a committee composed of the budget director and such high-level executives as the controller, treasurer, production manager, and sales manager. The process is initiated by requesting estimates of sales, production, and other operating data from the various administrative units concerned. It is important that all levels of management and all departments participate in the preparation and submission of

562

budget estimates. The involvement of all supervisory personnel engenders cooperation both within and among departments and also heightens awareness of each department's importance in the overall processes of the company. All levels of management are thus encouraged to establish goals and to control operations in a manner that strengthens the possibilities of achieving the goals.

The various estimates received by the budget committee are revised, reviewed, coordinated, cross-referenced, and finally assembled to form the *master budget*. The estimates submitted should not be substantially revised by the committee without first giving the originator an opportunity to defend his proposals. After agreement has been reached and the master budget has been adopted by the budget committee, copies of the pertinent sections are distributed to appropriate personnel in the chain of accountability. Periodic reports comparing actual results with the budget should likewise be distributed to all supervisory personnel.

SYSTEMS OF BUDGETARY CONTROL

The details of budgeting systems vary among enterprises; they are affected by the type and degree of complexity of the particular company, the volume of its revenues, the relative importance of its various divisions, and many other factors. Budget procedures employed by a large manufacturer of automobiles would obviously differ in many respects from a system designed for a small manufacturer of paper products. The differences between a system designed for factory operations of any type and a financial enterprise such as a bank would be even more marked.

As a framework for describing and illustrating budgeting, a small manufacturing enterprise will be assumed. The principal components of its master budget are as follows:

> Budgeted income statement
>> Sales budget
>> Cost of goods sold budget
>>> Production budget
>>> Direct materials purchases budget
>>> Direct labor cost budget
>>> Factory overhead cost budget
>> Operating expenses budget
>
> Budgeted balance sheet
>> Capital expenditures budget
>> Cash budget

BUDGET PERIOD

Budgets of operating activities ordinarily encompass the fiscal year of an enterprise. A year is short enough to make possible fairly dependable

563

estimates of future operations, and yet long enough to make it possible to view the future in a reasonably broad context. However, to achieve effective control the annual budgets must be subdivided into shorter time periods such as quarters of the year, months, or weeks. It is also necessary to review the budgets from time to time and make such revisions as are necessitated by unforeseen changes in business conditions, in the particular industry, or in the individual enterprise.

A frequent variant of fiscal year budgeting, sometimes called *continuous budgeting*, is to maintain at all times a twelve-month projection into the future. At the end of each time interval employed, the twelve-month budget is revised by removing the data for the currently elapsed period and adding the newly estimated budget data for the same period a year hence.

SALES BUDGET

The first budget to be prepared is customarily the sales budget. The estimate of the quantity of sales serves as the basis for the development of the other budgets and will, of course, have a material effect on all elements entering into the determination of income from operations.

The sales budget ordinarily indicates the quantity of each product expected to be sold, classified by area and/or salesman. The quantity estimates are based on an analysis of past sales and on forecasts of business conditions generally and for the specific industry. The anticipated sales revenue is then determined by multiplying the volume of forecasted sales by the expected unit sales price. A sales budget is illustrated below.

Dean Company
Sales Budget
For Year Ending December 31, 19--

PRODUCT AND AREA	UNIT SALES VOLUME	UNIT SELLING PRICE	TOTAL SALES
Product X:			
Area A	52,000	$ 6.60	$ 343,200
Area B	40,500	6.60	267,300
Area C	39,500	6.60	260,700
Total			$ 871,200
Product Y:			
Area A	27,900	$11.00	$ 306,900
Area B	19,700	11.00	216,700
Area C	22,400	11.00	246,400
Total			$ 770,000
Total revenue from sales			$1,641,200

Sales budget

If actual sales of each product are subsequently reported for each area, management can investigate any significant failures to achieve goals and take action to correct the causes of such failures.

PRODUCTION BUDGET

The number of units of each commodity expected to be manufactured to meet budgeted sales and inventory requirements is set forth in the production budget. The expected volume of production is determined by subtracting the estimated inventory at the beginning of the period from the sum of the units expected to be sold and the desired inventory at the end of the period. A production budget is illustrated below.

Dean Company
Production Budget
For Year Ending December 31, 19--

	UNITS	
	PRODUCT X	PRODUCT Y
Sales	132,000	70,000
Desired inventory, December 31, 19--.........	20,000	15,000
Total..................................	152,000	85,000
Less estimated inventory, January 1, 19--......	22,000	12,000
Total production.........................	130,000	73,000

Production budget

The production requirements must be carefully coordinated with the sales budget to assure that production and sales are kept in balance during the period. Ideally, manufacturing operations should be maintained at normal capacity with no idle time or overtime, nor should there be excessive inventories or inventories insufficient to fill sales orders.

565

DIRECT MATERIALS PURCHASES BUDGET

The production requirements indicated by the production budget combined with data on direct materials needed provide the data for the direct materials purchases budget. The direct materials purchases necessary to meet production requirements is determined by subtracting the quantity of materials on hand at the beginning of the period from

Dean Company
Direct Materials Purchases Budget
For Year Ending December 31, 19--

	DIRECT MATERIALS		
	A	B	C
Units required for production:			
Product X.........................	195,000	——	260,000
Product Y.........................	73,000	146,000	146,000
Desired inventory, December 31, 19--.....	40,000	20,000	60,000
Total.............................	308,000	166,000	466,000
Less estimated inventory, January 1, 19--.	51,500	22,000	56,000
Total units to be purchased.............	256,500	144,000	410,000
Unit price.........................	$ .20	$ .55	$ .35
Total direct materials purchases..........	$51,300	$79,200	$143,500

Direct materials purchases budget

the sum of the units expected to be needed to meet production requirements and the number of units desired in the inventory at the end of the period. The quantities of direct materials required are then multiplied by the expected unit purchase price to determine the total cost of direct materials purchases.

In the direct materials purchases budget illustrated on the preceding page, materials A and C are required for Product X and materials A, B, and C are required for Product Y.

The timing of the direct materials purchases requires close coordination between the purchasing and production departments so that inventory levels can be maintained within reasonable limits.

DIRECT LABOR COST BUDGET

The production requirements indicated by the production budget provide the starting point for the preparation of the direct labor cost budget. The direct labor hours necessary to meet production requirements multiplied by the estimated hourly rate yields the total direct labor cost. It was assumed for the direct labor cost budget illustrated below that manufacturing operations for Products X and Y are performed in two production departments.

Dean Company
Direct Labor Cost Budget
For Year Ending December 31, 19--

	DEPARTMENT 1	DEPARTMENT 2
Hours required for production:		
Product X............................	32,500	26,000
Product Y............................	18,250	29,200
Total...........................	50,750	55,200
Hourly rate...........................	$4	$5
Total direct labor cost.................	$203,000	$276,000

Direct labor cost budget

FACTORY OVERHEAD COST BUDGET

The factory overhead costs estimated to be necessary to meet production requirements are presented in the factory overhead cost budget. For use as a part of the master budget, the factory overhead cost budget ordinarily presents the total estimated cost for each item of factory overhead. Supplemental schedules are often prepared to present the factory overhead cost for each individual department. Such schedules enable each department foreman to confine his attention to those costs for which he is responsible. They also aid the production manager in evaluating performance in each department. A factory overhead cost budget is illustrated at the top of the next page.

Dean Company
Factory Overhead Cost Budget
For Year Ending December 31, 19--

Indirect factory wages...	$120,500
Supervisory salaries...	65,000
Power and light...	56,000
Depreciation of plant and equipment.............................	50,000
Indirect materials...	32,500
Maintenance..	24,000
Insurance and property taxes....................................	11,250
Total factory overhead cost.....................................	$359,250

Factory overhead cost budget

COST OF GOODS SOLD BUDGET

The budget for the cost of goods sold is prepared by combining the relevant estimates of quantities and costs presented in the direct materials purchases, direct labor cost, and factory overhead cost budgets, and adding data on estimated inventories. A cost of goods sold budget is illustrated below.

Dean Company
Cost of Goods Sold Budget
For Year Ending December 31, 19--

Finished goods inventory, January 1, 19--.......			$ 186,400
Work in process inventory, January 1, 19--......		$ 11,100	
Direct materials:			
Direct materials inventory, January 1, 19--....	$ 43,700		
Direct materials purchases...................	274,000		
Cost of direct materials available for use.......	$317,700		
Less direct materials inventory, December 31,			
19--....................................	40,000		
Cost of direct materials placed in production..	$277,700		
Direct labor................................	479,000		
Factory overhead...........................	359,250		
Total manufacturing costs....................		1,115,950	
Total work in process during period............		$1,127,050	
Less work in process inventory, December 31, 19--		11,000	
Cost of goods manufactured..................			1,116,050
Cost of finished goods available for sale........			$1,302,450
Less finished goods inventory, December 31, 19--.			198,750
Cost of goods sold...........................			$1,103,700

Cost of goods sold budget

OPERATING EXPENSES BUDGET

The estimated selling and general expenses are set forth in the operating expenses budget, in a format similar to the factory overhead cost budget illustrated earlier. Where feasible, detailed schedules based on departmental responsibility should be prepared for all major items in the budget. The advertising expense schedule, for example, should include such details as advertising media to be used (newspaper, direct mail, etc.), quantities (column inches, number of pieces, etc.), cost per unit, frequency of use, and sectional totals. It is only through careful attention to details that a realistic budget can be produced, and through assignment of responsibility to departmental supervisors that effective controls can be achieved.

BUDGETED INCOME STATEMENT

A budgeted income statement can ordinarily be prepared from the data presented in the budgets for sales, cost of goods sold, and operating expenses, with the addition of data on other income, other expense, and income tax. It need not differ in form and arrangement from an income statement based on actual data in the accounts and hence is not illustrated.

The budgeted income statement brings together in condensed form the projection of all profit-making phases of operations and enables management to weigh the effects of the individual budgets on the profit plan for the year. If the budgeted net income in relationship to sales or to stockholders' equity is disappointingly low, additional review of all causative factors should be undertaken in an attempt to improve the plans.

CAPITAL EXPENDITURES BUDGET

The capital expenditures budget summarizes future plans for acquisition of plant facilities and equipment. Substantial expenditures may be required to replace machinery and other plant assets as they wear out, become obsolete, or for other reasons fall below minimum standards of efficiency. In addition, an expansion of plant facilities may be planned to keep pace with increasing demand for a company's product or to provide for additions to the product line.

It is evident that the useful life of most capital expenditures is likely to cover a relatively long period of time and the magnitude of such expenditures is likely to vary considerably from year to year. The customary practice, therefore, is to project the plans for a number of years into the future in preparing the capital expenditures budget. A five-year capital expenditures budget is illustrated below.

Dean Company
Capital Expenditures Budget
For Five Years Ending December 31, 1978

Item	1974	1975	1976	1977	1978
Machinery — Department 1	$50,000			$ 70,000	$60,000
Machinery — Department 2	45,000	$65,000	$40,000	50,000	
Office equipment		22,500			15,000
Total	$95,000	$87,500	$40,000	$120,000	$75,000

Capital expenditures budget

The various proposals recognized in the capital expenditures budget must be considered in preparing certain operating budgets. For example, the expected amount of depreciation on new equipment to be acquired in the current year must be taken into consideration when preparing the budgets for factory overhead and operating expenses. The manner in which the proposed expenditures are to be financed will also affect the cash budget.

CASH BUDGET

The cash budget presents the expected inflow and outflow of cash for a day, week, month, or longer period. Receipts are classified by source and disbursements by purpose. The expected cash balance at the end of the period is then compared with the amount established as the minimum balance and the difference is the anticipated excess or deficiency for the period.

The minimum cash balance represents a safety buffer for miscalculations in cash planning and for unforeseen contingencies. However, the amount designated as the minimum balance need not remain fixed; it should perhaps be larger during periods of "peak" business activity than during the "slow" season.

The interrelationship of the cash budget with other budgets may be observed from the illustration below. Data from the sales budget, the various budgets for manufacturing costs and operating expenses, and the capital expenditures budget affect the cash budget. Consideration must also be given to dividend policies, plans for equity or long-term debt financing, and other projected plans that will affect cash.

569

Dean Company
Cash Budget
For Three Months Ending March 31, 19--

	JANUARY	FEBRUARY	MARCH
Estimated cash receipts from:			
Cash sales....................................	$ 28,000	$ 30,000	$ 25,000
Collections of accounts receivable...............	116,500	119,500	91,500
Other sources (issuance of securities, interest, etc.).	——	——	1,500
Total cash receipts........................	$144,500	$149,500	$118,000
Estimated cash disbursements for:			
Manufacturing costs.........................	$ 90,200	$ 92,700	$ 84,000
Operating expenses..........................	25,300	25,300	23,400
Capital expenditures.........................	——	27,000	18,500
Other purposes (notes, income tax, etc.).........	7,500	3,000	31,500
Total cash disbursements....................	$123,000	$148,000	$157,400
Cash increase or decrease*......................	$ 21,500	$ 1,500	$ 39,400*
Cash balance at beginning of month..............	78,000	99,500	101,000
Cash balance at end of month...................	$ 99,500	$101,000	$ 61,600
Minimum cash balance........................	75,000	75,000	75,000
Excess or deficiency*.........................	$ 24,500	$ 26,000	$ 13,400*

Cash
budget

The importance of accurate cash budgeting can scarcely be over-emphasized. An unanticipated lack of cash can result in loss of discounts, unfavorable borrowing terms on loans, and damage to the credit rating. On the other hand, an excess amount of idle cash is also indicative of poor management. When the budget indicates periods of excess cash, such funds should be used to reduce loans or they should be invested in readily marketable income-producing securities. Reference to the illustration on the preceding page indicates excess cash during January and February, and a deficiency during March.

BUDGETED BALANCE SHEET

The budgeted balance sheet presents estimated details of financial condition at the end of a budget period, assuming that all budgeted operating and financing plans are fulfilled. It need not differ in form and arrangement from a balance sheet based on actual data in the accounts and hence is not illustrated. If the budgeted balance sheet reveals weaknesses in financial position, such as an abnormally large amount of current liabilities in relation to current assets, or excessive long-term debt in relation to stockholders' equity, the relevant factors should be given further study with a view to taking corrective action.

570

BUDGET PERFORMANCE REPORTS

A budget performance report comparing actual results with the budgeted figures should be prepared periodically for each budget. All significant variations should be investigated immediately to determine their cause and to seek means of preventing their recurrence. If corrective action cannot be taken because of changed conditions that have occurred since the budget was prepared, future budget figures should be revised accordingly. A budget performance report is illustrated below.

Dean Company
Budget Performance Report — Factory Overhead Cost, Department 1
For Month Ended June 30, 19--

	Budget	Actual	Over	Under
Indirect factory wages...............	$ 5,050	$ 5,065	$ 15	
Supervisory salaries..................	2,600	2,600		
Power and light.....................	2,375	2,355		$20
Depreciation of plant and equipment...	2,000	2,000		
Indirect materials...................	1,250	1,375	125	
Maintenance.......................	1,000	990		10
Insurance and property taxes.........	525	525		
	$14,800	$14,910	$140	$30

Budget performance report

The amounts reported in the "budget" column were obtained from supplemental schedules accompanying the master budget. The amounts in the "actual" column are the costs actually incurred. The last two columns indicate the amounts by which actual costs exceeded or were below budgeted figures. As indicated in the illustration, there were variations between the actual and budgeted amounts for some of the items of overhead cost. The cause of the variation in indirect materials cost should be investigated, and an attempt made to find means of corrective action.

FLEXIBLE BUDGETS

Implicit in the discussion of budget systems has been the assumption that the volume of sales and manufacturing activity achieved during a period approximated the goals established in the budgets. When substantial changes in expectations occur during a budget period, the budgets should be revised to give effect to such changes. Otherwise they will be of questionable value as incentives and instruments for controlling costs and expenses.

The effect of fluctuations in volume of activity can be "built-in" to the system by what are termed *flexible budgets*. Particularly useful in estimating and controlling factory overhead costs and operating expenses, a flexible budget is in reality a series of budgets for varying rates of activity. To illustrate, assume that because of extreme variations in demand and other uncontrollable factors the output of a particular manufacturing enterprise fluctuates widely from month to month. In such circumstances the total factory overhead costs incurred during periods of high activity are certain to be greater than during periods of low activity. It is equally certain, however, that fluctuations in total factory overhead costs will not be exactly proportionate to the volume of production. For example, if $100,000 of factory overhead costs are ordinarily incurred during a month in which production totals 10,000 units, the factory overhead for a month in which only 5,000 units are produced would unquestionably be more than $50,000.

Items of factory cost and operating expense that tend to remain constant in amount regardless of variations in volume of activity may be said to be *fixed*. Real estate taxes, property insurance, and depreciation expense on buildings are examples of fixed costs; the amounts incurred are substantially independent of the level of operations. Costs and expenses which tend to fluctuate in amount in accordance with variations in volume of activity are designated *variable*. Supplies and indirect materials used and salesmen's commissions are examples of variable costs and expenses. The degree of variability is not the same for all variable items; few, if any, vary in exact proportion to sales or production. The terms *semivariable* or *semifixed* are sometimes applied to items that have both fixed and variable characteristics to a significant degree. An example is electric power, for which there is often an initial

571

flat fee, for example $500 for the first 10,000 kw-hrs consumed during a month and a lower rate, such as $.03 per kw-hr for additional usage.

A flexible budget for factory overhead cost is illustrated below. A single manufacturing department and a single product are assumed, with budgeted costs stated at three different levels of production. In practice, the number of production levels and the interval between levels will vary with the range of production volume. For example, instead of budgeting for 8,000, 9,000, and 10,000 units of product, it might be necessary to provide for levels, at intervals of 500, from 6,000 to 12,000 units. Alternative bases may also be used in measuring volume of activity, such as hours of departmental operation or direct labor man hours.

W. Mann and Company
Monthly Factory Overhead Cost Budget

Units of product	8,000	9,000	10,000
Variable cost:			
Indirect factory wages	$ 32,000	$ 36,000	$ 40,000
Electric power	24,000	27,000	30,000
Indirect materials	12,000	13,500	15,000
Total variable cost	$ 68,000	$ 76,500	$ 85,000
Fixed cost:			
Supervisory salaries	$ 40,000	$ 40,000	$ 40,000
Depreciation of plant and equipment	25,000	25,000	25,000
Property taxes	15,000	15,000	15,000
Insurance	12,000	12,000	12,000
Electric power	10,000	10,000	10,000
Total fixed cost	$102,000	$102,000	$102,000
Total factory overhead cost	$170,000	$178,500	$187,000

572

Flexible budget for factory overhead cost

STANDARD COSTS

The determination of the unit cost of products manufactured is fundamental to cost accounting. The process cost and job order cost systems discussed in the preceding chapters were designed to determine *actual* or *historical* unit costs. The aim of both systems is to provide timely data on actual manufacturing costs and to facilitate cost control and profit maximization.

The use of budgetary control procedures is often extended to the point of unit cost projections for each commodity produced. Cost systems employing detailed estimates of each element of manufacturing cost entering into the finished product are sometimes referred to as *standard cost systems*. The use of such estimates enables management to determine how much a product should cost (standard), how much it does cost (actual), and the cause of any differences (variances) between the two. Standard costs thus serve as a measuring device for determination of efficiency. If the standard cost of a product is $5 per unit and its current actual cost is $5.50 per unit, the factors responsible for the excess cost can be determined and remedial measures taken. Thus supervisors have a device for controlling costs, and employees become more cost-conscious.

Standard costs may be used in either the process type of production or the job order type of production. For most effective control, standard costs should be used for each department or cost center in the factory. It is possible, however, to use standard costs in some departments and actual costs in others.

The establishment of standards requires exhaustive research. Motion and time studies are made of each operation, and the work force is trained to use the most efficient methods. Direct materials and productive equipment are subjected to detailed study and tests in an effort to achieve maximum productivity at minimum cost. A wide variety of management skills are needed in setting standards, requiring the joint effort of accounting, engineering, personnel administration, and other managerial areas.

VARIANCES FROM STANDARDS

Production management's goal is the attainment of properly determined standards. Differences between the standard cost of a department or product and the actual costs incurred are termed *variances*. If actual cost incurred is less than standard cost, the variance is favorable; if actual cost exceeds standard cost, the variance is unfavorable. When actual costs are compared with standard costs, only the "exceptions" or variances are reported to the individual responsible for cost control. This reporting by the "principle of exceptions" enables the one responsible for cost control to concentrate on the cause and on the correction of the variances.

573

The total variance for a particular period is ordinarily a composite of a number of variances, some of which may be favorable and some unfavorable. There may be variances from standards in direct materials costs, in direct labor costs, and in factory overhead costs. The remainder of the chapter is devoted to illustrations and analyses of these variances for a hypothetical manufacturing enterprise. In actual practice a wide variety of direct materials might be used, there could be a substantial number of processing departments, and two or more classes of commodities would probably be produced. For illustrative purposes, however, it is assumed that only one type of direct material is used, that there is a single processing department, and that Product X is the only commodity manufactured.

DIRECT MATERIALS COST VARIANCE

Two principal factors enter into the determination of standards for direct materials cost: (1) the quantity (usage) standard and (2) the price standard. If actual quantity of direct materials used in producing a commodity differs from the standard quantity, there is a *quantity variance*; if the actual unit price of the materials differs from the standard price, there is a *price variance*. To illustrate, assume that the standard direct materials cost of producing 10,000 units of Product X and the direct materials cost actually incurred during the month of June were as follows:

Standard: 20,000 pounds at $.50. . . . . $10,000
Actual: 20,600 pounds at $.52. 10,712

It is readily apparent that the unfavorable variance of $712 resulted in part from an excess usage of 600 pounds of direct materials and in part from an excess cost of $.02 per pound. The analysis of the materials cost variance is as follows:

QUANTITY VARIANCE:
   Actual quantity. . . . . .20,600 pounds
   Standard quantity. . . . . .20,000 pounds
      Variance — unfavorable. . .   600 pounds × standard price, $.50. . . . . . . $300

PRICE VARIANCE:
   Actual price. . . . . $.52 per pound
   Standard price. . . . .   .50 per pound
      Variance — unfavorable. . . $.02 per pound × actual quantity, 20,600. . 412
TOTAL DIRECT MATERIALS COST VARIANCE — unfavorable. $712

574

Direct materials cost variance

The physical quantity and the dollar amount of the quantity variance should be reported to the factory superintendent and other personnel responsible for production. If excessive amounts of direct materials were used because of the malfunction of equipment or some other failure within the production department, those responsible should correct the situation. However, an unfavorable direct materials quantity variance is not necessarily the result of inefficiency within the production department. If the excess usage of 600 pounds in the example above had been caused by inferior materials, the purchasing department should be held responsible.

The unit price and the total amount of the materials price variance should be reported to the purchasing department, which may or may not be able to control this variance. If the materials could have been purchased from another supplier at the standard price, the variance was controllable. On the other hand, if the variance resulted from a market-wide price increase, the variance was not subject to control.

DIRECT LABOR COST VARIANCE

As in the case of direct materials, two principal factors enter into the determination of standards for direct labor cost: (1) the time (usage or efficiency) standard, and (2) the rate (price or wage) standard. If the actual direct labor hours spent producing a product differ from the standard hours, there is a *time variance*; if the wage rate paid differs from the standard rate, there is a *rate variance*. The standard cost and the actual cost of direct labor in the production of 10,000 units of Product **X** during June are assumed to be as shown below.

Standard: 8,000 hours at $2.00........... $16,000
Actual: 7,900 hours at 2.10........... 16,590

The unfavorable direct labor variance of $590 is a composite of a favorable time variance and an unfavorable rate variance, as indicated below.

TIME VARIANCE:
  Standard time..............8,000 hours
  Actual time................7,900 hours
    Variance — favorable...... 100 hours × standard rate, $2.............$200

RATE VARIANCE:
  Actual rate.................$2.10 per hour
  Standard rate............... 2.00 per hour
    Variance — unfavorable...$ .10 per hour × actual time, 7,900 hours.... 790
TOTAL DIRECT LABOR COST VARIANCE — unfavorable.....................$590

Direct labor cost variance

The control of direct labor cost is often in the hands of production foremen. To assist them in the control of direct labor costs, daily or weekly reports analyzing the cause of any direct labor variance are often prepared. A comparison of standard direct labor hours and actual direct labor hours will provide the basis for an investigation into the efficiency of direct labor (time variance). A comparison of the rates paid for direct labor with the standard rates highlights the efficiency of the foremen or personnel department in selecting the proper grade of direct labor for production (rate variance).

ESTABLISHING STANDARDS FOR FACTORY OVERHEAD COST

Some of the difficulties encountered in allocating factory overhead costs among products manufactured have been considered in earlier chapters. These difficulties stem from the great variety of costs that are included in factory overhead and their nature as indirect costs. For the same reasons, the procedures employed in determining standards and variances for factory overhead cost are more complex than those used for direct materials cost and direct labor cost.

A flexible budget is employed to establish the standard factory overhead rate and to assist in determining subsequent variations from standard. The standard rate is determined by dividing what the factory overhead costs should be by the standard amount of productive activity, generally expressed in direct labor hours, direct labor cost, or machine hours. A flexible budget indicating the standard factory overhead rate for June is presented at the top of the next page.

Nelson Manufacturing Company
Factory Overhead Cost Budget
For Month Ending June 30, 19 − −

Percent of normal productive capacity..	80%	90%	100%	110%
Direct labor hours..................	8,000	9,000	10,000	11,000
Budgeted factory overhead:				
Variable cost:				
Indirect factory wages............	$ 6,400	$ 7,200	$ 8,000	$ 8,800
Power and light................	2,800	3,150	3,500	3,850
Indirect materials...............	1,600	1,800	2,000	2,200
Maintenance....................	1,200	1,350	1,500	1,650
Total variable cost............	$12,000	$13,500	$15,000	$16,500
Fixed cost:				
Supervisory salaries.............	$ 2,250	$ 2,250	$ 2,250	$ 2,250
Depreciation of plant and equipment	2,750	2,750	2,750	2,750
Insurance and property taxes......	1,000	1,000	1,000	1,000
Total fixed cost...............	$ 6,000	$ 6,000	$ 6,000	$ 6,000
Total factory overhead cost...........	$18,000	$19,500	$21,000	$22,500

Factory overhead
cost budget
indicating
standard factory
overhead rate

Factory overhead rate per direct labor hour ($21,000 ÷ 10,000)... $2.10

The standard factory overhead cost rate is determined on the basis of the projected factory overhead costs at 100% of normal productive capacity, where this level of capacity represents the general expectation of business activity under normal operating conditions. In the illustration above, the standard factory overhead rate is $2.10 per direct labor hour. This rate can be subdivided into $1.50 per hour for variable factory overhead ($15,000 ÷ 10,000 hours) and $.60 per hour for fixed factory overhead ($6,000 ÷ 10,000 hours).

FACTORY OVERHEAD COST VARIANCE

Variances from standard for factory overhead cost result (1) from operating at a level above or below 100% of normal capacity, which is called the *volume variance*; and (2) from incurring a total amount of factory overhead cost greater or less than the amount budgeted for the level of operations achieved, which is called the *controllable variance*. To illustrate, assume that the standard cost and the actual cost of factory overhead for the production of 10,000 units of Product X during June were as follows:

Standard:	8,000 hours at $2.10.............		$16,800
Actual:	Variable factory overhead........	$12,300	
	Fixed factory overhead..........	6,000	18,300

The unfavorable factory overhead cost variance of $1,500 is composed of a volume variance and a controllable variance as indicated in the tabulation presented at the top of the next page.

VOLUME VARIANCE:

Normal productive capacity of 100%....................	10,000 hours	
Standard for product produced........................	8,000 hours	
Productive capacity not used.........................	2,000 hours	
Standard fixed factory overhead cost rate................	× $.60	
Variance — unfavorable...		$1,200

CONTROLLABLE VARIANCE:

Actual factory overhead cost incurred...................	$18,300	
Budgeted factory overhead for standard product produced..	18,000	
Variance — unfavorable..		300
TOTAL FACTORY OVERHEAD COST VARIANCE — unfavorable..............		$1,500

Factory
overhead cost
variance

Volume variance. The volume variance is a measure of the penalty of operating at less than 100% of normal productive capacity or the benefit from operating at a level above 100% of normal productive capacity. In determining the amount of the variance, the productive capacity not used (or the productive capacity used in excess of 100% of capacity) is multiplied by the standard fixed factory overhead cost rate. In the illustration, the 2,000 hours of idle productive capacity was multiplied by $.60, the standard fixed factory overhead cost rate. It should be noted that the variable portion of the factory overhead cost rate was ignored in determining the volume variance. Variable factory overhead costs vary with the level of production; thus, a curtailment of production should be accompanied by a comparable reduction of such costs. On the other hand, the fixed factory overhead costs are not affected by fluctuations in the volume of production. The fixed factory overhead costs therefore represent the costs of providing the capacity for production and the volume variance measures the amount of the fixed factory overhead cost attributed to the variance between capacity used and 100% of capacity. In the illustration the volume variance was unfavorable. This unfavorable volume variance of $1,200 can be viewed as the cost of the available but unused production capacity.

The idle time may be due to such factors as failure to maintain an even flow of work, machine breakdowns or repairs causing work stoppages, and failure to obtain enough sales orders to keep the factory operating at full capacity. Management should then ascertain the causes of the idle time and should take corrective action. A volume variance caused by failure of foremen to maintain an even flow of work, for example, can be remedied. Volume variances caused by lack of sales orders may be corrected through increased advertising or other sales effort, or it may be advisable to develop other means of utilizing the excess plant capacity.

Controllable variance. The controllable variance is the difference between the actual amount of factory overhead incurred and the amount

577

of factory overhead budgeted for the level of production achieved during the period. In the illustration, the standard direct labor hours for the product manufactured during June was 8,000, which represents 80% of normal productive capacity. According to the flexible budget on page 576, the factory overhead budgeted at this level of production is $18,000. The excess of the $18,300 of factory overhead costs actually incurred over the $18,000 budgeted yields the unfavorable controllable variance of $300.

The amount and the direction of the controllable variance indicate the degree of efficiency in keeping the factory overhead costs within the limits established by the budget. Most of the controllable variance is related to the cost of the variable factory overhead items because generally there is little or no variation in the costs incurred for the fixed factory overhead items. Therefore, responsibility for the control of this variance generally rests with department foremen.

Reporting factory overhead cost variance. The most effective means of presenting standard factory overhead cost variance data is through a factory overhead cost variance report. Such a report, illustrated below, can present both the controllable variance and the volume variance in a format that pinpoints the causes of the variance and facilitates placing the responsibility for control.

Nelson Manufacturing Company
Factory Overhead Cost Variance Report
For Month Ended June 30, 19--

| | | | VARIANCES | |
	BUDGET	ACTUAL	FAVORABLE	UNFAVORABLE
Normal production capacity for the month..........................				10,000 hours
Actual production for the month...................................				8,000 hours
Variable cost:				
Indirect factory wages.............	$ 6,400	$ 6,510		$ 110
Power and light..................	2,800	2,790	$10	
Indirect materials................	1,600	1,800		200
Maintenance.....................	1,200	1,200		
Total variable cost.............	$12,000	$12,300		
Fixed cost:				
Supervisory salaries...............	$ 2,250	$ 2,250		
Depreciation of plant and equipment	2,750	2,750		
Insurance and property taxes.......	1,000	1,000		
Total fixed cost................	$ 6,000	$ 6,000		
Total factory overhead cost..........	$18,000	$18,300		
Total controllable variances.........			$10	$ 310
Net controllable variance — unfavorable.........................				$ 300
Volume variance — unfavorable:				
Idle hours at the standard rate for fixed factory overhead—2,000 × $.60				1,200
Total factory overhead cost variance — unfavorable.................				$1,500

Factory
overhead cost
variance report

The variance in many of the individual cost items in factory overhead can be subdivided into quantity and price variances, as were the variances in direct materials and direct labor. For example, the indirect factory wages variance may include both time and rate variances and the indirect materials variance may be composed of both a quantity variance and a price variance.

The foregoing brief introduction to analysis of factory overhead cost variance suggests the many ramifications and complexities that may be encountered in actual practice. The rapid increase of automation in factory operations has been accompanied by increased attention to factory overhead costs. The use of predetermined standards, and the analysis of variances from such standards, provides management with the best possible means of establishing responsibility and controlling factory overhead costs.

STANDARDS IN THE ACCOUNTS

Although standard costs can be employed solely as a statistical device apart from the ledger, it is generally considered preferable to incorporate them in the accounts. When this plan is adopted, the work in process account is debited for the actual costs of direct materials, direct labor, and factory overhead entering into production. The same account is credited for the standard cost of the product completed and transferred to the finished goods account. The balance remaining in the work in process account is then a composite of the ending inventory of work in process and the variances of actual cost from standard cost. In the illustrative accounts presented below there is assumed to be no ending inventory of work in process, hence the balance in the account is the sum of the variances (unfavorable) between standard and actual costs.

579

WORK IN PROCESS

DATE		ITEM	DEBIT	CREDIT	BALANCE DEBIT	BALANCE CREDIT
June	30	Direct materials (actual)....	10,712		10,712	
	30	Direct labor (actual).......	16,590		27,302	
	30	Factory overhead (actual)...	18,300		45,602	
	30	Units finished (standard)....		42,800		
	30	Balance (variances)........			2,802	

FINISHED GOODS

DATE		ITEM	DEBIT	CREDIT	BALANCE DEBIT	BALANCE CREDIT
June	1	Inventory (standard).......			39,800	
	30	Units finished (standard)...	42,800		82,600	
	30	Units sold (standard).......		40,700	41,900	

Variances from standard costs are ordinarily not reported to stockholders and others outside the management group. However, it is customary to disclose the variances on income statements prepared for management. An interim monthly income statement prepared for internal use is illustrated below.

Nelson Manufacturing Company
Income Statement
For Month Ended June 30, 19—

	FAVORABLE	UNFAVORABLE	
Sales..................................			$77,900
Cost of goods sold—at standard.............			40,700
Gross profit on sales—at standard...........			$37,200
Less variances from standard cost:	FAVORABLE	UNFAVORABLE	
Direct materials quantity................		$ 300	
Direct materials price...................		412	
Direct labor time......................	$200		
Direct labor rate......................		790	
Factory overhead volume................		1,200	
Factory overhead controllable............		300	2,802
Gross profit on sales....................			$34,398
Operating expenses:			
Selling expenses.......................		$14,500	
General expenses......................		9,125	23,625
Income before income tax................			$10,773

At the end of the fiscal year, the variances from standard are usually transferred to the cost of goods sold account. However, if the variances are significant or if many of the products manufactured are still on hand, the variances should be allocated to the work in process, finished goods, and cost of goods sold accounts. The result of such an allocation is to convert these account balances from standard cost to actual cost.

RESPONSIBILITY ACCOUNTING

One of the basic functions of management is to direct operations in such a manner as to achieve as nearly as possible the predetermined objectives of the enterprise. Prerequisite to establishing effective control over operations is the assignment of definite responsibilities to personnel at the various managerial levels. Accounting assists management by providing relevant revenue and expense data for use in measuring actual performance on the basis of the responsibilities assigned.

A term frequently applied to this process of accumulating and reporting operating data by areas of responsibility is *responsibility accounting*. Budgets and budget performance reports are designed in accordance with the plan of responsibility for each operating area, department, or other designated segment. Similarly, the application of responsibility accounting procedures in a standard cost system provides the factory superintendent, department heads, and foremen with cost data essential to the control of manufacturing costs.

QUESTIONS

1. Name the two basic functions of management.

2. What is a budget?

3. How does a budget aid management in the discharge of its basic functions?

4. What is a budget performance report?

5. Why should all levels of management and all departments participate in the preparation and submission of budget estimates?

6. What is meant by *continuous* budgeting?

7. Why should the production requirements as set forth in the production budget be carefully coordinated with the sales budget?

8. Why should the timing of direct materials purchases be closely coordinated with the production budget?

9. What is a capital expenditures budget?

10. (a) Discuss the purpose of the cash budget. (b) If the cash budget for the first quarter of the fiscal year indicates excess cash at the end of each of the first two months, how might the excess cash be used?

11. What is a flexible budget?

12. Which of the following costs incurred by a manufacturing enterprise tend to be fixed and which tend to be variable: (a) property taxes on factory building, (b) salary of factory superintendent, (c) insurance on factory building, (d) electric power (purchased) to operate manufacturing machinery, (e) cost of steel tubing entering into finished product, (f) direct labor, and (g) depreciation of factory building.

13. The Roland Corporation uses flexible budgets. For each of the following variable operating expenses, indicate whether there has been a saving or an excess of expenditures, assuming actual sales were $1,000,000.

Expense Item	Actual Amount	Budget Allowance Based on Sales
Store supplies expense	$20,300	2%
Uncollectible accounts expense	29,550	3%

14. What are the basic objectives in the use of standard costs?

15. As the term is used in reference to standard costs, what is a *variance*?

16. (a) What are the two types of variances between actual cost and standard cost for direct materials? (b) Discuss some possible causes of these variances.

17. (a) What are the two types of variances between actual cost and standard cost for direct labor? (b) Who generally has control over the direct labor cost?

18. Describe the two variances between actual costs and standard costs for factory overhead.

19. Where do the variances for direct materials, direct labor, and factory overhead appear on interim income statements prepared for management?

20. What is meant by responsibility accounting?

EXERCISES

22-1. Sharp Company manufactures two models of adding machines, A and B. Based on the following production and sales data for the month of May of the current year, prepare (a) a sales budget and (b) a production budget.

	A	B
Estimated inventory (units), May 1.	4,500	2,250
Desired inventory (units), May 31..	5,000	2,000
Expected sales volume (units):		
Area I......................	3,250	1,800
Area II.....................	4,400	2,200
Unit sales price.................	$75	$120

22-2. Brooks Company uses flexible budgets. Prepare a flexible operating expenses budget for June of the current year for sales volumes of $400,000, $450,000 and $500,000, based upon the following data:

Salesmen's commissions.......	10% of sales
Advertising expense..........	$20,000 for $400,000 of sales
	$21,500 for $450,000 of sales
	$22,500 for $500,000 of sales
Miscellaneous selling expense..	$ 1,000 + 1% of sales
Office salaries..............	$12,000
Office supplies expense.......	$\frac{1}{2}$ of 1% of sales
Miscellaneous general expense.	$750 + $\frac{1}{2}$ of 1% of sales

22-3. The operating expenses incurred during June of the current year by Brooks Company were as follows:

Salesmen's commissions.......	$45,000
Advertising expense..........	21,850
Miscellaneous selling expense..	5,650
Office salaries..............	12,000
Office supplies expense.......	2,100
Miscellaneous general expense.	2,800

Assuming that the total sales for June were $450,000, prepare a budget performance report for operating expenses on the basis of the data presented above and in Exercise 22-2.

22-4. The following data relating to direct materials cost are taken from the records of Kline Manufacturing Company for the month of November of the current year:

Quantity of direct materials used...................	30,000 lbs.
Unit cost of direct materials.......................	$3 per lb.
Units of finished product manufactured.............	9,800 units
Standard direct materials per unit of finished product.	3 lbs.
Direct materials quantity variance — unfavorable....	$1,950
Direct materials price variance — favorable.........	$7,500

Determine the standard direct materials cost per unit of finished product, assuming that there was no inventory of work in process at either the beginning or the end of the month. Present your computations.

22-5. Standard costs and actual costs for direct materials, direct labor, and factory overhead incurred for the manufacture of 1,000 units of product were as shown on the next page.

	Standard Costs	Actual Costs
Direct materials.....	1,000 units at $15	990 units at $15.50
Direct labor........	2,500 hours at $ 5	2,600 hours at $ 4.80
Factory overhead....	Rates per direct labor hour, based on normal capacity of 3,000 labor hours:	
	Variable cost, $2.50	$6,450 variable cost
	Fixed cost, $1.00	$3,000 fixed cost

Determine (a) the quantity variance, price variance, and total direct materials cost variance; (b) the time variance, rate variance, and total direct labor cost variance; and (c) the volume variance, controllable variance, and total factory overhead cost variance.

22-6. The Carr Manufacturing Company prepared the following factory overhead cost budget for Department C for April of the current year. The company expected to operate the department at normal capacity of 20,000 direct labor hours.

Variable cost:		
Indirect factory wages.............	$ 5,400	
Power and light..................	2,500	
Indirect materials................	1,200	
Total variable cost.............		$ 9,100
Fixed cost:		
Supervisory salaries...............	$ 4,250	
Depreciation of plant and equipment.	1,800	
Insurance and property taxes........	1,150	
Total fixed cost.................		7,200
Total factory overhead cost...........		$16,300

During April the department was operated for 19,000 direct labor hours, and the factory overhead costs incurred were: indirect factory wages, $5,275; power and light, $2,310; indirect materials, $1,165; supervisory salaries, $4,250; depreciation of plant and equipment, $1,800; and insurance and property taxes, $1,150.

Prepare a standard factory overhead variance report for April. To be useful for cost control, the budgeted amounts should be based on 19,000 direct labor hours.

22-7. Prepare an income statement for presentation to management from the following data taken from the records of Stark Manufacturing Company for the month of January of the current year:

Cost of goods sold (at standard).....................	$167,500
Direct materials quantity variance — unfavorable.....	1,650
Direct materials price variance — favorable..........	950
Direct labor time variance — favorable..............	750
Direct labor rate variance — unfavorable............	500
Factory overhead volume variance — unfavorable.....	2,000
Factory overhead controllable variance — unfavorable.	200
Selling expenses..................................	40,800
General expenses.................................	29,400
Sales..	277,600

583

PROBLEMS

The following additional problems for this chapter are located in Appendix B: 22-1B, 22-3B, 22-4B.

22-1A. Manson Company prepared the following factory overhead cost budget for the Sanding Department for July of the current year:

Manson Company
Factory Overhead Cost Budget — Sanding Department
For Month Ending July 31, 19—

Direct labor hours:		
Normal productive capacity..................		10,000
Hours budgeted............................		8,000
Variable cost:		
Indirect factory wages......................	$ 5,200	
Indirect materials...........................	3,600	
Power and light............................	3,200	
Total variable cost........................		$12,000
Fixed cost:		
Supervisory salaries..........................	$ 7,500	
Indirect factory wages........................	4,000	
Depreciation of plant and equipment..........	2,800	
Insurance....................................	1,300	
Power and light............................	1,020	
Property taxes...............................	880	
Total fixed cost...........................		17,500
Total factory overhead cost....................		$29,500

Instructions:

(1) Prepare a flexible budget for the month of August indicating capacities of 8,000, 9,000, 10,000, and 11,000 direct labor hours and the determination of a standard factory overhead rate per direct labor hour.

(2) Prepare a standard factory overhead cost variance report for August. The Sanding Department was operated for 9,000 direct labor hours and the following factory overhead costs were incurred:

Indirect factory wages...............	$ 9,700
Supervisory salaries..................	7,500
Power and light......................	4,870
Indirect materials....................	4,100
Depreciation of plant and equipment...	2,800
Insurance............................	1,300
Property taxes.......................	880
Total factory overhead costs incurred.	$31,150

22-2A. The budget director of Miller Company requests estimates of sales, production, and other operating data from the various administrative units every month. Selected information submitted for the month of June of the current year concerning sales and production are summarized as follows:

(a) Estimated sales for June by sales territory:
    East:
        Product A . . . .   12,000 units at $50 per unit
        Product B . . . .   5,000 units at $75 per unit
    Midwest:
        Product A . . . .   20,000 units at $50 per unit
        Product B . . . .   8,000 units at $75 per unit
    West:
        Product A . . . .   18,000 units at $50 per unit
        Product B . . . .   7,000 units at $75 per unit

(b) Estimated inventories at June 1:
    Direct materials:
        Material M: 75,000 lbs.
        Material N: 21,000 lbs.
        Material O: 22,500 lbs.
        Material P: 9,500 lbs.
    Finished products:
        Product A: 25,000 units
        Product B: 9,000 units

(c) Desired inventories at June 30:
    Direct materials:
        Material M: 80,000 lbs.
        Material N: 20,000 lbs.
        Material O: 25,000 lbs.
        Material P: 10,000 lbs.
    Finished products:
        Product A: 30,000 units
        Product B: 10,000 units

585

(d) Direct materials used in production:
    In manufacture of Product A:
        Material M: 2 lbs. per unit of product
        Material N: .5 lb. per unit of product
        Material O: 1 lb. per unit of product

    In manufacture of Product B:
        Material M: 2 lbs. per unit of product
        Material N: .5 lb. per unit of product
        Material P: 1 lb. per unit of product

(e) Anticipated purchase price for direct materials:
    Material M: $1.25 per lb.
    Material N: $5.00 per lb.
    Material O: $2.50 per lb.
    Material P: $6.00 per lb.

(f) Direct labor requirements:
    Product A:
        Department 1: 1 hour at $4 per hour
        Department 2: 2 hours at $5 per hour
    Product B:
        Department 1: 1 hour at $4 per hour
        Department 3: 3 hours at $6 per hour

Instructions:
(1) Prepare a sales budget for June.
(2) Prepare a production budget for June.
(3) Prepare a direct materials purchases budget for June.
(4) Prepare a direct labor cost budget for June.

22-3A. Decker Manufacturing, Inc., maintains perpetual inventory accounts for materials, work in process, and finished goods and uses a standard cost system based upon the following data:

		Standard Cost Per Unit
Direct materials..	2 pounds at $2.50 per lb.	$ 5
Direct labor......	2 hours at $5 per hr.....	10
Factory overhead.	$2 per direct labor hour.	4
Total............................		$19

There was no inventory of work in process at the beginning or end of January, the first month of the current year. The transactions relating to production completed during January are summarized as follows:

(a) Materials purchased on account, $24,500.

(b) Direct materials used, $23,030. This represented 9,400 pounds at $2.45 per pound.

(c) Direct labor paid, $44,880. This represented 8,800 hours at $5.10 per hour. There were no accruals at either the beginning or the end of the period.

(d) Factory overhead incurred during the month was composed of indirect labor, $9,600; depreciation on plant and equipment, $6,000; insurance, $1,200; and miscellaneous factory costs, $1,450. The indirect labor and miscellaneous factory costs were paid during the period, and the insurance represents an expiration of prepaid insurance. Of the total factory overhead of $18,250, fixed costs amounted to $7,500 and variable costs were $10,750.

(e) Goods finished during the period, 4,500 units.

Instructions:

(1) Prepare entries in general journal form to record the transactions, assuming that the work in process account is debited for actual production costs and credited with standard costs for goods finished.

(2) Prepare a T account for Work in Process and post to the account, using the identifying letters as dates.

(3) Prepare schedules of variances for direct materials cost, direct labor cost, and factory overhead cost. Normal productive capacity for the plant is 10,000 direct labor hours.

(4) Total the amount of the standard cost variances and compare this total with the balance of the work in process account.

22-4A. The treasurer of Cullen Company instructs you to prepare a monthly cash budget for the next three months. He presents you with the following budget information:

	March	April	May
Sales..............	$660,000	$560,000	$700,000
Manufacturing costs.	378,000	321,000	411,000
Operating expenses..	210,000	201,000	240,000
Capital expenditures.	—	75,000	—

The company expects to sell about 20% of its merchandise for cash. Of sales on account, 75% are expected to be collected in full in the month following the sale and the remainder the next following month. Depreciation, insurance, and property taxes represent $15,000 of the estimated monthly manufacturing costs and $6,000 of the probable monthly operating expenses. Insurance and property taxes are paid in January and July respectively. Of the remainder of the manufacturing costs and operating expenses, two thirds are expected to be paid in the month in which they are incurred and the balance in the following month.

Current assets of March 1 are composed of cash of $110,000, marketable securities of $75,000, and accounts receivable of $540,000 ($400,000 from February sales and $140,000 from January sales). Current liabilities as of March 1 are composed of a $50,000, 8%, 90-day note payable due March 20, $110,000 of accounts payable incurred in February for manufacturing costs, and accrued liabilities of $60,000 incurred in February for operating expenses.

It is expected that $750 in dividends will be received in April. An estimated income tax payment of $32,500 will be made in April. Cullen Company's regular semiannual dividend of $50,000 is expected to be declared in April and paid in May. Management desires to maintain a minimum cash balance of $75,000.

Instructions:
(1) Prepare a monthly cash budget for March, April, and May.
(2) On the basis of the cash budget prepared in (1), what recommendation should be made to the treasurer?

22-5A. As a preliminary to requesting budget estimates of sales, costs, and expenses for the fiscal year beginning January 1, 1974, the following tentative trial balance as of December 31 of the preceding year is prepared by the accounting department of Young Manufacturing Company:

Cash.	34,500	
Accounts Receivable.	76,000	
Finished Goods.	61,200	
Work in Process.	30,750	
Materials.	21,000	
Prepaid Expenses.	3,200	
Plant and Equipment.	675,000	
Accumulated Depreciation — Plant and Equipment		175,800
Accounts Payable.		60,250
Income Tax Payable.		26,000
Common Stock, $25 par.		500,000
Retained Earnings.		139,600
	901,650	901,650

Factory output and sales for 1974 are expected to total 40,000 units of product, which are to be sold at $25 per unit. The quantities and costs of the inventories (lifo method) at December 31, 1974, are expected to remain unchanged from the balances at the beginning of the year.

Budget estimates of manufacturing costs and operating expenses for the year are summarized at the top of the next page.

Balances of accounts receivable, prepaid expenses, and accounts payable at the end of the year are expected to differ from the beginning balances by only inconsequential amounts. The liability for income tax listed in the tentative trial balance is due on March 15, 1974.

For purposes of the problem, assume federal income tax liability of $76,000 on taxable income of 1974 of which $46,000 will be payable during the year in four installments, and the remainder on March 15, 1975. Regular quarterly cash dividends of $1 a share are expected to be declared and paid in February,

	Estimated Costs and Expenses	
	Fixed (Total for Year)	Variable (Per Unit Sold)
Cost of goods manufactured and sold:		
Direct materials.....................	——	$3.75
Direct labor........................	——	6.25
Factory overhead:		
Depreciation of plant and equipment..	$40,000	——
Other factory overhead..............	95,000	1.50
Selling expenses:		
Sales salaries and commissions..........	20,000	1.50
Advertising.........................	22,000	——
Miscellaneous selling expense...........	7,500	.50
General expenses:		
Office and officers' salaries............	75,000	.25
Supplies............................	1,100	.10
Miscellaneous general expense..........	8,500	.25

May, August, and November. It is anticipated that plant and equipment will be purchased for $50,000 cash in November.

Instructions:

(1) Prepare a budgeted income statement for 1974.

(2) Prepare a budgeted balance sheet as of December 31, 1974.

Chapter 23

INCOME TAXES AND THEIR EFFECT ON BUSINESS DECISIONS

NATURE OF INCOME TAXES

Income taxes are assessed against *taxable income*, which, in general, is gross income less various exclusions and deductions specified by the statutes and administrative regulations. The principal economic entities against which a tax on annual income is levied are individuals, corporations, estates, and trusts. The federal government and more than three fourths of the states levy an income tax. Some states permit enactment of an income tax by municipalities or other political subdivisions.

The data required for the determination of income tax liability is supplied by the taxpayer on official forms and supporting schedules that are referred to collectively as a *tax return*. Failure to receive the forms from the governmental agency or failure to maintain adequate records does not relieve taxpayers of their legal obligation to file an annual tax return and pay the amount due. Willful failure to comply with the income tax laws may result in the imposition of severe penalties, both civil and criminal.

A common characteristic of income taxes, particularly those assessed against individuals, is the provision for a graduated series of tax rates, successively higher rates being applied to successive segments of income. It is because of this progression of rates that an income tax is sometimes termed a *progressive tax*. The highest rate applied to the income of any particular taxpayer is sometimes referred to as his *marginal tax rate*.

RELATIONSHIP TO ACCOUNTING

Because of the intricacies of income determination, it is inevitable that accounting and income taxes should be closely interrelated. An understanding of any but the simplest aspects of income taxes is almost impossible without some knowledge of accounting concepts.

One of the major concerns in tax planning is tax minimization. Managers of business enterprises make few decisions about proposals for new ventures or about significant changes in business practices without first giving careful consideration to the tax consequences.

There are many situations in which an enterprise or an individual taxpayer may choose from among two or more optional accounting methods. Examples of such situations described in earlier chapters are cost-flow assumptions for inventories (first-in, first-out; last-in, first-out; etc.), depreciation methods (straight-line, declining-balance, etc.), and revenue recognition practices (point of sale, installment method, etc.). The particular method elected may have a substantial effect on the amount of income tax, not only in the year in which the election is made but also in subsequent years.

Prerequisite to a meaningful discussion of the impact of income taxes on business decisions is an acquaintance with the basic structure of the federal income tax. The explanations and illustrations of the federal system presented in this chapter are of necessity brief and relatively free of the many complexities encountered in actual practice.

FEDERAL INCOME TAX SYSTEM

The present system of federal income tax originated with the Revenue Act of 1913, which was enacted soon after the ratification of the Sixteenth Amendment to the Constitution. All current income tax statutes, as well as other federal tax laws, are now codified in the Internal Revenue Code (abbreviated "Code" or "IRC").

The executive branch of the government charged with responsibility in tax matters is the Treasury Department. The branch of the Department concerned specifically with enforcement and collection of the income tax is the Internal Revenue Service (abbreviated IRS), headed by the Commissioner of Internal Revenue. Interpretations of the law and directives formulated in accordance with express provisions of the Code are issued in various forms. The most important and comprehensive are the "Regulations" which comprise over two thousand pages.

Taxpayers alleged by the IRS to be deficient in reporting or paying their tax may, if they disagree with the determination, present their case in informal conferences at district and regional levels. Unresolved disputes may be taken to the federal courts for adjudication. The taxpayer may seek relief in the Tax Court or he may pay the disputed amount and sue to recover it, either in the appropriate District Court or the Court of Claims. Either party may appeal an adverse decision to the Court of Appeals of the appropriate circuit, and thence to the Supreme Court.

The income tax is not imposed upon business units as such, but upon taxable entities. Business enterprises organized as sole proprietorships are not taxable entities. The net income or the net loss of a sole proprietorship is reported by the owner as an individual, together with his income from other sources, his allowable deductions, and his personal exemptions. Partnerships are not taxable entities but are required to report in an informational return the details of their revenues, expenses, and allocations to partners. Each partner then reports in his individual return the amount of net income and other special items allocated to him on the partnership return.

Corporations engaged in business for profit are generally treated as distinct taxable entities. However, it is possible for two or more corporations with common ownership to join in filing a consolidated return. Subchapter S of the Code also permits a closely held corporation that conforms to specified requirements to elect to be treated in a manner similar to a partnership. The effect of the election is to tax the individual stockholders on their respective distributive shares of the corporation's net income. The corporation itself is not taxed and, of course, distributions of once-taxed earnings in the form of dividends are tax-free to the shareholders.

ACCOUNTING METHODS

Although neither the Code nor the Regulations provide uniform systems of accounting for use by all taxpayers, detailed procedures are prescribed in specified situations. In addition the IRS has the authority to prescribe accounting methods where those employed by a taxpayer fail to yield a fair determination of taxable income. In general, taxpayers have the option of using either the cash basis or the accrual basis.

591

Cash basis. Because of its greater simplicity, the cash method of determining taxable income is usually adopted by individuals whose sources of income are limited to salary, dividends, and interest. Employers are required to use the cash basis in determining the salary amounts which they report to their employees and also to the IRS in connection with the withholding of income tax. Payments of interest and dividends by business enterprises are also required to be reported in accordance with the cash method. Copies of such notifications, supplemented by check stubs, sales tickets, and other memorandums, frequently provide all of the information needed by an individual to determine his tax base.

Professional and other service enterprises (e.g., physicians, attorneys, insurance agencies, employment agencies) also ordinarily employ the cash basis in determining net income. One of the advantages is that the fees charged to clients or customers are not considered to be earned until payment is received. Accordingly, no provisions need be made for uncollectible accounts expense; write-offs are reductions in anticipated revenue rather than an expense. Similarly, it is not necessary to accrue expenses incurred but not paid within the tax year; rent, electricity, wages, and other items of expense are recorded only at the time of cash payment. It is not permissible, however, to treat the entire cost of long-lived assets as wholly expense of the period in which the cash payment is made. Deductions for depreciation on equipment and buildings used for business purposes may be claimed in the same manner as under the accrual basis, regardless of when payment is made. Similarly, when advance payments for insurance premiums or rentals on business property exceed a period of one year, the total cost must be prorated over the life of the contract.

Recognition of revenue in accordance with the cash method is not always contingent upon the actual receipt of cash. Gross income is said to be *constructively received* at the time it becomes available to the taxpayer, regardless of when it is actually converted to cash. For example, a check for services rendered which is received before the end of a taxable year is income of such year even though the check is not deposited or cashed until the following year. Other examples of constructive receipt are bond interest coupons due within the taxable year and interest credited to a savings account as of the last day of the taxable year.

Accrual basis. For businesses in which production or trading in commodities is a material factor, purchases and sales must be accounted for on the accrual basis. Thus, revenues from sales must be reported as such in the year in which the goods are sold, regardless of when the cash is received. Similarly, the cost of commodities purchased must be reported in the year in which the liabilities are incurred, regardless of when payment is made. The usual adjustments must also be made for the beginning and ending inventories in order to determine the cost of goods sold and the gross profit on sales. However, manufacturing and mercantile enterprises are not required to extend the accrual basis to every other phase of their operations. A considerable degree of hybridization of accounting methods is permissible, provided they yield reasonable results and are used consistently from year to year.

Methods of accounting in general, as well as many of the regulations affecting the determination of net business or professional income, are not affected by the legal nature or the organizational structure of the taxpayer. On the other hand, the tax base and the rate structure for individuals differ markedly from those applicable to corporations.

TAX BASE OF INDIVIDUALS

The tax base to which tax rates for individuals are applied is identified by the Code as *taxable income*. The starting point in the computation is the determination of the amount of *gross income* to be reported. Amounts subtracted from gross income are divided into two principal categories. The first category is composed of expenses of operating a business or profession and certain other expenses related to the earning of revenues. Subtraction of these *deductions from gross income* yields an intermediate balance identified as *adjusted gross income*. The second category is subdivided into (1) so-called *nonbusiness* expenses and specified expenses that are primarily of a personal nature, and (2) arbitrary allowances known as *exemptions*. The procedures are summarized in the following computations:

Gross income...............................		$37,600
Deductions from gross income:		
Expenses (related to business or specified revenue)..		15,200
Adjusted gross income...........................		$22,400
Deductions from adjusted gross income:		
Expenses (nonbusiness and personal)[1]...........	$2,640	
Exemptions...............................	1,500	4,140
Taxable income...............................		$18,260

GROSS INCOME AND FILING REQUIREMENTS

Gross income is defined in Section 61(a) of the Internal Revenue Code as follows:

> Except as otherwise provided in this subtitle, gross income means all income from whatever source derived, including (but not limited to) the following items: (1) compensation for services, including fees, commissions, and similar items; (2) gross income derived from business; (3) gains derived from dealings in property; (4) interest; (5) rents; (6) royalties; (7) dividends; (8) alimony and separate maintenance payments; (9) annuities; (10) income from life insurance and endowment contracts; (11) pensions; (12) income from discharge of indebtedness; (13) distributive share of partnership gross income; (14) income in respect of a decedent; and (15) income from an interest in an estate or trust.

Statutory items of gross income are sometimes referred to as *taxable gross income* or *includable gross income*. Exceptions to the general rule quoted above are frequently termed *nontaxable gross income* or *excludable gross income*. Examples of common items of gross income inclusions and exclusions of individuals are presented at the top of the next page. They are illustrative only and should not be considered to be exhaustive lists.

Wholly excludable items of gross income, such as interest on state bonds, are not reported on the tax return. Partly excludable items, such as dividends on corporation stocks and annuity benefits, are reported in their entirety and the excludable portion is then deducted.

Partnerships and corporations organized for profit are required to file annual income tax returns regardless of the amount of their gross income. Individuals must file a return if their (taxable) gross income is equal to or exceeds a specified amount, depending on age, marital status, and the joint return election. Single individuals under 65 years of age

593

---

[1]Instead of itemizing these deductions, an alternative *standard deduction* may be elected. The alternative is described later in the chapter.

Taxable Items	Nontaxable Items
Wages and other remuneration from employer.	Federal and state old-age pensions.
Tips and gratuities for services rendered.	State unemployment benefits.
Interest on United States obligations.	Value of property received as a gift.
Interest on commercial and industrial obligations.	Value of property received by bequest, devise, or inheritance.
Dividends in excess of $100 on stock.	Dividends of $100 or less on stock.[2]
Portion of pensions, annuities, and endowments representing income.	Life insurance proceeds received because of death of insured.
Rents and royalties.	Interest on obligations of a state or political subdivision.
Gross profit from a business.	Undergraduate scholarships for which no services are required.
Taxable gains from the sale of real estate, securities, and other property.	Portion of pensions, annuities, and endowments representing return of capital invested.
Distributive share of partnership income.	Compensation for injuries or for damages related to personal or family rights.
Income from an estate or trust.	Workmen's compensation insurance for sickness or injury.
Prizes won in contests.	Limited sick pay benefits.
Gains from wagering.	

as of the last day of the year must file a return if their gross income for the year is $2,050 or more; those age 65 or over need file only if their gross income is $2,800 or more. Married individuals both under 65 years of age, filing jointly, must file if their gross income is $2,800 or more; the limit is increased by $750 for each spouse who is 65 or over. Married individuals filing separately must file if their gross income is $750 or more.

DEDUCTIONS FROM GROSS INCOME

Business expenses and other expenses connected with earning certain types of revenue are deducted from gross income to yield adjusted gross income. The categories of such expenses that are of general applicability are described in the following paragraphs.

Business expenses other than as an employee. Ordinary and necessary expenses incurred by the taxpayer in the operation of his own unincorporated business or profession are deductible from gross income. The tax forms provide spaces for reporting sales, cost of goods sold, gross profit, salaries, taxes, depreciation, and other business expenses, and finally net income, which is the adjusted gross income derived from the business.

Business expenses of an employee. The types of expenses that an employee may deduct from salary and similar remuneration are circumscribed by the statutes and regulations. The broad term "ordinary and necessary expense" used in the preceding paragraph does not apply to

---

[2] In a joint return of husband and wife the exclusion is $200. However, neither may use any part of the other's exclusion.

employees. The types of employment-related expenses that an employee may deduct from his salary or wages in determining adjusted gross income are briefly described below.

Transportation expenses, which are the costs of public transportation and the cost of operating an employee-owned automobile. The cost of commuting from home to the place of employment is not deductible.

Travel expenses, which in addition to transportation expenses include the cost of meals and lodging if incurred when away from home overnight or when rest and recuperation are required during the day.

Outside salesmen's expenses, which in addition to transportation and travel, include other expenses incurred in soliciting business away from the employer's establishment, such as telephone, secretarial help, meals for customers, and entertainment.

Moving expenses, which are the expenses incurred by an employee[3] in changing his place of residence in connection with beginning work in a new location, either because of a transfer in an existing job, or for new employment. The distance moved and the length of time employed in the new location must meet specified minimum requirements.

Reimbursed expenses, which include all employment-connected expenses incurred by the employee for which he receives reimbursement from the employer. If expenses of any of the four types described above exceeds the amount of the reimbursement, the excess is deductible. If the amount of the reimbursement exceeds the expenses incurred, the excess is includable in gross income.

Expenses attributable to rents and royalties. Expenses that are directly connected with earning rent or royalty income are allowable as deductions from gross income in determining adjusted gross income. Expenses commonly incurred in connection with rental properties include depreciation, taxes, repairs, wages of custodian, and interest on indebtedness incurred to purchase the income-producing property.

Losses from sale or exchange of property. Losses from the sale or the exchange of property are deductible from gross income provided the property was acquired or held for the production of income. Thus, losses from the sale of rental property or of investments in stocks and bonds are deductible; losses from the sale of the taxpayer's residence or of his family automobile are not deductible.

ADJUSTED GROSS INCOME

Each category of expenses described in the preceding section is deducted from the amount of related gross income to yield adjusted gross income. If the adjusted gross income from a particular source is a nega-

595

---

[3]Also may be incurred by a self-employed individual who performs personal services.

tive amount, such as a net loss from business operations or from property rentals, it is deducted from the positive amounts in the other categories. The system of assembling data for each type of gross income and its related deductions is illustrated by the following summary for a hypothetical single taxpayer:

SUMMARY OF GROSS INCOME AND RELATED DEDUCTIONS		ADJUSTED GROSS INCOME
Salary from employment	$18,600	
Deductions	700	$17,900
Rental income	$ 2,700	
Deductions	2,900	(200)
Dividends from corporation stocks	$ 820	
Exclusion	100	720
Interest on savings deposits		300
Total adjusted gross income		$18,720

DEDUCTIONS FROM ADJUSTED GROSS INCOME

In addition to the deductions from gross income to yield adjusted gross income, there are other specified expenditures and arbitrary allowances that are deductible from adjusted gross income. The remainder is the so-called "taxable income," the base to which the progressive tax rates are applied. These allowable deductions may be classified as follows:

1. Specified expenditures and losses.
    A. Nonbusiness expenses.
    B. Charitable contributions, and other personal expenses and losses unrelated to income-producing activities.
2. Exemptions.

The deductions from adjusted gross income that are of general applicability are described in the paragraphs that follow.

Nonbusiness expenses. Expenses in this category are those related to the production or conservation of income which do not qualify as "business" expenses or other categories of expenses that are are deductible from gross income in determining adjusted gross income. Specifically, nonbusiness expenses are the expenses which are attributable (1) to the production or collection of income, (2) to the maintenance or management of income-producing property, or (3) to the determination, collection, or refund of any tax but do not qualify as deductions from gross income. For example, job-related travel expenses and labor union dues are both attributable to the "production of income," but only the former is deductible from *gross income*; the latter is deductible from *adjusted gross income* as a nonbusiness expense. Other examples of nonbusiness expenses are fees paid for the preparation of a personal income tax return, the cost of investment advisory services and subscriptions to financial periodicals, and the cost of uniforms worn on the job that are unsuitable for street wear.

Charitable contributions. Contributions made by an individual to domestic organizations created exclusively for religious, charitable, scientific, literary, or educational purposes, or for the prevention of cruelty to children or animals, are deductible provided the organization is nonprofit and does not devote a substantial part of its activities to influencing legislation. Contributions to domestic governmental units and to organizations of war veterans are also deductible.

The limitation on the amount of qualified contributions that may be deducted ranges from 20% of adjusted gross income for private foundations to 50% of adjusted gross income for public charities, with 50% being the overall maximum. There are other intermediate limitations related to contributions of various types of property other than cash.

Interest expense. Interest expense of an entirely personal nature, such as on indebtedness incurred to buy a home, household appliances, or an automobile, is deductible.

Taxes. Most of the taxes levied by the federal government are not deductible from adjusted gross income. Federal excise taxes are deductible only when the expense to which they relate qualifies as a deductible nonbusiness expense. Some of the taxes of a nonbusiness or personal nature levied by states or their political subdivisions are deductible from adjusted gross income. The deductible status of state and local taxes of general applicability is as follows:

Deductible: Real estate taxes, personal property taxes, income taxes, general sales taxes, gasoline taxes.

Nondeductible: Gift, inheritance, and estate taxes, automobile and drivers' licenses, cigarette and alcoholic beverages taxes.

Medical expenses. One half of the premiums paid for medical care insurance, but not in excess of $150 a year, is deductible from adjusted gross income. The remaining amount of such premiums is combined with other medical expenses, which are deductible to the extent that they exceed 3% of adjusted gross income. Amounts paid for medicines and drugs may be included in medical expenses only to the extent that they exceed 1% of adjusted gross income. To illustrate, assume that the medical expenses of a taxpayer with adjusted gross income of $16,000 were medical care insurance of $260, medicines and drugs of $180, and other medical expenses (doctor's fees, hospital expenses, etc.) of $475. The computation of the taxpayer's deduction is presented at the top of the next page.

597

One half of medical care insurance premium ($260).		$130
Total cost of medicines and drugs..................	$180	
Less 1% of adjusted gross income ($16,000)......	160	$ 20
Other medical expenses (including $130 insurance premium).....................................		605
Total.....................................		$625
Less 3% of adjusted gross income ($16,000)........		480 145
Medical expense deduction....................		**$275**

Casualty and theft losses. Property losses in excess of $100 resulting from fire, storm, automobile accident or other casualty, or theft are deductible to the extent not compensated for by insurance. The $100 exclusion applies to each occurrence rather than to total losses for the year. It should be noted that payments to another person for property damage or personal injury caused by the taxpayer do not constitute casualty losses.

"Child care" expenses. Taxpayers who maintain a household are allowed a deduction of up to $400 a month for expenses involved in the care, including household expenses, of a dependent child under age 15, a dependent relative who is physically or mentally disabled, or a disabled spouse, provided the expenses are incurred to enable the taxpayer to be gainfully employed. If children are cared for in a child-care facility outside the home, the deduction is limited to $200 a month for one child, $300 for two, and $400 for three or more. In no event may the total deduction for expenses (inside or outside the home) exceed $400 a month. If the taxpayer's adjusted gross income exceeds $18,000, the maximum deduction is reduced by one half of the amount of the excess over $18,000. For example, if a taxpayer with adjusted gross income of $20,000 had incurred otherwise deductible expenses of $4,800 ($400 per month), the allowable deduction would be $3,800 ($4,800 − ½ [$20,000 − $18,000]).

Political contributions. Taxpayers may deduct up to $50 ($100 for joint returns) for contributions to a candidate or candidates for election or to a political committee. In lieu of the deduction, a credit against the tax liability may be claimed for one half of the contributions, with a maximum credit of $12.50 ($25 for joint returns). Thus, a single taxpayer who makes a political contribution of $25 during the year may either (1) claim $25 as a deduction from adjusted gross income or (2) deduct $12.50 from the income tax shown on the tax return.

Exemptions. In addition to the allowable deductions from adjusted gross income described above, every individual taxpayer is entitled to a *personal* exemption of $750 for himself plus an additional exemption of the same amount for each *dependent*.

In general, a dependent is a person who satisfies all of the following requirements: (1) is closely related to the taxpayer, (2) received over one half of his support from the taxpayer during the year, (3) had less than $750 of gross income during the year, and (4) if married, does not file a joint return with his or her spouse. However, the $750 limitation on gross income does not apply to a child of the taxpayer who is either under 19 years of age at the close of the taxable year or who has been a full-time student at an educational institution during each of five months of the year.

An additional exemption is allowed to a taxpayer who is 65 years of age or older on the last day of the taxable year. An additional exemption is also allowed to a taxpayer who is blind at the close of the taxable year.

Standard deduction. Instead of itemizing their allowable deductions from adjusted gross income, taxpayers may in general elect the *standard deduction*, which is the larger of (1) the *percentage standard deduction* or (2) the *low income allowance*. The percentage standard deduction for single taxpayers and married taxpayers filing a joint return[4] is equal to 15% of their adjusted gross income, with a maximum deduction of $2,000; the low income allowance amounts to $1,300.

Taxpayers who can be claimed as a dependent (child under 19 or a student) by another taxpayer may claim the standard deduction only to the extent of their wages or other compensation for personal services (earned income). Unearned income, such as dividends and interest, may not be used as a basis for electing the standard deduction.

Except for taxpayers whose standard deduction is reduced in accordance with the limitation described in the preceding paragraph, taxpayers with adjusted gross income of less than $10,000 who elect the standard deduction are required to determine their income tax by reference to a "tax table" applicable to their number of exemptions. A portion of Table 2, for tax returns claiming two exemptions, is reproduced on page 601. The amount of income tax listed for each interval of adjusted gross income is determined by applying the percentage standard deduction or the low income allowance, whichever yields the larger deduction.

The percentage standard deduction will always yield a larger standard deduction than the low income allowance for adjusted gross income of $10,000 or more. For example, the standard deduction for $10,000 of adjusted gross income is 15% of $10,000, or $1,500; for $12,000 it is 15% of $12,000, or $1,800; and for $13,333.33 or more it is the maximum of $2,000.

599

---

[4]Married persons usually file joint returns. For this reason the special rules applicable to separate returns of married persons are not described in this chapter.

COMPUTING THE INCOME TAX

If the deductions from adjusted gross income are itemized, the tax is computed by applying the appropriate schedule of rates to the amount of taxable income reported on the tax return. If the standard deduction is elected, the same procedure is followed if the amount of adjusted gross income reported is $10,000 or more; if the adjusted gross income reported is less than $10,000, the tax is determined from the appropriate tax table.

There are four tax rate schedules for individuals, classified as follows: (1) for single taxpayers, (2) for married taxpayers filing a joint return, (3) for married taxpayers filing separate returns and (4) for unmarried taxpayers who qualify as heads of household. The first two schedules are presented below.

SINGLE TAXPAYERS

If the taxable income is: / The tax is:

Not over $500.................14% of taxable income

Over	But not over	The tax is:	of excess over
$ 500 —	$ 1,000..	$ 70, plus 15% —	$ 500
1,000 —	1,500..	145, plus 16% —	1,000
1,500 —	2,000..	225, plus 17% —	1,500
2,000 —	4,000..	310, plus 19% —	2,000
4,000 —	6,000..	690, plus 21% —	4,000
6,000 —	8,000..	1,110, plus 24% —	6,000
8,000 —	10,000..	1,590, plus 25% —	8,000
10,000 —	12,000..	2,090, plus 27% —	10,000
12,000 —	14,000..	2,630, plus 29% —	12,000
14,000 —	16,000..	3,210, plus 31% —	14,000
16,000 —	18,000..	3,830, plus 34% —	16,000
18,000 —	20,000..	4,510, plus 36% —	18,000
20,000 —	22,000..	5,230, plus 38% —	20,000
22,000 —	26,000..	5,990, plus 40% —	22,000
26,000 —	32,000..	7,590, plus 45% —	26,000
32,000 —	38,000..	10,290, plus 50% —	32,000
38,000 —	44,000..	13,290, plus 55% —	38,000
44,000 —	50,000..	16,590, plus 60% —	44,000
50,000 —	60,000..	20,190, plus 62% —	50,000
60,000 —	70,000..	26,390, plus 64% —	60,000
70,000 —	80,000..	32,790, plus 66% —	70,000
80,000 —	90,000..	39,390, plus 68% —	80,000
90,000 —	100,000..	46,190, plus 69% —	90,000
100,000 —	....	53,090, plus 70% —	100,000

MARRIED TAXPAYERS — JOINT RETURN

If the taxable income is: / The tax is:

Not over $1,000.................14% of taxable income

Over	But not over	The tax is:	of excess over
$ 1,000 —	$ 2,000..	$ 140, plus 15% —	$ 1,000
2,000 —	3,000..	290, plus 16% —	2,000
3,000 —	4,000..	450, plus 17% —	3,000
4,000 —	8,000..	620, plus 19% —	4,000
8,000 —	12,000..	1,380, plus 22% —	8,000
12,000 —	16,000..	2,260, plus 25% —	12,000
16,000 —	20,000..	3,260, plus 28% —	16,000
20,000 —	24,000..	4,380, plus 32% —	20,000
24,000 —	28,000..	5,660, plus 36% —	24,000
28,000 —	32,000..	7,100, plus 39% —	28,000
32,000 —	36,000..	8,660, plus 42% —	32,000
36,000 —	40,000..	10,340, plus 45% —	36,000
40,000 —	44,000..	12,140, plus 48% —	40,000
44,000 —	52,000..	14,060, plus 50% —	44,000
52,000 —	64,000..	18,060, plus 53% —	52,000
64,000 —	76,000..	24,420, plus 55% —	64,000
76,000 —	88,000..	31,020, plus 58% —	76,000
88,000 —	100,000..	37,980, plus 60% —	88,000
100,000 —	120,000..	45,180, plus 62% —	100,000
120,000 —	140,000..	57,580, plus 64% —	120,000
140,000 —	160,000..	70,380, plus 66% —	140,000
160,000 —	180,000..	83,580, plus 68% —	160,000
180,000 —	200,000..	97,180, plus 69% —	180,000
200,000 —	....	110,980, plus 70% —	200,000

Income tax rate schedules

Although the tax rates are changed by Congress from time to time, the progressive characteristic is a permanent feature of the income tax system. The manner in which a rate schedule is used may be illustrated as follows, assuming taxable income of $15,300 for a single person:

Tax on $14,000........	$3,210
Tax on $ 1,300 at 31%.	403
Total income tax......	$3,613

The rates in the lower brackets of the four schedules were used in constructing the optional tax tables for taxpayers with adjusted gross income of less than $10,000 who elect the standard deduction. There are thirteen tax tables, for returns claiming from one to thirteen exemptions respectively. The tax liability shown in each bracket of each table was computed on the basis of the adjusted gross income at the midpoint of the respective bracket. The larger of the percentage standard deduction or the low income allowance, plus the exemptions, were then deducted from the midpoint and the tax was computed by applying the appropri-

600

ate rate schedule and rounding the result to the nearest dollar. To illustrate the procedure, the tax liability indicated in the partial tax table below for a joint return with adjusted gross income of $9,750 to $9,800 was determined as follows:

Midpoint of $9,750–$9,800 bracket.................		$9,775.00
Larger of low income allowance, $1,300, or 15% of $9,775......................................	$1,466.25	
Exemptions, 2 at $750..........................	1,500.00	2,966.25
Taxable income..................................		$6,808.75
Tax on $4,000...................................	$ 620.00	
Tax on $2,808.75 at 19%.......................	533.66	
Total...		$1,153.66
Income tax, rounded to nearest dollar.............		$1,154.00

For the two years following the year in which a married person dies, the surviving spouse may continue to determine the tax as though it were a joint return, provided however that the surviving spouse (1) maintains as his or her home a household in which a dependent son or daughter resides and (2) does not remarry.

The tax rates for heads of household (not illustrated) are between those applicable to single taxpayers and those applicable to married taxpayers filing jointly. To qualify as a head of household, an individual must be unmarried at the close of the taxable year and must, in general, maintain as his or her home a household in which at least one of the following persons lives: (1) an unmarried son, daughter, or descendent, (2) a married son, daughter, or descendent who qualifies as a dependent of the taxpayer, or (3) any other close relative who qualifies as a dependent of the taxpayer. The head of household status may also be claimed by an unmarried taxpayer who maintains his or her dependent mother or father in a separate household.

TABLE 2 — Returns claiming TWO exemptions (and not itemizing deductions)

If adjusted gross income is —		And you are —		
At least	But less than	Single, not head of house-hold	Head of house-hold	Married filing joint return
		Your tax is —		
2,775	2,800	0	0	0
2,800	2,825	2	2	2
2,825	2,850	5	5	5
2,850	2,875	9	9	9
2,875	2,900	12	12	12
5,250	5,300	400	386	366
5,300	5,350	410	395	374
5,350	5,400	419	404	382
5,400	5,450	429	413	390
5,450	5,500	438	422	398
9,750	9,800	1,304	1,218	1,154
9,800	9,850	1,314	1,227	1,162
9,850	9,900	1,325	1,237	1,170
9,900	9,950	1,335	1,246	1,178
9,950	10,000	1,345	1,255	1,186

601

Partial tax table for returns claiming two exemptions

CAPITAL GAINS AND LOSSES

Gains and losses of individuals resulting from the sale or the exchange of certain types of assets, called *capital assets*, are accorded special treatment for income tax purposes. Capital assets most commonly owned by taxpayers are stocks and bonds. Under certain conditions, land, buildings, and equipment used in business may also be treated as capital assets.

The gains and losses from the sale or exchange of capital assets held for six months or less are classified as *short-term*. Gains and losses from those held for more than six months are classified as *long-term*. The aggregate of all short-term gains and losses during a taxable year is called a *net short-term capital gain* (or *loss*) and the aggregate of all long-term gains and losses is similarly identified as a *net long-term capital gain* (or *loss*). The net short-term and net long-term results are then combined to form the *net capital gain* (or *loss*).

Net capital gain. If there is a net capital gain it is reported as gross income. To the extent that a net capital gain is composed of an excess of a net long-term gain over a net short-term loss (if any), 50% of such excess is deducted from gross income to yield adjusted gross income from this source. The application of the foregoing provisions is demonstrated by the following illustration:

	A	B	C
Net short-term capital gain (loss).........	($2,000)	$8,000	$3,000
Net long-term capital gain (loss).........	8,000	(2,000)	3,000
Net capital gain — gross income..........	$6,000	$6,000	$6,000
Long-term capital gain deduction........	3,000	—	1,500
Adjusted gross income from capital gain.	$3,000	$6,000	$4,500

It should be noted that although the net capital gain is $6,000 in each of the three examples, the adjusted gross income from capital gain is $3,000, $6,000, and $4,500 respectively.

Further consideration of the composition of the adjusted gross income attributable to net capital gain is required in order to determine its taxable status. To the extent that it is composed of long-term gain of less than $50,000 the tax is limited to 50% of such gain included in adjusted gross income, regardless of the marginal rate of the taxpayer. This tax ceiling may be advantageous if the taxpayer is (1) single or head of household, with taxable income exceeding $38,000 or (2) married and filing jointly, with taxable income exceeding $52,000. The additional analysis of the three examples above is presented below:

	A	B	C
Adjusted gross income from capital gain.....	$3,000	$6,000	$4,500
Taxable status:			
Short-term gain, taxed as ordinary income	—	$6,000	$3,000
Long-term gain, tax limited to 50%.......	$3,000	—	1,500

Net capital loss. When the taxpayer's transactions in capital assets during the year result in a net capital loss instead of a gain, it can be applied in the reduction of gross income but only to the extent of $1,000. Here again the composition of the "net figure" must be considered. If it is composed of short-term loss, each dollar of loss provides an equivalent dollar deduction from gross income. If it is composed of long-term loss, two dollars of loss are required to yield one dollar of deduction. If there is both a net short-term loss and a net long-term loss, the former is applied to gross income first. The excess of net capital loss is carried over and may be used in future years. The application of these provisions is illustrated as follows:

	A	B	C
Net short-term capital gain (loss)..........	($8,000)	$2,000	($3,000)
Net long-term capital gain (loss)..........	2,000	(8,000)	(3,000)
Net capital (loss).......................	($6,000)	($6,000)	($6,000)
Capital loss used to reduce adjusted gross income by $1,000.......................	(1,000)	(2,000)	(1,000)
Capital loss carryover to future years:			
Short-term carryover.................	($5,000)	—	($2,000)
Long-term carryover.................	—	($4,000)	(3,000)

PAYMENT OF TAX; FILING RETURNS

603

The income tax withheld from an employee's earnings by his employer represents current payments on account. An individual whose income is not subject to withholding, or only partially so, or an individual whose income is fairly large must estimate his income tax in advance and file a tax form known as a *Declaration of Estimated Income Tax*. The estimated tax for the year, after deducting the estimated amount to be withheld and any credit for overpayment from prior years, must be paid currently, usually in four installments.

Annual income tax returns must be filed within 3½ months following the end of the taxpayer's taxable year. Any balance owed must accompany the return. If there has been an overpayment of the tax liability the taxpayer indicates the portion, if any, that he wishes to have refunded, and the portion, if any, that he wishes to have credited to his estimated tax for the following year.

DETERMINATION OF INCOME TAX OF INDIVIDUALS

The method of assembling income tax information and determining tax liability is illustrated on the next page. The data are for a married couple who file a joint return. The husband owns and operates a retail enterprise. The wife owns a building, which she leases; she also works as a secretary part-time. Each is entitled to one personal exemption and there are two additional exemptions for their dependent children. Sources and amounts of includable gross income, itemized deductions, exemptions, and other data are presented in condensed form below. In practice, the data would be reported in considerably greater detail on official tax forms.

James R. and Carol B. Hall
Summary of Federal Income Tax Data
For Calendar Year 19—

GROSS INCOME AND DEDUCTIONS FROM GROSS INCOME:

Salary			$ 3,750
Dividends on corporation stocks:			
Owned by husband	$ 570		
Owned by wife	80	$ 650	
Exclusion ($100 for husband, $80 for wife)		180	470
Rents:			
Gross income		$ 9,600	
Expenses		5,400	4,200
Business:			
Sales		$180,000	
Cost of merchandise sold		117,000	
Gross profit		$ 63,000	
Expenses		34,400	28,600
Capital gains and losses:			
Net long-term capital gain		$ 4,000	
Net short-term capital loss		1,000	
Net capital gain		$ 3,000	
Long-term capital gain deduction		1,500	1,500
Adjusted gross income			$38,520

DEDUCTIONS FROM ADJUSTED GROSS INCOME:

Interest on residence mortgage note	$1,310		
Charitable contributions	1,130		
Real estate tax on residence	996		
State income tax	825		
State sales tax	249		
State gasoline tax	98		
Safe-deposit box rental	12	$ 4,620	
Exemptions (4 × $750)		3,000	7,620
Taxable income			$30,900

INCOME TAX LIABILITY:

On $28,000		$ 7,100	
On $ 2,900 at 39%		1,131	
Total tax			$ 8,231

ADVANCE PAYMENTS:

Tax withheld from salary		$ 255	
Payments of estimated tax		7,600	
Total payments			7,855
Balance due			$ 376

Federal income tax data summary

INCOME AVERAGING

Individual taxpayers whose taxable income for a taxable year is unusually large in comparison with the average taxable income of the four preceding years may elect to compute the income tax by the averaging method. The averaging method permits part of the unusually large income to be taxed in lower brackets, resulting in a reduction of the overall amount of tax due. There is a special form designed for use in determining the tax by the averaging method.

The tabulation below indicates the amount of current taxable income needed (joint return), based on assumed amounts of income of past years, to achieve a tax saving of $100. For larger amounts of taxable income in the taxable year the averaging method would, of course, yield additional tax savings.

AVERAGE TAXABLE INCOME OF PRECEDING 4 YEARS	TAXABLE INCOME OF CURRENT YEAR	TAX SAVED BY INCOME AVERAGING
$ 12,000	$ 19,333	$100
20,000	31,333	100
40,000	55,333	100
60,000	79,333	100
100,000	145,000	100

MAXIMUM TAX ON EARNED INCOME

Individual taxpayers may elect to apply the maximum marginal tax rate of 50% to their *earned taxable income* if they are (1) single or head of household, with earned income in excess of $38,000; or (2) married, filing jointly, with earned taxable income in excess of $52,000. Earned taxable income is that portion of taxable income attributable to *earned income* less the related deductible expenses.

Earned income generally includes wages, salaries, professional fees or other compensation for personal services. A taxpayer engaged in a business where both personal service and capital investment are a material income-producing factor may consider not more than 30% of the business income as being "earned."

As with income averaging, the formula for determining the maximum tax on earned taxable income is complex. The effect is to treat earned taxable income as the first income earned for purposes of applying the graduated tax rates. Other taxable income is considered the last income earned and the tax rates applied are those that would be applied if none of the taxable income had been "earned." To illustrate, assume that married taxpayers, filing jointly, have taxable income of $120,000, of which $100,000 is earned taxable income and $20,000 is attributable to other taxable income such as interest, dividends, rents, or business income not considered earned. Determination of the tax may be illustrated as shown on the next page, though it does not follow the more complex procedure provided in the special tax form.

Income tax on earned taxable income of $100,000:		
First $52,000, on which the marginal rate is 50%......	$18,060	
Remaining $48,000, at the rate of 50%...............	24,000	$42,060
Income tax on other taxable income of $20,000:		
At 62%, the rate in the $100,000 to $120,000 bracket.		12,400
Income tax liability..................................		$54,460

Continuing the illustration, the tax on taxable income of $120,000, computed without regard to the maximum tax, would have been $57,580 (see tax schedule for joint return, page 600). Thus the election effected a tax saving of $3,120. Taxpayers who elect the income averaging method of computing the tax may not elect the alternative computation limiting the tax to 50% of earned taxable income.

TAXABLE INCOME OF CORPORATIONS

Certain classes of corporations are accorded special treatment because the sources and nature of their income differ from that of general business corporations. Included in the special categories are insurance companies, mutual savings banks, regulated investment companies, farm cooperatives, and corporations specifically exempt by statute.

Excluding the special classes from consideration, the taxable income of a corporation is determined, in general, by deducting its ordinary business expenses from the total amount of its includable gross income. Of the numerous variations from this general procedure there are three of broad applicability that merit brief consideration.

Dividends received deduction. All dividends received on shares of stock in other corporations are includable in gross income. However, 85% of such dividends is ordinarily allowed as a special deduction from gross income. Certain small corporations may deduct the entire amount of dividends received.

Charitable contributions. The deduction for charitable contributions is limited to 5% of taxable income, computed without regard to the contributions and the special deduction for dividends received. Contributions in excess of the 5% limitation may be carried over to the five succeeding years, deductions in the succeeding years also being subject to the 5% maximum.

Capital gains and losses. As in the case of individuals, capital gains and losses of corporations are classified as short-term (assets held for six months or less) and long-term (assets held for more than six months). The excess of a net long-term capital gain over a net short-term capital loss is included in its entirety in taxable income. However, the tax thereon is limited to a maximum of 30%. No part of a net capital loss may be deducted from ordinary income. However, it may be carried back to the third year preceding the year of the loss and applied against net capital gain of such year. Any unused amount of the carryback is then carried to the succeeding years to the extent of a five year carryover from the loss year.

CORPORATION INCOME TAX

Corporations in general are subject to a *normal tax* on the amount of their taxable income and to a *surtax* on taxable income in excess of $25,000. Procedures for determining taxable income and the income tax are summarized in the tabulation below, assuming a normal tax rate of 22% and a surtax rate of 26%.

Gross income (including dividends of $20,000).		$200,000
Deductions.		90,000
Taxable income before special deduction.		$110,000
Special deduction for dividends received, 85% of $20,000.		17,000
Taxable income		$ 93,000
Normal tax, 22% of $93,000.	$20,460	
Surtax, 26% of ($93,000 − $25,000).	17,680	
Total income tax.		$ 38,140
Payments of estimated tax.		31,000
Balance due.		$ 7,140

There are two additional taxes designed to limit the use of the corporate form as a means of avoiding income tax on individuals. Although the statutes which provide for these "loophole closing" taxes are too voluminous for detailed explanations, their basic nature merits brief consideration.

Accumulated earnings tax. An additional income tax may be assessed against corporations that accumulate earnings with intent to avoid the income tax that would be levied on shareholders if such earnings were distributed as dividends. Accumulated earnings of up to $100,000 are exempt from this tax; additional accumulations are subject to the additional tax unless it can be proved by a preponderance of evidence that they are not in excess of the reasonable needs of the business. The tax rate is 27.5% of the first $100,000 of accumulated taxable income and 38.5% of the excess over $100,000.

Personal holding company tax. The statutory definition of a personal holding company is quite technical. In general, the special tax is designed to discourage individuals from transferring their investment properties to a corporation in exchange for its stock, or to "incorporate" their personal talents or services. The additional tax, which is levied at the rate of 70% of the undistributed personal holding company income, is an effective deterrent to the use of this device for the accumulation of "tax-sheltered" income.

MINIMIZING INCOME TAXES

There are various legal means of minimizing or reducing federal income taxes, some of which are of broader applicability than others. Much depends upon the volume and the sources of a taxpayer's gross income, the nature of his expenses and other deductions, and the accounting methods employed.

The amount of income tax that may be saved by any particular proposal can be determined by estimating the total tax assuming that the proposal is to be adopted, and comparing that amount with the estimated tax according to the alternative proposals under consideration. In many cases it is possible to determine the tax effect of a proposal by merely computing the tax at the *marginal* rate on the amount of taxable income differential. To illustrate the latter procedure, assume that a married couple filing a joint return will report taxable income of $42,000 if they claim the standard deduction of $2,000. According to the applicable rate schedule on page 600 their marginal tax rate, which is the rate for the segment of taxable income in the $40,000 to $44,000 bracket, is 48%. If an analysis of their check stubs and other records should disclose allowable deductions of $3,400, they would save $672 (48% of $1,400) by itemizing their deductions.

It should be noted that the value of a tax saving exceeds the value of additional taxable earnings of the same amount. If instead of saving $672 of income tax in the foregoing example the taxpayer had earned additional taxable income of $672, there would have been a tax liability on the additional income. The $672 saving is the equivalent of approximately $1,292 of additional earnings ($672 ÷ [100% − 48%]).

FORM OF BUSINESS ORGANIZATION

One of the most important considerations in selecting the form of organization to use in operating a business enterprise is the impact of the federal income tax. If the business is a sole proprietorship, the owner must report the income on his personal income tax returns. In a partnership each individual partner is taxed on his distributive share of the business income in much the same manner as a sole proprietor. If the business is incorporated, the corporation must pay an income tax on its earnings, and the remaining earnings are again taxed to the owners (shareholders) when they are distributed in the form of dividends.

The double taxation feature of the corporate form might seem to outweigh any possible advantages of employing it for a family enterprise or other closely held business. This is not necessarily the case, however. For most business enterprises there are likely to be both advantages and disadvantages in the corporate form. Among the many factors that need to be considered are the following: (1) magnitude of net income, (2) fluctuations in net income from year to year, (3) disposition of after-tax income (withdrawn from the enterprise or used for expansion), (4) method of financing, (5) number of owners and shares of ownership, and (6) income of owners from other sources. The type of analysis required to appraise the relative merits of alternative forms of organization is described in the paragraphs that follow. For purposes of illustration, assume that a married couple engaged in a business enterprise organized as a partnership are considering incorporation. The business, in which personal services and capital investment are material income-producing

Organized as a Partnership

Tax on individuals:

Business income..		$65,000
Other income..		16,000
Adjusted gross income............................		$81,000
Deductions:		
Nonbusiness and personal........................	$4,250	
Exemptions (5)................................	3,750	8,000
Taxable income....................................		$73,000
Income tax liability:		
On $64,000......................................		$24,420
On $ 9,000 at 55%.............................		4,950
Total income tax — partnership form...............		**$29,370**

Organized as a Corporation

Tax on corporation:

Taxable income, $65,000 − $30,000 (salary expense)...		$35,000
Income tax liability:		
Normal tax, 22% of $35,000......................	$ 7,700	
Surtax, 26% of ($35,000 − $25,000)..............	2,600	$10,300

Tax on individuals:

Salary..		$30,000
Other income....................................		16,000
Adjusted gross income............................		$46,000
Deductions:		
Nonbusiness and personal........................	$4,250	
Exemptions (5)................................	3,750	8,000
Taxable income....................................		$38,000
Income tax liability:		
On $36,000......................................		$10,340
On $ 2,000 at 45%.............................		900
		11,240
Total income tax — corporation form...............		**$21,540**

factors, has been yielding adjusted gross income of $65,000, other investments yield income of $16,000, and nonbusiness and personal deductions from adjusted gross income total approximately $4,250. They are entitled to five exemptions and they file a joint return. Partners' withdrawals from the business totaling $30,000 a year would be treated as salary expense if the enterprise were to be incorporated. The federal income tax consequences under the two forms of organization are presented on the preceding page, using the tax rates presented in this chapter.

Comparison of the two tax liabilities indicates that an annual tax saving of approximately $8,000 ($29,370 − $21,540) could be effected by adopting the corporate form. However, the possible distribution of the corporation's net income as dividends was not taken into consideration. If the corporation's after-tax net income of $24,700 were to be paid to the owners as dividends, their taxable income would total $62,700 instead of $38,000. The resulting increase in their personal income tax amounting to approximately $12,500 would convert the expected $8,000 advantage of the corporate form to a $4,500 disadvantage.

Earnings accumulated by the corporation in the foregoing example might at some future time become available to the stockholders through sale of their stock. They would thus be converted into long-term capital gains, of which only one half would be included in taxable income. However, retention of earnings beyond the $100,000 exemption could result in imposition of the accumulated earnings tax. If additional accumulations were beyond the reasonable needs of the business, the shareholders might then elect partnership treatment under Subchapter S and thus avoid the double tax on corporate earnings. Additional information about the intentions of the owners and prospects for the future would be needed to explore additional ramifications of the problem.

It is readily apparent that the best form of organization, from the standpoint of the federal income tax, can be determined only by a careful detailed analysis of the particular situation. Generalizations are likely to be of little benefit and may even be misleading. The impact of state and local taxes also varies according to the form of business organization, and the importance of such nontax factors as limited liability and transferability of ownership should be weighed.

TIMING OF TRANSACTIONS AND REPORTING

"Timing" is an important element in the effect of management's decisions on liability for income tax. The selection of the fiscal year, the choice of accounting methods, and acceleration or deferment of gross income or expense are some of the time factors that need to be considered. Applications of timing considerations to relatively common situations are described in the paragraphs that follow.

Cash basis v. accrual basis. Corporations that regularly have taxable income in excess of the $25,000 surtax exemption are unlikely to be greatly affected by their choice of the cash or accrual basis of accounting. A small corporation whose taxable income tends to fluctuate above and below the $25,000 amount from year to year may be better able to control the fluctuation if the cash basis is used. For example, near the close of a taxable year in which taxable income is likely to exceed $25,000, some of the excess, which will be subject to the surtax (26%) may be shifted to the succeeding year. It may be possible to postpone the receipt of gross income by delayed billings for services, or expenses may be increased by payment of outstanding bills prior to the end of the year. The timing of expenditures and payment for such expenses as redecorating, repairs, and advertising may also be readily subject to control.

Unincorporated businesses may also be able to reduce fluctuations in net income, with a consequent lowering of the marginal tax rate of the owners. Even individual taxpayers whose income is primarily from salary may have opportunities to save a modest amount by careful planning of payment of deductible items. For example, if a substantial amount of medical expense is incurred near the end of the year, it would be preferable to pay all such bills before the end of the year if by so doing the medical expense deduction and other itemized deductions will exceed the standard deduction. Conversely, if early payment would not yield a reduction in taxes for the current year, postponement of payment to the following year might be beneficial.

A closely related technique is to alternate from year to year between electing the standard deduction and claiming actual deductions. Because of differences between the taxable year of the individual, which is usually the calendar year, and the fiscal year of charitable organizations and local taxing authorities, it is often possible to pay two fiscal-year amounts in a single calendar year. To illustrate, assume that a married couple with average annual adjusted gross income of $15,000 has average annual deductions of $1,850, exclusive of their two exemptions. Use of the standard deduction of $2,000 would reduce taxable income by $150, which at their marginal tax rate of 22% would yield a tax saving of $33. However, if they could schedule their cash payments so as to alternate $800 of deductible expenses from year to year they could then alternate between itemizing deductions of $2,650 ($1,850 + $800) and claiming the standard deduction of $2,000. By so doing they would realize an additional tax saving of $143 in alternate years (22% of [$2,650 − $2,000]).

Installment method. The installment method of determining gross income from sales of merchandise on the installment plan, which was described in Chapter 14, is widely used for income tax purposes. The

611

method may also be employed in reporting the net gain from a sale of real estate or from a casual sale of personal property at a price in excess of $1,000, provided the payments received in the year of sale do not exceed 30% of the selling price.

Tax savings may be effected by reporting gain on the sale of a capital asset by the installment method, particularly if the amount of the gain is substantial in relation to other income. Care must be used in so arranging the sale contract that not more than 30% of the selling price is received in the year of sale. If payment of a larger portion of the selling price in the year of sale is preferred, it may be possible for the seller to achieve a tax saving by use of the averaging method of computation.

Capital gains and losses. The timing of capital gains and losses is ordinarily subject to a high degree of control because the taxpayer is able to sell capital assets or to refrain from selling them, as he chooses. Postponement of a sale by only a single day can result in a substantial tax saving. To illustrate, assume that the only sale of a capital asset by an individual during the taxable year is the sale of listed stocks that had been held for exactly six months, realizing a gain of $4,000. The gain would be classified as a short-term capital gain and taxed as ordinary income. Assuming that the taxpayer's marginal tax rate is 60%, the tax on the $4,000 gain would be $2,400. Alternatively, if the individual had held the securities at least one additional day before selling them, the $4,000 gain (assuming no change in selling price) would have qualified as a long-term capital gain, of which only half would be taxed, at a rate not higher than 50%. Thus, if the sale had occurred at least one day later, there would have been a tax saving of $1,400 ($2,400 − [50% of $2,000]).

When a taxpayer owns various lots of an identical security that were acquired at different dates and at different prices, it may be possible to choose between realizing a gain and realizing a loss, and perhaps to a limited extent to govern the amount realized. For example, a taxpayer who has realized gains from the sale of securities may wish to offset them, in whole or in part, by losses from the sale of other securities. To illustrate, assume that a taxpayer who owns three 100-share lots of common stock in the same corporation, purchased at $40, $48, and $60 a share respectively, plans to sell 100 shares at the current market price of $52. Depending upon which of the three 100-share lots is sold, he will realize a gain of $1,200, a gain of $400, or a loss of $800. If the identity of the particular lot sold cannot be determined, the first-in, first-out cost flow assumption must be applied; the use of average cost is not permitted.

Accelerated depreciation. The declining-balance and sum-of-the-years-digits methods of computing depreciation were described and illustrated in Chapter 10. The Code specifically authorizes the use of these methods for new items of tangible personal property having a useful life of at least three years.

Taxpayers may also elect to deduct additional first-year depreciation of 20% on up to $10,000 ($20,000 on a joint return) of tangible personal property having a useful life of at least six years. The 20% "extra" depreciation is computed without regard to the period of time the asset has been held during the year or to the residual value. Taxpayers electing to claim the additional deduction must identify the specific assets to which it is applied, and they must deduct the extra depreciation from the asset cost before computing the "regular" depreciation. To illustrate the application of this provision, the extra and regular depreciation on a $10,000 item of equipment is computed below. The asset is expected to have a useful life of six years; it was acquired near the end of the third month of the taxable year; and the declining-balance method, at twice the straight-line rate, is elected.

Extra depreciation, 20% of $10,000...............................	$2,000
Declining-balance depreciation on $10,000 − $2,000,	
9/12 of (33⅓% of $8,000)...................................	2,000
Total depreciation..	$4,000

613

The accelerated write-off of depreciable assets does not, of course, effect a long-run net saving in income tax. The tax reduction of the early years of use is offset by higher taxes as the annual depreciation expense diminishes. The ever-present possibility of changes in tax rates in future years adds to the uncertainty of the real merits of accelerated depreciation. Nevertheless, the additional funds made available by current tax savings are usually considered to be sufficiently advantageous to justify the election of accelerated depreciation.

EQUALIZATION AMONG TAXABLE ENTITIES

In some situations a saving in income taxes may be effected by transfers of income-producing properties among members of a family group. For example, if a taxpayer with a high marginal tax rate gives securities or other income-producing properties to his children, grandchildren, or other close relatives of modest means, the income from the gift will be taxed to the owner at a lower rate. It is also possible to accomplish a reduction in income taxes by establishing trust funds.

IMPACT OF INCOME TAXES GENERALLY

The foregoing description of the federal income tax system and discussion of tax minimization, together with explanations in other chapters, demonstrates the importance of income taxes to business enterprises. The most important factor influencing a business decision is often the federal income tax. Many accountants, in both private and public practice, devote their entire attention to tax planning for their employers or their clients. The statutes and the administrative regulations, which change frequently, must be studied continuously by anyone who engages in this phase of accounting.

QUESTIONS

1. Who initially determines the amount of a taxpayer's *taxable income*?

2. Does the failure to maintain adequate records qualify as a legitimate means of tax avoidance? Discuss.

3. A particular individual owns three unincorporated business enterprises, maintaining a separate accounting system for each. (a) Is a separate income tax return required for each enterprise? (b) May the owner elect to file a separate return and determine the tax on each enterprise separately?

4. Describe briefly the system employed in subjecting the income of partnerships to the federal income tax.

5. The adjusted gross income of a sole proprietorship for the year was $30,000, of which the owner withdrew $20,000. What amount of income from the business enterprise must the owner report in his income tax return?

6. Do corporations electing partnership treatment (Subchapter S) pay federal income tax? Discuss.

7. Which of the two methods of accounting, cash or accrual, is more commonly used by individual taxpayers?

8. During the year an attorney who uses the cash basis of determining taxable income spends $300 for a new office desk and determines that a $200 fee billed to a client during the year is uncollectible. Discuss the status of these two items as allowable deductions.

9. Describe *constructive* receipt of gross income, as it applies to (a) salary check received from employer, (b) interest credited to a savings account, and (c) bond interest coupons.

10. Arrange the following in their proper sequence for the determination of the income tax base of an individual:

(a) Adjusted gross income
(b) Personal exemptions
(c) Expenses (nonbusiness and personal)
(d) Taxable income
(e) Gross income
(f) Expenses (related to business or specified revenue)

11. Which of the following items are includable in gross income by an individual in determining his taxable income?

    (1) Scholarship received from State University by a sophomore.
    (2) Wages received for farm labor.
    (3) Insurance proceeds received by beneficiary because of death of insured.
    (4) Cash received from a friend in repayment of a non-interest-bearing loan.
    (5) Shares of corporation stocks received as a gift.
    (6) Dividends in excess of $100 on stock acquired in (5).
    (7) Receipts from rental of room in taxpayer's home.
    (8) Interest on municipal bonds.

12. Which of the following are required to file an income tax return?

    (a) Unmarried man, 70 years old, with gross income of $2,700.
    (b) Child, 14 years old, with gross income of $1,800 from investments.
    (c) Corporation, with net loss of $6,000.
    (d) College student, 20 years old, supported by father, with gross income of $2,100.
    (e) Husband with gross income of $16,000; wife with gross income of $650; each entitled to one exemption. Answer for both separate returns and a joint return.

13. Classify the following items paid by an individual operating a business as a sole proprietorship as: (a) deductible from gross income in determining adjusted gross income, (b) deductible from adjusted gross income in determining taxable income, or (c) not deductible. (Ignore any possible limitations on the amount of the deduction.)

615

    (1) Fire insurance on taxpayer's residence.
    (2) State sales taxes on commodities purchased for family use.
    (3) Loss incurred on sale of corporation securities.
    (4) Property taxes on apartment building held as an investment.
    (5) State license tax on family automobile.
    (6) Transportation expenses incurred for the business enterprise.
    (7) Storm damage to family residence, not covered by insurance.
    (8) Interest on money borrowed for use in the business enterprise.
    (9) Contribution to State University by the business enterprise.
    (10) Federal excise tax on commodities purchased for family use.
    (11) State income tax.
    (12) Property tax on residence.
    (13) State cigarette tax.
    (14) State tax on gasoline used in family automobile.

14. May an unmarried taxpayer with adjusted gross income of $8,500 deduct his exemption and the larger of the percentage standard deduction or the low income allowance and determine his tax by reference to the graduated tax rate schedule for single taxpayers? Explain.

15. Is it permissible for a taxpayer with adjusted gross income of less than $10,000 to itemize his deductions from adjusted gross income and determine his tax by reference to the appropriate tax rate schedule?

16. An acquaintance is considering whether he should reject an opportunity to easily earn an additional thousand dollars, on the grounds that doing so would "put him in a higher tax bracket." How should you advise him?

17. An unmarried son of the taxpayer, 22 years of age, was a full-time student at a university until his graduation in August; his gross income for the year was

$2,300. (a) What requirement must be met to enable the taxpayer to claim the son as a dependent? (b) If the son was married during the year, would there be an additional requirement? Discuss.

18. According to the tax rate schedule for single taxpayers appearing in this chapter, the tax on taxable income of $20,000 is $5,230. (a) What is the approximate percentage of the tax to the $20,000 of taxable income? (b) What is the marginal tax rate at this level of taxable income?

19. A single taxpayer had a net long-term capital gain of $12,000 and a net short-term capital loss of $2,000 during the year. (a) What is the amount of his adjusted gross income from net capital gain? (b) Assuming that the taxpayer's taxable income, exclusive of capital gains and losses, is $120,000 (marginal tax rate of 70%), what is the amount of income tax on the net capital gain?

20. An individual taxpayer had a net short-term capital gain of $2,000 and a net long-term capital loss of $10,000 during the year. What is the amount of (a) the net capital loss, (b) the allowable deduction from adjusted gross income, and (c) the carryover?

21. Is it true that "earned taxable income" of an individual is taxed at the uniform rate of 50%? Explain.

22. What terms are applied to the two basic income tax rates levied against corporations?

23. The president and major stockholder of X Corporation receives in salary and income from other investments an amount which places him in the 64% income tax bracket. (a) Which corporate policy would be more advantageous to him, retention of earnings or distribution in dividends? (b) Describe the deterrent to retention of earnings provided by the Code.

EXERCISES

23-1. An employee who does not qualify as an outside salesman received a salary of $18,000 during the year and incurred the following unreimbursed expenses related to his employment: (a) automobile, $400, and lunches, $175, incurred while calling on customers within the city in which he lives; (b) travel away from home overnight, $800; and (c) customer entertainment, $460. Determine his adjusted gross income from salary.

23-2. Determine the adjusted gross income from salary of employees A, B, and C, assuming that none of them is an outside salesman and that no travel expenses were incurred.

	A	B	C
Salary................................	$12,000	$14,000	$18,000
Reimbursement allowance received from employer for entertainment expenses.	600	900	1,200
Entertainment expenses incurred and paid by the employee.....................	450	1,000	1,200

23-3. Taxpayer husband and wife, each entitled to one exemption, with two dependent children, have adjusted gross income of $13,000 for the year. Amounts paid for medical expenses during the year were as follows: medical care insurance premiums, $330; medicines and drugs, $165; other medical expenses, $520. (a) Determine the amount of their allowable deduction for medical expenses. (b) Determine the maximum amount that they may claim as a standard deduction. (c) Assuming that they claim the standard deduction, determine their income tax, applying the appropriate schedule of rates appearing in this chapter.

23-4. The capital gains and losses of an individual taxpayer during the year are listed below. Losses are identified by parentheses.

Short-term: $5,000, $2,000, ($4,000)
Long-term: $7,000, ($3,000), $6,000

Determine the following: (a) net short-term capital gain or loss; (b) net long-term capital gain or loss; (c) net capital gain or loss; (d) long-term capital gain deduction, if any; (e) adjusted gross income from net capital gain; and (f) amount of capital gain subject to the tax rate limitation of 50%.

23-5. Unmarried taxpayer, not head of household, is entitled to one exemption for himself and one exemption for his younger brother for whom he contributes over half the cost of support. His adjusted gross income for the year is $9,850 and his allowable deductions from adjusted gross income (exclusive of exemptions) total $550. Determine his income tax (a) claiming itemized deductions and (b) electing the standard deduction, applying data appearing in this chapter.

23-6. Taxpayer husband and wife, entitled to one exemption each and three additional exemptions for dependents, file a joint return. Other summary data related to their income tax return are as follows:

Includable gross income $26,000
Allowable deductions from gross income 1,250
Allowable itemized deductions from adjusted gross income . 1,420
Tax withheld from salary 2,524
Payments of estimated tax 1,200

Determine the following: (a) adjusted gross income; (b) taxable income; (c) income tax liability, using the appropriate schedule of rates appearing in this chapter; and (d) overpayment or balance due.

23-7. The data required for the determination of a particular corporation's income tax for the current year are summarized below.

Dividends received from other corporations. . . . . $ 20,000
Net short-term capital loss 4,000
Net long-term capital gain 20,000
Includable gross income from ordinary operations (i.e., in addition to the three items listed above). 180,000
Allowable deductions, exclusive of special deduction for dividends received 70,000

Determine the corporation's total income tax for the year, using the rates appearing in this chapter (assume an 85% dividends received deduction).

23-8. An unmarried taxpayer (not head of household) has taxable income of $130,000, of which $100,000 is "earned taxable income." Determine the following amounts, using the appropriate schedule of rates appearing in this chapter: (a) income tax on the $100,000 of earned taxable income, (b) income tax on the taxable income of $130,000, (c) income tax on taxable income of $130,000 assuming that there had been no earned taxable income, and (d) tax saving effected by electing the alternative computation.

PROBLEMS

The following additional problems for this chapter are located in Appendix B: 23-1B, 23-2B, 23-3B.

23-1A. G. T. Shaw owns a small office building from which he receives rental income. He uses the cash method of determining income, depositing all rents received from tenants in a special bank account. All disbursements related to the building, as well as occasional unrelated disbursements, are paid by checks drawn on the same account. During the current taxable year ending December 31, he deposited $35,000 of rent receipts in the special account.

Disbursements from the special bank account during the current year are summarized as follows:

Wages of custodian:		
Withheld for FICA tax and paid to IRS	$ 390	
Withheld for income tax and paid to IRS	582	
Paid to custodian	5,528	$6,500
Real estate tax		2,630
Payments of personal income tax:		
Applicable to preceding year		1,500
Applicable to current year		4,500
Interest on mortgage note payable on land and office building		1,450
Installment payments of principal on mortgage note payable		3,000
Utilities expense		960
Air-conditioning units installed in two offices not previously air-conditioned		2,860
Repainting interior of two offices		820
Premium on a three-year insurance policy on the building, effective January 5		690
Repairs to heating and plumbing equipment		515
Payroll tax expense		503
Contributions:		
United Fund		300
State University		500
Political committee		100
Miscellaneous expenses incurred in earning rentals		592
Purchases of various stocks		6,280

In addition to the foregoing data, you determine from other records and the tax return for the preceding year that the allowable deduction for depreciation expense is $4,200 and that current expirations of insurance premiums paid in earlier years total $518.

Instructions:

Prepare a statement of adjusted gross income from rents, identifying each of the allowable deductions from gross income.

23-2A. Mark L. Martin, unmarried and entitled to one exemption for himself, is an architect. He uses the cash method of determining taxable income and reports on the calendar-year basis. A summary of his record of cash receipts and disbursements for the current calendar year is presented below.

The automobile was used 40% of the time for professional purposes. It is to be depreciated by the declining-balance method at twice the straight-line rate, assuming an estimated life of 3 years. Allocate 40% of the depreciation and other automobile expenses to professional purposes.

CASH RECEIPTS

Professional fees....................................	$63,200
Borrowed from bank (professional purposes)..............	5,000
Inheritance from uncle's estate..........................	4,000
Dividends on corporation stocks.........................	516

CASH DISBURSEMENTS

Wages of employees..................................	$15,210
Payroll taxes.......................................	1,107
Fees to collaborating engineers.........................	5,630
Office rent...	4,920
Telephone expense (office)............................	710
Electricity (office)...................................	365
Blueprints...	535
Office supplies expense...............................	195
Insurance on office equipment (3-year policy, dated January 1)...	210
Partial repayment of bank loan (see receipts).............	2,000
Interest on bank loan................................	350
Charitable contributions..............................	750
Payment on principal of residence mortgage note...........	1,200
Interest on residence mortgage note.....................	820
Personal property tax on office equipment................	45
Real estate tax on home..............................	688
State sales tax on purchases for personal use.............	175
Political contribution................................	100
New automobile (purchased January 10)...................	4,800
Office equipment (purchased at various times during year)..	1,000
Automobile operating expenses (exclusive of depreciation)...	640
Purchase of 100 shares of Miami Corporation stock........	1,860
Payments of estimated income tax for current year.........	8,400

619

The cost of the office equipment owned at the beginning of the year was $2,400, the additions made during the year are indicated above, and none of the equipment was disposed of during the year. Use a composite depreciation rate of 10%, based on the average of the beginning and ending balances.

Instructions:

> Prepare a summary of federal income tax data for Martin, applying the appropriate schedule of tax rates presented in this chapter.

23-3A. The preliminary income statement of H. M. Riley's Valley Record Shop presented on the next page was prepared as of the end of the calendar year in which the business was established. You are engaged to examine the statement, review the business records, revise the accounting system to the extent necessary, and determine the adjusted gross income.

Sales.............		$98,760
Purchases.........		76,545
Gross profit on sales.		$22,215
Operating expenses:		
Salaries.........	$18,320	
Rent...........	3,300	
Taxes..........	976	
Store equipment..	7,400	
Advertising......	538	
Fuel...........	382	
Utilities.........	365	
Insurance.......	780	
Donations.......	162	
Miscellaneous....	741	32,964
Net loss...........		$10,749

You obtain the following information during your examination:

(a) The preliminary income statement is a summary of cash receipts and disbursements. Sales on account are not recorded until cash is received; in the meantime they are evidenced only by duplicate sales tickets. Similarly, invoices for merchandise and other purchases are not recorded until payment is made; in the meantime they are filed in an unpaid file.

(b) Uncollected sales to customers on account at December 31 amount to $1,858.

(c) Unpaid invoices at December 31 for expenditures of the past year are summarized as follows:

Merchandise.........	$5,416
Fuel................	67
Utilities.............	52

(d) The inventory of merchandise on hand at December 31 amounted to $18,432.

(e) Withdrawals of $6,600 by the owner of the enterprise were included in the amount reported as Salaries.

(f) The agreement with the three part-time salesclerks provides for a bonus equal to 1% of cash collected on sales during the year, payable in January of the following year. (Figure to nearest dollar.)

(g) The rent for January of the following year ($300) was paid and recorded in December.

(h) Accrued taxes as of the end of the year amount to $325.

(i) The store equipment reported in the preliminary income statement was installed on April 5. It has an estimated life of 10 years and no residual value. Depreciation is to be claimed for 9 months, using the declining-balance method at twice the straight-line rate.

(j) A total of $450 of insurance premiums was unexpired at December 31.

(k) Payments classified as Donations were contributions to charitable, religious, and educational organizations.

(l) Payments classified as Miscellaneous included $185 of personal expenses of the owner.

Instructions:

Prepare a statement of adjusted gross income from the business for submission with the income tax return of H. M. Riley, the owner, employing the accrual method of accounting.

23-4A. Three married individuals, designated as A, B, and C, who are engaged in related types of businesses as sole proprietors, plan to combine their enterprises to form Dee Co. They have discussed the relative merits of the partnership and the corporation form of organization, exclusive of the effect of the federal income tax. You are engaged to assemble and analyze the relevant data and to determine the immediate income tax consequences to each of them of the two forms of organization. The consolidation is planned to take effect as of next January 1, the beginning of the company's fiscal year.

The combined annual net income of the three separate enterprises has typically totaled $110,000. It is anticipated that economies of operation and other advantages of the consolidation will have the immediate effect of increasing annual net income by $30,000, making a total of $140,000 before deducting owners' salaries totaling $70,000.

Each of the owners is to be assigned managerial duties as a partner or, alternatively, to be designated an officer of the corporation. In either event, each is to be paid an annual salary, which is to be treated as an operating expense of the enterprise. In addition, they plan to distribute $20,000 of earnings annually, which are to be allocated among them in accordance with their original investments. It is anticipated that the remaining earnings will be retained for use in expanding operations. The agreed capital investments, salaries, and distributions of earnings are to be as follows:

	A	B	C	Total
Capital investment.......	$120,000	$200,000	$ 80,000	$400,000
Salary.................	30,000	15,000	25,000	70,000
Distribution of earnings.	6,000	10,000	4,000	20,000

The estimated adjusted gross income from sources other than Dee Co., for each individual and his wife, and other pertinent data are reported below. The amount of income reported for each includes dividends on various corporation stocks in excess of the allowable exclusion, and each files a joint return for the calendar year prepared in accordance with the cash method.

	A	B	C
Ordinary adjusted gross income, exclusive of salary and net income of Dee Co....	$26,000	$ 2,000	$24,000
Allowable deductions from adjusted gross income, including exemptions........	5,000	3,000	6,000

Instructions:
(1) Present the following reports of estimated results of the first year of operations, based on the assumption that Dee Co. is to be organized as a partnership: (a) Estimated capital statement of the partners of Dee Co. (b) Statement of estimated federal income tax of A, B, and C, applying the appropriate schedule of tax rates presented in this chapter.
(2) Present the following reports of estimated results of the first year of operations, based on the assumption that Dee Co. is to be organized as a corporation: (a) Statement of estimated federal income tax of Dee Co., applying the corporation tax rates presented in this chapter. (b) Estimated statement of stockholders' equity of each of the stockholders in Dee Co., allocating each increase and decrease in the manner employed in (1a) above. (c) Estimated federal income tax of A, B, and C, applying the appropriate schedule of tax rates presented in this chapter.

621

(3) Present a report comparing the estimated federal income tax effects of the two methods of organization on each of the three individuals. For purposes of this report, the income tax on the corporation should be allocated among the individuals, as in (2b) above.

23-5A. Robert and Janet Reed, each of whom is entitled to one exemption, have 2 dependent children. The older child, 18 years of age, earned $900 during the year, and the younger child earned $210. Mr. Reed also contributed more than half of the cost of supporting his mother, who received gross income of $800 during the year. During the current year ended December 31, Mr. Reed realized a net short-term capital gain of $1,800 and incurred a net long-term capital loss of $2,800. Other details of their receipts and disbursements during the year are presented below. They also suffered windstorm damages of $400 to their residence.

Cash Receipts

Robert Reed:

Salary as sales manager of Astrasonic Co..	$28,690
(Earnings, $48,000. Withholding: income tax, $12,770; FICA tax, $540; purchases of Astrasonic stock, $6,000)	
Interest on bonds of City of Sacramento.	900
Dividends on corporation stocks.	820

Janet Reed:

Withdrawals of net income from Burton & Associates, a partnership in which she is a partner (distributive share of the net income for the year, $10,200).	5,400
Rent from property owned.	7,200
Insurance proceeds (death of father).	20,000
Dividends on corporation stock.	90
Interest on U.S. Treasury bills.	523

Cash Disbursements

Robert Reed:

Charitable contributions.	2,580
Political contribution.	150
Interest on mortgage on residence.	899
Automobile license fees (family cars).	42
Real estate tax on residence.	1,286
State sales tax on items purchased for personal or family use.	320
State gasoline tax (family cars).	124
Federal tax on residence telephone service.	21
Damages for accidental injury suffered by visitor, not compensated by insurance.	1,500
Payments of estimated income tax for current year.	5,400

Janet Reed:

Rental property:

Real estate tax.	815
Insurance (one-year policies).	370
Painting and repairs.	220

Mortgage note payments:

Principal.	3,000
Interest.	1,124
(Building was acquired several years ago at a cost of $80,000 and is being depreciated at the rate of 4%)	
Charitable contributions.	485

Instructions:

Prepare a summary of federal income tax data for the Reeds, applying the appropriate schedule of tax rates presented in this chapter.

Chapter 24

COST AND REVENUE RELATIONSHIPS FOR MANAGEMENT

ALTERNATIVE CONCEPTS OF COST AND REVENUE

One of the primary objectives of accounting is the determination of net income. For this purpose costs are classified as either assets or expenses. The costs of properties and prepaid services owned at any particular time represent assets. As the assets are sold or consumed, they become expenses. This concept of cost has been explored in detail in earlier chapters. Various criteria for determining when revenues should be recognized and reported in the income statement were also described and discussed.

Another important objective of accounting is to provide data that will be useful to management in analyzing and resolving current problems and making plans for the future. For any particular business problem or proposed project there may be a variety of possible courses of action, only one of which can be selected. Much of the analysis involved in consideration of alternatives is concerned with costs and revenues. Useful data on past costs and revenues may be available in the ledger, but data relevant to some situations, particularly those related to proposed new projects, cannot always be found there. In any case, the record of past events alone is seldom an adequate basis for a decision affecting the future. The more important cost and revenue concepts and relationships, and their application to decision making, are described in this chapter.

HISTORICAL COST AND REPLACEMENT COST

As used in a broad generic sense, the term "cost" means the amount of money or other property expended, or liability or other obligation incurred, for goods or services purchased. References to the amount of property expended or liability incurred for goods or services may be expressed by the shorter phrase "cash or equivalent." The element of time is important in discussions of cost, often necessitating the use of the adjective "historical" or "replacement."

Historical cost is the cash or equivalent outlay for goods or services actually acquired. An alternative term, *actual cost*, is often used when making comparisons with estimated or standard cost. Historical costs are recorded in the ledgers and other basic accounting records; the expired portions are reported as expenses in the income statement and the unexpired portions are reported as assets in the balance sheet. Historical costs are relevant in the determination of periodic net income and current financial status. However, they may be of only slight consequence or completely irrelevant in planning for the future.

Replacement cost is the cost of replacing an asset at current market prices. In many planning situations the cost of replacing an asset is of greater significance than its historical cost. To illustrate, assume that an offer is received for goods to be manufactured at a specific price. Assume also that there is a sufficient quantity of unprocessed materials in stock that were acquired at a considerably higher cost than current market prices. In deciding whether to accept the offer, it is the replacement cost of the materials that is significant. It might be advisable to accept the offer even though, on the basis of historical costs, a loss is likely to result.

Replacement cost analysis is useful in planning the replacement of worn-out or obsolete plant assets. The cost of the replacement asset is likely to differ from the cost of the original asset, in part because of changes in price levels. In addition, because of technological improvements and other changes in physical characteristics, new equipment is rarely identical with the asset it replaces. It is often useful to compare annual depreciation expense based on historical cost with depreciation based on estimated replacement cost. The difference between the two represents the estimated amount of operating income that should be retained in order to maintain the productive capacity of the physical plant. If, for example, depreciation expense recorded for the year is $120,000 and depreciation based on estimated replacement cost is $200,000, it may be prudent for the board of directors to authorize an $80,000 appropriation of retained earnings for "replacement of facilities." In any event there should be a realization by management that if the replacement of facilities is not to be financed in part by earnings, it may be necessary to issue more stock or debt obligations.

The significance of replacement cost, adjusted for depreciation, in the admission or the withdrawal of a partner was considered in an earlier chapter. Similar analyses play a significant role in negotiations for the purchase and sale of a going business and in the merging of two separate enterprises. In such situations the values finally placed on plant assets are greatly influenced by the bargaining process, but consideration of replacement cost is often the starting point.

ABSORPTION COSTING AND VARIABLE COSTING

The cost of manufactured products is customarily considered to be composed of direct materials, direct labor, and factory overhead. All such costs ultimately become a part of the finished goods inventory and remain there as an asset until the goods are sold. This is the conventional treatment of manufacturing costs. It is sometimes referred to as *absorption costing* because all costs are "absorbed" into finished goods. Although the concept is indispensable in the determination of historical cost and taxable income, another costing concept may be more useful to management in making decisions.

The concept of *variable costing*, which is also termed *direct costing*, considers the cost of products manufactured to be composed only of those manufacturing costs that increase or decrease as the volume of production rises or falls. According to this point of view, the cost of finished goods includes, in addition to direct materials and direct labor, only those factory overhead costs which vary with the rate of production. The remaining factory overhead costs, which are the nonvariable or fixed items, are related to the productive capacity of the manufacturing plant and are not affected by changes in the quantity of product manufactured. Accordingly, the nonvariable factory overhead does not become a part of the costs of finished goods but is considered to be an expense of the period.

625

VARIABLE COSTING AND THE INCOME STATEMENT

The arrangement of data in the variable costing income statement differs considerably from the format of the conventional income statement. Variable costs and expenses are presented as distinct categories separate from fixed costs and expenses, with significant summarizing amounts inserted at intermediate points. The differences between the two forms may be observed by comparing two income statements prepared from the following basic information:

	Total Cost or Expense	Number of Units	Unit Cost
Manufacturing costs:			
Variable................	$ 75,000	15,000	$5
Fixed.................	30,000	15,000	2
Total...............	$105,000		$7
Selling and general expenses:			
Variable................	$ 12,000		
Fixed.................	10,000		
Total...............	$ 22,000		

The two types of income statement based on the assumed data are illustrated below. Arithmetical memorandums are inserted parenthetically as an aid to understanding.

ABSORPTION COSTING INCOME STATEMENT

Sales...		$120,000
Cost of goods sold:		
Cost of goods manufactured (15,000 × $7).................	$105,000	
Less ending inventory (3,000 × $7)......................	21,000	
Cost of goods sold..................................		84,000
Gross profit on sales....................................		$ 36,000
Selling and general expenses ($12,000 + $10,000)............		22,000
Income from operations................................		$ 14,000

VARIABLE COSTING INCOME STATEMENT

Sales...		$120,000
Variable cost of goods sold:		
Variable cost of goods manufactured (15,000 × $5)..........	$ 75,000	
Less ending inventory (3,000 × $5)......................	15,000	
Variable cost of goods sold............................		60,000
Manufacturing margin....................................		$ 60,000
Variable selling and general expenses.......................		12,000
Marginal income.......................................		$ 48,000
Fixed costs and expenses:		
Fixed manufacturing costs.............................	$ 30,000	
Fixed selling and general expenses......................	10,000	40,000
Income from operations................................		$ 8,000

In the absorption costing income statement, both fixed and variable manufacturing costs are included in cost of goods sold, and the excess of sales over cost of goods sold is identified as gross profit on sales. In the variable costing income statement, only the variable manufacturing costs are included in cost of goods sold; the excess of sales over the variable cost of goods sold is termed *manufacturing margin*. Deduction of the variable selling and general expenses from manufacturing margin yields *marginal income*, which is the remaining amount of revenue available for fixed manufacturing costs, fixed expenses, and operating income. The fixed costs and expenses are then deducted from marginal income to yield income from operations.

When the level of inventory fluctuates from period to period, the operating income reported under absorption costing differs from that reported under variable costing. The difference in operating income arises because absorption costing, by including the fixed factory overhead as a part of the cost of the product produced, defers to another period that portion of the fixed factory overhead included in inventory on hand, whereas variable costing includes all the fixed factory overhead costs incurred during the period as expenses of the period. For a period in which the amount of inventory increases, such as in the illustration on the preceding page, the operating income reported by absorption costing will be larger than the operating income reported by variable costing. In the illustration this difference of $6,000 ($14,000 − $8,000) is composed of the $2 unit cost of fixed factory overhead multiplied by the 3,000 units of product remaining in the inventory. When the inventory decreases during a period, the effect is reversed; that is, a smaller operating income will be reported if absorption costing is used.

VARIABLE COSTING AS A MANAGERIAL AID

Many concepts of cost and revenue are useful to management in making decisions. Some of these concepts, however, are not acceptable for published financial statements which report the results of operations and financial condition to stockholders, creditors, and others outside the management group. Variable costing is one such concept.[1] Although it cannot be used for published financial statements or generally for federal income tax purposes, variable costing can be very useful to management in making decisions relating to cost control, product pricing, production planning, and other management functions.

627

VARIABLE COSTING AS AN AID IN COST CONTROL

All costs are controllable by someone within the firm, but they are not all controllable at the same level of management. For example, a plant foreman has control over the use of materials in his department, but he cannot control the cost of insurance on the building that houses his department. For a specific level of management, *controllable costs* are costs that it controls directly, and *uncontrollable costs* are costs that another level of management controls. This distinction, as applied to specific levels of management, is useful in fixing the responsibility for incurrence of costs and then for reporting the cost data to those responsible for cost control.

Variable manufacturing costs are responsive to the control of the operating level of management because they vary with changes in production. By including only the variable manufacturing costs in the cost of the product, variable costing provides a product cost figure that is subject to control by operating management. The fixed factory overhead costs are ordinarily the responsibility of a higher echelon of

[1]*Accounting Research and Terminology Bulletins — Final Edition*, "No. 43, Restatement and Revision of Accounting Research Bulletins" (New York: American Institute of Certified Public Accountants, 1961), pp. 28–29.

management. When the fixed factory overhead costs are reported as a separate item in the variable costing income statement, they are easier to identify and control than when they are spread among units of product as in absorption costing.

As is the case with the fixed and variable manufacturing costs, the control of the variable and fixed operating expenses are ordinarily the responsibility of different echelons of management. Under variable costing, the variable selling and general expenses are reported in a separate category from the fixed selling and general expenses. Because they are reported in this manner, both types of operating expenses are easier to identify and control than is the case under absorption costing where they are not reported separately.

VARIABLE COSTING AS AN AID IN PRICING

Many factors enter into the determination of the selling price of a product. The cost of making the product is obviously a significant factor. Microeconomic theory deduces, from a set of restrictive assumptions, that income is maximized by expanding output to the volume where the revenue realized by the sale of the final unit (marginal revenue) is equaled by the cost of that unit (marginal cost). Although the degree of exactitude assumed in economic theory is rarely attainable, the concepts of marginal revenue and marginal cost are useful in establishing selling prices.

In the short run an enterprise is committed to the existing capacity of its manufacturing facilities, and the pricing decision should be based upon making the best use of such capacity. The fixed costs and expenses cannot be avoided, but the variable costs and expenses can be eliminated if the company does not manufacture the product. The selling price of a product therefore should not be less than the variable costs and expenses of making and selling it. Any revenue above this minimum selling price contributes toward covering fixed costs and expenses and providing operating income. Variable costing procedures yield data that emphasize these relationships.

In the long run, plant capacity can be increased or decreased, and if an enterprise is to continue in business, the selling prices of its products must be sufficient to cover all costs and expenses and provide a reasonable operating income. Hence, in establishing pricing policies for the long run, information provided by absorption costing procedures is needed.

There are no simple solutions to most pricing problems; consideration must be given to many factors of varying importance. Accounting can contribute by preparing analyses of various pricing plans for both the short run and the long run.

VARIABLE COSTING AS AN AID IN PRODUCTION PLANNING

Production planning also has both short-run and long-run implications. In the short run, production is limited to existing capacity, and operating decisions must be made promptly before opportunities are lost. For example, a company manufacturing products with a seasonal demand may have an opportunity to obtain an off-season order that will not compete with regular products. The relevant factors for such a short-run decision are the revenues and the variable costs and expenses. If the revenues from the special order will provide marginal income, the order should be accepted because it will increase the company's operating income. For long-run planning, management must also consider the fixed costs and expenses.

ADDITIONAL MANAGERIAL USES OF VARIABLE COSTING

To control and plan operations, management needs information on the profitability of the various segments of its business, such as types of products and sales territories. Variable costing makes a significant contribution to management decision making in providing data for effective profit planning in such areas. Two aspects of profit planning are (1) determination of the most profitable sales mix of a company's products and (2) determination of the contribution being made by each sales territory.

Sales mix studies. *Sales mix* is generally defined as the relative distribution of sales among the various products. Ordinarily some lines are more profitable than others, and management should concentrate its sales efforts on those products that will provide the maximum total operating income. The marginal income and the amount of production facilities required to produce each product are two important factors for management to consider in selecting the products that should be emphasized in sales promotion.

The illustrative statement presented below is an example of the type of data needed for an evaluation of sales mix. The hypothetical enterprise, which manufactures two products and is operating at full capacity, is considering the advisability of changing the emphasis of its advertising and other promotional efforts.

Marginal Income by Unit of Product
April 15, 19--

	PRODUCT A	PRODUCT B
Sales price...............................	$6.00	$8.50
Variable cost of goods sold..........................	3.50	5.50
Manufacturing margin............................	$2.50	$3.00
Variable selling and general expenses..................	1.00	1.00
Marginal income...............................	$1.50	$2.00

Marginal income statement — unit of product

629

The statement indicates that Product B yields a greater amount of marginal income per unit than Product A and hence provides the larger contribution to the recovery of fixed costs and expenses and the realization of operating income. If the amount of production facilities devoted to each product is assumed to be equal, it is obvious that it would be desirable to increase the sales of Product B. However, if it is assumed that Product B requires twice the amount of production facilities that are devoted to Product A, the conclusion would be different. Under the latter assumption, the production of one additional unit of Product B would require a decrease of two units of Product A. The effect on marginal income would be an increase of $2 (Product B) and a decrease of $3 (Product A), or a net decrease of $1. Under such circumstances, a change in sales mix designed to increase sales of Product A would be desirable.

Sales mix studies are based on assumptions, such as the ability to sell one product in place of another and the ability to convert production facilities to accommodate manufacture of one product instead of another. Proposed changes in the sales mix often affect only small segments of a company's total operations. In such cases, changes in sales mix may be possible within the limits of existing capacity, and the presentation of cost and revenue data in the variable costing form is useful in achieving the most profitable sales mix.

Contribution of sales territories. An income statement presenting the marginal income by sales territories is often useful to management in appraising past performance and in directing future efforts. An income statement prepared in such a format is illustrated below in abbreviated form.

Marginal Income Statement by Sales Territory

For Month Ended July 31, 19--

	TERRITORY A	TERRITORY B	TOTAL
Sales.	$210,000	$335,000	$545,000
Less variable costs and expenses.	126,000	167,500	293,500
Marginal income.	$ 84,000	$167,500	$251,500
Less fixed costs and expenses.			198,000
Income from operations			$ 53,500

Marginal income
statement —
sales territories

In addition to sales volume and marginal income, the marginal income ratio for each territory is useful in comparing sales territories, evaluating performance, and directing operations toward more profitable activities. For Territory A the ratio is 40% ($84,000 ÷ $210,000), and for Territory B it is 50% ($167,500 ÷ $335,000).

DIFFERENTIAL ANALYSIS

Planning for future operations is chiefly decision making. For some decisions, revenue and cost information drawn from the general ledger and other basic accounting records is very useful. For example, historical cost data in the absorption costing format are helpful in setting pricing policies for the long run, and historical cost data in the variable costing format are useful for pricing decisions affecting the short run. However, the revenue and cost data needed to evaluate courses of future operations or to choose among competing alternatives are often not available in the basic accounting records.

The relevant revenue and cost data in the analysis of future possibilities are the differences between the alternatives under consideration. The amounts of such differences are called *differentials* and the area of accounting concerned with the effect of alternative courses of action on revenues and costs is called *differential analysis*.

Differential revenue is the amount of increase or decrease in revenue expected from a particular course of action as compared with an alternative. To illustrate, assume that certain equipment is being used to manufacture a product that provides revenue of $50,000. If the equipment could be used to manufacture another product that would provide revenue of $60,000, the differential revenue from the alternative would be $10,000.

Differential cost is the amount of increase or decrease in cost that is expected from a particular course of action as compared with an alternative. For example, if an increase in advertising expenditures from $100,000 to $150,000 is contemplated, the differential cost of the undertaking would be $50,000.

Differential analyses can be used advantageously by management in arriving at decisions on a variety of alternatives, such as (1) whether equipment should be leased or sold, (2) whether or not to accept additional business at a special price, (3) whether to discontinue an unprofitable endeavor, (4) whether to manufacture or purchase a needed part, (5) whether to replace usable plant assets, (6) whether to expand or contract production capacity, and (7) whether to introduce new products or abandon old products. The following sections relate to the use of differential analysis in analyzing some of these alternatives.

631

LEASE OR SELL

The principal advantage of differential analysis, as illustrated in this first example, is its selection of relevant revenues and costs related to alternative courses of action. Differential analysis reports emphasize the significant factors bearing on the decision, help to clarify the issues, and conserve the time of the reader.

Assume that an enterprise is considering the disposal of an item of equipment that is no longer needed in the business. Its original cost is $100,000 and accumulated depreciation to date totals $60,000. A tentative offer has been received to lease the machine for a number of years for a total of $80,000, after which the machine would be sold as scrap for a negligible amount. The repair, insurance, and property tax expenses during the period of the lease are estimated at $17,500. Alternatively, the equipment can be sold through a broker for $50,000 less a 6% commission. The decision to be made is whether the equipment should be leased or sold. The report of the analysis is presented below:

Proposal to Lease or Sell Equipment
June 22, 19—

Differential revenue from alternatives:		
Revenue from lease......................................	$80,000	
Proceeds from sale.....................................	50,000	
Differential revenue from lease.........................		$30,000
Differential cost of alternatives:		
Estimated repair, insurance, and property tax expenses during lease...	$17,500	
Commission expense on sale.............................	3,000	
Differential cost of lease...............................		14,500
Net advantage of lease alternative.........................		**$15,500**

Differential analysis report — lease or sell

It should be noted that it was not necessary to consider the $40,000 book value ($100,000 − $60,000) of the equipment. The $40,000 is a *sunk cost*, that is, it is a cost that will not be affected by subsequent decisions. In the illustration, the expenditure to acquire the equipment had already been made, and the choice is now between leasing or selling the equipment. The relevant factors to be considered are the differential revenues and differential costs associated with the lease or sell decision; the undepreciated cost of the equipment is irrelevant. The validity of the foregoing report can be verified by the following conventional analysis:

Lease alternative:			
Revenue from lease.............................		$80,000	
Depreciation expense...........................	$40,000		
Estimated repair, insurance, and property tax expense	17,500	57,500	
Net gain.....................................			$22,500
Sell alternative:			
Sale price.....................................		$50,000	
Book value of equipment	$40,000		
Commission expense............................	3,000	43,000	
Net gain.....................................			7,000
Net advantage of lease alternative.................			**$15,500**

The alternatives presented in the illustration were relatively uncomplicated. Regardless of the number and complexity of the additional factors that may be involved, the approach to differential analysis remains basically the same. Two factors that frequently need to be considered are (1) the differential revenue from investing the funds generated by the alternatives and (2) the income tax differential. In the example above there would undoubtedly be a differential advantage to the immediate investment of the $47,000 net proceeds from the sale over the investment of the net proceeds from the lease arrangement, which would become available over a period of years. The income tax differential would be that related to the differences in timing of the income from the alternatives and the differences in the amount of investment income.

ACCEPTANCE OF BUSINESS AT A SPECIAL PRICE

In considering the advisability of accepting additional business at a special price, management must consider the differential revenue that would be provided and the differential cost that would be incurred. If the company is operating at full capacity, the additional production will increase both fixed and variable production costs; but if the normal production of the company is below full capacity, additional business may be undertaken without increasing fixed production costs. In the latter case, the variable costs will be the differential cost of the additional production; they are the only costs pertinent in making a decision to accept or reject the order. If the operating expenses are subject to change, these differentials must also be considered.

633

To illustrate, assume that the usual monthly production of an enterprise is 10,000 units of a particular commodity. At this level of operation, which is well below capacity, the manufacturing cost is $6.50 per unit, composed of variable costs of $4 and fixed costs of $2.50. The selling price of the product in the domestic market is $10. The manufacturer receives an offer from an exporter for 5,000 units of the product at $6 each. Production can be spread over a three-month period without interfering with normal production or incurring overtime costs. Pricing policies in the domestic market will not be affected. Comparison of a sales price of $6 with the present unit cost of $6.50 would indicate the advisability of rejecting the offer. However, if attention is confined to the differential cost, which in this case is composed of the variable costs and expenses, the conclusion is quite different. The essentials of the analysis can be presented in the brief report as illustrated on the next page.

Proposals to sell an increased output in the domestic market at a reduced price may necessitate additional considerations of a complex nature. It would clearly be inadvisable to increase sales volume in one

Proposal to Sell to Exporter
March 10, 19--

Differential revenue from acceptance of offer:
Revenue from sale of 5,000 additional units at $6..................... $30,000

Differential cost of acceptance of offer:
Variable costs and expenses of 5,000 additional units at $4.............. 20,000

Gain from acceptance of offer.................................... **$10,000**

territory by means of a price reduction if sales volume would thereby be jeopardized in other areas. Manufacturers must also exercise care to avoid violations of the Robinson-Patman Act, which prohibits price discrimination within the United States unless the difference in price can be justified by a difference in the cost of serving different customers.

DISCONTINUANCE OF AN UNPROFITABLE ENDEAVOR

If a department, branch, territory, or other segment of an enterprise is operating at a loss, management may be faced with the decision of whether or not to eliminate the unprofitable endeavor. It might be assumed that the operating income of the enterprise as a whole will be increased by discontinuing the unsuccessful activity. Discontinuance of the losing venture will eliminate the variable costs and expenses of the activity. However, if the losing venture represents a relatively minor segment of the enterprise, the fixed costs and expenses such as depreciation, property taxes, and insurance will continue even though the operation is terminated. It is entirely possible in this situation for the total operating income of a company to be reduced rather than increased by eliminating an unprofitable endeavor. As a basis for illustrating this type of situation, an income statement for the year just ended, which was a normal year, is presented below. For purposes of the illustration it is assumed that

Condensed Income Statement
For Year Ended August 31, 19--

| | PRODUCT | | | |
	A	B	C	TOTAL
Sales........................	$400,000	$500,000	**$100,000**	$1,000,000
Cost of goods sold:				
Variable costs....................	$200,000	$220,000	**$ 60,000**	$ 480,000
Fixed costs......................	80,000	120,000	**20,000**	220,000
Total cost of goods sold..........	$280,000	$340,000	**$ 80,000**	$ 700,000
Gross profit on sales................	$120,000	$160,000	**$ 20,000**	$ 300,000
Operating expenses:				
Variable expenses.................	$ 60,000	$ 95,000	**$ 25,000**	$ 180,000
Fixed expenses....................	20,000	25,000	**6,000**	51,000
Total operating expenses.........	$ 80,000	$120,000	**$ 31,000**	$ 231,000
Income (loss) from operations........	$ 40,000	$ 40,000	**$(11,000)**	$ 69,000

discontinuance of Product C, on which losses are incurred annually, will have no effect on the aggregate fixed costs and expenses.

Data on the estimated differential revenue and differential cost associated with discontinuing Product C, on which an operating loss of $11,000 was incurred during the past year, may be assembled in a report as shown below.

Proposal to Discontinue Product C
September 29, 19--

Differential revenue from annual sales of product:		
Revenue from sales.....................................		$100,000
Differential cost of annual sales of product:		
Variable cost of goods sold.............................	$60,000	
Variable operating expenses............................	25,000	85,000
Annual differential income from sales of Product C..........		**$ 15,000**

Differential analysis report — discontinuance of unprofitable endeavor

Instead of an increase in annual operating income to $80,000 (Product A, $40,000; Product B, $40,000) that might seem to be indicated by the income statement, the discontinuance of Product C would reduce operating income to an estimated $54,000 ($69,000 − $15,000). If plant capacity made available by discontinuance of a losing operation can be utilized in some other manner or if plant capacity can be reduced with a consequent reduction in fixed costs and expenses, additional analysis would, of course, be required.

In decisions involving the elimination of an unprofitable endeavor, management must also consider such other factors as its effect on employees and customers. If a segment of the business is discontinued, some employees may have to be discharged and others may have to be relocated and retrained. Also important is the possible decline in sales of the more profitable products to customers who were attracted to the firm by the discontinued product.

MAKE OR BUY

The assembly of numerous parts is often a substantial element in manufacturing operations. Many of the large factory complexes of automobile manufacturers are specifically designated as assembly plants. Some of the components of the finished automobile, such as the motor, are produced by the automobile manufacturer, while other parts, such as tires, are often purchased from other manufacturers. Even in manufacturing the motors, such items as spark plugs, nuts and bolts, and other items may be acquired from suppliers in their finished state. When parts or components are purchased, it is generally because management has evaluated the question of "make or buy" and has concluded that a savings in cost results from buying the part rather than manufacturing it. However, "make or buy" options are likely to arise anew when a

635

manufacturer has excess productive capacity with attendant unused equipment, space, and labor.

As a basis for illustrating make or buy alternatives, assume that a manufacturer has been purchasing a component, Part X, for $5 a unit. The factory is currently operating at 80% of capacity and no significant increase in production is anticipated in the near future. The cost of manufacturing Part X, determined by absorption costing methods, is estimated at $1 for direct materials, $2 for direct labor, and $3 for factory overhead (at the predetermined rate of 150% of direct labor cost), or a total of $6. The decision based on a simple comparison of a "make" price of $6 with a "buy" price of $5 is obvious. However, to the extent that unused capacity could be used in manufacturing the part, there would be no increase in the total amount of fixed factory overhead costs; hence only the variable factory overhead costs need to be considered. Variable factory overhead costs such as power, lubricants, and maintenance are determined to amount to approximately 65% of direct labor cost. The cost factors to be considered are summarized in the report below.

Proposal to Manufacture Part X
February 15, 19--

Differential analysis report — make or buy

Purchase price of part...		$5.00
Estimated cost to manufacture part:		
Direct materials..	$1.00	
Direct labor..	2.00	
Variable factory overhead..................................	1.30	4.30
Cost reduction from manufacturing Part X......................		**$ .70**

Other possible effects of a change in policy should also be considered, such as the possibility of a future increase in volume of production that would necessitate the use of the currently idle capacity of 20%. The possible effect of the alternatives on employees and on future business relations with the supplier of the part, who may be providing other essential components, are additional factors that might require study.

EQUIPMENT REPLACEMENT

The usefulness of plant assets may be impaired long before they are considered to be "worn-out." Equipment may no longer be ideally adequate for the purpose for which it is used, but on the other hand it may not have reached the point of complete inadequacy. Similarly, the point in time when equipment becomes obsolete may be difficult to determine. Decisions to replace usable plant assets should be based on studies of relevant costs rather than on caprice or subjective opinions. The costs to be considered are the alternative future costs of retention as opposed to replacement. Sunk costs are irrelevant.

To illustrate some of the factors involved in replacement decisions, assume that an enterprise is contemplating the disposal for $25,000 of several identical machines having a total book value of $100,000 and an estimated remaining life of five years. The old equipment would be replaced by a single high-speed machine at a cost of $250,000, with an estimated useful life of five years and negligible residual value. Analysis of the specifications of the new machine and of accompanying changes in manufacturing methods indicate an estimated annual reduction in variable manufacturing costs from $225,000 to $150,000. No other changes in the manufacturing costs or the operating expenses are expected. The basic data to be considered may be summarized in a report similar to that illustrated below.

Proposal to Replace Equipment
November 28, 19--

Annual variable costs associated with present equipment.......	$225,000	
Annual variable costs associated with proposed new equipment..	150,000	
Annual reduction in variable costs........................	$ 75,000	
Number of years applicable...............................	× 5	
Cost reduction attributable to difference in variable costs.......	$375,000	
Proceeds from sale of present equipment....................	25,000	$400,000
Cost of new equipment....................................		250,000
Net cost reduction anticipated from replacement, 5-year total...		$150,000
Annual cost reduction anticipated........................		$ 30,000

637

Differential analysis report — equipment replacement

Complicating features could be added to the foregoing illustration, such as a disparity between the remaining useful life of the old equipment and the estimated life of the new equipment, or possible improvement in the product attributable to the new machine, with consequent increase in selling price or volume of sales. Another factor that should be considered is the importance of alternative uses for the cash outlay necessary to acquire the new equipment. The amount of income that would result from the best available alternative to the proposed use of resources is sometimes called *opportunity cost*. If, for example, it is assumed that the use of the $225,000 of additional funds required to replace the equipment would yield a 10% return, the opportunity cost of the replacement proposal would be $22,500.

It should be noted that the term "opportunity cost" introduces a new concept of "cost." In reality it is not a cost in any usual sense of the word; instead it represents the foregoing of possible income associated with a lost opportunity. Nevertheless, the term is unquestionably useful in analyses involving choices between alternative courses of action.

QUESTIONS

1. (a) Differentiate between historical cost and replacement cost. (b) Why would replacement costs be more useful than historical costs in preparing a capital expenditures budget?

2. What types of costs are customarily included in the cost of manufactured products under (a) the *absorption costing* concept and (b) the *variable costing* concept?

3. Which of the following costs would be included in the cost of a product manufactured according to the variable costing concept? (a) insurance on factory equipment, (b) direct labor, (c) property taxes on factory building, (d) direct materials, (e) depreciation on factory equipment, and (f) electricity purchased to operate factory equipment.

4. How are the fixed factory overhead (fixed manufacturing) costs reported on the variable costing income statement?

5. What term is commonly used to describe the amount reported on the variable costing income statement as the excess of sales over variable cost of goods sold?

6. How is *marginal income* determined on the variable costing income statement?

7. What costs and expenses are included in the fixed costs and expenses category on income statements prepared on the basis of variable costing?

8. If the level of inventory has increased during a period, will the amount of income from operations determined by absorption costing be greater than or less than the amount determined by variable costing? Explain.

9. Is variable costing generally acceptable for use in (a) published financial statements and (b) federal income tax returns?

10. Inasmuch as all costs of operating a business are controllable, what is the significance of the term *uncontrollable cost*?

11. A company, operating at full capacity, manufactures two products with Product X requiring 50% more production facilities than does Product Y. Marginal income is $10 per unit for Product X and $6 per unit for Product Y. How much would the total marginal income be increased or decreased for the coming year if the sales of Product X could be increased by 1,000 units by changing the emphasis of promotional efforts?

12. Discuss how the use of financial data prepared on the basis of variable costing can assist management in the development of short-run pricing policies.

13. What term is applied to the type of analysis that emphasizes the difference between the revenues and costs for proposed alternate courses of action?

14. Explain the meaning of (a) *differential revenue* and (b) *differential cost.*

15. Acme Lumber Company incurs a cost of $18 per thousand board feet in processing a certain "rough-cut" lumber which it sells for $80 per thousand board feet. An alternative is to produce a "finished-cut" at a total processing cost of $25 per thousand board feet which can be sold for $90 per thousand board feet. What is the amount of (a) the differential revenue and (b) the differential cost associated with the alternative?

16. (a) What is meant by *sunk costs*? (b) A company is contemplating replacing an old piece of machinery which cost $35,000 and has accumulated depreciation to date of $25,000 with a new machine costing $50,000. What is the sunk cost in this situation?

17. The condensed income statement for Wallace Company for the current year is presented below.

	Product			
	X	Y	Z	Total
Sales....................	$ 70,000	$425,000	$350,000	$845,000
Less variable costs and expenses..	52,500	265,000	255,000	572,500
Marginal income..............	$ 17,500	$160,000	$ 95,000	$272,500
Less fixed costs and expenses.....	25,000	132,500	80,000	237,500
Income (loss) from operations....	$ (7,500)	$ 27,500	$ 15,000	$ 35,000

Management decided to discontinue the manufacture and sale of Product X. Assuming that the discontinuance will have no effect on the aggregate fixed costs and expenses or on the sales of Products Y and Z, has management made the correct decision? Explain.

18. (a) What is meant by *opportunity cost*? (b) Dunham Company is currently earning 6% on $100,000 invested in marketable securities. It proposes to use the $100,000 to acquire plant facilities to manufacture a new product that is expected to add $7,500 annually to net income. What is the opportunity cost involved in the decision to manufacture the new product?

639

EXERCISES

24-1. Boswell Company is contemplating the expansion of its operations through the purchase of the net assets of Landis Lumber Company. Included among the assets is lumber which was purchased for $87,500 and which has a replacement cost of $102,500. (a) At what amount should the inventory of lumber be included on the balance sheet of Landis Lumber Company? Briefly explain the reason for your answer. (b) How much might Boswell Company be expected to pay for the inventory if it purchases the net assets of Landis Lumber Company? Briefly explain the reason for your answer.

24-2. Clark Company began operations on April 1 and operated at 100% of capacity during the first month. The following data summarizes the results for April:

Sales (7,500 units)...........................		$112,500
Production costs (10,000 units):		
Direct materials...........................	$40,000	
Direct labor..............................	30,000	
Variable factory overhead..................	20,000	
Fixed factory overhead....................	14,000	104,000

Selling and general expenses:
Variable selling and general expenses......... $11,600
Fixed selling and general expenses............ 8,500   20,100

(a) Prepare an income statement in accordance with the absorption costing concept. (b) Prepare an income statement in accordance with the variable costing concept. (c) What is the reason for the difference in the amount of operating income reported in (a) and (b)?

24-3. Lang Company expects to operate at 80% of productive capacity during the month of March. The total manufacturing costs for March for the production of 4,000 grinders are budgeted as follows:

Direct materials.....................................	$160,000
Direct labor..	102,000
Variable factory overhead.............................	58,000
Fixed factory overhead...............................	40,000
Total manufacturing costs...........................	$360,000

The company has an opportunity to submit a bid for 500 grinders to be delivered by March 31 to a governmental agency. If the contract is obtained, it is anticipated that the additional activity will not interfere with normal production during March or increase the selling or general expenses. (a) What is the present unit product cost on an absorption costing basis? (b) What is the present unit product cost on a variable costing basis? (c) What is the unit cost below which the Lang Company should not go in bidding on the government contract? (d) Is a unit cost figure based on absorption costing or one based on variable costing more useful in arriving at a bid on this contract? Explain.

24-4. Downing Manufacturing Company has a plant capacity of 100,000 units and current production is 85,000 units. Monthly fixed costs and expenses are $115,000 and variable costs and expenses are $7.50 per unit. The present selling price is $10 per unit. On May 2 the company received an offer from Walter Company for 10,000 units of the product at $9 each. The Walter Company will market the units in Canada under its own brand name. The additional business is not expected to affect the regular selling price or quantity of sales of Downing Manufacturing Company. (a) Prepare a differential analysis report for the proposed sale to Walter Company. (b) Briefly explain the reason why the acceptance of this additional business will increase operating income. (c) What is the minimum price per unit that would produce marginal income?

24-5. An income statement by product line for Carter Manufacturing Company indicated an operating loss for Product P of $25,000 for the past year. Because of this operating loss, management is considering the elimination of the unprofitable endeavor. The operating loss resulted from sales of $175,000, cost of goods sold of $115,000, and operating expenses of $85,000. It is estimated that 20% of cost of goods sold represents fixed factory overhead costs and that 30% of operating expenses is fixed. Since Product P is only one of many products, the fixed costs and expenses will not be materially affected if the product is discontinued. (a) Prepare a differential analysis report dated January 25 of the current year for the proposed discontinuance of Product P. (b) Should Product P be retained? Explain.

24-6. Edwards Company has been purchasing carrying cases for its portable typewriters at a delivered cost of $7.50 per unit. The company, which is currently operating below full capacity, charges factory overhead to production at the rate of 80% of direct labor cost. The direct materials and direct labor costs per unit to produce comparable carrying cases are expected to be $3 and $2.50 respectively. If the carrying cases are made, fixed factory overhead costs will not increase and variable factory overhead costs associated with the manufacture of the cases are expected to be 60% of direct labor costs. (a) Prepare a differential analysis report dated April 10 of the current year for the make or buy decision. (b) On the basis of the data presented, would it be advisable to make or to continue buying the carrying cases? Explain.

24-7. Fowler Company produces a commodity by applying a shaping machine and direct labor to the direct material. The original cost of the shaping machine is $60,000, the accumulated depreciation is $30,000, the remaining useful life of the machine is 4 years, and its salvage value is negligible. On January 7, a proposal was made to replace the present manufacturing procedure with a fully automatic machine that will cost $145,000. The automatic machine has an estimated useful life of 4 years and no significant salvage value. For use in evaluating the proposal, the accountant accumulated the following annual data on present and proposed operations.

	Present Operations	Proposed Operations
Sales.....................................	$150,000	$150,000
Direct materials.........................	65,500	65,500
Direct labor.............................	44,750	———
Power and maintenance....................	5,000	6,500
Taxes, insurance, etc....................	2,850	3,750
Selling and general expenses.............	17,500	17,500

641

(a) Prepare a differential analysis report for the proposal to replace the machine. Include in the analysis both the net reduction in costs and expenses anticipated over the 4 years and the annual reduction in costs and expenses anticipated. (b) Based only on the data presented, should the proposal be accepted? (c) What are some of the other factors that should be considered before a final decision is made?

24-8. On November 25 of the current year, Wilson Company is considering leasing a building and purchasing the necessary equipment to operate a public warehouse. The project would be financed by selling $100,000 of 6% U.S. Treasury bonds that mature in 10 years. The bonds were purchased at face value and are currently selling at face value. The following data have been assembled:

Cost of equipment.......................................	$100,000
Life of equipment.......................................	10 years
Estimated residual value of equipment...................	$ 5,000
Yearly costs to operate the warehouse, in addition to depreciation of equipment.......................................	$ 22,500
Yearly expected revenues — first 3 years................	$ 30,000
Yearly expected revenues — next 7 years................	$ 45,000

(a) Prepare a differential analysis report presenting the differential revenue and the differential cost associated with the proposed operation of the warehouse for the 10 years compared with present conditions. (b) Based upon the results disclosed by the differential analysis, should the proposal be accepted? (c) If the proposal is accepted, what is the total estimated income from operation of the warehouse for the 10 years?

PROBLEMS

The following additional problems for this chapter are located in Appendix B: 24-1B, 24-2B, 24-4B.

24-1A. Universal Chemical Company refines Product M in batches of 100,000 gallons, which it sells for $.20 per gallon. The associated unit costs and expenses are currently as follows:

	Per Gallon
Direct materials....................	$.085
Direct labor.......................	.035
Variable factory overhead............	.020
Fixed factory overhead..............	.015
Salesmen's commissions.............	.012
Fixed selling and general expenses.....	.005

The company is presently considering a proposal to put Product M through several additional processes to yield Products M and N. Although the company had determined such further processing to be unwise, new processing methods have now been developed. Existing facilities can be used for the additional processing, but inasmuch as the factory is operating at full 8-hour day capacity, the processing would have to be performed at night. Additional costs of processing would be $4,500 per batch and there would be an evaporation loss of 10%, with 40% of the processed material evolving as Product M and 50% as Product N. Selling price of Product N is $.35 per gallon. Salesmen's commissions are a uniform percentage based on the sales price.

Instructions:

(1) Prepare a differential analysis report as of August 11 presenting the differential revenue and the differential cost per batch associated with the processing to produce Products M and N compared with processing to produce Product M only.

(2) Briefly report your recommendation.

24-2A. Midwest Industries purchased a machine at a cost of $240,000 which is depreciated at $30,000 yearly based on an 8-year useful life and no residual value. The company's manufacturing costs for a normal year, exclusive of depreciation, total $450,000, operating expenses are $195,000 yearly, and revenues total $750,000 yearly.

Two years after the original purchase, a new type of machine priced at $400,000 becomes available. It has an estimated life of 6 years, with no salvage value, and its use is expected to reduce the company's manufacturing costs, exclusive of depreciation, to $380,000 yearly. The old machine can be sold for only $100,000. Revenues and operating expenses will not be affected by substitution of the new machine for the old.

Instructions:

(1) Prepare a differential analysis report as of June 27 of the current year, comparing operations utilizing the new machine with operations using the present equipment. The analysis should indicate the net cost reduction or net cost increase that would result over the 6-year period if the new machine is acquired.

(2) List other factors that should be considered before a final decision is reached.

24-3A. Larson Company is planning a one-month campaign for June to promote sales of one of its two products. A total of $250,000 has been budgeted for advertising, contests, redeemable coupons, and other promotional activities. The following data have been assembled for their possible usefulness in deciding which of the products to select for the campaign.

	Product P	Product Q
Unit selling price.....................	$150	$100
Unit production costs:		
Direct materials....................	$40	$25
Direct labor.......................	30	15
Fixed factory overhead...............	15	10
Variable factory overhead............	20	15
Total unit production costs...........	$105	$ 65
Unit variable operating expenses.........	25	15
Unit fixed operating expenses...........	10	5
Total unit costs and expenses.........	$140	$ 85
Operating income per unit.............	$ 10	$ 15

No increase in facilities would be necessary to produce and sell the increased output. It is anticipated that 25,000 additional units of Product P or 20,000 additional units of Product Q could be sold without changing the unit selling price of either product.

Instructions:
(1) Prepare a differential analysis report as of May 3 of the current year, presenting the additional revenue and additional costs and expenses anticipated from the promotion of (a) Product P and (b) Product Q.
(2) The sales manager had tentatively decided to promote Product Q, because by so doing he estimated that operating income would be increased by $50,000 ($15 operating income per unit for 20,000 units, less promotion expenses of $250,000). He also believed that the selection of Product P would have no effect on operating income ($10 operating income per unit for 25,000 units, less promotion expenses of $250,000). State briefly your reasons for supporting or opposing the tentative decision.

24-4A. Product A is one of numerous products manufactured by Murray Company. The demand for Product A has dropped sharply because of recent competition from a similar product. The company's chemists are currently completing tests of various new formulas, and it is anticipated that the manufacture of a superior product can be started on July 1, one month hence. No changes will be needed in the present production facilities to manufacture the new product because only the mixture of the various materials will be changed.

The controller has been asked by the president of the company for advice on whether to continue production during June or to suspend the manufacture of Product A until July 1. The controller has assembled the following pertinent data:

The estimated production costs and selling and general expenses based on a production of 15,000 units are as follows:

Direct materials................................	$6.00 per unit
Direct labor....................................	3.75 per unit

643

Variable factory overhead......................	1.75 per unit
Variable selling and general expenses............	4.00 per unit
Fixed factory overhead........................	$52,500 for May
Fixed selling and general expenses...............	$35,000 for May

Murray Company
Estimated Income Statement — Product A
For Month Ending May 31, 19--

Sales (15,000 units).................................	$300,000
Less cost of goods sold.............................	225,000
Gross profit on sales................................	$ 75,000
Less selling and general expenses.....................	95,000
Loss from operations...............................	$ 20,000

Sales for June are expected to drop about 30% below those of the preceding month. No significant changes are anticipated in the production costs or operating expenses. No extra costs will be incurred in discontinuing operations in the portion of the plant associated with Product A. The inventory of Product A at the beginning and end of June is expected to be inconsequential.

Instructions:

(1) Prepare an estimated income statement in absorption costing form for June for Product A, assuming that production continues during the month.
(2) Prepare an estimated income statement in variable costing form for June for Product A, assuming that production continues during the month.
(3) State the estimated amount of operating loss arising from the activities associated with Product A for June if production is temporarily suspended.
(4) Prepare a brief statement of the advice you think the controller should give.

24-5A. Holmes Company manufactures three styles of folding chairs, A, B, and C. The income statement has consistently indicated a net loss for Style C and management is considering three proposals: (1) continue Style C, (2) discontinue Style C and reduce total output accordingly, or (3) discontinue Style C and conduct an advertising campaign to expand the sales of Style B so that the entire plant capacity can continue to be used. The sales, costs, and expenses have been relatively stable over the past few years and they are expected to remain so for the foreseeable future. The income statement for the past year is:

	Style			
	A	B	C	Total
Sales.......................	$525,000	$350,000	$105,000	$980,000
Cost of goods sold:				
Variable costs...............	$280,000	$210,000	$ 75,000	$565,000
Fixed costs.................	110,000	60,000	20,000	190,000
Total cost of goods sold.......	$390,000	$270,000	$ 95,000	$755,000
Gross profit on sales...........	$135,000	$ 80,000	$ 10,000	$225,000

Less operating expenses:				
Variable expenses............	$ 52,500	$ 35,000	$ 10,500	$ 98,000
Fixed expenses..............	30,000	15,000	9,500	54,500
Total operating expenses......	$ 82,500	$ 50,000	$ 20,000	$152,500
Income from operations........	$ 52,500	$ 30,000	$(10,000)	$ 72,500

If Style C is discontinued and production curtailed, the annual fixed production costs and fixed operating expenses could be reduced by $5,000 and $1,500 respectively. It is anticipated that an additional annual expenditure of $8,000 for advertising Style B would yield an increase of 30% in its sales volume; also that the increased production of Style B would utilize the plant facilities released by the discontinuance of Style C.

Instructions:

(1) Prepare an income statement in the variable costing format, indicating the projected annual operating income under each of the three proposals.

(2) Why would total operating income be reduced below its present level if Proposal 2 is accepted?

(3) Why would total operating income increase above its present level if Proposal 3 is accepted?

645

Chapter 25

MANAGEMENT REPORTS AND SPECIAL ANALYSES

PURPOSE OF MANAGEMENT REPORTS AND SPECIAL ANALYSES

A basic function of accounting is to provide the data needed to report the results of the economic activities of an enterprise to all interested parties. One group making extensive use of accounting data is operating management. The manager of even a very small business needs factual data to assist him in making decisions. As the size and the complexity of businesses increase, the importance of accounting as a tool in directing operations becomes more apparent.

In assisting management, the accountant relies upon a variety of methods of analysis. The use of cost accounting and of cost relationships as they affect planning and controlling operations was discussed in earlier chapters. In this chapter additional reports and analyses for the use of management will be explained and illustrated.

The term *management reports* is applied generally to various statements, schedules, and summaries prepared solely for the use of management. There are no standardized patterns for such reports. They may be devoted to a very small segment of the activities of the enterprise or to special problems confronting management. They often contain forecasts rather than historical data, and timeliness is more important than complete accuracy.

Reports prepared for the top echelon of management should ordinarily be broad in scope, presenting summaries of data rather than minute details. They should be departmentalized to the extent necessary to assign responsibility. On the other hand, reports for personnel at the lower end of the managerial range should ordinarily be narrow in scope and contain detailed data. To illustrate, assume that a manufacturer records direct labor idle time and classifies it according to such causes as machine breakdown, inferior materials, absenteeism, and accidents. Such data are of little if any value unless reported to the responsible persons with authority to take action. The report to the executive vice president or other appropriate officer should summarize the data by departments and causes so that he can identify the persons responsible. The superintendent of maintenance is not concerned with absenteeism or faulty materials, but he needs to know the details of machine breakdowns. It is equally evident that the foremen of the various factory departments should be supplied with detailed data on idle time within the departments for which they are held responsible.

RATE OF RETURN ON ASSETS

The rate of return on assets, sometimes referred to as the rate of return on investment (ROI), is a useful measure of the relative efficiency of assets employed in earning income. It can be computed for an enterprise as a single unit, but its usefulness is enhanced if segments of income can be identified with specific groups of assets. This basic determination may be difficult or it may be fairly simple, as in computing the rate of return on the stocks and bonds owned by a business enterprise. For example, if an investment portfolio of $100,000 yields dividends and interest for the year of $5,700, the rate of return on the assets is 5.7% ($5,700 ÷ $100,000).

Even in such relatively clear-cut situations as the foregoing, complicating factors may be introduced. The amount of administrative expense that should be allocated to the investment earnings is not subject to exact determination. The portion of the income tax allocable to the earnings could also be deducted in order to yield the net rate of return. There may also be alternatives in selecting the asset value to be used in the computation. There was an unstated assumption in the illustration that the composition of the investments remained unchanged during the year. Any material fluctuations in the amount of the portfolio should be taken into consideration and an average computed.

The rate of return on assets is often computed on a departmental basis for the purpose of measuring relative operating performance. For such computations the interest on borrowed funds and income taxes is ordinarily not taken into consideration. In evaluating a segment of a business, such nonoperating items as interest on borrowed funds should not be considered because the return on assets is basically a measure of the efficiency with which the assets have been used. The nonoperating items are not relevant to the evaluation of divisional management efficiency because such items are beyond the control of the division managers.

To illustrate, assume that for the past year the two operating divisions of a business had about the same volume of sales and approximately the same amount of operating income. Assume also that there was a substantial difference in the amounts of assets employed by each division.

647

The following report points out the significance of this disparity.

Rate of Return on Assets
For Year Ended December 31, 19—

	DIVISION A	DIVISION B
Sales.............................	$400,000	$435,000
Operating expenses.................	350,000	380,000
Income from operations.............	$ 50,000	$ 55,000
Average assets employed.............	$500,000	$300,000
Rate of return on assets.............	10%	18.3%

Information such as that presented in the report above would alert management to the far greater effectiveness of Division B in the employment of assets. It would indicate the need for a careful study of the operating policies of the two divisions and the causes of the variation in rate of return.

The rate of return on assets can also be used as a control device by the establishment of a minimum rate of return and then by comparison of rates actually achieved with this minimum. The measure can be used in new product pricing by making it possible to determine the price necessary to earn a certain rate of return on the assets employed. It is also useful in profit planning and in evaluating proposed purchases of machinery and equipment and other capital expenditures.

ANALYSIS OF PROPOSED CAPITAL EXPENDITURES

With the accelerated growth of American industry in recent years, increasing attention has been given to accounting analyses designed to evaluate plans requiring substantial outlays for plant replacement, improvement, and expansion. Three types of analysis commonly employed in evaluating proposals for major capital expenditures are described.

Average rate of return. The expected *average rate of return* is a measure of the anticipated profitability of an investment in plant assets. The amount of income expected to be earned from the investment is stated as an annual average over the number of years the asset is to be used. The amount of the investment may be considered to be the original cost of the plant assets, or recognition may be given to the effect of depreciation on the amount of the investment. According to the latter view, the investment gradually declines from the original cost to the estimated residual value at the end of its useful life. Assuming straight-line depreciation and no residual value, the average investment would be equal to one half of the original expenditure.

To illustrate, assume that management is considering the acquisition of a particular machine at a cost of $50,000, that it is expected to have a useful life of 4 years with negligible residual value, and that its use during

648

the 4 years is expected to yield total income of $20,000. The expected average annual income is therefore $5,000 ($20,000 ÷ 4) and the average investment is $25,000 ($50,000 ÷ 2). Accordingly, the expected average rate of return on the average investment is 20%, computed as follows:

$$\frac{\$20,000 \div 4}{\$50,000 \div 2} = 20\% \text{ average rate of return}$$

Comparison of this expected rate of return with the rate established by management as the minimum reward for the risks involved will indicate the comparative attractiveness of the proposed expenditure. If the foregoing analysis had been based on original cost of the equipment instead of the average investment, the rate of return would have been computed as 10% ($5,000 ÷ $50,000) instead of 20% ($5,000 ÷ $25,000).

A significant objection to the use of this measure is its disregard of the effect (1) of the timing of the expected recovery of the amount invested in plant assets, or (2) of the timing of the income that such investment is expected to produce. Funds derived from the recovery of the cost of a capital expenditure and from the income that it generates can be reinvested in other income-producing activities. Therefore, a project that recovers a high proportion of its investment and yields high income early in its life is more desirable than a project with the same average rate of return but with lower cost recovery and income in the earlier years.

649

Cash payback period. The expected period of time that will elapse between the date of a capital expenditure and a complete recoupment in cash or equivalent is called the *cash payback period*. To simplify the analysis, the revenues and the out-of-pocket operating expenses expected to be associated with the operation of the plant assets are assumed to be entirely in the form of cash. The excess of the cash flowing in from revenue over the cash flowing out for expenses is termed *net cash flow*. The time required for the net cash flow to equal the initial outlay for the plant asset is the payback period.

For purposes of illustration, assume that the proposed expenditure for a plant asset with an 8-year life is $200,000 and that the annual net cash flow is expected to be $40,000. The estimated cash payback period for the expenditure is 5 years, computed as follows:

$$\frac{\$200,000}{\$40,000} = 5\text{-year cash payback period}$$

The cash payback concept is widely used in evaluating proposals for expansion and for investment in new projects. A relatively short payback period is desirable, because the sooner the cash is recovered the sooner it becomes available for reinvestment in other projects. In addition, there is likely to be less possibility of loss from changes in economic conditions and other unavoidable risks when the commitment is short-term. The cash payback concept is also of interest to bankers and other creditors who may be dependent upon net cash flow for the repayment of claims associated with the initial capital expenditure.

The principal limitation of the cash payback period as a basis for decisions is its failure to take into consideration the expected profitability of a proposal. A project with a very short payback period coupled with relatively poor profitability would be less desirable than one for which the investment was committed for a longer period but with satisfactory profitability.

Discounted cash flow. An expenditure for plant and equipment may be looked upon as the acquisition of a series of future net cash flows composed of two elements: (1) recovery of the initial expenditure and (2) income. Both the absolute and the relative amounts of these two elements are obviously important. The period of time over which the net cash flows will be received is also important. Any specified amount of cash that is to be received at some date in the future is not the equivalent of the same amount of cash held at an earlier date. Cash on hand can be immediately employed. The income that can be earned by earlier investment may be an important factor to consider. This element of timing is given recognition in *discounted cash flow* analysis. The expected future net cash flows originating from proposed present capital expenditures are reduced to their present values.

The concept of present value of future payments was noted in earlier chapters in connection with discounting promissory notes, determination of the issuance price of bonds, and amortization of bond discount and premium. Application of the concept of discounted cash flow analysis may be illustrated by computing the amount to be deposited at a given rate of interest that will yield a specified sum at a later date. If the rate of interest is 6% and the sum to be accumulated in one year is $1,000, the amount to be invested is $943.40 ($1,000 ÷ 1.06). If the funds were to be invested a year earlier, with the interest compounded at the end of the first year, the amount of the deposit would be $890.00 ($943.40 ÷ 1.06).

Instead of determining the present value of future sums by a series of divisions in the manner just illustrated, it is customary to find the present value of 1 from a table of present values and to multiply it by the amount of the future sum. Reference to the partial table presented on page 651 indicates that the present value of $1 to be received two years hence, with interest at the rate of 6% a year, is .890. Multiplication of .890 by $1,000 yields the same amount that was determined in the preceding paragraph by two successive divisions.

YEARS	6%	10%	15%	20%	
1	.943	.909	.870	.833	
2	.890	.826	.756	.694	
3	.840	.751	.658	.579	
4	.792	.683	.572	.482	
5	.747	.621	.497	.402	
6	.705	.564	.432	.335	
7	.665	.513	.376	.279	Present
8	.627	.467	.327	.233	value of 1
9	.592	.424	.284	.194	at compound
10	.558	.386	.247	.162	interest

The particular rate of return selected in discounted cash flow analysis is affected by the nature of the business enterprise and its relative profitability, the purpose of the capital expenditure, and other related factors. If the present value of the net cash flow expected from a proposed expenditure, at the selected rate, equals or exceeds the amount of the expenditure, the proposal is desirable. For purposes of illustration, assume a proposal for the acquisition of $200,000 of equipment with an expected useful life of 5 years, and a minimum desired rate of return of 10%. The anticipated net cash flow for each of the 5 years and the analysis of the proposal are presented below. The report indicates that the proposal is expected to recover the investment and provide more than the minimum rate of return.

651

Analysis of Proposal to Acquire Equipment
June 30, 19--

YEAR	PRESENT VALUE OF 1 AT 10%	NET CASH FLOW	PRESENT VALUE OF NET CASH FLOW	
1	.909	$ 70,000	$ 63,630	
2	.826	60,000	49,560	
3	.751	50,000	37,550	
4	.683	40,000	27,320	
5	.621	40,000	24,840	
Total		$260,000	$202,900	Discounted cash flow analysis report — equipment acquisition

Amount to be invested in equipment.................. 200,000

Excess of present value over amount to be invested....$ 2,900

Each of the three methods of analyzing proposals for capital expenditures has both advantages and limitations. It is often advisable to employ a combination of methods in evaluating the various economic aspects of major projects. It is obvious, of course, that estimates play a substantial role in all analyses of future expectations. Such factors as product pricing, improvements in products, availability and training of personnel, marketing procedures, and severity of competition must also be given consideration in arriving at decisions.

GROSS PROFIT ANALYSIS

Gross profit on sales is frequently considered to be the most significant intermediate figure in the income statement. It is customary to determine its percentage relationship to sales and to make comparisons with prior periods. However, the mere knowledge of the percentages and the degree and direction of change from prior periods is insufficient; management needs information about the underlying factors. The procedure employed in developing such information is termed *gross profit analysis*.

Inasmuch as gross profit is the excess of sales over the cost of goods sold, it follows that a change in the amount of gross profit can be caused by (1) an increase or decrease in amount of sales and (2) an increase or decrease in the amount of cost of goods sold. An increase or decrease in either element may in turn be attributable to (1) a change in the number of units sold and (2) a change in the unit price. The effect of these two factors on either sales or cost of goods sold may be expressed as follows:

1. *Quantity factor.* The effect of a change in the number of units sold, assuming no change in unit price.
2. *Price factor.* The effect of a change in unit price on the number of units sold.

The data to be used as the basis for illustrating gross profit analysis are presented below. For the sake of simplicity, a single commodity is

	1974	1973	INCREASE DECREASE*
Sales.....................	$225,000	$200,000	$ 25,000
Cost of goods sold..........	162,500	140,000	22,500
Gross profit on sales.........	$ 62,500	$ 60,000	$ 2,500
Number of units sold........	125,000	100,000	25,000
Unit sales price.............	$1.80	$2.00	$.20*
Unit cost price..............	$1.30	$1.40	$.10*

assumed. The amount of detail entering into the analysis would be greater if a number of different commodities were sold, but the basic principles would not be affected.

The analysis of the foregoing data is presented on the next page. The report indicates that the favorable increase in the number of units sold was partially offset by a decrease in unit selling price, and that the increase in the cost of goods sold attributable to increased quantity was partially offset by a decrease in unit cost.

The data presented in the report may be useful both in evaluating past performance and in planning for the future. The importance of the

652

Analysis of Increase in Gross Profit
For Year Ended December 31, 1974

Increase in amount of sales attributed to:				
Quantity factor:				
Increase in number of units sold in 1974.........	25,000			
Unit sales price in 1973......................	×	$2	$50,000	
Price factor:				
Decrease in unit sales price in 1974.............	$.20			
Number of units sold in 1974..................	×125,000	25,000		
Net increase in amount of sales..................			$25,000	
Increase in amount of cost of goods sold attributed to:				
Quantity factor:				
Increase in number of units sold in 1974.........	25,000			
Unit cost price in 1973........................	×	$1.40	$35,000	
Price factor:				
Decrease in unit cost price in 1974..............	$.10			
Number of units sold in 1974..................	×125,000	12,500		
Net increase in amount of cost of goods sold.......			22,500	
Increase in gross profit on sales..................			$ 2,500	

Gross profit
analysis
report

cost reduction of $.10 a unit is quite evident. If the unit cost had remained unchanged from the preceding year, the net increase in amount of sales ($25,000) would have been more than offset by the increase in cost of goods sold ($35,000), causing a decrease in gross profit of $10,000. The $2,500 increase in gross profit actually attained was made possible, therefore, by the ability of management to reduce the unit cost.

653

The means by which the reduction in the unit cost of the commodity was accomplished is also significant. If it was attributable to the spreading of fixed factory overhead costs over the larger number of units produced, the decision to reduce the sales price in order to achieve a larger volume was probably wise. On the other hand, if the $.10 reduction in unit cost was attributable to operating efficiencies entirely unrelated to the increased production, the $.20 reduction in the unit sales price was ill-advised. The accuracy of the conclusion is demonstrated by the following analysis, which indicates the possible loss of an opportunity to have realized an additional gross profit of $7,500 ($70,000 − $62,500):

	ACTUAL		HYPOTHETICAL	
Number of units sold.........	125,000		100,000	
Unit sales price.............	$1.80		$2.00	
Sales.......................		$225,000		$200,000
Unit cost price..............	$1.30		$1.30	
Cost of goods sold...........		162,500		130,000
Gross profit on sales.........		$ 62,500		$ 70,000

If the reduction in unit cost had been achieved by a combination of the two means, the approximate effects of each could be determined by additional analyses. The methods employed in gross profit analysis may also be extended, with some modifications, to the analysis of changes in selling and general expenses.

COST-VOLUME-PROFIT RELATIONSHIPS

The determination of the selling price of a product is a complex matter that is often affected by forces partially or entirely beyond the control of management. Nevertheless, management must formulate pricing policies within the bounds permitted by the market place. Accounting can play an important role in the development of policy by supplying management with special reports on the relative profitability of its various products, the probable effects of contemplated changes in selling price, and other cost-volume-profit relationships.

The unit cost of producing a commodity is affected by such factors as the inherent nature of the product, the efficiency of operations, and the volume of production. An increase in the quantity produced is ordinarily accompanied by a decrease in unit cost, provided the volume attained remains within the reasonable limits of plant capacity.

Quantitative data relating to the effect on income of changes in unit selling price, sales volume, production volume, production costs, and operating expenses help management to improve the relationship among these variables. If a change in selling price appears to be desirable or, because of competitive pressure, unavoidable, the possible effect of the change on sales volume and product cost needs to be studied. Inquiry into the likely effect on income of a promotional sales campaign is another example of special studies that may be undertaken.

A requisite of cost-volume-profit analysis is that all costs and expenses be subdivided into two categories: (1) fixed and (2) variable. Analyses of this type are facilitated by the use of variable costing procedures, which require that costs and expenses be so classified. When conventional absorption costing systems are employed, it is necessary first to divide the relevant cost data between the fixed and variable categories. Types of analyses employed in appraising the interactions of selling price, sales and production volume, variable cost and expense, fixed cost and expense, and income are described and illustrated in the next three sections.

BREAK-EVEN ANALYSIS

The point in the operations of an enterprise at which revenues and expired costs are exactly equal is called the *break-even point*. At this level of operations an enterprise will neither realize an operating income nor incur an operating loss. Break-even analysis can be applied to past periods, but it is most useful when applied to future periods as a guide to business planning, particularly if either an expansion or a curtailment of operations is anticipated. In such cases it is concerned with future prospects and future operations and hence relies upon estimates. Obviously the reliability of the analysis is greatly influenced by the accuracy of the estimates.

The break-even point can be computed by means of a mathematical formula or it can be ascertained from a graphic presentation of the relationship between revenue, costs, and volume of productive capacity. In either case the data required are (1) total estimated fixed costs and expenses for a future period, such as a year, and (2) the total estimated variable costs and expenses for the same period, stated as a percent of net sales. To illustrate, assume that fixed costs and expenses are estimated at $90,000 and that variable costs and expenses are expected to amount to 60% of sales. The break-even point is $225,000 of sales revenue, computed as follows:

Break-Even Sales (in \$) = Fixed Costs (in \$) + Variable Costs (as % of Break-Even Sales)

$$S = \$90,000 + 60\%S$$
$$40\% \ S = \$90,000$$
$$S = \$225,000$$

Break-even analysis may also be employed in estimating the sales volume required to yield a specified amount of operating income. The formula stated above can be modified for use in this computation by the addition at the end of the equation of the desired amount of operating income. For example, the sales volume required to yield operating income of $40,000 for the enterprise assumed above would be $325,000, computed as follows:

$$\text{Sales} = \text{Fixed Costs} + \text{Variable Costs} + \text{Operating Income}$$
$$S = \$90,000 + 60\%S + \$40,000$$
$$40\% \ S = \$130,000$$
$$S = \$325,000$$

655

A break-even chart, based on the foregoing data, is illustrated on the following page. It is constructed in the following manner:

1. Percentages of productive capacity of the enterprise are spread along the horizontal axis, and dollar amounts representing operating data are spread along the vertical axis. The outside limits of the chart represent 100% of productive capacity and the maximum sales potential at that level of production.

2. A diagonal line representing sales is drawn from the lower left corner to the upper right corner.

3. A point representing fixed costs is plotted on the vertical axis at the left and a point representing total costs at maximum capacity is plotted at the right edge of the chart. A diagonal line representing total costs at various percentages of capacity is then drawn connecting these two points. In the illustration, the fixed costs are $90,000 and the total costs at

maximum capacity amount to $330,000 ($90,000 plus variable costs of 60% of $400,000).

4. Horizontal and vertical lines are drawn at the point of intersection of the sales and cost lines, which is the break-even point, and the areas representing operating income and operating loss are identified.

Projected Break-Even Chart
For Year Ending December 31, 19– –

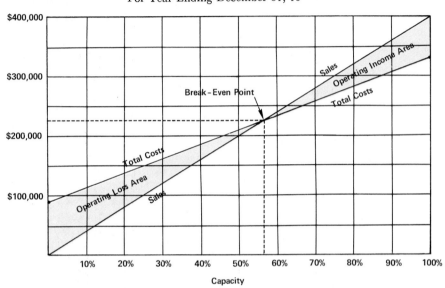

Break-even
chart

Presentation of break-even analysis in the chart form is frequently preferred over the equation form. From such a chart the approximate operating income or operating loss associated with any given sales volume or percentage of capacity can be readily determined.

Relying as it does on rigid assumptions concerning the behavior of sales and costs, break-even analysis should be employed with caution. If the selling price of a product is increased or decreased or if the amount of cost changes, the analysis prepared prior to such action will no longer be valid. In addition, the assumptions underlying the classification of costs as fixed or variable must be recognized. Among these is the assumption of relatively stable use of plant facilities. For example, in the foregoing illustration it is quite possible that at 80% and 100% of capacity the fixed costs would be $90,000, while if production were only 10% of capacity the fixed costs would be less than $90,000. Under conditions of substantial change in the use of plant facilities, very few costs would be fixed. Since substantial changes in the use of plant facilities are relatively rare in practice, break-even analysis can often be used quite effectively in decision making.

It should also be noted that a break-even chart for an enterprise selling two or more products must be based on a specified "product-mix."

Changes in the mix would necessitate additional analysis and construction of a new chart. Recognition of the inherent assumptions and the limitations of break-even analysis is essential to the effective use of studies of this type in management planning.

MARGIN OF SAFETY

Business enterprises do not adopt the break-even point as their goal for future operations. Rather, they seek to achieve the largest possible volume of sales above the break-even point. The difference between the current sales revenue and the sales at the break-even point is called the *margin of safety*. It represents the possible decrease in sales revenue that may occur before an operating loss results, and it may be expressed either in terms of dollars or as a percentage of sales. For example, if the volume of sales is $250,000 and sales at the break-even point amount to $200,000, the margin of safety is $50,000 or 20% as indicated by the following computation:

$$\text{Margin of Safety} = \frac{\text{Sales} - \text{Sales at Break-Even Point}}{\text{Sales}}$$

$$\text{Margin of Safety} = \frac{\$250,000 - \$200,000}{\$250,000} = 20\%$$

The margin of safety is useful in evaluating past operations and as a guide to business planning. For example, if the margin of safety is low, management should carefully evaluate forecasts of future sales revenue because even a small decline in sales revenue will result in an operating loss.

657

MARGINAL INCOME RATIO

Another relationship between costs, volume, and profits that is especially useful in business planning because it gives an insight into the profit potential of a firm is the *marginal income ratio*, sometimes referred to as the *profit-volume ratio*. This ratio indicates the percentage of each sales dollar available to cover the fixed expenses and to provide operating income. For example, if the volume of sales is $250,000 and variable expenses amount to $175,000, the marginal income ratio is 30% as indicated by the following calculation:

$$\text{Marginal Income Ratio} = \frac{\text{Sales} - \text{Variable Expenses}}{\text{Sales}}$$

$$\text{Marginal Income Ratio} = \frac{\$250,000 - \$175,000}{\$250,000} = 30\%$$

The marginal income ratio permits the quick determination of the effect on operating income of an increase or a decrease in sales volume. To illustrate, assume that the management of a firm with a marginal income ratio of 30% is evaluating the effect on operating income of the addition of $25,000 in sales orders. Multiplying the ratio (30%) by the change in sales volume ($25,000) indicates an increase in operating income of $7,500 if the additional orders are obtained. In employing the analysis in such a situation, factors other than sales volume, such as the amount of fixed expenses, the percentage of variable expenses to sales, and the unit sales price, are assumed to remain constant. If these factors are not constant, the effect of any change in these factors must be considered in applying the analysis.

The marginal income ratio is also useful in setting business policy. For example, if the marginal income ratio of a firm is large and production is at a level below 100% capacity, a comparatively large increase in operating income can be expected from an increase in sales volume. Conversely, a comparatively large decrease in operating income can be expected from a decline in sales volume. A firm in such a position might decide to devote considerable effort to additional sales promotion because of the substantial change in operating income that will result from changes in sales volume. On the other hand, a firm with a small marginal income ratio will probably want to devote considerable attention to reducing costs and expenses before concentrating large efforts on additional sales promotion.

MANAGERIAL USES OF QUANTITATIVE TECHNIQUES

Each of the previously discussed uses of accounting data in planning and controlling business operations has been concerned with a restricted number of objectives or variables. In recent years, more sophisticated quantitative techniques have been developed to assist management in solving problems. This framework of quantitative techniques, sometimes referred to as *operations research*, often utilizes mathematical and statistical models encompassing a large number of interdependent variables. The accounting system is the source of much of the quantitative data required by many operations research techniques.

One of the areas for which operations research is often utilized is inventory control. For each category of materials in the inventory it is important to know the ideal quantity to be purchased in a single order and the minimum and maximum quantities to be on hand at any time. Such factors as economies of large-scale buying, storage costs, work interruption due to shortages, and seasonal and cyclical variations in production schedules need to be considered. Two quantitative techniques that may be employed to assist in inventory control are (1) the economic order quantity formula and (2) linear programming.

Economic order quantity formula. The economic order quantity (EOQ) is the optimum quantity of specified inventoriable materials to be ordered at one time. Significant factors to be considered in determining the optimum quantity are the costs incurred in processing an order for the materials and the costs incurred in storing the materials.

The annual cost of processing orders for a specified material (cost of placing orders, verifying invoices, processing payments, etc.) increases as the number of orders placed increases. On the other hand, the annual cost of storing the materials (taxes, insurance, occupancy of storage space, etc.) decreases as the number of orders placed increases. The economic order quantity is therefore that quantity that will minimize the combined annual costs of ordering and storing materials.

The combined annual cost incurred in ordering and storing materials can be computed under various assumptions as to the number of orders to be placed during a year. To illustrate, assume the following data for an inventoriable material which is used at a uniform rate during the year:

MATERIAL A732

Units required during the year...	1,200
Ordering cost, per order placed..	$10.00
Storage cost, per unit...........	.60

If a single order were placed for the entire year's needs, the cost of ordering the 1,200 units would be $10. The average number of units held in inventory during the year would therefore be 600 (1,200 units ÷ 2) and would result in an annual storage cost of $360 (600 units × $.60). The combined order and storage costs for placing only one order during the year would thus be $370 ($10 + $360). If, instead of a single order, two orders were placed during the year, the order cost would be $20 (2 × $10), 600 units would need to be purchased on each order, the average inventory would be 300 units, and the annual storage costs would be $180 (300 units × $.60). Accordingly, the combined order and storage costs for placing two orders during the year would be $200 ($20 + $180). Successive computations, adding an order each time, will disclose the EOQ when the combined cost reaches its lowest point and starts upward. The following tabulation indicates an optimum of 200 units of material per order, with 6 orders per year, at a combined cost of $120.

659

NUMBER OF ORDERS	NUMBER OF UNITS PER ORDER	AVERAGE UNITS IN INVENTORY	ORDER AND STORAGE COSTS		
			ORDER COST	STORAGE COST	COMBINED COST
1	1,200	600	$10	$360	$370
2	600	300	20	180	200
3	400	200	30	120	150
4	300	150	40	90	130
5	240	120	50	72	122
6	200	100	60	60	120
7	171	86	70	52	122

The economic order quantity may also be determined by a formula based on differential calculus. The formula and its application to the illustration is as follows:

$$EOQ = \sqrt{\frac{2 \times \text{Annual Units Required} \times \text{Cost per Order Placed}}{\text{Storage Cost per Unit}}}$$

$$EOQ = \sqrt{\frac{2 \times 1{,}200 \times \$10}{\$.60}}$$

$$EOQ = \sqrt{40{,}000}$$

$$EOQ = 200 \text{ units}$$

The annual requirement of 1,200 units would require the placement of six orders (1,200 ÷ 200) for the EOQ of 200 units.

The foregoing brief introduction to the determination of the economic order quantity suggests the many ramifications of inventory control that may be encountered in actual practice. Formulas can be developed to incorporate such factors as economies of large-scale buying and seasonal and cyclical variations in volume of production.

Linear programming. One of the techniques employed in selecting the most favorable course of action from among feasible alternatives is referred to as *linear programming*. It is sometimes used in solving business problems in which there are many variables and alternative courses of action. The technique ordinarily utilizes numerous algebraic expressions. The following simplified illustration demonstrates the essential nature of linear programming without the use of algebra.

A manufacturing company purchases Part P for use at both its West Branch and East Branch. Part P is available in limited quantities from two suppliers. The total unit cost price varies considerably for parts acquired from the two suppliers principally because of differences in transportation charges. The relevant data bearing upon the decision as to the most economical purchase arrangement are summarized in the diagram below.

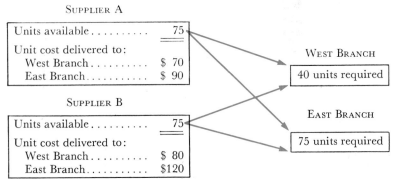

It might appear that the most economical course of action would be to purchase (1) the 40 units required by West Branch from Supplier A at $70 a unit, (2) 35 units for East Branch from Supplier A at $90 a unit, and (3) the remaining 40 units required by East Branch from Supplier B at $120 a unit. If this course of action were followed, the total cost of the parts required by the two branches would amount to $10,750, as indicated by the computation below.

	COST OF PURCHASE		
	FOR WEST BRANCH	FOR EAST BRANCH	TOTAL
From Supplier A:			
40 units at $70.............	$2,800		$ 2,800
35 units at $90.............		$3,150	3,150
From Supplier B:			
40 units at $120............		4,800	4,800
Total.....................	$2,800	$7,950	$10,750

Although many alternative purchasing programs are possible, the most economical course of action would be to purchase (1) the 75 units required by East Branch from Supplier A at $90 a unit and (2) the 40 units required by West Branch from Supplier B at $80 a unit. If this plan were adopted, the total cost of the parts would be $9,950, even though no units were purchased at the lowest available unit cost, as illustrated below.

661

	COST OF PURCHASE		
	FOR WEST BRANCH	FOR EAST BRANCH	TOTAL
From Supplier A:			
75 units at $90.............		$6,750	$6,750
From Supplier B:			
40 units at $80.............	$3,200		3,200
Total.....................	$3,200	$6,750	$9,950

This simplified illustration demonstrates the importance of considering all of the variables and all of the possible solutions to a particular problem. Linear programming and other operations research techniques employ electronic computers to determine the most favorable course of action in many situations that involve numerous variables and offer many alternatives.

QUESTIONS

1. What are management reports?

2. What does the rate of return on assets measure?

3. Why is interest on borrowed funds ordinarily not considered in computing the rate of return on assets for the various operating divisions of a business?

4. What is a significant objection to the use of the average rate of return method in evaluating capital expenditure proposals?

5. (a) As used in analysis of proposed capital expenditures, what is the cash payback period? (b) Discuss the principal limitation of this method for evaluating capital expenditure proposals.

6. Which method of evaluating capital expenditure proposals reduces the expected future net cash flows originating from the proposals to their present values?

7. Discuss the two factors affecting both sales and cost of goods sold to which a change in gross profit can be attributed.

8. The gross profit of the McDaniel Company increased by $20,000 over the preceding year. Discuss possible unfavorable occurrences that might have accompanied the increase.

9. The analysis of increase in gross profit report for Ashby Company includes the effect that an increase in quantity of goods sold has had on sales. How is this figure determined?

10. (a) What is the break-even point? (b) How can the break-even point be determined?

11. (a) If fixed costs and expenses are $250,000 and variable costs and expenses are 50% of sales, what is the break-even point? (b) What sales are required to realize operating income of $100,000 under the conditions described in (a)?

12. What is the advantage of presenting break-even analysis in the chart form over the equation form?

13. Both the Benton Company and the Yoder Company had the same sales, total costs and expenses, and operating income for the current fiscal year, yet the Benton Company had a lower break-even point than the Yoder Company. Explain the reason for this difference in break-even points.

14. (a) What is meant by the term "margin of safety"? (b) If sales are $750,000, net income $60,000, and sales at the break-even point $600,000, what is the margin of safety?

15. What ratio indicates the percentage of each sales dollar that is available to cover fixed costs and expenses and to provide a profit?

16. (a) If sales are $1,000,000 and variable costs and expenses $600,000, what is the marginal income ratio? (b) What is the marginal income ratio if variable costs and expenses are 70% of sales?

17. An examination of the accounting records of Boone Company disclosed a high marginal income ratio and production at a level below maximum capacity. Based on this information, suggest a likely means of improving operating income. Explain.

18. What is operations research?

EXERCISES

25-1. The sales, income from operations, and asset investments of two divisions in the same company are as follows:

	Division C	Division D
Sales.	$ 750,000	$525,000
Income from operations.	75,000	52,500
Assets.	1,500,000	350,000

(a) What is the percentage of operating income to sales for each division?
(b) What is the rate of return on assets for each divison?
(c) As far as the data permit, comment on the relative performance of these two divisions.

25-2. Potter Company is considering the acquisition of machinery at a cost of $50,000. The machinery has an estimated life of 4 years and no salvage value. It is expected to provide yearly income of $7,500 and yearly net cash flows of $20,000. The company's minimum desired rate of return for discounted cash flow analysis is 15%. Compute the following:

(a) The average rate of return, giving effect to depreciation on investment.
(b) The cash payback period.
(c) The excess or deficiency of present value over the amount to be invested as determined by the discounted cash flow method. Use the table of present values appearing in this chapter.

25-3. From the following data for the Mercer Company, prepare an analysis of the decrease in gross profit for the year ended December 31, 1974.

	1974		1973	
Sales	60,000 units @ $7	$420,000	75,000 units @ $6.50	$487,500
Cost of goods sold	60,000 units @ $5	300,000	75,000 units @ $4.50	337,500
Gross profit on sales		$120,000		$150,000

25-4. Kramer Company anticipates for the coming year fixed costs and expenses of $150,000 and variable costs and expenses equal to 40% of sales.

(a) Compute the anticipated break-even point.
(b) Compute the sales required to realize operating income of $60,000.
(c) Construct a break-even chart, assuming sales of $400,000 at full capacity.
(d) Determine the probable operating income if sales total $320,000.

25-5. Friedman Company operated at full capacity during the past year. Fixed costs and expenses were $275,000, variable costs and expenses were 45% of sales, and sales totaled $600,000. Management proposed to expand plant capacity by 50%, which will increase fixed costs and expenses by $110,000 yearly but will not affect the ratio of variable costs and expenses to sales.

(a) Compute the operating income under present conditions.
(b) Compute the break-even point under present and proposed conditions.
(c) Compute the sales necessary under proposed conditions to reach current operating income.
(d) Compute the maximum operating income under proposed conditions.

25-6. (a) If Reynolds Company, with a break-even point at $450,000 of sales, has actual sales of $600,000, what is the margin of safety expressed (1) in dollars and (2) as a percentage of sales?

(b) If the margin of safety for Hayden Company was 20%, fixed costs and expenses were $195,000, and variable costs and expenses were 35% of sales, what was the amount of actual sales?

25-7. (a) If Dugan Company budgets sales of $400,000, fixed costs and expenses of $225,000, and variable costs and expenses of $140,000, what is the anticipated marginal income ratio?

(b) If the marginal income ratio for Fogarty Company is 60%, sales were $850,000, and fixed costs and expenses were $425,000, what was the operating income?

25-8. For the past year Ballard Company had sales of $750,000, a margin of safety of 30%, and a marginal income ratio of 40%. Compute:

(a) The break-even point.
(b) The variable costs and expenses.
(c) The fixed costs and expenses.
(d) The operating income.

25-9. For 1973 Lindsey Company had sales of $2,500,000, fixed costs and expenses of $855,000, a margin of safety of 24%, and a marginal income ratio of 45%. During 1974 the variable costs and expenses were 55% of sales, the fixed costs and expenses did not change from the previous year, and the margin of safety was 20%.

(a) What was the operating income for 1973?
(b) What was the break-even point for 1974?
(c) What was the amount of sales for 1974?
(d) What was the operating income for 1974?

25-10. McCracken Company estimates that 3,000 units of material M will be required during the coming year. Past experience indicates the storage costs are $1 per unit and the cost to place an order is $15. Determine the economic order quantity to be purchased.

PROBLEMS

The following additional problems for this chapter are located in Appendix B: 25-1B, 25-3B, 25-4B, 25-6B.

25-1A. Bowers Manufacturing Company is considering the addition of a new product to its line. For 1973, production was at 90% of capacity, the assets employed were $4,000,000 (original cost), and the income statement showed an operating income of $440,000, computed as follows:

Sales...		$5,000,000
Less: Cost of goods sold....................	$3,475,000	
Selling expenses.....................	775,000	
General expenses....................	310,000	4,560,000
Operating income......................		$ 440,000

If the new product is added, market research indicates that 10,000 units can be sold in 1974 at an estimated selling price of $50 per unit. The idle capacity will be utilized to produce the product, but an additional $500,000 in plant assets will be required. The cost data per unit for the new product are presented at the top of the next page.

Direct materials.	$18.50
Direct labor.	10.50
Factory overhead (includes depreciation on additional invest- ment).	6.50
Selling expenses.	5.00
General expenses.	2.00
	$42.50

Instructions:

(1) Prepare an estimated income statement for 1974 for the new product.
(2) Prepare a schedule indicating the rate of return on assets under present conditions and for the new product. Use the original cost of the assets in your computations.
(3) Would you recommend addition of the new product? Would you require other data before you make your decision? If so, what data would you require?

25-2A. The chief accountant of Garner Company prepares weekly reports of idleness of direct labor employees for the plant superintendent. These reports classify the idle time by departments. Idle time data for the week ended September 23 of the current year are as follows:

Department	Standard Hours	Productive Hours
1	1,600	1,520
2	800	712
3	1,400	1,400
4	1,000	880

The hourly direct labor rates are $5.00, $5.75, $4.75 and $4.50 respectively for Departments 1 through 4. The idleness was caused by a lack of sales orders in Department 1, a shortage of materials in Department 2, and a machine breakdown in Department 4.

665

Instructions:

Prepare an idle time report classified by departments for the week ended September 23 for the plant superintendent. Use the following columnar headings for the report:

	Production			Idle Time		
Dept.	Standard Hours	Actual Hours	Percentage of Standard	Hours	Cost of Idle Time	Remarks

25-3A. The capital expenditures budget committee is considering two projects. The estimated operating income and net cash flows from each project are presented below:

	Project A		Project B	
Year	Operating Income	Net Cash Flow	Operating Income	Net Cash Flow
1	$ 9,000	$19,000	$ 5,000	$15,000
2	8,000	18,000	6,000	16,000
3	6,000	16,000	7,000	17,000
4	4,000	14,000	7,000	17,000
5	3,000	13,000	5,000	15,000
	$30,000	$80,000	$30,000	$80,000

Each project requires an investment of $50,000 with no residual value expected. The committee has selected a rate of 15% for purposes of the discounted cash flow analysis.

Instructions:

(1) Compute the following:

    (a) The average rate of return for each project, giving effect to depreciation on the investment.

    (b) The excess or deficiency of present value over amount to be invested as determined by the discounted cash flow method for each project. Use the present value table appearing in this chapter.

(2) Prepare a brief report for the budget committee, advising it on the relative merits of the two projects.

25-4A. Palmer Company expects to maintain the same inventories at the end of 1974 as at the beginning of the year. The total of all production costs for the year is therefore assumed to be equal to the cost of goods sold. With this in mind, the various department heads were asked to submit estimates of the expenses for their departments during 1974. A summary report of these estimates is presented below.

	Estimated Fixed Expense	Estimated Variable Expense (per unit sold)
Production costs:		
Direct materials..................	$ ——	$4.50
Direct labor......................	——	3.00
Factory overhead.................	150,000	.80
Selling expenses:		
Sales salaries and commissions......	45,000	.30
Advertising......................	37,500	——
Travel..........................	15,000	——
Miscellaneous selling expenses......	9,000	.20
General expenses:		
Office and officers' salaries.........	90,000	.10
Supplies........................	7,500	.05
Miscellaneous general expenses.....	6,000	.05
	$360,000	$9.00

It is expected that 75,000 units will be sold at a selling price of $15 a unit. Capacity output is 80,000 units.

Instructions:

(1) Determine the break-even point (a) in dollars of sales, (b) in units, and (c) in terms of capacity.

(2) Prepare an estimated income statement for 1974.

(3) Construct a break-even chart, indicating the break-even point in dollars of sales.

(4) What is the expected margin of safety?

(5) What is the expected marginal income ratio?

25-5A. Collins Company manufactures only one product. In 1973 the plant operated at full capacity. At a meeting of the board of directors on December 3, 1973, it was decided to raise the price of this product from its price of $9, which had prevailed for the past few years, to $10, effective January 1, 1974. Although the cost price was expected to rise about $.60 per unit in 1974 because of a direct materials and direct labor wage increase, the increase in selling price was expected to cover this increase and also add to operating income. The comparative income statement for 1973 and 1974 is presented below.

	1974		1973	
Sales................................		$400,000		$450,000
Cost of goods sold — variable........	$144,000		$150,000	
fixed...........	100,000	244,000	100,000	250,000
Gross profit on sales................		$156,000		$200,000
Operating expenses — variable.......	$ 60,000		$ 67,500	
fixed.........	70,000	130,000	70,000	137,500
Operating income.................		$ 26,000		$ 62,500

Instructions:

(1) Prepare a gross profit analysis report for the year 1974.
(2) At a meeting of the board of directors on February 10, 1975, the president, after reading the gross profit analysis report, made the following comment:
   "It looks as if the increase in unit cost price was $1.10 and not the anticipated $.60. The failure of operating management to keep these costs within the bounds of those in 1973, except for the anticipated $.60 increase in direct materials and direct labor cost, was a major factor in the decrease in gross profit."
Do you agree with this analysis of the increase in unit cost price? Explain.

667

25-6A. Powell Company operated at full capacity during 1973. Its income statement appears below.

Sales.....................		$800,000
Cost of goods sold...........		500,000
Gross profit on sales.........		$300,000
Operating expenses:		
Selling expenses...........	$160,000	
General expenses..........	65,000	
Total operating expenses.		225,000
Operating income..........		$ 75,000

An analysis of costs and expenses reveals the following division of costs and expenses between fixed and variable.

	Fixed	Variable
Cost of goods sold............	30%	70%
Selling expenses..............	35%	65%
General expenses.............	60%	40%

The management of Powell Company is considering a plant expansion program that will permit an increase of $200,000 in yearly sales. The expansion will increase fixed costs and expenses by $50,000 but will not affect the relationship between sales and variable costs and expenses.

Instructions:

(1) Determine for present capacity (a) the total fixed costs and expenses and (b) the total variable costs and expenses.
(2) Determine the percentage of total variable costs and expenses to sales.
(3) Compute the break-even point under present conditions.
(4) Compute the break-even point under the proposed program.
(5) Determine the amount of sales that would be necessary under the proposed program to realize the $75,000 of operating income that was earned in 1973.
(6) Determine the maximum operating income possible with the expanded plant.
(7) If the proposal is accepted and sales remain at the 1973 level, what will the operating income be for 1974?
(8) Based upon the data given, would you recommend accepting the proposal? Explain.

Chapter 26

STATEMENT OF CHANGES IN FINANCIAL POSITION

REPORTING FINANCIAL POSITION

The financial position of an enterprise as of a specific point in time is reported on its balance sheet. It does not disclose the changes in financial position that have occurred during the preceding fiscal period. Indications of such changes can be determined by comparing the individual items on the current balance sheet with the related amounts on the earlier statement. The income statement and retained earnings statement, both of which encompass a fiscal period, reveal some of the details of changes in stockholders' equity. However, significant changes in financial position may be overlooked in the process of examining and comparing the statements and still other changes may be completely undisclosed by the statements. For example, if items of equipment or other plant assets were retired and other items acquired during the period, comparison of the balance sheets will disclose only the net amount of the change.

669

The usefulness of a concise statement devoted exclusively to changes in financial position has become increasingly apparent during the past several decades. There has been much experimentation and discussion among accountants concerning the scope, format, and terminology to be employed, and the inclusion of such statements in financial reports to stockholders has steadily increased. Guidelines for their preparation were issued by the Accounting Principles Board in 1963.[1] Considerable variation in form and content of the statement was sanctioned and, although not required, its inclusion as a basic statement in annual financial reports was encouraged. A wide variety of titles has been employed, including *Statement of Source and Application of Funds*, *Statement of Resources Provided and Applied*, and *Statement of Changes in Working Capital*. The term frequently used as a convenience in discussing the

[1]*Opinions of the Accounting Principles Board*, *No. 3*, "The Statement of Source and Application of Funds" (New York: American Institute of Certified Public Accountants, 1963).

statement is *funds statement*. This shorter term will often be employed in the discussions that follow.

The 1963 pronouncement of the Accounting Principles Board was superseded by a more definitive opinion in 1971. In addition to broadening the scope of the funds statement the Board directed that it be considered a basic financial statement for all profit-oriented enterprises and recommended the adoption of the more descriptive title *Statement of Changes in Financial Position*.[2]

CONCEPTS OF FUNDS

In accounting and financial usage the term "fund" has a variety of meanings. It was first used in this book to denote segregations of cash for a special purpose, as in "change fund" and "petty cash fund." Later it was employed to designate the amount of cash and marketable investments segregated in a "sinking fund" for the purpose of liquidating bonds or other long-term obligations at maturity. When used in the plural form, "funds" is often a synonym for cash, as when a drawee bank refuses to honor a check and returns it to the depositor with the notation "not sufficient funds."

The concept employed in funds statements has varied somewhat in practice, with resulting variation in the content of the statements. "Funds" can be interpreted broadly to mean "working capital" or, more narrowly, to mean "cash" or "cash and marketable securities." Regardless of which of the concepts is adopted for a specific funds statement, financial position may also be affected by transactions that do not involve funds. If such transactions have occurred during the period, their effect, if significant, should also be reported in the funds statement.[3]

WORKING CAPITAL CONCEPT OF FUNDS

The excess of an enterprise's total current assets over its total current liabilities at the same point in time may be termed its "net current assets" or *working capital*. To illustrate, assume that a corporate balance sheet lists current assets totaling $550,000 and current liabilities totaling $230,000. The working capital of the corporation at the balance sheet date is $550,000 − $230,000, or $320,000. The comparative schedule shown at the top of the next page includes the major categories of current assets and current liabilities.

The increase or decrease in each item is reported in the third column of the schedule. The increase of $50,000 in total current assets during the year tended to increase the working capital. The decrease of $30,000

---

[2]*Opinions of the Accounting Principles Board, No. 19*, "Reporting Changes in Financial Position" (New York: American Institute of Certified Public Accountants, 1971).
[3]*Ibid*, par. 8.

| | DECEMBER 31 | | INCREASE |
	1974	1973	DECREASE*
Current assets:			
Cash............................	$ 30,000	$ 35,000	$ 5,000*
Marketable securities..............	60,000	40,000	20,000
Receivables (net).................	100,000	115,000	15,000*
Inventories......................	350,000	295,000	55,000
Prepaid expenses.................	10,000	15,000	5,000*
Total.......................	$550,000	$500,000	$50,000
Current liabilities:			
Notes payable....................	$ 55,000	$ 50,000	$ 5,000
Accounts payable................	120,000	145,000	25,000*
Income tax payable..............	30,000	40,000	10,000*
Dividends payable................	25,000	25,000	——
Total.......................	$230,000	$260,000	$30,000*
Working capital...................	$320,000	$240,000	$80,000

671

in total current liabilities also tended to increase the working capital. The combined effect was an increase of $80,000 in working capital. It should be noted that working capital is a "net" concept. An increase or decrease in working capital cannot be determined solely by the amount of change in total current assets nor solely by the amount of change in total current liabilities.

The magnitude of most of the items classified as current assets and current liabilities varies from one balance sheet date to another. Many of the items fluctuate daily. Inventories are increased by purchases on account, which also increase accounts payable. Accounts payable are reduced by payment, which also reduces cash. As merchandise is sold on account, inventories decrease and accounts receivable increase. In turn the collections from customers increase cash and reduce accounts receivable. An understanding of this continuous cycle of interplay among the various current assets and current liabilities is essential to an understanding of the concept of working capital and analyses related to it. In the illustration, for example, the absence of increase or decrease in the amount of dividends payable between balance sheet dates should not be construed as an indication that the account balance remained unchanged throughout the year. If dividends were paid quarterly, four separate liabilities would have been created and four would have been liquidated during the period. It may also be noted that the amount of working capital is neither increased nor decreased by a transaction (1) that affects only current assets (such as a purchase of marketable securities for cash), (2) that affects only current liabilities (such as issuance of a short-term note to a creditor on account), or (3) that affects only current assets and current liabilities (such as payment of an account payable).

WORKING CAPITAL FLOW

The working capital schedule on the preceding page indicates an increase of $80,000 in working capital, which may be significant in evaluating financial position. However, the schedule gives no indication of the source of the increase. It could have resulted from the issuance of common stock, from the sale of treasury stock, from operating income or from a combination of these and other sources. It is also possible that working capital would have increased by considerably more during the year had it not been for the purchase of plant assets, the retirement of bonded indebtedness, an adverse judgment as defendant in a damage suit, or other occurrences with a similar effect on working capital.

Both the inward flow and the outward flow of funds are reported in a funds statement. Those flowing into the enterprise, classified as to source, form the first section of the funds statement. Funds flowing out of the enterprise, classified according to the manner of their use or application are reported in the second section of the statement. Ordinarily the totals of the two sections are unequal. If the inflow (sources) has exceeded the outflow (applications), the excess is the amount of the increase in working capital. When the reverse situation occurs, the excess of outflow is a measure of the amount by which working capital has decreased. Accordingly, the difference between the total of the sources and the applications sections of the funds statement is identified as an increase or a decrease in working capital. The details of this balancing amount are frequently presented in a subsidiary section of the statement or in a separate schedule.

Some of the data needed in preparing a funds statement can be obtained from comparing items on the current balance sheet with those on the preceding balance sheet. Information regarding net income may be obtained from the current income statement and dividend data are available in the retained earnings statement. However, there may be sources and applications of funds that are not disclosed by these statements. Some of the relevant data can be obtained only from an examination of accounts in the ledger or from journal entries.

Although there are many kinds of transactions that affect funds, consideration will be limited here to the most common sources and applications. As a matter of convenience in the discussion that follows, all asset accounts other than current assets will be referred to as "noncurrent assets" and all liability accounts other than current liabilities will be referred to as "noncurrent liabilities."

SOURCES OF WORKING CAPITAL

The amount of inflow of working capital from various sources can be determined without the necessity of reviewing and classifying every transaction that occurred during the period. There is also no need to determine the individual effects of a number of similar transactions; summary figures are sufficient. For purposes of discussion, transactions that provide working capital are classified in terms of their effect on noncurrent accounts, as follows:

1. Transactions that decrease noncurrent assets.
2. Transactions that increase noncurrent liabilities.
3. Transactions that increase stockholders' equity.

Decreases in noncurrent assets. The sale of long-term investments, equipment, buildings, land, patents, or other noncurrent assets for cash or on account provides working capital. However, the reduction in the balance of the noncurrent asset account between the beginning and end of the period is not necessarily the amount of working capital provided by the sale. For example, if a patent carried in the ledger at $20,000 is sold during the year for $50,000, the patents account will decrease by $20,000 but the funds provided by the transaction amounted to $50,000. Similarly, if the long-term investments carried at $100,000 at the beginning of the year are sold for $75,000 cash, the transaction provided funds of $75,000 instead of $100,000.

673

Increases in noncurrent liabilities. The issuance of bonds or long-term notes is a common source of working capital. For example, if during the year bonds with a face value of $500,000 are sold at 100 for cash, the amount of funds provided by the transaction would be indicated by a $500,000 increase in the bonds payable account. If the bonds were issued at a price above or below 100, it would be necessary to refer to the bond premium or discount account, in addition to the bonds payable account, in order to determine the amount of funds provided by the transaction. For example, if the $500,000 of bonds had been issued at 90 instead of 100, the funds provided would have been $450,000 instead of $500,000.

Increases in stockholders' equity. Often the largest and most frequently recurring source of working capital is profitable operations. Revenues realized from the sale of commodities or services are accompanied by increases in working capital. On the other hand, many of the expenses incurred are accompanied by decreases in working capital. Inasmuch as the significant details of revenues and expenses appear in the income statement, they need not be repeated in the funds statement. However, the amount of income from normal operations reported on the income statement is not necessarily equivalent to the working capital actually provided by operations. Such expenses as depreciation of plant assets and amortization of patents are deducted from revenue but have no effect on current assets or current liabilities. Similarly, the amortization of premium on bonds payable increases operating income but does not affect current assets or current liabilities. The amount reported on the income statement as income from normal operations must therefore be adjusted upward or downward to determine the amount of working capital so provided. Items reported as "extraordinary" on the income statement should be stated separately on the funds statement.

If capital stock is sold during the period, the amount of working capital provided will not necessarily coincide with the amount of the increase in the capital stock account; consideration must also be given to accompanying debits or credits to other paid-in capital accounts. There also may be entries in stockholders' equity accounts that do not affect financial position, such as a transfer of retained earnings to paid-in capital accounts in the issuance of a stock dividend. Similarly, transfers between the retained earnings account and appropriations accounts have no effect on financial position.

APPLICATIONS OF WORKING CAPITAL

As in the case of working capital sources, it is convenient to classify applications according to their effects on noncurrent accounts. Transactions affecting the outflow or applications of working capital may be described as follows:

1. Transactions that **increase noncurrent assets.**
2. Transactions that **decrease noncurrent liabilities.**
3. Transactions that **decrease stockholders' equity.**

Increases in noncurrent assets. Working capital may be applied to the purchase of equipment, buildings, land, long-term investments, patents, or other noncurrent assets. However, the amount of funds used for such purposes is not necessarily indicated by the net increases in the related accounts. For example, if the debits to the equipment account for acquisitions during the year totaled $100,000 and the credits to the same account for retirements amounted to $25,000, the net change in the account would be $75,000. Such facts can be determined only by reviewing the details in the account.

Decreases in noncurrent liabilities. The liquidation of bonds or long-term notes represents an application of working capital. The amount applied would be indicated by the decrease in the balance of the liability account if the face value was paid at maturity. If the obligations were redeemed prior to maturity, it would be necessary to consider any unamortized premium or discount and any gain or loss on the transaction.

Decreases in stockholders' equity. Probably the most frequent application of working capital in reduction of stockholders' equity results from the declaration of cash dividends. Funds may also be applied to the redemption of preferred stock or to the purchase of treasury stock. As indicated earlier, the issuance of stock dividends does not affect working capital or financial position.

OTHER CHANGES IN FINANCIAL POSITION

In accordance with the broadened concept of the funds statement, significant transactions affecting financial position should be reported even though they do not affect funds.[4] For example, if an enterprise issues bonds or capital stock in exchange for land and buildings, the transaction has no effect on working capital. Nevertheless, because of the significant effect on financial position, both the increase in the plant assets and the increase in long-term liabilities or stockholders' equity should be reported on the statement. A complete catalog of the kinds of non-fund transactions that ordinarily have a significant effect on financial position is beyond the scope of the discussion here. The following are illustrative of the many possibilities: preferred or common stock may be issued in liquidation of long-term debt, common stock may be issued in exchange for convertible preferred stock, long-term investments may be exchanged for machinery and equipment, and land and buildings may be received from a municipality as a gift.

Transactions of the type indicated in the preceding paragraph may be reported on the funds statement as though there were in reality two transactions: (1) a source of funds and (2) an application of funds. The relationship of the source and the application should be disclosed by appropriate phraseology in the descriptive captions or by footnote. To illustrate, assume that common stock of $100,000 par is issued in exchange for $100,000 face amount of bonds payable, on which there is no unamortized discount or premium. The issuance of the common stock should be reported in the source section of the statement somewhat as follows: "Issuance of common stock at par in retirement of bonds payable, $100,000." The other part of the transaction could be described in the applications section as follows: "Retirement of bonds payable by the issuance of common stock at par, $100,000."

675

ASSEMBLING DATA FOR THE FUNDS STATEMENT BASED ON WORKING CAPITAL

Much of the information on funds flow is obtained in the process of preparing the balance sheet, the income statement, and the retained earnings statement. When the volume of data is substantial, experienced accountants may first assemble all relevant facts in working papers designed for the purpose. Specialized working papers are not essential, however. Because of their complexity they tend to obscure the basic

---

[4]*Opinions of the Accounting Principles Board, No. 19, ibid.,* par. 8.

concepts of funds analysis for anyone who is not already familiar with the subject. For this reason special working papers will not be used in this text for assembling the data needed for the funds statement; instead, a thorough understanding of the basic analyses will be emphasized.

In the illustration that follows, the information will be obtained from (1) a comparative balance sheet and (2) ledger accounts for noncurrent assets, noncurrent liabilities, and stockholders' equity. The comparative balance sheet in simplified form appears below; ledger accounts will be presented contemporaneously with the discussion of the related data. Descriptive notations have been inserted in the accounts to facilitate the explanations; otherwise it would be necessary to refer to supportive journal entries to determine the complete effect of some of the transactions.

Fairview Corporation
Comparative Balance Sheet
December 31, 1974 and 1973

	1974	1973	Increase Decrease*
Assets			
Cash...	$ 48,000	$ 26,000	$22,000
Trade receivables (net)........................	70,000	65,000	5,000
Inventories.....................................	171,000	180,000	9,000*
Prepaid expenses...............................	4,000	3,000	1,000
Investments (long-term)........................	——	50,000	50,000*
Equipment......................................	157,000	138,000	19,000
Accumulated depreciation — equipment...........	(41,000)	(40,000)	(1,000)
Building..	100,000	100,000	——
Accumulated depreciation — building............	(34,000)	(30,000)	(4,000)
Land...	25,000	5,000	20,000
Total assets....................................	$500,000	$497,000	$ 3,000
Liabilities			
Accounts payable (merchandise creditors).........	$ 40,000	$ 32,000	$ 8,000
Dividends payable...............................	10,000	6,000	4,000
Income tax payable.............................	2,500	4,000	1,500*
Bonds payable..................................	75,000	150,000	75,000*
Total liabilities................................	$127,500	$192,000	$64,500*
Stockholders' Equity			
Common stock..................................	$270,000	$250,000	$20,000
Retained earnings..............................	102,500	55,000	47,500
Total stockholders' equity.......................	$372,500	$305,000	$67,500
Total liabilities and stockholders' equity...........	$500,000	$497,000	$ 3,000

Inasmuch as only the noncurrent accounts reveal sources and applications of funds, it is not necessary to examine the current asset or the current liability accounts. The first of the noncurrent accounts listed on the comparative balance sheet of the Fairview Corporation is Investments.

Investments. The comparative balance sheet indicates that investments decreased by $50,000. The notation in the investments account reproduced below indicates that the investments were sold for $70,000 cash. The $20,000 gain on the sale appears on the income statement as an extraordinary item less applicable income tax of $6,000; hence, the sale should be reported on the statement as a source of $64,000 ($70,000 − $6,000) of working capital. The notation is accordingly as follows:

Source of working capital:
Sale of investments............................ $64,000

INVESTMENTS

DATE		ITEM	DEBIT	CREDIT	BALANCE DEBIT	BALANCE CREDIT
1974						
Jan.	1	Balance			50,000	
June	8	Sold for $70,000 cash		50,000	—	

Equipment. The comparative balance sheet indicates that the cost of equipment increased $19,000. The equipment account and the accumulated depreciation account illustrated below reveal that the net change of $19,000 was the result of two separate transactions, the discarding of equipment that had cost $8,000 and the purchase of equipment for $27,000. The equipment discarded had been fully depreciated, as indicated by the debit of $8,000 in the accumulated depreciation account, and no salvage was realized from its disposal. Hence, the transaction had no effect on working capital and is not reported on the funds statement. The effect on funds of the purchase of equipment for $27,000 was as follows:

Application of working capital:
Purchase of equipment......................... $27,000

The credit in the accumulated depreciation account had the effect of reducing the investment in equipment by $9,000 but caused no change

EQUIPMENT

DATE		ITEM	DEBIT	CREDIT	BALANCE DEBIT	BALANCE CREDIT
1974						
Jan.	1	Balance			138,000	
May	9	Discarded, no salvage		8,000		
July	7	Purchased for cash	27,000		157,000	

ACCUMULATED DEPRECIATION — EQUIPMENT

DATE		ITEM	DEBIT	CREDIT	BALANCE DEBIT	BALANCE CREDIT
1974						
Jan.	1	Balance				40,000
May	9	Discarded, no salvage	8,000			
Dec.	31	Depreciation for year		9,000		41,000

677

in working capital. Further attention will be given to depreciation in a later paragraph.

Building. According to the comparative balance sheet there was no change in the $100,000 balance between the beginning and end of the year. Reference to the building account in the ledger confirms the absence of entries during the year and hence the account is not shown here. Although the credit in the related accumulated depreciation account reduced the investment in building, working capital was not affected.

ACCUMULATED DEPRECIATION — BUILDING

DATE		ITEM	DEBIT	CREDIT	BALANCE DEBIT	BALANCE CREDIT
1974						
Jan.	1	Balance				30,000
Dec.	31	Depreciation for year		4,000		34,000

Land. The comparative balance sheet indicates that land increased by $20,000. The notation in the land account, which is reproduced below, indicates that the land was acquired by issuance of common stock at par. Although working capital was not involved in this transaction, the acquisition represents a significant change in financial position which may be noted as follows:

> Application of working capital:
> Purchase of land by issuance of common stock at par. $20,000

LAND

DATE		ITEM	DEBIT	CREDIT	BALANCE DEBIT	BALANCE CREDIT
1974						
Jan.	1	Balance			5,000	
Dec.	28	Acquired by issuance of				
		common stock at par	20,000		25,000	

Bonds payable. The next noncurrent item listed on the balance sheet, bonds payable, decreased $75,000 during the year. Examination of the bonds payable account, which appears below, indicates that half of the bonds payable were retired by payment of the face amount. The effect on funds is noted as follows:

> Application of working capital:
> Retirement of bonds payable..................... $75,000

BONDS PAYABLE

DATE		ITEM	DEBIT	CREDIT	BALANCE DEBIT	BALANCE CREDIT
1974						
Jan.	1	Balance				150,000
June	30	Retired by payment of cash				
		at face amount	75,000			75,000

Common stock. The increase of $20,000 in the common stock account is identified as having been issued in exchange for land valued at $20,000. This change in financial position should be reported on the funds statement and may be noted as follows:

Source of working capital:
Issuance of common stock at par for land........... $20,000

COMMON STOCK

DATE		ITEM	DEBIT	CREDIT	BALANCE	
					DEBIT	CREDIT
1974						
Jan.	1	Balance				250,000
Dec.	28	Issued at par in exchange for land		20,000		270,000

Retained earnings. According to the comparative balance sheet, there was an increase of $47,500 in retained earnings during the year. The retained earnings account, which is reproduced below, reveals a credit of $67,500 transferred from the income summary account and a debit of $20,000 transferred from the cash dividends account.

RETAINED EARNINGS

DATE		ITEM	DEBIT	CREDIT	BALANCE	
					DEBIT	CREDIT
1974						
Jan.	1	Balance				55,000
Dec.	31	Net income, including extraordinary gain of $14,000 ($20,000 less applicable income tax of $6,000)		67,500		
	31	Cash dividends	20,000			102,500

The memorandum in the account indicates that the $67,500 of net income includes $14,000 of extraordinary income on the sale of investments. The net amount realized from their sale is reported separately as a source of working capital. Hence, to avoid double counting of the extraordinary income, the $14,000 must be deducted from $67,500, yielding income from normal operations of $53,500.

Unlike most operating expenses, depreciation of plant assets is not accompanied by a decrease in current assets or an increase in current liabilities. Although it is a proper deduction from revenue in determining net income, it causes an understatement of the amount of working capital provided by operations. Accordingly, it is necessary to add back depreciation expense of $9,000 on the equipment and $4,000 on the building.

The data to be reported as working capital provided by normal operations is noted as shown at the top of the next page.

679

Source of working capital:
Operations during the year:
Income exclusive of
extraordinary item................... $53,500
Add deduction not decreasing
working capital during the year:
Depreciation..................... 13,000 $66,500

The effect of the declaration of cash dividends of $20,000 recorded as a debit in the retained earnings account is indicated as follows:

Application of working capital:
Declaration of cash dividends.................... $20,000

It should be noted that working capital is applied to cash dividends at the time the current liability is incurred, regardless of when the dividends are actually paid.

FORM OF THE FUNDS STATEMENT BASED ON WORKING CAPITAL

Although there are many possible variations in the form and the content of the funds statement, the first section is customarily devoted to the source of funds, followed by the section on the application or use of funds. There is frequently a third section in which changes in the amounts of the current assets and the current liabilities are reported. Income from normal operations should be presented as the first item in the statement.[5] A funds statement for the Fairview Corporation is illustrated at the top of the next page.

Changes in components of working capital. The difference between the totals of the source section and the application section of the funds statement is identified as the increase or the decrease in working capital. The net change in the amount of working capital reported on the statement should be supported by details of the changes in each of the working capital components.[6] The information may be presented in a third section of the statement, as in the illustration on the next page, or it may be presented as a separate tabulation accompanying the statement. The data required in either case are readily obtainable from the comparative balance sheet. The two amounts identified as the increase or decrease in working capital ($8,500 increase in the illustration) obviously must agree.

ANALYSIS OF CASH

When *cash*[7] is employed as the concept of funds, the analysis is devoted to the movement of cash rather than to the inflow and outflow

---

[5]*Opinions of the Accounting Principles Board, No. 19, ibid.,* par. 10.
[6]*Opinions of the Accounting Principles Board, No. 19, ibid.,* par. 12.
[7]The concept may be expanded to include temporary investments that are readily convertible into cash.

Fairview Corporation
Statement of Changes in Financial Position
For Year Ended December 31, 1974

Source of working capital:

Operations during the year:

Income exclusive of extraordinary item...........	$53,500		
Add deduction not decreasing working capital during the year:			
Depreciation..............................	13,000	$66,500	
Sale of investments.......................................		64,000	
Issuance of common stock at par for land..................		20,000	$150,500

Application of working capital:

Purchase of equipment................................	$27,000	
Purchase of land by issuance of common stock at par.........	20,000	
Retirement of bonds payable............................	75,000	
Declaration of cash dividends............................	20,000	142,000
Increase in working capital................................		$ 8,500

Changes in components of working capital:

Increase (decrease) in current assets:

Cash...	$22,000	
Trade receivables (net)...............................	5,000	
Inventories.......................................	(9,000)	
Prepaid expenses..................................	1,000	$ 19,000

Increase (decrease) in current liabilities:

Accounts payable.....................................	$ 8,000	
Dividends payable....................................	4,000	
Income tax payable...................................	(1,500)	10,500
Increase in working capital................................		$ 8,500

Statement of
changes in
financial
position —
based on
working capital

of working capital. The portion of the statement devoted to normal operations may report the total revenue that provided cash, followed by deductions for operating costs and expenses requiring the outlay of cash. The usual practice, however, is to begin with income from operations (exclusive of extraordinary items) as was done in the preceding illustration. This basic amount is then adjusted for increases and decreases of all working capital items except cash, in accordance with procedures demonstrated later in the chapter.

There has been much experimentation in the methodology of cash-flow analysis and in the form of the related funds statement. The approach that will be employed here is patterned after the procedures used in the preceding discussion and illustrations. Although the working capital concept of funds discussed earlier is more commonly used, particularly in preparing funds statements for reports to stockholders, the cash concept is useful in evaluating financial policies and current cash position. It is especially useful to management in preparing cash budgets.

The format of a funds statement based on the cash concept may be quite similar to the form illustrated above. It is ordinarily divided into two principal sections, source of cash and application of cash. The difference between the totals of the two sections is the cash increase or decrease for the period. The principal parts of the report may be followed by a listing of the cash balance at the beginning of the period, at the end of the period, and the net change. A variant is to begin the statement with the beginning cash balance, add the total of the source section, subtract the total of the application section, and conclude with the cash balance at the end of the period.

ASSEMBLING DATA FOR THE FUNDS STATEMENT BASED ON CASH

The comparative balance sheet of Fairview Corporation on page 676 and the related accounts presented on succeeding pages will be used as the basis for illustration. Reference to the earlier analysis discloses that the sale of investments yielded cash and that there were cash outlays for equipment and the retirement of bonds. These transactions may be noted as follows:

Source of cash:
Sale of investments. $64,000

Application of cash:
Purchase of equipment. $27,000
Retirement of bonds payable.   75,000

The earlier analysis also indicated that land was acquired by the issuance of common stock. Although the transaction did not involve cash, it resulted in a significant change in financial position and should be reported on the statement. It is as if the common stock had been issued for cash and the cash received had then been expended for the parcel of land. The following notation indicates the manner in which the transaction is to be reported in the statement:

Source of cash:
Issuance of common stock at par for land. $20,000

Application of cash:
Purchase of land by issuance of common stock at par. $20,000

The amount of cash provided by normal operations ordinarily differs from the amount of income before extraordinary items. The amount of cash applied to the payment of dividends may also differ from the amount of cash dividends declared. The determination of these amounts is discussed in the paragraphs that follow.

Cash provided by normal operations. The starting point in the analysis of the effect of operations on cash is income for the period, exclusive of extraordinary items. This amount was reported for Fairview Corporation on page 679 as $53,500. As in the earlier analysis, depreciation expense of $13,000 must be added to the $53,500 because depreciation expense did not decrease the amount of cash during the year. In addition, it is necessary to recognize the relationship of the accrual method of accounting to the movement of cash. Ordinarily a portion of some of the other costs and expenses reported on the income statement, as well as a portion of the revenue earned, are not accompanied by cash outflow or inflow.

There is frequently a time differential between the accrual of a revenue and the receipt of the related cash. Perhaps the most common example is the sale of merchandise or a service on account, for which payment is received at a later point in time. Hence, the amount reported on the income statement as revenue from sales is not likely to correspond with the amount of the related cash inflow for the same period.

Timing differences between the incurrence of an expense and the related cash outflow must also be considered in determining the amount of cash provided by normal operations. For example, the amount reported on the income statement as insurance expense is the amount of insurance premiums expired rather than the amount of premiums paid during the period. Similarly, supplies paid for in one year may be consumed and thus converted to an expense in a later year. Conversely, a portion of some of the expenses incurred near the end of one period, such as wages and taxes, may not require a cash outlay until the following period.

The effect of timing differences is indicated by the amount of change in the balances of the asset and liability accounts affected by normal operations. Decreases in such assets and increases in such liabilities during the period must be added to the amount reported as income from normal operations. Conversely, increases in such assets and decreases in such liabilities must be deducted from the amount reported as income from normal operations.

The Fairview Corporation balance sheet (page 676) data indicating the effect of timing differences on the amount of cash inflow and outflow from normal operations are listed below, followed by an explanation of each item.

| | DECEMBER 31 | | INCREASE |
ACCOUNTS	1974	1973	DECREASE*
Trade receivables (net).	$ 70,000	$ 65,000	$5,000
Inventories.	171,000	180,000	9,000*
Prepaid expenses.	4,000	3,000	1,000
Accounts payable (merchandise creditors).	40,000	32,000	8,000
Income tax payable.	2,500	4,000	1,500*

Trade receivables (net) increase. The additions to trade receivables for sales on account during the year exceeded by $5,000 the deductions for amounts collected from customers on account. The amount reported on the income statement as sales therefore included $5,000 that did not

683

yield cash inflow during the year. Accordingly, $5,000 must be deducted from income to determine the amount of cash provided by operations.

Inventories decrease. The $9,000 decrease in inventories indicates that the merchandise sold exceeded the cost of the merchandise purchased by $9,000. The amount reported on the income statement as a deduction from revenue therefore included $9,000 that did not require cash outflow during the year. Accordingly, $9,000 must be added to income to determine the amount of cash provided by operations.

Prepaid expenses increase. The outlay of cash for prepaid expenses exceeded by $1,000 the amount deducted from revenue as expense during the year. Hence, $1,000 must be deducted from income to determine the amount of cash provided by operations.

Accounts payable increase. The effect of the increase in the amount owed creditors for goods and services was to include in expired costs and expenses the sum of $8,000 for which there had been no cash outlay during the year. Income was thereby reduced by $8,000, though there was no cash outlay. Hence, $8,000 must be added to income to determine the amount of cash provided by operations.

Income tax payable decrease. The outlay of cash for income taxes exceeded by $1,500 the amount of income tax deducted from revenue during the period. Accordingly, $1,500 must be deducted from income to determine the amount of cash provided by operations.

The foregoing adjustments to income may be summarized as follows in a format suitable for the funds statement:

Source of cash:			
Operations during the year:			
Income exclusive of extraordinary item.....			$53,500
Add deductions not decreasing cash during the year:			
Depreciation.................	$13,000		
Decrease in inventories.........	9,000		
Increase in accounts payable....	8,000	30,000	
		$83,500	
Deduct additions not increasing cash during the year:			
Increase in trade receivables....	$ 5,000		
Increase in prepaid expenses....	1,000		
Decrease in income tax payable.	1,500	7,500	$76,000

Cash applied to payment of dividends. According to the retained earnings account of Fairview Corporation (page 679), cash dividends of $20,000 were declared during the year. In the earlier funds flow analysis this was noted as the amount of working capital applied to the declaration of cash dividends. However, the amounts reported as dividends payable on Fairview Corporation's comparative balance sheet (page 676) are $10,000 and $6,000 respectively, revealing a timing difference between declaration and payment.

According to the dividends payable account, which is reproduced below, dividend payments during the year totaled $16,000.

DIVIDENDS PAYABLE

DATE		ITEM	DEBIT	CREDIT	BALANCE DEBIT	BALANCE CREDIT
1974						
Jan.	1	Balance				6,000
	10	Cash paid	6,000			—
June	20	Dividend declared		10,000		10,000
July	10	Cash paid	10,000			—
Dec.	20	Dividend declared		10,000		10,000

The amount of cash applied to dividend payments may be noted as follows:

Application of cash:
Cash dividends declared................ $20,000
Deduct increase in dividends payable...... 4,000 $16,000

FORM OF THE FUNDS STATEMENT BASED ON CASH

685

The illustrative statement presented on the next page is comparable in form to the funds statement illustrated earlier (page 681). The statement may conclude with the amount of increase or decrease in cash or it may be supported by a reconciliation such as that appearing in the illustration.

Comparison of the two statements reveals the similarity of format. The greatest difference between them is in the section devoted to funds provided by operations. Two statements, one based on working capital and the other on cash, may be prepared for the use of management, but only one statement is ordinarily presented in published financial reports.

CASH FLOW FROM OPERATIONS

The term *cash flow* is sometimes encountered in reports to stockholders. It may be mentioned in a company president's letter to stockholders, in operating summaries, or elsewhere in the published financial report. Although there are variations in the method of determination, cash flow is approximately equivalent to income from normal operations plus depreciation, depletion, and any other expenses that had no effect on working capital during the period. A variety of terms has been employed to describe the amount so determined, including "cash flow from operations," "cash income," "cash earnings," and "cash throw-off."

Fairview Corporation
Statement of Changes in Financial Position
For Year Ended December 31, 1974

Source of cash:				
Operations during the year:				
Income exclusive of extraordinary item............		$53,500		
Add deductions not decreasing cash during the year:				
Depreciation.......................	$13,000			
Decrease in inventories..............	9,000			
Increase in accounts payable.........	8,000	30,000		
		$83,500		
Deduct additions not increasing cash during the year:				
Increase in trade receivables.........	$ 5,000			
Increase in prepaid expenses.........	1,000			
Decrease in income tax payable......	1,500	7,500	$76,000	
Sale of investments.....................................			64,000	
Issuance of common stock at par for land...................			20,000	$160,000
Application of cash:				
Purchase of land by issuance of common stock at par.........			$20,000	
Purchase of equipment................................			27,000	
Retirement of bonds payable...........................			75,000	
Payment of dividends:				
Cash dividends declared......................		$20,000		
Deduct increase in dividends payable............		4,000	16,000	138,000
Increase in cash.......................................				$ 22,000
Change in cash balance:				
Cash balance, December 31, 1974........................				$ 48,000
Cash balance, December 31, 1973........................				26,000
Increase in cash.......................................				$ 22,000

Statement of
changes in
financial
position —
based on
cash

The amount of cash flow from operations for a period may be useful to internal financial management in considering the possibility of retiring long-term debt, in planning replacement of plant facilities, or in formulating dividend policies. However, when it is presented without reference to the funds statement and its importance stressed in reporting operations to stockholders, it is likely to be misunderstood. The reporting of so-called cash flow per share of stock may be even more misleading, particularly when the amount is larger, which it usually is, than the net income per share. Readers are quite likely to substitute cash flow for net income in appraising the relative success of operations. Guidelines for determining acceptable terminology and practice are expressed in the following admonition and recommendation:

The amount of working capital or cash provided from operations is not a substitute for or an improvement upon properly determined net income as a measure of results of operations and the consequent effect on financial position. Terms referring to "cash" should not be used to describe amounts provided from operations unless all non-cash items have been appropriately adjusted. . . . The Board strongly recommends that isolated statistics of working capital or cash provided from operations, especially per-share amounts, not be presented in annual reports to shareholders. If any per-share data relating to flow of working capital or cash are presented, they should as a minimum include amounts for inflow from operations, inflow from other sources, and total outflow, and each per-share amount should be clearly identified with the corresponding total amount shown in the Statement.[8]

QUESTIONS

1. (a) Does a balance sheet as of a single specified date disclose changes in financial position that have occurred during a period of time? (b) Is it possible to determine the changes in financial position during a period by comparing data on balance sheets as of the beginning and the end of the period?

2. What is the shorter term often employed in referring to the statement of changes in financial position?

3. The word *fund* may be used to mean (a) cash segregated for a special purpose or (b) a combination of cash and securities segregated for a special purpose. Give an example of each usage.

4. What are the principal concepts of the term *funds*, as employed in referring to the statement of changes in financial position.

5. (a) What is meant by *working capital*? (b) Name another term, other than "funds," that has the same meaning.

6. State the effect of each of the following transactions, considered individually, on working capital:
  (a) Purchased $3,000 of merchandise on account, terms 2/10, n/30.
  (b) Sold for $500 cash merchandise that had cost $350.
  (c) Borrowed $10,000 cash, issuing a 60-day, 6% note.
  (d) Issued a $5,000, 30-day note to a creditor in temporary settlement of an account payable.
  (e) Received $250 from a customer in payment of his account.
  (f) Purchased office equipment for $2,000 on account.
  (g) Issued 1,000 shares of common stock for $25 a share, receiving cash.

7. What is the effect on working capital of writing off $1,500 of uncollectible accounts against Allowance for Doubtful Accounts?

8. Give examples of (a) "noncurrent" asset accounts and (b) "noncurrent" liability accounts.

9. A corporation issued $1,000,000 of 10-year bonds for cash at 102. (a) Did the transaction provide funds or apply funds? (b) What was the amount of funds involved? (c) Was working capital affected? (d) Was cash affected?

---

[8]*Opinions of the Accounting Principles Board, No. 19, op. cit.*, par. 15.

10. Long-term investments with a cost of $80,000 were sold for $60,000 cash. (a) What was the gain or loss on the sale? (b) What was the effect of the transaction on working capital? (c) How should the transaction be reported in the funds statement?

11. Fully depreciated plant equipment costing $12,000 was discarded and no salvage was realized. What was the effect of the transaction on working capital?

12. The board of directors declared a cash dividend of $25,000 near the end of the fiscal year which ends on December 31, payable in January. (a) What was the effect of the declaration on working capital? (b) Did the declaration represent a source or an application of working capital? (c) Did the payment of the dividend in January affect working capital, and if so, how?

13. (a) What is the effect on working capital of the declaration and issuance of a stock dividend? (b) Does the stock dividend represent a source or an application of working capital?

14. For the current year a company reported a loss of $20,000 from normal operations on its income statement and an increase of $10,000 in working capital from operations, exclusive of extraordinary items, on its statement of changes in financial position. Explain the seeming contradiction between the loss and the increase in working capital.

15. What is the effect on working capital of an appropriation of retained earnings for plant expansion?

16. A loss of $18,000 from normal operations is reported on the income statement. The only revenue or expense item reported on the statement that did not affect working capital was depreciation expense of $8,000. Will the change in financial position attributed to normal operations appear in the funds statement as a source or as an application of working capital, and at what amount?

17. A corporation acquired as a long-term investment all of the capital stock of another corporation, valued at $10,000,000, by the issuance of $10,000,000 of its own long-term bonds. Where should the transaction be reported on the statement of changes in financial position, (a) if the working capital concept of funds is employed, and (b) if the cash concept of funds is employed?

18. A retail enterprise employing the accrual method of accounting owed merchandise creditors (accounts payable) $200,000 at the beginning of the year and $150,000 at the end of the year. What adjustment for the $50,000 decrease must be made to income from normal operations in determining the amount of cash provided by operations? Explain.

19. If revenue from sales amounted to $600,000 for the year and trade receivables totaled $50,000 and $30,000 at the beginning and end of the year respectively, what was the amount of cash received from customers during the year?

20. The board of directors declared cash dividends totaling $200,000 during the current year. The comparative balance sheet indicates dividends payable of $40,000 at the beginning of the year and $50,000 at the end of the year. What was the amount of cash disbursed to stockholders during the year?

EXERCISES

26-1. On the basis of the schedule of current assets and current liabilities of Burton Corporation presented below, prepare the section of the statement of changes in financial position entitled changes in components of working capital.

	End of Year	Beginning of Year
Cash...................	$ 32,500	$ 31,500
Accounts receivable (net).	51,000	53,000
Notes receivable.........	10,000	6,000
Inventories.............	144,000	147,500
Prepaid expenses........	2,800	2,500
Accounts payable.......	45,000	41,200
Dividends payable.......	20,000	16,000
Salaries payable........	7,800	10,500

26-2. The net income (no extraordinary items) reported on the income statement of Adams Corporation for the current year was $86,400. Adjustments required to determine the amount of working capital provided by operations, as well as some other data used for the year-end adjusting entries, are described below. Prepare the working capital provided by operations section of the statement of changes in financial position.

(a) Depreciation expense, $19,400.
(b) Uncollectible accounts expense, $2,400.
(c) Amortization of patents, $2,000.
(d) Interest accrued on notes receivable, $500.
(e) Income tax payable, $15,600.
(f) Wages accrued but not paid, $1,700.

689

26-3. On the basis of the details of the plant asset account presented below, assemble in memorandum form the data needed to prepare a statement of changes in financial position, employing the working capital concept of funds.

LAND

DATE		ITEM	DEBIT	CREDIT	BALANCE DEBIT	BALANCE CREDIT
19—						
Jan.	1	Balance			100,000	
June	20	Purchased for cash	25,000		125,000	
Dec.	10	Purchased with long-term mortgage note	90,000		215,000	

26-4. On the basis of the stockholders' equity accounts presented below and on the next page, assemble in memorandum form the items, exclusive of net income, to be reported as a source of working capital and as an application of working capital on the statement of changes in financial position.

COMMON STOCK, $10 PAR

DATE		ITEM	DEBIT	CREDIT	BALANCE DEBIT	BALANCE CREDIT
19—						
Jan.	1	Balance, 25,000 shares				250,000
July	1	5,000 shares issued for cash		50,000		300,000
Dec.	15	1,500 share stock dividend		15,000		315,000

PREMIUM ON COMMON STOCK

DATE		ITEM	DEBIT	CREDIT	BALANCE DEBIT	BALANCE CREDIT
19—						
Jan.	1	Balance				90,000
July	1	5,000 shares issued for cash		60,000		150,000
Dec.	15	Stock dividend		21,000		171,000

RETAINED EARNINGS

DATE		ITEM	DEBIT	CREDIT	BALANCE DEBIT	BALANCE CREDIT
19—						
Jan.	1	Balance				195,000
Dec.	15	Stock dividend	36,000			159,000
	31	Net income		75,000		234,000
	31	Cash dividends	20,000			214,000

26-5. The net income (no extraordinary items) reported on the income statement of Runyon Company for the current year was $32,000. Depreciation recorded on equipment and building for the year amounted to $11,000. Balances of the current asset and current liability accounts at the end and beginning of the year are listed below. Prepare the cash provided by operations section of a statement of changes in financial position.

	End	Beginning
Trade receivables.....................	$38,000	$31,000
Inventories.........................	45,000	35,000
Prepaid expenses....................	3,000	2,400
Accounts payable (merchandise creditors).	36,500	42,500
Salaries payable.....................	4,550	3,500

26-6. Based on the comparative balance sheet of M. J. Carter, Inc., presented below, and the following notes, prepare a statement of changes in financial position, employing the working capital concept of funds: (a) there were no disposals of equipment during the year, (b) the investments were sold for $88,000 cash less applicable income tax of $8,000, (c) equipment and land were acquired for cash, (d) the common stock was issued for cash, (e) there was a $78,000 credit to Retained Earnings, composed of $60,000 of income from normal operations and $18,000 of extraordinary gain from sale of investments (net of applicable income tax), and (f) there was a $25,000 debit to Retained Earnings for cash dividends declared.

	June 30 Current Year	June 30 Preceding Year
Cash..................................	$ 75,000	$ 34,500
Trade receivables (net).................	70,000	50,000
Inventories...........................	91,000	53,000
Investments...........................	——	62,000
Equipment...........................	200,000	115,000
Accumulated depreciation...............	(55,000)	(40,000)
Land.................................	50,000	30,000
	$431,000	$304,500

	June 30	
	Current Year	Preceding Year
Accounts payable (merchandise creditors).	$ 60,000	$ 52,000
Dividends payable.....................	10,000	4,500
Common stock, $25 par.................	200,000	150,000
Premium on common stock..............	10,000	———
Retained earnings.....................	151,000	98,000
	$431,000	$304,500

26-7. From the data presented in Exercise 26-6, prepare a statement of changes in financial position, employing the cash concept of funds.

PROBLEMS

The following additional problems for this chapter are located in Appendix B: 26-1B, 26-2B, 26-3B, 26-4B, 26-5B.

26-1A. The comparative balance sheet of the Benton Corporation at June 30 of the current year and the preceding year appears below in condensed form.

Assets	Current Year	Preceding Year
Cash...............................	$ 21,900	$ 28,100
Accounts receivable (net).............	32,000	29,700
Merchandise inventory................	82,400	94,500
Prepaid expenses.....................	2,600	2,950
Plant assets.........................	198,000	150,000
Accumulated depreciation — plant assets.	(46,000)	(64,000)
	$290,900	$241,250

Liabilities and Stockholders' Equity		
Accounts payable....................	$ 46,800	$ 26,900
Mortgage note payable...............	———	50,000
Common stock, $10 par...............	150,000	100,000
Premium on common stock............	10,000	———
Retained earnings....................	84,100	64,350
	$290,900	$241,250

Additional data for the current year obtained from the income statement and from an examination of the noncurrent asset, noncurrent liability, and stockholders' equity accounts in the ledger are as follows:

(a) Net income (no extraordinary items), $49,750.
(b) Depreciation reported on the income statement, $12,000.
(c) An addition to the building was constructed at a cost of $78,000, and fully depreciated equipment costing $30,000 was discarded, no salvage being realized.
(d) The mortgage note payable was not due until 1978, but the terms permitted earlier payment without penalty.
(e) 5,000 shares of common stock were issued at 12 for cash.
(f) Cash dividends declared, $30,000.

Instructions:

(1) On the basis of the comparative balance sheet and the other information, assemble in memorandum form the data needed to prepare a funds statement (working capital concept) for the current year ended June 30.

(2) Prepare a statement of changes in financial position, including a section on changes in components of working capital.

26-2A. The comparative balance sheet of the Hull Corporation at December 31 of the current year and the preceding year appears below in condensed form:

Assets	Current Year	Preceding Year
Cash.....................................	$ 14,900	$ 23,500
Trade receivables (net)......................	48,600	41,400
Inventories................................	91,300	102,500
Prepaid expenses..........................	1,500	2,200
Buildings.................................	220,400	110,400
Accumulated depreciation — buildings..............	(40,100)	(36,900)
Machinery and equipment.......................	75,000	75,000
Accumulated depreciation—machinery and equipment.	(27,000)	(15,000)
Land.....................................	30,000	30,000
Patents...................................	48,000	51,000
	$462,600	$384,100

Liabilities and Stockholders' Equity		
Accounts payable (merchandise creditors)...........	$ 25,300	$ 33,000
Dividends payable............................	6,900	4,500
Salaries payable.............................	4,500	3,400
Mortgage note payable........................	50,000	——
Bonds payable..............................	——	60,000
Common stock, $10 par........................	230,000	180,000
Premium on common stock.....................	33,000	23,000
Retained earnings............................	112,900	80,200
	$462,600	$384,100

An examination of the income statement and the accounting records revealed the following additional information applicable to the current year:

(a) Net income (no extraordinary items), $55,800.

(b) Depreciation expense reported on the income statement: buildings, $3,200; machinery and equipment, $12,000.

(c) Patent amortization reported on the income statement, $3,000.

(d) A mortgage note for $50,000, due in 1984, was issued in connection with the construction of a building costing $110,000; the remainder was paid in cash.

(e) 5,000 shares of common stock were issued at $12 in exchange for the bonds payable.

(f) Cash dividends declared, $23,100.

Instructions:

(1) On the basis of the information presented above, assemble in memorandum form the data needed to prepare a funds statement (working capital concept) for the current year ended December 31.

(2) Prepare a statement of changes in financial position, including a section for changes in components of working capital.

26-3A. The comparative balance sheet of Hull Corporation and other data necessary for the analysis of the corporation's funds flow are presented in Problem 26-2A.

Instructions:

(1) On the basis of the information presented in Problem 26-2A, assemble in memorandum form the data needed to prepare a funds statement (cash concept) for the current year ended December 31 (notations prepared for Problem 26-2A that are applicable to this problem need not be repeated).

(2) Prepare a statement of changes in financial position, including a summary of the change in cash balance.

26-4A. The comparative balance sheet of Brock & Dolan, Inc., at December 31 of the current year and the preceding year, in condensed form, and the noncurrent asset accounts, the noncurrent liability accounts, and the stockholders' equity accounts for the current year are presented below and on pages 694 and 695.

Assets	Current Year	Preceding Year
Cash..................................	$ 79,750	$ 49,500
Trade receivables (net).................	84,200	67,300
Inventories...........................	235,820	248,350
Prepaid expenses.....................	6,250	5,350
Investments..........................	——	40,000
Equipment...........................	445,500	375,500
Accumulated depreciation — equipment..	(86,000)	(75,000)
Buildings............................	431,000	241,000
Accumulated depreciation — buildings....	(31,100)	(22,750)
Land................................	50,000	50,000
	$1,215,420	$979,250

693

Liabilities and Stockholders' Equity		
Accounts payable (merchandise creditors).	$ 34,250	$ 90,030
Income tax payable....................	17,600	15,500
Notes payable........................	200,000	——
Discount on long-term notes payable.....	(9,150)	——
Common stock, $25 par................	618,000	600,000
Premium on common stock.............	55,800	45,000
Appropriation for contingencies.........	50,000	30,000
Retained earnings.....................	248,920	198,720
	$1,215,420	$979,250

INVESTMENTS

DATE		ITEM	DEBIT	CREDIT	BALANCE DEBIT	BALANCE CREDIT
19—						
Jan.	1	Balance			40,000	
Nov.	17	Realized $65,000 cash from sale, after deducting applicable income tax		40,000	—	—

EQUIPMENT

DATE		ITEM	DEBIT	CREDIT	BALANCE DEBIT	BALANCE CREDIT
19—						
Jan.	1	Balance			375,500	
Apr.	12	Discarded, no salvage		25,000		
July	17	Purchased for cash	60,000			
Nov.	18	Purchased for cash	35,000		445,500	

ACCUMULATED DEPRECIATION — EQUIPMENT

DATE		ITEM	DEBIT	CREDIT	BALANCE DEBIT	BALANCE CREDIT
19—						
Jan.	1	Balance				75,000
Apr.	12	Equipment discarded	25,000			
Dec.	31	Depreciation for year		36,000		86,000

BUILDINGS

DATE		ITEM	DEBIT	CREDIT	BALANCE DEBIT	BALANCE CREDIT
19—						
Jan.	1	Balance			241,000	
July	1	Acquired with notes payable	190,000		431,000	

ACCUMULATED DEPRECIATION — BUILDINGS

DATE		ITEM	DEBIT	CREDIT	BALANCE DEBIT	BALANCE CREDIT
19—						
Jan.	1	Balance				22,750
Dec.	31	Depreciation for year		8,350		31,100

LAND

DATE		ITEM	DEBIT	CREDIT	BALANCE DEBIT	BALANCE CREDIT
19—						
Jan.	1	Balance			50,000	

LONG-TERM NOTES PAYABLE

DATE		ITEM	DEBIT	CREDIT	BALANCE DEBIT	BALANCE CREDIT
19—						
July	1	Issued 5-year notes		200,000		200,000

DISCOUNT ON LONG-TERM NOTES PAYABLE

DATE		ITEM	DEBIT	CREDIT	BALANCE DEBIT	BALANCE CREDIT
19—						
July	1	Notes issued	10,000		10,000	
Dec.	31	Amortization		850	9,150	

COMMON STOCK, $25 PAR

DATE		ITEM	DEBIT	CREDIT	BALANCE DEBIT	BALANCE CREDIT
19—						
Jan.	1	Balance				600,000
Dec.	10	Stock dividend		18,000		618,000

PREMIUM ON COMMON STOCK

DATE		ITEM	DEBIT	CREDIT	BALANCE DEBIT	BALANCE CREDIT
19—						
Jan.	1	Balance				45,000
Dec.	10	Stock dividend		10,800		55,800

694

APPROPRIATION FOR CONTINGENCIES

DATE		ITEM	DEBIT	CREDIT	BALANCE DEBIT	BALANCE CREDIT
19—						
Jan.	1	Balance				30,000
Dec.	31	Appropriation		20,000		50,000

RETAINED EARNINGS

DATE		ITEM	DEBIT	CREDIT	BALANCE DEBIT	BALANCE CREDIT
19—						
Jan.	1	Balance				198,720
Dec.	10	Stock dividend	28,800			
	31	Net income		135,000		
	31	Cash dividends	36,000			
	31	Appropriated	20,000			248,920

Instructions:

(1) On the basis of the comparative balance sheet and the accounts of Brock & Dolan, Inc., assemble in memorandum form the data needed to prepare a funds statement (working capital concept) for the current year ended December 31. (The gain on the sale of investments was reported on the income statement as an extraordinary item, less applicable income tax.)

(2) Prepare a statement of changes in financial position, including a section for changes in components of working capital.

26-5A. The comparative balance sheet of Brock & Dolan, Inc., and other data necessary for the analysis of the corporation's funds flow are presented in Problem 26-4A.

Instructions:

(1) On the basis of the information presented in Problem 26-4A, assemble in memorandum form the data needed to prepare a funds statement (cash concept) for the current year ended December 31. (Notations prepared for Problem 26-4A that are applicable to this problem need not be repeated.)

(2) Prepare a statement of changes in financial position, including a summary of the change in cash balance.

26-6A. A comparative balance sheet and income statement of Frazer Company, both in condensed form, are presented on the next page.

The following additional information on funds flow during the year was obtained from an examination of the ledger:

(a) Marketable securities were purchased for $45,250 cash.

(b) Investments (long-term) were sold for $100,000 cash, which yielded $91,000 after deducting applicable income tax of $9,000 on the capital gain.

(c) Equipment was purchased for $27,500 cash. There were no disposals.

(d) A building valued at $95,000 and land valued at $5,000 were acquired by a cash payment of $20,000 and issuance of a five-year mortgage note payable for the balance.

(e) Bonds payable of $50,000 were retired by payment of their face amount.

(f) 2,000 shares of common stock were issued for cash at 14.

(g) Cash dividends of $30,000 were declared.

695

Comparative Balance Sheet
December 31, Current and Preceding Year

Assets	Current Year	Preceding Year
Cash.	$ 47,500	$ 24,500
Marketable securities.	45,250	———
Trade receivables (net).	39,900	46,600
Inventories.	120,000	105,400
Prepaid expenses.	2,250	1,750
Investments.	———	70,000
Equipment.	287,500	260,000
Accumulated depreciation — equipment. . . .	(105,400)	(80,750)
Buildings.	285,000	190,000
Accumulated depreciation — buildings.	(60,500)	(53,000)
Land.	35,000	30,000
	$696,500	$594,500

Liabilities and Stockholders' Equity

	Current Year	Preceding Year
Accounts payable (merchandise creditors).	$ 34,000	$ 37,500
Income tax payable.	13,000	6,000
Dividends payable.	7,500	5,000
Mortgage note payable.	80,000	———
Bonds payable.	150,000	200,000
Common stock, $10 par.	270,000	250,000
Premium on common stock.	43,000	35,000
Retained earnings.	99,000	61,000
	$696,500	$594,500

Income Statement
For Current Year Ended December 31

Sales.		$945,000
Cost of goods sold.		667,500
Gross profit on sales.		$277,500
Operating expenses (including depreciation of $32,150).		187,000
Income from operations.		$ 90,500
Interest income.		400
		$ 90,900
Interest expense.		6,900
Income before income tax.		$ 84,000
Income tax.		37,000
Income before extraordinary item.		$ 47,000
Extraordinary item:		
Gain on sale of investments.	$30,000	
Less applicable income tax.	9,000	21,000
Net income.		$ 68,000

Instructions:
(1) Prepare a statement of changes in financial position (working capital concept), including a section for changes in components of working capital.
(2) Prepare a statement of changes in financial position (cash concept), including a summary of the change in cash balance.

Chapter 27

CONSOLIDATED STATEMENTS AND OTHER STATEMENTS

The history of business organization in the United States has been characterized by continuous growth in the size of business entities and the combining of separate enterprises to form even larger operating units. The trend toward combining individual businesses engaged either in similar types of activity or in wholly dissimilar pursuits has been influenced by such objectives as efficiencies of large-scale production, broadening of markets and sales volume, reduction of competition, diversification of product lines, and savings in income taxes.

The methods and procedures employed in combining separate corporations into larger operating units are varied and complex. The discussion that follows is intended to be only of an introductory nature, with particular emphasis on the financial statements of business combinations. Combinations may be effected through a fusion of two or more corporations to form a single unit or through common control of two or more corporations by means of stock ownership.

MERGERS AND CONSOLIDATIONS

When one corporation acquires the properties of another corporation and the latter then dissolves, the fusion of the two enterprises is called a *merger*. Ordinarily all of the assets of the acquired company, as well as its liabilities, are taken over by the acquiring company, which continues its operations as a single unit. Payment may be in the form of cash, obligations, or capital stock of the acquiring corporation, or there may be a combination of several types of consideration. In any event the consideration received by the dissolving corporation is distributed to its stockholders in final liquidation.

When two or more corporations transfer their assets and liabilities to a corporation which has been created for purposes of the take-over, the combination is called a *consolidation*. The new corporation ordinarily issues its own securities in exchange for the properties acquired, and the original corporations are dissolved.

There are many legal, financial, managerial, and accounting problems associated with mergers and consolidations. Perhaps the most crucial matter is the determination of the class and amount of securities to be issued to the owners of the dissolving corporations. In resolving this problem a number of factors are considered, including the relative value of the net assets contributed, the relative earning capacities, and the market prices of the securities of the respective companies. Bargaining between the parties to the combination may also affect the final outcome to a significant degree.

PARENT AND SUBSIDIARY CORPORATIONS

In addition to effecting business combinations through the fusion of previously separate corporations, it has been quite common to achieve similar business objectives through ownership by one corporation of a controlling share of the outstanding voting stock of one or more other corporations. When this method is employed in combining corporate enterprises, none of the participants dissolves; all continue as separate legal entities. The corporation owning all or a majority of the voting stock of another corporation is known as the *parent* company and the corporation that is controlled is known as the *subsidiary* company. Although each corporation maintains its separate legal identity, the relationship between parent and subsidiary is somewhat like that between the home office of an enterprise and one of its branch offices. Two or more corporations closely related through stock ownership are sometimes referred to as *affiliated* or *associated* companies.

The relationship of parent-subsidiary may be accomplished by "purchase" or by a "pooling of interests."[1] When a corporation acquires a controlling share of the voting common stock of another corporation in exchange for cash, other assets, issuance of notes or other debt obligations, or by a combination of the foregoing, the transaction is treated as a purchase; it is accounted for by the *purchase method*. When this method of effecting a parent-subsidiary affiliation is employed, the stockholders of the acquired company transfer their stock to the parent corporation.

Alternatively, when two corporations become affiliated by means of an exchange of voting common stock of one corporation (the parent) for substantially all of the voting common stock of the other corporation (the subsidiary), the transaction is termed a pooling of interests; it is accounted for by the *pooling of interests method*. When this method of

698

---

[1]*Opinions of the Accounting Principles Board, No. 16,* "Business Combinations" (New York: American Institute of Certified Public Accountants, 1970), par. 42.

effecting a parent-subsidiary affiliation is employed, the former stock-holders of the subsidiary become stockholders of the parent company.

The accounting implications of the two affiliation methods are markedly different. The method first described constitutes a "sale-purchase" transaction in contrast to the second method in which there is a "joining of ownership interests" in the two companies.

ACCOUNTING FOR PARENT-SUBSIDIARY AFFILIATIONS

Although the corporations composing a parent-subsidiary affiliation may operate as a single economic unit, they continue to maintain separate accounting records and prepare their own periodic financial reports. The parent corporation employs the equity method of accounting, described on pages 461–462, for its investment in the stock of a subsidiary.

After the parent-subsidiary relationship has been established, the investment account of the parent is periodically increased by its share of the subsidiary's net income and decreased by its share of dividends received from the subsidiary. The balance in the investment account is reported on the parent's balance sheet as a long-term investment, and its share of the subsidiary's net income is reported on the parent's income statement.

In addition to the interrelationship through stock ownership, there are usually other intercorporate transactions which have a reciprocal effect on the financial statements of both the parent and the subsidiary. For example, either may own bonds or other evidences of indebtedness issued by the other and either may purchase or sell commodities or services to the other.

Because of the central managerial control factor and the intertwining of relationships, it is usually considered desirable to present the results of operations and the financial position of a parent company and its subsidiaries as if the group were a single company with one or more branches or divisions. Such statements are likely to be more meaningful to stockholders of the parent company than separate statements for each corporation. However, separate statements are preferable for a subsidiary whose business operations are wholly unlike those of the parent (as when the parent is engaged in manufacturing and the subsidiary is a bank, insurance company, or finance company) or because control over the subsidiary's assets and operations is uncertain (as in a subsidiary located outside the United States subject to foreign government controls).

The financial statements resulting from the combining of parent and subsidiary statements are referred to generally as *consolidated* statements. Specifically, such statements may be identified by the addition of "and subsidiary(ies)" to the name of the parent corporation or by modifica-

699

tion of the title of the respective statement, as in *consolidated balance sheet*, *consolidated income statement*,[2] etc.

BASIC PRINCIPLES OF CONSOLIDATION OF FINANCIAL STATEMENTS

The basic principles applicable to the consolidation of the statements of a parent corporation and its subsidiaries are similar to those described earlier for combining the statements of a home office and its branch offices. The ties of relationship between the separate corporations are evidenced by the reciprocal accounts appearing in their respective ledgers and financial statements. It is necessary to eliminate these reciprocals from the statements that are to be consolidated. The remaining items on the financial statements of the subsidiaries are then combined with the like items on the financial statements of the parent.

Unlike the relationship between a home office and its branch offices, the intercompany accounts of a parent and its subsidiaries may not be entirely reciprocal in amount. Disparities may be caused by the manner in which the parent-subsidiary relationship was created, by the extent of the parent's ownership of the subsidiary, or by the nature of their subsequent intercompany transactions. Such factors must be considered when consolidating the financial statements of affiliated corporations.

700

Affiliation by purchase. When a parent-subsidiary affiliation is effected as a purchase, the parent corporation is deemed to have purchased all or a major portion of the subsidiary corporation's net assets. Accordingly, the assets of the subsidiary should be reported on the consolidated balance sheet at their cost to the parent, as measured by the amount of the consideration given in acquiring the stock. Such cost is likely to differ from the amounts reported on the subsidiary's balance sheet. The disparity between the two amounts must be given recognition on the consolidated balance sheet.

Income from an investment in assets does not accrue to an investor until after the assets have been purchased. Therefore, subsidiary company earnings accumulated prior to the date of the parent-subsidiary purchase affiliation must be excluded from the consolidated balance sheet and the income statement. Only those earnings of the subsidiary realized subsequent to the affiliation are includable in the consolidated statements.

Affiliation effected as a pooling of interests. When a parent-subsidiary affiliation is effected as a pooling of interests, the ownership of the two companies is joined together in the parent corporation. Consequently, no change is required in the amounts at which the subsidiary's assets should be stated in the consolidated balance sheet; they are reported as they appear in the subsidiary's separate balance sheet.

---

[2]Examples of consolidated statements are presented in Appendix C.

In accordance with the concept of continuity of ownership interests, earnings accumulated prior to the affiliation should be combined with those of the parent on the consolidated balance sheet. It is as though there had been a single economic unit from the time the enterprises had begun.

CONSOLIDATED BALANCE SHEET — PURCHASE METHOD

The stock of a subsidiary purchased by the parent is recorded at cost in an investment account in the parent company's ledger. The reciprocal of the investment account in the subsidiary's ledger at the date of acquisition is the composite of all of its stockholders' equity accounts. Attention will first be directed to consolidating the balance sheets immediately after the relationship of parent and subsidiary has been established. The illustrative companies will be identified merely as Parent and Subsidiary.

Consolidation at date of acquisition. In order to direct attention more effectively to the basic concepts, most of the data appearing in financial statements will be omitted from the illustrations and the term "net assets" will be used as a substitute for the specific assets and liabilities that appear on the balance sheet. Explanations will also be simplified by using the term "book equity" in referring to the monetary amount of the stockholders' equity of the subsidiary acquired by the parent.

Wholly owned subsidiary acquired at a cost equal to book equity. Assume that Parent creates Subsidiary, transferring to it $120,000 of assets and $20,000 of liabilities, and taking in exchange 10,000 shares of $10 par common stock of Subsidiary. The effect of the transaction on Parent is to replace net assets of $100,000 with a single item: Investment in Subsidiary, $100,000. This effect on the balance sheet of Parent, together with the balance sheet of Subsidiary prepared immediately after the transaction, is depicted below.

	Assets	Capital
PARENT:		
Investment in subsidiary, 10,000 shares..............	$100,000	
SUBSIDIARY:		
Net assets......................................	$100,000	
Common stock, 10,000 shares, $10 par..............		$100,000

In consolidating the balance sheets of the two corporations, the reciprocal accounts Investment in Subsidiary and Common Stock are offset against each other, or eliminated. The individual assets (Cash, Equipment, etc.) and the individual liabilities (Accounts payable, etc.) comprising the $100,000 of net assets on the balance sheet of Subsidiary are then added to the corresponding items on the balance sheet of Parent. The consolidated balance sheet is completed by listing Parent's capital stock and other paid-in capital balances, and retained earnings.

Wholly owned subsidiary acquired at a cost above book equity. Instead of organizing a subsidiary corporation, a corporation may acquire an established business by purchasing the stock of an existing company. In such cases the cost of the stock to the parent company ordinarily differs from the book equity of the stock. To illustrate, assume that Parent acquires for $180,000 all of the outstanding stock of Subsidiary, a going concern, from Subsidiary's stockholders. Assume further that the capital, or stockholders' equity, of Subsidiary is composed of 10,000 shares of $10 par common stock and retained earnings of $50,000. Parent records the investment at its cost of $180,000, regardless of the amount of the book equity of Subsidiary. It should also be noted that the $180,000 paid to subsidiary's stockholders has no effect on the assets, liabilities, or capital of Subsidiary. The situation immediately after the transaction may be presented as follows:

	Assets	Capital
PARENT:		
Investment in subsidiary, 10,000 shares..............	$180,000	
SUBSIDIARY:		
Net assets.......................................	$150,000	
Common stock, 10,000 shares, $10 par..............		$100,000
Retained earnings................................		50,000

It is readily apparent that the reciprocal items on the separate balance sheets differ by $30,000. If the reciprocals were eliminated, as in the preceding illustration, and were replaced solely by Subsidiary's net assets of $150,000, the consolidated balance sheet would obviously be out of balance.

If the additional amount above book equity paid by Parent for Subsidiary's stock was attributable to an excess of fair value over book value of Subsidiary's assets, the values of the appropriate assets should be revised upward by $30,000. However, if the additional amount paid for the stock was attributable to Subsidiary's high earning power, the $30,000 should be reported on the consolidated balance sheet as "Goodwill." When there are elements of both factors, the excess of cost over book equity should be allocated accordingly.[3] For combinations effected prior to the directives of APB Opinion No. 16, it is customary to describe the excess of cost over book equity on consolidated balance sheets as "Excess of cost of businesses acquired over related net assets," or a variant with similar meaning.

Wholly owned subsidiary acquired at a cost below book equity. When all of the stock of a corporation is acquired from its stockholders at a cost which is less than book equity, the situation is the reverse of that described in the preceding section. For purposes of illustration, assume that the stock in Subsidiary is acquired for $130,000 and that the composition of

702

---

[3]*Opinions of the Accounting Principles Board, No. 16, op. cit.,* par. 87.

the capital of Subsidiary is the same as in the preceding illustration. Parent records the investment at its cost of $130,000. The situation immediately after the transaction is as follows:

	ASSETS	CAPITAL
PARENT:		
Investment in subsidiary, 10,000 shares..............	$130,000	
SUBSIDIARY:		
Net assets......................................	$150,000	
Common stock, 10,000 shares, $10 par..............		$100,000
Retained earnings................................		50,000

Elimination of the reciprocal accounts and reporting the $150,000 of net assets of Subsidiary on the consolidated balance sheet creates an imbalance of $20,000. The possible reasons for the apparent "bargain" purchase are somewhat the reverse of those given in explaining acquisition at a price higher than book equity.

In actuality a "bargain" purchase is highly unlikely. The more logical view is that the assets of Subsidiary are overvalued. Regardless of the circumstances, the net assets acquired should be reported on the consolidated balance sheet at their cost to Parent. Accordingly, the fair value of Subsidiary's assets should be determined. If the excess of the $20,000 overvaluation is not wholly absorbed, the remainder should be prorated among all of the noncurrent assets except any long-term investments with a readily determinable market value. If this procedure should reduce such noncurrent assets to zero without fully absorbing the remaining overvaluation, the remainder should be listed on the consolidated balance sheet as a deferred credit.[4] The amount should be identified as "Excess of fair value of net assets over cost of investment in subsidiary," or a variant with similar meaning.

Partially owned subsidiary acquired at a cost above or below book equity. When one corporation seeks to achieve control over another by purchase of its stock, it is not necessary and often not feasible to acquire all of the stock. To illustrate this situation, assume that Parent acquires 80% of the 10,000 shares of $10 par common stock of Subsidiary, whose total stockholders' equity is $180,000. The 8,000 shares are purchased from the stockholders of Subsidiary at a total cost of $190,000. The relevant data immediately after the acquisition of the stock are presented below.

	ASSETS	CAPITAL
PARENT:		
Investment in subsidiary, 8,000 shares...............	$190,000	
SUBSIDIARY:		
Net assets......................................	$180,000	
Common stock, 10,000 shares, $10 par..............		$100,000
Retained earnings................................		80,000

The explanation of the $10,000 imbalance in the reciprocal items in this illustration is more complex than in the preceding two illustrations.

703

---

[4]*Ibid.*, par. 91.

Parent acquired 8,000 shares, or 80%, of the 10,000 outstanding shares of Subsidiary, hence only 80% of the stockholders' equity accounts of Subsidiary can be eliminated. The remaining 20% of the stock is owned by outsiders, who are referred to collectively as *minority interest*. The partial elimination of Subsidiary's common stock and retained earnings and the determination of the amount of the minority interest are computed as follows:

SUBSIDIARY:

Common stock....................................	$100,000	
Eliminate 80% of Subsidiary stock...............	80,000	$ 20,000
Retained earnings.................................	$ 80,000	
Eliminate 80% of Subsidiary retained earnings.....	64,000	16,000
Minority interest.....................................		$ 36,000

The minority interest of $36,000, which is the amount of Subsidiary's book equity allocable to outsiders, is reported on the consolidated balance sheet, usually preceding the stockholders' equity accounts of Parent.

The difference between the $190,000 paid by Parent for the stock of Subsidiary and the book equity acquired is determined as follows:

PARENT:

Investment in subsidiary..........................	$190,000	
Eliminate 80% of Subsidiary stock...............	$ 80,000	
Eliminate 80% of Subsidiary retained earnings.....	64,000	
Excess of cost over book equity of Subsidiary interest......		$ 46,000

The excess cost of $46,000 is reported on the consolidated balance sheet as goodwill or is absorbed by increased valuations of other assets, as explained earlier.

In the foregoing analysis it should be noted that the two eliminations from the stockholders' equity accounts of Subsidiary ($80,000 and $64,000) are exactly matched by the two eliminations from Parent's investment account.

Consolidation subsequent to acquisition. Subsequent to acquisition of a subsidiary, a parent company's investment account is increased periodically for its share of the subsidiary's earnings and decreased for the related dividends received. Correspondingly, the retained earnings account of the subsidiary will be increased periodically by the amount of its net income and reduced by dividend distributions. Because of these periodic changes in the balances of the reciprocal accounts, the eliminations required in preparing a consolidated balance sheet will change each year.

To illustrate consolidation of balance sheets subsequent to acquisition, assume that Subsidiary in the preceding illustration earned net income of $50,000 and paid dividends of $20,000 during the year subsequent to Parent's acquisition of 80% of its stock. The net effect of the year's transactions on Subsidiary were as follows:

SUBSIDIARY:	NET ASSETS	COMMON STOCK	RETAINED EARNINGS
Date of acquisition......................	$180,000	$100,000	$ 80,000
Add net income........................	50,000		50,000
Deduct dividends......................	(20,000)		(20,000)
Date subsequent to acquisition.............	$210,000	$100,000	$110,000

The effect of Subsidiary's operations on Parent's investment account is a net increase of $24,000, as indicated by the following entries to record 80% of Subsidiary's net income and dividends:

Parent:

Investment in Subsidiary.............................	40,000	
Income of Subsidiary.............................		40,000
Cash...	16,000	
Investment in Subsidiary...........................		16,000

The net effect of the foregoing entries on Parent's investment account is to increase the balance by $24,000. Details of the account are as follows:

PARENT:

Investment in subsidiary, 8,000 shares

Date of acquisition.......................................	$190,000
Add 80% of Subsidiary's net income.......................	40,000
Deduct 80% of Subsidiary's dividends.....................	(16,000)
Date subsequent to acquisition............................	$214,000

Continuing the illustration, the eliminations from the partially reciprocal accounts and determination of the amounts to be reported on the consolidated balance sheet are as follows:

SUBSIDIARY:

Common stock......................................	$100,000	
Eliminate 80% of Subsidiary stock.................	80,000	$ 20,000
Retained earnings....................................	$110,000	
Eliminate 80% of Subsidiary retained earnings......	88,000	22,000
Minority interest......................................		$ 42,000

PARENT:

Investment in subsidiary............................	$214,000	
Eliminate 80% of Subsidiary stock................	$ 80,000	
Eliminate 80% of Subsidiary retained earnings......	88,000	
Excess of cost over book equity of Subsidiary interest........		$ 46,000

In comparing the above computations with the analysis as of the date of acquisition (page 704), note (1) that the minority interest increased by $6,000 ($36,000 to $42,000) which is equivalent to 20% of the $30,000 net increase in Subsidiary's retained earnings and (2) that the excess of cost over book equity of the subsidiary interest remained unchanged at $46,000. For the sake of simplicity, it is assumed that the $46,000 excess had not been assigned to goodwill or to other assets subject to depreciation or amortization.[5]

CONSOLIDATED BALANCE SHEET — POOLING OF INTERESTS METHOD

When a parent-subsidiary affiliation is effected by a pooling of interests, the parent corporation deems its investment in the subsidiary to be equal to the carrying amount of the subsidiary's net assets. Any disparity that may exist between such carrying amount and the fair value of the subsidiary's assets does not affect the amount recorded as the investment.

The credit to the parent company's capital accounts for the stock issued in exchange for the subsidiary company's stock corresponds, of course, to the amount debited to the investment account. In addition to the common stock account, the paid-in capital accounts may be affected, as well as the retained earnings account.

The fundamental principles involved in effecting a pooling of interests and the consolidation of the related balance sheets are illustrated in the subsections immediately following. Inasmuch as poolings must involve substantially all (90% or more)[6] of the stock of the subsidiary, the illustration will assume an exchange of 100% of the stock. In practice it may be necessary to pay cash for fractional shares or for shares of the subsidiary held by dissenting stockholders.

Consolidation at date of affiliation. To illustrate the procedure for consolidating the balance sheets of two corporations by the pooling of interests method, their respective financial positions immediately prior to the exchange of stock are assumed to be as follows:

	Assets	Capital
PARENT:		
Net assets....................................	$230,000	
Common stock, 20,000 shares, $5 par..............		$100,000
Retained earnings................................		130,000
SUBSIDIARY:		
Net assets....................................	$150,000	
Common stock 10,000 shares, $10 par..............		$100,000
Retained earnings................................		50,000

It is assumed further that the fair value of the net assets of both companies is greater than the amounts reported above and that there appears

---

[5]Any portion of the excess of cost over book equity assigned to goodwill must be amortized in accordance with *Opinions of the Accounting Principles Board, No. 17*, "Intangible Assets," issued in 1970. Similarly, any excess of cost over book equity assigned to plant assets of limited life must be gradually reduced by depreciation. The application of such amortization and depreciation techniques to consolidated statements goes beyond the scope of the discussion here.

[6]*Opinions of the Accounting Principles Board, No. 16, op. cit.*, par. 47b.

to be an element of goodwill in both cases. Based on recent price quotations for the common stock of each it is agreed that for purposes of the issuance of Parent's stock for Subsidiary's stock the former is to be valued at $9 a share and the latter at $18 a share. In accordance with the agreement Parent issues 20,000 shares of its $5 par stock, valued at $180,000, to Subsidiary's stockholders for the 10,000 shares of Subsidiary's $10 par stock, also valued at $180,000. The additional $30,000 value assigned to the net assets of Subsidiary may be ignored and the investment recorded as follows:

Parent:

Investment in Subsidiary.........................	150,000	
Common Stock.................................		100,000
Retained Earnings.............................		50,000

After the foregoing entry has been recorded, the basic balance sheet data of the two companies are as follows:

	ASSETS	CAPITAL
PARENT:		
Investment in subsidiary, 10,000 shares...............	$150,000	
Other net assets...................................	230,000	
Common stock, 40,000 shares, $5 par...............		$200,000
Retained earnings.................................		180,000
SUBSIDIARY:		
Net assets..	$150,000	
Common stock, 10,000 shares, $10 par..............		$100,000
Retained earnings.................................		50,000

707

To consolidate the balance sheets of the two companies, Parent's investment account and Subsidiary's common stock and retained earnings accounts are eliminated. The net assets of the two companies ($230,000 and $150,000) are then combined without any changes in valuation and consolidated capital is composed of common stock and retained earnings ($200,000 and $180,000).

Consolidation subsequent to affiliation. The equity method is employed by the parent corporation in recording changes in its investment account subsequent to acquisition. Thus the account is increased by the subsidiary's earnings and decreased by its dividends. Continuing the illustration of the preceding section, assume that Subsidiary's net income and dividends paid during the year subsequent to affiliation with Parent are $20,000 and $5,000 respectively. After Parent has recorded Subsidiary's net income and dividends, the relevant account balances are as follows:

	ASSETS	CAPITAL
PARENT:		
Investment in subsidiary, 10,000 shares...............	$165,000	
SUBSIDIARY:		
Net assets..	$165,000	
Common stock, 10,000 shares, $10 par..............		$100,000
Retained earnings.................................		65,000

In consolidating the balance sheets of the affiliated corporations, the reciprocal accounts are eliminated and the $165,000 of net assets of Subsidiary are combined with those of Parent.

CONSOLIDATED INCOME STATEMENT AND OTHER STATEMENTS

Consolidation of income statements and other statements of affiliated companies usually presents fewer complexities than those encountered in balance sheet consolidations. The difference is largely because of the inherent nature of the statements. The balance sheet reports cumulative effects of all transactions from the very beginning of an enterprise to a current date, whereas the income statement, the retained earnings statement, and the statement of changes in financial position are restricted to selected transactions only and are for a limited period of time, usually a year.

The principles applicable to the consolidation of the income statements of a parent and its subsidiaries are the same, regardless of whether the affiliation is deemed to be a purchase or a pooling of interests. The consolidation is accomplished primarily by combining the amounts of sales, cost of goods sold, operating expenses, and other revenues and expenses reported on the income statements of the affiliated corporations. All amounts resulting from intercompany transactions, such as management fees or interest on loans charged by one affiliate to another, must be eliminated. Any intercompany profit included in inventories must also be eliminated in determining consolidated gross profit. The eliminations required in consolidating the retained earnings statement and any other statements are based largely on data assembled in consolidating the balance sheet and the income statement.

ALTERNATIVE FORMS OF PRINCIPAL FINANCIAL STATEMENTS[7]

Conventional forms of the principal financial statements were described and illustrated in earlier chapters. There are many possible variations in the general format of such statements as well as differences in terminology employed and the extent to which details are presented. Some of the variations in the form of published statements are described and illustrated in the sections that follow.

Financial position form of balance sheet. The arrangement of assets on the left-hand side of the statement, with the liabilities and stockholders' equity on the right-hand side, is the traditional and still the customary form of the balance sheet. If the entire statement is confined to a single page, it is customary to present the three sections in a downward sequence with the total of the assets section equaling the combined

[7]Examples of some of the alternative forms described in this section are presented in Appendix C.

totals of the other two sections. Two variations from the customary forms are encountered with sufficient frequency to justify brief consideration. Both are sometimes referred to as the *financial position* or *financial condition* form of the balance sheet. In one of the variations the total of the liabilities section is subtracted from the total of the assets section to yield stockholders' equity. The other variant emphasizes the working capital position of an enterprise by deducting current liabilities from current assets. The illustration below was severely condensed to focus attention on its principal features. Such condensation is not an essential characteristic of the form.

Electronic Products, Inc.
Statement of Financial Position
September 30, 19--

Current assets		$420,600
Deduct:		
Current liabilities.		180,400
Working capital.		$240,200
Add:		
Investments	$150,000	
Plant assets (net).	522,300	672,300
Total assets less current liabilities.		$912,500
Deduct:		
Long-term liabilities.		200,000
Net assets		$712,500
Stockholders' equity:		
Common stock, $10 par.		$400,000
Retained earnings.		312,500
Total stockholders' equity		$712,500

709

Financial position
form of
balance sheet

In addition to the specific disclosure of the amount of working capital, the financial position form presents the amount of the excess of total assets over current liabilities and the amount of the excess of total assets over total liabilities. The balancing amounts in the statement are thus the net assets and the total stockholders' equity. The principal advantage claimed for this form is its emphasis on working capital, which is a significant factor in judging financial stability. A major criticism is its failure to present the total of the assets and the total of the liabilities.

Single-step form of income statement. The *single-step* form of income statement derives its name from the fact that the total of all expenses is deducted from the total of all revenues. This is in contrast to the multiple-step form, which contains conventional groupings of items, with intermediate balances, before concluding with the net income balance. A single-step form of income statement, severely condensed, is illustrated at the top of the next page.

Electronic Products, Inc.
Income Statement
For Year Ended September 30, 19--

Revenues:		
Sales		$940,000
Interest income		27,500
Total revenues		$967,500
Expenses:		
Cost of merchandise sold	$530,000	
Selling expenses	146,800	
General expenses	120,400	
Interest expense	10,500	
Income tax	70,200	
Total expenses		877,900
Net income (per share, $2.24)		$ 89,600

Single-step form of income statement

The use of the single-step form, in many cases varying slightly from the illustration, has steadily increased during the past two decades. It has the advantage of simplicity and also emphasizes total revenues and total expenses as the determinants of net income. The most common variation from the form illustrated is to present income tax as a separate deduction from income. If there are extraordinary items to be reported, they should also be shown in a separate last section. The arrangement of the additional sections may be identical to the format illustrated on page 429 for a multiple-step statement. An objection to the single-step form is that such relationships as gross profit to sales and operating income to sales are not as readily determinable as when the conventional groupings and intermediate balances are shown.

Combined income and retained earnings statement. It is not unusual to add the analysis of retained earnings at the bottom of the income statement to form a *combined* income and retained earnings statement. The income statement portion of the combined statement may be presented either in multiple-step form or in a single-step form, as in the illustration at the top of the next page.

The combined statement form emphasizes net income as the connecting link between the income statement and the retained earnings portion of the stockholders' equity and thus facilitates understanding by the reader. A possible criticism of the combined statement is the fact that net income, a very significant figure, is buried in the body of the statement. If a portion of retained earnings is appropriated for various purposes, or if there have been other increases or decreases of an unusual nature, separate statements may be preferable.

MONEY AS A UNIT OF MEASUREMENT

The effects of business transactions are recorded in the accounts of an enterprise in terms of money. Because of the homogeneity of money and

Electronic Products, Inc.
Income and Retained Earnings Statement
For Year Ended September 30, 19--

Revenues:		
Sales.	$940,000	
Interest income.	27,500	
Total revenues	$967,500	
Expenses:		
Cost of merchandise sold.	$530,000	
Selling expenses.	146,800	
General expenses.	120,400	
Interest expense.	10,500	
Income tax.	70,200	
Total expenses.		877,900
Net income (per share, $2.24).		$ 89,600
Retained earnings, October 1, 19--.		262,900
		$352,500
Deduct cash dividends declared.		40,000
Retained earnings, September 30, 19--.		$312,500

Combined
income and
retained earnings
statement

its use as a standard of value, it is the only practicable medium for recording and reporting financial data. A balance sheet containing only detailed descriptions of inventories and plant assets would impart information of scant usefulness. Furthermore, such statements would be lacking in qualities of comparability, either between different points in time or between different enterprises.

It was noted in an earlier chapter that as a means of measurement money lacks the stability of the standards used in measuring time and the weight, dimensions, and other physical properties of matter. The dollar is an abstraction that has relevance only when related to a particular level of prices.

An early attempt to recognize the effects of inflation in the accounts proved to be unacceptable. During the inflationary period 1920–29 many corporations revised their plant asset accounts to bring them up to their appraised value. The offsetting credits to stockholders' equity accounts were identified by such titles as "Appraisal Capital" and "Revaluation Capital." Most of the appraisal write-ups were subsequently reversed during the severe deflationary period that followed.

The problems created by increasing price levels in planning for the replacement of inventories and plant assets have been described in earlier chapters. The use of the lifo method of inventory determination and of accelerated depreciation methods provide some relief, particularly through income tax reductions. The accompanying increase in the amount of funds available to an enterprise is advantageous, but such devices are only partial solutions. They do not resolve the financial reporting problems.

711

EFFECT OF CHANGES IN PRICE LEVEL

Changes in price level may also be viewed as changes in purchasing power. An increase in the general price level (inflationary trend) is equivalent to a decrease in the purchasing power of money. Conversely, if the general price level decreases (deflationary trend), there is an equivalent increase in the purchasing power of money.

Changes in the general price level do not affect all assets and liabilities in the same manner. For discussion purposes it is helpful to classify all balance sheet items as either *monetary* or *nonmonetary*.

Monetary assets are composed of cash and all claims which are to be settled in cash such as accounts receivable, notes receivable, and bonds receivable. Monetary liabilities include virtually all debts, such as accounts payable, notes payable, and bonds payable, because settlement is usually to be made in cash. Monetary assets and liabilities are determined by law or contract and consequently remain fixed in terms of dollars regardless of changes in the price level.

Nonmonetary assets are composed of all assets that are not classified as monetary, such as inventories, plant assets, patents, and investments in stocks. Nonmonetary assets change with changes in the price level. The ownership equity of a business enterprise (stockholders, partners, or a sole proprietor) fluctuates in accordance with the change in nonmonetary assets. The discussion and illustrations that follow are inflation oriented; the effects and conclusions indicated would be reversed, of course, if a deflationary period were assumed.

Monetary items. Changes in price levels produce purchasing power gains or losses in monetary assets and liabilities. A long-term note will be used to illustrate the effect of an increase in general price level on monetary items, first as an asset (note receivable) and then as a liability (note payable). Assume that ten years ago a $100,000 ten-year note receivable was acquired in connection with a sale of property, that the note is now due, and is paid in full.[8] Inasmuch as the number of dollars received is exactly the same as the number of dollars loaned, it might appear that the lender has been restored to his original position (i.e., ten years earlier). This would be the case only if there had been no change in the general price level between the date of the note and the date of its repayment. If a 50% increase in price level between the two dates is assumed, the holder of the note has incurred a *price-level loss* of $50,000 during the period. The amount of the loss is measured by the difference between the amount needed to maintain the original purchasing power, which is $150,000 (150% of $100,000) and $100,000, the actual amount of money received.

_____

[8]To simplify the illustration the periodic interest payments will be excluded from consideration.

It is evident that the effect of the assumed change in price level on the debtor would be the reverse of the effect on the creditor. During the ten-year period the purchasing power of the $100,000 originally owed had increased to $150,000 but only $100,000 was needed to satisfy the obligation; hence, a *price-level gain* of $50,000 was realized.

Although conventional accounting on a historical-dollar basis does not give formal recognition to price-level gains or losses, they are a factor to be considered in business planning. Generalizations that may be derived from the foregoing illustration, assuming an inflationary trend, are as follows:

1. Ownership of monetary assets tends to result in price-level losses.
2. Maintenance of liabilities tends to result in price-level gains.

Nonmonetary items. Changes in price levels do not produce gains or losses in nonmonetary assets and liabilities. To illustrate the effect of an increase in price level on a nonmonetary asset, assume that ten years ago a plot of unimproved land was purchased as a speculation for $10,000. Assume also, as in the preceding illustration, that during the period the general price level has increased by 50%. The present cost of the land in terms of current dollars is therefore $15,000 (150% of $10,000). The $5,000 increase from the original investment of $10,000 to the present equivalent cost of $15,000 is not in any sense a realized gain.

Furthermore, it cannot be said that the land is worth $15,000 in the usual sense of "worth," nor is there any certainty that it can be sold for $15,000. This particular plot of land, influenced by local real estate developments, by population growth, by economic conditions in the area, etc., might be appraised at far in excess of $15,000 or even at far below $10,000. The price at which the land could be sold currently is irrelevant, however, within our frame of reference. The concern is solely with the conversion of acquisition cost of a nonmonetary asset from historical (original) dollars to equivalent current dollars, thereby giving recognition to the change in the purchasing power of the dollar.

Nonmonetary liabilities are composed of unearned revenues, such as advances received on sales contracts and liabilities for rent collected in advance. Nonmonetary liabilities are relatively rare in comparison with nonmonetary assets.

To generalize from the illustration, conversion of the cost of nonmonetary assets and liabilities from historical dollars to current dollars gives recognition to the changing value of the dollar, without recognition of gain or loss.

PRICE-LEVEL INDEXES

The changes in price level referred to in the preceding section were based on assumptions. In order to prepare financial statements that recognize changes in price levels, it is necessary to know the direction and extent of the change. Price-level data are systematically collected by governmental agencies and converted into price-level indexes. The differing opinions as to which of several such indexes most accurately measures the movement of the general price level need not concern us here. It is sufficient merely to note that some indexes are broader in scope than others and that it is a "general" price-level index rather than a "specific" index, such as the price-level index for fuel oil, that should be used.

A price-level index is a ratio of the total price of a group of commodities prevailing at a particular time to the total price of the same group of commodities at a selected base period. The prices at the base period time are assigned a value of 100 and the indexes for all other items or periods are expressed as a ratio to 100. For example, if the composite cost of a selected group of commodities amounted to $2,000 for the base period and $2,200 for a later period, the index for the base period would be 100 and for the later period it would be 110 (2,200 ÷ 2,000 × 100). The manner in which a price-level index is used to convert the cost of nonmonetary assets from original dollars to dollars of another time is demonstrated below, based on the following index:

YEAR	INDEX
19X 1	100
19X 2	103
19X 8	140
19X 9	143
19X10	150

The dollars expended for a nonmonetary asset can be converted to equivalent dollars at a later period by use of a multiplier in which the index for the later period is the numerator and the index for the earlier period is the denominator. Thus if the hypothetical plot of land in the preceding example had been acquired in 19X 1, the monetary equivalent in 19X 8 can be determined as follows:

$$\frac{(19X\ 8)}{(19X\ 1)}\ \frac{140}{100} \times \$10,000 = \$14,000$$

Determination of the equivalent dollars in 19X10 can be based either (1) on the $14,000 obtained above or (2) on the $10,000 of original cost, as follows:

$$(1)\ \frac{(19X10)}{(19X\ 8)}\ \frac{150}{140} \times \$14,000 = \$15,000,\ \text{or}$$

$$(2)\ \frac{(19X10)}{(19X\ 1)}\ \frac{150}{100} \times \$10,000 = \$15,000$$

PRESENTATION OF GENERAL PRICE-LEVEL FINANCIAL INFORMATION

In 1953 a committee of the AICPA considered the possibility of introducing price-level adjustments to plant assets reported in financial statements. Although the proposal was rejected, the committee stated that it "gives its full support to the use of supplementary financial schedules, explanations or footnotes by which management may explain the need for retention of earnings" (in the face of rising general price levels and the related problems of asset replacement).[9]

Discussions by the Accounting Principles Board of the AICPA of the effects on accounting of price-level changes, beginning in 1960, led to a thoroughgoing study of the problem which ultimately resulted in a 278-page publication.[10] Based on the conclusions of this study and additional investigations and discussions, the Accounting Principles Board issued a 72-page statement in 1969 describing the problem and recommending guidelines for preparing general price-level statements.[11]

The position taken relative to the necessity of presenting price-level financial statements is as follows:

> The Board believes that general price-level financial statements or pertinent information extracted from them present useful information not available from basic historical-dollar financial statements. General price-level information may be presented in addition to the basic historical-dollar financial statements, but general price-level financial statements should not be presented as the basic statements. The Board believes that general price-level information is not required at this time for fair presentation of financial position and results of operations in conformity with generally accepted accounting principles in the United States.[12]

715

There appears to be little likelihood that price-level financial statements will replace historical-cost statements in the foreseeable future, if ever. However, it is quite possible that the use of separate schedules or charts and narrative explanations related to price-level changes may become commonplace. Thus far relatively few companies in the United States have seen fit to include in their published reports details of the effects of inflation on operations and financial position. Of the annual reports of 600 industrial and commercial corporations included in a recent survey, none presented financial statements adjusted for changes in the general price level. However, references to economic price-level

---

[9]*Accounting Research and Terminology Bulletins, Final Edition,* "No. 43, Restatement and Revision of Accounting Research Bulletins" (New York: American Institute of Certified Public Accountants, 1961), Chapter 9A, par. 17.

[10]*Reporting the Financial Effects of Price-Level Changes,* Accounting Research Study No. 6 (New York: American Institute of Certified Public Accountants, 1963).

[11]*Statement of the Accounting Principles Board, No. 3,* "Financial Statements Restated for General Price-Level Changes" (New York: American Institute of Certified Public Accountants, 1969).

[12]*Ibid.,* par. 25.

changes or inflation were included in the annual reports of 68 of the corporations.[13]

The references and brief discussions touched on various aspects of inflation-related problems, including advances in wage rates, increases in costs and expenses generally, necessity of increasing prices of the products manufactured, and inadequacy of depreciation charges based on historical cost. The following excerpt is from a recent annual report of a manufacturer of heavy equipment:

> The generally accepted accounting principle followed with respect to buildings, machinery, and equipment is the systematic allocation to each year's operations of a portion of the *original* cost of these facilities. The plant assets currently in use were acquired over many years at price levels which were lower than current price levels. The portion of the original cost of these assets allocated to each year and used in determining profit was, therefore, substantially lower than if a provision had been made on the current replacement price levels.

The discussion of the merits and techniques of reporting the effect of price-level changes on financial statements is likely to continue as long as inflation is a material factor in management decisions and government policies. Whether presenting readers of financial statements with additional complexities in the form of supplemental statements would be helpful or only increase their perplexities is also subject to debate.

QUESTIONS

1. If Corporation A acquires the assets and assumes the liabilities of Corporation B and the latter is then dissolved, is the combination termed a *merger* or a *consolidation*?

2. What terms are applied to the following: (a) a corporation that owns a controlling interest in the voting stock of another corporation; (b) a corporation that is controlled by another corporation through ownership of a controlling interest in its stock; (c) a group of corporations related through stock ownership?

3. What are the two methods by which the relationship of parent-subsidiary may be accomplished?

4. Parent Corporation owns 90% of the outstanding common stock of Subsidiary Corporation, which has no preferred stock. Net income of Subsidiary for the year was $100,000 and cash dividends declared and paid during the year amounted to $40,000. What entries should be made by Parent to record its share of Subsidiary's (a) net income and (b) dividends? (c) What is the amount of the net increase in the equity of the remaining 10% stock interest? (d) What is the term applied to the remaining 10% interest?

---

[13]*Accounting Trends and Techniques, 1972* (New York: American Institute of Certified Accountants, 1972), p. 66.

5. Parent Corporation purchases for $2,000,000 the entire outstanding common stock of Subsidiary. What type of accounts on Subsidiary's balance sheet are reciprocal to the investment account on Parent's balance sheet?

6. Are the eliminations of the reciprocal accounts in consolidating the balance sheets of Parent and Subsidiary in Question 5 recorded in the respective ledgers of the two companies?

7. Parent purchased from stockholders the entire outstanding stock of Subsidiary for a total of $3,900,000 in cash. At the date of acquisition Subsidiary had $400,000 of liabilities and total stockholders' equity of $3,300,000. (a) As of the acquisition date what was the total amount of Subsidiary's assets? (b) As of the acquisition date what was the amount of Subsidiary's net assets? (c) What is the amount of difference between the investment account and the book equity of the subsidiary interest acquired by Parent?

8. What is the possible explanation of the difference determined in Question 7 (c) and how will it affect the reporting of the difference on the consolidated balance sheet?

9. (a) If in Question 7 Parent had paid only $2,600,000 for Subsidiary's stock, what would the difference in part (c) have been? (b) How would it be treated in preparing a consolidated balance sheet as of the date of acquisition?

10. At the close of the fiscal year the amount of notes receivable and notes payable reported on the respective balance sheets of a parent and its wholly owned subsidiary are as follows:

	Parent	Subsidiary
Notes Receivable.....	$145,000	$60,000
Notes Payable.......	80,000	35,000

If $40,000 of Subsidiary's notes receivable are owed by Parent, determine the amount of notes receivable and notes payable to be reported on the consolidated balance sheet.

11. Sales and purchases of merchandise by a parent corporation and its wholly owned subsidiary during the year were as follows:

	Parent	Subsidiary
Sales.............	$3,000,000	$600,000
Purchases.........	1,800,000	400,000

If $200,000 of the sales of Parent were made to Subsidiary, determine the amount of sales and purchases to be reported on the consolidated income statement.

12. The relationships of parent and subsidiary were established by the transactions described below. Identify each as a "purchase" or a "pooling of interests."

(a) Company A receives 90% of the voting common stock of Company B in exchange for cash.
(b) Company A receives 100% of the voting common stock of Company B in exchange for cash and long-term bonds payable.
(c) Company A receives 95% of the voting common stock of Company B in exchange for voting common stock of Company A.
(d) Company A receives 75% of the voting common stock of Company B in exchange for voting common stock of Company A.

13. Which of the following procedures for consolidating the balance sheet of a parent and wholly owned subsidiary are characteristic of acquisition of control by purchase and which are characteristic of a pooling of interests? (a) Assets are not revalued. (b) Retained earnings of subsidiary at date of acquisition are eliminated. (c) Goodwill may be recognized. (d) Retained earnings of subsidiary at date of acquisition are combined with retained earnings of parent.

14. On June 30, Penfield Corp. issued 10,000 shares of its $10 par common stock, with a total market value of $140,000, to the stockholders of Sunray, Inc., in exchange for all of Sunray's common stock. Penfield Corp. records its investment at $110,000. The net assets and stockholders' equities of the two companies just prior to the affiliation are summarized below.

	Penfield Corp.	Sunray Inc.
Net assets........	$190,000	$110,000
Common stock....	$180,000	$ 80,000
Retained earnings.	10,000	30,000
	$190,000	$110,000

(a) At what amounts would the following be reported on the consolidated balance sheet as of June 30, applying the pooling of interests method: (1) Net assets, (2) Retained earnings?

(b) Assume that, instead of issuing shares of stock, Penfield Corp. had given $140,000 in cash and long-term notes. At what amounts would the following be reported on the consolidated balance sheet as of June 30: (1) Net assets, (2) Retained earnings?

15. How does the financial position form of balance sheet differ from a conventional balance sheet?

16. What two financial statements are frequently combined and presented as a single statement?

17. What effect does a general increase in the price level have on the purchasing power of the dollar?

18. Classify the following as monetary items or nonmonetary items: (a) Cash, (b) Investment in common stock, (c) Bonds payable, (d) Accounts receivable, (e) Plant asset.

19. Explain the meaning of "price-level index."

20. Does a price-level gain or loss result from (a) holding cash and receivables or (b) from maintaining liabilities during a period of inflation?

21. Six hundred shares of common stock of MFG Corporation were purchased for $40,000 at a time when the price-level index was 100. Six years later the price-level index is 120 and the market price of the six hundred shares is $55,000. (a) If the stock is sold for $55,000, how much gain would be considered to be realized according to conventional accounting? (b) How much of the gain may be attributed to a change in price level? (c) How much of the gain may be considered a true gain in terms of current dollars?

EXERCISES

27-1. On the last day of the fiscal year, Pioneer Company purchased 80% of the common stock of Shawnee Company for $350,000, at which time Shawnee Company reported the following on its balance sheet: assets, $580,000; liabilities, $170,000; common stock, $10 par, $300,000; retained earnings, $110,000. In negotiating the stock sale, it was determined that the book carrying amounts of Shawnee's recorded assets and equities approximated their current market values.

(a) Indicate for each of the following the section, title of the item, and amount to be reported on the consolidated balance sheet as of the date of acquisition:

(1) Difference between cost and book equity of subsidiary interest.
(2) Minority interest.

(b) During the following year Pioneer Company realized net income of $650,000, exclusive of the income of the subsidiary, and Shawnee Company realized net income of $100,000. In preparing a consolidated income statement for the year, in what amounts would the following be reported:

(1) Minority interest's share of net income.
(2) Consolidated net income.

27-2. On December 31 of the current year Peerless Corporation purchased 90% of the stock of Sanders Corporation. The data reported on their separate balance sheets immediately after the acquisition are reported below. The fair value of Sanders Corporation's assets correspond to their book carrying amounts, except for equipment, which is valued at $175,000. Prepare a consolidated balance sheet as of that date, in report form, omitting captions for current assets, plant assets, etc.

Assets	Peerless Corporation	Sanders Corporation
Cash.	$ 22,000	$ 8,000
Accounts receivable (net)	35,000	21,000
Inventories	143,000	46,000
Investment in Sanders Corporation	250,000	———
Equipment (net)	400,000	165,000
	$850,000	$240,000
Liabilities and Stockholders' Equity		
Accounts payable	$ 50,000	$ 13,000
Common stock, $10 par	500,000	150,000
Retained earnings	300,000	77,000
	$850,000	$240,000

27-3. As of December 31 of the current year, Paramount Corporation exchanged 10,000 shares of its $10 par common stock for the 4,000 shares of Saginaw Corporation $25 par common stock held by Saginaw stockholders. The separate balance sheets of the two corporations immediately after the exchange of shares are presented at the top of the next page. Prepare a consolidated balance sheet as of December 31, in report form, omitting captions for current assets, plant assets, etc.

Assets	Paramount Corporation	Saginaw Corporation
Cash.	$ 27,000	$ 11,000
Accounts receivable (net).	40,000	26,000
Inventories.	148,000	51,000
Investment in Saginaw Corporation.	187,000	——
Equipment (net).	385,000	132,000
	$787,000	$220,000
Liabilities and Stockholders' Equity		
Accounts payable.	$ 61,000	$ 33,000
Common stock.	460,000	100,000
Retained earnings.	266,000	87,000
	$787,000	$220,000

27-4. The results of operations of Carter Corporation and its wholly owned subsidiary, Duncan Enterprises, for the current year ended June 30 are presented below. During the year Carter sold merchandise to Duncan for $70,000; the merchandise was sold by Duncan to nonaffiliated companies for $100,000. Carter's interest income was realized from a long-term loan to Duncan.

	Carter Corporation		Duncan Enterprises	
Sales.		$620,000		$300,000
Cost of goods sold.	$420,000		$190,000	
Selling expenses.	75,000		30,000	
General expenses.	60,000		40,000	
Interest income.	(8,000)		——	
Interest expense.	——	547,000	8,000	268,000
		$ 73,000		$ 32,000

(a) Prepare a consolidated income statement for the current year for Carter and its subsidiary. Use the single-step form and disregard income taxes.

(b) If none of the merchandise sold by Carter to Duncan had been sold during the year to nonaffiliated companies, and assuming that Carter's cost of the merchandise had been $50,000, determine the amounts that would have been reported on the consolidated income statement for the following items:

(1) Sales, (2) Cost of goods sold, (3) Net income.

27-5. Summary financial data for the Maxwell Corporation at December 31 of the current year are as follows: common stock, no par, $140,000; current assets, $200,000; current liabilities, $110,000; investments, $35,000; long-term liabilities, $50,000; plant assets (net), $195,000; and retained earnings, $130,000.

(a) Prepare a financial position form of balance sheet disclosing the amount of working capital.

(b) What is the advantage and disadvantage of this form of balance sheet?

27-6. Summary operating data for the H. F. Conrad Company during the current year ending December 31 are as follows: cost of goods sold, $240,000; general expenses, $50,000; income tax, $28,000; interest expense, $12,000; rent income, $15,000; sales, $410,000; and selling expenses, $65,000. At December 31, there were 20,000 shares of $25 par common stock outstanding.

(a) Prepare a single-step income statement, listing income tax as an item in the expenses section.
(b) What advantage and disadvantage does the single-step income statement have in comparison to the multiple-step statement?

27-7. Convert the account balances listed below to current price-level equivalents according to each of the following assumptions:
(a) The price-level index at the time the assets were acquired was 90 and currently it is 120.
(b) The price-level index at the time the assets were acquired was 120 and currently it is 90.

Account Balances

Investments in common stock.	$ 36,000
Building.	240,000
Accumulated depreciation. . . .	30,000
Land.	25,200

PROBLEMS

The following additional problems for this chapter are located in Appendix B: 27-1B, 27-3B, 27-4B, 27-5B.

721

27-1A. On June 30 Peptone Corporation purchased 90% of the outstanding stock of Sigman Company for $475,000. Balance sheet data for the two corporations immediately after the transaction are presented below.

Assets	Peptone Corp.	Sigman Co.
Cash and marketable securities.	$ 50,700	$ 35,700
Accounts receivable.	85,000	57,500
Allowance for doubtful accounts.	(3,000)	(2,000)
Inventories.	345,800	187,800
Investment in Sigman Company stock.	475,000	————
Equipment and building.	600,800	337,400
Accumulated depreciation.	(170,300)	(70,400)
Land.	60,000	32,000
	$1,444,000	$578,000

Liabilities and Stockholders' Equity		
Accounts payable.	$ 146,800	$ 67,800
Income tax payable.	89,600	30,200
Bonds payable (due in 1990).	300,000	————
Common stock, $10 par.	700,000	————
Common stock, $5 par.	————	400,000
Retained earnings.	207,600	80,000
	$1,444,000	$578,000

Instructions:

(1) Prepare in report form a detailed consolidated balance sheet as of the date of acquisition. The fair value of Sigman Company's assets

are deemed to correspond to their book carrying amounts, except for land, which is to be increased by $18,000.

(2) Assuming that Sigman Company earns net income of $80,000 and pays cash dividends of $30,000 during the ensuing fiscal year and that Peptone Corporation records its share of the earnings and dividends, determine the following as of the end of the year:

(a) The net amount added to Peptone Corporation's investment account as a result of Sigman Company's earnings and dividends.

(b) The amount of the minority interest.

27-2A. Several years ago Porter Corporation purchased 9,000 of the 10,000 outstanding shares of stock of Sutton Company. Since the date of acquisition, Porter Corporation has debited the investment account for its share of the subsidiary's earnings and has credited the account for dividends declared. Balance sheet data for the two corporations as of November 30 of the current year appear below. Sutton Company holds $30,000 of short-term notes of Porter Corporation, on which there is accrued interest of $1,500. Sutton Company owes Porter Corporation $15,000 for a management advisory fee for the second half of the year. It has been recorded by both corporations in their respective accounts payable and accounts receivable accounts.

Assets	Porter Corp.	Sutton Co.
Cash..	$ 62,800	$ 28,000
Notes receivable..............................	20,000	35,000
Accounts receivable...........................	137,500	44,300
Interest receivable...........................	900	1,800
Dividends receivable..........................	4,500	———
Inventories...................................	199,340	93,200
Prepaid expenses..............................	3,600	2,000
Investment in Sutton Co. stock, 9,000 shares...	233,860	———
Equipment and building........................	440,000	135,000
Accumulated depreciation......................	(141,000)	(40,000)
Land..	40,000	30,000
	$1,001,500	$329,300

Liabilities and Stockholders' Equity		
Notes payable.................................	$ 35,000	———
Accounts payable..............................	82,400	$ 40,700
Income tax payable............................	21,000	8,200
Dividends payable.............................	13,500	5,000
Interest payable..............................	1,600	———
Common stock, $25 par.........................	450,000	———
Common stock, $10 par.........................	———	100,000
Premium on common stock.......................	———	50,000
Retained earnings.............................	398,000	125,400
	$1,001,500	$329,300

Instructions:

Prepare in report form a detailed consolidated balance sheet as of November 30 of the current year. The excess of book equity in Sutton Company over the balance of the Porter Corporation's investment account is attributable to overvaluation of Sutton Company's land.

27-3A. On January 1 of the current year Pence Corporation exchanged 35,000 shares of its $10 par common stock for 12,000 shares (the entire issue) of Shilling Company's $20 par common stock. Later in the year Shilling Company purchased from Pence Corporation $50,000 of its $200,000 issue of bonds payable, at face amount. All of the items for "interest" appearing on the balance sheets and income statements of both corporations are related to the bonds.

During the year Pence Corporation sold finished goods with a cost of $120,000 to Shilling Company for $150,000, all of which was sold by Shilling Company before the end of the year.

Pence Corporation has correctly recorded the income and dividends reported for the year by Shilling Company. Data for the balance sheets of both companies as of the end of the current year and for their income statements for the current year are presented below.

BALANCE SHEET DATA

Assets	Pence Corp.	Shilling Co.
Cash.....................................	$ 69,000	$ 24,700
Accounts receivable (net).................	84,200	52,600
Dividends receivable.....................	12,000	——
Interest receivable.......................	——	2,000
Inventories..............................	416,000	196,000
Investment in Shilling Co. stock, 12,000 shares.	440,100	——
Investment in Pence Corp. bonds, at face amount.	——	50,000
Plant and equipment......................	584,000	224,400
Accumulated depreciation.................	(97,000)	(46,800)
	$1,508,300	$502,900

Liabilities and Stockholders' Equity		
Accounts payable.........................	$ 95,200	$ 46,800
Income tax payable.......................	10,000	4,000
Dividends payable........................	17,500	12,000
Interest payable..........................	8,000	——
Bonds payable, 8% (due in 1983)...........	200,000	——
Common stock, $10 par...................	700,000	——
Common stock, $20 par...................	——	240,000
Premium on common stock................	——	60,000
Retained earnings........................	477,600	140,100
	$1,508,300	$502,900

INCOME STATEMENT DATA

Revenue:		
Sales.....................................	$1,470,000	$520,000
Income of subsidiary.....................	79,300	——
Interest income..........................	——	2,000
	$1,549,300	$522,000
Expenses:		
Cost of goods sold........................	$ 955,500	$310,000
Selling expenses..........................	130,000	40,000
General expenses.........................	98,000	32,000
Interest expense..........................	8,000	——
Income tax...............................	131,000	60,700
	$1,322,500	$442,700
Net income...............................	$ 226,800	$ 79,300

723

Instructions:

(1) Determine the amounts to be eliminated from the following items in preparing the consolidated balance sheet as of December 31 of the current year: (a) Dividends receivable and dividends payable; (b) Interest receivable and interest payable; (c) Investment in Shilling Co. stock and stockholders' equity; (d) Investment in Pence Corp. bonds and bonds payable.

(2) Prepare a detailed consolidated balance sheet in report form.

(3) Determine the amounts to be eliminated from the following items in preparing the consolidated income statement for the current year ended December 31: (a) Sales and cost of goods sold; (b) Interest income and interest expense; (c) Income of subsidiary and net income.

(4) Prepare a single-step consolidated income statement, inserting the earnings per share as a parenthetical notation on the same line with net income.

(5) Determine the amount of the reduction in consolidated inventories, net income, and retained earnings if Shilling Company's inventory had included $40,000 of the finished goods purchased from Pence Corporation.

27-4A. The balances in the accounts of Apex, Inc., after adjustment at September 30, the close of the current fiscal year, are as follows:

Accounts Payable		$ 62,400
Accounts Receivable	$ 76,200	
Accumulated Depreciation — Buildings		20,700
Accumulated Depreciation — Equipment		37,900
Allowance for Doubtful Accounts		4,000
Bond Sinking Fund	46,500	
Bonds Payable (due 1985)		100,000
Buildings	65,500	
Cash Dividends	28,000	
Cash in Bank	50,300	
Common Stock, $5 par		200,000
Cost of Goods Sold	248,500	
Dividends Payable		7,000
Equipment	152,700	
General Expenses	41,400	
Income Tax	48,800	
Income Tax Payable		6,000
Interest Expense	6,000	
Interest Income		4,500
Inventories	144,600	
Land	47,500	
Prepaid Insurance	3,700	
Retained Earnings		103,500
Sales		473,500
Salaries Payable		3,100
Selling Expenses	62,900	
	$1,022,600	$1,022,600

The number of shares of stock outstanding remained unchanged during the year.

Instructions:
(1) Prepare a combined income and retained earnings statement using the single-step form, listing income tax as an item in the expenses section. Insert the earnings per share as a parenthetical notation on the same line with net income.
(2) Prepare a detailed balance sheet in financial position form, disclosing the amount of working capital.

27-5A. The balances of selected ledger accounts of an enterprise as of the end of the year are listed below. The price level at the beginning of the year was 110 and at the end of the year it was 132. The marketable securities, which are stated at cost, are common stocks purchased at the beginning of the year. Merchandise inventory is stated at cost, employing the fifo flow assumption. It is assumed to have been acquired when the price level index was 121, midway between the beginning and end of the year. The equipment was acquired a number of years ago, at which time the price level index was 100.

Account Title	Account Balance
Cash....................	$15,200
Marketable Securities.....	20,400
Accounts Receivable......	28,800
Merchandise Inventory....	33,000
Equipment..............	76,500
Accumulated Depreciation.	37,000
Accounts Payable.........	52,000

Instructions:
(1) Convert the account balances to current price-level equivalents as of the end of the period, presenting the details indicated by the following captions:

Account Title	Account Balance	Conversion Multiplier	Converted Balance

(2) Determine the price-level gain or loss during the year on each of the monetary items, assuming that the account balances were the same at the beginning and end of the year.

725

Chapter 28

FINANCIAL STATEMENT ANALYSIS

NEED FOR ANALYSIS

The financial condition and the results of operations of business enterprises are of interest to various groups, including owners, managers, creditors, governmental agencies, employees, and prospective owners and creditors. The principal statements, together with supplementary statements and schedules, present much of the basic information needed to form opinions and to make decisions regarding the business.

Most of the items in these statements are of limited significance when considered individually. Users of financial statements often gain a clearer picture through studying relationships and comparisons of items (1) within a single year's financial statements, (2) in a succession of financial statements, and (3) with other enterprises. The selection and the preparation of analytical aids are a part of the work of the accountant.

It will be readily recognized that particular aspects of financial condition or of operations are of greater significance to some interested groups than to others. In general, all groups are interested in the ability of a business to pay its debts as they come due and to earn a reasonable amount of income. These two aspects of the status of an enterprise are sometimes referred to as factors of *solvency* and *profitability* respectively. An enterprise that cannot meet its obligations to its creditors on a timely basis is likely to experience difficulty in obtaining credit, which may lead to a diminution in its profitability. Similarly, an enterprise whose earnings are comparatively less than those of its competitors is likely to be at a disadvantage in obtaining credit or new capital from stockholders. In addition to keeping in mind this interrelationship between solvency and profitability, it is important to recognize that analysis of historical data is useful in assessing both the past performance of an enterprise and in forecasting its future performance.

Earlier chapters have included references to several types of financial analysis. For example, break-even analysis, gross profit analysis, and the statement of changes in financial position were all forms of analysis. In this chapter, additional types of financial analysis will be discussed.

BASIC ANALYTICAL PROCEDURES

The analytical measures obtained from financial statements are usually expressed as ratios or percentages. For example, the relationship of $150,000 to $100,000 ($150,000/$100,000 or $150,000:$100,000) may be expressed as 1.5, 1.5:1, or 150%.

Analytical procedures may be used to compare the amount of specific items on a current statement with the corresponding amounts on earlier statements. For example, in comparing cash of $150,000 on the current balance sheet with cash of $100,000 on the balance sheet of a year earlier, the current amount may be expressed as 1.5 or 150% of the earlier amount. The relationship may also be expressed in terms of change, that is, the increase of $50,000 may be stated as a 50% increase.

Analytical procedures are also widely used to indicate relationships of individual items to each other and of individual items to totals on a single statement. To illustrate, assume that included in the total of $1,000,000 of assets on a balance sheet are cash appearing at $50,000 and inventories at $250,000. In relative terms, the cash balance is 5% of total assets and the inventories represent 25% of total assets. Individual items in the current asset group could also be related to total current assets. Assuming that the total of current assets in the example is $500,000, cash represents 10% of the total and inventories represent 50% of the total.

It should be noted that increases or decreases in items may be expressed in percentage terms only when the base figure is positive. If the base figure is zero or a negative value, the amount of change cannot be expressed as a percentage. For example, if comparative balance sheets indicate no liability for notes payable on the first, or base, date and a liability of $10,000 on the later date, the increase of $10,000 cannot be stated as a percent of zero. Similarly, if a net loss of $10,000 in a particular year is followed by a net income of $5,000 in the succeeding year, the increase of $15,000 cannot be stated as a percent of the loss of the base year.

In the discussion and the illustrations of analytical procedures that follow, the basic significance of the various measures will be emphasized. It should be borne in mind that the measures developed are not ends in themselves; they are only guides to the evaluation of financial and operating data. Many other factors, such as trends in the industry, changes in price levels, and general economic conditions and prospects may also need consideration in arriving at sound conclusions.

727

HORIZONTAL ANALYSIS

The percentage analysis of increases and decreases in corresponding items in comparative financial statements is sometimes referred to as *horizontal analysis*. The amount of each item on the most recent statement is compared with the corresponding item on one or more earlier statements. The increase or the decrease in the amount of the item is then listed, together with the percent of increase or decrease. When the comparison is made between two statements, the earlier statement is used as the base. If the analysis includes three or more statements, there are two alternatives in the selection of the base: the earliest date or period may be used as the basis for comparing all subsequent dates or periods, or each statement may be compared with the immediately preceding statement. The two alternatives are illustrated below.

BASE: EARLIEST YEAR

				INCREASE OR DECREASE*			
				1972–73		1972–74	
ITEM	1972	1973	1974	AMOUNT	PERCENT	AMOUNT	PERCENT
A	$100,000	$150,000	$200,000	$ 50,000	50%	$100,000	100%
B	100,000	200,000	150,000	100,000	100%	50,000	50%

BASE: PRECEDING YEAR

				INCREASE OR DECREASE*			
				1972–73		1973–74	
ITEM	1972	1973	1974	AMOUNT	PERCENT	AMOUNT	PERCENT
A	$100,000	$150,000	$200,000	$ 50,000	50%	$ 50,000	33%
B	100,000	200,000	150,000	100,000	100%	50,000*	25%*

Comparison of the amounts in the last two columns of the first analysis with the amounts in the corresponding columns of the second analysis reveals the effect of the base year on the direction of change and the amount and percent of change.

A condensed comparative balance sheet for two years, with horizontal analysis, is presented at the top of the next page.

The significance of the various increases and decreases cannot be fully determined without additional information. Although total assets at the end of 1974 were $91,000 (7.4%) less than at the beginning of the year, liabilities were reduced by $133,000 (30%) and capital increased $42,000 (5.3%.) It would appear that the reduction of $100,000 in long-term liabilities was accomplished, for the most part, through the sale of long-term investments. A statement of changes in financial condition would, of course, provide more definite information about the changes in the composition of the balance sheet items.

The foregoing balance sheet may be expanded to include the details of the various categories of assets and liabilities, or the details may be

Martin Company
Comparative Balance Sheet
December 31, 1974 and 1973

	1974	1973	INCREASE OR DECREASE*	
			AMOUNT	PERCENT
Assets				
Current assets...............	$ 550,000	$ 533,000	$ 17,000	3.2%
Long-term investments........	95,000	177,500	82,500*	46.5%*
Plant assets (net).............	444,500	470,000	25,500*	5.4%*
Intangible assets.............	50,000	50,000	——	
Total assets.................	$1,139,500	$1,230,500	$ 91,000*	7.4%*
Liabilities				
Current liabilities.............	$ 210,000	$ 243,000	$ 33,000*	13.6%*
Long-term liabilities..........	100,000	200,000	100,000*	50.0%*
Total liabilities..............	$ 310,000	$ 443,000	$133,000*	30.0%*
Stockholders' Equity				
Preferred 6% stock, $100 par...	$ 150,000	$ 150,000	——	——
Common stock, $10 par.......	500,000	500,000	——	——
Retained earnings............	179,500	137,500	$ 42,000	30.5%
Total stockholders' equity......	$ 829,500	$ 787,500	$ 42,000	5.3%
Total liab. & stockholders' equity	$1,139,500	$1,230,500	$ 91,000*	7.4%*

presented on separate schedules. Opinions differ as to which method presents the clearer picture. The form of supporting schedules is illustrated by the following comparative schedule of current assets with horizontal analysis:

729

Martin Company
Comparative Schedule of Current Assets
December 31, 1974 and 1973

	1974	1973	INCREASE OR DECREASE*	
			AMOUNT	PERCENT
Cash......................	$ 90,500	$ 64,700	$ 25,800	39.9%
Marketable securities.........	75,000	60,000	15,000	25.0%
Accounts receivable (net)......	115,000	120,000	5,000*	4.2%*
Merchandise inventory........	264,000	283,000	19,000*	6.7%*
Prepaid expenses.............	5,500	5,300	200	3.8%
Total current assets..........	$550,000	$533,000	$ 17,000	3.2%

The changes in the composition of the current assets would appear to be favorable, particularly in view of the increase in sales shown on the income statement illustrated on the next page. The reduction in accounts receivable may have come about through changes in credit terms or improved collection policies. Similarly, a reduction in the merchandise inventory during a period of increased sales probably indicates an improvement in management of inventory.

A comparative income statement and a comparative retained earnings statement with horizontal analysis appear on pages 730 and 731. Examination of the income statement reveals an increase of 24.8% in

Martin Company
Comparative Income Statement
For Years Ended December 31, 1974 and 1973

	1974	1973	INCREASE OR DECREASE* AMOUNT	PERCENT
Sales......................	$ 1,530,500	$ 1,234,000	$ 296,500	24.0%
Sales returns and allowances....	32,500	34,000	1,500*	4.4%*
Net sales...................	$ 1,498,000	$ 1,200,000	$ 298,000	24.8%
Cost of merchandise sold.......	1,043,000	820,000	223,000	27.2%
Gross profit on sales...........	$ 455,000	$ 380,000	$ 75,000	19.7%
Selling expenses..............	$ 191,000	$ 147,000	$ 44,000	29.9%
General expenses.............	104,000	97,400	6,600	6.8%
Total operating expenses......	$ 295,000	$ 244,400	$ 50,600	20.7%
Operating income...........	$ 160,000	$ 135,600	$ 24,400	18.0%
Other income................	8,500	11,000	2,500*	22.7%*
	$ 168,500	$ 146,600	$ 21,900	14.9%
Other expense................	6,000	12,000	6,000*	50.0%*
Income before income tax......	$ 162,500	$ 134,600	$ 27,900	20.7%
Income tax..................	71,500	58,100	13,400	23.1%
Net income.................	$ 91,000	$ 76,500	$ 14,500	19.0%

net sales. An increase in sales, considered alone, is not necessarily favorable. The increase in sales was accompanied by a somewhat greater percentage increase in the cost of merchandise sold, which indicates a narrowing of the gross profit margin. Selling expenses increased markedly and general expenses increased slightly, making an overall increase in operating expenses of 20.7% as contrasted with a 19.7% increase in gross profit.

Obviously, the increase in operating income and in the final net income figure is favorable. It would be erroneous for the management to conclude, however, that its operations were at maximum efficiency. A study of fixed and variable expenses and additional analysis and comparisons of individual expense accounts should be made.

The income statement illustrated is in condensed form. Such a condensed statement ordinarily provides sufficient information for all interested groups except management. If desired, the statement may be expanded or supplemental schedules may be prepared to present details of the cost of merchandise sold, selling expenses, general expenses, other income, and other expenses.

Martin Company
Comparative Retained Earnings Statement
For Years Ended December 31, 1974 and 1973

	1974	1973	INCREASE OR DECREASE* AMOUNT	PERCENT
Retained earnings, Jan. 1......	$ 137,500	$ 100,000	$ 37,500	37.5%
Net income for year..........	91,000	76,500	14,500	19.0%
Total......................	$ 228,500	$ 176,500	$ 52,000	29.5%
Dividends:				
On preferred stock..........	$ 9,000	$ 9,000	——	——
On common stock..........	40,000	30,000	$ 10,000	33.3%
Total....................	$ 49,000	$ 39,000	$ 10,000	25.6%
Retained earnings, Dec. 31.....	$ 179,500	$ 137,500	$ 42,000	30.5%

VERTICAL ANALYSIS

Percentage analysis may also be used to show the relationship of the component parts to the total in a single statement. This type of analysis is sometimes called *vertical analysis*. As in horizontal analysis, the statements may be prepared in either detailed or condensed form. In the latter case, additional details may be presented in supporting schedules. Although the analysis is confined within each individual statement, the significance of both the amounts and the percents is increased by preparing comparative statements. A condensed comparative balance sheet, with vertical analysis, is presented below.

731

Martin Company
Comparative Balance Sheet
December 31, 1974 and 1973

	1974 AMOUNT	1974 PERCENT	1973 AMOUNT	1973 PERCENT
Assets				
Current assets................	$ 550,000	48.3%	$ 533,000	43.3%
Long-term investments........	95,000	8.3	177,500	14.4
Plant assets (net).............	444,500	39.0	470,000	38.2
Intangible assets..............	50,000	4.4	50,000	4.1
Total assets.................	$ 1,139,500	100.0%	$ 1,230,500	100.0%
Liabilities				
Current liabilities.............	$ 210,000	18.4%	$ 243,000	19.7%
Long-term liabilities..........	100,000	8.8	200,000	16.3
Total liabilities..............	$ 310,000	27.2%	$ 443,000	36.0%
Stockholders' Equity				
Preferred 6% stock...........	$ 150,000	13.2%	$ 150,000	12.2%
Common stock...............	500,000	43.9	500,000	40.6
Retained earnings............	179,500	15.7	137,500	11.2
Total stockholders' equity......	$ 829,500	72.8%	$ 787,500	64.0%
Total liab. & stockholders' equity	$ 1,139,500	100.0%	$ 1,230,500	100.0%

Each asset item is stated as a percent of total assets, and each liability and stockholders' equity item is stated as a percent of total liabilities and stockholders' equity. The major relative changes in assets were in the current asset and long-term investment groups. In the lower half of the balance sheet the greatest relative change was in long-term liabilities and retained earnings. Stockholders' equity increased from 64% of total liabilities and stockholders' equity at the close of 1973 to 72.8% at the close of 1974, with a corresponding decrease in the claims of creditors. Supporting schedules may be prepared to provide additional details of the changes in the various categories. If supporting schedules are prepared, the percentage analysis may be based on either the total of the schedule or the balance sheet total.

In vertical analysis of the income statement, each item is stated as a percent of net sales. A condensed comparative income statement, with vertical analysis, appears below.

Care must be used in judging the significance of differences between percentages for the two years. For example, the decline of the gross profit rate from 31.7% in 1973 to 30.4% in 1974 is only 1.3%. In terms of dollars of potential gross profit, however, it represents a decline of approximately $19,000 (1.3% × $1,498,000).

Martin Company
Comparative Income Statement
For Years Ended December 31, 1974 and 1973

	1974		1973	
	AMOUNT	PERCENT	AMOUNT	PERCENT
Sales....................	$ 1,530,500	102.2%	$ 1,234,000	102.8%
Sales returns and allowances....	32,500	2.2	34,000	2.8
Net sales.................	$ 1,498,000	100.0%	$ 1,200,000	100.0%
Cost of merchandise sold.......	1,043,000	69.6	820,000	68.3
Gross profit on sales..........	$ 455,000	30.4%	$ 380,000	31.7%
Selling expenses.............	$ 191,000	12.8%	$ 147,000	12.3%
General expenses............	104,000	6.9	97,400	8.1
Total operating expenses......	$ 295,000	19.7%	$ 244,400	20.4%
Operating income............	$ 160,000	10.7%	$ 135,600	11.3%
Other income..............	8,500	.6	11,000	.9
	$ 168,500	11.3%	$ 146,600	12.2%
Other expense..............	6,000	.4	12,000	1.0
Income before income tax......	$ 162,500	10.9%	$ 134,600	11.2%
Income tax.................	71,500	4.8	58,100	4.8
Net income.................	$ 91,000	6.1%	$ 76,500	6.4%

COMMON-SIZE STATEMENTS

Horizontal and vertical analyses with both dollar and percentage figures are helpful in disclosing relationships and trends in financial condition and operations of individual enterprises. Vertical analysis with both dollar and percentage figures is also useful in comparing one company with another or with industry averages. Such comparisons may be facilitated by the use of *common-size* statements, in which all items are expressed only in relative terms (percentages of a common base).

Common-size statements may be prepared to compare percentages of a current date or period with past dates or periods, to compare individual businesses, or to compare one business with industry percentages published by trade associations and financial information services. A comparative common-size income statement for two enterprises is presented below. Examination of the statement reveals that although Martin Company has a slightly higher rate of gross profit than Grant Corporation, the advantage is more than offset by its higher percentage of both selling and general expenses. As a consequence the operating income of Martin Company is 10.7% of net sales as compared with 14.4% for Grant Corporation, an unfavorable difference of 3.7%.

733

Martin Company and Grant Corporation
Condensed Common-Size Income Statement
For Year Ended December 31, 1974

	MARTIN COMPANY	GRANT CORPORATION
Sales..	102.2%	102.3%
Sales returns and allowances....................	2.2	2.3
Net sales......................................	100.0%	100.0%
Cost of merchandise sold.......................	69.6	70.0
Gross profit on sales...........................	30.4%	30.0%
Selling expenses...............................	12.8%	11.5%
General expenses..............................	6.9	4.1
Total operating expenses.......................	19.7%	15.6%
Operating income..............................	10.7%	14.4%
Other income..................................	.6	.6
	11.3%	15.0%
Other expense.................................	.4	.5
Income before income tax......................	10.9%	14.5%
Income tax....................................	4.8	5.5
Net income...................................	6.1%	9.0%

OTHER ANALYTICAL MEASURES

In addition to the percentage analyses discussed above, there are a number of other relationships that may be expressed in ratios and percentages. The items used in the measures are taken from the accounting statements of the current period and hence are a further development of vertical analysis. Comparison of the items with corresponding measures of earlier periods constitutes an extension of horizontal analysis.

Some of the most significant and commonly used ratios are discussed in the sections that follow, the examples being based on the illustrative statements presented earlier. In a few instances, data from the hypothetical company's statements of the preceding year are also used.

CURRENT POSITION ANALYSIS

To be useful, ratios must express significant relationships. One such relationship is the expression of the company's ability to meet its currently maturing debts. This expression or analysis is referred to as *current position* analysis. This analysis is of particular interest to short-term creditors.

Working capital. The excess of the current assets of an enterprise over its current liabilities at a particular moment of time is referred to as *working capital*. The absolute amount of working capital and the flow of working capital during a period of time as reported by a statement of changes in financial position are often used in evaluating a company's ability to meet currently maturing obligations. Although useful for making intraperiod comparisons for a company, these absolute amounts are difficult to use in comparing companies of different sizes or in comparing such amounts with industry figures. For example, working capital of $100,000 may be very adequate for a small building contractor specializing in residential construction, but it may be completely inadequate for a large building contractor specializing in industrial and commercial construction.

Current ratio. Another means of expressing the relationship between current assets and current liabilities is through the *current ratio*, sometimes referred to as the *working capital ratio* or *bankers' ratio*. The ratio is computed by dividing the total of current assets by the total of current liabilities. The determination of working capital and the current ratio is illustrated below.

	1974	1973
Current assets.	$550,000	$533,000
Current liabilities.	210,000	243,000
Working capital.	$340,000	$290,000
Current ratio.	2.6:1	2.2:1

The current ratio is a more dependable indication of solvency than is working capital. To illustrate, assume that as of December 31, 1974 the working capital of a competing corporation is substantially greater than $340,000 but that its current ratio is only 1.3:1. Considering these factors alone, the Martin Company, with its current ratio of 2.6:1 is in a more favorable position to obtain short-term credit than the corporation with the greater amount of working capital.

Acid-test ratio. The amount of working capital and the current ratio are two indicators of a company's ability to meet currently maturing obligations. However, these two measures do not take into account the composition of the various items making up the current assets. To illustrate the significance of this additional factor, the current position data for two hypothetical companies are presented below.

	ALBERT CORPORATION	BAILEY COMPANY
Current assets		
Cash......................................	$ 200,000	$ 550,000
Marketable securities......................	100,000	100,000
Receivables (net).........................	200,000	200,000
Inventories..............................	800,000	450,000
Total current assets....................	$1,300,000	$1,300,000
Current liabilities........................	650,000	650,000
Working capital.........................	$ 650,000	$ 650,000
Current ratio...........................	2:1	2:1

735

Both companies have working capital of $650,000 and a current ratio of 2 to 1. But the ability of the two companies respectively to meet their currently maturing debts is vastly different. Albert Corporation has a large portion of its current assets in inventories, which must be sold and the receivables collected before the current liabilities can be paid in full. A considerable amount of time may be required to convert these inventories into cash in the normal operating processes. Declines in market prices and a reduction in demand could also impair the ability to pay current liabilities. Bailey Company has almost enough cash on hand to meet its current liabilities.

A ratio that measures the "instant" debt-paying ability of a company is called *acid-test ratio* or *quick ratio*. It is the ratio of the sum of cash, receivables, and marketable securities, which are sometimes called *quick assets*, to current liabilities. The computation of the acid-test ratio of Martin Company is presented on the next page.

A thorough analysis of a firm's current position would include the determination of the amount of working capital, the current ratio, and the acid-test ratio. These ratios are most useful when viewed together and when compared with similar ratios for previous periods and with those of other firms in the industry.

	1974	1973
Quick assets		
Cash...	$ 90,500	$ 64,700
Marketable securities............................	75,000	60,000
Receivables (net)...............................	115,000	120,000
Total.......................................	$280,500	$244,700
Current liabilities................................	$210,000	$243,000
Acid-test ratio	1.3:1	1.0:1

ACCOUNTS RECEIVABLE ANALYSIS

The magnitude and composition of accounts receivable change continually during business operations. The amount is increased by sales on account and reduced by collections. Firms that grant long credit terms tend to have relatively greater amounts tied up in accounts receivable than those granting short credit terms. Increases or decreases in the volume of sales also affect the amount of outstanding accounts.

Accounts receivable yield no revenue, hence it is desirable to keep the amount invested in them at a minimum. The cash made available by prompt collection of receivables may be employed to reduce bank loans and thus yield a saving of interest, to purchase merchandise in larger quantities at a lower price, to pay dividends, or for other purposes. Prompt collection also reduces the risk of loss from uncollectible accounts.

Accounts receivable turnover. The relationship between credit sales and accounts receivable may be stated as the *accounts receivable turnover*. It is computed by dividing net sales on account by the average net accounts receivable. It is preferable to base the average on monthly balances, which gives effect to seasonal fluctuations. When such data are not available, it is necessary to use the average of the balances at the beginning and the end of the year. If there are trade notes receivable as well as accounts, the two should be combined. The data used in computing the accounts receivable turnover are presented below. All sales were made on account.

	1974	1973
Net sales on account............................	$1,498,000	$1,200,000
Accounts receivable (net):		
Beginning of year..............................	$ 120,000	$ 140,000
End of year....................................	115,000	120,000
Total..	$ 235,000	$ 260,000
Average.......................................	$ 117,500	$ 130,000
Accounts receivable turnover....................	12.7	9.2

The increase in the accounts receivable turnover for Martin Company for 1974 indicates that there has been an acceleration in the collection of receivables, due perhaps to improvement in either the granting of credit or the collection practices employed, or both.

Number of days' sales in receivables. Another means of expressing the relationship between credit sales and accounts receivable is the *number of days' sales in receivables.* This measure is determined by dividing the accounts receivable at the end of the year by the average daily sales on account (net sales on account divided by 365), which is illustrated below.

	1974	1973
Accounts receivable, end of year................	$ 115,000	$ 120,000
Net sales on account.........................	$1,498,000	$1,200,000
Average daily sales on account.................	$ 4,104	$ 3,288
Number of days' sales in receivables...........	28.0	36.5

The number of days' sales in receivables gives a rough measure of the length of time the accounts receivable have been outstanding. A comparison of this measure with the credit terms, with figures for comparable firms in the same industry, and with figures of Martin Company for prior years will help reveal the efficiency in collecting receivables and the trends in the management of credit.

737

MERCHANDISE INVENTORY ANALYSIS

Although an enterprise must maintain sufficient inventory quantities to meet the demands for its merchandise, it is desirable to keep the amount invested in inventory to a minimum. Inventories in excess of the needs of the business tie up funds that could be used in other ways to better advantage and may cause increases in the amount of insurance, property taxes, storage, and other expenses. There is also added risk of loss through price declines and deterioration or obsolescence of the merchandise.

Merchandise inventory turnover. The relationship between the volume of merchandise sold and merchandise inventory may be stated as the *merchandise inventory turnover.* It is computed by dividing the cost of merchandise sold by the average inventory. If monthly data are not available, it is necessary to use the average of the inventories at the beginning and the end of the year. Given monthly figures for purchases and sales, the interim monthly inventories can be estimated by the gross profit method described in Chapter 8. Data used in computing the merchandise inventory turnover for Martin Company are presented on the next page.

The improvement in the turnover resulted from an increase in the cost of merchandise sold, combined with a decrease in average inventory.

	1974	1973
Cost of merchandise sold........................	$1,043,000	$820,000
Merchandise inventory:		
Beginning of year............................	$ 283,000	$311,000
End of year.................................	264,000	283,000
Total.......................................	$ 547,000	$594,000
Average....................................	$ 273,500	$297,000
Merchandise inventory turnover.................	3.8	2.8

The variation in types of merchandise is too great to permit any broad generalizations as to what constitutes a satisfactory turnover. For example, a firm selling food should have a much higher turnover than one selling furniture or jewelry, and the perishable foods department of a supermaket should have a higher turnover than the soaps and cleaners department. However, for each business or each department within a business there is a reasonable turnover rate. A turnover below this rate means that the company or the department is incurring extra expenses such as those for administration and storage, increasing its risk of loss because of obsolescence and adverse price changes, and incurring interest charges in excess of those considered necessary or failing to free funds for other uses.

Number of days' sales in merchandise inventory. Another means of expressing the relationship between the cost of merchandise sold and merchandise inventory is the *number of days' sales in merchandise inventory.* This measure is determined by dividing the merchandise inventory at the end of the year by the average daily cost of merchandise sold (cost of merchandise sold divided by 365), which is illustrated below.

	1974	1973
Merchandise inventory, end of year...............	$ 264,000	$283,000
Cost of merchandise sold........................	$1,043,000	$820,000
Average daily cost of merchandise sold............	$ 2,858	$ 2,274
Number of days' sales in inventory..............	92.4	124.5

The number of days' sales in inventory gives a rough measure of the length of time it takes to acquire, sell, and then replace the average merchandise inventory. Although there was a substantial improvement in the second year, comparison of the measure with those of earlier years and of comparable firms is an essential element in judging the effectiveness of Martin Company's inventory control.

As with many attempts to analyze financial data, it is possible to determine more than one measure to express the relationship between the cost of merchandise sold and merchandise inventory. Both the merchandise inventory turnover and number of days' sales in merchandise inventory are useful for evaluating the efficiency in the management of inventory. Whether both measures are used or whether one measure is preferred over the other, is a matter for the individual analyst to decide.

RATIO OF STOCKHOLDERS' EQUITY TO LIABILITIES

Claims against the total assets of an enterprise are divided into two basic groups, those of the creditors and those of the owners. The relationship between the total claims of the two groups provides an indication of the margin of safety of the creditors and the ability of the enterprise to withstand adverse business conditions. If the claims of the creditors are large in proportion to the equity of the stockholders, there are likely to be substantial charges for interest payments. If earnings decline to the point of inability to meet interest payments, control of the business may pass to the creditors.

The relationship between stockholder and creditor equity is shown in the vertical analysis of the balance sheet. For example, the balance sheet of Martin Company presented on page 731 indicates that on December 31, 1974, stockholders' equity represented 72.8% and liabilities represented 27.2% of the sum of the liabilities and stockholders' equity (100.0%). Instead of expressing each item as a percent of the total, the relationship may be expressed as a ratio of one to the other, as follows:

739

	1974	1973
Total stockholders' equity.........................	$829,500	$787,500
Total liabilities...................................	$310,000	$443,000
Ratio of stockholders' equity to liabilities...........	2.7:1	1.8:1

By referring to the balance sheet of Martin Company it may be seen that the principal factor affecting the change in the ratio was the $100,000 reduction in long-term liabilities during 1974. The ratio at both dates indicates a substantial margin of safety for the creditors.

RATIO OF PLANT ASSETS TO LONG-TERM LIABILITIES

Long-term notes and bonds are frequently secured by mortgages on plant assets. The ratio of total plant assets to long-term liabilities provides a measure of the margin of safety of the noteholders or bondholders. It also gives an indication of the potential ability of the enterprise to borrow additional funds on a long-term basis. The ratio of plant assets to long-term liabilities of Martin Company is as follows:

	1974	1973
Plant assets (net)................................	$444,500	$470,000
Long-term liabilities.............................	$100,000	$200,000
Ratio of plant assets to long-term liabilities.........	4.4:1	2.4:1

RATIO OF NET SALES TO ASSETS

The ratio of net sales to assets is a measure of the effectiveness of the utilization of assets. Assume that two competing enterprises have equal amounts of assets but that the amount of the sales of one is double the amount of the sales of the other. Obviously, the former is making better use of its assets. In computing the ratio, any long-term investments should be excluded from total assets as they are wholly unrelated to sales of commodities or services. Assets used in determining the ratio may be the total at the end of the year, the average at the beginning and the end of the year, or the average of the monthly totals. The basic data and the ratio of net sales to assets for Martin Company are as follows:

	1974	1973
Net sales.....................................	$1,498,000	$1,200,000
Total assets (excluding long-term investments):		
Beginning of year............................	$1,053,000	$1,010,000
End of year..................................	1,044,500	1,053,000
Total.......................................	$2,097,500	$2,063,000
Average.....................................	$1,048,750	$1,031,500
Ratio of net sales to assets	1.4:1	1.2:1

RATE EARNED ON TOTAL ASSETS

The rate earned on total assets is a measure of the productivity of the assets, without regard to the equity of creditors and stockholders in the assets. The rate is therefore not affected by differences in methods of financing an enterprise.

The rate earned on total assets is derived by adding interest expense to net income and dividing this sum by total assets. By adding interest expense to net income, the productivity of the assets is determined without considering the means of financing the acquisition of the assets. The rate earned by Martin Company on total assets appears below.

	1974	1973
Net income....................................	$ 91,000	$ 76,500
Plus interest expense...........................	6,000	12,000
Total.......................................	$ 97,000	$ 88,500
Total assets:		
Beginning of year............................	$1,230,500	$1,187,500
End of year..................................	1,139,500	1,230,500
Total.......................................	$2,370,000	$2,418,000
Average.....................................	$1,185,000	$1,209,000
Rate earned on total assets	8.2%	7.3%

It is sometimes considered preferable to determine the rate of operating income (income before nonoperating income, nonoperating expense, extraordinary items, and income tax) to total assets. If nonoperating income is excluded from consideration, the investments yielding such income should be excluded from the assets. The use of income before income tax eliminates the effect of changes in the tax structure on the rate of earnings. When considering published data on rates earned on assets, it is obviously important that the reader take note of the exact nature of the measure.

RATE EARNED ON STOCKHOLDERS' EQUITY

Another relative measure of earnings is obtained by dividing net income by the total stockholders' equity. In contrast to the rate earned on total assets, this measure emphasizes the income yield in relationship to the amount invested by the stockholders.

The amount of the total stockholders' equity varies throughout the year; additional stock may be issued, a class of stock may be retired, dividends may be paid, and net income accrues gradually. If monthly figures are not available, the average of the stockholders' equity at the beginning and the end of the year is used, as in the following illustration.

	1974	1973
Net income.................................	$ 91,000	$ 76,500
Stockholders' equity:		
Beginning of year............................	$ 787,500	$ 750,000
End of year..................................	829,500	787,500
Total.......................................	$1,617,000	$1,537,500
Average....................................	$ 808,500	$ 768,750
Rate earned on stockholders' equity	11.3%	10.0%

The rate earned by a thriving enterprise on the equity of its stockholders is ordinarily higher than the rate earned on total assets. The reason for the variance is that the amount earned on assets equivalent in amount to the total claims of creditors exceeds the interest charges on such claims. This tendency of the rate on stockholders' equity to vary disproportionately from the rate on total assets is sometimes referred to as *leverage*. The Martin Company rate of 11.3% for 1974, shown above, compares favorably with the rate of 8.2% earned on total assets, as reported on the preceding page. The leverage factor of 3.1% (11.3% − 8.2%) for 1974 also compares favorably with the 2.7% (10.0% − 7.3%) differential for the preceding year.

RATE EARNED ON COMMON STOCKHOLDERS' EQUITY

When a corporation has both preferred and common stock outstanding, the holders of the common stock have the residual claim on earnings. The net income for the period, reduced by the preferred dividend requirements, may be stated as a percent of the average equity of the common stockholders.

Martin Company has $150,000 of preferred 6% nonparticipating stock outstanding at both balance sheet dates, hence annual preferred dividends amount to $9,000. The common stockholders' equity is the total stockholders' equity reduced by the par of the preferred stock ($150,000). The data are presented below.

	1974	1973
Net income...................................	$ 91,000	$ 76,500
Preferred dividends............................	9,000	9,000
Remainder — identified with common stock.........	$ 82,000	$ 67,500
Common stockholders' equity:		
Beginning of year............................	$ 637,500	$ 600,000
End of year..................................	679,500	637,500
Total.......................................	$1,317,000	$1,237,500
Average.....................................	$ 658,500	$ 618,750
Rate earned on common stockholders' equity	12.5%	10.9%

EARNINGS PER SHARE ON COMMON STOCK

One of the financial measures most commonly quoted in the financial press and included in the income statement in corporate annual reports is earnings per share on common stock. If there is only one class of stock, the earnings per share are determined by dividing net income by the number of shares outstanding. If there are both preferred and common stock outstanding, the net income must be reduced first by the amount necessary to meet the preferred dividend requirements.

Any changes in the number of shares outstanding during the year, such as would result from stock dividends or stock splits, should be disclosed in quoting earnings per share on common stock. Also if net income includes extraordinary items, the per share amounts should be presented for (1) income before extraordinary items, (2) extraordinary items (less applicable income tax), and (3) net income.

The data on the earnings per share of common stock of Martin Company are as follows:

	1974	1973
Net income...	$91,000	$76,500
Preferred dividends.................................	9,000	9,000
Remainder — identified with common stock..............	$82,000	$67,500
Shares of common stock outstanding....................	50,000	50,000
Earnings per share on common stock..................	$1.64	$1.35

Earnings per share on common stock is commonly used by the investor or prospective investor in evaluating past operating performance of a business enterprise, in attempting to project its future potential, and in weighing the merits of one investment opportunity in comparison with those of others.

SELECTION OF ANALYTICAL MEASURES

The analytical measures that have been discussed and illustrated are representative of many that can be developed for a medium-size merchandising enterprise. Some of them might well be omitted in analyzing a specific firm or additional measures could be developed. The type of business activity, the capital structure, and the size of the enterprise usually affect the measures employed. For example, in analyzing railroads, public utilities, and other corporations with a high ratio of debt to stockholders' equity, it is customary to express the relative risk of the bondholders in terms of the number of times the interest charges are earned during the year. The higher the ratio, the greater the assurance of continued interest payments in the event of decreased earnings. The measure also provides an indication of general financial strength, which is of concern to stockholders and employees, as well as to creditors.

In the data for a hypothetical corporation presented below, it should be noted that the amount available to meet interest charges is not affected by taxes on net income.

	1974	1973
Income before income tax.....................	$ 900,000	$ 800,000
Add interest charges.........................	300,000	250,000
Amount available to meet interest charges......	$1,200,000	$1,050,000
Number of times interest charges earned........	4	4.2

Analyses similar to the above can be applied to dividends on preferred and common stock. The number of times preferred dividends are earned indicates the relative assurance of continued dividend payments to preferred stockholders. For corporations with a policy of regular dividends on common stock, the number of times the common dividend is earned provides a similar measure for the common stockholders. In addition, it is a measure of the extent to which the corporation is retaining its earnings for use in the business.

Percentage analyses, ratios, turnovers, and other measures of financial position and operating results are useful analytical devices. They are helpful in appraising the present performance of an enterprise and in forecasting its future. They are not, however, a substitute for sound judgment nor do they provide definitive guides to action. In selecting and interpreting analytical indexes, appropriate consideration should be given to any conditions peculiar to the particular enterprise or to the industry of which the enterprise is a part. The possible influence of the general economic and business environment should also be weighed.

The interrelationship of the measures employed in appraising a particular enterprise should be carefully studied, as should comparable indexes of earlier fiscal periods, to ascertain trends. Data from competing

743

enterprises may also be helpful in determining the relative efficiency of the firm being analyzed. In making such comparisons, however, it is important to consider the effect of any significant differences in their accounting methods.

QUESTIONS

1. In analysis of the status of an enterprise, what is meant by *solvency*?

2. J. W. Moore Company and Parker, Inc., are both department stores. For the current year, they reported net income (after income tax) of $350,000 and $550,000 respectively. Is Parker, Inc., a more profitable company than J. W. Moore Company? Discuss.

3. Illustrate (a) horizontal analysis and (b) vertical analysis, using the following data taken from a comparative balance sheet:

	Current Year	Preceding Year
Cash............	$ 450,000	$ 300,000
Total current assets.	1,500,000	1,200,000

4. What is the advantage of using comparative statements for financial analysis rather than statements for a single date or period?

5. The current year's amount of net income (after income tax) is 10% larger than that of the preceding year. Does this indicate an improved operating performance? Discuss.

6. What are common-size financial statements?

7. (a) Name three measures or ratios that are useful in the analysis of a firm's current position. (b) Why is the analysis of current position of particular interest to short-term creditors?

8. Company A and Company B have working capital of $200,000 and $100,000 respectively. Does this mean that Company A has a higher current ratio than Company B? Explain.

9. The working capital for Mills Company at the end of the current year exceeds the working capital at the end of the preceding year, by $25,000 as reported below. Does this mean that the current position has improved? Explain.

	Current Year	Preceding Year
Current assets:		
Cash, marketable securities, and accounts receivable.	$100,000	$100,000
Merchandise inventory.........................	200,000	75,000
Total current assets.........................	$300,000	$175,000
Current liabilities............................	200,000	100,000
Working capital.............................	$100,000	$ 75,000

10. A company that grants terms of n/30 on all sales has an accounts receivable turnover for the year, based on monthly averages, of 6. Is this a satisfactory turnover? Discuss.

11. What does a decrease in the number of days' sales in receivables ordinarily indicate about the credit and collection policy of the firm?

12. (a) Why is it advantageous to have a high merchandise inventory turnover? (b) Is it possible for a merchandise inventory turnover to be too high? Discuss.

13. What does an increase in the ratio of stockholders' equity to liabilities indicate about the margin of safety for the firm's creditors and the ability of the firm to withstand adverse business conditions?

14. In determining the rate earned on total assets, why is interest expense added to net income before dividing by total assets?

15. Explain why the rate earned on stockholders' equity by a thriving enterprise is ordinarily higher than the rate earned on total assets?

16. The net income (after income tax) of Baldwin Company was $3 per common share in the latest year and $5 per common share for the preceding year. At the beginning of the latest year, the number of shares outstanding was doubled by a stock split. There were no other changes in the amount of stock outstanding. What were the earnings per share in the preceding year, adjusted to place them on a comparable basis with the latest year?

17. Favorable business conditions may bring about certain seemingly unfavorable ratios, and unfavorable business operations may result in apparently favorable ratios. For example, Wallace Company increased its sales and net income substantially for the current year, yet the current ratio at the end of the year is lower than at the beginning of the year. Discuss some possible causes of the apparent weakening of the current position while sales and net income have increased substantially.

745

EXERCISES

28-1. Revenue and expense data for Dawkins Company are presented below:

	1974	1973
Sales.	$700,000	$600,000
Cost of merchandise sold.	420,000	366,000
Selling expense.	105,000	120,000
General expense.	70,000	54,000
Income tax.	42,000	24,000

(a) Prepare an income statement in comparative form stating each item for both 1974 and 1973 as a percent of sales.
(b) Comment upon the significant changes disclosed by the comparative income statement.

28-2. The following data were abstracted from the balance sheet of Geltner Company:

Cash.	$ 95,000
Marketable securities.	40,000
Accounts and notes receivable (net).	135,000
Merchandise inventory.	172,500
Prepaid expenses.	7,500
Accounts and notes payable (short-term).	185,000
Accrued liabilities.	40,000

(a) Determine (1) working capital, (2) current ratio, and (3) acid-test ratio. (Present figures used in your computations.)
(b) What conclusions can be drawn from these data as to the company's ability to meet its currently maturing debts?

28-3. The following data are from the financial statements for Murray Company:

	Current Year	Preceding Year
Accounts receivable, end of year..........	$ 315,600	$ 290,000
Monthly average accounts receivable (net).	300,000	275,000
Net sales on account...................	2,400,000	1,925,000

Terms of all sales are 1/10, n/60.

(a) Determine for each year (1) the accounts receivable turnover and (2) the number of days' sales in receivables.

(b) What conclusions can be drawn from these data concerning the composition of accounts receivable?

28-4. The following data are from the income statements of Roth Corporation:

	Current Year	Preceding Year
Sales...................	$2,590,000	$2,350,000
Beginning inventory.......	300,000	260,000
Purchases..............	1,350,000	1,240,000
Ending inventory.........	350,000	300,000

(a) Determine for each year (1) the merchandise inventory turnover and (2) the number of days' sales in merchandise inventory.

(b) What conclusions can be drawn from these data concerning the composition of the merchandise inventory?

746

28-5. The data presented below were taken from the financial statements of Fred Robeson and Co. for the current fiscal year.

Plant assets (net).....................		$ 687,500
Liabilities:		
Current liabilities..................		$ 175,000
Mortgage note payable, 7%, due 1990..		275,000
Total liabilities....................		$ 450,000
Stockholders' equity:		
Preferred 6% stock, $100 par, cumulative, nonparticipating (no change during year).........................		$ 100,000
Common stock, $20 par (no change during year)......................		500,000
Retained earnings:		
Balance, beginning of year..........	$252,550	
Net income......................	88,450	$341,000
Preferred dividends................	$ 6,000	
Common dividends...............	35,000	41,000
Balance, end of year..............		300,000
Total stockholders' equity............		$ 900,000
Net sales..........................		$1,485,000
Interest expense......................		19,250

Determine the following, presenting figures used in your computations: (a) ratio of stockholders' equity to liabilities, (b) ratio of plant assets to long-term liabilities, (c) ratio of net sales to assets, (d) rate earned on total assets, (e) rate earned on stockholders' equity, (f) rate earned on common stockholders' equity.

28-6. The net income reported on the income statement of Benton Products, Inc., was $2,000,000. There were 250,000 shares of $20 par common stock and 50,000 shares of $100 par 6% preferred stock outstanding throughout the year. The income statement included a gain on the sale of long-term investments of $1,000,000 and a fire loss of $500,000, both after applicable income tax. Determine the per share figures for common stock for (a) income before extraordinary items, (b) extraordinary items (less applicable income tax), and (c) net income.

28-7. The balance sheet for Dugan Corporation at the end of the current fiscal year indicated the following:

Total current liabilities (non-interest bearing).....	$300,000
Bonds payable, 7% (issued in 1970, due in 1990).	500,000
Preferred 6% stock, $100 par...................	200,000
Common stock, $5 par......................	500,000
Premium on common stock...................	100,000
Retained earnings.........................	400,000

Income before income tax was $175,000 and income taxes were $80,000 for the current year. Determine each of the following: (a) rate earned on total assets, (b) rate earned on stockholders' equity, (c) rate earned on common stockholders' equity, (d) number of times bond interest charges were earned, (e) number of times preferred dividends were earned, (f) earnings per share on common stock.

747

PROBLEMS

The following additional problems for this chapter are located in Appendix B: 28-1B, 28-3B, 28-4B.

28-1A. Data pertaining to the current position of P. A. Finch and Company are presented below.

Cash..........................	$120,000
Marketable securities.............	50,000
Accounts and notes receivable (net).	220,000
Merchandise inventory............	248,000
Prepaid expenses................	12,000
Accounts payable................	185,000
Notes payable (short-term).........	40,000
Accrued liabilities................	35,000

Instructions:

(1) Compute (a) working capital, (b) current ratio, and (c) acid-test ratio.
(2) Consider each of the following transactions separately and assume that only that transaction affects the data given above.

    (a) Purchased merchandise on account, $60,000
    (b) Paid notes payable, $40,000.
    (c) Received cash on account, $100,000.
    (d) Paid accounts payable, $75,000.
    (e) Declared a cash dividend, $25,000.
    (f) Declared a common stock dividend on common stock, $50,000

(g) Issued additional shares of stock for cash, $100,000.
(h) Borrowed cash from bank on a long-term note, $100,000.
(i) Paid cash for store supplies, $2,500.
(j) Sold marketable securities, $25,000.

State the effect of each transaction (increase, decrease, or no effect) on working capital, current ratio, and acid-test ratio. Use the following column headings for recording your answers:

	Effect on		
Item	Working Capital	Current Ratio	Acid-Test Ratio

28-2A. Presented below for the current calendar year are revenue and expense data for Hayden Paper Company and for the paper industry. The Hayden Paper Company data are expressed in dollars; the paper industry averages are expressed in percentages.

	Hayden Paper Company	Paper Industry Average
Sales.....................	$3,333,000	100.5%
Sales returns and allowances.	33,000	.5%
Cost of merchandise sold.....	2,343,000	69.0%
Selling expenses...........	267,300	9.8%
General expenses..........	231,000	8.2%
Other income............	19,800	.5%
Other expense............	46,200	1.5%
Income tax	198,000	5.5%

Instructions:

(1) Prepare a common-size income statement comparing the results of operations for Hayden Paper Company with the industry average.
(2) As far as the data permit, comment on significant relationships revealed by the comparisons.

28-3A. For 1974, Cross Company initiated an extensive sales promotion campaign that included the expenditure of an additional $50,000 for advertising. At the end of the year, Ralph Cross, the president, is presented with the following condensed comparative income statement:

Cross Company
Comparative Income Statement
For Years Ended December 31, 1974 and 1973

	1974	1973
Sales..	$714,000	$555,500
Sales returns and allowances......................	14,000	5,500
Net sales......................................	$700,000	$550,000
Cost of merchandise sold........................	434,000	330,000
Gross profit on sales.............................	$266,000	$220,000
Selling expenses................................	$140,000	$ 82,500
General expenses...............................	33,600	27,500
Total operating expenses.........................	$173,600	$110,000
Operating income...............................	$ 92,400	$110,000

	1974	1973
Other income..................................	2,800	2,750
Income before income tax.......................	$ 95,200	$112,750
Income tax.....................................	42,000	50,600
Net income....................................	$ 53,200	$ 62,150

Instructions:

(1) Prepare a comparative income statement for the two-year period, presenting an analysis of each item in relationship to net sales for each of the years.
(2) To the extent the data permit, comment on significant relationships revealed by the vertical analysis prepared in (1).

28-4A. The comparative financial statements of A. D. Conrad Company are presented below and on the following page.

A. D. Conrad Company
Comparative Balance Sheet
For Years Ended December 31, 1974 and 1973

Assets	1974	1973
Current assets:		
Cash.......................................	$ 140,000	$ 160,000
Marketable securities.......................	90,000	75,000
Accounts receivable (net)...................	340,000	210,000
Merchandise inventory......................	480,000	360,000
Prepaid expenses...........................	12,000	20,000
Total current assets........................	$1,062,000	$ 825,000
Long-term investments......................	200,000	175,000
Plant assets................................	1,938,000	1,800,000
Total assets................................	$3,200,000	$2,800,000
Liabilities		
Current liabilities..........................	$ 620,000	$ 500,000
Long-term liabilities:		
Mortgage note payable, due 1989.............	$ 200,000	——
Bonds payable, 6%, due 1995.................	600,000	$ 600,000
Total long-term liabilities..................	$ 800,000	$ 600,000
Total liabilities............................	$1,420,000	$1,100,000
Stockholders' Equity		
Preferred 6% stock, $100 par...................	$ 500,000	$ 500,000
Common stock, $10 par........................	500,000	500,000
Retained earnings............................	780,000	700,000
Total stockholders' equity....................	$1,780,000	$1,700,000
Total liabilities and stockholders' equity...........	$3,200,000	$2,800,000

Instructions:

Determine for 1974 the ratios, turnovers, and other measures listed below and on page 750, presenting the figures used in your computations:

(1) Working capital.
(2) Current ratio.

A. D. Conrad Company
Comparative Income Statement
For Years Ended December 31, 1974 and 1973

	1974	1973
Sales..	$3,075,000	$2,652,000
Sales returns and allowances....................	75,000	52,000
Net sales....................................	$3,000,000	$2,600,000
Cost of merchandise sold......................	2,100,000	1,705,000
Gross profit on sales..........................	$ 900,000	$ 895,000
Selling expenses..............................	$ 420,000	$ 390,000
General expenses..............................	170,000	176,800
Total operating expenses......................	$ 590,000	$ 566,800
Operating income.............................	$ 310,000	$ 328,200
Other income................................	15,000	14,400
	$ 325,000	$ 342,600
Other expense (interest).......................	46,000	36,000
Income before income tax......................	$ 279,000	$ 306,600
Income tax...................................	133,000	146,600
Net income..................................	$ 146,000	$ 160,000

A. D. Conrad Company
Comparative Retained Earnings Statement
For Years Ended December 31, 1974 and 1973

	1974	1973
Retained earnings, January 1.....................	$700,000	$595,000
Add net income for year........................	146,000	160,000
Total..	$846,000	$755,000
Deduct dividends:		
On preferred stock............................	$ 30,000	$ 30,000
On common stock.............................	36,000	25,000
Total....................................	$ 66,000	$ 55,000
Retained earnings, December 31..................	$780,000	$700,000

(3) Acid-test ratio.
(4) Accounts receivable turnover.
(5) Number of days' sales in receivables.
(6) Merchandise inventory turnover.
(7) Number of days' sales in merchandise inventory.
(8) Ratio of plant assets to long-term liabilities.
(9) Ratio of stockholders' equity to liabilities.
(10) Rate earned on total assets.
(11) Rate earned on stockholders' equity.
(12) Rate earned on common stockholders' equity.
(13) Ratio of net sales to assets.
(14) Earnings per share on common stock.

28-5A. John Robinson is considering making a substantial investment in A. D. Conrad Company. The company's comparative financial statements for 1974 and 1973 were given in Problem 28-4A. To assist in the evaluation of the company, Mr. Robinson secured the following additional data taken from the balance sheet at December 31, 1972:

Accounts receivable (net)...............................	$ 190,000
Merchandise inventory....................................	300,000
Long-term investments...................................	150,000
Total assets..	2,700,000
Total stockholders' equity (preferred and common stock outstanding same as in 1973)....................................	1,595,000

Instructions:

Prepare a report for Mr. Robinson based on an analysis of the financial data presented above. In preparing your report, include all ratios and other data that will be useful in arriving at a decision regarding the investment.

Appendix A

CONTINUING DEVELOPMENT OF ACCOUNTING STANDARDS

In March of 1971 the American Institute of Certified Public Accountants (AICPA) appointed a seven-man group to make a "Study on Establishment of Accounting Principles." Instructions to the study group, headed by former SEC Commissioner Francis M. Wheat, were "to examine the organization of the Accounting Principles Board (APB) and determine what changes are necessary to attain better results faster." In March 1972 the study group issued its conclusions and recommendations in a 105-page report entitled "Establishing Financial Accounting Standards."

The recommendations embodied in the report were adopted by the governing body of the AICPA and are expected to be fully implemented by early 1973. At the heart of the proposals is the replacement of the eighteen-member APB by a seven-member Financial Accounting Standards Board (FASB). All of the members of the APB were members of the AICPA, they continued their affiliations with their firms or institutions, they served part time, and they served without pay. In contrast, only four of the members of the FASB are required to be CPAs drawn from public practice, they must resign from the firm or institution with which they have been affiliated, they are to serve full time, and they will receive a salary. Appointments are for a term of five years with a possible renewal for a second term.

In accordance with the study group's recommendations, a new nonprofit institution called the Financial Accounting Foundation was established in 1972. The principal duties of its nine trustees are to appoint the members of the FASB and to arrange financing for the multimillion dollar a year program. Membership of the Board of Trustees of the Foundation includes the President of the AICPA as an ex officio trustee. Of the other eight trustees, who serve three-year terms, four are CPAs drawn from public practice; two are experienced as financial executives, one nominated by the Financial Executives Institute and one nominated by the National Association of Accountants; one experienced as a financial analyst, nominated by the Financial Analysts Federation; and one experienced as an accounting educator, nominated by the American Accounting Association. Appointments to the Board of Trustees are made by the Board of Directors of the AICPA.

The FASB is to be assisted by an Advisory Council of approximately twenty members, appointed by the Board of Trustees of the Financial Accounting Foundation. Members of the Council are appointed for one-year terms and ordinarily are to serve no more than four consecutive terms. Major responsibilities of the Advisory Council include recommendations to the FASB as to its priorities and agenda, and the review of its plans, activities, and statements proposed for issuance.

The FASB will appoint Task Forces to study and make recommendations on specific matters under consideration. Assistance to the FASB will also be provided by a research staff and an administrative staff.

The salient features of the structure of the Financial Accounting Foundation are summarized in the chart on the next page.

754

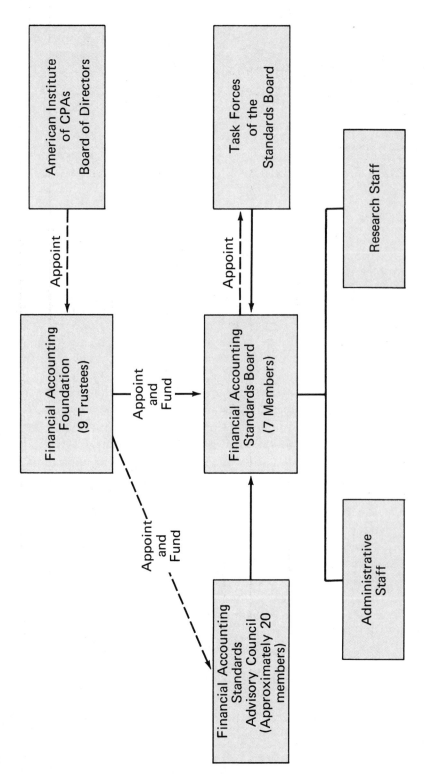

Financial Accounting
Foundation
organizational
chart

Appendix B

SERIES B PROBLEMS

Numbers assigned to the problems in this appendix correspond to the numbers of the comparable problems presented at the end of the chapters, with the substitution of the letter "B" for the letter "A." For example, Problem 1-2B presented below is the alternate for Problem 1-2A presented on page 25. The working papers correlating with the textbook are designed for use either for the series A problems at the end of the chapters or for the series B problems in this appendix.

CHAPTER 1

1-2B. On January 1, the *beginning* of the current year, Ritter Corporation had capital stock of $75,000 and retained earnings of $36,000. During the year the corporation paid cash dividends of $40,000. The amounts of the corporation's assets and liabilities at December 31, the *end* of the current year, and of its revenue and expenses for the year ended on that date are as stated below, listed in alphabetical order.

Accounts payable	$ 6,240
Accounts receivable	14,850
Accumulated depreciation — building	3,800
Accumulated depreciation — equipment	5,540
Advertising expense	4,370
Building	84,640
Cash	11,420
Depreciation expense — building	1,200
Depreciation expense — equipment	1,790
Equipment	25,950
Insurance expense	990
Land	7,420
Miscellaneous expense	1,780
Prepaid insurance	2,590
Salaries payable	840
Salary expense	40,520
Sales	128,740
Supplies	1,890
Supplies expense	2,620
Taxes expense	13,750
Taxes payable	2,780
Utilities expense	3,160

Instructions:

(1) Prepare an income statement for the current year ending December 31, exercising care to include each item of expense listed.

(2) Prepare a retained earnings statement for the current year ending December 31.

(3) Prepare a balance sheet as of December 31 of the current year. There was no change in the amount of capital stock during the year.

1-3B. B. J. Shaw operates a sole proprietorship known as Model Dry Cleaners. The actual work of dry cleaning is done by another company at wholesale rates. The assets and the liabilities of the business on August 1 of the current year are as follows: Cash, $1,800; Accounts Receivable, $550; Supplies, $110; Equipment, $5,200; Accumulated Depreciation, $900; Accounts Payable, $1,020. Business transactions during August are summarized below.

(a) Paid rent for the month, $240.

(b) Purchased supplies on account, $65.

(c) Received cash from cash customers for dry cleaning sales, $2,500.

(d) Paid creditors on account, $920.

(e) Charged customers for dry cleaning sales on account, $820.

(f) Received monthly invoice for dry cleaning expense for August (to be paid on September 10), $1,320.

(g) Paid the following: wages expense, $330; truck expense, $85; utilities expense, $50; miscellaneous expense, $80.

(h) Purchased an item of equipment on account, $180.

(i) Received cash from customers on account, $780.

(j) Paid personal expenses by checks drawn on the business, $340, and withdrew $100 in cash for personal use.

(k) Reimbursed a customer $50 for a garment lost by the cleaning company, which agreed to deduct the amount from the invoice received in transaction (f).

(l) Determined by taking an inventory the cost of supplies used during the month, $25.

(m) Estimated depreciation of truck and other equipment for the month, $110.

Instructions:

(1) State the assets, liabilities, and capital as of August 1 in equation form similar to that shown in this chapter.

(2) Record, in tabular form below the equation, the increases and decreases resulting from each transaction, indicating the new balances after each transaction. Explain the nature of each increase and decrease in capital by an appropriate notation at the right of the amount.

(3) Prepare (a) an income statement, (b) a capital statement, and (c) a balance sheet.

CHAPTER 2

2-1B. John D. Cramer established an enterprise to be known as Moderne Decorators, on April 16 of the current year. During the remainder of the month he completed the business transactions described on the next page.

April 16. Cramer transferred cash from a personal bank account to an account to be used for the business, $3,500.

16. Purchased supplies for cash, $90.

16. Paid rent for period of April 16 to end of month, $165.

17. Purchased a truck for $4,200, paying $1,100 cash and giving a note payable for the remainder.

18. Purchased equipment on account, $530.

19. Received cash for job completed, $315.

22. Purchased supplies on account, $340.

23. Paid wages of employees, $650.

25. Paid premiums on property and casualty insurance, $403.

26. Paid creditor for equipment purchased on April 18, $530.

27. Recorded sales on account and sent invoices to customers, $4,305.

28. Received cash for job completed, $379. This sale had not been recorded previously.

29. Received an invoice for truck expenses, to be paid in May, $76.

29. Paid utilities expense, $39.

29. Paid miscellaneous expenses, $41.

30. Received cash from customers on account, $2,835.

30. Paid wages of employees, $650.

30. Withdrew cash for personal use, $500.

Instructions:

(1) Open a ledger of two-column accounts for Moderne Decorators, using the following titles and account numbers: Cash, 11; Accounts Receivable, 12; Supplies, 13; Prepaid Insurance, 14; Truck, 16; Equipment, 18; Notes Payable, 21; Accounts Payable, 22; John D. Cramer, Capital, 31; John D. Cramer, Drawing, 32; Sales, 41; Wages Expense, 51; Rent Expense, 53; Truck Expense, 54; Utilities Expense, 55; Miscellaneous Expense, 59.

(2) Record each transaction in a two-column journal, referring to the above list of accounts or to the ledger in selecting appropriate account titles to be debited and credited. (Do *not* insert the account numbers in the journal at this time.)

(3) Post the journal to the ledger, inserting appropriate posting references as each item is posted.

(4) Determine the balances of the accounts in the ledger, pencil footing all accounts having two or more debits or credits. A memorandum balance should also be inserted in accounts having both debits and credits, in the manner illustrated on page 39. For accounts with entries on one side only (such as Sales) there is no need to insert the memorandum balance in the item column. Accounts containing only a single debit and a single credit (such as Accounts Receivable) need no pencil footings; the memorandum balance should be inserted in the appropriate item column. Accounts containing a single entry only (such as Prepaid Insurance) need neither a pencil footing nor a memorandum balance.

(5) Prepare a trial balance for Moderne Decorators as of April 30.

If the working papers correlating with the textbook are not used, omit Problem 2-3B.

2-3B. The following records of Ace TV Service are presented in the working papers:

Journal containing entries for the period January 1–31.
Ledger to which the January entries have been posted.
Preliminary trial balance as of January 31, which does not balance.

Locate the errors, supply the information requested, and prepare a corrected trial balance, proceeding in accordance with the detailed instructions presented below. The balances recorded in the accounts as of January 1 and the entries in the journal are correctly stated. If it is necessary to correct any posted amounts in the ledger, a line should be drawn through the erroneous figure and the correct amount inserted above. Although corrections to memorandum pencil footings and balances are ordinarily accomplished through erasures, any such errors discovered may be corrected by crossing out the erroneous amount and substituting the correct figure. Corrections or other notations may be inserted on the preliminary trial balance in any manner desired. It is not necessary to complete all of the instructions if equal trial balance totals can be obtained earlier. However, the requirements of instructions (9) and (10) should be completed in any event.

Instructions:

(1) Verify the totals of the preliminary trial balance, inserting the correct amounts in the schedule provided in the working papers.
(2) Compute the difference between the trial balance totals.
(3) Determine whether the difference obtained in (2) is evenly divisible by 9.
(4) If the difference obtained in (2) is an even number, determine half the amount.
(5) Scan the amounts in the ledger to determine whether a posting has been omitted or erroneously posted to the wrong side of an account.
(6) Compare the listings in the trial balance with the memorandum balances appearing in the ledger.
(7) Verify the accuracy of the memorandum footings and balances of each account in the ledger.
(8) Trace the postings in the ledger back to the journal, using small check marks to identify items traced. (Correct any memorandum amounts in the ledger that may be necessitated by errors in posting.)
(9) Journalize as of January 31 the purchase of an item of equipment at a cost of $682.40, paying cash of $182.40 and issuing a note payable for the balance. The transaction had occurred on January 31 but was inadvertently omitted from the journal. Post to the ledger. (Revise any memorandum amounts necessitated by posting this entry.)
(10) Prepare a new trial balance.

2-4B. The following business transactions were completed by Outdoor Theatre Corporation during September of the current year:

Sept. 3. Received and deposited in a bank account $32,000 cash received from stockholders for capital stock.
      4. Purchased the Valley Drive-In Theatre for $55,000, allocated as

follows: equipment, $22,000; buildings, $15,000; land, $18,000. Paid $20,000 in cash and gave a mortgage note for the remainder.

Sept. 5. Paid premiums for property and casualty insurance policies, $1,520.

7. Paid for September billboard and newspaper advertising, $475.

8. Purchased supplies, $310, and equipment, $1,400, on account.

9. Cash received from admissions for the week, $2,450.

11. Paid miscellaneous expenses, $93.

15. Paid semimonthly wages, $1,900.

16. Cash received from admissions for the week, $2,730.

16. Entered into a contract for the operation of the refreshment stand concession at a rental of 10% of the concessionaire's sales, with a guaranteed minimum of $320 a month, payable in advance. Received cash of $160 as the advance payment for the second half of the month of September.

18. Paid miscellaneous expenses, $67.

20. Returned portion of equipment purchased on September 8 to the supplier, receiving full credit for its cost, $275.

22. Paid cash to creditors on account, $1,365.

23. Cash received from admissions for the week, $2,810.

24. Purchased supplies for cash, $44.

25. Paid for advertising leaflets for September, $62.

28. Recorded invoice of $2,320 for rental of film for September. Payment is due on October 5.

29. Paid electricity and water bills, $329.

30. Paid semimonthly wages, $2,300.

30. Cash received from admissions for remainder of the month, $2,919.

30. Recorded additional amount owed by the concessionaire for the second half of September, whose sales for that period totaled $2,050. Rental charges in excess of the advance payment of $160 are not due and payable until October 10.

759

Instructions:

(1) Open a ledger of four-column accounts for Outdoor Theatre Corporation, using the following account titles and numbers: Cash, 11; Accounts Receivable, 12; Prepaid Insurance, 13; Supplies, 14; Equipment, 17; Buildings, 18; Land, 19; Accounts Payable, 21; Mortgage Note Payable, 24; Capital Stock, 31; Admissions Income, 41; Concession Income, 42; Wages Expense, 51; Film Rental Expense, 52; Advertising Expense, 53; Electricity & Water Expense, 54; Miscellaneous Expense, 59.

(2) Record the transactions in a two-column journal.

(3) Post the journal to the ledger, extending the month-end balances to the appropriate balance columns after all posting is completed.

(4) Prepare a trial balance as of September 30.

(5) Determine the following:

(a) Amount of total revenue recorded in the ledger.

(b) Amount of total expenses recorded in the ledger.

(c) Amount of net income for September, assuming that additional unrecorded expenses were as follows: Supplies expense, $130; Insurance expense, $75; Depreciation expense — equipment, $200; Depreciation expense — buildings, $90; Interest expense (on mortgage note), $180.

(d) The understatement or overstatement of net income for September that would have resulted from failure to record the invoice for film rental until it was paid in October. (See transaction of September 28.)

(e) The understatement or overstatement of liabilities as of September 30 that would have resulted from failure to record the invoice for film rental in September. (See transaction of September 28.)

2-6B. The following trial balance for Superior Household Services as of May 31 of the current year does not balance because of a number of errors:

Cash.	3,120	
Accounts Receivable.	2,360	
Supplies.	1,076	
Prepaid Insurance.	398	
Equipment.	7,390	
Notes Payable.		1,200
Accounts Payable.		1,030
Harold Long, Capital.		3,860
Harold Long, Drawing.	300	
Sales.		15,215
Wages Expense.	4,800	
Rent Expense.	600	
Advertising Expense.	41	
Gas, Electricity, and Water Expense.	202	
	20,287	21,305

In the process of comparing the amounts in the trial balance with the ledger, recomputing the balances of the accounts, and comparing the postings with the journal entries, the errors described below were discovered.

(a) The balance of cash was understated by $100.

(b) A cash payment of $820 was posted as a credit to Cash of $280.

(c) A debit of $90 to Accounts Receivable was not posted.

(d) A return of $39 of defective supplies was erroneously posted as a $93 credit to Supplies.

(e) An insurance policy acquired at a cost of $136 was posted as a credit to Prepaid Insurance.

(f) A credit of $300 in Notes Payable was overlooked when determining the balance of the account.

(g) The balance of Accounts Payable was overstated by $100.

(h) A debit of $200 for a withdrawal by the owner was posted as a credit to the capital account.

(i) The balance of $410 in Advertising Expense was entered as $41 in the trial balance.

(j) Miscellaneous Expense, with a balance of $473, was omitted from the trial balance.

Instructions:

Prepare a corrected trial balance as of May 31 of the current year.

CHAPTER 3

3-1B. The trial balance of Newport Launderette at December 31, the end of the current fiscal year, and data needed to determine year-end adjustments are presented on the next page.

Newport Launderette
Trial Balance
December 31, 19—

Cash.....................	1,267	
Laundry Supplies.........	2,185	
Prepaid Insurance........	622	
Laundry Equipment.......	23,800	
Accumulated Depreciation.		4,800
Accounts Payable.........		476
Alice Shafer, Capital......		13,661
Alice Shafer, Drawing.....	6,300	
Laundry Revenue.........		26,910
Wages Expense...........	8,245	
Rent Expense............	1,500	
Utilities Expense..........	1,310	
Miscellaneous Expense....	618	
	45,847	45,847

Adjustment data:
(a) Inventory of laundry supplies at December 31. $ 295
(b) Insurance premiums expired during the year.. 430
(c) Depreciation on equipment during the year... 2,150
(d) Wages accrued but not paid at December 31.. 82

Instructions:
(1) Record the trial balance on an eight-column work sheet.
(2) Complete the work sheet.
(3) Prepare an income statement, a capital statement (no additional investments were made during the year), and a balance sheet.
(4) On the basis of the adjustments data in the work sheet, journalize the adjusting entries.
(5) On the basis of the data in the work sheet or in the income and capital statements, journalize the closing entries.
(6) Compute the following:
    (a) Percent of net income to sales.
    (b) Percent of net income to the capital balance at the beginning of the year.

3-2B. As of August 31, the end of the current fiscal year, the accountant for Graham Company prepared a trial balance, journalized and posted the adjusting entries, prepared an adjusted trial balance, prepared the statements, and completed the other procedures required at the end of the accounting cycle. The two trial balances as of August 31, one before adjustments and the other after adjustments, are presented at the top of the next page.

Instructions:
(1) Present the eight journal entries that were required to adjust the accounts at August 31. None of the accounts was affected by more than one adjusting entry.
(2) Present the journal entries that were required to close the accounts at August 31.
(3) Prepare a capital statement for the fiscal year ended August 31. There were no additional investments during the year.

Graham Company
Trial Balance
August 31, 19—

	Unadjusted		Adjusted	
Cash.................................	1,720		1,720	
Supplies.............................	2,365		375	
Prepaid Rent.........................	3,150		1,050	
Prepaid Insurance....................	730		205	
Automobile..........................	4,900		4,900	
Accumulated Depreciation — Automobile.		825		1,915
Equipment...........................	14,100		14,100	
Accumulated Depreciation — Equipment.		3,675		5,025
Accounts Payable.....................		460		540
Salaries Payable......................		—		130
Taxes Payable........................		—		65
John Graham, Capital.................		12,950		12,950
John Graham, Drawing.................	13,425		13,425	
Service Fees Earned...................		38,800		38,800
Salaries Expense......................	14,710		14,840	
Rent Expense.........................	—		2,100	
Supplies Expense......................	—		1,990	
Depreciation Expense — Equipment......	—		1,350	
Depreciation Expense — Automobile......	—		1,090	
Utilities Expense......................	595		675	
Taxes Expense........................	575		640	
Insurance Expense....................	—		525	
Miscellaneous Expense.................	440		440	
	56,710	56,710	59,425	59,425

If the working papers correlating with this textbook are not used, omit Problem 3-3B.

3-3B. The ledger and trial balance of Todd Machine Repairs as of October 31, the end of the first month of its current fiscal year, is presented in the working papers. The accounts had been closed on September 30.

Instructions:

(1) Complete the eight-column work sheet. Data needed to determine the necessary adjusting entries are as follows:

Inventory of supplies at October 31................	$265.00
Insurance premiums expired during October........	79.40
Depreciation on the truck during October..........	145.00
Depreciation on equipment during October.........	97.00
Wages accrued but not paid at October 31.........	102.00

(2) Prepare an income statement, a capital statement, and a balance sheet.

(3) Journalize and post the adjusting entries, inserting balances in the accounts affected.

(4) Journalize and post the closing entries. Indicate closed accounts by inserting a line in both balance columns opposite the closing entry. Insert the new balance of the capital account.

(5) Prepare a post-closing trial balance.

CHAPTER 4

4-1B. Kendall Sales Co. was established in June of the current year. Its sales of merchandise on account and related returns and allowances during the remainder of the month are described below. Terms of all sales were n/30, FOB destination.

June 17. Sold merchandise on account to Carter & Co., Invoice No. 1, $1,390.
   18. Sold merchandise on account to Matson & Palmer, Invoice No. 2, $860.
   20. Sold merchandise on account to Superior Corp., Invoice No. 3, $770.
   22. Issued Credit Memorandum No. 1 for $50 to Carter & Co. for merchandise returned.
   22. Sold merchandise on account to R. T. Jordan, Inc., Invoice No. 4, $1,040.
   25. Sold merchandise on account to B. J. Weaver Co., Invoice No. 5, $1,980.
   26. Issued Credit Memorandum No. 2 for $60 to Matson & Palmer for merchandise returned.
   27. Sold merchandise on account to Carter & Co., Invoice No. 6, $310.
   28. Issued Credit Memorandum No. 3 for $40 to B. J. Weaver Co. for damages to merchandise caused by faulty packing.
   30. Sold merchandise on account to Matson & Palmer, Invoice No. 7, $1,230.

Instructions:

(1) Open the following accounts in the general ledger, using the account numbers indicated: Accounts Receivable, 113; Sales, 411; Sales Returns and Allowances, 412.

(2) Open the following accounts in the accounts receivable ledger: Carter & Co.; R. T. Jordan, Inc.; Matson & Palmer; Superior Corp.; B. J. Weaver Co.

(3) Record the transactions for June, posting to the customers' accounts in the accounts receivable ledger and inserting the balance *immediately* after recording each entry. Use a sales journal similar to the one illustrated on page 93 and a two-column general journal.

(4) Post the general journal and the sales journal to the three accounts opened in the general ledger, inserting the account balances only after the last postings.

(5) (a) What is the sum of the balances of the accounts in the subsidiary ledger?
   (b) What is the balance of the controlling account?

If the working papers correlating with the textbook are not used, omit Problem 4-2B.

4-2B. Three journals, the accounts receivable ledger, and portions of the general ledger of Lanham Company are presented in the working papers. Sales invoices and credit memorandums were entered in the journals by an assistant. Terms of sales on account are 2/10, n/30, FOB shipping point. Transactions in which cash and notes receivable were received during May of the current year are as follows:

May 1. Received $1,225 cash from John Hill & Co. in payment of April 22 invoice, less discount.
   2. Received $816 cash in payment of a $800 note receivable and interest of $16.

Post transactions of May 1, 3, and 4 to accounts receivable ledger.

May 8. Received $1,764 cash from Daniel G. Weber in payment of April 29 invoice, less discount.
   9. Received $900 cash from James B. Riley Corp. in payment of April 9 invoice, no discount.

Post transactions of May 8, 9, 10, 12, and 15 to accounts receivable ledger.

15. Cash sales for first half of May totaled $8,241.
17. Received $220 cash refund for return of defective equipment purchased for cash in April.
19. Received $1,127 cash from John Hill & Co. in payment of balance due on May 10 invoice, less discount.
22. Received $637 cash from James B. Riley Corp. in payment of May 12 invoice, less discount.

Post transactions of May 18, 19, 22, 23, 24, 25 and 26 to accounts receivable ledger.

29. Received $13 cash for sale of store supplies at cost.
30. Received $188 cash and a $750 note receivable from H. L. Abbott, Inc., in settlement of the balance due on the invoice of May 3, no discount. (Record receipt of note in the general journal.)
31. Cash sales for second half of May totaled $9,432.

Post transactions of May 30 to accounts receivable ledger.

Instructions:

764

(1) Record the cash receipts in the cash receipts journal and the note in the general journal. *Before recording a receipt of cash on account, determine the balance of the customer's account.* Post the entries from the three journals, in date sequence, to the *accounts receivable* ledger in accordance with the instructions inserted in the narrative of transactions. Insert the new balance after each posting to an account.
(2) Post the appropriate individual entries from the cash receipts journal and the general journal to the *general* ledger.
(3) Add the columns of the sales journal and the cash receipts journal and post the appropriate totals to the *general* ledger. Insert the balance of each account after the last posting.
(4) Prepare a schedule of the accounts receivable as of May 31 and compare the total with the balance of the controlling account.

4-3B. Transactions related to sales and cash receipts completed by Hatcher Company during the period January 16–31 of the current year are described below. The terms of all sales on account are 2/10, n/30, FOB shipping point, with delivery charges prepaid and debited to the customers' accounts.

Jan. 16. Received cash from Boyd & Cole for the balance due on its account, less discount.
   17. Issued Invoice No. 399 to Todd & Co., $2,084; delivery, $42; total, $2,126.
   18. Issued Invoice No. 400 to T. B. Porter Co., $1,750; delivery, $35; total, $1,785.
   19. Issued Invoice No. 401 to Henry Kirk, $1,361; delivery, $28; total, $1,389.

Post all journals to the accounts receivable ledger.

Jan. 22. Received cash from Henry Kirk for the balance owed on January 16; no discount.
   24. Issued Credit Memo No. 19 to Todd & Co., $34.
   24. Issued Invoice No. 402 to T. B. Porter Co., $2,639; delivery, $63; total $2,702.
   25. Received $684 cash in payment of a $675 note receivable and interest of $9.

   Post all journals to the accounts receivable ledger.

   27. Received cash from Todd & Co. for the balance due on invoice of January 17, less discount.
   28. Received cash from T. B. Porter Co. for invoice of January 18, less discount.
   29. Issued Invoice No. 403 to Boyd & Cole, $1,920; delivery, $58; total, $1,978.
   31. Recorded cash sales for the second half of the month, $5,925.
   31. Issued Credit Memo No. 20 to Boyd & Cole, $71.

   Post all journals to the accounts receivable ledger.

Instructions:

(1) Open the following accounts in the general ledger, inserting the balances indicated, as of January 1:

111 Cash.............	$1,973	412 Sales Returns and Allowances.	———
112 Notes Receivable....	2,000	413 Sales Discount..............	———
113 Accounts Receivable.	3,654	615 Delivery Expense...........	———
411 Sales.............	———	811 Interest Income...........	———

765

(2) Open the following accounts in the accounts receivable ledger, inserting the balances indicated, as of January 16: Boyd & Cole, $1,193, including a delivery charge of $43; Henry Kirk, $1,651, including a delivery charge of $51; T. B. Porter Co.; Todd & Co. Make a notation of the amount of the delivery charges in the item section of the first two accounts.

(3) Insert the amounts stated below in a sales journal similar to the one illustrated on page 93, a sales returns and allowances journal, similar to the one illustrated on page 96, and a cash receipts journal similar to the one illustrated on page 99. Insert on the first line of each journal "Jan. 16 Totals Forwarded √" and the following dollar figures in the amount columns, reading from left to right:

   Sales journal: 3,468; 68; 3,400
   Sales returns and allowances journal: 26
   Cash receipts journal: 217; 6,230; 4,252; 63; 10,636

(4) Record the transactions for the remainder of January, posting to the *accounts receivable* ledger and inserting the balances, at the points indicated in the narrative of transactions. *Determine the balance in the customer's account before recording a cash receipt.*

(5) Add the columns of the journals and post the individual entries and totals to the general ledger. Insert account balances after the last posting.

(6) Determine that the subsidiary ledger agrees with the controlling account.

CHAPTER 5

5-2B. Tucson Squire Shop was established in March of the current year. Transactions related to purchases, returns and allowances, and cash payments during the remainder of the month are described below.

Mar. 16. Issued Check No. 1 in payment of rent for March, $450.
16. Purchased store equipment on account from Ritter Supply Corp., $9,550.
17. Purchased merchandise on account from Vanguard Clothes, Inc., $1,500.
17. Issued Check No. 2 in payment of store supplies, $56, and office supplies, $31.
19. Purchased merchandise on account from Lane Clothing Co., $2,492.
20. Purchased merchandise on account from Brady & Co., $1,450.
21. Received a credit memorandum from Lane Clothing Co. for returned merchandise, $42.

Post the journals to the accounts payable ledger.

24. Issued Check No. 3 to Ritter Supply Corp. in payment of invoice of $9,550.
25. Received a credit memorandum from Brady & Co. for defective merchandise, $37.
26. Issued Check No. 4 to Vanguard Clothes, Inc., in payment of invoice of $1,500, less 2% discount.
27. Issued Check No. 5 to a cash customer for merchandise returned, $19.
28. Issued Check No. 6 to Lane Clothing Co. in payment of the balance owed, less 2% discount.
28. Purchased merchandise on account from Brady & Co., $1,242.

Post the journals to the accounts payable ledger.

29. Purchased the following from Ritter Supply Corp. on account: store supplies, $48; office supplies, $42; office equipment, $3,420.
30. Issued Check No. 7 to Brady & Co. in payment of invoice of $1,450, less the credit of $37.
30. Purchased merchandise on account from Vanguard Clothes, Inc., $3,929.
31. Issued Check No. 8 in payment of incoming transportation charges on merchandise delivered during March, $214.
31. Issued Check No. 9 in payment of sales salaries, $1,025.
31. Received a credit memorandum from Ritter Supply Corp. for defect in office equipment, $25.

Post the journals to the accounts payable ledger.

Instructions:

(1) Open the following accounts in the general ledger, using the account numbers indicated.

111 Cash	412 Sales Returns and Allowances
116 Store Supplies	511 Purchases
117 Office Supplies	512 Purchases Discount
121 Store Equipment	611 Sales Salaries
122 Office Equipment	712 Rent Expense
211 Accounts Payable	

(2) Open the following accounts in the accounts payable ledger:

Brady & Co.; Lane Clothing Co.; Ritter Supply Corp.; Vanguard Clothes, Inc.

(3) Record the transactions for March, using a purchases journal similar to the one illustrated on pages 118 and 119, a cash payments journal similar to the one illustrated on page 124, and a two-column general journal. Post to the *accounts payable ledger* at the points indicated in the narrative of transactions.

(4) Post the appropriate individual entries to the *general ledger*. (Sundry Accounts columns of the purchases journal and the cash payments journal; both columns of the general journal.)

(5) Add the columns of the purchases journal and the cash payments journal, and post the appropriate totals to the general ledger. (Because of omission from the problem of transactions related to cash receipts, the cash account in the ledger will have a credit balance.)

(6) Prepare a schedule of accounts payable.

If the working papers correlating with the textbook are not used, omit Problem 5-3B.

5-3B. Fresno Specialty Co. uses carbon copies of its sales invoices as a sales journal, posting to the accounts receivable ledger directly from the invoices. At the end of the month the invoices are totaled and the appropriate entry is recorded in the general journal and posted to the general ledger. Purchases on account are recorded in a similar manner, the invoices being used as a purchases journal.

Invoices for the month of March, the first month of the current fiscal year, are listed and summarized below.

Sales Invoices

Mar.	4. Henry Parker Co.	$ 2,200
	6. Waldon & Kline, Inc.	960
	10. A. Clark & Co.	1,830
	16. Hamilton Corp.	749
	17. A. Clark & Co.	2,682
	22. Waldon & Kline, Inc.	1,595
	Total	$10,016

Purchases Invoices

Mar.	2. T. Altman & Co.; store supplies, $105; office supplies, $36.	$ 141
	3. Kirby Corp.; merchandise	2,710
	11. Dixon-Elliott, Inc.; merchandise	2,190
	18. Quincy Manufacturing Co.; store equipment	3,250
	19. Scott & Young, Inc.; merchandise	937
	29. T. Altman & Co.; store supplies	23
	31. Dixon-Elliott, Inc.; merchandise	1,586
	Total	$10,837
	Analysis: Purchases	$ 7,423
	Store supplies	128
	Office supplies	36
	Store equipment	3,250
	Total	$10,837

The other transactions completed during the month have already been recorded in a cash receipts journal, a cash payments journal, and a 4-column general journal with special columns for debits to Sales Returns and Allowances and credits to Accounts Receivable. The three journals are presented in the working papers. The accounts receivable ledger, the accounts payable ledger, and the general ledger are also presented in the working papers, with March 1 balances. There have been no postings to any of the accounts during the month of March.

Instructions:

(1) Post the sales invoices to the accounts receivable ledger and the purchases invoices to the accounts payable ledger. The posting reference columns of the accounts in the subsidiary ledgers may be left blank.

(2) Post the appropriate entries in the three journals to the accounts receivable ledger and the accounts payable ledger, in the following order: (a) general journal, (b) cash receipts journal, (c) cash payments journal. (If the customary practice of daily posting were followed, the postings would be in chronological order; imperfect date sequence is immaterial in this problem. It is also unnecessary to extend account balance after each posting.)

(3) Record the appropriate sales and purchases data (see summaries of the sales invoices and purchases invoices) in the four-column general journal. Add each of the four columns.

(4) Post all entries in the Sundry Accounts columns of the three journals to the general ledger, proceeding in the order indicated in instruction (2).

(5) Post the appropriate columnar totals of the three journals, proceeding in the order indicated in instruction (2).

(6) Prepare a trial balance of the general ledger.

(7) Determine the sum of the balances in (a) the accounts receivable ledger and (b) the accounts payable ledger; compare the amounts with the balances of the related accounts in the general ledger.

5-4B. The transactions completed by Snyder's during June, the first month of the current fiscal year, were as follows:

June 1. Issued Check No. 698 for June rent, $650.
 2. Purchased merchandise on account from Roth-Engle Corp., $2,240.
 3. Purchased equipment on account from Gibson Supply, Inc., $1,832.
 3. Issued Invoice No. 527 to L. B. Shannon, Inc., $1,221.
 5. Received check for $2,548 from Allen & Cramer in payment of $2,600 invoice, less discount.
 5. Issued Check No. 699 for miscellaneous selling expense, $103.
 5. Received credit memorandum from Roth-Engle Corp. for merchandise returned to them, $40.
 8. Issued Invoice No. 528 to Zimmer Corp., $915.
 9. Issued Check No. 700 for $3,038 to Bader Manufacturing Co. in payment of $3,100 balance, less 2% discount.
 9. Received check for $931 from Hartman & Co. in payment of $950 invoice, less discount.
 10. Issued Check No. 701 to Layton & Co. in payment of invoice of $997, no discount.
 10. Issued Invoice No. 529 to Allen & Cramer, $2,862.
 11. Issued Check No. 702 to Ward & Halter, Inc., in payment of account, $1,522, no discount.

June 12. Received check from L. B. Shannon, Inc., on account, $922, no discount.
   14. Issued credit memorandum to Allen & Cramer for damaged merchandise, $112.
   15. Issued Check No. 703 for $2,156 to Roth-Engle Corp. in payment of $2,200 balance, less 2% discount.
   15. Issued Check No. 704 for $468 for cash purchase of merchandise.
   15. Cash sales for June 1–15, $4,792.
   17. Purchased merchandise on account from Layton & Co., $2,435.
   18. Received check for return of merchandise that had been purchased for cash, $38.
   18. Issued Check No. 705 for miscellaneous general expense, $182.
   22. Purchased the following on account from Gibson Supply, Inc.: store supplies, $25; office supplies, $46.
   22. Issued Check No. 706 in payment of advertising expense, $350.
   23. Issued Invoice No. 530 to Hartman & Co., $2,163.
   24. Purchased the following on account from Bader Manufacturing Co.; merchandise, $1,510; store supplies, $27.
   25. Issued Invoice No. 531 to Zimmer Corp., $1,625.
   25. Received check for $2,695 from Allen & Cramer in payment of $2,750 balance, less discount.
   26. Issued Check No. 707 to Gibson Supply, Inc., in payment of invoice of June 3, $1,832, no discount.
   29. Issued Check No. 708 to Frank Snyder as a personal withdrawal, $900.
   30. Issued Check No. 709 for monthly salaries as follows: sales salaries, $1,580; office salaries, $670.
   30. Cash sales for June 16–30, $4,183.
   30. Issued Check No. 710 for transportation on commodities purchased during the month as follows: merchandise, $142; equipment, $39.

Instructions:

(1) Open the following accounts in the general ledger, entering the balances indicated as of June 1:

111	Cash	$ 6,840	411	Sales
113	Accounts Receivable	4,472	412	Sales Returns and Allowances
114	Merchandise Inventory	25,960	413	Sales Discount
115	Store Supplies	215	511	Purchases
116	Office Supplies	145	512	Purchases Discount
117	Prepaid Insurance	1,320	611	Sales Salaries
121	Equipment	19,827	612	Advertising Expense
121.1	Accumulated Depreciation	4,394	619	Miscellaneous Selling Expense
211	Accounts Payable	5,619	711	Office Salaries
311	Frank Snyder, Capital	48,766	712	Rent Expense
312	Frank Snyder, Drawing		719	Miscellaneous General Expense

(2) Record the transactions for June, using a sales journal (as on page 93), a purchases journal (as on pages 118 and 119), a cash receipts journal (as on page 99), a cash payments journal (as on page 124), and a 2-column general journal. The terms of all sales on account are FOB shipping point, 2/15, n/60. Assume that an assistant makes daily postings to the individual accounts in the accounts receivable ledger and the accounts payable ledger.

(3) Post the appropriate individual entries to the general ledger.

(4) Add the columns of the special journals and post the appropriate totals to the general ledger.

769

(5) Prepare a trial balance.
(6) Balances in the accounts in the subsidiary ledgers as of June 30 are listed below. Verify the agreement of the ledgers with their respective controlling accounts.

> Accounts Receivable: Balances of $2,163; $1,221; $2,540.
> Accounts Payable: Balances of $1,537; $71; $2,435.

CHAPTER 6

6-1B. The accounts in the ledger of Midland Corporation, with the unadjusted balances on August 31, the end of the current fiscal year, are as follows:

Cash....................	$ 5,370	Income Summary.........	——
Accounts Receivable.......	23,900	Sales....................	$215,000
Merchandise Inventory.....	54,700	Purchases................	136,000
Prepaid Insurance.........	2,480	Sales Salaries.............	24,000
Store Supplies.............	610	Advertising Expense.......	2,240
Store Equipment..........	25,100	Depreciation Expense —	
Accumulated Depreciation —		Store Equipment.......	——
Store Equipment........	2,650	Delivery Expense.........	1,450
Accounts Payable..........	5,900	Store Supplies Expense....	——
Salaries Payable...........	——	Rent Expense............	8,700
Capital Stock.............	50,000	Office Salaries............	7,550
Retained Earnings.........	25,380	Insurance Expense........	——
Dividends................	5,000	Misc. General Expense....	1,590
		Loss on Disposal of Equip..	240

The data needed for year-end adjustments on August 31 are as follows:

Merchandise inventory on August 31..	$52,600
Insurance expired during the year....	1,210
Store supplies inventory on August 31.	220
Depreciation for the current year.....	1,980
Accrued salaries on August 31:	
Sales salaries.............. $360	
Office salaries............. 120	480

Instructions (corporation income tax is excluded from consideration):

(1) Prepare an eight-column work sheet for the fiscal year ended August 31, listing all of the accounts in the order given.
(2) Prepare an income statement.
(3) Prepare a retained earnings statement.
(4) Prepare a balance sheet.
(5) Compute the following:
  (a) Percent of income from operations to sales.
  (b) Percent of net income to total capital as of the beginning of the year.

If the working papers correlating with this textbook are not used, omit Problem 6-2B.

6-2B. The general ledger of Plaza Appliances, Inc., with account balances as of December 1, is presented in the working papers. The company's journals, in which transactions for the month of December have been recorded, are also presented in the working papers. The fiscal year ends on December 31. (Corporation income tax is excluded from consideration.)

Instructions:

(1) Post the journals to the general ledger accounts, following the order indicated below. Balances need not be inserted in the balance columns of the accounts until all journals have been posted. Assume that entries to the subsidiary ledgers have been posted by an assistant.

POSTING ORDER

(a) Individual items in Sundry Accounts columns:
(1) General Journal, (2) Purchases Journal, (3) Cash Receipts Journal, (4) Cash Payments Journal.
(b) Column totals:
(1) Sales Journal, (2) Purchases Journal, (3) Cash Receipts Journal, (4) Cash Payments Journal.

(2) Complete the trial balance as of December 31. The account titles are listed on an eight-column work sheet presented in the working papers.

(3) Complete the work sheet. Adjustment data are:

Merchandise inventory at December 31.	$42,620
Insurance expired during the year......	1,432
Store supplies on hand at December 31.	260
Depreciation for the current year on:	
Store equipment..................	1,740
Office equipment.................	364
Accrued taxes at December 31........	3,410

(4) Prepare an income statement, a retained earnings statement, and a balance sheet.
(5) Journalize the adjusting entries and post.
(6) Journalize the closing entries and post. Indicate closed accounts by inserting a line in both balance columns.
(7) Complete the post-closing trial balance presented in the working papers.
(8) Journalize the reversing entry or entries as of January 1 and post.

771

6-4B. A portion of the work sheet of Grafton Co. for the current year ending December 31 is presented below and on the next page.

Account Title	Income Statement Debit	Income Statement Credit	Balance Sheet Debit	Balance Sheet Credit
Cash...............................			12,400	
Accounts Receivable...............			38,600	
Merchandise Inventory.............			51,000	
Prepaid Rent......................			1,200	
Prepaid Insurance.................			1,310	
Supplies..........................			430	
Store Equipment...................			17,700	
Accumulated Depr. — Store Equip...				5,100
Office Equipment..................			3,900	
Accumulated Depr. — Office Equip..				1,610
Accounts Payable..................				25,600
Sales Salaries Payable.............				290
Mortgage Note Payable.............				15,000
John Grafton, Capital..............				53,120

Account Title	Income Statement Debit	Income Statement Credit	Balance Sheet Debit	Balance Sheet Credit
John Grafton, Drawing.............			12,000	
Income Summary.................	48,000	51,000		
Sales...........................		290,000		
Sales Returns and Allowances........	3,100			
Purchases......................	196,000			
Purchases Discount................		2,200		
Sales Salaries....................	26,200			
Delivery Expense.................	5,300			
Supplies Expense..................	560			
Depreciation Expense — Store Equip.	1,820			
Miscellaneous Selling Expense.......	860			
Office Salaries....................	11,600			
Rent Expense....................	7,200			
Insurance Expense................	1,420			
Depreciation Expense — Office Equip.	840			
Miscellaneous General Expense......	1,580			
Interest Expense..................	900			
	305,380	343,200	138,540	100,720

Instructions:

(1) From the partial work sheet presented above and on the preceding page, determine the eight entries that appeared in the adjustments columns and present them in general journal form. The only accounts affected by more than a single adjusting entry were Merchandise Inventory and Income Summary. The balance in Prepaid Rent before adjustment was $8,400, representing a prepayment for 14 months' rent at $600 a month.

(2) Determine the following:

    (a) Amount of net income for the year.

    (b) Amount of the owner's capital at the end of the year.

CHAPTER 7

7-1B. The following were selected from among the transactions completed by Turner Co. during the current year:

Jan. 12. Purchased merchandise on account from Feldman & Co., $800.

    22. Paid Feldman & Co. for the invoice of January 12, less 2% discount.

Feb. 10. Purchased merchandise on account from L. V. Blair Co., $1,400.

Mar. 12. Issued a 30-day, 8% note for $1,400 to L. V. Blair Co. on account.

Apr. 11. Paid L. V. Blair Co. the amount owed on the note of March 12.

May 26. Issued a 60-day, non-interest-bearing note for $12,000 to Second National Bank. The bank discounted the note at the rate of 7%.

July 25. Paid Second National Bank the amount due on the note of May 26.

Aug. 8. Borrowed $4,000 from Merchants Bancorporation, issuing a 60-day, 7½% note for that amount.

Oct. 7. Paid Merchants Bancorporation the interest due on the note of August 8 and renewed the loan by issuing a new 30-day, 7½% note for $4,000. (Record both the debit and the credit to the notes payable account.)

Nov. 6. Paid Merchants Bancorporation the amount due on the note of October 7.

Dec. 1. Purchased office equipment from Central Equipment Co. for $6,800, paying $800 and issuing a series of ten 8% notes for $600 each, coming due at 30-day intervals.

    31. Paid the amount due Central Equipment Co. on the first note in the series issued on December 1.

Instructions:

(1) Record the transactions in general journal form.

(2) Determine the total amount of interest accrued as of December 31 on the nine notes owed to Central Equipment Co.

(3) Assume that a single note for $6,000 had been issued on December 1 instead of the series of ten notes, and that its terms required principal payments of $600 each 30 days, with interest at 8% on the principal balance before applying the $600 payment. Determine the amount that would have been due and payable on December 31.

7-2B. The following were selected from among the transactions completed by John Williams & Co. during the current year:

Jan. 8. Sold merchandise on account to Madden Co., $1,200.

  18. Accepted a 30-day, 7% note for $1,200 from Madden Co. on account.

Feb. 17. Received from Madden Co. the amount due on the note of January 18.

Mar. 10. Sold merchandise on account to Gilman & Hardy, $800, charging an additional $20 for prepaid transportation costs.

  20. Received from Gilman & Hardy the amount due on the invoice of March 10, less 2% discount.

Apr. 28. Loaned $500 cash to Fred Wiley, receiving a 30-day, 8% note.

May 28. Received the interest due from Fred Wiley and a new 60-day, 6% note as a renewal of the loan. (Record both the debit and the credit to the notes receivable account.)

July 27. Received from Fred Wiley the amount due on his note.

Aug. 16. Sold merchandise on account to R. B. Olson, Inc., $4,000.

Sept. 17. Received from R. B. Olson, Inc., a 60-day, 8% note for $2,100, dated September 15.

  25. Discounted the note from R. B. Olson, Inc., at the Bank of Commerce at 7%.

Nov. 14. Received notice from Bank of Commerce that R. B. Olson, Inc., had dishonored its note. Paid the bank the maturity value of the note.

Dec. 4. Received from R. B. Olson, Inc., the amount owed on the dishonored note, plus interest for 20 days at 8% computed on the maturity value of the note.

Instructions:

Record the transactions in general journal form.

7-3B. The transactions, adjusting entries, and closing entries described below are related to uncollectible accounts. All were completed during the current fiscal year ended December 31.

Jan. 26. Wrote off the $512 balance owed by Yost Corp., which has no assets.

Apr. 10. Reinstated the account of Fred Fisher that had been written off in the preceding year and received $80 cash in full payment.

773

July 17. Received 9% of the $500 balance owed by Hansen & Co., a bankrupt, and wrote off the remainder as uncollectible.

Oct. 3. Reinstated the account of Gary Carver that had been written off two years earlier and received $62 cash in full payment.

Dec. 27. Wrote off the following accounts as uncollectible (compound entry): Roger Frost, $295; Hart & Cooper, $815; Monroe Corp., $977; M. G. Watson, Inc., $530.

31. On the basis of an analysis of the $123,580 of accounts receivable, it was estimated that $3,520 will be uncollectible. Recorded the adjusting entry.

31. Recorded the entry to close the appropriate account to Income Summary.

Instructions:

(1) Open the following selected accounts, recording the credit balance indicated as of January 1 of the current fiscal year:

114.1	Allowance for Doubtful Accounts.	$3,600
313	Income Summary.............	——
718	Uncollectible Accounts Expense..	——

(2) Record in general journal form the transactions and the adjusting and closing entries described above. After each entry, post to the three selected accounts affected and extend the new balances.

(3) Determine the expected realizable value of the accounts receivable as of December 31.

(4) Assuming that, instead of basing the provision for uncollectible accounts on an analysis of receivables, the adjusting entry on December 31 had been based on an estimated loss of 1/2 of 1% of net sales for the year of $750,000, determine the following:

(a) Uncollectible accounts expense for the year.

(b) Balance in the allowance account after the adjustment of December 31.

(c) Expected realizable value of the accounts receivable as of December 31.

If the working papers correlating with the textbook are not used, omit Problem 7-4B.

7-4B. The following transactions, all of which are related to receivables and payables, were selected from among the transactions completed by Layton Co. during the current fiscal year.

Jan. 9. Issued to Pierce Co. a 2-month, 8% note for $4,350, on account.

22. Received from Globe Co., a 90-day, non-interest-bearing note for $2,400, dated January 21, on account.

Feb. 20. Discounted at Manufacturers Trust Co. at 7% the note received from Globe Co., dated January 21.

Mar. 9. Issued Check No. 416 to Pierce Co. in payment of the note issued on January 9.

18. Received from Black & Co. the amount due on a March 8 invoice for $1,600, less 2% discount.

Apr. 4. Wrote off against the allowance account the $158 owed by Corbin & Son.

24. Borrowed $4,000 from Manufacturers Trust Co., issuing a 7%, 90-day note.

May 12. Received from Newton, Inc., a 90-day, 7% note for $3,600, dated May 11, on account.
18. Purchased land for a building site from County Development Co. for $60,000, issuing Check No. 533 for $12,000 and a 7% mortgage note for the balance. The contract provides for payments of $6,000 of principal plus accrued interest at intervals of six months. (Record entire transaction in the cash payments journal.)
June 10. Discounted at Columbia National Bank at 6% the note received from Newton, Inc., dated May 11.
July 3. Received from Myron Kane on account a 30-day, 6% note for $400, dated July 2.
23. Issued Check No. 579 to Manufacturers Trust Co. for the amount due on the note dated April 24.
Aug. 1. Myron Kane dishonored his note dated July 2. Charged the principal and interest to his account.
10. Received notice from Columbia National Bank that Newton, Inc., had dishonored the note due on August 9. Issued Check No. 687 for the amount due on the note, plus a protest fee of $3.
Sept. 2. Received from Myron Kane the amount due on the note dishonored on August 1, plus $2.01 interest for 30 days on the maturity value of the note.
15. Reinstated the account of Joel Fields that had been written off against the allowance account in the preceding year, and received cash in full payment, $76.
Oct. 9. Received from Newton, Inc., the amount due on the note dishonored on August 9, plus $42.77 interest for 60 days on the maturity value of the note plus protest fee.
Nov. 18. Issued Check No. 776 for principal and interest due on the mortgage note issued on May 18.

775

Instructions:

(1) Record the selected entries in the three journals provided in the working papers: Cash Receipts, Cash Payments, and a General Journal. No posting is required.

(2) At the end of the year, Accounts Receivable has a debit balance of $110,400. The distribution of the accounts, by age intervals, is presented in the working papers, together with the percent of each class estimated to be uncollectible. Determine the amount of the accounts estimated to be uncollectible.

(3) Prior to adjustment at the end of the year, Allowance for Doubtful Accounts has a credit balance of $462. Record the adjusting entry in the general journal as of December 31.

(4) Present the data on accounts receivable as they will appear in the balance sheet as of December 31.

CHAPTER 8

8-1B. Robert Ford's Television employs the periodic inventory system. Details regarding their inventory of television sets at January 1, purchase invoices during the year, and the inventory count at December 31 are summarized at the top of the next page.

| | | Purchase Invoices | | | Inventory |
Model	Inventory Jan. 1	1st	2d	3d	Count Dec. 31
C23	7 at $110	4 at $110	4 at $110	5 at $114	6
E17	9 at 65	10 at 65	10 at 65	8 at 65	6
G29	2 at 275	2 at 280	2 at 280	2 at 285	3
K11	4 at 190	6 at 185	6 at 185	4 at 185	4
P39	8 at 224	4 at 226	6 at 230	4 at 235	6
R18	——	2 at 350	2 at 360	——	2
X47	6 at 305	3 at 310	3 at 316	4 at 321	5

Instructions:

(1) Determine the cost of the inventory on December 31 by the first-in, first-out method. Present data in columnar form, using the columnar headings indicated below. If the inventory of a particular model is composed of an entire lot plus a portion of another lot acquired at a different unit price, use a separate line for each lot.

Model	Quantity	Unit Cost	Total Cost

(2) Determine the cost of the inventory on December 31 by the last-in, first-out method, following the procedures indicated in instruction (1).

(3) Determine the cost of the inventory on December 31 by the weighted average method, using the columnar headings indicated in instruction (1).

8-2B. The beginning inventory of Commodity 592D and data on purchases and sales for a three-month period are presented below.

April	1.	Inventory......	6 units at $16.00	$ 96.00
	8.	Purchase......	10 units at 16.25	162.50
	18.	Sale..........	8 units at 25.00	200.00
	26.	Sale..........	4 units at 25.00	100.00
May	7.	Purchase......	8 units at 16.50	132.00
	11.	Sale..........	4 units at 25.00	100.00
	19.	Sale..........	3 units at 25.00	75.00
	27.	Purchase......	7 units at 16.50	115.50
June	5.	Sale..........	6 units at 25.00	150.00
	13.	Sale..........	3 units at 25.00	75.00
	20.	Purchase......	10 units at 17.00	170.00
	28.	Sale..........	5 units at 26.00	130.00

Instructions:

(1) Record the inventory, purchase, and cost of merchandise sold data in a perpetual inventory record similar to the one illustrated on page 197, using the first-in, first-out method.

(2) Determine the total sales and the total cost of Commodity 592D sold for the period, and express their effect on the general ledger by two entries in general journal form. Assume that all sales were on account.

(3) Determine the gross profit from sales for Commodity 592D for the period.

(4) Determine the cost of the inventory at June 30, assuming that the periodic system of inventory had been employed and that the inventory cost had been determined by the last-in, first-out method.

8-3B. Selected data on merchandise inventory, purchases, and sales for the Dawkins Co. and the Milton Co. are presented below.

DAWKINS CO.

	Cost	Retail
Merchandise inventory, March 1....	$350,970	$540,780
Transactions during March:		
Purchases.....................	125,678⎫	189,740
Purchases discount.............	1,810⎭	
Sales.......................		224,280
Sales returns and allowances......		3,840

MILTON CO.

Merchandise inventory, June 1......	$185,000
Transactions during June and July:	
Purchases.....................	220,500
Purchases discount.............	2,600
Sales.......................	305,000
Sales returns and allowances......	4,100
Estimated gross profit rate........	30%

Instructions:

(1) Determine the estimated cost of the merchandise inventory of the Dawkins Co. on March 31 by the retail method, presenting details of the computations.
(2) Estimate the cost of the merchandise inventory of the Milton Co. on July 31 by the gross profit method, presenting details of the computations.

777

If the working papers correlating with the textbook are not used, omit Problem 8-4B.

8-4B. Data on the physical inventory of Powell Corporation as of June 30, the close of the current fiscal year, are presented in the working papers. The quantity of each commodity on hand has been determined and recorded on the inventory sheet; unit market prices have also been determined as of June 30 and recorded on the sheet. The inventory is to be determined at cost and also at the lower of cost or market, using the first-in, first-out method. Quantity and cost data from the last purchase invoice of the year and the next-to-the-last purchase invoice are summarized below and on the next page.

	Last Purchase Invoice		Next-to-the-Last Purchase Invoice	
Description	Quantity Purchased	Unit Cost	Quantity Purchased	Unit Cost
31FT	50	$ 20	30	$ 19
1542E	75	9	100	10
OP37	25	215	25	225
SE72	300	12	200	10
31VX	40	45	60	47
57ABC	175	15	125	15
WD71	12	410	10	425
C775	500	6	500	7
814B	90	8	60	7
259LC	5	250	4	260

	Last Purchase Invoice		Next-to-the-Last Purchase Invoice	
Description	Quantity Purchased	Unit Cost	Quantity Purchased	Unit Cost
XX75	25	$230	25	$220
1954D	300	13	200	12
BD111	8	48	10	47
AD65	175	8	100	9
G17H	360	5	220	5
KK22	100	30	100	28
PX86	96	20	120	21
MK630	50	90	30	92

Instructions:

Record the appropriate unit costs on the inventory sheet and complete the pricing of the inventory. When there are two different unit costs applicable to a commodity, proceed as follows:

(1) Draw a line through the quantity and insert the quantity and unit cost of the last purchase.

(2) On the following line insert the quantity and unit cost of the next-to-the-last purchase. The first item on the inventory sheet has been completed as an example.

8-5B. The preliminary income statement of Reeder Company presented below was prepared before the accounts were adjusted or closed at the end of the fiscal year. The company uses the periodic inventory system.

Reeder Company
Income Statement
For Year Ended December 31, 19—

Sales (net)...................................		$394,700
Cost of merchandise sold:		
Merchandise inventory, January 1, 19—.....	$ 78,750	
Purchases (net)..........................	261,150	
Merchandise available for sale.............	$339,900	
Less merchandise inventory, December 31, 19—	71,600	
Cost of merchandise sold.................		268,300
Gross profit on sales........................		$126,400
Operating expenses........................		90,150
Net income................................		$ 36,250

The following errors in the ledger and on inventory sheets were discovered by the independent CPA retained to conduct the annual audit:

(a) A number of errors were discovered in pricing inventory items, in extending amounts, and in footing inventory sheets. The net effect of the corrections, exclusive of those described below, was to decrease by $1,700 the amount stated as the ending inventory on the income statement above.

(b) An item of office equipment, received on December 30, was erroneously included in the December 31 merchandise inventory at its cost of $1,250. The invoice had been recorded correctly.

(c) A purchase invoice for merchandise of $500, dated December 28, had been received and correctly recorded, but the merchandise was not received until January 3 and had not been included in the December 31 inventory. Title had passed to Reeder Company on December 28.

(d) A purchase invoice for merchandise of $950, dated December 30, was not received until January 4 and had not been recorded by December 31. However, the merchandise, to which title had passed, had arrived and had been included in the December 31 inventory.

(e) A sales order for $2,000, dated December 30, had been recorded as a sale on that date, but title did not pass to the purchaser until shipment was made on January 3. The merchandise, which had cost $1,375, was excluded from the December 31 inventory.

(f) A sales invoice for $2,200, dated December 31, had not been recorded. The merchandise was shipped on December 31, FOB shipping point, and its cost, $1,600, was excluded from the December 31 inventory.

Instructions:

(1) Journalize the entries necessary to correct the general ledger accounts as of December 31, inserting the identifying letters in the date column. All purchases and sales were made on account.

(2) Determine the correct inventory for December 31, beginning your analysis with the $71,600 shown on the preliminary income statement. Assemble the corrections in two groupings, "Additions" and "Deductions," allowing six lines for each group. Identify each correction by the appropriate letter.

(3) Prepare a revised income statement.

779

CHAPTER 9

9-1B. The accounts listed below appear in the ledger of Pierce Company at December 31, the end of the current fiscal year. None of the year-end adjustments have been recorded.

113 Interest Receivable	$——	411 Rental Income		$95,700
114 Supplies	405	511 Salary and Commissions		
115 Prepaid Insurance	1,150	Expense		19,100
116 Prepaid Advertising	——	513 Advertising Expense		3,250
117 Prepaid Interest	——	514 Insurance Expense		——
213 Salaries and Commissions		515 Supplies Expense		——
Payable	——	611 Interest Income		205
215 Unearned Rent	——	711 Interest Expense		425
313 Income Summary	——			

The following information relating to adjustments at December 31 is obtained from physical inventories, supplementary records, and other sources:

(a) Interest accrued on notes receivable at December 31, $50.

(b) Inventory of supplies at December 31, $125.

(c) The insurance record indicates that $550 of insurance has expired during the year.

(d) Of a prepayment of $500 for advertising space in a local newspaper, 80% has been used and the remainder will be used in the following year.

(e) A short-term non-interesting-bearing note payable was discounted at a bank in December. The amount of the total discount of $200 applicable to December is $120.

(f) Salaries and commissions accrued at December 31, $725.

(g) Rent collected in advance that will not be earned until the following year, $5,500.

Instructions:

(1) Open the accounts listed and record the balances in the appropriate balance columns, as of December 31.

(2) Journalize the adjusting entries and post to the appropriate accounts after each entry, extending the balances. Identify the postings by writing "Adjusting" in the item columns.

(3) Prepare a compound journal entry to close the revenue accounts and another compound entry to close the expense accounts.

(4) Post the closing entries, inserting a short line in both balance columns of accounts that are closed. Identify the postings by writing "Closing" in the item columns.

(5) Prepare the reversing journal entries that should be made on January 1 and post to the appropriate accounts after each entry, inserting a short line in both balance columns of accounts that are now in balance. Write "Reversing" in the item columns.

9-2B. Higgins Co. closes its accounts annually as of December 31, the end of the fiscal year. All relevant data regarding notes payable and related interest from November 16 through February 14 of the following year are presented below. (All notes are dated as of the day they are issued.)

Nov. 16. Issued a $9,000, 8%, 90-day note on account.

Dec. 1. Issued a $6,000, 8%, 60-day note on account.

7. Paid principal, $7,000, and interest, $105, on note payable due today.

16. Borrowed $12,000 from Citizens National Bank, issuing a 7%, 60-day note.

31. Recorded an adjusting entry for the interest accrued on the notes dated November 16, December 1, and December 16. There are no other notes outstanding on this date.

31. Recorded the entry to close the interest expense account.

Jan. 1. Recorded a reversing entry for the accrued interest.

10. Issued a $4,500, 8%, 30-day note on account.

30. Paid $6,080 on the note issued on December 1.

Feb. 9. Paid $4,530 on the note issued on January 10.

14. Paid $9,180 on the note issued on November 16.

14. Paid $12,140 on the note issued on December 16.

Instructions:

(1) Open accounts for Interest Payable (Account No. 214) and Interest Expense (Account No. 711), and record a debit balance of $1,300 in the latter account as of November 16 of the current year.

(2) Present entries in general journal form to record the transactions and other data described above, posting to the two accounts after each entry affecting them.

(3) If the reversing entry had not been recorded as of January 1, indicate how each interest payment in January and February should be allocated. Submit the data in the form illustrated at the top of the next page.

(4) Do the February 14 balances of Interest Payable and Interest Expense obtained by use of the reversing entry technique correspond to

Note (Face Amount)	Total Interest Paid	Dr. Interest Payable	Dr. Interest Expense
$ 6,000	$	$	$
4,500			
9,000			
12,000			
Total	$	$	$

the balances that would have been obtained by the more laborious process of analyzing each payment?

If the working papers correlating with the textbook are not used, omit Problem 9-3B.

9-3B. Allen Company prepares interim financial statements at the end of each month and closes its accounts annually on December 31. Its income statement for the two-month period, January and February of the current year, is presented in the working papers. In addition, the trial balance of the ledger as of one month later is presented on an eight-column work sheet in the working papers. Data needed for adjusting entries at March 31, the end of the three-month period, are as follows:

(a) Uncollectible accounts expense is estimated at $\frac{1}{2}$ of 1% of net sales for the three-month period.
(b) Estimated merchandise inventory at March 31, $58,750.
(c) Insurance expired during the three-month period:
    Allocable as selling expense, $225.
    Allocable as general expense, $100.
(d) Estimated inventory of store supplies at March 31, $250.
(e) Depreciation for the three-month period:
    Store equipment, $450.
    Office equipment, $135.
(f) Estimated property tax of $140 a month for January and February was recorded in the accounts. The tax statement, which was received in March, indicates a liability of $1,740 for the calendar year.
(g) Salaries accrued at March 31:
    Sales salaries, $285.
    Office salaries, $100.
(h) The notes payable balance of $15,000 is composed of the following:
    $9,000, 90-day, non-interest-bearing note discounted at Winters Trust Co. on March 1. The $180 discount was debited to Interest Expense. (Record adjustment in work sheet before considering the other note.)
    $6,000, 6-month, 8% note dated December 1 of the preceding year. (Accrue interest for 4 months.)

Instructions:

(1) Complete the eight-column work sheet for the three-month period ended March 31 of the current year.
(2) Prepare an income statement for the three-month period, using the last three-column group of the nine-column form in the working papers.
(3) Prepare an income statement for the month of March, using the middle three-column group of the nine-column form in the working papers.
(4) Prepare a capital statement for the three-month period. There were no additional investments during the period.

781

(5) Prepare a balance sheet as of March 31.

(6) Determine the amount of interest expense on each note allocable to the month of March and compare the total with the amount reported as interest expense in the income statement for March.

9-4B. The Andersen Co. prepares interim statements at the end of each month and closes its accounts annually on December 31. Property taxes are assessed for fiscal years beginning on July 1 and ending on June 30. Selected transactions and property tax allocations for the period July 1 to December 31 of one year and of January 1 to June 30 of the following year are presented below.

July 31. Property tax allocation for July based on estimated property tax of $10,200 for the taxing authority's fiscal year beginning July 1.

Sept. 30. Property tax allocation for September, based on tax statement dated September 20 indicating a tax assessment of $9,600.

Oct. 15. Paid first half of tax assessment, $4,800.

31. Property tax allocation for October.

Dec. 31. Property tax allocation for December.

Jan. 31. Property tax allocation for January.

May 15. Paid second half of tax assessment, $4,800.

31. Property tax allocation for May.

June 30. Property tax allocation for June.

Instructions:

(1) Present in general journal form the entries to record the selected tax allocations and payments, assuming in all cases that appropriate entries have been recorded in the accounts for all intervening months.

(2) Indicate the amount of prepaid property tax and property tax payable that would be reported on the balance sheets prepared as of (a) November 30, (b) December 31, and (c) April 30. In each case list the section in which the item would appear (Current assets, etc.), the account title (Prepaid Property Tax, etc.), and the amount.

9-7B. Selected accounts from the ledger of Beeman Co., with the account balances before and after adjustment, at the close of the fiscal year are presented below:

	Un-adjusted Balance	Adjusted Balance		Un-adjusted Balance	Adjusted Balance
Interest Receivable...	$——	$ 225	Rent Income........	$ 9,600	$ 8,800
Supplies............	1,240	605	Wages Expense......	24,340	24,750
Prepaid Insurance....	1,860	750	Supplies Expense.....	——	635
Prepaid Property Tax.	450	——	Property Tax Expense	2,250	2,700
Prepaid Interest......	——	75	Insurance Expense...	——	1,110
Wages Payable......	——	410	Interest Income......	400	625
Interest Payable.....	——	125	Interest Expense.....	360	410
Unearned Rent......	——	800			

Instructions:

(1) Journalize the adjusting entries that were posted to the ledger at the close of the fiscal year.

(2) Insert the letter "R" in the date column opposite each adjusting entry that should be reversed as of the first day of the following fiscal year.

CHAPTER 10

10-1B. The following expenditures and receipts are related to land, land improvements, and buildings acquired for use in a business enterprise. The receipts are identified by an asterisk.

(a)	Cost of real estate acquired as a plant site: Land........	$ 65,000
	Building......	35,000
(b)	Fee paid to attorney for title search....................	475
(c)	Delinquent real estate taxes on property, assumed by purchaser...	2,750
(d)	Architect's and engineer's fees for plans and supervision...	52,000
(e)	Cost of razing and removing the building...............	4,500
(f)	Premium on 1-year insurance policy during construction..	5,600
(g)	Cost of land fill and grading...........................	2,000
(h)	Paid to building contractor for new building............	700,000
(i)	Cost of paving parking lot to be used by customers.......	4,900
(j)	Cost of repairing windstorm damage during construction..	1,250
(k)	Cost of trees and shrubbery, planted...................	2,200
(l)	Special assessment paid to city for extension of water main to the property...................................	400
(m)	Real estate taxes accrued during construction...........	2,500
(n)	Interest accrued on building loan during construction....	18,000
(o)	Cost of floodlights on parking lot, installed.............	2,900
(p)	Cost of repairing vandalism damage during construction..	250
(q)	Proceeds from sale of salvage materials from old building.	1,000*
(r)	Money borrowed to pay building contractor............	450,000*
(s)	Proceeds from insurance company for windstorm damage.	1,150*
(t)	Refund of premium on insurance policy (f) canceled after 11 months..	300*
		$447,275

Instructions:

(1) Assign each expenditure and receipt (indicate receipts by an asterisk) to Land (permanently capitalized), Land Improvements (limited life), Building, or "Other Accounts." Identify each item by letter and list the amounts in columnar form, as follows:

Item	Land	Land Improvements	Building	Other Accounts
	$	$	$	$

(2) Total the amount columns.

10-2B. An item of new equipment acquired at a cost of $65,000 at the beginning of a fiscal year has an estimated life of 5 years and an estimated trade-in value of $5,000. The manager requested information (details given in Instruction 1) regarding the effect of alternative methods on the amount of depreciation expense deductible each year for federal income tax purposes.

783

Upon the basis of the data presented to the manager in accordance with Instruction 1, the declining-balance method was elected. In the first week of the fourth year the equipment was traded in for similar equipment priced at $80,000. The trade-in allowance on the old equipment was $15,000, cash of $15,000 was paid, and a note payable was issued for the balance.

Instructions:

(1) Determine the annual depreciation for each of the estimated 5 years of use, the accumulated depreciation at the end of each year, and the book value of the equipment at the end of each year by (a) the straight-line method, (b) the declining-balance method (at twice the straight-line rate), and (c) the sum-of-the-years-digits method. The following columnar headings are suggested for each schedule:

Year	Depreciation Expense	Accumulated Depreciation End of Year	Book Value End of Year

(2) Present the debits and credits required, in general journal form, to record the exchange at the beginning of the fourth year, assuming that the gain or loss on the disposal is to be recognized.

(3) Present the debits and credits required, in general journal form, to record the exchange at the beginning of the fourth year, assuming that the gain or loss on the disposal is not to be recognized.

(4) What is the cost basis of the new equipment, for purposes of computing the amount of depreciation allowable for income tax purposes?

(5) Assuming that the trade-in allowance had been $10,000 instead of $15,000, determine the cost basis of the new equipment for purposes of computing the amount of depreciation allowable for income tax purposes, solving by two methods.

If the working papers correlating with the textbook are not used, omit Problem 10-3B.

10-3B. Fleming Printing Co. maintains a subsidiary equipment ledger for the printing equipment and accumulated depreciation accounts in the general ledger. A small portion of the subsidiary ledger, the two controlling accounts, and a general journal are presented in the working papers. The company computes depreciation on each individual item of equipment. Transactions and adjusting entries affecting the printing equipment are described below.

1973
Oct. 1. Purchased a power cutter (Model 2-C, Serial No. 41772) from Stevens Typograph Co. on account for $5,000. The estimated life of the asset is 10 years, it is expected to have no residual value, and the straight-line method of depreciation is to be used. (This is the only transaction of the year that directly affected the printing equipment account.)

Dec. 31. Recorded depreciation for the year in subsidiary accounts 125-77 to 125-79, and inserted the new balances. (An assistant recorded the depreciation and the new balances in accounts 125-1 to 125-76.)

31. Journalized and posted the annual adjusting entry for depreciation on printing equipment. The depreciation for the year recorded in subsidiary accounts 125-1 to 125-76 totaled $16,027 to which was added the depreciation entered in accounts 125-77 to 125-79.

784

1974

June 29. Purchased a Model TR-3 rotary press from Bower Press, Inc., priced at $35,620, giving the Model C8 flatbed press (Account No. 125-77) in exchange plus $7,590 cash and a series of eight $2,500 notes payable, maturing at 6-month intervals. The estimated life of the new press is 8 years, it is expected to have a residual value of $2,000, and the straight-line method of depreciation is used. (Recorded depreciation to date in 1974 on item traded in; gain or loss on the disposal was not recognized.)

Instructions:

(1) Journalize the transaction of October 1. Post to Printing Equipment in the general ledger and to Account No. 125-79 in the subsidiary ledger.

(2) Journalize the adjusting entries required on December 31 and post to Accumulated Depreciation — Printing Equipment in the general ledger.

(3) Journalize the entries required by the purchase of printing equipment on June 29. Post to Printing Equipment and to Accumulated Depreciation — Printing Equipment in the general ledger and to Accounts Nos. 125–77 and 125–80 in the subsidiary ledger.

(4) If the rotary press purchased on June 29 had been depreciated by the declining-balance method, at twice the straight-line rate, determine the depreciation on this press for the fiscal years ending (a) December 31, 1974, and (b) December 31, 1975.

785

10-4B. The following transactions, adjusting entries, and closing entries were completed by Robeson's Department Store during a 3-year period. All are related to the use of delivery equipment. The declining-balance method (twice the straight-line rate) of depreciation is used.

1973

Apr. 2. Purchased a used delivery truck for $3,700, paying cash.
      9. Paid $300 for major repairs to the truck.
Nov. 7. Paid garage $40 for miscellaneous repairs to the truck.
Dec. 31. Recorded depreciation on the truck for the fiscal year. The estimated life of the truck is 4 years, with a trade-in value of $325.
     31. Closed the appropriate accounts to the income summary account.

1974

June 29. Traded in the used truck for a new truck priced at $5,750, receiving a trade-in allowance of $1,600 and paying the balance in cash. (Record depreciation to date in 1974; gain or loss on exchange is not to be recognized.)
Oct. 9. Paid garage $50 for miscellaneous repairs to the truck.
Dec. 31. Recorded depreciation on the truck. It has an estimated trade-in value of $625 and an estimated life of 5 years.
     31. Closed the appropriate accounts to the income summary account.

1975

Oct. 1. Purchased a new truck for $6,000, paying cash.
      3. Sold the truck purchased in 1974 for $3,100. (Record depreciation.)
Dec. 31. Recorded depreciation on the remaining truck. It has an estimated trade-in value of $800 and an estimated life of 6 years.
     31. Closed the appropriate accounts to the income summary account.

Instructions:

(1) Open the following accounts in the ledger:

122   Delivery Equipment
122.1 Accumulated Depreciation — Delivery Equipment
616   Depreciation Expense — Delivery Equipment
617   Truck Repair Expense
912   Loss on Disposal of Plant Assets

(2) Record the transactions and the adjusting and closing entries in general journal form. Post to the accounts and extend the balances after each posting.

10-6B. The trial balance of W. W. Roe Corporation at the end of the current fiscal year, before adjustments, is as follows:

W. W. Roe Corporation
Trial Balance
September 30, 19—

Cash..	20,770	
Accounts Receivable...........................	23,239	
Allowance for Doubtful Accounts.................		1,125
Merchandise Inventory.........................	93,750	
Prepaid Expenses..............................	6,190	
Office Equipment..............................	7,700	
Accumulated Depreciation — Office Equipment......		3,010
Store Equipment..............................	25,250	
Accumulated Depreciation — Store Equipment.......		12,750
Delivery Equipment...........................	22,900	
Accumulated Depreciation — Delivery Equipment....		7,225
Buildings.....................................	110,000	
Accumulated Depreciation — Buildings.............		40,500
Land...	25,000	
Accounts Payable..............................		65,000
Notes Payable (short-term)......................		10,000
Capital Stock.................................		100,000
Retained Earnings.............................		49,189
Dividends....................................	15,000	
Sales (net)...................................		960,750
Purchases (net)...............................	749,290	
Operating Expenses (control account)..............	149,710	
Interest Expense..............................	750	
	1,249,549	1,249,549

Data needed for year-end adjustments:

(a) Merchandise inventory at September 30, $91,500.
(b) Insurance and other prepaid operating expenses expired during the year, $3,850.
(c) Estimated uncollectible accounts at September 30, $1,925.
(d) Depreciation is computed at composite rates on the average of the beginning and the ending balances of the plant asset accounts. The beginning balances and rates are as follows:
Office equipment, $6,900; 8%   Delivery equipment, $23,100; 20%
Store equipment, $24,750; 10%   Buildings, $90,000; 2½%
(e) Accrued liabilities at the end of the year, $1,135, of which $125 is for

the interest on the notes and $1,010 is for wages and other operating expenses.

Instructions (corporation income tax is excluded from consideration):

(1) Prepare an income statement for the current year.
(2) Prepare a balance sheet in report form, presenting the plant assets in the manner illustrated in this chapter.

CHAPTER 11

11-1B. The cash in bank account for C. A. Bowers and Son at June 30 of the current year indicated a balance of $7,560.70 after both the cash receipts journal and the check register for June had been posted. The bank statement indicated a balance of $9,148.85 on June 30. Comparison of the bank statement and the accompanying canceled checks and memorandums with the records revealed the following reconciling items:

(a) A deposit of $1,825.36 representing receipts of June 30 had been made too late to appear on the bank statement.
(b) Checks outstanding totaled $2,976.16.
(c) The bank had collected for C. A. Bowers and Son $515 on a note left for collection. The face of the note was $500.
(d) A check drawn for $10 had been erroneously charged by the bank as $100.
(e) A check for $57 returned with the statement had been recorded in the check register as $75. The check was for the payment of an obligation to Dodson Equipment Company for the purchase of office equipment on account.
(f) Bank service charges for June amounted to $5.65.

Instructions:

(1) Prepare a bank reconciliation.
(2) Journalize the necessary entries. The accounts have not been closed. The voucher system is used.

11-2B. Fern Company had the following vouchers in its unpaid voucher file at June 30 of the current year.

Due Date	Voucher No.	Creditor	Date of Invoice	Amount	Terms
July 5	904	Ames, Inc.	June 25	$1,000	1/10, n/30
July 13	885	Wells Co.	June 13	450	n/30
July 21	901	Dow Co.	June 21	800	n/30

The vouchers prepared and the checks issued during the month of July were as listed on the next page.

Instructions:

(1) Set up a four-column account for Accounts Payable, Account No. 211, and record the balance of $2,250 as of July 1.
(2) Record the July vouchers in a voucher register similar to the one illustrated in this chapter, with the following amount columns:

Accounts Payable Cr., Purchases Dr., Store Supplies Dr., Office Supplies Dr., and Sundry Accounts Dr. Purchase invoices are recorded at the gross amount.

(3) Record the July checks in a check register similar to the one illustrated in this chapter, but omit the Bank Deposits and Balance columns. As each check is recorded in the check register, the date and check number should be inserted in the appropriate columns of the voucher register. (Assume that notations for payment of June vouchers are made in the voucher register for June.)

(4) Total and rule the registers and post to the accounts payable account.

(5) Prepare a schedule of unpaid vouchers.

Vouchers

Date	Voucher No.	Payee	Amount	Terms	Distribution
July 2	920	John Carr Co.	$ 750	2/10, n/30	Purchases
3	921	Orr Supply	1,500	n/30	Store equipment
5	922	B. B. Lee, Inc.	400	1/10, n/30	Purchases
9	923	Neff and Son	36	cash	Store supplies
12	924	Mason Co.	1,100	2/10, n/30	Purchases
17	925	Root Co.	450	2/10, n/30	Purchases
18	926	Cook Co.	725	n/30	Office equipment
19	927	Ryan Trust Co.	5,100		Note payable, $5,000 Interest, $100
19	928	W. Feld Co.	600	2/10, n/30	Purchases
22	929	Kane Supply	85	cash	Store supplies
25	930	Morton Courier	64	cash	Advertising expense
27	931	Myers Co.	250	1/10, n/30	Purchases
29	932	Petty Cash	76		Office supplies, $26 Store supplies, $21 Delivery expense, $8 Miscellaneous selling expense, $12 Miscellaneous general expense, $9

Checks

Date	Check No.	Payee	Voucher Paid	Amount
July 5	960	Ames, Inc.	904	$ 990
9	961	Neff and Son	923	36
12	962	John Carr Co.	920	735
13	963	Wells Co.	885	450
15	964	B. B. Lee, Inc.	922	396
19	965	Ryan Trust Co.	927	5,100
21	966	Dow Co.	901	800
22	967	Kane Supply	929	85
22	968	Mason Co.	924	1,078
25	969	Morton Courier	930	64
27	970	Root Co.	925	441
29	971	W. Feld Co.	928	588
29	972	Petty Cash	932	76

If the working papers correlating with the textbook are not used, omit Problem 11-3B.

11-3B. Portions of the following accounting records of P. D. Connors Co. are presented in the working papers:

Voucher Register	General ledger accounts:
Check Register	Prepaid Insurance
General Journal	Notes Payable
Insurance Register	Accounts Payable
Notes Payable Register	

Expenditures, cash disbursements, and other selected transactions completed during the period March 24–31 of the current year are described below.

Mar. 24. Recorded Voucher No. 627 payable to Carson Co. for merchandise, $2,500, terms 2/10, n/30. (Purchase invoices are recorded at the gross amount.)

24. Issued Check No. 877 to Wilcox Co. in payment of Voucher No. 615 for $2,000, less cash discount of 1%.

26. Issued a 90-day, 8% note (No. 52), dated today to Alton Co. in settlement of Voucher No. 611, $6,500. The note is payable to Miami County Bank.

26. Recorded Voucher No. 628 payable to United Automobile Insurance Co. for the following insurance policy, dated today: No. 7083D, automobiles, 1 year, $1,134.

26. Issued Check No. 878 in payment of Voucher No. 628.

26. Recorded Voucher No. 629 payable to First National Bank for note payable (No. 48), $5,000.

26. Issued Check No. 879 in payment of Voucher No. 629.

28. Recorded Voucher No. 630 payable to Palmer Co. for merchandise, $3,500, terms n/30.

28. Recorded Voucher No. 631 payable to Macon Gazette for advertising, $400.

28. Issued Check No. 880 in payment of Voucher No. 631.

29. Recorded Voucher No. 632 payable to Petty Cash for $172.25, distributed as follows: Office Supplies, $44.60; Advertising Expense, $11.65; Delivery Expense, $31.20; Miscellaneous Selling Expense, $54.55; Miscellaneous General Expense, $30.25.

29. Issued Check No. 881 in payment of Voucher No. 632.

31. Issued Check No. 882 to Denton Products Co. in payment of Voucher No. 612 for $2,800, less cash discount of 2%.

31. Recorded Voucher No. 633 payable to Mid-American Insurance Co. for the following insurance policy, dated today: No. 6B71, building, $100,000, 3 years, $1,908.

31. Issued Check No. 883 in payment of Voucher No. 633.

789

After the journals are posted at the end of the month, the cash in bank account has a debit balance of $15,814.65.

The bank statement indicates a March 31 balance of $22,284.40. Comparison of paid checks returned by the bank with the check register reveals that Nos. 878, 882, and 883 are outstanding. Check No. 849 for $720, which appeared on the February reconciliation as outstanding, is still outstanding. A debit memorandum accompanying the bank statement indicates a charge of $92.25 for a check drawn by B. D. Carter, a customer, which was returned because of insufficient funds.

Instructions:

(1) Record the transactions for March 24–31 in the appropriate journals. Immediately after recording a transaction, post individual items, where appropriate, to the three general ledger accounts given.

(2) Enter the necessary notations in the notes payable register and the insurance register, rounding insurance expirations to the nearest month.

(3) Total and rule the voucher register and the check register, and post totals to the accounts payable account.

(4) Complete the schedule of unpaid vouchers. (Compare the total with the balance of the accounts payable account as of March 31.)

(5) Prepare a bank reconciliation and journalize any necessary entries.

(6) Total the Expired Premium column for March in the insurance register, journalize the adjusting entry, and post to the prepaid insurance account. (Determine the balance of prepaid insurance as of March 31 from the columns in the insurance register and compare it with the balance of the prepaid insurance account as of the same date.)

(7) Determine the amount of interest accrued as of March 31 on notes payable (Nos. 50 and 52). (Assume 28 days in February.)

(8) Determine the amount of interest prepaid as of March 31 on notes payable (No. 51). (The non-interest-bearing note was discounted by the bank.)

790

11-5B. Black Company employs the voucher system in controlling expenditures and disbursements. All cash receipts are deposited in a night depository after banking hours each Wednesday and Friday. The data required to reconcile their bank statement as of April 30 of the current year have been abstracted from various documents and records and are reproduced below and on pages 791 and 792. To facilitate identification, the sources of the data are printed in capital letters.

CASH IN BANK ACCOUNT

Balance as of April 1................................ $5,166.90

CASH RECEIPTS JOURNAL

Total of Cash in Bank Debit column for month of April... 6,061.44

DUPLICATE DEPOSIT TICKETS

Date and amount of each deposit in April:

Date	Amount	Date	Amount	Date	Amount
April 2	$567.17	April 14	$699.10	April 23	$591.69
7	670.33	16	749.89	28	742.12
9	791.12	21	620.84	30	629.18

BANK STATEMENT FOR APRIL

Balance as of April 1................................ $5,156.88
Deposits and other credits........................... 6,727.96
Checks and other debits.............................. 5,484.19
Balance as of April 30............................... $6,400.65

CHECK REGISTER

Number and amount of each check issued in April:

Check No.	Amount	Check No.	Amount	Check No.	Amount
722	$ 65.37	729	$315.04	736	$320.13
723	37.29	730	32.87	737	272.10
724	361.04	731	627.59	738	572.65
725	631.21	732	300.60	739	89.49
726	517.62	733	Void	740	76.60
727	47.30	734	717.26	741	511.21
728	266.29	735	315.40	742	147.76

Total amount of checks issued in April.................... $6,224.82

Date and amount of each deposit in April:

Date	Amount	Date	Amount	Date	Amount
April 1	$680.70	April 10	$791.12	April 22	$620.84
3	567.17	15	699.10	24	591.69
8	670.33	17	749.89	29	742.12

CHECKS ACCOMPANYING BANK STATEMENT FOR APRIL

Number and amount of each check, rearranged in numerical sequence:

Check No.	Amount	Check No.	Amount	Check No.	Amount
690	$ 78.20	726	$517.62	735	$315.40
720	410.93	727	47.30	736	320.13
721	89.50	728	266.29	737	272.10
722	65.37	729	315.04	739	89.49
723	37.29	730	32.87	741	511.21
724	361.04	731	627.59	742	147.76
725	631.21	732	300.60		

BANK MEMORANDUMS ACCOMPANYING BANK STATEMENT FOR APRIL

Date, description, and amount of each memorandum:

Date	Description	Amount
April 20	Bank credit memo for note collected:	
	Principal...	$600.00
	Interest..	15.00
27	Bank debit memo for check returned because of insufficient funds..	52.15
30	Bank debit memo for service charges.................	4.10

BANK RECONCILIATION FOR PRECEDING MONTH

Black Company
Bank Reconciliation
March 31, 19—

Balance per bank statement....................	$5,156.88
Add: Deposit of March 31, not recorded by bank.	680.70
	$5,837.58

Deduct: Outstanding checks:

No. 690	$ 78.20	
716	92.05	
720	410.93	
721	89.50	670.68
Adjusted balance		$5,166.90
Balance per depositor's records		$5,170.15
Deduct: Service charges		3.25
Adjusted balance		$5,166.90

Instructions:

(1) Prepare a bank reconciliation as of April 30. If errors in recording deposits or checks are discovered, assume that the errors were made by the company.
(2) Journalize the necessary entries. The accounts have not been closed.
(3) What is the amount of cash in bank that should appear on the balance sheet as of April 30?

CHAPTER 12

12-1B. The Powell Corporation has seven employees. They are paid on an hourly basis, receiving time-and-one-half pay for all hours worked in excess of 40 a week. The record of time worked for the week ended December 10 of the current year, together with other relevant information, is summarized below:

Name	Total Hours	Hourly Rate	Income Tax Withheld	Bond Deductions	Cumulative Earnings, December 3
A	20	$3.00	$ 3.50	$1.50	$ 2,400
B	44	4.25	18.50	1.75	8,750
C	40	3.75	15.25	——	7,900
D	42	5.25	23.10	——	11,900
E	45	5.00	26.90	7.50	12,150
F	40	4.25	16.70	2.00	8,220
G	48	5.20	34.50	1.75	4,140

In addition to withholding for income tax, FICA tax, and bond purchases, $25 is to be withheld from G for partial payment of his account receivable.

A and C are office employees, the others are salesmen. The following tax rates and limitations are assumed: FICA, 6% on maximum of $12,000; state unemployment (employer only), 2.2% on maximum of $4,200; federal unemployment, .5% on maximum of $4,200.

Instructions:

(1) Prepare the payroll register for the week, using a form like the one illustrated on pages 302 and 303.
(2) Journalize the entry to record the payroll for the week.
(3) The company uses a voucher system and pays by regular check. Give the necessary entries in *general journal form* to record the payroll voucher and the issuance of the checks.

(4) Complete the payroll register by inserting the check numbers, beginning with No. 912.

(5) Journalize the entry to record the employer's payroll taxes for the week.

If the working papers correlating with the textbook are not used, omit Problem 12-2B.

12-2B. The payroll register for W. C. Wilson Company for the week ending November 27 of the current fiscal year is presented in the working papers.

Instructions:

(1) Journalize the entry to record the payroll for the week.

(2) Assuming the use of a voucher system and payment by regular check, present the entries, in *general journal form*, to record the payroll voucher and the issuance of the checks to employees.

(3) Journalize the entry to record the employer's payroll taxes for the week. Assume the following tax rates: FICA, 6%; state unemployment, 1.8%; federal unemployment, .5%.

(4) Present the entries, in *general journal form*, to record the following transactions selected from those completed by W. C. Wilson Company:

Dec. 13. Prepared a voucher, payable to American National Bank, for employees income taxes, $912.70, and FICA taxes, $710.40, on salaries paid in November.

13. Issued a check to American National Bank in payment of the above voucher.

793

12-3B. The following information relative to the payroll for the week ended December 29 was abstracted from the payroll register and other records of A. B. Simon, Inc.:

Salaries:		Deductions:	
Sales salaries.............	$31,350	Income tax withheld......	$3,630
Warehouse salaries.......	6,440	U.S. savings bonds........	310
Office salaries...........	4,100	Group insurance..........	170
	$41,890	FICA tax withheld is assumed to total the same amount as the employer's tax.	

Tax rates assumed:

FICA, 6%
State unemployment (employer only), 2%
Federal unemployment, .5%

Instructions:

(1) Assuming that the payroll for the last week of the year is to be paid on December 31, present the following entries:

(a) December 29, to record the payroll. Of the total payroll for the last week of the year, $20,200 is subject to FICA tax and $2,900 is subject to unemployment compensation taxes.

(b) December 29, to record the employer's payroll taxes on the payroll to be paid on December 31.

(2) Assuming that the payroll for the last week of the year is to be paid on January 2 of the following fiscal year, present the following entries:

(a) December 31, to record the payroll.

(b) January 2, to record the employer's payroll taxes on the payroll to be paid on January 2.

12-5B. Rockwell Company began business on January 2 of last year. Salaries were paid to employees on the last day of each month and both FICA tax and federal income tax were withheld in the required amounts. All required payroll tax reports were filed and the correct amount of payroll taxes was remitted by the company for the calendar year. Before the Wage and Tax Statements (Form W-2) could be prepared for distribution to employees and filing with the Internal Revenue Service, the employees' earnings records were inadvertently destroyed.

Data on dates of employment, salary rates, and employees' income taxes withheld, which are summarized below, were obtained from personnel records and payroll registers. None of the employees resigned or were discharged during the year and there were no changes in salary rates. The FICA tax was withheld at the rate of 6% on the first $12,000 of salary.

Employee	Date First Employed	Monthly Salary	Monthly Income Tax Withheld
A	Jan. 2	$1,125	$150.10
B	Mar. 1	550	56.30
C	Jan. 2	875	97.20
D	Oct. 16	550	68.10
E	Jan. 2	1,000	117.00
F	Feb. 1	480	52.10
G	July 1	725	78.00

Instructions:

(1) Determine the amounts to be reported on each employee's Wage and Tax Statement (Form W-2) for the year, arranging the data in the following form:

Employee	Gross Earnings	Federal Income Tax Withheld	Earnings Subject to FICA Tax	FICA Tax Withheld

(2) Determine the total FICA tax withheld from employees during the year.

(3) Determine the following payroll taxes for the year paid by the employer: (a) FICA; (b) state unemployment compensation at 1.8% on first $4,200; (c) federal unemployment compensation at .5% on first $4,200; (d) total.

(4) In a manner similar to the illustrations in this chapter, develop four algorithms to describe the computations required to determine the four amounts in part (1), using the symbols shown below and at the top of the next page.

$$n = \text{Number of payroll periods}$$
$$g = \text{Monthly gross earnings}$$
$$f = \text{Monthly federal income tax withheld}$$

G = Total gross earnings
F = Total federal income tax withheld
T = Total earnings subject to FICA tax
S = Total FICA tax withheld

CHAPTER 13

13-1B. Barton Tea Company is a newly organized enterprise. The list of asset, liability, and capital accounts to be opened in the general ledger is presented below, arranged in alphabetical order. The accounts are to be arranged in balance sheet order and account numbers assigned. Each account number is to be composed of three digits; the first digit is to indicate the major classification ("1" for assets, etc.), the second digit is to indicate the subclassification ("11" for current assets, etc.), and the third digit is to identify the specific account ("111" for Cash in Bank, etc.).

Accounts Payable
Accounts Receivable
Accumulated Depr. — Building
Accumulated Depr. — Del. Equip.
Accum. Depr. — Office Equip.
Accum. Depr. — Store Equip.
Allowance for Doubtful Accounts
Building
Cash in Bank
Delivery Equipment
Capital Stock
Dividends
Interest Payable

Land
Merchandise Inventory
Mortgage Note Payable (long-term)
Notes Payable (short-term)
Office Equipment
Office Supplies
Petty Cash
Prepaid Insurance
Prepaid Taxes
Retained Earnings
Salaries Payable
Store Equipment
Store Supplies
Taxes Payable

Instructions:
    Construct a chart of accounts for the accounts listed.

13-2B. Western Ohio Water Co. employs an automated system for billing customers for water. There are two rate structures, residential and industrial. A master file of customers is maintained on punched cards, with name, address, and appropriate rate structure indicated. At the end of each billing period the meter readers are given prepunched and printed cards containing the name, address, and last meter reading for each customer on their route. The current meter readings are recorded on the cards by the meter readers with a special pencil. The reproducer converts the pencil markings to holes in the card and the cards are then matched by the collator against the master file to assure that a current billing card has been prepared for each customer. The current billing cards are then processed by an electronic computer that computes the amount of the billing and prints the sales journal. The journal is then subjected to clerical review before processing is continued.

Instructions:

Construct a flow chart of the following computer operations: read a current billing card; compute the amount of billing, including provision to employ the appropriate rate structure; print an entry in the sales journal; and continue the processing until the last current billing card has been processed.

If the working papers correlating with the textbook are not used, omit Problem 13-4B.

13-4B. Foster Supply Company employs punched card machines in processing much of its accounting data. This problem requires the manual processing of a portion of the data normally processed by the machines.

Instructions:

(1) Remove from the working papers and separate the 15 punched cards. Note that the cards numbered 1–3 represent customers' account balances at April 30, the cards numbered 4–6 represent receipts on account from customers at various dates during May, and the cards numbered 7–15 represent sales made to customers on account at various dates in May. Record on the top line of the cards numbered 13–15 the following additional sales data:

	Customer No.	Date	Salesman No.	Invoice No.	Commodity No.	Quantity Sold	Unit Sales Price	Amount
13.	115	5/20	3	17189	212	25	5.00	125.00
14.	110	5/25	1	17190	202	100	1.75	175.00
15.	115	5/30	3	17191	208	200	1.25	250.00

(2) Sort the cards into numerical order according to customer number.
(3) Sort the cards for each customer according to date, placing the earliest date on top.
(4) Using the data recorded on the cards, prepare the three customers' statements of account.
(5) Resort cards numbered 7–15 into numerical order according to salesman number. Prepare for the sales manager a report of sales by salesmen during May.
(6) Resort cards numbered 7–15 into numerical order by commodity number. Prepare for the store manager, who also acts as buyer, a report of the quantity of each commodity sold during May.

CHAPTER 14

14-1B. You are engaged to review the accounting records of Ennis Company prior to closing of the revenue and expense accounts as of December 31, the end of the current fiscal year. The following information comes to your attention during the review:

(a) Accounts receivable include $1,250 owed by P. M. Baker Co., a bankrupt. There is no prospect of collecting any of the receivable. The allowance method of accounting for receivables is employed.
(b) No interest has been accrued on a $15,000, 8%, 90-day note receivable, dated December 1 of the current year.

(c) Merchandise inventory on hand at December 31 of the current year has been recorded in the accounts at cost, $99,200. Current market price of the inventory is $102,490.

(d) The store supplies account has a balance of $1,350. The cost of the store supplies on hand at December 31, as determined by a physical count, was $525.

(e) Since net income for the current year is expected to be considerably less than it was for the preceding year, depreciation on equipment has not been recorded. Depreciation for the year on equipment, determined in a manner consistent with the preceding year, amounts to $17,750.

(f) Land recorded in the accounts at a cost of $20,000 was appraised at $35,000 by two expert appraisers.

(g) The company is being sued for $50,000 by a customer who claims damages for personal injury apparently caused by a defective product. Company attorneys feel extremely confident that the company will have no liability for damages resulting from this case.

Instructions:

Journalize any entries required to adjust or correct the accounts, identifying each entry by letter.

14-3B. Lambert Construction Company began construction on three contracts during 1973. The contract prices and construction activities for 1973, 1974, and 1975 were as follows:

		1973		1974		1975	
Contract	Contract Price	Costs Incurred	Percent Completed	Costs Incurred	Percent Completed	Costs Incurred	Percent Completed
A	$3,000,000	$1,250,000	50%	$1,300,000	50%	———	——
B	4,000,000	680,000	20%	2,040,000	60%	$ 735,000	20%
C	2,800,000	234,000	10%	702,000	30%	1,170,000	50%

Instructions:

Determine the amount of revenue and income to be recognized from the contracts for each of the following years: 1973, 1974, and 1975. Revenue is to be recognized by the degree-of-contract-completion method. Present computations in good order.

14-4B. Morgan Company was organized on January 1, 1972. During its first three years of operations, the company determined uncollectible accounts expense by the direct write-off method, the cost of the merchandise inventory at the end of the period by the first-in, first-out method, and depreciation expense by the straight-line method. The amounts of net income reported and the amounts of the foregoing items for each of the three years were as follows:

	First Year	Second Year	Third Year
Net income reported..........	$19,750	$31,500	$40,500
Uncollectible accounts expense.	400	1,350	2,600
Ending merchandise inventory.	33,500	44,750	48,900
Depreciation expense.........	8,100	8,700	9,000

The firm is considering the possibility of changing to the following methods in determining net income for the fourth and subsequent years: provision for doubtful accounts through the use of an allowance account, last-in, first-out inventory, and declining-balance depreciation at twice the straight-line rate.

In order to consider the probable future effect of these changes on the determination of net income, the management requests that net income of the past
three years be recomputed on the basis of the proposed methods. The uncollectible accounts expense, inventory, and depreciation expense, for the past
three years, computed in accordance with the proposed methods, are as follows:

	First Year	Second Year	Third Year
Uncollectible accounts expense.	$ 1,200	$ 1,900	$ 2,400
Ending merchandise inventory.	34,100	42,750	45,250
Depreciation expense.........	16,200	15,500	14,600

Instructions:

Recompute the net income for each of the three years,
presenting the figures in an orderly manner.

14-6B. John Powers owns and manages The Art Fair on a full-time basis.
He also maintains the accounting records. At the close of the first year of
operations, he prepared the following income statement and balance sheet.

The Art Fair
Income Statement
For Year Ended December 31, 19—

Sales.....................		$72,250
Purchases.................		63,000
Gross profit on sales.......		$ 9,250
Operating expenses:		
Salary expense............	$9,600	
Rent expense.............	4,875	
Utilities expense..........	1,600	
Miscellaneous expense.....	1,750	
Total operating expenses.		17,825
Net loss..................		$ 8,575

The Art Fair
Balance Sheet
December 31, 19—

Cash.....................	$ 3,425
Equipment................	8,000
John Powers..............	$11,425

Because of the large net loss reported by the income statement, Powers is
considering discontinuing operations. Before making a decision, he asks you to
review the accounting methods employed and, if material errors are found, to
prepare revised statements. The following information is elicited during the
course of the review:

(a) The only transactions recorded have been those in which cash was
received or disbursed.
(b) The accounts have not been closed for the year.
(c) The business was established on January 3 by an investment of $12,500
in cash by the owner. An additional investment of $7,500 was made in
cash on July 1.
(d) The equipment listed on the balance sheet at $8,000 was purchased for

cash on January 3. Equipment purchased July 2 for $2,000 in cash was debited to Purchases. Equipment purchased on December 27 for $2,500, for which a 90-day non-interest-bearing note was issued, was not recorded.

(e) Depreciation on equipment has not been recorded. The equipment is estimated to have a useful life of 10 years and no salvage value. (Use straight-line method.)

(f) Accounts receivable from customers at December 31 total $3,850.

(g) Uncollectible accounts are estimated at $275.

(h) The merchandise inventory at December 31, as nearly as can be determined, has a cost of $13,000.

(i) Insurance premiums of $750 were debited to Miscellaneous Expense during the year. The unexpired portion at December 31 is $350.

(j) Supplies of $900 purchased during the year were debited to Purchases. An estimated $300 of supplies were on hand at December 31.

(k) A total of $4,000 is owed to merchandise creditors on account at December 31.

(l) Rent Expense includes an advance payment of $375 for the month of January in the subsequent year.

(m) Salaries owed but not paid on December 31 total $350.

(n) The classification of operating expenses as "selling" and "general" is not considered to be sufficiently important to justify the cost of the analysis.

(o) The proprietor made no withdrawals during the year.

Instructions:

(1) On the basis of the financial statements presented above, prepare an unadjusted trial balance as of December 31, on an eight-column work sheet.

(2) Record the adjustments and the corrections in the Adjustments columns and complete the work sheet.

(3) Prepare an income statement, a capital statement, and a balance sheet.

799

CHAPTER 15

15-1B. Ralph Feld and James Gove have decided to form a partnership. They have agreed that Feld is to invest $20,000 and that Gove is to invest $30,000. Feld is to devote full time to the business and Gove is to devote one-half time. The following plans for the division of income are being considered:

(a) Equal division.

(b) In the ratio of original investments.

(c) In the ratio of time devoted to the business.

(d) Interest of 6% on original investments and the remainder in the ratio of 2:1.

(e) Interest of 6% on original investments, salaries of $10,000 to Feld and $5,000 to Gove, and the remainder equally.

(f) Plan (e), except that Feld is also to be allowed a bonus equal to 20% of the amount by which net income exceeds the salary allowances.

Instructions:

Determine the division of the net income under each of the following assumptions: net income of $30,000 and net income of $15,000. Present the data in tabular form, using the following columnar headings:

	$30,000		$15,000	
Plan	Feld	Gove	Feld	Gove

15-2B. On July 1 of the current year C. K. Owen and R. C. Powers form a partnership.

Owen invests certain business assets at valuations agreed upon, transfers business liabilities, and contributes sufficient cash to bring his total capital to $40,000. Details regarding the book values of the business assets and liabilities, and the agreed valuations, follow:

	Owen's Ledger Balance	Agreed Valuation
Accounts Receivable....................	$11,200	$11,200
Allowance for Doubtful Accounts........	600	850
Merchandise Inventory.................	18,000	19,250
Equipment..........................	27,500⎱	
Accumulated Depreciation — Equipment.	17,500⎰	14,500
Accounts Payable....................	8,600	8,600
Notes Payable.......................	5,000	5,000

Powers agrees to invest merchandise inventory priced at $15,000 and $5,000 in cash.

The articles of partnership include the following provisions regarding the division of net income: interest on original investment at 8%, salary allowances of $8,000 and $12,000 respectively, and the remainder equally.

Instructions:

(1) Give the entries, in general journal form, to record the investments of Owen and Powers in the partnership accounts.
(2) Prepare a balance sheet as of July 1, the date of formation of the partnership.
(3) After adjustments and the closing of revenue and expense accounts at June 30, the end of the first full year of operations, the income summary account has a credit balance of $31,500 and the drawing accounts have debit balances of $7,000 (Owen) and $11,500 (Powers). Present the journal entries to close the income summary account and the drawing accounts at June 30.

15-5B. Burns, Cox, and Davis decide to discontinue business operations as of March 31 and liquidate their partnership. The firm's post-closing trial balance at that date appears on the next page.

The partners share net income and losses in the ratio 2:1:2. The realization and liquidation transactions are summarized as follows:

(a) Collected $7,600 of accounts receivable; the remainder are worthless.
(b) Collected $5,000 on notes receivable.
(c) Sold the merchandise for $22,275 cash.
(d) Realized $400 cash from cancellation of the insurance policies.
(e) Sold the supplies for $350.
(f) Sold the equipment for $5,575 cash.

(g) Sold the land and building for $27,000, purchaser paying $7,000 cash and assuming the mortgage note. The mortgage holder released the partners from further liability.

(h) Paid miscellaneous expenses in connection with the sale of the assets, $600. (Charge to Loss and Gain on Realization.)

(i) Distributed the loss on realization to the partners' capital accounts.

(j) Paid the accounts payable in full.

(k) Distributed remaining cash to the partners.

Burns, Cox, and Davis
Post-Closing Trial Balance
March 31, 19—

Cash...............................	8,100	
Accounts Receivable..................	9,250	
Allowance for Doubtful Accounts........		650
Notes Receivable.....................	5,000	
Merchandise Inventory................	26,500	
Prepaid Insurance....................	475	
Supplies............................	450	
Equipment..........................	13,500	
Accumulated Depreciation — Equipment.		7,425
Building............................	30,000	
Accumulated Depreciation — Building...		12,500
Land...............................	6,000	
Accounts Payable....................		7,500
Mortgage Note Payable...............		20,000
Frank Burns, Capital.................		21,300
James Cox, Capital...................		11,100
Roger Davis, Capital.................		18,800
	99,275	99,275

801

Instructions:

(1) Open T accounts for Cash; Loss and Gain on Realization; Frank Burns, Capital; James Cox, Capital; and Roger Davis, Capital, and record the March 31 balances in the respective accounts.

(2) Present entries, in general journal form, to record the liquidation, posting to the appropriate T accounts after each journal entry. (None of the five T accounts should have a balance after the final entry is posted.)

(3) Assuming that there had been a net loss of $47,000, instead of the amount determined above, prepare a complete summary of the liquidation in the form illustrated in the chapter. No entries are required.

(4) Assuming that there had been a net loss of $50,000, instead of the amount determined above, prepare a complete summary of the liquidation in the form illustrated in the chapter. No entries are required.

CHAPTER 16

16-2B. The annual dividends declared by Belmont Company during a six-year period are presented in the table at the top of the next page. During the entire period the outstanding stock of the company was composed of 2,000 shares of cumulative, participating, 7% preferred stock, $50 par, and 40,000 shares of common stock, $10 par. The preferred stock contract provides that the preferred stock shall participate in distributions of additional dividends after allowance of a $1 dividend per share on the common stock, the additional dividends to be divided among common and preferred shares on the basis of the total par of the stock outstanding.

Year	Total Dividends	Preferred Dividends		Common Dividends	
		Total	Per Share	Total	Per Share
1970	$27,000				
1971	43,000				
1972	57,000				
1973	62,000				
1974	4,800				
1975	9,000				

Instructions:

(1) Determine the total dividends and the per share dividends declared on each class of stock for each of the six years, using the headings presented above. There were no dividends in arrears on January 1, 1970.

(2) Determine the average annual dividend per share for each class of stock for the six-year period.

(3) Assuming that the preferred stock was sold at par and the common stock was sold at $12 at the beginning of the six-year period, determine the percentage return on initial shareholders' investment based on the average annual dividend per share (a) for preferred stock, and (b) for common stock.

16-3B. Selected data from the balance sheets of six corporations, identified by letter, are presented below and on the next page.

A. Common stock, $5 par....... $1,800,000
   Premium on common stock... 130,000
   Deficit.................... 346,000

B. Preferred 5% stock, $50 par.. $1,000,000
   Premium on preferred stock.. 150,000
   Common stock, $25 par...... 2,000,000
   Discount on common stock... 250,000
   Deficit.................... 348,000

   Preferred stock has prior claim to assets on liquidation to the extent of par.

C. Preferred 7% stock, $25 par.. $ 750,000
   Common stock, $50 par...... 1,000,000
   Premium on common stock... 50,000
   Retained earnings........... 308,000

   Preferred stock has prior claim to assets on liquidation to the extent of par.

D. Preferred 6% stock, $40 par.. $1,200,000
   Premium on preferred stock.. 50,000

Common stock, $100 par..... 3,000,000
Deficit..................... 170,000

Preferred stock has prior claim to assets on liquidation to the extent of 105% of par.

E. Preferred 5% stock, $100 par. $ 900,000
Common stock, $5 par....... 1,250,000
Premium on common stock... 250,000
Retained earnings.......... 63,000

Dividends on preferred stock are in arrears for 2 years including the dividend passed during the current year. Preferred stock is entitled to par plus unpaid cumulative dividends upon liquidation to the extent of retained earnings.

F. Preferred 8% stock, $25 par.. $ 500,000
Discount on preferred stock... 20,000
Common stock, $10 par...... 1,500,000
Deficit..................... 55,000

Dividends on preferred stock are in arrears for 3 years including the dividend passed during the current year. Preferred stock is entitled to par plus unpaid cumulative dividends upon liquidation, regardless of the availability of retained earnings.

Instructions:

Determine for each corporation the equity per share of each class of stock, presenting the total stockholders' equity allocated to each class and the number of shares outstanding.

803

16-5B. The stockholders' equity and related accounts appearing in the ledger of Marlin Corporation on November 1, the beginning of the current fiscal year, are listed below.

Preferred 6% Stock Subscriptions Receivable.. $ 40,000
Preferred 6% Stock, $100 par (20,000 shares authorized, 8,000 shares issued)........... 800,000
Preferred 6% Stock Subscribed (1,500 shares). 150,000
Premium on Preferred Stock............... 60,000
Common Stock, $5 par (500,000 shares authorized, 400,000 shares issued).............. 2,000,000
Premium on Common Stock............... 1,600,000
Retained Earnings...................... 1,100,000

During the year the corporation completed a number of transactions affecting the stockholders' equity. They are summarized below.

(a) Received balance due on preferred stock subscribed and issued the certificates.
(b) Purchased 5,000 shares of treasury common for $65,000.
(c) Sold 3,000 shares of treasury common for $45,000.
(d) Received subscriptions to 2,000 shares of preferred 6% stock at $110, collecting 25% of subscription price.
(e) Issued 20,000 shares of common stock at $9, receiving cash.
(f) Sold 1,000 shares of treasury common for $9,000.

Instructions:

(1) Prepare entries in general journal form to record the transactions listed above. Identify each entry by letter. (Use of T accounts for the stockholders' equity accounts will facilitate the determination of the amounts needed in recording some of the transactions and in completing instruction (2).)

(2) Prepare the stockholders' equity section of the balance sheet as of October 31. Net income for the year amounted to $520,000. Cash dividends declared and paid during the year totaled $290,000.

CHAPTER 17

17-1B. Differences in accounting methods between those applied to its accounts and financial reports and those used in determining taxable income yielded the following amounts during the first four years of a corporation's operations:

	First Year	Second Year	Third Year	Fourth Year
Income before income tax.	$210,000	$230,000	$220,000	$200,000
Taxable income..........	160,000	190,000	230,000	210,000

The income tax rate for each of the four years was 45% of taxable income and each year's taxes were promptly paid.

Instructions:

(1) Determine for each year the amounts described in the following columnar captions, presenting the information in the form indicated:

Year	Income Tax Deducted on Income Statement	Income Tax Payments for the Year	Deferred Income Tax Payable	
			Year's Addition (Deduction)	Year-End Balance

(2) Total the first three amount columns.

17-2B. Selected transactions completed by the Banner Corporation during the current fiscal year are as follows:

Jan. 12. Purchased 2,000 shares of own common stock at $23, recording the stock at cost. (Prior to the purchase there were 50,000 shares of $10 par common stock outstanding.)

April 14. Discovered that a receipt of $300 cash on account from H. T. Brown had been posted in error to the account of H. T. Braun. The transaction was recorded correctly in the cash receipts journal.

May   8. Declared a semiannual dividend of $2 on the 10,000 shares of preferred stock and a 60¢ dividend on the common stock to stockholders of record on May 22, payable on June 10.

June 10. Paid the cash dividends.

Sept. 30. Sold 500 shares of treasury stock at $29, receiving cash.

Nov.   8. Declared semiannual dividends of $2 on the preferred stock and 60¢ on the common stock. In addition, a 4% common stock dividend was declared on the common stock outstanding, to be capitalized at the approximate fair market value of the common stock which is $31.

Dec. 10. Paid the cash dividends and issued the certificates for the common stock dividend.

31. Recorded $74,800 additional federal income tax allocable to net income for the year. Of this amount, $69,800 is a current liability and $5,000 is deferred.

31. The board of directors authorized the appropriation necessitated by the holding of treasury stock.

Instructions:

Record the transactions above in general journal form.

17-4B. The following data were selected from the records of Hibbard, Inc., for the current fiscal year ended August 31:

Merchandise inventory (September 1)...........	$ 75,900
Merchandise inventory (August 31).............	66,200
Advertising expense...........................	12,550
Depreciation expense — store equipment.........	5,200
Sales..	740,000
Sales salaries...............................	60,300
Sales commissions............................	28,650
Office salaries..............................	25,700
Purchases....................................	446,500
Rent expense.................................	18,000
Delivery expense.............................	4,600
Store supplies expense.......................	1,350
Office supplies expense......................	1,260
Insurance expense............................	3,850
Depreciation expense — office equipment.........	2,520
Miscellaneous selling expense.................	2,500
Miscellaneous general expense.................	2,970
Interest expense.............................	2,850
Uninsured flood loss.........................	30,000
Gain on sale of investments..................	40,000
Income tax:	
Net of amounts allocable to extraordinary items.	47,020
Reduction applicable to uninsured flood loss....	14,400
Applicable to gain on sale of investments.......	12,000

Instructions:

Prepare an income statement, concluding with a section for earnings per share in the form illustrated in this chapter. There were 10,000 shares of common stock (no preferred) outstanding throughout the year.

17-5B. The stockholders' equity accounts of Slade Industries, Inc., with balances on January 1 of the current fiscal year are as follows:

Common Stock, stated value $10 (100,000 shares	
authorized, 60,000 shares issued).............	$600,000
Paid-In Capital in Excess of Stated Value......	240,000
Appropriation for Retirement of Debt.........	50,000
Appropriation for Treasury Stock.............	22,000
Retained Earnings............................	195,000
Treasury Stock (2,000 shares, at cost).........	22,000

The following selected transactions occurred during the year:

Jan. 10. Paid cash dividends of 40¢ per share on the common stock. The dividend had been properly recorded when declared on December 10 of the preceding fiscal year.

Mar. 15. Sold all of the treasury stock for $42,000 cash.

Apr. 4. Issued 5,000 shares of common stock for $110,000 cash.

     4. Received land with an estimated fair market value of $25,000 from the Midwest Industrial Park Council as a donation.

June 15. Declared a 5% stock dividend on common stock, to be capitalized at the market price of the stock, which is $21 a share.

July 10. Issued the certificates for the dividend declared on June 15.

Nov. 8. Purchased 2,000 shares of treasury stock for $39,000.

Dec. 1. Declared a 40¢ per share dividend on common stock.

     15. The board of directors authorized the addition of $50,000 to the appropriation for retirement of debt.

     15. Increased the appropriation for treasury stock to $39,000.

     31. Closed the credit balance of the income summary account, $162,450.

     31. Closed the two dividends accounts to Retained Earnings.

Instructions:

(1) Open T accounts for the stockholders' equity accounts listed and enter the balances as of January 1. Also open T accounts for the following: Paid-In Capital from Sale of Treasury Stock; Donated Capital; Stock Dividend Distributable; Stock Dividends; Cash Dividends.

(2) Prepare entries in general journal form to record the selected transactions and post to the eleven selected accounts.

(3) Prepare the stockholders' equity section of the balance sheet as of December 31 of the current fiscal year.

CHAPTER 18

18-1B. The board of directors of Cameron Industries, Inc., is planning an expansion of plant facilities expected to cost $1,000,000. The board is undecided about the method of financing this expansion and is considering two plans:

Plan 1. Issue an additional 25,000 shares of no-par common stock at $40 per share.

Plan 2. Issue $1,000,000 of 20-year, 8% bonds at face amount.

The condensed balance sheet of the corporation at the end of the most recent fiscal year is presented below.

Cameron Industries, Inc.
Balance Sheet
December 31, 19--

Assets		Liabilities and Capital	
Current assets	$ 850,000	Current liabilities	$ 640,000
Plant assets................	3,150,000	Common stock (100,000 shares issued).................	2,500,000
		Retained earnings.........	860,000
Total assets................	$4,000,000	Total liabilities and capital...	$4,000,000

Net income has remained relatively constant over the past several years. The expansion program is expected to increase yearly income before bond interest and income tax, from $450,000 to $600,000. Assume an income tax rate of 50%.

Instructions:

(1) Prepare a tabulation indicating the expected earnings per share on common stock under each plan.

(2) List factors other than earnings per share that the board should consider in evaluating the two plans.

(3) Which plan offers the greater benefit to the present stockholders? Give reasons for your opinion.

18-2B. The following transactions were completed by Peoples Electric Co.:

1974

Sept. 30. Issued $5,000,000 of 20-year, 7% callable bonds dated September 30, 1974, for cash of $4,505,180. Interest is payable semiannually on September 30 and March 31.

Dec. 31. Recorded the adjusting entry for interest payable.

    31. Recorded amortization of $2,605 discount on the bonds.

    31. Closed the interest expense account.

1975

Jan. 1. Reversed the adjusting entry for interest payable.

Mar. 31. Paid the semiannual interest on the bonds.

Sept. 30. Paid the semiannual interest on the bonds.

Dec. 31. Recorded the adjusting entry for interest payable.

    31. Recorded amortization of $10,835 discount on the bonds.

    31. Closed the interest expense account.

1989

Sept. 30. Called the bonds at 101¾. Recorded amortization of discount for the 9-month period, $24,045, leaving a balance of $202,770 in the discount account. Recorded the redemption of the bonds.

Instructions:

(1) Record the foregoing transactions in general journal form.

(2) Indicate the amount of the interest expense in (a) 1974 and (b) 1975.

(3) Determine the effective interest rate (divide the interest expense for 1974 by the bond carrying amount at time of issuance) and express as an annual rate.

(4) Determine the carrying amount of the bonds as of December 31, 1975.

18-3B. During 1974 and 1975 Midland Construction Company completed the transactions described below and on the next page, relating to its $3,000,000 issue of 10-year, 9% bonds dated March 1, 1974. Interest is payable on March 1 and September 1. The corporation's fiscal year is the calendar year.

1974

Mar. 1. Sold the bond issue for $3,203,855 cash.

Sept. 1. Paid the semiannual interest on the bonds.

Dec. 31. Recorded the adjusting entry for interest payable.

    31. Recorded amortization of $11,592 of bond premium.

    31. Deposited $189,000 in a bond sinking fund.

    31. Appropriated $250,000 of retained earnings for bonded indebtedness.

    31. Closed the interest expense account.

1975

Jan. 1. Reversed the adjustment for interest payable.

Jan. 10. Purchased various securities with sinking fund cash, cost $187,230.
Mar. 1. Paid the semiannual interest on the bonds.
Sept. 1. Paid the semiannual interest on the bonds.
Dec. 31. Recorded the receipt of $10,298 of income on sinking fund securities, depositing the cash in the sinking fund.
    31. Recorded the adjusting entry for interest payable.
    31. Recorded amortization of $14,910 of bond premium.
    31. Deposited $228,000 cash in the sinking fund.
    31. Appropriated $300,000 of retained earnings for bonded indebtedness.
    31. Closed the interest expense account.

Instructions:

(1) Record the foregoing transactions in general journal form.
(2) Prepare a columnar table, using the headings presented below, and list the information for each of the two years.

				Account Balances at End of Year			
	Bond Interest Expense for Year	Sinking Fund Income for Year	Bonds Payable	Premium on Bonds	Sinking Fund		Appropriation for Bonded Indebtedness
Year					Cash	Investments	

18-5B. The following transactions relate to certain securities acquired by R. J. Lehman and Company, whose fiscal year ends on December 31:

1974
Apr. 1. Purchased $150,000 of Benton Company 10-year, 8% coupon bonds dated April 1, 1974, directly from the issuing company for $160,660.
June 25. Purchased 500 common shares of Pace Corporation at 45½ plus commission and other costs of $205.
Aug. 15. Received the regular cash dividend of 40¢ a share on Pace Corporation stock.
Oct. 1. Deposited the coupons for semiannual interest on Benton Company bonds.
Nov. 15. Received the regular cash dividend of 40¢ a share plus an extra dividend of 60¢ on Pace Corporation stock.
Dec. 31. Recorded the adjustment for interest receivable on the Benton Company bonds.
    31. Recorded the amortization of premium of $572 on the Benton Company bonds.

(Assume that all intervening transactions and adjustments have been recorded properly, and that the number of bonds and shares of stocks owned have not changed from December 31, 1974, to December 31, 1977.)

1978
Jan. 1. Reversed the adjustment of December 31, 1977, for interest receivable on the Benton Company bonds.
Feb. 1. Received the regular cash dividend of 40¢ a share and a 5% stock dividend on the Pace Corporation stock.
Apr. 1. Deposited coupons for semiannual interest on the Benton Company bonds.
May 1. Received the regular cash dividend of 50¢ a share on the Pace Corporation stock.
June 1. Sold one half of the Benton Company bonds at 102⅜ plus accrued interest. The broker deducted $262.75 for commission, etc., remitting the balance. Before recording the sale, premium amortization of $203

on one half of the bonds was recorded, reducing the carrying amount of those bonds to $78,542.

Sept. 2. Sold 100 shares of Pace Corporation stock at 52⅞. The broker deducted commission and other costs of $48.50, remitting the balance.

Oct. 1. Deposited coupons for semiannual interest on the Benton Company bonds.

Dec. 31. Recorded the adjustment for interest receivable on the Benton Company bonds.

31. Recorded the amortization of premium of $497 on the Benton Company bonds.

Instructions:

(1) Record the foregoing transactions in general journal form.

(2) Determine the amount of interest earned on the bonds in 1974.

(3) Determine the amount of interest earned on the bonds in 1978.

CHAPTER 19

19-1B. Midway Radio and TV operates two sales departments: Department R for radios and Department T for television. The following trial balance was prepared at the end of the current fiscal year after all adjustments, including the adjustments for merchandise inventory, were recorded and posted:

Midway Radio and TV
Trial Balance
March 31, 19—

Cash	77,700	
Accounts Receivable	47,800	
Merchandise Inventory — Department R	9,700	
Merchandise Inventory — Department T	26,000	
Prepaid Insurance	1,700	
Store Supplies	550	
Store Equipment	48,800	
Accumulated Depreciation — Store Equipment		19,200
Accounts Payable		31,700
Income Tax Payable		6,200
Common Stock		100,000
Retained Earnings		32,750
Cash Dividends	10,000	
Income Summary	31,300	35,700
Sales — Department R		150,000
Sales — Department T		450,000
Sales Returns and Allowances — Department R	3,150	
Sales Returns and Allowances — Department T	11,400	
Purchases — Department R	108,500	
Purchases — Department T	360,000	
Sales Salaries	27,750	
Advertising Expense	10,000	
Depreciation Expense — Store Equipment	4,800	
Store Supplies Expense	700	
Miscellaneous Selling Expense	1,000	
Office Salaries	10,000	
Rent Expense	9,600	

Heating and Lighting Expense................	3,600	
Property Tax Expense......................	2,000	
Insurance Expense.........................	900	
Uncollectible Accounts Expense..............	600	
Miscellaneous General Expense..............	500	
Interest Expense...........................	1,200	
Income Tax................................	16,300	
	825,550	825,550

Merchandise inventories at the beginning of the year were as follows: Department R, $9,100; Department T, $22,200.

The bases to be used in apportioning expenses, together with other essential information, are as follows:

Sales salaries — payroll records: Department R, $7,750; Department T, $20,000.

Advertising expense — usage: Department R, $2,000; Department T, $8,000.

Depreciation expense — average cost of equipment. Balances at beginning of year: Department R, $18,200; Department T, $26,000. Balances at end of year: Department R, $19,000; Department T, $29,800.

Store supplies expense — requisitions: Department R, $200; Department T, $500.

Office salaries — Department R, 20%; Department T, 80%.

Rent expense and heating and lighting expense — floor space: Department R, 1,200 sq. ft.; Department T, 6,000 sq. ft.

Property tax expense and insurance expense — average cost of equipment plus average cost of merchandise inventory.

Uncollectible accounts expense, miscellaneous selling expense, and miscellaneous general expense — volume of gross sales.

Instructions:

Prepare an income statement departmentalized through income from operations.

19-2B. Webb's, a department store, has 18 departments. Those with the least sales volume are Department A and Department B, which were established about a year ago on a trial basis. The board of directors feels that it is now time to consider the retention or the termination of these two departments. The adjusted trial balance, severely condensed, as of January 31, the end of the first month of the current fiscal year, is presented below and on the next page. January is considered to be a typical month. The income tax accrual has no bearing on the decision and is excluded from consideration.

Webb's
Trial Balance
January 31, 19—

Current Assets..............................	406,350	
Plant Assets................................	325,500	
Accumulated Depreciation — Plant Assets.......		187,750
Current Liabilities..........................		144,500
Common Stock.............................		200,000
Retained Earnings..........................		143,650
Cash Dividends.............................	18,000	
Sales — Department A.......................		18,750

Sales — Department B........................		12,450
Sales — Other Departments...................		855,900
Cost of Merchandise Sold — Department A.....	13,800	
Cost of Merchandise Sold — Department B......	9,450	
Cost of Merchandise Sold — Other Departments.	567,800	
Direct Expenses — Department A..............	3,750	
Direct Expenses — Department B..............	4,750	
Direct Expenses — Other Departments.........	121,500	
Indirect Expenses..........................	86,500	
Interest Expense...........................	5,600	
	1,563,000	1,563,000

Instructions:

(1) Prepare an income statement for January departmentalized through departmental margin.

(2) State your recommendations concerning the retention of Departments A and B, giving reasons.

19-5B. R. M. Carr and Son opened a branch office in Dover on May 1 of the current year. Summaries of transactions, adjustments, and year-end closing for branch operations of the current year ended December 31 are described below.

(a) Received cash advance, $40,000, and merchandise (billed at cost), $65,000, from the home office.
(b) Purchased equipment on account, $25,000.
(c) Purchased merchandise on account, $105,000.
(d) Sales on account, $110,000; cash sales, $50,000.
(e) Received cash from customers on account, $95,000.
(f) Paid creditors on account, $110,000.
(g) Paid operating expenses, $18,100 (all expenses are charged to Operating Expenses, a controlling account).
(h) Sent $40,000 cash to home office.
(i) Recorded accumulated depreciation, $1,600 and allowance for doubtful accounts, $500.
(j) Merchandise inventory at December 31, $47,500.
(k) Closed revenue and expense accounts.

Instructions:

(1) Present, in general journal form, the entries for the branch to record the foregoing. Post to the following T accounts: Cash, Accounts Receivable, Allowance for Doubtful Accounts, Merchandise Inventory, Equipment, Accumulated Depreciation, Accounts Payable, Home Office, Income Summary, Sales, Shipments from Home Office, Purchases, and Operating Expenses.

(2) Prepare an income statement for the year and a balance sheet as of December 31 for the branch.

(3) Present, in general journal form, the entries required on the home office records. Post to a T account entitled Dover Branch.

CHAPTER 20

If the working papers correlating with the textbook are not used, omit Problem 20-1B.

20-1B. The work sheet for Creative Builders, Inc., for the current year ended December 31 is presented in the working papers. Data concerning account titles, trial balance amounts, and selected adjustments have been entered on the work sheet.

Instructions:

(1) Enter the six adjustments required for the inventories on the work sheet. Additional adjustment data are:

Finished goods inventory at December 31	$51,150
Work in process inventory at December 31	39,200
Direct materials inventory at December 31	30,100

(2) Complete the work sheet.
(3) Prepare a statement of cost of goods manufactured.
(4) Prepare an income statement.

20-2B. Walton Company manufactures Product P. Material A is placed in process in Department 1 where it is ground and partially refined. The output of Department 1 is transferred to Department 2, where Material B is added at the beginning of the process and the refining is completed. On July 1, Walton Company had the following inventories:

Finished goods (2,500 units)	$60,000
Work in process — Department 1	—
Work in process — Department 2 (900 units, $\frac{2}{3}$ completed)	19,650
Materials	9,750

Departmental accounts are maintained for factory overhead and there is one service department, factory office. Manufacturing operations for the month of July are summarized as follows:

(a) Materials purchased on account $13,500

(b) Materials requisitioned for use:
Material A	$ 8,250
Material B	4,400
Indirect materials — Department 1	625
Indirect materials — Department 2	410

(c) Labor used:
Direct labor — Department 1	$13,750
Direct labor — Department 2	9,600
Indirect labor — Department 1	1,450
Indirect labor — Department 2	800
Factory office	400

(d) Miscellaneous costs incurred on account:
Department 1	$ 2,750
Department 2	1,875
Factory office	975

(e) Expiration of prepaid expenses:
Department 1	$ 375
Department 2	310
Factory office	75

(f) Depreciation charged on plant assets:

Department 1 .... $ 5,000

Department 2   2,800

Factory office   250

(g) Distribution of factory office costs:

Department 1 .... 40% of total factory office costs

Department 2 .... 60% of total factory office costs

(h) Application of factory overhead costs:

Department 1 .... 80% of direct labor cost

Department 2 .... 75% of direct labor cost

(i) Production costs transferred from Department 1 to Department 2:
2,200 units were fully processed and there was no inventory of work in process in Department 1 at July 31.

(j) Production costs transferred from Department 2 to finished goods:
2,300 units were fully processed including the inventory at July 1.
800 units were ½ completed at July 31.

(k) Cost of goods sold during July:
3,000 units (use the first-in, first-out method in crediting the finished goods account).

Instructions:

Present entries in general journal form to record the foregoing operations. Identify each entry by letter.

20-4B. Benson Company manufactures Product P by a series of four processes, all materials being introduced in Department 1. From Department 1 the materials pass through Departments 2, 3, and 4, emerging as finished Product P. All inventories are priced at cost by the first-in, first-out method.

The balances in the accounts Work in Process — Department 4 and Finished Goods were as follows on May 1:

Work in Process — Department 4

750 units, ⅔ completed $15,875

Finished Goods

1,200 units at $24 a unit   28,800

The following costs were charged to Work in Process — Department 4 during May:

Direct materials transferred from Department 3: 2,000 units at

$15 a unit $30,000

Direct labor   11,100

Factory overhead   7,400

During the month of May, 2,250 units of P were completed and 2,500 units were sold. Inventories on May 31 were as follows:

Work in process — Department 4: 500 units, ⅕ completed

Finished Goods: 950 units

Instructions:

(1) Determine the following, presenting the computations in good order:

(a) Equivalent units of production for Department 4 during May.

(b) Unit processing cost for Department 4 for May.

(c) Total and unit cost of Product P started in a prior period and finished in May.

(d) Total and unit cost of Product P started and finished in May.

(e) Total cost of goods transferred to finished goods.

813

    (f) Work in process inventory for Department 4, May 31.

    (g) Cost of goods sold (indicate number of units and unit costs).

    (h) Finished goods inventory, May 31.

(2) Prepare a cost of production report for Department 4 for May.

20-6B. A process cost system is used to record the costs of manufacturing Product P-37, which requires a series of four processes. The inventory of Work in Process — Department 4 on May 1 and debits to the account during May were as follows:

Balance, 1,500 units, ½ completed	$ 6,000
From Department 3, 8,000 units	16,800
Direct labor	21,200
Factory overhead	10,600

During May the 1,500 units in process on May 1 were completed, and of the 8,000 units entering the department, all were completed except 1,200 units, which were ⅓ completed.

Charges to Work in Process — Department 4 for the month of June were as follows:

From Department 3, 7,000 units	$15,050
Direct labor	18,260
Factory overhead	9,130

During June the units in process at the beginning of the month were completed, and of the 7,000 units entering the department, all were completed except 1,600 units, which were ¼ completed.

Instructions:

(1) Set up an account for Work in Process — Department 4. Enter the balance as of May 1 and the debits and the credits to the account in May. Present computations for determination of (a) equivalent units of production, (b) unit processing cost, (c) cost of goods finished, differentiating between units started in the prior period and units started and finished in May, and (d) work in process inventory.

(2) Enter the transactions for June into the account. Present the computations listed in instruction (1).

(3) Determine the difference in unit cost between the product started and completed in May and the product started and completed in June. Determine also the amount of the difference attributable collectively to operations in Departments 1 through 3 and the amount attributable to operations in Department 4.

CHAPTER 21

21-1B. Stines Printing Company uses a job order cost system. The following data summarize the operations related to production for March, the first month of operations:

(a) Materials purchased on account, $18,500.

(b) Materials requisitioned and factory labor used:

	Materials	Factory Labor
Job No. 1.	$1,175	$ 950
Job No. 2.	2,425	1,800
Job No. 3.	2,700	1,450
Job No. 4.	3,500	2,750
Job No. 5.	1,075	900
Job No. 6.	1,250	1,050
For general factory use.	400	550

(c) Depreciation of machinery and equipment, $1,050.
(d) Factory overhead costs incurred on account, $4,250.
(e) The factory overhead rate is 60% of direct labor cost.
(f) Jobs completed: Nos. 1, 2, 3, and 5.
(g) Jobs Nos. 1, 2, and 3 were shipped and customers were billed for $3,000, $7,950, and $7,500 respectively.

Instructions:

(1) Prepare entries in general journal form to record the foregoing summarized operations.
(2) Open T accounts for Work in Process and Finished Goods and post the appropriate entries, using the identifying letters as dates.
Insert memorandum account balances as of the end of the month.
(3) Prepare a schedule of unfinished jobs to support the balance in the work in process account.
(4) Prepare a schedule of completed jobs on hand to support the balance in the finished goods account.

815

If the working papers correlating with the textbook are not used, omit Problem 21-2B.

21-2B. Wallace Furniture Company repairs, refinishes, and reupholsters furniture. A job order cost system was installed recently to facilitate (1) the determination of price quotations to prospective customers, (2) the determination of actual costs incurred on each job, and (3) cost reductions.

In response to a prospective customer's request for a price quotation on a job, the estimated cost data are inserted on an unnumbered job order cost sheet. If the offer is accepted, a number is assigned to the job and the costs incurred are recorded in the usual manner on the job order cost sheet. After the job is completed, reasons for the variances between the estimated and actual costs are noted on the sheet. The data are then available to management in evaluating the efficiency of operations and in preparing quotations on future jobs.

On May 3, an estimate of $270 for reupholstering a couch was given to Robert Pace. The estimate was based upon the following data:

Estimated direct materials:	
10 yards at $12 per yard.	$120
Estimated direct labor:	
14 hours at $5 per hour.	70
Estimated factory overhead (50% of direct labor cost).	35
Total estimated costs.	$225
Markup (20% of production costs).	45
Total estimate.	$270

On May 8, the couch was picked up from the residence of Robert Pace at 1022 Holly Drive, Oakdale, with a commitment to return it on May 22. The job was completed on May 21.

The materials requisition and time tickets relating to the job are summarized below:

Materials Requisition No.	Description	Amount
371	10 yards at $12	$120
372	1 yard at $12	12

Time Ticket No.	Description	Amount
602	8 hours at $5	$ 40
603	7 hours at $5	35

Instructions:

(1) Complete that portion of the job order cost sheet that would be completed when the estimate is given to the customer.

(2) Assign number 437-P to the job, record the costs incurred, and complete the job order cost sheet. In commenting upon the variances between actual costs and estimated costs, assume that 1 yard of material was spoiled and that the factory overhead rate has been proved to be satisfactory.

21-5B. Selected accounts for Anderson Products are presented below and on the next page. For the purposes of this problem, some of the debits and credits have been omitted.

ACCOUNTS RECEIVABLE

July 1 Balance	37,250	July 31 Collections	42,750
31 Sales	(A)		

MATERIALS

July 1 Balance	7,800	July 31 Requisitions	(B)
31 Purchases	12,500		

WORK IN PROCESS

July 1 Balance	7,400	July 31 Goods finished	(E)
31 Direct materials	(C)		
31 Direct labor	21,500		
31 Factory overhead	(D)		

FINISHED GOODS

July 1 Balance	19,750	July 31 Cost of goods sold	(G)
31 Goods finished	(F)		

FACTORY OVERHEAD

July 1 Balance	100	July 31 Applied (75% of direct labor cost)	(H)
1–31 Costs incurred	16,200		

COST OF GOODS SOLD

July 31	(I)

SALES

| | July 31 | (J) |

Selected balances at July 31:

Accounts receivable......	$38,000
Finished goods.........	17,900
Work in process........	7,500
Materials.............	5,850

Materials requisitions for July included $600 of materials issued for general factory use. All sales are made on account, terms n/30.

Instructions:

(1) Determine the amounts represented by the letters (A) through (J), presenting your computations.
(2) Determine the amount of factory overhead overapplied or under-applied as of July 31.

CHAPTER 22

22-1B. Davis Company prepared the following factory overhead cost budget for the Finishing Department for June of the current year:

Davis Company
Factory Overhead Cost Budget — Finishing Department
For Month Ending June 30, 19—

Direct labor hours:		
Normal productive capacity.........		10,000
Hours budgeted..................		8,000
Variable cost:		
Indirect factory wages..............	$5,600	
Indirect materials.................	4,000	
Power and light..................	3,200	
Total variable cost..............		$12,800
Fixed cost:		
Supervisory salaries...............	$7,800	
Indirect factory wages.............	4,100	
Depreciation of plant and equipment.	2,750	
Insurance.......................	1,450	
Power and light..................	1,025	
Property taxes....................	875	
Total fixed cost.................		18,000
Total factory overhead cost..........		$30,800

Instructions:

(1) Prepare a flexible budget for the month of July indicating capacities of 8,000, 9,000, 10,000, and 11,000 direct labor hours and the determination of a standard factory overhead rate per direct labor hour.

(continued)

(2) Prepare a standard factory overhead cost variance report for July. The Finishing Department was operated for 9,000 direct labor hours and the following factory overhead costs were incurred:

Indirect factory wages................	$10,250
Supervisory salaries..................	7,800
Power and light......................	4,875
Indirect materials...................	4,600
Depreciation of plant and equipment...	2,750
Insurance............................	1,450
Property taxes.......................	875
Total factory overhead costs incurred.	$32,600

22-3B. Roland Manufacturing, Inc., maintains perpetual inventory accounts for materials, work in process, and finished goods and uses a standard cost system based upon the following data:

		Standard Cost Per Unit
Direct materials..	2½ pounds at $2 per lb....	$ 5
Direct labor......	2 hours at $6 per hr.......	12
Factory overhead.	$2.50 per direct labor hour.	5
Total.....................................		$22

There was no inventory of work in process at the beginning or end of January, the first month of the current year. The transactions relating to production completed during January are summarized as follows:

(a) Materials purchased on account, $43,500.
(b) Direct materials used, $45,920. This represented 22,400 pounds at $2.05 per pound.
(c) Direct labor paid, $105,020. This represented 17,800 hours at $5.90 per hour. There were no accruals at either the beginning or the end of the period.
(d) Factory overhead incurred during the month was composed of depreciation on plant and equipment, $22,000; indirect labor, $15,500; insurance, $6,000; and miscellaneous factory costs, $5,250. The indirect labor and miscellaneous factory costs were paid during the period, and the insurance represents an expiration of prepaid insurance. Of the total factory overhead of $48,750, fixed costs amounted to $30,000 and variable costs were $18,750.
(e) Goods finished during the period, 9,000 units.

Instructions:

(1) Prepare entries in general journal form to record the transactions, assuming that the work in process account is debited for actual production costs and credited with standard costs for goods finished.
(2) Prepare a T account for Work in Process and post to the account, using the identifying letters as dates.
(3) Prepare schedules of variances for direct materials cost, direct labor cost, and factory overhead cost. Normal productive capacity for the plant is 20,000 direct labor hours.
(4) Total the amount of the standard cost variances and compare this total with the balance of the work in process account.

22-4B. The treasurer of Vincent Company instructs you to prepare a monthly cash budget for the next three months. He presents you with the following budget information:

	May	June	July
Sales...............	$700,000	$610,000	$840,000
Manufacturing costs.	381,000	324,000	414,000
Operating expenses..	209,000	200,000	239,000
Capital expenditures.	——	75,000	——

The company expects to sell about 10% of its merchandise for cash. Of sales on account, 80% are expected to be collected in full in the month following the sale and the remainder the next following month. Depreciation, insurance, and property taxes represent $18,000 of the estimated monthly manufacturing costs and $5,000 of the probable monthly operating expenses. Insurance and property taxes are paid in March and September respectively. Of the remainder of the manufacturing costs and operating expenses, two thirds are expected to be paid in the month in which they are incurred and the balance in the following month.

Current assets of May 1 are composed of cash of $100,000, marketable securities of $75,000, and accounts receivable of $550,000 ($400,000 from April sales and $150,000 from March sales). Current liabilities as of May 1 are composed of a $50,000, 8%, 90-day note payable due May 10, $110,000 of accounts payable incurred in April for manufacturing costs, and accrued liabilities of $60,000 incurred in April for operating expenses.

It is expected that $600 in dividends will be received in June. An estimated income tax payment of $32,500 will be made in June. Vincent Company's regular semiannual dividend of $20,000 is expected to be declared in June and paid in July. Management desires to maintain a minimum cash balance of $90,000.

Instructions:

(1) Prepare a monthly cash budget for May, June, and July.
(2) On the basis of the cash budget prepared in (1), what recommendation should be made to the treasurer?

CHAPTER 23

23-1B. L. R. Bonner owns a small office building from which he receives rental income. He uses the cash method of determining income, depositing all rents received from tenants in a special bank account. All disbursements related to the building, as well as occasional unrelated disbursements, are paid by checks drawn on the same account. During the current taxable year ending December 31, he deposited $40,000 of rent receipts in the special account.

Disbursements from the special bank account during the current year are summarized as follows:

Wages of custodian:		
Withheld for FICA tax and paid to IRS..........	$ 468	
Withheld for income tax and paid to IRS........	622	
Paid to custodian............................	6,710	$7,800
Real estate tax.......................................		2,750

Payment of personal income tax:

Applicable to preceding year.................................	1,600
Applicable to current year...................................	4,800
Interest on mortgage note payable on land and office building.	1,800
Installment payments of principal on mortgage note payable..	3,600
Utilities expense..	1,040
Air-conditioning units installed in two offices not previously air-	
conditioned...	3,240
Repainting interior of two offices...........................	960
Premium on a three-year insurance policy on the building, effec-	
tive January 5...	1,230
Repairs to heating and plumbing equipment................	620
Payroll taxes expense.......................................	756

Contributions:

United Fund...	250
State University...	600
Political committee......................................	100
Miscellaneous expenses incurred in earning rentals...........	543
Purchases of various stocks................................	7,650

In addition to the foregoing data, you determine from other records and the tax return for the preceding year that the allowable deduction for depreciation expense is $4,500 and that current expirations of insurance premiums paid in earlier years total $415.

Instructions:

Prepare a statement of adjusted gross income from rents, identifying each of the allowable deductions from gross income.

23-2B. John T. Nolan, unmarried and entitled to one exemption for himself, is an architect. He uses the cash method of determining taxable income and reports on the calendar-year basis. A summary of his record of cash receipts and disbursements for the current calendar year is presented below and on the next page.

The automobile was used 40% of the time for professional purposes. It is to be depreciated by the declining-balance method at twice the straight-line rate, assuming an estimated life of 3 years. Allocate 40% of the depreciation and other automobile expenses to professional purposes.

Cash Receipts

Professional fees...	$71,400
Borrowed from bank (professional purposes)................	6,000
Inheritance from uncle's estate............................	5,000
Dividends on corporation stocks...........................	605

Cash Disbursements

Wages of employees..	$18,340
Payroll taxes..	1,680
Fees to collaborating engineers............................	6,210
Office rent..	5,760
Telephone expense (office).................................	940
Electricity (office)..	420
Blueprints..	610
Office supplies expense....................................	185
Insurance on office equipment (3-year policy, dated January 1)	240
Partial repayment of bank loan (see receipts)..............	2,000

Interest on bank loan...............................	420
Charitable contributions.............................	1,210
Payment on principal of residence mortgage note..........	1,500
Interest on residence mortgage note.....................	760
Personal property tax on office equipment.................	55
Real estate tax on home.............................	693
State sales tax on purchases for personal use..............	190
Political contribution...............................	100
New automobile (purchased January 10).................	4,500
Office equipment (purchased at various times during year)..	1,200
Automobile operating expenses (exclusive of depreciation)...	680
Purchase of 100 shares of Miami Corporation stock.........	1,920
Payments of estimated income tax for current year.........	9,200

The cost of the office equipment owned at the beginning of the year was $2,800, the additions made during the year are indicated above, and none of the equipment was disposed of during the year. Use a composite depreciation rate of 10%, based on the average of the beginning and ending balances.

Instructions:

Prepare a summary of federal income tax data for Nolan, applying the appropriate schedule of tax rates presented in this chapter.

23-3B. The preliminary income statement of L. B. Garvin's College Shop presented below was prepared as of the end of the calendar year in which the business was established. You are engaged to examine the statement, review the business records, revise the accounting system to the extent necessary, and determine the adjusted gross income.

821

Sales..............		$102,640
Purchases..........		78,310
Gross profit on sales.		$ 24,330
Operating expenses:		
Salaries...........	$19,140	
Rent.............	3,410	
Taxes............	1,050	
Store equipment..	8,580	
Advertising.......	542	
Fuel.............	418	
Utilities..........	394	
Insurance........	920	
Donations........	195	
Miscellaneous....	782	35,431
Net loss...........		$ 11,101

You obtain the following information during your examination:

(a) The preliminary income statement is a summary of cash receipts and disbursements. Sales on account are not recorded until cash is received; in the meantime they are evidenced only by duplicate sales tickets. Similarly, invoices for merchandise and other purchases are not re-recorded until payment is made; in the meantime they are filed in an unpaid file.

(b) Uncollected sales to customers on account at December 31 amount to $1,970

(c) Unpaid invoices at December 31 for expenditures of the past year are summarized as follows:

Merchandise.	$6,118
Fuel........	74
Utilities.....	31

(d) The inventory of merchandise on hand at December 31 amounted to $20,400.

(e) Withdrawals of $7,200 by the owner of the enterprise were included in the amount reported as Salaries.

(f) The agreement with the three part-time salesclerks provides for a bonus equal to 1% of cash collected on sales during the year, payable in January of the following year. (Figure to nearest dollar.)

(g) The rent for January of the following year ($310) was paid and recorded in December.

(h) Accrued taxes as of the end of the year amount to $298.

(i) The store equipment reported in the preliminary income statement was installed on March 2. It has an estimated life of 10 years and no residual value. Depreciation is to be claimed for 10 months, using the declining-balance method at twice the straight-line rate.

(j) A total of $390 of insurance premiums was unexpired at December 31.

(k) Payments classified as Donations were contributions to charitable, religious, and educational organizations.

(l) Payments classified as Miscellaneous included $125 of personal expenses of the owner.

Instructions:

Prepare a statement of adjusted gross income from the business for submission with the income tax return of L. B. Garvin, the owner, employing the accrual method of accounting.

CHAPTER 24

24-1B. Allied Chemical Products refines Product P in batches of 200,000 gallons, which it sells for $.25 per gallon. The associated unit costs and expenses are currently as follows:

	Per Gallon
Direct materials.................	$.105
Direct labor....................	.045
Variable factory overhead........	.020
Fixed factory overhead...........	.015
Salesmen's commissions..........	.025
Fixed selling and general expenses.	.010

The company is presently considering a proposal to put Product P through several additional processes to yield Products P and Q. Although the company had determined such further processing to be unwise, new processing methods have now been developed. Existing facilities can be used for the additional processing, but inasmuch as the factory is operating at full 8-hour-day capacity, the processing would have to be performed at night. Additional costs of processing would be $7,500 per batch and there would be an evaporation loss of 10%, with 40% of the processed material evolving as Product P and 50% as Product Q. Selling price of Product Q is $.40 per gallon. Salesmen's commissions are a uniform percentage based on the sales price.

Instructions:

(1) Prepare a differential analysis report as of November 4 presenting the differential revenue and the differential cost per batch associated with the processing to produce Products P and Q compared with processing to produce Product P only.

(2) Briefly report your recommendation.

24-2B. Fuller Company purchases a machine at a cost of $175,000 which is depreciated at $25,000 yearly based on a 7-year useful life and no residual value. The company's manufacturing costs for a normal year, exclusive of depreciation, total $375,000, operating expenses are $167,500 yearly, and revenues total $625,000 yearly.

Two years after the original purchase, a new type of machine priced at $270,000 becomes available. It has an estimated life of 5 years, with no residual value, and its use is expected to reduce the company's manufacturing costs, exclusive of depreciation, to $315,000 yearly. The old machine can be sold for only $50,000. Revenues and operating expenses will not be affected by substitution of the new machine for the old.

Instructions:

(1) Prepare a differential analysis report as of June 23, comparing operations utilizing the new machine with operations using the present equipment. The analysis should indicate the net cost reduction or net cost increase that would result over the 5-year period if the new machine is acquired.

(2) List other factors that should be considered before a final decision is reached.

823

24-4B. Product A-7 is one of numerous products manufactured by Wilcox Company. The demand for Product A-7 has dropped sharply because of recent competition from a similar product. The company's chemists are currently completing tests of various new formulas, and it is anticipated that the manufacture of a superior product can be started on May 1, one month hence. No changes will be needed in the present production facilities to manufacture the new product because only the mixture of the various materials will be changed.

The controller has been asked by the president of the company for advice on whether to continue production during April or to suspend the manufacture of Product A-7 until May 1. The controller has assembled the following pertinent data:

Wilcox Company
Estimated Income Statement — Product A-7
For Month Ending March 31, 19—

Sales (10,000 units)	$270,000
Cost of goods sold	205,000
Gross profit on sales	$ 65,000
Selling and general expenses	80,000
Loss from operations	$ 15,000

The estimated production costs and selling and general expenses based on a production of 10,000 units are listed at the top of the next page.

Direct materials.	$5.00 per unit
Direct labor.	6.25 per unit
Variable factory overhead.	1.75 per unit
Variable selling and general expenses.	4.00 per unit
Fixed factory overhead.	$75,000 for March
Fixed selling and general expenses. . . .	$40,000 for March

Sales for April are expected to drop about 25% below those of the preceding month. No significant changes are anticipated in the production costs or operating expenses. No extra costs will be incurred in discontinuing operations in the portion of the plant associated with Product A-7. The inventory of Product A-7 at the beginning and end of April is expected to be inconsequential.

Instructions:

(1) Prepare an estimated income statement in absorption costing form for April for Product A-7, assuming that production continues during the month.

(2) Prepare an estimated income statement in variable costing form for April for Product A-7, assuming that production continues during the month.

(3) State the estimated amount of operating loss arising from the activities associated with Product A-7 for April if production is temporarily suspended.

(4) Prepare a brief statement of the advice you think the controller should give.

CHAPTER 25

25-1B. Watson Manufacturing Company is considering the addition of a new product to its line. For 1973, production was at 85% of capacity, the assets employed were $5,000,000 (original cost), and the income statement showed an operating income of $550,000, computed as follows:

Sales.		$5,000,000
Less: Cost of goods sold.	$3,375,000	
Selling expenses.	765,000	
General expenses.	310,000	4,450,000
Operating income.		$ 550,000

If the new product is added, market research indicates that 15,000 units can be sold in 1974 at an estimated selling price of $30 per unit. The idle capacity will be utilized to produce the product, but an additional $500,000 in plant assets will be required. The cost data per unit for the new product are as follows:

Direct materials.	$10.25
Direct labor.	6.25
Factory overhead (includes depreciation on additional investment).	4.00
Selling expenses.	3.20
General expenses.	1.30
	$25.00

Instructions:
(1) Prepare an estimated income statement for 1974 for the new product.
(2) Prepare a schedule indicating the rate of return on assets under present conditions and for the new product. Use the original cost of the assets in your computations.
(3) Would you recommend addition of the new product? Would you require other data before you make your decision? If so, what data would you require?

25-3B. The capital expenditures budget committee is considering two projects. The estimated operating income and net cash flows from each project are presented below:

	Project A		Project B	
Year	Operating Income	Net Cash Flow	Operating Income	Net Cash Flow
1	$10,000	$20,000	$ 4,000	$14,000
2	7,500	17,500	6,000	16,000
3	5,000	15,000	7,000	17,000
4	3,500	13,500	7,000	17,000
5	2,000	12,000	4,000	14,000
	$28,000	$78,000	$28,000	$78,000

Each project requires an investment of $50,000 with no residual value expected. The committee has selected a rate of 15% for purposes of the discounted cash flow analysis.

Instructions:
(1) Compute the following:
  (a) The average rate of return for each project, giving effect to depreciation on the investment.
  (b) The excess or deficiency of present value over amount to be invested as determined by the discounted cash flow method for each project. Use the present value table appearing in this chapter.
(2) Prepare a brief report for the budget committee advising it on the relative merits of the two projects.

25-4B. Cowan Company expects to maintain the same inventories at the end of 1974 as at the beginning of the year. The total of all production costs for the year is therefore assumed to be equal to the cost of goods sold. With this in mind, the various department heads were asked to submit estimates of the expenses for their departments during 1974. A summary report of these estimates is presented below and on the next page.

	Estimated Fixed Expense	Estimated Variable Expense (per unit sold)
Production costs:		
Direct materials..............	$ ——	$2.00
Direct labor.................	——	1.25
Factory overhead.............	160,000	.75

Selling expenses:

Sales salaries and commissions..	42,500	.20
Advertising.................	32,500	———
Travel.....................	12,500	———
Miscellaneous selling expenses..	7,500	.10
General expenses:		
Office and officers' salaries.....	90,000	.10
Supplies....................	9,000	.05
Miscellaneous general expenses.	6,000	.05
	$360,000	$4.50

It is expected that 140,000 units will be sold at a selling price of $7.50 a unit. Capacity output is 160,000 units.

Instructions:

(1) Determine the break-even point (a) in dollars of sales, (b) in units, and (c) in terms of capacity.
(2) Prepare an estimated income statement for 1974.
(3) Construct a break-even chart, indicating the break-even point in dollars of sales.
(4) What is the expected margin of safety?
(5) What is the expected marginal income ratio?

25-6B. Dever Company operated at full capacity during 1973. Its income statement appears below.

Sales......................		$1,000,000
Cost of goods sold...........		600,000
Gross profit on sales.........		$ 400,000
Operating expenses:		
Selling expenses...........	$200,000	
General expenses..........	100,000	
Total operating expenses.		300,000
Operating income...........		$ 100,000

An analysis of costs and expenses reveals the following division of costs and expenses between fixed and variable.

	Fixed	Variable
Cost of goods sold.	30%	70%
Selling expenses...	30%	70%
General expenses..	60%	40%

The management of Dever Company is considering a plant expansion program that will permit an increase of $250,000 in yearly sales. The expansion will increase fixed costs and expenses by $60,000 but will not affect the relationship between sales and variable costs and expenses.

Instructions:

(1) Determine for present capacity (a) the total fixed costs and expenses and (b) the total variable costs and expenses.
(2) Determine the percentage of total variable costs and expenses to sales.
(3) Compute the break-even point under present conditions.

(4) Compute the break-even point under the proposed program.
(5) Determine the amount of sales that would be necessary under the proposed program to realize the $100,000 of operating income that was earned in 1973.
(6) Determine the maximum operating income possible with the expanded plant.
(7) If the proposal is accepted and sales remain at the 1973 level, what will the operating income be for 1974?
(8) Based upon the data given, would you recommend accepting the proposal? Explain.

CHAPTER 26

26-1B. The comparative balance sheet of the Arbor Corporation at September 30 of the current year and the preceding year appears below in condensed form.

Assets	Current Year	Preceding Year
Cash..................................	$ 31,800	$ 38,100
Accounts receivable (net)...............	42,100	39,700
Merchandise inventory.................	92,200	104,500
Prepaid expenses......................	3,600	2,950
Plant assets...........................	298,000	250,000
Accumulated depreciation — plant assets.	(96,000)	(114,000)
	$371,700	$321,250

Liabilities and Stockholders' Equity		
Accounts payable.....................	$ 41,800	$ 36,900
Mortgage note payable................	——	60,000
Common stock, $5 par.................	200,000	150,000
Premium on common stock.............	10,000	——
Retained earnings.....................	119,900	74,350
	$371,700	$321,250

Additional data for the current year obtained from the income statement and from an examination of the noncurrent asset, noncurrent liability, and stockholders' equity accounts in the ledger are as follows:

(a) Net income (no extraordinary items), $65,550.
(b) Depreciation reported on the income statement, $14,000.
(c) An addition to the building was constructed at a cost of $80,000, and fully depreciated equipment costing $32,000 was discarded, no salvage being realized.
(d) The mortgage note payable was not due until 1979, but the terms permitted earlier payment without penalty.
(e) 10,000 shares of common stock were issued at 6 for cash.
(f) Cash dividends declared, $20,000.

Instructions:

(1) On the basis of the comparative balance sheet and the other information, assemble in memorandum form the data needed to prepare

827

a funds statement (working capital concept) for the current year ended September 30.

(2) Prepare a statement of changes in financial position, including a section on changes in components of working capital.

26-2B. The comparative balance sheet of the Ballard Corporation at December 31 of the current year and the preceding year appears below in condensed form.

Assets	Current Year	Preceding Year
Cash..	$ 44,600	$ 33,500
Trade receivables (net)........................	58,500	51,300
Inventories....................................	101,200	112,500
Prepaid expenses..............................	2,100	2,700
Buildings.....................................	330,400	210,400
Accumulated depreciation — buildings..........	(93,200)	(86,900)
Machinery and equipment......................	175,000	175,000
Accumulated depreciation—machinery and equipment.	(82,000)	(65,000)
Land...	30,000	30,000
Patents.......................................	51,000	55,000
	$617,600	$518,500

Liabilities and Stockholders' Equity		
Accounts payable (merchandise creditors)...........	$ 35,600	$ 42,000
Dividends payable..............................	13,000	10,000
Salaries payable...............................	5,100	3,200
Mortgage note payable.........................	60,000	—
Bonds payable.................................	—	100,000
Common stock, $10 par.........................	280,000	200,000
Premium on common stock......................	40,000	20,000
Retained earnings..............................	183,900	143,300
	$617,600	$518,500

An examination of the income statement and the accounting records revealed the following additional information applicable to the current year:

(a) Net income (no extraordinary items), $83,600.

(b) Depreciation expense reported on the income statement: buildings, $6,300; machinery and equipment, $17,000.

(c) Patent amortization reported on the income statement, $4,000.

(d) A mortgage note for $60,000, due in 1985, was issued in connection with the construction of a building costing $120,000; the remainder was paid in cash.

(e) 8,000 shares of common stock were issued at 12½ in exchange for the bonds payable.

(f) Cash dividends declared, $43,000.

Instructions:

(1) On the basis of the information presented above, assemble in memorandum form the data needed to prepare a funds statement (working capital concept) for the current year ended December 31.

(2) Prepare a statement of changes in financial position, including a section for changes in components of working capital.

828

26-3B. The comparative balance sheet of Ballard Corporation and other data necessary for the analysis of the corporation's funds flow are presented in Problem 26-2B.

Instructions:

(1) On the basis of the information presented in Problem 26-2B, assemble in memorandum form the data needed to prepare a funds statement (cash concept) for the current year ended December 31 (notations prepared for Problem 26-2B that are applicable to this problem need not be repeated).

(2) Prepare a statement of changes in financial position, including a summary of the change in cash balance.

26-4B. The comparative balance sheet of Spencer & Thomas, Inc., at December 31 of the current year and the preceding year, in condensed form, and the noncurrent asset accounts, the noncurrent liability accounts, and the stockholders' equity accounts for the current year are presented below and on pages 830 and 831.

Assets	Current Year	Preceding Year
Cash....................................	$ 80,750	$ 89,400
Trade receivables (net)..................	94,400	77,200
Inventories.............................	285,600	248,350
Prepaid expenses........................	5,120	6,240
Investments............................	———	50,000
Equipment.............................	468,500	420,500
Accumulated depreciation — equipment.....	(91,000)	(78,000)
Buildings..............................	391,000	191,000
Accumulated depreciation — buildings......	(51,420)	(43,600)
Land..................................	40,000	40,000
	$1,222,950	$1,001,090

Liabilities and Stockholders' Equity

	Current Year	Preceding Year
Accounts payable (merchandise creditors)...	$ 22,110	$ 80,630
Income tax payable.....................	17,800	14,500
Long-term notes payable.................	210,000	———
Discount on long-term notes payable........	(9,250)	———
Common stock, $25 par..................	780,000	750,000
Premium on common stock...............	80,000	60,000
Appropriation for contingencies...........	40,000	20,000
Retained earnings......................	82,290	75,960
	$1,222,950	$1,001,090

INVESTMENTS

DATE		ITEM	DEBIT	CREDIT	BALANCE DEBIT	BALANCE CREDIT
19—						
Jan.	1	Balance			50,000	
Nov.	17	Realized $67,000 cash from sale, after deducting applicable income tax		50,000	—	—

829

EQUIPMENT

DATE		ITEM	DEBIT	CREDIT	BALANCE DEBIT	BALANCE CREDIT
19—						
Jan.	1	Balance			420,500	
Apr.	12	Discarded, no salvage		30,000		
July	17	Purchased for cash	50,000			
Nov.	18	Purchased for cash	28,000		468,500	

ACCUMULATED DEPRECIATION—EQUIPMENT

DATE		ITEM	DEBIT	CREDIT	BALANCE DEBIT	BALANCE CREDIT
19—						
Jan.	1	Balance				78,000
Apr.	12	Equipment discarded	30,000			
Dec.	31	Depreciation for year		43,000		91,000

BUILDINGS

DATE		ITEM	DEBIT	CREDIT	BALANCE DEBIT	BALANCE CREDIT
19—						
Jan.	1	Balance			191,000	
July	1	Acquired with notes payable	200,000		391,000	

ACCUMULATED DEPRECIATION—BUILDINGS

DATE		ITEM	DEBIT	CREDIT	BALANCE DEBIT	BALANCE CREDIT
19—						
Jan.	1	Balance				43,600
Dec.	31	Depreciation for year		7,820		51,420

LAND

DATE		ITEM	DEBIT	CREDIT	BALANCE DEBIT	BALANCE CREDIT
19—						
Jan.	1	Balance			40,000	

LONG-TERM NOTES PAYABLE

DATE		ITEM	DEBIT	CREDIT	BALANCE DEBIT	BALANCE CREDIT
19—						
July	1			210,000		210,000

DISCOUNT ON LONG-TERM NOTES PAYABLE

DATE		ITEM	DEBIT	CREDIT	BALANCE DEBIT	BALANCE CREDIT
19—						
July	1	Notes issued	10,000		10,000	
Dec.	31	Amortization		750	9,250	

COMMON STOCK, $25 PAR

DATE		ITEM	DEBIT	CREDIT	BALANCE DEBIT	BALANCE CREDIT
19—						
Jan.	1	Balance				750,000
Dec.	10	Stock dividend		30,000		780,000

PREMIUM ON COMMON STOCK

DATE		ITEM	DEBIT	CREDIT	BALANCE DEBIT	BALANCE CREDIT
19—						
Jan.	1	Balance				60,000
Dec.	10	Stock dividend		20,000		80,000

APPROPRIATION FOR CONTINGENCIES

DATE		ITEM	DEBIT	CREDIT	BALANCE DEBIT	BALANCE CREDIT
19—						
Jan.	1	Balance				20,000
Dec.	31	Appropriation		20,000		40,000

RETAINED EARNINGS

DATE		ITEM	DEBIT	CREDIT	BALANCE DEBIT	BALANCE CREDIT
19—						
Jan.	1	Balance				75,960
Dec.	10	Stock dividend	50,000			
	31	Net income		136,330		
	31	Cash dividends	60,000			
	31	Appropriated	20,000			82,290

Instructions:

(1) On the basis of the comparative balance sheet and the accounts of Spencer & Thomas, Inc., assemble in memorandum form the data needed to prepare a funds statement (working capital concept) for the current year ended December 31. (The gain on the sale of investments was reported on the income statement as an extraordinary item, less applicable income tax.)

(2) Prepare a statement of changes in financial position, including a section for changes in components of working capital.

26-5B. The comparative balance sheet of Spencer & Thomas, Inc., and other data necessary for the analysis of the corporation's funds flow are presented in Problem 26-4B.

Instructions:

(1) On the basis of the information presented in Problem 26-4B, assemble in memorandum form the data needed to prepare a funds statement (cash concept) for the current year ended December 31. (Notations prepared for Problem 26-4B that are applicable to this problem need not be repeated.)

(2) Prepare a statement of changes in financial position, including a summary of the change in cash balance.

CHAPTER 27

27-1B. On September 30 Parker Corporation purchased 90% of the outstanding stock of Sparks Company for $600,000. Balance sheet data for the two corporations immediately after the transaction are presented at the top of the next page.

Assets	Parker Corp.	Sparks Corp.
Cash and marketable securities.	$ 92,300	$ 36,500
Accounts receivable.	88,000	58,600
Allowance for doubtful accounts.	(6,000)	(2,500)
Inventories.	418,600	192,400
Investment in Sparks Company stock.	600,000	——
Equipment and building.	660,200	378,950
Accumulated depreciation.	(95,100)	(73,000)
Land.	50,000	12,750
	$1,808,000	$603,700

Liabilities and Stockholders' Equity		
Accounts payable.	$ 141,800	$ 69,200
Income tax payable.	23,700	7,000
Bonds payable (due in 1992).	500,000	——
Common stock, $5 par.	800,000	——
Common stock, $10 par.	——	400,000
Retained earnings.	342,500	127,500
	$1,808,000	$603,700

Instructions:

(1) Prepare in report form a detailed consolidated balance sheet as of the date of acquisition. The fair value of Sparks Company's assets are deemed to correspond to their book carrying amounts, except for land, which is to be increased by $25,250.

(2) Assuming that Sparks Company earns net income of $100,000 and pays cash dividends of $40,000 during the ensuing fiscal year and that Parker Corporation records its share of the earnings and dividends, determine the following as of the end of the year:

    (a) The net amount added to Parker Corporation's investment account as a result of Sparks Company's earnings and dividends.

    (b) The amount of the minority interest.

27-3B. On January 1 of the current year Procter Corporation exchanged 32,000 shares of its $10 par common stock for 60,000 shares (the entire issue) of Shaw Company's $5 par common stock. Later in the year Shaw purchased from Procter Corporation $100,000 of its $300,000 issue of bonds payable, at face amount. All of the items for "interest" appearing on the balance sheets and income statements of both corporations are related to the bonds.

During the year Procter Corporation sold finished goods with a cost of $140,000 to Shaw Company for $200,000, all of which was sold by Shaw Company before the end of the year.

Procter Corporation has correctly recorded the income and dividends reported for the year by Shaw Company. Data for the balance sheets of both companies as of the end of the current year and for their income statements for the current year are presented on the next page.

Instructions:

(1) Determine the amounts to be eliminated from the following items in preparing the consolidated balance sheet as of December 31 of the current year: (a) Dividends receivable and dividends payable; (b) Interest receivable and interest payable; (c) Investment in Shaw

BALANCE SHEET DATA

Assets	Procter Corporation	Shaw Company
Cash.....................................	$ 76,400	$ 32,500
Accounts receivable (net).................	98,200	56,200
Dividends receivable......................	15,000	——
Interest receivable.......................	——	4,000
Inventories..............................	510,300	204,100
Investment in Shaw Co. stock, 60,000 shares...	550,700	——
Investment in Procter Corp. bonds, at face amount................................	——	100,000
Plant and equipment......................	639,600	275,300
Accumulated depreciation..................	(82,400)	(51,100)
	$1,807,800	$621,000

Liabilities and Stockholders' Equity		
Accounts payable.........................	$ 97,600	$ 49,300
Income tax payable.......................	13,000	6,000
Dividends payable........................	24,000	15,000
Interest payable..........................	12,000	——
Bonds payable, 8% (due in 1985)............	300,000	——
Common stock, $10 par....................	800,000	——
Common stock, $5 par.....................	——	300,000
Premium on common stock.................	——	60,000
Retained earnings........................	561,200	190,700
	$1,807,800	$621,000

833

INCOME STATEMENT DATA

Revenue:		
Sales.....................................	$1,640,000	$620,400
Income of subsidiary.....................	111,300	——
Interest income..........................	——	4,000
	$1,751,300	$624,400
Expenses:		
Cost of goods sold.......................	1,032,600	$325,000
Selling expenses.........................	150,000	60,000
General expenses........................	102,000	38,000
Interest expense.........................	12,000	——
Income tax..............................	160,200	90,100
	$1,456,800	$513,100
Net income..............................	$ 294,500	$111,300

Co. stock and stockholders' equity; (d) Investment in Procter Corp. bonds and bonds payable.

(2) Prepare a detailed consolidated balance sheet in report form.
(3) Determine the amounts to be eliminated from the following items in preparing the consolidated income statement for the current year ended December 31: (a) Sales and cost of goods sold; (b) Interest income and interest expense; (c) Income of subsidiary and net income.
(4) Prepare a single-step consolidated income statement, inserting the earnings per share as a parenthetical notation on the same line with net income.

(continued)

(5) Determine the amount of the reduction in consolidated inventories, net income, and retained earnings if Shaw Company's inventory had included $50,000 of the finished goods purchased from Procter Corporation.

27-4B. The balances in the accounts of Barcus, Inc., after adjustment at December 31, the close of the current fiscal year, are as follows:

Accounts Payable........................		$ 61,800
Accounts Receivable.....................	$ 77,400	
Accumulated Depreciation — Buildings.....		31,100
Accumulated Depreciation — Equipment....		41,300
Allowance for Doubtful Accounts...........		5,000
Bond Sinking Fund......................	47,300	
Bonds Payable (due 1987)................		100,000
Buildings..............................	85,600	
Cash Dividends.........................	40,000	
Cash in Bank..........................	53,600	
Common Stock, $10 par.................		200,000
Cost of Goods Sold.....................	251,600	
Dividends Payable......................		10,000
Equipment............................	176,400	
General Expenses.......................	42,700	
Income Tax............................	72,300	
Income Tax Payable.....................		8,000
Interest Expense........................	8,000	
Interest Income.........................		6,200
Inventories............................	167,200	
Land.................................	27,500	
Prepaid Insurance......................	4,500	
Retained Earnings......................		127,800
Sales.................................		524,600
Salaries Payable........................		2,600
Selling Expenses.......................	64,300	
	$1,118,400	$1,118,400

The number of shares of stock outstanding remained unchanged during the year.

Instructions:

(1) Prepare a combined income and retained earnings statement using the single-step form, listing income tax as an item in the expenses section. Insert the earnings per share as a parenthetical notation on the same line with net income.
(2) Prepare a detailed balance sheet in financial position form, disclosing the amount of working capital.

27-5B. The balances of selected ledger accounts of an enterprise as of the end of the year are listed at the top of the next page. The price level at the beginning of the year was 120 and at the end of the year it was 130. The marketable securities, which are stated at cost, are common stocks purchased at the beginning of the year. Merchandise inventory is stated at cost, employing the fifo flow assumption. It is assumed to have been acquired when the price-level index was 125, midway between the beginning and end of the year. The equipment was acquired a number of years ago, at which time the price-level index was 90.

Account Title	Account Balance
Cash....................	$ 43,200
Marketable Securities.....	58,320
Accounts Receivable......	50,400
Merchandise Inventory....	120,000
Equipment.............	148,500
Accumulated Depreciation.	71,460
Accounts Payable.........	72,000

Instructions:

(1) Convert the account balances to current price-level equivalents as of the end of the period, presenting the details indicated by the following captions:

Account Title	Account Balance	Conversion Multiplier	Converted Balance

(2) Determine the price-level gain or loss during the year on each of the monetary items, assuming that the account balances were the same at the beginning and end of the year.

CHAPTER 28

28-1B. Data pertaining to the current position of P. A. Finch and Company are presented below.

Cash...........................	$110,000
Marketable securities..............	25,000
Accounts and notes receivable (net).	165,000
Merchandise inventory............	225,000
Prepaid expenses.................	15,000
Accounts payable................	220,000
Notes payable (short-term).........	50,000
Accrued liabilities...............	30,000

Instructions:

(1) Compute (a) working capital, (b) current ratio, and (c) acid-test ratio.
(2) Consider each of the following transactions separately and assume that only that transaction affects the data given above.

    (a) Purchased merchandise on account, $40,000.
    (b) Paid accounts payable, $100,000.
    (c) Received cash on account, $75,000.
    (d) Paid notes payable, $50,000.
    (e) Declared a cash dividend, $25,000.
    (f) Declared a common stock dividend on common stock, $50,000.
    (g) Borrowed cash from bank on a long-term note, $100,000.

(h) Issued additional shares of stock for cash, $100,000.

(i) Sold marketable securities, $25,000.

(j) Paid cash for store supplies, $2,000.

State the effect of each transaction (increase, decrease, or no effect) on working capital, current ratio, and acid-test ratio. Use the following column headings for recording your answers.

	Effect on		
Item	Working Capital	Current Ratio	Acid-Test Ratio

28-3B. For 1974, Lambert Company initiated an extensive sales promotion campaign that included the expenditure of an additional $40,000 for advertising. At the end of the year, Frank Lambert, the president, is presented with the following condensed comparative income statement:

Lambert Company
Comparative Income Statement
For Years Ended December 31, 1974 and 1973

	1974	1973
Sales......................................	$612,000	$454,500
Sales returns and allowances.................	12,000	4,500
Net sales..................................	$600,000	$450,000
Cost of merchandise sold....................	369,000	270,000
Gross profit on sales.......................	$231,000	$180,000
Selling expenses............................	$123,000	$ 67,500
General expenses...........................	28,800	22,500
Total operating expenses....................	$151,800	$ 90,000
Operating income..........................	$ 79,200	$ 90,000
Other income..............................	2,400	2,250
Income before income tax...................	$ 81,600	$ 92,250
Income tax................................	36,000	41,400
Net income................................	$ 45,600	$ 50,850

Instructions:

(1) Prepare a comparative income statement for the two-year period, presenting an analysis of each item in relationship to net sales for each of the years.

(2) To the extent the data permit, comment on the significant relationships revealed by the vertical analysis prepared in (1).

28-4B. The comparative financial statements of R. N. Monroe Company are presented on pages 837 and 838.

Instructions:

Determine for 1974 the ratios, turnovers, and other measures listed below, presenting the figures used in your computations:

(1) Working capital.

(2) Current ratio.

(3) Acid-test ratio.

(*continued on page 838*)

R. N. Monroe Company
Balance Sheet
December 31, 1974 and 1973

	1974	1973
Assets		
Current assets:		
Cash..	$ 135,000	$ 100,000
Marketable securities........................	75,000	75,000
Accounts receivable (net)....................	330,000	270,000
Merchandise inventory........................	400,000	360,000
Prepaid expenses.............................	20,000	20,000
Total current assets.........................	$ 960,000	$ 825,000
Long-term investments.........................	200,000	175,000
Plant assets..................................	1,840,000	1,800,000
Total assets..................................	$3,000,000	$2,800,000
Liabilities		
Current liabilities............................	$ 600,000	$ 600,000
Long-term liabilities:		
Mortgage note payable, due 1985..............	$ 150,000	——
Bonds payable, 7%, due 1990.................	500,000	$ 500,000
Total long-term liabilities...................	$ 650,000	$ 500,000
Total liabilities.............................	$1,250,000	$1,100,000
Stockholders' Equity		
Preferred 5% stock, $100 par..................	$ 500,000	$ 500,000
Common stock, $10 par........................	500,000	500,000
Retained earnings............................	750,000	700,000
Total stockholders' equity....................	$1,750,000	$1,700,000
Total liabilities and stockholders' equity...........	$3,000,000	$2,800,000

R. N. Monroe Company
Comparative Income Statement
For Years Ended December 31, 1974 and 1973

	1974	1973
Sales.......................................	$3,045,000	$2,652,000
Sales returns and allowances.....................	45,000	52,000
Net sales......................................	$3,000,000	$2,600,000
Cost of merchandise sold.......................	2,090,000	1,705,000
Gross profit on sales...........................	$ 910,000	$ 895,000
Selling expenses...............................	$ 430,000	$ 390,000
General expenses...............................	170,000	176,800
Total operating expenses.......................	$ 600,000	$ 566,800
Operating income..............................	$ 310,000	$ 328,200
Other income..................................	15,000	14,400
	$ 325,000	$ 342,600
Other expense (interest)........................	45,050	35,000
Income before income tax......................	$ 279,950	$ 307,600
Income tax....................................	133,950	147,600
Net income....................................	$ 146,000	$ 160,000

837

R. N. Monroe Company
Comparative Retained Earnings Statement
For Year Ended December 31, 1974 and 1973

	1974	1973
Retained earnings, January 1	$ 700,000	$ 636,000
Add net income for year	146,000	160,000
Total	$ 846,000	$ 796,000
Deduct dividends:		
On preferred stock	$ 25,000	$ 25,000
On common stock	71,000	71,000
Total	$ 96,000	$ 96,000
Retained earnings, December 31	$ 750,000	$ 700,000

(4) Accounts receivable turnover.
(5) Number of days' sales in receivables.
(6) Merchandise inventory turnover.
(7) Number of days' sales in merchandise inventory.
(8) Ratio of plant assets to long-term liabilities.
(9) Ratio of stockholders' equity to liabilities.
(10) Rate earned on total assets.
(11) Rate earned on stockholders' equity.
(12) Rate earned on common stockholders' equity.
(13) Ratio of net sales to assets.
(14) Earnings per share on common stock.

Appendix C

SPECIMEN CORPORATION STATEMENTS

MONSANTO COMPANY AND SUBSIDIARIES

STATEMENT OF CONSOLIDATED FINANCIAL POSITION
(Dollars in millions, except per share)

ASSETS

	December 31, 1971	December 31, 1970
Current Assets:		
Cash..	$ 34.2	$ 28.9
Marketable securities, at cost which approximates market........	40.4	50.9
Receivables, less allowances....................................	402.9	383.1
Inventories...	395.4	392.1
	872.9	855.0
Investments and Miscellaneous Assets, at Cost or Less:		
Investment in and advances to associates........................	16.0	15.0
Miscellaneous investments and receivables......................	54.1	64.5
	70.1	79.5
Property, Plant and Equipment, at Cost:		
Land..	32.4	30.5
Buildings...	408.4	397.2
Machinery and equipment..	2,172.5	2,083.5
Phosphate deposits...	12.1	12.1
Oil and gas properties..	109.7	113.4
	2,735.1	2,636.7
Less accumulated depreciation and depletion, etc................	1,564.8	1,466.8
Net property....................................	1,170.3	1,169.9
Deferred Charges..	40.2	40.3
	$2,153.5	$2,144.7

LIABILITIES

	December 31, 1971	December 31, 1970
Current Liabilities:		
Accounts payable and accruals..................................	$ 247.2	$ 249.5
Income taxes..	63.3	18.2
Current portion of long-term debt...............................	15.8	49.4
	326.3	317.1
Long-Term Debt — Less Current Portion Above.....................	558.2	589.3
Other Liabilities and Deferred Credits:		
Deferred income taxes...	27.5	31.2
Miscellaneous..	12.9	10.4
	40.4	41.6
Minority Interests in Subsidiary Companies......................	2.9	2.5
Shareowners' Equity:		
Preferred stock — authorized, 10,000,000 shares without par value, issuable in series; outstanding, 2,320,410 shares in 1971 and 2,313,910 shares in 1970..............................	5.2	5.2
Common stock — authorized, 50,000,000 shares, par value $2 each; issued, 33,155,500 shares in 1971 and 33,088,362 shares in 1970..	66.3	66.2
Paid-in surplus...	586.5	583.5
Retained earnings..	580.2	551.6
	1,238.2	1,206.5
Less common stock in treasury, at cost (306,543 shares in 1971 and 301,741 shares in 1970)..................................	12.5	12.3
	1,225.7	1,194.2
	$2,153.5	$2,144.7

The above statement should be read in conjunction with pages 17 through 20 of this report.

ADDRESSOGRAPH MULTIGRAPH AND SUBSIDIARY COMPANIES

CONSOLIDATED BALANCE SHEET

AS OF JULY 31	1972	1971
ASSETS		
CURRENT ASSETS:		
Cash and short-term securities	$ 34,655,000	$ 34,225,000
Accounts receivable, less allowance for doubtful accounts of $4,804,000 in 1972 and $3,905,000 in 1971	116,473,000	109,318,000
Inventories	112,751,000	108,523,000
Prepaid income taxes and expenses	11,758,000	12,609,000
	275,637,000	264,675,000
LEASE CONTRACTS RECEIVABLE, due after one year, less unearned finance charges	15,127,000	12,364,000
PLANT AND EQUIPMENT, AT COST:		
Land	4,528,000	4,524,000
Buildings	61,983,000	62,394,000
Machinery and equipment	83,977,000	79,082,000
Rental machines	38,302,000	38,186,000
Leasehold improvements, less amortization	3,098,000	2,330,000
	191,888,000	186,516,000
Less accumulated depreciation	104,466,000	101,504,000
	87,422,000	85,012,000
OTHER ASSETS:		
Excess of cost of businesses acquired over related net assets	4,017,000	3,768,000
Deferred charges	5,807,000	4,517,000
	9,824,000	8,285,000
	$388,010,000	$370,336,000

840

	1972	1971
LIABILITIES AND SHAREHOLDERS' EQUITY		
CURRENT LIABILITIES:		
Bank loans	$ 3,869,000	$ 10,716,000
Accounts payable	27,202,000	17,601,000
Supply and service contract obligations, etc.	22,460,000	23,520,000
Federal, state and foreign income taxes	10,812,000	9,399,000
Accrued taxes, commissions, payroll, etc.	20,668,000	17,092,000
Long-term debt due within one year	463,000	2,217,000
	85,474,000	80,545,000
LONG-TERM DEBT	83,415,000	85,425,000
DEFERRED INCOME TAXES	8,213,000	6,039,000
INTERNATIONAL OPERATIONS RESERVE	2,902,000	2,152,000
SHAREHOLDERS' EQUITY:		
Common stock, par value $2.50		
Authorized: 15,000,000 shares (10,000,000 in 1971)		
Outstanding: 8,037,169 shares (8,036,994 shares in 1971)	20,093,000	20,092,000
Capital in excess of par value	69,125,000	69,121,000
Retained earnings, per accompanying statements	118,788,000	106,962,000
	208,006,000	196,175,000
	$388,010,000	$370,336,000

841

Consolidated Balance Sheet

Chesebrough-Pond's Inc.
and Subsidiaries

Assets

	December 31, 1971	December 31, 1970
Current Assets:		
Cash	$ 6,317,000	$ 7,357,000
Short-term investments, at cost which approximates market	5,539,000	7,369,000
Accounts receivable	61,728,000	54,172,000
Inventories—lower of cost (first-in, first-out) or market:		
Finished goods	24,364,000	20,747,000
Raw materials and work-in-process	36,616,000	26,446,000
Prepaid expenses	5,856,000	5,777,000
Total current assets	140,420,000	121,868,000
Property, Plant and Equipment:		
At cost	78,399,000	66,895,000
Less accumulated depreciation	28,689,000	25,724,000
Net property, plant and equipment	49,710,000	41,171,000
Other Assets, at cost	3,834,000	5,036,000
Deferred Taxes	589,000	802,000
Goodwill and Trademarks, at cost	40,325,000	34,638,000
	$234,878,000	$203,515,000

842

See accompanying notes.

Liabilities and Stockholders' Equity

	December 31, 1971	December 31, 1970*
Current Liabilities:		
Notes payable and foreign bank overdrafts	**$ 14,812,000**	$ 8,432,000
Accounts payable and accrued liabilities	**34,771,000**	26,623,000
Federal and foreign income taxes	**10,600,000**	5,672,000
Long-term obligations due within one year	**1,801,000**	1,861,000
Total current liabilities	**61,984,000**	42,588,000
Long-Term Obligations	**41,726,000**	45,523,000
Deferred Executive Incentive Compensation	**1,922,000**	1,746,000
Other Non-Current Liabilities	**1,562,000**	1,469,000
Minority Interest in Consolidated Subsidiaries	**—**	1,118,000
Stockholders' Equity:		
Preferred stock—$1.00 par value Authorized and unissued—1,000,000 shares	**—**	—
Common stock—$1.00 par value Authorized—15,000,000 shares Issued—12,184,468 shares (1970—12,019,550)	**12,184,000**	12,020,000
Capital surplus	**19,496,000**	13,974,000
Retained earnings	**97,711,000**	86,841,000
	129,391,000	112,835,000
Less 56,080 shares of treasury stock (1970—57,943), at cost	**1,707,000**	1,764,000
Total stockholders' equity	**127,684,000**	111,071,000
	$234,878,000	$203,515,000

843

*Reclassified to conform with 1971 presentation.
See accompanying notes.

R. H. Macy & Co., Inc. and consolidated subsidiaries

Consolidated Statement of Financial Condition

Assets	July 29, 1972	July 31, 1971
Current Assets:		
Cash	$ 23,076,552	$ 25,240,714
Short-term investments, at amortized cost (approximate market)	36,873,148	41,226,301
Customers' accounts receivable, per statement on page 14	74,191,144	68,253,938
Other receivables	9,548,147	7,664,526
Merchandise inventories (Note 2—page 16)	130,903,767	117,743,941
Prepaid expenses and supplies	8,357,341	8,690,626
Total current assets	282,950,099	268,820,046
Other Assets:		
Investment in Macy Credit Corp., at equity, per statement on page 18	31,074,144	28,499,004
Investments in, at equity, and advances to 50% owned shopping centers and affiliated companies	14,404,323	12,547,255
Deferred pension charges	4,172,666	2,399,828
Miscellaneous, including unamortized deferred charges of $3,151,387 and $3,441,709	5,671,758	6,303,864
	55,322,891	49,749,951
Property and Equipment, at cost:		
Land	44,253,414	49,947,411
Buildings and improvements on owned properties	129,585,454	116,214,121
Buildings and improvements on leased properties and leaseholds	78,702,928	74,409,649
Fixtures and equipment	139,910,056	127,583,575
Construction in progress	13,395,676	24,536,638
	405,847,528	392,691,394
Accumulated depreciation	107,469,832	95,540,133
	298,377,696	297,151,261
	$636,650,686	$615,721,258

844

See notes to financial statements on pages 16 and 17.

Liabilities and Investment of Shareholders	July 29, 1972	July 31, 1971
Current Liabilities:		
Accounts payable and accrued liabilities	$108,588,706	$110,227,128
Federal income taxes (Note 3—page 16)—		
Current	7,224,500	3,343,500
Deferred	37,826,100	36,940,300
Due to Macy Credit Corp.	1,012,147	3,607,016
Long-term debt due within one year (Note 8—page 17)	14,655,219	30,094,068
Total current liabilities	169,306,672	184,212,012
Deferred Credits:		
Deferred Federal and state taxes (Note 3—page 16)	39,385,409	36,881,453
Deferred investment credit ($5,340,675 and		
$4,990,675) and unamortized capital gains on		
sales and leasebacks	8,135,529	7,886,542
Deferred contingent compensation	4,532,826	3,890,205
	52,053,764	48,658,200
Long-Term Debt, due after one year, per statement		
on page 14:		
R. H. Macy & Co., Inc.	31,259,265	44,207,629
Real estate subsidiaries	112,628,801	86,888,236
	143,888,066	131,095,865
Investment of Shareholders:		
Cumulative preferred shares, 500,000 authorized;		
par value $100 per share—		
4¼ % Series A—165,600 shares issued; 12,240		
and 5,990 in treasury; 153,360 and 159,610		
outstanding, callable at $107.50 per share	15,336,000	15,961,000
4% Series B—100,000 shares issued; 80,000 and		
100,000 outstanding (Note 4—page 16)	8,000,000	10,000,000
Preference shares, $5.00 par value per share—		
1,000,000 authorized and unissued	—	—
Common shares, $0.25 par value, assigned value		
$3.75 per share—20,000,000 authorized; 9,861,952		
and 9,693,416 issued; 15,756 in treasury; leaving		
9,846,196 and 9,677,660 outstanding (Notes 5 and 6		
—page 16)	36,923,235	36,291,225
Additional paid-in capital, per statement on page 14	39,977,549	35,844,817
Earnings reinvested in the business, per statement		
on page 11; at July 29, 1972, $77,600,000 is not		
distributable to common shareholders under terms		
of long-term debt agreements	171,165,400	153,658,139
Total investment of shareholders	271,402,184	251,755,181
	$636,650,686	$615,721,258

845

Standard Oil Company (New Jersey)

Consolidated statement of financial position, December 31, 1971—1970

Assets

Current assets	1971	1970
Cash	$ 421,063,000	$ 366,150,000
Marketable securities, at cost, which approximates market	1,198,276,000	1,173,203,000
Notes and accounts receivable, less estimated doubtful amounts of $87,846,000 and $87,886,000	3,130,683,000	3,076,646.000
Inventories		
Crude oil, products, and merchandise	1,460,230,000	1,372,536,000
Materials and supplies	215,786,000	193,478,000
Prepaid taxes and other expenses	364,469,000	345,734,000
Total current assets	6,790,507,000	6,527,747,000
Investments and advances	1,184,411,000	1,105,662,000
Property, plant, and equipment, at cost, less depreciation and depletion	11,930,428,000	11,305,267,000
Deferred charges and other assets	409,903,000	303,108,000
Total assets	20,315,249,000	19,241,784,000

Liabilities

Current liabilities		
Notes and loans payable	1,186,284,000	1,349,934,000
Accounts payable and accrued liabilities	2,402,376,000	2,127,279,000
Income taxes payable	741,081,000	762,845,000
Total current liabilities	4,329,741,000	4,240,058,000
Long-term debt	2,679,177,000	2,443,166,000
Annuity, insurance, and other reserves	548,978,000	512,195,000
Deferred income tax credits	593,938,000	552,548,000
Other deferred credits	76,274,000	71,789,000
Equity of minority shareholders in affiliated companies	494,219,000	471,383,000
Total liabilities	8,722,327,000	8,291,139,000

Shareholders' equity

Capital	2,640,576,000	2,608,369,000
Earnings reinvested	8,952,346,000	8,342,276,000
Total shareholders' equity	$11,592,922,000	$10,950,645,000

The financial information on pages 27, 28, 29, and 30 is an integral part of these statements.

United States Steel Corporation

Consolidated Statement of Financial Position

	Dec. 31, 1971	Dec. 31, 1970
CURRENT ASSETS		
Cash	$ 218,531,673	$ 217,686,393
Marketable securities, at cost (approximates market)	54,977,259	11,529,302
Receivables, less estimated bad debts	580,487,511	617,204,941
Inventories *(details on page 24)*	840,774,573	923,458,156
Total	1,694,771,016	1,769,878,792
Less		
CURRENT LIABILITIES		
Notes and accounts payable	785,782,871	753,992,126
Accrued taxes	264,617,949	248,157,996
Dividend payable	21,667,095	32,490,357
Long-term debt due within one year............................	53,796,999	38,082,506
Total	1,125,864,914	1,072,722,985
WORKING CAPITAL...	568,906,102	697,155,807
Marketable securities, at cost (approximates market), set aside for plant and equipment additions and replacements	255,000,000	255,000,000
Investments in realty, leasing and finance operations *(details on page 25)* ...	63,500,443	62,598,249
Long-term receivables and other investments, less estimated losses	179,726,420	171,819,531
Plant and equipment, less depreciation *(details on page 25)*	4,077,929,561	3,922,961,695
Operating parts and supplies	58,290,299	54,083,796
Costs applicable to future periods	79,441,461	74,695,801
TOTAL ASSETS LESS CURRENT LIABILITIES	5,282,794,286	5,238,314,879
Deduct		
Long-term debt *(details on page 25)*	1,444,070,597	1,398,684,573
Reserves and deferred taxes on income *(details on page 24)*	331,560,086	389,480,530
EXCESS OF ASSETS OVER LIABILITIES AND RESERVES	$3,507,163,603	$3,450,149,776
OWNERSHIP EVIDENCED BY		
Common stock (authorized 90,000,000 shares; outstanding 54,169,462 shares)		
Par value $30 per share	$1,625,083,860	$1,625,083,860
Income reinvested in business	1,882,079,743	1,825,065,916
(see page 22 for addition of $57,013,827 in 1971 and $17,529,669 in 1970)		
Total	$3,507,163,603	$3,450,149,776

847

hayes-albion corporation
and subsidiaries

CONSOLIDATED STATEMENT OF EARNINGS *Fiscal years ended July 31*

	1972	1971
Net sales	$114,496,568	$81,172,103
Cost of sales	93,911,479	69,297,291
Gross profit	20,585,089	11,874,812
Selling, general and administrative expenses	7,959,730	6,945,940
Operating profit	12,625,359	4,928,872
Other income (expense):		
Interest income	148,182	171,825
Interest expense	(473,298)	(587,736)
Sundry, net	(341,540)	132,650
	(666,656)	(283,261)
Earnings before Federal and State income taxes	11,958,703	4,645,611
Federal and State income taxes (note 4)	5,952,000	2,150,000
Net earnings	$ 6,006,703	$ 2,495,611
Earnings per common share	$1.88	$.78

See accompanying notes to consolidated financial statements.

848

ACCOUNTANTS' REPORT

The Board of Directors and Stockholders
Hayes-Albion Corporation:

We have examined the consolidated balance sheet of Hayes-Albion Corporation and subsidiaries as of July 31, 1972 and the related statements of earnings, stockholders' equity and changes in financial position for the year then ended. Our examination was made in accordance with generally accepted auditing standards, and accordingly included such tests of the accounting records and such other auditing procedures as we considered necessary in the circumstances.

In our opinion, such financial statements present fairly the consolidated financial position of Hayes-Albion Corporation and subsidiaries at July 31, 1972, the results of their operations and the changes in financial position for the year then ended, in conformity with generally accepted accounting principles applied on a basis consistent with that of the preceding year.

Peat, Marwick, Mitchell & Co.

Detroit, Michigan
September 13, 1972

Standard Oil Company of California

Chevron

Consolidated Statement of Income

REVENUES:	1971	1970
Sales and other operating revenues	$5,727,931,000	$4,961,562,000
Equity in net income of certain affiliated companies	168,977,000	121,672,000
Other income	32,862,000	24,775,000
	5,929,770,000	5,108,009,000
COSTS AND OTHER DEDUCTIONS:		
Purchased crude oil and products	1,978,957,000	1,660,292,000
Operating expenses	1,068,622,000	874,119,000
Selling, general and administrative expenses	483,831,000	476,912,000
Depreciation, depletion and amortization	344,212,000	325,442,000
Taxes	1,477,222,000	1,270,612,000
Interest and debt expense	65,834,000	45,815,000
	5,418,678,000	4,653,192,000
NET INCOME	$ 511,092,000	$ 454,817,000
NET INCOME PER SHARE OF COMMON STOCK	$6.02	$5.36

849

Consolidated Statement of Earned Surplus

	1971	1970
BALANCE AT BEGINNING OF YEAR	$2,786,153,000	$2,568,765,000
NET INCOME FOR YEAR	511,092,000	454,817,000
CASH DIVIDENDS ON COMMON STOCK —		
$2.80 per share in 1971 and 1970	(237,388,000)	(237,429,000)
BALANCE AT END OF YEAR	$3,059,857,000	$2,786,153,000

(See Accompanying Notes to Financial Statements)

Koppers

Koppers Company, Inc. and Consolidated Subsidiaries

Consolidated Statement of Income and Earnings Retained in the Business

Years ended December 31, 1971 and 1970 (See accompanying notes)

	1971	1970
Net sales	**$598,443,870**	$532,840,834
Operating expenses (Note 2):		
Cost of sales	**470,953,925**	421,682,328
Depreciation and depletion	**23,222,587**	20,826,346
Taxes, other than income taxes	**11,433,060**	10,695,013
Selling, research, general and administrative expenses	**54,079,558**	53,709,895
	559,689,130	506,913,582
Operating Profit	**38,754,740**	25,927,252
Other income (Note 1):		
Dividends, interest, etc.	**1,550,163**	1,120,755
Provision for decline in value of investments	**(1,000,000)**	—
Profit on sales of capital assets	**2,425,092**	845,783
Equity in earnings of company approximately 50% owned, dividends received 1971—none; 1970—$11,520	**713,229**	890,640
	3,688,484	2,857,178
	42,443,224	28,784,430
Interest expense	**7,856,984**	8,741,460
	34,586,240	20,042,970
Provision for income taxes:		
Federal (Note 3):		
Currently payable	**8,285,741**	4,865,790
Deferred	**3,924,000**	1,473,000
State and foreign	**3,842,163**	2,001,734
	16,051,904	8,340,524
Income before extraordinary items	**18,534,336**	11,702,446
Extraordinary items, net of applicable income taxes (Note 6)	**159,000**	—
Net income for the year	**18,693,336**	11,702,446
Earnings retained in the business at beginning of period	**124,814,229**	121,615,813
Decrease resulting from pooling of interests (Note 1)	**(94,420)**	—
	143,413,145	133,318,259
Cash dividends paid:		
On preferred stock, $4.00 per share	**600,000**	600,000
On common stock, $1.60 per share	**8,787,756**	7,904,030
	9,387,756	8,504,030
Earnings retained in the business at end of period	**$134,025,389**	$124,814,229
Average number of shares of common stock outstanding during year	**5,491,965**	5,151,401
Per share of common stock:		
Earnings before extraordinary items	**$3.26**	$2.16
Extraordinary items	**.03**	—
Net earnings	**$3.29**	$2.16

850

GENERAL ⊛ ELECTRIC

Statement of Current and Retained Earnings

General Electric Company and consolidated affiliates   *(In millions)*

For the year	1971	1970
Sales of products and services to customers	$9,425.3	$8,726.7
Other income	152.0	106.8
	9,577.3	8,833.5

Costs

Employee compensation, including benefits	3,885.3	3,776.4
Materials, supplies, services and other costs	4,484.0	4,073.9
Depreciation	273.6	334.7
Taxes, except those on income	101.8	88.8
Interest and other financial charges	96.9	101.4
Provision for income taxes	317.1	220.6
Deduct increase in inventories during the year	(56.4)	(96.0)
	9,102.3	8,499.8

Earnings before interest of other share owners	475.0	333.7
Deduct interest of other share owners in net results of affiliates	(3.2)	(5.2)
Net earnings applicable to common stock	471.8	328.5
Deduct dividends declared	(249.7)	(235.4)
Amount added to retained earnings	222.1	93.1
Retained earnings at January 1	1,874.1	1,781.0
Retained earnings at December 31	$2,096.2	$1,874.1

Earnings per common share *(In dollars)*	$2.60	$1.81
Dividends declared per common share *(In dollars)*	$1.38	$1.30

Per-share amounts have been adjusted for the two-for-one stock split in April 1971.

The 1971 Financial Summary beginning on page 26 and ending on page 35 is an integral part of this statement.

851

COMMERCIAL SOLVENTS CORPORATION

Consolidated Earnings and Summary of Earnings Retained in Business

	Year Ended December 31,	
	1971	**1970**
Revenues		
Net sales	$89,346,470	$90,772,978
Other income (net)	539,855	663,228
	89,886,325	91,436,206
Costs and Expenses		
Cost of sales	67,760,458	67,899,840
Selling, research and administrative expenses	12,879,949	13,063,003
Depreciation, depletion and amortization (principally straight-line method)	5,452,969	6,058,566
Interest on borrowings	1,015,948	1,175,021
	87,109,324	88,196,430
Earnings from Consolidated Operations before Federal and Foreign Income Taxes	2,777,001	3,239,776
Federal and Foreign Income Taxes	903,566	1,441,084
Earnings from Consolidated Operations	1,873,435	1,798,692
Northwest Nitro-Chemicals Ltd. Operations (after income tax benefits of $942,984)	—	(1,003,516)
Equity in Earnings of Non-Consolidated Foreign Subsidiary and Investments	213,100	83,315
Earnings before Extraordinary Items	2,086,535	878,491
Extraordinary Items Net of Income Taxes	—	(6,623,897)
Net Earnings (Loss)	2,086,535	(5,745,406)
Earnings Retained in Business at Beginning of Year	39,212,322	46,291,985
	41,298,857	40,546,579
Dividends Paid		
Preferred stock ($.90 per share)	121,169	121,169
Common stock ($.40 per share)	1,213,088	1,213,088
	1,334,257	1,334,257
Earnings Retained in Business at End of Year	$39,964,600	$39,212,322
Per Share of Common Stock		
Earnings before extraordinary items	$.65	$ .25
Extraordinary items	—	(2.18)
Net earnings (loss)	$.65	$(1.93)

See accompanying notes to financial statements.

SHERWOOD MEDICAL INDUSTRIES INC. AND SUBSIDIARIES

Consolidated Statements of Earnings

FOR THE YEARS ENDED DECEMBER 31, 1971 AND 1970

	1971	1970
NET SALES (Notes 1 and 7)	$111,134,000	$95,422,000
COST AND EXPENSES (Note 7):		
Cost of sales	$ 67,562,000	$58,476,000
Selling and administrative expenses	25,581,000	21,627,000
	$ 93,143,000	$80,103,000
Income from operations	$ 17,991,000	$15,319,000
INTEREST EXPENSE, net (Note 7)	(1,388,000)	(938,000)
EARNINGS BEFORE INCOME TAXES	$ 16,603,000	$14,381,000
PROVISION FOR INCOME TAXES (Note 9):		
Current	$ 7,601,000	$ 6,936,000
Deferred	169,000	184,000
	$ 7,770,000	$ 7,120,000
NET EARNINGS FOR THE YEAR	$ 8,833,000	$ 7,261,000
EARNINGS PER COMMON SHARE	$1.76	$1.45

853

Consolidated Statements of Shareholders' Equity

FOR THE YEARS ENDED DECEMBER 31, 1971 AND 1970

	Common Stock Shares	Common Stock Amount	Additional Paid-In Capital	Retained Earnings
BALANCE DECEMBER 31, 1969	5,000,000	$5,000,000	$1,666,000	$19,925,000
Net earnings for year 1970	—	—	—	7,261,000
BALANCE DECEMBER 31, 1970	5,000,000	$5,000,000	$1,666,000	$27,186,000
Shares issued for land and buildings transferred from Brunswick Corporation (Note 7)	41,411	41,000	2,061,000	—
Net earnings for year 1971	—	—	—	8,833,000
BALANCE DECEMBER 31, 1971	5,041,411	$5,041,000	$3,727,000	$36,019,000

The accompanying notes to consolidated financial statements are an integral part of these statements.

INDIANA TELEPHONE CORPORATION ....

ITC

Statement of Income

YEAR ENDED DECEMBER 31

	Column A Historical Cost		Column B Historical Cost Restated for Changes in Purchasing Power of Dollar	
	1971	1970	1971	1970
OPERATING REVENUES:				
Local service ....$	5,744,356	$5,384,154	$ 5,788,990	$ 5,695,270
Toll service	4,852,156	4,350,496	4,889,858	4,601,883
Miscellaneous	304,522	234,979	306,888	248,557
Total operating revenues	10,901,034	9,969,629	10,985,736	10,545,710
OPERATING EXPENSES:				
Depreciation provision, Note 2	1,943,551	1,541,560	2,497,078	2,026,211
Maintenance	1,486,495	1,427,487	1,505,457	1,523,311
Traffic	1,226,906	1,157,565	1,237,139	1,224,453
Commercial	511,661	449,104	515,637	475,054
General and administrative	1,055,318	1,170,198	1,068,682	1,278,407
State, local and miscellaneous Federal taxes.......	912,601	648,996	919,692	686,497
Federal income taxes, Note 2.....................				
Currently payable	1,132,500	1,127,087	1,141,300	1,192,215
Deferred until future years	315,800	295,000	318,254	312,047
Deferred investment tax credit (net)	9,708	(14,997)	3,262	(21,018)
Total operating expenses	8,594,540	7,802,000	9,206,501	8,697,177
OPERATING INCOME	2,306,494	2,167,629	1,779,235	1,848,533
INCOME DEDUCTIONS:				
Interest on funded debt..........................	651,195	659,567	656,255	697,679
Other deductions	36,828	21,355	40,229	24,583
Interest charged to construction (credit)	(63,905)	(30,442)	(64,402)	(32,201)
Other income (credit)	(95,974)	(98,759)	(96,720)	(104,466)
Gain from retirement of long-term debt through operation of sinking fund (credit)	(15,192)	(15,865)	(15,310)	(16,781)
Price level gain from retirement of long-term debt (credit), Note 1	—	—	(61,137)	(55,175)
Gain from retirement of preferred stock through operation of sinking fund (credit), Note 1	(5,055)	(5,515)	(5,094)	(5,834)
Price level gain from retirement of preferred stock (credit), Note 1	—	—	(12,908)	(12,029)
Price level loss from other monetary items	—	—	87,508	118,125
Total income deductions	507,897	530,341	528,421	613,901
NET INCOME, Note 1.............................	1,798,597	1,637,288	1,250,814	1,234,632
Preferred stock dividends applicable to the period..	96,209	97,541	96,957	103,178
EARNINGS APPLICABLE TO COMMON STOCK.......$	1,702,388	$1,539,747	$ 1,153,857	$ 1,131,454
EARNINGS PER COMMON SHARE ....$	3.49	$ 3.16	$ 2.37	$ 2.32
BOOK VALUE PER SHARE ....$	21.45	$ 18.29	$ 20.19	$ 18.14
Stations in service at end of year...................	75,015	72,569	75,015	72,569

The accompanying notes are an integral part of this statement.

Amstar Corporation and Subsidiaries

Consolidated statements of changes in financial position for the years ended June 30	1972	1971
Source of funds:		
Net income	$16,645,000	$20,700,000
Charges to income not requiring cash disbursements:		
Depreciation	10,409,000	9,962,000
Deferred taxes	1,231,000	792,000
Funds provided from operations	28,285,000	31,455,000
Proceeds from issuance of Common Stock—employee stock options	159,000	3,832,000
Stated value of Junior Preferred Stock converted into Common Stock	114,000	696,000
Other	486,000	550,000
Total source of funds	29,044,000	36,533,000
Application of funds:		
Additions to plant and equipment	17,319,000	13,194,000
Dividends paid to shareholders	8,963,000	8,695,000
Reduction of long-term debt	2,111,000	4,833,000
Purchase of stock for treasury	9,000	172,000
Par value of Common Stock issued on		
conversion of Junior Preferred Stock	114,000	696,000
Total application of funds	28,516,000	27,590,000
Increase in working capital	$ 528,000	$ 8,943,000
Summary of changes in working capital—increase (decrease)		
Cash and marketable securities	($ 5,580,000)	$ 7,345,000
Accounts receivable	(843,000)	6,122,000
Inventories	(6,103,000)	21,133,000
Current assets	(12,526,000)	34,600,000
Notes payable	(2,251,000)	13,658,000
Payable to suppliers and others	(4,945,000)	9,068,000
Accrued expenses	(1,385,000)	3,394,000
Federal income taxes	(4,473,000)	(463,000)
Current liabilities	(13,054,000)	25,657,000
Increase in working capital	$ 528,000	$ 8,943,000

855

The accompanying notes to financial statements are an integral part of these statements.

G. D. Searle & Co.

Consolidated Statement of Changes in Financial Position

For the years ended December 31, 1971 and 1970 (dollars in thousands)

	1971	1970
Sources of Working Capital		
Net earnings	$ 36,004	$ 31,930
Add—Expenses not requiring outlay of working capital in the current period:		
Depreciation and amortization	5,987	5,192
Deferred income taxes	5,901	2,179
Other	1,469	——
Provided from operations	$ 49,361	$ 39,301
Sale of 8.70% debentures due in 1995	——	30,000
Additions to long-term debt	7,961	61
Decrease in marketable securities maturing after one year	2,507	4,520
Issuance of common stock upon conversion of 4¾% convertible debentures	5,461	——
Other, net	2,545	513
	$ 67,835	$ 74,395
Uses of Working Capital		
Dividends	$ 18,485	$ 18,362
Property, plant, and equipment additions	11,098	12,967
Increase in investments in and advances to affiliates and unconsolidated subsidiaries	7,125	686
Property, plant and equipment from company acquisitions	——	561
Conversion of 4¾% convertible debentures	5,461	——
	$ 42,169	$ 32,576
Net increase in working capital	$ 25,666	$ 41,819
The net increase in working capital is summarized as follows:		
Increases in current assets		
Cash and marketable securities	$ 15,789	$ 14,745
Receivables	2,795	10,033
Inventories	7,790	8,091
Prepaid expenses	138	672
	$ 26,512	$ 33,541
Increase (decrease) in current liabilities	846	(8,278)
Net increase	$ 25,666	$ 41,819

Consolidated Statement of Changes in Financial Position

Standard Brands Incorporated and Subsidiary Companies

	Year Ended December 31	
	1971	**1970**
Sources of Working Capital:		
From Operations		
Net Income	$39,693,460	$37,456,254
Depreciation	18,118,904	16,955,024
Deferred Federal Income Taxes	4,427,153	3,455,143
	62,239,517	57,866,421
Long Term Debt	47,051,060	(7,957,906)
Disposition of Property, Plant and Equipment	2,890,155	2,221,223
Other Items—Net	3,977,006	(217,717)
	116,157,738	51,912,021
Uses of Working Capital:		
Additions to Property, Plant and Equipment	33,909,269	29,250,706
Dividends	21,645,811	21,258,679
Cost of Acquisitions less Working Capital Acquired	22,588,629	9,614,395
	78,143,709	60,123,780
Increase (Decrease) in Working Capital	$38,014,029	($8,211,759)
Changes in Working Capital:		
Current Assets		
Cash and Marketable Securities	$31,626,857	$ 7,456,096
Receivables	3,269,025	9,180,810
Inventories	7,186,405	17,991,232
Prepaid Expenses	1,093,305	761,559
	43,175,592	35,389,697
Current Liabilities		
Bank Loans	27,899,042	(39,166,144)
Current Maturities—Long Term Debt	(203,020)	(104,613)
Accounts Payable and Accrued Expenses	(26,500,129)	(3,025,542)
United States and Foreign Taxes on Income	(6,357,456)	(1,305,157)
	(5,161,563)	(43,601,456)
Increase (Decrease) in Working Capital	$38,014,029	($8,211,759)

857

Auditors' Report

To the Stockholders and Board of Directors of Standard Brands Incorporated:

We have examined the consolidated balance sheet of Standard Brands Incorporated (a Delaware corporation) and subsidiaries as of December 31, 1971, and 1970, and the related consolidated statements of income, retained earnings and changes in financial position for the years then ended. Our examinations were made in accordance with generally accepted auditing standards, and accordingly included such tests of the accounting records and such other auditing procedures as we considered necessary in the circumstances.

In our opinion, the accompanying consolidated financial statements present fairly the financial position of Standard Brands Incorporated and subsidiaries as of December 31, 1971, and 1970, and the results of their operations and the changes in financial position for the years then ended, in conformity with generally accepted accounting principles consistently applied during the periods.

New York, N.Y.,
February 24, 1972.

ARTHUR ANDERSEN & CO.

Statement of Changes
in Financial Position
for the Years Ended December 31, 1971 and 1970
Minnesota Mining and Manufacturing Company
and Consolidated Subsidiaries

	1971	1970
Funds Provided By		
Operations		
Net income for the year	$210,715,000	$187,665,000
Depreciation — generally determined on the straight-line method	83,192,000	72,602,000
Deferred taxes	8,000,000	6,000,000
Borrowing		
Long-term debt	55,070,000	32,268,000
Short-term loans	12,261,000	23,249,000
Current liabilities	50,656,000	1,937,000
Common stock issued		
Employee stock plans (1971 - 110,451 shares; 1970 - 41,026 shares)	9,918,000	3,357,000
Other (71,340 shares)	1,880,000	
Investments	3,072,000	(2,809,000)
Minority interest in subsidiaries	429,000	291,000
	435,193,000	324,560,000
Funds Used For		
Dividends	103,970,000	98,140,000
Property additions		
Plant and equipment	127,567,000	131,553,000
Equipment for lease and other property	44,238,000	31,159,000
Book value of disposals	(11,094,000)	(8,798,000)
Current asset additions		
Receivables	36,602,000	17,492,000
Inventories	1,313,000	27,488,000
Other	5,124,000	(4,361,000)
Deferred pension costs	33,123,000	
	340,843,000	292,673,000
Increase in funds	94,350,000	31,887,000
Cash and marketable securities, beginning of year	135,268,000	103,381,000
Cash and marketable securities, end of year	$229,618,000	$135,268,000

Accountants' Opinion

To the Stockholders of
Minnesota Mining and
Manufacturing Company:

We have examined the balance sheet of Minnesota Mining and Manufacturing Company and consolidated subsidiaries as of December 31, 1971 and 1970 and the related statements of income and net income retained for use in the business and of changes in financial position for the years then ended. Our examination was made in accordance with generally accepted auditing standards, and accordingly included such tests of the accounting records and such other auditing procedures as we considered necessary in the circumstances.

In our opinion, the accompanying financial statements present fairly the financial position of the companies at December 31, 1971 and 1970 and the results of their operations and the changes in their financial position for the years then ended, in conformity with generally accepted accounting principles applied on a consistent basis.

Haskins & Sells
Certified Public Accountants

Saint Paul, Minnesota
February 14, 1972

Index

860

861

—— D ——

E

F

G

863

H

I

J - K

864

L

M

Q

R

866

S

867